www.wadsworth.com

wadsworth.com is the World Wide Web site for Wadsworth and is your direct source to dozens of online resources.

At *wadsworth.com* you can find out about supplements, demonstration software, and student resources. You can also send email to many of our authors and preview new publications and exciting new technologies.

wadsworth.com
Changing the way the world learns®

TENTH EDITION

ANTHROPOLOGY

William A. Haviland

University of Vermont

With the assistance of
Harald Prins and Dana Walrath
Technical Consultants

Australia • Canada • Mexico • Singapore • Spain
United Kingdom • United States

THOMSON
WADSWORTH

Anthropology Editor: Lin Marshall
Assistant Editor: Analie Barnett
Editorial Assistants: Amanda Santana, Reilly O'Neal
Technology Project Manager: Dee Dee Zobian
Marketing Manager: Diane McOscar
Project Manager, Editorial Production: Jerilyn Emori
Print/Media Buyer: Barbara Britton
Permissions Editor: Sandra Lord
Production Service: Robin Lockwood Productions
Photo Researcher: Sandra Lord
Copy Editor: Jennifer Gordon
Illustrators: Carol Zuber-Mallison, Magellan Geographix
Cover Designer: Hiroko Chastain/Cuttriss & Hambleton
Cover Images: Getty Images/Stone, Getty Images/PhotoDisc
Cover Printer: Phoenix Color Corp.
Compositor: New England Typographic Service, Inc.
Printer: R.R. Donnelley/Willard

Printed in the United States of America
1 2 3 4 5 6 7 06 05 04 03 02

For more information about our products, contact us at:
Thomson Learning Academic Resource Center
1-800-423-0563

For permission to use material from this text, contact us by:
Phone: 1-800-730-2214
Fax: 1-800-730-2215
Web: http://www.thomsonrights.com

Library of Congress Control Number: 2002105833

ISBN 0-534-61020-X

Wadsworth/Thomson Learning
10 Davis Drive
Belmont, CA 94002-3098
USA

Asia
Thomson Learning
5 Shenton Way #01-01
UIC Building
Singapore 068808

Australia
Nelson Thomson Learning
102 Dodds Street
South Melbourne, Victoria 3205
Australia

Canada
Nelson Thomson Learning
1120 Birchmount Road
Toronto, Ontario M1K 5G4
Canada

Europe/Middle East/Africa
Thomson Learning
High Holborn House
50/51 Bedford Row
London WC1R 4LR
United Kingdom

Latin America
Thomson Learning
Seneca, 53
Colonia Polanco
11560 Mexico D.F.
Mexico

Spain
Paraninfo Thomson Learning
Calle/Magallanes, 25
28015 Madrid, Spain

To my three sons:

Thomas Philip Haviland

Wallace de Laguna Haviland

Theodore William John Haviland

ABOUT THE AUTHOR

William A. Haviland, Professor Emeritus of Anthropology at the University of Vermont, earned his BA, MA, and PhD degrees at the University of Pennsylvania. He began his career as a physical anthropologist at the Philadelphia Center for Research in Child Growth and as a research assistant for its director, Dr. Wilton M. Krogman. He subsequently went on to teach at Hunter College and Barnard College in New York City, and then at the University of Vermont, Burlington, VT, where he founded the anthropology department.

Dr. Haviland's first field experience was as a member of a Smithsonian Institution field crew doing archaeology on the Lower Brule Indian Reservation in South Dakota. A year later, he became a member of the University of Pennsylvania's archaeological project at the ancient Maya city of Tikal, Guatemala, where he explored prehistoric settlement and served as physical anthropologist. After six seasons there, he helped establish a program of Cultural Resource Management in Vermont, where he also began research on the archaeology, ethnography, and ethnohistory of the region's Native American inhabitants. In 1989, he served as expert witness for Vermont's Abenakis in a landmark case involving aboriginal fishing rights, and has frequently testified before legislative committees on their behalf. During this same period, he also investigated Anglo-American settlement in a Maine coastal community over the 200 years since the community was established.

Dr. Haviland is a member of several professional societies and has served on the board of the American Anthropological Association's general Anthropology Division. He has published many research articles in North American, British, and Mexican journals. Besides his three college texts published by Harcourt College Publishers, he has several other books to his credit, including technical monographs on his work at Tikal and *The Original Vermonters,* of which he is senior author. His professional publications cover three of the four subfields of anthropology.

Now retired, Dr. Haviland is heavily involved in writing and continues as co-editor of the University of Pennsylvania Museum's series of Tikal Reports. He spends much of his spare time in his wooden lobster boat on the waters of Penobscot Bay with his wife, sons, and grandchildren.

TABLE OF CONTENTS

PREFACE

PURPOSE

The purpose of a textbook is to transmit and register ideas and information, to induce the readers to see old things in new ways, and then to ask readers to think about what they see. A book may be the most elegantly written, most handsomely designed, most lavishly illustrated text available on the subject, but if it is not interesting, clear, and comprehensible to the student, it is valueless as a teaching tool. The trick is not just to present facts and concepts; the trick is to make them *memorable.* This is what I have tried to do in *Anthropology,* an introductory text that presents the key concepts and terminology for the basic divisions of anthropology—physical anthropology and cultural anthropology, including ethnology and linguistics, and prehistoric archaeology.

Most anthropology instructors have two goals for their introductory classes: to provide an overview of the principles and processes of anthropology, and to plant a seed of cultural awareness in their students that will enable them to see other cultures as not-so-strange and to challenge their ethnocentrism, long past the end of the semester.

All 10 editions of *Anthropology* have tried to support and further these goals. The majority of our students come to class intrigued with the subject of anthropology, but they have little more than a vague sense of what the field is about. The first and most obvious aim of the text, therefore, is to give students a comprehensive introduction to anthropology. Because it draws from the research and ideas of a number of schools of anthropological thought, the text exposes students to a balanced presentation of such key theoretical approaches as evolutionism, historical particularism, diffusionism, functionalism, French structuralism, structural functionalism, and behavioral ecology. This inclusiveness reflects my conviction that different approaches all have important things to say about human behavior. To restrict oneself to one approach, at the expense of the others, is to cut oneself off from significant insights.

If most students have little substantive concept of anthropology, they often have less clear—and potentially more destructive—views of the primacy of their own culture and its place in the world. A secondary goal of the text, then, is to persuade our students to understand and appreciate the true complexity and breadth of human behavior and culture. Debates in North America and Europe regarding the "naturalness" of the nuclear family, the place of nonstandard English dialects in public education, and the nature of racial differences and gender roles all greatly benefit from the perspectives gained through anthropology. This questioning aspect of anthropology is perhaps the most relevant gift we can pass on to our students. Indeed, debunking is close to the spirit of anthropology, and questioning the superiority of European (and European American) peoples and cultures is something anthropologists have always done especially well. Anthropology is, in this sense, a tool to enable students to think both in and out of their own cultural context.

ORGANIZATION OF THE BOOK

A Unifying Theme

I have found in my own teaching that introductory students often lack a sense of the bigger picture in their studies of human beings. The best solution seems to be the use of a common theme that unifies chapters but that also allows students to make sense of each chapter and part introduction, regardless of the order in which they are read. For want of a better term, I refer to this common theme as one of *adaptation,* although not in the sense of simple behavioral responses to environmental stimuli. Of course, people do not react to an environment as a given; rather, they react to it as they perceive it, and different groups of people may perceive the same environment in dramatically different ways. People also react to things other than the environment: their own biological natures, for one, and their beliefs, attitudes, and the consequences of their behavior, for others. All of these factors present them with problems, and people maintain cultures to deal with problems or matters that concern them. To be sure, their cultures must produce behavior that is generally adaptive, or at least not maladaptive, but this is far from saying that cultural practices necessarily arise because they are adaptive in a particular environment.

Many Messages, Many Media

For most of the discipline's history, anthropologists have relied upon print resources to share information, especially the very linear genre of ethnography, occasionally supplemented with photographs and, in fewer cases, film and analog recordings. However, many of the people anthropologists have studied and worked with have different "literacies" that they draw upon. Indeed, cultural anthropologists work with numerous guises of human behavior, ranging from oral narrative, to music, to ritual dance, weaving, and spray-paint graffiti. Anthropology, therefore, is arguably among the most inherently multimedia of all studies. Today's students are quite familiar with multimedia, and the 10th edition of *Anthropology* uses nonprint media as some of the many potential paths students can take to explore the techniques, processes, and findings of anthropology. The art program is an important part of the text's narrative, while a selection of videos (discussed in more detail below) show culture in motion and bring action and life to the ideas presented in the book. Guides to the World Wide Web (also discussed in more detail below) build skills for analysis and research and move the content of the text away from standard linear textbook format to a multimedia package. Instructors will find the PowerPoint slides and overhead transparencies helpful in bringing the ideas and art of the text into the classroom. And of course, the Classic Readings and Bibliography continue to provide students with a rich library of anthropological resources. Anthropology has been an archive of human behavior, and it is important that the discipline show the richness and diversity of humanity through the appropriate media.

SPECIAL FEATURES OF THE BOOK

Readability

The readability of the text is enhanced by the writing style; even the most difficult concepts are presented in prose that is clear, straightforward, and easy for today's first- and second-year students to understand, without feeling that they are being "spoken down to." Where technical terms are necessary, they appear in bold-faced type, are carefully defined in the text, and defined again in the running glossary in simple, clear language.

The Selection of Cross-Cultural Examples

Because much learning is based on analogy, numerous and engaging examples have been utilized to illustrate, emphasize, and clarify anthropological concepts. Cross-cultural perspectives infuse the text, comparing cultural practices in a great variety of societies, often including the student's own. But these examples have been chosen with the knowledge that although students should be aware that anthropology has important statements to make about the student's own culture and society, the emphasis in introductory anthropology should be on non-Western societies and cultures for illustrative purposes. Why?

It is a fact of life that North Americans share the same planet with great numbers of people who are not only not North American but are non-Western as well. Moreover, North Americans constitute a minority, for they account for far less than one-quarter of the world's population. Yet traditional school curricula in North America emphasize their own surroundings and backgrounds, saying little about the rest of the world. More than ever, as recent events involving Afghanistan and the Middle East make clear, college students need to acquire knowledge about the rest of the world and its peoples. Such a background gives them the global perspective they need to better understand their own culture and society and their place in today's world. Anthropology, of all disciplines, has a long-standing commitment to combating ethnocentrism, and instructors have a unique obligation to provide this perspective.

Maps, Photographs, and Other Illustrations

In this text, numerous four-color photos have been used to make important anthropological points by catching the students' eyes and minds. Many are unusual in the sense that they are not "standard" anthropological textbook photographs; each has been chosen because it complements the text in some distinctive way. And many photographs are shown within groups so students can contrast and compare their messages. In the 10th edition, for instance, Chapter 27 has two photos that compare colonial and modern violence against indigenous people in Guatemala. The success of these photographs can be measured in the number of comments I have received from students and other instructors over the years about the vividness of particular selections.

In addition, the line drawings, maps, charts, and tables were selected especially for their usefulness in illustrating, emphasizing, or clarifying particular anthropological concepts and have also proved to be valuable and memorable teaching aids. Maps in particular have been a popular aid through each edition of *Anthropology,* and the 10th edition builds on this success. Many of the locator maps are new or have been revised. And we have returned to one feature initially utilized in the first edition: placing a world map (a Robinson projection) in the front matter that shows where all of the cultures mentioned in the text are located.

Original Studies

A special feature of this text is the Original Study that appears in each chapter. These studies consist of selections from ethnographies and other original works by women and men who have done, or are doing, work of anthropological significance. Each study, integrated within the flow of the text, sheds additional light on an important anthropological concept or subject area found in the chapter. Their content is not extraneous or supplemental. The Original Studies bring specific concepts to life through specific examples. And a number of Original Studies also demonstrate the anthropological tradition of the case study, albeit in abbreviated form.

The idea behind the Original Studies is to coordinate the two halves of the human brain, which have different functions. Whereas the left (dominant) hemisphere is logical and processes verbal inputs in a linear manner, the right hemisphere is creative and less impressed with linear logic. Psychologist James V. McConnell describes the brain as "an analog computer of sorts—a kind of intellectual monitor that not only handles abstractions, but also organizes and stores material in terms of Gestalts [that] include the emotional relevance of the experience." Logical thinking, as well as creative problem solving, occurs when the two sides of the brain cooperate. The implication for textbook writers is obvious: To be truly effective, they must reach both sides of the brain. The Original Studies help to do this by conveying some "feel" for humans and their behavior and how anthropologists actually study them. For example, in Chapter 16's Original Study, adapted from "The Blessed Curse" by R. K. Williamson, students hear the author describe growing up as an "intersexed" person and the clash of her parents' fundamentalist Christian worldview with that of her Cherokee grandmother regarding her identity. Her state of existence "between" genders is considered alternately as a blessing and a curse. As with other Original Studies, the striking nature of her experiences drives the discussion of a host of issues deeply relevant to students and anthropology.

Integrated Gender Coverage

Unlike many introductory texts, the 10th edition of *Anthropology* integrates rather than separates gender coverage. Thus, material on gender-related issues is included in every chapter. This approach gives the 10th edition a very large amount of gender-related material: the equivalent of three full chapters. This much content far exceeds the single chapter most introductory textbooks contain.

Why is the gender-related material integrated? Anthropology is itself an integrative discipline; concepts and issues surrounding gender are almost always too complicated to remove from their context. Moreover, spreading this material through all of the chapters emphasizes how considerations of gender enter into virtually everything people do. Much of the new content for the 10th edition (listed below) relates to gender in some way. These changes generally fall into at least one of three categories: changes in thinking about gender within the discipline, examples that have important ramifications for gender in a particular society or culture, and cross-cultural implications about gender and gender relations. Examples of new material range from an expanded discussion of homosexual identity and same-sex marriage to current thinking on the role of females in ape societies and recent news in regard to female genital mutilation. Through a steady drumbeat of such coverage, the 10th edition avoids "ghettoizing" gender to a single chapter that is preceded and followed by resounding silence.

Previews and Summaries

An old and effective pedagogical technique is repetition: "Tell 'em what you're going to tell 'em, tell 'em, and then tell 'em what you've told 'em." To do this, each chapter begins with preview questions that set up a framework for studying the contents of the chapter. At the end of the chapter is a summary containing the kernels of the more important ideas presented in the chapter. The summaries provide handy reviews for students without being so long and detailed as to seduce students into thinking they can get by without reading the chapter itself.

Web Links

The Internet has proved to be an increasingly important means of communication and will no doubt continue to grow in relevance and complexity. The 10th edition draws upon the World Wide Web both as an instructional tool and as a vehicle for providing new examples of culture and cultural change. Every chapter contains Cyber Road

Trips that refer the student and instructor to the book's companion Web site, found at **http://www.wadsworth.com /product/053461020X,** where Web links and accompanying interactive exercises can be found for each chapter.

Classic Readings and Bibliography

Each chapter includes a list of classic readings that will supply the inquisitive student with further information about specific anthropological points. The books suggested are oriented toward the general reader and the interested student who wishes to explore further the more technical aspects of the subject. In addition, the bibliography at the end of the book contains a listing of more than 500 books, monographs, and articles from scholarly journals and popular magazines on virtually every topic covered in the text that a student might wish to investigate further.

Glossary

The running glossary is designed to catch the students' eyes as they read, reinforcing the meaning of each newly introduced term. It is also useful for chapter review, as the student may readily isolate the new terms from those introduced in earlier chapters. A new, complete glossary is also included at the back of the book for easy reference. In the glossaries each term is defined in clear, understandable language. As a result, less class time is required going over terms, leaving instructors free to pursue matters of greater interest.

Length

Careful consideration has been given to the length of this book. On the one hand, it had to be of sufficient length to avoid superficiality or misrepresentation of the discipline by ignoring or otherwise slighting some important aspect of anthropology. On the other hand, it could not be so long as to present more material than can be reasonably dealt with in the space of a single semester, or to be prohibitively expensive. The resultant text is comparable in length to introductory texts in the sister disciplines of economics, psychology, and sociology, even though there is more ground to be covered in an introduction to general anthropology.

The 10th Edition

Every chapter in the 10th edition has been thoroughly updated, edited, and fine-tuned with the help of two expert consultants. Major changes for the 10th edition include:

CHAPTER 1

New discussion of anthropology's relevance illustrated with discussion of racism in the United States, the issue of same-sex marriage, and the common confusion of "nation" with "state." There is a revised discussion of ethics illustrated by the author's work, and a new example of ethnographic fieldwork.

CHAPTER 3

Completely rewritten with greatly expanded coverage of human genetics.

CHAPTER 4

New discussion of chimpanzee culture.

CHAPTER 5

Extensive revision; material on macroevolution was moved to this chapter, and the discussion of fossil primates was simplified.

CHAPTER 6

Revised discussion of *Australopithecus* and new material on *Ardipithecus, Kenyanthropus,* and *Orrorin tugenensis.*

CHAPTER 7

Revised discussion of Oldowan tools.

CHAPTER 8

Revised discussion of Acheulean tools; new discussion of comparable technology from China; new material on implications of stone tool technology for language origins.

CHAPTER 9

New material on Neandertal DNA; new discussion of the controversial "Neandertal flute"; expanded section on Neandertals and spoken language.

CHAPTER 10

New emphasis on difficulty of defining "anatomically modern"; rewritten and expanded discussion of the peopling of the Americas; removal (to Chapter 11) of section on the Mesolithic.

CHAPTER 11

Placement of section on the Mesolithic at the start of the chapter; new material on early domestication of goats.

CHAPTER 12

Expanded discussion of Çatalhöyük; new material on early writing; expanded section on "Civilization and Its

Discontents," including material on genetic diseases (cystic fibrosis and Tay-Sachs).

CHAPTER 16

New discussion of changing concepts of normality and abnormality in the United States.

CHAPTER 17

New material on relation of ritual to agriculture in Bali and revised discussion of birth control among food foragers.

CHAPTER 18

New examples of cross-cultural misunderstandings in business.

CHAPTER 19

Expanded material on primate sexuality in general and human sexuality in particular; new material on both polygyny and same-sex marriage in the United States, discussion of the relation between rising divorce rates and rising life expectancy in the United States.

CHAPTER 21

New chapter conclusion raises the issue of reproductive technologies and their effects on kinship.

CHAPTER 22

New discussion of lowered participation in traditional common-interest associations and rise of "virtual" associations via cyberspace.

CHAPTER 24

A revised discussion of shamanism and its origins in trance experience.

New Original Studies

Six of the 27 Original Studies are new to the 10th edition:

Chapter 1: Encountering Environmentalism in Rural Costa Rica, by Luis Vivanco (2000)

Chapter 3: The Unsettling Nature of Variational Change, by Stephen Jay Gould (2000)

Chapter 4: The Culture of Chimpanzees, by A. Whitten and C. Boesch (2001)

Chapter 5: Will the Real Human Ancestor Please Stand Up? by Dana Walrath (2002)

Chapter 20: The Ever-Changing Family in North America, by Linda Stone (1998)

Chapter 22: Digital Revolution: Indigenous Peoples in Cyberia, by Harald E. L. Prins (2000)

New Anthropology Applied and Bio Boxes

Four new Anthropology Applied boxes are:

Chapter 3: Anthropology and the Ethical, Legal, and Social Implications of the Human Genome Project, by Dana Walrath

Chapter 17: Agricultural Development and the Anthropologist

Chapter 18: Anthropology and the World of Business, with a section by Dureen Hughes

Chapter 26: Development Anthropology and Dams

In addition, the Anthropology Applied boxes for Chapters 1, 13, 21, and 23 have been updated and revised.

Two new Bio Boxes are:

Chapter 3: Gregor Mendel

Chapter 13: Ashley Montagu

SUPPLEMENTS FOR INSTRUCTORS

In keeping with the 10th edition's recognition that the use of many messages requires many media, the selection of ancillaries accompanying *Anthropology* should meet most instructor's needs.

Technology Demo CD-ROM for *Anthropology*

The Technology Demo CD-ROM introduces and demonstrates all of the key technology supplements that Wadsworth offers. The demos provide instructors with an overview of each supplement and a more detailed demonstration of exactly how to use each product. The Technology Demo CD-ROM comes in each Instructor's Edition of the text.

Instructor's Manual

This supplement provides student learning objectives, a chapter review, brief descriptions of chapter feature pieces, key terms, lecture and class activity suggestions, as well as a list of additional resources that correspond to each chapter of the textbook. Concise user guides for InfoTrac® College Edition and WebTutor are provided as appendixes.

Test Bank

Each chapter of the Test Bank features approximately 40–70 multiple-choice questions; 10–15 true/false questions; and many matching, short-answer, and essay questions. In addition to answers and page references, all test questions are followed by codes that indicate the type of question, whether the question focuses on the main narrative of the text or on a feature piece, and if a similar question can be found in the Study Guide and Workbook.

ExamView Computerized and Online Testing

Create, deliver, and customize tests and study guides (both print and online) in minutes with this easy-to-use assessment and tutorial system. *ExamView* offers both a Quick Test Wizard and an Online Test Wizard that guide you step by step throughout the process of creating tests, while its unique "WYSIWYG" capability allows you to see the test you are creating on screen exactly as it will print or display online. Using *ExamView*'s complete word processing capabilities, you can enter an unlimited number of new questions or edit existing questions.

CLASSROOM PRESENTATION TOOLS FOR INSTRUCTORS

Wadsworth's Cultural Anthropology Transparency Acetates 2003

A set of four-color acetates from Wadsworth's cultural anthropology texts is available to help prepare lecture presentations.

Wadsworth's Physical Anthropology Transparency Acetates 2003

A set of four-color acetates from Wadsworth's physical anthropology texts is available to help prepare lecture presentations.

Multimedia Manager for Anthropology: A Microsoft PowerPoint Link Tool 2003 CD-ROM

This *2003 CD-ROM* contains digital media and PowerPoint presentations for all of Wadsworth's 2003 introductory anthropology texts—placing images, lectures, and video clips at instructors' fingertips. Start with our preassembled PowerPoint Presentations, which include chapter outlines and key terms. Then easily add video and images from Wadsworth's anthropology texts all included on the CD-ROM. Instructors can also add their own lecture notes and images to create a custom-made lecture presentation. The NEW Wadsworth Multimedia Manager also includes an exciting Earthwatch Institute Research Feature!

Wadsworth Anthropology Video Library

Qualified adopters may select full-length videos from an extensive library of offerings drawn from excellent educational video sources such as *Films for the Humanities and Sciences.*

Faces of Culture Video Series

Prepared by Coast Telecourses in Fountain Valley, California, through the Coast Community College District, this video series (for which Haviland served as technical consultant) has been an important part of anthropology since 1983. Most of the 26 half-hour programs focus on key anthropological concepts, while several episodes are devoted to presenting rich ethnographic detail on specific cultures. These videos are available for stand-alone use or in the context of a telecourse. A Telecourse Student Study Guide is also available. Instructors can obtain information on the Telecourse and order an Instructor's Manual and Testbank by calling Coast Telelearning directly at (800) 547-4748 or via email at coastlearning@cccd.edu.

CNN Today Anthropology Video Series, Volume I
CNN Today Cultural Anthropology Video Series, Volumes I–V
CNN Today Physical Anthropology Video Series, Volumes I–IV

The *CNN Today Anthropology* video series is an exclusive series jointly created by Wadsworth and CNN for the anthropology course. Each video in the series consists of approximately 45 minutes of footage originally broadcast on CNN within the last several years. The videos are broken into short 2–7 minute segments, which are perfect for classroom use as lecture launchers or to illustrate key anthropological concepts. An annotated table of contents accompanies each video with descriptions of the segments and suggestions for their possible use within the course.

Visual Anthropology Video and Guide

This video consists of 16 clips, each 3–4 minutes in length, from some of the best-known ethnographic films. The shortness of the clips makes for maximum flexibility. Documentary Educational Resources produced the video exclusively for Wadsworth Publishing. Derive the most benefit from the Visual Anthropology video by using it in conjunction with *A Guide to Visual Anthropology*. The *Guide* describes the films on the video, suggests related topic areas, provides a brief summary, and includes classroom questions for discussion.

SUPPLEMENTS FOR STUDENTS

Anthropology Student CD-ROM

This student CD-ROM comes automatically with every copy of the text. On the CD, students will find the following features for each field of anthropology:

Meet the Scientist Read interviews with scientists who talk about their field research projects, including project goals, personal anecdotes, and discoveries. See actual photos of fieldwork and learn what each principal investigator has to say about the exciting contributions anthropology is making today. Includes well-known Earthwatch scientists and field research expeditions from around the world.

Live From the Field Watch CNN broadcast video clips that take you on a journey around the world. See anthropologists' research and fieldwork on contemporary anthropological issues. Critical thinking questions follow each video clip and can be answered and emailed to your instructor.

Interactive Exercises Experience the fun of learning—test your knowledge by placing fossils correctly on a map, completing historical timelines, and labeling skeletons. Identify the similarities and differences of simple words between languages, click on words in Shinzwani to hear how they are pronounced, and much more.

Online Research Learn how to research a specific topic in any field of anthropology. This section will help you prepare for class, complete course assignments, write your research paper.

Exploring Further Explore a wealth of anthropology resources. See the latest breaking news in anthropology, read essays on agricultural and economic development, learn about cultural survival, and find facts and advice about anthropology careers.

Study Guide and Workbook

This guide includes chapter synopses, chapter goals, lists of key terms and people, and questions to guide students in their reading of chapter material. Each chapter also includes practice tests consisting of fill-in-the-blank, multiple-choice, matching, true/false, and essay questions.

Researching Anthropology on the Internet, Second Edition

Written by David Carlson, this useful guide is designed to assist anthropology students in all of their needs when doing research on the Internet. Part One contains general information necessary to get started and answers questions about security, the type of material available on the Internet, the sites with information that is reliable and the sites that are not, the best ways to find research, and the best links to take students where they want to go. Part Two looks at each main discipline in anthropology and refers students to sites where the most enlightening research can be obtained.

WEB RESOURCES AND SUPPLEMENTS FOR INSTRUCTORS AND STUDENTS

Anthropology Online: Wadsworth's Anthropology Resource Center

The Wadsworth Anthropology Resource Center contains a wealth of information and useful tools for both instructors and students. After logging on to the Wadsworth home page at **http://anthropology.wadsworth.com,** click on Course Materials, Anthropology, and the *Haviland* book cover. Proceed to the Student Resources section by clicking For Students. There, students will find many exciting chapter specific resources such as CNN video clips, crossword puzzles, Internet Exercises, InfoTrac College Edition Exercises, practice quizzes that calculate results that can then be emailed to instructors, and much more. Instructors too will find a wealth of materials such as an online Instructor's Manual and PowerPoint lecture slides.

A Virtual Tour of Applying Anthropology

This special section of the Web site serves as an online resource center for the anthropology student. Students will find Applied Anthropologists at Work, Graduate Studies Info, Job Boards, Internships and Fieldwork, and an Essay on Careers with video.

InfoTrac College Edition

Ignite discussions or augment lectures with the latest developments in anthropology and societal change. InfoTrac College Edition (available as a free option with newly purchased texts) gives instructors and students 4-months' free access to an easy-to-use online database of reliable, full-length articles (not abstracts) from hundreds of top academic journals and popular sources. Among the journals that are available 24 hours a day, seven days a week, *American Anthropologist, Current Anthropology, Canadian Review of Sociology and Anthropology.* Contact your Wadsworth/Thomson Learning representative for more information.

WebTutor Advantage™ on WebCT and Blackboard

For students, WebTutor Advantage offers real-time access to a full array of study tools, including chapter summaries, flashcards (with audio), practice quizzes, interactive maps and timelines, online tutorials, and Web links. Professors can use WebTutor Advantage to provide virtual office hours, post syllabi, set up threaded discussions, track student progress with quizzing material, and more. WebTutor Advantage provides rich communication tools, including a course calendar, asynchronous discussion, "real-time" chat, a whiteboard, and an integrated email system.

ACKNOWLEDGMENTS

Many people assisted in the preparation of this book, some of them directly, some of them indirectly. In the latter category are all of the anthropologists under whom I was privileged to study at the University of Pennsylvania: Robbins Burling, William R. Coe, Carleton S. Coon, Robert Ehrich, Loren Eisley, J. Louis Giddings, Ward H. Goodenough, A. Irving Hallowell, Alfred V. Kidder II, Wilton M. Krogman, Froelich Rainey, Ruben Reina, and Linton Satterthwaite. A similar debt is owed to all those anthropologists with whom I have worked or discussed teaching, research interests, and the field in general. There are far too many of them to list here, but surely they have had an important impact on my own thinking and so on this book. Finally, the influence of all those who assisted in the preparation of the first nine editions continues to linger in this new one. They are all listed in the prefaces to the earlier editions, and the 10th edition benefits from their past influence.

The 10th edition owes a special debt to anthropologists Harald E. L. Prins of Kansas State University and Dana Walrath of the University of Vermont College of Medicine. In addition to careful reviewing, Harald completely rewrote his piece for the Anthropology Applied box in Chapter 21, wrote a new Original Study for Chapter 22, and supplied the Cyber Road Trips for the cultural chapters. Dana also carefully reviewed material and wrote the Anthropology Applied box in Chapter 3 and the Original Study for Chapter 5. She also prepared the timelines for Chapters 5 through 10, and supplied the Cyber Road Trips for Chapters 2 through 13. Both colleagues did a careful review of my initial revisions, certainly strengthening the final product. Harald, Dana, and I share some common research interests, as well as similar visions of what anthropology is (and should be) all about, and I look forward to their expanded participation in future editions of this book.

This revision also benefits from my continued association with valued colleagues at the University of Vermont: Deborah Blom, Robert Gordon, Carroll M. P. Lewin, Stephen L. Pastner, James Peterson, Jeanne Shea, Luis Vivanco, and A. Peter Woolfson. All have responded graciously at one time or another to my requests for sources and advice in their various fields of expertise. We all share freely our successes and failures in trying to teach anthropology to introductory students. In addition, Luis was kind enough to write a short Original Study for this edition; it appears in Chapter 1. Thanks are also due the anthropologists who made suggestions for this edition. They include: Jeffrey A. Behm, University of Wisconsin, Oshkosh; Gregory R. Campbell, University of Montana; James G. Flanagan, University of Southern Mississippi; Jim Merryman, Wilkes University; H. Lyn Miles, University of Tennessee, Chattanooga; and William H. Thomas, Marquette University.

All of their comments were carefully considered; how I have responded to them has been determined by my own perspective of anthropology, as well as my 36 years of experience with undergraduate students. Therefore, neither they nor any of the other anthropologists mentioned here should be held responsible for any shortcomings in this book. I also wish to acknowledge my debt to a number of nonanthropologists who helped me with this book. The influence of David Boynton, winner of the 1985 Distinguished Service Award of the American Anthropological Association and my editor at Holt, Rinehart, & Winston until his retirement in 1983, I am sure lingers on. Helpful in seeing this edition through to publication have been my editors at Harcourt: Tracy Napper and Parrish Glover; and my editors at Wadsworth: Lin Marshall, Analie Barnett, and Robin Lockwood. I also wish to thank the skilled design and production team headed by Jerilyn Emori.

The greatest debt of all is owed my wife, Anita de Laguna Haviland, who not only has put up with my preoccupation with this revision, but has taken care of all of the word processing as well. Her suggestions for topics to include and ways to express concepts have enormously benefited the book.

PUTTING THE WORLD IN PERSPECTIVE

Although all humans that we know about are capable of producing accurate sketches of localities and regions with which they are familiar, CARTOGRAPHY (the craft of mapmaking as we know it today) had its beginnings in 13th century Europe, and its subsequent development is related to the expansion of Europeans to all parts of the globe. From the beginning, there have been two problems with maps: the technical one of how to depict on a two-dimensional, flat surface a three-dimensional spherical object, and the cultural one of whose worldview they reflect. In fact, the two issues are inseparable, for the particular projection one uses inevitably makes a statement about how one views one's own people and their place in the world. Indeed, maps often shape our perception of reality as much as they reflect it.

In cartography, a PROJECTION refers to the system of intersecting lines (of longitude and latitude) by which part or all of the globe is represented on a flat surface. There are more than 100 different projections in use today, ranging from polar perspectives to interrupted "butterflies" to rectangles to heart shapes. Each projection causes distortion in size, shape, or distance in some way or another. A map that shows the shape of land masses correctly will of necessity misrepresent the size. A map that is accurate along the equator will be deceptive at the poles.

Perhaps no projection has had more influence on the way we see the world than that of Gerhardus Mercator, who devised his map in 1569 as a navigational aid for mariners. So well suited was Mercator's map for this purpose that it continues to be used for navigational charts today. At the same time, the Mercator projection became a standard for depicting land masses, something for which it was never intended. Although an accurate navigational tool, the Mercator projection greatly exaggerates the size of land masses in higher latitudes, giving about two-thirds of the map's surface to the northern hemisphere. Thus, the lands occupied by Europeans and European descendants appear far larger than those of other people. For example, North America (19 million square kilometers) appears almost twice the size of Africa (30 million square kilometers), while Europe is shown as equal in size to South America, which actually has nearly twice the land mass of Europe.

A map developed in 1805 by Karl B. Mollweide was one of the earlier equal-area projections of the world. Equal-area projections portray land masses in correct relative size, but, as a result, distort the shape of continents more than other projections. They most often compress and warp lands in the higher latitudes and vertically stretch land masses close to the equator. Other equal-area projections include the Lambert Cylindrical Equal-Area Projection (1772), the Hammer Equal-Area Projection (1892), and the Eckert Equal-Area Projection (1906).

The Van der Grinten Projection (1904) was a compromise aimed at minimizing both the distortions of size in the Mercator and the distortion of shape in equal-area maps such as the Mollweide. Allthough an improvement, the lands of the northern hemisphere are still emphasized at the expense of the southern. For example, in the Van der Grinten, the Commonwealth of Independent States (the former Soviet Union) and Canada are shown at more than twice their relative size.

The Robinson Projection, which was adopted by the National Geographic Society in 1988 to replace the Van der Grinten, is one of the best compromises to date between the distortion of size and shape. Although an improvement over the Van der Grinten, the Robinson projection still depicts lands in the northern latitudes as proportionally larger at the same time that it depicts lands in the lower latitudes (representing most third-world nations) as proportionally smaller. Like European maps before it, the Robinson projection places Europe at the center of the map with the Atlantic Ocean and the Americas to the left, emphasizing the cultural connection between Europe and North America, while neglecting the geographical closeness of northwestern North America to northeast Asia.

The following pages show four maps that each convey quite different "cultural messages." Included among them is the Peters Projection, an equal-area map that has been adopted as the official map of UNESCO (the United Nations Educational, Scientific, and Cultural Organization), and a map made in Japan, showing us how the world looks from the other side.

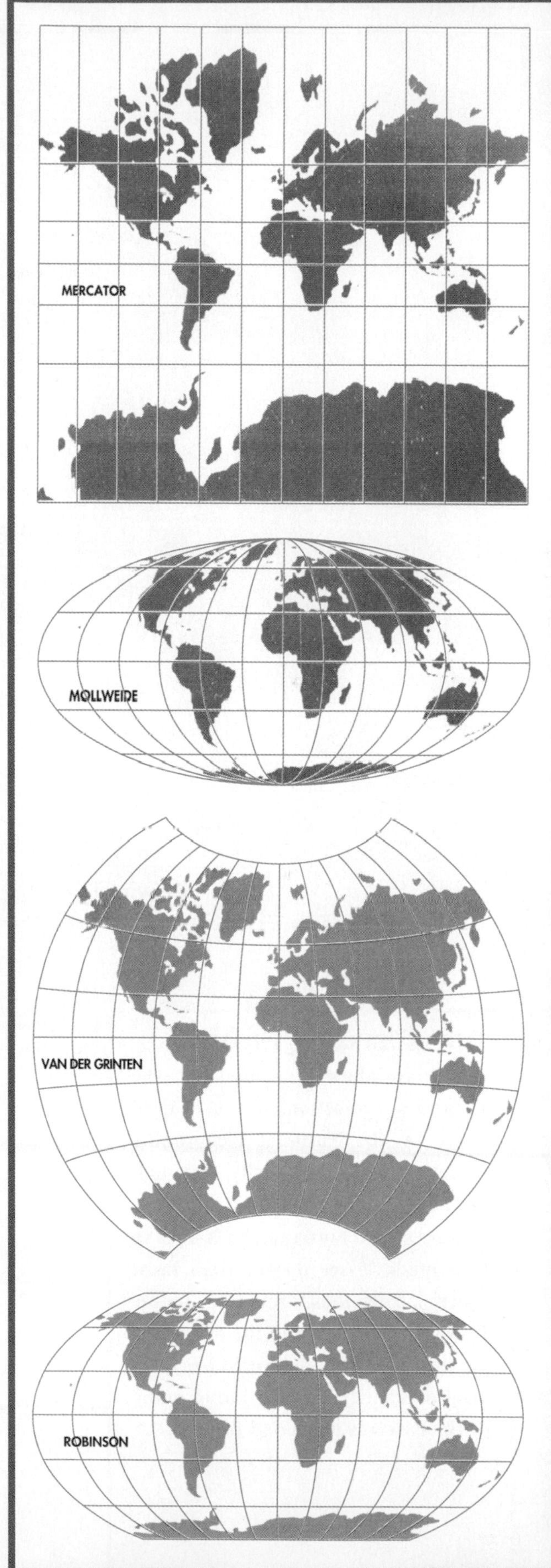

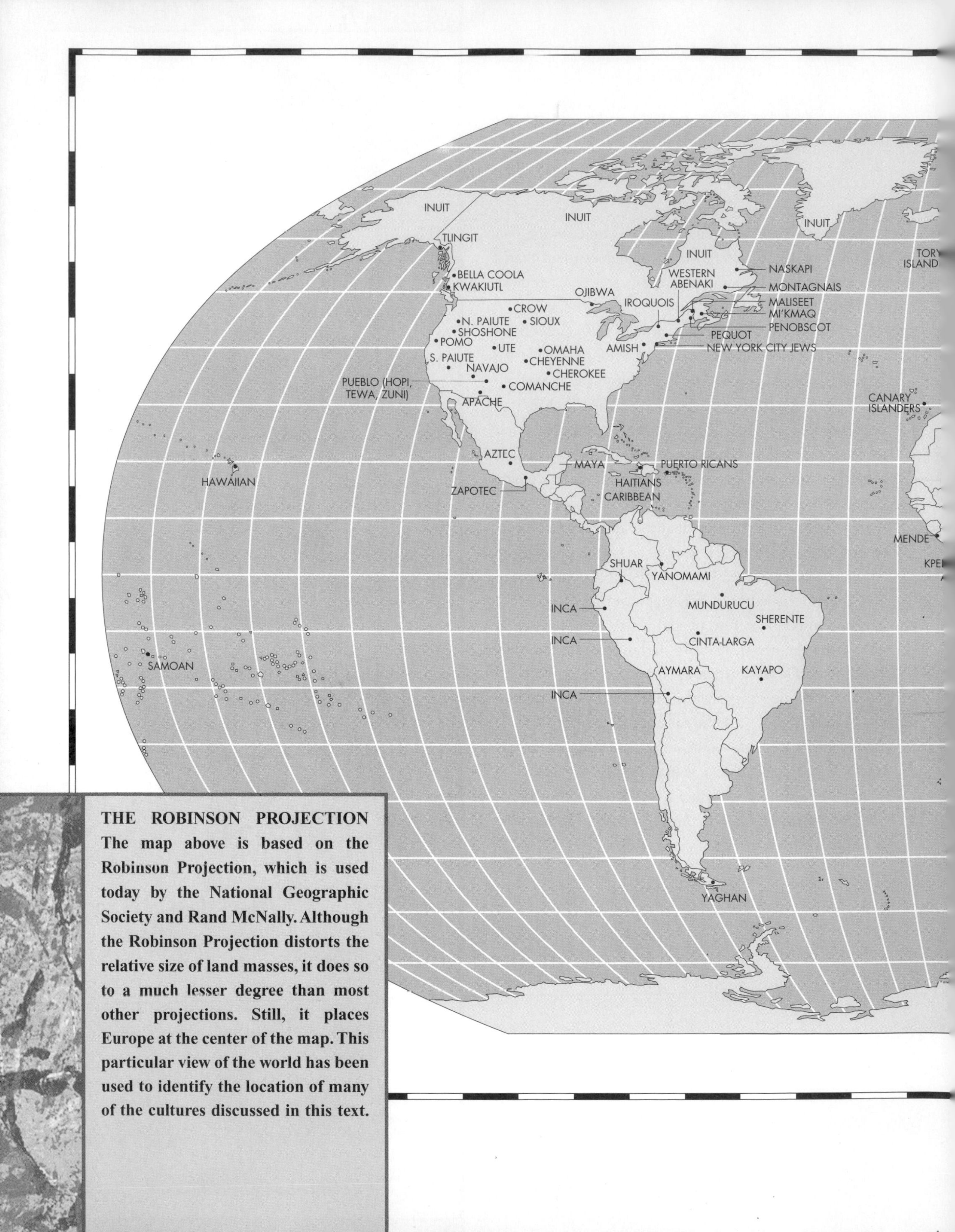

THE ROBINSON PROJECTION The map above is based on the Robinson Projection, which is used today by the National Geographic Society and Rand McNally. Although the Robinson Projection distorts the relative size of land masses, it does so to a much lesser degree than most other projections. Still, it places Europe at the center of the map. This particular view of the world has been used to identify the location of many of the cultures discussed in this text.

SAAMI (SKOLT LAPPS)
INUIT
CROATS
SERBS
BOSNIANS
CHECHENS
KURDS
JAPANESE
ISRAELIS
BAKHTIARI
TIBETANS
MELEMCHI
CHINESE
AWLAD ALI BEDOUINS
EGYPTIANS
CHENCHU
KAREN
TAIWANESE
TRUK
NUER
YORUBA
BENIN
IBIBIO
AFAR & TEGREANS
NAYAR
KOTA AND KURUMBA
KAPAUKU
AZANDE
TURKANA
NANDI
SOMALI
MBUTI
MONGO
TODA AND BADAGA
WAPE
ENGA
TSEMBAGA
YAKO
HUTU AND TUTSI
GUSII
MASAI
TIRIKI
MINANGKABAU
HADZA
BALINESE
ARAPESH
MELANESIANS
TROBRIANDERS
DOBU
JU/'HOANSI
BUSHMEN
SWAZI
ABORIGINES
TASMANIANS

THE PETERS PROJECTION

The map above is based on the Peters Projection, which has been adopted as the official map of UNESCO. While it distorts the shape of continents (countries near the equator are vertically elongated by a ratio of two to one), the Peters Projection does show all continents according to their correct relative size. Though Europe is still at the center, it is not shown as larger and more extensive than the third world.

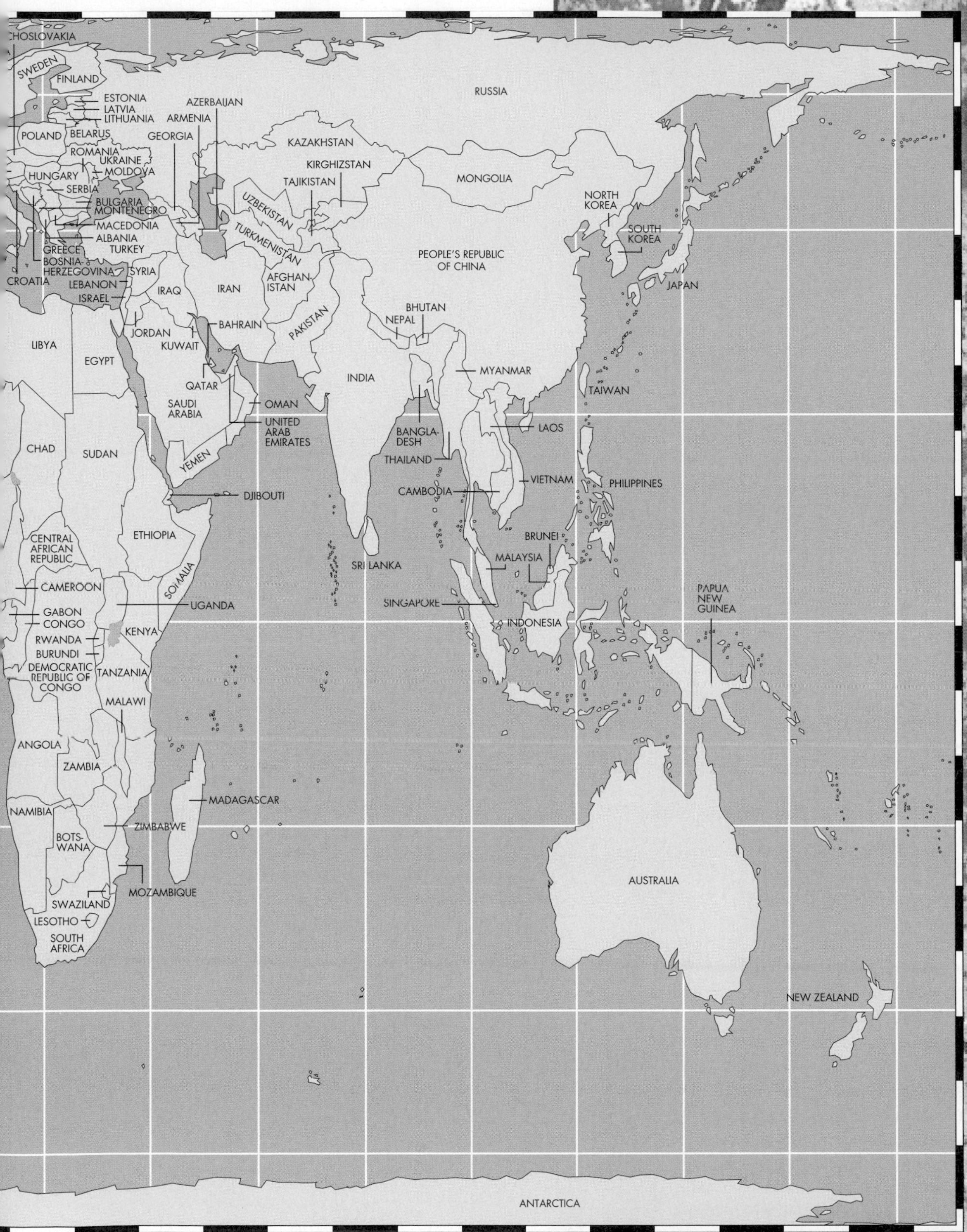

CHOSLOVAKIA
SWEDEN
FINLAND
ESTONIA
LATVIA
LITHUANIA
POLAND
BELARUS
ROMANIA
UKRAINE
MOLDOVA
HUNGARY
SERBIA
BULGARIA
MONTENEGRO
MACEDONIA
ALBANIA
GREECE
TURKEY
BOSNIA-HERZEGOVINA
CROATIA
SYRIA
LEBANON
ISRAEL
AZERBAIJAN
ARMENIA
GEORGIA
RUSSIA
KAZAKHSTAN
KIRGHIZSTAN
TAJIKISTAN
UZBEKISTAN
TURKMENISTAN
MONGOLIA
NORTH KOREA
SOUTH KOREA
JAPAN
PEOPLE'S REPUBLIC OF CHINA
IRAQ
IRAN
AFGHAN-ISTAN
PAKISTAN
BHUTAN
NEPAL
JORDAN
BAHRAIN
KUWAIT
LIBYA
EGYPT
QATAR
SAUDI ARABIA
OMAN
UNITED ARAB EMIRATES
INDIA
MYANMAR
TAIWAN
BANGLA-DESH
LAOS
THAILAND
YEMEN
CHAD
SUDAN
VIETNAM
PHILIPPINES
CAMBODIA
DJIBOUTI
ETHIOPIA
BRUNEI
CENTRAL AFRICAN REPUBLIC
MALAYSIA
SRI LANKA
SOMALIA
CAMEROON
SINGAPORE
PAPUA NEW GUINEA
GABON
CONGO
UGANDA
KENYA
INDONESIA
RWANDA
BURUNDI
DEMOCRATIC REPUBLIC OF CONGO
TANZANIA
MALAWI
ANGOLA
ZAMBIA
MADAGASCAR
NAMIBIA
ZIMBABWE
BOTS-WANA
MOZAMBIQUE
AUSTRALIA
SWAZILAND
LESOTHO
SOUTH AFRICA
NEW ZEALAND
ANTARCTICA

JAPANESE MAP
Not all maps place Europe at the center of the world, as this Japanese map illustrates. Besides reflecting the importance the Japanese attach to themselves in the world, this map has the virtue of showing the geographic proximity of North America to Asia, a fact easily overlooked when maps place Europe at their center.

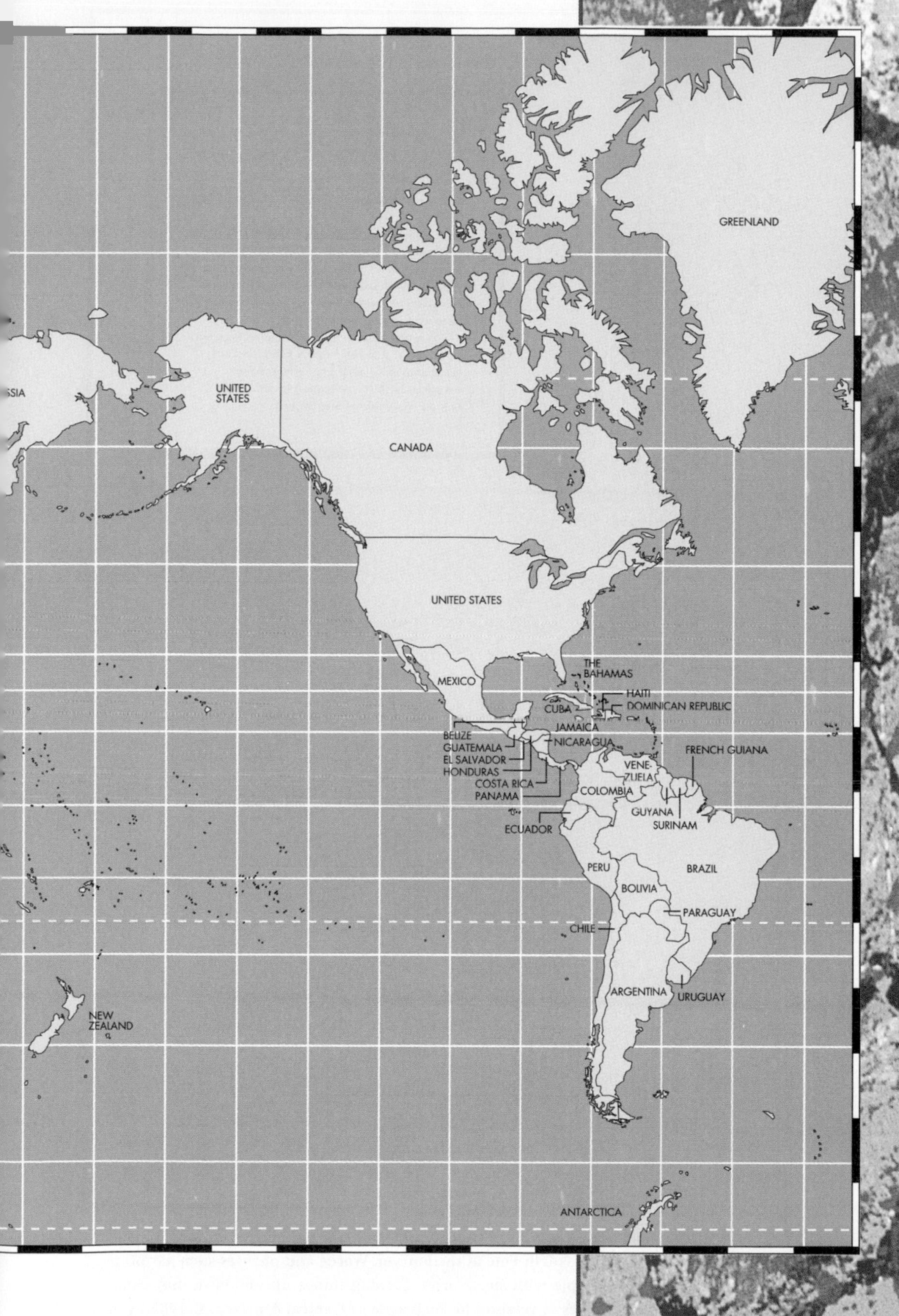

GREENLAND
UNITED STATES
CANADA
SSIA
UNITED STATES
MEXICO
THE BAHAMAS
HAITI
DOMINICAN REPUBLIC
CUBA
JAMAICA
BELIZE
GUATEMALA
EL SALVADOR
HONDURAS
NICARAGUA
COSTA RICA
PANAMA
VENE-ZUELA
FRENCH GUIANA
COLOMBIA
GUYANA
SURINAM
ECUADOR
PERU
BRAZIL
BOLIVIA
PARAGUAY
CHILE
ARGENTINA
URUGUAY
NEW ZEALAND
ANTARCTICA

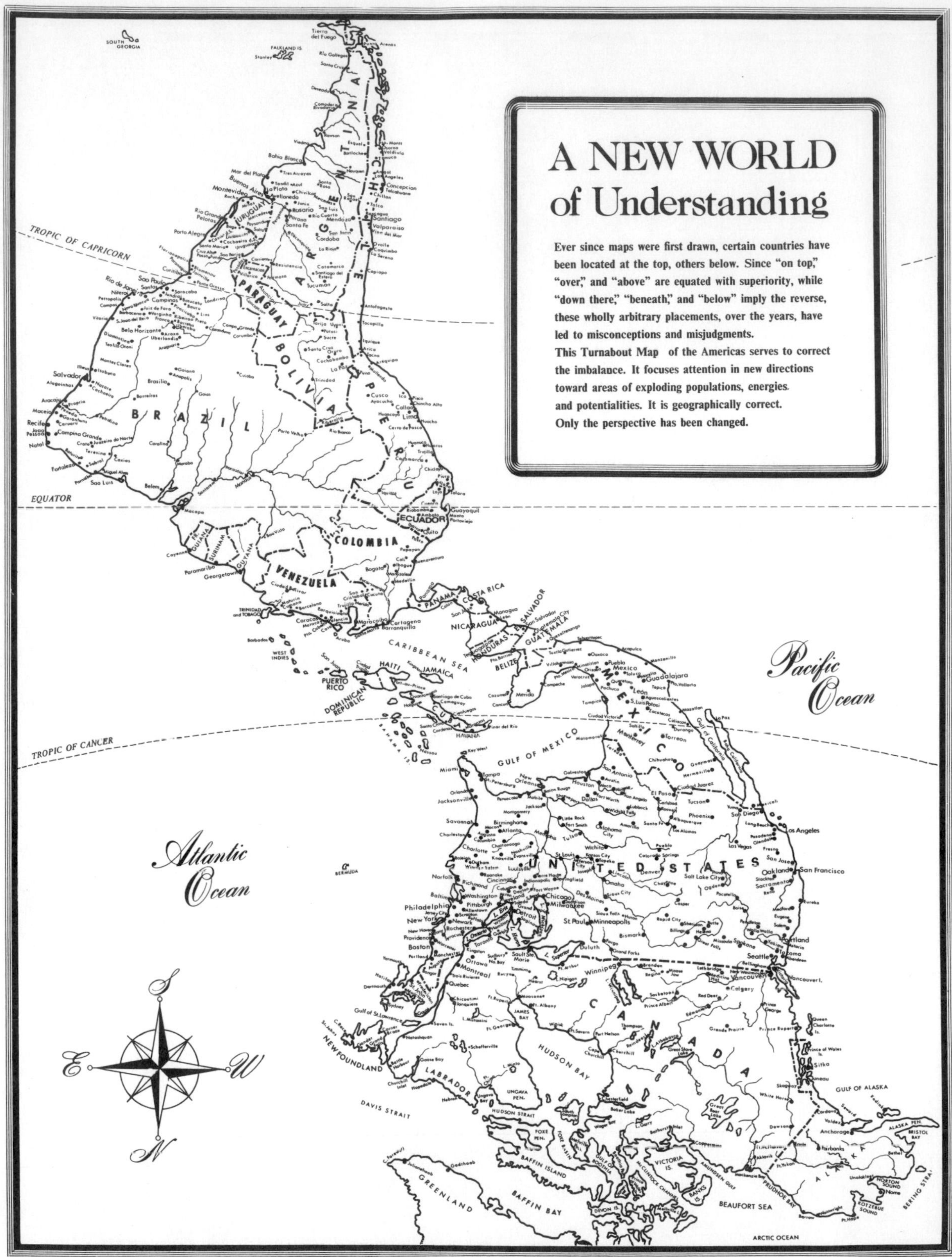

THE TURNABOUT MAP The way maps may reflect (and influence) our thinking is exemplified by the "Turnabout Map," which places the South Pole at the top and the North Pole at the bottom. Words and phrases such as "on top," "over," and "above" tend to be equated by some people with superiority. Turning things upside down may cause us to rethink the way North Americans regard themselves in relation to the people of Central America. © 1982 by Jesse Levine Turnabout Map™ —Dist. by Laguna Sales, Inc., 7040 Via Valverde, San Jose, CA 95135

ANTHROPOLOGY

PART I

THE STUDY OF HUMANKIND

INTRODUCTION

Anthropology is the most liberating of all the sciences. Not only has it exposed the fallacies of racial and cultural superiority, but also its devotion to the study of all peoples, regardless of where and when they lived, has cast more light on human nature than all the reflections of the sages or the studies of laboratory scientists. If this sounds like the assertion of an overly enthusiastic anthropologist, it is not; it was all said long ago in 1941 by the philosopher Grace de Laguna in her presidential address to the Eastern Division of the American Philosophical Association.

The subject matter of anthropology is vast, as we shall see in this book: It includes everything that has to do with human beings, past and present. Of course, many other disciplines are concerned in one way or another with human beings. Some, such as anatomy and physiology, study humans as biological organisms. The social sciences are concerned with the distinctive forms of human relationships, while the humanities examine the great achievements of human culture. Anthropologists are interested in all of these things, too, but they try to deal with them all together, in all places and times. It is this unique, broad perspective that equips anthropologists so well to deal with that elusive thing called human nature.

No single anthropologist is able to investigate personally everything that has to do with people. For practical purposes, the discipline is divided into various subfields, and individual anthropologists specialize in one or more of these. Whatever their specialization, though, they retain a commitment to a broader overall perspective on humankind. For example, cultural anthropologists specialize in the study of human ideas, values, and behavior, whereas physical anthropologists

specialize in the study of humans as biological organisms. Yet neither can afford to ignore the work of the other, for human culture and nature are inextricably intertwined, with each affecting the other in important ways. We can see, for example, how biology affects a cultural practice such as color-naming behavior. Human populations differ in the density of pigmentation within the eye itself, which in turn affects people's ability to distinguish the color blue from green, black, or both. Consequently, a number of cultures identify blue with green, black, or both. We can see also how a cultural practice may affect human biology, as exemplified by abnormal forms of hemoglobin, the substance that transports oxygen in the blood. In certain parts of Africa and Asia, when humans took up the practice of farming, they altered the ecology in a way that, by chance, created ideal conditions for the breeding of mosquitoes. As a result, malaria became a serious problem (mosquitoes carry the malarial parasite), and a biological response to this was the spread of certain genes that, in those people who inherit the gene from one parent, produced a built-in resistance to the disease. Although those who inherit the gene from both parents contract a potentially lethal anemia, such as sickle-cell anemia, those without the gene are apt to succumb to malaria. (We will take up this topic in Chapter 3.)

To begin our introduction to the study of anthropology, we will look closely at the nature of the discipline. In Chapter 1 we will see how the field of anthropology is subdivided, how the subdivisions relate to one another, and how they relate to the other sciences and humanities. Chapter 1 introduces us as well to the methods anthropologists use to study human cultures, especially those of today, or the very recent past. However, because the next two parts of the book take us far back into the human past, to see where we came from and how we got to be the way we are today, further discussion of methods used to study contemporary cultures is deferred to Parts V and VIII (especially Chapter 14). The very different methods used to find out about the ancient past are the subject of Chapter 2, which discusses the nature of fossils and archaeological materials, where they are found, how they are (quite literally) unearthed, and how they are dealt with once unearthed. From this, one can begin to appreciate what the evidence can tell us if handled properly, as well as its limitations. To understand what fossils have to tell us about our past, we need some knowledge of how biological evolution works. But fossils, unlike flesh-and-blood people, do not speak for themselves, and so they must be interpreted. If we are to have confidence in an interpretation of a particular fossil, we must be sure the interpretation is consistent with what we know about the workings of evolution; therefore, Chapter 3 is devoted to a discussion of evolution. With this done, we will have set the stage for our detailed look at human biological and cultural evolution in Parts II, III, and IV. ■

CHAPTER 1

THE NATURE OF ANTHROPOLOGY

In 1534, Jacques Cartier explored the St. Lawrence River for France, bringing him in contact with members of several native groups. Such contacts sparked the curiosity about other peoples that led to the development of anthropology.

CHAPTER PREVIEW

1

What Is Anthropology?

Anthropology, the study of humankind everywhere, throughout time, seeks to produce reliable knowledge about people and their behavior, both about what makes them different and about what they all have in common.

2

What Do Anthropologists Do?

Physical anthropologists study humans as biological organisms, tracing the evolutionary development of the human animal and looking at biological variation within the species, past and present. Cultural anthropologists are concerned with human cultures, or the ways of life in societies. Within the field of cultural anthropology are archaeologists, who seek to explain human behavior by studying material objects, usually from past cultures; linguists, who study languages, by which cultures are maintained and passed on to succeeding generations; and ethnologists, who study cultures as they have been observed, experienced, and discussed with people from those cultures.

How Do Anthropologists Do What They Do?

Anthropologists are concerned with the description and explanation of reality. By formulating and testing hypotheses, they hope to develop reliable theories—explanations supported by bodies of data—although they recognize that no theory is ever completely beyond challenge. To frame objective hypotheses that are as free of cultural bias as possible, anthropologists typically develop them through fieldwork that allows them to become so familiar with details of situations that they can recognize patterns inherent in the data. It is also through fieldwork that anthropologists test existing hypotheses and explain what is going on.

A common part of the mythology of all peoples is a legend that explains the appearance of humans on earth. Such myths, for example, are the accounts of creation recorded in the Bible's Book of Genesis. Another vastly different example, which nonetheless serves the same function, is the belief of the Nez Perce (a people native to the American Northwest) that humanity is the creation of Coyote, one of the animal people that inhabited the earth before humans. Coyote chased the giant beaver monster, Wishpoosh, in an epic chase whose trail formed the Columbia River. When Coyote caught Wishpoosh, he killed him and dragged his body to the riverbank. Ella Clark retells the story:

> With his sharp knife Coyote cut up the big body of the monster.
>
> "From your body, mighty Wishpoosh," he said, "I will make a new race of people. They will live near the shores of Big River and along the streams which flow into it."
>
> From the lower part of the animal's body, Coyote made people who were to live along the coast. "You shall live near the mouth of Big River and shall be traders."
>
> "You shall live along the coast," he said to others. "You shall live in villages facing the ocean and shall get your food by spearing salmon and digging clams. You shall always be short and fat and have weak legs."
>
> From the legs of the beaver monster he made the Klickitat Indians. "You shall live along the rivers that flow down from the big white mountain north of Big River. You shall be swift of foot and keen of wit. You shall be famous runners and great horsemen."
>
> From the arms of the monster he made the Cayuse Indians. "You shall be powerful with bow and arrows and with war clubs."
>
> From the ribs he made the Yakima Indians. "You shall live near the new Yakima River, east of the mountains. You shall be the helpers and the protectors of all the poor people."
>
> From the head he created the Nez Perce Indians. "You shall live in the valleys of the Kookooskia and Wallowa rivers. You shall be men of brains, great in council and in speech making. You shall also be skillful horsemen and brave warriors."
>
> Then Coyote gathered up the hair and blood and waste. He hurled them far eastward, over the big mountains. "You shall be the Snake River Indians," said Coyote. "You shall be people of blood and violence. You shall be buffalo hunters and shall wander far and wide."[1]

For as long as they have been on earth, people have sought answers to questions about who they are, where they come from, and why they act as they do. Throughout most of their history, though, people relied on myth and folklore for their answers to these questions, rather than the systematic testing of data obtained through careful observation. Anthropology, over the last 200 years, has emerged as a scientific approach to answering these questions. Simply stated, **anthropology** is the study of humankind in all places, and throughout time. The anthropologist is concerned primarily with a single species—*Homo sapiens*—the human species, its ancestors, and near relatives. Because anthropologists are members of the species being studied, it is difficult for them to maintain a scientific detachment toward those they study. This, of course, is part of a larger problem in science. As one of our leading scientists puts it,

> Nature is objective, and nature is knowable, but we can only view her through a glass darkly—and many clouds upon our vision are of our own making: social and cultural biases, psychological preferences, and mental limitations (in universal modes of thought, not just human stupidity).
>
> The human contribution to this equation of difficulty becomes ever greater as the subject under investigation comes closer to the heart of our practical and philosophical concerns.[2]

Since nothing comes closer to the heart of our practical and philosophical concerns than ourselves and others of our kind, can we ever hope to gain truly objective knowledge about peoples' behavior? Anthropologists worry about this a great deal but have found that by maintaining a critical awareness of their assumptions and constantly testing their conclusions against new sources of data, they can achieve a useful understanding of human behavior. By scientifically

[1]Clark, E. E. (1966). *Indian legends of the Pacific Northwest* (p. 174). Berkeley: University of California Press.

[2]Gould, S. J. (1996). *Full house* (p. 8). New York: Harmony Books.

Anthropology. The study of humankind, in all times and places.

FRANK HAMILTON CUSHING (1857–1900)
MATILDA COXE STEVENSON (1849–1915)

In the United States anthropology began in the 19th century when a number of dedicated amateurs went into the field to gain a better understanding of what many European Americans still regarded as "primitive people." Exemplifying their emphasis on firsthand observation is Frank Hamilton Cushing, who lived among the Zuni Indians for 4 years (he is shown here in full dress as a war chief).

Among these founders of North American anthropology were a number of women, whose work was highly influential among those who spoke out in the 19th century in favor of women's rights. One of these pioneering anthropologists was Matilda Coxe Stevenson, who also did fieldwork among the Zuni. In 1885, she founded the Women's Anthropological Society, the first professional association for women scientists. Three years later, she was hired by the Bureau of American Ethnology, making her one of the first women in the United States to hold a full-time position in science. The tradition of women being active in anthropology continues, and since World War II more than half the presidents of the American Anthropological Association have been women.

approaching how people live, anthropologists have learned an enormous amount, both about human differences and about the common humanity underlying those differences.

THE DEVELOPMENT OF ANTHROPOLOGY

Although works of anthropological significance have a considerable antiquity—two examples being the accounts of other peoples by the Greek historian Herodotus (written in the 5th century B.C.) or the North African scholar Arab Ibn Khaldun (written in the 14th century A.D.)—anthropology as a distinct field of inquiry is a relatively recent product of Western civilization. In the United States, for example, the first course in general anthropology to carry credit in a college or university (at the University of Rochester) was not offered until 1879. If people have always been concerned about themselves and their origins, and those of other people, why then did it take such a long time for a systematic discipline of anthropology to appear?

The answer to this is as complex as human history. In part, it relates to the limits of human technology. Throughout most of history, people have been restricted in their geographical horizons. Without the means of traveling to distant parts of the world, observation of cultures and peoples far from one's own was a difficult—if not impossible—venture. Extensive travel was usually the exclusive prerogative of a few; the study of foreign peoples and cultures was not likely to flourish until adequate modes of transportation and communication could be developed.

This is not to say that people have always been unaware of the existence of others in the world who look and act differently from themselves. The Old and New Testaments of the Bible, for example, are full of references to diverse peoples, among them Jews, Egyptians, Hittites, Babylonians, Ethiopians, Romans, and so forth. The differences between these peoples pale by comparison to those between any of them on the one hand and, for example, indigenous people of Australia, the Amazon forest, or arctic North America. With the means to travel to truly faraway places, it became possible to meet for the first time such radically different people. It was the massive encounter with hitherto unknown peoples, which came as Europeans sought to extend their trade and political domination to all parts of the world, that focused attention on human differences in all their glory.

Another significant element that contributed to the slow growth of anthropology was that Europeans only gradually came to recognize that beneath all the differences, they might share a basic humanity with people everywhere. Societies that did not share the fundamental cultural values of Europeans were labeled "savage" or "barbarian." It was not until the mid-18th century that a significant number of Europeans considered the behavior of such people to be at all relevant to an understanding of themselves. This growing interest in human diversity, coming at a time when there were increasing efforts to explain things in terms of natural laws, cast doubts on the traditional explanations based on authoritative texts such as the Torah, Bible, or Qu'ran.

Although anthropology originated within the historical context of European culture, it has long since gone global. Today, it is an exciting, transnational discipline whose practitioners are drawn from diverse societies all across the globe. Even societies that have long been studied by European and North American anthropologists—several African and Native American societies, for example—have produced anthropologists who continue to make their mark on the discipline. Their distinct perspectives help shed new light not only on their own cultures, but also on others, including Western societies.

Anthropologists are not all men, nor are they all European or European American. Mamphela Ramphele is a native South African anthropologist who studied the migrant labor hostels of Cape Town before moving on to high administration positions at the University of Cape Town and the World Bank.

ANTHROPOLOGY AND THE OTHER SCIENCES

It would be incorrect to conclude from the foregoing that serious attempts were never made to analyze human diversity before the 18th century. Anthropologists are not the only scholars who study people. In this respect they share their objectives with the other social and natural scientists. Anthropologists do not consider their findings in isolation from those of psychologists, economists, sociologists, or biologists; rather, they welcome the contributions these other disciplines have to make to the common goal of understanding humanity, and they gladly offer their own findings for the benefit of these other disciplines. Anthropologists do not expect, for example, to know as much about the structure of the human eye as anatomists, or as much about the perception of color as psychologists. As synthesizers, however, they are better prepared than any of their fellow scientists to understand how these relate to color-naming behavior in different human societies. Because they look for the broad basis of human ideas and practices without limiting themselves to any single social or biological aspect, anthropologists can acquire an especially broad and inclusive overview of the complex biological and cultural organism that is the human being.

THE DISCIPLINE OF ANTHROPOLOGY

Anthropology is traditionally divided into four fields: physical anthropology and the three branches of cultural anthropology: archaeology, linguistic anthropology, and ethnology. **Physical anthropology** is concerned primarily with humans as biological organisms, whereas **cultural anthropology** deals with humans as a culture-making species. Both are closely related; we cannot understand what people think and do unless we know how

Physical anthropology. The systematic study of humans as biological organisms. • **Cultural anthropology.** The branch of anthropology that focuses on humans as a culture-making species.

Anthropology Applied

Forensic Anthropology

In the public mind, anthropology is often identified with the recovery of the bones of remote human ancestors, the unearthing of ancient campsites and lost cities, or the study of present-day tribal peoples whose way of life is erroneously seen as being something out of the past. What people are often unaware of are the many practical applications of anthropological knowledge. One field of applied anthropology–known as **forensic anthropology**–specializes in the identification of human skeletal remains for legal purposes. Forensic anthropologists are routinely called upon by police and other authorities to identify the remains of murder victims, missing persons, or people who have died in disasters such as plane crashes or the terrorist attacks on the World Trade Center and the Pentagon. From skeletal remains, the forensic anthropologist can establish the age, sex, population affiliation, and stature of the deceased, and often whether they were right- or left-handed, exhibited any physical abnormalities, or had evidence of trauma (broken bones and the like). In addition, some details of an individual's health and nutritional history can be read from the bones.

Forensic anthropologist Laura Fulginiti gives advice on a human skull to an artist with the Maricopa County Sheriff's Department in Phoenix, Arizona.

One well-known forensic anthropologist is Clyde C. Snow, who has been practicing in this field for over 35 years, first for the Federal Aviation Administration and more recently as a freelance consultant. In addition to the usual police work, Snow has studied the remains of General George Armstrong Custer and his men from the 1876 battlefield at Little Big Horn, and in 1985, he went to Brazil, where he identified the remains of the notorious Nazi war criminal Josef Mengele. He was also instrumental in establishing the first forensic team devoted to documenting cases of human rights abuses around the world. This began in 1984 when he went to Argentina at the request of a newly elected civilian government as part of a team to help with the identification of remains of the *desaparecidos,* or "disappeared ones"–the 9,000 or more people who were eliminated by government death squads during 7 years of military rule. A year later, he returned to give expert testimony at the trial of nine junta members and to teach Argentineans how to recover, clean, repair, preserve, photograph, x-ray, and analyze bones. Besides providing factual accounts of the fate of victims to their surviving kin and refuting the assertions of revisionists that the massacres never happened, the work of Snow and his Argentinean associates was crucial in convicting several military officers of kidnapping, torture, and murder.

Since Snow's pioneering work, forensic anthropologists have become increasingly involved in the investigation of human rights abuses in all parts of the world–from Chile, to Guatemala, to Haiti, to the Philippines, to Iraqi Kurdistan, to Rwanda, to (most recently) Bosnia, Kosovo, and East Timor. Meanwhile, they continue to do important work for regular clients in the United States. Snow, for example, is regularly

Forensic anthropology. Field of applied physical anthropology that specializes in the identification of human skeletal remains for legal purposes.

consulted by the medical examiners' offices of Oklahoma; Cook County, Illinois; and the Federal Bureau of Investigation. Although not all cases he investigates involve abuse of police powers, when this is an issue, evidence provided by forensic anthropologists is often crucial for bringing the culprits to justice. To quote Snow: "Of all the forms of murder, none is more monstrous than that committed by a state against its own citizens. And of all murder victims, those of the state are the most helpless and vulnerable since the very entity to which they have entrusted their lives and safety becomes their killer."* Thus, it is especially important that states be called to account for their deeds.

*Joyce, C. (1991). *Witnesses from the grave: The stories bones tell.* Boston: Little, Brown.

people are made. And we want to know how biology does and does not influence culture, as well as how culture affects biology.

Physical Anthropology

Physical anthropology, also called *biological anthropology,* focuses on humans as biological organisms, and one of its many interests is human evolution. Whatever distinctions people may claim for themselves, they are mammals—specifically primates—and, as such, they have a common ancestry with other primates, most specifically apes and monkeys. Through analysis of fossils and observation of living primates, physical anthropologists try to reconstruct the ancestry of the human species in order to understand how, when, and why we became the kind of animal we are today.

Another major specialty of physical anthropology is the study of present-day human variation. Although we are all members of a single species, we differ from one another in many obvious and not so obvious ways. We differ not only in such visible traits as the color of our skin or the shape of our nose, but also in such biochemical factors as our blood type and our susceptibility to certain diseases. The physical anthropologist applies all the techniques of modern molecular biology to achieve fuller understanding of human variation and the ways in which it relates to the different environments in which people have lived.

Cultural Anthropology

Because the capacity for culture is rooted in our biological natures, there is an important link between physical and cultural anthropology. In order to understand the work of the cultural anthropologist, we must clarify what we mean when we speak of culture. The subject will be taken up in more detail in Chapter 14, but for our purposes here, we may think of culture as the often unconscious standards by which societies—structured groups of people—operate. These standards are socially learned rather than acquired through biological inheritance. Because they determine, or at least guide, the day-to-day behavior of the members of a society, human behavior is above all cultural behavior. The manifestations of culture may vary considerably from place to place, but no person is "more cultured" in the anthropological sense than any other.

Just as physical anthropology is closely related to the other biological sciences, cultural anthropology is closely related to the other social sciences. The one to which it has most often been compared is sociology, since the business of both is the description and explanation of behavior of people within a social context. Sociologists, however, have concentrated heavily on studies of people living in industrialized North American and European societies, thereby increasing the probability that their theories of human behavior will be **culture-bound:** that is, based on assumptions about the world and reality that are part of the sociologists' own Western culture. Because cultural anthropologists are largely products of the culture with which they grew up, they are also capable of culture-bound theorizing. However, they constantly seek to minimize the problem of bias by studying the whole of humanity in all times and places, and they do not limit themselves to the study of recent Western peoples; anthropologists have found that to fully understand the complex of human ideas and behavior, all humans, past and present, must be studied. More than any other feature, this unique cross-cultural and long-term historical perspective distinguishes cultural anthropology from the other social sciences. It provides anthropology with a far richer body of data than that of

Culture-bound. Theories about the world and reality based on the assumptions and values of one's own culture.

Sociologists conduct structured interviews and administer questionnaires to *respondents,* whereas psychologists experiment with *subjects.* Anthropologists, by contrast, learn from *informants.*

any other discipline that studies humankind, and it can also be applied to any current issue. As a case in point, consider the way infants in the United States are routinely made to sleep apart from their parents, their mothers in particular. To most North Americans, this may seem quite normal, but cross-cultural studies show that "co-sleeping" is the rule. Only in the past 200 years, generally in Western industrialized societies, has it been considered proper for mother and infant to sleep apart. In fact, it amounts to a cultural experiment in child rearing.

Recent studies have shown that this unusual degree of separation of mother and infant in Western societies has important consequences for both biology and behavior. For one thing, it increases the length of the infant's crying bouts, which may last in excess of 3 hours a day in the child's second and third month. Some mothers incorrectly interpret the cause as a deficiency in breast milk and switch to less healthy bottle-fed formulas, and in extreme cases, the crying may provoke physical abuse, sometimes with lethal effects. But the benefits of co-sleeping go beyond significant reductions in crying; infants also nurse more often and three times as long per feeding; they receive more stimuli (important for neurological development); and they are apparently less susceptible to sudden infant death syndrome ("crib death"). But there are benefits to the mother as well: Frequent nursing prevents early ovulation after childbirth, and she gets at least as much sleep as mothers who sleep apart from their infants.[3]

These benefits may lead one to ask: Why do so many mothers continue to sleep apart from their infants? In North America the cultural values of independence and consumerism come into play. To begin building unique individual identities, babies are provided with rooms (or at least space) of their own. At the same time, this provides a place to put all the toys, furniture, and other paraphernalia that signify that the parents are "good" and "caring" (and help keep the consumer economy humming along).

The emphasis cultural anthropology places on studies of ancient and more recent non-Western cultures has often led to findings that run counter to existing beliefs derived from Western studies. Thus, cultural anthropologists were the first to demonstrate "that the world does not divide into the pious and the superstitious; that there are sculptures in jungles and paintings in deserts; that political order is possible without centralized power and principled justice without codified rules; that the norms of reason were not fixed in Greece, the evolution of morality not consummated in England. We have, with no little success, sought to keep the world off balance; pulling out rugs, upsetting tea tables, setting off firecrackers. It has been the office of others to reassure; ours to unsettle."[4] Although the findings of cultural anthropologists have often challenged the conclusions of sociologists, psychologists, and economists, anthropology is absolutely indispensable to them, as it is the only consistent check against culture-bound assertions. In a sense, anthropology is to these disciplines what the laboratory is to physics and chemistry: an essential testing ground for their theories.

Cultural anthropology may be divided into the areas of archaeology, linguistic anthropology, and ethnology

[3]Barr, R. G. (1997, October). The crying game. *Natural History,* 47. Also McKenna, J. J. (1997, October). Bedtime story. *Natural History,* 50.

[4]Geertz, C. (1984). Distinguished lecture: Anti anti-relativism. *American Anthropologist, 86,* 275.

(often called sociocultural anthropology; see Figure 1.1). Although each has its own special interests and methods, all deal with cultural data. The archaeologist, the linguist, and the ethnologist take different approaches to the subject, but each gathers and analyzes data that are useful in explaining similarities and differences among human cultures, as well as the ways that cultures everywhere develop, adapt, and continue to change.

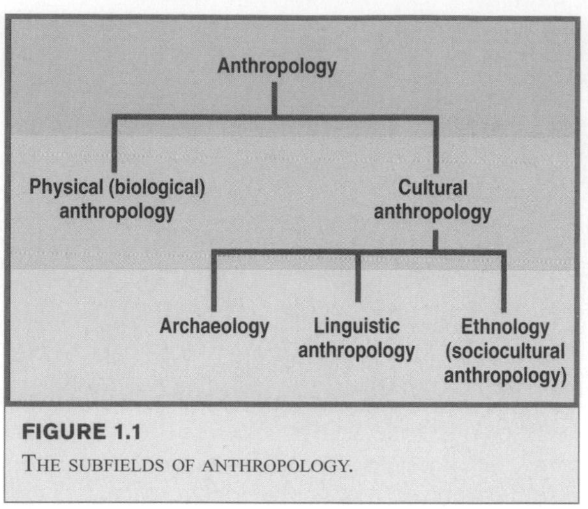

FIGURE 1.1
THE SUBFIELDS OF ANTHROPOLOGY.

Archaeology

Archaeology is the branch of cultural anthropology that studies material remains in order to describe and explain human behavior. Traditionally, it has focused on the human past, for material products and traces of human practices, rather than the practices themselves, are all that survive of that past. The archaeologist studies the tools, pottery, and other enduring features such as hearths and enclosures that remain as the testimony of earlier cultures, some of them 2.5 million years old. Such objects, and the way they were left in the ground, reflect aspects of human behavior. For example, shallow, restricted concentrations of charcoal that include oxidized earth, bone fragments, and charred plant remains, and near which are pieces of fire-cracked rock, pottery, and tools suitable for food preparation, are indicative of cooking and associated food processing. From such remains much can be learned about a people's diet and subsistence practices. Thus the archaeologist is able to find out about human behavior in the past, far beyond the mere 5,000 years to which historians are ultimately limited by their dependence upon written records. But archaeologists are not limited to the study of prehistoric societies; they may also study those for which historical documents are available to supplement the material remains that people left behind. In most literate societies, written records are associated with governing elites rather than with people at the grass roots. Thus, although they can tell archaeologists

The discovery by geologists in the 18th and 19th centuries that the world was far older than most Europeans thought paved the way for the anthropological exploration of past cultures and peoples.

Archaeology. The study of material remains, usually from the past, to describe and explain human behavior.

Although history tells us something of the horrors of slavery in North America, the full horror is revealed only by archaeological investigation of the African burial ground in New York. Even young children were worked so far beyond their ability to endure that their spines actually fractured.

much that they might not know from archaeological evidence alone, it is equally true that archaeological remains can tell historians much about a society that is not apparent from its written documents.

Although most archaeologists have concentrated on the human past, some are concerned with the study of material objects in contemporary settings. One example is the University of Arizona's "Garbage Project," which, by a carefully controlled study of household waste, continues to produce information about contemporary social issues. Among its accomplishments, the project has tested the validity of interview-survey techniques, upon which sociologists, economists, other social scientists, and policymakers rely heavily for their data. The tests clearly show a significant difference between what people believe or say they do and what garbage analysis shows they actually do. For example, in 1973, conventional techniques were used to construct and administer a questionnaire to find out about the rate of alcohol consumption in Tucson. In one part of town, 15 percent of respondent households affirmed consumption of beer, but no household reported consumption of more than eight cans a week. Analysis of garbage from the same area, however, demonstrated that some beer was consumed in over 80 percent of households, and 50 percent discarded more than eight empty cans a week. Another interesting finding of the Garbage Project is that when beef prices reached an all-time high in 1973, so did the amount of beef wasted by households (not just in Tucson but in other parts of the country as well). Although common sense would lead us to suppose just the opposite, high prices and scarcity correlate with more, rather than less, waste. Obviously, such findings are important, for they demonstrate that ideas about human behavior based on conventional interview-survey techniques alone can be seriously in error. Likewise, they show that what people actually do does not always match with what they think they do.

In 1987, the Garbage Project began a program of test excavations in landfills in different parts of the country. From this work came the first reliable data on what materials actually go into landfills and what happens to them there. And once again, common beliefs turn out to be at odds with the actual situation. For example, biodegradable materials such as newspapers take far longer to decay when buried in deep compacted landfills than anyone had previously expected. Needless to say, this kind of information is vital if the United States is ever to solve its waste-disposal problems.

Linguistic Anthropology

Perhaps the most distinctive feature of humanity is the ability to speak. Humans are not alone in the use of symbolic communication. Studies have shown that the sounds and gestures made by some other animals—especially by apes—may serve functions comparable to those of human speech; yet no other animal has developed a system of symbolic communication as complex as that of humans. Ultimately, language is what allows people to preserve and transmit their culture from generation to generation.

The branch of cultural anthropology that studies human languages is called **linguistic anthropology.** Linguists may deal with the description of a language (the way a sentence is formed or a verb conjugated) or with the history of languages (the way languages develop and change one another with the passage of time). Both approaches yield valuable information, not only about how people communicate but also about how they understand the world around them. The everyday language of English-speaking North Americans, for example, includes a number of slang words, such as *dough, greenback, dust, loot, cash, bucks, change,* and *bread,* to identify what an indigenous native of Papua New Guinea would recognize only as "money." Such phenomena help identify things that are considered of special importance to a culture. Through the study of language in its social setting, the anthropologist is able to understand how people perceive themselves and the world around them.

Anthropological linguists may also make a significant contribution to our understanding of the human past. By working out the genealogical relationships among languages and examining the distributions of those languages, they may estimate how long the speakers of those languages have lived where they do. By identifying those words in related languages that have survived from an ancient ancestral tongue, they can also suggest both where and how the speakers of the ancestral language lived.

Ethnology

As the archaeologist has commonly concentrated on cultures of the past, so the **ethnologist,** or sociocultural anthropologist, concentrates on cultures of the present. And unlike the archaeologist, who focuses on the study of material objects to learn about human behavior, the ethnologist concentrates on the study of human ideas and practices as they can be seen, experienced, and even discussed with those whose culture is to be understood.

Fundamental to the ethnologist's approach is **ethnography.** Whenever possible, the ethnologist becomes ethnographer by living among the people under study. The intent of such fieldwork is not just to describe their culture but to explain as well relationships among its various aspects. Through **participant observation**—eating a people's food, speaking their language, and personally experiencing their habits and customs—the ethnographer seeks to understand their way of life to a far greater extent than any nonparticipant anthropologist or other social scientist ever could; one learns a culture best by learning how to behave acceptably in the society in which one is doing fieldwork. To become a participant observer in the culture under study does not mean that the ethnographer must join in a people's battles in order to study a culture in which warfare is prominent; but by living among a warlike people, the ethnographer should be able to understand how warfare fits into the overall cultural framework. He or she must be a careful observer in order to get an in-depth overview of a culture without placing undue emphasis on one of its parts at the expense of another. Only by discovering how all cultural institutions—social, political, economic, religious—relate to one another can the ethnographer begin to understand the cultural system. Anthropologists refer to this as the **holistic perspective,** and it is one of the fundamental principles of anthropology. Robert Gordon, an anthropologist from Namibia, speaks of it this way: "Whereas the sociologist or the political scientist might examine the beauty of a flower petal by petal, the anthropologist is the person that stands on the top of the mountain and looks at the beauty of the field. In other words, we try and go for the wider perspective."[5]

When participating in an unfamiliar culture, the ethnographer does not just blunder about blindly but enlists the assistance of individual **informants.** These are members of the society in which the anthropologist as ethnographer is working, with whom she or he develops close relationships, and who help the anthropologist as a newcomer in the community unravel whatever activities are taking place. As a child learns proper behavior from its parents, so do informants help the anthropologist in the field unravel the mysteries of what is, at first, a strange culture.

[5]Gordon, R. (1981, December). [Interview for Coast Telecourses, Inc.]. Los Angeles.

Linguistic anthropology. The branch of cultural anthropology that studies human language. • **Ethnologist.** An anthropologist who studies cultures from a comparative or historical point of view, utilizing ethnographic accounts. • **Ethnography.** The systematic description of a particular culture based on firsthand observation. • **Participant observation.** In ethnography, the technique of learning a people's culture through direct participation in their everyday life over an extended period of time. • **Holistic perspective.** A fundamental principle of anthropology, that the various parts of culture must be viewed in the broadest possible context in order to understand their interconnections and interdependence. • **Informants.** Members of a society in which the ethnographer works who help interpret what she or he sees taking place.

So basic is ethnographic fieldwork to ethnology that the British anthropologist C. G. Seligman once asserted, "Field research in anthropology is what the blood of the martyrs is to the church."[6] Something of its flavor is conveyed by the experience of Luis Vivanco, a young anthropologist working in the field for the first time. In particular, the following Original Study illustrates the impossibility of going into the field free of all naïveté, the importance of "the unexpected" in the field, how such events lead to new understanding, and the importance of freeing oneself from the assumptions and biases of one's own culture. It is also illustrative of anthropology's interest in global issues.

[6]Lewis, I. M. (1976). *Social anthropology in perspective* (p. 27). Harmondsworth, England: Penguin.

Encountering Environmentalism in Rural Costa Rica[7]

Original Study

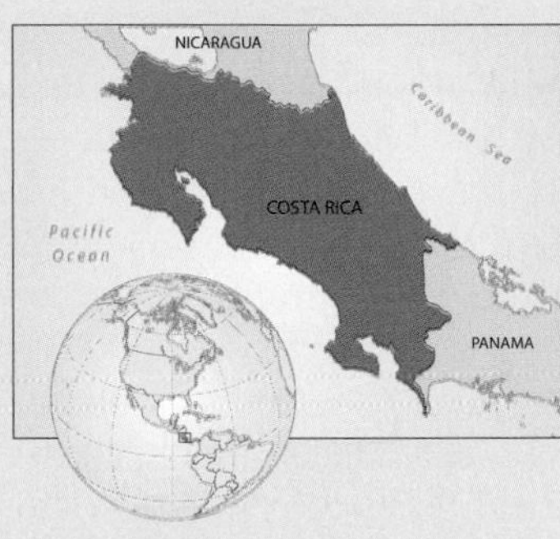

Several weeks into my first ethnographic fieldwork project in rural Costa Rica, I woke up one morning, rolled over in bed and groaned to myself "I hope nothing happens today!" This was not so much because I wanted a day off from work, but because of all the "work" I needed to do, especially writing up all those raw fieldnotes piling up next to my laptop. It seemed as though one moment I was trying desperately to record or figure out the significance of something I just heard or saw, when something new would happen. I would find myself hurtling off on some other inquiry or follow-up, wondering if it would be a dead-end or take me far from my accumulating collection of investigative loose ends and unfinished notes. To my frustration, something did happen that day, and more notes had to be written. I learned to live with this persistent ambivalence, but then I had one of those occasional epiphanies in which one of these unexpected events has a curious way of circling around and helping to reel in some of the loose ends floating around.

Late one afternoon, a couple of months after that desperate morning, my friend Manuel Azofeifa and I returned from working at the Reserva San Miguel cloud forest preserve as we usually did, walking the six kilometers by dirt road to the village of San Miguel where we lived. There were no tourists in their rental cars from whom we could hitch a ride—one of the few forms of motorized transportation on this quiet back road—and we settled into the routine of brisk walk and conversation (in other words, an uninterrupted chance to ask questions related to my research on the cultural dynamics of nature conservation and ecotourism, an opportunity I now relished as the road unfolded in front of us). Several kilometers ahead we heard the

Anthropologist Luis Vivanco, with cloud forest in the background.

[7]Vivanco, L. M. (2000). ***Encountering environmentalism in rural Costa Rica.*** © by author, Department of Anthropology, University of Vermont, Burlington.

Original Study

sounds of motorcycles and cars on the road, and his (not my) hopes for a ride rose. Within a couple of minutes the vehicles sped by us, heading purposefully in the direction from which we came, toward the Reserva San Miguel. We knew the motorcycle riders, one of whom was a naturalist tour guide and the other a forest guard for an area of the cloud forest preserve. Following closely behind them was the local Rural Police officer, who sped by in his jeep with a preoccupied look on his face. We wondered where they could be going, especially since the Reserva San Miguel was closed for the day, and aside from the cloud forest preserve there were only a few dairy farms in the area.

Several minutes later, two middle-aged San Miguel residents pulled up in a jeep, and upon recognizing us, they stopped to greet us. They were excited, even giddy. One of them asked us if we had heard about the *len que estaba encaramado* (the puma that was driven up a tree) on Pedro Solrzano's land, a dairy *finca* (farm) several kilometers from Reserva San Miguel in a remote area known as Bajos de Santa Clara. We admitted that we had no idea, and they invited us to join them to go see it. In the car, one of the men, Don Eugenio, explained that the word around San Miguel was that a puma had attacked some of Solrzano's farm animals and that his dog chased it up a tree, where it still remained this afternoon. Apparently Solrzano had threatened to kill the animal, but had contacted regional environmental conservation organizations. Their representatives had been out there all day trying to prevent him from killing the cat. For this reason, the excitement in the jeep had a tinge of nervousness, knowing the harsh fines and possible prison sentence for Solrzano if he killed the animal.

When we arrived at the entrance to Solrzano's property, a North American man building an ecotourism hotel nearby confronted us and announced that he would not allow us to enter the farm, since the policeman asked him to keep people out. Even though the North American was holding a gun (an unusual sight here) and seemed suspicious of our intentions, Don Eugenio and companions scoffed—they had known Solrzano for many years, and this guy was a newcomer—and we entered the farm. After several minutes walking across pastures and squeezing through barbed-wire fences, we approached a patch of cloud forest on the edge of which several forest guards were sitting and laughing loudly. No one was surprised or offended that we had arrived, and after hearty greetings they motioned us to enter the forest where seven or eight other people were milling about, periodically looking up. They too were not surprised we had come, although unlike the joviality on the forest edge, the tension here was palpable. About thirty feet up, sure enough, was the puma, a large male that was nervously peering down on us from a moss-covered tree branch.

There was a feeling of expectation in the assembled crowd, each of us waiting for something to happen. True to his reputation as a locally famous hunter, the policeman turned to Don Eugenio and in a low voice remarked (wistfully, I thought) that he could hit it using his rifle, as he had done several times before with cats at this distance. But then he explained in a louder voice that it was against the law for anyone, including himself, to kill a puma. This animal was *patrimonio nacional* (national patrimony), defined as such by recently passed wildlife protection laws. But the reason Solrzano called all these people to his farm was not to tangle with the law. As Solrzano said, he too is a *conservacionista*, and "it would hurt me to have to kill the puma, because we aren't here to destroy things." At the same time, however, he felt that someone needed to take responsibility for his losses and to compensate him for not taking revenge on the cat: "We *campesinos* have been damaged by animals for a long time, and it would set a good example if the environmentalists would help us live with these animals." The traditional reaction to situations like this in rural Costa Rica, my companions told me, had always been to unceremoniously kill the puma. But Solrzano chose to call the San Miguel Conservation Association because he knew that it had paid financial compensations for losses to jaguars and pumas to *campesinos* like himself on several occasions in the past. Association employees who were involved were aware of the previous precedents of financial compensation, but also were aware of the steep fiscal crisis their organization, once deluged with foreign funds, was experiencing as those funds dried up. Costa Rica, it seems, was not so hot anymore for international conservation investments, and Association employees were nervous Solrzano would ask for money.

After we waited around for another half-hour, the president of the San Miguel Conservation Association's board of directors, who is a North American biologist, entered the forest patch with an air of authority, followed by a small entourage of subordinates and an older foreign man that nobody recognized. The biologist-president introduced Solrzano to the older man, a Swiss national who owns a small zoo in the Guanacaste lowlands (several hours away) that rehabilitates and maintains large cats and shows them to tourists. A circle formed in the center of the forest patch, around Solrzano and the Swiss man. Recognizing his opportunity, Solrzano histrionically pointed at the cat above, and declared, "I hear you buy pumas. Well, I have one and I want to sell it! You pay in dollars or *colones*?!" (Colones are the Costa Rican national currency.) Amidst the ensuing laughter, the man responded that he already had four pumas. He added that he was in no position to buy this one since the Costa Rican government would fine him for illegally trading in wildlife. Solrzano asked him how much he thought the cat was worth. The Swiss man responded that it would be difficult to get it down: even though they had access to a gun that shoots tranquilizer darts, it would not be wise to shoot the cat since it would be hurt by the fall. He then admonished Solrzano, "You should want the cat to go free since it belongs to no one and it would serve conservation. If you want my counsel, learn to live with it." Again, Solrzano pushed, "It's an expensive cat, but I can give you a good deal!" More laughter.

Solrzano quickly grew impatient with the man's lack of spirit for dealing. As the Swiss man began to lecture the rest of us on puma behavior, Solrzano stalked away to survey the cat's half-eaten victims again, taking the biologist-president with him. The biologist told me later that it was then that they reached a solution to the dilemma. Both of them knew the Conservation Association could not pay damages, but he also recognized Solrzano's problem and felt that if North Americans and environmentalists like him wanted to help save Costa Rican wildlife and wilderness they would have to be willing to make some compromises. So he ended up taking money from his own account to help Solrzano build some new cages to protect his remaining animals, hoping this would not encourage too many other farmers to make claims for lost animals.

When I got home late that night, I felt troubled by what I had witnessed—wondering what would happen to the puma and Solrzano, and why the environmentalists had seemed so unable or unwilling to do anything. I determined to do some follow-up research and interviews, honoring my gut feeling that something significant had just happened. After talking to the different actors and beginning to mentally connect this situation to others I had observed or researched, I realized that this encounter on Solrzano's farm was a power-laden negotiation, not simply over the life of a puma, but over the meanings of nature, its conservation, and who counts as an environmentalist. As I had seen happening in other social contexts in San Miguel, but had not yet been able to articulate, Solrzano had approached a boundary (one that tends to define him and other rural Costa Rican farmers not as environmentalists, but commonly as enemies of nature) and was trying to redefine what counts as an "environmental" issue so that it includes his needs. By turning the negotiation over a puma into a negotiation over compensation, both he and the biologist were recognizing that as long as people like himself live in the fluid boundaries between nature and society, others (such as the neighbor building his ecotourism hotel) are making a profit at his expense. And, perhaps uncharacteristically for some environmental activists, this biologist entered the negotiation on the farmer's terms instead of balking at it.

My initial ambivalence with fieldwork, I also realized, was based on an unexamined assumption that I could understand the dynamics of "culture" by taking snapshots of it, or seeing these dynamics as frozen bits and pieces. But ethnographic knowledge grows in increments and by fits and starts, and one does not just fill in the gaps that exist between snapshots. Like culture itself, fieldwork is an open-ended and emergent process, where such power-laden, but accidental and unexpected, encounters like this one lead to more complicated understandings and bring diverse loose ends together. Not that I never again woke up to roll over and groan, "I hope nothing happens today," but that was because that pile of raw fieldnotes never seemed to disappear.

The End

The popular image of ethnographic fieldwork is that it takes place among far-off, exotic peoples. To be sure, much ethnographic work has been done in places like Africa, the islands of the Pacific Ocean, the deserts of Australia, and so on. One very good reason for this is that non-Western peoples have been ignored too often by other social scientists. Still, anthropologists have recognized from the start that an understanding of human behavior depends upon knowledge of all cultures and peoples, including their own. During the years of the Great Depression and World War II, for example, many anthropologists in the United States worked in settings ranging from factories to whole communities. One of the landmark studies of this period was W. Lloyd Warner's study of "Yankee City" (Newburyport, Massachusetts). Less well known is that it was Philleo Nash, an anthropologist who was on the White House staffs of Presidents Roosevelt and Truman, who was instrumental in desegregating the armed forces and moving the federal government into the field of civil rights. Nash put his anthropological expertise to work to accomplish a particular goal, an example of **applied anthropology.** Later he served as lieutenant governor of Wisconsin and as Indian Affairs Commissioner in President Kennedy's administration. Today, numerous anthropologists work outside of academic settings as applied anthropologists, and examples of their work are provided in succeeding chapters of this book.

In the 1950s, the availability of large sums of money for research in foreign lands diverted attention from work at home. Later, as political unrest made fieldwork increasingly difficult to carry out, there was renewed awareness of important anthropological problems that need to be dealt with in North American society. Many of these problems involve people whom anthropologists have studied in other settings. Thus, as people from South and Central America have moved into the cities and suburbs of the United States, or as refugees have arrived from Haiti, Southeast Asia, and other places, anthropologists have been there not just to study them but to help them adjust to their new circumstances. Simultaneously, anthropologists are applying the same research techniques that served them so well in the study of non-Western peoples to the study of such diverse things as street gangs, corporate bureaucracies, religious cults, health care delivery systems, schools, and how people deal with consumer complaints.

An important discovery from such research is that it produces knowledge that usually does not emerge from the kinds of research done by other social scientists. For example, the theory of cultural deprivation arose during the 1960s as a way of explaining the educational failure of many children of ethnic minorities. In order to account for their lack of educational achievement, some social scientists proposed that such children were "culturally deprived." They then proceeded to "confirm" this idea by studying children—mostly from Native American, African American, and Hispanic populations—interpreting the results through the framework of their theory. By contrast, ethnographic research on the cultures of "culturally deprived" children reveals a different story. Far from being culturally deprived, they have elaborate, sophisticated, and adaptive cultures that are simply different from the ones espoused by the educational system. Although some still cling to it, the cultural-deprivation theory is culture-bound and is merely a way of saying that people are "deprived" of "my culture." One cannot argue that such children do not speak adequate Spanish, African American vernacular English (sometimes called Ebonics or Black English), or whatever; clearly they do well the things that are considered important in *their* cultures.

Much though it has to offer, the anthropological study of one's own culture is not without its own special problems. Sir Edmund Leach, a major figure in British anthropology, once put it this way:

> Surprising though it may seem, fieldwork in a cultural context of which you already have intimate firsthand experience seems to be much more difficult than fieldwork which is approached from the naïve viewpoint of a total stranger. When anthropologists study facets of their own society their vision seems to become distorted by prejudices which derive from private rather than public experience.[8]

Although the ethnographer strives to get an inside view of another culture, he or she does so very self-consciously as an outsider. The most successful anthropological studies of their own culture by North Americans have been done by those who first worked in some other

[8] Leach, E. (1982). *Social anthropology* (p. 24). Glasgow, Scotland: Fontana Paperbacks.

Applied anthropology. The use of anthropological knowledge and methods to solve practical problems, often for a specific client.

culture. Lloyd Warner, for example, had studied the Murngin aborigines of Australia before he tackled Newburyport, Massachusetts. The more one learns of other cultures, the more one gains a different perspective on one's own. Put another way, as other cultures come to be seen as less exotic, the more exotic one's own becomes. In addition to getting ourselves outside of our own culture before trying to study it ourselves (so that we may see ourselves as *others* see us), much is to be gained by encouraging anthropologists from Africa, Asia, and South America to do fieldwork in North America. From their outsiders' perspective come insights all too easily overlooked by an insider. This is not to say that the special difficulties of studying one's own culture cannot be overcome; what is required is an acute awareness of those difficulties.

Although ethnographic fieldwork is basic to ethnology, it is not the sole occupation of the ethnologist. Largely descriptive in nature, ethnography provides the basic data the ethnologist (who is more theoretically oriented) may then use to study one particular aspect of a culture by comparing it with that same aspect in others. Anthropologists constantly make such cross-cultural comparisons, and this is another hallmark of the discipline. Interesting insights into one's own beliefs and practices may come from cross-cultural comparisons, as when one compares the time that people devote to what North Americans consider to be "housework." In the United States, there is a widespread belief that the ever-increasing output of household appliance consumer goods has resulted in a steady reduction in housework, with a consequent increase in leisure time. Thus, consumer appliances have become important indicators of a high standard of living. Anthropological research among food foragers (people who rely on wild plant and animal resources for subsistence), however, has shown that they work far less at household tasks, and indeed less at all subsistence pursuits, than do people in industrialized societies. Aboriginal Australian women, for example, devote an average of approximately 20 hours per week to collecting and preparing food, as well as other domestic chores. By contrast, women in the rural United States in the 1920s, without the benefit of laborsaving appliances, devoted approximately 52 hours a week to their housework. One might suppose that this has changed over the decades since, yet some 50 years later, urban U.S. women who were not working for wages outside their homes were putting 55 hours a week into their housework; this despite all their "laborsaving" dishwashers, washing machines, clothes dryers, vacuum cleaners, food processors, and microwave ovens.[9]

Cross-cultural comparisons highlight alternative ways of doing and thinking about things and so have much to offer North Americans, large numbers of whom, opinion polls show, continue to worry about the effectiveness of their own ways of doing things. In this sense, one may think of ethnology as the study of alternative ways of doing things. At the same time, by making systematic cross-cultural comparisons of cultures, ethnologists seek to arrive at valid conclusions concerning the nature of culture in all times and places.

ANTHROPOLOGY AND SCIENCE

The foremost concern of all anthropologists is the detailed and comprehensive study of humankind. Anthropology has been called a social or a behavioral science by some, a natural science by others, and one of the humanities by still others. Can the work of the anthropologist properly be labeled "scientific"? What exactly do we mean by the term *science*?

Science is a carefully honed way of producing knowledge that seeks to explain or understand the underlying logic, the structural processes, that make the world tick. Science is a creative endeavor that seeks testable explanations for observed phenomena, ideally in terms of the workings of hidden but universal and immutable principles, or laws. Two basic ingredients are essential for this: imagination and skepticism. Imagination, though capable of leading us astray, is required in order that we may recognize unexpected ways phenomena might be ordered and think of old things in new ways. Without it, there can be no science. Skepticism is what allows us to distinguish **fact** from fancy, to test our speculations, and to prevent our imaginations from running away with us.

In their search for explanations, scientists do not assume that things are always as they appear on the surface. After all, what could be more obvious than that the earth is a stable entity, around which the sun travels every day? And yet, it isn't so. Religious and metaphysical

[9]Bodley, J. H. (1985). *Anthropology and contemporary human problems* (2nd ed., p. 69). Palo Alto, CA: Mayfield.

Fact. An observation verified by several observers skilled in the necessary techniques of observation.

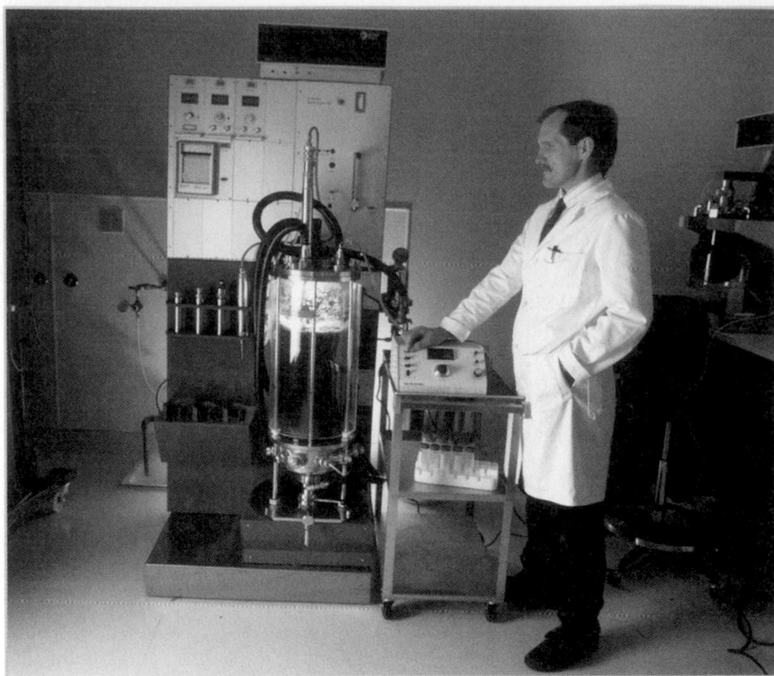

To many people, a scientist is someone (usually a White male) who works in a laboratory, carrying out experiments with the aid of specialized equipment. Contrary to the stereotypical image, not all scientists work in laboratories, nor is experimentation the only technique they use (nor are scientists invariably White males in lab coats).

explanations are rejected, as are all explanations and appeals to any authority that are not supported by strong empirical (observational) evidence. Because explanations are constantly challenged by new observations and novel ideas, science is self-correcting; that is, inadequate explanations are sooner or later shown up as such, to be replaced by more reliable explanations.

The scientist begins with a **hypothesis,** or a hunch about the possible relationship between certain observed facts. By gathering various kinds of data that seem to support such generalizations, and, equally important, by showing that alternative hypotheses may be proved wrong or eliminated from consideration, the scientist arrives at a system of validated hypotheses, or **theory.** Thus a theory, contrary to popular use of the term, is more than mere speculation; it is a carefully tested explanation of observed reality. Even so, no theory is ever considered to be beyond challenge. Truth in science is not considered to be absolute but rather a matter of varying degrees of probability; what is considered to be true is what is most probable. This is just as true in anthropology as it is in biology or physics. But although nothing can be proved to be absolutely true, incorrect assumptions can be proved false. Indeed, if a theory (or hypothesis) is not potentially falsifiable, it cannot be considered scientific. So it is that, as our knowledge expands, the odds in favor of some theories over others are generally increased, even though old truths sometimes must be discarded as alternative theories are shown to be more probable.

By way of illustration, we may compare two competing theories that sought to explain the fact of biological evolution: those of Charles R. Darwin and his predecessor, Jean Baptiste Lamarck. The latter's theory "explained" how evolution worked through inheritance of acquired characteristics, as opposed to Darwin's theory of natural selection. Experiments such as those of August Weismann near the start of the 20th century effectively laid to rest Lamarck's theory. Breeding 20 generations of mice, Weismann cut off the tails in each generation, only to find them still present in the 21st. By contrast, not only have countless attempts to falsify Darwin's theory failed to do so, but as our knowledge of genetics, geology, and paleontology has improved in the 20th century, our understanding of how natural selection works has advanced accordingly. Thus, although Lamarck's theory had to be abandoned, evidence has increased the probability that Darwin's is correct.

Hypothesis. A tentative explanation of the relation between certain phenomena. • **Theory.** In science, an explanation of natural phenomena, supported by a reliable body of data.

FRANZ BOAS (1858–1942)
FREDRIC WARD PUTNAM (1839–1915)
JOHN WESLEY POWELL (1834–1902)

In North America, anthropology among the social sciences has a unique character, owing in large part to the natural science (rather than social science) background of the three men pictured here. Franz Boas (top), educated in physics, was not the first to teach anthropology in the United States, but it was he and his students, with their insistence on scientific rigor, who made such courses a common part of college and university curricula. Putnam (middle), a zoologist specializing in the study of birds and fishes, and permanent secretary of the American Association for the Advancement of Science, made a decision in 1875 to devote himself to the promotion of anthropology. It was through his efforts that many of the great anthropology museums were established: at the University of California (now the Phoebe Hearst Museum), at Harvard University (the Peabody Museum), and the Field Museum in Chicago; in New York he founded the anthropology department of the American Museum of Natural History. Powell (bottom) was a geologist and founder of the United States Geological Survey, but he also carried out ethnographic and linguistic research (his classification of Indian languages north of Mexico is still consulted by scholars today). In 1879, he founded the Bureau of American Ethnology (ultimately absorbed by the Smithsonian Institution), thereby establishing anthropology within the U.S. government.

Difficulties of the Scientific Approach

Straightforward though the scientific approach may seem, there are serious difficulties in its application in anthropology. One problem is that once one has stated a hypothesis, one is strongly motivated to verify it, and this can lead to unwittingly overlooking negative evidence as well as other unexpected discoveries. This is a familiar problem in science; as paleontologist Stephen Jay Gould puts it, "The greatest impediment to scientific innovation is usually a conceptual lock, not a factual lock."[10] In the fields of cultural anthropology there is a further difficulty: In order to arrive at useful theories concerning human behavior, one must begin with hypotheses that are as objective and as little culture-bound as possible. And here lies a major—some would say insurmountable—problem: It is difficult for someone who has grown up in one culture to frame hypotheses about others that are not culture-bound.

[10]Gould, S. J. (1989). *Wonderful life* (p. 226). New York: Norton.

As one example of this sort of problem, we may look at attempts by archaeologists to understand the nature of settlement in the Classic period of Maya civilization. This civilization flourished between A.D. 250 and 900 in what is now northern Guatemala, Belize, and adjacent portions of Mexico and Honduras. Today much of this region is covered by a dense tropical forest of the sort that people of European background find difficult to manage. In recent times this forest has been inhabited by few people, who sustain themselves through slash-and-burn farming. (After cutting and burning the natural vegetation, crops are grown for 2 years or so before fertility is exhausted, and a new field must be cleared.) Yet numerous archaeological sites, featuring temples sometimes as tall as modern 20-story buildings, other sorts of monumental architecture, and carved stone monuments are to be found there. Because of their cultural bias against tropical forests as places to prosper, and against slash-and-burn farming as a means of raising sufficient food, North American and European archaeologists asked the question: How could the Maya have maintained large, permanent settlements on the basis of slash-and-burn farming? The answer seemed self-evident—they couldn't; therefore, the great archaeological sites must have been ceremonial centers inhabited by few, if any, people. Periodically a rural peasantry, scattered in small hamlets over the countryside, must have gathered in these centers for rituals or to provide labor for their construction and maintenance.

This view was the dominant one for several decades, and it was not until 1960 that archaeologists working at Tikal, one of the largest of all Maya sites, decided to ask the simplest and least biased questions they could think of: Did anyone live at this particular site on a permanent basis? If so, how many, and how were they supported? Working intensively over the next decade, with as few preconceived notions as possible, the archaeologists were able to establish that Tikal was a large settlement inhabited on a permanent basis by tens of thousands of people, who were supported by forms of agriculture more productive than slash-and-burn alone. It was this work at Tikal that proved wrong the older culture-bound ideas and paved the way for a new understanding of Classic Maya civilization.

By recognizing the potential problems of framing hypotheses that are not culture-bound, anthropologists have relied heavily on a technique that has proved successful in other fields of the natural sciences. As did the archaeologists working at Tikal, they immerse themselves in the data to the fullest extent possible. By doing so, they become so thoroughly familiar with the minute details that they can begin to see patterns inherent in the data, many of which might otherwise have been overlooked. These patterns are what allow the anthropologist to frame hypotheses, which then may be subjected to further testing.

This approach is most easily seen in ethnographic fieldwork, but it is just as important in archaeology. Unlike many social scientists, the ethnographer usually does not go into the field armed with prefigured questionnaires; rather, he or she recognizes that there are probably all sorts of unexpected issues, to be found out only by maintaining as open a mind as one can. This is not to say that anthropologists never use questionnaires, for sometimes they do. Generally, though, they use them as a means of supplementing or clarifying information gained through other means. As the fieldwork proceeds, ethnographers sort their complex observations into a meaningful whole, sometimes by formulating and testing limited or low-level hypotheses, but as often as not by making use of intuition and playing hunches. What is important is that the results are constantly scrutinized for consistency, for if the parts fail to fit together in a manner that is internally consistent, then the ethnographer knows that a mistake has been made and that further work is necessary.

Two studies of a village in Peru illustrate the contrast between the anthropological and other social-science approaches. One was carried out by a sociologist who, after conducting a survey, concluded that people in the village invariably worked together on one another's individually owned plots of land. By contrast, an anthropologist who lived in the village for over a year (during which the sociologist did his study) observed the practice only once. Although a belief in exchange relations was important for the people's understanding of themselves, it was not an economic fact.[11] This is not to say that all sociological research is bad and all anthropological research is good; merely, reliance on questionnaire surveys is a risky business, no matter who does it. The problem is that questionnaires all too easily embody the concepts and categories of outsiders rather than those of the people under study. The misfit between the concepts of professionals from industrialized societies and those of a different people is likely to be great, and the questions asked often construct artificial chunks of knowledge that bear little relation to the reality experienced by other people. Even where this is not a problem, questionnaire surveys alone are not good ways of identifying causal relationships. Correlations alone say nothing definite about cause, nor do they effectively explore such social relationships as reciprocity, dependence, exploitation, and so on. They tend to concentrate on what is measurable, answerable, and accept-

[11]Chambers, R. (1983). *Rural development: Putting the last first* (p. 51). New York: Longman.

able as a question, rather than probing less tangible and more qualitative aspects of society. Moreover, for a host of reasons—fear, prudence, wishful thinking, ignorance, exhaustion, hostility, hope of benefit—people may give slanted or false information.[12] Finally, to the degree that extensive questionnaire surveys preempt resources, using up staff as well as funds, they prevent other approaches.

Another problem in scientific anthropology is the matter of validity. In the other natural sciences, replication of observations and/or experiments is a major means of establishing the reliability of a researcher's conclusions. The problem in ethnology is that observational access is far more limited. As anthropologist Paul Roscoe notes,

> In the natural sciences, the ubiquity of the physical world, coupled with liberal funding, traditionally has furnished a comparatively democratic access to observation and representation: the solar spectrum, for example, is accessible to, and describable by, almost any astronomer with access to the requisite equipment.[13]

Thus, one can see for oneself if one's colleague has "gotten it right." Access to a non-Western culture, by contrast, is constrained by the difficulty of getting there and being accepted, the limited number of ethnographers, often inadequate funding, the fact that conditions and cultures change so that what could be observed at one time in one particular context cannot be at others, and so on. Thus, one can not easily confirm for oneself the reliability or completeness of the ethnographer's account. For this reason, an ethnographer bears a special responsibility for accurate reporting. In the final record, the ethnographer must be clear about three things: What did he or she do in the field, and why? Who did he or she talk to and learn from? And what was brought back to document it? Without these, one cannot judge the validity of the account.[14]

COMPARISON IN ANTHROPOLOGY

The end result of archaeological or ethnographic fieldwork, if properly carried out, is a coherent statement about a culture that provides an explanatory framework for understanding the ideas and actions of the people who have been studied. And this, in turn, is what permits the anthropologist to frame broader hypotheses about human behavior. Plausible though such hypotheses may be, however, the consideration of a single society is generally insufficient for their testing. Without some basis for comparison, the hypothesis grounded in a single case may be no more than a historical coincidence. On the other hand, a single case may be enough to cast doubt on, if not refute, a theory that previously had been held to be valid. The discovery in 1948 that aborigines living in Australia's northern Arnhem Land put in an average workday of less than 6 hours, while living well above a level of bare sufficiency, was enough to call into question the widely accepted notion that food-foraging peoples are so preoccupied with finding food that they lack time for any of life's more pleasurable activities. Even today, economists are prone to label such peoples as "backward," even though the observations made in the Arnhem Land study have since been confirmed many times over in various parts of the world.

Hypothetical explanations of cultural phenomena may be tested by the comparison of archaeological, historical, and/or ethnographic data for several societies found in a particular region. Carefully controlled comparison provides a broader context for understanding cultural phenomena than does the study of a single culture. The anthropologist who undertakes such a comparison may be more confident that the conditions believed to be related really are related, at least within the region that is under investigation; however, an explanation that is valid in one region is not necessarily so in another.

Ideally, theories in cultural anthropology are generated from worldwide comparisons. The cross-cultural researcher examines a worldwide sample of societies in order to discover whether or not hypotheses proposed to explain cultural phenomena seem to be universally applicable. Ideally the sample should be selected at random, thereby enhancing the probability that the conclusions of the cross-cultural researcher will be valid; however, the greater the number of societies being compared, the less likely it is that the investigator will have a detailed understanding of all the societies encompassed by the study. The cross-cultural researcher depends upon other ethnographers for data. It is impossible for any single individual personally to perform in-depth analyses of a broad sample of human cultures throughout the world.

In anthropology, cultural comparisons need not be restricted to ethnographic data. Anthropologists can, for example, turn to archaeological or historical data to test hypotheses about culture change. Cultural characteristics thought to be caused by certain specified conditions can be tested archaeologically by investigating situations

---

[12]Ibid., p. 51.

[13]Roscoe, P. B. (1995). The perils of "positivism" in cultural anthropology. *American Anthropologist, 97,* 497.

[14]Sanjek, R. (1990) On ethnographic validity. In R. Sanjek (Ed.), *Fieldnotes* (p. 395). Ithaca, NY: Cornell University Press.

GEORGE PETER MURDOCK (1897–1985)

Modern cross-cultural studies in anthropology derive from efforts of this man to develop a rigorous methodology. Educated at Yale University, Murdock was strongly influenced by the firm belief of his mentor, Albert Keller, in history's "lawfulness" (in the sense of scientific laws). Influenced as well by a pioneering attempt at statistical comparison by the early British anthropologist Sir Edward B. Tylor, in 1937 Murdock instituted the Cross Cultural Survey in Yale's Institute of Human Relations. This later became the Human Relations Area File (HRAF), a catalogue of cross-indexed ethnographic data filed under uniform headings. In a landmark book, *Social Structure* (published in 1949), he demonstrated the utility of this tool for researching the ways in which human societies were structured and changed. Later in life, Murdock used HRAF as the model for his *World Ethnographic Sample* (1957) and (after he moved to the University of Pittsburgh) *An Ethnographic Atlas*. The latter is a database of over 100 coded cultural characteristics in almost 1,200 societies.

The value of HRAF (now available at many colleges and universities) and other such research tools is that they permit a search for correlations that suggest possible causal relationships, utilizing statistical techniques to provide testable generalizations. To cite one example, anthropologist Peggy Reeves Sanday examined a sample of 156 societies drawn from HRAF in an attempt to answer such questions as: Why do women play a more dominant role in some societies than others? Why, and under what circumstances, do men dominate women? Her study, published in 1981 (*Female Power and Male Dominance*), besides disproving the common myth that women are universally subordinate to men, shed important light on the way men and women relate to one another in human societies, and ranks as a major landmark in the study of gender (so important is this topic, since gender considerations enter into just about everything that people do, that it is included in every chapter of this book).

Valuable though HRAF is, the files are not without their problems. Although they permit blind searches for correlations among customs, such correlations say nothing about cause and effect. All too easily they are rationalized by construction of elaborate causal chains that may amount to little more than "just so" stories. What is required is further historical analysis of particular practices. The strength of Sanday's study is that she did not ignore the particular historical contexts of the societies in her sample.

Other problems consist of errors in the files from inadequate ethnographies or unsystematic sources; from the nonrandom nature of the sample (cultures are included or rejected in accordance with the quality of available literature); and from the fact that items are wrenched out of context. In short, HRAF and similar databases are useful tools, but they are not foolproof; they can lead to false conclusions unless carefully (and critically) used.

where such conditions actually occurred. Also useful are data provided by the ethnohistorian. **Ethnohistory** is a kind of historical ethnography that studies cultures of the recent past through oral histories, the accounts of explorers, missionaries, and traders; and analysis of such records as land titles, birth and death records, and other archival materials. The ethnohistorical analysis of cultures, like archaeology, is a valuable approach to understanding change. By examining the conditions believed to have caused certain phenomena, we can discover whether or not those conditions truly precede those phenomena.

Ethnohistorical research is also valuable for assessing the reliability of data used for making cross-cultural comparisons. For example, anthropologists working with data

Ethnohistory. The study of cultures of the recent past through oral histories; accounts left by explorers, missionaries, and traders; and analysis of such records as land titles, birth and death records, and other archival materials.

from such resources as the Human Relations Area Files (see the biography of George Peter Murdock in this chapter) have sometimes concluded that, among food foragers, it is (and was) the practice for married couples to live in or near the household of the husband's parents (anthropologists call this *patrilocal residence*). To be sure, this is what many ethnographers reported. But what this fails to take into account is the fact that most such ethnographies were done among food foragers whose traditional practices had been severely altered by pressures set into motion (usually) by the expansion of Europeans to all parts of the globe. For example, the Western Abenaki people of northwestern New England are asserted to have practiced patrilocal residence prior to the actual invasion of their homeland by English colonists. What ethnohistorical research shows, however, is that their participation in the fur trade with Europeans, coupled with increasing involvement in warfare to stave off invasions by outsiders, led to increased importance of men's activities and a change from more flexible to patrilocal residence patterns.[15] Upon close examination, other cases of patrilocal residence among food foragers turn out to be similar responses to circumstances associated with the rise of colonialism. Rather than wives regularly going to live with their husbands in proximity to the latter's male relations, food-foraging peoples originally seem to have been far more flexible in their postmarital residence arrangements.

Ethnohistorical research, like the field studies of archaeologists, is valuable for testing and confirming hypotheses about culture. And like much of anthropology, it has practical utility as well. In the United States, ethnohistorical research has flourished, for it often provides the key evidence necessary for deciding legal cases involving Native American land claims and hunting and fishing rights. And here again is an example of a practical application of anthropological knowledge.

ANTHROPOLOGY AND THE HUMANITIES

Although the sciences and humanities are often thought to be mutually exclusive approaches to learning, they share methods for critical thinking, mental creativity, and innovation.[16] In anthropology, both come together, which is why, for example, anthropological research is funded not only by such "hard science" agencies as the National Science Foundation but also by such organizations as the National Endowment for the Humanities. To paraphrase Roy Rappaport, a past president of the American Anthropological Association,[17] the combination of scientific and humanistic approaches is and always has been a source of tension. It has been crucial to anthropology because it truly reflects the condition of a species that lives and can only live in terms of meanings that it must construct in a world devoid of intrinsic meaning, yet subject to natural law. Without the continued grounding in careful observation that scientific aspects of our tradition provide, our interpretive efforts may float off into literary criticism and speculation. But without the interpretive tradition, the scientific tradition that grounds us will never get off the ground.

The humanistic side of anthropology is perhaps most immediately evident in its concern with other cultures' languages, values, achievements in the arts and literature (including oral literature among peoples who lack writing), and how they make sense of their lives. Beyond this, anthropologists remain committed to the proposition that one cannot fully understand another culture by simply observing it; as the term *participant observation* implies, one must *experience* it as well. Thus, ethnographers spend prolonged periods of time living with the people they study, sharing their joys and suffering their hardships, including sickness and, sometimes, premature death. They are not so naïve as to believe that they can be, or even should be, dispassionate about the people whose trials and tribulations they share. As Robin Fox puts it, "our hearts, as well as our brains, should be with our men and women."[18] Nor are anthropologists so self-deceived as to believe that they can avoid dealing with the moral and political consequences of their findings. Indeed, anthropology has a long tradition of protecting and promoting the rights of indigenous peoples, a topic to which we shall return in later chapters of this book.

The humanistic side of anthropology is evident as well in its emphasis on qualitative, as opposed to quantitative, research. This is not to say that anthropologists are unaware of the value of quantification and statistical procedures; they do make use of them for various purposes. Nevertheless, reducing people and the things they do to numbers may have a definite dehumanizing effect (it is easier to

---

[15]Haviland, W. A., & Power, M. W. (1994). *The original Vermonters* (Rev. and exp. ed., pp. 174–175, 215–216, 297–299). Hanover, NH: University Press of New England.

[16]Shearer, R. R., & Gould, S. J. (1999). Of two minds and one nature. *Science, 286,* 1093.

[17]Rappaport, R. A. (1994). Commentary. *Anthropology Newsletter, 35,* 76.

[18]Fox, R. (1968). *Encounter with anthropology* (p. 290). New York: Dell.

ignore the concerns of impersonal numbers than it is those of flesh-and-blood human beings) and keep us from dealing with important issues less susceptible to numeration. For all these reasons, anthropologists tend to place less emphasis on numerical data than do other social scientists.

Given their intense involvement with other peoples, it should come as no surprise that anthropologists have amassed as much information about human weakness and greatness—the stuff of the humanities—as any other discipline. Small wonder, too, that above all they intend to avoid allowing a coldly scientific approach to blind them to the fact that human societies are made up of individuals with rich assortments of emotions and aspirations that demand respect. Anthropology has sometimes been called the most human of the sciences, a designation in which anthropologists take considerable pride.

QUESTIONS OF ETHICS

The kinds of research carried out by anthropologists, and the settings within which they work, raise a number of important moral questions about the use and abuse of our knowledge. Who will make use of the findings of anthropologists, and for what purposes? Who, if anyone, will profit from them? In the case of a hostile minority, for example, will governmental or corporate interests use anthropological data to suppress that minority? And what of traditional communities around the world? Who is to decide what changes should, or should not, be introduced for community "betterment"? By whose definition is it betterment—the community's, that of some remote national government, or an international agency like the World Bank? Then there is the problem of privacy. Anthropologists deal with people's private and sensitive matters, including things that people would not care to have generally known about them. How does one write about such matters and at the same time protect the privacy of informants? Not surprisingly, because of these and other questions, there has been much discussion among anthropologists over the past two decades on the subject of ethics.[19]

Anthropologists recognize that they have obligations to three sets of people: those whom they study, those who fund the research, and those in the profession who expect us to publish our findings so that they may be used to further our knowledge. Because fieldwork requires a relationship of trust between fieldworker and informants, the anthropologist's first responsibility clearly is to his or her informants and their people. Everything possible must be done to protect their physical, social, and psychological welfare and to honor their dignity and privacy. In other words, *do no harm*. Although early ethnographers often provided colonial administrators with the kind of information needed to control the "natives," they have long since ceased to be comfortable with such work and regard as basic a people's right to their own culture.

As an example of how these issues play out, I turn to my own work with the Western Abenakis of northwestern New England. In writing a book about them, I made a point of having them see the manuscript to ensure that I did not violate anyone's confidences or privacy, or misrepresent them in any way. I also had to be sensitive to legal matters having to do with federal recognition, traditional hunting and fishing rights, and potential land claims. I had to be careful to present information in such a way that the state could not use it unfairly against them. Recognizing an obligation to "give back," I have done this in various ways. These include signing over the book's royalties to the Abenakis, responding to their requests in various ways, giving countless presentations to a wide range of schools, public and civic organizations, testifying on the Abenaki's behalf before legislative committees, and providing expert testimony in court over native fishing rights. Truly this has been a long-term relationship. With regard to those funding my work—the National Endowment for the Humanities, the Vermont Historical Society, and the University of Vermont—publication of the book satisfied their requirements. Finally, my obligations to the profession have been met not only through the book but by publication of supplementary articles in specialist journals as well.

ANTHROPOLOGY AND CONTEMPORARY LIFE

Anthropology, with its long-standing commitment to understanding people in all parts of the world, past and present, coupled with its holistic perspective, is better equipped than any other discipline to grapple with a problem of overriding importance for all of humanity at the beginning of the 21st century. An inescapable fact of life is that North Americans—a small minority of the world's people—live in a global community in which all of those people are interdependent. There is now widespread awareness of this in the business community, which relies on foreign sources

[19] American Anthropological Association. (1998). Code of ethics of the American Anthropological Association. *Anthropology Newsletter, 39*(6), 19–20.

Ignorance of other cultures can have serious consequences. When George W. Bush responded to attacks on targets in New York and Arlington, VA, he spoke of a crusade against terrorism, which the Department of Defense dubbed "Operation Infinite Justice." This caused problems with Islamic countries, where the word *crusade* reminds people of invasions of Islamic lands by Christians from Europe, and where only Allah can dispense "infinite justice."

for raw materials, sees the non-Western world as its major area for market expansion, and more and more is manufacturing its products abroad. Nevertheless, citizens of the United States are on the whole as ignorant about the cultures of the rest of the world as they have ever been. This is true not just of average citizens but highly educated people. In Guatemala, for example, where over half the population is made up of Maya Indians, U.S. Foreign Service personnel are largely ignorant of the literature—most of it by anthropologists—pertaining to these people.[20] As a result, too many of us are poorly equipped to handle the demands of living in the modern world.

The relevance of anthropological knowledge for the contemporary world may be illustrated by three quite different examples. In the United States today, discrimination based on notions of race continues to be a serious problem affecting economic, political, and social relations. What anthropology has shown, as we shall see in Chapter 13, is the fallacy of racial categories themselves. Far from being the biological reality it is thought to be, the concept of race emerged in the 18th century as a device for justifying the dominance of Europeans and their descendants over Africans, American Indians, and other people of color. In fact, differences of skin color are adaptations to differing amounts of ultraviolet radiation and have nothing to do with other traits. Nor do they covary with other biological characteristics; a northern European, for example, may have more in common with a "black" from southern Africa than with someone from Greece or Italy, depending on what genetically based characteristics other than skin color are considered. Moreover, one finds far more biological variation *within*

[20]Nance, C. R. (1997). Review of Haviland's *Cultural Anthropology* (p. 2).

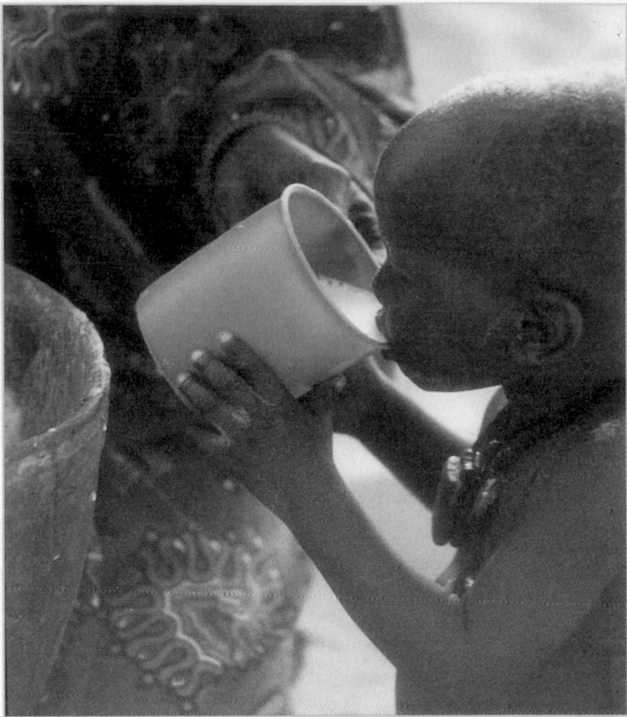

Though their skin colors differ, this northern European and East African cattle herder share the genetically based ability to digest milk, something that sets them apart from many central Europeans and central Africans. Because their differences are distributed independently, humans cannot be classified into races having any biological validity.

any given human population than *between* them. In short, human races are nothing more than folk categories, and the sooner this is recognized, the better off we will all be.[21]

A second example involves the issue of same-sex marriage. As this is written, two countries have made moves toward allowing such unions: Brazil, by recognizing "stable unions" between same-sex partners, and the Netherlands, which is about to recognize same-sex marriages called *homohuwelijk* by national law. In the United States, California is debating and Vermont has legalized "civil unions" between same-sex couples. Those opposed to same-sex unions frequently argue that marriage has always been between one man and one woman and that only heterosexual relations are natural. Yet, as we will see in succeeding chapters of this book (especially Chapters 16 and 19), neither assertion is true. Anthropologists have documented same-sex marriages in many human societies in various parts of the world, where they are regarded as perfectly acceptable under appropriate circumstances.

These people are protesting Vermont's civil union legislation. Their objections are based on beliefs that anthropologists have proved are without foundation.

[21]American Anthropological Association. (1998). Statement on "race." Available: *www.ameranthassn.org*.

HIGHWAY 1
American Anthropological Association
www.aaanet.org/about_aaa.htm

HIGHWAY 2
Indiana University Anthropology Department
www.indiana.edu/~anthro/home.html

As for homosexual behavior, it is quite common in the animal world, including among humans.[22] The only difference between people and other animals is that human societies specify when, where, how, and with whom it is appropriate (just as they do for heterosexual behavior).

A final example relates to the common confusion of *nation* with *state*. The distinction is important: States are politically organized territories, whereas nations are socially organized bodies of people. As we will see in later chapters (especially Chapters 23 and 27), states and nations rarely coincide, nations being split among different states, and states typically being controlled by members of one nation who commonly use their control to gain access to the land, resources, and labor of other nationalities. Rarely is the consent of the other nationals obtained, nor are their interests given much (if any) consideration by those who control the government. As a consequence, oppressed nationals often resort to force to defend their land, resources, and even their very identities, feeling they have no other options. Most of the armed conflicts in the world today are of this sort and are not mere outbreaks of "tribalism," as commonly asserted. Nor should they be confused with acts of terrorism carried out by religious or other extremists. For example, the conflict in Chechnya is one between Chechan nationals on the one hand against domination by Russian nationals on the other. The attacks on the New York World Trade Center and the Pentagon, by contrast, were carried out by a transnational organization of religious extremists.

In numerous ways, our ignorance about other peoples and their ways is a cause of serious problems. It is as true today as when Edwin Reischauer, a former ambassador, said it some years ago: "Education is not moving rapidly enough in the right directions to produce the knowledge about the outside world and attitudes toward other peoples that may be essential for human survival."[23] What anthropology has to contribute to contemporary life, then, are an understanding of, and way of looking at, the world's peoples, which are nothing less than basic skills for survival in the modern world.

[22]Kirkpatrick, R. C. (2000). The evolution of human homosexual behavior. *Current Anthropology, 41,* 384.

[23]Quoted in Haviland, W. A. (1997). Cleansing young minds, or what should we be doing in introductory anthropology? In C. P. Kottak, J. J. White, R. H. Furlow, & P. C. Rice (Eds.), *The teaching of anthropology: Problems, issues, and decisions* (p. 35). Mountain View, CA: Mayfield.

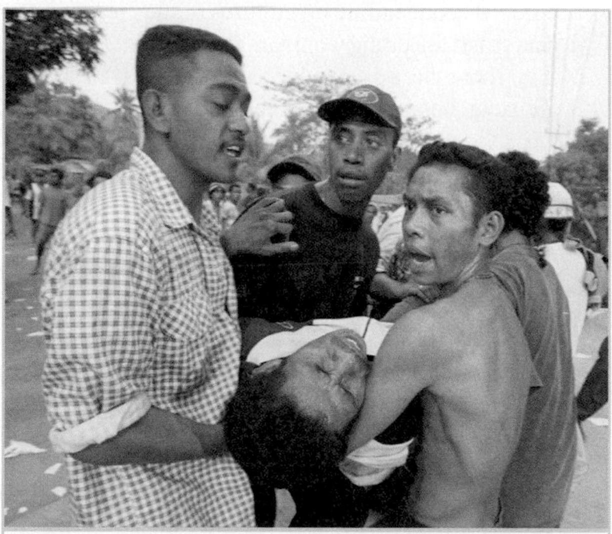

Violence triggered by East Timor's vote for independence exemplifies the problem of multinational states in which members of one nationality try to control those of another through all possible means.

CHAPTER SUMMARY

Throughout human history, people have needed to know who they are, where they came from, and why they behave as they do. Traditionally, myths and legends provided the answers to these questions. Anthropology, as it has emerged over the last 200 years, offers another approach to answering the questions people ask about themselves.

Anthropology is the study of humankind. In employing a scientific approach, anthropologists seek to produce a reasonably objective understanding of both human diversity and those things all humans have in common. The two major branches of anthropology are physical and cultural anthropology. Physical anthropology focuses on humans as biological organisms. Particular emphasis is given by physical anthropologists to tracing the evolutionary development of the human animal and studying biological variation within the species today. Cultural anthropologists study humans in terms of their cultures, the often unconscious standards by which societies operate.

Three areas of cultural anthropology are archaeology, anthropological linguistics, and ethnology. Archaeologists study material objects, usually from past cultures, to explain human behavior. Linguists, who study human languages, may deal with the description of a language, with the history of languages, or how they are used in particular social settings. Ethnologists concentrate on cultures of the present or recent past; in doing comparative studies of culture, they focus on a particular aspect of it, such as religious or economic practices, or as ethnographers, they may go into the field to observe, describe, and explain human behavior as it can be seen, experienced, and discussed with persons whose culture is to be understood.

Anthropology is unique among the social and natural sciences in that it is concerned with formulating explanations of human diversity based on a study of all aspects of human biology and behavior in all known societies, past and present, rather than in recent European and North American societies alone. Thus, anthropologists have devoted much attention to the study of ancient and contemporary non-Western peoples.

Anthropologists are concerned with the objective and systematic study of humankind. The anthropologist employs the methods of other scientists by developing hypotheses, or assumed explanations, using other data to test these hypotheses, and ultimately arriving at theories—explanations supported by reliable bodies of data. The data used by the cultural anthropologist may be from a single society or from numerous societies, which are then compared.

In anthropology, the humanities and sciences come together into a genuinely human science. Anthropology's link with the humanities can be seen in its concern with people's beliefs, values, languages, arts, and literature—oral as well as written—but above all in its attempt to convey the experience of living as other people do. As both science and humanity, anthropology has essential skills to offer the modern world, where understanding the other people with whom we share the globe has become a matter of survival.

CLASSIC READINGS

Lett, J. (1987). *The human enterprise: A critical introduction to anthropological theory.* Boulder, CO: Westview.

Part 1 examines the philosophical foundations of anthropological theory, paying special attention to the nature of scientific inquiry and the mechanisms of scientific progress. Part 2 deals with the nature of social science as well as the particular features of anthropology.

Peacock, J. L. (1986). *The anthropological lens: Harsh light, soft focus.* New York: Cambridge University Press.

This lively and innovative book manages to give the reader a good understanding of the diversity of activities undertaken by anthropologists, while at the same time identifying the unifying themes that hold the discipline together.

Sanjek, R. (Ed.). (1990). *Fieldnotes: The making of anthropology.* Ithaca, NY: Cornell University Press.

This book goes right to the heart of the ethnographic enterprise. What, how, and why do fieldworkers write down what they do and how do they deal with it all? How do others assess the credibility of the ethnographer?

Spradley, J. P. (1979). *The ethnographic interview.* New York: Holt, Rinehart & Winston.

This contains one of the best discussions of the nature and value of ethnographic research to be found. The bulk of the book is devoted to a step-by-step, easy-to-understand account of how one carries out ethnographic research with the assistance of informants. Numerous examples drawn from the author's own research in such diverse settings as Skid Row, courtrooms, and bars make for interesting reading. A companion volume, *Participant Observation,* is also highly recommended.

Vogt, F. W. (1975). *A history of ethnology.* New York: Holt, Rinehart & Winston.

This history of cultural anthropology attempts to describe and interpret the major intellectual strands, in their cultural and historical contexts, that influenced the development of the field. The author tries for a balanced view of this subject rather than one that would support a particular theoretical position.

CHAPTER 2

METHODS OF STUDYING THE HUMAN PAST

This excavation is of an old Stone Age campsite in France. Vertical strings are markers for a grid by which excavators keep track of exact locations of objects found. Without such meticulous records, the finds tell us nothing about the human past.

CHAPTER PREVIEW

1

What Are Archaeological Sites and Fossil Localities, and How Are They Found?

Archaeological sites are places containing the remains of past human activity. They are revealed by the presence of artifacts as well as soil marks, changes in vegetation, and irregularities of the surface. Fossil localities contain actual remains of organisms that lived in the past. They are revealed by the presence of fossils—any trace or impression of an organism of past geological time that has been preserved in the earth. Although fossils are sometimes found in archaeological sites, not all archaeological sites contain fossils, and localities are often found apart from archaeological sites.

2

How Are Sites and Localities Investigated?

Archaeologists and paleoanthropologists face something of a dilemma. The only way to thoroughly investigate a site or locality is by excavation, which results in its destruction. Thus, every attempt is made to excavate in such a way that the location of everything found, no matter how small, is precisely recorded. Without such records little sense can be made of the data, and the potential of the site or locality to contribute to our knowledge of the past would be lost forever.

3

How Are Archaeological or Fossil Remains Dated?

Remains can be dated in relative terms by noting their stratigraphic position, by measuring the amount of fluorine contained in fossil bones, or by associating them with different floral or faunal remains. More precise dating is achieved by counting the tree rings in wood from archaeological contexts, by measuring the amount of carbon 14 remaining in organic materials, or by measuring the percentage of potassium that has decayed to argon in volcanic materials. Where problems exist in applying these standard techniques, other specialized methods are available.

A popular stereotype of anthropologists is that they are concerned exclusively with the human past. This is not the case, as should now be evident; not even archaeologists and physical anthropologists, those most likely to be engaged in the study of the past, devote all of their time to such pursuits. As explained in Chapter 1, some archaeologists study the refuse of modern peoples, and many physical anthropologists engage in research on such issues as present-day human variation and adaptation. Nevertheless, the study of the human past is an important *part* of anthropology, given its concern with peoples in all places and times. Moreover, knowledge of the human past is essential if we are to understand what it was that made us distinctively human, as well as how the processes of change—both biological and cultural—affect the human species. Indeed, given the radical changes taking place in the world today, one may say that an understanding of the nature of change has never been more important. Although it is not their sole concern, archaeology and physical anthropology are the two branches of anthropology most involved in the study of the human past.

Archaeologists (apart from those engaged in the analysis of modern garbage) study things left behind by people who lived in historic or prehistoric times—tools, trash, traces of shelters, and the like. As the British archaeologist Stuart Piggot put it, "Archaeology is the science of rubbish."[1] Most of us are familiar with some kind of archaeological material: the coin dug out of the earth, the fragment of an ancient jar, the spear point used by some ancient hunter. The finding and cataloguing of such objects is often thought by laypeople to be the chief goal of archaeology. While this was true in the 19th century, the situation changed in the 20th. Today, the aim is to use archaeological remains to reconstruct human societies that can no longer be observed firsthand, in order to understand and explain human behavior. Although it may look as if the archaeologist is digging up things, he or she is really digging up human behavior.

The actual remains of our ancestors, as opposed to the things they lost or discarded, are the concern of physical anthropologists. Those physical anthropologists engaged in the recovery and study of the fossil evidence for human evolution, as opposed to those who study present-day peoples, are generally known as **paleoanthropologists.** Unlike paleontologists, who study all forms of past life, paleoanthropologists confine their attention to humans, near humans, and other ancient primates, the group to which humans belong. Just as the finding and cataloguing of objects was once the chief concern of the archaeologist, so the finding and cataloguing of human and other primate fossils was once the chief concern of the paleoanthropologist. But, again, there has been a major change in the field; although recovery, description, and organization of fossil materials are still important, the emphasis since the 1950s has been on what those fossils can tell us about the processes at work in human biological evolution. It is not so much a case of what you find, but what you find out.

In Chapter 1, we surveyed at some length just what it is that anthropologists do and why they do it. We also looked briefly at the ethnographic methods used by anthropologists to study the cultures of living peoples. Other methods are required, however, when studying peoples of the past—especially those of the prehistoric past, before the existence of written records. The term **prehistoric** is a conventional one that, while not denying the existence of history, recognizes that *written* history is absent. Since the next two parts of this book are about the prehistoric past, in this chapter we shall look at how archaeologists and paleoanthropologists go about their study of the human past.

METHODS OF DATA RECOVERY

Archaeologists, one way or another, work with **artifacts:** any object fashioned or altered by humans—a flint chip, a basket, an axe, a pipe, or such nonportable things as house ruins or walls. An artifact expresses a facet of human culture. Because it is something that someone made, archaeologists like to say that an artifact is a product of human behavior or, in more technical words, that it is a material representation of an abstract ideal.

Just as important as the artifacts themselves is the way they were left in the ground. What people do with the things they have made, how they dispose of them, and how they lose them also reflect important aspects of human behavior. Furthermore, the context in which the artifacts were found tells us which objects were contemporary with which other objects, which are older, and which are younger.

[1]Quoted in Fagan, B. M. (1995). The quest for the past. In L. L. Hasten (Ed.), *Annual editions 95/96, Archaeology* (p. 10). Guilford, CT: Dushkin.

Paleoanthropologist. An anthropologist who studies human evolution from fossil remains. • **Prehistoric.** A conventional term used to refer to the period of time before the appearance of written records. Does not deny the existence of history, merely of *written* history. • **Artifact.** Any object fashioned or altered by humans.

Without this information, the archaeologist is in no position at all even to identify, let alone understand, specific cultures of the past. This importance of context cannot be overstated; without context, the archaeologist in effect knows nothing! Unfortunately, such information is easily lost if the materials have been disturbed, whether by bulldozers or by the activities of relic collectors.

While archaeologists work with artifacts, paleoanthropologists work with human or other primate fossils—the remains of past forms of life. And just as the context of a find is as important to the archaeologist as the find itself, so is the context of a fossil absolutely critical to the paleoanthropologist. Not only does it tell which fossils are earlier or later in time than other fossils, but also by noting the association of human fossils with other nonhuman remains, the paleoanthropologist may go a long way toward reconstructing the environmental setting in which the human lived.

The Nature of Fossils

Broadly defined, a **fossil** is any trace or impression of an organism of past geologic time that has been preserved in the earth's crust. Fossilization typically involves the hard parts of an organism: Bones, teeth, shells, horns, and the woody tissues of plants are the most successfully fossilized materials. Although the soft parts of an organism are rarely fossilized, the casts or impressions of footprints, and even whole bodies, have sometimes been found. Because dead animals quickly attract meat-eating scavengers and bacteria that cause decomposition, they rarely survive long enough to become fossilized. What is required is that they be covered by some protective substance soon after death.

An organism or part of an organism may be preserved in a number of ways. The whole animal may be frozen in ice, like the famous mammoths found in Siberia, safe from the actions of predators, weathering, and bacteria. Or it may be enclosed in a fossil resin such as amber. Specimens of spiders and insects dating back millions of years have been preserved in the Baltic Sea area, which is rich in resin-producing conifers. It may be preserved in the bottoms of lakes and sea basins, where the accumulation of chemicals renders the environment antiseptic. The entire organism may also be mummified or preserved in tar pits, peat, oil, or asphalt bogs, in which the chemical environment prevents the growth of decay-producing bacteria. Such **unaltered fossils,** although not common, are often quite spectacular and may be particularly informative. As an example, consider the recovery in 1994 of the remains of a young girl in Barrow, Alaska.

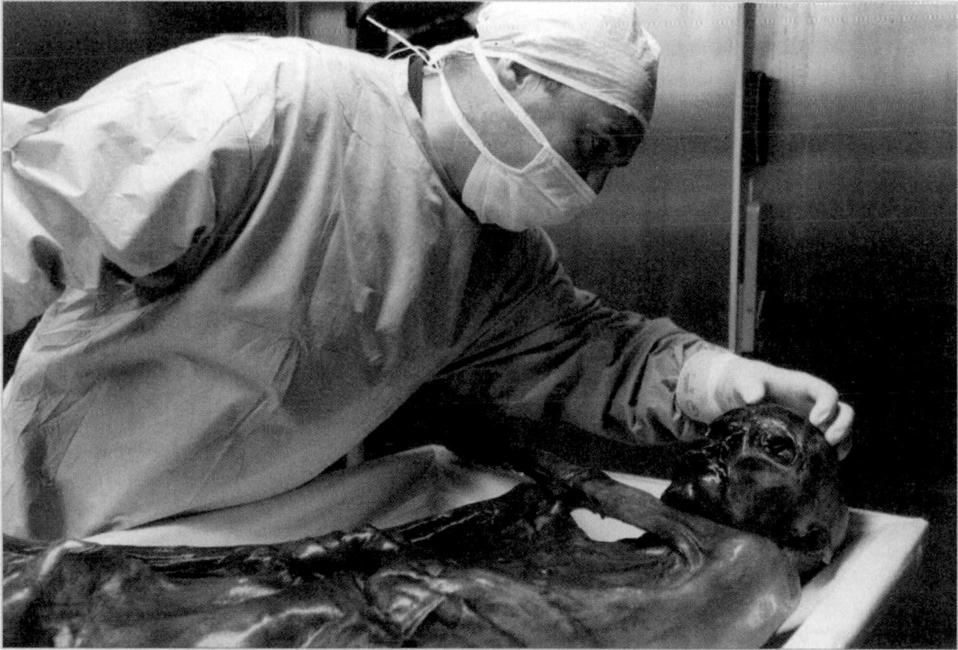

In rare circumstances, human bodies are so well preserved that they could be mistaken for recent corpses. Such is the case of the 5,200-year-old "Ice Man," exposed by the melting of an alpine glacier in northern Italy in 1991.

Fossil. The preserved remains of plants and animals that lived in the past. • **Unaltered fossil.** Remains of plants and animals that lived in the past and that have not been altered in any significant way.

Original Study

Whispers from the Ice[2]

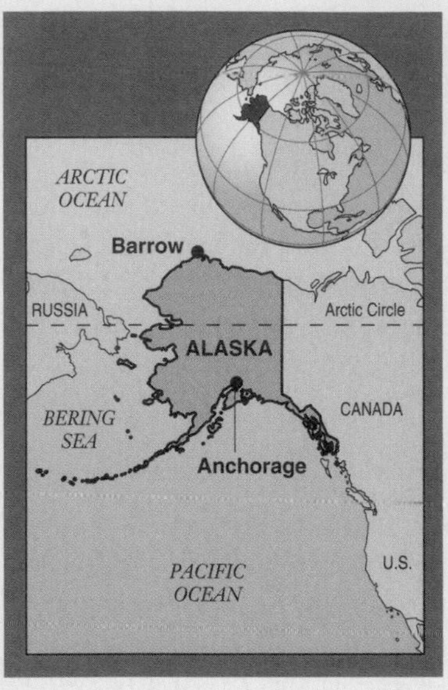

People grew excited when a summer rainstorm softened the bluff known as Ukkuqsi, sloughing off huge chunks of earth containing remains of historic and prehistoric houses, part of the old village that predates the modern community of Barrow. Left protruding from the slope was a human head. Archaeologist Anne Jensen happened to be in Barrow buying strapping tape when the body appeared. Her firm, SJS Archaeological Services, Inc., was closing a field season at nearby Point Franklin, and Jensen offered the team's help in a kind of archaeological triage to remove the body before it eroded completely from the earth. The North Slope Borough hired her and Glenn Sheehan, both associated with Pennsylvania's Bryn Mawr College, to conduct the work. The National Science Foundation, which supported the 3 year Point Franklin project, agreed to fund the autopsy and subsequent analysis of the body and artifacts. The Ukkuqsi excavation quickly became a community event. In remarkably sunny and calm weather, volunteers troweled and picked through the thawing soil, finding trade beads, animal bones, and other items. Teen-age boys worked alongside grandmothers. The smell of sea mammal oil, sweet at first then corrupt, mingled with ancient organic odors of decomposed vegetation. One man searched the beach for artifacts that had eroded from the bluff, discovering such treasures as two feather parkas. Elder Silas Negovanna, originally of Wainwright, visited several times, "more or less out of curiosity to see what they have in mind," he says. George Leavitt, who lives in a house on the bluff, stopped by one day while carrying home groceries and suggested a way to spray water to thaw the soil without washing away valuable artifacts. Tour groups added the excavation to their rounds.

"This community has a great interest in archaeology up here just because it's so recent to their experience," says oral historian Karen Brewster, a tall young woman who interviews elders as part of her work with the North Slope Borough's division of Inupiat History, Language, and Culture. "The site's right in town, and everybody was really fascinated by it."

Slowly, as the workers scraped and shoveled, the earth surrendered its historical hoard: carved wooden bowls, ladles, and such clothing as a mitten made from polar bear hide, birdskin parkas, and mukluks. The items spanned prehistoric times, dated in Barrow to before explorers first arrived in 1826.

The work prompted visiting elders to recall when they or their parents lived in traditional sod houses and relied wholly on the land and sea for sustenance. Some remembered sliding down the hill as children, before the sea gnawed away the slope. Others described the site's use as a lookout for whales or ships. For the archaeologists, having elders stand beside them and identify items and historical context is like hearing the past whispering in their ears. Elders often know from experience, or from stories, the answers to the scientists' questions about how items were used or made. "In this instance, usually the only puzzled people are the archaeologists," jokes archaeologist Sheehan.

A modern town of 4,000, Barrow exists in a cultural continuum, where history is not detached or remote but still pulses through contemporary life. People live, hunt, and fish where their ancestors did, but they can also buy fresh vegetables at the store and jet to other places. Elementary school classes include computer and Inupiaq language studies. Caribou skins, still ruddy with blood, and black brant

[2]Adapted from Simpson, S. (1995, April). Whispers from the ice. *Alaska,* 23–28.

Among the objects found at Ukkuqsi are these wooden devices for throwing spears.

carcasses hang near late-model cars outside homes equipped with television antennas. A man uses power tools to work on his whaling boat. And those who appear from the earth are not just bodies, but relatives. "We're not a people frozen in time," says Jana Harcharek, an Inupiat Eskimo who teaches Inupiaq and nurtures her culture among young people. "There will always be that connection between us [and our ancestors]. They're not a separate entity."

The past drew still closer as the archaeologists neared the body. After several days of digging through thawed soil, they used water supplied by the local fire station's tanker truck to melt through permafrost until they reached the remains, about 3 feet below the surface. A shell of clear ice encased the body, which rested in what appeared to be a former meat cellar. With the low-pressure play of water from the tanker, the archaeologists teased the icy casket from the frozen earth, exposing a tiny foot. Only then did they realize they had uncovered a child. "That was kind of sad, because she was about my daughter's size," says archaeologist Jensen.

The girl was curled up beneath a baleen toboggan and part of a covering that Inupiat elder Bertha Leavitt identified as a kayak skin by its stitching. The child, who appeared to be 5 or 6, remained remarkably intact after her dark passage through time. Her face was cloaked by a covering that puzzled some onlookers. It didn't look like human hair, or even fur, but something with a feathery residue. Finally they concluded it was a hood from a feather parka made of bird skins. The rest of her body was delineated muscle that had freeze-dried into a dark brick-red color. Her hands rested on her knees, which were drawn up to her chin. Frost particles coated the bends of her arms and legs.

"We decided we needed to go talk to the elders and see what they wanted, to get some kind of feeling as to whether they wanted to bury her right away, or whether they were willing to allow some studies in a respectful manner—studies that would be of some use to residents of the North Slope," Jensen says. Working with community elders is not a radical idea to Jensen or Sheehan, whose previous work in the Arctic has earned them high regard from local officials who appreciate their sensitivity. The researchers feel obligated not only to follow community wishes, but to invite villagers to sites and to share all information through public presentations. In fact, Jensen is reluctant to discuss findings with the press before the townspeople themselves hear it.

"It seems like it's a matter of simple common courtesy," she says. Such consideration can only help researchers, she points out. "If people don't get along with you, they're not going to talk to you, and they're liable to throw you out on your ear." In the past, scientists were not terribly sensitive about such matters, generally regarding human remains—and sometimes living Natives—as artifacts themselves. Once, the girl's body would have

Original Study

been hauled off to the catacombs of some university or museum, and relics would have disappeared into exhibit drawers in what Sheehan describes as "hit-and-run archaeology."

"Grave robbers" is how Inupiat Jana Harcharek refers to early Arctic researchers. "They took human remains and their burial goods. It's pretty gruesome. But, of course, at the time they thought they were doing science a big favor. Thank goodness attitudes have changed."

Today, not only scientists but municipal officials confer with the Barrow Elders Council when local people find skeletons from traditional platform burials out on the tundra, or when bodies appear in the house mounds. The elders appreciate such consultations, says Samuel Simmonds, a tall, dignified man known for his carving. A retired Presbyterian minister, he presided at burial ceremonies of the famous "frozen family" that ancient Inupiats discovered in Barrow 13 years ago. "They were part of us, we know that," he says simply, as if the connection between old bones and bodies and living relatives is self-evident. In the case of the newly discovered body, he says, "We were concerned that it was reburied in a respectful manner. They were nice enough to come over and ask us."

The elders also wanted to restrict media attention and prevent photographs of the body except for a few showing her position at the site. They approved a limited autopsy to help answer questions about the body's sex, age, and state of health. She was placed in an orange plastic body bag in a stainless steel morgue with the temperature turned down to below freezing.

With the help of staff at the Indian Health Service Hospital, Jensen sent the girl's still-frozen body to Anchorage's Providence Hospital. There she assisted with an autopsy performed by Dr. Michael Zimmerman of New York City's Mount Sinai Hospital. Zimmerman, an expert on prehistoric frozen bodies, had autopsied Barrow's frozen family in 1982, and was on his way to work on the prehistoric man recently discovered in the Alps.

The findings suggest the girl's life was very hard. She ultimately died of starvation, but also had emphysema caused by a rare congenital disease—the lack of an enzyme that protects the lungs. She probably was sickly and needed extra care all her brief life. The autopsy also found soot in her lungs from the family's sea mammal oil lamps, and she had osteoporosis, which was caused by a diet exclusively of meat from marine mammals.

The girl's stomach was empty, but her intestinal tract contained dirt and animal fur. That remains a mystery and raises questions about the condition of the rest of the family. "It's not likely that she would be hungry and everyone else well fed," Jensen says.

That the girl appears to have been placed deliberately in the cellar provokes further questions about precontact burial practices, which the researchers hope Barrow elders can help answer. Historic accounts indicate the dead often were wrapped in skins and laid out on the tundra on wooden platforms, rather than buried in the frozen earth. But perhaps the entire family was starving and too weak to remove the dead girl from the house, Jensen speculates. "We probably won't ever be able to say, 'This is the way it was,'" she adds. "For that you need a time machine."

The scientific team reported to the elders that radiocarbon dating places the girl's death in about A.D. 1200. If correct—for dating is technically tricky in the Arctic—the date would set the girl's life about 100 years before her people formed settled whaling villages, Sheehan says.

Following the autopsy and the body's return to Barrow in August, one last request by the elders was honored. The little girl, wrapped in her feather parka, was placed in a casket and buried in a small Christian ceremony next to the grave of the other prehistoric bodies. Hundreds of years after her death, an Inupiat daughter was welcomed back into the midst of her community.

The "rescue" of the little girl's body from the raw forces of time and nature means researchers and the Inupiat people will continue to learn still more about the region's culture. Sheehan and Jensen returned to Barrow in winter 1994 to explain their findings to townspeople. "We expect to learn just as much from them," Sheehan said before the trip. A North Slope

Cultural Center scheduled for completion in 1996 will store and display artifacts from the dig sites.

Laboratory tests and analysis also will contribute information. The archaeologists hope measurements of heavy metals in the girl's body will allow comparisons with modern-day pollution contaminating the sea mammals that Inupiats eat today. The soot damage in her lungs might offer health implications for Third World people who rely on oil lamps, dung fires, and charcoal for heat and light. Genetic tests could illuminate early population movements of Inupiats. The project also serves as a model for good relations between archaeologists and Native people. "The larger overall message from this work is that scientists and communities don't have to be at odds," Sheehan says. "In fact, there are mutual interests that we all have. Scientists have obliga-tions to communities. And when more scientists realize that, and when more communities hold scientists to those standards, then everybody will be happier."

The End

Cases in which an entire organism of any sort, let alone a human, is preserved in a relatively unaltered state are especially rare and comprise possibly less than 1 percent of all fossil finds. Most **fossils** have been **altered** in some way. They generally consist of such things as scattered teeth and fragments of bones found embedded in the earth's crust as part of rock deposits. Thousands, and even millions, of years ago, the organisms died and were deposited in the earth; they may then have been covered by sediments and silt, or sand. These materials gradually hardened, forming a protective shell around the skeleton of the organism. The internal cavities of bones or teeth and other parts of the skeleton are generally filled in with mineral deposits from the sediment immediately surrounding the specimen. Then the external walls of the bone decay and are replaced by calcium carbonate or silica.

Fossils are not always found in the ground. In this picture, paleoanthropologist Donald Johanson searches for fossils in a gully in Ethiopia. The fossils in the foreground were once buried beneath sediments on an ancient lake bottom, but rains in more recent times have eroded the sediments from around them so that they lie exposed on the surface.

Fossilization is most apt to occur among marine animals and other creatures that live near water, because their remains accumulate on shallow sea, river, or lake bottoms, away from waves and tidal action. These concentrations of shells and other parts of organisms are covered and completely enclosed by the soft waterborne sediments that eventually harden into shale and limestone.

Terrestrial animals that do not live near lakes, rivers, or the sea are less likely to be fossilized unless they happened to die in a cave, or their remains were dragged there by some other meat-eating animal. In caves, conditions are often excellent for fossilization, as minerals contained in water dripping from the ceiling may harden over bones left on the cave floor. In northern China, for example, many fossils of *Homo erectus* (discussed in Chapter 8)

Altered fossils. Remains of plants and animals that lived in the past that have been altered, as by the replacement of organic material by calcium carbonate or silica.

and other animals were found in a cave at a place called Zhoukoudian, in deposits consisting of consolidated clays and rock that had fallen from the cave's limestone ceiling. The cave had been frequented by both humans and predatory animals, who left remains of many a meal there.

Unless protected in some way, the bones of a land dweller, having been picked clean and often broken by predators and scavengers, are then scattered and exposed to the deteriorating influence of the elements. The fossil record for many primates, for example, is poor, because organic materials decay rapidly in the tropical forests in which they lived. The records are much more complete in the case of primates that lived on the grassy plains, or savannas, where conditions are far more favorable to the formation of fossils. This is particularly true in places where ash deposited from volcanic eruptions or waterborne sediments along lakes and streams could quickly cover over the skeletons of primates that lived there. At several localities in Ethiopia, Kenya, and Tanzania in East Africa, numerous fossils important for our understanding of human evolution have been found near ancient lakes and streams, often sandwiched between layers of volcanic ash.

SITES AND FOSSIL LOCALITIES

Given that archaeologists and paleontologists work with artifacts and fossils, the question is: Where are they found? Places containing archaeological remains of previous human activity are known as **sites.** There are many kinds of sites, and sometimes it is difficult to define their boundaries, for remains may be strewn over large areas. Some examples are hunting campsites, from which hunters went out to hunt game; kill sites, in which game was killed and butchered; village sites, in which domestic activities took place; and cemeteries, in which the dead, and sometimes their belongings, were buried.

Sometimes human fossil remains are present at archaeological sites. This is the case, for example, at certain early sites in East Africa. Sometimes, though, human remains are found at other localities. For example, in South Africa the fossil remains of early human ancestors have been found in rock fissures, where their remains were dropped by such predators as leopards and eagles. Such places are usually referred to as **fossil localities.**

Stone blocks and notched logs suggest that this site may have been a human habitation prior to the flooding of the Black Sea, ca. 5600 B.C. This site was found along the submerged coast 25 km to the west of Ince Burun on the Sinop peninsula.

Site. In archaeology, a place containing remains of previous human activity. • **Fossil locality.** In paleoanthropology, a place where fossils are found.

Site and Locality Identification

Archaeological sites, particularly very old ones, frequently lie buried underground, and therefore the first task for the archaeologist is actually finding sites to investigate. Most sites are revealed by the presence of artifacts. Chance may play a crucial role in the discovery, as in the previously discussed case of the site at Barrow, Alaska. Usually, however, the archaeologist will have to survey a region in order to plot the sites available for excavation. A survey can be made from the ground, but nowadays more and more use is made of remote sensing techniques, many of them byproducts of space-age technology. Aerial photographs have been used off and on by archaeologists since the 1920s and are widely used today. Among other things, they were used for the discovery and interpretation of the huge geometric and zoomorphic markings on the coastal desert of Peru. More recently, use of high-resolution aerial photographs, including satellite imagery, resulted in the astonishing discovery of over 500 miles of prehistoric roadways connecting sites in the four-corners region (where Arizona, New Mexico, Colorado, and Utah meet) with other sites in ways that archaeologists had never suspected. This led to a new understanding of prehistoric Pueblo Indian economic, social, and political organization. Evidently, large centers like Pueblo Bonito were able to exercise political control over a number of satellite communities, mobilize labor for large public works, and see to the regular redistribution of goods over substantial distances.

On the ground, sites can be spotted by **soil marks,** or stains, that often show up on the surface of recently plowed fields. From soil marks, many Bronze Age burial mounds were discovered in northern Hertfordshire and southwestern Cambridgeshire, England. The mounds hardly rose out of the ground, yet each was circled at its core by chalky soil marks. Sometimes the very presence of certain chalky rock is significant. A search for Stone Age cave sites in Europe would be simplified with the aid of a geological map showing where limestone—a mineral necessary in the formation of caves—is to be found.

Some sites may be spotted by the kind of vegetation they grow. For example, the topsoil of ancient storage and refuse pits is often richer in organic matter than that of the surrounding areas, and so it grows a distinct vegetation.

Some archaeological features are best seen from the air, such as this figure of a hummingbird made in prehistoric times on the Nazca Desert of Peru.

Soil marks. Stains that show up on the surface of recently plowed fields that reveal an archaeological site.

Revealed by unusually low water levels are these remains of a 1,700-year-old fish weir, for trapping fish, in Maine. Until their discovery, submersion beneath the water preserved the lower portions of wooden stakes.

At Tikal, an ancient Maya site in Guatemala (Chapter 12), breadnut trees usually grow near the remains of ancient houses, so that an archaeologist looking for the remains of houses at Tikal would do well to search where these trees grow. In England, a wooden monument of the Stonehenge type at Darrington, Wiltshire, was discovered from an aerial photograph showing a distinct pattern of vegetation growing where the ancient structure once stood.

Documents, maps, folklore—ethnohistorical data—are also useful to the archaeologist. Heinrich Schliemann, the famous (and controversial) 19th-century German archaeologist, was led to the discovery of Troy after a reading of Homer's *Iliad.* He assumed that the city described by Homer as Ilium was really Troy. Place-names and local lore often are an indication that an archaeological site is to be found in the area. Archaeological surveys in North America depend a great deal upon amateur collectors who are usually familiar with local history.

Sometimes sites in eastern North America are exposed by natural agents, such as soil erosion or droughts. Many prehistoric Indian shell refuse mounds have been exposed by the erosion of river banks. A whole village of stone huts was exposed at Skara Brae in Britain's Orkney Islands by the action of wind as it blew away sand. And during the long drought of 1853–1854, a well-preserved prehistoric village was exposed when the water level of Lake Zurich, Switzerland, fell dramatically. In 1991, the mummified body of a man who lived 5,200 years ago was found in the Tyrolean Alps, where it had been released by glacial melting.

Often, archaeological remains are accidentally discovered in the course of some other human activity. Plowing sometimes turns up bones, fragments of pots, and other archaeological objects. Stone quarrying at Swanscombe, Kent, in England revealed an important site of the Old Stone Age, with human remains thought to be about 250,000 years old. In 1995, strip mining near the town of Schoningen in Germany led to the discovery of 400,000-year-old spears of *Homo erectus* (see Chapter 8). So frequently do construction projects uncover archaeological remains that in many countries, including the United States, projects that require government approval will not be authorized unless measures are first taken to identify and protect archaeological remains on the construction sites. Archaeological surveys in the United States are now routinely carried out as part of the envi-

Sometimes archaeological sites are marked by dramatic ruins, as shown here. This temple stands at the heart of the ancient Maya city of Tikal. Built by piling up rubble and facing it with limestone blocks held together with mortar, it served as the funerary monument of a king, whose body was placed in a tomb beneath the pyramidal base.

ronmental review process for federally funded or licensed construction projects.

Conspicuous sites, such as the great mounds or "tells" of the Middle East, are easy to spot, for the country is open. But it is difficult to locate ruins, even those that are well above ground, where there is a heavy forest cover. Thus, the discovery of archaeological sites is strongly affected by local geography.

Although archaeological sites may be found just about anywhere, the same is not true for fossil localities. One will find fossils only in geological contexts where conditions are known to have been right for fossilization. Once the paleoanthropologist has identified such regions, specific localities are identified in much the same ways as archaeological sites. Indeed, the discovery of ancient stone tools may lead to the discovery of human fossil remains. For example, it was the presence of very crude stone tools in Olduvai Gorge, East Africa, that prompted Mary and Louis Leakey to search there for the human fossils (discussed in Chapters 6 and 7) they eventually found.

Site and Locality Excavation

Before the archaeologist or paleoanthropologist plans an excavation, he or she must ask the question, "Why am I digging?" Then he or she must consider the amount of time, money, and labor that can be committed to the enterprise. The recovery of archaeological and fossil material long ago ceased to be the province of the enlightened amateur, as it once was when any enterprising collector went out to dig for the sake of digging. A modern excavation is carefully planned and rigorously conducted; it should not only shed light on the human past but should also help us to understand cultural and evolutionary processes in general.

ARCHAEOLOGICAL EXCAVATION

Once a site is located that is likely to contribute to the solution of some important research problem, the next step is to plan and carry out excavation. To begin, the land is cleared, and the places to be excavated are plotted. This is usually done by means of a **grid system.**

Grid system. A system for recording data from an archaeological excavation.

Anthropology Applied: Cultural Resource Management

In June 1979, on a knoll next to a river not far from Lake Champlain, a survey crew working for Peter A. Thomas of the University of Vermont's Consulting Archaeology Program discovered archaeological materials unlike any found before in the region. The following June, Thomas returned to the site with a crew of five in order to excavate a portion of it. What they found were the remains of an 8,000-year-old hunting-and-fishing camp that had been occupied for up to a few months in the spring or fall by perhaps one or two families. From the site they recovered a distinctive tool inventory never recognized before, as well as data related to hunting and fishing subsistence practices, butchery or hide processing, cooking, tool manufacture, and a possible shelter. Because many archaeologists had previously believed the region to be devoid of human occupation 8,000 years ago, recovery of these data was especially important.

What sets this work apart from traditional archaeological research is that it was conducted as part of cultural resource management activities required by state and federal laws to preserve important aspects of the country's prehistoric and historic heritage. In this case, the Vermont Agency of Transportation planned to replace an inadequate highway bridge with a new one. Because the project was partially funded by the U.S. government, steps had to be taken to identify and protect any significant prehistoric or historic resources that might be adversely affected. To do so, the Vermont Agency of Transportation hired Thomas—first to see if such resources existed in the project area, and then to retrieve data from the endangered portions of the one site that was found. As a result, an important contribution was made to our knowledge of the prehistory of northeastern North America.

Since passage of the Historic Preservation Act of 1966, the National Environmental Policy Act of 1969, and the Archaeological and Historical Preservation Act of 1974, the field of cultural resource management has flourished. Today, most archaeological fieldwork in the United States is carried out as cultural resource management. Consequently, many archaeologists are employed by such agencies as the Army Corps of Engineers, the National Park Service, the U.S. Forest Service, and the U.S. Soil and Conservation Service to assist in the preservation, restoration, and salvage of archaeological resources. Archaeologists are also employed by state historic preservation agencies. Finally, they do a considerable amount of consulting work for engineering firms to help them prepare environmental impact statements. Some of these archaeologists, like Thomas, operate out of universities and colleges, while others are on the staffs of independent consulting firms.

The surface of the site is divided into squares, each square being numbered and marked with stakes. Each object found may then be located precisely in the square from which it came. (Remember, in archaeology, context is everything!) The starting point of a grid system may be a large rock, the edge of a stone wall, or an iron rod sunk into the ground. The starting point is also known as the reference or **datum point.** At a large site covering several square miles, this kind of grid system is not feasible because of the large size of the ruins. In such cases, the plotting may be done in terms of individual structures, numbered according to the square of a "giant grid" in which they are found (Figure 2.1).

In a gridded site, each square is dug separately with great care. Trowels are used to scrape the soil, and screens are used to sift all the loose soils so that even the smallest artifacts, such as flint chips or beads, are recovered.

A technique employed when looking for very fine objects, such as fish scales or very small bones, is called **flotation.** Flotation consists of immersing soil in water,

Datum point. The starting, or reference, point for a grid system. • **Flotation.** An archeological technique employed to recover very tiny objects by immersion of soil samples in water to separate heavy from light particles.

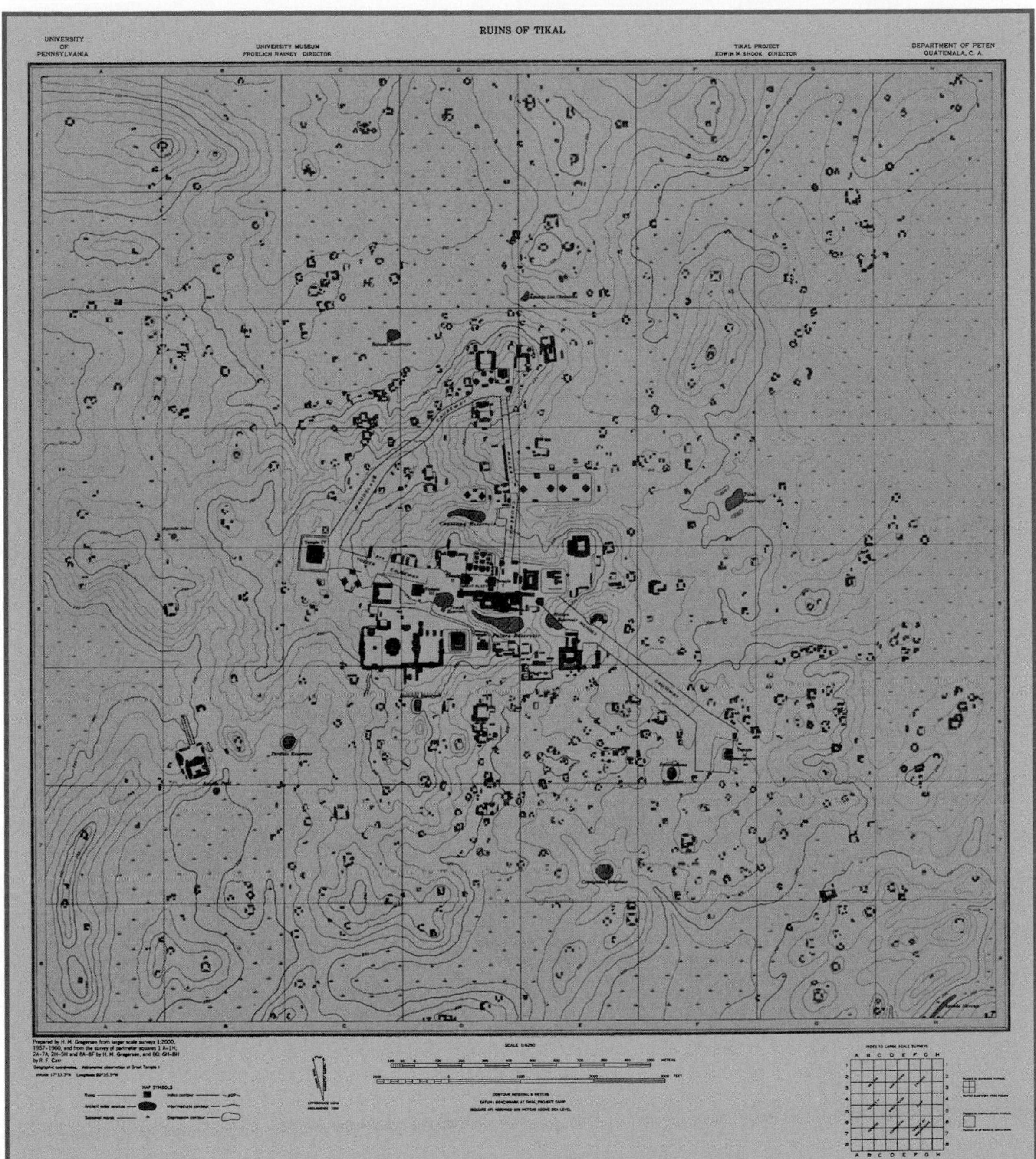

FIGURE 2.1

AT LARGE SITES COVERING SEVERAL SQUARE MILES, A GIANT GRID IS CONTRUCTED, AS SHOWN IN THIS MAP OF THE CENTER OF THE ANCIENT MAYA CITY OF TIKAL. EACH SQUARE OF THE GRID IS ONE-QUARTER OF A SQUARE KILOMETER; INDIVIDUAL STRUCTURES ARE NUMBERED ACCORDING TO THE SQUARE IN WHICH THEY ARE FOUND. THE TEMPLE SHOWN ON PAGE 43 CAN BE LOCATED NEAR THE CENTER OF THE MAP, ON THE EAST EDGE OF THE GREAT PLAZA.

To recover very small objects easily missed in excavation, archaeologists routinely screen the earth they remove.

causing the particles to separate. Some will float, others will sink to the bottom, and the remains can be easily retrieved. If the site is **stratified**—that is, if the remains lie in layers one upon the other—each layer, or stratum, will be dug separately. Each layer, having been laid down during a particular span of time, will contain artifacts deposited at the same time and belonging to the same culture. Culture change can be traced through the order in which artifacts were deposited. But, say archaeologists Frank Hole and Robert F. Heizer, "because of difficulties in analyzing stratigraphy, archaeologists must use the greatest caution in drawing conclusions. Almost all interpretations of time, space, and culture contexts depend on stratigraphy. The refinements of laboratory techniques for analysis are wasted if archaeologists cannot specify the stratigraphic position of their artifacts."[3] If no stratification is present, then the archaeologist digs by arbitrary levels. Each square must be dug so that its edges and profiles are straight; walls between squares are often left standing to serve as visual correlates of the grid system.

This photo shows a section excavated through a building at the ancient Maya site of Tikal and illustrates stratigraphy. Inside the building's base are the remains of walls and floors for earlier buildings. Oldest are the innermost and deepest walls and floors. As time wore on, the Maya periodically demolished upper portions of older buildings, the remains of which were buried beneath new construction.

EXCAVATION OF FOSSILS

Excavating for fossils is in many ways like archaeological excavation, although there are some differences. The paleoanthropologist must be particularly skilled in the techniques of geology, or else have ready access to geological expertise, because a fossil is of little value unless its temporal place in the sequence of rocks that contain it can be determined. In addition, the paleoanthropologist must be able to identify the fossil-laden rocks, their deposition, and other geological details. In order to provide all the necessary expertise, paleoanthropological expeditions these days generally are made up of teams of experts in various fields in addition to physical anthropology. A great deal of skill and caution is required to remove a

[3]Hole, F., & Heizer, R. F. (1969). *An introduction to prehistoric archeology* (p. 113). New York: Holt, Rinehart & Winston.

Stratified. Layered; said of archaeological sites where the remains lie in layers, one upon another.

fossil from its burial place without damage. An unusual combination of tools and materials is usually contained in the kit of the paleoanthropologist—pickaxes, enamel coating, burlap for bandages, and plaster of paris.

To remove newly discovered bones, the paleoanthropologist begins uncovering the specimen, using pick and shovel for initial excavation, then small camel-hair brushes and dental picks to remove loose and easily detachable debris surrounding the bones. Once the entire specimen has been uncovered (a process that may take days of back-breaking, patient labor), the bones are covered with shellac and tissue paper to prevent cracking and damage during further excavation and handling.

Both the fossil and the earth immediately surrounding it, or the matrix, are prepared for removal as a single block. The bones and matrix are cut out of the earth (but not removed), and more shellac is applied to the entire block to harden it. The bones are covered with burlap bandages dipped in plaster of paris. Then the entire block is enclosed in plaster and burlap bandages, perhaps splinted with tree branches, and allowed to dry overnight. After it has hardened, the entire block is carefully removed from the earth, ready for packing and transport to a laboratory. Before leaving the discovery area, the investigator makes a thorough sketch map of the terrain and pinpoints the find on geological maps to aid future investigators.

State of Preservation of Archaeological and Fossil Evidence

What is recovered in the course of excavation depends upon the nature of the remains as much as upon the excavator's digging skills. Inorganic materials such as stone and metal are more resistant to decay than organic ones such as wood and bone. Often an archaeologist comes upon an assemblage—a collection of artifacts—made of durable inorganic materials, such as stone tools, and traces of organic ones long since decomposed, such as woodwork (Figure 2.2), textiles, or food.

State of preservation is affected by climate; under favorable climatic conditions, even the most perishable objects may survive over vast periods of time. For example, predynastic Egyptian burials consisting of shallow pits in the sand often yield well-preserved corpses. Because these bodies were buried long before mummification was ever practiced, their preservation can only be the result of rapid desiccation in the very warm, dry climate. The tombs of dynastic Egypt often contain wooden furniture, textiles, flowers, and papyri barely touched by time, seemingly as fresh looking as they were when deposited in the tomb 3,000 years ago—a consequence of the dryness of the atmosphere.

The dryness of certain caves is also a factor in the preservation of fossilized human or animal feces. Human feces are a source of information on prehistoric foods and

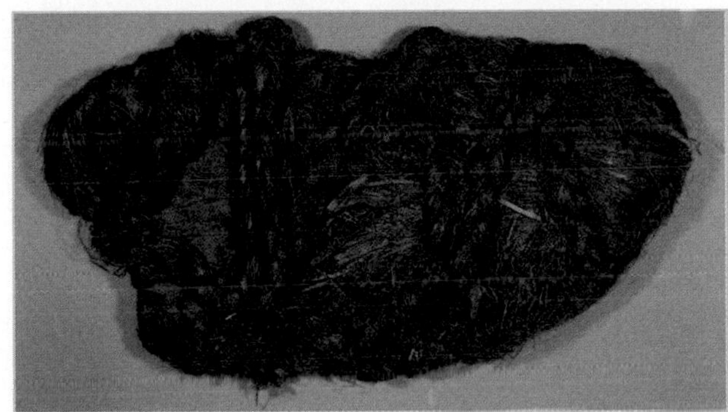

This sandal, made of plant fibers, is over 8,000 years old, making it North America's oldest known footwear. In most soils, objects made of such materials would have long since decayed. This one survived only because of the dry condition of the cave (Arnold Research Cave in Missouri) in which it was found.

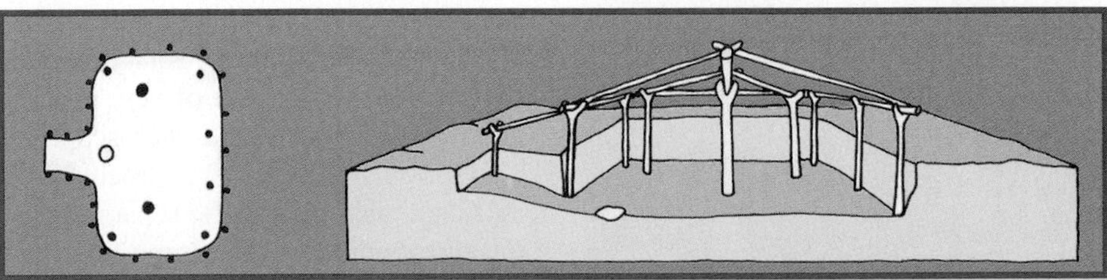

FIGURE 2.2

ALTHOUGH THE WOODEN POSTS OF A HOUSE MAY HAVE LONG SINCE DECAYED, THEIR POSITIONS MAY STILL BE MARKED BY DISCOLORATION OF THE SOIL. THE PLAN SHOWN ON THE LEFT, OF AN ANCIENT POSTHOLE PATTERN AND DEPRESSION AT SNAKETOWN, ARIZONA, PERMITS THE HYPOTHETICAL HOUSE RECONSTRUCTION ON THE RIGHT.

can be analyzed for dietary remains. From such analysis archaeologists can determine not only what the inhabitants ate but also how the food was prepared. Because many sources of food are available only in certain seasons, it is even possible to tell the time of year in which the food was eaten and the excrement deposited.

Certain climates can soon obliterate all evidence of organic remains. Maya ruins found in the very warm and moist tropical rain forests of Mesoamerica are often in a state of collapse—notwithstanding that many are massive structures of stone—as a result of the pressure exerted upon them by the heavy forest vegetation. The rain and humidity soon destroy almost all traces of woodwork, textiles, or basketry. Fortunately, impressions of these artifacts can sometimes be preserved in plaster, and some objects made of wood or plant fibers are depicted in stone carvings and pottery figurines. Thus, even in the face of complete decay of organic substances, something may still be learned about them.

The cultural practices of ancient humans may also account for the preservation of archaeological remains. The ancient Egyptians believed that eternal life could be achieved only if the dead person were buried with his or her worldly possessions. Hence, their tombs are usually filled with a wealth of artifacts. Many skeletal remains of Neandertals (Chapter 9) are known because they practiced burial, perhaps because they, too, believed in some sort of afterlife. By contrast, skeletal remains of pre-Neandertal peoples are rare and when found usually consist of mere fragments rather than complete skeletons.

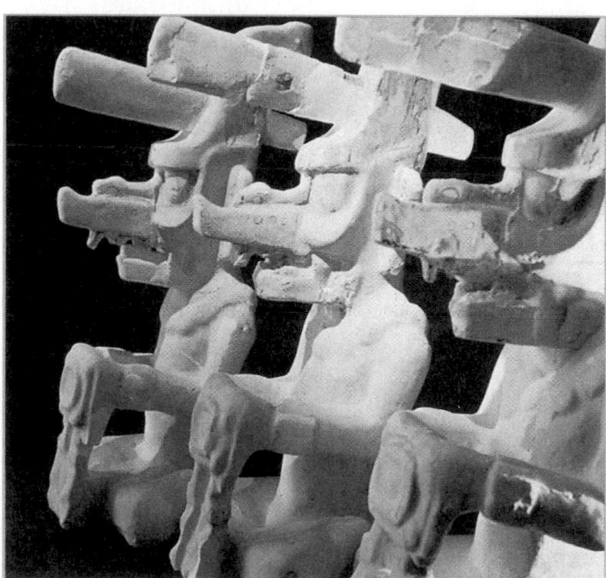

At the Maya site of Tikal, these manikin sceptre figures originally made of wood were recovered from a king's tomb by pouring plaster into a cavity in the soil, left when the original organic material decayed.

SORTING OUT THE EVIDENCE

It cannot be stressed too strongly that the value of archaeological materials is virtually destroyed if an accurate and detailed record of the excavations is not kept. As one eminent anthropologist has put it:

> The fundamental premise of excavation is that all digging is destructive, even that done by experts. The archaeologist's primary responsibility, therefore, is to record a site for posterity as it is dug because there are no second chances.[4]

Excavation records include a scale map of all the features, the stratification of each excavated square, a description of the exact location and depth of every artifact or bone unearthed, and photographs and scale drawings of the objects. This is the only way archaeological evidence can later be pieced together so as to arrive at a plausible reconstruction of a culture. Although the archaeologist may be interested only in certain kinds of remains, every aspect of the site must be recorded, whether it is relevant to the particular investigation or not, because such evidence may be useful to others and would otherwise be permanently lost. One must remember that archaeological sites are nonrenewable resources, and that their destruction, whether by proper excavation or by looting, is permanent.

After photographs and scale drawings are made, the materials recovered are processed in the laboratory. In the case of fossils, the block in which they have been removed from the field is cut open, and the fossil is separated from the matrix. Like the initial removal from the earth, this is a long, painstaking job involving a great deal of skill and special tools. This task may be done with hammer and chisel, dental drills, rotary grinders, or pneumatic chisels, and, in the case of very small pieces, with awls and tiny needles under a microscope.

Chemicals, such as hydrochloric and hydrofluoric acids, are also used in the separation process to dissolve the surrounding matrix. Some fossils require processing by other methods. For example, precise identification

---

[4]Fagan, B. M. (1995). *People of the earth* (8th ed.; p. 19). New York: HarperCollins.

This ancient Sumerian Tell in Iraq has been so extensively looted that it resembles a moonscape. Such looting destroys irreplaceable evidence.

can be obtained by examining thin, almost transparent strips of some fossils under a microscope. Casts of the insides of skulls (**endocasts**) are made by filling the skull wall with an acid-resistant material, then removing the wall with acid. A skull may be cleaned out and the inside painted with latex. After the latex hardens, it is removed in a single piece, revealing indirect evidence of brain shape and outer appearance. Such endocasts are helpful in determining the size and complexity of ancient brains.

Archaeologists, as a rule of thumb, plan on at least 3 hours of laboratory work for each hour of fieldwork. In the lab, artifacts that have been recovered must first be cleaned and catalogued—often a tedious and time-consuming job—before they are ready for analysis. From the shapes of the artifacts and from the traces of manufacture and wear, archaeologists can usually determine their function. For example, the Russian archaeologist S. A. Semenov devoted many years to the study of prehistoric technology. In the case of a flint tool used as a scraper, he was able to determine, by examining the wear patterns of the tool under a microscope, that the prehistoric individuals who used it began to scrape from right to left and then scraped from left to right, and in so doing avoided straining the muscles of the hand.[5] From the work of Semenov and others, we now know that most stone tools were made by right-handed individuals, a fact that has implications for brain structure (see also Figure 2.3).

[5]Semenov, S. A. (1964). *Prehistoric technology.* New York: Barnes & Noble.

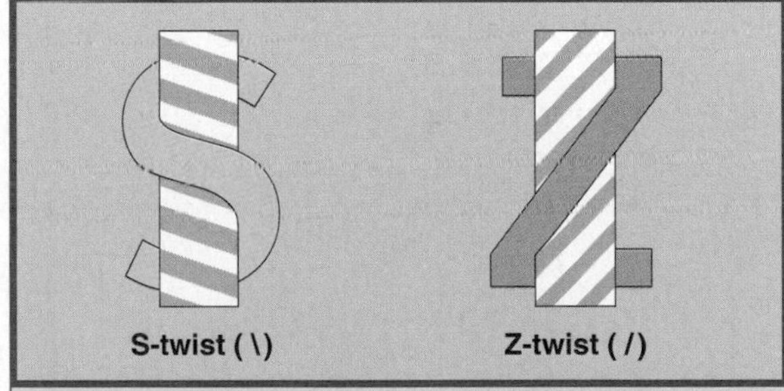

FIGURE 2.3
IN NORTHERN NEW ENGLAND, PREHISTORIC POTTERY WAS OFTEN DECORATED BY IMPRESSING THE DAMP CLAY WITH A CORD-WRAPPED STICK. EXAMINATION OF CORD IMPRESSIONS REVEALS THAT COASTAL PEOPLE TWISTED FIBERS USED TO MAKE CORDAGE TO THE LEFT (Z-TWIST), WHILE THOSE LIVING INLAND DID THE OPPOSITE (S-TWIST). THE NONFUNCTIONAL DIFFERENCES REFLECT MOTOR HABITS SO DEEPLY INGRAINED AS TO SEEM COMPLETELY NATURAL TO THE CORDAGE MAKERS. FROM THIS, WE MAY INFER TWO DISTINCTIVELY DIFFERENT POPULATIONS.

Endocast. A cast of the inside of a skull; helps determine the size and shape of the brain.

Analysis of vegetable and animal remains provides clues about the environment and the economic activities of the occupants of a site (Figure 2.4). Such analysis may help clarify peoples' relationship to their environment and its influence upon the development of their **technology**—the knowledge they employ to make and use objects. For example, we know that the people responsible for Serpent Mound in Ontario, Canada (a mound having the form of a serpent, consisting of burials and discarded shells), were there only in the spring and early summer, when they came to collect shellfish and perform their annual burial rites; apparently they moved elsewhere at the beginning of summer to pursue other seasonal subsistence activities. Archaeologists have inferred that the mound was unoccupied in winter, because this is the season when deer shed their antlers, yet no deer antlers were found on the site. Nor were duck bones found, and so archaeologists conclude that the mound was also unoccupied in the fall, when ducks stopped on their migratory route southward to feed on the wild rice that grew in the region.

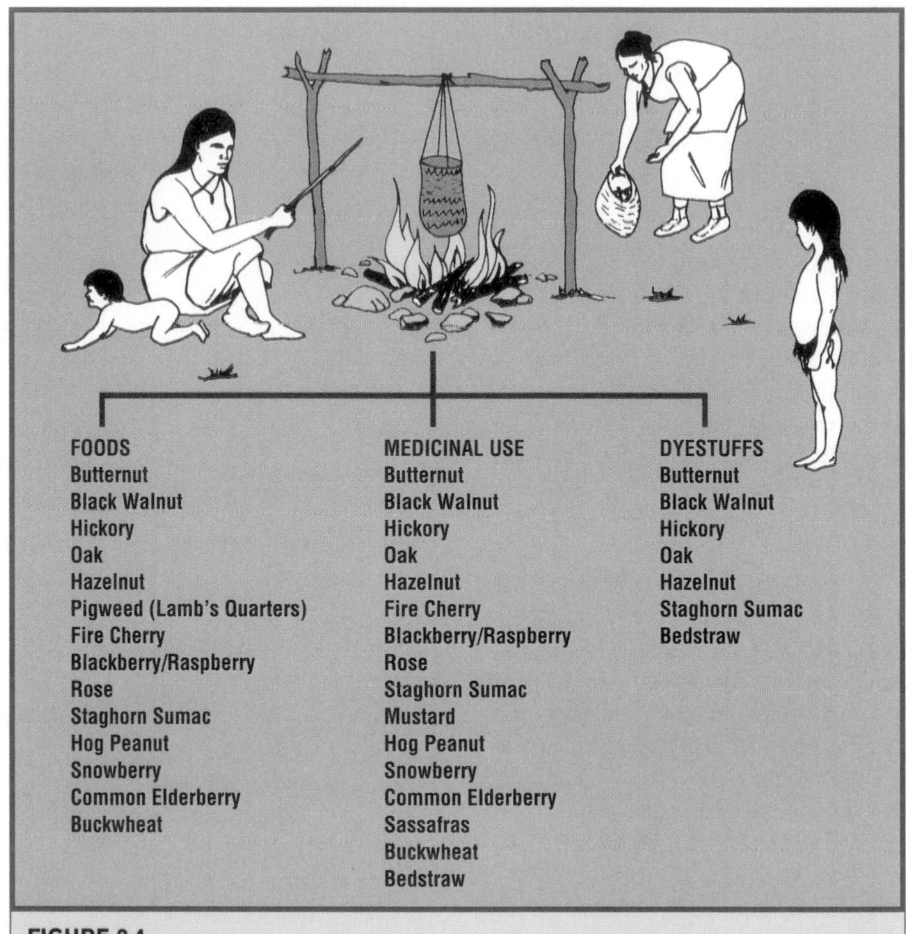

FIGURE 2.4

Plant remains recovered from hearths used by people between 1,000 and 2,000 years ago at an archaeological site in Vermont may have been utilized as shown here, based on our knowledge of how the same plants were used by Indians in the region when first encountered by Europeans. Occupation of the site must have been in the summer and fall, the seasons when these plants are available.

Technology. The knowledge that people employ to make and use objects.

Analysis of human skeletal material also provides important insights into ancient peoples' diets. Microscopic wear patterns on teeth, for example, may reveal whether abrasive plants were important foods. Similarly, people who eat more plants than meat will have a higher ratio of strontium to calcium in their bones. At the ancient Maya city of Tikal, analysis of human skeletons showed that elite members of society had access to better diets than lower ranking members of society, allowing them to reach their full growth potential with greater regularity. Important insights into life expectancy, mortality, and health status also emerge from the study of human skeletal remains. Unfortunately, such studies have become more difficult to carry out, especially in the United States, as Native American communities demand (and federal law requires) the return of skeletons from archaeological excavations for reburial. Archaeologists find themselves in something of a quandary over this requirement; as scientists, they know the importance of the information that can be gleaned from studies of human skeletons, but as anthropologists, they are bound to respect the feelings of those whose ancestors those skeletons represent. Currently (as illustrated in the Original Study in this chapter), archaeologists are consulting with representatives of Native American communities to work out procedures with which both parties can live.

Some ancient societies devised precise ways of recording dates that archaeologists have been able to correlate with our own calendar. Here is the tomb of an important ruler, Stormy Sky, at the ancient Maya city of Tikal. The glyphs painted on the wall give the date of the burial in the Maya calendar, which is the same as March 18th, A.D. 457, in our calendar.

Dating the Past

With accurate and detailed records of their excavations in hand, archaeologists and paleoanthropologists are able to deal with a question crucial to their research: the question of age. As we have seen, without knowledge of which materials are contemporary, older, or younger, no meaningful analysis is possible. How, then, are objects and events from the past reliably dated? Because archaeologists and paleoanthropologists deal so often with peoples and events in times far removed from our own, the calendar of historic times is of little use to them. Therefore, they must rely on two kinds of dating: relative and "absolute." **Relative dating** consists simply of finding out if an event or object is younger or older than another. **"Absolute"** or (more properly) **chronometric dates** are dates based upon solar years and are reckoned in "years before the present" (B.P., with "present" defined as A.D. 1950). Many relative and chronometric techniques are available; here, there is space to discuss only the ones most often relied upon (others will be touched on as necessary in succeeding chapters). Ideally, archaeologists try to utilize as many methods as are appropriate, given the materials available to work with and the funds at their disposal. By doing so, they significantly reduce the risk of arriving at erroneous dates.

Relative dating. In archaeology and paleoanthropology, designating an event, object, or fossil as being older or younger than another. • **"Absolute" or chronometric dates.** In archaeology and paleoanthropology, dates for archaeological materials based on solar years, centuries, or other units of absolute time.

Methods of Relative Dating

Of the many relative dating techniques available, **stratigraphy** is probably the most reliable. Stratigraphy is based on the simple principle that the oldest layer, or stratum, was deposited first (it is the deepest) whereas the newest layer was deposited last (in undisturbed situations, it lies at the top). Therefore, in an archaeological site the evidence is usually deposited in chronological order. The lowest stratum contains the oldest artifacts and/or fossils, whereas the uppermost stratum contains the most recent ones. Thus, even in the absence of precise dates, one knows the *relative* age of objects in one stratum compared with the ages of those in other strata.

Another method of relative dating is the **fluorine test.** It is based on the fact that the amount of fluorine deposited in bones is proportional to their age. The oldest bones contain the greatest amount of fluorine, and vice versa. The fluorine test is useful in dating bones that cannot be ascribed with certainty to any particular stratum and cannot be dated according to the stratigraphic method. A shortcoming of this method is that the rate of fluorine formation is not constant, but varies from region to region.

Relative dating can also be done on the evidence of botanical and animal remains. A common method, known as **palynology,** involves the study of pollen grains. The kind of pollen found in any geologic stratum depends on the kind of vegetation that existed at the time that stratum was deposited. A site or locality can therefore be dated by determining what kind of pollen was found associated with it. In addition, palynology is also an important technique for reconstructing past environments in which people lived.

Another method, involving faunal analysis, relies on our knowledge of paleontology. Sites containing the bones of extinct animal species are usually older than sites in which the remains of these animals are absent. Very early North American Indian sites have yielded the remains of mastodons and mammoths—animals now extinct—and on this basis the sites can be dated to a time before these animals died out, roughly 10,000 years ago. Even in the absence of extinct animal remains, faunal assemblages may provide clues to dating. Since the end of the Ice Age, climates have continued to change, in response to natural cycles as well as human activity. The resultant changes in ecology are reflected in the kinds of animal remains to be found. As one learns the sequence of changes, the presence or absence of particular animal species can give at least an approximate age for associated archaeological materials.

Methods of Chronometric Dating

One of the most widely used methods of "absolute" or chronometric dating is **radiocarbon analysis.** It is based on the fact that all living organisms absorb radioactive carbon (known as carbon 14), maintaining equilibrium with the level of this isotope in the atmosphere, and that this absorption ceases at the time of death. It is possible to measure in the laboratory the amount of radioactive carbon left in even a few milligrams of a given organic substance, because radioactive substances break down or decay slowly and at a constant rate over a fixed period of time. Carbon 14 begins to disintegrate, returning to nitrogen 14, emitting radioactive (beta) particles in the process. At death, about 15 beta radiations per minute per gram of material are emitted. The rate of decay is known as "half-life," and the half-life of carbon 14 is 5,730 years. This means that it takes 5,730 years for one-half of the original amount of carbon 14 to decay into nitrogen 14. Beta radiation will be about 7.5 counts per minute per gram. In another 5,730 years, one-half of this amount of carbon 14 will also have decayed. In other words, after 11,460 years, only one-fourth of the original amount of carbon 14 will be present. Thus the age of an organic substance such as charcoal, wood, shell, or bone can be measured by counting the beta rays emitted by the remaining carbon 14. The radiocarbon method can adequately date organic materials up to 70,000 years old and is the standard method of dating such materials. Of course, one has to be sure that the association between organic remains and archaeological materials is valid. For example, charcoal found on a site may have gotten there from a recent

Stratigraphy. In archaeology and paleoanthropology, the most reliable method of relative dating by means of strata. • **Fluorine test.** In archaeology or paleoanthropology, a technique for relative dating based on the fact that the amount of fluorine in bones is proportional to their age. • **Palynology.** In archaeology and paleoanthropology, a method of relative dating based on changes in fossil pollen over time. • **Radiocarbon analysis.** In archaeology and paleoanthropology, a technique for chronometric dating based on measuring the amount of radioactive carbon (C-14) left in organic materials found in archaeological sites.

forest fire, rather than more ancient activity; or wood used to make something by the people who lived at a site may have been retrieved from some older context.

Because there is always a certain amount of error involved, radiocarbon dates are not as absolute as is sometimes thought. This is why any stated date always has a plus-or-minus (±) factor attached to it. For example, a date of 5,200 ± 120 years ago means that there is a 2 out of 3 chance that the true date falls somewhere within the 240 years between 5,080 and 5,320 radiocarbon years ago. The qualification "radiocarbon years" is necessary, because we have discovered that radiocarbon years are not precisely equivalent to calendar years.

The discovery that radiocarbon years are not precisely equivalent to calendar years was made possible by another method of "absolute" dating, **dendrochronology.** Originally devised for dating Pueblo Indian sites in the North American Southwest, this method is based on the fact that in the right kind of climate, trees add one (and only one) new growth ring to their trunks every year (Figure 2.5). The rings vary in thickness, depending upon the amount of rainfall received in a year, so that climatic fluctuation is registered in the growth ring. By taking a sample of wood, such as a beam from a Pueblo Indian house, and by comparing its pattern of rings with those in the trunk of a tree known to be as old as the artifact, archaeologists can date the archaeological material. Dendrochronology is applicable only to wooden objects. Furthermore, it can be used only in regions in which trees of great age, such as the giant sequoias and the bristlecone pine, are known to grow. On the other hand, radiocarbon dating of wood from bristlecone pines that have been dated by dendrochronology allows us to correct carbon-14 dates so as to bring them into agreement with calendar dates.

Potassium-argon analysis, another commonly used method of "absolute" dating, is based on a technique similar to that of radiocarbon analysis. Following intense heating, as from a volcanic eruption, radioactive potassium decays at a known rate to form argon, any previously existing argon having been released by the heating. The half-life of radioactive potassium is 1.3 billion years. Deposits that are millions of years old can now be dated by measuring the ratio of potassium to argon in a given rock. Volcanic debris, such as at Olduvai Gorge and other localities in East Africa, is routinely dated by potassium-argon analysis; thus we know when the volcanic eruption occurred. If fossils or artifacts are found sandwiched between layers of volcanic ash, as they are at Olduvai and other sites in East Africa, they can therefore be dated with some precision. But as with radiocarbon dates, there are limits to that precision, and potassium-argon dates are always stated with a plus-or-minus margin of error attached.

Amino acid racemization dating, yet another chronometric technique, is of potential importance

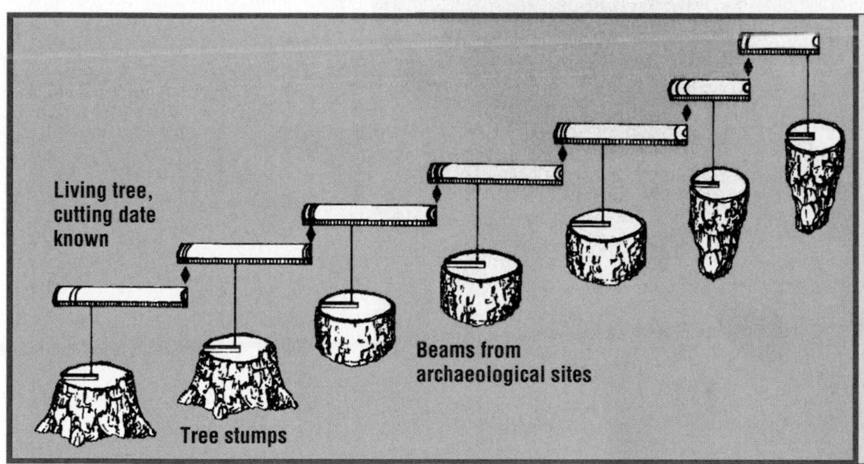

FIGURE 2.5
CHRONOMETRIC DATING BASED ON TREE RINGS IS CALLED *DENDROCHRONOLOGY.* STARTING WITH A SAMPLE OF KNOWN AGE, RING PATTERNS TOWARD THE INNER PART ARE MATCHED WITH THOSE FROM THE OUTER PART OF THE OLDER SAMPLE, AND SO ON, BACK IN TIME.

Dendrochronology. In archaeology, a method of chronometric dating based on the number of rings of growth found in a tree trunk. • **Potassium-argon analysis.** In archaeology and paleoanthropology, a technique for chronometric dating that measures the ratio of radioactive potassium to argon in volcanic debris associated with human remains. • **Amino acid racemization dating.** In archaeology and paleoanthropology, a technique for chronometric dating that measures the ratio of right- to left-handed amino acids.

because it bridges a time gap between the effective ranges of the radiocarbon and potassium-argon methods. It is based on the fact that amino acids trapped in organic materials gradually change, or "racemize" after death, from left-handed forms to right-handed forms. Thus, the ratio of left- to right-handed forms should indicate the specimen's age. Unfortunately, in substances like bone, moisture and acids in the soil can leach out the amino acids, thereby introducing a serious source of error. However, ostrich eggshells have proved immune to this problem, the amino acids being so effectively locked up in a tight mineral matrix that they are preserved for thousands of years. Because ostrich eggs were widely used as food, and the shells as containers in Africa and the Middle East, they provide a powerful means of dating sites of the middle part of the Old Stone Age (Paleolithic), between 40,000 and 180,000 years ago.

Radiocarbon, potassium-argon, and amino acid racemization dating are only three of several high-tech dating methods that have been developed in the past few decades. Radiocarbon and potassium-argon, in particular, are the chronometric methods most heavily relied on by archaeologists and paleoanthropologists; nevertheless, other methods are increasingly used as a check on accuracy and to supplement dates determined by other means. To cite one example, a technique called **electron spin resonance** measures the trapped electron population in bone or shell (the number of trapped electrons indicates the specimen's age). Because electron spin resonance dates derived from an important Middle Paleolithic skull from Qafzeh, Israel (discussed in Chapter 9), agree with those based on amino acid racemization, we can have confidence that the dating is correct. Because other methods of chronometric dating are often complicated, they tend to be expensive; many can be carried out only on specific kinds of materials, and in the case of some, are so new that their reliability is not yet unequivocally established. It is for these reasons that they have not been as widely used as radiocarbon and potassium-argon.

CHANCE AND THE STUDY OF THE PAST

It is important to understand the imperfect nature of the archaeological and fossil records. They are imperfect, first of all, because the chance circumstances of preservation have determined what has and what has not sur-

In this photo, geologist Carl Swisher orients a rock sample for paleomagnetic dating. This method of dating is based on the fact that the earth's magnetic pole has shifted over time. For example, magnetically charged particles in sediments between 1.8 and 1.6 million years old document a reversal, and fossils found in such sediments can be dated accordingly.

Electron spin resonance. In archaeology and paleoanthropology, a technique for chronometric dating that measures the number of trapped electrons in bone or shell.

HIGHWAY 1

Visit the award-winning interactive Web site of the University of Pennsylvania's Museum of Archaeology and Anthropology and experience the museum's fabulous collections. You can tour everything from virtual excavations being conducted by Penn faculty in places such as Mesoamerica and Central Asia, to the treasures housed in the Egyptian gallery, to virtual exhibits on the origins and ancient history of wine.
www.upenn.edu/museum/

HIGHWAY 2

A trip to this site goes underwater to visit the State of Florida's Underwater Archaeological Preserves. Visit the shipwrecked remains of battleships, steamers, and sailboats. Each shipwreck site contains a location map and a complete site plan as well as ways to become involved in Florida's Underwater Archaeology Program.
http://dhr.dos.state.fl.us/bar/uap/

vived the ravages of time. Thus, cultures must be reconstructed on the basis of incomplete and, possibly, unrepresentative samples of artifacts. The problems are further compounded by the large role chance continues to play in the discovery of prehistoric remains. Therefore, one must always be cautious when trying to interpret the human past. No matter how elegant a particular theory may be about what happened in the past, new evidence may at any time force its reexamination and modification, or even rejection, in favor of some better theory.

CHAPTER SUMMARY

Archaeology and physical anthropology, though they do not neglect the present, are the two branches of anthropology most involved in the study of the human past. Archaeologists study material remains to describe and explain human behavior; physical anthropologists called paleoanthropologists study fossil remains to understand and explain the processes at work in human biological evolution. Each specialty contributes to the other's objectives, as well as its own, and the two share many methods of data recovery.

Artifacts are objects fashioned or altered by humans, such as a flint chip, a pottery vessel, or even a house. A fossil is any trace of an organism of past geological time that has been preserved in the earth's crust. Fossilization typically involves the hard parts of an organism and may take place through freezing in ice, preservation in bogs or tar pits, immersion in water, or inclusion in rock deposits. Fossilization is most apt to occur among animals and other organisms that live in or near water because of the likelihood that their corpses will be buried and preserved on sea, lake, and river bottoms. On land, conditions in caves or near active volcanic activity may be conducive to fossilization.

Places containing archaeological remains of previous human occupation are known as sites. Sometimes human fossils are present at archaeological sites, but they may occur by themselves at fossil localities. Sites and localities are generally located by a survey of a region. While fossil localities are revealed by the presence of fossils, archaeological sites are revealed by the presence of artifacts. Irregularities of the ground surface, unusual soil discoloration, and unexpected variations in vegetation type and coloring may also indicate the location of a site. Ethnohistorical data—maps, documents, and folklore—may provide further clues to the location of archaeological sites. Sometimes both fossils and archaeological remains are discovered accidentally, for example, in plowing, quarrying, or in building construction.

Once a site or locality has been selected for excavation, the area is divided and carefully marked with a grid system; the starting point of the dig is called the datum point. Each square within the grid is carefully excavated, and any archaeological or fossil remains are recovered through employment of various tools and screens; for very fine objects, the method of flotation is employed. The location of each artifact when found must be carefully noted. Once excavated, artifacts and fossils undergo further cleaning and preservation in the laboratory with the use of specialized tools and chemicals.

The durability of archaeological evidence depends upon climate and the nature of the artifacts. Inorganic materials are more resistant to decay than organic ones. However, given a very dry climate, even organic materials may be well preserved. Warm, moist climates as well as thick vegetation act to decompose organic material quickly, and even inorganic material may suffer from the effects of humidity and vegetation growth. The durability of archaeological evidence is also dependent upon the social customs of ancient people.

Because excavation in fact destroys a site, the archaeologist must maintain a thorough record in the form of maps, descriptions, scale drawings, and photographs of every aspect of the excavation. All artifacts must be cleaned and classified before being sent to the laboratory for analysis. Often the shape and markings of artifacts can determine their function, and the analysis of vegetable and animal remains may provide information.

There are two kinds of methods for dating archaeological and fossil remains. Relative dating is a method of determining the age of objects relative to one another and includes the method of stratigraphy, based on the position of the artifact or fossil in relation to different layers of soil deposits. The fluorine test is based on the determination of the amount of fluorine deposited in the bones. The analysis of floral remains (including palynology) and faunal deposits is also widely employed. Methods of "absolute," or chronometric, dating include radiocarbon analysis, which measures the amount of carbon 14 that remains in organic objects; potassium-argon analysis, which measures the percentage of radioactive potassium that has decayed to argon in volcanic material; dendrochronology, dating based upon tree rings; and amino acid racemization, based on changes from left- to right-handed amino acids in organic materials, especially eggshells. Other chronometric methods exist, such as electron spin resonance, but are not as widely used, because of limited applicability, difficulty of application, expense, or (as-yet) unproven reliability.

CLASSIC READINGS

Fagan, B. M. (1998). *People of the earth: An introduction to world prehistory* (9th ed.). New York: Longman.

There are a number of good texts that, like this one, try to summarize the findings of archaeologists on a worldwide scale. This book, being one of the more recent ones, is reasonably up to date.

Feder, K. L. (1999). *Frauds, myths, and mysteries* (3rd ed.). Mountain View, CA: Mayfield.

This very readable book is written to enlighten readers about the many pseudo-scientific and even crackpot theories about past cultures that all too often have been presented to the public as "solid" archaeology.

Joukowsky, M. (1980). *A complete field manual of archaeology: Tools and techniques of fieldwork for archaeologists.* Englewood Cliffs, NJ: Prentice-Hall.

This book, encyclopedic in its coverage, explains for the novice and professional alike all of the methods and techniques used by archaeologists in the field. Two concluding chapters discuss fieldwork opportunities and financial aid for archaeological research.

Sharer, R. J., & Ashmore, W. (1993). *Archaeology: Discovering our past* (2nd ed.). Palo Alto, CA: Mayfield.

One of the best presentations of the body of method, technique, and theory that most archaeologists accept as fundamental to their discipline. The authors confine themselves to the operational modes, guiding strategies, and theoretical orientations of anthropological archaeology in a manner well designed to lead the beginner into the discipline.

Shipman, P. (1981). *Life history of a fossil: An introduction to taphonomy and paleoecology.* Cambridge, MA: Harvard University Press.

In order to understand what a fossil has to tell us, one must know how it came to be where the paleoanthropologist found it (taphonomy). In this book, anthropologist-turned-science-writer Pat Shipman explains how animal remains are acted upon and altered from death to fossilization.

Thomas, D. H. (1998). *Archaeology* (3rd ed.). Fort Worth, TX: Harcourt Brace.

Some books tell us how to do archaeology, some tell us what archaeologists have found out, but this one tells us why we do archaeology. It does so in a coherent and thorough way, and Thomas's blend of ideas, quotations, biographies, and case studies makes for interesting reading.

CHAPTER 3

BIOLOGY AND EVOLUTION

Evolution has produced a variety of primates, ranging all the way from lemurs to humans. Such variety is not the result of progressive change, but rather the adaptation of organisms to local conditions. Because these conditions change, essentially at random, so too do adaptations.

CHAPTER PREVIEW

1

What Forces Are Responsible for the Diversity of Primates in the World Today?

Although all primates—lemurs, lorises, tarsiers, monkeys, apes, and humans—share a common ancestry, they have come to differ through the operation of evolutionary forces that have permitted them to adapt to a variety of environments in a variety of ways. Although biologists agree upon the fact of evolution, they are still unraveling the details of how it has proceeded.

2

What Is Evolution?

Biological evolution is descent with modification, as descendant populations come to differ from ancestral ones. Evolution happens as differential reproduction changes the frequency of a population's genetic variants from one generation to another over time.

3

What Are the Forces Responsible for Evolution?

Evolution works as mutation produces genetic variation, which is acted upon by drift (accidental changes in frequencies of gene variants in a population), gene flow (the introduction of new gene variants from other populations), and natural selection. Natural selection is the adaptive mechanism of evolution, favoring individuals with genetic variants that are adaptive and who produce more offspring than those without.

Humans have long had close contact with other animals. Some—such as dogs, horses, and cows—have lived close to people for so long that little attention is paid to their behavior. We are interested only in how well they do what they were bred for—companionship, racing, milk production, or whatever. Domestic animals are so dependent on humans that they have lost many of the behavioral traits of their wild ancestors. Except to a small child, perhaps, and a dairy farmer, a cow is not a very interesting animal to watch.

By contrast, wild animals, especially exotic ones, have always fascinated people, as the popularity of circuses and zoos attests. In cultures very different from those of the industrialized countries of the world—those of some American Indians, for example—people can have a special relationship with particular animals, believing their fates to be intertwined. Such companion animals may be called upon for assistance to serve as messengers, or the person may be able to transfer his or her state of being into the animal's body.

A curious feature of this interest is the desire of humans to see animals as mirror images of themselves, a phenomenon known as **anthropomorphism.** Stories in which animals talk, wear clothes, and exhibit human virtues and vices go back to antiquity. Many children today learn of Mickey Mouse or Kermit the Frog and Miss Piggy; the animals created by Walt Disney, Jim Henson, and many others have become an integral part of contemporary North American culture. Occasionally one sees on television trained apes dressed like humans eating at a table, pushing a stroller, or riding a tricycle. They are amusing because they look so "human."

Over the ages, people have trained animals to perform tricks, making them mimic human behavior. But in the Western world people never suspected the full extent of the relationship they have with animals. For centuries, Christianity—the dominant religion of the West—preached that humans and animals were quite separate from one another. Nevertheless, the close biological tie between humans and the other **primates**—the group of animals that, besides humans, includes lemurs, lorises, tarsiers, monkeys, and apes—is now better understood. The diversity of primates existing today is the product of **evolution,** defined by Darwin in his most famous book as *descent with modification.* Over time the operation of evolutionary forces permitted primates to adapt to environments in a variety of ways. These evolutionary forces are the subject of this chapter.

THE CLASSIFICATION OF LIVING THINGS

Crucial to our understanding of the place of humanity among the animals was the invention by the 18th-century Swedish naturalist Carl von Linné of a system to classify living things. The problem the Linnaean system addressed was simply to create order in the great mass of confusing biological data that had accumulated in the wake of European exploration and exploitation of foreign lands. At the same time, discovering and naming the multitude of creatures was seen as a means of demonstrating the glory of God's creation.

Von Linné—or Linnaeus, as he is generally called—classified living things on the basis of overall similarities into small groups, or species. Modern classification, while retaining the structure of the Linnaean system, has gone beyond this by distinguishing superficial similarities among organisms—called **analogies**—from basic ones—called **homologies.** The latter are possessed by organisms that share a common ancestry; even though homologous structures may serve different functions (the hand of a human and the front paw of a dog, for instance), they arise in similar fashion and pass through similar stages in embryonic development prior to their ultimate differentiation. By contrast, analogous structures look similar and may serve the same purpose (the wings of birds and butterflies, for example), but they are built from different parts, do not pass through similar stages in embryonic development, nor do the organisms share a common ancestry.

On the basis of homologies, as in Linnaeus' original system, groups of like **species** (a species is defined today as a population or group of populations capable of interbreeding that is reproductively isolated from other such populations) are organized into larger, more inclusive groups, called **genera** (the singular term is *genus*). The

Anthropomorphism. The ascription of human attributes to nonhuman beings. • **Primates.** The group of mammals that includes lemurs, lorises, tarsiers, monkeys, apes, and humans. • **Evolution.** Descent with modification. • **Analogies.** In biology, structures that are superficially similar; the result of convergent evolution. • **Homologies.** In biology, structures possessed by two different organisms that arise in similar fashion and pass through similar stages during embryonic development. • **Species.** In biology, a population or group of populations that is capable of interbreeding but that is reproductively isolated from other such populations. • **Genera; genus.** In the system of plant and animal classification, a group of like species.

Birds and butterflies exemplify analogy: Both have wings that are used for flight, but the wings are built differently.

characteristics on which Linnaeus based his system were the following:

1. *Body structure:* A Guernsey cow and a Holstein cow are of the same species because they have identical body structure. A cow and a horse do not.
2. *Body function:* Cows and horses bear their young in the same way. Although they are of different species, they are closer than either cows or horses are to chickens, which lay eggs and have no mammary glands.
3. *Sequence of bodily growth:* Both cows and chickens give birth to—or hatch out of the egg—fully formed young. They are therefore more closely related to each other than either one is to the frog, whose tadpoles undergo a series of changes before attaining adult form.

Modern taxonomy (scientific classification) is based on more than body structure, function, and growth. One must also compare chemical reactions of blood, protein structure, and the genetic material itself. Even comparison of parasites is useful, for they tend to show the same degree of relationship as the forms they infest.

Through careful comparison and analysis, Linnaeus and those who have come after him have been able to classify specific animals into a series of larger and more inclusive groups up to the largest and most inclusive of all, the animal kingdom. In Table 3.1 are the main categories of the Linnaean system applied to the classification of the human species, with a few of the more important distinguishing features noted for each category. (Other categories of primates will be dealt with in Chapter 4.)

THE DISCOVERY OF EVOLUTION

As Linnaeus and his contemporaries went about their business of classification, no thought was given to the possibility that species might not be fixed and unchangeable.

An example of homology: Fish have gills but humans do not. Gill structures do develop in the human embryo but then are modified to serve other purposes. From the rudimentary, gill-like structures are built such things as the jaw, bones of the inner ear, thymus, and parathyroid glands.

TABLE 3.1 Classification of Humans

Kingdom	Animalia	Do not make their own food, but depend on intake of living food.
Phylum	Chordata	Have at some stage gill slits as well as **notochord** (a rodlike structure of cartilage) and nerve chord running along the back of the body.
Subphylum*	Vertebrata	Notochord replaced by vertebral column ("backbone") to form internal skeleton along with skull, ribs, and limb bones.
Class	Mammalia	Maintain constant body temperature; young nourished after birth by milk from mother's mammary glands.
Order	Primates	Hands and feet capable of grasping; tendency to erect posture; acute development of vision rather than sense of smell; tendency to large brains.
Superfamily	Hominoidea	Rigid bodies, broad shoulders, and long arms; ability to hang vertically from arms; no tail.
Family	Hominidae	As above but 98% identical at genetic level.
Subfamily	Homininae	Ground-dwelling with bipedal locomotion.
Genus	*Homo*	Large brains; reliance on cultural, as opposed to biological adaption.
Species	*sapiens*	Brains of modern size; relatively small faces.

*Most categories can be expanded or narrowed by adding the prefix "sub" or "super." A family could thus be part of a superfamily, and in turn contain two or more subfamilies.

Rather, species were seen as being just as they had always been since the time of creation. But as the process of classification continued, naturalists became increasingly aware of continuities between different forms of life. At the same time, earth-moving for construction and mining associated with developing industrialism brought to light all sorts of fossils of past life that had to be dealt with. And with industrialization, the idea of progress became ever more prominent in European thought.

In hindsight, it seems inevitable that someone would hit upon the idea of evolution. So it was that, by the start of the 19th century, many naturalists had come to accept the idea that life had evolved, even though they were not clear about how it happened. It remained for Charles Darwin, midway through the century, to discover how evolution worked. Interestingly, he was not alone in his discovery. A Welshman, Alfred Russell Wallace, independently came up with the same idea at the same time. That idea was **natural selection,** and it is based on two observations: All organisms display a range of variation,

As more and more fossils were recovered in the 18th and 19th centuries, it became evident that life forms of past times were not the same as those of the present and that change had occurred.

Natural selection. The evolutionary process through which factors in the environment exert pressure that favors some individuals over others to produce the next generation. • **Notochord.** A rodlike structure of cartilage that, in vertebrates, is replaced by the vertebral column.

CHARLES R. DARWIN (1809–1882)

Grandson of Erasmus Darwin (a physician, scientist, poet, and originator of a theory of evolution himself), Charles Darwin began the study of medicine at the University of Edinburgh. Finding himself unfitted for this profession, he then went to Christ's College, Cambridge, to study theology. Upon completion of his studies there, he took the position of naturalist and companion to Captain Fitzroy on the *HMS Beagle,* which was about to embark on an expedition to various poorly mapped parts of the world. The voyage lasted for close to 5 years, taking Darwin along the coasts of South America, over to the Galapagos Islands, across the Pacific to Australia, and then across the Indian and Atlantic oceans back to South America before returning to England. The observations he made on this voyage, his readings of Sir Charles Lyell's *Principles of Geology,* and the arguments he had with the orthodox and dogmatic Fitzroy had a powerful influence on the development of the ideas culminating in Darwin's most famous book, *On the Origin of Species,* which was published in 1859.

Contrary to what many people seem to think, Darwin did not "discover" or "invent" evolution. The general idea of evolution had been put forward by a number of writers, including his grandfather, long before Darwin's time. Nor is evolution a theory, as some people seem to believe, any more than gravity is a theory. To be sure, there are competing theories of gravity—the Newtonian and Einsteinian—that seek to explain its workings, but the evidence in favor of gravity is overwhelming. Similarly, the evidence in favor of evolution is overwhelming, so much so that evolution is now understood in biology as the organizing principle at all levels of life. But, as with gravity, there have been competing theories that seek to explain how evolution works.

Darwin's contribution was one such theory—that of evolution through natural selection. His was the theory that was best able to account both for change within species and for the emergence of new species in purely naturalistic terms. As is usually the case with pioneering ventures, there were weaknesses in Darwin's original theory. Ultimately, however, his basic ideas were vindicated, and modern biology has not only confirmed but (as with all good theories) extended and amplified those ideas. Today, we can say that the evidence in favor of natural selection is about as good as we had for the theory that the earth is spherical, until we were able to put up an astronaut who could see with his own eyes that this indeed is the case.

and all have the ability to expand beyond their means of subsistence. It follows that, in their "struggle for existence," organisms with advantageous variations for survival in a particular environment will do better than those without them, thereby reproducing with greater success. Thus, as generation succeeds generation, nature selects the most advantageous variations, and species evolve. So obvious did the idea seem in hindsight that Thomas Huxley, one of the pillars of 19th-century British science, remarked, "How extremely stupid of me not to have thought of that."[1]

If Darwin's idea was so straightforward, why did it arouse such controversy? It wasn't so much that species were no longer seen as changeless entities that were set at the time of divine creation (as Linnaeus and his contemporaries thought); after all, emerging evolutionary ideas recognized that species were not fixed and immutable. But, before Darwin, evolution could still be seen as progressive, leading inexorably and predictably to humans, who stood at the pinnacle. After Darwin, this was no longer possible, as paleontologist Stephen Jay Gould explains in the following Original Study.

[1]Quoted in Durant, J. C. (2000, April 23). Everybody into the gene pool. *New York Times Book Review,* p. 11.

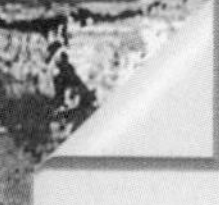

Original Study

The Unsettling Nature of Variational Change[2]

The Darwinian principle of natural selection yields temporal change—evolution in the biological definition—by the twofold process of producing copious and undirected variation within a population and then passing along only a biased (selected) portion of this variation to the next generation. In this manner, the variation within a population at any moment can be converted into differences in mean values (average size, average braininess) among successive populations through time. For this fundamental reason, we call such theories of change *variational* as opposed to the more conventional, and more direct, models of *transformational* change imposed by natural laws that mandate a particular trajectory based on inherent (and therefore predictable) properties of substances and environments. (A ball rolling down an inclined plane does not reach the bottom because selection has favored the differential propagation of moving versus stable elements of its totality but because gravity dictates this result when round balls roll down smooth planes.)

To illustrate the peculiar properties of variational theories like Darwin's in an obviously caricatured, but not inaccurate, description: Suppose that a population of elephants inhabits Siberia during a warm interval before the advance of an ice sheet. The elephants vary, at random, and in all directions, in their amount of body hair. As the ice advances and local conditions become colder, elephants with more hair will tend to cope better, by the sheer good fortune of their superior adaptation to changing climates—and they will leave more offpring on average. (This differential reproductive success must be conceived as broadly statistical and not guaranteed in every case: In any generation, the hairiest elephant of all may fall into a crevasse and die.) Because offspring inherit their parents' degree of hairiness, the next generation will contain a higher proportion of more densely clad elephants (who will continue to be favored by natural selection as the climate becomes still colder). This process of increasing hairiness may continue for many generations, leading to the evolution of woolly mammoths.

This little fable can help us understand how peculiar and how contrary to all traditions of Western thought and explanation the Darwinian theory of evolution, and variational theories of historical change in general, must sound to the common ear. All the odd and fascinating properties of Darwinian evolution—the sensible and explainable but quite unpredictable nature of the outcome (dependent upon complex and contingent changes in local environments), the nonprogressive character of the alteration (adaptive only to these unpredictable local circumstances and not inevitably building a "better" elephant in any cosmic or general sense)—flow from the variational basis of natural selection.

Transformational theories work in a much simpler and more direct manner. If I want to go from A to B, I will have so much less conceptual (and actual) trouble if I can postulate a mechanism that will push me there directly than if I must rely upon the selection of "a few good men" from a random cloud of variation about point A, then constitute a new generation around an average point one step closer to B, then generate a new cloud of random variation about this new point, then select "a few good men" once again from this new array—and then repeat this process over and over until I finally reach B.

When one adds the oddity of variational theories in general to our strong cultural and psychological resistance against their application to our own evolutionary origin (as an unpredictable and not necessary progressive little twig on life's luxuriant tree), then we can better understand why Darwin's revolution surpassed all other scientific discoveries in reformatory power and why so many people still fail to understand, and may even

[2]Gould, S. J. (2000). What does the dreaded "E" word mean, anyway? *Natural History, 109*(1), 34–36.

resist, its truly liberal content. (I must leave the issue of liberation for another time, but once we recognize that the specification of morals and the search for a meaning to our lives cannot be accomplished by scientific study in any case, then Darwin's variational mechanism will no longer seem threatening and may even become liberating in teaching us to look within ourselves for answers to these questions and to abandon a chimerical search for the purpose of our lives, and for the source of our ethical values, in the external workings of nature.)

The End

In order for natural selection to occur, vast time is necessary for gradual changes to accumulate, and it was not until the early 19th century that the idea of vast time took hold as the field of geology developed. It was this that made Darwin and Wallace's formulation possible. Still, there was a problem: No one knew how variation arose in the first place, nor were the mechanisms of heredity understood. This gave Darwin difficulty for the rest of his life, and by the end of his century, Darwin's theory was rejected by many. Ironically, the information he needed was available by 1865, when an obscure monk in what is now the Czech Republic discovered the basic laws of heredity. Even so, it was not until well into the 20th century that genetics and Darwinian theory were reconciled.

HEREDITY

In order to understand how evolution works, one has to have some understanding of the mechanics of heredity, because heritable variation constitutes the raw material for evolution. Our knowledge of the mechanisms of heredity is fairly recent; most of the fruitful research into the molecular level of inheritance has taken place in the past five decades. Although some aspects remain puzzling, the outlines by now are reasonably clear.

The Transmission of Genes

Biologists call the actual units of heredity **genes**, a term that comes from the Greek word for "birth." The presence and activity of genes were originally deduced rather than observed by the Augustine monk, Gregor Mendel, in the 19th century. Working at the time of publication of Darwin's theory of evolution, Mendel sought to answer some of the riddles of heredity by experimenting with garden peas to determine how various traits are passed from one generation to the next. Specifically, he discovered that inheritance was *particulate,* rather than *blending,* as Darwin and many others thought. That is, the units controlling the expression of visible traits retain their separate identities over the generations. This was the basis of Mendel's **law of segregation.** Another of his laws, that of **independent assortment,** was that what we now call genes, controlling different traits, are inherited independently of one another.

In the first half of the 20th century, much was learned about what genes did, but it was not until 1953 that James Watson and Francis Crick discovered that genes are actually portions of molecules of deoxyribonucleic acid, or **DNA.** DNA is a complex molecule with an unusual shape, rather like two strands of a rope twisted around each another. These strands are formed by alternating sugars and phosphates and are connected by four base pairs: adenine, thymine, guanine, and cytosine (usually written as A, T, G, and C). The connections are between complementary bases: A with T and G with C (Figure 3.1). This confers upon genes the unique property of being able to make exact copies of themselves. This happens as a single strand attracts the appropriate bases—A to T, T to A, C to G, and G to C—and forms a new strand. This new strand, by the same process, produces an exact copy of the original. As long as no errors are made in this replication process, new organisms will contain genetic material exactly like that in ancestral organisms.

Genes. Portions of DNA molecules that direct the synthesis of proteins. DNA molecules have the unique property of being able to produce exact copies of themselves. • **Law of segregation.** Variants of genes for a particular trait retain their separate identities through the generations. • **Law of independent assortment.** Genes controlling different traits are inherited independently of one another. • **DNA.** The genetic material, deoxyribonucleic acid; a complex molecule with information to direct the synthesis of proteins. DNA molecules have the unique property of being able to produce exact copies of themselves.

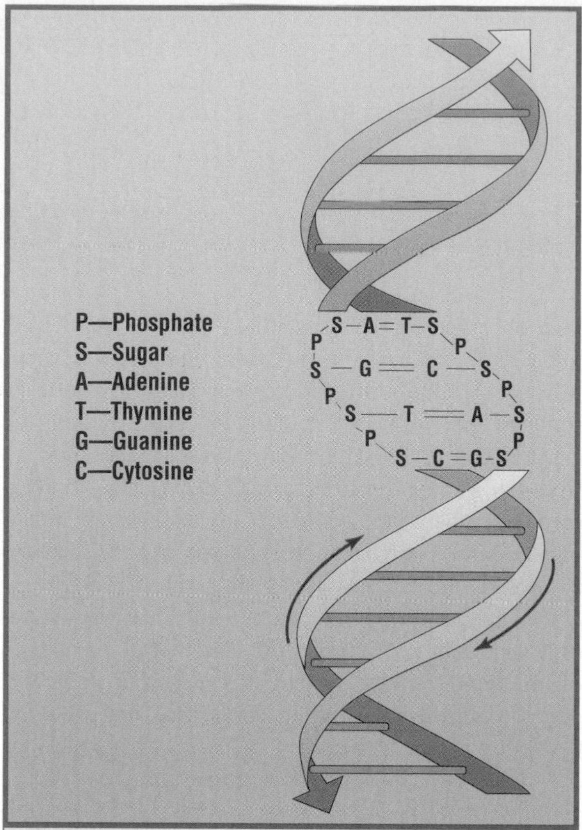

FIGURE 3.1

THIS DIAGRAMMATIC REPRESENTATION OF A PORTION OF A DEOXYRIBONUCLEIC ACID (DNA) MOLECULE REPRESENTS THE DOUBLE HELIX STRANDS AND THE CONNECTING NITROGENOUS BASE PAIRS. THE HELIX STRANDS ARE FORMED BY ALTERNATING SUGAR AND PHOSPHATE GROUPS. THE CONNECTION IS PRODUCED BY COMPLEMENTARY BASES—ADENINE WITH THYMINE, CYTOSINE WITH GUANINE—AS SHOWN FOR A SECTION OF THE MOLECULE.

The chemical bases of DNA constitute a recipe for making proteins. As science writer Matt Ridley puts it, "Proteins . . . do almost every chemical, structural, and regulatory thing that is done in the body: they generate energy, fight infection, digest food, form hair, carry oxygen, and so on and on."[3] Almost everything in the body is made *of* or *by* proteins.

How is the DNA recipe converted into a protein? Through a somewhat complicated series of intervening steps, each three-base sequence of a gene, called a **codon,** specifies production of a particular amino acid, strings of which build proteins. Because DNA cannot leave the cell's nucleus (Figure 3.2), the directions for a specific protein are first converted into ribonucleic acid or **RNA** in a process called **transcription.** RNA differs from DNA in the structure of its sugar phosphate backbone and in the presence of the base uracil rather than thymine. Next the RNA travels to the **ribosomes,** the cellular structure (see Figure 3.2) where **translation** of the directions found in the codons into proteins occurs. For example, the sequence of CGA specifies the amino acid arginine, GCG alanine, CAG glutamine, and so on. There are 20 amino acids, which are strung together in different amounts and sequences to produce an almost infinite number of different proteins. This is the so-called **genetic code,** and it is the same for every living thing, whether it be a worm or a human being. Some simple living things without nucleated cells, such as the retrovirus that causes AIDS, contain their genetic information only as RNA.

GENES

A gene is a portion of the DNA molecule containing several base pairs that directs the production of a particular protein. Thus, when we speak of the gene for a human blood type in the A-B-O system, we are referring to the portion of a DNA molecule that is 1,062 "letters" long—a medium-sized gene—that specifies production of an **enzyme,** a particular kind of protein that initiates and directs a chemical reaction. This particular enzyme causes molecules involved in immune responses to attach to the surface of red blood cells. Genes, then, are not really separate structures, as had once been imagined, but locations, like dots on a map. These genes provide the recipe for the many proteins that keep us alive and healthy.

[3]Ridley, M. (1999). *Genome: The autobiography of a species in 23 chapters* (p. 40). New York: HarperCollins.

Codon. Three-base sequence of a gene that specifies production of an amino acid. • **RNA.** Ribonucleic acid; similar to DNA but with uracil substituted for the base thymine. Carries instructions from DNA to produce amino acids for protein building. • **Transcription.** Process of conversion of instructions from DNA into RNA. • **Ribosomes.** Structures in the cell where translation occurs. • **Translation.** Process of conversion of RNA instructions into proteins. • **Genetic code.** The sequence of DNA bases that specifies production of a particular amino acid. • **Enzyme.** Proteins that initiate and direct chemical reactions in an organism.

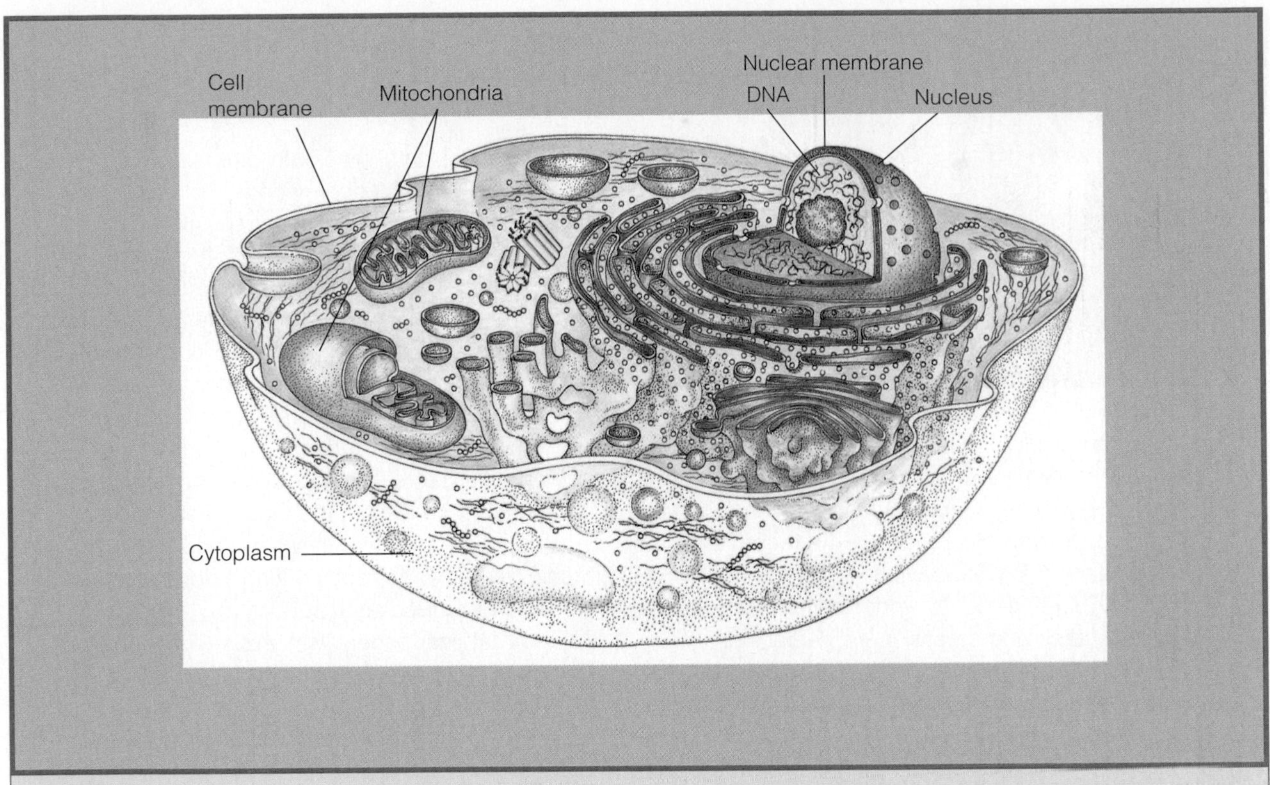

FIGURE 3.2
STRUCTURE OF A GENERALIZED EUKARYOTIC CELL, ILLUSTRATING THE CELL'S THREE-DIMENSIONAL NATURE.

Interestingly, the human **genome**—the complete sequence of human DNA—contains 3 billion chemical bases, with about 30,000 functioning genes. This is a mere three times as many genes as in the lowly fruit fly. How this seemingly modest difference in numbers of genes can produce so much complexity in humans is suggested by the following analogy: A combination lock with two wheels can display almost 100 combinations, but a similar lock with 6 wheels—"only" three times as many—can generate just under 1 million.[4] Those 30,000 human genes account for only 1 to 1.5 percent of the entire genome. As Jerold Lowenstein puts it, our DNA, "like daytime television, is nine-tenths junk."[5] The genes themselves are split by long stretches of this "junk" DNA. The 1,062 bases of the A-B-O blood group gene, for example, are interrupted by five such longish stretches. In the course of producing proteins, "junk" DNA is metaphorically "snipped out" and left on the "cutting room floor."

Some of this seemingly useless, noncoding DNA was inserted by retroviruses; these are some of the most diverse and widespread infectious entities of vertebrates (they are responsible for many diseases that affect humans, such as immunodeficiencies—including AIDS—hepatitis, anemias, and some neurological disorders).[6] There are several thousand nearly complete viral genomes integrated into our own. Now inert or missing a gene, they account for 1.3 percent of the human genome. Other

[4] Solomon, R. (2001, February 20). Genome's riddle. *New York Times,* p. D3.

[5] Lowenstein, J. M. (1992). Genetic surprises. *Discover, 13*(12), 86.

[6] Amábile-Cuevas, C. F., & Chicurel, M. E. (1993). Horizontal gene transfer. *American Scientist, 81,* 338.

Genome. The complete sequence of DNA for a species.

GREGOR MENDEL (1822–1884)

Johann Mendel, as he was christened, was raised on a farm in Moravia and attended the local grammar school. Having done well as a student, he became an Augustine monk in order to further his education. As Brother Gregor, he went on to serve as a parish priest but without much success. Since he had previously studied science at the University of Vienna, he thought of becoming a science teacher but failed the examination. So it was that he retreated to the monastery in Bruno, in what is now the Czech Republic. There, he put to work two talents: a flair for mathematics and a passion for gardening.

As with all farmers of his time, Mendel had an intuitive understanding of biological inheritance. He went a step further, though, in that he recognized the need for a more systematic understanding. Thus, at age 34, he began carefully thought-out breeding experiments in the monastery garden, first with pea plants, then with others.

For 8 years, Mendel worked, planting over 30,000 plants, controlling their pollination, observing the results, and figuring out the mathematics behind it all. This allowed him to predict the outcome of hybridization over successive generations. His findings were published in 1866 in a respected scientific journal found in all the best libraries of Europe. But despite Mendel's straightforward presentation, no one else picked up on the importance of his work until 1900. By then, understanding of cell biology had advanced to the point where rediscovery of Mendel's laws was inevitable, and in that year three European botanists, working independently of one another, rediscovered not only the laws but also Mendel's original paper. With this rediscovery, the science of genetics took off. Still, it would be another 53 years before science understood the true nature of genes, the discreet units of inheritance, the existence of which Mendel had deduced from his experiments.

"junk" DNA consists of decaying hulks of once-useful but now functionless genes; damaged genes that have been "turned off" or stopped being used. All of this litter continues to exist because it is still very good at getting itself replicated. As it does so, mistakes are fairly frequently made, often adding or subtracting repeats of the four bases: A, C, G, and T. This happens with sufficient speed that it is different in every individual, but not so fast that people mostly have the same repeat lengths of their parents. Because there are thousands of series, the result is a unique set of numbers for each person: his or her unique DNA fingerprint.

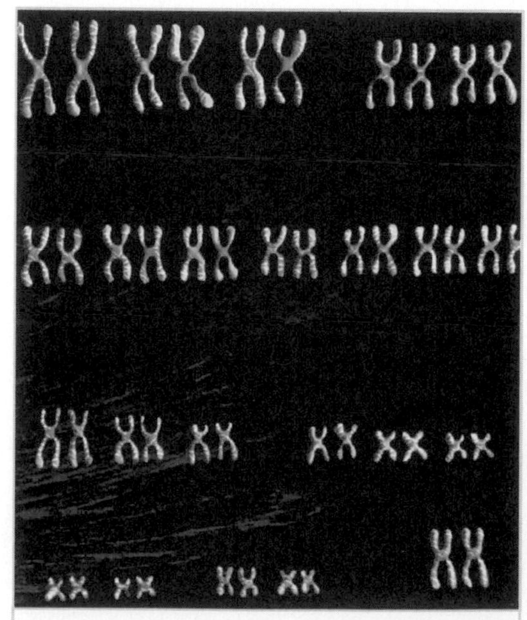

This is a photomicrograph of human chromosomes.

CHROMOSOMES

Most DNA molecules do not float freely about in our bodies but are organized into structures called **chromosomes** found in the nucleus of each cell. Chromosomes, discovered early in the 20th century, are nothing more than long strands of DNA combined with protein to produce structures that can be seen under a conventional light

Chromosome. In the cell nucleus, long strands of DNA combined with a protein that can be seen under the microscope.

Anthropology Applied

The Ethical, Legal, and Social Implications of the Human Genome Project*

The Human Genome Project, an effort to sequence the entire human genetic code, may well be the most massive cooperative scientific undertaking in the history of the natural sciences. The project officially began in 1990 with support from the U.S. Congress. Planners estimated a 15-year time frame and a $3 billion price tag to map the human genetic blueprint. A "working draft" of the human genome has now been completed several years ahead of schedule through a collaboration between government-funded and private researchers.

Though the Human Genome Project will certainly contribute to an understanding of our evolutionary history, the main motivation for this enormous investigation is a hope that detailed genetic knowledge will have revolutionary practical applications for human health. Scientists are currently developing gene therapy models for diseases such as cystic fibrosis and muscular dystrophy that affect tens of thousands of people. Genes that predispose to breast and colon cancer have been identified so that family members can be tested for the presence of these heritable conditions when their loved ones are diagnosed. An increasing number of hereditary conditions can also be diagnosed before birth as new "disease genes" are continually identified. In short, the Human Genome Project is leading to a massive geneticization of our society's health care practices and in turn to the way we think about ourselves. Today, genetics is embedded in our day-to-day lives.

From the Human Genome Project's first conception, scientists were aware that the genetic knowledge they were generating had far-reaching consequences for individuals and society. Therefore, the National Institutes of Health formed a special investigative group to study the ethical, legal, and social implications (ELSI) of the Human Genome Project. The ELSI research program currently has an annual budget of over $12 million and is the largest source of bioethics research. Anthropologists have brought their unique biocultural perspective to the study of the societal effects of knowledge generated from the new genetics.

A primary ELSI research area concerns the study of human genetic variation as the study of the human genome is completed. Initially this DNA sequence will not capture the enormous variation present at the genetic level due to multiple alleles, or alternate forms, that are found for many genes. Anthropologists are contributing to a more complete understanding of this variation through their examination of worldwide genetic diversity so that North Americans are not the only humans represented in the human genome. Ethical issues have been raised by global genetic investigation, such as whether scientists or indigenous people own the patent rights to beneficial genes discovered through such investigations.

A global understanding of genetic diversity raises additional ELSI questions. For instance, how can genetic diversity be examined without falling into the trap of grouping such differences by race? As anthropologists have shown, the concept of race has no validity as a biological concept when applied to humans (see Chapter 13). However, in health care, the field where practical applications of genetic knowledge are most promising, race is often mistakenly considered a biological feature rather than a social feature of an individual. As individual and population variation for specific genes is understood, anthropologists will play an important role in assuring that this information does not lead to the construction of false biological categories. In this way, social determinants of health and disease will not be mistaken for biological difference.

Anthropologists are also uniquely poised to examine how social factors such as race, gender, class, and ethnicity influence the use of clinical genetic services; the understanding and interpretation of genetic information; and the development of public policy about these new genetic technologies. For example, these social factors influence whether an individual will choose to have prenatal genetic testing to assess a fetus' genetic blueprint. Some expectant parents might consider "undesirable" a gene or condition that other parents easily embrace. Cultures and individuals differ as to whether such testing is valuable, ethical, or moral. In a pluralistic society like ours, no simple answer exists to these complex questions. Detailed anthropological study of human beliefs and practices related to the new genetic technology are vital for the development of respectful and fair public policy surrounding this new genetic technology.

---

*Walrath, D. E. (2001). *Anthropology and the ethical, legal, and social implications of the human genome project.* © by author, College of Medicine, University of Vermont, Burlington.

microscope. Each kind of organism has a characteristic number of chromosomes, which are usually found in pairs. For example, the body cells of the fruit fly each contain 4 pairs of chromosomes; those of humans contain 23 pairs; those of some brine shrimp have as many as 160 pairs. The two chromosomes in each pair contain genes for the same traits. The gene for one's A-B-O blood group, for instance, will be found on each chromosome of a particular pair (Chromosome 9 in this instance), but there may be variant forms of these genes. There are three such variants of the A-B-O gene that determine whether one's blood type is A, B, AB, or O. Forms of genes that are located on paired chromosomes and that code for different versions of the same trait are called **alleles.** The difference between the A and B blood alleles is a mere 7 chemical bases out of the total 1,062.

CELL DIVISION

In order to grow and maintain good health, the body cells of an organism must divide and produce new cells. Cell division is initiated when the chromosomes, and hence the genes, replicate, forming a second pair that duplicates the original pair of chromosomes in the nucleus. To do this, the DNA metaphorically "unzips" between the base pairs—adenine from thymine and guanine from cytosine—following which each base on each now-single strand attracts its complementary base, reconstituting the second half of the double helix. Each new pair is surrounded by a membrane and becomes the nucleus that directs the activities of a new cell. This kind of cell division is called **mitosis,** and it produces new cells that have exactly the same number of chromosome pairs, and hence genes, as did the parent cell.

Like most animals, humans reproduce sexually. The reason sex is so popular, from an evolutionary perspective, is that it brings beneficial alleles together, purges the genome of harmful ones, and allows beneficial alleles to spread without being held back by the baggage of disadvantageous variants of other genes. Without sexual reproduction, we would lack genetic diversity, without which we would be more open to attack by various viruses than we already are. Nor would we be able to adapt to changing environments.

When new individuals are produced through sexual reproduction, the process involves the merging of two cells, one from each parent. If two regular body cells, each containing 23 pairs of chromosomes, were to merge, the result would be a new individual with 46 pairs of chromosomes; such an individual surely could not survive. But this increase in chromosome number does not occur, because the sex cells that join to form a new individual are the product of a different kind of cell division, called **meiosis.**

Although meiosis begins like mitosis, with the replication and doubling of the original genes and chromosomes, it proceeds to divide that number into four new

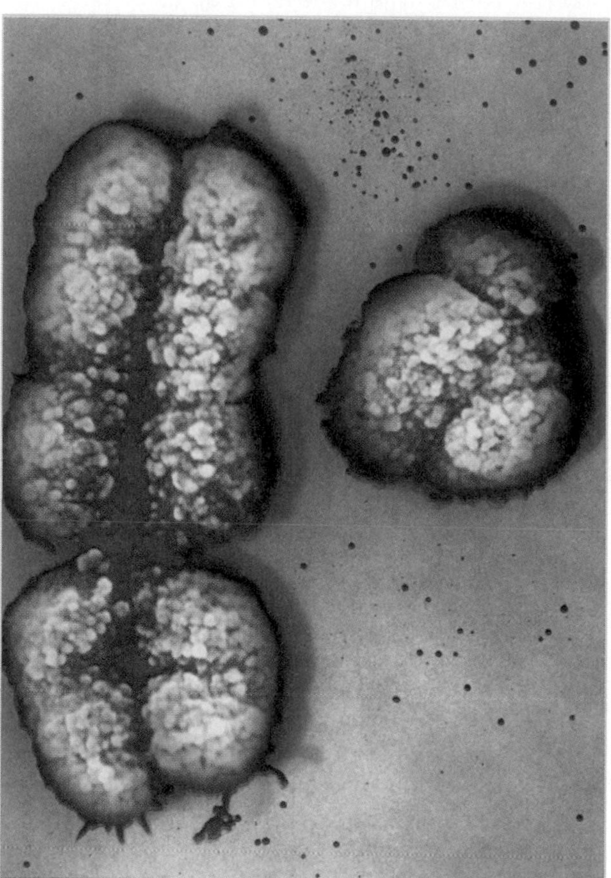

In humans as in all mammals, sex is determined by the male, as everyone inherits an X chromosome (left) from their mother, but has a 50-50 chance of inheriting an X or Y chromosome (right) from their father. Hence, about equal numbers of males as females are born. Compared to the other chromosomes, the Y is tiny and carries little genetic information. The X carries a "normal" complement of genes.

Alleles. Alternate forms of a single gene. • **Mitosis.** A kind of cell division that produces new cells having exactly the same number of chromosome pairs, and hence genes, as the parent cell. • **Meiosis.** A kind of cell division that produces the sex cells, each of which has half the number of chromosomes, and hence genes, as the parent cell.

cells rather than two (Figure 3.3). Thus each new cell has only half the number of chromosomes with their genes found in the parent cell. Human eggs and sperm, for example, have only 23 single chromosomes (half of a pair), whereas body cells have 23 pairs, or 46 chromosomes.

The process of meiotic division has important implications for genetics. Because paired chromosomes are separated, two different types of new cells will be formed; two of the four new cells will have one-half of a pair of chromosomes, and the other two will have the second half of the original chromosome pair. At the same time, corresponding portions of one chromosome may "cross over" to the other one, somewhat scrambling the genetic material compared to the original chromosomes. Of course, none of this will make any difference if the original pair was **homozygous,** possessing identical alleles

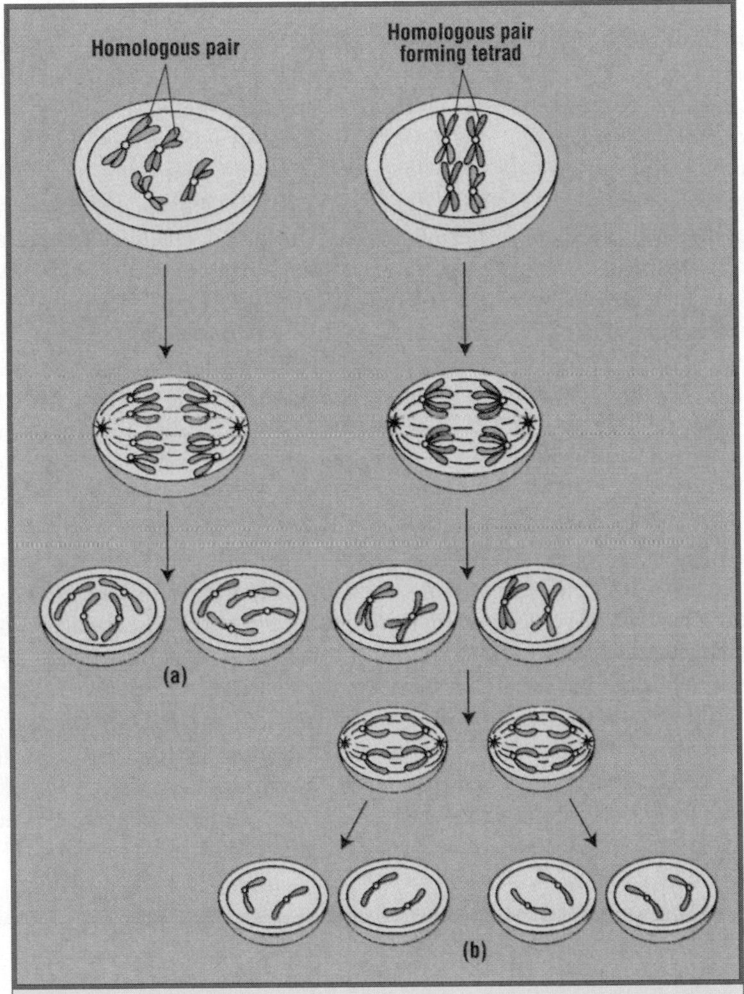

FIGURE 3.3
IN CELL DIVISION BOTH MITOSIS (A) AND MEIOSIS (B) CREATE NEW CELLS. HOWEVER, IN MITOSIS THE NEW CELL HAS THE SAME NUMBER OF CHROMOSOMES AS THE PARENT CELL, WHEREAS IN MEIOSIS THERE ARE HALF OF THE CHROMOSOMES. CHROMOSOMES IN BLUE ORIGINALLY CAME FROM ONE PARENT, THOSE IN PINK FROM THE OTHER.

Homozygous. Refers to a chromosome pair that bears identical alleles for a single gene.

for a specific gene. For example, if in both chromosomes of the original pair the gene for A-B-O blood type was represented by the allele for Type A blood, then all new cells will have the "A" allele. But if the original pair was **heterozygous,** with the "A" allele on one chromosome and the allele for Type O blood on the other, then half of the new cells will contain only the "O" allele; the offspring have a 50-50 chance of getting either one. It is impossible to predict any single individual's **genotype,** or genetic composition, but (as Mendel originally discovered) statistical probabilities can be established.

What happens when a child inherits the allele for Type O blood from one parent and that for Type A from the other? Will the child have blood of Type A, O, or some mixture of the two? Many of these questions were answered by Mendel's original experiments.

Mendel discovered that certain alleles are able to mask the presence of others; one allele is dominant, whereas the other is recessive. This is his **law of dominance and recessiveness.** Actually, it is the traits that are dominant or recessive, rather than the alleles themselves; geneticists merely speak of dominant and recessive alleles for the sake of convenience. Thus, one might speak of the allele for Type A blood as being dominant to the one for Type O. An individual whose blood type genes are heterozygous, with one "A" and one "O" allele, will have Type A blood. In other words, the heterozygous condition (AO) will show exactly the same physical characteristic, or **phenotype,** as the homozygous (AA), even though the two have a somewhat different genetic composition, or genotype. Only the homozygous recessive genotype (OO) will show the phenotype of Type O blood.

The dominance of one allele does not mean that the recessive one is lost or in some way blended. A Type A heterozygous parent (AO) will produce sex cells containing both "A" and "O" alleles. (This is an example of Mendel's law of segregation, that alleles retain their separate identities.) Recessive alleles can be handed down for generations before they are matched with another recessive in the process of sexual reproduction and show up in the phenotype. The presence of the dominant allele simply renders the recessive allele inactive.

All of the traits Mendel studied in garden peas showed this dominant-recessive relationship, and so for some years it was believed that this was the only relationship possible. Later studies, however, have indicated that patterns of inheritance are not always so simple. In some cases, neither allele is dominant; they are both co-dominant. An example of co-dominance in human heredity can be seen also in the inheritance of blood types. Type A is produced by one allele; Type B by another. A heterozygous individual will have a phenotype of AB, because neither allele can dominate the other.

The inheritance of blood types points out another complexity of heredity. The number of alleles is by no means limited to two; certain traits have three or more allelic forms. Of course, only one allele can appear on each of the pairs of chromosomes, so each individual is limited to two alleles.

Another example of co-dominance is the alleles for normal **hemoglobin** (the protein that carries oxygen in the red blood cells) and the abnormal hemoglobin that is responsible for **sickle-cell anemia** in humans. The abnormality is caused by a change in a single base pair in the DNA of the hemoglobin gene, producing a single amino acid substitution in the protein. Individuals who are homozygous for this particular allele contract sickle-cell anemia, as their red blood cells take on a characteristic sickle shape, causing them to collapse and clump together, blocking the capillaries and so causing tissue damage. With their severe anemia, such individuals commonly die before reaching adulthood. The homozygous dominant condition (Hb^AHb^A; normal hemoglobin is known as hemoglobin A, not to be confused with blood Type A) produces only normal molecules of hemoglobin whereas the heterozygous condition (Hb^AHb^S) produces 50 percent normal and 50 percent abnormal molecules; except under low-oxygen or some other stressful conditions, such individuals suffer no ill effects. We shall return to the sickle-cell condition later, for we now know that under certain conditions the heterozygous condition is actually more advantageous than is the "normal" homozygous condition.

POLYGENETIC INHERITANCE

So far, we have spoken as if the traits of organisms are single-gene traits—that is, the alleles of one particular gene determine one particular trait. Certainly this is the

Heterozygous. Refers to a chromosome pair that bears different alleles for a single gene. • **Genotype.** The actual genetic makeup of an organism. • **Law of dominance and recessiveness.** Certain alleles are able to mask the presence of others. • **Phenotype.** The physical appearance of an organism that may or may not reflect a particular genotype because the latter may or may not include recessive alleles. • **Hemoglobin.** The protein that carries oxygen in the red blood cells. • **Sickle-cell anemia.** An inherited form of anemia caused by the red blood cells assuming a sickled shape.

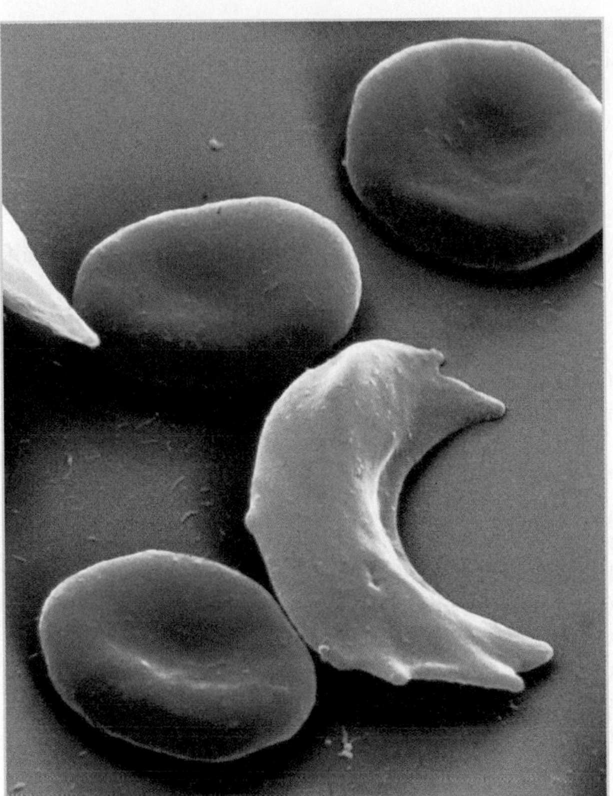

Sickle-cell anemia is caused by an abnormal hemoglobin, called hemoglobin S. Those afflicted by the disease are homozygous for the allele S; heterozygotes are not afflicted. Shown here is a sickle cell among normal red blood cells.

case with the A-B-O blood groups and some other things, but in humans, the most obvious traits are usually not ones controlled by a single gene. Skin color, for example, is programmed by the action of many genes, each of which produces a small effect. In such cases, we speak of **polygenetic inheritance,** where two or more genes (as opposed to just two or more alleles) work together to effect one particular phenotypic character. Because so many genes are involved, each of which may have alternative alleles, it is difficult to unravel the genetic underpinnings of a trait like skin color. Theoretically, the observed range of variation in human skin color seems to require the presence of at least three, if not as many as six, separate genes, each of which produces a small additive effect. For this reason, characteristics controlled by multiple genes exhibit a continuous range of variation in their phenotype expression.

POPULATION GENETICS

At the level of the individual, the study of genetics shows how traits are transmitted from one generation to the next and enables a prediction about the chances that any given individual will display some phenotypic characteristic. At the level of the group, the study of genetics takes on additional significance, revealing mechanisms that support evolutionary interpretations of the diversity of life.

A key concept in genetics is that of the **population,** or a group of individuals within which breeding takes place. It is within populations that natural selection takes place, as some members produce more than their share of the next generation, while others produce less than their share. Thus, over a period of generations, the population shows a measure of adaptation to its environment as a consequence of this evolution.

The Stability of the Population

In theory, the characteristics of any given population should remain remarkably stable. And indeed, generation after generation, thc bullfrogs in my farm pond, for example, look much alike, have the same calls, and exhibit the same behavior when breeding. Another way to look at this remarkable consistency is to say that the **gene pool** of the population—the genetic variants available to that population—seems to remain the same.

The theoretical stability of a population's gene pool is not only easy to observe; it is also easy to understand. As Mendel's experiments with garden peas revealed, and subsequent genetic experiments have confirmed, although some alleles may be dominant to others, the recessive alleles are not just lost or destroyed. Statistically, a heterozygous individual has a 50 percent chance of passing on to the next generation the dominant allele; he or she also has a 50 percent chance of passing on the recessive allele. The recessive allele may again be masked by the presence of a dominant allele in the next generation, but it is there nonetheless and will be passed on again.

Polygenetic inheritance. When two or more genes work together to effect a single phenotypic character. • **Population.** In biology, a group of similar individuals that can and do interbreed. • **Gene pool.** The genetic variants available to a population.

Because alleles are not "lost" in the process of reproduction, the frequency with which certain ones occur in the population should remain exactly the same from one generation to the next. The **Hardy-Weinberg principle,** named for the English mathematician and the German physician who worked it out (in 1908) soon after the rediscovery of Mendel's laws, demonstrates algebraically that the percentage of individuals that are homozygous for the dominant allele, homozygous for the recessive allele, and heterozygous will remain the same from one generation to the next provided that certain specified conditions are met: that mating is entirely random; that the population is sufficiently large for statistical averages to express themselves; that no new variants will be introduced into the population's gene pool; and that all individuals are equally successful at surviving and reproducing. In real life, however, these conditions are rarely met, as geographical, physiological, or behavioral factors may favor matings between certain individuals over others; as populations—on islands, for example—may be quite small; as new genetic variants may be introduced through mutation, interspecies gene transfer, or gene flow; and as natural selection may favor the carriers of some alleles over others. Thus, changes in the gene pools of populations, without which there could be no evolution, can and do take place.

EVOLUTIONARY FORCES

Mutation

The ultimate source of change is **mutation** of genes. This happens when copying mistakes are made during cell division. It may involve a change in a single base of a DNA sequence, or at the other extreme, relocation of large segments of DNA. In any event, genes are altered, producing new alleles—ones not inherited from an ancestor, but heritable by descendants. The fact is, every second that you read this page, the DNA in each cell of your body is being damaged.[7] Fortunately, DNA repair enzymes exist that constantly scan DNA for mistakes, slicing out damaged segments and patching up gaps. Were it not for this repair mechanism, we would have diseases like cancer at a much higher frequency than we do, nor would we get a faithful copy of our parental inheritance (from an evolutionary perspective, the only mutations that count are those in sex cells). Not only would we not live long, but our species would not exist for long. But because the repair mechanism itself is not perfect, not all mistakes are corrected; otherwise, there would be no possibility for evolution to occur.

Geneticists have calculated the rate at which various types of mutant genes appear. In human populations, they run from a low of about 5 mutations per million sex cells formed, in the case of a gene abnormality that leads to the absence of an iris in the eye, to a high of about 100 per million, in the case of a gene involved in a form of muscular dystrophy. (Note that the human male ejaculates hundreds of millions of sperm cells at a single time.) The average is about 30 mutants per million. Because of the repeated replication needed to supply fresh sperm throughout life, the mutation rate throughout the genome is five times higher in men than in women. Although mutations sometimes produce marked abnormalities, the great majority of them produce more subtle effects. Still, they are more often harmful than not.

Research with a variety of organisms indicates that certain factors increase the rate at which mutations occur. These include a number of chemicals, such as some dyes, certain antibiotics, and some chemicals used in the preservation of food. Another important cause of increased mutation rates is irradiation. The ultraviolet rays of sunshine are capable of producing mutations, as are x-rays and other radiation. In at least some organisms, there is even evidence stress can crank up mutation rates, increasing the diversity necessary for selection if successful adaptation is to occur.[8]

In humans, as in all multicelled animals, the very nature of the genetic material itself ensures that mutations will occur. For instance, the fact that genes are split by stretches of "junk" DNA increases the chances that a simple editing mistake in the process of copying DNA will cause significant gene mutations. To cite one exam-

[7]Culotta, E., & Koshland, D. E., Jr. (1994). DNA repair works its way to the top. *Science, 266,* 1926.

[8]Chicurel, M. (2001). Can organisms speed their own evolution? *Science, 292,* 1824–1827.

Hardy-Weinberg principle. Demonstrates algebraically that the percentage of individuals that are homozygous for the dominant allele, homozygous for the recessive allele, and heterozygous should remain constant from one generation to the next, provided that certain specified conditions are met. • **Mutation.** Chance alteration of a gene that produces a new allele.

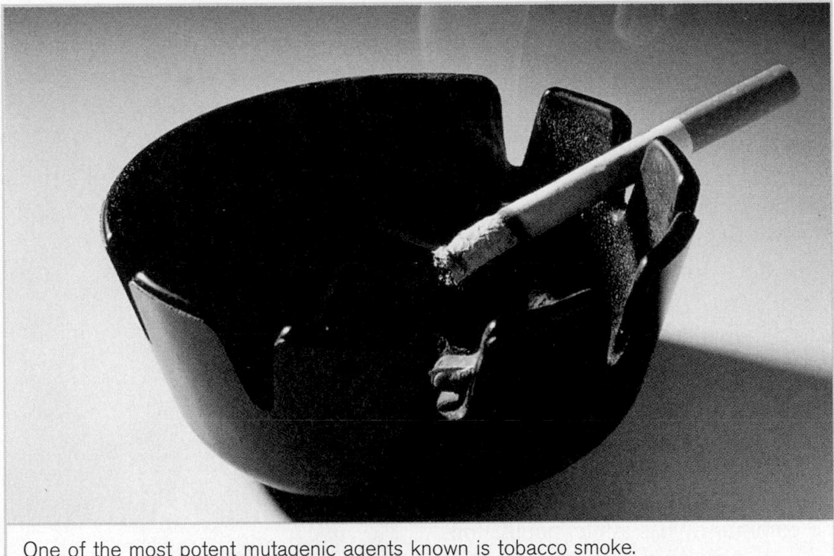

One of the most potent mutagenic agents known is tobacco smoke.

ple, the gene for collagen (the main structural protein of the skin, bones, and teeth) is fragmented by no fewer than 50 segments of "junk" DNA. As a consequence, there are 50 chances for error each time the gene is copied. One result of this seemingly inefficient if not dangerous situation is that it becomes possible to shuffle the gene segments themselves like a deck of cards, putting together new proteins with new functions. Although individuals may suffer as a result (the French artist Henri Toulouse-Lautrec's growth abnormality resulted from a mutation of the collagen gene), it does make it possible for an evolving species to adapt more quickly to a new environment. Another source of genetic remodeling from within is the movement of whole DNA sequences from one locality or chromosome to another. This may disrupt the function of other genes or, in the case of so-called jumping genes, carry important functional messages of their own. In humans, about 1 in every 700 mutations is caused by "jumping genes."

One recent finding is that humans have longer strings of repetitious DNA within and between genes than do other primates, so it is not surprising that we have a higher mutation rate. And a consequence of this is an increased incidence of such genetic disorders as Huntington's disease and Fragile X syndrome (a form of mental retardation).[9]

It is important to realize that mutations do not arise out of need for some new adaptation. Indeed, there is no tendency for the frequency of a particular mutation to correlate with the direction in which a population is evolving. They are purely chance events; what happens once they occur depends on whether they happen (by chance) to enhance the survival and reproductive success of the individuals who carry them.

French artist Henri Toulouse-Lautrec, whose growth abnormality resulted from a mutation of the collagen gene.

[9] Glausiusz, J. (1995). Micro gets macro. *Discover, 16*(11), 40.

Genetic Drift

Each individual is subject to a number of chance events that determine life or death. For example, an individual squirrel in good health and possessed of a number of advantageous traits may be killed in a forest fire; a genetically well-adapted baby cougar may not live longer than a day if its mother gets caught in an avalanche, whereas the weaker offspring of a mother that does not die may survive. In a large population, such accidents of nature are unimportant; the accidents that preserve individuals with certain alleles will be balanced out by the accidents that destroy them. However, in small populations, such averaging out may not be possible. Because human populations today are so large, we might suppose that human beings are unaffected by chance events. Although it is true that a rock slide that kills 5 campers whose home community has a total population of 100,000 is not statistically significant, a rock slide that kills 5 hunters from a small group of food foragers could significantly alter frequencies of alleles in the local gene pool. The average size of local groups of historically known food foragers (people who hunt, fish, and gather other wild foods for subsistence) varies between about 25 and 50.

Another sort of chance event may occur when an existing population splits up into two or more new ones, especially if one of these new populations is founded by a particularly small number of individuals. What this amounts to is a sampling error; in such cases, it is unlikely that the gene frequencies of the smaller population will duplicate those of the larger one. Even if a population does not split in this way, in a small population, the same sort of sampling error may occur as, by chance, parental alleles may not be passed on to the next generation in the same frequencies. If, for example, a person's genotype for blood type is AO, but he or she has only one offspring, only one of those alleles will be passed on.

The effect of chance events on the gene pool of small populations is called **genetic drift.** Genetic drift plays an important role in causing the sometimes striking characteristics found in isolated island populations. On the isolated island of Tristan de Cuna, for example, over 20 percent of the human population have overt symptoms of asthma, despite living in an environment free of the pollution and other triggers that lead to asthma. Because asthma tends to run in families (regardless of what triggers asthma) and because the underlying biochemical events involved are the same, it is clear that an underlying genetic component exists. Thus, it appears that Tristan de Cuna was populated by descendants of an asthma-susceptible person.[10] Drift is also likely to have been an important factor in human evolution, because until 10,000 years ago all humans were food foragers who probably lived in relatively small, self-contained populations.

The 1998 Casitas Volcano mudslide in Nicaragua, triggered by the rains of Hurricane Mitch, buried a village, killing over 1,200 people. This is one kind of accident that can produce chance alterations of allele frequency in human gene pools.

Gene Flow

Another factor that brings change to the gene pool of a population is **gene flow,** or the introduction of new alleles from nearby populations. Gene flow occurs when

[10]Ridley, M. (1999). *Genome: The autobiography of a species in 23 chapters* (p. 71). New York: HarperCollins.

Genetic drift. Chance fluctuations of allele frequencies in the gene pool of a population. • **Gene flow.** The introduction of alleles from the gene pool of one population into that of another.

In Central America, gene flow between Native Americans (upper left), Spaniards (upper right), and Africans (lower left) has contributed to genetic diversity.

previously separated groups are once again able to interbreed, as, for example, when a river that once separated two populations of small mammals changes course. Migration of individuals or groups into the territory occupied by others may also lead to gene flow. This genetic change has been observed in several North American rodents that have been forced to leave their territory due to changes in environmental conditions. Gene flow has been an important factor in human evolution, both in terms of early human or near-human groups and in terms of current so-called racial variation. For example, the last 400 years have seen the introduction of alleles into Central and South American populations from both the Spanish colonists and the Africans whom Europeans imported as slaves. The result has been an increase in the range of phenotypic variation.

Interspecies Gene Transfer

A recent discovery is that the transfer of genes can occur between unrelated organisms. Unlike gene flow, however, it does not take place by interbreeding but through other means. Hence, like mutation, it is a source of random variation. Such **interspecies gene transfer** is well known between different kinds of bacteria, but seems to take place even among vertebrate animals. In some cases, the agent of transfer can be a retrovirus; how this takes place is depicted in Figure 3.4.

Natural Selection

Although the factors discussed above may produce change in a population, that change would not necessarily make the population better adapted to its biological and social environment. **Adaptation** means both a process, by which organisms achieve a beneficial adjustment to an available environment, and the results of that process, the characteristics of organisms that fit them to the particular set of conditions of the environment in which they are generally found. Genetic drift, for example, often produces strange characteristics that have no survival value; mutant genes may be either helpful or harmful to survival, or simply neutral. So we return to the subject of natural selection, for it is this process that makes evolutionary change adaptive.

Natural selection refers to the evolutionary process through which the environment exerts pressure that

Interspecies gene transfer. Transfer of DNA as when retroviruses insert DNA into the cells of one species from another. • **Adaptation.** A process by which organisms achieve a beneficial adjustment to an available environment; also the results of that process—the characteristics of organisms that fit them to the particular set of conditions of the environment in which they are generally found.

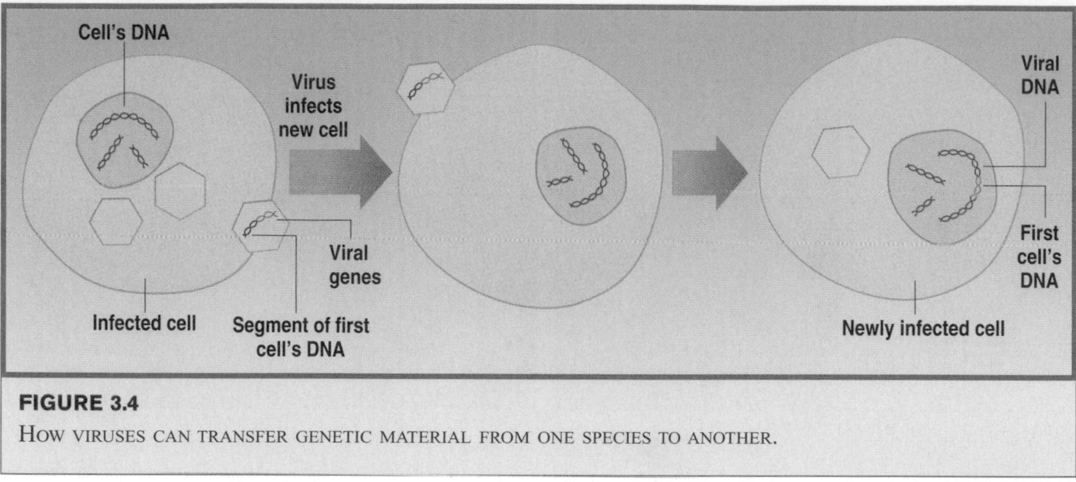

FIGURE 3.4
HOW VIRUSES CAN TRANSFER GENETIC MATERIAL FROM ONE SPECIES TO ANOTHER.

selects some individuals over others to reproduce the next generation of the group. In other words, instead of a completely random selection of individuals whose traits will be passed on to the next generation, there is selection by the forces of nature. In the process, the frequency of genetic variants for harmful or maladaptive traits within the population is reduced while the frequency of genetic variants for adaptive traits is increased.

In popular writing, natural selection is often thought of as "survival of the fittest," a phrase coined by British philosopher Herbert Spencer but never used by Darwin. The phrase implies that the physically weak, being unfit, are eliminated from the population by disease, predation, or starvation. Obviously, the survival of the fittest has some bearing on natural selection; one need hardly point out that the dead do not reproduce. But there are many cases in which individuals survive, and even do quite well, but do not reproduce. They may be incapable of attracting mates, or they may be sterile, or they may produce offspring that do not survive after birth. For example, among the Uganda Kob, a kind of antelope native to eastern Africa, males that are unable to attract females form all-male herds in which they live out their lives. As members of a herd, they are reasonably well protected against predators, and so they may survive to relatively ripe old ages. They do not, however, pass on their genes to succeeding generations.

Change brought about by natural selection in the frequency with which certain genetic variants appear in a population is actually a very slow process. For example, the present frequency of the sickle-cell allele is 0.05 in the entire U.S. population. A 5-percent reduction per generation (about 25 years) would take about 2,000 years to reach a frequency of 0.01, assuming complete selection against those homozygous for the allele. Yet given the great time span involved—life on earth has existed for 3 to 4 billion years—even such small and slow changes will have a significant cumulative impact on both the genotypes and phenotypes of any population.

Natural selection may act to promote change in frequencies of genetic variants, or act to promote stability, rather than change. **Stabilizing selection** occurs in populations that are already well adapted or where change would be disadvantageous. In humans, for instance, there has been no significant change in brain size for the last 200,000 years or so. Stabilizing selection seems to be operating here, as the human birth canal is not adequate for the birth of larger-brained offspring. In cases where change is disadvantageous, natural selection will favor the retention of allele frequencies more or less as they are. The qualification "more or less" is necessary, as "stable" does not mean "static." Still, the evolutionary history of most forms of life is not one of constant change, proceeding as a steady, stately progression over vast periods of time; rather, it is one of prolonged periods of relative stability or gradual change punctuated by shorter periods of more rapid change (or extinction) when altered conditions require new adaptations or when a new mutation

Stabilizing selection. Natural selection as it acts to promote stability, rather than change, in a population's gene pool.

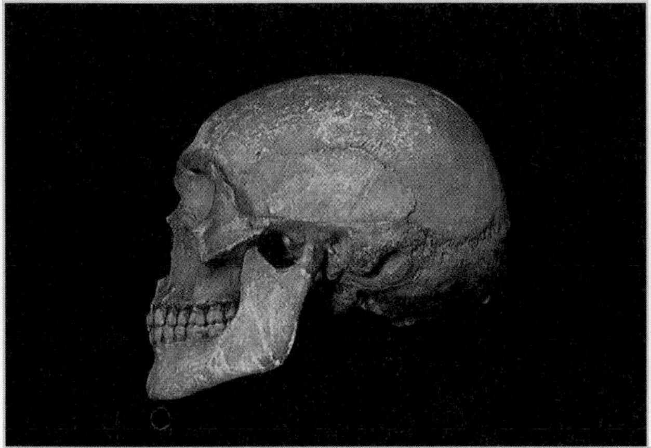
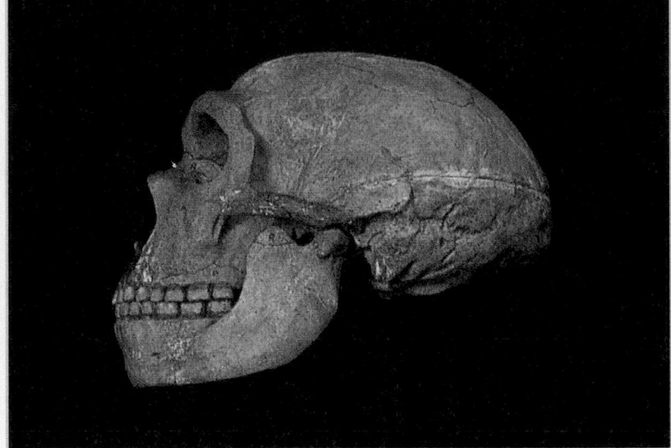

An example of stabilizing selection: The brain of the modern skull on the left is no bigger relative to body mass than that in the ca. 50,000-year-old skull on the right, even though the outer appearance of the skulls has changed.

produces an opportunity to adapt to some other available environment. According to the fossil record, most species survive somewhere between 3 and 5 million years.[11]

Discussions of the action of natural selection typically focus on anatomical or structural changes, such as the evolutionary change in the types of teeth found in primates; ample evidence (fossilized teeth, for example) exists to interpret such changes. By extrapolation, biologists assume that the same mechanisms work on behavioral traits as well. It seems reasonable that individuals in a group of Vervet monkeys capable of warning one another of the presence of predators would have a significant survival advantage over those without this capability. Such situations have constituted an enigma for evolutionary biologists; individuals are typically seen as "survival machines," acting always selfishly in their own interest, but by giving an alarm call, an individual calls attention to itself, thereby becoming an obvious target for the predator. How, then, could the kind of behavior evolve in which individuals place themselves at risk for the good of the group? One biologist's simple solution substitutes money for fitness to illustrate one way in which such cooperative behavior may come about:

> You are given a choice. Either you can receive $10 and keep it all or you can receive $10 million if you give $6 million to your next door neighbor. Which would you do? Guessing that most selfish people would be happy with a net gain of $4 million, I consider the second option to be a form of selfish behavior in which a neighbor gains an incidental benefit. I have termed such selfish behavior benevolent.[12]

Natural selection of beneficial social traits was probably a particularly important influence on human evolution, since in the primates, some degree of cooperative social behavior became important for food-getting, defense, and mate attraction. Indeed, anthropologist Christopher Boehm argues that, "If human nature were merely selfish, vigilant punishment of deviants would be expected, whereas the elaborate prosocial prescriptions that favor altruism would come as a surprise."[13]

ADAPTATION

As a consequence of the process of natural selection, those populations that do not become extinct generally become well adapted to their environments. Anyone who has ever looked carefully at the plants and animals that survive in the deserts of the western United States can cite many instances of adaptation. For example, members of the cactus family have extensive root networks close to the surface of the soil, enabling them to soak up the slightest bit of moisture; they are able to store large

[11]Thomson, K. S. (1997). Natural selection and evolution's smoking gun. *American Scientist, 85,* 516.

[12]Nunney, L. (1998). Are we selfish, are we nice, or are we nice because we are selfish? *Science, 281,* 1619.

[13]Boehm, C. (2000). The evolution of moral communities. *School of American Research, 2000 Annual Report,* 7.

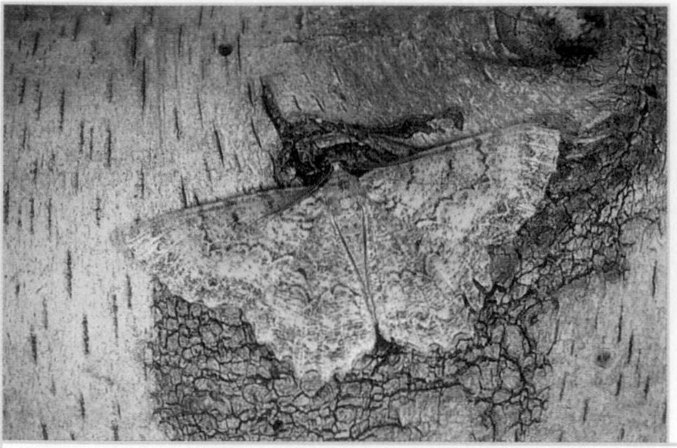

The moths shown in these two pictures are varieties of a single species. Although the mottled brown variant is well-camouflaged on relatively clean tree trunks, it is readily visible on sooty tree trunks and is subject to increased predation. The reverse is true for the black variant, which became especially common when coal fueled British industry.

quantities of water whenever it is available; they are shaped so as to expose the smallest possible surface to the dry air and are generally leafless as adults, thereby preventing water loss through evaporation; and a covering of spines discourages animals from chewing into the juicy flesh of the plant.

Desert animals are also adapted to their environment. The kangaroo rat can survive without drinking water; many reptiles live in burrows where the temperature is lower; most animals are nocturnal or active only in the cool of the night. Many of the stories traditionally offered to explain observable cases of adaptation rely heavily on the purposeful acts of a world creator. The legend of Coyote and Wishpoosh (Chapter 1) is one such example; the belief popular among Europeans early in the 19th century that God created each animal separately to occupy a specific place in a hierarchical ladder of being is another.

The adaptability of organic structures and functions, no matter how much a source of wonder and fascination, nevertheless falls short of perfection. This is so because natural selection can only work with what the existing store of genetic variation provides; it cannot create something entirely new. That exquisite design is not the rule is illustrated by the pains of aching backs, the annoyances of hernias, and problems with hemorrhoids that we humans must endure because the body of a four-footed vertebrate, designed for horizontal posture, has been jury-rigged to be held vertically above the two hind limbs. And surely, truly intelligent design from scratch could have produced an eye without a blind spot. Yet, these defects have been perpetuated by natural selection, because they are outweighed by other aspects of human adaptation that enhance the reproductive success of the species as a whole.

The Case of Sickle-Cell Anemia

Among human beings, a particularly well-studied case of an adaptation paid for by the misery of many individuals brings us back to the case of sickle-cell anemia. This disorder first came to the attention of geneticists when it was observed that most North Americans who suffer from it are of African ancestry. Investigation traced the abnormality to populations that live in a clearly defined belt throughout central Africa (although brought to North America from central Africa, the condition also exists in some non-African populations, as will be noted below).

Geneticists were curious to know why such a deleterious hereditary disability persisted in these populations. According to the theory of natural selection, any alleles that are harmful will tend to disappear from the group, because the individuals who are homozygous for the abnormality generally die—are "selected out"—before they are able to reproduce. Why, then, had this seemingly harmful condition remained in populations from central Africa?

The answer to this mystery began to emerge when it was noticed that the areas in which sickle-cell anemia is prevalent are also areas in which falciparum malaria is common (Figure 3.5). This severe form of malaria causes high fevers that significantly interfere with the reproductive abilities of those who do not actually die from

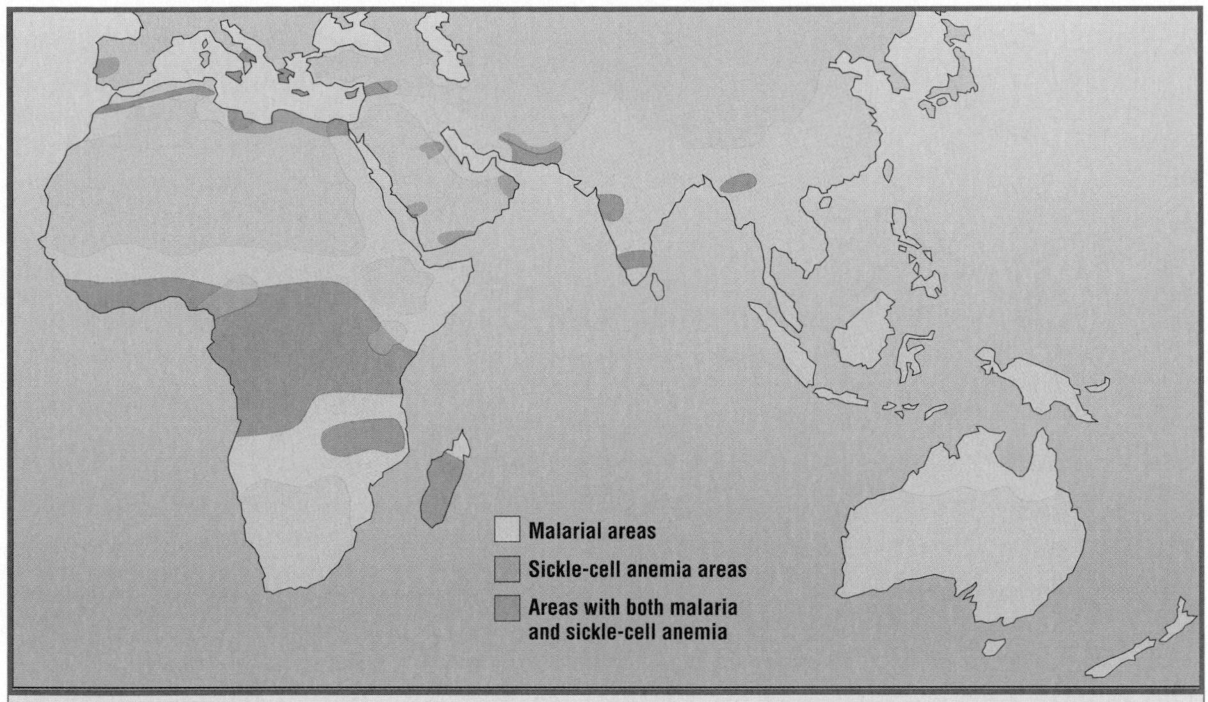

FIGURE 3.5
THE ALLELE THAT, IN HOMOZYGOTES, CAUSES SICKLE-CELL ANEMIA MAKES HETEROZYGOTES RESISTANT TO FALCIPARUM MALARIA. THUS, THE ALLELE IS MOST COMMON IN POPULATIONS NATIVE TO REGIONS WHERE THIS STRAIN OF MALARIA IS COMMON.

the disease. Moreover, it was discovered that the same hemoglobin abnormalities are found in people living in parts of the Arabian Peninsula, Greece, Algeria, and Syria as well as in certain East Indians, all of whom also are native to regions where falciparum malaria is common.

Further research established that the abnormal hemoglobin was associated with an increased ability to survive the effects of the malarial parasite; it seems that the effects of the abnormal hemoglobin in limited amounts were less injurious than the effects of the malarial parasite.

Thus, selection favored heterozygous individuals (Hb^AHb^S). The loss of alleles for abnormal hemoglobin caused by the death of those homozygous for it (from sickle-cell anemia) was balanced out by the loss of alleles for normal hemoglobin, as those homozygous for it experienced reproductive failure.

This example also points out how adaptations tend to be specific; the abnormal hemoglobin was an adaptation to the particular parts of the world in which the malarial parasite flourished. When Africans adapted to that region came to North America, where falciparum malaria is unknown, what had been an adaptive characteristic became an injurious one. Where there is no malaria to attack those with normal hemoglobin, the abnormal hemoglobin becomes comparatively disadvantageous. Although the rates of sickle-cell trait are still relatively high among African Americans—about 9 percent show the sickling trait—this represents a significant decline from the approximately 22 percent who are estimated to have shown the trait when the first slaves were brought from Africa. A further decline over the next several generations is to be expected, as selection pressure continues to work against it.

This example also illustrates the important role culture may play even with respect to biological adaptation. In West Africa, falciparum malaria was not a significant problem until humans abandoned food foraging for farming a few thousand years ago. In order to farm, they had to clear areas of the natural forest cover. In the forest, decaying vegetation on the forest floor had imparted an absorbent quality to the ground so that the heavy rainfall of the region rapidly soaked into the soil. But once stripped of its natural vegetation, the soil lost this quality.

HIGHWAY 1

A trip to this site, designed by students of Connecticut College, follows the route of Charles Darwin's historical voyage on the *HMS Beagle.* Learn about everything from the giant tortoises and finches on the Galapagos Islands to Darwin's thoughts about slavery from his voyage diary.
http://camel2.conncoll.edu/academics/departments/philosophy/courses/beagle/index

HIGHWAY 2

Learn how the genetics revolution is changing the practice of medicine. This site describes the story of the hunt for a cure for the genetic disease cystic fibrosis through gene therapy and also features a great tutorial in genetics.
www.hhmi.org/genetictrail/front/fwd.htm

HIGHWAY 3

The National Institutes of Health maintains this information-packed site that includes all the latest research about the Human Genome Project including its program on the ethical, legal, and social issues.
www.ornl.gov/hgmis/

Furthermore, the forest canopy was no longer there to break the force of the rainfall, and so the impact of the heavy rains tended to compact the soil further. The result was that stagnant puddles commonly formed after rains, and these were perfect for the breeding purposes of the type of mosquito that is the host to the malarial parasite. These mosquitoes then began to flourish and transmit the malarial parasite to humans. Thus, humans unwittingly created the kind of environment that made a hitherto disadvantageous trait, the abnormal hemoglobin associated with sickle-cell anemia, advantageous.

Although it is true that all living organisms have many adaptive characteristics, it is not true that all characteristics are adaptive. All male mammals, for example, possess nipples, even though they serve no useful purpose. To female mammals, however, nipples are essential to reproductive success, which is why males have them. The two sexes are not separate entities, shaped independently by natural selection but are variants upon a single ground plan, elaborated in later embryology. Precursors of mammary glands are built in all mammalian fetuses, enlarging later in the development of females, but remaining small and without function in males.

Nor is it true that current utility is a reliable guide to historical origin. For one thing, nonadaptive characters may be co-opted for later utility following origins as developmental consequences of changing patterns in embryonic and postnatal growth. The unusually large size of a kiwi's egg, for example, enhances the survivability of kiwi chicks, in that they are particularly large and capable when hatched. Nevertheless, kiwi eggs probably did not evolve such large size because it is adaptive. Kiwis evolved from large, moa-sized ancestors, and in birds, egg size reduces at a slower rate than does body size. Therefore, the out-sized eggs of kiwi birds seem to be no more than a developmental

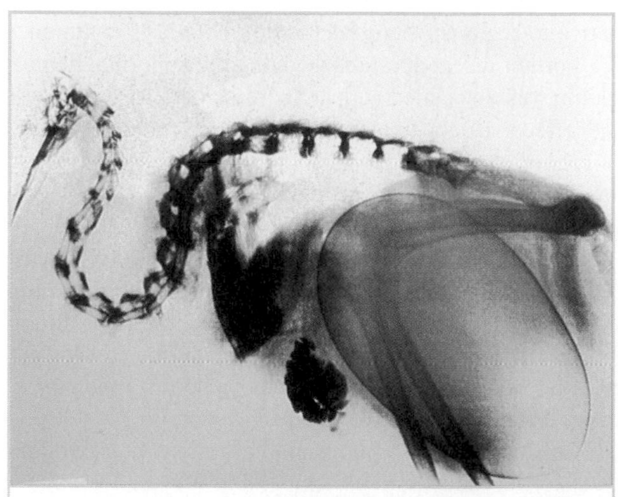

This x-ray illustrates the unusually large size of a kiwi's egg.

byproduct of a reduction in body size.[14] Similarly, an existing adaptation may come under strong selective pressure for some new purpose, as did insect wings. These did not arise so that insects might fly, but rather as gills that were used to "row," and later skim, across the surface of the water.[15] Later, the larger ones by chance proved useful for purposes of flight. In both these cases, what we see is natural selection operating as "a creative scavenger, taking what is available and putting it to new use."[16]

[14]Gould, S. J. (1991). *Bully for brontosaurus* (pp. 109–123). New York: Norton.

[15]Kaiser, J. (1994). A new theory of insect wing origins takes off. *Science, 266,* 363.

[16]Doist, R. (1997). Molecular evolution and scientific inquiry, misperceived. *American Scientist, 85,* 475.

CONCLUSION

As primatologist Frans de Waal notes, "Evolution is a magnificent idea that has won over essentially everyone in the world willing to listen to scientific arguments."[17] We will return to the topic in Chapter 5, as we look at how the primates evolved to produce the many species in the world today. First, however, we will survey the living primates (in Chapter 4) in order to understand the kinds of animals they are, what they have in common, and what distinguishes the various forms.

[17]de Waal, F. (2001). Sing the song of evolution. *Natural History, 110*(8), 77.

CHAPTER SUMMARY

In the 18th century, Carl von Linné (Linnaeus) devised a system to classify the great variety of living things then known. On the basis of similarities in body structure, body function, and sequence of bodily growth, he grouped organisms into small groups, or species. Modern taxonomy still uses his basic system but now looks at such characteristics as chemical reactions of blood, protein structure, and the makeup of the genetic material itself. Although Linnaeus regarded species as fixed and unchangeable, this idea was challenged by the finding of fossils, the idea of progress, and the many continuities among different species.

Evolution may be defined as descent with modification, which occurs as genetic variants in the gene pool of a population change in frequency. Genes, the actual units of heredity, are segments of molecules of DNA (deoxyribonucleic acid), and the entire sequence of DNA is known as the genome. DNA is a complex molecule resembling two strands of rope twisted around each other. Connecting the two strands are four chemical bases, adenine always pairing with thymine and guanine with cytosine. The sequence of these bases along the molecules are recipes that direct the production of proteins. These in turn direct the development of such identifiable traits as blood type. Just about everything in the human body is made of or by proteins, and human DNA provides the instructions for the thousands of proteins that keep us alive and healthy. DNA molecules have the unique property of being able to produce exact copies of themselves. As long as no errors are made in the process of replication, new organisms will contain genetic material exactly like that in ancestral organisms.

DNA molecules are located on chromosomes, structures found in the nucleus of each cell. Each kind of organism has a characteristic number of chromosomes, which are usually found in pairs. Humans have 23 pairs. Genes that are located on paired chromosomes and coded for different versions of the same trait are called alleles.

Mitosis, one kind of cell division, begins when the chromosomes (hence the genes) replicate, forming a second pair that duplicates the original pair of chromosomes in the nucleus. It results in new cells with exactly the same number of chromosome pairs as the parent cell. Meiosis, a different kind of cell division, is involved in sexual reproduction. It begins with the replication of original chromosomes, but these are divided into four cells, each containing 23 single chromosomes.

The Augustine monk Gregor Mendel studied the mechanism of inheritance with garden peas. He discovered the particulate nature of heredity and that some alleles are able to mask the presence of others. They are called dominant. The allele not expressed is recessive. The allele for Type A blood in humans, for example, is dominant to the allele for Type O blood. Alleles that are both expressed when present are termed *co-dominant.* An individual with the alleles for Type A and Type B blood has the AB blood type.

Phenotype refers to the physical characteristics of an organism, whereas genotype refers to its genetic composition. Two organisms may have the same phenotype but different genotypes.

A key concept is that of population, or a group of individuals within which most breeding takes place. It is populations, rather than individuals, that evolve. The total number of different alleles of genes available to a population is called its gene pool. The frequency with which certain alleles occur in the same gene pool theoretically remains the same from one generation to another; this is known as the Hardy-Weinberg principle. Nonetheless, change does take place in gene pools as a result of several factors.

The ultimate source of genetic variation is mutation. These are accidents that cause changes in sequences of DNA. Although mutations are inevitable given the nature of cellular chemistry, extrinsic factors—such as heat, certain chemicals, or various kinds of radiation—can increase the mutation rate. Another source of variation is interspecies gene transfer, as retroviruses can introduce DNA from one species into the genome of another.

The effects of chance events (other than mutations and interspecies transfer) on the gene pool of a small population is called genetic drift. Genetic drift may have been an important factor in human evolution because until 10,000 years ago all humans probably lived in relatively small populations. Another factor that brings change to the gene pool of a population is gene flow, or the introduction of new variants of genes from nearby populations. Gene flow occurs when previously separated groups are able to breed again.

Natural selection is the force that makes evolutionary change adaptive. It reduces the frequency of alleles for harmful or maladaptive traits within a population and increases the frequency of alleles for adaptive traits. The term *adaptation* means both the process by which organisms achieve a beneficial adjustment to an available environment and the results of the process—the characteristics of organisms that fit them to the particular set of conditions of the environment in which they are generally found. A well-studied example of adaptation through natural selection in humans is inheritance of the trait for sickling red blood cells. The sickle-cell trait, caused by the inheritance of an abnormal form of hemoglobin, is an adaptation to life in regions in which falciparum malaria is common. In these regions, the sickle-cell trait plays a beneficial role, but in other parts of the world, the sickling trait is no longer advantageous, while the associated sickle-cell anemia remains injurious. Geneticists predict that as malaria is brought under control, within several generations, there will be a decline in the number of individuals who carry the allele responsible for sickle-cell anemia.

CLASSIC READINGS

Berra, T. M. (1990). *Evolution and the myth of creationism.* Stanford, CA.: Stanford University Press.

Written by a zoologist, this book is a basic guide to the facts in the debate over evolution. It is not an attack on religion but a successful effort to assist in understanding the scientific basis for evolution.

Edey, M. A., & Johanson, D. (1989). *Blueprints: Solving the mystery of evolution.* Boston: Little, Brown.

This book is about the evolution of the idea of evolution, told as a scientific detective story. As much about the discoverers of evolution as it is about their discoveries, the book provides insights into the workings of science and gives readers the information they need to ponder the significance of our newfound ability, through genetic engineering, to actually direct the evolution of living things, including ourselves.

Gould, S. J. (1996). *Full house: The spread of excellence from Plato to Darwin.* New York: Harmony.

In this highly readable book, Gould explodes the misconception that evolution is inherently progressive. In the process, he shows how trends should be read as changes in variation within systems.

Ridley, M. (1999). *Genome: The autobiography of a species in 23 chapters.* New York: HarperCollins.

Written just as the mapping of the human genome was about to be announced, this book made *The New York Times* best-seller list. The 23 chapters discuss DNA on each of the 23 human chromosomes. A word of warning, however: The author uncritically accepts some ideas (one example relates to IQ). Still, there's much food for thought here.

Zimmer, C. (2001). *Evolution: The triumph of an idea.* New York: HarperCollins.

This is the companion volume to the seven part television series broadcast by PBS in fall 2001. Covered are a range of topics in modern evolutionary biology in a readable manner. Its drawback is that it pays too much attention to the tension between contemporary biblical literalism and the life sciences.

PART II

PRIMATE EVOLUTION AND THE EMERGENCE OF THE HOMININES

INTRODUCTION

In Chapter 1, we saw how the Nez Perce Indians of North America explained their existence in the world. Indeed, all human cultures of which we have record have grappled with such age-old questions as: Where do we come from? What is our place in the overall scheme of things? Each culture has answered these questions in its own way, through bodies of myth and folklore, as did the Nez Perce. It was not until the 20th century that hard scientific evidence was available to apply to these questions. In particular, as physical anthropologists and archaeologists have unearthed the bones and tools of our earliest ancestors, we have begun to glimpse the outline of a fantastic saga in which a tropics-dwelling apelike creature is transformed into a creative being capable of inventing solutions to problems of existence, rather than passively accepting what the environment and its own biology dictate.

This is not to say that humans represent the pinnacle of evolution, for they do not. We are, understandably, fascinated by our own origins, but in the overall scheme of things, we are nothing more than one small twig among many on the evolutionary tree of life. And as we shall see, there was nothing inevitable about our appearance: We are simply one more primate, successful for the moment as others have been in the

past (and some, like baboons and macaques, still are) but with no guarantee that our success will be any more lasting than the successes of others from the past.

This section of the book discusses developments that set the stage for the human transformation. We begin, in Chapter 4, with a review of the modern primates (the zoological order to which humans belong), in order to understand how much we humans are like the other primates. In particular, we can begin to appreciate that many of the physical characteristics we think of as distinctively human are simply our own peculiar versions of characteristics common to other primates. For example, primate brains tend to be large and heavy relative to body size and weight; in humans, this trait is realized to a greater degree than it is in other primates. We can begin to appreciate as well the kind of behavioral versatility of which present-day members of this order are capable. In the range of modern primate behavior patterns, we find clues to patterns that were characteristic of primates that lived in the past, from which humans descended.

Knowledge of the modern primates sets the stage for a review of the fossil evidence for primate evolution. In Chapter 5, key fossils are interpreted in light of evolutionary theory, our understanding of the biological variation of modern primates, and the behavioral correlates of that variation. This brings us to the apelike creatures of 8 to 16 million years ago, from some of which human ancestors evolved. Our early apelike ancestors seem to have spent more and more time on the ground and probably possessed mental abilities more or less equivalent to those of modern great apes. Because they were small and vulnerable, we think that the greatest measure of reproductive success came to those that were able to rear up on their hind limbs and scan the savanna, threaten predators with their forelimbs, transport food to a tree or other place where it could be eaten in relative safety, and transport offspring instead of relying on them to hang on by themselves, all the while managing to keep cool in the heat of the day.

With the appearance by 4 million years ago of *Australopithecus*, one of the earliest true hominines, the stage was set for the human transformation. *Australopithecus* may best be thought of as an apelike human; it walked bipedally in a fully human manner, but its mental abilities do not seem to have differed greatly from those of its ancestors of a few million years earlier. This implies essentially apelike behavior patterns, and it is appropriate to complete this section of the book with a chapter on *Australopithecus*. ■

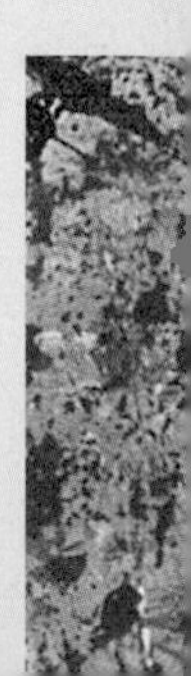

CHAPTER 4

MONKEYS, APES, AND HUMANS: THE MODERN PRIMATES

Monkeys and apes have long fascinated humans, owing to our many shared anatomical and behavioral characteristics. The study of other primates provides us with important clues as to what life may have been like for our own ancestors.

CHAPTER PREVIEW

What Is the Place of Humanity Among the Other Animals?

Humans are classified by biologists as belonging to the primate order, a group that also includes lemurs, lorises, tarsiers, monkeys, and apes. They are so classified on the basis of shared characteristics of anatomy, physiology, protein structure, and even the genetic material itself. Among the primates, humans resemble monkeys, but most closely resemble apes.

2

What Are the Implications of the Shared Characteristics Between Humans and the Other Primates?

The similarities on which the modern classification of animals is based are indicative of evolutionary relationships. Therefore, by studying the anatomy, physiology, and molecular structure of the other primates, we can gain a better understanding of what human characteristics we owe to our general primate ancestry and what traits are uniquely ours as humans. Such studies indicate that many of the differences between apes and humans are differences of degree rather than kind.

Why Do Anthropologists Study the Social Behavior of Monkeys and Apes?

By studying the behavior of monkeys and apes living today—especially those most closely related to us—we may find essential clues from which to reconstruct the adaptations and behavior patterns involved in the emergence of our earliest ancestors.

All living creatures—be they great or small, fierce or timid, active or inactive—face a fundamental problem in common: that of survival. Simply put, unless they are able to adapt themselves to some available environment, they cannot survive. Adaptation requires the development of behavior patterns that will help an organism utilize the environment to its advantage—to find food and sustenance, avoid hazards, and, if the species is to survive, reproduce its own kind. In turn, organisms need to have the biological equipment that makes possible the development of appropriate patterns of behavior. For the hundreds of millions of years that life has existed on earth, biological adaptation has been the primary means by which the problem of survival has been solved. This is accomplished through natural selection as those organisms of a particular species whose biological equipment is best suited to a particular way of life produce more offspring than those whose equipment is not so adapted. In this way, advantageous characteristics become more common in succeeding generations, while less advantageous ones become less common.

In this chapter, we will look at the biological equipment possessed by the primates, the group of animals to which humans belong. By doing so, we will gain a firmer understanding of those characteristics we share with other primates, as well as those that distinguish us from them and make us distinctively human. We shall also sample the behavior made possible by the biological equipment of primates. The study of that behavior is important in our quest to understand something of the origins of human culture and the origin of humanity itself.

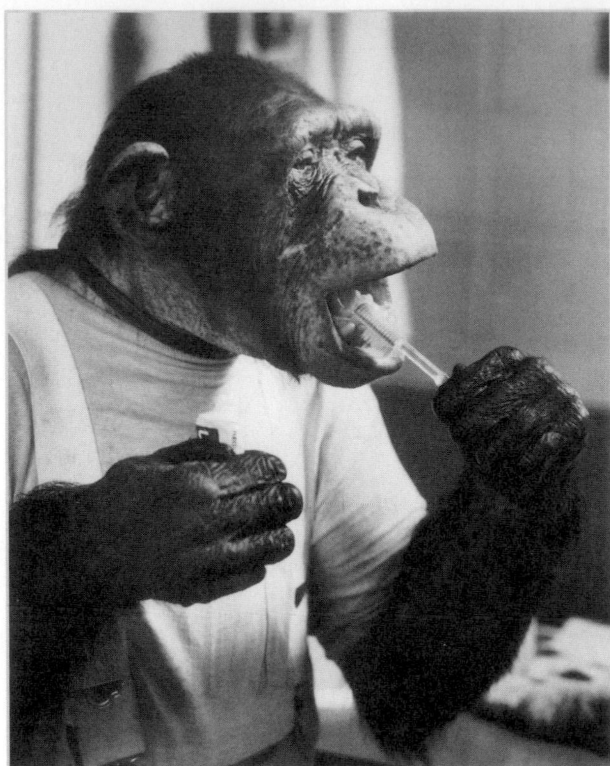

The traditional (but mistaken) Western notion of an unbridgeable gap between humans and animals is implicitly exemplified by the practice of dressing apes as humans and laughing at their behavior; that is, you can dress 'em up like us, but they sure don't behave like us!

THE PRIMATE ORDER

The primate order (see Table 4.1) is only one of several mammalian orders, such as rodents, carnivores, ungulates (hoofed mammals), and so on. As such, primates share a number of features with other mammals. Generally speaking, mammals are intelligent animals, having more in the way of brains than reptiles or other sorts of vertebrates. In most species, the young are born live, the egg being retained within the womb of the female until the embryo achieves an advanced state of growth. Once born, the young are nourished by their mothers with milk provided from the mammary glands, from which the class Mammalia gets its name. During this period of infant dependency, young mammals are able to learn some of the things that they will need for survival as adults. Overall, these characteristics make for more flexible behavior than found among nonmammal vertebrates.

Mammals are also active animals. This is made possible by their relatively constant body temperature, an efficient respiratory system featuring a separation between the nasal and mouth cavities (allowing them to breathe while they eat), a diaphragm to assist in drawing in and letting out breath, and an efficient four-chambered heart that prevents mixing of oxygenated and deoxygenated blood. It is facilitated as well by a skeleton in which the limbs are positioned beneath the body, rather than out at the sides, for ease and economy of movement. The bones of the limbs have joints constructed so as to permit growth in the young while simultaneously providing strong, hard joint surfaces that will stand up to the stresses of sustained activity. In return, they have given up the ability, possessed by reptiles, for bone growth throughout life.

The skeleton of most mammals is simplified, compared to that of most reptiles, in that it has fewer bones. For example, the lower jaw consists of a single bone, rather than several. The teeth, however, are another matter. Instead of the relatively simple, pointed, peglike teeth of reptiles,

TABLE 4.1 THE PRIMATE ORDER

Order	Suborder	Infraorder	Superfamily	Family
			Lemuroidea	
Primates	Strepsirhini	Lemuriformes		Five families of lemurs and lemurlike animals
			Lorisoidea	Three families of lorises
	Haplorhini	Tarsii	Tarsioidea	One family, represented solely by tarsiers
		Platyrrhini	Ceboidea	Three families of New World Monkeys
		Catarrhini	Cercopithecoidea	One family with two subfamilies of Old World monkeys
			Hominoidea	Hylobatidae (small apes)
				Pongidae (Asian great apes)
				Hominidae (African apes, humans, and near humans)

mammals have special teeth for special purposes: incisors for nipping, gnawing, and cutting; canines for ripping, tearing, killing, and fighting; premolars that may either slice and tear or crush and grind (depending on the kind of animal); and molars for crushing and grinding. This enables mammals to eat a wide variety of food—an advantage to them, since they require more food than do reptiles to sustain their high activity. But they pay a price: Reptiles have unlimited tooth replacement, whereas mammals are limited to two sets. The first set serves the immature animal and is replaced by the permanent or adult dentition.

The primate order is divided into two suborders (Table 4.1), of which one is the **Strepsirhini** (from the Greek for "turned nose"). This includes lemurs and lorises (all members of the infraorder **Lemuriformes**). On the whole, strepsirhines are cat-sized or smaller, although there have been some larger forms in the past. Generally, they do not exhibit the characteristics of their order as obviously as do the members of the other suborder, the **Haplorhini** (from the Greek for "simple nose"). The strepsirhines also retain certain features common among nonprimate mammals, such as claws and moist, naked skin on their noses, that have not been retained by the haplorhines.

The haplorhine suborder is divided into three infraorders: the **Tarsii,** or tarsiers; the **Platyrrhini,** or New World monkeys; and the **Catarrhini,** consisting of the superfamilies Cercopithecoidea (Old World monkeys) and Hominoidea. Within the Hominoidea are the families Hylobatidae (small apes, like the gibbon), Pongidae, and Hominidae. Although the traditional classification of primates placed all great apes (bonobo, chimpanzee, gorilla, and orangutan) together in the pongid family, and humans alone as hominids, molecular evidence has demonstrated that this way of grouping apes and humans violates evolutionary relationships. Because the way we classify is supposed to reflect evolutionary genealogies, recent classifications restrict the Pongidae to orangutans, whereas bonobos, chimps, and gorillas are included with humans in the Hominidae, as a reflection of their closer relation to one another than to orangs. Unfortunately, old habits die hard, and it is still common to find scientists using the family names in the outmoded way. But because it misleads, this obsolete practice should be dropped; therefore, in this book we shall use classificatory terminology more reflective of evolutionary genealogy. Only at the level of the subfamily will humans (homininae) be separated from bonobos, chimps, and gorillas, although

Strepsirhini. A primate suborder that includes the single infraorder Lemuriformes. • **Lemuriformes.** A strepsirhine infraorder that includes lemurs and lorises. • **Haplorhini.** A primate suborder that includes tarsiers, monkeys, apes, and humans. • **Tarsii.** A haplorhine infraorder that includes tarsiers. • **Platyrrhini.** A haplorhine infraorder that includes the New World monkeys. • **Catarrhini.** A haplorhine infraorder that includes Old World monkeys, apes, and humans.

Hands that grasp and eyes that see in three dimensions enable primates, like these South American monkeys, to live effectively in the trees.

a case can be made that the separation should be made below even the level of the subfamily.[1]

CHARACTERISTICS

Although the living primates are a varied group of animals, they do have a number of features in common (Table 4.2). We humans, for example, can grasp, throw things, and see stereoscopically because we are primates. Primate features are, however, displayed in varying degree by the different members of this order; in some they are barely detectable, while in others they are greatly elaborated. All are useful in one way or another to **arboreal,** or tree-dwelling, animals, although (as any squirrel knows) they are not essential to life in the trees. For animals preying upon the many insects living on the fruit and flowers of trees and shrubs, however, such primate characteristics as manipulative hands and keen vision would have been enormously adaptive. Probably, it was as arboreal animals relying on visual predation of insects that primates got their start in life.

The Primate Brain

By far the most outstanding characteristic of primate evolution has been the enlargement of the brain among members of the order. Primate brains tend to be large, heavy in proportion to body weight, and very complex. The cerebral hemispheres (the areas of conscious thought) have enlarged dramatically and, in catarrhines, completely cover the cerebellum, which is the part of the brain that coordinates the muscles and maintains body equilibrium.

The reasons for this important change in brain size are many, but it likely began as the earliest primates, along with many other mammals, began to carry out their activities in the daylight hours. Prior to 65 million years ago, mammals seem to have been nocturnal in their habits, but with the extinction of the dinosaurs, inconspicuous, nighttime activity was no longer the key to survival. With the change to diurnal or daytime activity, the sense of vision took on greater importance, and so visual acuity was favored by natural selection. Unlike reptile vision, where the information-processing neurons are in the retina, mammalian vision is processed in the brain, permitting integration with information received by hearing and smelling.

If the evolution of visual acuity led to larger brains, it is likely that the primates' insect predation in an arboreal setting also played a role in enlargement of the brain. This would have required great agility and muscular coordination, favoring development of the brain centers. Thus it is of interest that much of the higher mental faculties are apparently developed in an area alongside the motor centers of the brain.[2]

Another related hypothesis that may help account for primate brain enlargement involves the use of the hand

[1]Goodman, M., Bailey, W. J., Hayasaka, K., Stanhope, M. J., Slighton J., & Czelusniak, J. (1994). Molecular evidence on primate phylogeny from DNA sequences. *American Journal of Physical Anthropology, 94,* 7.

[2]Romer, A. S. (1945). *Vertebrate paleontology* (p. 103). Chicago: University of Chicago Press.

Arboreal. Tree-dwelling.

TABLE 4.2 PRIMATE ANATOMY VARIATION AND SPECIALIZATION

Suborder, Infraorder, Superfamily	Skull and Face	Dental Pattern and Specializations	Locomotor Pattern and Morphology	Tail and Other Skeletal Specializations
Strepsirhini	Complete ring of bone around eye orbit	2-1-3-3	Hind leg dominance for vertical clinging and leaping	Tail present
Lemuriformes		Dental comb for grooming		"Toilet claw" for grooming
Lorisiformes	Upper lip bound down to gum			
Haplorhini	Forward facing orbit fully enclosed in bone Free upper lip Shorter snout			
Tarsiiformes Tarsiers		2-1-3-3	Hind leg dominance	Tail present
Platyrrhini New World Monkeys		2-1-3-3	Quadrupedal	Prehensile tail
Catarrhini Old World Monkeys		2-1-2-3 4-cusped molars	Quadrupedal	Tail present
Apes		2-1-2-3 Y5 molars	Suspensory hanging apparatus	No tail

as a tactile organ to replace the teeth and jaws or snout. The hands assumed some of the grasping, tearing, and dividing functions of the snout, again requiring development of the brain centers for more complete coordination. Thus, while the skull and brain expanded, the teeth and jaws grew smaller. Certain areas of the brain became more elaborate and intricate. One of these areas is the cortex, considered to be the center of an animal's intelligence; it receives impressions from the animal's various sensory receptors, analyzes them, and sends responses back down the motor nerves to the proper receptor.

The enlarged cortex not only served the primates well in the daily struggle for survival but also gave them the basis for more complex cerebration, or thought. Flexibility of thought probably played a decisive role in the evolution of the primates from which human beings emerged.

Primate Sense Organs

Catching insects in the trees, as the early primates did and many still do, demands quickness of movement and the ability to land in the right place without falling. Thus, they had to be adept at judging depth, direction, distance, and the relationships of objects in space—abilities that remain useful to animals that travel through the trees (as most primates still do today), even though they may have given up most insect eating in favor of fruits and leaves. In the haplorhines, these abilities are provided by their binocular **stereoscopic vision,** the ability to see the world in three dimensions—height, width, and depth. It requires two eyes set apart from each other on the same plane, so that each eye views an object from a slightly different angle (binocular vision). In addition, nerve fibers from each eye go to each side of the brain. The result is that

Stereoscopic vision. Three-dimensional vision.

the object assumes a three-dimensional appearance, indicating spatial relationships. Stereoscopic vision is one of the most important factors in primate evolution, for it evidently led to increased brain size in the visual area and a great complexity at nerve connections.

Visual acuity, however, varies throughout the primate order. Lemuriformes, for example, are the most visually primitive of the primates. With binocular but not stereoscopic vision, their eyes look out from either side of their muzzle or snout with some overlap of visual fields, but their nerve fibers do not cross from each eye to both halves of the brain. Nor do they possess color vision, an advantage for nocturnal animals as it enhances night vision. All other primates possess both color and stereoscopic vision, as well as a unique structure called the **fovea centralis,** or central pit in the retina of each eye. Like a camera lens, this feature enables the animal to focus on a particular object for acutely clear perception, without sacrificing visual contact with the object's surroundings.

The primates' emphasis on visual acuity came at the expense of their sense of smell. One reason is that smell is processed in the snout, and a large protruding snout may interfere with stereoscopic vision. But smell is an expendable sense to tree-dwelling animals in search of insects; they no longer needed to live a "nose-to-the-ground" existence, sniffing close to the ground in search of food. The haplorhines especially have the least-developed sense of smell of all land animals. Strepsirhines still rely on it to a degree, scent marking objects in their territories.

Primate sense of touch also became highly developed as a result of arboreal living. Primates found useful an effective feeling and grasping mechanism to grab their insect prey and to prevent them from falling and tumbling while moving through the trees. The primitive mammals from which primates descended possessed tiny tactile hairs that gave them extremely sensitive tactile capacities. In primates, these hairs were replaced by informative pads on the tips of the animals' fingers and toes.

Primate Dentition

Although they have added other things than insects to their diets, primates have retained less specialized teeth than other mammals. According to primatologist W. E. LeGros Clark,

> An arboreal life obviates the necessity for developing highly specialized grinding teeth, since the diet available to most tree-living mammals in the tropics, consisting of leaves, shoots, soft fruits, and insects, can be adequately masticated by molar teeth of relatively simple structure.[3]

In most primates (humans included), on each side of each jaw, in front, are two straight-edged, chisel-like broad teeth called incisors (Figure 4.1). Behind the incisors is a canine, which in many mammals is large, flaring, and fanglike and is used for defense as well as for tearing and shredding food. Among some catarrhines the

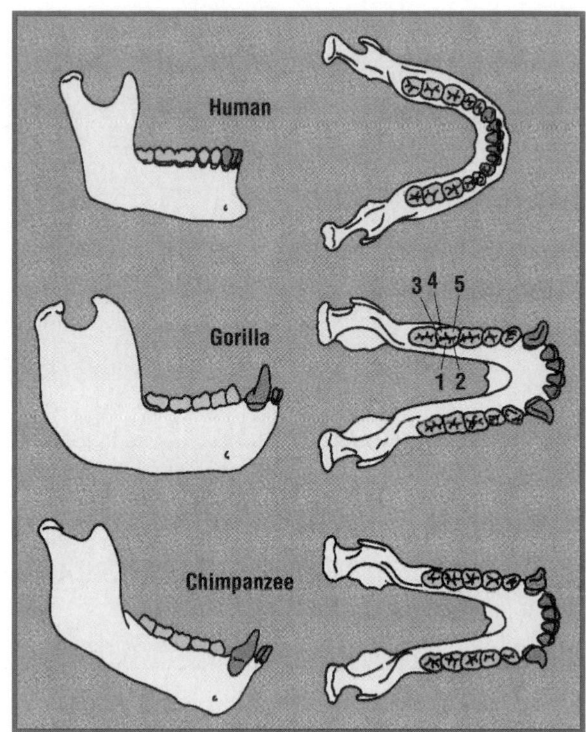

FIGURE 4.1
IN THIS DEPICTION OF THE LOWER JAWS OF A HUMAN, A GORILLA, AND A CHIMPANZEE, INCISORS ARE SHOWN IN BLUE, CANINES IN RED, AND PREMOLARS AND MOLARS IN YELLOW. ON ONE OF THE GORILLA MOLARS, THE CUSPS ARE NUMBERED TO FACILITATE THEIR IDENTIFICATION.

[3]LeGros Clark, W. E. (1966). *History of the primates* (5th ed., p. 271). Chicago: University of Chicago Press.

Fovea centralis. A shallow pit in the retina of the eye that enables an animal to focus on an object while maintaining visual contact with its surroundings.

canine is somewhat reduced in size, especially in females, though it is still large in males. In humans, though, incisors and canines are practically indistinguishable, although the canine has an oversized root, suggestive of larger canines some time back in our ancestry. Behind the canines are the premolars. Last come the molars, usually with four or five cusps, used mostly for crushing or grinding food. This basic dentition contrasts sharply with that of nonprimate mammals.

Comparative anatomy and the fossil record point to the existence of an early primate ancestor that possessed three incisors, one canine, five premolars, and three molars (expressed as the dental formula 3-1-5-3) on each side of the jaw, top and bottom, for a total of 48 teeth. In the early stages of primate evolution, four incisors (one on each side of each jaw) were lost. This change differentiated the primates, with their two incisors on each side of each jaw, from other mammals. The canines of most primates develop into long, daggerlike teeth that enable them to rip open tough husks of fruit and other foods. In a combat situation, male baboons, apes, and other primates flash these formidable teeth at their enemies, intending to scare them off. Only infrequently, when this bluffing action fails, are teeth used to inflict bodily harm.

Other evolutionary changes in primate dentition involve the premolar and molar teeth. Over the millennia, three premolars became smaller and eventually disappeared altogether, while the two remaining premolars grew larger with the addition of a second pointed projection, or cusp, thus becoming "bicuspid." In humans, all eight premolars are bicuspid, but in apes, the lower first premolar is not. Instead, it is a specialized, single cusped tooth with a sharp edge to act with the upper canine as a shearing mechanism. The molars, meanwhile, evolved from a three-cusp pattern to one with four and even five (in apes and humans) cusps. This kind of molar economically combined the functions of grasping, cutting, and grinding in one tooth.

The evolutionary trend for primate dentition has generally been toward economy, with fewer, smaller, more efficient teeth doing more work. Thus our own 32 teeth (a 2-1-2-3 dental formula shared with the Old World monkeys and apes) are fewer in number than those of some, and more generalized than those of most, primates. Indeed, the absence of third molars in many individuals indicates that the human dentition is undergoing further reduction.

The Primate Skeleton

The skeleton gives an animal its basic shape or silhouette, supports the soft tissues, and helps protect the vital internal organs. In primates (Figure 4.2), for example, the

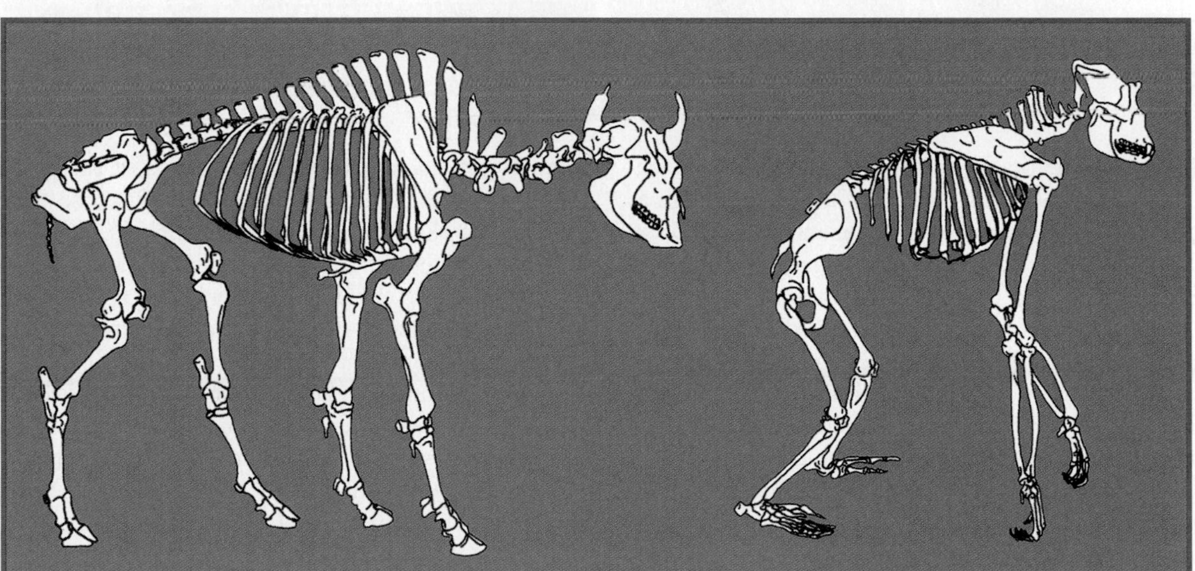

FIGURE 4.2

NOTE WHERE THE SKULLS AND VERTEBRAL COLUMNS ARE JOINED IN THESE SKELETONS OF A BISON (LEFT) AND A GORILLA (RIGHT). IN THE BISON (AS IN MOST MAMMALS) THE SKULL PROJECTS FORWARD FROM THE VERTEBRAL COLUMN, BUT IN THE SEMIERECT GORILLA, THE VERTEBRAL COLUMN IS FURTHER BENEATH THE SKULL. NOTE ALSO THE SPECIALIZED FOOT SKELETON OF THE BISON, COMPARED TO THE GENERALIZED FOOT OF THE GORILLA.

Humans owe their flat facial profile and erect posture to their catarrhine ancestry.

skull protects the brain and the eyes. A number of factors are responsible for the shape of the primate skull as compared with those of most other mammals: changes in dentition, changes in the sensory organs of sight and smell, and increased brain size. The primate brain case, or **cranium,** tends to be high and vaulted. A solid partition exists in most primate species (including humans) between the eye and the temple, affording maximum protection to the eyes from the contraction of the chewing muscles positioned directly next to the eyes.

The **foramen magnum** (the large opening in the skull through which the spinal cord passes and connects to the brain) is an important clue to evolutionary relationships. In most mammals, as in dogs and horses, this opening faces directly backward, with the skull projecting forward from the vertebral column. In humans, by contrast, the vertebral column joins the skull toward the center of its base, thereby placing the skull in a balanced position as required for habitual upright posture. Other primates, though they frequently cling, sit, or hang with their bodies upright, are not as fully committed to such posture as humans, and so their foramen magnum is not as far forward.

In most primates, the snout or muzzle portion of the skull has grown smaller as the acuity of the sense of smell declined. The smaller snout offers less interference with stereoscopic vision; it also enables the eyes to be placed in the frontal position. As a result, primates have flatter faces than other mammals. Below the primate skull and the neck is the **clavicle,** or collarbone, a holdover from primitive mammal ancestors. Though reduced in quadru-

Cranium. The brain case of the skull. • **Foramen magnum.** A large opening in the skull through which the spinal cord passes and connects to the brain. • **Clavicle.** The collarbone.

Humans are able to grasp and throw things as they do because of characteristics of their hands and shoulders inherited from ape ancestors.

pedal primates like monkeys, in apes and humans it serves as a strut that prevents the arm from collapsing inward when brought across the front of the body. It allows for great maneuverability of the arms, permitting them to swing sideways and outward from the trunk of the body. The clavicle also supports the **scapula** (shoulder blade) and allows for the muscle development that is required for flexible, yet powerful, arm movement, particularly in hominoids, whose shoulders are especially broad. This shoulder and limb structure is associated with considerable acrobatic agility and, in the case of all apes and a few New World monkeys, the ability to **brachiate**—use their arms to swing and hang beneath the branches of trees with the body in a vertical (upright) position.

Primates have retained also the characteristic, found in early mammals, of **pentadactyly.** Pentadactyly, which means possessing five digits, is an ancient characteristic that proved to be of special advantage to tree-dwelling primates. Their grasping feet and hands (Figure 4.3) have

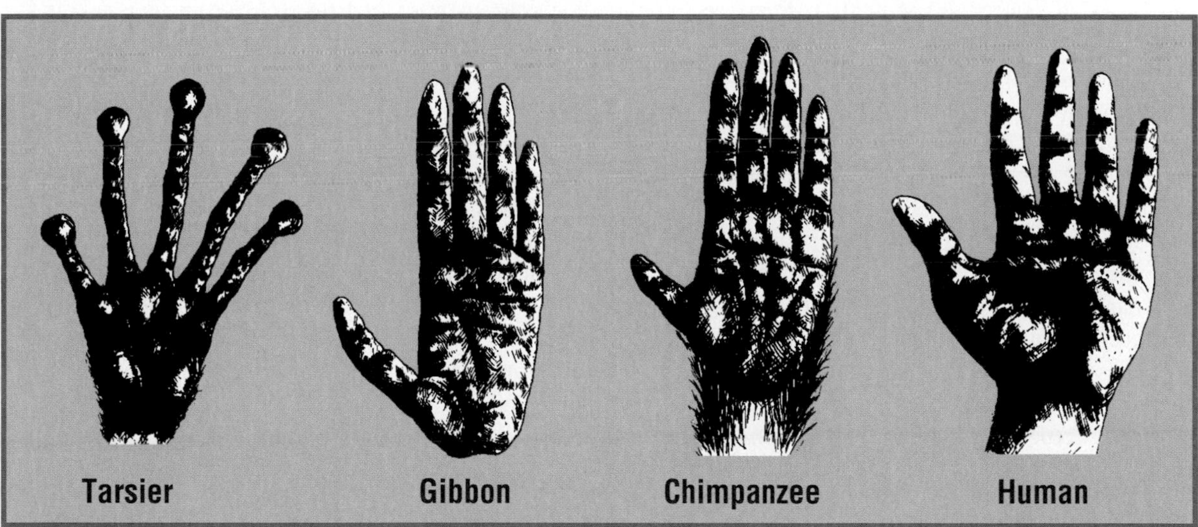

FIGURE 4.3

THE HANDS OF PRIMATES ARE SIMILAR. HOWEVER, HUMAN HANDS ARE DISTINGUISHED BY PROMINENT THUMBS THAT CAN BE USED IN OPPOSITION TO THE FINGERS. THE HIGHLY SPECIALIZED HANDS OF THE BRACHIATORS (GIBBONS AND CHIMPANZEES) ARE CHARACTERIZED BY LONG FINGERS AND LESS PROMINENT THUMBS.

Scapula. The shoulder blade. • **Brachiate.** To use the arms to move from branch to branch, with the body hanging suspended beneath the arms. • **Pentadactyly.** Possessing five digits (fingers and toes).

sensitive pads at the tips of their digits, backed up (except in some strepsirhines) by flattened nails. This unique combination of pad and nail provides the animal with an excellent **prehensile** (grasping) device for use when moving from branch to branch. The structural characteristics of the primate foot and hand make grasping possible; the digits are extremely flexible, the big toe is fully opposable to the other digits in all but humans and their immediate ancestors, and the thumb is opposable to the other digits to varying degrees.

Hindsight indicates that the flexible, unspecialized primate hand was to prove a valuable asset for future evolution of this group. Had they not had generalized grasping hands, early hominines (members of the human subfamily) would not have been able to manufacture and utilize tools and thus embark on the new and unique evolutionary pathway that led to the revolutionary ability to adapt through culture.

Reproduction and Care of Young

The breeding of most mammals occurs once or twice a year, but many primate species are able to breed at any time during the course of the year. Generally, the male is ready to engage in sexual activity whenever females are in **estrus,** around the time of ovulation. The female's receptivity is cyclical, corresponding to her period of estrus, which occurs once each month.

This is not to say that females are receptive regularly each month. Rather, the average adult female monkey or ape spends most of her time either pregnant or nursing, at which times she is not sexually receptive. But after her infant is weaned, she will come into estrus for a few days each month, until she becomes pregnant again. Because this can happen at any time, it is advantageous to have males present throughout the year. This is promoted in some species by lack of visual signs of estrus. Thus, sex plays a role in keeping both sexes constantly together, except among some orangutans, among whom adults may only come together when females are in estrus. In most species, however, sex is not the only, or even the most important, cause of males and females remaining together.

Among primates, as among some other mammals, females give birth to few offspring at a time. In the case of lemurs, the primates closest to the ancestral condition, two or three young are produced at each birth. By contrast, catarrhines (humans included), usually produce but a single offspring at a time. Natural selection may have favored single births among primate tree dwellers because the primate infant, which has a highly developed grasping ability (the grasping reflex can also be seen in human infants), must be transported about by its mother, and more than one clinging infant would seriously encumber her as she moved about the trees (where twinning is seen, fathers as well as mothers transport offspring). Moreover, a female pregnant with a large litter would be unable to lead a very active life as a tree dweller.

Because primates bear few young at a time, they must devote more time and effort to their care if the species is to survive. This usually means a longer period during which the infant is dependent upon its mother. As a general rule, the more closely related to humans the species is, the smaller, more helpless, and more immature the newborn offspring tend to be. For example, a lemur is dependent upon the mother for only a few months after birth; an ape, for 4 or 5 years; and a human for more than a decade. Prolonged infancy is typically associated with an increase in longevity (Figure 4.4). If the breeding life of primates had not extended, the lengthened infancy could have led to a decrease in numbers of individuals. Something approaching this can be seen in the great apes: A female chimpanzee, for example, does not reach sexual maturity until about the age of 10, and once she produces her first live offspring, there is a period of 5 or 6 (on average 5.6) years before she will bear another. Furthermore, a chimpanzee infant cannot survive if its mother dies before it reaches the age of 4 at the very least. Thus, assuming that none of her offspring die before adulthood, a female chimpanzee must survive for at least 20 or 21 years just to maintain the size of chimpanzee populations at existing levels. In fact, chimpanzee infants and juveniles do die from time to time, and not all females live full reproductive lives. This is one reason why apes are far less abundant in the world today than are monkeys.

The young of catarrhine, and especially hominoid, species are born with relatively underdeveloped nervous systems; moreover, they lack the social knowledge that guides behavior. Thus they depend upon adults not only for protection but also for instruction, as they must learn how to survive. The longer period of dependence in these primates makes possible a longer period of learning, which appears to be a distinct evolutionary advantage.

Prehensile. Having the ability to grasp. • **Estrus.** In primate females, the time of sexual receptivity during which ovulation takes place.

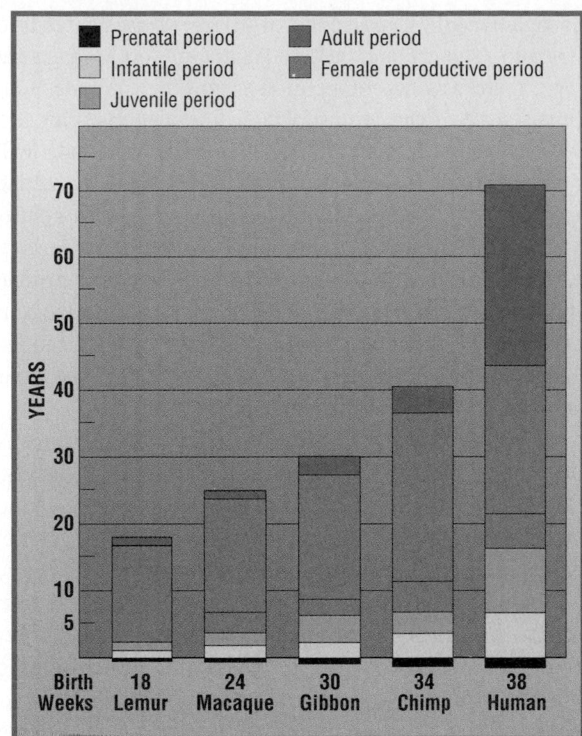

FIGURE 4.4

PRIMATES ARE BORN AT EARLIER STAGES OF DEVELOPMENT THAN MANY OTHER ANIMALS. HUMANS ARE BORN AT A PARTICULARLY EARLY STAGE BECAUSE OF THEIR LARGER BRAIN; IF BORN LATER, THE BABY'S HEAD WOULD BE TOO LARGE FOR THE MOTHER'S PELVIS.

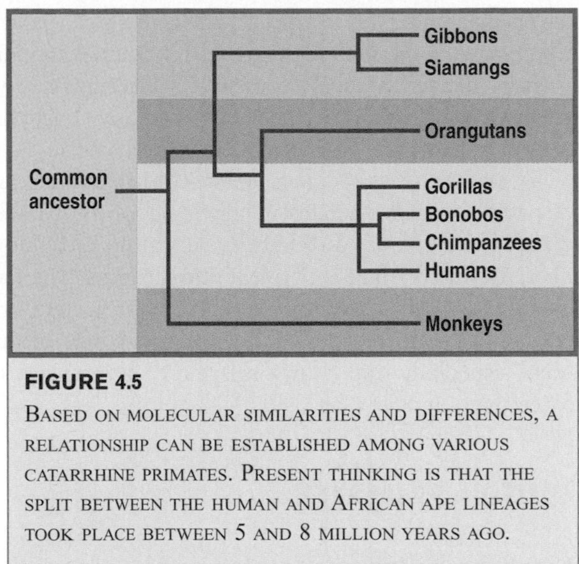

FIGURE 4.5

BASED ON MOLECULAR SIMILARITIES AND DIFFERENCES, A RELATIONSHIP CAN BE ESTABLISHED AMONG VARIOUS CATARRHINE PRIMATES. PRESENT THINKING IS THAT THE SPLIT BETWEEN THE HUMAN AND AFRICAN APE LINEAGES TOOK PLACE BETWEEN 5 AND 8 MILLION YEARS AGO.

Establishing Evolutionary Relationships

Most of the primate characteristics discussed so far are present at least in a rudimentary sort of way in the strepsirhines, but all are seen to a much greater degree in the haplorhines. The differences between humans and the other haplorhines, especially catarrhines, are rather like those between strepsirhines and haplorhines. In humans many of the characteristic primate traits are developed to a degree not realized by any other species. Among some strepsirhines, some of the distinctive primate traits are missing, whereas others are clearly present, so that the borderline between primate and nonprimate becomes blurred, and the difference is one of degree rather than kind. All of this is fully expectable, given an evolutionary history in which early primates having a rough resemblance to today's strepsirhines developed out of some other mammalian order and eventually gave rise to early haplorhines; from these emerged the catarrhines and, ultimately, hominids.

Similar though our appearance is to other primates, just how close our evolutionary relationship is to them is indicated most dramatically by molecular evidence. There is a striking similarity in blood and protein chemistry among the hominoids especially, indicating close evolutionary relationships. On the basis of tests with blood proteins, it has been shown that the bonobo, chimpanzee, and gorilla are closest to humans; next comes the orangutan; then the smaller apes (gibbons and siamangs); Old World monkeys; New World monkeys; and finally the strepsirhines. Measurements of genetic affinity confirm these findings, providing further evidence of humanity's close kinship to the great apes, especially those of Africa (Figure 4.5). The modern classification of humans, two species of genus *Pan* (bonobos and chimpanzees), and gorillas together in the family hominidae, distinct from the pongidae, reflects the fact that the three genera are more closely related to one another than any is to the orangutan.

At the genetic level, humans, bonobos, and chimpanzees are between 98 and 99 percent identical. The differences are that bonobos and chimps (like gorillas and orangs) have an extra pair of chromosomes; in humans, two medium-sized chromosomes have fused together in Chromosome 2 (the second largest of the human chromosomes). Of the other pairs, 18 are virtually identical between humans and the genus *Pan* whereas the remaining ones have been reshuffled. Overall, the differences are fewer than those between gibbons (with 44 chromosomes) and siamangs (50 chromosomes), which, in captivity, have produced live hybrid offspring. Although some studies of molecular similarities have suggested a closer relationship between *Pan* and humans than either has to gorillas, others disagree, and the safest course at the moment is to regard all three hominid genera as having an equal degree of relationship (the two species of genus *Pan* are, of course, more closely related to each other than either is to gorillas or humans).[4]

To sum up, what becomes apparent when humans are compared to other primates is how many of the characteristics we think of as distinctly human are no such thing; rather, they are variants of typical primate traits. The fact is, we humans look the way we do *because* we are primates, and the differences between us and others of this order—especially the apes—are more differences of degree than kind.

MODERN PRIMATES

The modern primates are mostly restricted to warm areas of the world. As already noted, they are divided into two suborders: Strepsirhini and Haplorhini. Strepsirhines are small Old World animals that do a lot of leaping and clinging; haplorhines include tarsiers, monkeys, apes, and humans.

Strepsirhines

The strepsirhines, the most primitive primates (that is, closest to the ancestral condition), are represented by the single infraorder Lemuriformes, within which are the lemurs and lorises. Although lemurs are restricted to the island of Madagascar (off the east coast of Africa), lorises range from Africa to southern and eastern Asia. Only on Madagascar, where there was no competition from other primates until humans arrived, are lemuriformes diurnal; lorises by contrast, are all nocturnal. All these animals are small, with none larger than a good-sized dog. In general body outline, they resemble rodents and insectivores, with short pointed snouts, large pointed ears, and big eyes. In the anatomy of the upper lip and snout, lemuriformes resemble nonprimate mammals, in that the upper lip is bound down to the gum and the naked skin on the nose around the nostrils is moist. They also have long tails, with that of a ring-tail lemur somewhat like the tail of a raccoon.

In brain structure, lemuriformes are clearly primates, and they have characteristically primate "hands," although they use them in pairs, rather than one at a time. Their legs are longer than their forelimbs, and when they move on all fours, the forelimbs are in a "palms down" position. They also leap and cling in near vertical positions to branches. Although they retain a claw on their second toe, which they use for scratching and grooming, all other digits are equipped with flattened nails. Also for grooming is a structure unique to lemuriformes: a dental comb made up of the lower incisors and canines, which project forward from the jaw. With their distinctive mix of characteristics, strepsirhine primates appear to occupy a place between the haplorhines and insectivores (the mammalian order that includes moles and shrews).

Haplorhines

The suborder Haplorhini is divided into three infraorders: the Tarsii (tarsiers), Platyrrhini (New World monkeys), and Catarrhini (Old World monkeys, apes, and humans). Most

[4]Rogers, J. (1994). Levels of the genealogical hierarchy and the problem of hominid phylogeny. *American Journal of Physical Anthropology, 94,* 81.

Modern strepsirhines represent highly evolved variants of an early primate model.

haplorhines are bigger than the strepsirhines and are strikingly humanlike in appearance. Actually, it is more accurate to say that humans are remarkably like monkeys, but even more like apes, in appearance. The defining traits of the strepsirhines—large cranium, well-developed brain, acute vision, chisel-like incisors, prehensile digits—are especially evident in the haplorhines. Most haplorhines generally move on all four limbs but sit with the body erect, and many stand erect to reach fruit hanging in trees: Some apes even walk occasionally on two feet. Monkeys are often highly arboreal, and New World species have prehensile tails that wrap around a tree branch, freeing the forelimbs to grasp food. A few New World monkeys brachiate; Old World monkeys never do.

All apes may once have been fully arboreal brachiators, but among modern apes, only the gibbon and siamang still are. The larger bonobo, chimpanzee, and gorilla spend most of their time on the ground but sleep in the trees and may also find food there. Orangutans, too, spend time down on the ground, but are more arboreal than the African apes. When on the ground, they move mostly on all fours.

TARSIERS

Tarsiers are the haplorhine primates most like the lemuriformes, and in the past they were usually classified in the same suborder with them. Molecular evidence, however, indicates a closer relationship to the other haplorhines. The head, eyes, and ears of these kitten-sized arboreal creatures are huge in proportion to the body. They have the remarkable ability to turn their heads 180 degrees, so they can see where they have been as well as where they are going. The digits end in platelike, adhesive discs. Tarsiers are named for the elongated tarsal, or foot bone, that provides leverage for jumps of 6 feet or more. Tarsiers are mainly nocturnal insect eaters. In the structure of the nose and lips, and the part of the brain governing vision, tarsiers resemble monkeys.

Tarsiers are distinctive for their large eyes, adapted for their nocturnal habitat.

NEW WORLD MONKEYS

New World monkeys live in forests and swamps of South and Central America. They are characterized by flat noses with widely separated, outward flaring nostrils, from which comes their name of platyrrhine (platy = flat; rhine = nose) monkeys. All are arboreal, and some have long, prehensile tails by which they hang from trees. These features and a 2-1-3-3 dental formula (three, rather than two, premolars on each side of each jaw) distinguish them from the Old World monkeys, apes, and humans. Platyrrhines walk on all fours with their palms down and scamper along tree branches in search of fruit, which they eat sitting upright. Spider monkeys are accomplished brachiators as well. Although other New World monkeys spend much of their time in the trees, they rarely hang or swing from limb to limb by their arms and have not developed the extremely long forelimbs and broad shoulders characteristic of brachiators.

OLD WORLD MONKEYS

Old World, or catarrhine, monkeys are characterized by noses with closely spaced, downward-pointing nostrils, a 2-1-2-3 dental formula (two, rather than three, premolars on each side of each jaw), and their lack of prehensile tails. They may be either arboreal or terrestrial. The arboreal species include the guereza monkey, the Asiatic langur, and the strange-looking proboscis monkey. Some are equally at home on the ground and in the trees, such as the macaques, of which some 19 species range from Gibraltar (the misnamed "Barbary ape") to Japan.

Several species of baboons are largely terrestrial, living in the savannas, deserts, and highlands of Africa. They have long, fierce faces and move quadrupedally, with all fours in the palms-down position. Like all monkeys, their forelimbs and hindlimbs are of equal length. Their diet consists of leaves, seeds, insects, and lizards, and they live in large, well-organized troops consisting of related females and adult males that have transferred out of other troops. Because baboons have abandoned trees (except for sleeping and refuge) and live in environments like that in which humans may have originated, they are of great interest to primatologists.

SMALL AND GREAT APES

The apes are the closest living relatives we humans have in the animal world. Their general appearance and way of life are related to their semierect posture. In their body chemistry, the position of their internal organs, and even their diseases, they are remarkably close to humans. They are arboreal to varying degrees, but their generally greater size and weight are obstacles to swinging and jumping as freely as monkeys. The exception is the small, lithe gibbon, which can both climb and swing freely through the trees and so spends virtually all of its time in them. At the opposite extreme are gorillas, who climb trees, using their prehensile hands and feet to grip the trunk and branches. Their swinging is limited to leaning outward as they reach for fruit, clasping a limb for support. Most of their time is spent on the ground.

The apes, like humans, have no external tail. Also shared with us are broad shoulders, unlike the narrow ones of monkeys. But, unlike humans, their arms are longer than their legs, indicating that their ancestors specialized for arboreal brachiation in a way that our own did not. In moving on the ground, the African apes "knuckle-walk" on the backs of their hands, resting their weight on the middle joints of the fingers. They stand erect when reaching for fruit, looking over tall grass, or in any activity where they find an erect position advantageous. The semierect position is natural in apes when on the ground because the curvature of their vertebral

Gibbons and orangutans are Southeast Asian apes. Gibbons are brachiators that use their long arms and hands to swing through the trees. Although orangutans sometimes brachiate, their legs move like arms and their feet are like hands; thus, much of their movement is by four-handed climbing.

column places their center of gravity, which is high in their bodies, in front of their hip joint. Thus, they are both "top heavy" and "front heavy." Furthermore, the structure of the ape pelvis is not well suited to support the weight of the torso and limbs easily. Nor do apes have the arrangement of leg muscles that enables humans to stand erect and swing their legs freely before and behind.

Gibbons and siamangs, which are native to Southeast Asia and Malaya, have compact, slim bodies with extraordinarily long arms compared to their short legs, and stand about 3 feet high. Although their usual form of locomotion is brachiation, they can run erect, holding their arms out for balance. Gibbons and siamangs resemble monkeys in size and general appearance more than the other apes.

Orangutans are found in Borneo and Sumatra. They are somewhat taller than gibbons and siamangs and are much heavier, with the bulk characteristic of apes. In the closeness of the eyes and facial prominence, an orangutan looks a little like a chimpanzee, except that its hair is reddish. Orangs walk with their forelimbs in a fists-sideways or a palms-down position. They are, however, somewhat more arboreal than the African apes. Although sociable by nature, the orangs of upland Borneo spend most of their time alone (except in the case of females with young), as they have to forage over a wide area to obtain sufficient food. By contrast, fruits and insects are sufficiently abundant in the swamps of Sumatra to sustain groups of adults and permit coordinated group travel. Thus, gregariousness is a function of habitat productivity.[5]

Gorillas, found in equatorial Africa, are the largest of the apes; an adult male can weigh over 400 pounds. The body is covered with a thick coat of glossy black hair, and mature males have a silvery gray upper back. There is a strikingly human look about the face, and like humans, gorillas focus on things in their field of vision by directing the eyes rather than moving the head. Gorillas are mostly ground dwellers but may sleep in trees in carefully constructed nests. Because of their weight, brachiation is limited to raising and lowering themselves among the tree branches when searching for fruit. They knuckle-walk, using all four limbs with the fingers of the hand flexed, placing the knuckles instead of the palm of the hand on the ground. They will stand erect to reach for fruit, to see something more easily, or to threaten perceived sources of danger with their famous chest-beating displays. Although gorillas are gentle and tolerant, bluffing is an important part of their behavioral repertoire.

Chimpanzees and bonobos are two species of the same genus (*Pan*), bonobos being the least well known and restricted in their distribution to the rain forests of

[5]Normile, D. (1998). Habitat seen as playing larger role in shaping behavior. *Science, 279,* 1454.

Chimpanzees and gorillas are African apes.

the Democratic Republic of Congo. The common chimpanzee, by contrast, is widely distributed in the forested portions of sub-Saharan Africa. They are probably the best known of the apes and have long been favorites in zoos and circuses. Although thought of as particularly quick and clever, all four great apes are of equal intelligence, despite some differences in cognitive styles. More arboreal than gorillas, but less so than orangs, chimpanzees and bonobos forage on the ground much of the day, knuckle-walking like gorillas. At sunset, they return to the trees, where they build their nests. Those of chimps are more dispersed than those of bonobos, who prefer to build their nests close to one another.

THE SOCIAL BEHAVIOR OF PRIMATES

The physical resemblance of human beings to the other catarrhines is striking, but the most startling resemblance of all is in their social behavior. Because of their highly developed brains, monkeys and apes behave in ways that are far more complex than most other animals except humans. Only over the past four decades have primatologists made prolonged close-range observations of catarrhines in their natural habitats, and we are discovering much about social organization, learning ability, and communication among our closest relatives in the animal kingdom. In particular, we are finding that a number of behavioral traits that we used to think of as distinctively human are found to one degree or another among other primates, reminding us once again that many of the differences between us and them are differences of degree, rather than kind.

The range of behavior shown by living primates is great—too great to be adequately surveyed in this book. Instead, we shall look primarily at the behavior of those species most closely related to humans: bonobos, chimpanzees, and gorillas.

The Group

Primates are social animals, living and traveling in groups that vary in size from species to species. In most species, females and their offspring constitute the core of the social system. This is true of chimpanzees to a degree. In two Tanzanian communities studied, females often leave their natal group for another, although up to 50 percent do not.[6] In both cases, however, females in ovulation may temporarily leave their group to mate with males of another. But whatever the case, their sons, and often their daughters, remain in their mother's group for life. Among bonobos, females always transfer to another group, in which they establish bonds with females already there. Female bonobos are especially skilled at establishing such bonds with one another, so they are far more sociable than are their chimpanzee counterparts. Among the latter, the stronger bonds are between males, as young ones reaching maturity spend more and more time with the adult males of their group. In the case of gorillas, either sex may or may not leave its natal group for another.

Among chimps, the largest organizational unit is the community, composed of 50 or more individuals. Rarely, however, are all these animals together at a single time. Instead, they are usually found ranging singly or in small subgroups consisting of adult males together, females with their young, or males and females together with their young. In the course of their travels, subgroups may join forces and forage together, but sooner or later these will break up again into smaller units. When they do, members are often exchanged, so that new subunits are different in their composition from the ones that initially came together.

Although relationships among individuals within the community are relatively harmonious, dominance hierarchies exist. Generally, males outrank females, although high-ranking females may dominate low-ranking males. Physical strength and size help determine an animal's rank, but so too does the rank of its mother, its skill at building coalitions with other individuals, and, in the case of the male, its motivation to achieve high status. Highly motivated males, even though they may not be the biggest in their group, may bring considerable intelligence and ingenuity to bear in their quest for high rank. For example, in the community studied by Jane Goodall, a pioneer in the study of primate behavior, one chimp hit upon the idea of incorporating noisy kerosene cans into his charging displays, thereby intimidating all the other males.[7] As a result, he rose from relatively low status to the number one (alpha) position.

On the whole, bonobo females form stronger bonds with one another than do their chimpanzee counterparts. Moreover, the strength of the bond between mother and son is such as to interfere with that between males. Thus, instead of the male dominance characteristic of chimps, one sees female dominance. Not only do bonobo males defer to females in feeding, but alpha females have been observed chasing high-ranking males. Alpha males even yield to low-ranking females, and groups of females form

[6]Moore, J. (1998). Comment. *Current Anthropology, 39,* 412.

[7]Goodall, J. (1986). *The chimpanzees of Gombe: Patterns of behavior* (p. 424). Cambridge, MA: Belknap Press.

JANE GOODALL (b. 1934)

In July 1960 Jane Goodall arrived with her mother at the Gombe Chimpanzee Reserve on the shores of Lake Tanganyika in Tanzania. The first of three women Kenyan anthropologist Louis Leakey sent out to study great apes in the wild (the others were Dian Fossey and Birute Galdikas, who were to study gorillas and orangutans, respectively), her task was to begin a long-term study of chimpanzees. Little did she realize that more than 40 years later she would still be at it.

Though born in London, Jane grew up and was schooled in Bournemouth, England. At the age of 5, she realized that she was born to watch animals, when she entered a chicken coop to find out how eggs were made. Upon her graduation at age 18, she first enrolled in secretarial school and then worked in England before the opportunity came to go to Africa. Having always dreamed of going there to live among animals, when an invitation arrived to visit a friend in Kenya, she jumped at the chance. Quitting her regular job, Goodall worked as a waitress to raise the money for travel and was then on her way. Once in Kenya, she met Louis Leakey, who gave her a job as an assistant secretary. Before long, she was on her way to Gombe. Within a year, the outside world began to hear the most extraordinary things about this pioneering woman and her work: tales of toolmaking apes, cooperative hunts by chimpanzees, and what seemed like exotic chimpanzee rain dances. By the mid-1960s, her work had earned her a Ph.D. from Cambridge University, and Gombe was on its way to becoming one of the most dynamic field stations for the study of animal behavior anywhere in the world.

Although field studies of primates in their natural habitats had been undertaken prior to 1960, they were few in number, and most had produced extremely limited information. It was Goodall's particular blend of patience and determination that showed what could be achieved, and before long her field station became something of a Mecca for aspiring young students interested in primate behavior. The list of those who have worked with her at Gombe, many of them women, reads like a *Who's Who* of eminent scholars in primate behavior.

Although Goodall is still very much involved with her chimpanzees, she spends a good deal of time these days lecturing, writing, and overseeing the work of others. She also is heavily committed to primate conservation, and no one is more dedicated to efforts to halt the illegal trafficking in captive chimps nor a more eloquent champion for humane treatment of captive chimpanzees.

alliances in which they may cooperatively attack males, to the point of inflicting blood-drawing injuries.[8]

The gorilla group is a "family" of 5 to 20 individuals led by a mature, silver-backed male and including younger, black-backed males, females, the young, and sometimes other silverbacks. Subordinate males, however, are usually prevented by the dominant male from mating with the group's females, although he may occasionally allow access to lower ranking ones. Thus, young silverbacks often leave their natal family to start their own families by winning outside females. If the dominant male is weakening with age, however, one of his sons may remain with the group to succeed to his father's position. Alternatively, an outside male may take over the group. Unlike chimpanzees, gorillas rarely fight over food, territory, or sex, but will fight fiercely to maintain the integrity of the group.

Individual Interaction

One of the most notable primate activities is grooming, the ritual cleaning of another animal's coat to remove parasites, shreds of grass, or other matter. The grooming animal deftly parts the hair of the one being groomed and removes any foreign object, often eating it. Interestingly, different chimp communities have different styles of grooming. In one East African group, for example, the two animals groom each other face to face, with one hand, while the other clasps the

[8]de Waal, F., Kano, T., & Parish, A. R. (1998). Comments. *Current Anthropology, 39,* 408, 410, 413.

Grooming is an important activity among all catarrhine primates, as shown here. Such activity is important for strengthening bonds between individual members of the group.

partner's free hand. In another group 90 miles distant, the hand clasp is unknown. In East Africa, all communities incorporate leaves in their grooming, but in West Africa they do not. However hygienic it may be, it is as well an important gesture of friendliness, submission, appeasement, or closeness. Embracing, touching, and jumping up and down are forms of greeting behavior among chimpanzees. Touching is also a form of reassurance.

Gorillas, though gentle and tolerant, are also aloof and independent, and individual interaction among adults tends to be quite restrained. Friendship or closeness between adults and infants is more evident. Among bonobos, chimpanzees, and gorillas, as among most other primates, the mother-infant bond is the strongest and most long-lasting in the group. It may endure for many years—commonly for the lifetime of the mother. Gorilla infants share their mothers' nests and have been seen sharing nests with mature, childless females. Bonobo, chimpanzee, and gorilla males are attentive to juveniles and may share in parental responsibilities. Bonobo males seem most involved with their young and even carry infants on occasion, including those from different groups. Moreover, a male's interest in a youngster does not elicit the nervous reaction from the mother that it does among chimps. This latter relates to the regular, if infrequent, practice of infanticide on the part of chimpanzee males, a practice never observed among bonobos.

Sexual Behavior

Among the three foregoing species, as with humans, there is no fixed breeding season. Sexual activity between the sexes, however—initiated by either the male or the female—occurs frequently during the period when the female is receptive to impregnation. This is signaled, in the case of chimps, by vivid swelling of the skin around their genitals. Because this swelling continues even after conception up until youngsters are weaned (at about age 4), females continue to attract attention of males. Bonobo females, by contrast, are constantly swollen, concealing their time of ovulation by looking (and behaving) as if they are fertile at all times. Gorillas differ in that they show little interest in sex after conception. To a degree, chimps are promiscuous in their sexual behavior, and 12 to 14 males have been observed to have as many as 50 copulations in one day with a single female. Mostly, females mate with males of their own group and rarely with outsiders. Generally, dominant males try to monopolize females in full estrus, although cooperation from the female is usually required for this to succeed. By making herself scarce, she is able to exercise some choice, showing preference for a male who has previously shared food and groomed her. In the chimpanzee community studied by Jane Goodall, about half the infants were sired by low- or mid-level males. An alpha male, however, is able to monopolize the females to

Swelling of her sexual skin suggests that this female chimpanzee is in estrus and will attract the attention of males.

some extent, and some alphas have been seen to monopolize several estrus females at the same time.

Although mating behavior among bonobos resembles that of chimps, there are differences. For one thing, bonobo females are constantly swollen, making them constantly attractive to males. For another, forced copulation has never been observed among bonobos.[9] But their sexuality goes far beyond male-female mating, and something like three-quarters of their sexual activity has nothing to do with reproduction. Bonobos have been observed having sex in virtually all combinations of ages and sex.[10] The variety is remarkable, including sporadic oral sex, tongue-kissing, and massage of another's genitals. Male bonobos may mount each other or, standing back to back, one will rub his scrotum against another's. Bonobo males have also been observed "penis fencing," as two males hang from a branch facing each other while rubbing their erect penises together as if crossing swords. Among females genital rubbing is particularly common. The function of most of this sex, both hetero- and homosexual, is to reduce tensions. Whereas chimps often settle disputes by aggressive behavior, bonobos often do so through sex.

In gorilla families, the dominant silverback has exclusive breeding rights with the females, although he may allow a young silverback occasional access to a low-ranking female. In one group studied in Rwanda, in which there was more than one adult male, all but one of 10 juveniles were fathered by a single male.[11] So it is that a young silverback must leave "home" in order to have much of a sex life, usually by luring partners away from other established groups.

Although the vast majority of primate species are not "monogamous" in their mating habits, many smaller species of New World monkeys, a few island-dwelling populations of leaf-eating Old World monkeys, and all of the smaller apes (gibbons and siamangs) do mate for life with a single

[9]de Waal, F. (1998). Comment. *Current Anthropology, 39,* 407.

[10]de Waal, F. (2001). *The ape and the sushi master* (pp. 131–132). New York: Basic Books.

[11]Gibbons, A. (2001). Studying humans—and their cousins and parasites. *Science, 292,* 627.

Female bonobos frequently engage in genital rubbing, as here. Such sexual activity is an important means of reducing tension.

individual of the opposite sex. None of these species is closely related to human beings, nor do "monogamous" species ever display the degree of **sexual dimorphism**—anatomical differences between males and females—that is characteristic of our closest primate relatives, or that was characteristic of our own ancient ancestors.

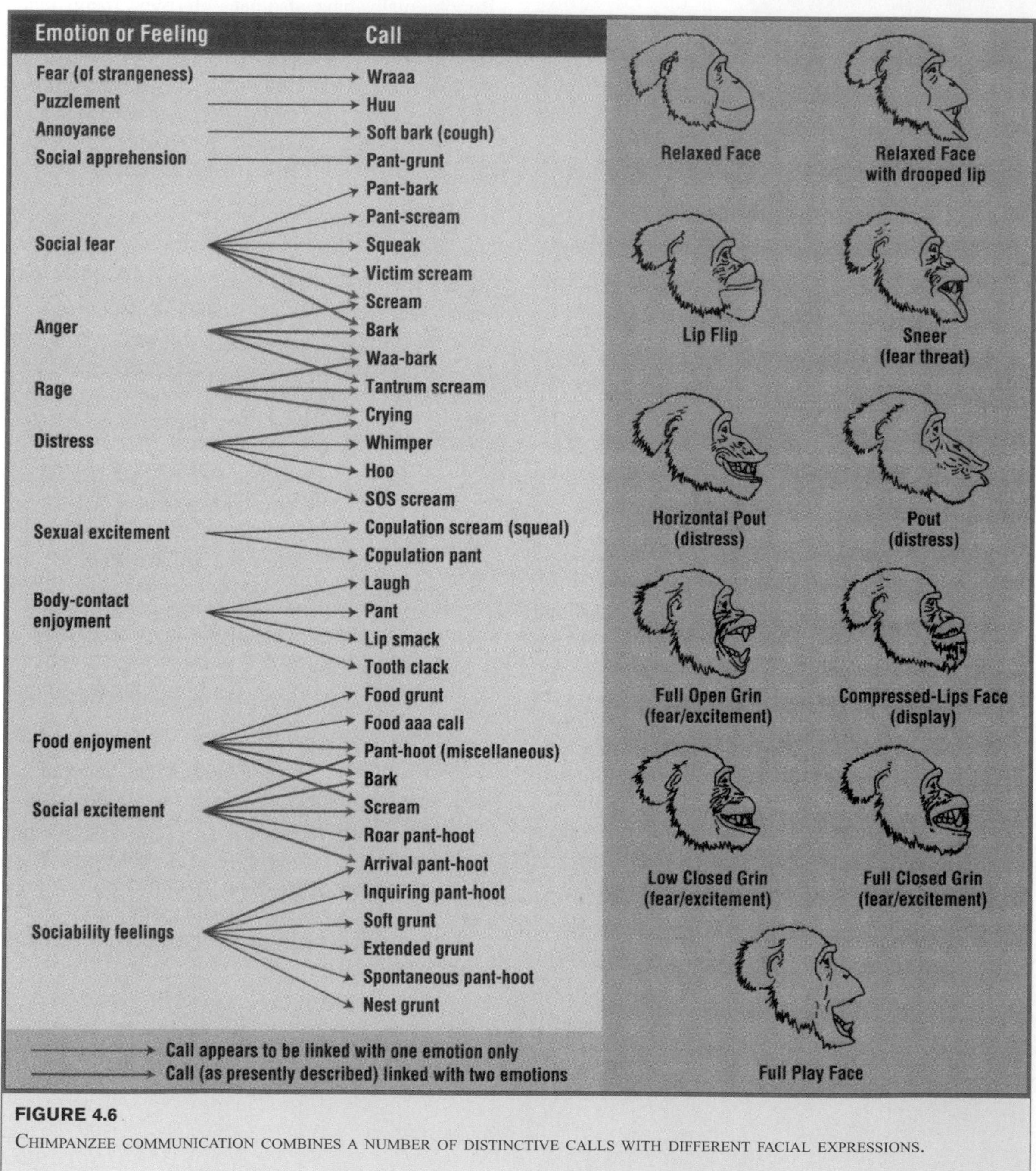

FIGURE 4.6
CHIMPANZEE COMMUNICATION COMBINES A NUMBER OF DISTINCTIVE CALLS WITH DIFFERENT FACIAL EXPRESSIONS.

Sexual dimorphism. Within a single species, the presence of marked anatomical differences between males and females.

Play

Frequent play activity among primate infants and juveniles is a means of learning about the environment, testing strength (rank in dominance hierarchies is based partially—but only partially—on size and strength), and generally learning how to behave as adults. Chimpanzee infants mimic the food-getting activities of their mothers, "attack" dozing adults, and "harass" adolescents.

Observers have watched young gorillas do somersaults, wrestle, and play tug-of-war, follow the leader, and king of the mountain. One juvenile, becoming annoyed at repeated harassment by an infant, picked it up, climbed a tree, and deposited it on a branch from which it was unable to get down on its own, and its mother had to retrieve it.

Communication

Primates, like many animals, vocalize. They have a great range of calls that are often used together with movements of the face or body to convey a message. Observers have not yet established the meaning of all the sounds, but a good number have been distinguished, such as warning calls, threat calls, defense calls, and gathering calls; the behavioral reactions of other animals hearing the call have also been studied. Among bonobos, chimpanzees, and gorillas, vocalizations are mainly emotional rather than propositional. Much of these species' communication takes place by the use of specific gestures and postures. Indeed, a number of these, such as kissing and embracing, are in virtually universal use today among humans, as well as apes.

Primatologists have classified numerous kinds of chimpanzee vocalization and visual communication (Figure 4.6). Together, these facilitate group protection, coordination of group efforts, and social interaction in general. One form of communication appears to be unique to bonobos: the use of trail markers. When foraging, the community breaks up into smaller groups, rejoining again in the evening to nest together. To keep track of each party's whereabouts, those in the lead will, at the intersections of trails or where downed trees obscure trails, deliberately stomp down the vegetation so as to indicate their direction, or rip off large leaves and place them carefully for the same purpose. Thus, they all know where to come together at the end of the day.[12]

[12]Recer, P. (1998, February 16). Apes shown to communicate in the wild. *Burlington Free Press,* p. 12A.

Experiments with captive apes, carried out over several decades, reveal that their communicative abilities exceed what they make use of in the wild. In some of these experiments, bonobos and chimpanzees have been taught to communicate using symbols, as in the case of Kanzi, a bonobo who uses a keyboard. Other chimpanzees, gorillas, and orangutans have been taught American Sign Language. Although this research provoked extreme controversy, it has become evident that all four apes are capable of understanding English quite well and are able to use a primitive grammar. They are able to generate original utterances, distinguish naming something from asking for it, ask questions, develop original ways to tell lies, coordinate their actions, and even spontaneously teach language to others. It is now clear that all of the great ape species can develop language skills to the level of a 2- to 3-year-old child.[13] From such knowledge, we may learn something about the origin of human language.

Home Ranges

Primates usually move about within circumscribed areas, or **home ranges,** which are of varying sizes, depending on the size of the group and on ecological factors such as availability of food. Ranges are often moved seasonally. The distance traveled by a group in a day varies but may include many miles. Some areas of a range, known as *core areas,* are used more often than others; they may contain water, food sources, resting places, and sleeping trees. The ranges of different groups may overlap, as among bonobos, where 65 percent of one territory may overlap with another.[14] By contrast, chimpanzee territories, at least in some regions, are exclusively occupied.

Gorillas do not defend their home ranges against incursions of others of their kind, and in the lowlands of Central Africa, it is not uncommon to find several families feeding in close proximity to one another,[15] although they certainly will defend their group if it is in any way threatened. In encounters with other communities, bonobos will defend their immediate space through vocalizations and

[13]Lestel, D. (1998). How chimpanzees have domesticated humans. *Anthropology Today, 14* (3); Miles, H. L. W. (1993). Language and the orangutan: The "old person" of the forest. In P. Cavalieri & P. Singer (Eds.), *The great ape project* (pp. 45–50). New York: St. Martin's Press.

[14]Parish, A. R. (1998). Comment. *Current Anthropology, 39,* 414.

[15]Parnell, R. (1999). Gorilla exposé. *Natural History, 108*(8), 43.

Home range. The area within which a group of primates usually moves.

Anthropology Applied: Primate Conservation

At present, no fewer than 76 species of primates are recognized as being in danger of extinction. Included among them are all of the great apes, as well as such formerly widespread and adaptable species as rhesus macaques. In the wild, these animals are threatened by habitat destruction in the name of development, by hunting for food and trophies, and by trapping for pets and research. Because monkeys and apes are so closely related to humans, they are regarded as essential for biomedical research in which humans cannot be used. Ironically, using live primates to supply laboratories can be a major factor in their local extinction.

Because of their vulnerability, the conservation of primates has become a matter of urgency. We can take two approaches to the problem, both of which require application of knowledge gained from studies of free-ranging animals. One is to maintain some populations in the wild, either by establishing preserves where animals are already living or by moving populations to places where suitable habitat exists. In either case, constant monitoring and management are necessary to ensure that sufficient space and resources remain available. The other approach is to maintain breeding colonies in captivity, in which case we must carefully provide the kind of physical and social environment that will encourage psychological and physical well-being, as well as reproductive success. Primates in zoos and laboratories do not successfully reproduce when deprived of such amenities as opportunities for climbing, materials to use for nest building, others to socialize with, and places for privacy.

The value of field studies for effective wild animal management is illustrated by Shirley Strum's relocation in 1984 of three troops of free-ranging baboons in Kenya. The troop she had been studying for 15 years had become a problem, raiding peoples' crops and garbage. Accordingly, it was decided to move this and two other local troops—130 animals in all—to more sparsely inhabited country 150 miles away. Knowing their habits, Strum was able to trap, tranquilize, and transport the animals to their new home; Strum's careful work did not disrupt their social relationships, cause them to abandon their new home, or block the transfer into their troops of new males, with their all-important knowledge of local resources. The success of her effort, which had never been tried with baboons, proves that relocation is a realistic technique for saving endangered primate populations.

displays, but rarely through fighting. Usually, they settle down and feed side by side, not infrequently grooming, playing, and engaging in sexual activity between groups as well. Chimpanzees, by contrast, have been observed patrolling their territories to ward off potential trespassers. Moreover, Goodall has recorded the destruction of one chimpanzee community by another that invaded the first one's turf. This sort of lethal intercommunity interaction has never been observed among bonobos. Some have interpreted this apparent territorial behavior as an expression of the supposedly violent nature of chimpanzees, but another interpretation is possible.[16] In Africa today, human encroachment is squeezing chimps into ever smaller pockets of forest. This places considerable stress on animals whose level of violence tends to increase in the absence of sufficient space. Perhaps the violence that Goodall witnessed was a response to crowding as a consequence of human encroachment. Another factor may be frustration engendered by artificial feeding. Among primates in general, the clearest territoriality appears in arboreal species, rather than in those that are more terrestrial in their habits.

Learning

Observation of monkeys and apes has shown that their learning abilities are remarkably humanlike. Numerous examples of inventive behavior have been observed among Japanese macaques, as well as among apes. One newly discovered example is a technique of food manipulation on the part of captive chimpanzees in the Madrid zoo. It began when a 5-year-old female rubbed apples against a sharp corner of a

[16]Power, M. G. (1995). Gombe revisited: Are chimpanzees violent and hierarchical in the "free" state? *General Anthropology, 2*(1), 5–9.

Nut cracking is an important activity among West African chimpanzees. Requiring the use of two objects as tools and complex eye-hand coordination, the task takes years for young chimps to learn from their elders.

concrete wall in order to lick the mashed pieces and juice left on the wall. From this youngster, the practice of "smearing" spread to her peers, and within 5 years, most group members were performing the operation frequently and consistently. The innovation has become standardized and durable, having transcended two generations in the group.[17]

Another dramatic example of learning is afforded by the way chimpanzees in West Africa crack open oil-palm nuts. For this they use tools: an anvil stone with a level surface on which to place the nut and a good-sized hammer stone to crack it. Not any stone will do; it must be of the right shape and weight, and the anvil may require leveling by placing smaller stones beneath one or more edges. Nor does random banging away do the job; the nut has to be hit at the right speed and the right trajectory, or else the nut simply flies off into the forest. Last but not least, the apes must avoid mashing their fingers, rather than the nut. According to fieldworkers, the expertise of the chimps far exceeds that of any human who tries cracking these hardest nuts in the world.

Youngsters learn this process by hanging around adults who are nut cracking, where their mothers share some of the food. This teaches them about the edibility of the nuts, but not how to get at what's edible. This they learn by observing and by "aping" (copying) the adults. At first they play with a nut or stone alone; later they begin to randomly combine objects. They soon learn, however, that placing nuts on anvils and hitting them with a hand or foot gets them nowhere. Only after 3 years of futile efforts do they begin to coordinate all of the multiple actions and objects, but even then it is only after a great deal of practice, by the age of 6 or 7 years, that they become proficient.

In short, after at least 3 years of failure, with no reward to reinforce their effort, they persevere. They do this for over 1,000 days without slacking off. Evidently, it is *social* motivation that keeps them going. At first, they are motivated by a desire to act like the mother; only later does the desire to feed on the tasty nut-meat take over.[18]

Use of Objects as Tools

The nut cracking just discussed is the most complex tool-use task known from the field, involving, as it does, both hands, two tools, and exact coordination. It is not, however, the only case of tool use among apes in the wild. Although gorillas do not make or use tools in any significant way, both chimpanzees and orangutans do. For our purposes, a **tool** may be defined simply as an object used to facilitate some task or activity. Here, a distinction must be made between simple tool use, as when one

[17]Fernandez-Carriba, S., & Loeches, A. (2001). Fruit smearing by captive chimpanzees: A newly observed food-processing behavior. *Current Anthropology, 42,* 143–147.

[18]de Waal, F.(2001). *The ape and the sushi master* (pp. 227–229). New York: Basic Books.

Tool. An object used to facilitate some task or activity. Although toolmaking involves intentional modification of the material of which it is made, tool use may involve objects either modified for some particular purpose or completely unmodified.

pounds something with a convenient stone when a hammer is not available, and toolmaking, which involves deliberate modification of some material for its intended use. Thus, otters that use unmodified stones to crack open clams may be tool users, but they are not toolmakers. Not only do chimpanzees modify objects to make them suitable for particular purposes, but chimps to some extent modify them to regular and set patterns. They also pick up, and even prepare, objects for future use at some other location, and they can use objects as tools to solve new and novel problems. Thus, chimps have been observed using stalks of grass, twigs that they have stripped of leaves, and even sticks up to 3 feet long that they have smoothed down to "fish" for termites. They insert the modified stick into a termite nest, wait a few minutes, pull the stick out, and eat the insects clinging to it, all of which requires considerable dexterity. Chimpanzees are equally deliberate in their nest building. They test the vines and branches to make sure they are usable. If they are not, the animal moves to another site.

Other examples of chimpanzee use of objects as tools involve leaves, used as wipes or as sponges, to get water out of a hollow to drink. Large sticks may serve as clubs or as missiles (as may stones) in aggressive or defensive displays. Twigs are used as toothpicks to clean teeth as well as to extract loose baby teeth. They use these dental tools not just on themselves but on other individuals as well.[19]

Interestingly, tool use to fish for termites or to crack open nuts is most often exhibited by females, whereas aimed throwing of rocks and sticks is most often exhibited by males. Such tool-using behavior, which (like nut cracking) young animals learn from their mothers and other adults in their group, may reflect one of the preliminary adaptations that, in the past, led to human cultural behavior.

In the wild, bonobos have not been observed making and using tools to the extent that chimpanzees do. However, the use of large leaves as trail markers may be considered a form of tool use. That these animals do have further capabilities is exemplified by a captive bonobo who has figured out how to make tools of stone that are remarkably like the earliest such tools made by our own ancestors.

Another interesting practice observed among chimps is the use of *Aspilia* leaves for medicinal purposes. When feeling a bit under the weather, they seek out these leaves, hold them in their mouths for a while, then swallow them whole. What this does is to remove parasites from their digestive tract.

[19]McGrew, W. C. (2000). Dental care in chimps. *Science, 288,* 1747.

Although gorillas (like bonobos and chimps) build nests, they are the only one of the four great apes that have not been observed to make and use other tools in the wild. The reason for this is probably not that gorillas lack the intelligence or skill to do so; rather, their easy diet of leaves and nettles makes tools of no particular use.

Hunting

The hunting, killing, and eating of small to medium-sized mammals, something that is seen only in a few primates, has been observed among bonobos and chimps, but not among gorillas. Although chimpanzee females sometimes hunt, males do so far more frequently. When on the hunt, they may spend up to 2 hours watching, following, and chasing intended prey. Moreover, in contrast to the usual primate practice of each animal finding food for itself, hunting frequently involves teamwork to trap and kill prey. The most sophisticated examples of this occur when hunting baboons; once a potential victim has been partially isolated from its troop, three or more adults will carefully position themselves so as to block off escape routes while another climbs toward the prey for the kill. Once a kill has been made, it is common for most of those present to get a share of the meat, either by grabbing a piece as the chance affords, or by sitting and begging for a piece. Whatever the nutritional value of meat, hunting is not done purely for dietary purposes, but for political and sociosexual reasons as well. The giving of meat helps cement alliances among males, and its sharing may be used also to entice a swollen female to have sex. In fact, males are more apt to hunt if a swollen female is present, and females in estrus are more successful at begging for meat.

Bonobos, too, hunt, but in their case it is usually the females who do so—duikers (a kind of small antelope) being the most frequent prey. The huntresses regularly share the carcasses with other females, but less often with males. Even when the most dominant male throws a tantrum nearby, he may still be denied a share.[20] Not only do females control the spoils of the hunt, they are unusual also in the degree to which they will share fruit. Otherwise, it is interesting to note that, in primates, as among many carnivores, increased cooperation seems to go hand in hand with predation and meat eating.

[20]Ingmanson, E. J. (1998). Comment. *Current Anthropology, 39,* 409.

THE QUESTION OF CULTURE

The more we learn of the behavior of our nearest primate relatives, the more we become aware of the importance to chimps of learned, socially shared practices and knowledge. This raises the question: Do chimpanzees (and perhaps other apes) have culture? This is a question that is now receiving a good deal of attention, as the following Original Study attests.

Original Study

The Culture of Chimpanzees[21]

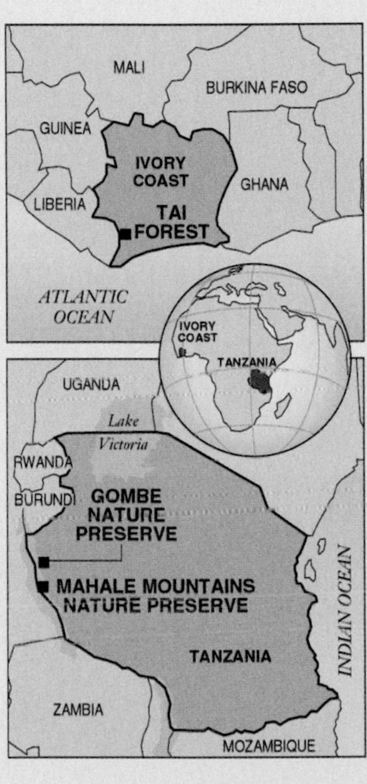

Homo sapiens and *Pan troglodytes* have coexisted for hundreds of millennia and share more than 98 percent of their genetic material, yet only 40 years ago we still knew next to nothing about chimpanzee behavior in the wild. That began to change in the 1960s, when Toshisada Nishida of Kyoto University in Japan and Jane Goodall began their studies of wild chimpanzees at two field sites in Tanzania. (Goodall's research station at Gombe—the first of its kind—is more famous, but Nishida's site at Mahale is the second-oldest chimpanzee research site in the world.)

In these initial studies, as the chimpanzees became accustomed to close observation, the remarkable discoveries began. Researchers witnessed a range of unexpected behaviors, including fashioning and using tools, hunting, meat eating, food sharing, and lethal fights between members of neighboring communities. In the years that followed, other primatologists set up camp elsewhere, and, despite all the financial, political, and logistical problems that can beset African fieldwork, several of these outposts became truly long-term projects. As a result, we live in an unprecedented time, when an intimate and comprehensive scientific record of chimpanzees' lives at last exists not just for one but for several communities spread across Africa.

As early as 1973, Goodall recorded 13 forms of tool use as well as eight social activities that appeared to differ between the Gombe chimpanzees and chimpanzee populations elsewhere. She ventured that some variations had what she termed a "cultural origin." But what exactly did Goodall mean by "culture"? According to the Oxford Encyclopedic English Dictionary, culture is defined as "the customs . . . and achievements of a particular time or people." The diversity of human cultures extends from technological variations to marriage rituals, from culinary habits to myths and legends. Animals do not have myths and legends, of course. But they do have the capacity to pass on behavioral traits from generation to generation—not through their genes but by learning. For biologists, this is the fundamental criterion for a cultural trait: It must be something that can be learned by observing the established skills of others and thus passed on to future generations.

By the 1990s the discovery of new behavioral differences among chimpanzees made it feasible to begin assembling comprehensive charts of cultural variations for these animals. William C. McGrew, in his 1992 book *Chimpanzee Material Cultures,* was able to list 19 different kinds of tool use in distinct communities. One of us (Boesch), along with colleague Michael Tomasello of the Max Planck Institute for Evolutionary Anthropology in Leipzig,

[21]Whitten, A., & Boesch, C. (2001). Cultures of chimpanzees. *Scientific American, 284*(1), 63–67.

Original Study

Germany, identified 25 distinct activities as potential cultural traits in wild chimpanzee populations.

The most recent catalogue of cultural variations results from a unique collaboration of nine chimpanzee experts (including the two of us) who pooled extensive field observations that, taken together, amounted to a total of 151 years of chimp watching. The list cites 39 patterns of chimpanzee behavior that we believe to have a cultural origin, including such activities as using sticks to "fish" for ants, making dry seats from leaves, and a range of social grooming habits. At present, these 39 variants put chimpanzees in a class of their own, with far more elaborate customs than any other animal studied to date. Of course, chimpanzees also remain distinct from humans, for whom cultural variations are simply beyond count. (We must point out, however, that scientists are only beginning to uncover the behavioral complexity that exists among chimpanzees—and so the number 39 no doubt represents a minimum of cultural traits.)

Multicultural Chimpanzees

When describing human customs, anthropologists and sociologists often refer to "American culture" or "Chinese culture"; these terms encompass a wide spectrum of activities—language, forms of dress, eating habits, marriage rituals and so on. Among animals, however, culture has typically been established for a single behavior, such as song dialects among birds. Ornithologists haven't identified variation in courtship patterns or feeding practices, for example, to go alongside the differences in dialect.

Chimpanzees, though, do more than display singular cultural traits: Each community exhibits an entire set of behaviors that differentiates it from other groups. As a result, we can talk about "Gombe culture" or "Taï culture." Indeed, once we observe how a chimpanzee behaves, we can identify where the animal lives. For instance, an individual that cracks nuts, leaf-clips during drumming displays, fishes for ants with one hand using short sticks,

Grooming is an activity seen in all chimpanzee communities, but styles differ between communities. Shown here is the hand clasping style characteristic of one East African community.

and knuckle-knocks to attract females clearly comes from the Taï Forest. A chimp that leaf-grooms and hand-clasps during grooming can come from the Kibale Forest or the Mahale Mountains, but if you notice that he also ant-fishes, there is no doubt anymore: He comes from Mahale.

In addition, chimpanzee cultures go beyond the mere presence or absence of a particular behavior. For example, all chimpanzees dispatch parasites found during grooming a companion. But at Taï they will mash the parasites against their forearms with a finger, at Gombe they squash them onto leaves, and at Budongo they put them on a leaf to inspect before eating or discarding them. Each community has developed a unique approach for accomplishing the same goal. Alternatively, behaviors may look similar yet be used in different contexts: at Mahale, males "clip" leaves noisily with their teeth as a courtship gesture, whereas at Taï chimpanzees incorporate leaf-clipping into drumming displays.

The implications of this new picture of chimpanzee culture are many. The information offers insight into our distinctiveness as a species. When we first published this work in the journal *Nature*, we found some people quite disturbed to realize that the characteristic that had appeared to separate us so starkly from the animal world—our capacity for cultural development—is not such an absolute difference after all.

But this seems a rather misdirected response. The differences between human customs and traditions, enriched and mediated by language as they are, are vast in contrast with what we see in the chimpanzee. The story of chimpanzee cultures sharpens our understanding of our uniqueness, rather than threatening it in any way that need worry us.

Human achievements have made enormous cumulative progress over the generations, a phenomenon Boesch and Tomasello have dubbed the "ratchet effect." The idea of a hammer—once simply a crude stone cobble—has been modified and improved on countless times until now we have electronically controlled robot hammers in our factories. Chimpanzees may show the beginnings of the ratchet effect—some that use stone anvils, for example, have gone a step further, as at Bossou, where they wedge a stone beneath their anvil when it needs leveling on bumpy ground—but such behavior has not become customary and is rudimentary indeed beside human advancements.

The cultural capacity we share with chimpanzees also suggests an ancient ancestry for the mentality that must underlie it. Our cultural nature did not emerge out of the blue but evolved from simpler beginnings. Social learning similar to that of chimpanzees would appear capable of sustaining the earliest stone-tool cultures of human ancestors living two million years ago.

The End

Primate Behavior and Human Evolution

Although not true of all humanity, in many societies there is an unfortunate tendency to erect what paleontologist Stephen Jay Gould refers to as "golden barriers" that set us apart from the rest of the animal kingdom.[22] It is unfortunate, for it blinds us to the fact that there are many continuities between "us" and "them" (animals). We have already seen that the physical differences between humans and apes are largely differences of degree, rather than kind. It now appears that the same is true with respect to behavior. As primatologist Richard Wrangham once put it, "Like humans, [chimpanzees] laugh, make up after a quarrel, support each other in times of trouble, medicate themselves with chemical and physical remedies, stop each other from eating poisonous foods, collaborate in the hunt, help each other over physical obstacles, raid neighboring groups, lose their tempers, get excited by dramatic weather, invent ways to show off, have family traditions and group traditions, make tools, devise plans, deceive, play tricks, grieve, and are cruel and are kind."[23]

This is not to say that we are "just" another ape; obviously, "degree" does make a difference. Nevertheless, the continuities between us and our primate kin are a reflection of a common evolutionary heritage; it is just that our later evolution has taken us in a somewhat different direction. But by looking at the range of practices displayed by contemporary apes and other catarrhines, we may find clues to the practices and capabilities possessed by our own ancestors as their evolutionary path diverged from those of the other hominids.

[22]de Waal, F. (2001). *The ape and the sushi master* (p. 235). New York: Basic Books.

[23]Quoted in Mydens, S. (2001, August 12). He's not hairy, he's my brother. *New York Times,* sec. 4, p. 5.

CHAPTER SUMMARY

The modern primates, like most mammals, are intelligent animals that bear their young live and then nourish them with milk from their mothers. Like other mammals, they maintain constant body temperature and have respiratory and circulatory systems that will sustain high activity. Their skeleton and teeth also resemble those of other mammals, although there are differences of detail.

Modern primates are divided into two suborders. The strepsirhines include lemurs and lorises, which resemble small rodents in body outline. The haplorhines include tarsiers, New and Old World monkeys, apes, and humans. To a greater degree among the haplorhines, and a lesser degree among the strepsirhines, primates show a number of characteristics that developed as adaptations to insect predation in the trees. These adaptive characteristics include a generalized set of teeth, suited to insect eating but also a variety of fruits and leaves. These teeth are fewer in number and set in a smaller jaw than in most mammals. Other evolutionary adaptations in the primate line include binocular stereoscopic vision, or depth perception, and an intensified sense of touch. This combination of developments had an effect upon the primate brain, resulting in larger size and greater complexity in later appearing species. There were also changes in the primate skeleton; in particular, a reduction of the snout, an enlargement of the brain case, and numerous adaptations for upright posture and flexibility of limb movement. In addition, changes in reproduction resulted in fewer offspring born to each female and a longer period of infant dependency than among most mammals.

The apes are humans' closest relatives. Apes include gibbons, siamangs, orangutans, gorillas, bonobos, and chimpanzees. In their outward appearance, the great apes seem to resemble each other more than they do humans, but their genetic structure and biochemistry reveal that bonobos, chimpanzees, and gorillas are closer to humans than to orangs and thus must share a more recent common ancestry.

The social life of primates is complex. Primates are social animals, and most species live and travel in groups. Among bonobos and chimpanzees, it is females that may transfer from one group to another, though not all do so; their sons and often their daughters remain with their mothers for life. Among gorillas, either males or females may transfer. In all three species, both males and females are organized into dominance hierarchies. In the case of females, the better food and reduced harassment that are a consequence of high rank enhance their ability to successfully raise offspring.

A characteristic primate activity is grooming, which is a sign of closeness between individuals. Among bonobos, gorillas, and chimpanzees, sexual interaction between adults of opposite sex generally takes place only when a female is in estrus. In bonobos, however, constant swelling of the female's genitals suggests constant estrus, whether or not she is actually fertile. Although dominant males try to monopolize females while they are in estrus, the cooperation of the females is usually required for this to succeed. Among bonobos, sex between both opposite and same-sex indivudials serves as a means of reducing tensions, as in the genital rubbing that frequently takes place between females. Primates have elaborate systems of communication based on vocalizations and gestures. In addition, bonobos employ trail signs to communicate their whereabouts to others. Usually primates move about within home ranges, rather than defended territories.

The diet of most primates is made up of a variety of fruits, leaves, and insects, but bonobos and chimpanzees sometimes hunt, kill, and eat animals as well. Among chimps, most hunting is done by males and may require considerable teamwork. By contrast, it is usually bonobo females that hunt. Once a kill is made, the meat is generally shared with other animals.

Among chimpanzees and other apes, learned behavior is especially important. From adults, juveniles learn to use a variety of tools and substances for various purposes. Innovations made by one individual may be adopted by other animals, standardized, and passed on to succeeding generations. Because practices are learned, socially shared, and often differ from one group to another, we may speak of chimpanzee culture.

HIGHWAY 1

See and hear living primates through this site that features a host of information about primate behavior, biology, and conservation from *Living Links: A Center for the Advanced Study of Ape and Human Evolution.* See classic videos from primate field research such as "Chimpanzee Conflict" and "Chimpanzee Food Sharing."
http://www.emory.edu/living_links/

HIGHWAY 2

The Gorilla Foundation: Conservation Through Communication site demonstrates the amazing lingusitic capacities of Koko the gorilla. Watch her communicate to humans through sign language, and learn how this project is working to protect all of the endangered ape species.
http://www.koko.org/

HIGHWAY 3

A trip to this site explains the action of a conservation group working to protect the endangered primate species being slaughtered for meat and medicine. The project mission states that "the Bushmeat Project has been established to develop and support community-based partnerships that will help the people of equatorial Africa to develop alternatives to unsustainable bushmeat. The programme is a long-term effort to provide economic and social incentive to protect great apes and other endangered wildlife."
http://bushmeat.net/

CLASSIC READINGS

de Waal, F. (1996). *Good natured: The origins of right and wrong in humans and other animals.* Cambridge, MA: Harvard University Press.

Primatologist Frans de Waal, though fully up on field studies of wild primates, has spent much of his career studying bonobos and chimpanzees in captivity. In this book he argues that moral behavior can be found in nonhuman animals, most clearly in apes but also in other primates and even nonprimate species. Written for a general audience, but with a strong scientific foundation, the book communicates its message in a clear and responsible way.

De Waal, F. (2001). *The ape and the sushi master.* New York: Basic Books.

Another by de Waal, one of the best observers of primate behavior in the business. In this book he deals with the question of animal culture in a manner guaranteed to provoke thought. The book is well written and, once begun, almost impossible to put down.

Fossey, D. (1983). *Gorillas in the mist.* Burlington, MA. Houghton Mifflin.

The late Dian Fossey is to gorillas what Jane Goodall is to chimpanzees. Fossey devoted years to the study of gorilla behavior in the field. This book is about the first 13 years of her study; as well as being readable and informative, it is well illustrated.

Goodall, J. (1990). *Through a window.* Boston: Houghton Mifflin.

This fascinating book is a personal account of Goodall's experiences over 35 years of studying wild chimpanzees in Tanzania. A pleasure to read and a fount of information on the behavior of these apes, the book is profusely illustrated as well.

LeGros Clark, W. E. (1966). *History of the primates* (5th ed.). Chicago: University of Chicago Press.

An old classic, this remains a fine introduction to the comparative anatomy of the primates.

Patterson, F., & Linden, E. (1981). *The education of Koko.* New York: Holt, Rinehart & Winston.

Several experiments with captive apes have sought to investigate the full potential of their communicative abilities, and one of the most interesting is that involving Koko the gorilla. This is a particularly readable account of those experiments and their results.

CHAPTER 5

MACROEVOLUTIO[N] AND THE EARLY PRIMATES

This is a reconstruction of what one of the earliest catarrhine primates, *Eosimias* of China, may have looked like. Although its bones indicate overall body form, its exterior appearance is pure speculation.

CHAPTER PREVIEW

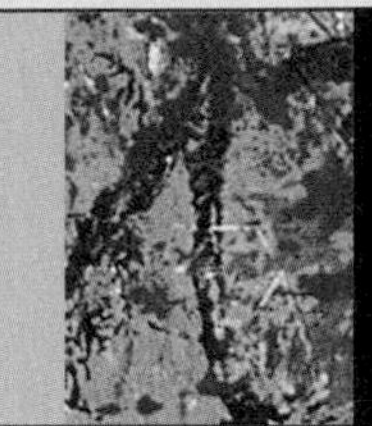

1

How Does Evolution Produce New Forms of Organisms?

Evolution may proceed in a branching manner, when isolating mechanisms prevent gene flow between separated populations. Then drift and selection may proceed in different ways, leading to the appearance first of divergent subspecies and then of separate species. In the absence of isolation, a species as a whole may evolve in a linear manner through variational change in response to environmental changes. As small changes accumulate from generation to generation, an older species may be transformed into a new one.

2

When Did the First Primates Appear, and What Were They Like?

The earliest primates had developed by 60 million years ago and became widespread in Africa, Eurasia, and North America. The initial adaptation of these small, arboreal insect eaters to life in the trees set the stage for the subsequent appearance of other primate models.

3

When Did the First Monkeys and Apes Appear, and What Were They Like?

By the late Eocene epoch, about 37 million years ago, small primates ancestral to monkeys and apes were living in Africa and Asia. By about 20 million years ago, they had proliferated and were common in many parts of the Old World. Some forms remained relatively small, while others became quite large, some even larger than present-day gorillas. Small versions of these apelike primates seem to have had the right kind of anatomy, and at least some were exposed to the right kind of selective pressures to transform them into primitive hominines.

Almost a century and a half ago, Charles Darwin shattered the surface calm of the Victorian world with his startling theory that humans are cousins of the living apes and monkeys and are descended from the same prehistoric ancestors. What would have been the public reaction, one wonders, if they had known, as we do, that even earlier ancestors were mouse-sized and smaller creatures that subsisted chiefly on insects and worms? Such primitive creatures date back about 60 million years. These ancient forebears of ours evolved over time into different species as mutations produced variation, which was acted upon by natural selection and genetic drift.

Although many of the primates discussed in this chapter no longer exist, their descendants, which were reviewed in Chapter 4, are to be found living throughout the world. The successful adaptation of the primates is believed to be due largely to their intelligence, a characteristic that provides for adaptive flexibility. Other physical traits, such as stereoscopic vision and a grasping hand, have also been instrumental in the success of the primates.

What is the justification for studying a form of life whose history is, at best, fragmentary and which existed millions of years ago? The study of these prehistoric primates tells us something we can use to interpret the evolution of the entire primate line, including ourselves. It gives us a better understanding of the physical forces that caused these early creatures to evolve into today's primates. Ultimately, the study of these ancient ancestors gives us a fuller knowledge of the processes through which an insect-eating, small-brained animal evolved into a toolmaker and thinker that is recognizably human.

SPECIATION

To understand how the primates evolved, we must first look at how the evolutionary forces discussed in Chapter 3 bring about the emergence of new species from old. As noted in that chapter, the term *species* is usually defined as a population or group of populations that is capable of interbreeding and that is reproductively isolated from other such populations. Thus the bullfrogs in my farm pond are the same species as those in my neighbor's pond, even though the two populations may never actually interbreed; in theory, they are capable of it if they are brought together. This definition is not altogether satisfactory, because isolated populations may be in the process of evolving into different species, and it is hard to tell exactly when they become separate. For example, all dogs belong to the same species, but a male Saint Bernard and a female Chihuahua would surely have trouble with the feat of copulation. On the other hand, Alaskan sled dogs are able to breed with wolves, even though they are of different species. In nature, however, wolves most often mate with their own kind. Although all species definitions are relative rather than absolute, the modern concept of species puts more stress on the question of whether breeding actually takes place in the wild than on the more academic question of whether breeding is technically feasible. After all, gibbons and siamangs, two different species of small apes, sometimes produce live offspring in captivity but do not in the wild.

Biologists define populations within species that are capable of interbreeding but may not regularly do so as **races,** or subspecies. Evolutionary theory suggests that species evolve from races through the accumulation of differences in the gene pools of the separated groups. This can happen, however, only in situations where one race is isolated from others of its species for prolonged periods of time. There is nothing inevitable about races evolving into new species. Because they are by definition genetically open—that is, members of different races are capable of interbreeding—races are impermanent and subject to reamalgamation. This is precisely what happens as long as gene flow remains open.

In the case of humans, as we shall see in Chapter 13, the race concept cannot be applied. For one thing, the human propensity for gene flow makes it impossible to define races with any biological validity. To make matters worse, there has been a deplorable tendency to confuse cultural with biological phenomena under the heading of "race." As applied to humans, races are nothing more than social categories.

Isolating Mechanisms

Certain factors, known as **isolating mechanisms,** separate breeding populations, leading to the appearance first of divergent races and then divergent species. This happens as mutations may appear in one of the isolated populations but not in the other, as genetic drift affects the two populations in different ways and as selective

Race. In biology, a subspecies; a population of a species that differs in allele frequencies from other such populations. Humans cannot be divided into racial categories that have any biological validity. • **Isolating mechanisms.** Factors that separate breeding populations, thereby preventing gene flow, creating divergent subspecies and ultimately (if maintained) divergent species.

Although horses and donkeys (two separate species) can mate and produce live offspring (mules, pictured here), sterility of mules maintains the reproductive isolation of the parental species.

pressures may come to differ slightly in the two places. Because isolation prevents gene flow, changes that affect the gene pool of one population cannot be introduced into the gene pool of the other.

Some isolating mechanisms are geographical—preventing contact, hence gene flow, between members of separated populations. Anatomical structure can also serve as an isolating mechanism, as we saw in the case of the Saint Bernard and the Chihuahua. Other physical isolating factors include early miscarriage of the offspring; weakness or presence of maladaptive traits that cause early death in the offspring; or, as in the case of horses and donkeys, sterility of the hybrid offspring (mules).

Although physical barriers to reproduction may develop in geographical isolation, as genetic differences accumulate in the gene pools of separate populations, they may also result from accidents as cells undergo meiosis. In the course of such accidents genetic material may be broken off, transposed, or transferred from one chromosome to another. Even a relatively minor mutation, if it involves a gene that regulates the growth and development of an organism, may have a major effect on its adult form. In this way, a kind of instantaneous genetic isolation may occur.

Regulator genes turn other genes on and off, and a mere change in their timing can cause significant evolutionary change. This may have a played a role in differentiating chimps and humans; for example, adult humans retain the flat facial profile of juvenile chimps.

Isolating mechanisms may also be social rather than physical. Speciation due to this mechanism is particularly common among birds. For example, cuckoos (birds that do not build nests of their own but lay their eggs in other birds' nests) attract mates by mimicking the song of the bird species whose nests they usurp; thus cuckoos that are physically capable of mating may have different courtship behavior, which effectively isolates them from others of their kind.

Social isolating mechanisms are thought to have been important factors in human evolution. They continue to play a part in the maintenance of so-called racial barriers. Although there are no physical barriers to mating between any two mature humans of the opposite sex, awareness of social and cultural differences often makes the idea distasteful, perhaps even unthinkable; in India, for example, someone of an upper caste would not think of marrying an "untouchable." This isolation results from the culturally implanted concept of a significant difference between "us" and "them." Yet, as evidenced by the blending of human populations—even hostile ones—that has so often taken place in the world, people are also capable of suspending or even reasoning away social isolating mechanisms that would, in the case of other animals, lead separate populations to evolve into separate species. Such speciation is extremely unlikely in *Homo sapiens*.

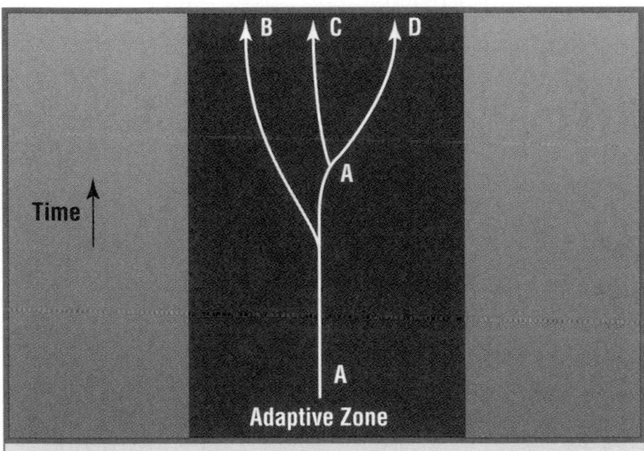

FIGURE 5.1
DIVERGENT EVOLUTION OCCURS AS DIFFERENT POPULATIONS OF AN ANCESTRAL SPECIES BECOME REPRODUCTIVELY ISOLATED. THROUGH DRIFT AND DIFFERENTIAL SELECTION, THE NUMBER OF DESCENDANT SPECIES INCREASES.

Divergence and Convergence

As just described, isolation may cause a single ancestral species to give rise to two or more descendant species. Such **divergent** or **branching evolution** (Figure 5.1) is probably responsible for much of the diversity of life to be observed today. This has happened repeatedly, for example, as the platelike segments of the earth on which the continents ride have shifted position, separating once adjacent land masses (Figure 5.2).

Sorting out evolutionary relationships may be complicated by a phenomenon called **convergence** in which two distant forms develop greater similarities—birds and bats, for example, because their structures serve similar functions. Among the primates, an example is hind-leg dominance in both lemurs and humans. In most primates, the

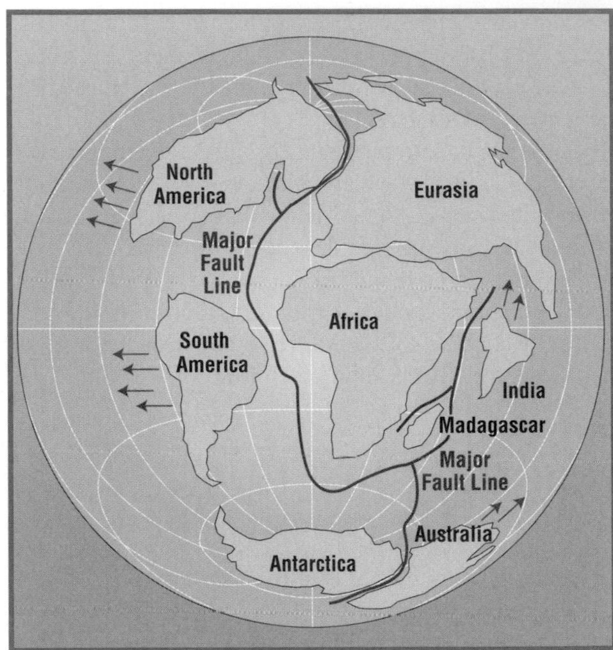

FIGURE 5.2
SEPARATION OF THE EARTH'S CONTINENTS RESULTED FROM MASSIVE SHIFTING IN THE PLATELIKE SEGMENTS OF THE CRUST AS ILLUSTRATED BY THE POSITION OF CONTINENTS AT THE END OF THE CRETACEOUS PERIOD SOME 65 MILLION YEARS AGO, THE TIME OF THE DINOSAUR'S EXTINCTION. THE SEAS, OPENED UP BY CONTINENTAL SEPARATION, CONSTITUTED ISOLATING BARRIERS BETWEEN MAJOR LAND MASSES.

Divergent or branching evolution. An evolutionary process in which an ancestral population gives rise to two or more descendant populations that differ from one another. • **Convergence.** A process by which unrelated populations develop similarities to one another.

hind limbs are either shorter or of the same length as the forelimbs. Lemurs and humans are not closely related to each other, but both have longer hind limbs due to aspects of their locomotion. Humans are bipedal while lemurs use their long legs to push off and propel them from tree to tree. Convergent evolution takes place in circumstances where an environment exerts similar pressures on different organisms, so that unrelated species become more like one another. Because the analogies produced by convergent evolution are not always easy to distinguish from the homologies that result from shared ancestry, it is often difficult to reconstruct the evolutionary history of any given species. As a case in point, humans and orangutans both have thick enamel on their molars, but African apes do not. Yet, molecular evidence reveals a closer human relationship to African apes than to orangs. Thus, thick molar enamel may be a case of analogy, rather than homology. Alternatively, thin enamel could have evolved separately in chimps and gorillas, and the presence of this feature in orangutans and humans could be retained from the ancestral condition.

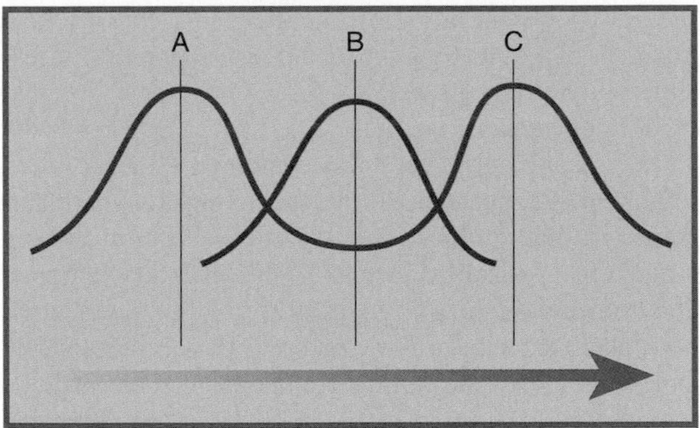

FIGURE 5.3
LINEAR EVOLUTION IS A PROCESS OF VARIATIONAL CHANGE THAT OCCURS AS RELATIVELY SMALL CHANGES THAT (BY CHANCE) ARE ADVANTAGEOUS ACCUMULATE IN A SPECIES' GENE POOL THROUGH GENE FLOW, DRIFT, AND SELECTION. OVER TIME, THIS MAY PRODUCE SUFFICIENT CHANGE TO TRANSFORM AN OLD SPECIES INTO A NEW ONE.

Linear Evolution

Another consequence of natural selection may be what appears to be a linear progression from one form to another without any evident branching. Although this may seem like a case of evolution heading in a particular direction, it is not. Rather, it is nothing more than variational change as discussed in the Original Study in Chapter 3. The example given there was of elephants becoming progressively hairier over time in response to climatic cooling. As generation succeeded generation, those elephants best adapted to cold enjoyed the highest reproductive success. The end result was the woolly mammoth. If, as such change proceeds, populations do not become isolated, then the species as a whole appears to evolve in a particular direction. **Linear evolution** may be defined, then, as a sustained directional change in a population's average characteristics (Figure 5.3).

As linear evolution proceeds, more recent populations may appear sufficiently changed from ancestral populations to be called different species. The difficulty arises because, given a reasonably good fossil record, one species will appear to grade into the other without any clear break. Thus, trying to assign a fossil to one species or the other can be an exercise in frustration.

Although linear evolution produces change, it generally does not transform a population into something radically different. Ultimately, stabilizing selection is likely to take over, as available alleles reach their most adaptive frequencies in a species' gene pool. There will be little change thereafter, as long as the adaptation remains viable. Ironically, a species may become extinct if it becomes too well adapted. If the environment changes for some reason, those organisms most highly adapted to the old environment will have the greatest difficulty surviving in a new one. Such changes took place a number of times during the course of vertebrate evolution; one of the most dramatic examples was the sudden extinction of the dinosaurs. In such cases, it is usually the more generalized organisms that survive; later they may give rise to new lines of specialists.

The Nondirectedness of Evolution

In the popular mind, evolution is often seen as leading in a predictable and determined way from one-celled organisms, through various multicelled forms, to humans, who occupy the top rung of a ladder of progress. To be sure, one-celled organisms appeared long before multicellular forms, but the latter could hardly emerge before the basic structure of the cell existed. Furthermore, single-celled organisms were not replaced by multicellular descendants, but remain today, as in the past, the dominant forms

Linear evolution. A sustained directional shift in a population's average characteristics.

of life. They exist in greater numbers and diversity than all forms of multicellular life and live in all habitats accessible to *any* form of life.[1]

As for humans, we are indeed recent arrivals in the world (though not as recent as some new strains of bacteria), but our appearance—like that of any kind of organism—was made possible only as a consequence of a whole string of historical accidents. To cite but one example, about 65 million years ago, some sort of extraterrestrial body slammed into earth where the Yucatan Peninsula now exists, disrupting the world's climate to such an extent as to cause the extinction of the dinosaurs (and numerous other species as well). For 100 million years, dinosaurs had ruled most terrestrial environments available for vertebrate animals and would probably have continued to do so were it not for this event. Although mammals appeared at about the same time as reptiles, they existed as small, inconspicuous creatures that an observer from outer space would probably have dismissed as insignificant. But with the demise of the dinosaurs, all sorts of opportunities became available, and mammals began their great expansion into new niches, including the one in which our own ancestors evolved. So it is that an essentially random event—the collision with a comet or asteroid—made possible our own existence. Had it not happened, or had it happened at some other time (before the existence of mammals), we would not be here, and there might not be any consciously intelligent life on earth.[2]

The history of any species is an outcome of many such contingencies. At any point in the chain of events, had any one element been different, the final result would be markedly different. As Stephen Jay Gould puts it, "All evolutionary sequences include . . . a fortuitous series of accidents with respect to future evolutionary success. Human brains and bodies did not evolve along a direct and inevitable ladder, but by a circuitous and tortuous route carved by adaptations evolved for different reasons, and fortunately suited to later needs."[3]

The history of life is not one of progressive advancement in complexity; if anything, it is one of proliferation of enormously varied designs that subsequently have been restricted to a few highly successful forms. Even at that, imperfections remain. As Gould so aptly puts it:

> Our world is not an optimal place, fine tuned by omnipotent forces of selection. It is a quirky mass of imperfections, working well enough (often admirably); a jury-rigged set of adaptations built of curious parts made available by past histories in different contexts.[4]

[1]Gould, S. J. (1996). *Full house: The spread of excellence from Plato to Darwin* (pp. 176–195). New York: Harmony Books.

[2]Gould, S. J. (1985). *The flamingo's smile: Reflections in natural history* (p. 409). New York: Norton.

[3]Ibid., p. 410.

[4]Ibid., p. 54.

For more than 260 million years, dinosaurs were the dominant land vertebrates. The later success of mammals was made possible by a chance event: the collision with the earth of an asteroid or comet, the effects of which brought about the dinosaurs' extinction.

EARLY MAMMALS

By 190 million years ago—the end of what geologists call the Triassic period—true mammals were on the scene. We know these and the mammals from the succeeding Jurassic (190–135 million years ago) and Cretaceous (135–65 million years ago) periods from hundreds of finds of mostly teeth and jaw parts. Because these structures are the most durable, they often outlast other parts of an animal's skeleton. Fortunately, investigators often are able to infer a good deal about the total animal on the basis of only a few teeth found lying in the earth. For example, knowledge of the way the teeth fit together indicates much about the operation of the jaws, suggesting the types of muscles needed. This in turn indicates how the skull must have been shaped to provide accommodation for the musculature. The shape of the jaws and details of the teeth also suggest the type of food that they were suited to deal with, indicating the probable diet of the specimen. Thus a mere jawbone reveals a great deal about the animal from which it came.

An interesting fact about the evolution of the mammals is that the diverse forms with which we are familiar today, including the primates, are the products of an **adaptive radiation,** the rapid increase in number of related species following a change in their environment. This did not begin until after mammals had been present on the earth for over 100 million years. Actually, the story of mammalian evolution starts as early as 280 to 230 million years ago (Figure 5.4). From deposits of this period, which geologists call the Permian, we have the remains of reptiles with features pointing in a distinctly mammalian direction. These mammal-like reptiles were slimmer than most other reptiles and were flesh eaters. In a series of graded fossils, we can see in them a reduction of bones to a more mammalian number, the shifting of limbs underneath the body, development of a separation between the mouth and nasal cavity, differentiation of the teeth, and so forth.

MILLIONS OF YEARS AGO	PERIODS	EPOCHS	LIFE FORMS
2		Pleistocene	
		Pliocene	First undoubted hominines
5		Miocene	
23		Oligocene	
34		Eocene	First undoubted monkey-ape ancestors
55		Paleocene	First undoubted primates
65	Cretaceous		
135	Jurassic		
180	Triassic		First undoubted mammals
230	Permian		Mammal-like reptiles
280	Carboniferous		First reptiles
345			

FIGURE 5.4

THIS TIMELINE HIGHLIGHTS SOME MAJOR MILESTONES IN THE EVOLUTION OF THOSE MAMMALS FROM WHICH HUMANS ARE DESCENDED.

All of these early mammals were small eaters of flesh—such things as insects, worms, and eggs. They seem to have been nocturnal in their habits, which is probably why the senses of smell and hearing became so developed in mammals. Although things cannot be seen as well in the dark as they can in the light, they can be heard and smelled just as well. Both sound and smell are more complex than sight. If something can be seen it is right there in the animal's line of vision. By contrast, it is possible to smell and hear things around corners and in other hidden places, and in addition to figuring out what it is that is smelled or heard and how far away it is, the animal must also figure out where it is. A further complication is the fact that smells linger, and so the animal must figure out if the cause of an odor is still there or, if not, how old the odor is.

As mammals' senses of hearing and smell became keener, they lost the ability (possessed by reptiles) to see in color. But the new, keener senses and the importance of outwitting both prey and predators served to improve

Adaptive radiation. Rapid diversification of an evolving population as it adapts to a variety of available niches.

their information-processing capacities and enlarge the part of the brain that handles these—the cerebral cortex—beyond that of reptiles. And to the extent that they become "brainier," they become more flexible in their behavior.

Because mammals were developing as such bright, active creatures, it may seem puzzling that reptiles continued to be the dominant land animals for more than 100 million years. After all, **warm-blooded** mammals, with their constant body temperature, can be active at any time, whereas **cold-blooded** reptiles, who take their body temperature from the surrounding environment, become more sluggish as the surrounding temperature drops. Furthermore, mammals provide care for their young, whereas most reptiles leave theirs to fend for themselves. But the mammals faced two limitations. For one, their high activity demanded more nutrition than did the less constant activity of reptiles. Such high-quality nutrition is provided by the fruits, nuts, and seeds of flowering plants, but these plants did not become common until late in the Cretaceous period. It is also provided by the flesh of other animals, but the mammals were small and therefore dependent particularly on small prey such as insects and worms. These were limited in numbers until flowers and fruits provided them with a host of new **ecological niches,** or functional positions in their habitats, to exploit.

The second limitation that affected mammals was the slight head start enjoyed by reptiles; this allowed them to preempt most available niches, which therefore were not available to mammals. With the mass extinction of many reptiles at the end of the Cretaceous, however, a number of existing niches became available to mammals; at the same time, whole new niches were opened up as the new grasses provided abundant food in arid places, and other flowering plants provided abundant, high-quality food elsewhere. By chance, the mammals had what it took in the way of biological equipment to take advantage of the new opportunities available to them.

The appearance of angiosperm plants provided not only highly nutritious fruits, seeds, and flowers but also a host of habitats for numerous edible insects and worms—just the sorts of foods required by mammals with their high metabolism.

RISE OF THE PRIMATES

Considering that primates have tended through the ages to live in environments where the conditions for fossilization are generally poor, we have a surprising number of fossils with which to work. What these fossils indicate is that the early primates emerged during a time of great change all over the world. The separation of continents was under way as the result of movement of the great platelike segments of the earth's crust on which they rest. The distribution of fossil primates across the earth makes sense only when one understands that the positions of the continents today differ tremendously from what was found in the past. Although Europe was still joined to North America, South America and India were isolated, while a narrow body of water separated Africa from Eurasia (see Figure 5.2). On the land itself the great dinosaurs had but recently become extinct, and the mammals were undergoing the great adaptive radiation that ultimately led to the development of the diverse forms with which we are familiar today. At the same time, the newly evolved grasses, ivies, shrubs, and other flowering plants were undergoing an enormous proliferation. This diversification, along with a milder climate, favored the spread of dense, lush tropical and subtropical forests over much of the earth, including North and South America and much of Eurasia and Africa. With the spread of these

Warm-blooded. Animals that maintain a relatively constant body temperature. • **Cold-blooded.** Animals whose body temperature rises or falls according to the temperature of the surrounding environment. • **Ecological niche.** A species' way of life considered in the context of its environment, including other species found in that environment.

huge belts of forest, the stage was set for the movement of some mammals from niches on the ground into the trees. Forests would provide our early ancestors with the ecological niches in which they would flourish.

The move to an arboreal existence brought for early primates a combination of the problems of earthbound existence with those of flight. In their move into the air, birds developed highly stereotyped behavior; primates, on the other hand, brought with them to the trees the flexible decision-making behavior characteristic of the mammals. The initial forays into the trees must have produced many misjudgments and errors of coordination, leading to falls that injured or killed the individuals poorly adapted to arboreal life. Natural selection favored those that judged depth correctly and gripped the branches strongly. It is quite likely that the early primates that took to the trees were in some measure preadapted, not just with behavioral flexibility but with better vision and more dexterous fingers than their contemporaries.

The relatively small size of the early primates allowed them to make use of the smaller branches of trees; larger, heavier competitors, and most predators, could not follow. The move to the smaller branches also gave them access to an abundant food supply; the primates were able to gather insects, leaves, flowers, and fruits directly rather than waiting for them to fall to the ground.

The strong selection to a new environment led to an acceleration in the rate of change of primate characteristics. Paradoxically, these changes eventually made possible a return to the ground on the part of some primates, including the ancestors of the genus *Homo.*

Paleocene Primates

Both genetics and anatomy suggest that the ancestry of primates lies with the insectivores, a diverse group of small mammals represented today by tree shrews, moles, and hedgehogs. Thus, we would expect to have difficulty distinguishing the earliest primate fossils from ancient insectivores. In fact, the earliest surely known primate fossils, 10 teeth from a site in Morocco, are about 60 million years old. These cheek teeth (molars and premolars) are very similar to the corresponding teeth of the modern mouse lemur, a tiny strepsirhine primate weighing a mere 2 ounces. They are sufficient to show that the primates were going their separate evolutionary way by 60 million years ago, having arisen as part of the great Paleocene adaptive radiation of mammals. Whether they originated in Africa or came from somewhere else is not known; certainly mammals that differed little from early primates were widespread at the time throughout what is now North America and Europe.

The abilities to judge depth correctly and grasp branches strongly are of obvious importance to animals as active in the trees as most primates.

Eocene Primates

The Eocene lasted from about 55 to 34 million years ago and began with an abrupt warming trend. With this, many older forms of mammals became extinct, to be replaced by recognizable progenitors of many of today's forms. Among the latter were numerous forms of lemurlike and tarsierlike primates, of which over 50 genera are known. Fossils of these creatures have been found in Africa, North America, Europe, and Asia, where the warm, wet conditions of the Eocene sustained extensive rain forests.

Most Eocene primates are classified into two families. One family consisted of mostly diurnal (active during daylight) creatures that generally ate fruit and leaves. Although for the most part small, some of these creatures were a bit larger than the smallest of today's monkeys. In many ways they were remarkably similar to modern lemurs and lorises, which likely are their descendants. Smaller in size were members of the other family, which were nocturnal eaters of fruits and insects. Tarsierlike in their anatomy, they are closely related to today's tarsier.

What the members of these early primate families have in common are somewhat enlarged brain cases, slightly reduced snouts, and a somewhat forward position of the eye orbits, which, though not completely walled in, are surrounded by a complete bony ring (Figure 5.5). Their dentition, however, was primitive and unlike that of modern forms in the total number of teeth. In their limb skeleton, they were well adapted to grasping, leaping, and perching. Moreover, nails like those possessed by modern primates, rather than claws, may be seen on some digits.

Other Eocene primates, represented by fossils from China and Egypt's Fayum depression, show unique mixes of lemurlike, tarsierlike, and platyrrhine-catarrhinelike characteristics and probably played a role in the ancestry of later monkeys and apes. The Chinese fossils, which are roughly 45 million years old, represent several species of tiny, insect-eating animals whose locomotion was by a combination of quadrupedalism and leaping. They include the smallest primates ever documented.[5] The Fayum fossils, not as old at 37 million years, are of a small leaf- or insect-eater. Although this creature's front teeth resemble those of the Eocene lemurlike primates, it has the catarrhinelike dental formula of two incisors, a canine, two premolars, and three molars on each side of the jaw, and the eye orbit has a complete wall, the latter being a feature of both catarrhine and platyrrhine primates. The foramen magnum has a somewhat forward position beneath the skull, and the brain was about 3.1 cubic centimeters in size.[6]

Although there is still much to be learned about these Eocene primates, it is clear that they were abundant, diverse, and widespread. Among them were ancestors of today's lemurs, as well as tarsiers and other haplorhines. The tarsierlike forms, with their large eyes, seem to have reverted to nocturnal habits, whereas the ancestors of platyrrhines and catarrhines did not. They shifted to a more herbivorous diet, with greater emphasis on arboreal quadrupedalism, in contrast to the emphasis on leaping seen in lemurlike and in tarsierlike forms.[7]

With the end of the Eocene, substantial changes took place among the primates, as among other mammals. In North America, now well isolated from Europe, primates became extinct, and elsewhere their range seems to have been reduced considerably. A driving force in all this was probably climatic change. Already, through the late Eocene, climates were becoming somewhat cooler and drier, but at the end temperatures took a sudden dive, sufficient to trigger formation of a substantial ice cap over previously forested Antarctica. The result was a marked reduction of the environments to which early primates were adapted. At the same time, some early primate niches may have been more effectively utilized by newly evolved rodent forms. Finally, the precursors of monkeys and apes, up to then overshadowed by lemurlike and

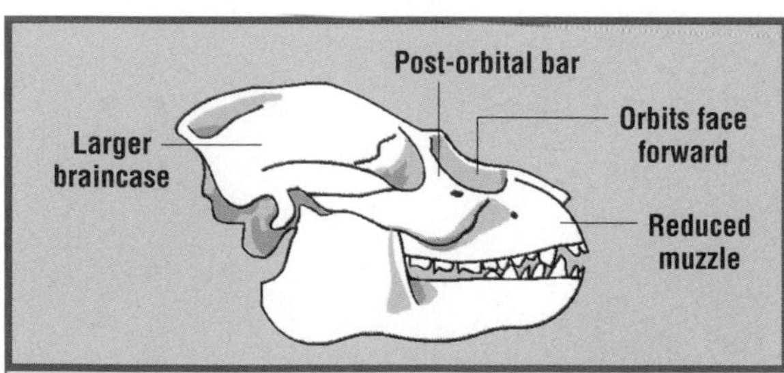

FIGURE 5.5

THE EOCENE GENUS *ADAPIS* IS A LEMURLIKE FORM. LIKE MODERN LEMURS, IT HAS A POSTORBITAL BAR, A BONY RING AROUND THE EYE ORBIT. NOTE THAT THE ORBIT IS OPEN BEHIND THE RING.

[5] Gebo, D. L., Dagosto, D., Beard, K. C., & Tao, Q. (2001). Middle Eocene primate tarsals from China: Implications for haplorhine evolution. *American Journal of Physical Anthropology, 116,* 83–107.

[6] Simons, E. (1995). Skulls and anterior teeth of *Catopithecus* (Primates: Anthropoidea) from the Eocene and anthropoid origins. *Science, 268,* 1,885–1,888.

[7] Kay, R. F., Ross, C., & Williams, B. A. (1997). Anthropoid origins. *Science, 275,* 803–804.

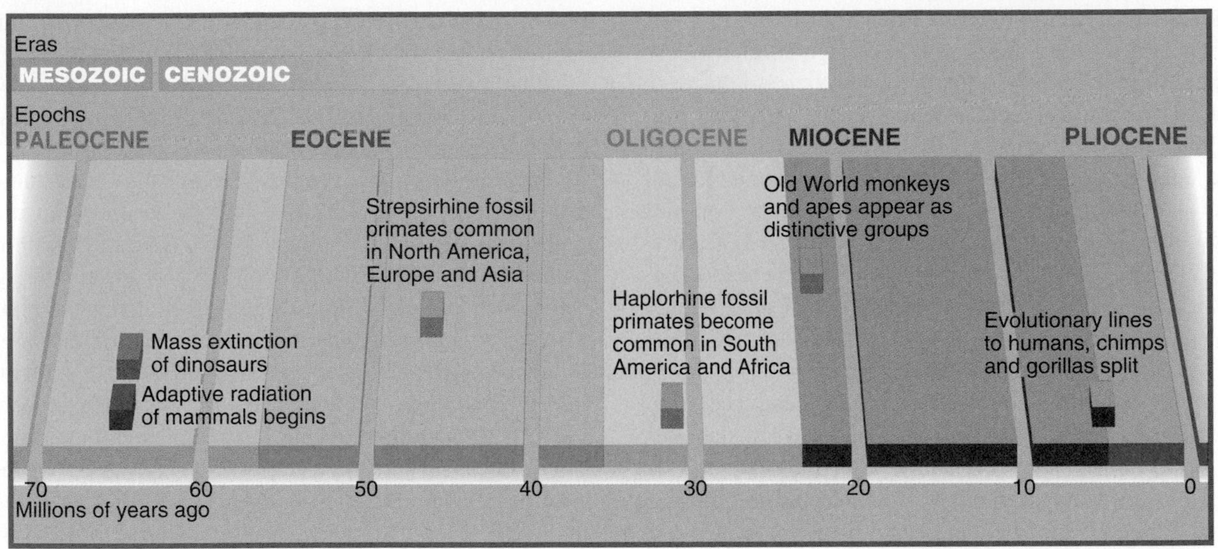

tarsierlike forms, may have been able to take over some other niches they formerly occupied.

Oligocene Monkeys and Apes

The Oligocene epoch began about 34 million and ended about 23 million years ago. Primate fossils that have thus far been discovered and definitely placed in the Oligocene are not common, but enough exist to prove that haplorhines were becoming quite prominent and diverse by this time. The scarcity of Oligocene primate fossils stems from the reduced habitat available to them and from the arboreal nature of primates then living, which restricted them to damp forest environments where conditions are exceedingly poor for fossil formation.

Fortunately, Egypt's Fayum depression has yielded sufficient fossils (more than 1,000) to reveal that by 33 million years ago, haplorhine primates existed in considerable diversity. Moreover, the cast of characters is growing, as new fossils continue to be found in the Fayum, as well as in newly discovered localities in Algeria and

Egypt's Fayum depression in the desert west of Cairo. Here, winds and flash floods have uncovered sediments more than 22 million years old, exposing the remains of a tropical rain forest that was home to a variety of primates that combine monkeylike and apelike features.

Oman. At present, we have evidence of at least 60 genera included in two families. All show a combination of monkeylike and apelike features, and their origins probably lie in the group of Eocene primates in which traits of platyrrhines and catarrhines are first evident. But in the Oligocene the tables have been turned; now lemurlike and tarsierlike forms have become far less prominent than forms that combine monkeylike and apelike features. Only on the island of Madagascar (off the coast of East Africa), which was devoid of haplorhines until humans arrived, did lemurs thrive. In their isolation, they underwent a further adaptive radiation.

Included among the smaller Oligocene haplorhine species may be the ancestors of true monkeys. In their dental formula and limb bones, these primates (about the size of a modern squirrel monkey) resemble platyrrhine monkeys. Some of them could easily have gotten to South America, which at the time was not attached to any other land mass, by means of floating masses of vegetation of the sort that originate even today in the great rivers of West and Central Africa. In the Oligocene, the distance between the two continents was far less than it is today; favorable winds and currents could easily have carried "floating islands" of vegetation across within the 13 days that platyrrhine ancestors could have survived, given an existing adaptation to seasonal variation in availability of fresh water.[8]

The earliest surely known true catarrhine monkey fossil comes from the Miocene epoch, but its ancestry may lie among the same primates that gave rise to the platyrrhines. This fossil's molars look as if they evolved from a similar form, and loss of one premolar on each side of the jaw would result in the typical catarrhine formula.

Given our obsession with our own ancestry, one particular genus of Oligocene catarrhine is worth a closer look. This is *Aegyptopithecus* ("Egyptian ape"). It is one of a number of genera with a specifically apelike dentition: Its lower molars have the five cusps of an ape, and the upper canine and lower first premolar exhibit the sort of shearing mechanism found in monkeys and apes. Its skull possesses eye sockets that are in a forward position and completely protected by a bony wall, as is typical of modern monkeys and apes. Evidently *Aegyptopithecus,* and probably its Fayum contemporaries as well, possessed vision superior to the lemurlike and tarsierlike primates of the Eocene. In fact, the inside of the skull of *Aegyptopithecus* reveals that its brain had a larger visual cortex and smaller olfactory lobes than do modern lemurs or tarsiers. Although the brain of *Aegyptopithecus* was smaller relative to body size than that of more recent catarrhines, this primate seems to have had a larger brain than any lemur or tarsier, past or present.

Aegyptopithecus, besides being the best-known Oligocene primate, is also of interest to us because its teeth suggest that it belongs in the ancestry of those Miocene forms that gave rise to both humans and today's African apes. Although no bigger than a modern house cat, *Aegyptopithecus* was nonetheless one of the larger Oligocene primates. Possessed of a monkeylike skull and body, with limb proportions not unlike those seen in some modern platyrrhine monkeys, and fingers and toes capable of powerful grasping, it evidently moved about in a quadrupedal monkeylike manner.[9] Differences between males and females include larger body size, more formidable canine teeth, and deeper mandibles (lower jaws) in the males. In modern catarrhines, species with these traits generally live in groups that include several adult females with one or more adult males.

Miocene Apes

The beginning of the Miocene epoch, which succeeded the Oligocene about 23 million years ago, saw a proliferation of apes in the forests that covered many parts of

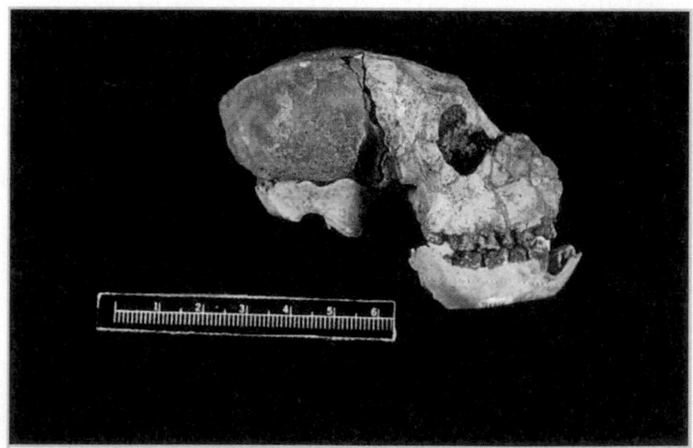

This *Aegyptopithecus* skull dates to the Oligocene epoch. The enclosed eye sockets and dentition mark it as a catarrhine primate, probably ancestral to *Proconsul.*

[8]Houle, A. (1999). The origin of platyrrhines: An evaluation of the Antarctic scenario and the floating island model. *American Journal of Physical Anthropology, 109,* 554–556.

[9]Ankel-Simons, F., Fleagle, J. G., & Chatrath, P. S. (1998). Femoral anatomy of *Aegyptopithecus zeuxis,* an early Oligocene anthropoid. *American Journal of Physical Anthropology, 106,* 421–422.

the Old World. Thus began a kind of golden age of apelike forms. East Africa is an area particularly rich in the fossils of apes from the early through the middle part of the Miocene. One of the earliest of these apes, *Proconsul* (Consul was the name of a chimpanzee prominent on the London vaudeville circuit), is one of the best known, owing to preservation of almost all elements of its skeleton. Four recognized species of *Proconsul* varied considerably in size, the smallest being no larger than a modern female baboon while the largest was the size of a female gorilla. That they were apes is clearly shown by their dentition, particularly the five-cusped lower molars. Moreover, their skull, compared to that of Oligocene proto-apes like *Aegyptopithecus,* shows a reduced snout and a fuller, more rounded brain case. Cranial capacity for one species is estimated at about 167 cubic centimeters, about 1.5 times larger than that typical of a mammal of comparable body size and relatively larger than in modern monkeys. Still, some features are reminiscent of monkeys, particularly the forward thrust and narrowness of the face.

Although its overall configuration is not quite like any living monkey or ape, the elbow, hip, knee, and foot anatomy of *Proconsul* is similar to what one sees in living apes, and like them, it had no tail (Figure 5.6). The wrist and pelvis, however, are monkeylike, and the lumbar vertebrae and leg bones show features that are intermediate between those of a gibbon and a monkey. Overall, the vertebral column was longer and more flexible and the torso narrower than in apes, but the hind limb was less monkeylike, being more mobile as are ape hind limbs. The consensus is that *Proconsul* represents

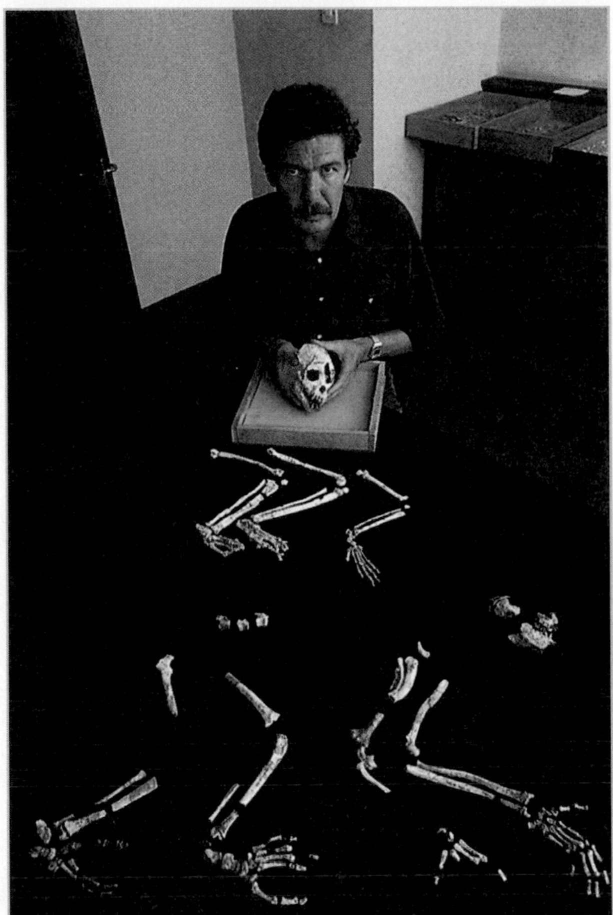

Paleoanthropologist Alan Walker displays bones of *Proconsul,* an unspecialized tree-dwelling, fruit-eating hominoid of the early Miocene.

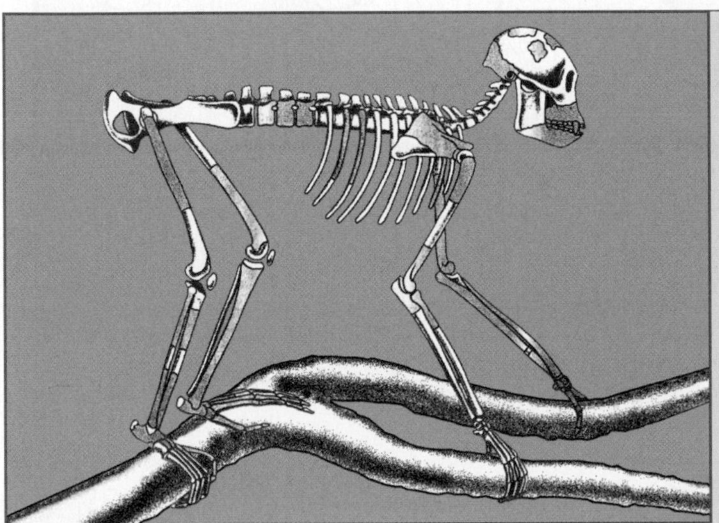

FIGURE 5.6

RECONSTRUCTED SKELETON OF *PROCONSUL.* NOTE APELIKE ABSENCE OF TAIL, BUT MONKEYLIKE LIMB AND BODY PROPORTIONS. *PROCONSUL,* HOWEVER, WAS CAPABLE OF GREATER ROTATION OF FORELIMBS THAN MONKEYS.

an unspecialized tree-dwelling, fruit-eating **hominoid** (the catarrhine superfamily to which modern apes and humans belong).

Some of *Proconsul*'s contemporaries were even more apelike. At least one species had a shoulder joint allowing suspension of the body when hanging by the arms. Its leg bones suggest strong climbing ability, and vertebrae are indicative of a stiff, apelike body. Otherwise, details of the teeth, face, and body are comparable to *Proconsul.*[10] Like *Proconsul,* this species is easily derivable from an animal like *Aegyptopithecus* and was almost certainly ancestral to hominoids of the middle Miocene. Like their probable ancestor as well as their descendants, *Proconsul* and other early Miocene apes were sexually dimorphic, the males being the larger sex with more formidable canine teeth.

Hominoids of the middle and late Miocene (from roughly 16 million to 5 million years ago) were a varied lot that ranged over a remarkably wide geographical area: Their fossils have been found in Europe, Asia, and Africa (by this time, Africa had collided with the Eurasian land mass, allowing faunal interchange). Such abundance and wide distribution indicates that these primates were very successful animals. With teeth and jaws very much like those of *Proconsul,* they seem to have been somewhat more apelike than monkeylike in their overall appearance; like some of *Proconsul*'s contemporaries, they had relatively rigid bodies as well as limb bones well adapted for suspension and climbing. Some species surely were ancestral to later large-bodied apes, including the **hominids**—the primate family in which the African apes and humans are placed. According to David Pilbeam, who has made the study of Miocene hominoids his lifework, "Any . . . would make excellent ancestors for the living hominoids: human bipeds, chimpanzee and gorilla knucklewalkers, Orangutan contortionists."[11] Figure 5.7 shows some important similarities and differences among hominoids. Over the years, these forms have been known by a confusing assortment of generic and specific names, not all of which have turned out to be justified, as the following Original Study explains.

[10]Gebo, D. L., MacLatchy, L., Kityo, R., Deino, A., Kingston, J., & Pilbeam, D. (1997). A hominoid genus from the early Miocene of Uganda. *Science, 276,* 401–404.

[11]Pilbeam, D. (1986). *Human origins* (p. 6). David Skamp Distinguished Lecture in Anthropology, Indiana University.

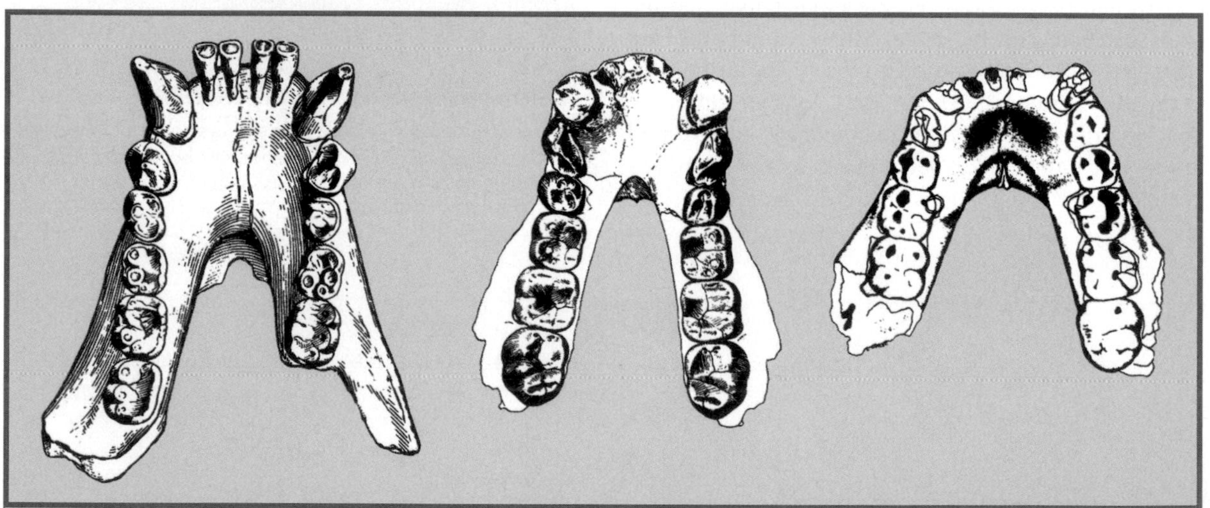

FIGURE 5.7

The lower jaws of two Miocene apes (A) and (B) and early *Australopithecus* (C), a hominine who lived 4 million years ago. Relative to the cheek teeth, all have comparatively small teeth at the front of the jaw. There is general similarity between A and B, as well as between B and C. The major difference between B and C is that the rows of cheek teeth are farther apart in the hominine.

Hominoid. A catarrhine primate superfamily that includes apes and humans. • **Hominid.** Hominoid family to which humans alone used to be assigned; now includes African apes and humans, with the latter assigned to the subfamily *Homininae.*

Will the Real Human Ancestor Please Stand Up?[12]

Original Study

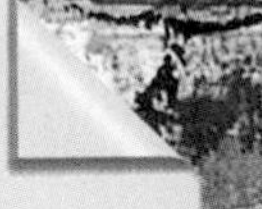

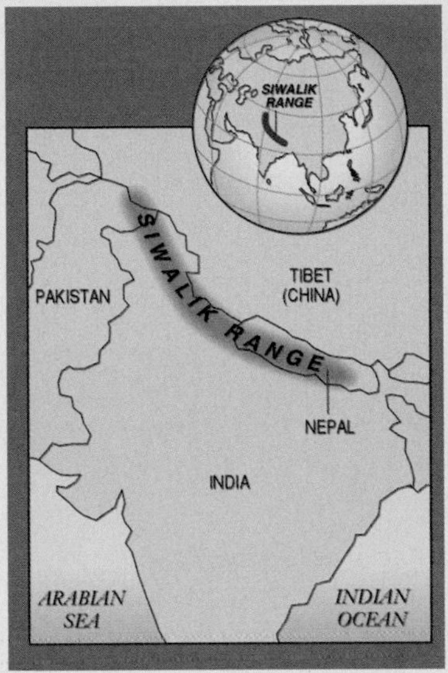

Today, humans are the only "ape" to have a global distribution. We inhabit every continent, including areas as inhospitable as the icy Antarctic or the scorching Sahara. Our closest living relatives, the other members of the superfamily *Hominoidea,* don't come close to occupying as much real estate. Instead these apes live in very circumscribed areas of the Old World tropical rain forest. Chimps, bonobos, and gorillas can be found only in portions of Central Africa. Orangutans are limited to the treetops on the islands of Sumatra and Borneo. Gibbons and siamangs swing through the branches only of the Southeast Asian forests.

This was not always the case. In the distant past, long before any human ancestor walked upon two legs, apes could be found throughout much of the Old World. True apes first appeared in the fossil record during the Miocene epoch, 5 to 23 million years ago. It was also during this time period that the African and Eurasian land masses made direct contact. For most of the preceding 100 million years, the Tethys Sea was a continuous body of water that more or less joined what are now the Mediterranean and Black Seas to the Indian Ocean. The Tethys Sea was a formidable barrier to migration. Once Africa and Eurasia were joined together through what is now the Middle East, Old World primate species that got their start in Africa could expand their ranges into Eurasia. Miocene ape fossil remains have been found everywhere from the caves of China, to the forests of France, to eastern Africa where the earliest fossil remains of bipeds have been found.

So varied and ubiquitous were the fossil apes of this period that the Miocene has even been labeled by some as the "golden age of the hominoids." The word *hominoid* comes from the Latin roots *Homo* and *Homin* (meaning "human being") and the suffix *oïdes* ("resembling"). As a group, the hominoids get their name from their resemblance to humans. The likeness between humans and the other apes bespeaks an important evolutionary relationship. One of the Miocene apes is the direct ancestor of the human lineage. Exactly which one is a question still to be resolved.

Looking at some of the history of the "contenders" for direct human ancestor among the Miocene apes illustrates how reconstructing evolutionary relationships draws on much more than bones alone. Fossil finds are always interpreted against the backdrop of scientific discoveries in a variety of fields as well as prevailing beliefs and biases. Interpretations are also affected by whether fossilization and discovery are likely to occur in any given region. Fortunately the self-correcting nature of scientific investigation allows evolutionary lineages to be redrawn in light of all new discoveries.

The first Miocene ape fossil remains were found in Africa in the 1930s and 1940s by A. T. Hopwood and the renowned paleoanthropologist Louis Leakey. These fossils turned up on one of the many islands in Lake Victoria, the 27,000-square-mile lake that separates Kenya, Tanzania, and Uganda. Impressed with the chimplike appearance of these fossil remains, Hopwood suggested that the new species be named *Proconsul* after a chimpanzee

[12]Walrath, D. E. (2001). *Will the real human ancestor please stand up?* © by author, College of Medicine, University of Vermont.

Original Study

who was performing on the London stage at the time. *Pro* is the Latin root for "before" and Consul was the stage name of the acting chimp. Dated to the early Miocene 17 to 21 million years ago, *Proconsul* has some of the classic hominoid features, namely no tail and the characteristic pattern of Y5 grooves in the lower molar teeth. However, the adaptations of the upper body seen in later apes (including humans) for hanging suspended below tree branches in search of ripe fruits were absent. In other words, *Proconsul* has some apelike features as well as some features of more generalized four-footed Old World monkeys. This mixture of ape and monkey features makes *Proconsul* a contender for a "missing link" between monkeys and apes but not as a connection between Miocene apes and bipeds. We know that the ape who stood was fully apelike in all the ways that humans are apes. Our broad shoulders and mobile upper limb joints are fully adapted for hanging from branches. A dentist would recognize the cusp pattern of human molars in the mouth of any hominoid.

At least seven groups besides *Proconsul* have been found in East Africa in the early to middle Miocene. But between 14 and 5 million years ago this fossil record thins out. It is not that all the apes suddenly moved from Africa to Eurasia, but rather that the geologic conditions for preservation of bones as fossils made it less likely that any of the African remains would survive. Tropical forests inhabited by chimps and gorillas today are just about the worst conditions for the preservation of bones. In order to become a fossil, bones must be quickly incorporated into the earth before any rotting or decomposition occurs. In tropical forests the heat, humidity, and the general abundance of life make this unlikely. The bones' organic matrix is consumed by other creatures before it can be fossilized.

Nevertheless, the scarcity of African fossil evidence for this time period fits well with prevailing notions about human origins. Two factors were at work to take the focus away from Africa. First, at this time no investigators thought that humans were any more closely related to the African apes than they were to the other intelligent great ape—the Asian orangutan. Chimps, bonobos, gorillas, and orangutans were thought to be more closely related to each other than any of them were to humans. Moreover, the construction of evolutionary relationships still relied upon visual similarities between species much as it did when Linnaeus developed the taxonomic scheme that grouped humans with other primates. Chimps, bonobos gorillas, and orangutans all possess the same basic body plan adapted to hanging by their arms from branches or knuckle-walking on the ground. Humans and their ancestors had an altogether different form of locomotion: walking upright on two legs. On an anatomical basis, it seemed as though the first Miocene ape to stand up and become a hominine could have come from any part of the vast Old World range of the Miocene apes.

The second factor at work to pull attention away from African origins was more subtle and embedded not in the bones from the earth but in the subconscious of the scientists of the day. It was hard for these scientists to imagine that humans originated entirely in Africa. Indeed, it took many years for the first bipedal hominine fossils discovered in South Africa in the 1920s to be accepted by the scientific community as a key part of the human line (see Chapter 6). Instead, human origins were imagined to involve a close link between those who invented the first tools and the people responsible for Western civilization. In this regard, a contender for a Miocene ape ancestor from southern Asia, near the ruins of the great Indus Valley civilization, may have been more palatable to anthropologists in the middle of the 20th century.

During the 1960s, it appeared as though this Miocene human ancestor lived in the Siwalkis, the foothills of the majestic Himalayan mountain range along the northern borders of India and Pakistan. The Himalayas are some of the youngest mountains of the world. They began forming during the Miocene when the Indian subcontinent collided with the rest of Eurasia and have been growing taller ever since.

In honor of the Hindu religion practiced in the region where the fossils were found, the contender was given the name *Ramapithecus*, after the Indian deity Rama and the Greek word for ape, *pithekos*. Rama is the avatar, or incarnation, of the Hindu god Vishnu, the preserver. He is meant to portray what a perfect human can be. He is benevolent, protects the weak, and embodies all noble human characteristics. Features like the relative delicacy and curvature of the jaw and palate as well as thick tooth enamel led paleoanthropologists David Pilbeam and Elwyn Simons to suggest that this was the first hominoid to become a hominine. They suggested that *Ramapithecus* was a bipedal tool-user—the earliest human ancestor. With these qualities, *Ramapithecus* was perfectly named.

Other Miocene apes were also present in the foothills of the Himalayas. *Sivapithecus* was named after the Hindu deity Siva, the god of destruction and regeneration. In the Hindu religion Siva is depicted as an asocial hermit who, when provoked, reduces his enemies to smoldering ashes in fits of rage. Though never an aspiring human ancestor, *Sivapithecus* also has the humanlike characteristic of thick molar tooth enamel (unlike the African apes). *Sivapithecus* also had large projecting canine teeth more suitable to a destroyer than to a human ancestor. The *Sivapithecus* and *Ramapithecus* fossils were dated to between 7 and 12 million years ago.

Fossils are not the only discoveries that have changed our understanding of human evolutionary history. By the 1970s, biochemical and genetic evidence was beginning to be used to establish evolutionary relationships. A Berkeley biochemist named Vince Sarich brought molecular techniques to evolutionary studies and developed the revolutionary concept of a "molecular clock." Such clocks help detect when the branching of related species from a common ancestor took place in the distant past.

Sarich used a molecular technique that had been around since the beginning of the 20th century: comparison of the blood proteins of living groups. He worked on serum albumin, a protein from the fluid portion of the blood that (like the albumin that forms egg whites) can be precipitated out of solution. One of the forces that will cause such precipitation is contact of this protein with antibodies directed against it, as in the immune response of the body when fighting an infection. The technique relies on the notion that the stronger the biochemical reaction between the protein and the antibody, the closer the evolutionary relationship, because the antibodies and proteins of closely related species will resemble one another more than the antibodies and proteins of distant species.

Sarich made immunological comparisons between a variety of species and suggested that he could establish a molecular clock by calculating a rate of change over time. By assuming a constant rate of change in the protein structure of each species over time, Sarich used these results to predict times of divergence between related groups. Each molecular clock needs to be set, or calibrated, by a known event such as the divergence between strepsirhine and haplorhine primates or Old World monkeys and apes. These dates are established directly by well-dated fossil specimens.

Using this technique, Sarich proposed a sequence of divergence for the living hominoids that showed that human, chimp, and gorilla lines split roughly 5 million years ago. He boldly stated that it was impossible to have a direct human ancestor before 7 million years ago "no matter what it looked like". In other words, anything that old would also have to be ancestral to chimps and gorillas. Because *Ramapithecus*, even with its humanlike jaws, was dated to between 7 and 12 million years ago, it could no longer be considered a human ancestor.

As recently as 1965, the renowned paleoanthropologist F. Clark Howell had described *Ramapithecus* as the earliest "manlike" primate, endorsing its direct place on the human line. However, the molecular evidence of the next decade did not strengthen this claim that, "the impressive thing about *Ramapithecus* is that each new piece of additional evidence about it has tended to strengthen rather than weaken the claim being made for it" as a human ancestor. Instead, the molecular data initiated an entirely new interpretation of the fossil evidence.

In the meantime, David Pilbeam and Elwyn Simons continued fossil hunting in the Himalayan foothills. Further specimens began to show that *Ramapithecus* was actually a smaller, perhaps

Original Study

female version of *Sivapithecus*. Eventually all the specimens referred to as *Ramapithecus* were "sunk" or absorbed into the *Sivapithecus* group so that today *Ramapithecus* no longer exists as a valid name for a Miocene ape. Instead of two distinct groups, one of which went on to evolve into humans, they are considered males and females of the sexually dimorphic species *Sivapithecus*. A spectacularly complete specimen found in the Potwar Plateau by David Pilbeam showed that *Sivapithecus* was undoubtedly the ancestor of living orangutans. This conclusion matched well with the molecular evidence that the separate line to orangutans originated 10–12 million years ago.

All of these changes might make paleoanthropologists seem fickle, but they are not. They are participants in an unusual kind of science. Paleoanthropology, like all paleontology, is a science of discovery. What is seen or discovered determines what interpretations can be made. As new discoveries come to light, interpretations inevitably change, making for better understanding of our evolutionary history. Today, discoveries can occur in the laboratory as easily as on the site of an excavation. Molecular studies provided a new line of evidence that can be seen in much the same way that fossils provide new data as they are unearthed. A discovery in the laboratory, like Sarich's molecular clocks, can drastically change the interpretation of the fossil evidence.

What we discover is also shaped by what we believe, since beliefs shape the search process itself. In the past, it seemed right to look for our Miocene ancestor in the foothills of the Himalayas. Today, though we still have very little fossil evidence from Africa between 5 and 14 million years ago, the molecular studies allow us to "see" that the human line got its start in Africa when chimps, gorillas, and hominines diverged.

As the human lineage developed since the Miocene, our closest living relatives—the chimpanzees and gorillas—followed their own separate evolutionary trajectories. Today they inhabit the tropical forested pockets of Central Africa leaving little trace of their evolutionary history behind. Hominines took a different course and have left behind a rich fossil record in eastern and southern Africa beginning about 5 million years ago. Several million years after the ability to walk on two feet appeared, hominines began to spread throughout the Old World. Today, humans inhabit every continent. The details of our evolutionary history will continue to be redrawn in light of new evidence that appears from the bones, the molecules, or some area yet to be discovered. Though we have not found the fossil remains of the common ancestor of chimps, gorillas, and hominines, we know from the molecules that Africa is the place where the first ape stood up.

The End

For many years, potential hominid ancestors were known exclusively from the remains of teeth and jaws. Relative to the size of the cheek teeth (premolars and molars), their incisor teeth are comparable in size to those of other large hominoids of the time, although they are placed a bit more vertically in the mouth. The canines are substantially larger in males than in females, but even in males they are significantly smaller relative to the cheek teeth than the canines of the other hominoids. Still, they do project beyond adjacent teeth so that, when closed, the jaws interlock. Furthermore, the shearing function of the upper canine with the first lower premolar is retained. The molars, which show the same five-cusp pattern as the other hominoids, have noticeably thicker enamel and low, rounded cusps. The tooth row tends to be slightly V-shaped, whereas that of the other hominoids is more like a U, with the rows of cheek teeth parallel to one another (see Figure 5.7). The palate, or roof of the mouth, is high and arched. Finally, the lower facial region is narrow, short, and deep. Overall, the dental apparatus was built for powerful chewing, especially on the back teeth.

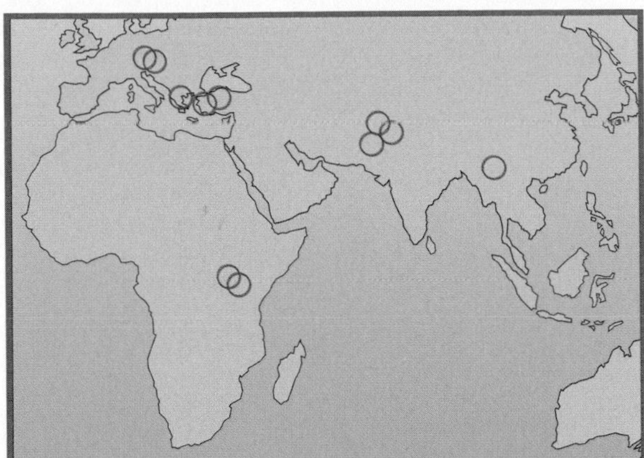

FIGURE 5.8
FOSSILS OF HOMINOIDS HAVE BEEN FOUND IN EAST AFRICA, EUROPE, AND ASIA THAT COULD BE ANCESTRAL TO LARGE APES AND HUMANS.

This *Sivapithecus* skull is remarkably similar to skulls of modern orangutans, so much so that an ancestor-descendant relationship is probable. The last common ancestor of chimpanzees, gorillas, and humans may not have differed greatly from *Sivapithecus*.

In the past three decades, our dependence on teeth and jaws for our knowledge of these hominoids has lessened as a number of their skull and limb bone fragments have been found in China, Greece, Hungary, Pakistan, and Turkey (Figure 5.8). In the best-known genus (*Sivapithecus*), the face is remarkably orangutanlike in its profile and a number of other details. The mandible, however, is only broadly rather than specifically similar to that of an orang, nor are the upper arm bones quite the same.

MIOCENE APES AND HUMAN ORIGINS

As long as several late Miocene apes were known only from fossils of teeth and jaws, it was easy to postulate some sort of relationship between them and ourselves. This was because a number of features—the position of the incisors, the reduced canines, the thick enamel of the molars, and the shape of the tooth row—seemed to point in a somewhat human direction. Some fossils (notably one from East Africa called *Kenyapithecus*) even show a shallow concavity above the position of the canine tooth, a feature not found in any recent ape but often found in humans. Indeed, some anthropologists went so far as to see such creatures as the earliest representatives of a human, as opposed to any ape lineage. This view was challenged when molecular evidence indicated a more recent split between apes and humans. The discovery of the orangutanlike skulls and apelike limb bones of *Sivapithecus* added fuel to the fire, leading many anthropologists to conclude that this and similar forms could have nothing to do with human origins. Rather, orangutans were seen as the sole modern survivors of an ancient group from which the line leading to the hominids (African apes and humans) had branched off, as molecular evidence suggested, some 18 to 12 million years ago.

Eventually, opinion shifted back to a middle position. Although a link between Miocene *Sivapithecus* and modern orangutans seems undeniable, this does not rule out the possibility of a link between other related late Miocene hominoids on the one hand and hominids on the other.[13] For example, some late Miocene species from

[13]Ciochon, R. L., & Fleagle, J. G. (1987). *Ramapithecus* and human origins. In R. L. Ciochon & J. G. Fleagle (Eds.), *Primate evolution and human origins* (p. 208). Hawthorne, NY: Aldine de Gruyter.

Although not identical, the modern ape most like *Sivapithecus* is the orangutan. Chimpanzees and gorillas, like humans, have come to differ more from the ancestral condition than have these Asian apes.

Africa seem closer in dental proportions and other features of their teeth to early **hominines** than do related Asian fossils.

That the ancestry of humans may ultimately be among late Miocene apes of Africa that show some resemblance to *Sivapithecus,* then, is consistent with dental evidence. It is consistent as well with estimates, based on molecular similarities and differences among humans, bonobos, chimpanzees, and gorillas, that they could not have separated from a common ancestral stock more than 8 million years ago. We know from the fossils that forms like *Sivapithecus* were still on the scene at that time (indeed, a form larger than a modern gorilla survived in Asia until about 300,000 years ago) and also that our own human ancestors were going their separate evolutionary way by at least 4.4 million, if not 6 million, years ago.

Hominoid Adaptations and Late Miocene Climatic Change

Molar teeth like those of some late Miocene apes that feature low crown relief, thick enamel, and surfaces poorly developed for cutting, are found in a number of modern primates.[14] Some of these species are terrestrial and some are arboreal, but all have one thing in common: They eat very hard nuts, fruits with very tough rinds, and some seeds. This provides them with a rich source of easily digested nutrients that are not accessible to species with thin molar enamel incapable of standing up to the stresses of tough rind removal or nut cracking. Thus these Miocene apes probably ate food similar to that eaten by these latter-day nut crackers.

Analysis of other materials from deposits in which these fossils have been found suggests utilization of a broad range of habitats, ranging from tropical rain forests to drier bush country. Of particular interest to us, from the standpoint of human origins, are those populations that lived in mosaic environments, where there was forested as well as some open country, where food could be obtained through foraging on the ground as well as in the trees of the forests. As it happened, a climatic shift was under way, associated with the geological events involved in the formation of East Africa's rift valleys. This caused a gradual but persistent breaking up of forested areas, with a consequent expansion of open grassland.[15] Under such circumstances, it seems likely that those populations of late Miocene hominoids living at the edge of forests were obliged to supplement food from the trees more and more with other foods readily available on

[14]Kay, R. F. (1981). The nut-crackers—A new theory of the adaptations of the Ramapithecinae. *American Journal of Physical Anthropology, 55,* 141–151.

[15]Conroy, G. C. (1997). *Reconstructing human origins: A modern synthesis* (pp. 84–86). New York: Norton.

Hominine. Member of the *Homininae,* the subfamily of hominids to which humans belong.

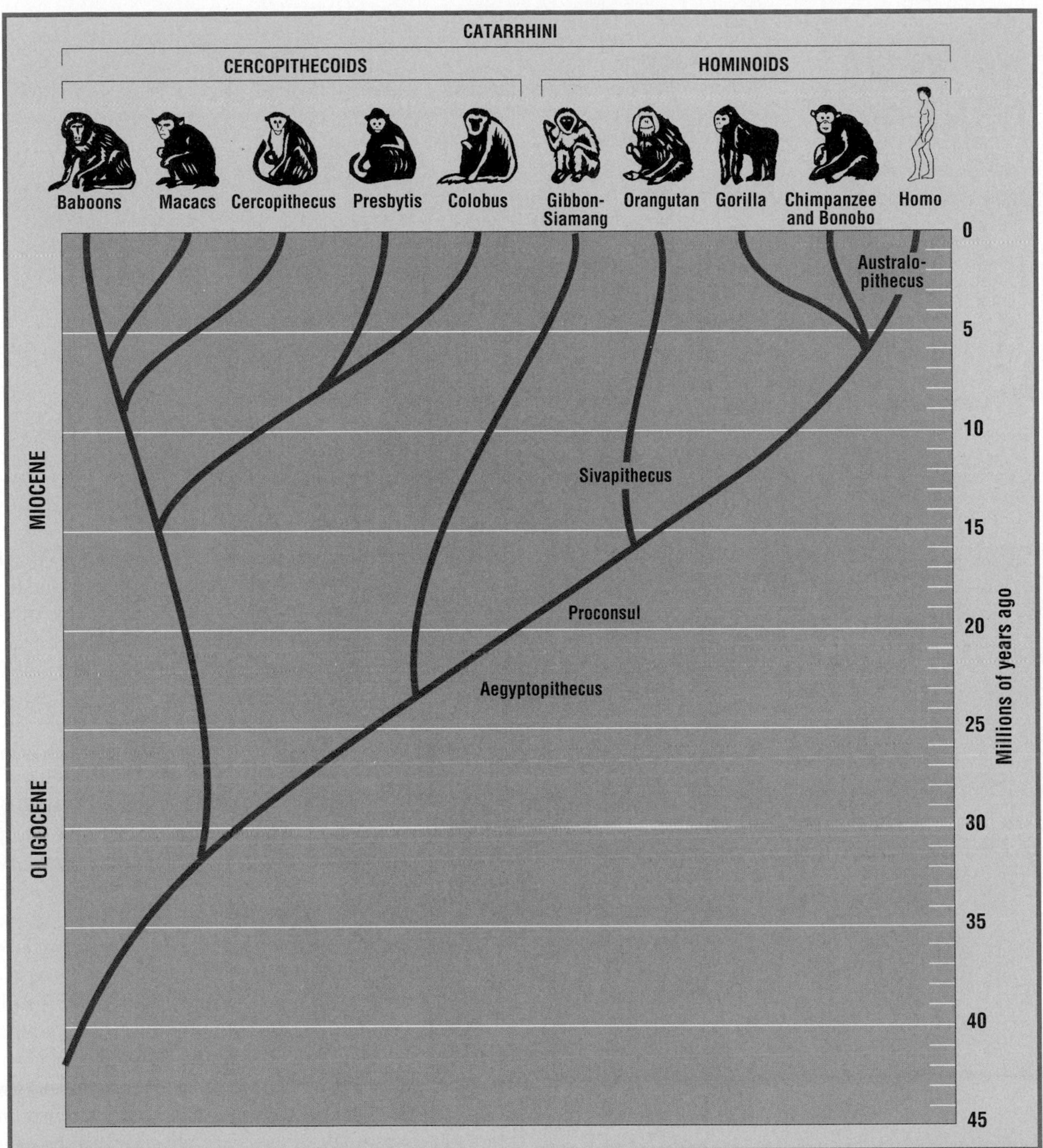

FIGURE 5.9

ALTHOUGH DEBATE CONTINUES OVER DETAILS, THIS CHART REPRESENTS A REASONABLE RECONSTRUCTION OF EVOLUTIONARY RELATIONSHIPS AMONG THE CATARRHINE PRIMATES. (NOT SHOWN ARE EXTINCT EVOLUTIONARY LINES.)

HIGHWAY 1
Find out about plate tectonics and continental drift from this nifty site created by NASA. Use interactive maps to understand how these phenomena shape our world and beyond.
http://kids.earth.nasa.gov/archive/pangaea/

HIGHWAY 2
This comprehensive primate evolution site provides a complete taxonomic listing of fossil primates as well as an excellent glossary of terms related to primate evolution.
http://members.tripod.com/cacajao/evolution.html

HIGHWAY 3
A trip to the Wisconsin Regional Primate Research Center's Primate Info Net opens the door to information about living and fossil primates as well as the people who study them. The site's search engine is a tremendous resource.
www.primate.wisc.edu/pin/

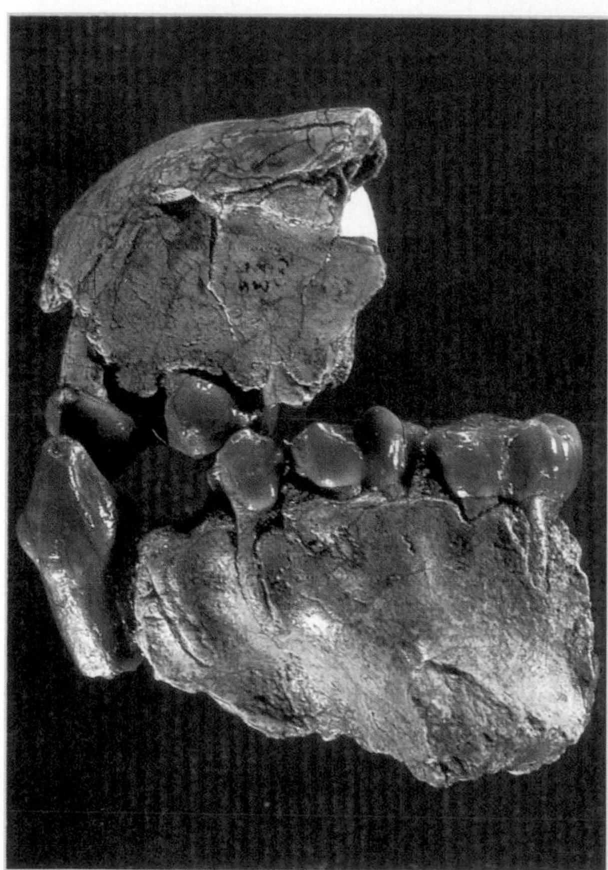

Kenyapithecus from East Africa is a Miocene ape that has relatively small canine teeth and a facial profile suitable for an ancestor of African apes and humans.

the ground in more open country. Consistent with this theory, late Miocene ape fossils are typically found in association with greater numbers of the remains of animals adapted to grasslands than are earlier ones.

Those Miocene apes that already had large, thickly enameled molars were capable of dealing with the tough and abrasive foods available on the ground when necessary. What they lacked, however, were canine teeth of sufficient size to have served as effective weapons of defense. By contrast, most modern monkeys and apes that spend much time down on the ground rely heavily for defense on the massive, fanglike canines possessed by the males. Because catlike predators were even more numerous on the ground than now, these Miocene apes, especially the smaller ones (which probably weighed no more than about 40 pounds[16]), would seem to have been especially vulnerable primates. Probably the forest fringe was more than just a source of foods different from those on the ground; its trees would have provided refuge when danger threatened. Yet, with continued expansion of open country, trees for refuge would have become fewer and farther between. Slowly, however, physical and behavioral changes must have improved these primates' chances for survival out in the open on the ground. For reasons discussed in the next chapter, bipedal locomotion was a key element in this new adaptation.

[16]Pilbeam, D. R. (1987). Rethinking human origins. In Ciochon & Fleagle, p. 217.

Ground-dwelling primates, like this male baboon, depend heavily on their massive canine teeth for protection from other animals. Some Miocene apes, by contrast, lacked such massive weapons of defense.

EARLY APES AND HUMAN EVOLUTION

Although some late Miocene apes display a number of features from which hominine characteristics may be derived, and some may occasionally have walked bipedally, they were much too apelike to be considered hominines. No matter how often some of them may have resorted to bipedalism, they had not yet developed the anatomical specializations for this mode of locomotion that are seen in the earliest known hominines. They were optional rather than obligatory bipeds. Nevertheless, existing anatomical and molecular evidence allows the hypothesis that apes and humans separated from a common evolutionary line sometime near the end of the Miocene, and some fossils, particularly the smaller hominoids, do possess traits seen in humans. Moreover, the Miocene apes possessed a limb structure less specialized for brachiation than modern apes; this structure could well have provided the basis for the development of human as well as ape limb types.

Clearly not all late Miocene apes evolved into hominines. Those that did might, in a sense, be regarded as losers, in that they were squeezed out of the most favorable forested habitat. It was just their good luck that their physical characteristics enabled them to make a go of it under changed conditions. Most contemporary hominoids, by contrast, remained in the forests and woodlands where they continued to develop as arboreal apes, although ultimately some of them, too, took up a more terrestrial life. These are the bonobos, chimpanzees, and gorillas, who have changed far more from the ancestral hominoid condition than have the still arboreal orangutans.

EARLY PRIMATE EVOLUTION: AN OVERVIEW

Looking back over the first several million years of primate evolution, what we see is an initial diversification of strepsirhine and some haplorhine forms as they adapt to life in the trees. Despite their initial success, however, the strepsirhines tended to lose out to competition from rodents and the haplorhines. The exceptions were those forms that made it to Madagascar, or that adapted to nocturnal niches. Meanwhile, haplorhines diversified into a large variety of monkeylike apes, from which developed true monkeys, true apes, and (later) humans. Like the strepsirhines before them, the apes did well at first but eventually took a back seat in the forests to monkeys. This happened at least in part because monkeys, with shorter reproductive cycles, can out-reproduce apes. At the same time, forests continued to shrink, with some apes eventually adopting more terrestrial lifestyles. But unfortunately for them, by the time they did this, ground-dwelling niches for primates were already occupied by baboons and humans.

CHAPTER SUMMARY

Over time, evolutionary forces act to produce new species from old ones. A species is a population or a group of populations that is capable of interbreeding. The concept of species is relative rather than absolute; whether breeding actually takes place in the wild or not is more important than the academic question of whether it is technically feasible. Biologists define populations within species that are capable of interbreeding but do so to a limited extent as subspecies or races. Although species are reasonably discreet and stable units in nature, races are impermanent and subject to reamalgamation. Among humans, it is not possible to define races with any biological validity.

Isolating mechanisms serve to separate breeding populations, creating first divergent races and then (if isolation continues) divergent species. Isolating mechanisms can be geographical; physical, as in the differing anatomical structures of the Saint Bernard and Chihuahua; or social, such as in the caste system of India.

As evolution proceeds it may be divergent (branching) or linear. The latter occurs as selection over time favors some variants over others, causing a change in a population's average characteristics. Convergence occurs when two unrelated species come to resemble each other owing to functional similarities.

Evolution is not a ladder of progress leading in a predictable and determined way to ever more complex forms. Rather, it has produced, through a series of accidents, a diversity of enormously varied designs that subsequently have been restricted to a lesser number of still less-than-perfect forms.

The primates arose as part of a great adaptive radiation, a branching of mammalian forms that began more than 100 million years after the appearance of the first mammals. The reason for this late diversification was that most ecological niches that mammals have since occupied were either preempted by the reptiles or were nonexistent until the flowering plants became widespread beginning about 65 million years ago.

The first primates were arboreal insect eaters, and the characteristics of all primates developed as adaptations to this initial way of life. Although some primates no longer inhabit the trees, it is certain that those adaptations that evolved in response to life in the trees were (by chance) preadaptive to the niche now occupied by the hominines.

The earliest primates had developed by 60 million years ago in the Paleocene epoch and were small arboreal creatures. A diversity of lemurlike and tarsierlike forms were common in the Eocene across what is now North America and Eurasia. By the late Eocene, perhaps 45 million years ago, small primates combining lemurlike and tarsierlike features with those seen in monkeys and apes were on the scene. In the Miocene epoch, apes proliferated and spread over many parts of the Old World. Among them were apparent ancestors of the large apes and humans. These appeared by 16 million years ago and were widespread even as recently as 8 million years ago. Details of dentition suggest that hominines, as well as the African apes, arose from these earlier apes. At least some populations of these primates lived in parts of Africa where the right kind of selective pressures existed to transform a creature just like it into a primitive hominine. Other populations remained in the forests, developing into today's bonobo, chimpanzee, and gorilla.

CLASSIC READINGS

Ciochon, R. L., & Fleagle, J. (Eds.). (1987). *Primate evolution and human origins.* Hawthorne, NY: Aldine de Gruyter.

Articles in Part IV of this book summarize recent knowledge of early catarrhine evolution, while those in Part V examine Miocene apes and their possible significance respecting human origins. Editors' introductions to each section provide the necessary overall perspective on the issues discussed in the articles.

Conroy, G. C. (1997). *Reconstructing human origins: A modern synthesis.* New York: Norton.

Though it says little about earlier primates, this book has an excellent, up-to-date chapter (3) on the Miocene hominoids. *Proconsul* and the other apes are discussed in the context of climate changes in Africa and elsewhere in the Old World.

Jones, S., Martin, R., & Pilbeam, D. (Eds.). (1992). *The Cambridge encyclopedia of human evolution.* New York: Cambridge University Press.

This useful reference work has good sections on primate evolution, molecular studies, and the geological context for primate evolution.

CHAPTER 6

THE EARLIEST HOMININES

Ethiopian paleoanthropologist Haile Selassie sifting sediments in which he found the remains of a hominine that lived between 5.6 and 5.8 million years ago. Although early hominines walked bipedally, their behavior was otherwise more apelike than human.

CHAPTER PREVIEW

1

When and Where Did the First Hominines Appear, and What Were They Like?

The earliest indisputable hominine, *Australopithecus,* appeared in Africa by 4 million years ago, although there are earlier candidates that date as early as 6 million years ago. *Australopithecus,* remarkably human from the waist down, had become fully adapted for moving about on the ground on its hind legs in the distinctive human manner. But from the waist up, *Australopithecus* was still essentially apelike, with a brain suggesting intellectual abilities roughly comparable to those of a modern-day African ape.

2

What Is the Relation Between the Various Forms of *Australopithecus*?

The earliest forms of *Australopithecus* preserve a number of features indicative of a more apelike ancestor. By 2.5 million years ago, this form gave rise to one whose chewing apparatus had become larger and more massive while its brain size remained relatively stable. For a while, this late form coexisted with a less radically altered version of the earlier form.

Why Had *Australopithecus* Become a Bipedal Walker?

Early hominines venturing out in the open on the ground would have been vulnerable in two ways: to damaging buildup of heat in the brain from direct exposure to the sun and to the many predators that prowled on the ground. Bipedal locomotion solves the heat problem by reducing the exposure of the body to direct solar radiation and positioning the body for most effective heat loss through convection. It also enabled *Australopithecus* to scan the savanna for danger, carry food to places where it could be consumed in safety, transport offspring, and grab hold of objects with which to threaten predators.

For a long time, the fossil evidence of the early stages of human evolution was both sparse and tenuous. Not until 1924 did the first important fossil come to light, from a site in South Africa. This unusual fossil, consisting of a partial cranium and natural brain cast, was brought to the attention of Professor Raymond Dart of the University of Witwatersrand in Johannesburg, and it was unlike any creature he had ever seen before in South Africa. Recognizing in this unusual fossil an intriguing mixture of simian and human characteristics, anatomist Dart named his discovery *Australopithecus africanus,* or southern ape of Africa. Based on the position of the foramen magnum, the large hole in the skull where the spinal cord enters, Dart claimed that *Australopithecus* was probably a biped.

In the scientific world, Dart's find was not greeted with enthusiasm. The problem was that fossils had already been found at Piltdown, England, that seemed to show that early humans had large-sized brains but retained apelike jaws. But according to Dart, his fossil had an ape-sized brain with humanlike jaws. Not until the 1950s was the Piltdown discovery shown to be a deliberate hoax, by which time other ***Australopithecus*** fossils had come to light from various South African sites. Overall, these finds confirmed the correctness of Dart's original claim.

With the advent of World War II, the search for early hominine fossils came to a halt. Although the search was resumed after the war, it was not until the 1960s that the real rush of paleoanthropologists into the field got under way. Numerous international expeditions—including over 100 researchers from Belgium, Great Britain, Canada, France, Israel, Kenya, the Netherlands, South Africa, and the United States—swarmed over parts of East and South Africa, where they unearthed unprecedented amounts of fossil material. The process continues today, and with so many fossils, coming fast and furiously, our ideas of early human evolution have had to be constantly revised. Nevertheless, there is widespread agreement over the broad outline, even though debate, often heated, continues over details. What is clear is that the course of human evolution has not been a simple, steady "advance" in the direction of modern humanity. Rather, it proceeded in fits and starts, sometimes producing divergent lines of hominines. In this chapter we will discuss some of these, beginning with the best-known fossils of *Australopithecus.* We will then see how they relate to earlier forms.

Raymond Dart, who described the first fossil of *Australopithecus* and correctly diagnosed its bipedal mode of locomotion.

AUSTRALOPITHECUS

Since Dart's original find, hundreds of other fossils of *Australopithecus* have been found, first in South Africa and later in Tanzania, Malawi, Kenya, Ethiopia, and Chad (Figure 6.1). As they were discovered, many were given a number of different specific and generic names, but now usually all are considered to belong to the single genus *Australopithecus.* Most anthropologists recognize at least four species of the genus, if not as many as seven (Table 6.1 and Figure 6.2). For our purposes, we may discuss them in terms of two broad categories: **gracile** and **robust** *Australopithecus.* The latter are notable for having jaws that are massive (robust) relative to the size of the brain case. The gracile forms are slightly smaller on average and lack such robust jaws.

Australopithecus. The first well-known hominine; lived between 4.2 and 1 million years ago. Characterized by bipedal locomotion when on the ground, but with an apelike brain; includes at least five species: *afarensis, africanus, anamensis, boisei,* and *robustus.* • **Gracile Australopithecines.** Smaller, more lightly built members of the genus *Australopithecus.* • **Robust Australopithecines.** Slightly larger and more robust than gracile members of genus *Australopithecus,* with larger, more powerful jaws.

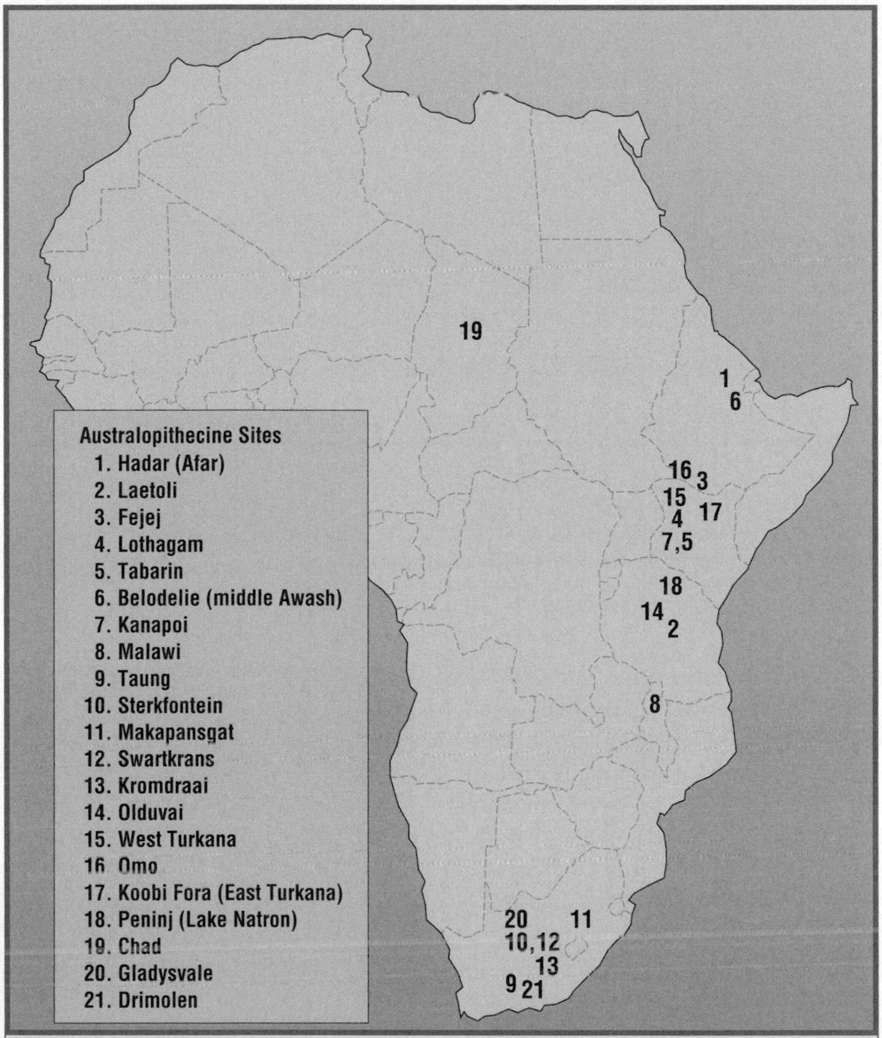

Australopithecine Sites
1. Hadar (Afar)
2. Laetoli
3. Fejej
4. Lothagam
5. Tabarin
6. Belodelie (middle Awash)
7. Kanapoi
8. Malawi
9. Taung
10. Sterkfontein
11. Makapansgat
12. Swartkrans
13. Kromdraai
14. Olduvai
15. West Turkana
16. Omo
17. Koobi Fora (East Turkana)
18. Peninj (Lake Natron)
19. Chad
20. Gladysvale
21. Drimolen

FIGURE 6.1

AUSTRALOPITHECINE FOSSILS HAVE BEEN FOUND IN SOUTH AFRICA, MALAWI, TANZANIA, KENYA, ETHIOPIA, AND CHAD.

Gracile Australopithecines

Included in this group are numerous fossils found beginning in the 1930s at Sterkfontein and Makapansgat in South Africa, in addition to Dart's original find from Taung (Figure 6.1). One unusually complete skeleton discovered in 1994 has been dated by paleomagnetism to about 3.5 million years ago. The other South African remains are difficult to date but seem to fit between 3 and 2.3 million years ago. Specimens from Ethiopia's Afar region, first discovered in 1970, are securely dated by potassium argon to between 3.9 and 2.9 million years ago. These include the famous "Lucy," represented by bones from almost all parts of a single skeleton, and "the First Family," a collection of bones from at least 13 individuals of both sexes, ranging in age from infancy to adulthood, who died together as a result of some single calamity. Also securely dated is material, close to 4 million years old, from Laetoli, in Tanzania, that is usually assigned to the same species as the Afar fossils. Thus, although there is overlap, the East African fossils seem for the most part to be earlier than those of South Africa.

Other pieces of gracile Australopithecines have been found at other East African sites that generally are

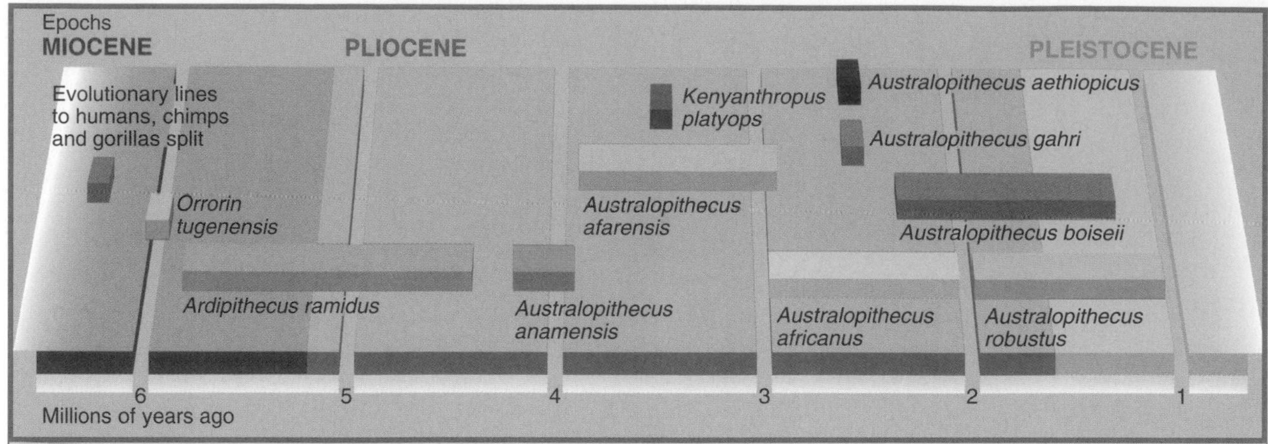

FIGURE 6.2

THE EARLIEST HOMININE FOSSILS AND THE SCIENTIFIC NAMES BY WHICH THEY HAVE BEEN KNOWN, ARRANGED ACCORDING TO WHEN THEY LIVED. *A. AETHIOPICUS, A. BOISEI,* AND *A. ROBUSTUS* ARE ALL ROBUST AUSTRALOPITHECINES; *A. AFARENSIS, A. AFRICANUS,* AND *A. ANAMENSIS* ARE GRACILE AUSTRALOPITHECINES. WHETHER ALL THE DIFFERENT SPECIES NAMES ARE WARRANTED IS HOTLY DEBATED.

2 million or more years old. The oldest so far found are some jaw and limb bones from Kenya that date to between 4.2 and 3.9 million years ago (see *Australopithecus anamensis* in Table 6.1 and Figure 6.2). All gracile species were erect, bipedal hominines about the size of modern pygmies (Figure 6.3), though far more powerfully built. Their stature ranged between 3.5 and 5 feet, and they are estimated to have weighed between 29 and 45 kilograms.[1]

TABLE 6.1 SPECIES OF *AUSTRALOPITHECUS**

Gracile Species	Location
A. afarensis	Ethiopia and Tanzania
A. africanus	South Africa
A. anamensis	Kenya
Robust Species	
A. aethiopicus	Kenya
A. boisei	Kenya
A. gahri	Ethiopia
A. robustus	South Africa

*Not all paleoanthropologists recognize as many as seven species; *A. aethiopicus,* for example, could be an early variety of *A. boisei.*

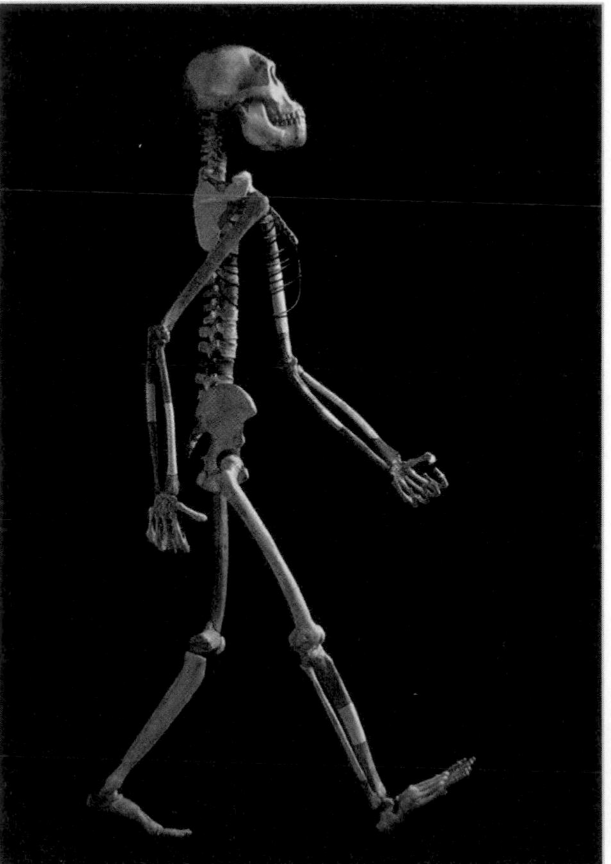

Sufficient parts of the skeleton of "Lucy" an Australopithecine that lived between 3.3 and 2.6 million years ago, survived to permit this reconstruction. Her hip and leg bones reveal that she walked about in a distinctively human manner.

[1]McHenry, H. M. (1992). Body size and proportions in early hominids. *American Journal of Physical Anthropology, 87,* 407.

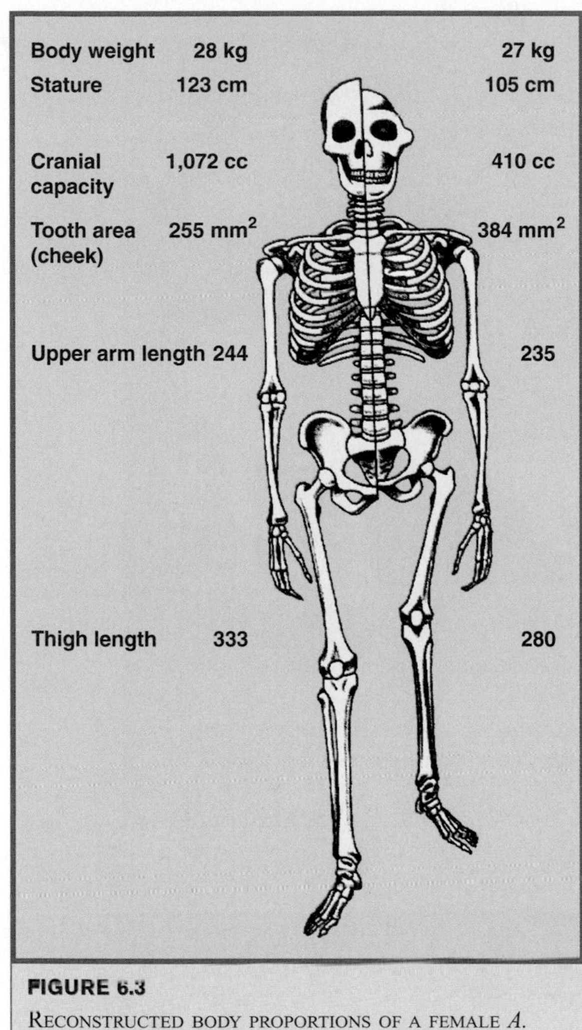

FIGURE 6.3

RECONSTRUCTED BODY PROPORTIONS OF A FEMALE *A. AFARENSIS* COMPARED TO A MODERN PYGMY.

Their physical appearance was unusual by our standards: They may be described as looking like an ape from the waist up and like a human from the waist down (Figure 6.4). Their cranium was relatively low, the forehead sloped backward, and the brow ridge that helps give apes such massive-looking foreheads was also present. The lower half of the face was chinless and accented by jaws that were quite large, relative to the size of the skull.

Much has been written about Australopithecine teeth. Speaking generally, the gracile forms possessed small incisors, short canines in line with adjacent teeth, and a rounded dental arch. The molars and premolars are larger in size but similar in form to modern human teeth (Figure 6.5). The molars are unevenly worn; the upper cheek teeth are worn from the inside, and the lower cheek teeth are worn from the outside. This indicates that both species chewed food in a hominine fashion, even though they were probably capable of 2 to 4 times the crushing force of modern human beings. Heavy wear indicates that the food chewed was high in tough plant fibers. There is usually no gap between the canines and the teeth next to them on the upper jaw, as there would be in apes. Further, the large mandible is very similar to that of the later hominine, *Homo erectus* (Chapter 8).

As one might expect, there are differences between the later South African fossils and the earlier ones from East Africa. The teeth of the Ethiopian specimens, but especially those from Laetoli, show numerous features reminiscent of some late Miocene apes that the later ones do not (see Figure 5.7). Generally, the incisors and canines are a bit larger in the earlier ones, there is sometimes a gap between upper lateral incisors and canines, the canines tend to project noticeably, the first lower premolars are less like molars and show more shearing wear, and the dental arch is less rounded. One jaw from Laetoli even shows a partial interlock of upper canines with lower canines and premolars. The oldest jaws of all, from Kenya (*A. anamensis*), are even more apelike with a shallow palate, large canines, and nearly parallel rows of cheek teeth.

In addition to differences between earlier and later gracile Australopithecines, there were also differences between the sexes. For one thing, males were about 1½ times the size of females. In this respect, they were somewhat like the Miocene apes, with sexual dimorphism greater than one sees in a modern chimpanzee but less than one sees in gorillas and orangs. Male canines, too, are significantly larger than those of females (Figure 6.6). There is as well a clear evolutionary trend for the first lower premolar of males to become more molarlike, through development of a second cusp. Those of females, by contrast, do not. By analogy with modern orangutans, such differences might be expected if male and female foraging patterns were not quite the same—for example, if females got more of their food from the trees, while males consumed large amounts of lower-quality food to be found on or near the ground. Consistent with this pattern, some features of the skeleton are somewhat better suited to climbing in females than in males.[2]

Although the brain is small and apelike and the general conformation of the skull seems nonhuman (even the semicircular canal, a part of the ear crucial to maintenance of balance, is apelike), the foramen magnum of these Australopithecines is placed forward and is downwardlooking, as it is in later bipedal hominines

[2]Simons, E. L. (1989). Human origins. *Science, 245,* 1,346.

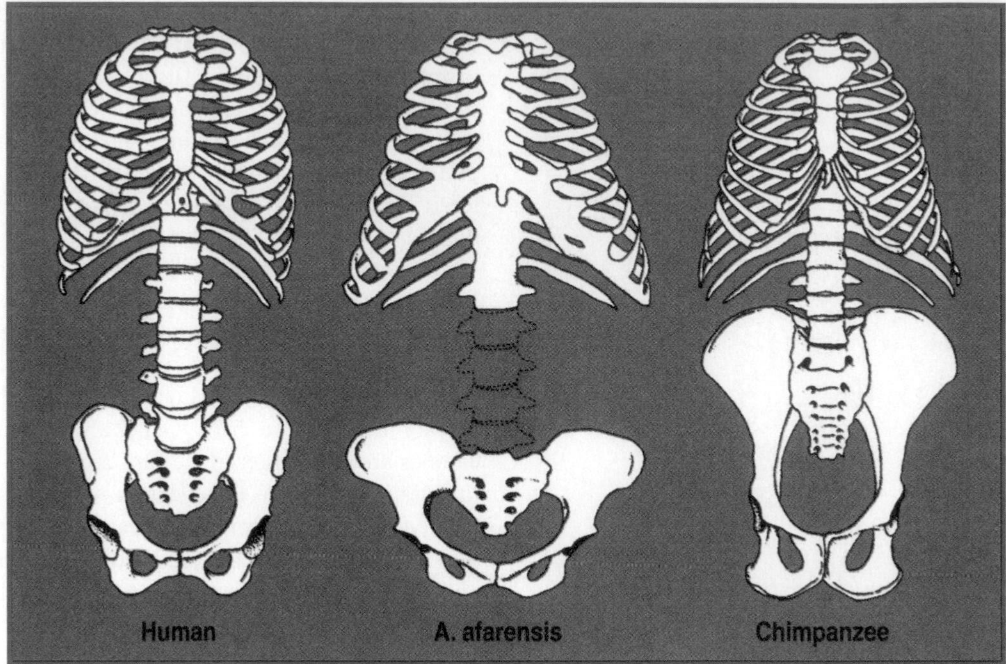

FIGURE 6.4
TRUNK SKELETONS OF MODERN HUMAN, GRACILE *AUSTRALOPITHECUS,* AND CHIMPANZEE, COMPARED. IN ITS PELVIS, THE AUSTRALOPITHECINE RESEMBLES THE MODERN HUMAN, BUT ITS RIB CAGE SHOWS THE PYRAMIDAL CONFIGURATION OF THE APE.

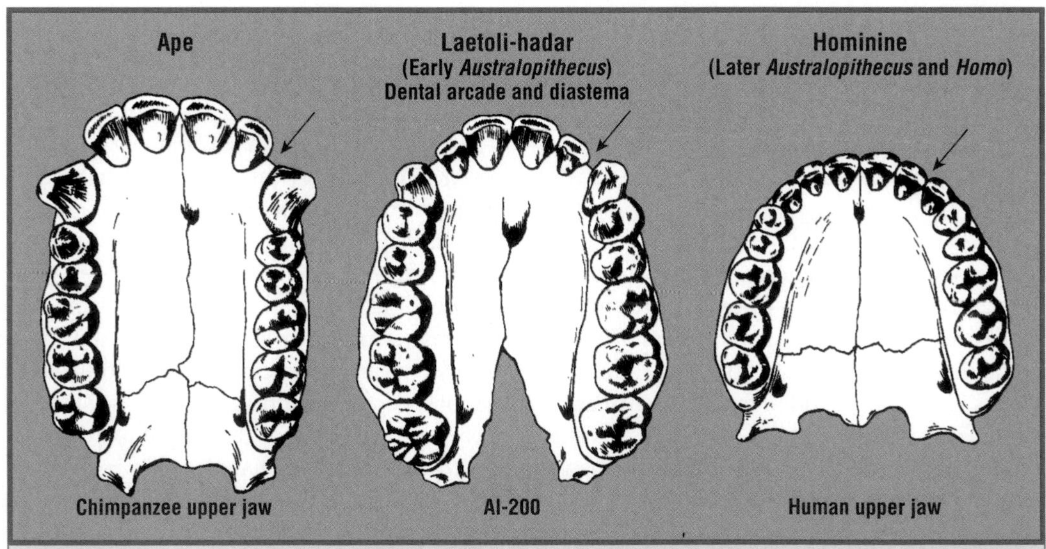

FIGURE 6.5
THE UPPER JAWS OF AN APE, *AUSTRALOPITHECUS,* AND MODERN HUMAN SHOW IMPORTANT DIFFERENCES IN THE DENTAL ARCH AND THE SPACING BETWEEN THE CANINES AND ADJOINING TEETH. ONLY IN THE EARLIEST AUSTRALOPITHECINES CAN A DIASTEMA (A LARGE GAP BETWEEN THE TEETH) BE SEEN.

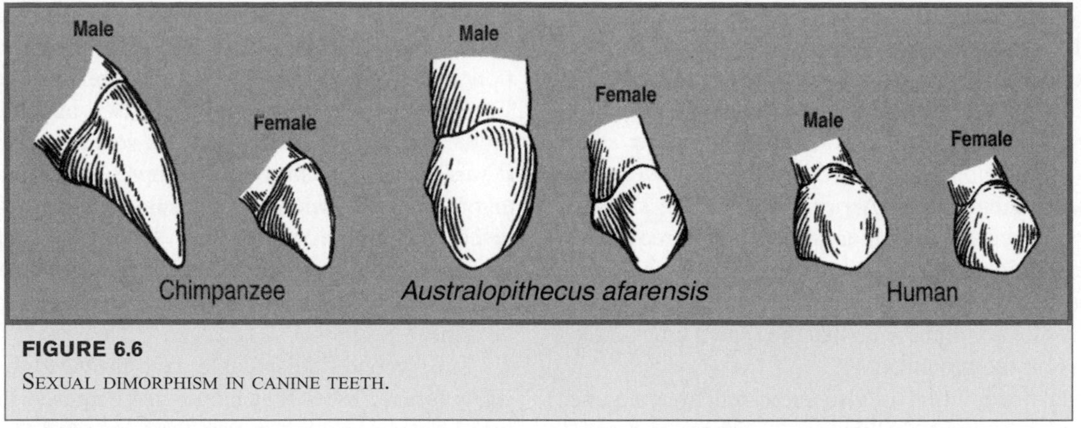

FIGURE 6.6
SEXUAL DIMORPHISM IN CANINE TEETH.

of the **genus *Homo*.** Cranial capacity, commonly used as an index of brain size, varied from 310 to 485 cubic centimeters in East African and 428 to 510 cubic centimeters in South African representatives,[3] roughly the size of a large chimpanzee brain. Although 3 times larger than the brain of any Miocene ape, it was only about a third the size of a modern human brain. Intelligence, however, is not indicated by absolute brain size alone but is roughly indicated by the ratio of brain to body size. Unfortunately, with such a wide range of adult weights it is not clear whether brain size was larger than a modern ape's relative to body size. Although some researchers think they see evidence for some expansion of the brain, others vigorously disagree. Moreover, the outside appearance of the brain, as revealed by casts of the insides of skulls, is more apelike than human, suggesting that cerebral reorganization toward a human condition had not yet occurred.[4] Consistent is the fact that the system for drainage of the blood from the cranium of the earlier Australopithecines is significantly different from that of the genus *Homo.* At the moment, the weight of the evidence favors mental capabilities for all gracile Australopithecines as being comparable to those of modern great apes.

[3]Grine, F. E. (1993). Australopithecine taxonomy and phylogeny: Historical background and recent interpretation. In R. L. Ciochon & J. G. Fleagle (Eds.), *The human evolution source book* (pp. 201–202). Englewood Cliffs, NJ: Prentice-Hall.

[4]Falk, D. (1989). Apelike endocast of "ape-man" Taung. *American Journal of Physical Anthropology, 80,* 339.

The fossil remains of gracile *Australopithecus* have provided anthropology with two indisputable facts. First, as early as 4 million years ago, this hominine was bipedal, walking erect. This is indicated first of all by the curvature of the spine, which is like that of humans rather than of apes. This served to place the center of gravity over, rather than in front of, the hip joint. In addition, a forearm bone from "Lucy," which is shorter than that of an ape, suggests that the upper limb was lighter and the center of gravity lower in the body than in apes. Still, the arms of Lucy and her kind are long compared to their

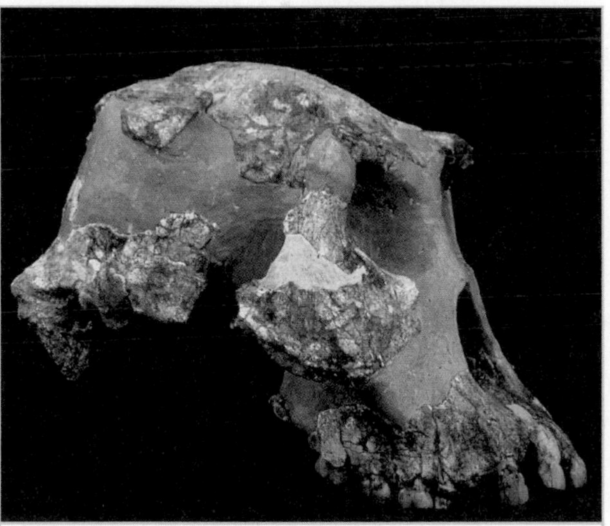

Shown here is the skull of a gracile *Australopithecine* from Ethiopia.

Genus *Homo.* Hominine genus characterized by expansion of brain, reduction of jaws, and reliance on cultural adaptation; includes at least three species: *habilis, erectus,* and *sapiens.*

relatively short legs. While these make for a shorter stride length than in *Homo,* they were well suited to vertical climbing. Moreover, the somewhat elevated position of the shoulder joint was more adapted to arboreal performance; fingers and toes show more curvature; and a partial foot skeleton between 3.5 and 3 million years old from Sterkfontein, South Africa (Figure 6.7), shows a long, flexible toe still useful for grabbing onto tree limbs.[5] The combination of traits indicate that the tree-climbing abilities of the gracile Australopithecines exceeded those of more recent hominines and that they spent time in trees as well as on the ground.

Bipedal locomotion is also indicated by a number of leg and hip remains (Figure 6.8). There is general agreement that even the relatively short legs are nonetheless much more human than apelike. In fact, a trait-by-trait comparison of individual bones shows that *Australopithecus* frequently falls within the range of modern *Homo,* even though the overall configuration is not exactly the same. But the most dramatic confirmation of *Australopithecus'* walking ability comes from Laetoli, where, nearly 4 million years ago, three individuals walked across newly fallen volcanic ash. Because it was damp, the ash took the impressions of their feet, and these were sealed beneath subsequent ash falls until discovered by Dr. Paul Abell in 1978. The shape of the footprints, the linear distance between the heels where they struck, and the amount of "toe off" are all quite human.

The second indisputable fact provided by gracile *Australopithecus* is that hominines acquired their erect bipedal position long before they acquired their highly enlarged brain. Not only is the latter more apelike than human in its size and structure, but also it is probable that *Australopithecus* did not have prolonged maturation as do modern humans; instead they grew up rapidly as do

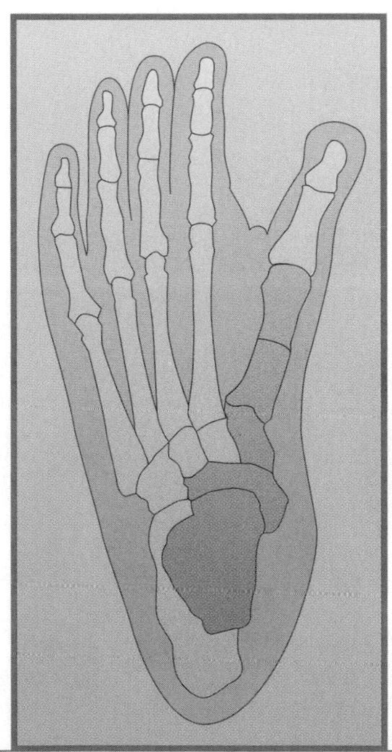

FIGURE 6.7

Drawing of the foot bones of a 3- to 3.5-million-year-old *Australopithecus* from Sterkfontein, South Africa, as they would have been in the complete foot. Note how long and flexible the first toe (at right) is.

These footprints from Laetoli, Tanzania, confirm that *Australopithecus* walked bipedally. They were made by three individuals, one of whom was careful to walk directly in the footsteps of one in front.

[5]Oliwenstein, L. (1995). New footsteps into walking debate. *Science, 269,* 476.

FIGURE 6.8

EXAMINATION OF THE UPPER HIP BONES AND LOWER LIMBS OF (FROM LEFT) *HOMO SAPIENS*, *AUSTRALOPITHECUS*, AND AN APE CAN BE USED TO DETERMINE MEANS OF LOCOMOTION. THE SIMILARITIES OF THE HUMAN AND AUSTRALOPITHECINE BONES ARE STRIKING AND ARE INDICATIVE OF BIPEDAL LOCOMOTION. (THE RECONSTRUCTION OF THE AUSTRALOPITHECINE LIMB IS BASED ON THE KNEE JOINT SHOWN IN THE PHOTOGRAPH.)

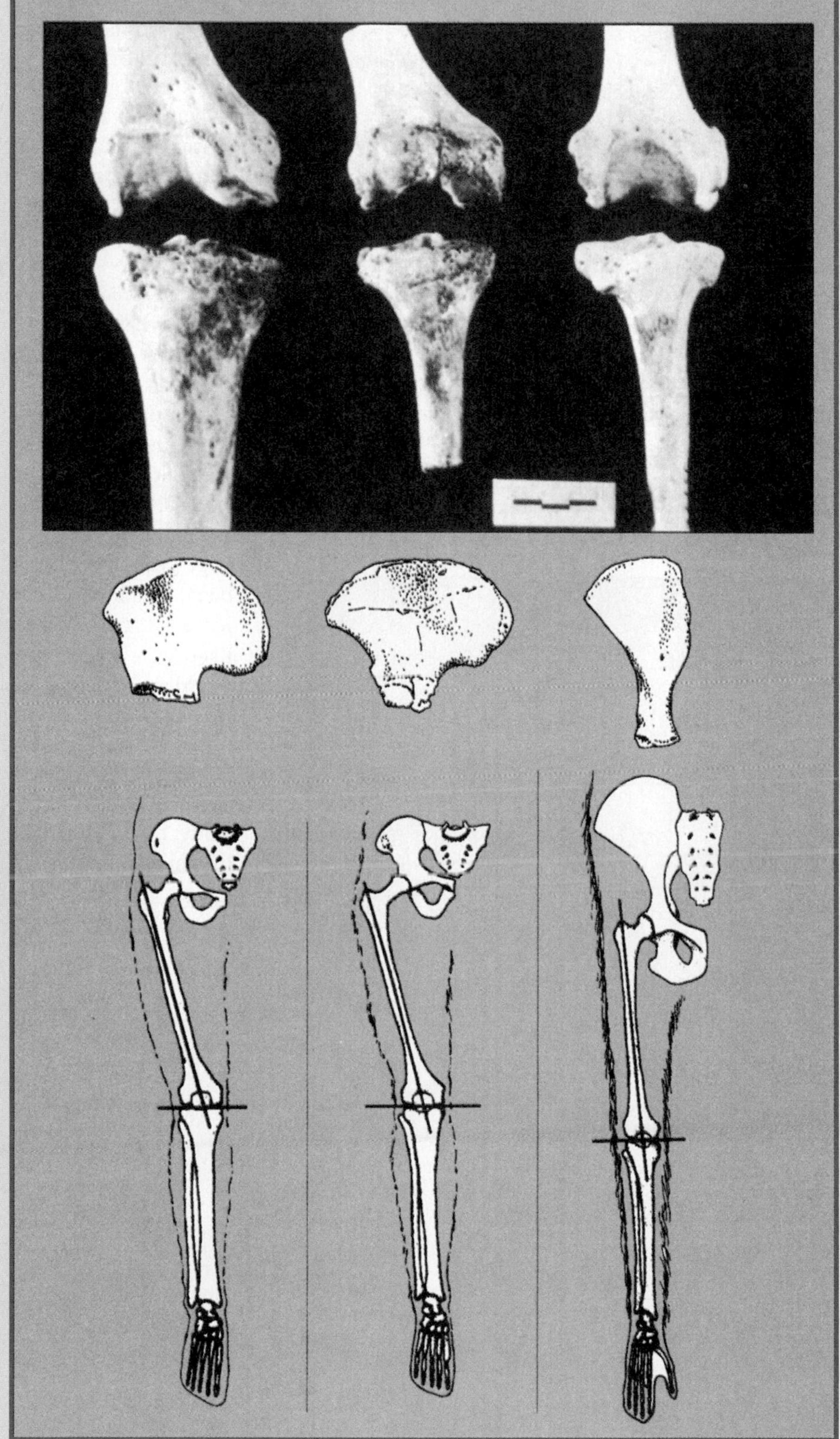

apes.[6] Thus, no matter how important bipedal locomotion may have been in setting the stage for the later expansion and elaboration of the human brain, it cannot by itself account for those developments.

Robust Australopithecines

The remains of robust Australopithecines were first found at Kromdraai and Swartkrans in South Africa by Robert Broom and John Robinson in 1948 in deposits that, unfortunately, cannot be securely dated. Current thinking puts them anywhere from 1.8 to 1.0 million years ago. Usually referred to as the species *A. robustus* (see Table 6.1 and Figure 6.2), it shared practically all of the traits listed for the species of gracile *Australopithecus* just discussed, especially the South African ones. Although of similar size, the bones of *robustus'* body were thick for their size, with prominent markings where their muscles attached. The skull of the robust form was thicker and larger than that of the graciles, with a slightly larger cranial capacity (around 530 cubic centimeters). Its skull also possessed a simianlike **sagittal crest** (more evident in males than in females) running from front to back along the top. This feature provides sufficient area on a relatively small braincase for attachment of the huge temporal muscles required to operate powerful jaws, such as robust *Australopithecus* possessed and gorillas have today; hence what we have here is an example of convergent evolution in gorillas and hominines.

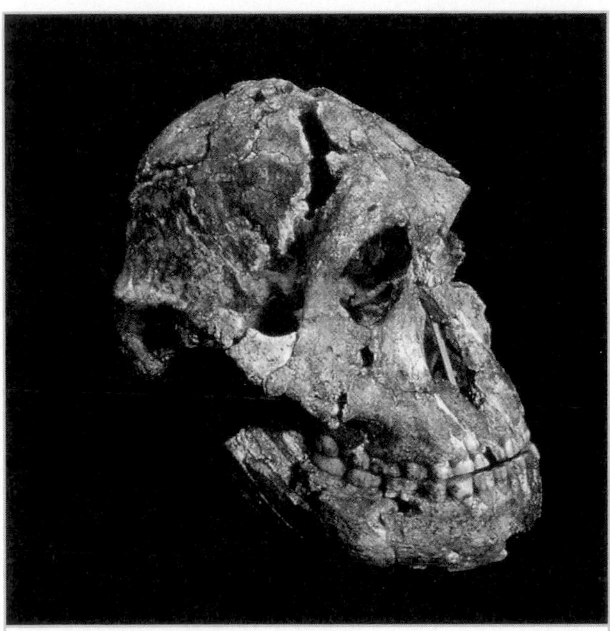

Sexual dimorphism was marked in the robust Australopithecines from South Africa. Although male skulls show a sagittal crest, female skulls like the one shown here do not.

The first robust Australopithecine to be found in East Africa was discovered by Mary Leakey in the summer of 1959, the centennial year of the publication of Darwin's *On the Origin of Species*. She found it in Olduvai Gorge, a fossil-rich area near Ngorongoro Crater, on the Serengeti Plain of Tanzania, East Africa. Olduvai is a huge gash in the earth, about 25 miles long and 300 feet deep, which cuts through Pleistocene and recent geological strata revealing close to 2 million years of the earth's history.

Mary Leakey's discovery was reconstructed by her husband, Louis, who gave it the name "*Zinjanthropus boisei*." At first, he thought this hominine seemed more humanlike than *Australopithecus* and extremely close to modern humans in evolutionary development. Further study, however, revealed that *Zinjanthropus*, the remains of which consisted of a skull and a few limb bones, was

Olduvai Gorge, Tanzania

[6]Tardieu, C. (1998). Short adolescence in early hominids: Infantile and adolescent growth of the human femur. *American Journal of Physical Anthropology, 107*, 173–174.

Sagittal crest. A crest running from front to back on the top of the skull in the midline.

LOUIS S. B. LEAKEY (1903–1972) MARY LEAKEY (1913–1996)

Few figures in the history of paleoanthropology discovered so many key fossils, received so much public acclaim, or stirred up as much controversy as Louis Leakey and his second wife, Mary Leakey. Born in Kenya of missionary parents, Louis received his early education from an English governess and subsequently was sent to England for a university education. He returned to Kenya in the 1920s to begin his career there.

It was in 1931 that Louis and his research assistant from England, Mary Nicol (whom he married in 1936), began working in their spare time at Olduvai Gorge in Tanzania, searching patiently and persistently for remains of early hominines. It seemed a good place to look, for there were numerous animal fossils, as well as crude stone tools lying scattered on the ground and eroding out of the walls of the gorge. Their patience and persistence were not rewarded until 1959, when Mary found the first hominine fossil. A year later, another skull was found, and Olduvai was on its way to being recognized as one of the most important sources of hominine fossils in all of Africa. While Louis reconstructed, described, and interpreted the fossil material, Mary made the definitive study of the Oldowan tools.

The Leakeys' important discoveries were not limited to those at Olduvai. In the early 1930s, they found the first fossils of Miocene apes in Africa at Rusinga Island in Lake Victoria. Also in the 1930s, Louis found a number of skulls at Kanjera, Kenya, that show a mixture of modern and more primitive features. In 1961, at Fort Ternan, Kenya, the Leakeys found the remains of a late Miocene ape with features that seemed appropriate for a hominine ancestor. After Louis' death, a member of an expedition led by Mary Leakey found the first footprints of *Australopithecus* at Laetoli, Tanzania.

In addition to their own work, Louis Leakey promoted a good deal of important work on the part of others. He made it possible for Jane Goodall to begin her landmark field studies of chimpanzees; later on, he was instrumental in setting up similar studies among gorillas (by Dian Fossey) and orangutans (by Birute Galdikas). Last but not least, the Leakey tradition has been continued by son Richard and his wife, Maeve.

Louis Leakey had a flamboyant personality and a way of making interpretations of fossil materials that frequently did not stand up well to careful scrutiny, but this did not stop him from publicly presenting his views as if they were the gospel truth. It was this aspect of the Leakeys' work that generated controversy. Nonetheless, the Leakeys accomplished and promoted more work that resulted in the accumulation of knowledge about human origins than anyone before them. Anthropology clearly owes them a great deal.

an East African representative of *Australopithecus*. Although similar in many ways to *A. robustus*, most commonly it is referred to as *Australopithecus boisei* (see Table 6.1 and Figure 6.2). Potassium-argon dating places this early hominine at about 1.75 million years old. Since the time of Mary Leakey's original find, numerous other fossils of this robust species have been found at Olduvai, as well as north and east of Lake Turkana in Ethiopia and Kenya. Although one (often referred to as the "Black Skull," sometimes as *A. aethiopicus*) is known to be as much as 2.5 million years old, some date to as recently as 1.3 million years ago.

The size of the teeth and certain cranial features of these East African fossils are reminiscent of the robust Australopithecines from South Africa. Molars and premolars are enormous, as are the mandible and palate. Even so, the anterior teeth (canines and incisors) are often crowded, owing to the room needed for the cheek teeth.

The heavy skull, more massive even than its robust South African relative's, has a sagittal crest and prominent brow ridges; cranial capacity ranges from about 500 to 530 cubic centimeters. Body size, too, is somewhat larger; whereas the robust South Africans are estimated to have weighed between 32 and 40 kilograms, the East Africans probably weighed from 34 to 49 kilograms.

Because the earliest robust skull from East Africa (2.5 million years), the so-called Black Skull from Kenya (*A. aethiopicus* in Table 6.1 and Figure 6.2), retains a number of primitive features shared with East African graciles, it is probable that it evolved from gracile ancestors, giving rise to the later robust East Africans. Whether the South African robusts represent a southern offshoot of the East African lineage or convergent evolution from a South African ancestor is so far not settled; arguments can be presented for both interpretations. In either case, what happened was that the later Australopithecines developed molars and premolars that are both absolutely and relatively larger than those of earlier gracile ones (though some tendency in this direction can be seen in the South African graciles). Larger teeth require more bone to support them, hence the prominent jaws of the robust Australopithecines. Finally, the larger jaws and the chewing of more food require more jaw musculature that attaches to the skull. The marked crests seen on skulls of the late Australopithecines provide for the attachment of such a musculature on a skull that has increased very little in size. In effect, robust Australopithecines had evolved into highly efficient chewing machines. Clearly, their immense cheek teeth and powerful chewing muscles bespeak the kind of heavy chewing a diet restricted to uncooked plant foods requires. Many anthropologists believe that, by becoming a specialized consumer of plant foods, the late Australopithecines avoided competing for the same niche with early *Homo,* with which they were contemporaries (see Figure 6.2). In the course of evolution, the **law of competitive exclusion** dictates that when two closely related species compete for the same niche, one will out-compete the other, bringing about the loser's extinction. That early *Homo* and late *Australopithecus* did not compete for the same niche is suggested by their coexistence for something like 1.5 million years.

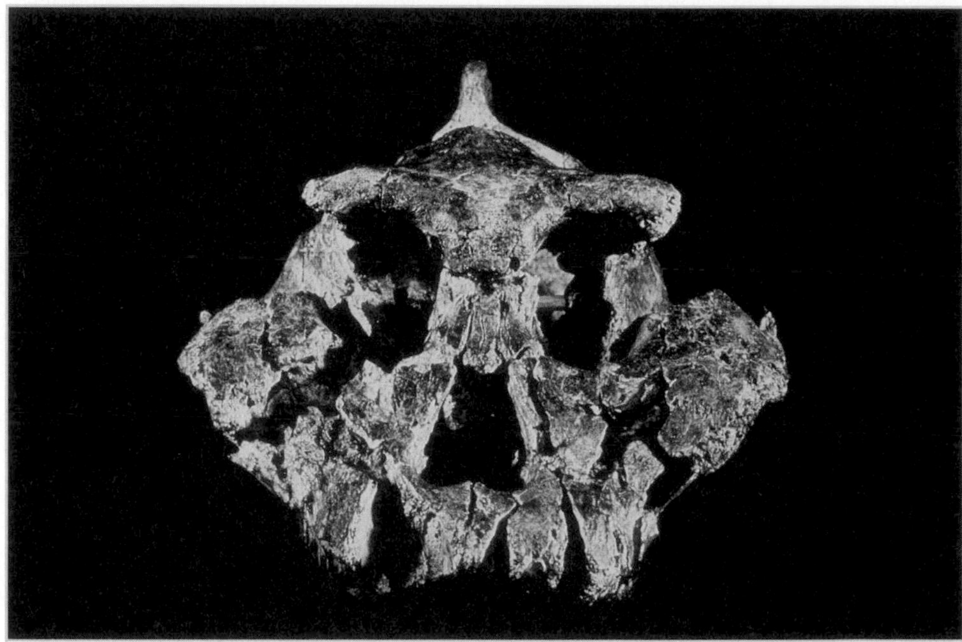

The so-called Black Skull, found at West Turkana, Kenya, is the earliest known robust *Australopithecus.* At 2.5 million years old, it appears ancestral to later robust Australopithecines from East Africa.

Law of competitive exclusion. When two closely related species compete for the same niche, one will out-compete the other, bringing about the latter's extinction.

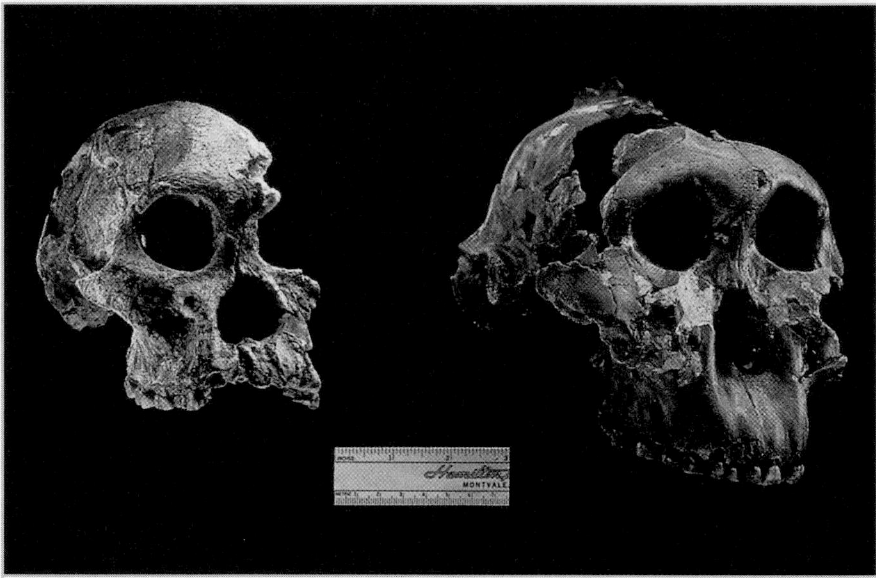

This photo contrasts gracile (left) and robust (right) Australopithecine skulls. Both were probably male; the gracile skull is from South Africa, the robust from East Africa.

AUSTRALOPITHECINE PREDECESSORS

Although the Australopithecines are now fairly well known, the same cannot be said about their immediate predecessors. As already noted, the earliest fossils of *Australopithecus* displayed a number of traits suggestive of an ancestry among the late Miocene apes. In addition to the features of the teeth, hands, and feet already noted, the earliest *Australopithecus* skulls are thick-boned and have a forward thrust to the face, large flaring cheek bones, and heavy cresting. But what about fossils that date between late Miocene apes on the one hand and early *Australopithecus* on the other?

Up until the 1990s, fossils from the crucial period of about 6 to 4 million years ago were so few and fragmentary that they provided scant information. Then in 1994, pieces of several individuals were discovered in 4.4 million-year-old deposits along Ethiopia's Awash River. Subsequent finds in the same region date between 5.8 and 5.2 million years. They are thought to represent early and later varieties of a single species, ***Ardipithecus ramidus*** (the name is fitting for an ultimate human ancestor as, in the local Afar language, *Ardi* means "floor" and *ramid* means "root"). Unfortunately, the task of freeing the actual fossils from their matrix has proved time-consuming and is not yet complete; hence a full description of this important material is not yet available.

Preliminary indications are that *Ardipithecus,* which was about the size of a modern chimpanzee, was more apelike than any Australopithecine. Although the large

These teeth and jaw fragment are from *Ardipithecus,* a hominine that lived between 5.8 and 4.4 million years ago in Ethiopia.

Ardipithecus ramidus. Probable early hominine; lived about 5.8 to 4.4 million years ago.

canines and lower first premolar resemble those of apes, chewing did not sharpen the upper canines as happens in apes. The thin-enameled molars are larger than in apes, and the diet included a greater variety of fibrous foods than typical of chimpanzees. Although the relative proportions of *Ardipithecus'* arms and legs appear chimplike, the foramen magnum is in the forward position consistent with bipedal locomotion. Consistent, too, is an upper arm bone that is not built to sustain the weight of a quadruped. Moreover, a toe bone is more like that of a human than an ape; unfortunately, it was not found in association with the other material. Still, it is likely that *Ardipithecus* walked bipedally when on the ground. But because it lived in a more forested environment than later hominines, it undoubtedly spent significant time in the trees.

Even earlier than *Ardipithecus* is the 6-million-year-old "Millennium Man," so called because its discovery was announced at the turn of the millennium (Figure 6.2). Its discoverers have dubbed it ***Orrorin tugenensis*** (*orrorin* means "original man" in the local dialect). Found in Kenya,[7] the remains include 13 pieces of lower jaw, teeth, and broken thigh bones. Because the head of the thigh bone is relatively large (though not as large as in modern humans), *Orrorin* may have walked bipedally, though this is by no means certain (the crucial knee joint, which would give this away, is missing). The molars, like those of *Australopithecus,* are thickly enameled but much smaller. At the moment, specialists are unsure what to make of this creature; some see it as the earliest human ancestor, whereas others doubt that it was even a hominine. It could even be on the line to chimps, or to an extinct side branch.

To further complicate matters, Maeve Leakey, daughter-in-law of Louis and Mary Leakey, announced the discovery in 1998 and 1999 of an almost complete cranium, parts of two upper jaws, and assorted teeth from a site in northern Kenya.[8] Contemporary with early East African *Australopithecus* (Figure 6.2), she sees this as a different species named ***Kenyanthropus platyops*** ("flat-faced man of Kenya"). Unlike contemporary *Australopithecus, Kenyanthropus* is said to have a small braincase and small molars set in a large, flat face. But

[7]Balter, M. (2001). Scientists spar over claims of earliest human ancestor. *Science, 291,* 1,460–1,461.

[8]Balter, M. (2001). Fossil tangles roots of human family tree. *Science, 291,* 2,289–2,291.

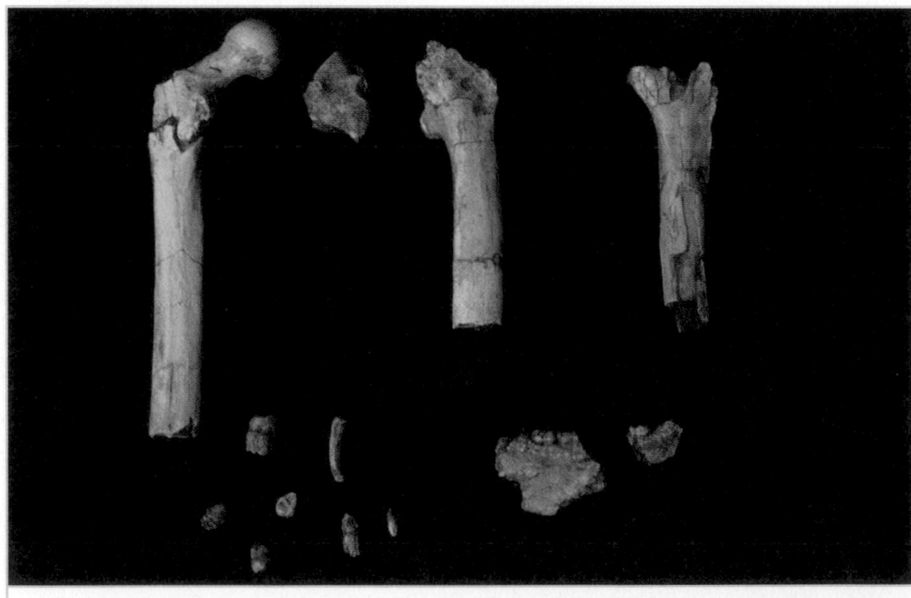

These 6-million-year-old bones are from a primate its discoverers claim to be the earliest hominine.

Orrorin tugenensis. Possible hominine; lived 6 million years ago. • ***Kenyanthropus platyops.*** Hominine contemporary with early Australopithecines; not certainly a separate species.

This 3- to 4-million-year-old skull could be an Australopithecine or a separate species its discoverer calls *Kenyanthropus platyops.*

again, there is controversy; Leakey sees her fossil as ancestral to the genus *Homo,* whereas others are not convinced it falls outside the range of variation for early gracile *Australopithecus.*

So what are we to make of these fossils? Until we have better samples, we will not know for sure. What seems likely on present evidence is that hominines evolved from late Miocene apes, becoming distinct by 5 million years ago. This move into a new primate niche probably saw the emergence of more than one bipedal model, but just how many is not known. Whether *Ardipithecus* or any other candidates for "human ancestor" discussed here really were ancestral to later humans, or side branches that went extinct, remains to be seen. The thin enamel of *Ardipithecus'* molars might suggest the latter. But out of this early hominine branching emerged *Australopithecus.*

Undoubtedly this evolution took place in fits and starts, rather than at a steady pace. For example, fragments of an *Australopithecus* skull 3.9 million years old are virtually identical to the corresponding parts of one 3 million years old. Evidently, once a viable bipedal adaptation was achieved, stabilizing selection took over, and there was little change for at least a million years. But 2.5 million years ago, change was again in the works, resulting in the branching out of new forms, including one or two robust species. But again, from about 2.3 million years until it became extinct around 1 million years ago, the East African robust species, at least, shows relatively little change.[9] Evidently, the pattern in early hominine evolution has been relatively short periods of marked change with diversification, separated by prolonged periods of relative stasis of surviving species.

ENVIRONMENT, DIET, AND AUSTRALOPITHECINE ORIGINS

Having described the fossil material, we may now consider *how* evolution transformed an early ape into *Australopithecus.* Because a major driving force in evolution is climatic change, we must take into account the effects of such changes in the late Miocene epoch that were profound enough to cause the temporary drying up of the Mediterranean Sea. On the land, tropical forests underwent reduction or, more commonly, broke up into mosaics where patches of forest were interspersed with savanna or other types of open country. The forebears of the hominine line lived in places where there was access to both trees and open country. With the breaking up of forests, these early ancestors of ours found themselves spending more and more time on the ground and had to adapt to this new, more open environment.

The most obvious problem facing these hominine ancestors in their new situation, other than getting from one patch of trees to another, was food getting. As the forest thinned or shrank, the traditional ape-type foods found in trees became less available to them, especially in seasons of reduced rainfall. Therefore, it became more and more necessary to forage on the ground for foods such as seeds, grasses, and roots. Associated with this change in diet is a change in their dentition; male canines (used by other primates as defensive weapons), not large to begin with, became as small as those of females (Figure 6.9), leaving both sexes relatively defenseless when down on the ground and easy targets for numerous carnivorous predators. That predators were a problem is revealed by the South African fossils, most of which are from individuals that were dropped into rock fissures by leopards or, in the case of Dart's original find, by an eagle.

Many investigators have argued that the hands of early hominines took over the weapon functions of the reduced canines, enabling them to threaten predators by using wooden objects as clubs and throwing stones. This set the

[9]Wood, B., Wood, C., & Konigsberg, L. (1994). *Paranthropus boisei:* An example of evolutionary stasis? *American Journal of Physical Anthropology, 95,* 134.

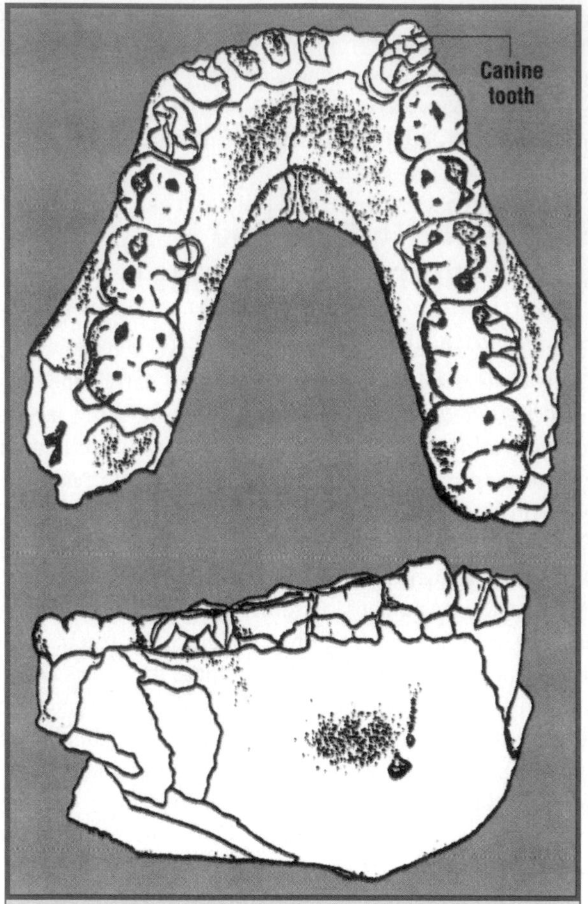

FIGURE 6.9
THIS LOWER JAW FROM LAETOLI, TANZANIA, IS BETWEEN 3.6 AND 3.8 MILLION YEARS OLD AND BELONGED TO *AUSTRALOPITHECUS.* ALTHOUGH ITS CANINE TOOTH PROJECTS A BIT BEYOND THE OTHER TEETH, IT IS A FAR CRY FROM THE PROJECTION SEEN IN MOST OTHER PRIMATES.

This bonobo figured out by himself how to make stone tools similar to those made by our ancestors 2.5 million years ago.

stage for the much later manufacture of more efficient weapons from bone, wood, and stone. Although the hands of the later Australopithecines were suitable for toolmaking, there is no evidence that any of them actually made stone tools. To illustrate the problem: Experiments with captive bonobos have shown that they are capable of making crude chipped stone tools, but they have never been known to do so under natural conditions. Thus, to be able to do something is not necessarily equivalent to doing it. In fact, the earliest known stone tools are at least 1.5 million years younger than the oldest undoubted fossils of *Australopithecus,* nor has anyone been able to establish a clear association between stone tools and later *Australopithecus* (as opposed to *Homo*). Considering the number of sites and fossils known (several hundred), this appears to be significant. However, *Australopithecus* certainly had no less intelligence and dexterity than do modern great apes, all of whom make use of tools when it is to their advantage to do so. Orangutans, bonobos, and chimpanzees have all been observed in the wild making and using simple tools such those described in Chapter 4. Gorillas seem not to do so in the wild only because they developed a diet of leaves and nettles that made tools pointless. Most likely, the ability to make and use simple tools is something that goes back to the last common ancestor of the Asian and African apes, before the appearance of hominines.

It is reasonable to suppose, then, that Australopithecines were tool users, though not toolmakers. Unfortunately, few tools that they used are likely to have survived for a million and more years, and any that did

Just as chimpanzees use wooden probes to fish for termites, so do orangutans use probes to extract termites, ants, or honey. Such tool use likely goes back to a time preceding the split between Asian and African hominoids, long before the appearance of hominines.

would be hard to recognize as such. Although we cannot be certain about this, in addition to clubs and missiles for defense, stout sticks may have been used to dig edible roots, and convenient stones may have been used (as some chimpanzees do) to crack open nuts. In fact, some animal bones from Australopithecine sites in South Africa show microscopic wear patterns suggesting their use to dig edible roots from the ground. We may also allow the possibility that, like chimpanzees, females may more often have used tools to get and process food than males, but the latter may more often have used tools as "weapons."[10]

Humans Stand on Their Own Two Feet

From an apelike carriage, the early hominines developed a fully erect posture; they became bipedal. Their late Miocene forebears seem to have been primates that combined quadrupedal climbing with at least some brachiation and, on the ground, were capable of assuming an upright stance, at least on occasion (optional, versus obligatory, bipedalism). On the basis of the few scrappy fossils that we have for the period of 2 or so million years between the last known African apes of the late Miocene and the first known *Australopithecus,* we may assume that those hominine ancestors that did exist during the period were evolving into fully erect bipeds.

We cannot understand the emergence of bipedalism as a means of locomotion without realizing its very serious drawbacks. For example, it makes an animal more visible to predators, exposes its soft underbelly, or gut, and interferes with the ability to change direction instantly while running. Nor does it make for particularly fast running; quadrupedal chimpanzees and baboons, for example, are 30 to 34 percent faster than we bipeds. For 100-meter distances, our best athletes today may attain speeds of 34–37 kilometers per hour, but the larger African carnivores can attain speeds up to 60–70 kilometers per hour. Other drawbacks include the frequent lower back problems, hernias, hemorrhoids, and other circulatory problems to which humans are prone by virtue of their bipedal specialization. Nor can we overlook the consequences of a serious leg or foot injury; a quadruped can do amazingly well on three legs, but a biped with only one functional leg is seriously hindered—an easy meal for some carnivore. Each of these drawbacks would have placed our early hominine ancestors at risk from

[10]Goodall, J. (1986). *The chimpanzees of Gombe: Patterns of behavior* (pp. 552, 564). Cambridge, MA: Belknap Press.

predators. And so, we must ask, what made bipedal locomotion worth paying such a high price? It is hard to imagine bipedalism becoming a viable adaptation in the absence of strong selective pressure in its favor.

One once-popular suggestion is that bipedal locomotion allowed males to gather food on the savanna and transport it back to females, who were restricted from doing so by the dependence of their offspring.[11] This explanation is unlikely, however, because female apes, not to mention women among food-foraging peoples, routinely combine infant care with foraging for food. Indeed, among food foragers, it is the women who commonly supply the bulk of the food eaten by both sexes. Moreover, the pair bonding (one male attached to one female) presumed by this model is not characteristic of terrestrial primates, nor of those displaying the degree of sexual dimorphism that was characteristic of *Australopithecus*. Nor is it really characteristic of *Homo sapiens;* in a substantial majority of recent human societies, including those in which people forage for their food, some form of polygamy—marriage to two or more people at the same time—is not only permitted, but preferred. And even in the supposedly monogamous United States, it is relatively common for an individual to marry two or more others (the only requirement is that he or she not be married to them at one and the same time).

Another suggestion, that bipedal locomotion arose as an adaptation for nonterritorial scavenging of meat,[12] is also unlikely. Although it is true that a biped is able to travel long distances without tiring, and that a daily supply of dead animal carcasses would have been available to hominines only if they were capable of ranging over vast areas, there is no evidence that hominines did much in the way of scavenging prior to about 2.5 million years ago. Furthermore, the heavy wear seen on Australopithecine teeth is indicative of a diet high in tough, fibrous plant foods. Thus, scavenging was likely an unforeseen byproduct of bipedal locomotion, rather than a cause of it.

Yet more recent is the suggestion that our ancestors stood up as a way to cope with heat stress out in the open.

[11] Lovejoy, C. O. (1981). The origin of man. *Science, 211,* 341–350.

[12] Lewin, R. (1987). Four legs good, two legs bad. *Science, 235,* 969–971.

Original Study

The Naked and the Bipedal[13]

Human beings are a peculiar species. Among other things, we're the only mostly hairless, consistently bipedal primate. Ever since Darwin, evolutionary biologists have wondered how we acquired these unique traits. Not long ago most would have argued that our upright stance evolved as part of a feedback loop that helped free our hands to use tools. But by the early 1980s a series of discoveries in Africa—including fossilized footprints and early hominine bones—made it clear that bipedalism preceded tool use by at least 2 million years. Lately a new theory has been gaining ground: It holds that our forebears reared up on two legs to escape the heat of the African savanna.

"The African savanna is one of the most thermally stressing habitats on the planet as far as large mammals are concerned," says Pete Wheeler, a physiologist at Liverpool John Moores University in England. For several years now Wheeler has been studying just how stressful such an environment would have been for the first primates to venture out of the shade of the forest. Among the apes, our ancestors are the only ones that managed the switch; no other ape today lives on the savanna full-time.

Most savanna animals, says Wheeler, cope with the heat by simply letting their body temperature rise during the day, rather than waste scarce water by sweating. (Some antelope allow their body temperature to climb above 110 degrees.) These animals have evolved elaborate ways of protecting the brain's delicate neural circuitry from overheating.

[13] Adapted from Folger, T. (1993). The naked and the bipedal. *Discover, 14*(11), 34–35.

Antelope, for instance, allow venous blood to cool in their large muzzles (the cooling results from water evaporation in the mucous lining), then run that cool blood by the arteries that supply the brain, thereby cooling it, too.

"But the interesting thing about humans and other primates," says Wheeler, "is that we lack the mechanisms other savanna animals have. The only way an ape wanting to colonize the savanna could protect its brain is by actually keeping the whole body cool. [See Figure 6.10.] We can't uncouple brain temperature from the rest of the body, the way an antelope does, so we've got to prevent any damaging elevations in body temperature. And of course the problem is even more acute for an ape, because in general, the larger and more complex the brain, the more easily it is damaged. So there were incredible selective pressures on early hominines favoring adaptations that would reduce thermal stress—pressures that may have favored bipedalism."

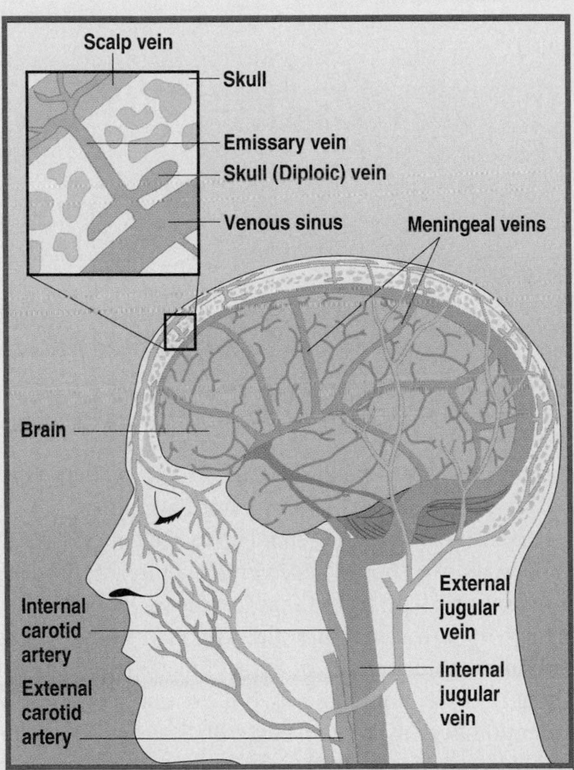

FIGURE 6.10

How the brain is cooled in modern humans: Blood from the face and scalp, instead of returning directly to the heart, may be shunted instead into the braincase, and then to the heart. Already cooled at the surface of the skin, it is able to carry away heat from the brain.

Just how would bipedalism have protected the brain from heat? And why did our ancestors become bipedal rather than evolve some other way to keep cool? Before moving out onto the savanna, says Wheeler, our forebears were preadapted to evolve into bipeds. Swinging from branch to branch in the trees, they had already evolved a body plan that could, under the right environmental pressures, be altered to accommodate an upright stance. Such a posture, says Wheeler, greatly reduces the amount of the body's surface area that is directly exposed to the intense midday sun. It thereby reduces the amount of heat the body absorbs.

Although this observation is not new, Wheeler has done the first careful measurements and calculations of the advantages such a stance would have offered the early hominines. His measurements were rather simple. He took a 1-foot-tall scale model of a hominine similar to Lucy—the 3-million year-old, chimp-size Australopithecine that is known from the structure of her pelvis and legs to have been at least a part-time biped. Wheeler mounted a camera on an overhead track and moved it in a semicircular arc above the model, mimicking the daily path of the sun. Every 5 degrees along that path—the equivalent of 20 minutes on a summer day—Wheeler stopped the camera and snapped a photograph of the model. He repeated this process with the model in a variety of postures, both quadrupedal and bipedal. To determine how much of the hominine's surface area would have been exposed to the sun's rays, Wheeler simply measured how much of the model's surface area was visible in the sun's-eye-view photos. He found that a quadrupedal stance would have exposed the hominine to about 60 percent more solar radiation than a bipedal one.

Not only does a biped expose less of its body to the sun, it also exposes more of its body to the cooler breezes a few feet above ground. The bottom line, says Wheeler, is that "on a typical savanna day, a knuckle-walking chimp-size hominine would

Original Study

require something in the region of five pints of water a day. Whereas simply by standing upright you cut that to something like three pints. In addition to that, you can also remain out in the open away from shade for longer, and at higher temperatures. So for an animal that was foraging for scattered resources in these habitats, bipedalism is really an excellent mode of locomotion."

Wheeler suspects that bipedalism also made possible two other uniquely human traits: our naked skin and large brains. "Our work suggests that you can't get a naked skin until you've become bipedal," he says.

"The problem has always been explaining why we don't see naked antelope or cheetahs. The answer appears to be that in those conditions in which animals are exposed to high radiation loads, the body hair acts as a shield. We always think of body hair as keeping heat in, but it also keeps heat out. If you take the fleece off a sheep and stand the animal out in the desert in the outback of Australia, the sheep will end up gaining more heat than you're helping it to dissipate. However, if you do that to a bipedal ape, because the exposure to solar radiation is so much less, it helps the ape lose more heat. Bipedalism, by reducing exposure to the sun, is tipping the balance and turning hair loss, which in quadrupeds would be a disadvantage, into an asset."

We bipeds maximize our heat loss, says Wheeler, by retaining a heat shield only on our most exposed surface—the top of our skull—and by exposing the rest of our body to cooling breezes. And bipedalism and naked skin together, he says, probably allowed us to evolve our oversize brains.

"The brain is one of the most metabolically active tissues in the body," he explains. "In the case of humans it accounts for something like 20 percent of total energy consumption. So you've got an organ producing a lot of heat that you've got to dump. Once we'd become bipedal and naked and achieved this ability to dump heat, that may have allowed the expansion of the brain that took place later in human evolution. It didn't cause it, but you can't have a large brain unless you can cool it."

The End

An objection to the above scenario might be that when bipedalism developed, savanna was not as extensive in Africa as it is today (Figure 6.11). In both East and South Africa, environments included both closed and open bush and woodlands. Moreover, fossil flora and fauna found with *Ardipithecus* are typical of a moist, closed, wooded habitat. Yet this may not tell us much, as we cannot rule out the possibility that *Ardipithecus* represents a side branch of hominine evolution that moved back into the forest from more open country. Alternatively, even today, similar floral and faunal elements can be found in the otherwise rather desolate region where *Ardipithecus* once lived,[14] and between 5 and 4 million years ago, the environments of eastern and southern Africa can best be described as a mosaic of both open and closed country. Although climbing ability would still have been useful to hominine ancestors, inevitably they would have had to spend significant amounts of time out in the open, away from trees.

Persuasive though the "stand up to keep cool" hypothesis may be, we should not overlook other life-or-death considerations. The fact is that the causes of bipedalism are likely to have been multiple. Although we may reject as culture-bound the idea of male "breadwinners" provisioning "stay-at-home moms," it is true that bipedal locomotion does make transport of bulky foods possible. A fully erect biped on the ground—whether male or female—has the ability to gather such foods for transport back to a tree or other place of safety for consumption; the animal does not have to remain out in the open, exposed and vulnerable, to do all of its eating. But food may not have been the only thing transported. As we saw in Chapter 4, primate infants must be able to cling to their mothers in order to be transported; because the mother is using her forelimbs in locomotion, to either walk or swing by, she can't very well carry her infant. Chimpanzee infants, for example, must cling for themselves to

[14]Conroy, G. C. (1997). *Reconstructing human origins: A modern synthesis* (p. 152). New York: Norton.

HIGHWAY 1

Learn about the most famous hoax in the history of science through a trip to this site about Piltdown Man. Learn who was thought to be behind this hoax and how it interfered with the acceptance of Australopithecines as human ancestors when they were discovered.
www.talkorigins.org/faqs/piltdown.html

HIGHWAY 2

Visit this site to use the interactive evolutionary tree and figure out the relationships among the ancestral hominine groups.
www.pbs.org/wgbh/aso/tryit/evolution/#

HIGHWAY 3

Visit the Institute of Human Origins Web site and discover more about Lucy and other fossil hominines, as well as the people who discovered them. Also visit the institute's educational site *www.becominghuman.org/*.
www.asu.edu/clas/iho/

HIGHWAY 4

A trip to National Geographic's Committee for Research and Exploration site follows the trail of paleoanthropologist Lee Berger as he searches for human origins in Botswana.
www.nationalgeographic.com/research/index.html

their mother, and even at the age of 4, they make long journeys on their mothers' backs. Injuries caused by falling from the mother are a significant cause of infant mortality. Thus, mothers able to carry their infants would have made a significant contribution to the survivorship of their offspring, and the ancestors of *Australopithecus* would have been capable of doing just this.

Besides making food transport possible, bipedalism could have facilitated the food quest in other ways. With their hands free and body upright, the animals could reach otherwise unobtainable food on thorn trees too flimsy and too spiny to climb. Furthermore, with both hands free, they could gather other small foods twice as fast. And in times of scarcity, their ability to travel far without tiring would help get them between widely distributed sources of food. Because the head is positioned higher than in a quadrupedal stance, sources of food and water are easier to spot from afar, thereby facilitating their location.

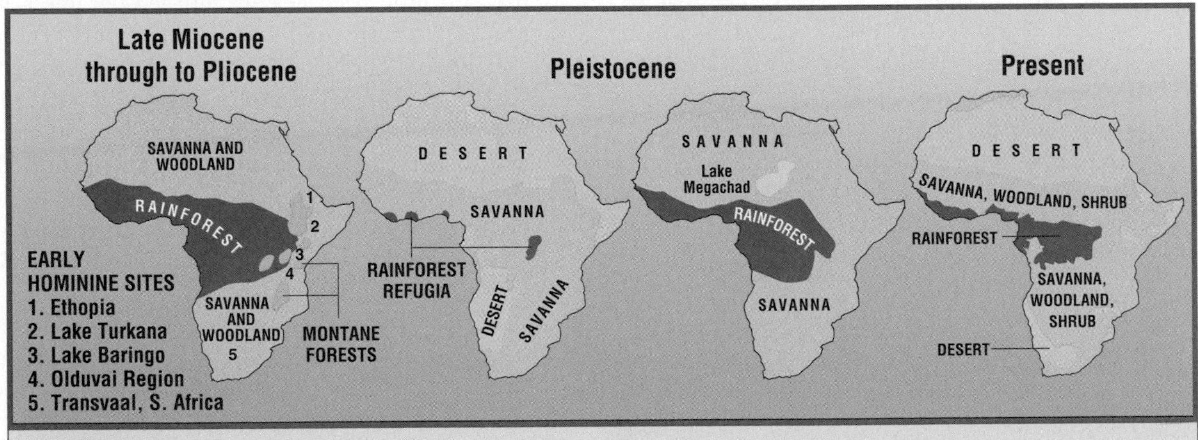

FIGURE 6.11

SINCE THE LATE MIOCENE, THE VEGETATION ZONES OF AFRICA HAVE CHANGED CONSIDERABLY.

Because apes do not normally walk bipedally, they cannot easily hold on to their infants when moving about. By holding on to their infants while walking bipedally, our own ancestors probably reduced the risk of fatal falls for their infants.

Still other advantages of bipedalism would have enhanced survivability. With their heads well up above the ground, bipeds are more likely to spot predators before they get too close for safety. Finally, if hominines did get caught away from a safe place of refuge by a predator, manipulative and dexterous hands freed from locomotion provided them with a means of protecting themselves by brandishing and throwing objects at their attackers. But, as the fate of the South African specimens attests, even this strategy was not foolproof.

CHAPTER SUMMARY

The course of hominine evolution, revealed by fossil finds, has not been a simple, steady advance in the direction of modern humans. One early hominine that appeared by 4 million years ago was *Australopithecus,* a genus that anthropologists divide into at least four and as many as seven species. All walked erect; the early gracile species were about the size of a modern human pygmy. They chewed food like humans, but their general appearance was that of an apelike human. The size and outward appearance of their brain suggest a degree of intelligence probably not greatly different from that of a modern bonobo, chimpanzee, or gorilla. Like most great apes, gracile Australopithecines may have made some use of objects as tools.

Robust Australopithecines shared practically all of the traits listed for the gracile species but were more highly specialized for the consumption of plant foods. The earliest Australopithecines exhibit traits reminiscent of some of the late Miocene apes of Africa. Fossils that fit time-wise between these apes and *Australopithecus* suggest the latter arose as part of an early diversification of bipeds.

During the late Miocene and Pliocene, the climate became markedly cooler and drier; many areas that had once been heavily forested became a mosaic of woodland and more open country. The ancestors of hominines likely found themselves spending more and more time on the ground; they had to adapt to this altered, more open environment, and food getting became a problem. As their diet changed, so did their dentition. On the whole, teeth became smaller, and many of the defensive functions once performed by the teeth seem to have been taken over by the hands.

Some of the Miocene apes are believed to have been part-time brachiators who may at times have walked erect. *Australopithecus* was a fully bipedal hominine with erect posture, and its immediate predecessors, such as *Ardipithecus,* may have also been.

Some disadvantages of bipedalism as a means of locomotion, besides anatomical and circulatory weaknesses, are that it makes an animal more visible to predators, exposes its "soft underbelly," slows the animal down, interferes with its ability to change direction instantly while walking or running, and leaves nothing to fall back on when one leg is injured. Its advantages are that it provides hominines with a means of keeping their brains from overheating, of protecting themselves and holding objects while running, of traveling long distances without tiring, and of seeing farther.

CLASSIC READINGS

Ciochon, R. L., & Fleagle, J. G. (Eds.). (1993). *The human evolution source book.* Englewood Cliffs, NJ: Prentice-Hall.

In the first four parts of this book, the editors have assembled articles to present data and survey different theories on the evolution and diversification of the earliest hominines. A short editors' introduction to each section places the various articles in context.

Conroy, G. C. (1997). *Reconstructing human origins: A modern synthesis.* New York: Norton.

This text devotes two chapters to *Australopithecus* that are reasonably up-to-date and are comprehensive in their description of the various fossils, discussion of environmental considerations, and coverage of competing interpretations of the material.

Johanson, D., & Edey, M. (1981). *Lucy: The beginnings of humankind.* New York: Simon & Schuster.

This book tells the story of the discovery of Lucy and the other fossils of *Australopithecus afarensis,* and how they have enhanced our understanding of the early stages of human evolution. It reads like a first-rate detective story, while giving an excellent description of Australopithecines and an accurate account of how paleoanthropologists analyze their fossils.

PART III

EVOLUTION OF THE GENUS *HOMO* AND THE DEVELOPMENT OF EARLY HUMAN CULTURE

INTRODUCTION

By 2.5 million years ago, long after the line of human evolution had branched off from that of apes, a new kind of evolutionary process was set in motion. Early hominines began to increase their manipulation of the physical world, inventing new solutions to the problems of human existence. With the passage of time, they came to intensify their reliance on cultural, rather than biological, adaptation as a more rapid and effective way of adjusting to environmental pressures. Even less than apes did they have to depend on physical attributes to survive. Moreover, as culture became more efficient at solving the problems of existence, human populations began to spread geographically, inhabiting new and even harsh environments, all of which is illustrated by human habitations of the cold regions of the world. Instead of being dependent on the evolution of humans capable of growing heavy coats of fur, as do other mammals that live in such regions, humans devised forms of

clothing and shelter that, coupled with the use of fire, enabled them to overcome the cold. Moreover, once this kind of cold adaptation was accomplished, it could readily be changed when circumstances required it. The fact is that cultural equipment and techniques can change rapidly, whereas biological change can be accomplished only over many generations.

The next four chapters discuss how evolving hominines developed the ability to invent their own solutions to the problems of existence and how this ingenuity gained primacy over biological change as the human mechanism for adapting to the environment. We begin, in Chapter 7, with the appearance of the genus *Homo.* Although the earliest members of this genus had far smaller brains than ours, they were significantly larger than those of *Australopithecus.* Their appearance is associated with a new way of surviving: Instead of foraging, as do most primates, on a more or less individual basis for vegetables and fruits, supplemented by eggs, grubs, lizards, and similar sources of animal protein, early *Homo* invented stone tools with which they could butcher the carcasses of larger animals than even chimpanzees can deal with. Thus, they were able to increase significantly the amount of meat in their diet. This made possible a degree of economic specialization; males scavenged for meat, and females gathered a wide variety of other wild foods. It also made possible new patterns of social interaction: Females and males began sharing the results of their food-getting activities on a regular basis.

Over the next nearly 2.5 million years—a period known as the Paleolithic, or Old Stone Age—the evolving genus *Homo* relied increasingly on expanded mental abilities for survival, as we shall see in Chapters 8, 9, and 10. In the process, hunting came to replace scavenging as the main means by which meat was procured, and other improvements of this food-foraging way of life took place. As a consequence, the human species, essentially a tropical one, was able to free itself from its tropical habitat and, through invention, adapt itself to colder climates. By 200,000 years ago, humans had acquired essentially modern brains. Shortly thereafter, they achieved the ability to survive under true Arctic conditions. To invent ways of surviving under such forbidding and difficult conditions ranks as no less an achievement than sending the first man to the moon. ■

CHAPTER 7

HOMO HABILIS AND CULTURAL ORIGINS

Though first found at Olduvai Gorge in Tanzania, some of the best finds of *Homo habilis* have come from Koobi Fora in Kenya (above). *Homo habilis,* the earliest maker of stone tools, was a scavenger of dead carcasses for meat and the first hominine to show evidence of significant increase in brain size beyond what is seen in apes.

CHAPTER PREVIEW

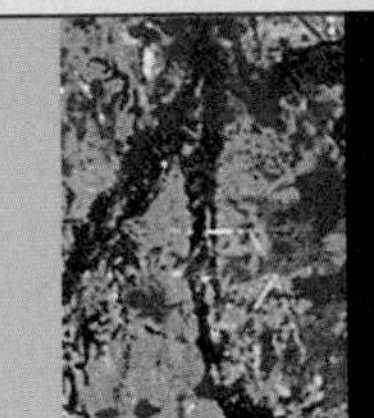

1

When, Where, and How Did Human Culture Develop?

Human culture appears to have developed in Africa, beyond what one sees in modern apes, as some populations of early hominines began making stone tools with which they could butcher animals for their meat. Actually, the earliest stone tools and evidence of significant meat eating date to about 2.6 million years ago, just prior to the appearance of the genus *Homo.*

2

When Did Reorganization and Expansion of the Human Brain Begin?

Reorganization and expansion of the human brain did not begin until at least 1.5 million years after the development of bipedal locomotion. It began in conjunction with scavenging and the making of stone tools. This marks the appearance of the genus *Homo,* an evolutionary offshoot of *Australopithecus.* The two forms coexisted for a million years or so, during the course of which *Australopithecus* relied on a vegetarian diet while developing a massive chewing apparatus. In contrast, *Homo* ate more meat and became brainier.

3

Why Did the Eating of More Meat Lead to Improved Brains?

The making of stone tools—needed to skin, butcher, and crack open the bones of animals for marrow—put a premium on improved eye-hand coordination and precision grip, both of which selected for more complex brains. Increased meat eating, too, led to changes in the subsistence activities of both females and males. These changes required both sexes to do more in the way of thinking and planning, which again selected for larger, more complex brains.

In 1931 when Louis and Mary Leakey began work at Olduvai Gorge, they did so because of the presence of crude stone tools in deposits dating back to very early in the Pleistocene epoch, which began almost 2 million years ago. When they found the bones of the robust *Australopithecus boisei* in 1959, in association with some of these tools, they thought they had found the remains of one of the toolmakers. They later changed their minds, however, and suggested that these tools were not produced by *A. boisei,* nor were the bones of the birds, reptiles, antelopes, and pigs found with the remains of *A. boisei* the remains of the latter's dinner. Instead, *A. boisei* may have been a victim of a rather different contemporary who created the tools, ate the animals, and possibly had the unfortunate *A. boisei* for dessert. That contemporary was called by the Leakeys ***Homo habilis*** ("handy man").

Of course we don't really know that the Leakey's *boisei* met its end in this way, but we do know that cut marks from a stone tool are present on a 2.4-million-year-old hominine from South Africa.[1] This was done, presumably, to remove the mandible, but for what purpose we do not know. Although it might have involved cannibalism, other possibilities include curation or just plain mutilation. In any event, it does lend credibility to the idea of *boisei* on occasion being dismembered by *H. habilis.*

EARLY REPRESENTATIVES OF THE GENUS *HOMO*

The Leakeys discovered the remains of this second hominine in 1960, only a few months after their earlier discovery, just a few feet below it. The remains, which were those of more than one individual, consisted of a few cranial bones, a lower jaw, a clavicle, some finger bones (Figure 7.1), and the nearly complete left foot of an adult (Figure 7.2). These fossils date from about 1.8 million years ago and represent a hominine with a cranial capacity in the 650 to 690 cubic centimeter range, a skull that lacks noticeable bony crests, and almost modern-looking hands and feet. Subsequent work at Olduvai has unearthed not only more skull fragments but other parts of the skeleton of *Homo habilis* as well. These indicated that, aside from their more modern-looking heads, hands, and feet, the skeleton of this hominine from the neck down does not differ greatly from that of the gracile Australopithecines. Overall size was about the same, as was the degree of sexual dimorphism (Figure 7.3), and they were equally adept at climbing trees.[2] Moreover, dental evidence suggests that, as with *A. afarensis* and *africanus,* the period of infancy and childhood in *H. habilis* was not prolonged, as it is in modern humans, but was more in line with apes.[3]

Since the late 1960s, fossils of the genus *Homo* that are essentially contemporaneous with those from Olduvai have been found elsewhere in Africa—in South Africa, in Kenya near Lake Baringo as well as east of Lake Turkana at Koobi Fora, and in Ethiopia just north of Lake Turkana. One of the best of these, known as KNM ER 1470, was discovered by the Leakeys' son Richard. (The letters *KNM* stand for Kenya National Museum; the *ER,* for East Rudolf, the former name for Lake Turkana.) The deposits in which it was found are about 1.9 million years old; these deposits, like those at Olduvai, also contain crude stone tools. The KNM ER 1470 skull is more modern in appearance than any *Australopithecus* skull and has a cranial capacity of 752 cubic centimeters. Furthermore, the inside of the skull shows a pattern in the left cerebral hemisphere that, in living people, is associated with a speech area.[4] This shape is in keeping with indications of brain asymmetry more like that of humans than apes, as is evident from wear patterns on tools used by early *Homo* that reveal that these hominines were predominately right-handed. In humans, the speech organs and the right hand are controlled by adjacent areas in the left cerebral hemisphere. Although this doesn't prove that early *Homo* had a spoken language, it does show that its brain was not only larger than that of *Australopithecus* but was reorganized along more human lines.

Although the 1470 skull and other early *Homo* fossils from localities other than Olduvai are frequently assigned to the same species, *H. habilis,* there are those who argue that a second distinct species (*H. Rudolfensis*) may be present. A rigorous evaluation of the arguments in favor of the two species hypothesis, however, by an independent investigator, failed to sustain them. The conclusion, then, is that "the data, at this point, are actually quite consistent

[1]White, T. D., & Toth, N. (2000). Cutmarks on a Plio-Pleistocene hominid from Sterkfontein, South Africa. *American Journal of Physical Anthropology, 111,* 579–584.

[2]Wood, B., & Collard, M. (1999). The human genus. *Science, 284,* 68.

[3]Ibid., p. 69.

[4]Ambrose, S. H. (2001). Paleolithic technology and human evolution. *Science, 291,* 1,750.

Homo habilis. Earliest representative of the genus *Homo;* lived between 2.4 and 1.6 million years ago. Characterized by expansion and reorganization of the brain, compared to *Australopithecus.*

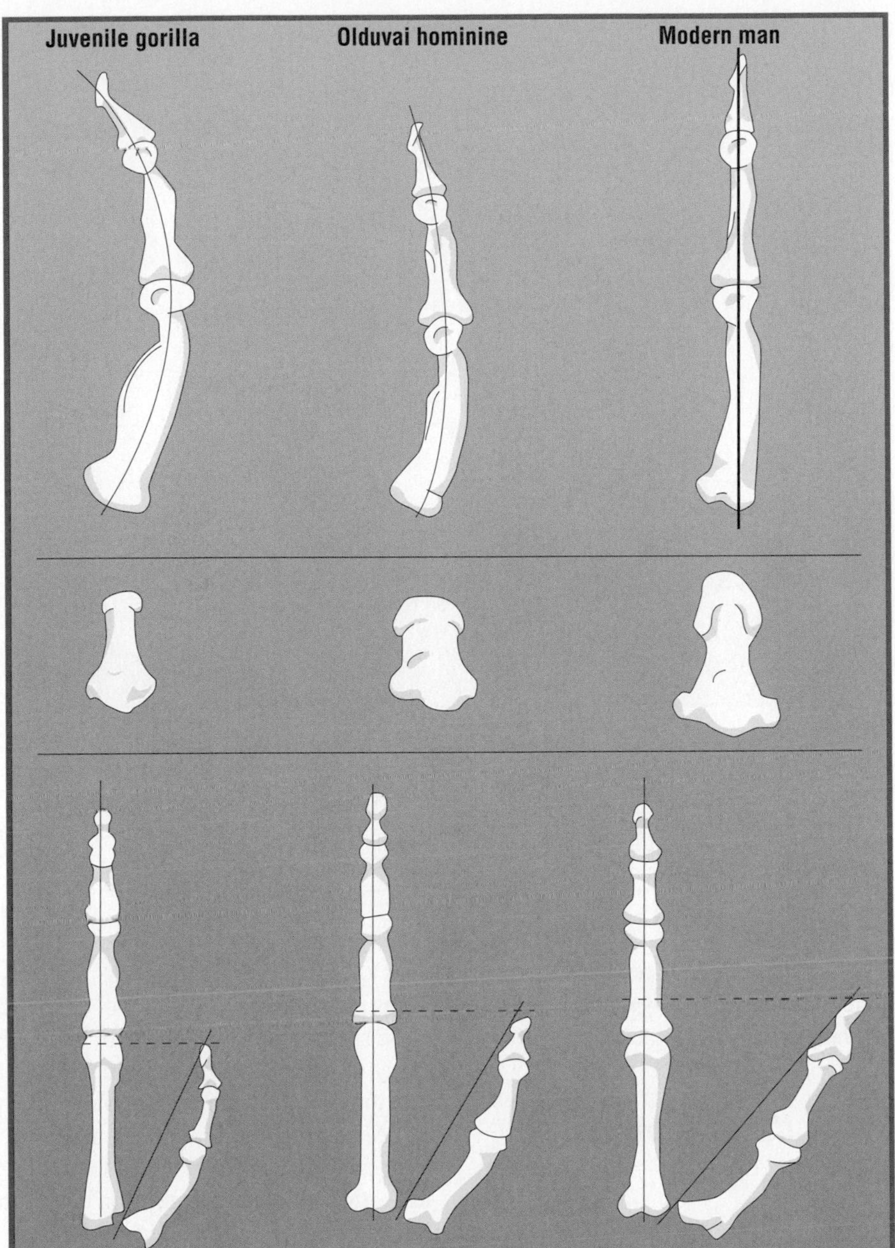

FIGURE 7.1

A comparison of hand bones of a juvenile gorilla, *Homo habilis* from Olduvai, and a modern human highlights important differences in the structure of fingers and thumbs. In the top row are fingers and in the second row are terminal thumb bones. Although terminal finger bones are more human, lower finger bones are more curved and powerful. The bottom row compares thumb length and angle relative to the index finger.

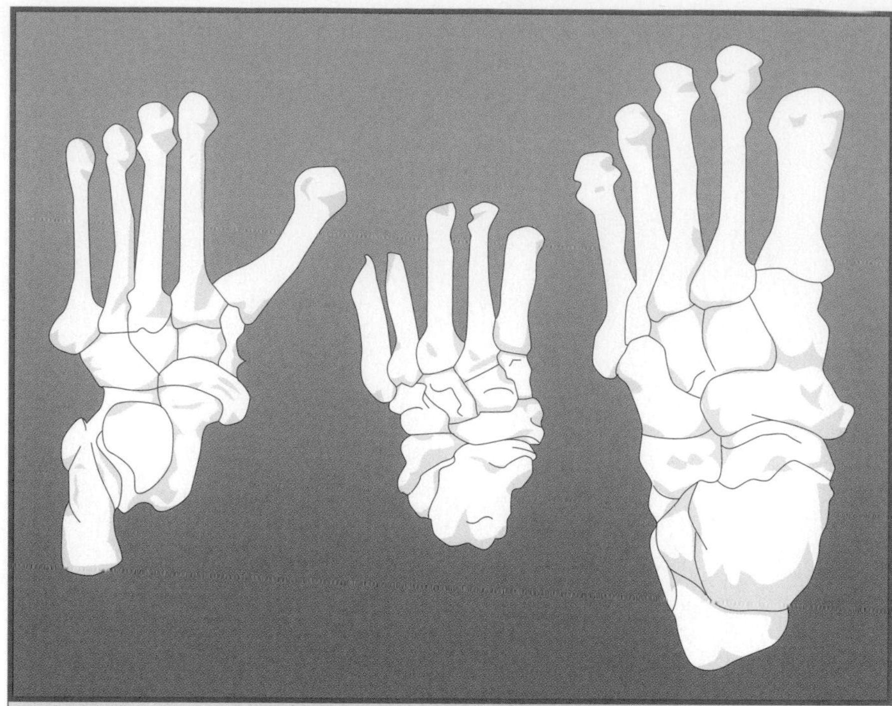

FIGURE 7.2

A PARTIAL FOOT SKELETON OF *HOMO HABILIS* (CENTER) IS COMPARED WITH THE SAME BONES OF A CHIMPANZEE (LEFT) AND MODERN HUMAN (RIGHT). NOTE HOW *HABILIS'* BONE AT THE BASE OF THE GREAT TOE IS IN LINE WITH THE OTHERS, AS IN MODERN HUMANS, MAKING FOR EFFECTIVE WALKING BUT POOR GRASPING.

in showing that the *H. habilis* sample is neither too great in degree nor too different in pattern of variation to warrant rejection of the single species hypothesis."[5]

Relations Between *Homo habilis* and *Australopithecus*

A consideration of brain size relative to body size clearly indicates that *Homo habilis* had undergone enlargement of the brain far in excess of values predicted on the basis of body size alone. This means that there was a marked increase in information-processing capacity over that of the Australopithecines. Because larger brains generate more heat, it is not surprising to find that *habilis'* brain was provided with a heat exchanger of a sort not seen in *Australopithecus,* save to a very rudimentary degree in the late gracile forms.[6] This heat-exchange system consists of small openings in the braincase through which veins pass allowing cooled blood from the face and scalp to be shunted to the brain, from which the blood can then carry off excess heat (see Figure 6.10). In this way, damage to the brain from excessive heat is prevented.

Although these hominines had teeth that are large by modern standards—or even by those of a half-million years ago—they are smaller in relation to the size of the skull than those of any Australopithecine. Because major brain-size increase and tooth-size reduction are important trends in the evolution of the genus *Homo,* but not of *Australopithecus,* it looks as if ER 1470 and similar hominines were becoming somewhat more human. Consistent with this are the indications that the brain of KNM ER 1470 was less apelike and more human in structure. It is probably no accident that the earliest fossils to exhibit these features appear by 2.4 million years ago (the age of the Baringo fossil), soon after the earliest evidence (to be discussed shortly) for stone toolmaking and increased consumption of meat.

[5]Miller, J. M. A. (2000). Craniofacial variation in *Homo habilis:* An analysis of the evidence for multiple species. *American Journal of Physical Anthropology, 112,* 122.

[6]Falk, D. (1993). A good brain is hard to cool. *Natural History, 102*(8), 65.

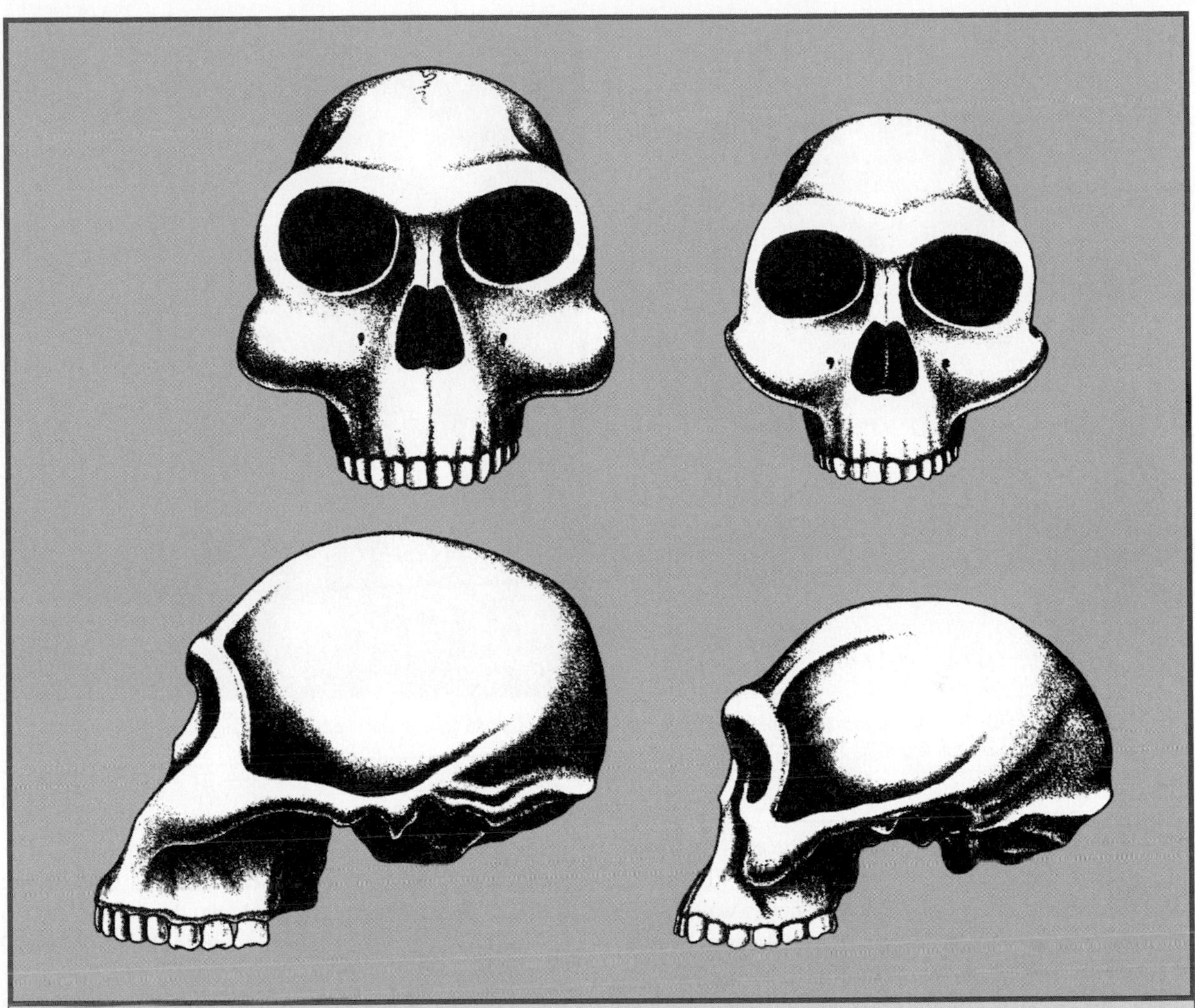

FIGURE 7.3

As these two skulls from Koobi Fora demonstrate, that of female *H. habilis* (right) was markedly smaller than that of the male (left).

As noted earlier, the Australopithecine diet seems to have consisted largely of plant foods, although the gracile species may have consumed limited amounts of animal protein as well. The later robust Australopithecines from East and South Africa evolved into more specialized "grinding machines" as their jaws became markedly larger (Figure 7.4), while their brain size did not. Nor is there firm evidence that they made stone tools. Thus, in the period between 2.5 and 1 million years ago, two kinds of hominines were headed in very different evolutionary directions.

If none of the robust species of *Australopithecus* belong in the direct line of human ancestry, what of earlier species of *Australopithecus*? From the standpoint of anatomy alone, it has long been recognized that either gracile species constitutes suitable ancestors for the genus *Homo,* and it now seems clear that the body of *Homo habilis* had changed little from that of either species. Precisely which of the two gave rise to *H. habilis* is vigorously debated. The arguments have become more complex with the discovery of *Kenyanthropus* (Chapter 6), which Maeve Leakey argues excludes all Australopithecines from the ancestry of *Homo.* At the moment, hers is a minority view. Most see the early East African graciles as sufficiently generalized to have given rise to both *Homo* and the robust *Australopithecus,* noting that the earliest skull to show the latter, the so-called Black Skull, nonetheless shows some holdovers from the earlier East Africans. This skull's age, 2.5 million years, is too old for any but the very earliest South African gracile

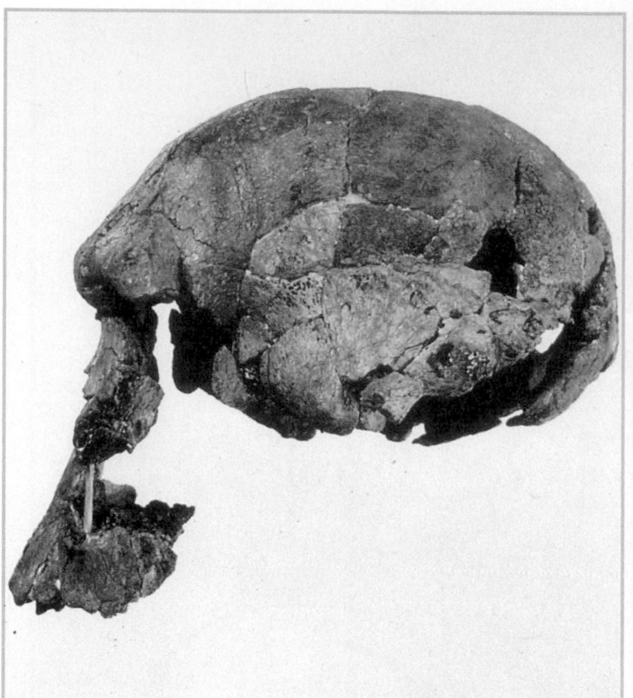

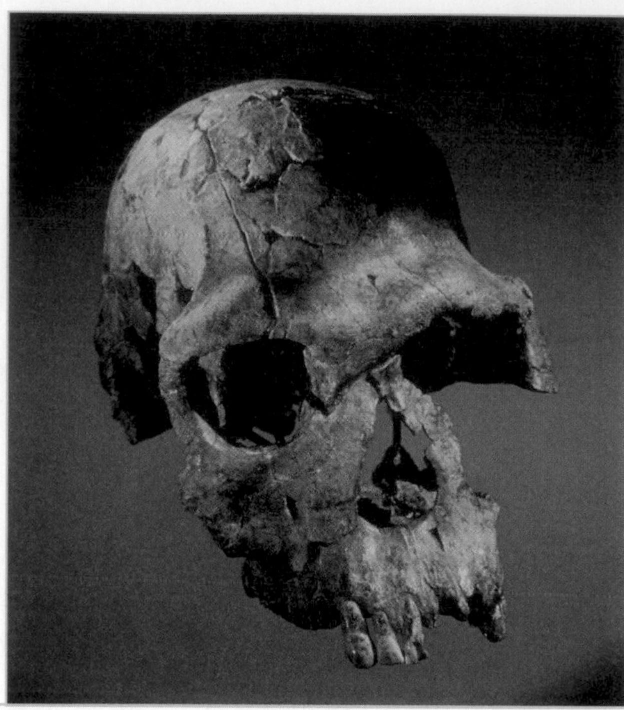

The ER 1470 skull (left): One of the most complete skulls of *Homo habilis* is close to 2 million years old and is probably a male; it contrasts with the ER 1813 skull (right), probably a female.

to have figured in its ancestry. Because the earliest *Homo habilis* skull is nearly as old, the same must be true for it. Evidently, at least a three-way split was under way by 2.5 million years ago, with the third line represented by late South African gracile *Australopithecus* (Figure 7.5). This persisted until about 2 million years ago (or later, if South African robusts are descended independently from graciles, rather than from East African robusts), by which time the other two lineages had become widespread in nonforested parts of Africa.

LOWER PALEOLITHIC TOOLS

The earliest tools known to have been made by hominines have been found in the vicinity of Lake Turkana in Kenya and southern Ethiopia, Olduvai Gorge in Tanzania, and Hadar in Ethiopia. Their appearance marks the beginning of the **Lower Paleolithic,** the first part of the Old Stone Age.

The makers of these early tools were highly skilled, consistently producing many well-formed flakes with few misdirected blows.[7] The object was to obtain large, sharp-edged flakes from available raw materials with the least effort. At Olduvai and Lake Turkana, these tools are close to 2 million years old; the Ethiopian tools are older at 2.6 million years.

Olduvai Gorge

What is now Olduvai Gorge was once a lake. Almost 2 million years ago, its shores were inhabited not only by numerous wild animals but also by groups of hominines, including robust Australopithecines and *Homo habilis* as well as the later *Homo erectus* (Chapter 8). The gorge, therefore, is a rich source of Paleolithic remains as well as a key site providing evidence of human evolutionary change. Among the finds are assemblages of stone tools that are about 2 million years old. These were found little

[7]Ambrose, p. 1,749.

Lower Paleolithic. The first part of the Old Stone Age; its beginning is marked by the appearance 2.6 million years ago of Oldowan tools.

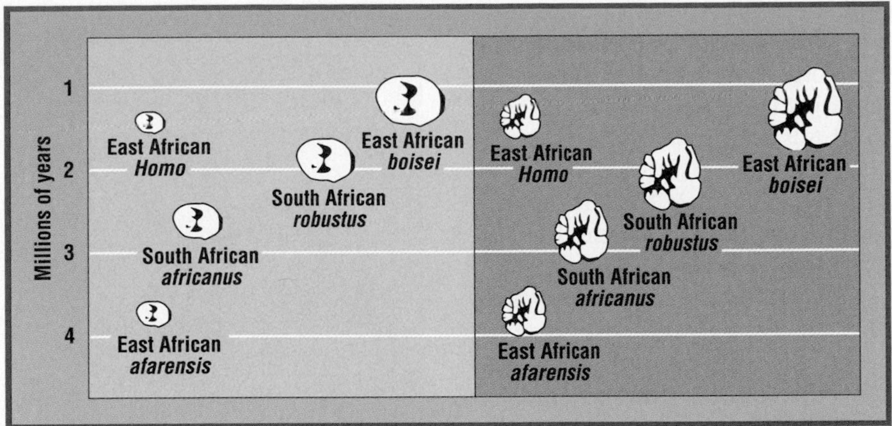

FIGURE 7.4

PREMOLARS (LEFT) AND MOLARS (RIGHT) OF *AUSTRALOPITHECUS* AND *HOMO HABILIS* COMPARED. THOUGH THERE IS LITTLE DIFFERENCE IN ABSOLUTE SIZE BETWEEN THE TEETH OF EARLY *AUSTRALOPITHECUS* (*AFARENSIS*) AND THOSE OF *HABILIS*, THOSE OF *AFARENSIS* ARE LARGER RELATIVE TO THE SIZE OF THE SKULL. MOREOVER, THE TEETH BECOME EVEN LARGER IN LATER SPECIES OF *AUSTRALOPITHECUS*.

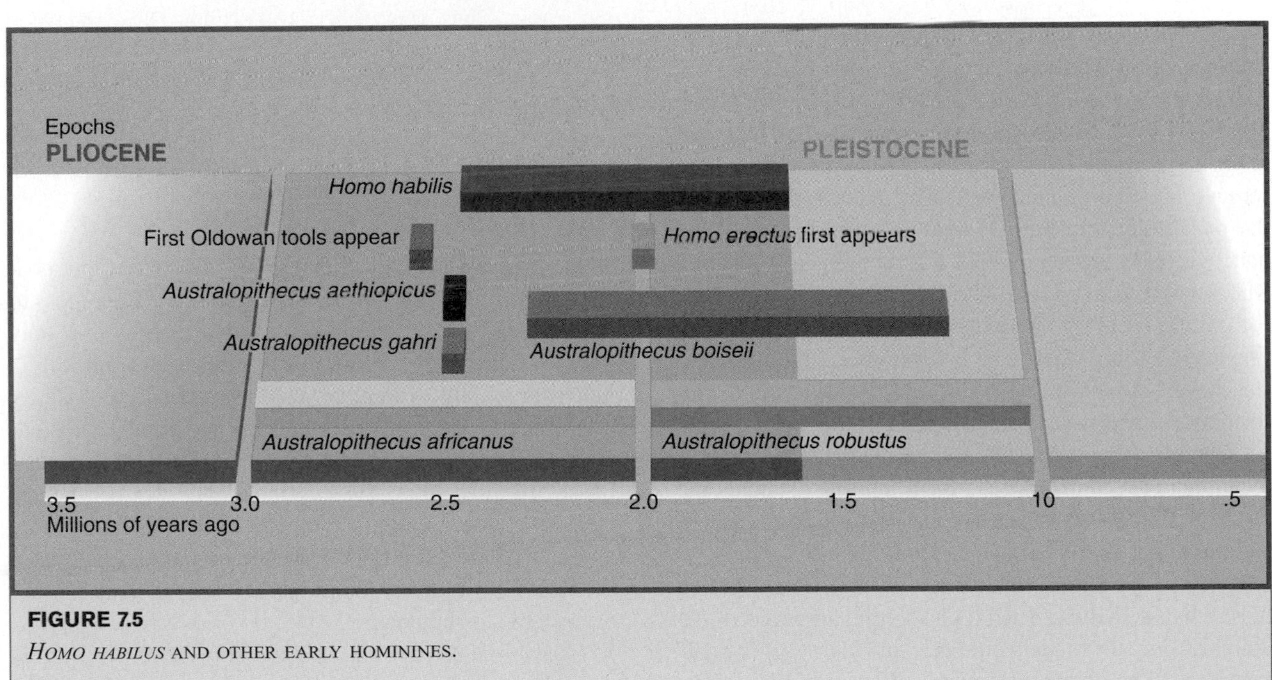

FIGURE 7.5

HOMO HABILUS AND OTHER EARLY HOMININES.

disturbed from when they were left, together with the bones of now-extinct animals that provided food. At one spot, in the lowest level of the gorge, the bones of an elephant lay in close association with more than 200 stone tools. Apparently, the animal was butchered here; there are no indications of any other activity. At another spot, on an occupation surface 1.8 million years old, basalt stones were found grouped in small heaps forming a circle. The interior of the circle was practically empty, while numerous tools and food debris littered the ground outside, right up to the edge of the circle. This was once interpreted as evidence for some sort of shelter, seeing the stone piles as supports for the framework of a protective fence of thorn branches, or perhaps a hut with a covering of animal skins or grass. Subsequence analysis suggests that the stones were "stockpiled" ahead of time, to be made into tools as needed, or to be hurled as missiles to hold off carnivorous animals while the hominines extracted meat, marrow, hide, and sinew from pieces of animal carcass.

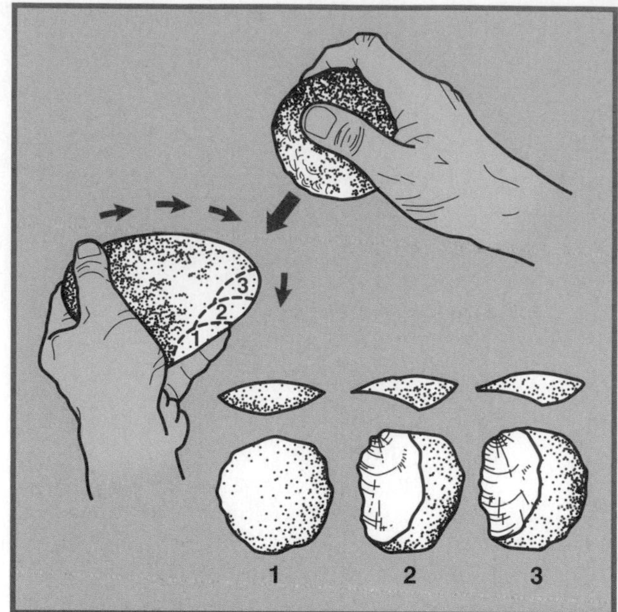

FIGURE 7.6

BY 2.6 MILLION YEARS AGO, HOMININES IN AFRICA HAD INVENTED THE PERCUSSION METHOD OF STONE TOOL MANUFACTURE. THIS DRAWING ILLUSTRATES HOW OLDOWAN TOOLMAKERS DETACHED FLAKES FROM A CORE USING THIS TECHNIQUE. A TECHNOLOGICAL BREAKTHROUGH, THE PRODUCTION OF STONE TOOLS BY PERCUSSION MADE POSSIBLE THE BUTCHERING OF MEAT FROM SCAVENGED CARCASSES.

Oldowan Tools

The oldest tools found at Olduvai Gorge belong to the **Oldowan tool tradition,** which is characterized by flakes struck from a stone (often a large, water-worn pebble) either by using another stone as a hammer (a hammerstone) or by striking the pebble against a large rock (anvil) to remove the flakes. This system of manufacture is called the **percussion method** (Figure 7.6). The finished flakes had two sharp edges, effective for cutting and scraping. Microscopic wear patterns show that these flakes were used for cutting meat, reeds, sedges, and grasses, and for cutting and scraping wood. The leftover cores, from which the flakes were struck, were also useful for bashing open bones for marrow and perhaps also defending the user.

Crude as they were, Oldowan tools mark an important technological advance for early hominines; previously, they depended on found objects requiring little or no modification, such as bones, sticks, or conveniently shaped stones. Oldowan tools made possible new additions to the diet, because, without such tools, hominines could eat few animals (only those that could be skinned by tooth or nail); therefore, their diet was limited in terms of animal proteins. The advent of Oldowan tools meant more than merely saving labor and time: They made possible the addition of meat to the diet on a frequent, rather than occasional, basis.

Much popular literature has been written about this penchant for meat, often with numerous colorful references to "killer apes." Such references are misleading, not only because hominines are not apes but also because killing has been greatly overemphasized. Meat can be obtained, after all, by scavenging or by stealing it from other predators. What is significant is that a dentition such as that possessed by *Australopithecus* and *Homo habilis* is poorly suited for meat eating. What is needed if substantial amounts of meat are to be eaten, without teeth like those possessed by carnivorous animals (or chimpanzees), are sharp tools for butchering.

The initial use of tools was probably the result of adaptation to an environment that we know was changing between 3 and 2 million years ago from forests to grasslands (see Figure 6.11). The physical changes that adapted hominines for spending increasing amounts of

Oldowan tool tradition. The earliest identifiable stone tools. • **Percussion method.** A technique of stone tool manufacture performed by striking the raw material with a hammerstone or by striking raw material against a stone anvil to remove flakes.

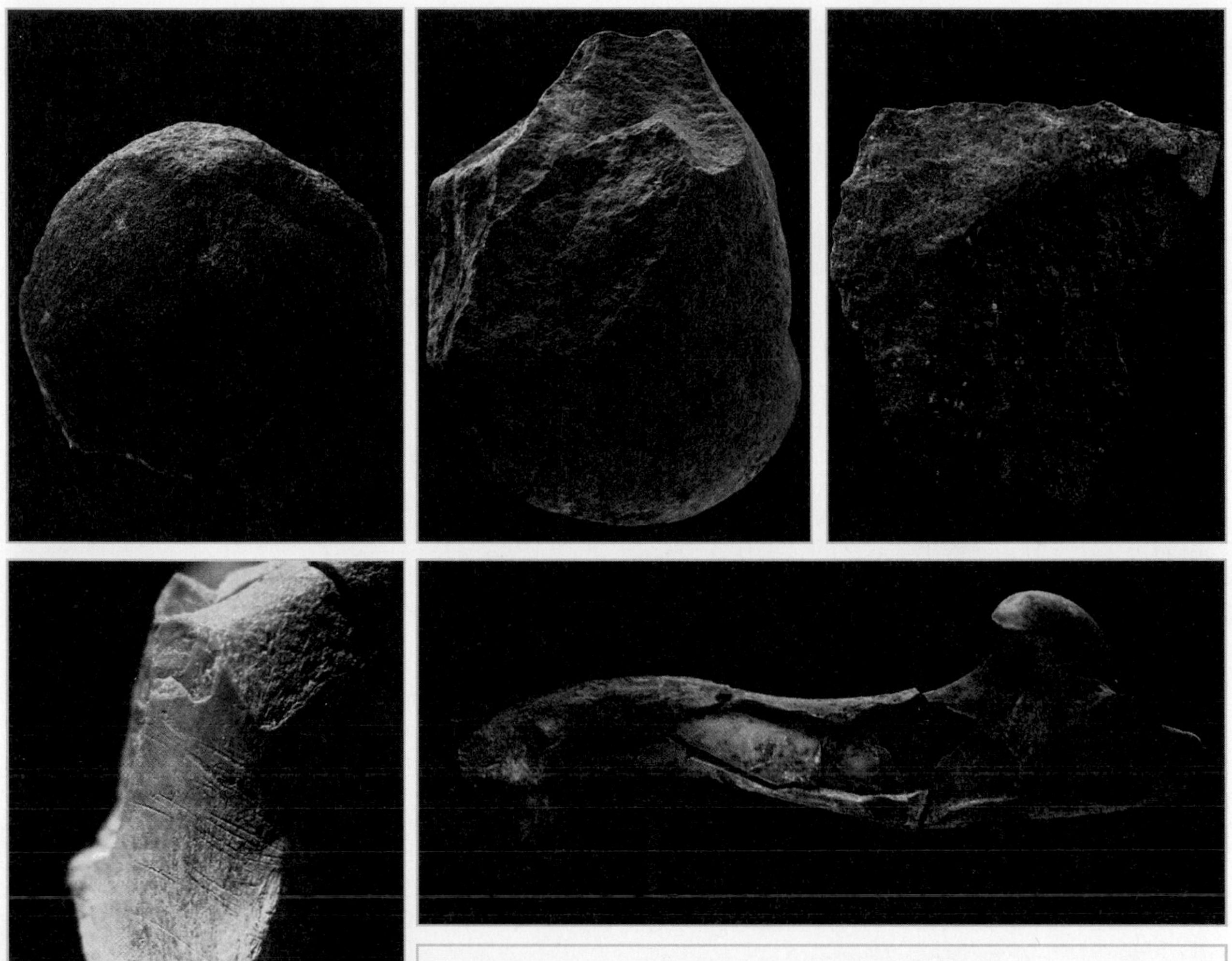

The stone tools used by *Homo habilis* included lava cobbles, choppers, and flakes like those shown here. Most choppers were probably the result of flakes being struck from one cobble by another. These flakes were used to remove meat from bones, leaving cut marks (lower left). The cobbles and choppers were used to break open bones (lower right) to get at the marrow.

time on the new grassy terrain encouraged toolmaking. It has been observed that monkeys and apes, for example, often use objects, such as sticks and stones, in their threat displays. The change to a nearly upright bipedal posture, coupled with existing flexibility at the shoulder, arms, and hands, allowed hominines to do so as well, helping them to compete successfully with the large predatory carnivores that shared their environment.

What else do these assemblages of Oldowan tools and broken animal bones have to tell us about the life of early *Homo*? First, they tell us that both *Homo habilis* and large carnivorous animals were active at these locations, for in addition to marks on the bones made by slicing, scraping, and chopping with stone tools, there are tooth marks from gnawing. Some of the gnawing marks overlie the butcher marks, indicating that enough flesh remained on the bones after the hominines were done with them to attract the other carnivores. In other cases, though, the butcher marks overlie the tooth marks of carnivores, indicating that the animals got there first. This is what we would expect if *H. habilis* were scavenging the kills of other animals, rather than doing its own killing. Consistent with this picture is that whole carcasses are not represented; evidently, only parts were transported away from the original location where they were obtained, again what we would expect if they were "stolen" from the kill of some other animal. The stone tools, too, were made of raw material procured at distances of up to 10 kilometers from where they were used to process the parts of carcasses. Finally, the incredible density of bones at some of the sites

Homo habilis filled the same niche on the ground that these vultures fill in the air: a nonterritorial scavenger.

and patterns of weathering indicate that, although *H. habilis* didn't linger longer than necessary at any one time (and for good reason—the carnivores attracted by the meat could have made short work of *habilis* as well), the sites were repeatedly used over periods guessed to be on the order of 5 to 15 years.

All of this is quite unlike the behavior of historically known food-foraging peoples, who bring whole carcasses back to camp, where they are completely processed; neither meat nor marrow is left (as they were at Oldowan sites), and the bones themselves are broken up not just to get at the marrow (as at Oldowan sites) but to fabricate tools and other objects of bone (unlike at Oldowan sites). Nor do historically known food foragers normally camp in thc midst of so much garbage. The picture that emerges of our Oldowan forebears, then, is of scavengers, getting

Becoming scavengers put *Homo habilis* in competition with formidable adversaries like hyenas.

their meat from the Lower Paleolithic equivalent of modern-day road kills, taking the spoils of their scavenging to particular places where tools, and the raw materials for making them (often procured from faraway sources), had been stockpiled in advance for the purpose of butchering. At these sites, the remains were quickly processed, so that those doing the butchering could clear out before their lives were endangered by carnivores attracted by the meat. Thus, the Oldowan sites were not campsites or "home bases" at all. Quite likely, *H. habilis* continued to sleep in trees or rocky cliffs, as do other small-bodied terrestrial or semiterrestrial primates, in order to be safe from predators. However, the advanced preparation for meat processing implied by the caching of stone tools, and the raw materials for making tools, attests to considerable foresight and ability to plan ahead.

Tools, Meat, and Brains

As we have seen, by 1.5 million years or so after early hominines became fully bipedal, the size and structure of the brain were beginning to change. Until about 2.5 million years ago, early hominines lived on foods that could be picked or gathered: plants, fruits, invertebrate animals such as ants and termites, and perhaps even an occasional piece of meat scavenged from kills made by other animals. After 2.5 million years ago, meat became more important in their diet, and they began to scavenge for it on a more regular basis.

Because early hominines lacked size and strength to drive off predators, or to compete directly with other scavengers attracted to kills, they must have had to rely on their wit and cunning for success. One may imagine them lurking in the vicinity of a kill, sizing up the situation as the predator ate its fill while hyenas and other scavengers gathered, and devising strategies to outwit them all so as to seize a piece of the carcass. A hominine depending on stereotyped instinctual behavior in such a situation would have been at a competitive disadvantage. One that could anticipate problems, devise distractions, bluff competitors into temporary retreat, and recognize, the instant it came, its opportunity to rush in and grab what it could of the carcass stood a much better chance of surviving, reproducing, and proliferating.

One means by which early hominines gained access to a reasonably steady supply of carcasses while at the same time minimizing the risks involved is suggested by recent field studies of leopards. How this could have worked and the arguments in favor of it are the subject of the following Original Study.

Original Study

Cat in the Human Cradle[8]

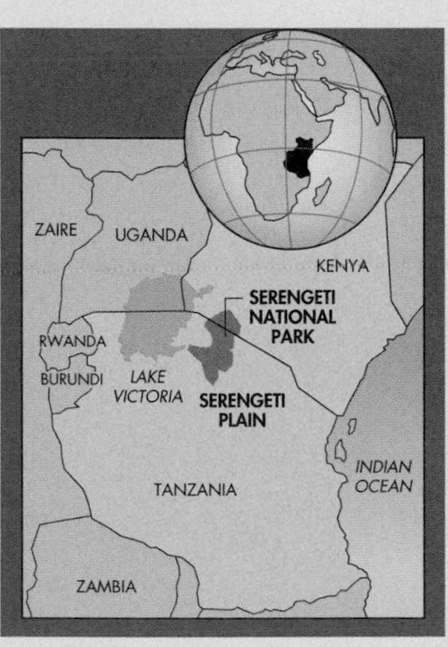

Recent evidence, such as marks on some of the Olduvai bones, indicates that animals the size of wildebeests or larger were killed, eaten, and abandoned by large predators such as lions, hyenas, and saber-toothed cats; hominines may have merely scavenged the leftovers. Several specialists now agree that early hominines obtained at least marrow mainly in this way. The picture with regard to the remains of smaller animals, such as gazelle-sized antelopes, is less certain. Paleoanthropologists Henry Bunn and Ellen Kroll believe that the cut-marked upper limb bones of small, medium-sized, and large animals found at Olduvai Gorge demonstrate that hominines were butchering the meaty limbs with cutting tools. Since modern-day lions and hyenas rapidly and completely consume small prey, leaving little or nothing for potential scavengers, Bunn and Kroll conclude that hominines must have acquired the smaller animals by hunting. But

[8]Adapted from Cavallo, J. A. (1990). Cat in the human cradle. *Natural History,* 54–56, 58–60.

Original Study

another scholar, Kay Behrensmeyer, suggests that a small group of hominines could have obtained these bones, not by hunting, but by driving off timid predators, such as cheetahs or jackals, from their kills.

Since carnivores play a key role in all these scenarios, three years ago I began thinking about studying their behavior and ecology. About the same time, a colleague directed me to a paper on the tree-climbing abilities of early hominines. The authors (anatomists Randall L. Susman, Jack T. Stern, and William L. Jungers) analyzed the limb bones of *Homo habilis* specimens from Olduvai Gorge, as well as those of the early hominine *Australopithecus afarensis* (better known as Lucy). They concluded that early hominines were probably not as efficient as we are at walking on two feet, but they were better than we are at climbing trees and suspending themselves from branches. At the very least, given their apparent lack of fire, early hominines must have used trees as refuges from large predators and as sleeping sites.

One evening, as I watched a documentary film by Hugh Miles about a female leopard and her cubs in Kenya's Masai Mara Reserve, carnivore behavior and early hominine tree climbing suddenly connected for me. In the film, a pack of hyenas attempt to scavenge an antelope that the mother leopard has killed. At the sight of the hyenas, the leopard grabs the prey in her jaws and carries it up a small tree. This striking behavior sparked my curiosity and sent me to the library the next morning to find out more about leopards.

I learned that the leopard differs from other large African carnivores in a variety of ways. Although it occasionally kills large animals, such as adult wildebeests and topi or young giraffes, the leopard preys primarily on smaller antelopes, such as Thomson's gazelles, impala, and Grant's gazelles, and on the young of both large and small species. Unable to defend its kills on the ground from scavenging by lions and spotted hyenas, both of which often forage in groups, the usually solitary leopard stores each kill in a tree, returning to feed but otherwise frequently abandoning it for varying lengths of time.

Although the leopard may not consume its entire prey immediately, the tree-stored kills are relatively safe from theft. (Even lions, which can climb trees, usually take little notice of this resource.) As a result, a kill can persist in a tree for several days. Also, leopard kills appear to be more predictably located than those of lions and hyenas because leopards tend to maintain a small territorial range for several years and occasionally

This leopard has carried part of a Thomson's gazelle up into a tree to prevent other scavengers from consuming what is left. Such tree-stored carcasses may have been the principal source of meat for *Homo habilis*.

reuse feeding trees. Finally, leopard kills are usually found in the woodlands near lakes and rivers, the habitat apparently preferred by early hominines. Such circumstances, I reasoned, might have once provided an ideal feeding opportunity for tree-climbing hominines, particularly *Homo habilis.* By scavenging from the leopard's temporarily abandoned larder, early hominines could have obtained the fleshy and marrow-rich bones of small- to medium-sized prey animals in relative safety.

Fossil evidence shows that ancestors of present-day leopards were contemporaneous with early hominines and shared the same habitats. The antiquity of tree-caching behavior is harder to prove, but it is supported by paleoanthropologist C. K. Brain's excavations of ancient caves in southern Africa's Sterkfontein Valley. In the vertical, shaftlike caves, Brain found the fossil remains of hominines, baboons, and antelopes, and of leopards and other large carnivores. The size of the prey animals and the selection of body parts, as well as puncture marks on some of the cranial bones of hominines and baboons, suggested that many of these fossils were the remains of leopard meals. Brain guessed that they had fallen into the caves from leopard-feeding trees growing out of the mouths of the caves.

Given its similarities to the ancient environments represented at the early archeological sites—extensive grasslands with wooded lakes, rivers, and streams—the Serengeti National Park in northern Tanzania seemed an ideal living laboratory in which to test my hypothesis. I traveled there in July 1987, accompanied by Robert J. Blumenschine, who had conducted an earlier study there on scavenging opportunities provided by lions and hyenas. Along the Wandamu River, a tributary of the Seronera, we were fortunate to find an adult female leopard and her 13-month-old (nearly full-grown) male cub that tolerated our Land-Rover. We spent a total of about 50 hours, during the day and at night, observing these leopards at three fresh, tree-stored kills of Thomson's gazelles. The leopards frequently left the carcasses unguarded between feedings. On one occasion, a complete young Thomson's gazelle, killed the previous evening, was abandoned for 9 daylight hours (we found the leopards resting approximately 2 miles away). Without directly confronting these predators, therefore, a creature able to climb trees could have easily carried off the same amount of flesh and marrow as it could obtain from hunting.

While Brain's work in South Africa implicates leopards as predators of early hominines, including the genus *Homo,* some hominines may have also benefited from living near these carnivores. Tree-stored leopard kills could have provided an important resource to early scavenging hominines and the sharp, broken limb bones from the partly eaten prey could have been used to peel back the hide, expose the flesh of the carcasses, and remove large muscle bundles. This activity may even have given early hominines the initial impetus to make and use tools in the extraction of animal nutrients.

Some paleoanthropologists have argued that scavenging was an unlikely subsistence strategy for early hominines, since large predators require expansive home ranges, and kills by these carnivores are rare in any particular area. They also contend that very little is left over from such kills after the predator is finished and that hominine competition with large carnivores for these leftovers would be a dangerous activity. My 1988 observations suggest something quite different. During approximately 2 months in the dry season, I documented 16 kills of small and medium antelopes made by my adult male and female leopards within an approximately 4-by-8-mile area. The majority of these kills, still retaining abundant flesh and marrow, were temporarily abandoned by the leopard for 3 to 8½ hours during a single day.

The tree-stored leopard kills consisted mainly of adult and juvenile Thomson's gazelles. Compared with kills of similar-sized prey made on the ground by Serengeti lions and hyenas, as recorded by Blumenschine, the tree-stored leopard kills lasted longer, offering large quantities of flesh and marrow for 2 or more days. In part this was because they were not subject to many scavengers. The leopard kills were also more predictably located on the landscape than those of lions in the same area. In modern leopard populations, a male maintains a relatively large territory that overlaps with the usually smaller territories of several females. This pattern often means that several tree-stored kills are available simultaneously during a given period of time within a relatively small area.

An obvious question is how leopards would have responded to repeated theft of their tree-stored kills

Original Study

by early hominines. Would they, perhaps, have abandoned portions of their ranges if such thefts occurred with sufficient regularity? Although I haven't yet tested this, I don't think they would have. According to my observations and those of other researchers, leopards are usually more successful at hunting larger prey, such as gazelles and impala, at night. This gives them the opportunity to consume part of such kills before the arrival of any daytime scavengers. They thus should be able to obtain enough nourishment to warrant remaining in a territory, despite some such losses.

Like modern baboons and chimpanzees, early hominines may have killed some small animals, such as newborn antelopes. But they could have acquired all sizes of animal carcasses without hunting if the prey killed by leopards is taken into account. The wide assortment of animal bones at sites like Olduvai Gorge, which have been attributed to ground-based hunting and scavenging, could instead be attributed to scavenging only, both in trees and on the ground. Leopard kills would then have provided much of the flesh consumed by early hominines, while carcasses abandoned on the ground by other large predators would have yielded primarily bone marrow. Additional flesh may have come from the remains of large kills made by saber-toothed cats or from the carcasses of animals that drowned when herds migrated across ancient lakes.

While we can't observe the behavior of our early ancestors, the present-day interactions between leopards and some other primate species can be instructive. Baboons, for example, often fall victim to leopards while they sleep at night in trees or caves. During the day, however, baboons regularly attack, displace, and according to one account, even kill leopards. In western Tanzania, a park ranger reported that during the day, a group of baboons saw a leopard in a tree with the carcass of an impala. Barking out alarm calls, the adult and adolescent male baboons chased the leopard for about 3/10 of a mile. The females and young baboons stayed with the carcass and began to eat, until the males returned and took possession of the kill.

Similarly, although chimpanzees in western Tanzania are the occasional prey of leopards, there is a report that one day some chimpanzees scavenged what was apparently a tree-stored leopard kill. On a more dramatic occasion, also during the day, a group of chimpanzees was observed noisily surrounding a leopard lair from which an adult leopard was heard growling. A male chimpanzee entered the lair and emerged with a leopard cub, which it and the others killed without reprisal from the adult leopard. This type of shifting day-night, predatory-parasitic relationship may once have existed between leopards and our early hominine ancestors.

The End

Although difficult to prove, several lines of evidence combine to suggest it was probably the early hominine males, rather than females, who did most of the scavenging. What predisposed them for such a division of labor may have been the foraging habits of the earlier Australopithecines. As already noted (in Chapter 6), dental and skeletal differences between males and females raise the possibility that males may have fed on the ground and lower levels of trees more heavily than females, who had a higher proportion of fruit in their diet.[9] Something like this pattern is seen today among orangutans, where it is a response to highly dispersed resources. As a consequence, males consume larger amounts of low-quality food such as bark than do females. A major difference, of course, is that orangutan males still forage in the forest, whereas male *Australopithecus* foraged in a mosaic woodland, bushland, and grassland environment. In such a situation, the latter may have been forced to try out supplementary sources of food on the ground, especially if existing sources became scarcer, as they likely did; in the crucial period between 3 and 2 million years ago climates became markedly cold and dry.[10] Already bipedal,

[9] Leonard, W. R., & Hegman, M. (1987). Evolution of P3 morphology in *Australopithecus afarensis. American Journal of Physical Anthropology, 73,* 60.

[10] Behrensmeyer, A. K., Todd, N. E., Potts, R., & McBrinn, G. E. (1997). Late Pliocene faunal turnover in the Turkana basin, Kenya and Ethiopia. *Science, 278,* 1,589–1,594.

ADRIENNE ZIHLMAN (b. 1940)

Up until the 1970s, the study of human evolution, from its very beginnings, was permeated by a deep-seated bias reflecting the privileged status enjoyed by men in Western society. Beyond the obvious labeling of fossils as particular types of "men," irrespective of the sex of the individual represented, it took the form of portraying males as the active players in human evolution. Thus, it was males who were seen as providers and innovators, using their wits to become ever more effective providers of food and protection for passive females. The latter were seen as spending their time getting pregnant and caring for offspring, while the men were getting ahead by becoming ever smarter. Central to such thinking was the idea of "man the hunter," constantly honing his wits through the pursuit and killing of animals. Thus, hunting by men was seen as the pivotal humanizing activity in evolution.

We now know, of course, that such ideas are culture-bound, reflecting the hopes and expectations of late-19th- and early-20th-century European and European American culture. This recognition came in the 1970s and was a direct consequence of the entry of a number of highly capable women into the profession of paleoanthropology. Up until the 1960s, there were few women in any field of physical anthropology, but with the expansion of graduate programs and changing attitudes toward the role of women in society, increasing numbers of them went on to earn a PhD. One of these was Adrienne Zihlman, who earned her doctorate at the University of California at Berkeley in 1967. Subsequently, she authored a number of important papers critical of "man the hunter" scenarios. She was not the first to do so; as early as 1971, Sally Linton had published a preliminary paper on "Woman the Gatherer," but it was Zihlman from 1976 on who especially elaborated on the importance of female activities for human evolution. Others have joined in the effort, including Zihlman's companion in graduate school and later colleague, Nancy Tanner, who collaborated with Zihlman on some of her papers and has produced important works of her own.

The work of Zihlman and her coworkers was crucial in forcing a reexamination of existing "man the hunter" scenarios, out of which came recognition of the importance of scavenging in early human evolution as well as the importance of female gathering and other activities. Although there is still plenty to learn about human evolution, thanks to these women we now know that it wasn't a case of women being "uplifted" as a consequence of their association with progressively evolving men. Rather, the two sexes evolved together with each making its own important contribution to the process.

Australopithecines were capable of covering, in an energetically efficient way, the considerable distances (on the order of 32 square miles, based on the Original Study) necessary to ensure a steady supply of meat.

Another consideration is that, without contraceptive devices and formulas that could be bottle-fed to infants, females in their prime, when not pregnant, must have had infants to nurse. Although this would not have restricted their local mobility, any more than it does a female ape or monkey or a woman among historically known food-foraging peoples, it would have been less easy for them than for males to range over the substantial distances required to search out carcasses. Also essential for the successful scavenger would have been the capacity for the massive bursts of energy needed to elude the many carnivores active on the savanna. Although anatomical and physiological differences between the sexes in humans today are relatively insignificant compared to *H. habilis,* as a general rule, men can still run faster than women (even though some women can certainly run faster than some men). Finally, even for the smartest and swiftest individuals, scavenging would still have been a risky business. To place early *Homo* females at risk would have been to place their offspring, actual and potential, at risk as well. Males, on the other hand, would have been relatively expendable, for, to put the matter bluntly, a very few males are capable of impregnating a large number of females. In evolutionary terms, the population that places its males at risk is less likely to jeopardize its chances for reproductive success than is the one that places its females at risk.

Early hominine females, as well as males, had to sharpen their wits in order to gain access to some of the meat scavenged. For the most part, females continued to gather the same kinds of foods that their ancestors had been eating all along. But instead of consuming all this food themselves as they gathered it (as other primates do), they provided some to the males who, in turn, provided the females with meat. To do this, they had to plan ahead so as to know where food would be found in sufficient quantities, devise means by which it could be transported to some agreed-upon location for division at the proper time, while at the same time preventing its loss through spoilage or to such animals as rats and mice. At the least, this may have required fabrication of carrying devices such as net bags and use of trail signs of the sort (described in Chapter 4) used by modern bonobos. Thus, female gathering played just as important a role in the development of larger, more complex brains as did male scavenging.

Evolving hominines' increased interest in meat is a point of major importance. Out on the savanna, it is hard for a primate with a digestive system like that of humans to satisfy its amino acid requirements from available plant resources. Moreover, failure to do so has serious consequences: growth depression, malnutrition, and ultimately death. The most readily accessible plant sources would have been the proteins available in leaves and legumes (nitrogen-fixing plants, familiar modern examples being beans and peas), but these are hard for primates like us to digest unless they are cooked. The problem is that leaves and legumes contain substances that cause the proteins to pass right through the gut without being absorbed.[11]

Chimpanzees have a similar problem when out on the savanna. In such a setting, they spend about 37 percent of their time on a yearly basis going after insects like ants and termites, while at the same time increasing their predation of eggs and vertebrate animals. Such animal foods not only are easily digestible, but they provide high-quality proteins that contain all the essential amino acids in just the right percentages. No one plant food does this by itself; only if the right combination is consumed can plants provide what meat does by itself in the way of amino acids. Moreover, there is abundant meat to be had on the savanna. All things considered, then, we should not be surprised if our own ancestors solved their protein problem in somewhat the same way that chimps on the savanna do today.

One means by which bonobos indicate to others where they are headed is to deliberately trample down the vegetation. *H. habilis* may have made use of similar trail signs.

Increased meat consumption on the part of early hominines did more than merely ensure an adequate intake of essential amino acids, important though this was. Animals that live on plant foods must eat large quantities of vegetation, and obtaining such foods consumes much of their time. Meat eaters, by contrast, have no need to eat so much, or so often. Consequently, meat-eating hominines may have had more leisure time available to explore and manipulate their environment; like lions and

[11]Stahl, A. B. (1984) Hominid dietary selection before fire. *Current Anthropology, 25,* 151–168.

Meat-eating animals, like these lions, do not have to spend as much time eating as do those that rely on plant foods alone. Consequently, they have more time available for play and exploration.

leopards, they would have time to spend lying around and playing. Such activity, coupled with the other factors already mentioned, may have been a stimulus to hominine brain development.

The importance of increased consumption of meat for early hominine brain development is suggested by the size of their brains: The cranial capacity of the largely plant-eating *Australopithecus* ranged from 310 to 530 cubic centimeters; that of the most primitive known meat eater, *Homo habilis* from East Africa, ranged from 580 to 752 cc; whereas *Homo erectus,* who eventually hunted as well as scavenged for meat, possessed a cranial capacity of 775 to 1,225 cc.

THE EARLIEST SIGNS OF CULTURE: TOOLS

The use of specially made tools of stone appears to have arisen out of a need for implements to butcher and prepare meat, because hominine teeth were inadequate for the task. Even chimpanzees, whose canine teeth are far larger and sharper, frequently have trouble tearing through the skin of other animals.[12] Besides overcoming this problem, the manufacture of stone tools must have played a role in the evolution of the human brain, first by putting a premium on manual dexterity and fine manipulation over mere power in the use of the hands. This in turn put a premium on improved organization of the nervous system. Second, the transformation of a lump of stone into a "chopper," "knife," or "scraper" is a far cry from what a chimpanzee does when it transforms a stick into a termite probe. Although the probe is not unlike the stick, the stone tool is (with the exception of hammerstones) quite unlike the lump of stone. Thus, the toolmaker must have in mind an abstract idea of the tool to be made, as well as a specific set of steps that will accomplish the transformation from raw material to finished product. Furthermore, only certain kinds of stone have the flaking properties that will allow the transformation to take place. The toolmaker must know about these, as well as where such stone can be found.

[12]Goodall, J. (1986) *The chimpanzees of Gombe: Patterns of behavior* (p. 372). Cambridge, MA: Belknap Press.

Chimpanzees' hunting and consumption of meat is made possible by their large, sharp canines. *Homo habilis,* by contrast, lacked such teeth.

A power grip (left) utilizes more of the hand, whereas the precision grip (right) relies on the fingers for control.

HIGHWAY 1

This Web site provides a comprehensive source of information about human evolutionary history and takes the evolution–creationism controversy head on. Search the site for excellent description of each of the fossil hominine species discovered.
www.talkorigins.org/faqs/homs/

HIGHWAY 2

The Leakey Foundation Web site is true to its mission to increase scientific knowledge and public understanding of human origins and evolution. The site provides an interactive timeline of key discoveries in paleoanthropology and documents the groundbreaking research conducted by the Leakey family and the investigators they have supported for over three decades.
www.leakeyfoundation.org/

HIGHWAY 3

This handsome Web site is packed with information about human evolution including each new discovery, a comprehensive glossary, and a perspective feature where new voices and ideas in the field can be heard.
www.archaeologyinfo.com/

COOPERATION AND SHARING

With an apelike brain and a diet like that of monkeys and apes when out in open country, *Australopithecus* probably behaved much like other hominoids. Like apes, adults probably foraged for their own food, which was not regularly shared with other adults. Among modern apes, however, there are two notable exceptions to this behavior. Among bonobos, females sometimes share meat and even fruits with one another and sometimes with males. Adult chimpanzees, by contrast, rarely share plant food with one another, but males almost always share meat, frequently with females. Increased consumption of meat on the part of *Homo habilis* may have promoted even more sharing among adults. Moreover, a regular supply of meat would have required that substantial amounts of time and energy be devoted to the search for carcasses, and food gathered by females and shared with males could have provided the latter with both.

Sharing and cooperation between the sexes need not necessarily have been between mated males and females, but may just as well have been between brothers and sisters and mothers and sons. On the other hand, the capacity to engage in sexual activity at any time the female deemed appropriate may have promoted sharing and cooperation between a male and one or more sex partners. Among most catarrhine primates, males attempt to monopolize females when the latter are at the height of sexual receptivity. Moreover, male chimpanzees frequently use the sharing of meat to entice females to have sex, and females in estrus are more successful at begging for meat from males. Males, too, are more apt to hunt if a sexually receptive female is present.[13] The willingness of human females to engage in sex at any time it suits them is shared with our nearest relatives (chimps and especially bonobos) and so probably is retained from our common ancestry. Hence, we can safely ascribe such behavior to the earliest hominines. Sharing with sex partners (who may have been multiple) therefore seems likely.

Although chimpanzees can and do hunt singly, they frequently cooperate in the task. In the case of *Homo habilis,* cooperation would seem to have been even more crucial to success in scavenging. It is hard to imagine a creature lacking the formidable canines of a chimpanzee competing on an individual basis with carnivores far more powerful than itself.

In summary, then, it seems reasonable to assume that *Homo habilis* engaged in more sharing and cooperative behavior than one sees among present-day chimpanzees. How much more is certainly not known, and certainly fell far short of what has been observed among any historically known food-foraging peoples. After all, *Homo habilis* was not just a different sort of hominine from *Australopithecus;* it was different from *Homo sapiens* as well.

---

[13]Moore, J. (1998). Comment. *Current Anthropology, 39,* 413.

LANGUAGE ORIGINS

The evident importance of cooperation, planning, and foresight in the life of *H. habilis* raises the issue of this species' ability to communicate. Modern apes communicate through a combination of calls and gestures, and humans, though we rely on spoken language, also use this gesture-call system. Like the apes, we have inherited this from ancient ancestors that predate the evolutionary split between hominids and pongids. After three decades of experiments by several different researchers with captive apes, there is a growing consensus that all great apes share an ability to develop language skills at least to the level of a 2- to 3-year-old.[14] Of course, they do not do so in the wild, even though the potential is there (just as bonobos do not make chipped stone tools in the wild, even though experiments show they are capable of it). Nor do they display these language skills through speech, but rather through use of gestures. Again, because this linguistic potential is shared, it must be one that the earliest hominines possessed as well. In view of these considerations, the previously noted features of the brain of *H. habilis* that in modern humans are associated with language take on added interest.

Moreover, the speech area is adjacent to and probably derived from that involved in precise hand control. This brings us back to the fact that the manufacture of Oldowan tools requires manual skills that go beyond those of chimpanzees, or even Kanzi: the bonobo.[15] And, as previously noted, the Oldowan toolmakers, like modern humans, were overwhelmingly right-handed; in making tools, they gripped the core in the left hand, striking flakes off with the right. Chimpanzees, by contrast, show no overall preference for right-handedness at the population level.[16] Handedness (whether right or left) is associated with lateralization of brain functions, that is, the two hemispheres specialize for different functions; rather than duplicating each other. Lateralization, in turn, is associated with language. Thus, toolmaking may have set the stage for language development. Putting this all together, we must at least allow the possibility that *H. habilis* had developed gestural language, though it may have been rudimentary. With the hands freed from locomotion to do other things, they were certainly more available for communication than are the hands of apes.

[14]Miles, H. L. W. (1993). Language and the orangutan: The old person of the forest. In P. Singer (Ed.), *The great ape project* (p. 46). New York: St. Martin's.

[15]Ambrose, p. 1,749.

[16]Ibid., p. 1,750

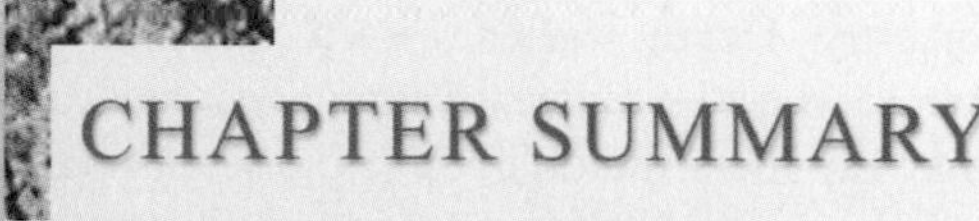

CHAPTER SUMMARY

Since 1960 a number of fossils have been found in East Africa at Olduvai Gorge, Lake Baringo, and east of Lake Turkana, and in South Africa at Sterkfontein and Swartkrans, which have been attributed to *Homo habilis,* the earliest representative of this genus. Among them is the well-known KNM ER 1470 skull, which is more modern in appearance than any *Australopithecus* skull. From the neck down, however, the skeleton of *Homo habilis* differs little from that of *Australopithecus.* Because it does show a significant increase in brain size and some reorganization of its structure, *Homo habilis'* mental abilities must have exceeded those of *Australopithecus.* By 2.4 million years ago, the evolution of *Homo* was proceeding in a direction different from that of *Australopithecus.*

The same geological strata that have produced *Homo habilis* have also produced the earliest known stone tools. These Lower Paleolithic artifacts from Olduvai Gorge, Lake Turkana, and sites in Ethiopia are simple in form but required considerable skill and knowledge for their manufacture.

Finds made at Olduvai Gorge have provided important evidence of human evolutionary development. The oldest Lower Paleolithic tools found at Olduvai are in the Oldowan tool tradition, which is characterized by all-purpose generalized flakes and chopping tools. Used to make them was the percussion method of manufacture. The simple but effective Oldowan choppers and flakes made possible the addition of meat to the diet on a regular basis because one could now butcher meat, skin any animal, and break open bones for marrow. Many Oldowan archaeological sites appear to be temporary places where meat was processed, rather than campsites.

Some changes in the brain structure of *Homo habilis* seem to have been associated with the changed diet. Increased consumption of meat, beginning about 2.5 million years ago, made new demands on their coordination and behavior. Successful procurement of meat through scavenging depended on *H. habilis'* ability to outthink far more powerful predators and scavengers. Obtaining animal food presented problems that very often had to be solved on the spot; a small scavenger depending on stereotyped instinctual behavior alone would have been at a competitive disadvantage in such a situation. Moreover, eaters of high-protein foods, such as meats, do not have to eat as often as vegetarians do. Consequently, meat-eating hominines may have had more leisure time available to explore and experiment with their environment.

Toolmaking and use also favored the development of a more complex brain. To make stone tools, one must have in mind at the beginning a clear vision of the tool to be made, one must know the precise set of steps necessary to transform the raw material into the tool, and one must be able to recognize the kind of stone that can be successfully worked. Complex eye-hand coordination is also required.

A prime factor in the success of early hominines may have been the development of some cooperation in the procurement of foods. Although the males probably supplied much of the meat, the females continued to gather the sorts of food eaten by other primates; however, instead of consuming what they gathered as they gathered it, they shared a portion with the males in exchange for meat. This required foresight and planning on the part of females, which played as important a role as male scavenging in favoring the development of larger, more complex brains. Food sharing with a sexual division of labor is characteristic of modern food foragers, and some hint of it can be seen among chimpanzees and bonobos, among whom meat is frequently shared.

The cooperation, planning, and foresight inferred for *Homo habilis* suggest the existence of some sort of rudimentary language, as do some features of this species' brain. Experiments with captive apes favor some sort of gestural language.

CLASSIC READINGS

Campbell, B. G., & Loy, J. D. (1995). *Humankind emerging* (7th ed.). New York: HarperCollins.

This well-written and lavishly illustrated text has excellent coverage of the earliest hominines.

Ciochon, R. L., & Fleagle, J. G. (Eds.). (1993). *The human evolution source book.* Englewood Cliffs, NJ: Prentice-Hall.

This collection of articles by specialists provides a more detailed look at the different theories on early hominine evolution.

Johanson, D., & Shreeve, J. (1989). *Lucy's child: The discovery of a human ancestor.* New York: Avon.

This sequel to *Lucy* is written in the same engaging style. Although it covers some of the same ground with respect to *Australopithecus,* its focus is on *Homo habilis.* Besides giving a good description of this earliest member of the genus *Homo,* it presents one of the best discussions of the issues concerning when (and why) *Homo* appeared.

CHAPTER 8

HOMO ERECTUS AND THE EMERGENCE OF HUNTING AND GATHERING

More "human" than *Homo habilis,* though less so than *Homo sapiens, Homo erectus* emerged about 1.8 million years ago, by which time the genus *Homo* was spreading to parts of Asia. Shown here is one of the most famous *Homo erectus* sites, at Zhoukoudian, China. Discovered in the 1920s, it is now included on UNESCO's World Heritage List.

CHAPTER PREVIEW

1

Who Was *Homo erectus*?

Homo erectus was the direct descendant of early members of the genus *Homo* as evidenced by findings in various parts of Africa. Populations of *Homo erectus* were widespread between about 1.8 million and 400,000 years ago, from Africa and Europe in the West, to Southeast Asia and China in the East.

2

What Were the Cultural Capabilities of *Homo erectus*?

Having a larger brain than its ancestors, *Homo erectus* became increasingly able to adapt to different situations through the medium of culture. This is reflected by better-made tools, a greater variety of tool types, regional diversification of tool kits, use of fire, and improved organizational skills.

3

What Were the Consequences of *Homo erectus'* Improved Abilities to Adapt Through Culture?

As culture became more important as the vehicle through which this species secured its survival, life became somewhat more secure than it had been. The result was increased reproductive success, allowing populations to grow, with "spillover" into previously uninhabited regions. This expansion in turn contributed to the further evolution of culture, as populations of *Homo erectus* had to find solutions to new problems of existence in newly inhabited regions.

In 1891, the Dutch army surgeon Eugene Dubois, intent upon finding the fossils of a "missing link" between humans and apes, set out for Indonesia (then the Dutch East Indies), which he considered to have provided a suitable environment for such a creature. At Trinil, on the island of Java, Dubois found what he was searching for: the fossil remains of a primitive kind of hominine, consisting of a skull cap, a few teeth, and a thighbone. Its features seemed to Dubois part ape, part human. Indeed Dubois at first thought the remains did not even belong to the same individual. The flat skull, for example, with its low forehead and enormous brow ridges, appeared to be like that of an ape; but it possessed a cranial capacity much larger than an ape's, even though small by modern human standards. The femur, or thighbone, was clearly human in shape and proportions and indicated the creature was a biped. Although Dubois called his find *Pithecanthropus erectus,* or "erect ape man," it has since been assigned to the species *Homo erectus.*

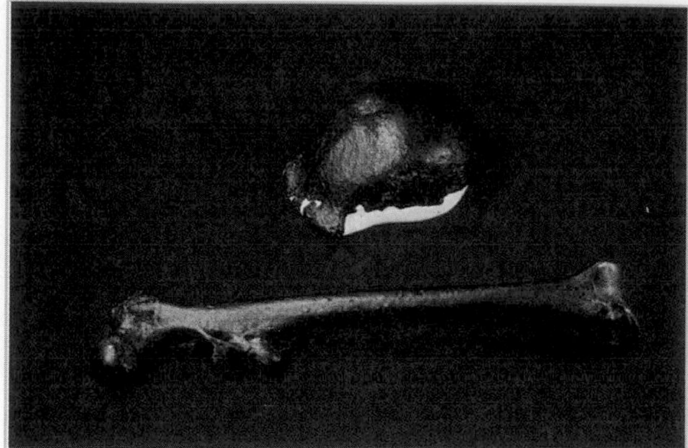

These casts of the skull cap and thighbone of *Homo erectus* were made from the original bones found by Eugene Dubois at Trinil, Java.

HOMO ERECTUS FOSSILS

Until 1.8 million years ago, hominines were not to be found living anywhere but in Africa. It was on this continent that hominines, and later the genus *Homo,* originated. It was also in Africa that the first stone tools were invented. But by the time of *Homo erectus,* hominines had spread far beyond the confines of their original homeland. Fossils of this species are now known from a number of localities not just in Africa, but in China, Europe, Georgia, and India, as well as Java (Figure 8.1). Although remains of this species have been found in many different places in three continents, the remains show very little significant physical variation. Evidence suggests, however, that populations of *H. erectus* in different regions of Africa, Asia, and Europe do show some differences from one another on a subspecific level.

Homo erectus from Java

For a long time, the scientific community was reluctant to accept Dubois' claim that his Javanese fossils were of human lineage. It was not until the 1930s, particularly when other fossils of *H. erectus* were discovered by G. H. R. von Königswald at Sangiran, Java, in the Early Pleistocene Djetis beds, that scientists almost without exception agreed that both discoveries were the remains of an entirely new kind of early hominine. Von Königswald found a small skull that fluorine analysis and (later) potassium-argon dating indicated to be older than Dubois' approximately 500,000- to 700,000-year-old Trinil specimen. Since 1960, additional fossils have been found in Java, and we now have remains of something like 40 individuals. A long continuity of *H. erectus* populations in Southeast Asia is indicated, from perhaps as many as 1.8 million to about 500,000 years ago. Interestingly, the teeth and jaws of some of the earliest Javanese fossils are in many ways quite similar to those of *Homo habilis.*[1]

[1]Tobias, P. V., & von Königswald, G. H. R. (1964). A comparison between the Olduvi hominines and those of Java and some implications for hominid phylogeny. *Nature, 204,* 515–518.

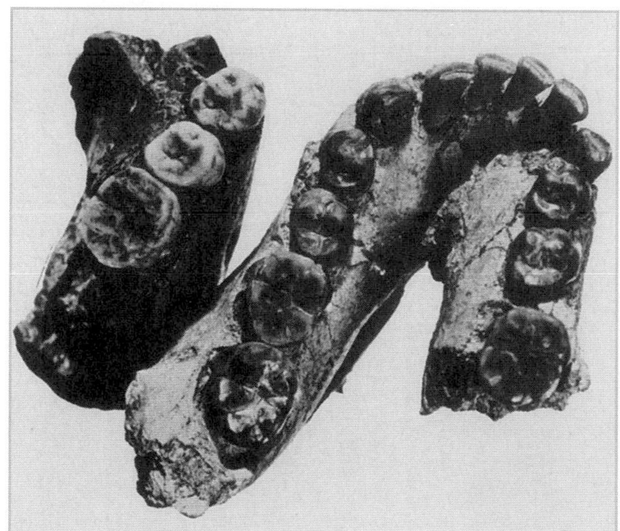

The fragment of the early *Homo erectus* jaw from Java on the left is nearly identical to the jaw of *Homo habilis* from Olduvai Gorge on the right.

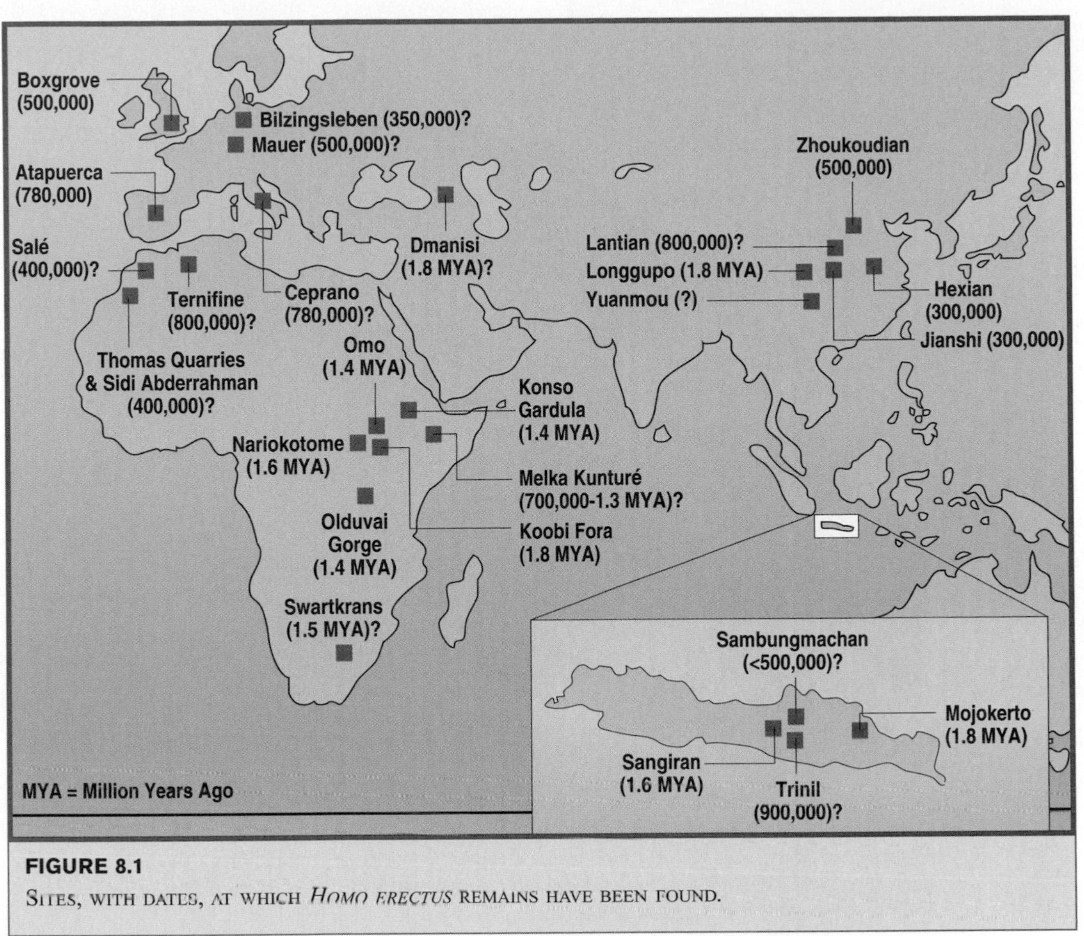

FIGURE 8.1
SITES, WITH DATES, AT WHICH *HOMO ERECTUS* REMAINS HAVE BEEN FOUND.

Homo erectus from China

A second population of *H. erectus* was found in the mid-1920s by Davidson Black, a Canadian anatomist then teaching at Peking Union Medical College. After purchasing in a Peking drugstore a few teeth for sale to local inhabitants for their supposed medicinal properties, Black set out for the nearby countryside to discover the owner of the teeth and perhaps a species of early hominine. At a place called Dragon Bone Hill in Zhoukoudian, 30 miles from Beijing, on the day before closing camp at the end of his first year of excavation, he found one molar tooth. Subsequently, a skull encased in limestone was found by W. C. Pei, Black's associate; and between 1929 and 1934, the year of his death, Black labored along with Pei in the fossil-rich deposits of Zhoukoudian, uncovering fragment after fragment of the hominine Black had named, on the basis of that first molar tooth, *Sinanthropus pekinensis,* or "Chinese man of Peking," now recognized as an East Asian representative of *H. erectus.*

After his death, Black's work was continued by Franz Weidenreich, a Jewish refugee from Nazi Germany. By 1938, the remains of more than 40 individuals, more than half of them women and children, had been dug out of the limestone. Most were represented by teeth, jawbones, and incomplete skulls. World War II brought a halt to the digging, and the original Zhoukoudian specimens were lost during the Japanese invasion of China. Fortunately, Weidenreich had made superb casts of most of the fossils and sent them to the United States. After the war, other specimens of *H. erectus* were discovered in China, at Zhoukoudian and at a number of other localities (Figure 8.1). The oldest skull is about 700,000 to 800,000 years old and comes from Lantian in Shensi Province. Even older is a fragment of a lower jaw from a cave in south-central China (Lunggupo) that is as old as the oldest Javanese fossils. Like some of their Javanese contemporaries, this Chinese fossil is reminiscent of African *H. habilis.* By contrast with these ancient remains, the original Zhoukoudian fossils appear to date between 600,000 and 300,000 years ago.

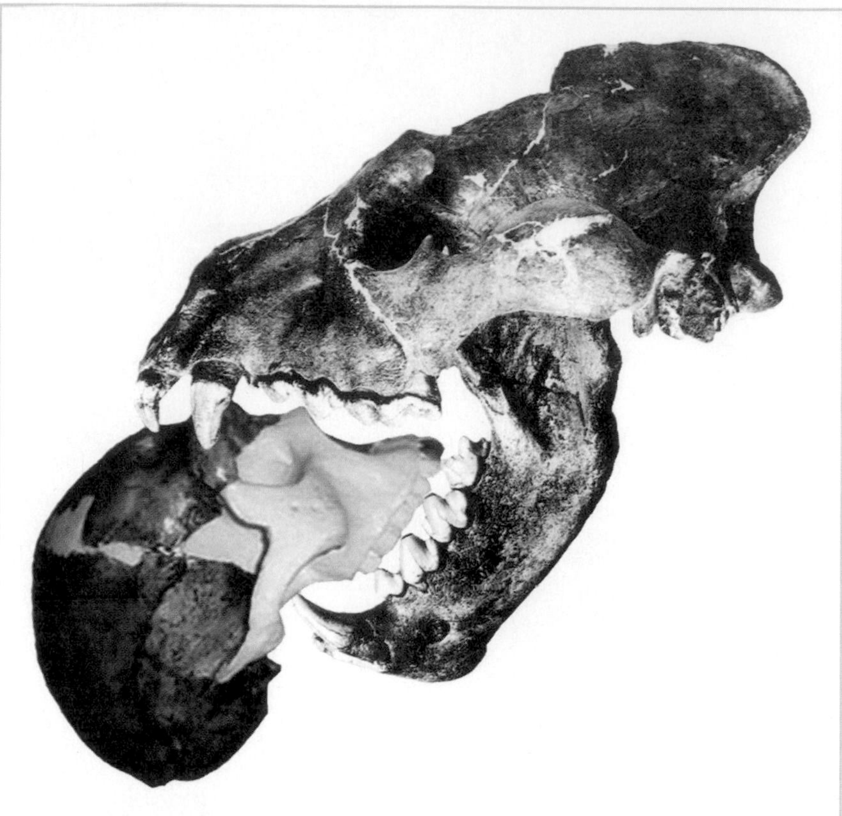

The fossils of *Homo erectus* from the cave at Dragon Bone Hill are the remains of individuals who were consumed in the cave by the now-extinct giant hyena. This composite shows how the giant hyena attacked the face.

Although the two populations overlap in time, the Chinese fossils are, on the whole, not quite as old as those from Java. Not surprisingly, Chinese *H. erectus* is a bit less "primitive" looking. Its average cranial capacity is about 1,000 cubic centimeters, compared to 900 cc for Javanese *H. erectus* (see Figure 8.2). The smaller teeth, short jaw, and lack of diastema in the lower dentition—a gap in the teeth to accommodate a large upper canine when the jaws are closed—of the Chinese are further evidence of their more modern status.

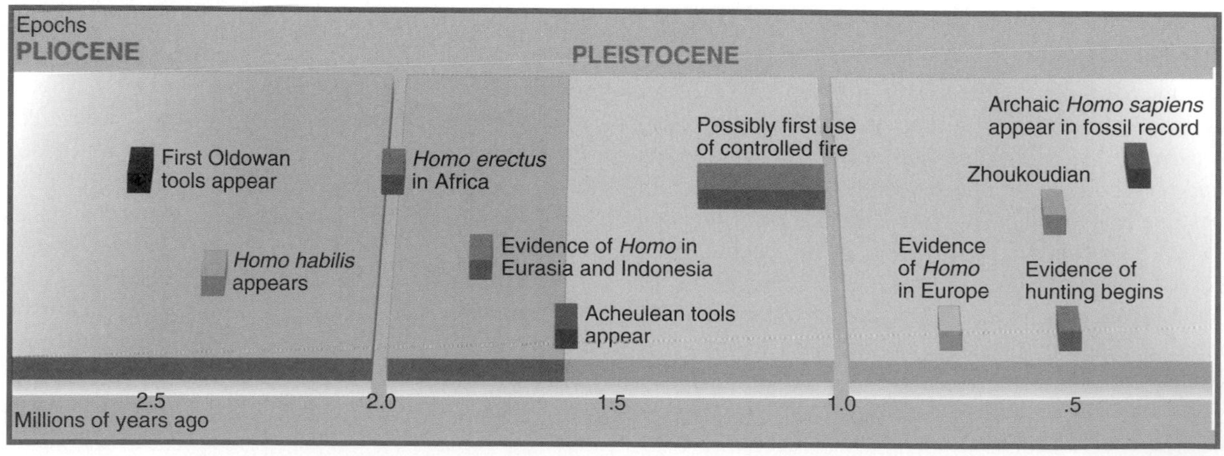

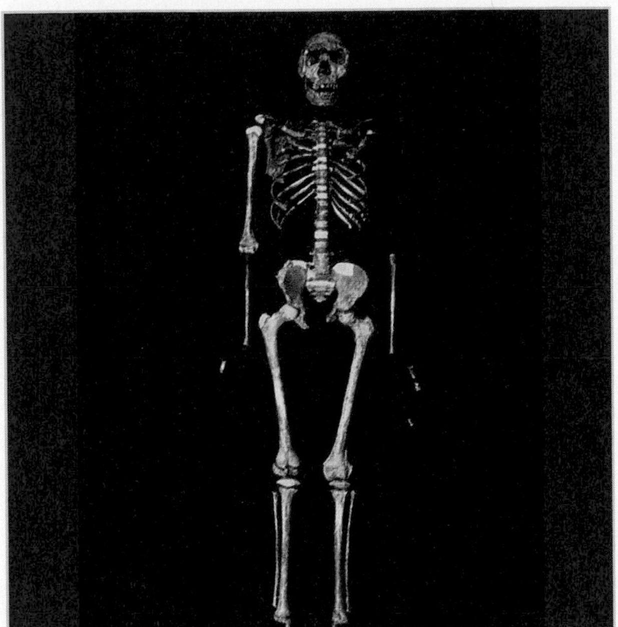

One of the oldest and certainly the most complete *Homo erectus* fossil is the Strapping Youth from Lake Turkana. The remains are those of a boy who died in his early teens.

Homo erectus from Africa

Although our samples of *H. erectus* from Asia remain among the best, several important specimens are now known from Africa. Fossils assigned to this species were discovered there as long ago as 1933, but the better-known finds have been made since 1960, at Olduvai and at Lake Turkana. Among them is the most complete *H. erectus* skeleton ever found, that of a boy who died 1.6 million years ago at about the age of 12. Another partial skeleton, that of an adult, had diseased bones, possibly the result of a massive overdose of vitamin A. This excess could have come from eating the livers of carnivorous animals, for they accumulate vitamin A in their livers at levels that are poisonous to human beings. Another possibility might have been heavy consumption of bee brood and other immature insects, producing the same result.

Generally speaking, African *H. erectus* skulls are similar to those from Asia; one difference is that their bones aren't quite as thick; another is that some Africans had smaller brow ridges. It may be, too, that individuals living in China were shorter and stockier, on the whole, than those living in Africa. Although some anthropologists

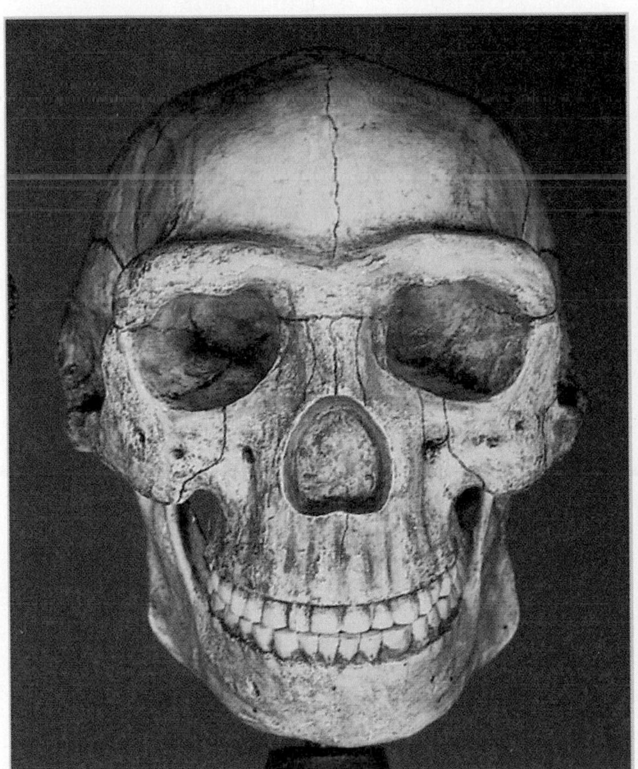

This photo of a reconstructed late *H. erectus* skull from Zhoukoudian, China, may be compared with the earlier African *erectus* skull shown at right.

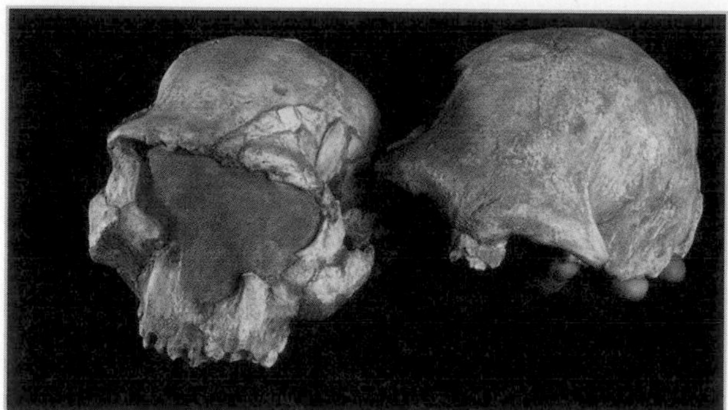

These two skulls of *Homo erectus* from Dmanisi, Georgia, are probably from a male and female. They are about 1.8 million years old and similar to contemporary fossils from Africa.

have argued that the African fossils represent a separate species (*H. ergaster*) and would restrict *H. erectus* to Asia, neither detailed anatomical comparisons nor measurements support such a separation.[2] Such differences as exist are minor and approximate the variation seen in *H. sapiens*. Consistent with this is the fact that a mandible almost 1.8 million years old from Dmanisi, Georgia—a region that lies between Africa on the one hand and Indonesia on the other—shows a mix of characters seen in African and Asian *erectus* populations.[3] Overall, it seems the Africans reveal no more significant physical variations from their Asian counterparts than are seen if modern human populations from East and West are compared. As in Asia, the most recent African fossils are less primitive in appearance, and the oldest fossils (up to 1.8 million years old) display features reminiscent of the earlier *Homo habilis*. Indeed, one of the problems is distinguishing early *H. erectus* from late *H. habilis*—precisely what one would expect if the one evolved from the other.

Homo erectus from Europe

Although Europe has been inhabited since at least 780,000 years ago, few fossils attributable to *H. erectus* have so far been found there. A robust shinbone from Boxgrove, England, and a large lower jaw from Mauer, Germany, are close to half a million years old. The jaw certainly came from a skull wide at the base, as is that of *H. erectus*. Older yet are fragments of four individuals from Atapuerca Hill in north-central Spain and a skull from Ceprano in southern Italy. As might be expected, these remains are similar to contemporary *erectus* material from North Africa. This finding, and the fact that the earliest evidence of hominines in Europe comes from Spain and Italy, suggests that they arrived there by crossing from North Africa.[4] At the time, a mere 6 or 7 kilometers separated Gibraltar from Morocco (compared to 13 kilometers today), and islands dotted the straits from Tunisia to Sicily. Still there was no land connection, requiring that open water be crossed, but evidence from Indonesia (discussed later in this chapter) demonstrates that *H. erectus* was capable of doing this by 800,000 years ago. And all of this evidence, in turn, undermines arguments made by some European researchers that the early Europeans represent a separate species from *H. erectus* (Table 8.1). Such

TABLE 8.1 NAMES SOMETIMES USED FOR *HOMO ERECTUS* FOSSILS FROM EUROPE

Name	Explanation
Homo antecessor	Coined for the earliest fossils from Spain; *antecessor* is Latin for "explorer" or "pioneer."
Homo heidelbergensis	Originally coined for the Mauer jaw (Mauer is not far from Heidelberg), this name is now used by some as a designation for all European fossils from about 500,000 years ago until the appearance of the Neandertals (Chapter 9).

Because multiple species coexisted in the early period of hominine evolution, some paleoanthropologists believe the same must have been true in later hominine evolution. Acting on this belief, they refer to the European fossils by different species names than contemporaries in Africa and Asia, which they refer to as *H. ergaster* and *H. erectus,* respectively. Such a belief, however, remains to be proved. Because all these fossils share a suite of characteristics as well as a common niche, and gene flow between populations seems likely, a reasonable interpretation is that they constitute a single species with regional variation.

[2]Rightmire, G. P. (1998). Evidence from facial morphology for similarity of Asian and African representatives of *Homo erectus. American Journal of Physical Anthropology, 106,* 61.

[3]Rosas, A., & Bermdez de Castro, J. M. (1998). On the taxonomic affinities of the Dmanisi mandible (Georgia). *American Journal of Physical Anthropology, 107,* 159.

[4]Balter, M. (2001). In search of the first Europeans. *Science, 291,* 1,724.

This skull, from Ceprano, Italy, is one of the oldest fossils of *H. erectus* from Europe. It is close to 800,000 years old.

speciation would require isolation of Europeans from other populations, but if ancient humans could cross between North Africa and southern Europe at least once, if not twice, they could do it any number of times and thus maintain at least a modicum of gene flow between populations.

Other European fossils are not as old as the Mauer and Boxgrove remains and display a mosaic of features characteristic of both *H. erectus* and subsequent archaic *H. sapiens*. Here, as in Africa and Asia, a distinction between late *erectus* and early *sapiens* is difficult to make.

Physical Characteristics of *Homo erectus*

Apart from its skull, the skeleton of *H. erectus* differs only subtly from that of modern humans. Although its bodily proportions are like ours, it was more heavily muscled, its rib cage was conical rather than barrel-shaped, and its hips were narrower. Stature seems to have been in the modern range, as the youth from Lake Turkana was about 5 feet 3 inches tall. Long legs and short toes made for effective long-distance walking. Compared to *Homo habilis, H. erectus* was notably larger but displayed significantly less sexual dimorphism.

Cranial capacity in *H. erectus* ranged from 700 to 1,225 cubic centimeters (average about 1,000 cc), which compares with 752 cc for the nearly 2-million-year-old KNM ER 1470 skull from East Africa and 1,000 to 2,000 cc (average 1,300 cc) for modern human skulls (Figure 8.2). The cranium itself had a low vault, and the head was long and narrow. When viewed from behind, its width was greater than its height, with its greatest width at the base. The skulls of modern humans when similarly viewed are higher than they are wide, with the widest dimension in the region above the ears. The shape of the inside of *H. erectus'* braincase showed near-modern development of the brain, especially in the speech area. Although some anthropologists argue that the vocal apparatus was not adequate for speech, others argue that asymmetries of the brain suggest the same pattern of right-handedness with left cerebral dominance that, in modern peoples, is correlated with the capacity for language.[5]

Massive ridges over the eyes gave this early hominine a somewhat simian, beetle-browed appearance. *H. erectus* also possessed a sloping forehead and a receding chin. Powerful jaws with large teeth, a protruding mouth, and huge neck muscles added to the generally rugged appearance. Nevertheless, the face, teeth, and jaws of this hominine are smaller than those of *Homo habilis.*

[5]Holloway, R. L. (1981). The Indonesian *Homo erectus* brain endocasts revisited. *American Journal of Physical Anthropology, 55,* 521.

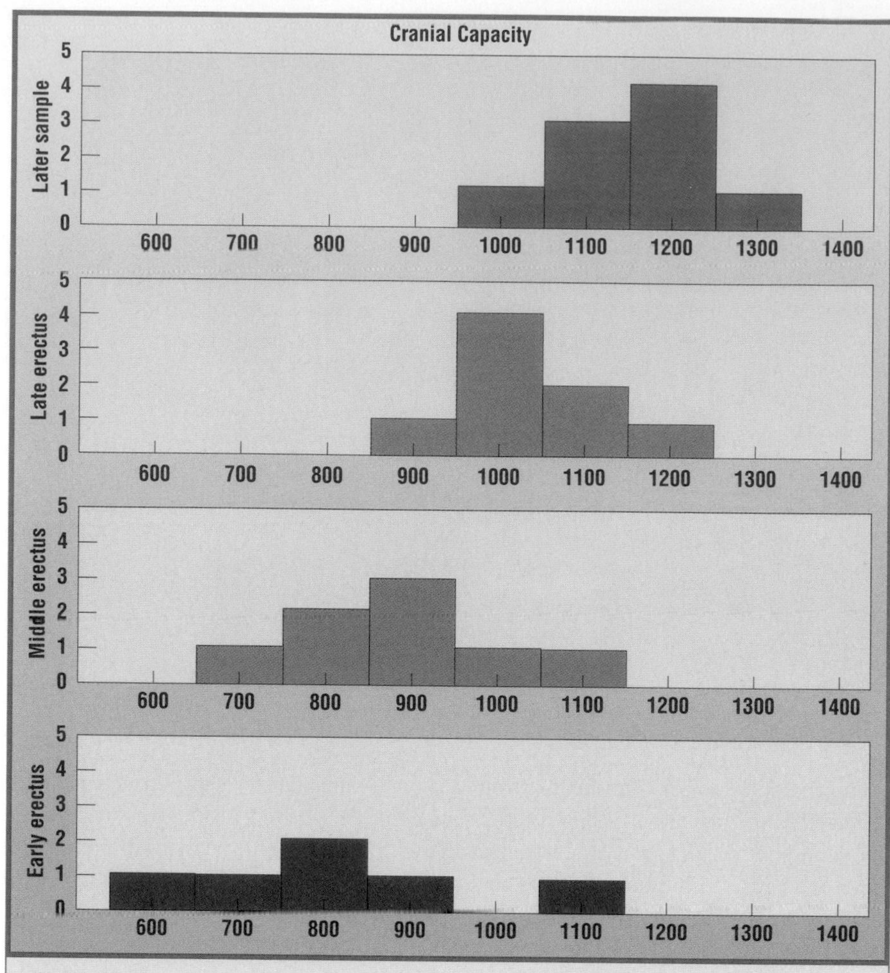

FIGURE 8.2

CRANIAL CAPACITY IN *HOMO ERECTUS* INCREASED OVER TIME, AS ILLUSTRATED BY THESE BAR GRAPHS, SHOWN IN CUBIC CENTIMETERS. THE TOP GRAPH DEPICTS CRANIAL CAPACITY IN SKULLS TRANSITIONAL FROM *ERECTUS* TO *SAPIENS*.

Relationship Between *Homo erectus* and *Homo habilis*

The smaller teeth and larger brains of *H. erectus* seem to mark continuation of a trend first seen in *Homo habilis*. What is new is the increased body size, reduced sexual dimorphism, and more "human" body form of *erectus*. Nonetheless, there is some resemblance to *habilis,* for example, in the conical shape of the rib cage, the long neck and low neck angle of the thighbone, the long low vault and marked constriction of the skull behind the eyes, and smaller brain size in the earliest *erectus* fossils. Indeed, as already noted, it is very difficult to distinguish between the earliest *erectus* and the latest *habilis* fossils (Figure 8.3). Presumably the one form evolved from the other, evidently fairly abruptly, in the period between 1.8 and 1.6 million years ago.

THE CULTURE OF *HOMO ERECTUS*

As one might expect given its larger brain, *H. erectus* outstripped its predecessors in cultural ability. In Africa, Europe, and Asia, there was refinement of the stone toolmaking technology begun by the makers of earlier flake and chopper tools. At some point, fire began to be used

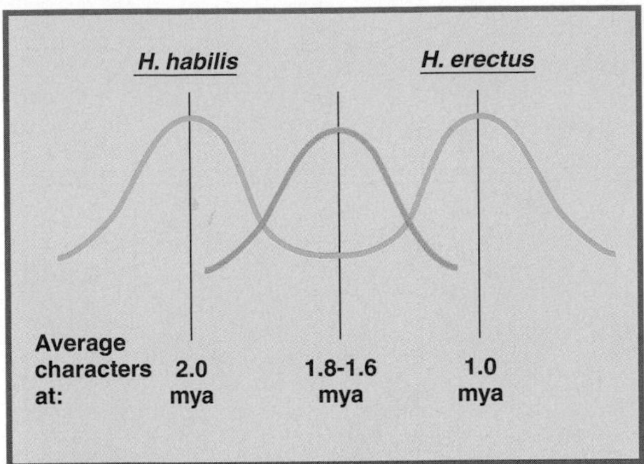

FIGURE 8.3
To understand the evolution of any species, the full range of variation must be considered, not merely typical representatives. The fact that fossils seemingly attributed to *H. habilis* and *H. erectus* coexisted between 1.8 and 1.6 million years ago (mya) need not mean coexistence of two separate species. If one evolved from the other, we would expect that at some point, the full range of variation included some individuals that still resembled *habilis*, whereas others were increasingly taking on the appearance of *erectus*.

Homo erectus made a variety of Acheulean handaxes.

for protection, warmth, and cooking, though precisely when is still a matter for debate. Finally, there is indirect evidence that the organizational and planning abilities of *H. erectus,* or at least the later ones, were improved over those of their predecessors.

The Acheulean Tool Tradition

Associated with the remains of *Homo erectus* in Africa, Europe, and Southwest Asia are tools of the **Acheulean tradition.** The signature piece of this tradition is the handaxe: a teardrop-shaped tool pointed at one end with a sharp cutting edge all around. In East Africa, the earliest handaxes are about 1.6 million years old; those found in Europe are no older than about 500,000 years. At the same time that handaxes appeared, archaeological sites in Europe became dramatically more common than earlier ones, suggesting an influx of people bringing with them Acheulean technology (and implying continued gene flow into Europe). Since the spread of the genus *Homo* from Africa took place before the invention of the handaxe, it is not surprising to find that different forms of tools were developed in East Asia.

That the Acheulean grew out of the Oldowan tradition is indicated by an examination of the evidence discovered at Olduvai. In Bed I, the lowest level, chopper tools were found along with remains of *Homo habilis.* In lower Bed II, the first crude handaxes were found intermingled with chopper tools. Acheulean handaxes having a more finished look about them appear in middle Bed II, together with *H. erectus* remains.

Early Acheulean tools represent a significant step beyond the generalized cutting, chopping, and scraping tools of the Oldowan tradition. The shapes of Oldowan tools were largely controlled by the original form, size, and mechanical properties of raw materials. The shapes of handaxes and some other Acheulean tools, by contrast, are more standardized, apparently reflecting arbitrary preconceived designs imposed upon a diverse range of primary forms.[6] Overall, sharper points and more regular cutting edges were produced, and more cutting edge was available from the same amount of stone.

[6]Ambrose, S. H. (2001). Paleolithic technology and human evolution. *Science, 291,* 1,750.

Acheulean tradition. The toolmaking tradition of *Homo erectus* in Africa, Europe, and Southwest Asia in which handaxes were developed from the earlier Oldowan chopper.

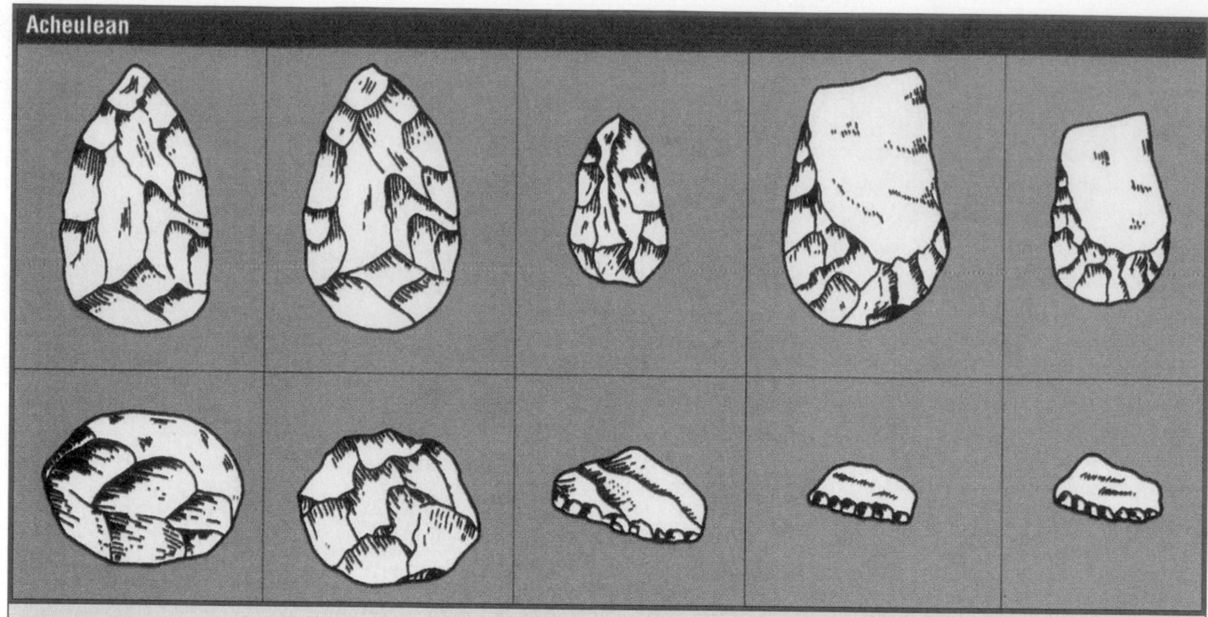

FIGURE 8.4
TEN PERCENT OF THE SHAPED TOOLS IN A TYPICAL ACHEULEAN ASSEMBLAGE ARE THE FORMS DRAWN HERE.

During this part of the ***Paleolithic,*** or Old Stone Age, tool kits began to diversify (Figure 8.4). Besides handaxes, *H. erectus* used tools that functioned as cleavers (these were handaxes with a straight, sharp edge where the point would otherwise be), picks and knives (variants of the handaxe form), and flake tools (generally smaller tools made by hitting a flint core with a hammerstone, thus knocking off flakes with sharp edges). Many flake tools were byproducts of handaxe and cleaver manufacture. Their sharp edges made them useful as is, but many were retouched to make points, scrapers, borers, and other sorts of tools. Diversification of tool kits is also indicated by the smaller numbers of handaxes in northern and eastern Europe, where people relied more on simple flaked choppers, a wide variety of unstandardized flakes, and supplementary tools of bone, antler,

HIGHWAY 1
Take a trip to the Sierra de Atapuerca and learn about the earliest hominines of Europe. See virtual fossils, learn about the research team, their excavation techniques, and the place of these recently discovered specimens in human evolutionary history.
www.ucm.es/info/paleo/ata/english/main.html

HIGHWAY 2
The Peking Man World Heritage Site at Zhoukoudian presents the history, fossils, and artifacts from this site known by locals as Dragon Bone Hill. Review the evidence for the use of fire and hunting and gathering by *Homo erectus.*
www.unesco.org/ext/field/beijing/whc/pkm-site.htm

Paleolithic. The Old Stone Age, characterized by manufacture and use of chipped stone tools.

The 803,000-year-old stone tool on the right is from the Bose Basin in southern China. Though not identical to Acheulean tools such as the handaxe on the left, the Bose Basin tools represent a comparable technology.

and wood. In eastern Asia, by contrast, people developed a variety of choppers, scrapers, points, and burins (chisel-like tools) different from those in the West. Besides direct percussion, anvil (striking the raw material against a stationary stone) and bipolar percussion (holding the raw material against an anvil, but striking it at the same time with a hammerstone) were used to make them. Although tens of thousands of stone tools have been found with *H. erectus* remains at Zhoukoudian, stone implements are not at all common in Southeast Asia. Here, favored materials likely were bamboo and other local woods, from which excellent knives, scrapers, and so on can be made.

Homo erectus and the Use of Bamboo[7]

Original Study

Bamboo provides, I believe, the solution to a puzzle first raised in 1943, when the late archaeologist Hallam Movius of Harvard began to publish his observations on Paleolithic (Old Stone Age) cultures of the Far East. In 1937 and 1938 Movius had investigated a number of archeological localities in India, Southeast Asia, and China. Although most of the archeological "cultures" that he recognized are no longer accepted by modern workers, he made another, more lasting contribution. This was the identification of the "Movius line" (which his colleague Carleton Coon named in his honor): a geographical boundary, extending through northern India, that separates two long-lasting Paleolithic cultures. West

[7]Adapted from Pope, G. C. (1989). Bamboo and human evolution. *Natural History, 10,* 50–54.

Original Study

of the line are found collections of tools with a high percentage of symmetrical and consistently proportioned handaxes (these are called Acheulean tools, after the French site of Saint Acheul). More or less similar tool kits also occur in Mongolia and Siberia, but with few exceptions (which are generally relatively late in time), not in eastern China or Southeast Asia, where more tools known as choppers and chopping tools prevail [Figure 8.5].

My own research on the Movius line and related questions evolved almost by accident. During the course of my work in Southeast Asia, I excavated many sites, studied a variety of fossil faunal collections, and reviewed the scientific literature dealing with Asia. As part of this research I compared fossil mammals from Asia with those recovered from other parts of the world. In the beginning, my purpose was biostratigraphic—to use the animals to estimate the most likely dates of various sites used by early hominines. On the basis of the associated fauna, for example, I estimate that Kao Pah Nam [a site in Thailand] may be as old as 700,000

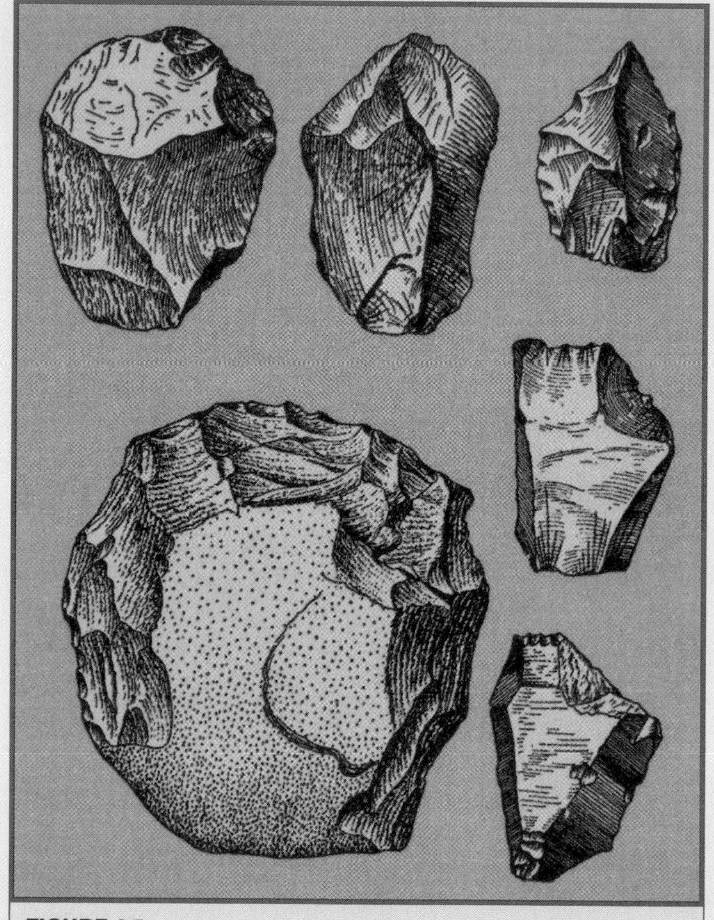

FIGURE 8.5
CHOPPERS AND FLAKES LIKE THESE WERE USED BY *HOMO ERECTUS* AT ZHOUKOUDIAN, CHINA.

years. After years of looking at fossil collections and faunal lists, I realized that something was very strange about the collections from Southeast Asia: There were no fossil horses of Pleistocene age or for a considerable time before that. The only exceptions were a few horse fossils from one place in southern China, the Yuanmou Basin which was and is a special small grassland habitat in a low, dry valley within the Shan-Yunnan Massif.

To mammalian biostratigraphers this is unusual, since members of the horse family are so common in both the Old and New World that they are a primary means of dating various fossil localities. Fossil horses have been reported from western Burma, but the last one probably lived there some 20 million years ago. Not a single fossil horse turns up later than that in Southeast Asia, although they are known from India to the west and China to the north and every other part of Europe and Asia.

I then began to wonder what other normally common animals might be missing. The answer soon became apparent: camels—even though they too were once widespread throughout the world—and members and relatives of the giraffe family. Pleistocene Southeast Asia was shaping up as a kind of "black hole" for certain fossil mammals! These animals—horses, camels, and giraffids—all dwell in open country. Their absence on the Southeast Asian mainland and islands (all once connected, along with the now inundated Sunda Shelf) is indicative of a forested environment. The mammals that are present—orangutans, tapirs, and gibbons—confirm this conclusion.

The significance of this is that most reconstructions of our evolutionary past have emphasized the influence of savanna grassland habitats, so important in Africa, the cradle of hominine evolution. Many anthropologists theorize that shrinking forests and spreading grasslands encouraged our primarily tree-dwelling ancestors to adapt to ground-dwelling conditions, giving rise to the unique bipedal gait that is the hallmark of hominines. Bipedalism, in turn, freed the hands for tool use and ultimately led to the evolution of a large-brained, cultural animal. Tropical Asia, instead, apparently was where early hominines had to readapt to tropical forest.

In studying the record, I noticed that the forested zone—the zone that lacked open-dwelling mammals—coincided generally with the distribution of the chopper-chopping tools. The latter appeared to be the products of a forest adaptation that, for one reason or another, deemphasized the utilization of standardized stone tools. At least this held for Southeast Asia; what at first I could not explain was the existence of similar tools in northern China, where fossil horses, camels, and giraffids were present. Finally, I came upon the arresting fact that the distribution of naturally occurring bamboo coincided almost directly with the distribution of chopper-chopping tools. The only exceptions that may possibly be of real antiquity—certain handaxe collections from Kehe and Dingcun, in China, and Chonggok-Ni, in Korea—fall on the northernmost periphery of the distribution of bamboo and probably can be attributed to fluctuation of the boundary.

Today there are, by various estimates, some 1,000 to 1,200 species of bamboo. This giant grass is distributed worldwide, but more than 60 percent of the species are from Asia. Only 16 percent occur in Africa, and those on the Indian subcontinent—to an unknown extent the product of human importation and cultivation—are discontinuous in distribution and low in diversity. By far, the greatest diversity occurs in East and Southeast Asia.

Based on these observations, I hypothesized that the early Asians relied on bamboo for much of their technology. At first I envisioned bamboo simply as a kind of icon representing all nonlithic technology. I now think bamboo specifically must have been an extremely important resource. This was not, in my opinion, because appropriate rock was scarce but because bamboo tools would have been efficient, durable, and highly portable.

There are few useful tools that cannot be constructed from bamboo. Cooking and storage containers, knives, spears, heavy and light projectile points, elaborate traps, rope, fasteners, clothing, and even entire villages can be manufactured from bamboo. In addition to the stalks, which are a source of raw material for the manufacture of a variety of artifacts, the seeds and shoots of many species can be eaten. In historical times, bamboo has been to Asian civilization what the olive tree was to the

Original Study

Greeks. In the great cities of the Far East, bamboo is still the preferred choice for the scaffolding used in the construction of skyscrapers. This incomparable resource is also highly renewable. One can actually hear some varieties growing, at more than 1 foot per day.

Some may question how bamboo tools would have been sufficient for killing and processing large and medium-size animals. Lethal projectile and stabbing implements can in fact be fashioned from bamboo, but their importance may be exaggerated. Large game accounts for a relatively small proportion of the diet of many modern hunters and gatherers. Furthermore, animals are frequently trapped, collected, killed, and then thrown on a fire and cooked whole prior to using bare hands to dismember the roasted carcass. There are many ethnographic examples among forest peoples of this practice.

The only implements that cannot be manufactured from bamboo are axes or choppers suitable for the working of hard woods. More than a few archaeologists have suggested that the stone choppers and resultant "waste" flakes of Asia were created with the objective of using them to manufacture and maintain nonlithic tools. Bamboo can be easily worked with stone flakes resulting from the manufacture of choppers (many choppers may have been a throwaway component in the manufacture of flakes).

The End

The greater variety and sophistication of tools found in the Acheulean and contemporary traditions is indicative of *H. erectus'* increased ability to deal with the environment. The greater the range of tools used, the greater the range of natural resources capable of being exploited in less time, with less effort, and with a higher degree of efficiency. For example, handaxes may have been used to kill game and dig up roots; cleavers to butcher; scrapers to process hides for bedding and clothes; and flake tools to cut meat and shape wooden objects. As argued in the Original Study, the differences between tool kits from the Far East and West are likely indicative of adaptation to specific regions. The same may be indicated by the differences between the tool kits of northern and eastern Europe on the one hand, and southern and western Europe on the other. One suggested explanation for this is that certain resources were scarcer in the latter region, which was more heavily forested than the former, and that this scarcity was a spur to increasing the efficiency of technology.[8]

[8]Gamble, C. (1986). *The paleolithic settlement of Europe* (p. 310). Cambridge, England: Cambridge University Press.

The improved technological efficiency of *H. erectus* is also evident in the selection of raw materials. Although Oldowan toolmakers frequently used coarse-grained stone such as basalt, their Acheulean counterparts generally used such stone only for their heavier implements, preferring flint or other stones with a high silica content for the smaller ones. During later Acheulean times, two techniques were developed that produced thinner, more elegant axes with straighter edges and more regular forms. The **baton method** of percussion manufacture involved using a bone or antler punch to strike the edge of the flint core. This method produced shallow flake scars, rather than the crushed edge that the hammerstone method produced on the earlier Acheulean handaxes. In later Acheulean times, the striking-platform method was also used to create sharper, thinner axes; the toolmakers would often strike off flakes to create a flat surface near the edge. These flat surfaces, or striking platforms, were set up along the edge of the tool perpendicular to its sides, so that the toolmaker could remove long, thin flakes stretching from the edge across each side of the tool.

Baton method. The technique of stone tool manufacture performed by striking the raw material with a bone or antler "baton" to remove flakes.

Large cutting tools, like this one (both sides are shown) from the Bose Basin of south China, were made and used in substantial numbers for only a brief period around 803,000 years ago. At the time, a large meteorite struck the region, igniting fires that caused widespread deforestation. The tools appear to be an adaptation to this event; once the vegetation recovered, early humans may have reverted to the use of bamboo for tools.

Experimentation on an elephant that died of natural causes demonstrates the effectiveness of Acheulean tools. Simple flint flakes easily slice through the thick hide, while handaxes sever large muscles. With such tools, two men working together can each butcher 100 pounds of meat in an hour.

Use of Fire

Another sign of *H. erectus'* developing technology is evidence of fires and cooking. Compelling evidence comes from the 700,000-year-old Kao Poh Nam rock shelter in Thailand, where a roughly circular arrangement of fire-cracked basalt cobbles was found in association with artifacts and animal bones. Because such rocks are not native to the rock shelter and are quite heavy, they probably had to have been carried in by hominines. The reason more readily available limestone rocks were not used for hearths is that, when burned, they produce a quicklime, which causes itchy and burning skin rashes.[9] The bones associated with the hearth (which was located near the rock shelter entrance, away from the deeper recesses favored by denning animals) show clear evidence of cut marks from butchering, as well as burning.

Homo erectus may have been using fire even earlier, based on evidence from Swartkrans, in South Africa. Here, in deposits estimated to date between 1.3 and 1 million years ago, bones have been found that had been heated to temperatures far in excess of what one would expect as the result of natural fires. Natural grass fires in the region will not heat bones above 212 degrees Fahrenheit, whereas coals in campfires reach temperatures from 900° to 1200° F. Consequently, bones thrown into such fires reach temperatures higher than 212° F. Furthermore, the burned bones do not occur in deeper deposits, even though natural grass fires would have been no less common. South African paleoanthropologists Andrew Sillen and C. K. Brain suggest that the purpose of the Swartkrans fires was protection from predators, as the bones were heated to such high temperatures that any meat on them would have been inedible.[10] Thus, fire may not have been "tamed" initially for cooking or to keep people warm; such uses may have come later.

[9]Pope, G. C. (1989). Bamboo and human evolution. *Natural History, 10,* 56.

[10]Sillen, A., & Brain, C. K. (1990). Old flame. *Natural History, 4,* 10.

Archaeologists excavate a hearth at a rock shelter in Kao Poh Nam, Thailand. This hearth testifies to human use of fire 700,000 years ago.

Whatever the reason for *Homo erectus'* original use of fire, it proved invaluable to populations that spread out of the tropics into regions with cooler climates. Not only did it provide warmth, but it may have assisted in the quest for food. In places like Europe and China, food would have been hard to come by in the long, cold winters, as edible plants were unavailable and the large herds of animals, whose mobility exceeded the potential of humans to maintain contact, dispersed and migrated. One solution could have been to search out the frozen carcasses of animals that had died naturally in the late fall and winter, using long wooden probes to locate them beneath the snow, wooden scoops to dig them out, and fire to thaw them so that they could be butchered and eaten.[11] Furthermore, such fire-assisted scavenging would have made available meat and hides of woolly mammoths, woolly rhinoceroses, and bison, which were probably beyond the ability of *H. erectus* to kill, at least until late in the species' career.

Perhaps it was the use of fire to thaw carcasses that led to the idea of cooking food, thereby altering the forces of natural selection, which previously favored individuals with heavy jaws and large, sharp teeth (food is tougher and needs more chewing when it is uncooked), thus favoring further reduction in tooth size along with supportive facial architecture. And it is a fact that, between early and late *H. erectus,* chewing-related structures undergo reduction at a rate markedly above the fossil vertebrate average.[12] Cooking did more than soften food, though. Cooking detoxifies a number of otherwise poisonous plants; alters digestion-inhibiting substances so that important vitamins, minerals, and proteins can be absorbed while in the gut, rather than just passing through it unused; and makes complex carbohydrates like starch—high-energy foods—digestible. With cooking, the nutritional resources available to humans were substantially increased and made more secure. The partial predigestion of food by cooking also may have caused a reduction in the size of the digestive tract. Despite its overall similarity of form to those of apes, the digestive tract of modern humans is substantially smaller. The advantage of this gut reduction is that it draws less energy to operate, thereby competing less with the high energy requirements of a larger brain. (Although a mere 2 percent of body weight, the brain accounts for about 20 to 25 percent of energy consumed at resting metabolism in modern human adults.[13])

Like tools, then, fire gave people more control over their environment. Possibly, *H. erectus* in Southeast Asia used fire, as have more recent populations living there, to keep areas in the forest clear for foot traffic. Certainly, the resistance to burning characteristic of many hardwood trees in this forest today indicates that fire has for a long time been important in their evolution. Fire may also have been used by *H. erectus,* as it was by subsequent hominines, not just for protection from animals out in the open but to frighten away cave-dwelling predators so that the fire-users might live in the caves themselves; and fire could then be used to provide warmth and light in these otherwise cold and dark habitations. Even more, it modified the natural succession of day and night, perhaps encouraging *H. erectus* to stay up after dark to review the day's events and plan the next day's activities. That *H. erectus* was capable of at least some planning is implied by the existence of populations in temperate climates, where the ability to anticipate the needs of the winter season by preparing in advance to protect against the cold would have been crucial to survival.[14]

OTHER ASPECTS OF *HOMO ERECTUS'* CULTURE

There is no evidence that populations of *H. erectus* lived anywhere outside the Old World tropics prior to a million years ago. Presumably, control of fire was a key element in permitting them to move into cooler regions like Europe and China. In cold winters, however, a fire is of little use without adequate shelter, and *H. erectus'* increased sophistication in the construction of shelters is suggested by three circular foundations of bone and stone 9 to 13 feet across at a 350,000-year-old site in Bilzingsleben, Germany. These could mark the bases of shelters of poles and grass similar to those used in recent times by people like the Bushmen of southern Africa. In the middle of one foundation was found a long elephant tusk, possibly used as a center post. Adjacent to these possible huts were hearths.

Keeping warm by the hearth is one thing, but keeping warm away from the hearth when procuring food or other necessities is another. Studies of modern humans

[11]Gamble, p. 387.

[12]Wolpoff, M. H. (1993). Evolution in *Homo erectus:* The question of stasis. In R. L. Ciochon & J. G. Fleagle (Eds.), *The human evolution source book* (p. 396). Englewood Cliffs, NJ: Prentice-Hall.

[13]Leigh, S. R., & Park, P. B. (1998). Evolution of human growth prolongation. *American Journal of Physical Anthropology, 107,* 347.

[14]Goodenough, W. H. (1990). Evolution of the human capacity for beliefs. *American Anthropologist, 92,* 601.

At some point, *H. erectus* ceased relying on scavenging as a source of meat, in favor of hunting live animals. One of those animals was the elephant hunted at Ambrona, Spain, where the tusk remains.

indicate that they can remain reasonably comfortable down to 50 degrees Fahrenheit with a minimum of clothing as long as they are active; below that temperature, the extremities cool to the point of pain;[15] thus the dispersal of early humans into regions where winter temperatures regularly went below 50° F, as they must have in China and Europe, was probably not possible without more in the way of clothing than hominines had hitherto worn. Unfortunately, clothing, like many other aspects of behavior, does not fossilize, so we have no direct evidence as to the kind of clothing worn by *H. erectus.* We only know that it must have been more sophisticated than before.

That *H. erectus* developed the ability to organize in order to hunt live animals is suggested by remains such as those from the 400,000-year-old sites of Ambrona and Torralba, in Spain. At the latter site, in what was an ancient swamp, were found the remains of several elephants, horses, red deer, wild oxen, and rhinoceroses. Their skeletons were dismembered, rather than in proper anatomical order, a fact that cannot be explained as a result of any natural geological process. Therefore, it is clear that these animals did not accidently get mired in a swamp where they simply died and decayed.[16] In fact, the bones are closely associated with a variety of stone tools—a few thousand of them. Furthermore, there is very little evidence of carnivore activity, and none at all for the really big carnivores. Clearly, hominines were involved—not just in butchering the animals but evidently in killing them as well. It appears that the animals were actually driven into the swamp so that they could be easily dispatched. The remains of charcoal and carbon, widely but thinly scattered in the vicinity, raises the possibility that grass fires were used to drive the animals into the swamp. In any event, what we have here is evidence for more than opportunistic scavenging; not only was *H. erectus* able to hunt, but considerable organizational and communicative skills are implied as well.

Additional evidence for hunting 400,000 years ago was discovered accidently in 1995 in the course of strip mining at Schöningen in northern Germany. Here were found five well-made and finely balanced spears made entirely of wood, the longest one measuring more than 7 feet in length. These are sophisticated weapons made by hunters who clearly knew what they were doing; no novices were they! The effectiveness of their weapons is attested by the butchered bones of more than a dozen horses nearby.

There is no reason to suppose that *H. erectus* became an accomplished hunter all at once. Presumably, the most ancient members of this species, like *Homo habilis* before them, got the bulk of their meat through scavenging. As their cultural capabilities increased, however, they could have devised ways of doing their own killing, rather than waiting for animals to die or be killed by other predators.

---

[15]Whiting, J. W. M., Sodergem, J. A., & Stigler, S. M. (1982). Winter temperature as a constraint to the migration of preindustrial peoples. *American Anthropologist, 84,* 289.

[16]Freeman, L. G. (1992). *Ambrona and Torralba: New evidence and interpretation.* Paper presented at the 91st Annual Meeting, American Anthropological Association, San Francisco.

Shown here are wooden spears made by *Homo erectus* 400,000 years ago. Found in a bog in northern Germany, they are anything but crude, testifying to the sophisticated toolmaking and hunting skills developed by then.

At Bilzingsleben, Germany, archaeologists have uncovered an arrangement of stones and bones suggesting pavement of an area, perhaps for group rituals.

As they became more proficient predators over time, they would have been able to count on a more reliable supply of meat.

Yet other evidence of *H. erectus'* capabilities comes from the island of Flores, in Indonesia. This island lies east of a deepwater strait that has acted as a barrier to the passage of animals to and from Southeast Asia. To get to Flores, even at times of lowered sea levels, required crossing open water: at minimum 25 kilometers from Bali to Sumbawa, with a further 19 kilometers to Flores. That early humans did just this is indicated by the presence of 800,000-year-old stone tools.[17] Precisely how they navigated across the deep, fast-moving water is not known, but at the least it required some sort of substantial raft.

Evidence for a developing symbolic life is suggested by the increased standardization and refinement of Acheulean handaxes over time. Moreover, at several sites in Europe deliberately marked objects of stone, bone, and ivory have been found in Acheulean contexts (see p. 212). These include several objects from Bilzingsleben, Germany, among them an elephant bone with a series of regular lines that appear to have been deliberately engraved. Though a far cry from the later Paleolithic cave art of France and Spain, these are among the earliest Paleolithic artifacts that have no obvious utility or model in the natural world. Such apparently symbolic artifacts became more common in later phases of the Paleolithic, as more modern forms of the genus *Homo* appeared on the scene. Similarly, the world's oldest known rock carvings are associated with Acheulean tools in a cave in India.[18] Alexander Marshack argues that the use of such

[17]Gibbons, A. (1998). Ancient island tools suggest *Homo erectus* was a seafarer. *Science, 279,* 1,635.

This 300,000-year-old ox rib from a site in France is one of several from the Lower Paleolithic that exhibit engraved designs.

symbolic images requires some sort of spoken language, not only to assign meaning to the images but to maintain the tradition they seem to represent.[19] That such a symbolic tradition did exist is suggested by similar motifs on later Paleolithic artifacts. It is also in late Acheulean contexts on three continents that we have our earliest evidence for the use of red ochre, a pigment that more modern forms of *Homo* employed to color symbolic as well as utilitarian artifacts, to stain the bodies of the dead, to paint the bodies of the living, and (ultimately) to make notations and paint pictures.

THE QUESTION OF LANGUAGE

We do not, of course, know anything definitive about *H. erectus'* linguistic abilities, but the evidence for a developing symbolic life, as well as the need to plan for seasonal changes and to coordinate hunting activities (and cross bodies of open water?), implies improving linguistic competence. In fact, the vocal tract and brain of *erectus* are intermediate between those of *H. sapiens* on the one hand and earlier *Australopithecus* on the other. Another clue is the size of the **hypoglossal canal,** the opening in the skull through which the nerve that controls tongue movements, so important for spoken language, passes from the skull (Figure 8.6). In modern humans this is twice the size that it is in any ape. It is in the skulls of late *H. erectus,* about 500,000 years ago, that we first see this characteristic in fossil remains.[20] Possibly, a changeover from gestural to spoken language was a driving force in these evolutionary changes. It also may have played a role in reduction of tooth and jaw size, thereby facilitating the ability to articulate speech sounds.

Certainly, the advantages of a spoken language over a gestural one seem to be obvious; not only does one *not* have to stop whatever one is doing with one's hands to "talk" (useful to a species increasingly dependent on tool use), but it is possible to talk in the dark, past opaque

[18]Bednarik, R. G. (1995). Concept-mediated marking in the lower Paleolithic. *Current Anthropology, 36,* 610–611.

[19]Marshack, A. (1976). Some implications of the paleolithic symbolic evidence for the origin of language. *Current Anthropology, 17,* 280.

[20]Cartmill, M. (1998). The gift of gab. *Discover 19*(11), 64.

Hypoglossal canal. The opening in the skull through which the tongue-controlling hypoglossal nerve passes.

objects, or among people whose gaze is concentrated on something else (potential prey, for example).

With *H. erectus,* then, we find a clearer manifestation of the interplay among cultural, physical, and environmental factors than ever before. However slowly, social organization, technology, and communication developed in tandem with an increase in brain size and complexity. In fact, the cranial capacity of late *H. erectus* is 31 percent greater than the mean for early *erectus,* a rate of increase more rapid than the average fossil vertebrate rate.[21] As a consequence of these, *H. erectus'* resource base was enlarged significantly; the supply of meat could be increased by hunting as well as by scavenging, and the supply of plant foods was increased as cooking allowed the consumption of vegetables that otherwise are toxic or indigestible. This, along with an increased ability to modify the environment in advantageous ways—for example, by using fire to provide warmth—undoubtedly contributed to a population increase and territorial expansion. In humans, as in other mammals, any kind of adaptation that enhances reproductive success causes population growth. This growth causes fringe populations to spill over into neighboring regions previously uninhabited by the species.

Thus, *Homo erectus* was able to move into areas that had never been inhabited by hominines before; first into the warm, southern regions of Asia, and ultimately into the cooler regions of China and Europe.

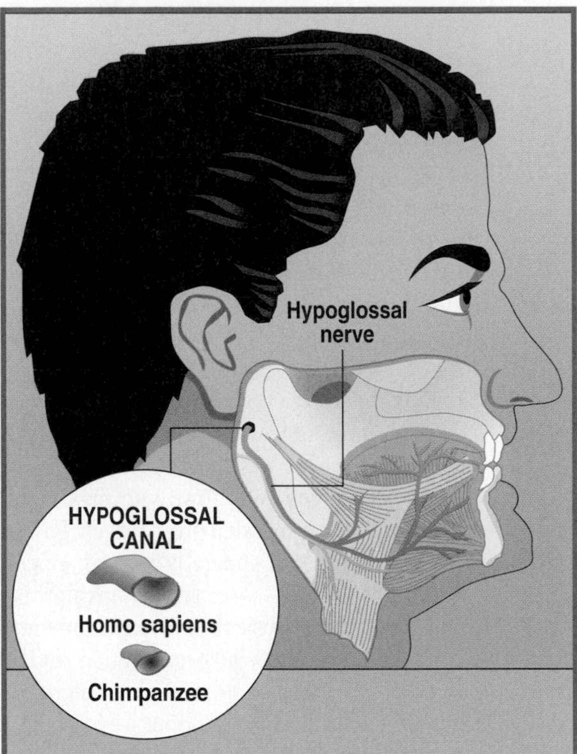

FIGURE 8.6

THE SIZE OF THE HYPOGLOSSAL CANAL IS MUCH LARGER IN HUMANS THAN IN CHIMPANZEES. THE NERVE THAT PASSES THROUGH THIS CANAL CONTROLS TONGUE MOVEMENT, AND COMPLEX TONGUE MOVEMENTS ARE INVOLVED IN SPOKEN LANGUAGE. ALL HOMININES AFTER ABOUT 500,000 YEARS AGO HAVE THIS ENLARGED HYPOGLOSSAL CANAL.

---

[21] Wolpoff, pp. 392, 396.

CHAPTER SUMMARY

The remains of *Homo erectus* have been found at several sites in Africa, Europe, China, and Java. The earliest is 1.6 million years old, and the species endured until about 400,000 years ago, by which time fossils exhibit a mosaic of features characteristic of both *H. erectus* and *H. sapiens. Erectus* appears to have evolved, rather abruptly, from *Homo habilis.* From the neck down, the body of *H. erectus* was essentially modern in appearance, and much larger than in earlier hominines. The brain, although small by modern standards, was larger than that of *H. habilis.* The skull was generally low, with maximum breadth near its base, and massive brow ridges. Powerful teeth and jaws added to a generally rugged appearance.

With *H. erectus* we find a greater interaction among cultural, physical, and environmental factors than ever before. Social organization and improved technology developed along with an increase in brain size. The Oldowan chopper evolved into the Acheulean handaxe. These tools, the earliest of which are about 1.4 million years old, are teardrop-shaped, with a pointed end and sharp cutting edges. They were remarkably standardized in form over large areas. During Acheulean times, tool cultures began to diversify. Along with handaxes, tool kits included cleavers, picks, scrapers, and flakes. Further signs of *H. erectus'* developing technology was the selection of different stone for different tools and the use of fires to provide protection, warmth, and light; thawing frozen carcasses; and cooking. Cooking is a significant cultural adaptation because it took the place of certain physical adaptations such as large, heavy jaws and teeth, because cooked food is easier to chew. Because it detoxifies various substances in plants, cooking also increased the food resources available and allowed reduction in the size of the digestive tract. Reduced jaw and tooth size may also correlate with a change from a gestural to spoken language. The complex tongue movements associated with speech are also indicated by features of the skull, and aspects of *H. erectus'* behavior imply improved communicative skills.

During later Acheulean times, *H. erectus* used the baton and striking-platform methods to make thinner axes with straighter, sharper cutting edges. From Germany comes evidence of the building of huts and the making of nonutilitarian artifacts; from Spain comes evidence of cooperative efforts to kill large amounts of game.

H. erectus' improved organizational, technological, and communicative abilities led to more effective hunting and a greater ability to modify the environment in advantageous ways. As a result, the populations of these early hominines increased and they expanded into new geographic areas.

CLASSIC READINGS

Campbell, B. G., & Loy, J. D. (1995). *Humankind emerging* (7th ed.). New York: HarperCollins.

This well-illustrated book has three good chapters on *Homo erectus* and their way of life.

Ciochon, R. L., & Fleagle, J. G. (Eds.). (1993). *The human evolution source book.* Englewood Cliffs, NJ: Prentice-Hall.

Part V of this book reproduces eight articles that deal with a variety of topics on the history of recovery, diversity, tempo, and mode of evolution and culture of *H. erectus.* An introduction by the editors puts the articles in context.

Gamble, C. (1986). *The Paleolithic settlement of Europe.* Cambridge, England: Cambridge University Press.

Although it does not deal exclusively with *Homo erectus,* this work does discuss material from Europe associated with this species. In doing so, it takes a critical stance as to conventional interpretations and offers novel explanations of *H. erectus'* behavior based on a better understanding of the process of archaeological site formation.

Rightmire, G. P. (1990). *The evolution of Homo erectus: Comparative anatomical studies of an extinct human species.* Cambridge, England: Cambridge University Press.

This is the standard work on our current understanding of *Homo erectus.*

White, E., & Brown, D., et al., and the editors of Time-Life. (1973). *The first men.* New York: Time-Life.

This magnificently illustrated volume in the Time-Life *Emergence of Man* series deals with *Homo erectus.* Its drawbacks are that it is not up-to-date, and it portrays early *H. erectus* as too much of a big game hunter; nevertheless, it remains a good introduction to many of the classic fossils, sites, and tools associated with this hominine.

CHAPTER 9

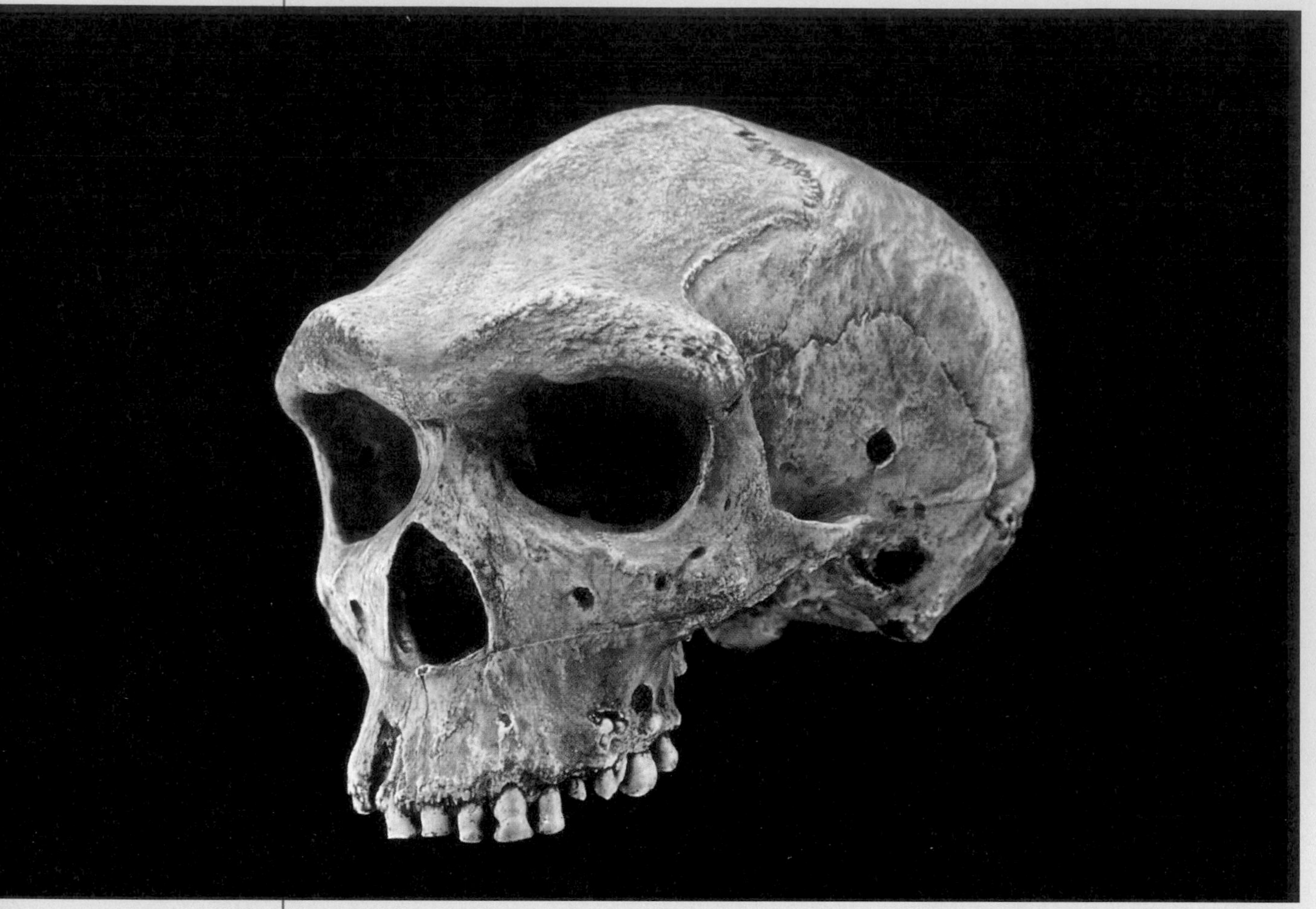

ARCHAIC *HOMO SAPIENS* AND THE MIDDLE PALEOLITHIC

This skull from Kabwe, in Zambia, is an example of archaic *Homo sapiens* from Africa. Like its contemporaries elsewhere in Africa, China, Europe, and Southeast Asia, it has a modern-sized brain in a skull that retains on the outside features of its *Homo erectus* ancestry.

CHAPTER PREVIEW

1

Who Was "Archaic" *Homo sapiens*?

"Archaic" *Homo sapiens* is the name used for members of this species with essentially modern-sized brains in skulls that still retained a number of ancestral features. Descended from *Homo erectus,* the transition took place between about 400,000 and 200,000 years ago. Best known of archaic *sapiens* are the Neandertals, who lived in Europe and western Asia between about 200,000 and 35,000 years ago. Other populations somewhat like them lived in Africa, China, and Southeast Asia.

2

What Was the Culture of Archaic *Homo sapiens* Like?

By 200,000 years ago, the human brain had reached its modern size, and by then human culture everywhere had become rich and varied. People not only made a wide variety of tools for special purposes, but they also made objects for purely symbolic purposes, engaged in ceremonial activities, and cared for the old and disabled.

3

What Became of the Neandertals?

Although there is some debate, the most likely explanation is that their contemporaries, and at least some of the Neandertals themselves, evolved into anatomically modern versions of *Homo sapiens*. This seems to have happened as different features of modern anatomy arose in different regional populations and were carried to others through gene flow. Thus, human populations on all three continents of the Old World seem to have contributed to the making of modern humans.

The anthropologist attempting to piece together the innumerable parts of the puzzle of human evolution must be as good a detective as a scholar, for the available evidence is often scant, enigmatic, or full of misleading clues. The quest for the origin of modern humans from more ancient representatives of the genus *Homo* has elements of a detective story, for it contains a number of mysteries concerning the emergence of humanity, none of which has been completely resolved to this day. The mysteries involve the appearance of the first fully sapient humans, the identity of the Neandertals, and the relationship of both to more modern forms.

THE APPEARANCE OF *HOMO SAPIENS*

At various sites in Europe and Africa, a number of hominine fossils—primarily skulls, jaws, and jaw fragments—have been found that seem to date roughly between 400,000 and 200,000 years ago. Most consist of parts of one or a very few individuals, the one exception consisting of a large number of bones and teeth from the Sierra de Atapuerca in northern Spain. Here, sometime between 325,000 and 205,000 years ago,[1] the remains of at least 32 individuals of both sexes, juveniles as well as adults, were deliberately dumped (after defleshing their skulls) by their contemporaries into a deep cave shaft known today as Sima de los Huesos ("Pit of the Bones"). This makes it the best population sample from this time period anywhere in the world. As expected of any population, this one displays a significant degree of variation; cranial capacity ranges, for example, from 1,125 to 1,390 cubic centimeters, overlapping the upper end of the range for *H. erectus* and the lower end of the range for *H. sapiens.* Overall, the bones display a mix of features, some typical of *erectus,* others of *sapiens,* including some incipient Neandertal characteristics. Of interest is the fact that, varied as it is, the sample shows no more sexual dimorphism than displayed by modern humans.[2]

Other remains from Africa and Europe dating between 400,000 and 200,000 years ago have sometimes been classified as *H. sapiens*—for example, skulls from Ndutu in Tanzania, Swanscombe in England, and Steinheim in Germany—and sometimes as *H. erectus,* as in the case of skulls from several African sites as well as Arago, France; Bilzingsleben, Germany; and Petralona, Greece. Yet all have cranial capacities that fit within the range exhibited by the Sima de los Huesos skulls, and all display the same mosaic of *erectus* and *sapiens* features. Compared to us, for instance, the Swanscombe and Steinheim skulls are large and robust, with their maximum breadth lower on the

[1] Parés, J. M., Perez-Gonzalez, A., Weil, A. B., & Arsuaga, J. L. (2000). On the age of hominid fossils at the Sima de los Huesos, Sierra de Atapuerca, Spain: Paleomagnetic evidence. *American Journal of Physical Anthropology,* 111, 451–461.

[2] Lorenzo, C., Carretero, J. M., Arsuaga, J. L., Gracia, A., & Martinez, I. (1998). Intrapopulational body size variation and cranial capacity variation in middle Pleistocene humans: The Sima de los Huesos sample (Sierra de Atapuerca, Spain). *American Journal of Physical Anthropology, 106,* 30.

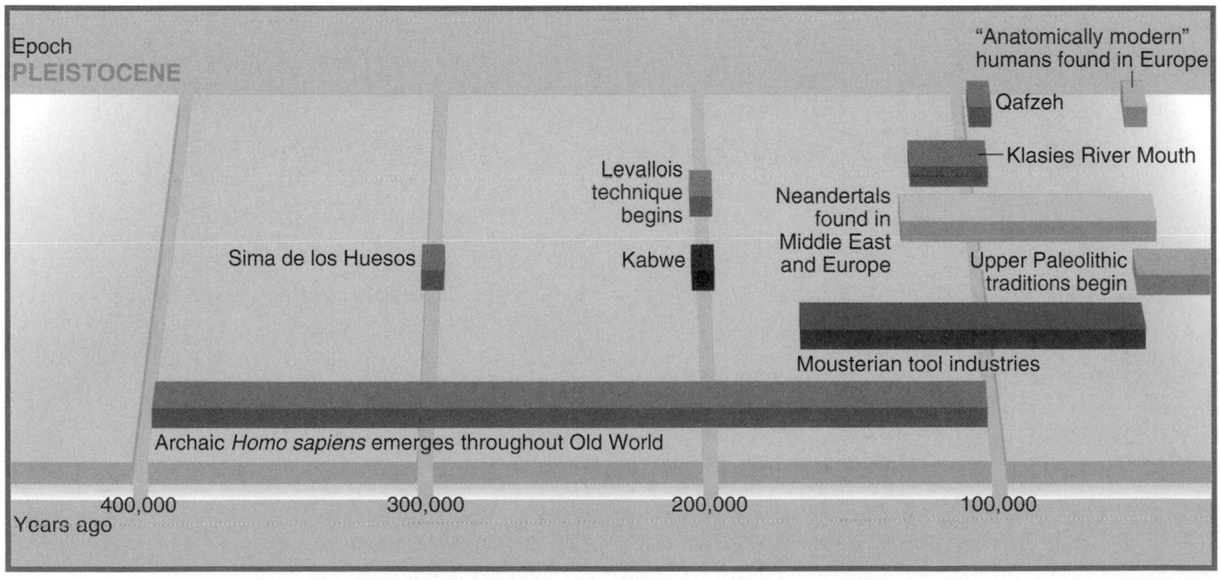

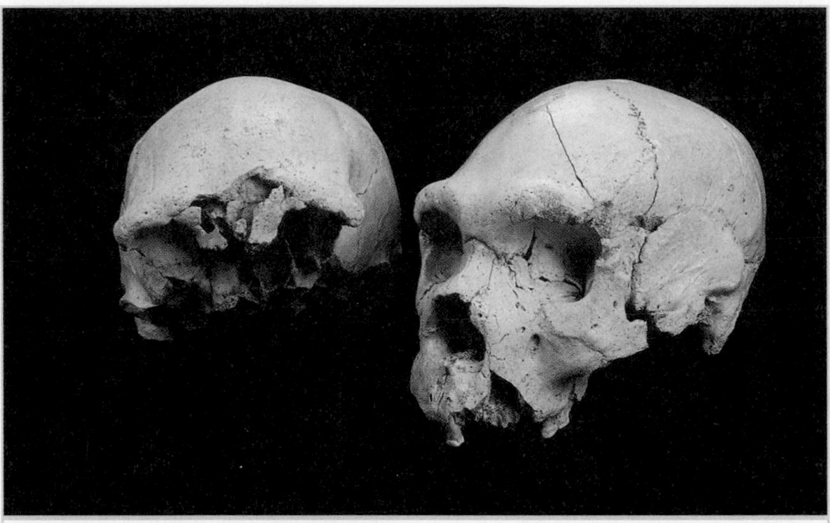

These two skulls are from the 300,000-year-old site of Sima de los Huesos in Spain and represent the transition from *H. erectus* to archaic *H. sapiens* in Europe.

skull, and they had more prominent brow ridges, larger faces, and bigger teeth. Similarly, the face of the Petralona skull resembles European Neandertals, but its back looks like *H. erectus*. Conversely, a skull from Salé in Morocco, which had a rather small brain for *H. sapiens* (930–960 cc), looks surprisingly modern from the back. Finally, various jaws from Morocco and France seem to combine features of *H. erectus* with those of the European Neandertals.

A similar situation exists in East Asia, where skulls from several sites in China exhibit the same sort of mix of *erectus* and *sapiens* characteristics. To call some of these early humans late *H. erectus* or early *H. sapiens* serves no useful purpose and merely obscures their apparently transitional status. Despite their retention of a number of features of *H. erectus*, their brain size shows a clear increase over that of even late representatives of that species (see Figure 8.2).

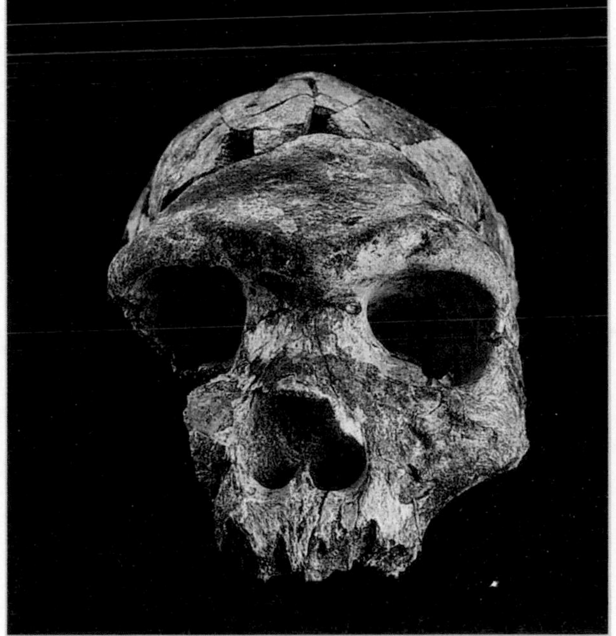

This skull from Ethiopia is one of several from Africa indicative of a transition from *Homo erectus* to *Homo sapiens*.

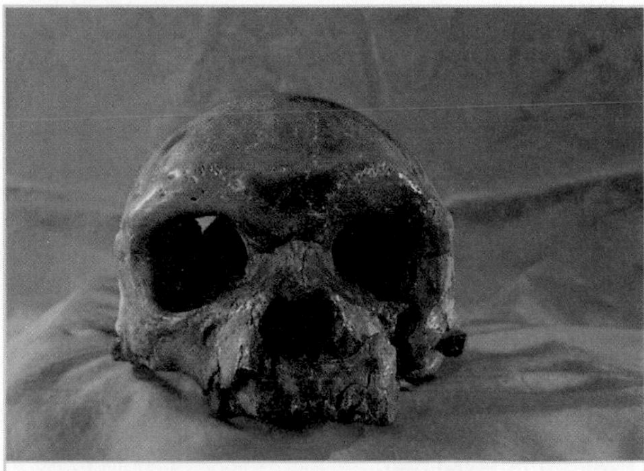

This skull from Dali, China, is representative of archaic *H. sapiens* in East Asia.

Levalloisian Technique

With the appearance of hominines transitional between *H. erectus* and *H. sapiens,* the pace of culture change began to accelerate. Although handaxes and other Acheulean tools were still made, a new method of flake manufacture was invented. This is the **Levalloisian technique,** and flake tools produced by this technique have been found widely in Africa, Europe, the Middle East, and even China. In the latter region, the technique could represent a case of independent invention, because eastern Asia is somewhat distinct culturally from the West. Or, it could represent the spread of ideas from one part of the inhabited world to another. In the Levalloisian technique, the core was shaped by removal of small flakes over its surface, following which a striking platform was set up by a crosswise blow at one end of the core of stone (Figure 9.1). Then the platform was struck, removing three or four long flakes, whose size and shape had been predetermined by the preceding preparation. What was left, besides small waste flakes, was a nodule that looked like a tortoise shell. This method produced a longer edge for the same amount of flint than the previous ones. The edges were sharper and could be produced in less time.

At about the same time, another technological breakthrough took place. This was the invention of hafting—the affixing of small stone bifaces and flakes in handles of wood—to make improved spears and knives. Unlike the older handheld tools made simply by reduction (flaking of stone or working of wood), these new composite tools involved three components: assembly of a handle or shaft, a stone insert, and binding materials. The acquisition and modification of each component involved planned sequences of actions that could be performed at different times and places.

With this new technology, regional stylistic and technological variants are clearly evident, suggesting emergence of more distinct cultural traditions and culture areas. At the same time, proportions of raw materials procured from faraway sources increases; whereas sources of stone for Acheulean tools were rarely more than 20 km away, Levalloisian tools are found up to 300 km from the sources of their stone.[3]

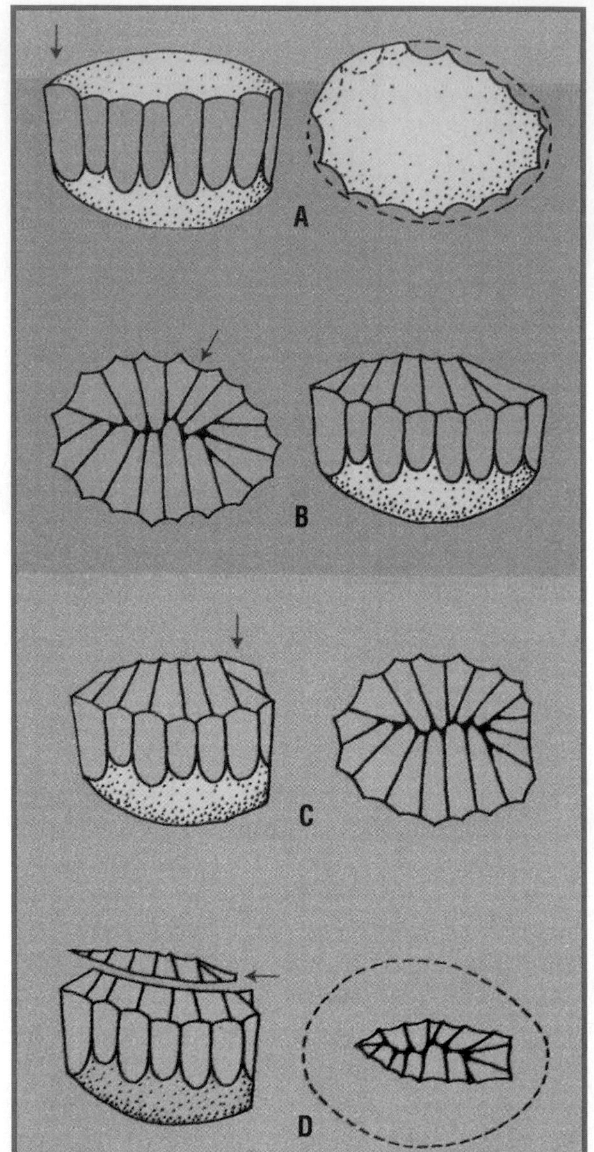

FIGURE 9.1
These drawings show top and side views of the steps in the Levalloisian technique. Drawing A shows the preparatory flaking of the stone core; B, the same of the top surface; C, the striking platform; and D, the final step of detaching a flake of a size and shape predetermined by the preceding steps.

[3]Ambrose, S. H. (2001). Paleolithic technology and human evolution. *Science, 291,* 1,752.

Levalloisian technique. Toolmaking technique by which three or four long triangular flakes were detached from a specially prepared core. Developed by humans transitional from *Homo erectus* to *Homo sapiens.*

Another development, in Africa, was the increasing use of yellow and red pigments of iron oxide, becoming especially common by 130,000 years ago.[4] This may signal a rise in ritual activity, as may the deliberate deposition of the human remains in the Sima de los Heusos, already noted. One possibility is that this involved ritual activity that presaged burial of the dead, a practice that became common after 100,000 years ago. Alternatively, the presence of other animal bones in the same pit with humans raises the possibility that all were eaten by the people who then simply dumped the bones.

Archaic *Homo sapiens*

Of all the remains of archaic *H. sapiens,* none have received more attention that those from Europe. The first publicized discovery came in 1856, 3 years before publication of Darwin's *On the Origin of Species*. In that year, the skeletal remains of a man were found in the Neander Valley—Neandertal in German—near Dusseldorf, Germany. Although the discovery was of considerable interest, the experts were generally at a loss as to what to make of it. Examination of the fossil skull, a few ribs, and some limb bones revealed that the individual was a human being, but it did not look "normal." Some people believed the bones were those of a sickly and deformed contemporary. Others thought the skeleton belonged to a soldier who had succumbed to "water on the brain" during the Napoleonic Wars. One prominent anatomist thought the remains were those of an idiot suffering from malnutrition, whose violent temper had gotten him into many scrapes, flattening his forehead and making his brow ridges bumpy.

The idea that **Neandertals,** as remains like this came to be called, were somehow deformed or aberrant was given impetus by an analysis of a skeleton found in 1908 near La Chapelle-Aux-Saints in France. The analysis mistakenly concluded that the specimen's brain was apelike and that it walked like an ape. Although a team of North American investigators subsequently proved that this French Neandertal specimen was that of an elderly *H. sapiens* who had suffered from malnutrition, severe arthritis, and other deformities, the apelike image has persisted. To many nonanthropologists, Neandertal has become the quintessential "caveman," portrayed by imaginative cartoonists as a slant-headed, stooped, dim-witted individual clad in animal skins and carrying a big club as he plods across the prehistoric landscape, perhaps dragging behind him an unwilling female or a dead leopard. The stereotype has been perpetuated in many a work of fiction, one of the more recent being John Darnton's *Neanderthal,* published in 1997. So it is that many people still think of Neandertals as brutish and incapable of spoken language, abstract or innovative thinking, or even thinking ahead.

Despite this popular stereotype, evidence was forthcoming that Neandertals were nowhere near as brutish and apelike as originally portrayed, and some scholars began to see them as no more than "less finished" versions of the anatomically modern populations that held exclusive sway in Europe and the Middle East after 30,000 years ago. For example, C. Loring Brace of the University of Michigan observes that such "classic" Neandertal features as a sloping forehead, a bunlike back of the skull, and a distinctively small, inward sloping mastoid process (behind the ear) are commonly present in medieval skulls from Denmark and Norway.[5] Nevertheless, Neandertals are somewhat distinctive, when compared to more recent populations. Although they held modern-sized brains (average cranial capacity 1,400 cc, versus 1,300 cc for modern *H. sapiens*), Neandertal skulls are notable in the projection of their noses and teeth and the swollen appearance of the mid-facial region. This is due at least in part to the large size of their front teeth, which were heavily used for tasks other than chewing. In many individuals, front teeth were worn down to the stubs of their roots by 35 to 40 years of age. The large noses, for their part, probably were necessary to warm frigid air to prevent damage to the lungs and brain, and to moisten and clean the dry, dusty air of the glacial climate. The eye sockets were also positioned well forward, with prominent brow ridges above them. At the back of the skull, a bunlike bony mass provided for

[4]Barham, L. S. (1998). Possible early pigment use in south-central Africa. *Current Anthropology, 39,* 703–710.

[5]Ferrie, H. (1997). An interview with C. Loring Brace. *Current Anthropology, 38,* 861.

Neandertals. Representatives of "archaic" *Homo sapiens* in Europe and western Asia, living from about 130,000 years ago to about 35,000 years ago.

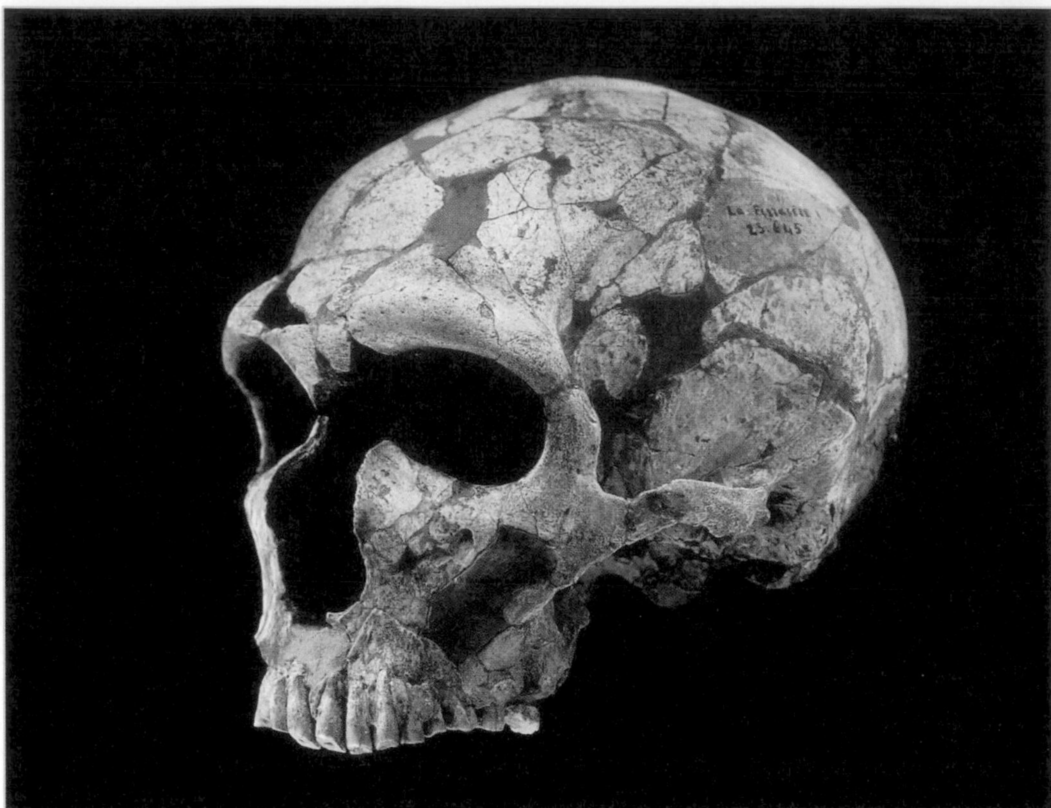

This Neandertal, from a site in France, shows the marked bony ridge above the eyes, receding forehead, and heavy wear on the front teeth that are common in these Europeans.

attachment of powerful neck muscles, needed to counteract the weight of a heavy face.

Both sexes were extraordinarily muscular, with extremely robust and dense limb bones. Relative to body mass, the limbs were relatively short (as they are in modern humans native to especially cold climates). Details of the shoulder blades indicate the importance of overarm and downward thrusting movements; their arms were exceptionally powerful, and pronounced attachments on their hand bones attest to a remarkably strong grip. It has been suggested that a healthy Neandertal could lift an average NFL linebacker over his head and throw him through the goalposts.[6] Their massive foot and leg bones (their shin bones, for example, were twice as strong as those of any recent human population) suggests a high level of endurance; evidently, Neandertals spent long hours walking and scrambling about. Because brain size is related to overall body mass as well as intelligence, the large average size of the Neandertal brain (compared to that of modern humans) is accounted for by their heavy, robust bodies.

The Neandertal pelvis, too, shows differences from that of anatomically modern humans, but these do not support suggestions that obstetric requirements were different for Neandertals than they are for modern humans. Dimensions of the pelvic outlet are fully consistent with those of a modern woman of the same size.[7] Differences in pelvic shape are easily accounted for as a consequence of posture-related biomechanics and deviation in modern humans from a shape characteristic of earlier hominines.

[6]Shreeve, J. (1995). *The Neandertal enigma: Solving the mystery of modern human origins* (p. 5). New York: William Morrow.

[7]Wolpoff, M. H. (1999). Review of Neandertals and modern humans in western Asia. *American Journal of Physical Anthropology, 109,* 418.

As this face-off between paleoanthropologist Milford Wolpoff and his reconstruction of a Neandertal shows, the latter did not differ all that much from modern humans of European descent.

African, Chinese, and Javanese Populations

Because Neandertal fossils are so numerous, have been known for so long, and are relatively well dated (30,000 to 130,000 years ago), they have received much more attention than have other populations of archaic *H. sapiens.* Nevertheless, outside Europe and western Asia, a number of skulls have been found in Africa, China, and Java that date to roughly the same time period.

Among them are 11 skulls that were found in the 1930s at Ngandong, Java. Though their dating was not precisely known, they were generally considered to be Southeast Asian equivalents of the Neandertals with modern-sized brains (from 1,013 to 1,252 ccs), while on the exterior they retained features of earlier Javanese *H. erectus*. With time, opinion on their dating changed, with scholars regarding them as considerably earlier than the Neandertals. This opinion focused attention on their resemblance to *erectus,* so that when their dating was recently revised (to sometime between 53,000 and 27,000 years ago) some concluded that this proved a late survival of *erectus* in Asia, contemporary with *H. sapiens* elsewhere. But the skulls remain what they always were: representatives of archaic *sapiens,* with modern brains in otherwise ancient-looking skulls.

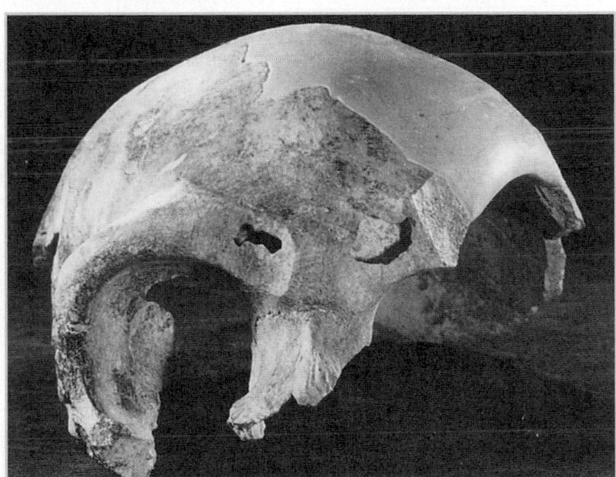

In China, the Maba skull is the one most like the Neandertals. Its round eye orbits are without precedent in the Far East and suggest gene flow from Western populations.

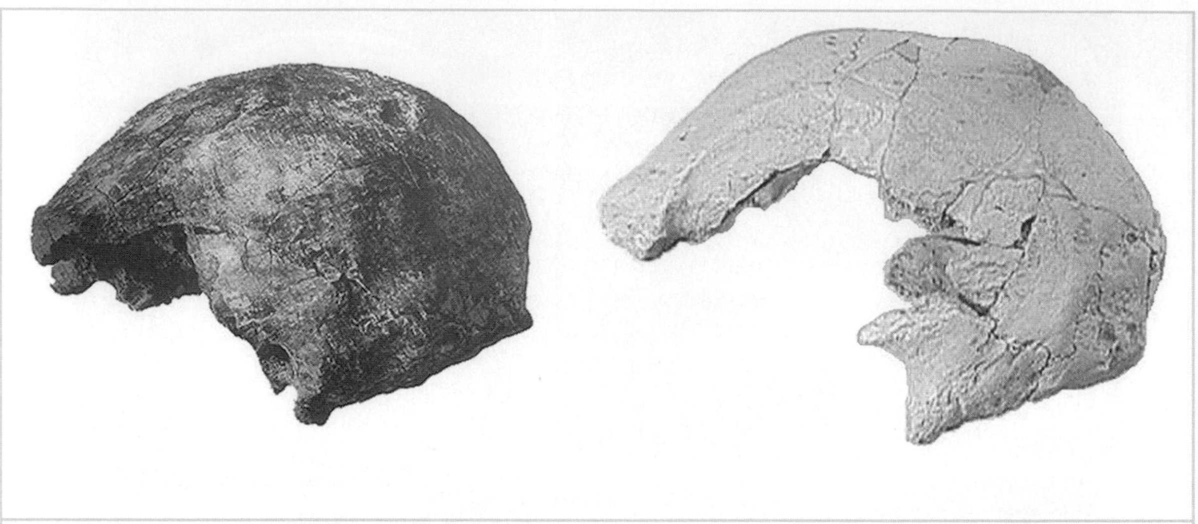

Shown on the left is one of the skulls of archaic *H. sapiens* from Ngandong, Java. On the right is an anatomically modern human skull from lake Mungo in Australia. A similarity between the two is obvious and suggests continuity of populations in Southeast Asia.

African and Asian contemporaries of the Neandertals differ from the Neandertals primarily in their lack of midfacial projection and massive muscle attachments on the back of the skull. Thus, the Neandertals represent an extreme form of archaic *sapiens*. Elsewhere, the archaics look like robust versions of the early modern populations that lived in the same regions or, if one looks backward, somewhat less primitive versions of the *H. erectus* populations that preceded them. All had fully modern-sized brains in skulls that still retained some older features on the outside.

THE CULTURE OF ARCHAIC *HOMO SAPIENS*

As the first hominines to possess brains of modern size, archaic *H. sapiens* had, as we would expect, greater cultural capabilities than their near ancestors. Such a brain made possible technological innovations as well as conceptual thought of considerable sophistication and, almost surely, communication by speech. In short, Neandertals and others like them were a fully sapient species of human being, relatively successful in surviving and thriving even in environments that would seem to us impossibly cold and hostile.

Middle Paleolithic

The improved toolmaking capabilities of archaic *H. sapiens* are represented by various **Middle Paleolithic** traditions, of which the best known are the Mousterian and Mousterianlike traditions of Europe, western Asia, and North Africa. These date between about 166,000 and 40,000 years ago. Comparable traditions are found as far east as China and Japan, where they arose independently from local predecessors. All these traditions represent a technological advance over what had preceded them. For example, the 16 inches of working edge that an Acheulean flint worker could get from a 2-pound core compares with the 6 feet the Mousterian could get from the same core.

THE MOUSTERIAN TRADITION

The **Mousterian tradition** is named after the Neandertal site of Le Moustier, France. The presence of Acheulean handaxes at Mousterian sites is one indication that this culture was ultimately rooted in the older Acheulean

Middle Paleolithic. The middle part of the Old Stone Age characterized by the emergence of archaic *H. sapiens* and the development of the Mousterian tradition of toolmaking. • **Mousterian tradition.** Toolmaking tradition of the Neandertals and their contemporaries of Europe, western Asia, and northern Africa, featuring flake tools that are lighter and smaller than earlier Levalloisian flake tools.

tradition. Neandertals and their contemporaries developed Levalloisian techniques to make Mousterian flake tools that are lighter and smaller than those of the Levalloisian. Whereas Levalloisian toolmakers obtained only two or three flakes from one core, Mousterian toolmakers obtained many more smaller flakes, which were then skillfully retouched and sharpened for special purposes.

The Mousterian tool kits contained a much greater variety of tool types than the previous traditions: handaxes, flakes, scrapers, borers, gravers, notched flakes for sawing and shredding wood, and many types of points that could be attached to wooden shafts to form thrusting spears. Many other tools also were hafted in handles of wood or bone, and some populations were experimenting with bitumen as a glue. With this new and varied tool kit, humans intensified their utilization of food resources and increased the availability and quality of clothing and shelter. For the first time, people could cope with the nearly arctic conditions that became prevalent in Europe as the glaciers began to expand about 70,000 years ago.

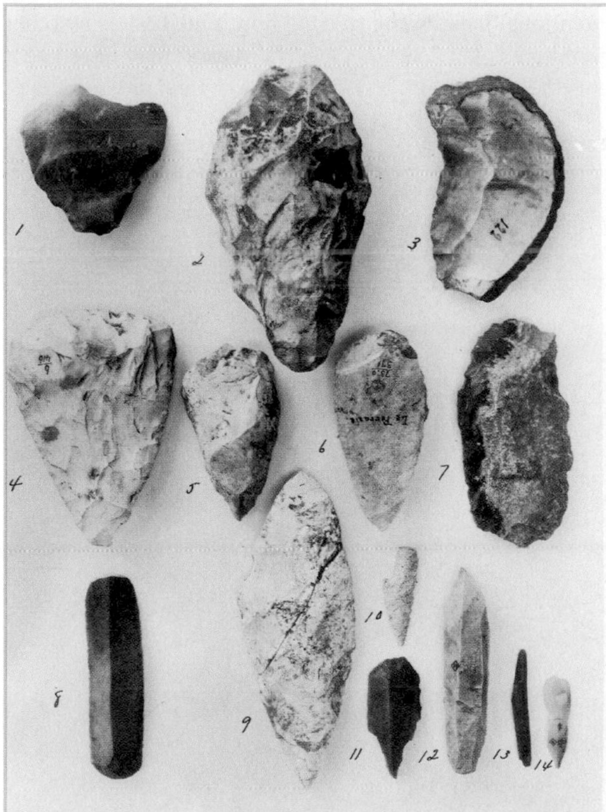

Tools such as 5, 6, and 7 are characteristic of the Mousterian tradition (1–4 are earlier, 8–14 later).

People likely came to live in cold climates as a result of a slow but steady population increase during the Paleolithic era. As this caused populations to gradually expand into previously uninhabited colder regions, humans developed a series of cold-climate adaptations that increased their cultural variability. Under near arctic conditions, vegetable foods are only rarely or seasonally available, and meat is the staff of life. In particular, animal fats, rather than carbohydrates, become the chief source of energy due to their slower rate of metabolism. Abundant animal fat in the diets of cold-climate meat eaters provides them with the extra energy needed for full-time hunting, as well as needed body heat. Insufficient fat in the diet produces lower resistance to disease, lassitude, and a loss of the will to work.

That meat was important to the makers of Mousterian tools is indicated by an abundance of associated animal bones, often showing clear cut marks. Frequently, the remains consist almost entirely of very large game—wild cattle (including bison), wild horses, and even mammoths and woolly rhinoceroses. At several sites there is striking evidence that particular species were singled out for the hunt. For example, at one site in the French Pyrenees, well over 90 percent of the faunal assemblage (representing at least 108 animals) consists of large members of the cattle family. These bones accumulated at the foot of a steep riverside escarpment, over which the animals were evidently stampeded. Similar mass hunting techniques are documented at other Mousterian sites: At La Quina in western France, a dense accumulation of cattle, horse, and reindeer bones (many with clear cut marks from butchering) occurred at the base of a steep cliff; at another site in the Channel Islands, dense deposits of mammoth and woolly rhinoceros bones indicate use of a deep coastal ravine for cliff-fall hunting. Clearly, the Neandertals were not mere unstructured or opportunistic hunters but engaged in a great deal of deliberate hunting of very large and potentially dangerous game.[8] This required careful planning, forethought, and logistical organization.

The importance of hunting to Mousterian peoples may also be reflected in their hunting implements, which are more standardized with respect to size and shape than are their domestic and maintenance implements (for maintaining necessary equipment). The complexity of the tool kit needed for survival in a cold climate may have played a role in lessening the mobility of the users of all these

[8]Mellars, P. (1989). Major issues in the emergence of modern humans. *Current Anthropology, 30,* 356–357.

possessions. That they were less mobile is suggested by the greater depth of deposits at Mousterian sites compared with those from the earlier ("Lower") Paleolithic. Similarly, evidence for long sequences of production, resharpening and discarding of tools, and large-scale butchering and cooking of game, along with evidence of efforts to improve accommodations in some caves and rock shelters through pebble paving, construction of simple walls, and the digging of postholes and artificial pits, all suggest that Mousterian sites were more than mere stopovers in peoples' constant quest for food. The large number of Mousterian sites uncovered in Europe and western Asia, as well as clear differences between them, is closely related to Neandertal's improved hunting techniques, based on superior technology in weapon and toolmaking and more efficient social organization than before. These, in turn, were closely related to Neandertal's fully modern brain size.

Neandertal society had developed, evidence shows, even to the point of being able to care for physically disabled members of the group. For the first time, the remains of "oldsters"—individuals well past their prime—are well represented in the fossil record. Furthermore virtually every elderly Neandertal skeleton that is reasonably complete shows evidence of trauma having been treated, with extensive healing of wounds and little or no infection.[9] Particularly dramatic examples include the remains of a blind man with a withered arm discovered in Shanidar Cave in Iraq, an individual found at Krapina in Croatia whose hand may have been surgically amputated, and a man badly crippled by arthritis unearthed at La Chapelle. The earliest example comes from a 200,000-year-old site in France, where a toothless man was able to survive probably because others in his group processed his food so he could swallow it. Whether or not this evidence indicates true compassion on the part of these early people is not known; what is certain is that culture had become more than barely adequate to ensure survival.

The Symbolic Life of Neandertals

Although earlier reports of evidence for some sort of "cave bear cult" have turned out to be far-fetched, indications of a symbolic life do exist. At several sites, there is clear evidence for deliberate burial of the dead. This is one reason for the relative abundance of reasonably complete Neandertal skeletons. To dig a grave large enough to receive an adult body without access to shovels suggests how important a social activity this was. Moreover, intentional positioning of dead hominine bodies by other hominines, whatever the specific reason may have been, nonetheless constitutes evidence of symbolism.[10] To date,

[9]Conroy, G. C. (1997). *Reconstructing human origins: A modern synthesis* (p. 427). New York: Norton.

[10]Schepartz, L. A. (1993). Language and modern human origins. *Yearbook of Physical Anthropology, 36,* 113.

This Neandertal skeleton from Shanidar Cave is of a man with a badly withered arm.

Anthropology Applied

Forensic Archaeology

Although the fields of Paleolithic and forensic archaeology might appear to have little in common, the two do share techniques of data recovery. The difference is that in one case what is recovered is evidence to be used in legal proceedings involving cases of murder, human rights abuses, and the like; in the other, the evidence is used to reconstruct ancient human behavior.

Forensic archaeologists commonly work closely with forensic anthropologists (Chapter 1). The relation between them is rather like that between a forensic pathologist, who examines a corpse to establish time and manner of death, and a crime scene investigator who searches the site for clues. While the forensic anthropologist deals with the human remains–often only bones and teeth–the forensic archaeologist controls the site, recording the position of all relevant finds and recovering any clues associated with the remains. In Rwanda, for example, a team assembled in 1995 to investigate a mass atrocity for the United Nations included archaeologists from the U.S. National Park Service's Midwest Archaeological Center. They performed the standard archaeological procedures of mapping the site, determining its boundaries, photographing and recording all surface finds, and excavating, photographing, and recording buried skeletons and associated materials in mass graves.*

In another example, Karen Burns of the University of Georgia was part of a team sent to northern Iraq after the Gulf War to investigate alleged atrocities. On a military base where there had been many executions, she excavated the remains of a man's body found lying on its side facing Mecca, conforming to Islamic practice. Although there was no intact clothing, two threads of polyester used to sew clothing were found along the sides of both legs. Although the threads survived, the clothing, because it was made of natural fiber, had decayed. "Those two threads at each side of the leg just shouted that his family didn't bury him," says Burns.† Proper though his position was, no Islamic family would bury their own in a garment sewn with polyester thread; proper ritual would require a simple shroud.

*Connor, M. (1996). The archaeology of contemporary mass graves. *SAA Bulletin, 14*(4), 6 & 31.

†Cornwell, T. (1995, November 10). Skeleton staff. *Times Higher Education*, p. 20.

at least 17 sites in Europe, South Africa, and Southwest Asia include Middle Paleolithic burials. To cite but two examples, at Kebara Cave in Israel, sometime between 64,000 and 59,000 years ago, a Neandertal male aged between 25 and 35 years was placed in a pit on his back, with his arms folded over his chest and abdomen. Some time later, after complete decay of attaching ligaments, the grave was reopened and the skull removed (a practice that, interestingly, is sometimes seen in burials in the same region roughly 50,000 years later). Another example is from Shanidar Cave in Iraq, where evidence was found of a burial accompanied by funeral ceremonies. In the back of the cave a Neandertal was buried in a pit. Pollen analysis of the soil around the skeleton indicated that flowers had been placed below the body and in a wreath about the head. Because the key pollen types were from insect-pollinated flowers, few if any of the pollen grains could have found their way into the pit via air currents. The flowers in question consist solely of varieties valued in historic times for their medicinal properties.

Other evidence for symbolic behavior in Mousterian culture comes from the use of two different naturally occurring pigments: manganese dioxide and red ocher. Finds of these in human trash reveal clear evidence of scraping to produce powder, as well as crayonlike facets from use. Thus, Mousterian peoples were clearly using these for applying color to things. An example is the carved and shaped section of a mammoth tooth, illustrated on page 228, that was worked by Mousterian peoples about 50,000 years ago. One of a number of carved and engraved objects that may have been made for purely symbolic purposes, it is similar to a number of plaques of bone and ivory made by later Paleolithic peoples, and it is also similar to the *churingas* made of wood by

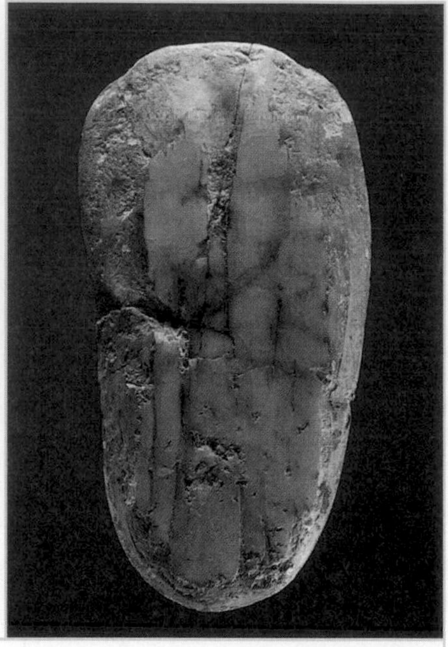

This carved symbolic plaque or *churinga* made from a section of a mammoth molar was excavated at the Mousterian site of Tata, Hungary. The edge is rounded and polished from long handling. The plaque has been symbolically smeared with red ocher. The reverse face of the plaque (right) shows the beveling and shaping of the tooth.

historic Australian aborigines for ritual purposes. The Mousterian object, which was once smeared with red ocher, has a highly polished face as if from long handling. Microscopic examination reveals that it was never provided with a working edge for any utilitarian purpose. As Alexander Marshack observes, "A number of researchers have indicated that the Neandertals did in fact have conceptual models and maps as well as problem-solving capacities comparable to, if not equal to, those found among anatomically modern humans."[11]

Evidence for symbolic activity on the part of Neandertals raises the possibility of the presence and use of musical instruments. One such may be a bone flute from a Mousterian site in Slovenia. The object consists of a hollow bone with perforations, and it has sparked controversy. Some see it as nothing more than a cave bear bone that was chewed on by carnivores—hence the perforations. Its discoverer, on the other hand, sees it as a flute. Unfortunately, the object is fragmentary; surviving are five holes, four on one side and one on the opposite side. The regular spacing of the four holes, the fact that they fit perfectly the fingers of a human hand, and the location of the fifth hole at the base of the opposite side, at the natural location of the thumb, all lend credence to the flute hypothesis. Furthermore, signs of gnawing by animals is superimposed on traces of human activity.[12] Thus, the object cannot be rejected as a flute. Were it found in a later Paleolithic context, it would probably be accepted without argument; only because it was clearly made by a Neandertal, who some are reluctant to accept as fully human, has it been called into question.

Neandertals and Spoken Language

Among modern humans, the sharing of thoughts and ideas, as well as the transmission of culture from one generation to the next, is dependent upon a spoken language. Because the Neandertals had modern-sized brains and a tool kit comparable to that being used in historic times by Australian aborigines, it might be supposed that they had some form of spoken language. And as pointed out

[11]Marshack, A. (1989). Evolution of the human capacity: The symbolic evidence. *Yearbook of Physical Anthropology, 32,* 22.

[12]Otte, M. (2000). On the suggested bone flute from Slovenia. *Current Anthropology, 41,* 271.

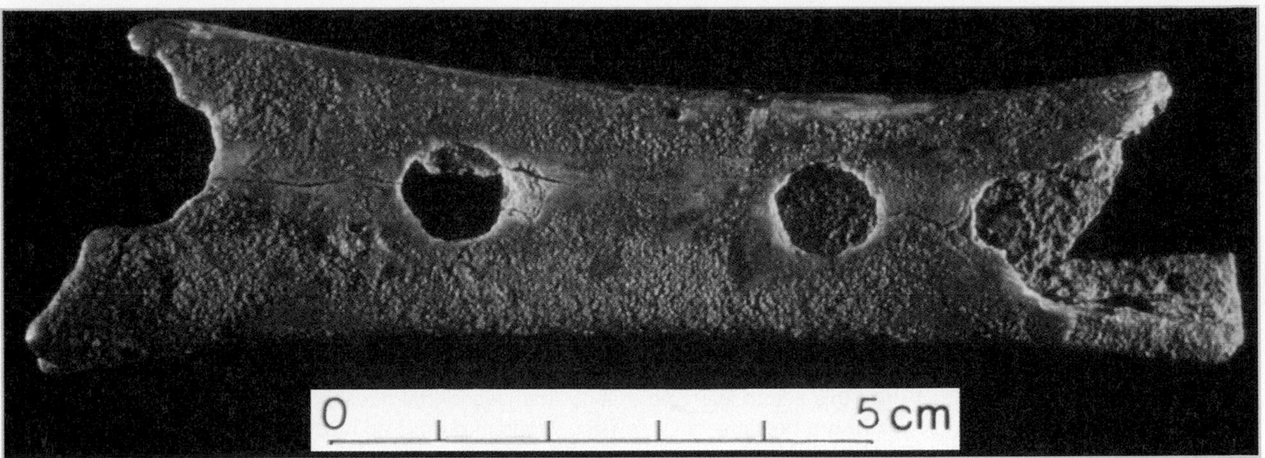

The first musical instrument? There is a strong possibility that this object, found in trash left by Neandertals, is all that remains of a flute made of bone.

by anthropologist Stanley Ambrose, the composite tools of Mousterian and contemporary peoples involved assembly of components in different configurations to produce functionally different tools. He likens this hierarchical assembly of parts into tools to grammatical language, "because hierarchical assemblies of sounds produce meaningful phrases and sentences, and changing word order changes meaning."[13] Furthermore, "a composite tool may be analogous to a sentence, but explaining how to make one is the equivalent of a recipe or a short story."[14] Talking Neandertals make a good deal of sense, too, in view of the evidence for the manufacture of objects of symbolic significance. Objects such as the mammoth tooth *churinga* already described would seem to have required some form of linguistic explanation.

Despite such considerations, some have argued that the Neandertals lacked the physical features necessary for spoken language. For example, the larynx was asserted to be higher in the throat than it is in modern humans, a reconstruction we now know to be faulty. In the skeleton from the Kebara Cave burial, for instance, the shape and position of the hyoid bone (the "wish bone," associated with the larynx) show that the vocal tract was quite adequate for speech. This is especially noteworthy, for humans pay a high price for the way their vocal tract is positioned. With the lowered position of our larynx, it is far easier for us to choke to death than it is for other mammals. (Before the Heimlich maneuver, choking on food was the sixth leading cause of accidental death in the United States.)[15] The only advantage worth such a price seems to be the ability to speak.

With respect to the brain, paleoneurologists, working from endocranial casts, are agreed that Neandertals had the neural development necessary for spoken language. Indeed, they argue that the changes associated with speech began even before the appearance of archaic *Homo sapiens.*[16] Consistent is the size of the hypoglossal canal, which in Neandertals is like that of modern humans and unlike that of apes.[17] As discussed in the last chapter, this feature is apparent in hominine fossils that are at least 400,000 years old and indicates an ability to make the tongue movements necessary for articulate speech. Consistent, too, is an expanded thoracic vertebral canal (the thorax is the upper part of the body), a feature Neandertals share with modern humans but not early *Homo erectus* (or any other primate). This feature suggests the increased breath control required for speech.[18] This control enables production of long phrases or single expirations of breath, punctuated with quick inhalations at meaningful linguistic breaks.

Another argument—that a relatively flat base in Neandertal skulls would have prevented speech—has no

[13]Ambrose, P. 1,751.

[14]Ibid.

[15]Shreeve, p. 273.

[16]Schepartz, p. 98.

[17]Cartmill, M. (1998). The gift of gab. *Discover, 19* (11), 62.

[18]MacLarnon, A. M. & Hewitt, G. P. (1999). The evolution of human speech: The role of enhanced breathing control. *American Journal of Physical Anthropology, 109,* 341–363.

HIGHWAY 1
Play "Name that Skull" and learn to identify fossil hominines and other primate species from their skulls. This site has three graded levels of play.
www.geocities.com/athens/acropolis/5579/knowyourskull.html

HIGHWAY 2
A trip to the site "Neandertals: A Cyber Perspective" provides comprehensive evidence about the Neandertals. Learn about their discovery, lifeways, tool kits, and ritual practices.
http://sapphire.indstate.edu/~ramanank/index.html

HIGHWAY 3
Visit this site to learn more about the Neandertal question including features about making a documentary television program on this controversial subject.
www.pbs.org/wgbh/nova/neanderthals/

merit, as some modern adults show as much flattening, yet have no trouble talking. Clearly, when the evidence is considered in its totality, there seems no compelling reason to deny Neandertals the ability to speak.

ARCHAIC *HOMO SAPIENS* AND MODERN HUMAN ORIGINS

One of the hot debates in paleoanthropology today is over the question: Did populations of archaic *H. sapiens* in most, if not all, parts of the Old World connected by gene flow, evolve together into anatomically modern humans (the multiregional hypothesis)? Or, was there a single, geographic place of origin, from which a new species, anatomically modern *H. sapiens,* spread to replace existing populations of the archaic species everywhere else (the "Eve" or "Out of Africa" hypothesis)? Based on the fossil evidence from Africa and some parts of Asia, a good case can be made for the former, as opposed to the latter, hypothesis.

The Multiregional Hypothesis

As several anthropologists have noted, African, Chinese, and Southeast Asian fossils of archaic *H. sapiens* imply local population continuity from *Homo erectus,* through archaic, to modern *Homo sapiens,*[19] lending strong support to the interpretation that there was genetic continuity in these regions. For example, in China hominine fossils consistently have small forward-facing cheeks and flatter faces than their contemporaries elsewhere, as is still true today. In Southeast Asia and Australia, by contrast, skulls are consistently robust, with huge cheeks and forward projection of the jaws.

Although the idea of continuity from the earliest European fossils through the Neandertals is widely accepted, the idea that Neandertals were involved in the ancestry of modern Europeans has been resisted by many. No earlier than 36,500 years ago[20] a new technology, known as the **Aurignacian tradition,** spread into Europe from Southwest Asia, where its appearance marks the start of the **Upper Paleolithic** period. In both regions, human skeletons associated with Aurignacian tools are usually modern in their features (but a notable exception is the central European site of Vindija, where Neandertals are associated with an Aurignacian split-bone point).[21]

[19]Wolpoff, M. H., & Caspari, R. (1997). *Race and human evolution.* New York: Simon & Schuster.

[20]Zilhão, J. (2000). Fate of the Neandertals. *Archaeology, 53*(4), 30.

[21]Karavani, I., & Smith, F. H. (2000). More on the Neanderthal problem: The Vindija case. *Current Anthropology, 41,* 839.

Aurignacian tradition. Toolmaking tradition in Europe and western Asia at the beginning of the Upper Paleolithic. • **Upper Paleolithic.** The last part of the Old Stone Age, characterized by the emergence of more modern-looking hominines and an emphasis on the blade technique of toolmaking.

FRANZ WEIDENREICH (1873–1948)

Franz Weidenreich was born and educated in Germany, where he later held professorships in anatomy, first at Strassburg and then at Heidelberg. Although his early work was primarily in hematology (the study of blood), his scientific work shifted to the study of bones and related tissues, and in 1926 he published his first study of a human fossil, an archaic *Homo sapiens* cranium from Ehringsdorf. Two years later, he was appointed professor of anthropology at the University of Frankfurt.

In 1935, he was sent by the Rockefeller Foundation to take up the study of fossils of *Homo erectus* from Zhoukoudian, China, following the death of their discoverer, Davidson Black. When the Japanese invasion of China forced Weidenreich to leave, he took with him to the United States several painstakingly prepared casts, as well as detailed notes on the actual fossils. From these he was able to prepare a major monograph that set new standards for paleoanthropological reports. For this alone, anthropology owes him a great debt, for the fossils themselves were among the casualties of World War II.

Unlike many physical anthropologists of his time or ours, Weidenreich had an extensive firsthand knowledge of extant human fossils from several parts of the Old World: Europe (where he had worked before going to China), China, and Southeast Asia (he collaborated in the 1930s study of *Homo erectus* and later fossils from Java). What struck him about the fossils in each of these regions was the evident continuity from the earliest to the latest specimens. From this observation, he developed his polycentric theory of human evolution, which received its first clear statement in a 1943 publication. In it, he argued the thesis that human populations of common ancestry thereafter evolved in the same direction in four different geographical regions (Africa was the fourth). Although some have (mis)understood this as the completely separate but parallel evolution of four lineages, Weidenreich was quite clear about the continued operation of gene flow in the process. As the number of human fossils has increased, and our knowledge of evolutionary processes has grown, Weidenreich's ideas have been taken up by others and developed into the modern multiregional theory of human evolution.

Nevertheless, fossils described as Neandertals are known from sites in western Europe that date to 35,000 to 33,000 years ago, in which case coexistence between the modern and archaic forms of *sapiens* would seem to be indicated. Given the anatomical differences between the two, some form of population replacement, rather than simple evolution from one to the other, may have occurred.

An alternate explanation is possible, however. If we think in terms of varied populations—as we should[22]—instead of ideal types, we find that features reminiscent of modern humans can be discerned in some of the latest Neandertals. A specimen from Saint Césaire in France, for example, has a higher forehead and chin. A number of other Neandertals, too, show incipient chin development as well as reduced facial protrusion and thinning of the brow ridges. Conversely, the earliest anatomically modern human skulls from Europe often exhibit features reminiscent of Neandertals (see Chapter 10). Accordingly, we might view the population of this region between 40,000 and 30,000 years ago as a varied one, with some individuals retaining a stronger Neandertal heritage than others, in whom modern characteristics are more prominent (Figure 9.2).

Nothing in the physical or mental makeup of Neandertals would have prevented them from leading a typical Upper Paleolithic way of life, as in fact the latest Neandertals of western, central, and eastern Europe did.[23] Out of the earlier Mousterian, they created their own Upper Paleolithic cultures (Figure 9.3). In some respects, they outdid their Aurignacian contemporaries, as in the

[22]Gould, S. J. (1996). *Full house: The spread of excellence from Plato to Darwin* (pp. 72–73). New York: Harmony Books.

[23]Mellars, p. 378.

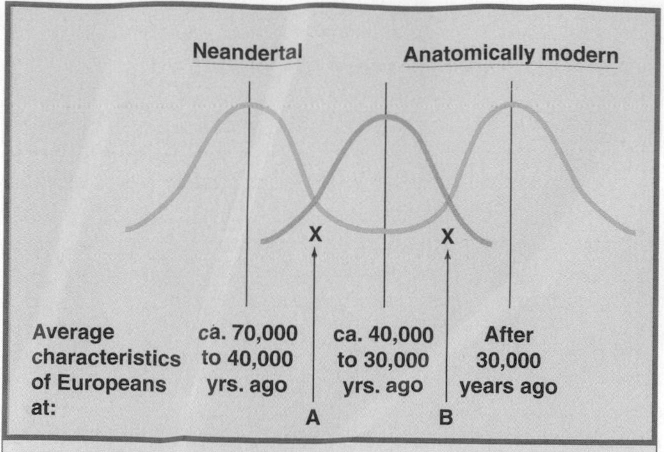

FIGURE 9.2

GRAPHICALLY PORTRAYED HERE IS A SHIFT IN AVERAGE CHARACTERISTICS OF AN OTHERWISE VARIED POPULATION OVER TIME FROM NEANDERTAL TO MORE MODERN FEATURES. BETWEEN 40,000 AND 30,000 YEARS AGO, WE WOULD EXPECT TO FIND INDIVIDUALS WITH CHARACTERISTICS SUCH AS THOSE OF THE SAINT CÉSAIRE "NEANDERTAL" (A) AND THE ALMOST (BUT NOT QUITE) MODERN CRO-MAGNON (B; THIS FOSSIL IS DISCUSSED IN CHAPTER 10).

use of red ocher, a substance less frequently used by the Aurignacians than by their late Neandertal neighbors.[24] This cannot be a case of borrowing ideas and techniques from Aurignacians, as these developments clearly predate the Aurignacian.[25]

Another often cited case of coexistence of the two forms is in Southwest Asia. Although Neandertal skeletons are clearly present at sites such as Kebara and Shanidar caves, skeletons from some older sites have been described as anatomically modern. At Qafzeh in Israel, for example, 90,000-year-old skeletons are said to show none of the Neandertal hallmarks; although their faces and bodies are large and heavily built by today's standards, they are nonetheless claimed to be within the range of living peoples. Yet, a statistical study comparing a number of measurements among Qafzeh, Upper Paleolithic, and Neandertal skulls found those from Qafzeh to fall in between the Aurignacian and Neandertal norms, though slightly closer to the Neandertals.[26] Nor is the dentition functionally distinguishable when Qafzeh and Neandertal are compared.[27]

At the nearby site of Skuhl, a skeleton similar to those from Qafzeh was part of a population whose continuous range of variation included individuals with markedly Neandertal characteristics. Furthermore, the idea of two distinctly different but coexisting populations receives no support from cultural remains, inasmuch as the people living at Skuhl and Qafzeh were making and using the same Mousterian tools as those at Kebara and Shanidar. Thus, there are no indications of groups with different cultural traditions coexisting in the same region. For that matter, the actual behaviors represented by Middle Paleolithic and early Upper Paleolithic cultures were not significantly different. For example, the Upper Paleolithic people who used Kebara Cave continued to live in exactly the same way as their Neandertal predecessors: They procured the same foods, processed them in the same way, used similar hearths, and disposed of their trash in the same way. The only evident difference is that the Neandertals did not bank their fires for warmth with small stones or cobbles as did their Upper Paleolithic successors.[28]

[24]Bednarik, R. G. (1995). Concept-mediated marking in the lower Paleolithic. *Current Anthropology, 36,* 606.

[25]Zilhão, p. 40.

[26]Corruccini, R. S. (1992). Metrical reconsideration of the Skhul IV and IX and Border Cave I crania in the context of modern human origins. *American Journal of Physical Anthropology, 87,* 433–445.

[27]Brace, C. L. (2000). *Evolution in an anthropological view* (p. 206). Walnut Creek, CA: Altamira.

[28]Corruccini, p. 436.

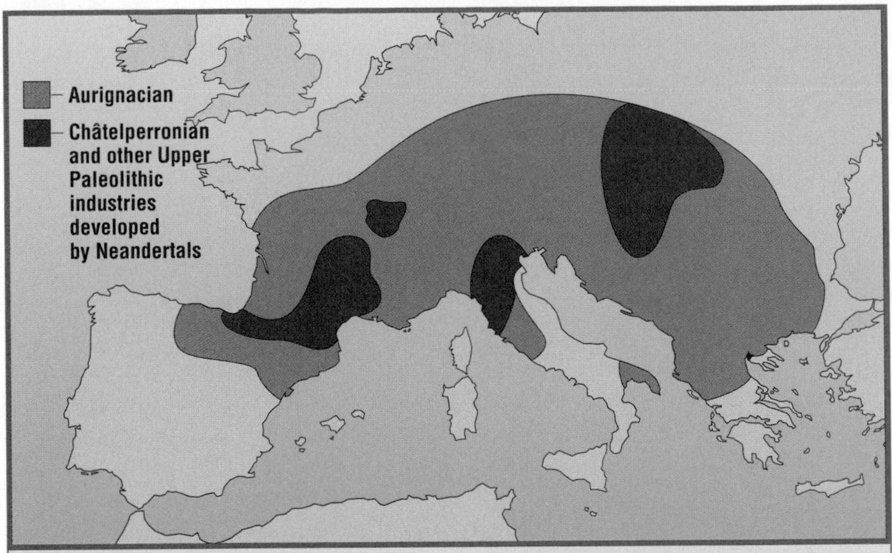

FIGURE 9.3

BETWEEN 36,500 AND 30,000 YEARS AGO, UPPER PALEOLITHIC INDUSTRIES DEVELOPED FROM THE MOUSTERIAN BY EUROPEAN NEANDERTALS COEXISTED WITH THE AURIGNACIAN INDUSTRY, USUALLY ASSOCIATED WITH ANATOMICALLY MODERN HUMANS.

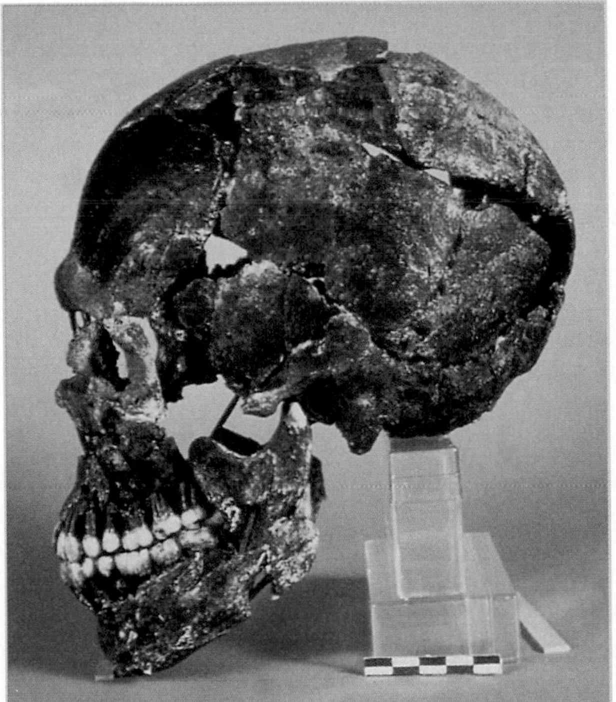

This *H. sapiens* skull from Qafzeh, Israel, is 90,000 years old. Though it looks more modern than a Neandertal, measurements taken on the skull fall slightly closer to those of the Neandertals than they do to those of more modern-looking Upper Paleolithic people.

The "Eve" or "Out of Africa" Hypothesis

This alternative to the multiregional hypothesis states that anatomically modern humans are descended from one specific population of *H. sapiens*, replacing not just the Neandertals, but other populations of archaic *H. sapiens* as our ancestors spread out of their original homeland. This idea came not from fossils but from a relatively new technique that uses mitochondrial DNA to reconstruct family trees. Unlike nuclear DNA (in the cell nucleus), mitochondrial DNA is located elsewhere in the cell, in compartments that produce the energy needed to keep cells alive. Because sperm does not contribute mitochondrial DNA to the fertilized egg, it is inherited only from one's mother and is not "rescrambled" with each succeeding generation. Therefore, it should be altered only by mutation. By comparing the mitochondrial DNA of living individuals from diverse geographical populations, anthropologists and molecular biologists seek to determine when and where modern *H. sapiens* originated. As widely reported in the popular press (including a cover story in *Newsweek*), preliminary results suggested that the mitochondrial DNA of all living humans could be traced back to a "Mitochondrial Eve" who lived in Africa (though some argued for Asia) some 200,000 years ago. If so, all other populations of archaic *H. sapiens,* as well as non-African *H. erectus,* would have to be ruled out of the ancestry of modern humans.

Most scholars today accept that fossils from Africa, scrappy though they are, exhibit the transition from *H. erectus* through archaic to anatomically modern *sapiens* on that continent. This by itself, however, offers no confirmation of the "Out of Africa" hypothesis. After all, proponents of the multiregional model also argue that the transition took place here, as in other parts of the Old World. If, however, anatomically modern fossils could be shown to be significantly older in Africa than elsewhere, this would bolster the argument for an African homeland for modern humanity. To date, the strongest candidates for such fossils consist of a skull from Border Cave and fragments of jaws of at least 10 people from a cave at the Klasies River mouth. Both sites are in South Africa. Unfortunately, the Border Cave skull is not adequately dated, nor is it as similar to modern African skulls as is often claimed.[29] The Klasies River material is well dated to between 120,000 and 90,000 years ago but is too fragmentary (the bones were cut and burned anciently, suggesting cannibalism) to permit categorical statements as to its modernity. Although one mandible displays what looks like a well-developed chin, this could be a result of loss of the front teeth, something that leads to resorption of supporting bone. This does not affect the bottom of the jaw, however, leaving it to protrude and appear more chinlike than it may have been.[30] Apart from this, chins are not entirely unknown in archaic *sapiens* (for example, some European Neandertals, as already discussed). Certainly, the Klasies remains are not inconsistent with the sort of wide variation just discussed for Southwest Asia.

[29]Bar-Yosef, O., Vandermeesch, B., Arensburg, B., Belfer-Cohen, A., Goldberg, P., Laville, H., Meignen, L., Rak, Y., Speth, J. D., Tchernov, E., Tillier, A. M., & Weiner, S. (1992). The excavations in Kebara Cave, Mt. Carmel. *Current Anthropology, 33,* 534.

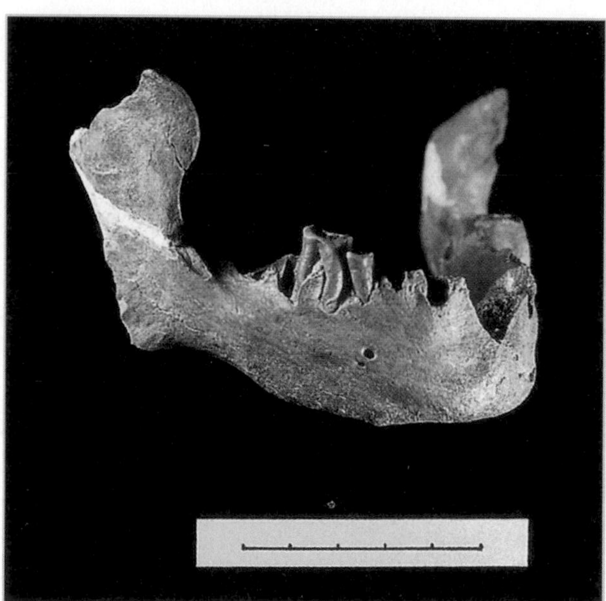

Because of its chin, this mandible from the Klasies River in South Africa has often been called "modern." Yet a number of archaic *sapiens* skulls, including several Neandertals, have this feature.

It is true that the people of Klasies River were culturally precocious. For one thing, they are the first people we know of to augment resources of the land with those from the sea; their gathering of shellfish led to the buildup of middens (refuse heaps) comparable to those left by later Upper Paleolithic peoples. Their technology was also advanced in the common production of blades—long parallel-sided flakes of a sort not commonly made in Europe until some 36,500 years ago. By 70,000 years ago, the people at Klasies River were blunting the backs of blades, much as later Europeans did, for hafting in composite tools. Some take these signs of cultural advancement as indicative of anatomically modern status. The fallacy of such argument, however, is revealed by the evidence from Europe and Southwest Asia that the cognitive abilities of archaic and modern *H. sapiens* were the same.

The fossil evidence presents other problems for the "Out of Africa" hypothesis as well. For one thing, we would expect an early replacement of archaic *sapiens* in Southwest Asia as more anatomically modern humans moved up out of Africa but, as we have already seen, we have no clear evidence for such a replacement. The same is true for East Asia, where evidence for continuity from regional *H. erectus,* through archaic, to anatomical *H. sapiens* populations is even better than it is in Africa. Consistent with this, the archaeological record of East Asia, though distinctly different from Europe, Africa, and western Asia, shows the same kind of continuity as do the fossils.[31] There is no sign of invasion by people possessing a superior, or even different, technology, as an "Out of Africa" scenario would require.

Given the problems in reconciling the "Out of Africa" hypothesis with the archaeological and fossil records, one may ask: What about the DNA analysis that gave birth to the hypothesis? Here, things are not as certain as proponents of "Out of Africa" maintain.

[30]Wolpoff & Caspari, p. 331.

[31]Pope, G. C. (1992). Craniofacial evidence for the origin of modern humans in China. *Yearbook of Physical Anthropology, 35,* 291.

Even older than the blades from the Klasies River mouth are these, from a site in Kenya. Struck from preshaped cores, they are about 240,000 years old, predating any known or possible fossils of anatomically modern humans.

African Origin or Ancient Population Size Differences?[32]

Original Study

The Eve theory depends on genetic evidence indicating an African origin for modern humanity, because . . . the fossil evidence is quite equivocal on this issue. But there is no particular reason to suggest Africa was the place of origin for the current mtDNA [mitochondrial DNA] lineages. The original studies suggesting an African origin were invalid because the computer program used in the analysis was not applied correctly. Then the greater genetic variability in Africans was taken to mean humans evolved there longer: The variation was thought to reflect more mutations and therefore a longer time span for their accumulation. Templeton [a geneticist] has argued that no statistical analysis shows that the genetic variation of Africans actually is greater than that of other populations; but even if it is, there is another, more compelling explanation.

Ancient population sizes expanded first and are larger in Africa than in other regions, which would have the same effect, creating more African variation. Consider what happens in an expanding population. Average family size is greater than two, and all variations have a good chance of being passed on; at least, if they are not selected against, they will probably not get lost by accident. But if a population is decreasing, drift can play a very active

[32]Wolpoff & Caspari, pp. 305–307.

Original Study

role since average family size is less than two. The role of drift is greatly amplified for mtDNA, because for transmission of this molecule the number of female offspring is important. Decreasing populations stand an excellent chance of losing mtDNA lineages.

Now, consider a small but stable population, neither increasing nor decreasing. Here, existing variations may each occur in only one individual. If it is a woman, and she has no female offspring, which can happen one-fourth of the time in a stable population, her unique variation is lost, her mtDNA lineage terminated. But in a large stable population with the same amount of genetic variability, it is likely each mtDNA variant is shared by many individuals. The odds are the same against one woman having no female offspring, but it is very unlikely all the women with a certain mtDNA variant will lack female offspring. It is much harder for mtDNA lines to end by accident in large populations.

These comparisons show that prehistoric population demography, how large or small populations were in the past and how much they fluctuated, can affect mtDNA evolution. Small, fluctuating populations will lose many mtDNA lines. The last common ancestor for the remaining mtDNA variations will be more recent because there is less remaining variation. Large or increasing populations will retain more variation. For them, the roots will be deeper and the last common ancestor will be farther in the past since more variations are retained.

Thus, ancient population size can dictate how long genetic lineages have existed, and therefore when they arose. Because ancient population size differences are an alternate explanation that unlinks the origin of genetic lineages from the origin of a population, it seems as though genetic analysis cannot help solve the problem of whether today's variation reflects African origin or ancient population size differences.

However, genetic analysis can indicate ancient population expansions. Henry Harpending and colleagues studied the probability distributions of pairwise mtDNA comparisons within populations for evidence of past population structure and size expansions. They conclude: "Our results show human populations are derived from separate ancestral populations that were relatively isolated from each other before 50,000 years ago." These studies clearly reveal there have been a series of recent, very significant, population expansions. Some of these are without question associated with the development and spread of agricultural revolutions. But others are earlier.

This means population size history by itself can explain the pattern of mtDNA variation. If, as we believe and as the archaeological record seems to show,

- there were more people living in Africa for most of human prehistory, and
- human populations outside of Africa were smaller and fluctuated more because of the changing ice-age environments,

we would expect just what we do see—African mtDNA has deeper roots, while in other places the coalescent time is more recent. But this explanation does not mean the populations living out of Africa have a more recent origin, or that they originated in Africa. MtDNA history, in other words, is not population history.

John Relethford and Henry Harpending examined the consequences of the possibility that greater African population size, and not greater time depth for modern humans in Africa, may account for their greater variation.

> Our results support our earlier contention that regional differences in population size can explain the genetic evidence pertaining to modern human origins. Our work thus far has involved examination of the classic genetic markers and craniometrics, but it also has implications for mitochondrial DNA. The greater mtDNA diversity in sub-Saharan African populations could also be a reflection of a larger long-term African population.

Moreover, they write, a unique African ancestry implies there was a bottleneck for the human species, as moderns would be able to trace their ancestry to only a small portion of humanity, as it existed then.

While this seems at first glance a reasonable notion, it soon becomes apparent that the actual effect of such a [bottleneck] event depends on both the magnitude and duration of a shift in population size. Rogers and Jorde show that given reasonable parameters for our species, the bottleneck would have to be more severe and long-lasting than considered plausible. We have to think of a population of 50 females for 6,000 years, for example.

The End

Other assumptions made by DNA analysts are problematic. For example, it is assumed that rates of mutation are steady, when in fact they can be notoriously uneven. Another assumption is that mtDNA is not subject to selection, when in fact variants have been implicated in epilepsy and a disease of the eye.[33] A third is that DNA is seen as traveling exclusively *from* Africa, when it is known that, over the past 10,000 years, there has been plenty of movement the other way. In fact, one study of DNA carried on the Y chromosome (and inherited exclusively in the male line) suggests that some DNA seen on the Y chromosome of some Africans was introduced from Asia, where it originated some 200,000 years ago.[34]

Since 1997, studies of mitochondrial DNA have not been limited to living people. In that year, mtDNA was extracted from the original German Neandertal, and two others have since been studied. Because the mtDNA of each of these differs substantially from modern Europeans, many have concluded that there can be no Neandertal ancestry in living humans and that Neandertals must constitute a separate species that went extinct. But as John Relethford (a specialist in anthropological genetics) points out, these conclusions are premature.[35] For one thing, the average differences are not as great as those seen among living subspecies of the single species of chimpanzee. For another, the differences between populations separated in time by tens of thousands of years tells us nothing about differences between populations contemporaneous with each other. More meaningful would be comparison of the DNA from a late Neandertal with an early Aurignacian European. Finally, if we are to reject Neandertals in the ancestry of modern Europeans because their DNA cannot be detected in their supposed ancestors, then we must also reject any connection between a 40,000- to 62,000-year-old skeleton from Australia (that everyone agrees is anatomically modern) and more recent native Australians. In this case, an mtDNA sequence present in an ancient human seems to have become extinct, in which case we must allow the same possibility for the Neandertals.[36]

In short, it is definitely premature to read out of the modern human ancestry all populations of archaic *sapiens* save those of Africa. Not even the Neandertals can be excluded. We shall return to this problem in the next chapter, but at the moment, the evidence seems to favor a multiregional emergence of anatomically modern humans. Still, the debate is by no means resolved.

[33]Shreeve, p. 121.

[34]Gibbons, A. (1997). Ideas on human origins evolve at anthropology gathering. *Science, 276,* 535–536.

[35]Relethford, J. H. (2001). Absence of regional affinities of Neandertal DNA with living humans does not reject multiregional evolution. *American Journal of Physical Anthropology, 115,* 95–98.

[36]Gibbons, A. (2001). The riddle of coexistence. *Science, 291,* 1,726

CHAPTER SUMMARY

At various sites in Europe, Africa, and East Asia, a number of fossils have been found that date between about 400,000 and 200,000 years ago and that show a mixture of traits of both *H. erectus* and *H. sapiens*. They are indicative of evolution from the older into the younger species. Their culture was enriched by development of a new technique of tool manufacture known as the Levalloisian.

By 200,000 years ago, populations of archaic *H. sapiens* lived in all parts of the inhabited world. In Europe and western Asia, archaic *H. sapiens* is represented by the Neandertals, some of whom, in Europe and western Asia, are said to have survived until at least 35,000 years ago. Alternatively, they may be members of varied populations in which some individuals show modern characteristics more strongly than others.

The brains of archaic *H. sapiens* were no different in size and organization than our own, although their skulls retained some ancestral characteristics. With a larger brain, they were able to utilize culture as a means of adaptation to a far greater extent than any of their predecessors; they were capable of complex technology and sophisticated conceptual thought.

The cultures of archaic *H. sapiens* are known as Middle Paleolithic, and the best known is the Mousterian of Europe, northern Africa, and western Asia. Mousterian tools included handaxes, flakes, scrapers, borers, wood shavers, and spears. These flake tools were lighter and smaller than those of the Levalloisian. Mousterian tools increased the availability and quality of food, shelter, and clothing. Archaeological evidence indicates that Mousterian peoples buried their dead, cared for the disabled, and made a variety of objects for purely symbolic purposes.

All populations of archaic *H. sapiens* are easily derivable from earlier populations of *H. erectus* from the same regions, and all could be ancestral to more modern populations in the same regions. Gene flow between populations would have prevented branching. An alternative hypothesis is that the transition from archaic to anatomically modern *H. sapiens* took place in one specific population, probably in Africa. From here, people spread to other regions, replacing older populations as they did so.

CLASSIC READINGS

Shreeve, J. (1995). *The Neandertal enigma: Solving the mystery of modern human origins.* New York: William Morrow.

Shreeve is a science writer who has written extensively about human evolution. This book is engagingly written and covers most of the major issues in the Neandertal-Modern debate.

Stringer, C. B., & McKie, R. (1996). *African exodus: The origins of modern humanity.* London: Jonathan Cape.

Chris Stringer of the British Museum is a leading champion of the "Out of Africa" hypothesis, and in this book one will find a vigorous presentation of his arguments.

Trinkaus, E., & Shipman, P. (1992). *The Neandertals: Changing the image of mankind.* New York: Alfred A. Knopf.

The senior author of this book is a long-time specialist on the Neandertals. Eminently readable, the book chronicles the changing interpretations of these fossils since the first recognized find in 1856. For a good look at what is known about the Neandertals, there is no better place to go than this.

Wolpoff, M., & Caspari, R. (1997). *Race and human evolution.* New York: Simon & Schuster.

One of the problems in evaluating the multiregional and "Out of Africa" hypotheses is that many writers misrepresent the former. That is no problem in this book, written by the leading champion of multiregionalism and his wife. The hypothesis is presented and defended in a straightforward and thorough way so that anyone can understand it.

CHAPTER 10

HOMO SAPIENS AND THE UPPER PALEOLITHIC

In the Upper Paleolithic period, evidence of human creativity becomes both widespread and dramatic, as this 32,000-year-old painting from the recently discovered (in 1994) Chauvet Cave in France shows. Equally old, and in some cases older, art is known from Africa and Australia.

CHAPTER PREVIEW

1

When Did Anatomically Modern Forms of *Homo sapiens* Appear?

The answer to this question depends on what is meant by "anatomically modern." Because all humans today are members of a single species, all are equally modern. Although populations of archaic *H. sapiens* such as the Neandertals are commonly seen as not anatomically modern, to exclude them requires exclusion of some modern populations—an obvious impossibility. Still, it is generally agreed that by 30,000 years ago, in the Upper Paleolithic period, populations in all parts of the inhabited world show some resemblance to more recent human populations.

2

What Was the Culture of Upper Paleolithic Peoples Like?

Upper Paleolithic cultures generally include a greater diversity of tools. Techniques of toolmaking became widespread, including the manufacture of blades, pressure flaking, and use of burins to fashion implements of bone and antler. In Europe, large game hunting was improved by invention of the spear-thrower, while net hunting allowed effective procurement of small game. In Africa the bow and arrow were invented. There was as well an explosion of creativity, represented by impressive works of art from Africa, Australia, and Europe.

What Were the Consequences of the New Upper Paleolithic Technologies?

First Upper Paleolithic and then Mesolithic technologies improved peoples' abilities to adapt through the medium of culture. This resulted in increased regionalism, as people refined their adaptations to local conditions, and further population growth promoted expansion into new regions, most dramatically Australia and the Americas. Biological consequences included final reduction of the human face to modern proportions, and the new hunting technologies led to reduction of body mass.

The remains of a Stone Age people who looked much like us were first discovered in 1868 at Les Eyzies in France, in a rock shelter together with tools of the Upper (late) Paleolithic. Consisting of eight skeletons, they are commonly referred to as **Cro-Magnons,** after the rock shelter in which they were found. The name was extended to 13 other specimens unearthed between 1872 and 1902 in the caves of the Côte d'Azur near the Italian Riviera, and since then, to other Upper Paleolithic skeletons discovered in other parts of Europe.

Because Cro-Magnons were found with Upper Paleolithic tools and seemed responsible for the production of impressive works of art, they were seen as particularly clever, when compared with the Neandertals. The idea that the latter were basically dim-witted fit comfortably with the prevailing stereotype of their brutish appearance, and their Mousterian tools were interpreted as evidence of cultural inferiority. Hence the idea was born of an anatomically modern people with a superior culture sweeping into Europe and replacing a primitive, local population.

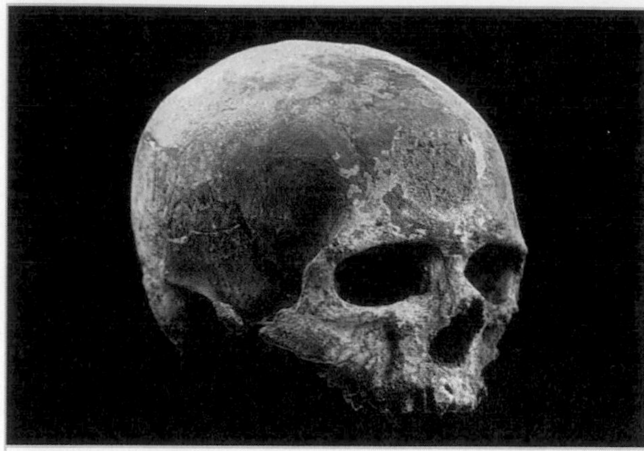

Though the original Cro-Magnon skull shows some resemblance to modern European skulls, it is not identical.

UPPER PALEOLITHIC PEOPLES: THE FIRST MODERN HUMANS

Much as Neandertals were stereotyped as particularly brutish, the Cro-Magnons of Europe were stereotyped as having a somewhat godlike appearance, epitomizing modern European ideals of beauty. This image found its way into popular culture, as in a best-selling novel of the 1970s, *The Clan of the Cave Bear.* In this book, the heroine is portrayed as a tall, slender, blonde-haired, blue-eyed beauty. But as Upper Paleolithic remains (from various parts of Africa and Asia as well as Europe) have become better understood, it has become clear that the differences from earlier populations have been greatly exaggerated. In the case of Europeans, for example, there is some resemblance between Cro-Magnons and later populations: in braincase shape, high broad forehead, narrow nasal openings, and common presence of chins. But Cro-Magnon faces were shorter and broader than those of modern Europeans, their brow ridges were a bit more prominent, and their teeth and jaws were as large as those of Neandertals. Some (a skull from the original Cro-Magnon site, for instance) even display the distinctive "occipital bun" of the Neandertals on the back of the skull.[1] Nor were they particularly tall, as their height of 5 feet 7 or 8 inches does not fall outside the Neandertal range.

Although the Cro-Magnons and Upper Paleolithic people from Africa and Asia are now routinely referred to as anatomically modern, it is surprisingly hard to be precise about what we mean by this. We think of people with brains the size of modern people, but this had already been achieved by archaic *H. sapiens,* among whom brain size actually peaked at 10 percent larger than ours. The reduction to today's size correlates with a reduction in brawn, as bodies have become less massive overall. Modern faces and jaws are, by and large, less massive as well, but there are exceptions. For example, anthropologists Milford Wolpoff and Rachel Caspari have pointed out that any definition of modernity that excludes Neandertals also excludes substantial numbers of recent and living native Australians, although they are, quite obviously, a modern people. The fact is, no multidimensional diagnosis of modern humans can be both exclusive of archaic populations and inclusive of all contemporary humans.[2]

The appearance of modern-sized brains in archaic *H. sapiens* no doubt was a consequence of increased reliance

[1]Brace, C. L. (1997). Cro-Magnons "Я" us? *Anthropology Newsletter, 38*(8), 1.

[2]Wolpoff, M., & Caspari, R. (1997). *Race and human evolution* (pp. 344–345, 393). New York: Simon & Schuster.

Cro-Magnons. Europeans of the Upper Paleolithic after about 36,000 years ago.

on cultural adaptation. Ultimately, this emphasis on cultural adaptation led to the development of more complex tool kits. Among Upper Paleolithic peoples, as specialized tools increasingly took over the cutting, softening, and clamping functions once performed by the front teeth, there followed a reduction in the size of the teeth and, eventually, the jaws. The cooking of food (which began with *H. erectus)* had already favored some reduction in size of the teeth and muscles involved in chewing; consequently, the jaws diminished in size, and robust sites for muscle attachment disappeared along with features like brow ridges that buttress the skull from the stresses and strains imposed by the action of massive jaw muscles.

Technological improvements also reduced the intensity of selective pressures that had previously favored especially massive, robust bodies. With new emphasis on elongate tools having greater mechanical advantages, more effective techniques of hafting, a switch from thrusting to throwing spears, and development of net hunting, there was a marked reduction in overall muscularity. Moreover, the skeletons of Upper Paleolithic peoples show far less evidence of trauma than do those of archaic *H. sapiens,* whose bones almost always show evidence of injury.

UPPER PALEOLITHIC TOOLS

The Upper Paleolithic was a time of great technological innovation. Typical were blades, flint flakes at least twice as long as they are wide. Although Middle Paleolithic toolmakers, especially in Africa, already made blades (some are illustrated in Chapter 9), they did not do so to the extent that their Upper Paleolithic successors did. What made this possible were new techniques of core preparation that allowed more intensive production of highly standardized blades. The toolmaker formed a cylindrical core, struck the blade off near the edge of the core, and repeated this procedure, going around the core in one direction until finishing near its center (Figure 10.1). The procedure is analogous to peeling long leaves off an artichoke. With this **blade technique,** an Upper Paleolithic flint knapper could get 75 feet of working edge from a 2-pound core; a Mousterian knapper could get only 6 feet from the same-sized core.

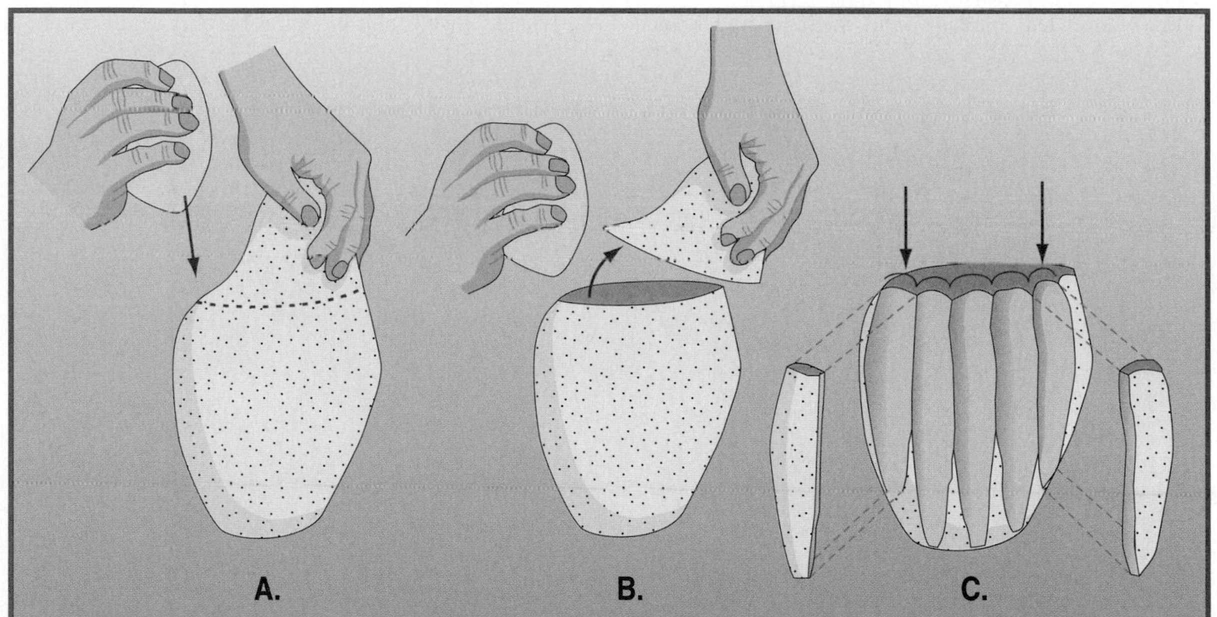

FIGURE 10.1

DURING THE UPPER PALEOLITHIC, A NEW TECHNIQUE WAS USED TO MANUFACTURE BLADES. THE STONE IS FLAKED TO CREATE A STRIKING PLATFORM; LONG, ALMOST PARALLEL-SIDED FLAKES THEN ARE STRUCK AROUND THE SIDES, PROVIDING SHARP-EDGED BLADES.

Blade technique. A technique of stone tool manufacture by which long, parallel-sided flakes are struck off the edges of a specially prepared core.

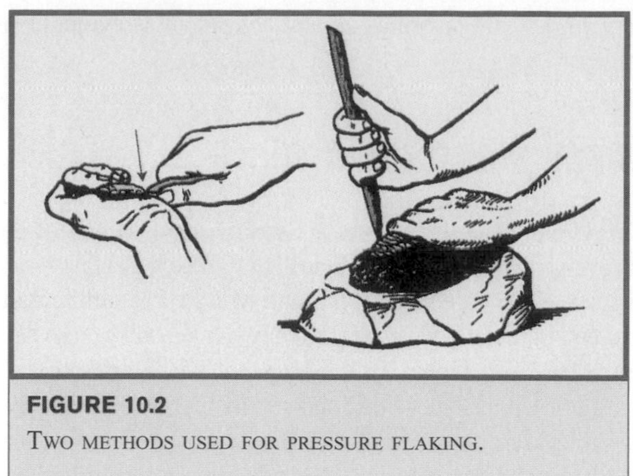

FIGURE 10.2
TWO METHODS USED FOR PRESSURE FLAKING.

Other efficient techniques of tool manufacture also came into common use at this time. One such method was **pressure flaking,** in which a bone, antler, or wooden tool was used to press rather than strike off small flakes as the final step in stone tool manufacture (Figure 10.2). The advantage of this technique was that the toolmaker had greater control over the final shape of the tool than is possible with percussion flaking alone. The so-called Solutrean laurel leaf blades found in Spain and France are examples of this technique. The longest of these blades is 13 inches in length but only about a quarter of an inch thick. Through pressure flaking, blades could be worked with great precision into a variety of final forms; and worn tools could be effectively resharpened over and over until they were too small for further use.

Another common Upper Paleolithic tool was the **burin,** although it too was invented earlier, in the Middle Paleolithic. These implements, with their chisel-like edges, facilitated the working of bone, horn, antler, and ivory into such useful things as fishhooks, harpoons, and eyed needles, all of which made life easier for *H. sapiens,* especially in northern regions. The spear-thrower, too, appeared at this time. Spear-throwers are wooden devices, one end of which is gripped in the hunter's hand, while the other end has a hole or hook, in or against which the end of the spear is placed (Figure 10.3). It is held so as to effectively extend the length of the hunter's arm, thereby increasing the velocity of the spear when thrown. Using a spear-thrower greatly added to the efficiency of the spear as a hunting tool. With handheld spears, hunters had to get close to their quarry to make the kill, and because many of the animals they hunted were quite large and fierce, this was a dangerous business. The need to approach closely, and the improbability of an instant kill,

Shown here is one of the Solutrean laurel leaf bifaces from Europe. Such fine flint work requires a high degree of skill.

Pressure flaking. A technique of stone tool manufacture in which a bone, antler, or wooden tool is used to press, rather than strike off, small flakes from a piece of flint or similar stone. • **Burins.** Stone tools with chisel-like edges used for working bone and antler.

exposed the spear hunter to considerable risk. But with the spear-thrower, the effective killing distance was increased; experiments demonstrate that the effective killing distance of a spear when used with a spear-thrower is between 18 and 27 meters (as opposed to 0.6 or 0.9 meters without).[3]

Another important innovation, net hunting, appeared some time between 29,000 and 22,000 years ago.[4] Knotted nets, made from the fibers of wild plants such as hemp or nettle, left their impression on the clay floors of huts when people walked on them. These impressions were baked in when the huts later burned, which is how we know that nets existed. Their use accounts for the high number of hare, fox, and other small mammal and bird bones at archaeological sites. Like historically known net hunters, everyone—men, women, and children—probably participated, frightening animals with loud noises to drive them to where hunters were stationed with their nets. In this way, large amounts of meat could be amassed in ways that did not put a premium on speed or strength.

A further improvement of hunting techniques came with the invention of the bow and arrow, which appeared first in Africa, but not until the end of the Upper Paleolithic in Europe. The greatest advantage of the bow is that it increases the distance between hunter and prey; beyond 18 to 27 meters, the accuracy and penetration of a spear thrown with a spear-thrower is quite poor, whereas even a poor bow will shoot an arrow farther, with greater accuracy and penetrating power. A good bow is effective even at 91 meters. Thus, hunters were able to maintain an even safer distance between themselves and dangerous prey, dramatically decreasing their chances of being seriously injured by an animal fighting for its life.

These changes in hunting weaponry and techniques likely were responsible for the less robust bodies of Upper Paleolithic people. Spear hunting, particularly where large, fierce animals are the prey as they often were in Europe, demands strength, power, and overall robusticity

[3]Frayer, D. W. (1981). Body size, weapon use, and natural selection in the European Upper Paleolithic and Mesolithic. *American Anthropologist, 83,* 58.

[4]Pringle, H. (1997). Ice Age communities may be earliest known net hunters. *Science, 277,* 1,203.

Anthropology Applied

Stone Tools for Modern Surgeons

When anthropologist Irven DeVore of Harvard University was to have some minor melanomas removed from his face, he did not leave it up to the surgeon to supply his own scalpels. Instead, he had graduate student John Shea make a scalpel. Making a blade of obsidian (a naturally-occurring volcanic "glass") by the same techniques used by Upper Paleolithic people to make blades, he then hafted this in a wooden handle, using melted pine resin as glue and then lashing it with sinew. After the procedure, the surgeon reported that the obsidian scalpel was superior to metal ones.*

DeVore was not the first to undergo surgery in which stone scalpels were used. In 1975, Don Crabtree, then at Idaho State University, prepared the scalpels that his surgeon would use in Crabtree's heart surgery. In 1980, Payson Sheets at the University of Colorado prepared obsidian scalpels that were used successfully in eye surgery. And in 1986, David Pokotylo of the Museum of Anthropology at the University of British Columbia underwent reconstructive surgery on his hand with blades he himself had made (the hafting was done by his museum colleague, Len McFarlane).

The reason for these uses of scalpels modeled on ancient stone tools is that the anthropologists realized that obsidian is superior in almost every way to materials normally used to make scalpels: It is 210 to 1,050 times sharper than surgical steel, 100 to 500 times sharper than a razor blade, and 3 times sharper than a diamond blade (which not only costs much more, but cannot be made with more than 3 mm of cutting edge). Obsidian blades are easier to cut with and do less damage in the process (under a microscope, incisions made with the sharpest steel blades show torn ragged edges and are littered with bits of displaced flesh).† As a consequence, the surgeon has better control over what she or he is doing and the incisions heal faster with less scarring and pain. Because of the supe-

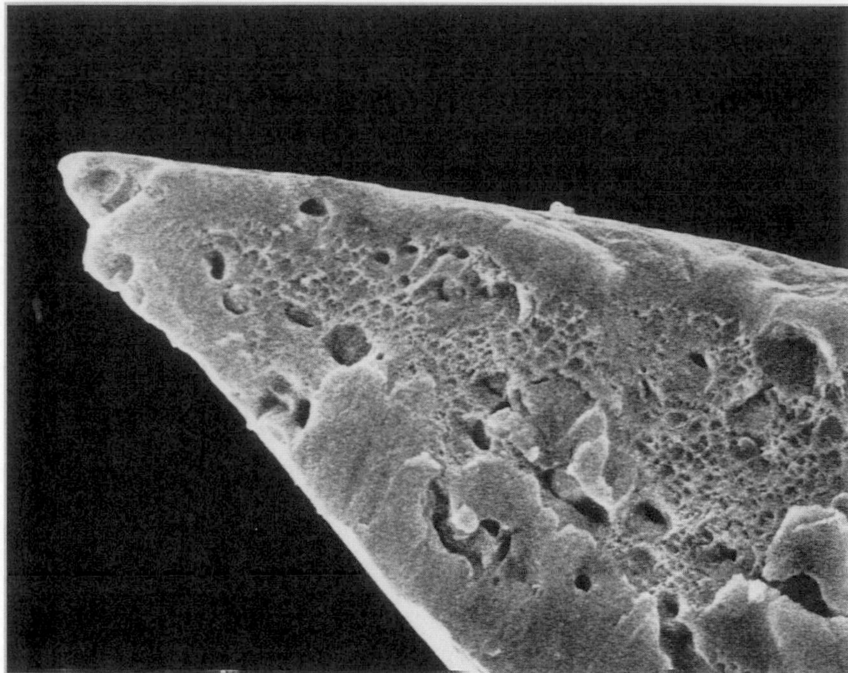

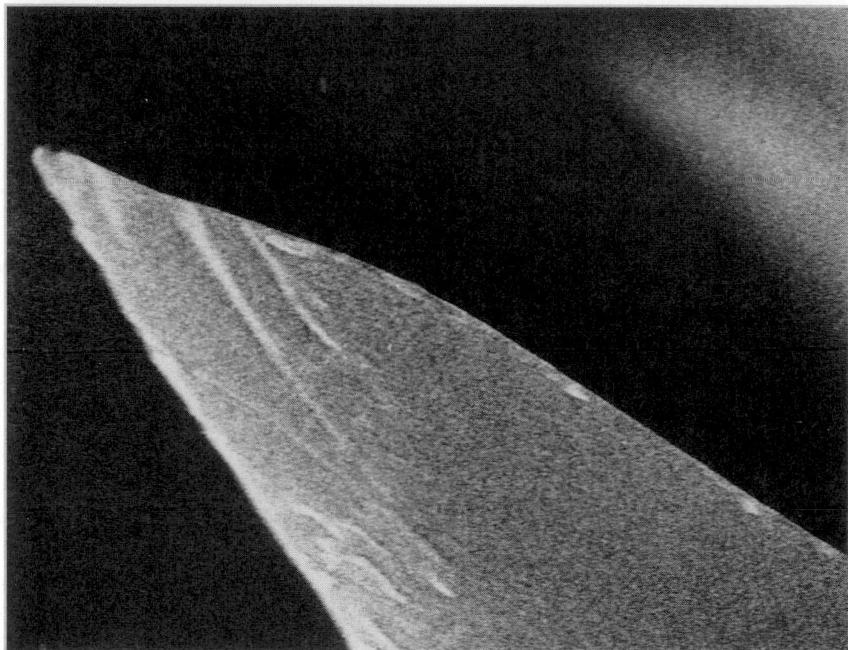

These microphotographs of an obsidian blade (bottom photo) and a modern steel scalpel (top photo) illustrate the superiority of the obsidian.

riority of obsidian scalpels, Sheets went so far as to form a corporation in partnership with Boulder, Colorado, eye surgeon Dr. Firmon Hardenbergh. Together, they developed a means of producing cores of uniform size from molten glass, as well as a machine to detach blades from the cores.

---

*Shreeve, J. (1995). *The Neandertal enigma: Solving the mystery of modern human origins* (p. 134). New York: William Morrow.

†Sheets, P. D. (1987). Dawn of a New Stone Age in eye surgery. In R. J. Sharer & W. Ashmore (Eds.), *Archaeology: Discovering our past* (p. 231). Palo Alto, CA: Mayfield.

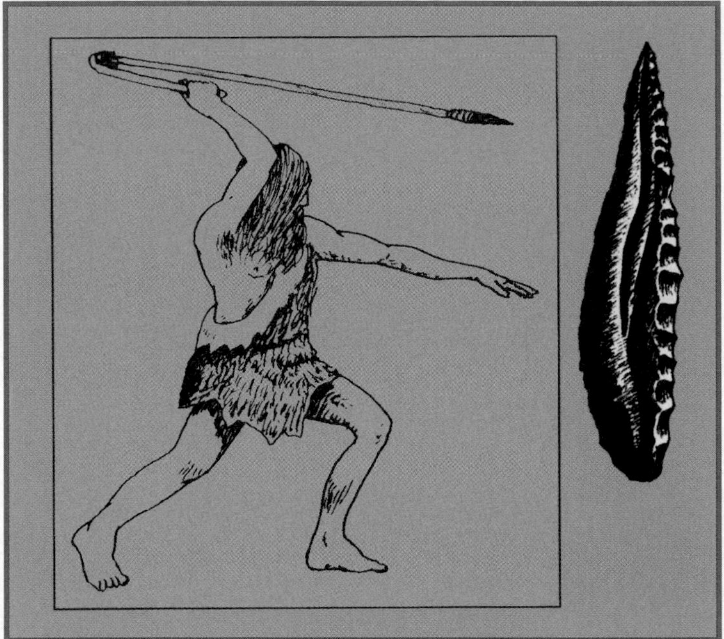

FIGURE 10.3
SHOWN HERE IS THE WAY AN UPPER PALEOLITHIC HUNTER WOULD THROW A SPEAR USING A SPEAR-THROWER, AS WELL AS A STONE POINT SUITABLE FOR THE SPEAR. THE HUNTER'S CLOTHING AND HAIR STYLE ARE PURE SPECULATION.

on the part of the hunter. Without them, the hunter is poorly equipped to withstand the rigors of close-quarter killing. A high nutritional price must be paid, however, for large, powerful, and robust bodies. Therefore, as speed and strength become less important for success, selection for them slacked off, and people tended to become weaker and less robust. As a consequence, nutritional requirements were reduced.

Upper Paleolithic peoples not only had better tools but also a greater diversity of types than earlier peoples (Figures 10.4 and 10.5). The highly developed Upper Paleolithic kit included tools for use during different seasons, and regional variation in tool kits was greater than ever before. Thus, it is really impossible to speak of an Upper Paleolithic culture, even in a relatively small peripheral region like Europe; instead, one must make note of the many different traditions that made it possible for people to adapt ever more specifically to the various environments in which they were living. Just how proficient (and even wasteful) people had become at securing a livelihood is indicated by boneyards containing thousands of skeletons. At Solutré in France, for example, Upper Paleolithic hunters killed 10,000 horses; at Predmost in Czechoslovakia, they were responsible for the deaths of 1,000 mammoths. The favored big game of European hunters, however, was reindeer, which they killed in even greater numbers.

UPPER PALEOLITHIC ART

Although the creativity of Upper Paleolithic peoples is evident in the tools and weapons they made, it is nowhere more evident than in their outburst of artistic expression. Some have argued that this was made possible by a newly evolved biological ability to manipulate symbols and make images, but in view of the modern-sized brains of archaic *sapiens* and increasingly compelling evidence that even the Neandertals were capable of speech, such an idea is hard to maintain. Like agriculture, which came later (see Chapter 11), the artistic explosion may have been no more than a consequence of innovations made by a people who had the capacity to make them for tens of thousands of years already.

In fact, just as many of the distinctive tools that were commonly used in Upper Paleolithic times first appear in the Middle Paleolithic, so too do objects of art. In Southwest Asia, a crude figurine of volcanic tuff is some 250,000 years

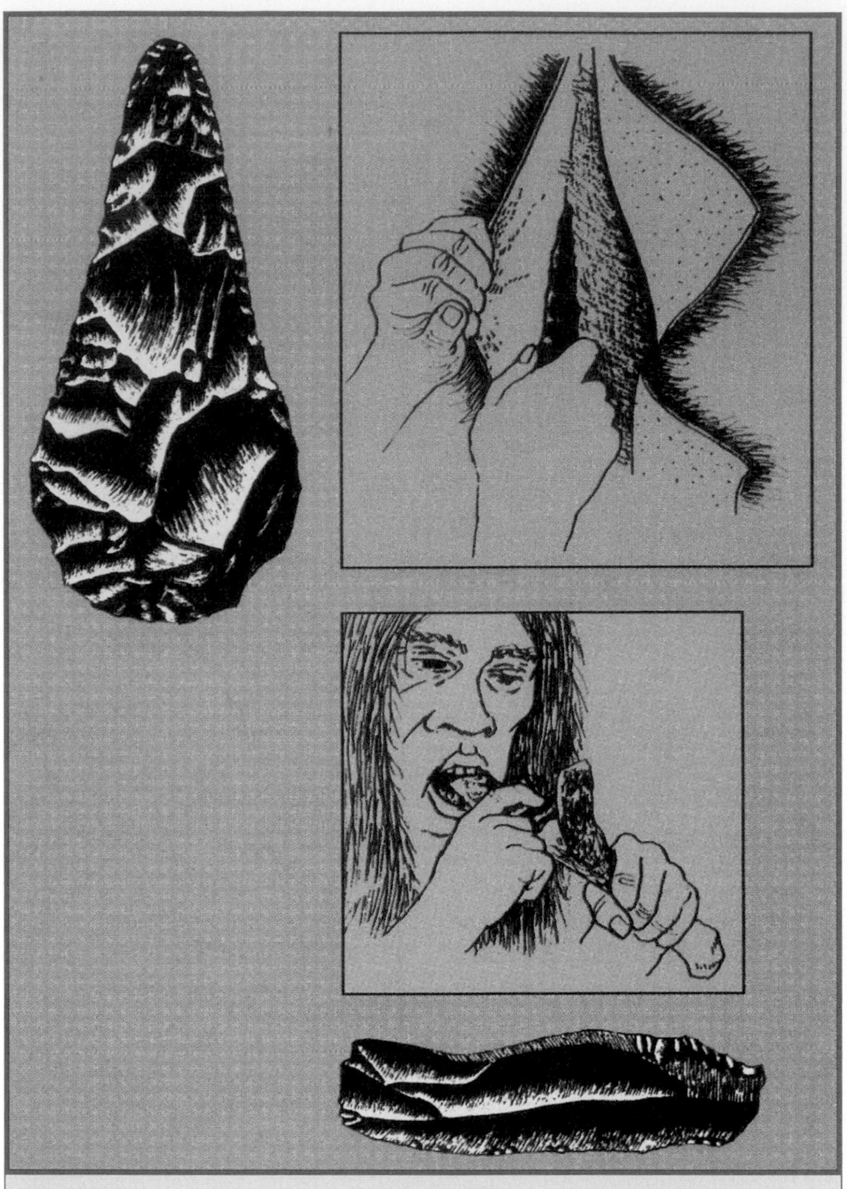

FIGURE 10.4
Two Upper Paleolithic stone tools, and how they might have been used to skin an animal and cut meat while eating.

old.[5] Although it is unusual, the fact that it exists at all indicates that people had the ability to carve all sorts of things from wood, a substance easier to work than volcanic tuff but rarely preserved for long periods of time. Furthermore, ocher "crayons" from Middle Paleolithic contexts in various parts of the world must have been used to decorate or mark something. In southern Africa, for example, regular use of yellow and red ocher goes back 130,000 years, with some evidence as old as 200,000 years.[6] Perhaps pigments were used on people's bodies, as well as objects, as the 50,000-year-old mammoth-tooth *churinga,* discussed and illustrated in Chapter 9, might suggest.

[5]Appenzeller, T. (1998). Art: Evolution or revolution? *Science, 282,* 1,452.

[6]Barham, L. S. (1998). Possible early pigment use in south-central Africa. *Current Anthropology, 39,* 709.

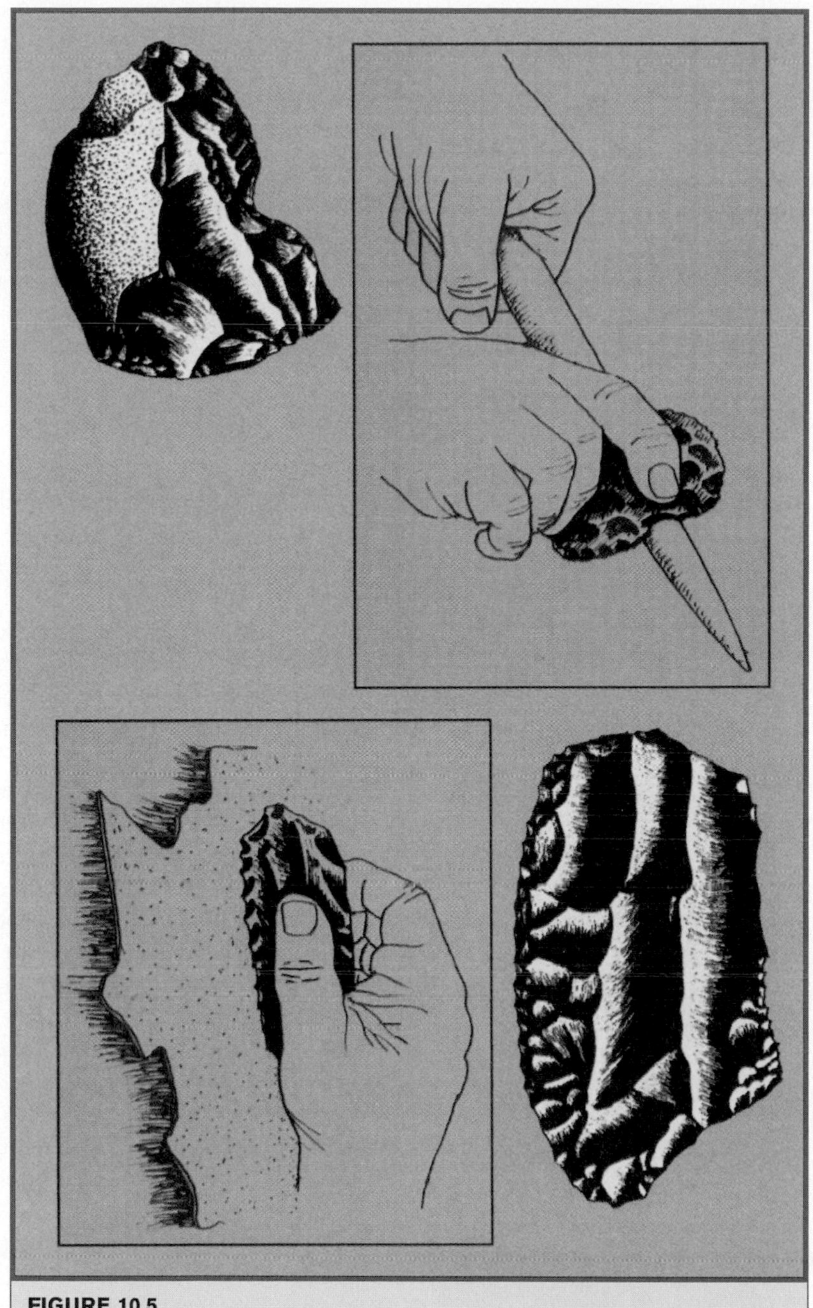

FIGURE 10.5
AN UPPER PALEOLITHIC "SPOKESHAVE" (TOP) AND SCRAPER (BOTTOM), AND THE WAYS THEY WERE USED.

That there was music in the lives of Upper Paleolithic peoples is indicated by the presence of bone flutes and whistles in sites, some up to 30,000 years old. But again, such instruments may have their origin in Middle Paleolithic prototypes, such as the probable "Neandertal flute" discussed in Chapter 9. Although we cannot be sure just where and when it happened, some genius discovered that bows could be used not just for killing, but to make music as well. Because the bow and arrow is an Upper Paleolithic invention, the musical bow likely is as well. We do know that the musical bow is the oldest of all stringed instruments, and its invention ultimately made

HIGHWAY 1

A trip to this site is a visual treat. It features cave rock art from Australia to Africa, some of which dates back to the Paleolithic.
www.bradshawfoundation.com/index.html

HIGHWAY 2

In order to protect the magnificent cave art at Lascaux Cave, only six people per day can go inside. To share this national treasure more widely, the French government has built an entire replica of the site as well as this Web site for a virtual tour.
www.culture.fr/culture/arcnat/lascaux/en/

Crude though it may be, this piece of tuff, carved some 250,000 years ago, looks like a woman if viewed from the right angle. It was found in 1980 on the Golan Heights in the Middle East.

possible the development of all of the stringed instruments with which we are familiar today.

The earliest evidence of figurative pictures goes back 32,000 years in Europe and is probably equally old in Africa. Both engravings and paintings are known from many rock shelters and outcrops in southern Africa, where they continued to be made by Bushman peoples up until about 100 years ago. Scenes feature both humans and animals, depicted with extraordinary skill, often in association with geometric and other abstract motifs.

Because this rock art tradition continued unbroken into historic times, it has been possible to discover what this art means. There is a close connection between the art and shamanism, and many scenes depict visions seen in states of trance. Distortions in the art, usually of human figures, represent sensations felt by individuals in a state of trance, whereas the geometric designs depict illusions that originate in the central nervous system in altered states of consciousness. These **entoptic phenomena** are luminous grids, dots, zigzags, and other designs that seem to shimmer, pulsate, rotate, and expand, and are seen as one enters a state of trance (sufferers of migraines experience similar hallucinations). The animals depicted in this art, often with startling realism, are not the ones most often eaten. Rather, they are powerful beasts like the eland, and this power is important to shamans—individuals skilled at manipulating supernatural powers and spirits for human benefit—who try to harness it for their rain-making and other rituals.

Rock art in Australia goes back at least 45,000 years, with the earliest examples consisting entirely of entoptic

Entoptic phenomena. Bright pulsating forms that are generated by the central nervous system and seen in states of trance.

In South Africa, rock art, like these engravings and paintings from Namibia, depict things seen by dancers while in states of trance.

motifs. But the Upper Paleolithic art that is most famous—largely because most students of prehistoric art are themselves of European background—is that of Europe. The earliest of this art took the form of sculpture and engravings often portraying such animals as reindeer, horses, bears, and ibexes, but there are also numerous portrayals of voluptuous women with exaggerated sexual and reproductive characteristics. Many appear to be pregnant, and some are shown in birthing postures. These so-called Venus figures have been found at sites from southwestern France to as far east as Siberia. Made of stone, ivory, antler, or baked clay, they differ little in style from place to place, testifying to the sharing of ideas over vast distances. Although some have interpreted the Venuses as objects associated with a fertility cult, others suggest that they may have been exchanged to cement alliances among groups.

Most spectacular are the paintings on the walls of 200 or so caves in southern France and northern Spain, the oldest of which date from about 32,000 years ago. Most common are visually accurate portrayals of Ice Age mammals, including bison, bulls, horses, mammoths, and stags, often painted one on top of another. Although well represented in other media, humans are not commonly portrayed in cave paintings, nor are scenes or depictions of events at all common. Instead, the animals are often abstracted from nature and rendered two-dimensionally without regard to the conformations of the surfaces they are on—no small achievement for these early artists. Sometimes, though, the artists did make use of bulges and other features of the rock to impart a more three-dimensional feeling. Frequently, the paintings are in hard-to-get-at places while suitable surfaces in more accessible places remain untouched. In some caves, the lamps by which the artists worked have been found; these are spoon-shaped objects of sandstone in which animal fat was burned. Experimentation has shown that such lamps would have provided adequate illumination over several hours.

The techniques used by Upper Paleolithic people to create their cave paintings were unraveled a decade ago through the experimental work of Michel Lorblanchet. Interestingly, they turn out to be the same ones used by native rock painters in Australia. Lorblanchet's experiments are described in the following Original Study by science writer Roger Lewin.

Upper Paleolithic art was quite varied: a carved antler spear-thrower ornamented by two headless ibexes (from Enlene Cave, France); a female Venus figurine of yellow steatite (from a cave at Liguria, Italy); and one of the sandstone lamps by which artists worked in caves (from Lascaux Cave, France).

Original Study

Paleolithic Paint Job[7]

Lorblanchet's recent bid to re-create one of the most important Ice Age images in Europe was an affair of the heart as much as the head. "I tried to abandon my skin of a modern citizen, tried to experience the feeling of the artist, to enter the dialogue between the rock and the man," he explains. Every day for a week in the fall of 1990 he drove the 20 miles from his home in the medieval village of Cajarc into the hills above the river Lot. There, in a small, practically inaccessible cave, he transformed himself into an Upper Paleolithic painter. And not just any Upper Paleolithic painter, but the one who 18,400 years ago crafted the dotted horses inside the famous cave of Pech Merle.

You can still see the original horses in Pech Merle's vast underground geologic splendor. You enter through a narrow passageway and soon find yourself gazing across a grand cavern to where the painting seems to hang in the gloom. "Outside, the

[7]Lewin, R. (1993). Paleolithic paint job. *Discover, 14*(7), 67–69.

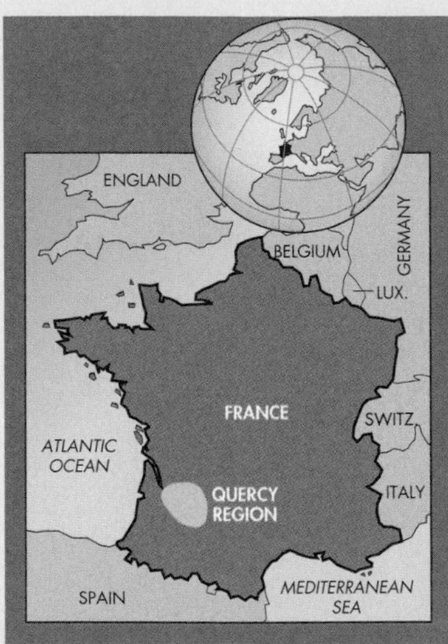

landscape is very different from the one the Upper Paleolithic people saw," says Lorblanchet. "But in here, the landscape is the same as it was more than 18,000 years ago. You see what the Upper Paleolithic people experienced." No matter where you look in this cavern, the eye is drawn back to the panel of horses.

The two horses face away from each other, rumps slightly overlapping, their outlines sketched in black. The animal on the right seems to come alive as it merges with a crook in the edge of the panel, the perfect natural shape for a horse's head. But the impression of naturalism quickly fades as the eye falls on the painting's dark dots. There are more than 200 of them, deliberately distributed within and below the bodies and arcing around the right-hand horse's head and mane. More cryptic still are a smattering of red dots and half-circles and the floating outline of a fish. The surrealism is completed by six disembodied human hands stenciled above and below the animals.

Lorblanchet began thinking about re-creating the horses after a research trip to Australia over a decade ago. Not only is Australia a treasure trove of rock art, but its aboriginal people are still creating it. "In Queensland I learned how people painted by spitting pigment onto the rock," he recalls. "They spat paint and used their hand, a piece of cloth, or a feather as a screen to create different lines and other effects. Elsewhere in Australia people used chewed twigs as paintbrushes, but in Queensland the spitting technique worked best." The rock surfaces there were too uneven for extensive brushwork, he adds—just as they are in Quercy.

When Lorblanchet returned home he looked at the Quercy paintings with a new eye. Sure enough,

This spotted horse in the French cave of Pech Merle was painted by an Upper Paleolithic artist.

Original Study

he began seeing the telltale signs of spit-painting—lines with edges that were sharply demarcated on one side and fuzzy on the other, as if they had been airbrushed—instead of the brushstrokes he and others had assumed were there. Could you produce lines that were crisp on both edges with the same technique, he wondered, and perhaps dots too? Archeologists had long recognized that hand stencils, which are common in prehistoric art, were produced by spitting paint around a hand held to the wall. But no one had thought that entire animal images could be created this way. Before he could test his ideas, however, Lorblanchet had to find a suitable rock face—the original horses were painted on a roughly vertical panel 13 feet across and 6 feet high. With the help of a speleologist, he eventually found a rock face in a remote cave high in the hills and set to work.

Following the aboriginal practices he had witnessed, Lorblanchet first made a light outline sketch of the horses with a charred stick. Then he prepared black pigment for the painting. "My intention had been to use manganese dioxide, as the Pech Merle painter did," says Lorblanchet, referring to one of the minerals ground up for paint by the early artists. "But I was advised that manganese is somewhat toxic, so I used wood charcoal instead." (Charcoal was used as pigment by Paleolithic painters in other caves, so Lorblanchet felt he could justify his concession to safety.) To turn the charcoal into paint, Lorblanchet ground it with a limestone block, put the powder in his mouth, and diluted it to the right consistency with saliva and water. For red pigment he used ocher from the local iron-rich clay.

He started with the dark mane of the right hand horse. "I spat a series of dots and fused them together to represent tufts of hair," he says, unself-consciously reproducing the spitting action as he talks. "Then I painted the horse's back by blowing the pigment below my hand held so"—he holds his hand flat against the rock with his thumb tucked in to form a straight line—"and used it like a stencil to produce a sharp upper edge and a diffused lower edge. You get an illusion of the animal's rounded flank this way."

He experimented as he went. "You see the angular rump?" he says, pointing to the original painting. "I reproduced that by holding my hand perpendicular to the rock, with my palm slightly bent, and I spat along the edge formed by my hand and the rock." He found he could produce sharp lines, such as those in the tail and in the upper hind leg, by spitting into the gap between parallel hands. The belly demanded more ingenuity; he spat paint into a V-shape formed by his two splayed hands, rubbed it into a curved swath to shape the belly's outline, then finger-painted short protruding lines to suggest the animals' shaggy hair. Neatly outlined dots, he found, could not be made by blowing a thin jet of charcoal onto the wall. He had to spit pigment through a hole made in an animal skin. "I spent seven hours a day for a week," he says. "Puff . . . puff . . . puff. . . . It was exhausting, particularly because there was carbon monoxide in the cave. But you experience something special, painting like that. You feel you are breathing the image onto the rock—projecting your spirit from the deepest part of your body onto the rock surface."

Was that what the Paleolithic painter felt when creating this image? "Yes, I know it doesn't sound very scientific," Lorblanchet says of his highly personal style of investigation, "but the intellectual games of the structuralists haven't got us very far, have they? Studying rock art shouldn't be an intellectual game. It is about understanding humanity. That's why I believe the experimental approach is valid in this case."

The End

Hypotheses to account for the early European cave art are difficult because they so often depend on conjectural and subjective interpretations. Some have argued that it is art for art's sake; but if that is so, why were animals so often painted over one another, and why were they so often placed in inaccessible places? The latter might suggest that they were for ceremonial purposes and that the caves served as religious sanctuaries. One suggestion is that the animals were drawn to ensure success in the hunt, another that their depiction was seen as a way to promote fertility and increase the size of the herds on which humans depended. In Altimira Cave in northern Spain, for example, the art shows a pervasive concern for the sexual reproduction of the bison.[8] In cave art generally, though, the animals painted bear little relationship to those most frequently hunted. Furthermore, there are few depictions of animals being hunted or killed, nor are there depictions of animals copulating or with exaggerated sexual parts as there are in the Venus figures. Another suggestion is that rites by which youngsters were initiated into adulthood took place in the painted galleries. In support of this idea, footprints, most of which are small, have been found in the clay floors of several caves, and in one, they even circle a modeled clay bison. The animals painted, so this argument goes, may have had to do with knowledge being transmitted from the elders to the youths. Furthermore, the transmission of information might be implied by countless so-called signs, apparently abstract designs that accompany much Upper Paleolithic art. Some have interpreted these as tallies of animals killed, a reckoning of time according to a lunar calendar, or both.

These abstract designs, including such ones as the spots on the Pech Merle horses, suggest yet another possibility. For the most part, these are just like the entoptic designs seen by subjects in experiments dealing with altered states of consciousness, and which are so consistently present in the rock art of southern Africa. Furthermore, the rock art of southern Africa shows the same painting of new images over older ones, as well as the same sort of fixation on large, powerful animals instead of the ones most often eaten. Thus, the cave art of Europe may well represent the same depictions of trance experiences, painted after the fact. Consistent with this interpretation, the caves themselves are conducive to the sort of sensory distortion that can induce trance.

Artistic expression, whatever its purpose may have been, was not confined to rock surfaces and portable objects alone. Upper Paleolithic peoples also ornamented their bodies with necklaces of perforated animal teeth, shells, beads of bone, stone, and ivory; rings; bracelets; and anklets. Clothing, too, was adorned with beads. This should alert us to the probability that quite a lot of art was executed in perishable materials—wood carving, paintings on bark or animal skins, and the like. Thus, the rarity or absence of Upper Paleolithic art in

[8]Halverson, J. (1989). Review of the book *Altimira revisited and other essays on early art. American Antiquity, 54,* 883.

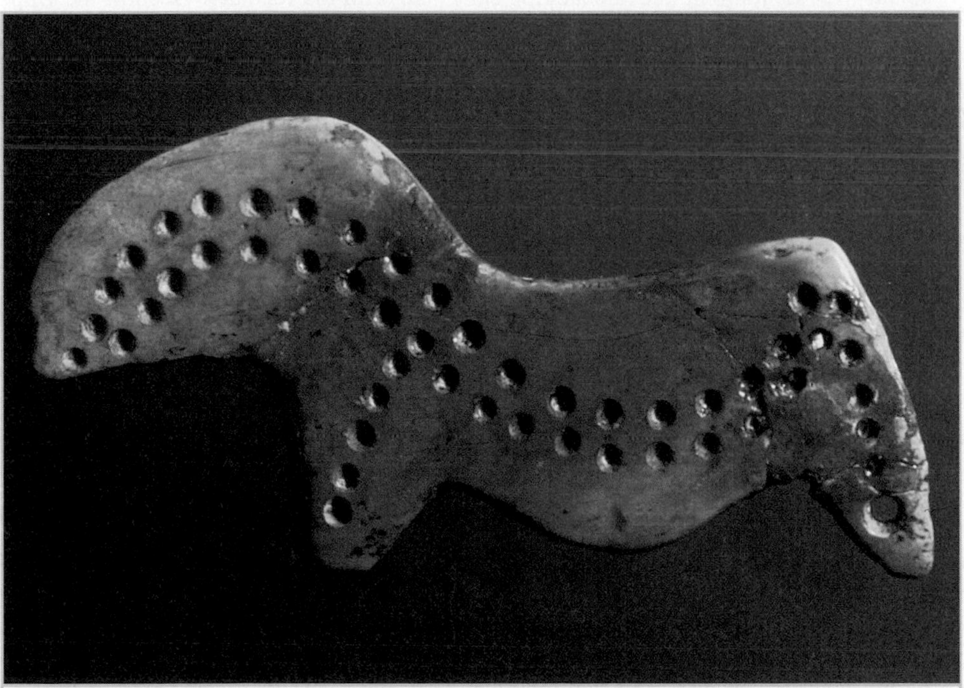

Dots are a common entoptic form, and in art depicting visions seen in trance, lines of dots are not uncommon, as on this 24,000-year-old ivory pendant from Sungir, Russia.

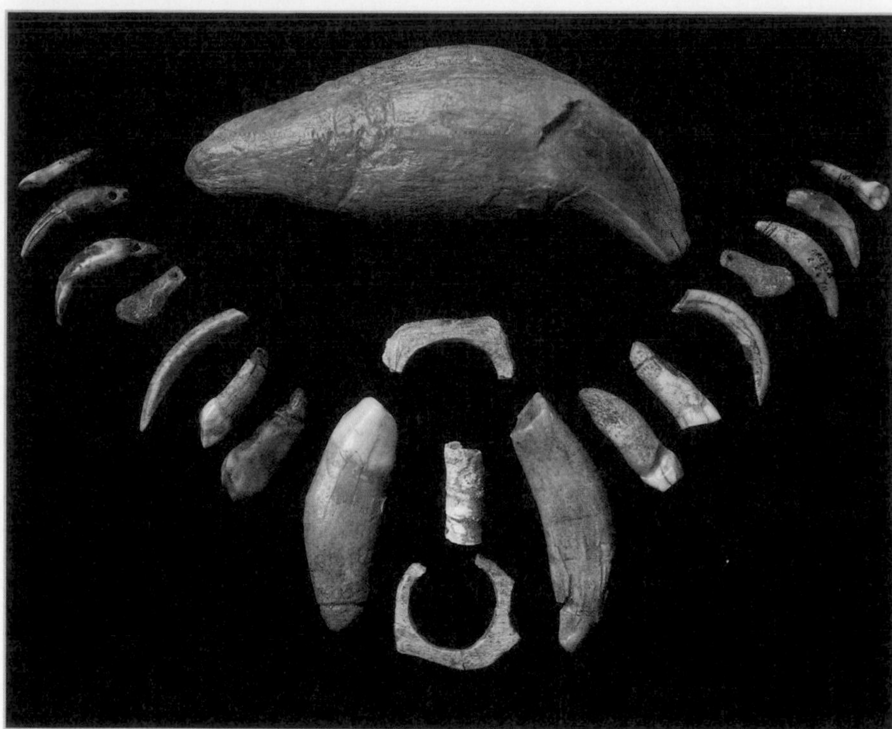

Pendants and beads for personal adornment became common in the Upper Paleolithic. In Europe, most were made by Cro-Magnons, but some—like those shown here—were made by Neandertals. The earliest undisputed items of personal adornment are some 40,000-year-old beads from Africa made from ostrich egg shell.

some parts of the inhabited world may be more apparent than real, as people elsewhere worked with materials unlikely to survive so long in the archaeological record.

OTHER ASPECTS OF UPPER PALEOLITHIC CULTURE

Upper Paleolithic peoples lived not only in caves and rock shelters, but also in structures built out in the open. In Ukraine, for example, the remains have been found of sizable settlements, in which huts were built on frameworks of intricately stacked mammoth bones. Where the ground was frozen, cobblestones were heated and placed in the earth to sink in, thereby providing sturdy, dry floors. Their hearths, no longer shallow depressions or flat surfaces that radiated back little heat, were instead stone-lined pits that conserved heat for extended periods and made for more efficient cooking. For the outdoors, they had the same sort of tailored clothing worn in historic times by the natives of Siberia, Alaska, and Canada. And they engaged in long-distance trade, as indicated, for example, by the presence of seashells and Baltic amber at sites several hundred kilometers from the sources of these materials. Although Middle Paleolithic peoples also made use of rare and distant materials, they did not do so with the regularity seen in the Upper Paleolithic.

THE SPREAD OF UPPER PALEOLITHIC PEOPLES

Such was the effectiveness of their cultures that Upper Paleolithic peoples were able to expand into regions previously uninhabited by their archaic forebears. Colonization of Siberia began about 42,000 years ago, although it took something like 10,000 years before they reached the northeastern part of that region. Much earlier, by 60,000 years ago, people managed to get to Australia and New Guinea. To do this, they had to use some kind of watercraft to make the difficult crossing of at least 90 kilometers of water that separated Australia and New Guinea (then a single landmass) from the Asian continent throughout Paleolithic times. Once in Australia, these people created some of the world's earliest sophisticated rock art, some 10,000 to 15,000 years earlier than the more famous European cave paintings. Other evidence for sophisticated ritual activity in early Australia is provided by the burial of a man at least 40,000 and

Reconstruction of an Upper Paleolithic hut with walls of interlocked mammoth mandibles.

possibly 60,000 years ago.[9] His fingers were intertwined around his penis and red ochre had been scattered over the body. It may be that this pigment had more than symbolic value; for example, its iron salts have antiseptic and deodorizing properties, and there are recorded instances in which red ochre is associated with prolonging life and is used medicinally to treat particular conditions or infections. One historically known native Australian society is reported to use ochre to heal wounds, scars, and burns, and a person with internal pain is covered with the substance and placed in the sun to promote sweating. What

[9]Rice, P. (2000). Paleoanthropology 2000—part 1. *General Anthropology, 7*(1), 11; Zimmer, C. (1999). New date for the dawn of dream time. *Science, 284,* 1,243.

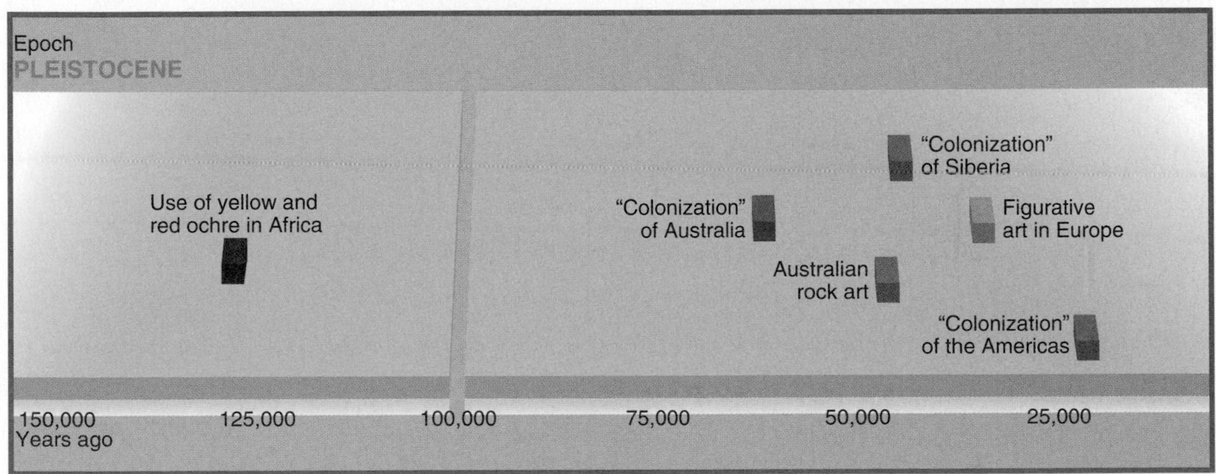

is especially interesting in view of the impressive accomplishments of native Australians is that the tools used by these people are remarkably similar to those of the Eurasian Middle Paleolithic. Clearly, simplicity of tool kits does not bespeak absence of sophisticated intellectual capabilities.

Just when people arrived in the Americas has been a matter of lively debate, but securely dated remains from Monte Verde, a site in south-central Chile, place people there by 12,500 years ago, if not earlier. Assuming the first populations spread from Siberia to Alaska, linguist Johanna Nichols suggests that the first people to arrive in North America did so by 20,000 years ago. She bases this estimate on the time it took various languages to spread from their homelands—Celtic languages in Europe, Eskimo languages in the Arctic, and Athabaskan languages from interior western Canada to New Mexico and Arizona (Navajo). Her conclusion is that it would have taken at least 7,000 years for people to reach south-central Chile.[10]

The conventional wisdom has long been that the first people spread into North America over dry land that connected Siberia to Alaska. This so-called land bridge was a consequence of the buildup of great continental glaciers. As these ice masses grew, there was a worldwide lowering of sea levels, causing an emergence of land in places like the Bering Straits where seas today are shallow. Thus, Alaska became, in effect, an eastward extension of Siberia (Figure 10.6).

Although ancient Siberians may indeed have spread eastward, it is now clear that their way south was blocked by massive glaciers until 13,000 years ago at the earliest.[11] By then, people were already living further south. Thus the question of how people first came to the Americas has been reopened. One possibility is that, like the first Australians, the first Americans may have come by boat, perhaps traveling between islands or ice-free pockets of coastline, from as far away as the Japanese islands and down North America's northwest coast. Hints of such voyages are provided by a handful of North

[10]The first Americans, ca. 20,000 B.C. (1998). *Discover, 19*(6), 24.

[11]Marshall, E. (2001). Preclovis sites fight for acceptance. *Science, 291,* 1,732.

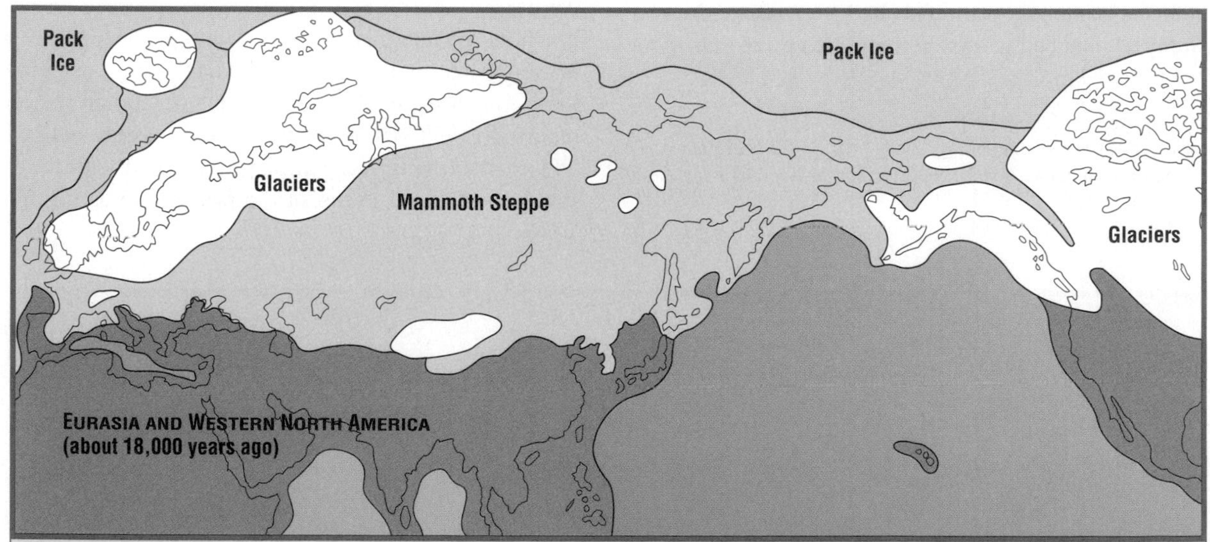

FIGURE 10.6

AS THIS MAP SHOWS, THE LAND CONNECTING SIBERIA AND ALASKA AT THE HEIGHT OF THE LAST GLACIATION WAS NOT SO MUCH A BRIDGE FOR PEOPLE TO CROSS INTO NORTH AMERICA AS IT WAS A PERIPHERAL PORTION OF A REGION INTO WHICH HUMAN POPULATIONS IN THE UPPER PALEOLITHIC SPREAD. OTHER POPULATIONS LIKELY MOVED BY BOAT ALONG THE COAST, ARRIVING IN NORTH AMERICA SOUTH OF THE ICE. ONCE THE ICE BARRIER BETWEEN LOWER NORTH AMERICA AND ALASKA RECEDED, OPPORTUNITIES FOR GENE FLOW BETWEEN NATIVE AMERICANS AND EAST ASIANS WOULD HAVE INCREASED.

Fluted points, such as these, tipped the spears of Paleoindian hunters in North America about 12,000 years ago.

American skeletons that bear a closer resemblance to the aboriginal Ainu people of Japan and their forebears than they do to other Asians or modern Native Americans. Unfortunately, because sea levels were lower than they are today, coastal sites used by early voyagers would now be under water.

The picture currently emerging, then, is of people, who did not look like modern American Indians, arriving by boat, spreading southward and eastward over time. There is no reason to suppose that contact back and forth between North America and Siberia ever stopped. In all probability, it became more common as the glaciers melted away. As a consequence, through gene flow as well as later arrivals of people from the East, those living in the Americas came to have the broad faces, prominent cheekbones, and round cranial vaults that characterize American Indians today.

Although the earliest technologies in the Americas remain poorly known, they gave rise in North America, about 12,000 years ago, to the distinctive fluted spear points of **Paleoindian** hunters of big game, such as mammoths, caribou, and now extinct forms of bison. Fluted points are finely made, with large channel flakes removed from one or both surfaces. This thinned section was inserted into the notched end of a spear shaft for a sturdy

Paleoindians, like their Upper Paleolithic contemporaries in Eurasia, were such accomplished hunters that they, too, could kill more animals than could possibly be used at one time. These bones are the remains of some 200 bison that Paleoindian hunters stampeded over a cliff 8,500 years ago.

Paleoindian. The earliest inhabitants of North America.

haft. Fluted points are found from the Atlantic seaboard to the Pacific coast, and from Alaska down into Panama. So efficient were the hunters who made these points that they may have hastened the extinction of the mammoth and other large Pleistocene mammals. By driving large numbers of animals over cliffs, they killed many more than they could possibly use, thus wasting huge amounts of meat.

WHERE DID UPPER PALEOLITHIC PEOPLE COME FROM?

As noted in Chapter 9, scholars still debate whether the transition from archaic to anatomically modern *H. sapiens* took place in one specific population or was the result of several populations living in Africa, Asia, and even Europe between 100,000 and 40,000 years ago evolving together. At the moment, though, the odds seem to favor the latter hypothesis. Even in Europe, where the argument for replacement of archaic by modern *sapiens* has been most strongly made, the most recent Neandertals display modern features, whereas the most ancient moderns show what appear to be Neandertal holdovers. For example, the Saint Césaire skull has the high forehead and chin of moderns. Similarly, a late Neandertal from Vindija, northern Croatia, shows a thinning of brow ridges toward their outer margins. Conversely, early Upper Paleolithic skulls from Brno, Mladec, and Predmosti, in the Czech Republic, retain heavy brow ridges and Neandertal-like muscle attachments on their backs.[12] As noted early in this chapter, some of the skulls from the Cro-Magnon rock shelter look Neandertal-like from the back. Of course, these features could all be the result of interbreeding between two populations that overlapped in time, rather than simple evolution from one into the other. Or, they could represent a single varied population whose average characters were shifting in a more "modern" direction. In either case, they do not fit with the idea of the complete extinction of the older population.

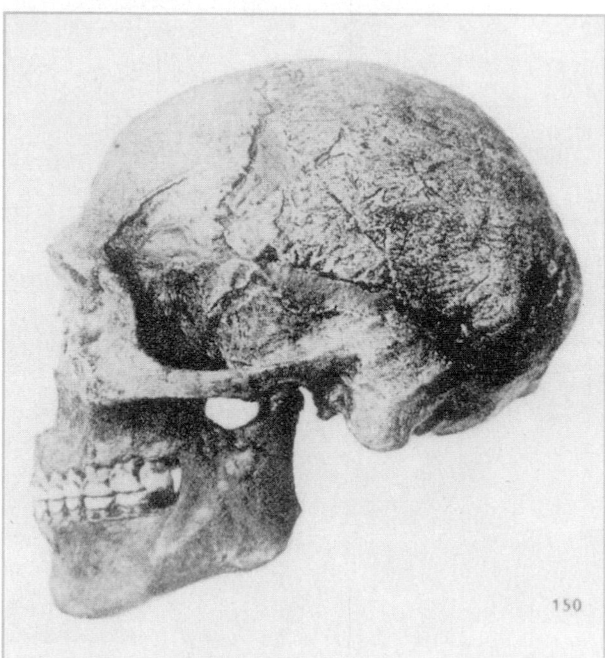

The bulge on the back of this Upper Paleolithic skull from Predmosti in the Czech Republic, along with its still prominent brow ridges, is reminiscent of the earlier Neandertals.

Looking at the larger picture, what we see in all regions of the Old World, since the time of *H. erectus,* is more and more emphasis placed on cultural, as opposed to biological, adaptation. To handle environmental stress, reliance was placed increasingly on the development of appropriate tools, clothes, shelter, use of fire, and so forth, as opposed to alteration of the human organism itself. This was true whether human populations lived in hot or cold, wet or dry, forest or grassland areas. Because culture is learned and not carried by genes, it is ultimately based on what might loosely be called "brain power" or, more formally, **cognitive capacity.** Although this includes intelligence in the IQ sense, it is broader than that, for it also includes such aptitudes as educability, concept formation, self-awareness, self-evaluation, reliability of performance under stress, attention span, sensitivity in discrimination, and creativity.

The major thrust in the evolution of the genus *Homo,* then, has been toward improved cognitive capacity through the evolution of the brain regardless of the environmental and climatic differences among the regions in

[12]Bednarik, R. G. (1995). Concept-mediated marking in the Lower Paleolithic. *Current Anthropology, 36,* 627; Minugh-Purvis, N. (1992). The inhabitants of Ice Age Europe. *Expedition, 34*(3), 33–34.

Cognitive capacity. A broad concept including intelligence, educability, concept formation, self-awareness, self-evaluation, attention span, sensitivity in discrimination, and creativity.

In 1998, this skeleton of a 4-year-old child was found in a Portuguese rock shelter, where it had been ritually buried. It displays a mix of Neandertal and Cro-Magnon traits, but its 25,000-year-old date makes it too recent to be the product of a chance encounter between two populations (by then, Neandertals were long gone). Instead, it bespeaks earlier extensive interbreeding, or else is one more example of an Upper Paleolithic European showing evidence of Neandertal ancestry. In either case, the idea of Neandertals and Cro-Magnons as separate species is effectively ruled out.

which populations of the genus lived. Hence, there has been a certain similarity of selective pressures in all regions. At the same time, gene flow among populations would have spread whatever genes happen to relate to cognitive capacity. In an evolving species, in the absence of isolating mechanisms, genes having survival value anywhere tend to spread from one population to another. As a case in point, wolves, like humans, have a wide distribution, ranging all the way from the Atlantic coast of Europe eastward across Eurasia and North America to Greenland. Yet, wolves constitute a single species—*Canis lupus*—and never in its 5- to 7-million-year evolutionary history has more than a single species coexisted.[13] That wolves never split into multiple species relates to the size of territories occupied by successful packs, and exchange of mates between packs. Both promoted gene flow across the species' entire range.

It is impossible to know just how much gene flow took place among ancient human populations, but that some took place is consistent with the sudden appearance of novel traits in one region later than their appearance somewhere else. For example, Upper Paleolithic remains from North Africa exhibit the kind of mid-facial flatness previously seen only in East Asian fossils; similarly, various Cro-Magnon fossils from Europe show the short upper jaws, horizontally oriented cheek bones, and rectangular eye orbits previously seen in East Asians. Conversely, the round orbits, large frontal sinuses, and thin cranial bones seen in some archaic *sapiens* skulls from China represent the first appearance there of traits that have greater antiquity in the West.[14] What appears to be happening, then, is that genetic variants from the East are being introduced into Western gene pools and vice versa. Support for this comes from studies of the

[13]Brace, C. L. (2000). *Evolution in an anthropological view* (p. 341). Walnut Creek, CA: Altamira.

[14]Pope, G. C. (1992). Craniofacial evidence for the origin of modern humans in China. *Yearbook of Physical Anthropology, 35,* 287–288.

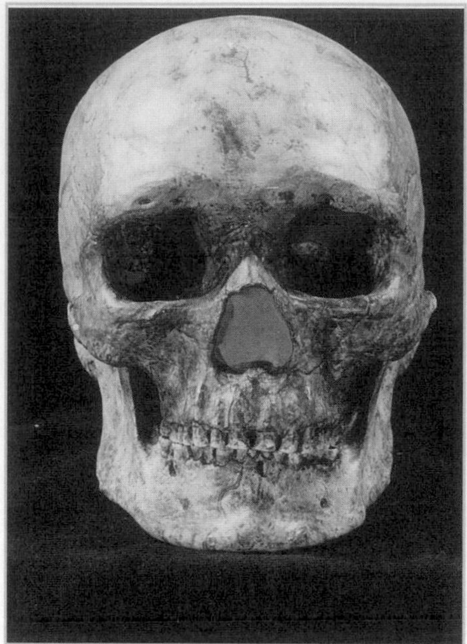

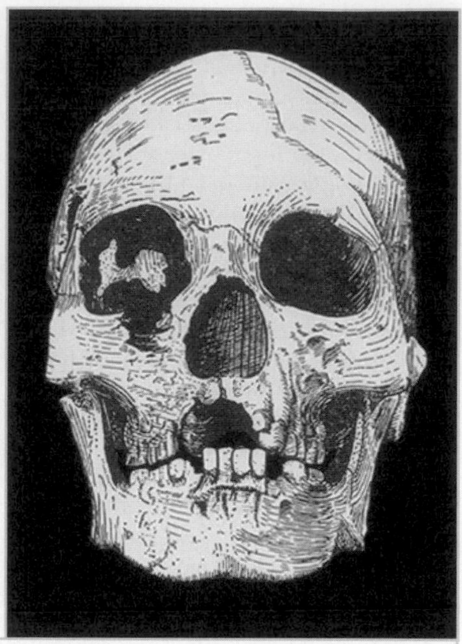

These Upper Paleolithic skulls from China (left) and Africa (right) are easily derivable from earlier archaic *sapiens* skulls in the same region.

Y chromosome in humans (found only in males). These studies indicate that some DNA carried by this chromosome originated in Asia at least 200,000 years ago and spread from there to Africa.[15] Not only is such gene flow consistent with the remarkable tendency historically known humans have to "swap genes" between populations, even in the face of cultural barriers to gene flow, it is also consistent with the tendency of other primates to produce hybrids when two subspecies (and sometimes even species) come into contact.[16] Moreover, without such gene flow, multiregional evolution inevitably would have resulted in the appearance of multiple species of modern humans, something that clearly has *not* happened. In fact, the low level of genetic differentiation among modern humans can be explained easily as a consequence of high levels of gene flow.[17]

[15]Gibbons, A. (1997). Ideas on human origins evolve at anthropology gathering. *Science, 276,* 535–536.

[16]Simons, E. L. (1989). Human origins. *Science, 245,* 1,349.

[17]Relethford, J. H., & Harpending, H. C. (1994). Craniometric variation, genetic theory, and modern human origins. *American Journal of Physical Anthropology, 95,* 265.

MAJOR PALEOLITHIC TRENDS

Certain trends stand out from the information anthropologists have gathered about the Old Stone Age, in most parts of the world. One was toward increasingly more sophisticated, varied, and specialized tool kits. Tools became progressively lighter and smaller, resulting in the conservation of raw materials and a better ratio between length of cutting edge and weight of stone. Tools became specialized according to region and function. Instead of crude all-purpose tools, more effective particularized devices were made to deal more effectively with the differing conditions of savanna, forest, and shore.

This more efficient tool technology enabled human populations to grow and spill over into more diverse environments; it also was responsible for the loss of heavy physical features, favoring instead decreased size and weight of face and teeth, the development of larger and more complex brains, and ultimately a reduction in body size and robusticity. This dependence on intelligence rather than bulk provided the key for humans' increased reliance on cultural rather than physical adaptation. As the brain became modernized, conceptual thought developed, as evidenced by symbolic artifacts and signs of ritual activity.

By the Upper Paleolithic, the amount of sexual dimorphism, too, was greatly reduced, as size differences between men and women were relatively slight compared to what they were in *Australopithecus, Homo habilis,* or (to a lesser extent) *Homo erectus.* This has important implications for gender relations. As noted in earlier chapters, among primates marked sexual dimorphism is associated with male dominance over females. Lack of sexual dimorphism, by contrast, correlates with a lack of such dominance. In evolving humans, it appears that a loss of male dominance went hand in hand with the ever-increasing importance of cooperative relationships. (Paradoxically, humans reinvented male dominance in the context of civilization, a relatively recent development that is the subject of Chapter 12.)

Through Paleolithic times, at least in the colder parts of the world, there appeared a trend toward the importance of and proficiency in hunting. Humans' intelligence enabled them to develop tools that exceeded other animals' physical equipment, as well as the improved social organization and cooperation so important for survival and population growth. As discussed in the next chapter, this trend was reversed during the Mesolithic, when hunting lost its preeminence, and the gathering of wild plants and seafood became increasingly important.

As human populations grew and spread, regionalism also became more marked. Tool assemblages developed in different ways at different times in different areas. General differences appeared between north and south, east and west. Although there are some indications of cultural contact and intercommunication, such as the development of long-distance trade in the Upper Paleolithic, regionalism was a dominant characteristic of Paleolithic times. The persistence of regionalism was probably due to two factors: a perceived need to distinguish symbolically one's own people from others and the need to adapt to differing environments. Paleolithic peoples eventually spread over all the continents of the world, including Australia and the Americas, and as they did so, changes in climate and environment called for new kinds of adaptations. Thus Paleolithic tool kits had to be altered to meet the requirements of many varying locations. In forest environments, people needed tools for working wood; on the open savanna and plains, they came to use the bow and arrow to hunt the game they could not stalk closely; the people in settlements that grew up around lakes and along rivers and coasts developed harpoons and hooks; in the subarctic regions they needed tools to work the heavy skins of seals and caribou. The fact that culture is first and foremost an adaptive mechanism meant that it was of necessity a regional thing.

CHAPTER SUMMARY

The Cro-Magnons and the other Upper Paleolithic peoples of the world, in addition to a full-sized brain, possessed a physical appearance somewhat similar to our own. The modernization of the face of Upper Paleolithic peoples is a result of a reduction in the size of the teeth and the muscles involved in chewing and relates to the fact that teeth were no longer being used as tools. Similarly, bodies became somewhat less massive and robust as improved technology reduced the need for brute strength.

Upper Paleolithic cultures evolved out of the Middle Paleolithic cultures of Africa, Asia, and Europe. The typical Upper Paleolithic tool was the blade. The blade technique of toolmaking was less wasteful of flint than Middle Paleolithic methods. Other efficient Upper Paleolithic toolmaking techniques were pressure flaking of stone and using chisel-like tools called burins to fashion bone, antler horn, and ivory into tools. The cultural adaptation of Upper Paleolithic peoples became specific; they developed different tools in different regions. Northern Upper Paleolithic cultures supported themselves by the hunting of large herd animals and catching smaller animals in nets. Hunting with the bow and arrow developed in Africa, spreading later to Europe and other regions. Upper Paleolithic cultures are the earliest in which artistic expression is common.

The emphasis in evolution of the genus *Homo* in all parts of the world was toward increasing cognitive capacity through development of the brain. This took place regardless of environmental or climatic conditions under which the genus lived. In addition, evolution of the genus *Homo* undoubtedly involved gene flow among populations. Lack of much genetic differentiation among human populations today bespeaks high levels of gene flow among populations in the past.

Three trends are evident in the Paleolithic period. First was a trend toward more sophisticated, varied, and specialized tool kits. This trend enabled people to increase their population and spread to new environments. It also had an impact on human anatomy, favoring decreased size and weight of face and teeth, the development of larger, more complex brains, and ultimately a reduction in body size, mass, and degree of sexual dimorphism. Second was a trend toward the importance of and proficiency in hunting. Third was a trend toward regionalism, as people's technology and life habits increasingly reflected their association with a particular environment.

CLASSIC READINGS

Campbell, B. G., & Loy, J. D. (1995). *Humankind emerging* (7th ed.). New York: HarperCollins.

Adapted in part from Time-Life's *Emergence of Man* and *Life Nature Library,* this is a richly illustrated, up-to-date account of the Paleolithic. In it, Campbell integrates paleontological and archaeological data with ethnographic data on modern food foragers to present a rich picture of evolving Paleolithic ways of life.

Pfeiffer, J. E. (1985). *The creative explosion.* Ithaca, NY: Cornell University Press.

A fascinating and readable discussion of the origins of art and religion. Its main drawback is its focus on European art.

Prideaux, T., et al. (1973). *Cro-Magnon man.* New York: Time-Life.

This beautifully illustrated volume in the Time-Life *Emergence of Man* series, though dated, is worth looking at for the illustrations. It also shows that, although our ideas about human evolution have changed over the past 30 years, some old biases still persist.

Wolpoff, M., & Caspari, R. (1997). *Race and human evolution.* New York: Simon & Schuster.

This book is a detailed but readable presentation of the multiregional hypothesis of modern human origins. Among its strengths is a discussion of the problem of defining what "anatomically modern" means.

PART IV

Human Biological and Cultural Evolution Since the Old Stone Age

INTRODUCTION

Up until the Middle Paleolithic, the story of the evolution of the genus *Homo* is one of a close interrelation between developing culture and developing humanity. The critical importance of culture as the human adaptive mechanism seems to have imposed selective pressures favoring a bigger, more elaborate brain, with greater cognitive power.

This in turn made possible improved cultural adaptation. Indeed, it seems fair to say that modern humans look the way they do today because cultural adaptation came to play such a vital role in the survival of our ancient ancestors.

By 200,000 years ago, the human brain had become as big as it would get, and there has been no subsequent increase in size. Human culture, by contrast, continued to change at an even faster pace than before. Hence, there was a kind of "disconnect" between culture and biology; as humans became modern in form, macroevolution came to a halt, even though microevolution continues to this day.

By 36,000 years ago, humans everywhere had developed cultures comparable to those of historically known food-foraging peoples. Although these cultures served humans well through tens of thousands of years of the Upper

Paleolithic, far-reaching changes began to take place in some parts of the world as early as 11,000 years ago. This second major cultural revolution consisted of the emergence of food production, the subject of Chapter 11. Eventually, most of the world's peoples became food producers, even though food foraging remained a satisfactory way of life for some.

At the present time, fewer than a quarter of a million people—less than 0.00005 percent of a world population of over 6 billion—remain food foragers. Just as the emergence of food foraging was followed by modifications and improvements leading to regional variants of this pattern, so the advent of food production opened the way for new cultural variants based upon it. Chapter 12 discusses the result: further cultural diversity, out of which developed civilization, the basis of modern life.

Despite the increasing effectiveness of culture as the primary mechanism by which humans adapt to diverse environments, and the lack of macroevolutionary change since the emergence of the modern human species, microevolutionary change has continued. In the course of their movement into other parts of the world, humans had already developed a certain amount of biological variation from one population to another. On top of this, populations of food producers were exposed to selective pressures of a different sort than those affecting food foragers, thereby inducing further changes in human gene pools. Such changes continue to affect humans today, even though we remain the same species now as at the end of the Paleolithic. Chapter 13 discusses how the variation to be seen in *Homo sapiens* today came into existence as the result of forces altering the frequencies of alleles in human gene pools and why such variation probably has nothing to do with intelligence. The chapter concludes with a look at forces apparently active today to produce further changes in those same gene pools.

CHAPTER 11

CULTIVATION AND DOMESTICATION

Beginning about 11,000 years ago, some of the world's people embarked on a new way of life based on food production. Though farming has changed dramatically in the millennia since then, all of the crops we rely on today originated with those earliest farmers.

CHAPTER PREVIEW

When and Where Did the Change from Food Foraging to Food Production Begin?

Independent centers of early plant and animal domestication exist in Africa, China, Mesoamerica, North and South America, as well as Southwest and Southeast Asia. From these places, food production spread to most other parts of the world. It began at more or less the same time in these different places—perhaps a bit earlier in Southwest Asia, but a bit later in Southeast Asia.

Why Did the Change Take Place?

Because food production by and large requires more work than hunting and gathering, it is not necessarily a more secure means of subsistence; and because it requires people to eat more of the foods that food foragers eat only when they have no other choice, it can be assumed that people probably did not become food producers through choice. Of various theories that have been proposed, the most likely is that food production came about as a consequence of a chance convergence of separate natural events and cultural developments.

What Were the Consequences of the Change to Food Production?

Although food production generally provides less leisure time than food foraging, it does permit some reallocation of the workload. Some people can produce enough food to support others who undertake other tasks, and so a number of technological developments, such as weaving and pottery making, generally accompany food production. In addition, it facilitates a sedentary way of life in villages, with more substantial housing. Finally, the new modes of work and resource allocation require new ways of organizing people, generally into lineages, clans, and common-interest associations.

Throughout the Paleolithic, people depended exclusively on wild sources of food for their survival. In cold northern regions, they came to rely on the hunting of large animals such as the mammoth, bison, and horse, but especially reindeer, as well as smaller animals such as hares, foxes, and birds. Elsewhere, they hunted, fished, or gathered whatever nature provided. There is no evidence in Paleolithic remains to indicate that livestock was kept or plants cultivated. Paleolithic people followed wild herds and gathered wild plant foods, relying on their wits and muscles to acquire what nature provided. Whenever favored sources of food became scarce, as sometimes happened, people adjusted by increasing the variety of food eaten and incorporating less favored food into their diets.

About 12,000 years ago, the subsistence practices of some people began to change in ways that were to transform radically their way of life, although no one involved had any way of knowing it at the time. Not until these changes were well advanced could people realize that their mode of subsistence differed from that of other cultures—that they had become farmers, rather than food foragers.[1] This change in the means of obtaining food had important implications for human development, for it meant that by taking matters into their own hands, people could lead a more sedentary existence. Moreover, by reorganizing the workload, some of them could be freed from the food quest to devote their energies to other sorts of tasks. With good reason, the **Neolithic period,** when this change took place, has been called a revolutionary one in human history. This period, and the changes that took place within it, are the subjects of this chapter.

THE MESOLITHIC ROOTS OF FARMING AND PASTORALISM

By 12,000 years ago, glacial conditions in the world were moderating, causing changes in human habitats. Throughout the world, sea levels were on the rise, ultimately flooding many areas that had been above sea level during periods of glaciation, such as the Bering Straits, parts of the North Sea, and an extensive area that had joined the eastern islands of Indonesia to Southeast Asia. In northern regions, milder climates brought about marked changes as, in some regions, tundras were replaced by hardwood forests. In the process, the herd animals upon which northern Paleolithic peoples had depended for much of their food, clothing, and shelter disappeared from many areas. Some, like the reindeer and musk ox, moved to colder climates; others, like the mammoths, died out completely. Thus, the northerners especially were forced to adapt to new conditions. In the new forests, animals were more solitary in their habits and so not as easy to hunt as they had been, and large, cooperative hunts were less productive than before. However, plant food was more abundant, and there were new and abundant sources of fish and other food around lake shores, bays, and rivers. Hence, human populations developed new and ingenious ways to catch and kill a variety of smaller birds and animals, while at the same time they devoted more energy to fishing and the collection of a broad spectrum of wild plant foods. This new way of life marks the end of the Paleolithic and the start of the **Mesolithic,** or Middle Stone Age.

Mesolithic Tools and Weapons

New technologies were developed for the changed postglacial environment. Ground stone tools, shaped and sharpened by grinding the tool against sandstone (often using sand as an additional abrasive), made effective axes and adzes. Such implements, though they do take longer to make, are less prone to breakage under heavy-duty usage than are those made of chipped stone. Thus, they were helpful in clearing forest areas and in the woodwork needed for the creation of dugout canoes and skin-covered boats. Although some kind of water craft had been developed early enough to get humans to the island of Flores (and probably Italy and Spain) by 800,000 years ago, sophisticated boats become prominent only in Mesolithic sites, indicating that human foraging for food frequently took place on the water as well as the land. Thus, it was possible to make use of deep-water resources as well as those of coastal areas.

The characteristic Mesolithic tool was the **microlith,** a small but hard, sharp blade. Although a microlithic

[1]Rindos, D. (1984). *The origins of agriculture: An evolutionary perspective* (p. 99). Orlando: Academic Press.

Neolithic period. The New Stone Age; began about 11,000 years ago in Southwest Asia. • **Mesolithic.** The Middle Stone Age of Europe and Southwest Asia; began about 12,000 years ago. • **Microlith.** A small blade of flint or similar stone, several of which were hafted together in wooden handles to make tools; widespread in the Mesolithic.

Two examples of ground stone tools used for heavy woodworking: an axe and a gouge. The groove on the axe was for hafting in a wooden handle. Gouges like this one were used to make dugout canoes.

tradition existed in Central Africa by about 40,000 years ago,[2] such tools did not become common elsewhere until the Mesolithic. Microliths could be mass produced because they were small, easy to make, and could be fashioned from materials other than flint. Also, they could be attached to arrow shafts by using melted resin as a binder. Thus, the bow and arrow with the microlith arrowhead became the deadliest and most common weapon of the Mesolithic.

The reliance of Mesolithic peoples on microliths provided them with an important advantage over their Upper Paleolithic forebears: The small size of the microlith enabled them to devise a wider array of composite tools made out of stone and wood or bone (Figure 11.1). Thus, they could make sickles, harpoons, arrows, and daggers by fitting microliths into slots in wood or bone handles. Later experimentation with these forms led to more sophisticated tools and weapons.

It appears that the Mesolithic was a more sedentary period for humans than earlier eras. Dwellings from this period seem more substantial, an indication of permanency. Indeed, this is a logical development. Most hunting cultures, and especially those depending on herd animals, are nomadic: To be successful, one must follow the game. This is not necessary for people who subsist on a diet of seafood and plants, as the location of shore and vegetation remains relatively constant.

Cultural Diversity in the Mesolithic

In the warmer parts of the world, the collection of wild plant foods had been more of an equal partner with hunting in subsistence activities in the Upper Paleolithic than had been the case in the colder north. Hence, in areas like Southwest Asia, the Mesolithic represents less of a

[2]Bednarik, R.G. (1995). Concept-mediated marking in the Lower Paleolithic. *Current Anthropology 36,* 606.

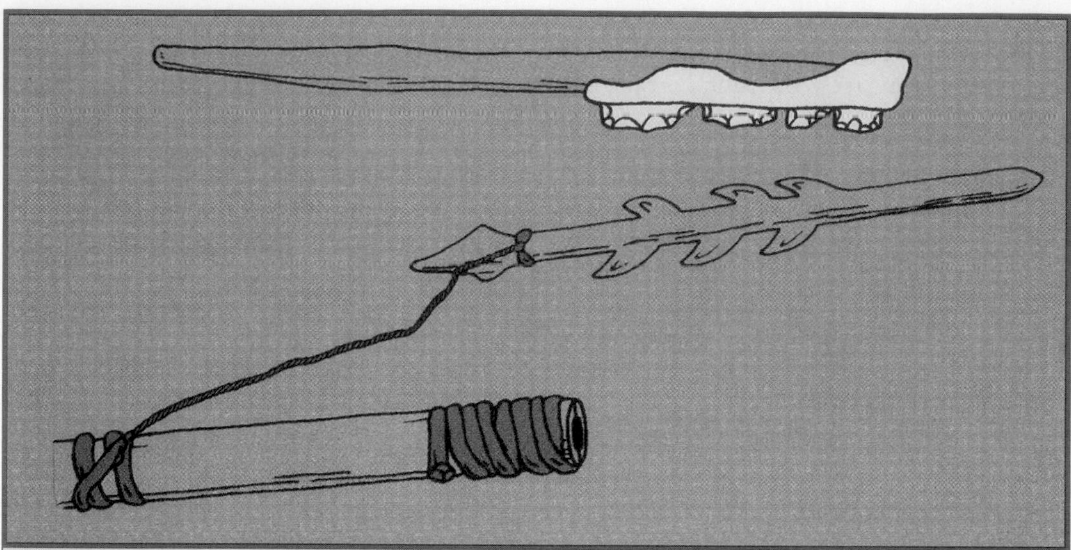

FIGURE 11.1

THIS DRAWING SHOWS A MESOLITHIC COMPOSITE TOOL CONSISTING OF MICROLITHS SET INTO A WOODEN HANDLE. ALSO SHOWN IS A BONE HARPOON HEAD WITH THE END OF ITS WOODEN SHAFT. HARPOONS ACTUALLY CAME INTO USE BEFORE THE MESOLITHIC.

changed way of life than was true in Europe. Here, the important **Natufian culture** flourished.

The Natufians were a people who lived between 12,500 and 10,200 years ago at the eastern end of the Mediterranean Sea in caves, rock shelters, and small villages with stone- and mud-walled houses. Nearby, their dead were buried in communal cemeteries, usually in shallow pits without grave goods or decorations. A small shrine is known from one of their villages, a 10,500-year-old settlement at Jericho. Basin-shaped depressions in the rocks found outside homes at Natufian sites are thought to have been storage pits. Plastered storage pits beneath the floors of the houses were also found, indicating that the Natufians were the earliest Mesolithic people known to have stored plant foods. Certain tools found among Natufian remains bear evidence that they were used to cut grain. These Mesolithic sickles, for that is what they were, consisted of small stone blades set in straight handles of wood or bone.

In the Americas, cultures comparable to Mesolithic cultures of the Old World developed, but here they are referred to as **Archaic cultures.** Outside of the Arctic, microlithic tools are not prominent in them, as they are in parts of the Old World, but ground stone tools such as axes, adzes, gouges, plummets, and spear-thrower weights are common. Archaic cultures were widespread in the Americas; one of the more dramatic was the **Maritime Archaic,** which began to develop about 7,000 years ago around the Gulf of St. Lawrence. These people developed an elaborate assortment of bone and ground slate tools with which they hunted a wide variety of sea mammals, including whales; fish, including swordfish; and sea birds. To get some of these, they regularly paddled their dugout canoes far offshore. To appreciate the skills this required, one need only recognize the difficulty of landing a 500-pound swordfish, as these are extremely aggressive fish. They are known historically to have driven their swords through the hulls of substantial wooden vessels. The Maritime Archaic people also developed the first elaborate burial cult in North America, involving the use of red ochre ("red paint") and the placement of finely made grave goods with the deceased.

Natufian culture. A Mesolithic culture of Israel, Lebanon, and western Syria, between about 12,500 and 10,200 years ago. • **Archaic cultures.** Term used to refer to Mesolithic cultures in the Americas. • **Maritime Archaic culture.** An Archaic culture of northeastern North America, centered on the Gulf of St. Lawrence, that emphasized the utilization of marine resources.

At Nulliak, Labrador, Maritime Archaic people lived in large, long houses with stone foundations. The alignments of stones seen in this photo are all that remain of one such house.

Varied though Mesolithic and Archaic cultures were, this new way of life generally offered more secure supplies of food and therefore an increased margin of survival. In some parts of the world, people started living in larger and more sedentary groups and cooperating with others outside the sphere of family or hunting band. They became settled village dwellers, and some of these settlements were shortly to expand into the first farming villages, towns, and (ultimately) cities.

THE NEOLITHIC REVOLUTION

The Neolithic, or New Stone Age, was characterized by the transition from foraging for food to dependence upon domesticated plants and animals. It was by no means a smooth or rapid transition; in fact, the switch to food production spread over many centuries—even millennia—and was a direct outgrowth of the preceding Mesolithic. Where to draw the line between the two periods is not always clear.

The term *New Stone Age* is derived from the polished stone tools that are characteristic of this period. But more important than the presence of these tools is the transition from a hunting, gathering, and fishing economy to one based on food production, representing a major change in the subsistence practices of early peoples. One of the first regions to undergo this transition, and certainly the most intensively studied, was Southwest Asia. The remains of domesticated plants and animals are known from parts of Israel, Jordan, Syria, Turkey, Iraq, and Iran, all before 8,000 years ago.

Domestication: What Is It?

Domestication is an evolutionary process whereby humans modify, either intentionally or unintentionally, the genetic makeup of a population of plants or animals, sometimes to the extent that members of the population are unable to survive and/or reproduce without human assistance. As such, it constitutes a special case of a kind

Domestication. An evolutionary process whereby humans modify, either intentionally or unintentionally, the genetic makeup of a population of plants or animals, sometimes to the extent that members of the population are unable to survive and/or reproduce without human assistance.

of relationship between different species frequently seen in the natural world, as in the case of one species that has come to depend for its protection and reproductive success on some other that feeds upon it. A particularly dramatic example is offered by species of New World ants that grow fungi in their nests, providing the ants with most of their nutrition. Like human farmers, the ants add manure to stimulate fungal growth and eliminate competing weeds both mechanically and through use of antibiotic herbicides. They propagate their crops vegetatively, as do humans for some of their crops (bananas, for example), and even share crops, as when one ant species borrows from another's nest or when several nests become disturbed and mixed. Finally, like human farming, ant farming did not develop just once, but at least five different times.[3]

Worker ants have made a path as they go out to cut pieces of leaf that they bring back to their nest to make the soil in which they plant their fungus gardens.

Looked at from the perspective of the fungi, the benefit gained is protection and ensured reproductive success. Turning from fungi to plants, we find that there are numerous species that rely on some type of animal—in some cases birds, in others mammals, and in yet others insects—for protection and dispersal of their seeds. The important thing is that both parties benefit from the arrangement; reliance on animals for seed dispersal ensures that the latter will be carried further afield than would otherwise be possible, thereby cutting down on competition for sun and nutrients between young and old plants and reducing the likelihood that any diseases or parasites harbored by one will be transmitted to the others. Added vigor is apt to come to plants that are freed from the need to provide themselves with built-in defensive mechanisms such as thorns, toxins, or chemical compounds that make them taste bad. This enhanced vigor may be translated into larger and more tasty edible parts to attract the animals that feed upon them, thereby cementing the relationship between the protected and protector.

Evidence of Early Plant Domestication

The characteristics of plants under human domestication that set them apart from their wild ancestors and have made them attractive to those who eat them include increased size, at least of edible parts; reduction or loss of natural means of seed dispersal; reduction or loss of protective devices such as husks or distasteful chemical compounds; loss of delayed seed germination (important to wild plants for survival in times of drought or other adverse conditions of temporary duration); and development of simultaneous ripening of the seed or fruit. Many of these characteristics can be seen in plant remains from archaeological sites; thus, paleobotanists can often tell the fossil of a wild plant species from a domesticated one, for example, by studying the seed of cereal grasses, such as barley, wheat, and maize (corn). Wild cereals have a very fragile stem, whereas domesticated ones have a tough stem. Under natural conditions, plants with fragile stems scatter their seed for themselves, whereas those with tough stems do not.

[3]Diamond, J. (1998). Ants, crops, and history. *Science, 281,* 1,974–1,975.

Wild wheat kernels from a site in Syria (left) are compared with those of a domestic variety grown in Greece 2,000 to 3,000 years later (right). Increased size of edible parts is a common feature of domestication.

The structural change from a soft to a tough stem in early domesticated plants involves a genetic change, undoubtedly the result of what Darwin referred to as **unconscious selection:** the preservation of valued individuals and the destruction of less valued ones, with no thought as to long-range consequences.[4] When the grain stalks were harvested, their soft stem would shatter at the touch of sickle or flail, and many of their seeds would be lost. Inevitably, most of the seeds that people harvested would have been taken from the tough plants. Early domesticators probably also tended to select seed from plants having few husks or none at all—eventually breeding them out—because husking prior to pounding the grains into meal or flour was much too time-consuming. Size of plants is another good indicator of the presence of domestication. For example, the large ear of corn (maize) we know today is a far cry from the tiny ears (about an inch long) characteristic of early maize. In fact, the ear of corn may have arisen as a simple gene mutation transformed male tassel spikes of the wild grass teosinte into small and primitive versions of the female corn ear.[5] Small and primitive though these were (an

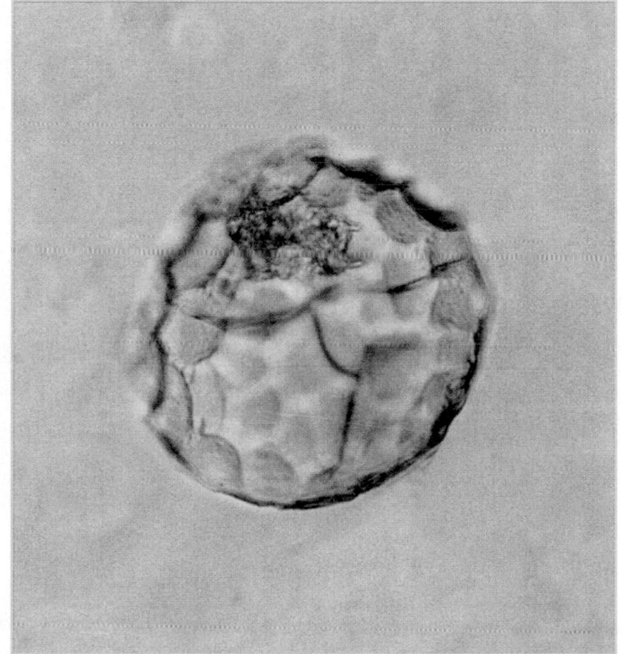

Shown here is a magnification of a phytolith of squash. Phytoliths are microscopic silica bodies formed as plants take up silica from groundwater. As the silica gradually fills plant cells, it assumes their distinctive size and shape. They are important for archaeologists, as they survive in humid climates where organic remains rapidly decay.

[4]Rindos, p. 86.

[5]Gould, S. J. (1991). *The flamingo's smile: Reflections in natural history* (p. 368). New York: Norton.

Unconscious selection. The preservation of valued variants of a plant or animal species and the destruction of less valued ones, with no thought as to the long-range consequences.

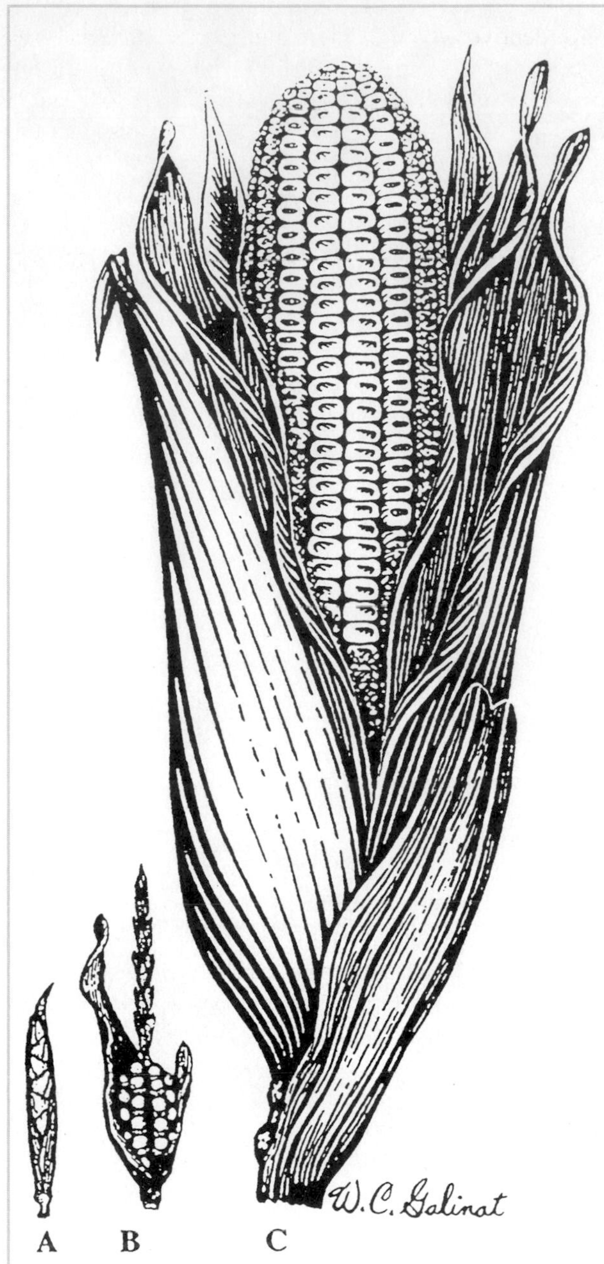

Teosinte (A), compared to the 5,500-year-old maize (B) and modern maize (C). The wild grass from which maize originated, teosinte is far less productive than maize and doesn't taste very good. Like most plants that were domesticated, it was not a first- or even second-choice food for foraging people.

entire ear contained less nourishment than a single kernel of modern maize), they were radically different in structure from the ears of teosinte.

Evidence of Early Animal Domestication

Domestication also produced changes in the skeletal structure of some animals. For example, the horns of wild goats and sheep differ from those of their domesticated counterparts (domesticated female sheep have none). Another structural change that occurred in domestication involves the size of the animal or its parts. For example, certain teeth of domesticated pigs are smaller than those of wild ones.

A study of age and sex ratios of butchered animals at a site may indicate whether or not animal domestication was practiced. Investigators have assumed that if the age and/or sex ratios at the site differ from those in wild herds, the imbalances are due to conscious selection. For example, at 10,000-year-old sites in the Zagros Mountains of Iran and Iraq, there was a sharp rise in the numbers of young male goats killed. Evidently, people were slaughtering the young males for food and saving the females for breeding. Although such herd management does not prove that the goats were fully domesticated, it does indicate a first step in the domestication process.[6]

In Peru, the prominence of bones of newborn llamas at archaeological sites (up to 72 percent at some), dating to around 6,300 years ago, is probably indicative of at least incipient domestication. Such high mortality rates for newborn animals are uncommon in wild herds but are common where animals are penned up. Under confined conditions, the inevitable buildup of mud and filth harbors bacteria that cause diarrhea and enterotoxemia, both of which are fatal to newborn animals.

Beginnings of Domestication

Over the past 30 years, a good deal of information has accumulated about the beginnings of domestication, primarily in Southwest Asia as well as Central and South America. We still do not have all the answers about how and why it took place. Nonetheless, some observations of general validity can be made that help us to understand how the switch to food production may have taken place.

The first of these observations is that the switch to food production was not the result of such discoveries

[6]Zeder, M. A., & Hesse, B. (2000). The initial domestication of goats *(Capra hircus)* in the Zagros Mountains 10,000 years ago. *Science, 287,* 2,254–2,257.

that seeds, if planted, grow into plants. Food foragers are far from ignorant about the forces of nature and are perfectly aware of the role of seeds in plant growth, that plants grow better under certain conditions than others, and so forth. Physiologist Jared Diamond calls such peoples "walking encyclopedias of natural history with individual names for as many as a thousand or more plant and animal species, and with detailed knowledge of those species' biological characteristics, distribution and potential uses."[7] What's more, they frequently apply their knowledge so as to manage actively the resources on which they depend. For example, Indians living in the northern part of Canada's Alberta Province put to use a sophisticated knowledge of the effects of fire to create local environments of their own design. Similarly, Indians in California used fire to perpetuate oak woodland savanna, to promote hunting and the collection of acorns. And in northern Australia, runoff channels of creeks were deliberately altered so as to flood extensive tracts of land, converting them into fields of wild grain. People do not remain food foragers through ignorance, but through choice.

A second observation is that a switch from food foraging to food production does not free people from hard work. The available ethnographic data indicate just the opposite—that farmers, by and large, work far longer hours than do most food foragers. Furthermore, it is clear that early farming required people not only to work longer hours but also to eat more "third-choice" food. Typically, food foragers divide potentially edible food resources into first-, second-, and third-choice categories; third-choice foods are eaten only by necessity, when there is no other option. And in Southwest Asia and Mexico, at least, the plants that were brought under domestication were clearly third-choice plants.

A final observation is that food production is not necessarily a more secure means of subsistence than food foraging. Seed crops in particular—of the sort domesticated in Southwest Asia, Mexico, and Peru—are highly productive but very unstable on account of low species diversity. Without constant human attention, their productivity suffers.

From all of this, it is little wonder that food foragers do not necessarily regard farming and animal husbandry as superior to hunting, gathering, and fishing. Thus, there are some people in the world who have remained food foragers down into the 1990s, although it has become increasingly difficult for them as food-producing peoples have deprived them of more and more of the land base necessary for their way of life. But as long as existing practices worked well, there was no need to abandon them. After all, their traditional way of life gave them all the food they needed and an eminently satisfactory way of living in small, intimate groups. Free from tedious routine, their lives were often more exciting than those of farmers. Food could be hunted, gathered, or fished for as needed, but in most environments they could relax when they had enough to eat. Why raise crops through backbreaking work when the whole family could camp under a tree bearing tasty and nutritious nuts? Farming brings with it a whole new system of human relationships that offers no easily understood advantages and disturbs an age-old balance between humans and nature as well as the people who live together.

WHY HUMANS BECAME FOOD PRODUCERS

In view of what has been said so far, we may well ask: Why did any human group abandon food foraging in favor of food production?

Several theories have been proposed to account for this change in human subsistence practices. One older theory, championed by V. Gordon Childe, is the desiccation, or oasis, theory based on climatic determinism. Its proponents advanced the idea that the glacial cover over Europe and Asia caused a southern shift in rain patterns from Europe to northern Africa and Southwest Asia. When the glaciers retreated northward, so did the rain patterns. As a result, northern Africa and Southwest Asia became dryer, and people were forced to congregate at oases for water. Because of the scarcity of wild animals in such an environment, people were driven by necessity to collect the wild grasses and seeds growing around the oases. Eventually they had to cultivate the grasses to provide enough food for the community. According to this theory, animal domestication began because the oases attracted hungry animals, such as wild goats, sheep, and also cattle, which came to graze on the stubble of the grain fields. People, finding these animals too thin to kill for food, began to fatten them up.

In spite of its initial popularity, evidence in support of the oasis theory was not immediately forthcoming. Moreover, as systematic fieldwork into the origins of domestication began in the late 1940s, other theories

[7] Diamond, J. (1997). *Guns, germs and steel* (p. 143). New York: Norton.

V. GORDON CHILDE (1892–1957)

This distinguished Australian, once the private secretary to the premier of New South Wales, became one of the most eminent British archaeologists of his time. His knowledge of the archaeological sequences of Europe and the Middle East was unsurpassed, enabling him to write two of the most popular and influential descriptions of prehistory ever written: *Man Makes Himself* in 1936 and *What Happened in History.* In these, he described two great "revolutions" that added measurably to the capacity of humans to survive: the Neolithic and urban revolutions. The first of these transformed food foragers into farmers and brought with it a drastic reordering of society; populations increased, a cooperative group spirit arose, trade began on a large scale, and new religions arose to ensure the success of crops. This set the stage for the urban revolution, which transformed society from one of egalitarianism with a simple age-sex division of labor into one of social classes and organized political bodies. The result of these ideas was to generate a whole new interest in the evolution of human culture in general.

gained favor. One of the pioneers in this work was Robert Braidwood of the University of Chicago, who proposed what is sometimes called the "hilly flanks" theory. Contrary to Childe, Braidwood argued that plants and animals were domesticated by people living in the hill country surrounding the Fertile Crescent (Figure 11.2). They had reached the point in their evolutionary development where they were beginning to "settle in"—that is, become more sedentary—a situation that allowed them to become intimately familiar with the plants and animals around their settlements. Given the human capacity and enthusiasm for experimentation, it was inevitable that they would have experimented with grasses and animals, bringing them under domestication. Problems with this theory include the ethnocentric notion that nonsedentary food foragers are not intimately familiar with the plants and animals on which they rely for survival and its projection onto all human cultures of the great value Western culture places on experimentation and innovation for its own sake. In short, the theory was culture-bound, strongly reflecting the notions of progress in which people in the Western world had such faith in the period following World War II.

Yet another theory that became popular in the 1960s is one in which population growth played a key role. In Southwest Asia, so this theory goes, people adapted to the cool, dry conditions of the last glacial period by developing a mixed pattern of resource utilization: They hunted such animals as were available, harvested wild cereal grasses, gathered nuts, and collected a wide variety of birds, turtles, snails, crabs, and mussels. They did so well that their populations grew, requiring the development of new ways of providing sufficient food. The result, especially in marginal situations where wild foods were least abundant, was to improve productivity through the domestication of plants and animals.

Just as there are problems with Braidwood's theory, so are there problems with this one. The most serious is that it requires an intentional decision on the part of the people involved to become producers of domestic crops, whereas, as we have already seen, domestication (as illustrated by ant farmers) does not require intentional design. Furthermore, prior to domestication, people could have had no way of knowing that plants and animals could be so radically transformed as to permit a food-producing way of life (even today, the long-term outcome of plant breeding cannot be predicted). Finally, even if people had wanted to become producers of their own food, there is no way such a decision could have had an immediate and perceptible effect; in fact, a complete switch to food production took more than a thousand years to accomplish. Although this may seem a relatively short period of time compared to the 200,000 or 300,000 years since the appearance of *H. sapiens,* it was still too long to have made any difference to people faced with immediate food shortages. Under such conditions, the usual response among food foragers is to make use of a wider variety of foods than before, which acts as a brake on domestication by diverting attention from potential domesticates, while alleviating the immediate problem.

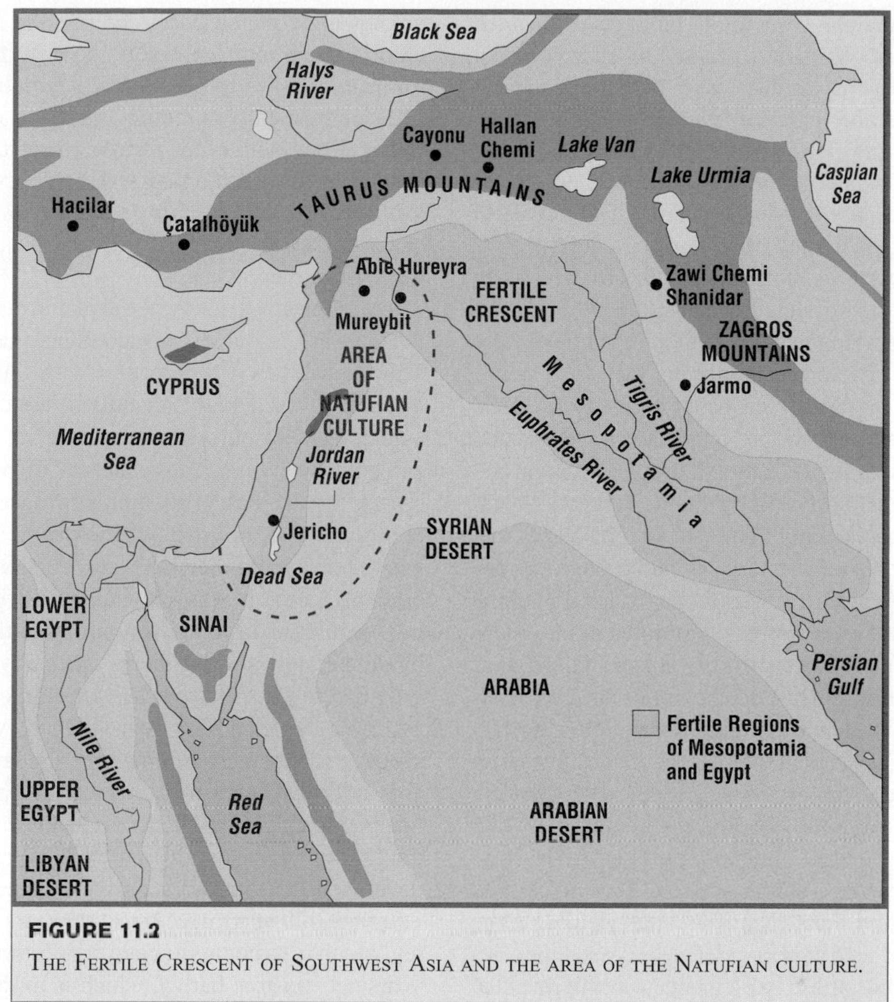

FIGURE 11.2
THE FERTILE CRESCENT OF SOUTHWEST ASIA AND THE AREA OF THE NATUFIAN CULTURE.

Another theory—in accord with the evidence as we now know it but also more in accord with the role played by chance both in evolution (Chapters 3 and 5) and in cultural innovation—takes us back to some of the ideas of Childe, who, as it turns out, guessed what the environmental circumstances were, even though he didn't fully understand the process. We now know that the earliest plant domestication took place in the lands just east of the Mediterranean Sea (Figure 11.2). As early as 13,000 years ago people living at a site (Abu Hureyra) east of Aleppo, Syria, were growing domestic rye, although they otherwise continued to rely heavily on wild plants and animals for food. Not until 3 millennia later did they become full-fledged farmers.[8] By 10,300 years ago, however, others in the region were also domesticating plants.

Evidently, the process was a consequence of a chance convergence of independent natural events and cultural developments.[9] The process is exemplified by the Natufians, whose culture we looked at earlier in this chapter. These people lived at a time of dramatically changing climates in the region. With the end of the last glaciation, climates not only became significantly warmer, but markedly seasonal as well. Between 12,000 and 6,000 years ago, the region experienced the most extreme seasonality in its history, with summer aridity significantly longer and more pronounced than today. As a consequence of increased evaporation, many shallow lakes dried up, leaving just three in the Jordan River

[8]Pringle, H. (1998). The slow birth of agriculture. *Science, 282,* 1,449.

[9]McCorriston, J., & Hole, F. (1991). The ecology of seasonal stress and the origins of agriculture in the Near East. *American Anthropologist, 93,* 46–69.

Valley. At the same time, the region's plant cover changed dramatically. Those plants best adapted to environmental instability and seasonal aridity were annuals, including wild cereal grains and legumes (plants that fix nitrogen in the soil, including peas, lentils, chickpeas, and bitter vetch). Such plants can evolve very quickly under unstable conditions, because they complete their life cycle in a single year. Moreover, they store their reproductive abilities for the next wet season in abundant seeds, which can remain dormant for prolonged periods.

The Natufians, who lived where these conditions were especially severe, adapted by modifying their subsistence practices in two ways: They probably regularly fired the landscape to promote browsing by red deer and grazing by gazelles, the main focus of their hunting activities; and they placed greater emphasis on the collection of wild seeds from the increasingly abundant annual plants that could be effectively stored to see people through the dry season. The importance of stored foods, coupled with the scarcity of reliable water sources, promoted more sedentary living patterns, reflected in the substantial villages of late Natufian times. The greater importance of seeds in Natufian subsistence was made possible by the fact that they already possessed sickles for harvesting grain and grinding stones for processing seeds. The grinding stones were used originally to process a variety of wild foods, whereas the sickles may originally have served to procure nonfood plants such as the sedges or reeds used to make baskets and mats (Natufian sites yielding large numbers of sickles tend to be located near coastal marshes and swamps).[10] Thus, these implements were not invented to enable people to become farmers, even though they turned out to be useful for that purpose.

The use of sickles to harvest grain turned out to have important consequences, again unexpected, for the Natufians. In the course of harvesting, it was inevitable that many easily dispersed seeds would be "lost" at the harvest site, whereas those from plants that did not readily scatter their seeds would mostly be carried back to where people processed and stored them.[11] Genetic mutations against easy dispersal would inevitably arise in the wild stocks, but they would be at a competitive disadvantage compared to variants that could readily disperse their seeds. However, the rate of this and other mutations potentially useful to human consumers might have been unknowingly increased by the periodic burning of vegetation carried out to promote the deer and gazelle herds, for heat is known to be an effective mutagenic agent, and fire can drastically and quickly change gene frequencies. In any event, with seeds for nondispersing variants being carried back to settlements, it was inevitable that some lost seeds would germinate and grow there on dump heaps and other disturbed sites (latrines, areas cleared of trees, or burned over).

As it turns out, many of the plants that became domesticated were colonizers, which do particularly well in disturbed habitats. Moreover, with people becoming increasingly sedentary, disturbed habitats became more extensive as resources in proximity to settlements were depleted over time; thus variants of plants particularly susceptible to human manipulation had more and more opportunity to flourish where people were living and where they would inevitably attract attention. Under such circumstances, it was inevitable that people sooner or later would begin to actively promote their growth, even by deliberately sowing them, especially as people otherwise had to travel farther afield to procure the resources that were depleted near their villages. An inevitable consequence of increased human manipulation would be the appearance of other mutant strains of particular benefit. For example, barley, which in its wild state can be tremendously productive but difficult to harvest and process, had developed the tougher stems that make it easier to harvest by 9,000 years ago; by 8,000 years ago "naked" barley, which is easier to process, was common, and by 7,500 years ago six-row barley, which is more productive than the original two-row, was widespread. Sooner or later, people realized that they could play a more active role in the process by deliberately trying to breed more useful strains. With this, domestication may be said to have shifted from a process that was unintentional to one that was intentional.

The development of animal domestication in Southwest Asia seems to have proceeded along somewhat similar lines but in the hilly country of southeastern Turkey, northern Iraq, and the Zagros Mountains of Iran (Figure 11.2). In the latter two regions were to be found large herds of wild sheep and goats, as well as much environmental diversity. From the low, alluvial plains of the valley of the Tigris and Euphrates rivers, for example, travel to the north or east takes one into the high country through three other zones: first steppe, then oak and pistachio woodlands, and, finally, high plateau country with grass, scrub, or desert vegetation. Valleys that run at right angles to the mountain ranges afford relatively easy access between these zones. Today, a number of

[10]Olszewki, D. I. (1991). Comment. *Current Anthropology, 32,* 43.

[11]Blumer, M. A., & Byrne, R. (1991). The ecological genetics and domestication and the origins of agriculture. *Current Anthropology, 32,* 30.

Today, deliberate attempts to create new varieties of plants take place in many a greenhouse, experiment station, or lab. But when first begun, the creation of domestic plants was not deliberate; rather, it was the unforeseen outcome of traditional food-foraging activities.

pastoral peoples in the region practice a pattern of **transhumance,** in which they graze their herds of sheep and goats on the low steppe in the winter and move to high pastures on the plateaus in the summer.

Moving 12,000 years backward in time to the Mesolithic, we find that the region was inhabited by peoples whose subsistence pattern, like that of the Natufians, was one of food foraging. Different plants were found in different ecological zones, and, because of the difference in altitude, plant foods matured at different times in different zones. The animals hunted for meat and hides by these people included several species, among them bear, fox, boar, and wolf. Most notable, though, were the hoofed animals: deer, gazelles, wild goats, and wild sheep. Their bones are far more common in human refuse piles than those of other animals. This is significant, for most of these animals are naturally transhumant in the region, moving back and forth from low winter pastures to high summer pastures. People followed these animals in their seasonal migrations, making use along the way of other wild foods in the zones through which they passed: dates in the lowlands; acorns, almonds, and pistachios higher up; apples and pears higher still; wild grains maturing at different times in different zones; woodland animals in the forested zone between summer and winter grazing lands. All in all, it was a rich, varied fare.

There was in hunting, then, a concentration on hoofed animals, including wild sheep and goats, which provided meat and hides. At first, animals of all ages and sexes were hunted. But, beginning about 11,000 years ago, the percentage of immature sheep eaten, for example, increased to about 50 percent of the total. At the same time, the percentage of females among animals eaten decreased. Apparently, people were learning that they could increase yields by sparing the females for breeding, while feasting on ram lambs. This marks the beginning of human management of sheep. As this management of flocks became more and more efficient, sheep were increasingly shielded from the effects of natural selection. Eventually, they were introduced into areas outside their natural habitat. So we find sheep and goats being kept by farmers at ancient Jericho, in the Jordan River Valley, 8,000 years ago (by which time farming, too, had spread widely, into Turkey to the north and into

Transhumance. Among pastoralists, the grazing of sheep and goats in low steppe lands in the winter and then moving to high pastures on the plateaus in the summer.

Although sheep and goats were first valued for their meat, hides, and sinew, the changes wrought by domestication made them useful for other purposes as well. This impression, from a 4,500-year-old seal, shows a goat being milked.

the Zagros Mountains in the east). As a consequence of this human intervention, variants that usually were not successful in the wild were able to survive and reproduce. Although variants that were perceived as being of immediate advantage would have attracted peoples' attention, they did not arise out of need, but independently of it at random, as mutations do. In such a way did those features characteristic of domestic sheep—such as greater fat and meat production, excess wool (Figure 11.3), and so on—begin to develop. By 9,000 years ago, the bones of domestic sheep had become distinguishable from those of wild sheep.

At about the same time that these events were happening, similar developments were taking place in southeastern Turkey, where pigs were the focus of attention.[12]

[12]Pringle, p. 1,448.

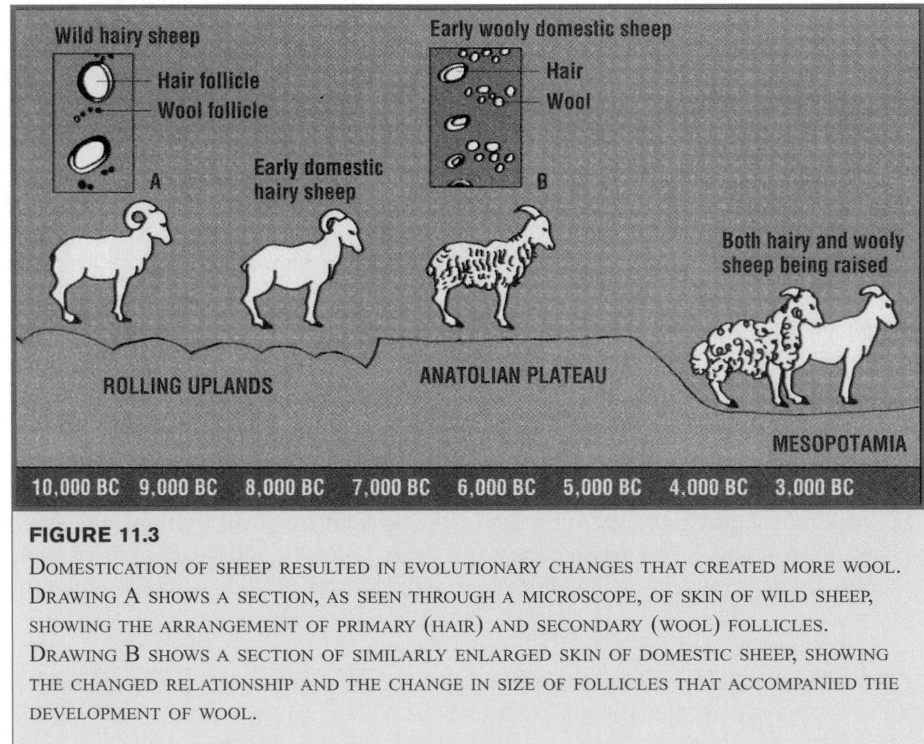

FIGURE 11.3

DOMESTICATION OF SHEEP RESULTED IN EVOLUTIONARY CHANGES THAT CREATED MORE WOOL. DRAWING A SHOWS A SECTION, AS SEEN THROUGH A MICROSCOPE, OF SKIN OF WILD SHEEP, SHOWING THE ARRANGEMENT OF PRIMARY (HAIR) AND SECONDARY (WOOL) FOLLICLES. DRAWING B SHOWS A SECTION OF SIMILARLY ENLARGED SKIN OF DOMESTIC SHEEP, SHOWING THE CHANGED RELATIONSHIP AND THE CHANGE IN SIZE OF FOLLICLES THAT ACCOMPANIED THE DEVELOPMENT OF WOOL.

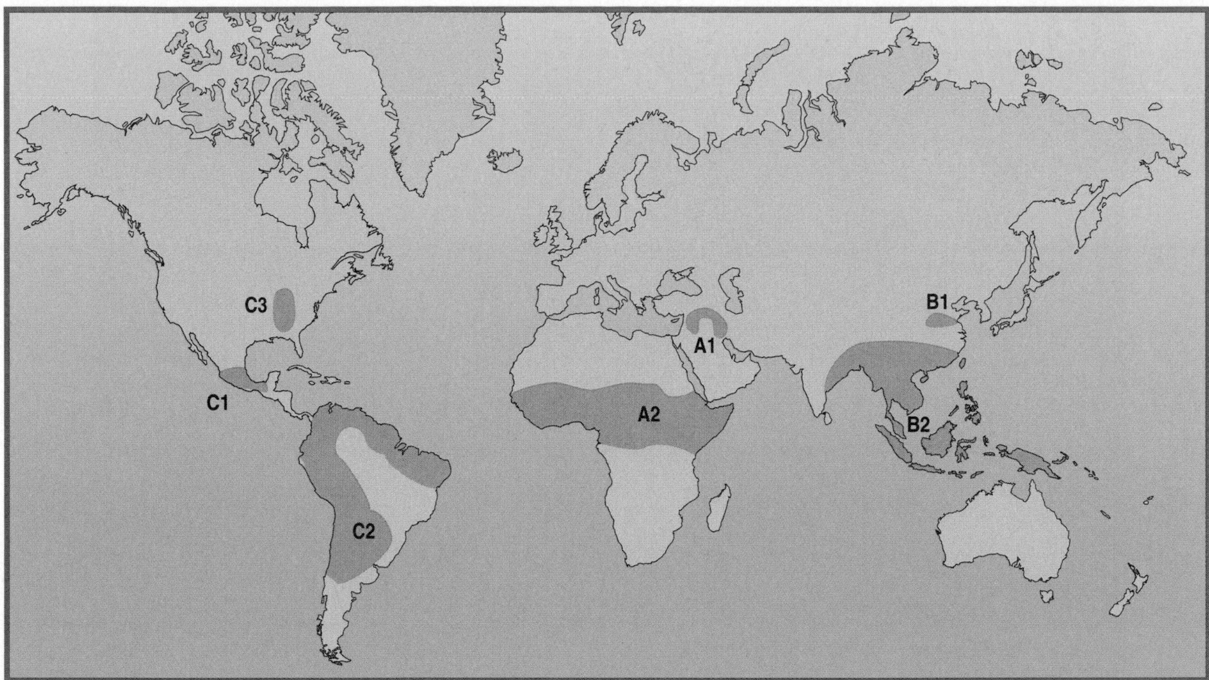

FIGURE 11.4

EARLY PLANT AND ANIMAL DOMESTICATION TOOK PLACE IN SUCH WIDELY SCATTERED AREAS AS SOUTHWEST ASIA (A1), CENTRAL AFRICA (A2), CHINA (B1), SOUTHEAST ASIA (B2), MESOAMERICA (C1), SOUTH AMERICA (C2), AND NORTH AMERICA (C3).

Here, an increase in pig bones in human trash, coupled with a heavy bias in favor of very young animals, is indicative of a taste for suckling pigs and the beginning of stock management by 10,500 years ago.

To sum up, the domesticators of plants and animals sought only to maximize the food sources available to them. They were not aware of the revolutionary consequences their actions were to have. But as the process continued, the productivity of the domestic species increased relative to wild species. Thus they became increasingly more important to subsistence, resulting in further intensification of interest in, and management of, the domesticates. Inevitably, the result would be further increases in productivity.

OTHER CENTERS OF DOMESTICATION

In addition to Southwest Asia, the domestication of plants and, in some cases, animals took place independently in Southeast Asia, parts of the Americas (southern Mexico, Peru, the tropical forests of South America, and eastern North America), northern China, and Africa (Figure 11.4). In China, domestication of rice was underway along the middle Yangtze River by about 11,000 years ago.[13] It was not until 4,000 years later, however, that domestic rice dominated wild rice to become the dietary staple.

In Southeast Asia the oldest domestic plant so far identified is rice, in pottery dated to some time between 8,800 and 5,000 years ago. What was distinctive in this region, however, was domestication of root crops, most notably yams and taro. Root crop farming, or **vegeculture,** typically involves the growing of many different species together in a single field. Because this approximates the complexity of the natural vegetation, vegeculture tends to be more stable than seed crop cultivation. Propagation (as in the case of the fungi-farming ants discussed earlier) is by vegetative means—the planting of cuttings—rather than the planting of seeds.

[13]Ibid., p. 1,449.

Vegeculture. The cultivation of domesticated root crops, such as yams and taro.

At this archaeological site in Diatonghuan Cave, China, archaeologists recover evidence of the transition from wild to domestic rice.

In the Americas, the domestication of plants began about as early as it did in these other regions. One species of domestic squash may have been grown as early as 10,000 years ago in the coastal forests of Ecuador at the same time another species was being grown in an arid region of highland Mexico.[14] Evidently, these developments were independent of one another. Other crops were eventually added later; the earliest occurrence of maize, for example, is from a site on the Gulf Coast of the Mexican state of Tobasco dated 7,700 years ago.[15] Because genetic evidence puts its place of origin somewhere in the highlands of western Mexico, it must have appeared somewhat earlier there. Ultimately, Native Americans domesticated over 300 food crops, including two of the four most important ones in the world today: potatoes and maize (the other two are wheat and rice). In fact, 60 percent of the crops grown in the world today were invented by American Indians, who not only remain the developers of the world's largest array of nutritious foods but are also the primary contributors to the world's varied cuisines.[16] After all, where would Italian cuisine be without tomatoes? Thai cooking without peanuts? Northern European cooking without potatoes? Or Chinese cooking without sweet potatoes (the daily food of peasants, but also used to make noodles rivaling in popularity those made of wheat)? Small wonder American Indians have been called the world's greatest farmers.[17]

Archaeological evidence for the beginning of farming in Mexico comes from the highland valleys of Oaxaca, Puebla, and Tamaulipas. In the Tehuacan Valley of Puebla, for example, crops such as maize, beans, and squash very gradually came to make up a greater percentage of the food eaten (Figure 11.5). Like the hill country of Southwest Asia, the Tehuacan Valley is environmentally diverse, and the people living there had a cyclical pattern of hunting and gathering that made use

[14]Ibid., p. 1,447.

[15]Piperno, D. R. (2001). On maize and the sunflower. *Science, 292,* 2,260.

[16]Weatherford, J. (1988). *Indian givers: How the Indians of the Americas transformed the world* (pp. 71, 115). New York: Fawcett Columbine.

[17]Ibid., p. 95.

Domestic plants were useful for purposes other than food. Although cotton was independently invented three times—in the Old World, Mesoamerica, and Peru—95 percent of the cotton grown in the world today is the Mesoamerican species, owing to its superiority.

CULTIGENS		Hunting	Horti-culture	Wild plant use
Squash Chili Amaranth Avocado	Cotton Maize Beans Gourd Sapote	29%		31%
Squash Chili Amaranth Avocado	Maize Beans Gourd Sapote	25%		50%
Squash Chili Amaranth Avocado	Maize Beans Gourd Sapote	34%		52%
Squash Chili Amaranth Avocado		54%		40%

FIGURE 11.5

SUBSISTENCE TRENDS IN TEHUACAN VALLEY SHOW THAT HERE, AS ELSEWHERE, DEPENDENCE ON HORTICULTURE CAME ABOUT GRADUALLY, OVER A PROLONGED PERIOD OF TIME.

of the resources of different environmental zones. In the course of their seasonal movements, people carried the wild precursors of future domesticates out of their native habitat, exposing them to different selective pressures. Under such circumstances, potentially useful (to humans) variants that did not do well in the native habitat would, by chance, do well in novel settings, again (as in Southwest Asia) attracting human attention.

The change to food production also took place in South America, including the highlands of Peru—again, an environmentally diverse region. Although a number of crops first grown in Mexico eventually came to be grown here, there was greater emphasis on root crops, the best known being potatoes (of which about 3,000 varieties were grown, versus the mere 250 grown today in North America), sweet potatoes, and manioc (originally developed in the tropics). South Americans domesticated guinea pigs, llamas, alpacas, and ducks, whereas the Mexicans never did much with domestic livestock. They limited themselves to dogs, turkeys, and bees.

Although the Native Americans living north of Mexico ultimately adopted several crops, such as maize and beans, from their southern neighbors, this occurred after they developed some of their own indigenous domesticates. These included local varieties of squash and sunflower (today, grown widely in Russia as a reliable source of edible oil). Other native crops such as lambs-quarter and sumpweed reverted to the wild as preferred foods appeared from Mexico.

Considering all of the separate innovations of domestic plants, it is interesting to note that in all cases people developed the same categories of foods. Everywhere,

Anthropology Applied

Archaeology for and by Native Americans

In the Americas, the practice of archaeology is closely tied to Native Americans because it is their ancestors who were responsible for the record those archaeologists seek to investigate. Yet, relationships between native people and archaeologists have not always been easy. Part of the problem has to do with power relationships: Archaeologists have been members of a dominant society with a long record of appropriating native lands and resources while denying native people political and even human rights. To have nonnative scholars appropriate their cultural heritage, while collecting their sacred objects and even the bodies of their ancestors, was the last straw. This is not to say that all archaeologists were insensitive to native concerns, but all too often the aims of the discipline and the interests of those whose past was being studied were at odds.

As a consequence, some native people today want nothing to do with archaeology and those who practice it. Others, however, recognize that archaeology can serve their own interests. Today, there are more than 43 tribes or native communities in 23 states that conduct their own archaeological research. At the same time, nonnative archaeologists have become more sensitive to native concerns and have been actively working to reconcile those interests with those of science. The result is that opportunities have been opened for fruitful collaboration. Today, a number of archaeologists are actually employed by native organizations, and programs have been set up to train native people themselves in archaeology.

One archaeologist who has worked for native organizations, including the Hopi tribe and the Pueblo of Zuni in Arizona and New Mexico, is T. J. Ferguson.* He points out that there are many reasons that American Indians need archaeology. A major one is that archeologists are needed to implement the National Historic Preservation Act and other federal legislation governing archaeological research. Many natives, too, are genuinely interested in uncovering their own history, using archaeological evidence to litigate land and water claims, attaining intellectual parity with non-Indian researchers, facilitating development on Indian lands, retaining financial benefits from mandated archaeology, and maintaining tribes' political sovereignty by controlling the management and protection of their own cultural resources and burials. There are benefits for the archaeologist as well. Ferguson has found working for native people to be personally rewarding, as it has resulted in modification of scientific values he learned in graduate school. This has not, however, prevented him from making important contributions to the profession. Moreover, it generates new and fruitful research questions to pursue.

*Ferguson, T. J. (1996, November). *Archaeology for and by Native Americans.* Paper presented at the 95th Annual Meeting of the American Anthropological Association, San Francisco.

starchy grains (or root crops) are accompanied by one or more legumes—wheat and barley with peas, chickpeas, bitter vetch, and lentils in Southwest Asia—maize with various kinds of beans in Mexico, for example. The starchy grains are the core of the diet and are eaten at every meal in the form of bread, some sort of food wrapper (like a tortilla), or a gruel or thickening agent in a stew along with one or more legumes. Being rather bland, these sources of carbohydrates and proteins are invariably combined with flavor-giving substances that help the food go down. In Mexico, for example, the flavor enhancer par excellence is the chili pepper; in other cuisines it may be a bit of meat, a dairy product, mushrooms, or whatever. Anthropologist Sidney Mintz refers to this as the core-fringe-legume pattern (CFLP), noting that only recently has it been upset by the worldwide spread of processed sugars and high-fat foods.[18]

[18]Mintz, S. (1996). A taste of history. In W. A. Haviland & R. J. Gordon (Eds.), *Talking about people* (2nd ed., pp. 81–82). Mountain View, CA: Mayfield.

In Mexico, chili peppers enhanced the flavor of foods and aided digestion. (They help break down cellulose in diets heavy in plant foods.) They had other uses as well: This illustration from a 16th-century Aztec manuscript shows a woman threatening her child with punishment by being exposed to smoke from chili peppers. Chili smoke was also used as a kind of chemical weapon in warfare.

THE SPREAD OF FOOD PRODUCTION

Although population growth and the need to feed more people cannot explain the origin of the food-producing way of life, it does have a lot to do with its subsequent spread. As already noted, domestication inevitably leads to higher yields, and higher yields make it possible to feed more people. In addition, unlike most food foragers, farmers have available a variety of foods that are soft enough to be fed to infants. Hence, farmers do not need to nurse their children so intensively nor for so many years. In humans, prolonged nursing, as long as it involves frequent stimulation of the nipple by the infant, has a dampening effect on ovulation. As a result, women in food-foraging societies are less likely to become fertile as soon after childbirth as they are in food-producing societies. Coupled with this, having too many children to care for at once interferes with the foraging activities of women in hunting, gathering, and fishing societies. Among farmers, however, numerous children are frequently seen as assets, to help out with the many household chores. Small wonder, then, that increased dependence on farming is associated with increased fertility across human populations.[19]

Paradoxically, although domestication increases productivity, so does it increase instability. This is so because those varieties with the highest yields become the focus of human attention, while other varieties are less valued and ultimately ignored. As a result, farmers become dependent on a rather narrow range of resources, compared to the wide range utilized by food foragers. Modern agriculturists, for example, rely on a mere dozen species for about 80 percent of the world's annual tonnage of all crops.[20] By contrast, the Bushmen of Africa's Kalahari Desert regard more than 100 species as edible. This dependence upon fewer varieties means that when a crop fails, for whatever reason, farmers have less to fall back on than do food foragers. Furthermore, the likelihood of failure is increased by the common farming practice of planting crops together in one locality, so that a disease contracted by one plant can easily spread to others. Moreover, by relying on seeds from the most productive plants of a species to establish next year's crop, farmers favor genetic uniformity over diversity. The result is that if some virus, bacterium, or fungus is able to destroy one plant, it will likely destroy them all. This is what happened in the famous Irish potato famine of 1845–1846, which sent waves of Irish immigrants to the United States.

---

[19]Sellen, D. W., & Mace, R. (1997). Fertility and mode of subsistence: A phylogenetic analysis. *Current Anthropology, 38,* 886.

[20]Diamond, p. 132.

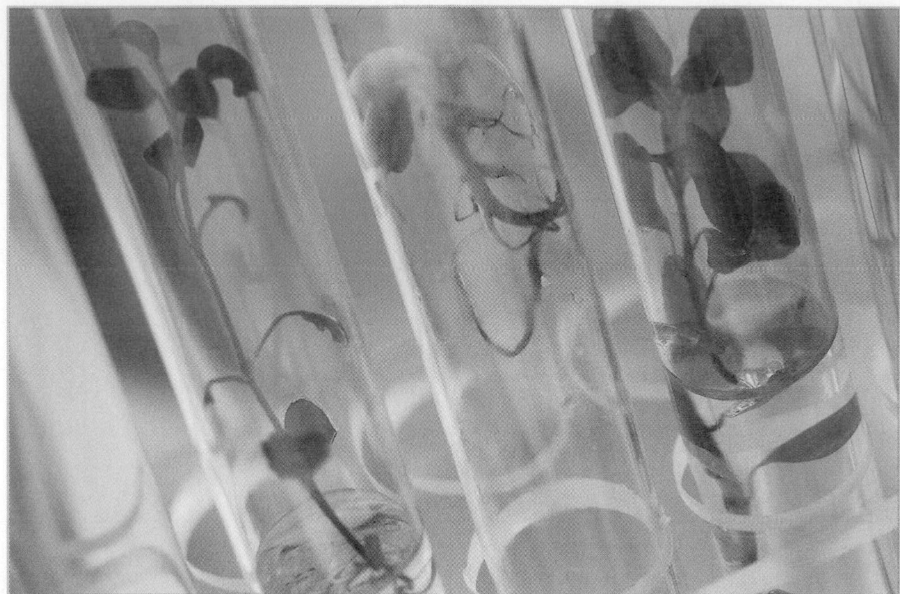

To the extent that genetic engineering strives to produce crops with uniform characteristics, genetic homogeneity will make them vulnerable to plant diseases and predators.

The Irish potato famine illustrates how the combination of increased productivity and vulnerability may contribute to the geographic spread of farming. Time and time again in the past, population growth followed by crop failures has triggered movements of people from one place to another, where they have reestablished the subsistence practices with which they were familiar. Thus, once farming came into existence, it was more or less guaranteed that it would spread to neighboring regions (Figure 11.6). From Southwest Asia, for instance, it spread to southeastern Europe by 8,000 years ago, reaching Central Europe and the Netherlands by 4,000 years ago, and England between 4,000 and 3,000 years ago. Those who brought crops to Europe brought other things as well, including new alleles for human gene pools. As a consequence, those modern Europeans who most resemble their Upper Paleolithic predecessors are to be found around the northern fringes of the region.[21] Early

[21]Brace, C. L. (1997). Cro-Magnons "Я" us? *Anthropology Newsletter, 38*(8), 2.

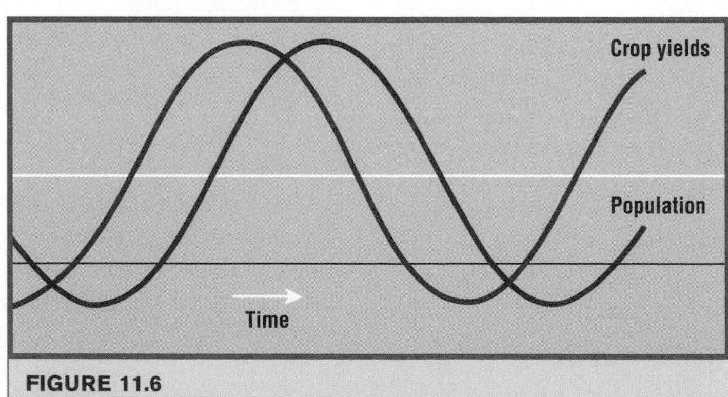

FIGURE 11.6

POPULATION GROWTH HAS A TENDENCY TO FOLLOW INCREASES IN FARMING YIELDS. INEVITABLY, THIS RESULTS IN TOO LARGE A POPULATION TO BE FED WHEN CROPS FAIL, AS THEY PERIODICALLY DO. THE RESULT IS AN OUTWARD MIGRATION OF PEOPLE TO OTHER REGIONS.

farmers likely introduced languages ancestral to most of today's European languages as well, leaving Basque (spoken today on the Atlantic coast where France and Spain meet) as the sole survivor of languages once spoken by earlier Mesolithic people.

From Southwest Asia, farming also spread westward in North Africa and eastward to India. Here, crops domesticated in the west met those spreading from Southeast Asia, some of which spread farther west. Facilitating this east-west exchange was the fact that localities shared the same seasonal variations in day length and more or less the same diseases, temperature, and rainfall.

In sub-Saharan Africa, a similar spread occurred and accounts for the modern distribution of speakers of Bantu languages. Crops including sorghum (so valuable today it is grown in hot, dry areas on all continents), pearl millet, watermelon, black-eyed peas, African yams, oil palms, and kola nuts (source of modern cola drinks) were first domesticated in West Africa but began spreading east by 5,000 years ago.

Between 3,000 and 2,000 years ago Bantu speakers with their crops reached the east coast, and a few centuries later, reached the Great Fish River, 500 miles east of Capetown. Being well adapted to summer rains, African crops spread no farther, for the Cape has a Mediterranean climate with winter rains.

In coastal Peru, the earliest domesticates were the nonedible bottle gourd (like the one shown here) and cotton. They were used to make nets and floats to catch fish, which was an important source of food.

In some instances, farming appears to have been adopted by food foragers from food-producing neighbors. By way of illustration, a crisis developed on the coast of Peru some 4,500 years ago as continental uplift caused lowering of the water table and destruction of marine habitats at a time of growing population; the result was an increasing shortage of the wild food resources on which people depended. Their response was to begin growing along the edges of rivers many of the domestic plants that their highland neighbors to the east had begun to cultivate a few thousand years earlier. Here, then, farming appears to have been a subsistence practice of last resort, which a food-foraging people took up only because they had no real choice.

CULTURE OF NEOLITHIC SETTLEMENTS

A number of Neolithic settlements have been excavated, particularly in Southwest Asia. The structures, artifacts, and food debris found at these sites have revealed much about the daily activities of their former inhabitants as they pursued the business of making a living.

Earliest Full-Fledged Farming Settlements

The earliest known sites containing domesticated plants and animals found in Southwest Asia date mostly between 10,300 and 9,000 years ago. These sites occur in a region extending from the Jordan Valley northward across the Taurus Mountains into Turkey, eastward across the flanks of the Taurus Mountains into northeastern Iran, and southward into Iraq and Iran along the hilly flanks of the Zagros Mountains. The sites contain evidence of domesticated barley, wheat, peas, chickpeas, bitter vetch, lentils, flax, goats, sheep, dogs, and pigs.

These sites are generally the remains of small village farming communities—small clusters of houses built of mud, each with its own storage pit and clay oven. Their occupants continued to use stone tools of Mesolithic type, plus a few new types of use in farming. Probably the people born into these communities spent their lives in them in a common effort to make their crops grow and their animals prosper. At the same time, they participated in long-distance trade networks. Obsidian found at Jarmo, Iraq, for instance, was imported from 300 miles away.

Stands of wild wheat are still to be found in parts of the Middle East.

Jericho: An Early Farming Community

At the Neolithic settlement that later grew to become the biblical city of Jericho, excavation has revealed the remains of a sizable farming community occupied as early as 10,350 years ago. Located in the Jordan River Valley, what made the site attractive was the presence of a bounteous spring and the rich soils of an Ice Age lake that had dried up some 3,000 years earlier. Here, crops could be grown almost continuously, because the fertility of the soil was regularly renewed by flood-borne deposits originating in the Judean Highlands, to the west. To protect their settlement against these floods and associated mudflows, the people of Jericho built massive walls of stone around it.[22] Within these walls, an estimated 400 to 900 people lived in houses of mud brick with plastered floors arranged around courtyards. In addition to these houses, a stone tower that would have taken 100 people 104 days to build was located inside one corner of the wall, near the spring. A staircase inside it probably led to a mud brick building on top. Nearby were mud brick storage facilities as well as peculiar structures of possible ceremonial significance. A village cemetery also reflects the sedentary life of these early people; nomadic groups, with few exceptions, rarely buried their dead in a single central location.

[22]Bar-Yosef, O. (1986) The walls of Jericho: An alternative interpretation. *Current Anthropology, 27,* 160.

Evidence of domestic plants and animals is scant at Jericho. However, indirect evidence in the form of harvesting tools and milling equipment has been uncovered at the site, and wheat, barley, and other domestic plants are known from sites of similar age in the region. We do know that the people of Jericho were keeping sheep and goats by 8,000 years ago, although some hunting still went on. Some of the meat from wild animals may have been supplied by food-foraging peoples whose campsites have been found everywhere in the desert of the Arabian peninsula. Close contacts between these people and the farmers of Jericho and other villages are indicated by common features in art, ritual, use of prestige goods, and burial practices. Other evidence of trade consists of obsidian and turquoise from Sinai as well as marine shells from the coast, all discovered inside the walls of Jericho.

Neolithic Technology

Early harvesting tools were made of wood or bone into which serrated flints were inserted. Later tools continued to be made by chipping and flaking stone, but during the Neolithic period, stone that was too hard to be chipped was ground and polished for tools (Figure 11.7). People developed scythes, forks, hoes, and plows to replace their simple digging sticks. Pestles and mortars were used for preparation of grain. Plows were later redesigned when, after 8,000 years ago, domesticated cattle became available for use as draft animals.

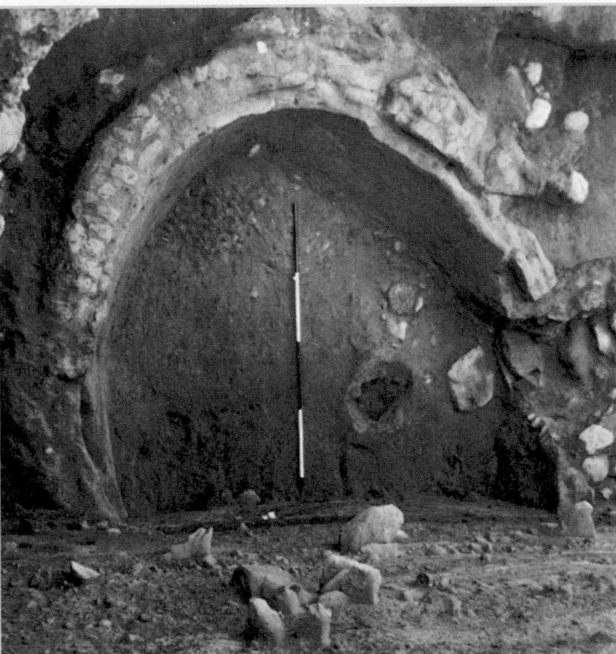

Neolithic farming communities, such as Jericho in the Jordan River Valley, were made possible by the result of the domestication of plants and animals. Jericho was surrounded by a stone wall as protection against floods. The wall included a tower (left). People lived in substantial houses (right).

Pottery

In addition to the domestication of plants and animals, one of the characteristics of the Neolithic period is the extensive manufacture and use of pottery. In food-foraging societies, most people are involved in the food quest. In food-producing societies, even though people have to work as long—if not longer—at subsistence activities than food foragers, the whole community need not be involved in the food quest. Hard work on the part of those producing the food may support other members of the society who devote their energies to other craft specialties. One such craft is pottery making, and different forms of pottery were created for transporting and storing food, artifacts, and other material possessions. Because pottery vessels are impervious to damage by insects, rodents, and dampness, they could be used for storing small grain, seeds, and other materials. Moreover, food can be boiled in pottery vessels directly over the fire rather than by such ancient techniques as dropping stones heated directly in the fire into the food being cooked. Pottery is also used for pipes, ladles, lamps, and other objects, and some cultures used large vessels for disposal of the dead. Significantly, pottery containers remain important for much of humanity today.

Widespread use of pottery, which is manufactured of clay and fired, is a good, though not foolproof, indication of a sedentary community. It is found in abundance in all but a few of the earliest Neolithic settlements. At ancient Jericho, for example, the earliest Neolithic people lacked pottery. Its fragility and weight make it impractical for use by nomads and hunters, who use baskets and hide containers. Nevertheless, there are some modern nomads who make and use pottery, just as there are farmers who lack it. In fact, food foragers in Japan were making pottery by 13,000 years ago, long before it was being made in Southwest Asia.

The manufacture of pottery is a difficult art and requires a high degree of technological sophistication. To make a useful vessel requires knowledge of clay, how to remove impurities from it, how to shape it into desired forms without it slumping, and how to dry it without cracking. Proper firing is tricky as well; it must be heated sufficiently that the clay will harden and resist future disintegration from moisture, but care must be taken to prevent the object from cracking or even exploding as it heats and later cools down.

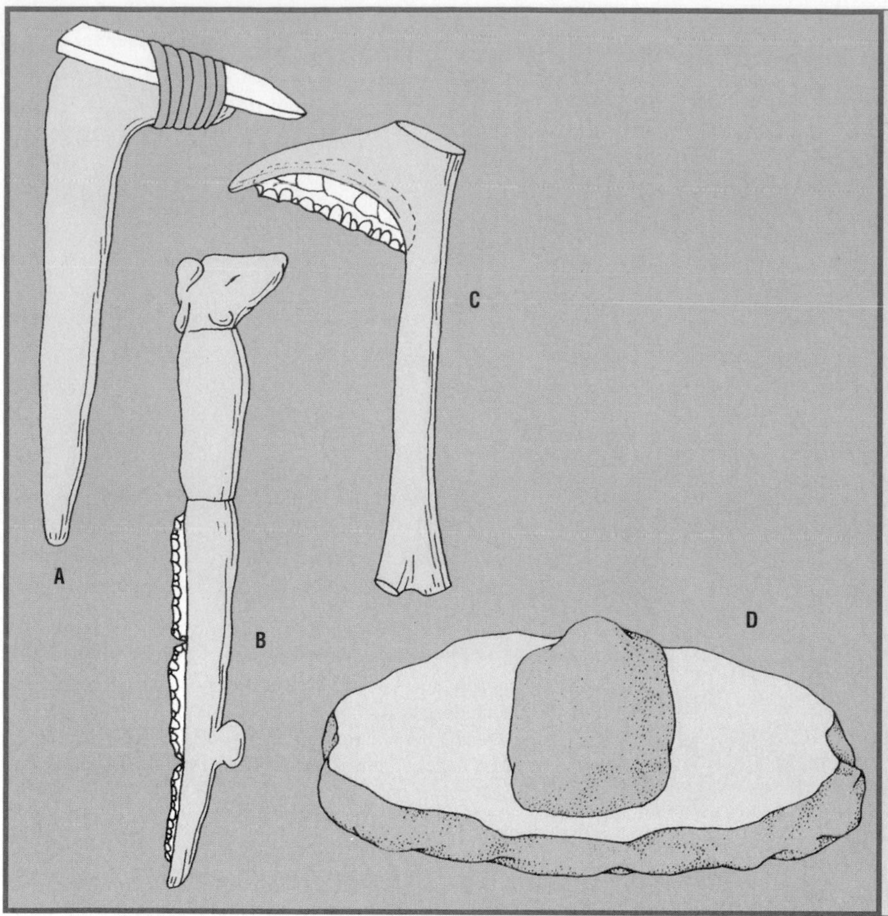

FIGURE 11.7
In Southwest Asia, many tools fabricated by Neolithic peoples made use of flint microliths in bone or wood handles, as well as ground and polished stone.

Coloration of the pot, too, is affected by the way it is fired; the presence of oxygen produces a reddish color, whereas absence of oxygen produces a darker color.

Pottery is decorated in various ways. For example, designs can be engraved on the vessel before firing, or special rims, legs, bases, and other details may be made separately and fastened to the finished pot. Painting is the most common form of pottery decoration, and there are literally thousands of painted designs found among the pottery remains of ancient cultures.

Housing

Food production and the new sedentary lifestyle engendered another technological development—house building. Permanent housing is of limited interest to most food foragers who frequently are on the move. Cave shelters, pits dug in the earth, and simple lean-tos made of hides and tree limbs serve their purpose of keeping the weather out. In the Neolithic, however, dwellings became more complex in design and more diverse in type. Some, like Swiss lake dwellings, were constructed of wood, housed several families per building, had doors, and contained beds, tables, and other furniture. In other places, more elaborate shelters were made of stone, sun-dried brick, or branches plastered together with mud or clay.

Although permanent housing frequently goes along with food production, there is evidence that one can have substantial houses without food production. For example, on the northwestern coast of North America, people lived in substantial houses made of heavy planks hewn from cedar logs. Yet their food consisted entirely of wild plants and animals, especially fish.

Clothing

During the Neolithic, for the first time in human history, clothing was made of woven textiles. The raw materials and technology necessary for the production of clothing came from several sources: flax and cotton from farm-

This pottery vessel from Turkey was made around 7,600 years ago. Pigs were under domestication as early as 10,500 to 11,000 years ago in southeastern Turkey.

ing, wool from domesticated sheep, silk from silk worms, and the spindle for spinning and the loom for weaving from the inventive human mind.

Social Structure

Evidence of all the economic and technological developments listed thus far has enabled archaeologists to draw certain inferences concerning the organization of Neolithic society. The general absence of elaborate buildings in all but a few settlements may suggest that neither religion nor government was yet a formally established institution able to wield real social power. Although there is evidence of ceremonial activity, little evidence of a centrally organized and directed religious life has been found. Burials, for example, show a marked absence of patterning; variation seems to have been common. Because early Neolithic graves were rarely constructed of or covered by stone slabs and rarely included elaborate grave goods, it is believed differences in social status were not great. Evidently, no person had attained the kind of exalted status that would have required an elaborate funeral. The smallness of most villages suggests that the inhabitants knew one another very well, so that most of their relationships were probably highly personal ones, charged with emotional significance.

The general picture that emerges is one of a relatively egalitarian society with minimal division of labor and probably little development of new and more specialized social roles. Villages seem to have been made up of several households, each providing for most of its own needs. The organizational needs of society beyond the household level were probably met by kinship groups and common-interest associations.

NEOLITHIC CULTURE IN THE NEW WORLD

Outside Mesoamerica (southern Mexico and northern Central America) and Peru, hunting, fishing, and the gathering of wild plant foods remained important elements in the economy of Neolithic peoples in the New World. Apparently, most American Indians never made a complete change from a food-foraging to a food-producing mode of life, even though maize and other domestic

Sometimes Neolithic villagers got together to carry out impressive communal works. Shown here is Stonehenge, the famous ceremonial and astronomical center in England, which dates back to about 2500 B.C. Its construction relates to the new attitudes toward the earth and forces of nature associated with food production.

crops came to be cultivated just about everywhere that climate permitted. Farming developed independently of Europe and Asia, with different crops and different technologies.

The Neolithic developed even more slowly in the New World than in the Old. For example, Neolithic agricultural villages were common in Southwest Asia between 9,000 and 8,000 years ago, but similar villages did not appear in the New World until about 4,500 years ago, in Mesoamerica and Peru. Moreover, pottery, which arose in the Old World shortly after plant and animal domestication, did not develop in the New World until about 4,500 years ago. Neither the potter's wheel nor the loom and spindle were used by early Neolithic people in the New World. Both pottery and textiles were manufactured by hand; evidence of the loom and spindle does not appear in the New World until 3,000 years ago. None of these absences indicate any backwardness on the part of New World peoples, who, as we have already seen, were highly sophisticated farmers and plant breeders. Rather, the effectiveness of existing practices was such that they continued to be satisfactory.

THE NEOLITHIC AND HUMAN BIOLOGY

Although we tend to think of the invention of food production in terms of its cultural impact, it obviously had a biological impact as well. From studies of human skeletons from Neolithic burials, physical anthropologists have found evidence for a somewhat lessened mechanical stress on peoples' bodies and teeth. Although there are exceptions, the teeth of Neolithic peoples show less wear, their bones are less robust, and osteoarthritis (the result of stressed joint surfaces) is not as marked as in the skeletons of Paleolithic and Mesolithic peoples. On the other hand, there is clear evidence for a marked deterioration in health and mortality. Anthropologist Anna Roosevelt sums up our knowledge of this in the following Original Study.

Original Study

History of Mortality and Physiological Stress[23]

Although there is a relative lack of evidence for the Paleolithic stage, enough skeletons have been studied that it seems clear that seasonal and periodic physiological stress regularly affected most prehistoric hunting-gathering populations, as evidenced by the presence of enamel hypoplasias [horizontal linear defects in tooth enamel] and Harris lines [horizontal lines near the ends of long bones]. What also seems clear is that severe and chronic stress, with high frequency of hypoplasias, infectious disease lesions, pathologies related to iron-deficiency anemia, and high mortality rates, is not characteristic of these early populations. There is no evidence of frequent, severe malnutrition, and so the diet must have been adequate in calories and other nutrients most of the time. During the Mesolithic, the proportion of starch in the diet rose, to judge from the increased occurrence of certain dental diseases, but not enough to create an impoverished diet. At this time, diets seem to have been made up of a rather large number of foods, so that the failure of one food source would not be catastrophic. There is a possible slight tendency for Paleolithic people to be healthier and taller than Mesolithic people, but there is no apparent trend toward increasing physiological stress during the Mesolithic. Thus, it seems that both hunter-gatherers and incipient agriculturalists regularly underwent population pressure, but only to a moderate degree.

During the periods when effective agriculture first comes into use, there seems to be a temporary upturn in health and survival rates in a few regions: Europe, North America, and the eastern Mediterranean. At this stage, wild foods are still consumed periodically and a variety of plants are cultivated, suggesting the availability of adequate amounts of different nutrients. Based on the increasing frequency of tooth disease related to high carbohydrate consumption, it seems that cultivated plants probably increased the storable calo-

[23]Roosevelt, A. C. (1984). Population, health, and the evolution of subsistence: Conclusions from the conference. In M. N. Cohen & G. J. Armelagos (Eds.), *Paleopathology at the origins of agriculture* (pp. 572–574). Orlando: Academic Press.

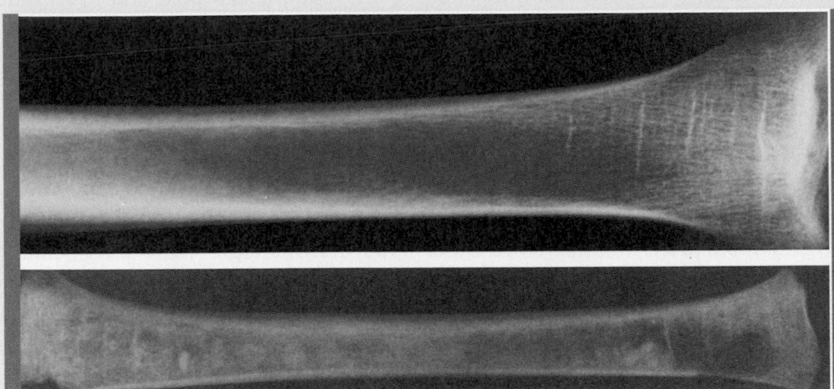

Harris lines near the ends of these youthful thigh bones, found in a prehistoric farming community in Arizona, are indicative of recovery after growth arrest, caused by famine or disease.

rie supply, removing for a time any seasonal or periodic problems in food supply. In most regions, however, the development of agriculture seems not to have had this effect, and there seems to have been a slight increase in physiological stress.

Stress, however, does not seem to have become common and widespread until after the development of high degrees of sedentism, population density, and reliance on intensive agriculture. At this stage in all regions the incidence of physiological stress increases greatly, and average mortality rates increase appreciably. Most of these agricultural populations have high frequencies of porotic hyperostosis and cribra orbitalia [bone deformities indicative of chronic iron-deficiency anemia], and there is a substantial increase in the number and severity of enamel hypoplasias and pathologies associated with infectious disease. Stature in many populations appears to have been considerably lower than would be expected if genetically determined height maxima had been reached, which suggests that the growth arrests documented by pathologies were causing stunting. Accompanying these indicators of poor health and nourishment, there is a universal drop in the occurrence of Harris lines, suggesting a poor rate of full recovery from the stress. Incidence of carbohydrate-related tooth disease increases, apparently because subsistence by this time is characterized by a heavy emphasis on a few starchy food crops. Populations seem to have grown beyond the point at which wild food resources could be a meaningful dietary supplement, and even domestic animal resources were commonly reserved for farm labor and transport rather than for diet supplementation.

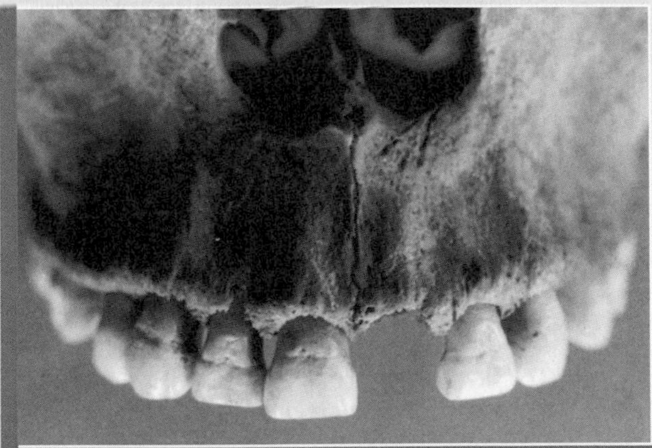

Enamel hypoplasias such as those shown on these teeth are indicative of arrested growth caused by disease or famine. The teeth are from an adult who lived in an ancient farming community in Arizona.

It seems that a large proportion of most sedentary prehistoric populations under intensive agriculture underwent chronic and life-threatening malnutrition and disease, especially during infancy and childhood. The causes of the nutritional stress are likely to have been the poverty of the staple crops in most nutrients except calories, periodic famines caused by the instability of the agricultural system, and chronic lack of food due to both population growth and economic expropriation by elites. The increases in infectious disease probably reflect both a poorer diet and increased interpersonal contact in crowded settlements, and it is, in turn, likely to have aggravated nutritional problems.

The End

For the most part, the crops on which Neolithic peoples came to depend were selected for their higher productivity and storability rather than their nutritional value. Moreover, as already noted, their nutritional shortcomings would have been exacerbated by their susceptibility to periodic failure, particularly as populations grew in size. Thus, the worsened health and mortality of Neolithic peoples is not surprising. Some have gone so far as to assert that the switch from food foraging to food production was the worst mistake that humans ever made!

Another key contributor to the increased incidence of disease and mortality was probably the new mode of life in Neolithic communities. Sedentary life in fixed villages brings with it sanitation problems as garbage and human waste accumulate. These are not a problem for small groups of people who move about from one campsite to another. Moreover, airborne diseases are more easily transmitted where people are gathered into villages. Another factor, too, was the close association between humans and their domestic animals, a situation conducive to the transmission of some animal diseases to humans. A host of life-threatening diseases, including smallpox, chicken pox, and in fact all of the infectious diseases of childhood that were not overcome by medical science until the latter half of the 20th century, were transmitted to humans through their close association with domestic animals (Table 11.1).

Another example of the biological impact of food production on human biology is that of the abnormal hemoglobin responsible for sickle-cell anemia, discussed in Chapter 3. Other abnormal hemoglobins are associated with the spread of farming from Southwest Asia westward around the Mediterranean as well as eastward to India, and also with the spread of farming in Southeast Asia. In all these regions, changes in human gene pools took place as a biological response to malaria, which had become a problem as a result of farming practices.

Higher mortality rates in Neolithic villages were offset by increased fertility, for population growth accelerated dramatically at precisely the moment that health and mortality worsened. The factors responsible for this increased natality have already been discussed in this chapter.

Crops bred for higher productivity and storability, rather than nutritional value, contributed to the poor health of Neolithic people. Even today, plants are still bred for nonnutritional characteristics: long shelf life, appearance, and the like. This is true, too, of genetically engineered crops, which are altered to survive massive applications of herbicides and pesticides and to not produce viable seed (the latter solidifies corporate control of the food system). One may only wonder what the long-term consequences of such practices will be.

THE NEOLITHIC AND THE IDEA OF PROGRESS

One of the more deeply held biases of Western culture is that human history is basically a record of steady progress over time. The transition from food foraging to food production is generally viewed as a great step upward on a

TABLE 11.1 DISEASES ACQUIRED FROM DOMESTICATED ANIMALS

Human Disease	Animal with Most Closely Related Pathogen
Measles	Cattle (rinderpest)
Tuberculosis	Cattle
Smallpox	Cattle (cowpox) or other livestock with related pox viruses
Influenza	Pigs, ducks
Pertussis ("whooping cough")	Pigs, dogs

Some of the diseases that humans have acquired from domestic animals. Close contact with animals provides a situation in which variants of animal pathogens may establish themselves in humans.

SOURCE: Diamond, J. (1997). *Guns, germs, and steel* (p. 207). New York: Norton.

HIGHWAY 1

This site spans time and space as it considers the global origins of agriculture and civilization as well as the ability of countries to feed their populations in the future.
www.mc.maricopa.edu/anthro/lost_tribes/hg_ag/

HIGHWAY 2

Visit this site to see the ruins and get a sense of what the ancient city of Jericho is like today.
www.visit-palestine.com/jericho/je-main.htm

supposed ladder of progress. To be sure, farming allowed people to increase the size of their populations, to live together in substantial sedentary communities, and to reorganize the workload in ways that permitted craft specialization. If one chooses to regard this as progress, that is fine—progress is, after all, whatever it is defined as, and different cultures define it differently.

Whatever the benefits of food production, however, a substantial price was paid. As anthropologists Mark Cohen and George Armelagos put it,

> Taken as a whole, indicators fairly clearly suggest an overall decline in the quality—and probably in the length—of human life associated with the adoption of agriculture. This decline was offset in some regions, but not in others, by a decline in physical demands on the body. The studies support recent ethnographic statements and theoretical arguments about the relatively good health and nutrition of hunter-gatherers. They also suggest that hunter-gatherers were relatively well buffered against episodic stress. These data call in question simplistic popular ideas about human progress. They also call in question models of human population growth that are based on assumed progressive increases in life expectancy. The data suggest that the well documented expansion of early farming populations was accomplished in spite of general diminution of both child and adult life expectancy rather than being fueled by increased survivorship.[24]

Rather than imposing ethnocentric notions of progress on the archaeological record, it is best to view the advent of food production as but one more factor contributing to the diversification of cultures, something that had begun in the Paleolithic. Although some societies continued to practice hunting, gathering, and fishing, others became **horticultural**—small communities of gardeners working with simple hand tools and using neither irrigation nor the plow. Horticulturists typically cultivate a variety of crops in small gardens they have cleared by hand. Some horticultural societies, however, developed **intensive agriculture.** Technologically more complex than the horticulturalists, intensive agriculturalists employ such techniques as irrigation, fertilizers, and the wooden or metal plow pulled by two harnessed draft animals, such as oxen or water buffalo, to produce food on larger plots of land. The distinction between horticulturalist and intensive agriculturalist is not always an easy one to make. For example, the Hopi Indians of the North American Southwest traditionally employed irrigation in their farming while at the same time using simple hand tools.

Some societies became specialized **pastoralists** in environments that were too dry, too grassy, too steep, or too

[24]Cohen, M. N., & Armelagos, G. J. (1984). Paleopathology at the origins of agriculture: Editors' summation. In *Paleopathology at the origins of agriculture* (p. 594). Orlando: Academic Press.

Horticulture. Cultivation of crops carried out with hand tools such as digging sticks or hoes. • **Intensive agriculture.** Intensive farming of large plots of land, employing fertilizers, plows, and/or extensive irrigation. • **Pastoralists.** People who rely on herds of domestic animals for their subsistence.

cold for effective horticulture or intensive agriculture. For example, the Russian steppes, with their heavy grass cover, were not suitable to farming without a plow, but they were ideal for herding. Thus, a number of peoples living in the arid grasslands and deserts that stretch from northwestern Africa into Central Asia kept large herds of domestic animals, relying on their neighbors for plant foods. A comparable development took place in the high, intermountain basins of Peru and Bolivia. Finally, some societies went on to develop civilizations—the subject of the next chapter.

CHAPTER SUMMARY

The end of the glacial period saw great physical changes in human habitats. Sea levels rose, vegetation changed, and herd animals disappeared from many areas. The European Mesolithic period marked a shift from big game hunting to the hunting of smaller game and gathering a broad spectrum of plants and aquatic resources. Increased reliance on seafood and plants made the Mesolithic a more sedentary period for people. Ground stone tools, including axes and adzes, responded to postglacial needs for new technologies. Many Mesolithic tools in the Old World were made with microliths—small, hard, sharp blades of flint or similar stone that could be mass produced and hafted with others to produce implements like sickles.

The change to food production, which (in Southwest Asia) was becoming widespread by 10,300 years ago, took place as people were becoming more sedentary and allowed reorganization of the workload, so that some people could pursue other tasks. From the end of the Mesolithic, human groups became larger and more permanent as people turned to animal breeding and crop growing.

A domesticated plant or animal is one that has become genetically modified as an intended or unintended consequence of human manipulation. Analysis of plant and animal remains at a site will usually indicate whether or not its occupants were food producers. Wild cereal grasses, for example, usually have fragile stems, whereas cultivated ones have tough stems. Domesticated plants can also be identified because their edible parts are usually larger than those of their wild counterparts. Domestication produces skeletal changes in some animals. The horns of wild goats and sheep, for example, differ from those of domesticated ones. Age and sex imbalances in herd animals may also indicate manipulation by human domesticators.

Several theories have been proposed to account for the changes in the subsistence patterns of early humans. One theory, the "oasis" or "desiccation" theory, is based on climatic determination. Domestication began because the oasis attracted hungry animals, which were domesticated instead of killed by early humans. Although once popular, this theory fell out of favor as systematic studies of the origins of domestication were begun in the late 1940s. One alternative idea was that domestication began in the hilly flanks of the Fertile Crescent because culture was ready for it. This somewhat culture-bound idea was replaced by theories, popular in the 1960s, that saw domestication as a response to population growth. However, this would require a deliberate decision on the part of people who could have had no prior knowledge of the long-range consequences of domestication. The most probable theory is that domestication came about as a consequence of a chance convergence of separate natural events and cultural developments. This happened independently even if at more or less similar times in Southwest and Southeast Asia, highland Mexico and Peru, South America's Amazon forest, eastern North America, China, and Africa. In all cases, however, people developed food complexes based on starchy grains and/or roots, that were consumed with protein-containing legumes plus some other flavor enhancers.

Two major consequences of domestication are that crops become more productive but also more vulnerable. This combination periodically causes population to outstrip food supplies, whereupon people are apt to move into new regions. In this way, farming has often spread from one region to another, as into Europe from Southwest Asia. Sometimes, food foragers will adopt the cultivation of crops from neighboring peoples, in response to a shortage of wild foods, as happened in ancient coastal Peru.

Among the earliest known sites containing domesticated plants and animals, about 10,300 to 9,000 years old, are those of Southwest Asia. These sites were mostly small villages of mud huts with individual storage pits and clay ovens. There is evidence not only of cultivation and domestication but also of trade. At ancient Jericho, remains of tools, houses, and clothing indicate the oasis was occupied by Neolithic people as early as 10,350 years ago. At its height, Neolithic Jericho had a population of 400 to 900 people. Comparable villages developed independently in Mexico and Peru by about 4,500 years ago.

During the Neolithic, stone that was too hard to be chipped was ground and polished for tools. People developed scythes, forks, hoes, and plows to replace simple digging sticks. The Neolithic was also characterized by the extensive manufacture and use of pottery. The widespread use of pottery is a good indicator of a sedentary community; it is found in all but a few of the earliest Neolithic settlements. The manufacture of pottery requires a knowledge of clay and the techniques of firing or baking. Other technological developments that accompanied food production and the sedentary life were the building of permanent houses and the weaving of textiles.

Archaeologists have been able to draw some inferences concerning the social structure of Neolithic society. No evidence has been found indicating that religion or government was yet a centrally organized institution. Society was probably relatively egalitarian, with minimal division of labor and little development of specialized social roles.

The development of food production had biological, as well as cultural, consequences. New diets, living arrangements, and farming practices led to increased incidence of disease and higher mortality rates. Increased fertility of women, however, more than offset mortality.

CLASSIC READINGS

Childe, V. G. (1951). *Man makes himself.* New York: New American Library.

In this classic, originally published in 1936, Childe presented his concept of the "Neolithic Revolution." He places special emphasis on the technological inventions that helped transform humans from food gatherers to food producers.

Coe, S. D. (1994). *America's first cuisines.* Austin: University of Texas Press.

Writing in an accessible style, Coe discusses some of the more important crops grown by Native Americans and explores their early history and domestication. Following this she describes how these foods were prepared, served, and preserved by the Aztec, Maya, and Incas.

Diamond, J. (1997). *Guns, germs, and steel.* New York: Norton.

This book, which won a Pulitzer Prize and became a best-seller, tries to answer the question: Why are wealth and power distributed as they are in the world today? For him, the answer requires an understanding of events associated with the origin and spread of food production. Although Diamond is a bit of an environmental determinist and falls into various ethnocentric traps, there is a great deal of solid information on the domestication and spread of crops and the biological consequences for humans. It is a lively book that can be read with pleasure.

MacNeish, R. S. (1992). *The origins of agriculture and settled life.* Norman: University of Oklahoma Press.

MacNeish was a pioneer in the study of the start of food production in the New World. In this book, he reviews the evidence from around the world in order to develop general laws about the development of agriculture and evolution of settled life.

Rindos, D. (1984). *The origins of agriculture: An evolutionary perspective.* Orlando: Academic Press.

This is one of the most important books on agricultural origins to appear in recent times. After identifying the weaknesses of existing theories, Rindos presents his own evolutionary theory of agricultural origins.

Zohary, D., & Hopf, M. (1993). *Domestication of plants in the Old World* (2nd ed.). Oxford: Clarenden Press.

This book deals with the origin and spread of domestic plants in western Asia, Europe, and the Nile Valley. Included is a species-by-species discussion of the various crops, an inventory of remains from archaeological sites, and a conclusion summarizing present knowledge.

CHAPTER 12

THE RISE OF CITIES AND CIVILIZATION

One of the hallmarks of a city is a well-defined nucleus. Shown here is the nucleus of Tikal, an ancient Maya city in Central America. In the foreground are the palaces where the city's rulers lived and carried out their administrative tasks. Beyond are the temples erected over the tombs of past kings.

CHAPTER PREVIEW

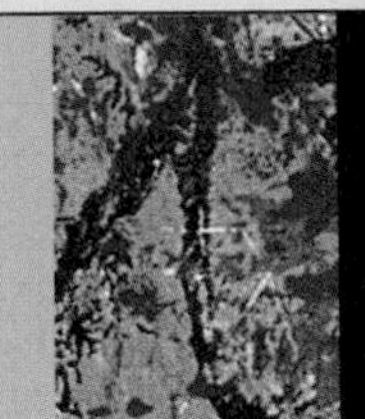

1

When and Where Did the World's First Cities First Develop?

Cities—urban settlements with well-defined nuclei, populations that are large, dense, and diversified both economically and socially—are characteristic of civilizations that developed initially between 6,000 and 4,500 years ago in China, the Indus and Nile valleys, Mesopotamia, Mesoamerica, and Peru. The world's oldest cities were those of Mesopotamia, but one of the world's largest was located in Mesoamerica.

2

What Changes in Culture Accompanied the Rise of Cities?

Four basic culture changes mark the transition from Neolithic village life to that in civilized urban centers. These are agricultural innovation, as new farming methods were developed; diversification of labor, as more people were freed from food production to pursue a variety of full-time craft specialties; the emergence of centralized governments to deal with the new problems of urban life; and the emergence of social classes as people were ranked according to the work they did or the position of the families into which they were born.

3

Why Did Civilizations Develop in the First Place?

A number of theories have been proposed to explain why civilizations develop. For example, some civilizations may have developed as populations grew, causing competition for space and scarce resources, which favored the development of centralized authority to control resources and organize warfare. Some civilizations, though, appear to have developed as a result of certain beliefs and values that brought people together. In some cases, too, the actions of powerful individuals to promote their own interests may have played a role. Thus, it may be that civilizations arose in different places for somewhat different reasons.

A walk down a street of a busy North American city brings us in contact with numerous activities that are essential to the well-being of North American society. The sidewalks are crowded with people going to and from offices and stores. The traffic of cars, taxis, and trucks is heavy, sometimes almost at a standstill. In a brief two-block stretch, there may be a department store; shops selling clothing, appliances, or books; a restaurant; a newsstand; a gasoline station; and a movie theater. Perhaps there will also be a museum, a police station, a school, a hospital, or a church. That is quite a number of services and specialized skills to find in such a small area.

Each of these services or places of business is dependent on others. A butcher shop, for instance, depends on slaughterhouses and beef ranches. A clothing store depends on designers, farmers who produce cotton and wool, and workers who manufacture synthetic fibers. Restaurants depend on refrigerated trucking and vegetable and dairy farmers. Hospitals depend on a great variety of other institutions to meet their more complex needs. All institutions, finally, depend on the public utilities—the telephone, gas, water, and electric companies. Although interdependence is not immediately apparent to the passerby, it is an important aspect of modern cities.

The interdependence of goods and services in a big city is what makes so many products readily available to people. For example, refrigerated air transport makes it possible to buy fresh Maine lobsters on the West Coast. This same interdependence, however, has undesirable effects if one service stops functioning, for example, because of strikes, bad weather, or acts of violence such as the attack on New York's World Trade Center. Thus, every so often, major North American cities have had to do without services as vital as newspapers, subways, schools, and trash removal. The question is not so much "Why does this happen?" but rather "Why doesn't it happen more often, and why does the city continue to function as well as it does when one of its services stops?" The answer is that services are not only interdependent, but they are also adaptable. When one breaks down, others take over its functions. During a long newspaper strike in New York City in the 1960s, for example, several new magazines were launched, and television expanded its coverage of news and events. Currently, we are adapting to changes in air travel in response to heightened terrorist activity.

On the surface, city life seems so orderly that we take it for granted; but a moment's reflection reminds us that the intricate fabric of city life did not always exist, and the goods that are widely accessible to us were once simply not available.

WHAT CIVILIZATION MEANS

This complicated system of goods and services available in such a small space is a mark of civilization itself. The history of civilization is intimately bound up with the history of cities. This does not mean that civilization is to be equated with modern industrial cities or with present-day European or North American society. People as diverse as the ancient preindustrial Aztecs of Mexico and the industrial North Americans of today are included in the term *civilization,* but each represents a very different kind. It was with the development of the earliest preindustrial cities, however, that civilization first developed (Figure 12.1). In fact, the word comes from the Latin *civis,* which refers to one who is an inhabitant of a city, and *civitas,* which refers to the community in which one dwells. The word *civilization* contains the idea of "citification," or "the coming-to-be of cities."

Civilization is one of those words that is used in different ways by different people. In everyday usage, it carries the notion of refinement and progress, two ethnocentric concepts that mean whatever a culture holds them to mean. In anthropology, by contrast, the term has a very precise meaning that avoids such culture-bound notions. As used by anthropologists, **civilization** refers to societies in which large numbers of people live in cities, are socially stratified, and are governed by centrally organized political systems called states. We shall elaborate on all of these points in the course of this chapter.

The world's first cities sprang up in some parts of the world as Neolithic villages of the sort discussed in Chapter 11 grew into towns, some of which in turn grew into cities. This happened first in Mesopotamia (in modern-day Iraq), then in Egypt and the Indus Valley, between 6,000 and 4,500 years ago. The inhabitants of Sumer, in southern Mesopotamia, developed the world's first civilization about 5,500 years ago. In China, civilization was under way by 5,000 years ago. Independent of these developments in the Old World, the first cities appeared in Peru around 4,000 years ago and in Mesoamerica about 2,000 years ago.

Civilization. In anthropology a type of society marked by the presence of cities, social classes, and the state.

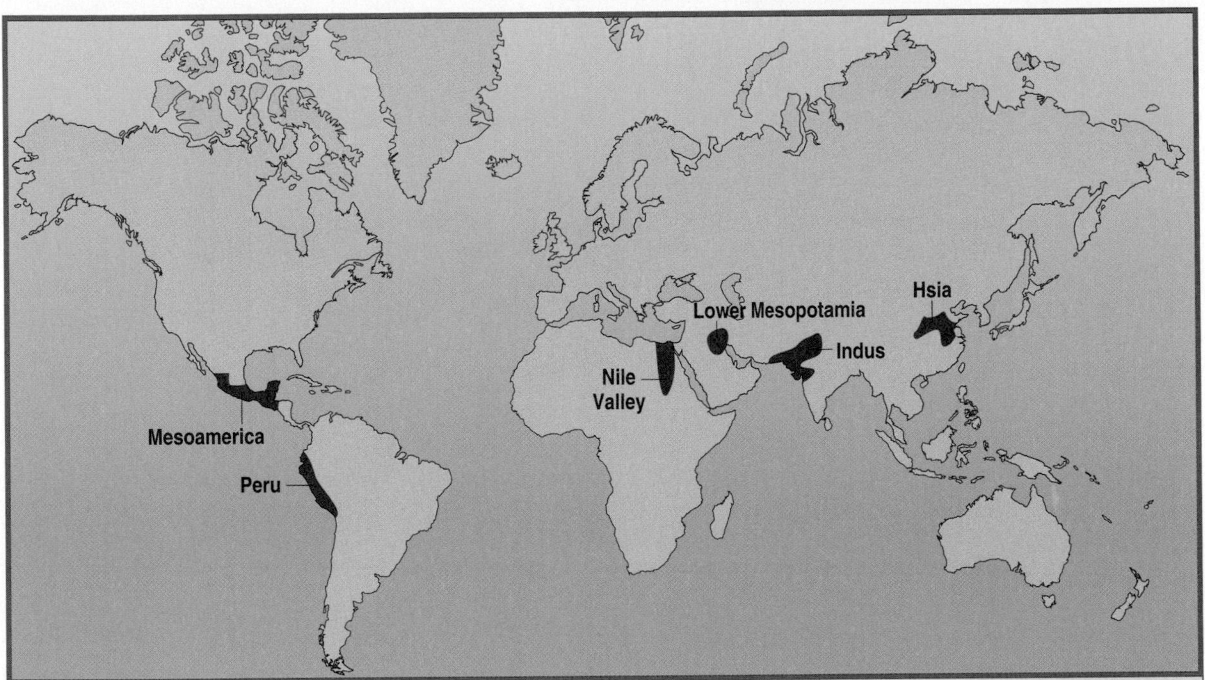

FIGURE 12.1

THE MAJOR EARLY CIVILIZATIONS SPRANG FROM NEOLITHIC VILLAGES IN VARIOUS PARTS OF THE WORLD. THOSE OF NORTH AND SOUTH AMERICA DEVELOPED WHOLLY INDEPENDENTLY OF THOSE IN AFRICA AND ASIA; CHINESE CIVILIZATION SEEMS TO HAVE DEVELOPED INDEPENDENTLY OF SOUTHWEST ASIA (INCLUDING THE NILE AND INDUS) CIVILIZATIONS.

What characterized these first cities? Why are they called the birthplaces of civilization? The first characteristic of cities—and of civilization—is their large size and population. But is this all that a city is? Consider the case of Çatalhöyük, a 9,500-year-old settlement in south-central Turkey (see Figure 11.2).[1] Home to 5,000 or more people, its houses were so tightly packed together in an area of roughly 12 hectares that there were no streets. To get into one's own house, one dropped through a hole in the roof, after having traversed the roofs of neighboring houses. For subsistence, people grew crops and tended livestock, but because the village was located in the middle of a swamp, these activities were carried out at locations at least 12 kilometers away. But there is no evidence for intensification of agriculture; furthermore, people's diets included significant amounts of food from wild plants and animals.

The reason for Çatalhöyük's location in the middle of a swamp may have been to take advantage of lime-rich clay that people used to plaster their walls, floors, and ovens. The walls were covered with all sorts of paintings, often of small men confronting outsize beasts, as well as reliefs of leopards, bulls, and female breasts. But there was little division of labor, nor is there any evidence of centralized authority. The houses are all pretty much alike, and there is no known public architecture. It is as if a

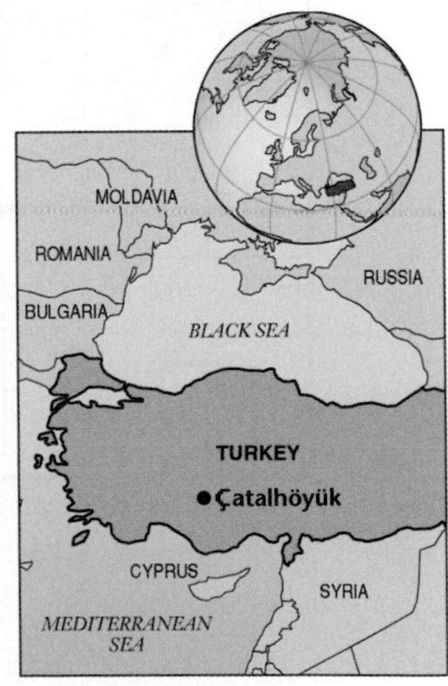

[1]Material on Çatalhöyük is drawn from Balter, M. (1998). Why settle down? The mystery of communities. *Science, 282,* 1,442–1,444; Balter, M. (1999). A long season puts Çatalhöyük in context. *Science, 286,* 890–891; Balter, M. (2001). Did plaster hold Neolithic society together? *Science, 294,* 2,278–2,281; Kunzig, R. (1999). A tale of two obsessed archaeologists, one ancient city and nagging doubts about whether science can ever hope to reveal the past. *Discover, 20*(5), 84–92.

Çatalhöyük in Turkey was a compact village, as suggested by this photo, but it was not a true city.

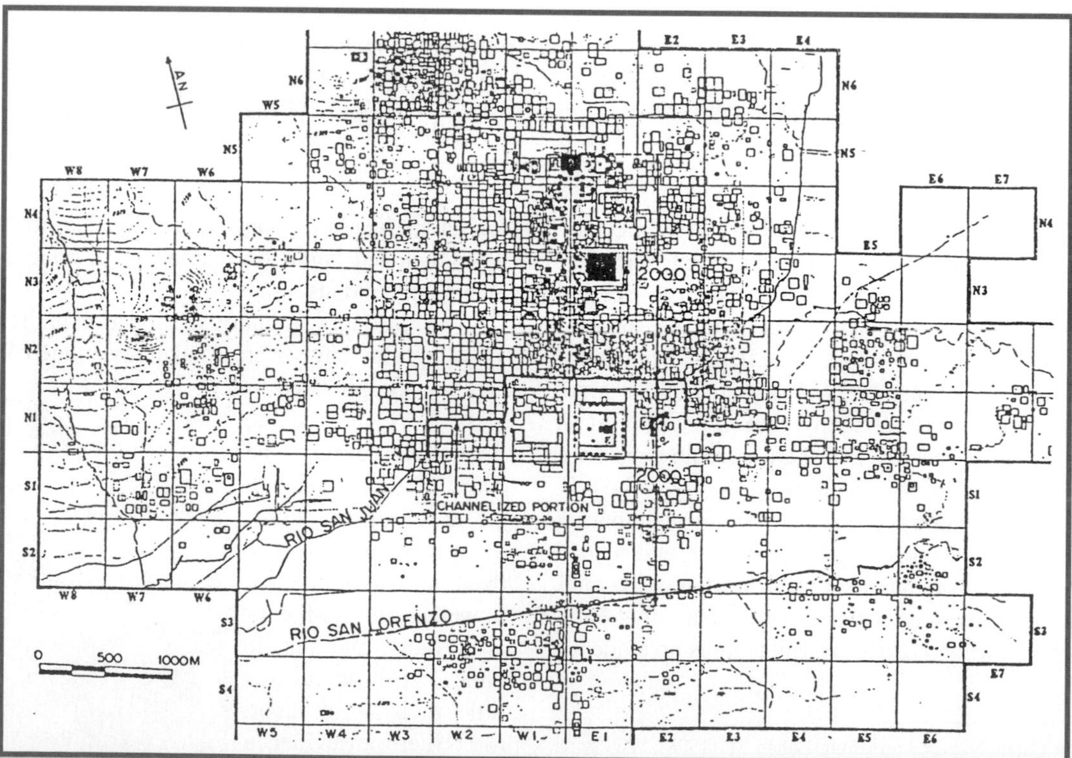

FIGURE 12.2

THE FOUNDERS OF TEOTIHUACAN IMPOSED AN AUDACIOUS PLAN ON SEVERAL SQUARE KILOMETERS OF LANDSCAPE IN CENTRAL MEXICO. AT THE CENTER IS THE AVENUE OF THE DEAD, RUNNING FROM THE TEMPLE OF THE MOON (NEAR TOP), PAST THE TEMPLE OF THE SUN AND, SOUTH OF THE RIO SAN JUAN, THE PALACE COMPOUND. NOTE THE GRIDDED LAYOUT OF SURROUNDING APARTMENT COMPOUNDS, AND THE CHANNELIZED RIO SAN JUAN.

number of what otherwise would be separate Neolithic villages were all crammed together in one place.

One may compare Çatalhöyük with Teotihuacan, America's first great experience in urbanism (Figure 12.2). Located in central Mexico, in the first 400 years after its founding 2,200 years ago, its population grew rapidly, until it reached perhaps 80,000 people. Slower growth thereafter brought this figure to around 100,000, all packed within an area of about 20 km^2. As revealed by regional surveys, one reason for the early rapid growth was that the population of the entire 5,000 km^2 Basin of Mexico (where modern Mexico City is located today) was removed and relocated to Teotihuacan. Furthermore, the layout of the city was planned from the very start. At its center is what is known as the Street of the Dead, a grand north-south axis along which are located the huge Sun and Moon pyramids as well as a royal palace compound (associated with the planet Venus) and other monumental construction. The Sun pyramid was built above a cave, seen as a portal to the underworld, home of deities associated with death. The street itself was deliberately oriented to an astronomical alignment east of true north. Surrounding this core were thousands of apartment compounds, separated from one another by narrow streets laid out in a grid, maintaining the east-of-north orientation throughout the city. Key linear dimensions of construction and distance between compounds seem to have translated calendrical numbers into a unified spatial pattern. So rigid was this layout that the Rio San Juan, where it runs through the city, was channelized to conform with the grid. Finally, there is clear evidence for both social and economic diversity. Some six levels of society can be recognized by variation in size and quality of apartment rooms. Those at and near the top of the social scale lived on or near the Street of the Dead. Exotic goods and raw materials were imported from afar to be worked by Teotihuacano artisans, and at least two enclaves housed people with foreign affiliations, one to Oaxaca, the other ("merchant's barrio") to the Gulf and Maya lowlands. Also resident in the city were farmers, whose labor in fields (some of them irrigated) supplied the food on which the city dwellers relied.[2]

[2]Cowgill, G. L. (1997). State and society at Teotihuacan, Mexico. *Annual Review of Anthropology, 26,* 129–161.

This photo looks south down Teotihuacan's principal avenue, the Street of the Dead, an urban axis unequaled in its scale until construction of such modern-day avenues as the Champs Elysées in Paris.

As this comparison shows, early cities were far more than expanded Neolithic villages. The changes that took place in the transition from village to city were so great that the emergence of urban living is considered by some to be one of the great revolutions in human culture. The following case study gives us a glimpse of another of the world's ancient cities, how it was studied by archaeologists, and how it may have grown from a smaller farming community.

TIKAL: A CASE STUDY

The ancient city of Tikal, one of the largest lowland Maya centers in existence, is situated in Central America about 200 miles by air north of Guatemala City. Tikal was built on a broad limestone terrace in a rain forest. Here the Maya settled in the 1st millennium B.C., and their civilization flourished until about A.D. 869 (dates were recorded by the Maya in their own calendar, which can be precisely correlated with our own).

At its height, Tikal covered about 120.5 km^2, and its nucleus, or "epicenter," was the Great Plaza, a large, paved area surrounded by about 300 major structures and thousands of houses (see the photo that opens this chapter). Starting from a small, dispersed population, the population of Tikal swelled to large proportions. By A.D. 550, the density of Tikal was on the order of 600 to 700 persons per square kilometer, 6 times that of the surrounding regions.

From 1956 through the 1960s, Tikal and the surrounding region were intensively explored under the joint auspices of the University of Pennsylvania Museum and the Guatemalan government. Until 1959, the Tikal Project had investigated only major temple and palace structures found in the vicinity of the Great Plaza, at the site's epicenter. It became evident, however, that in order to gain a balanced view of Tikal's development and composition, considerable attention would have to be devoted to hundreds of small mounds, thought to be the remains of dwellings, which surround the larger buildings. Just as one cannot get a realistic view of Washington, DC, by looking at its monumental public buildings alone, so one cannot obtain a realistic view of Tikal without examining the full range of ruins in the area.

It became evident that a long-range program of excavation of small structures, most of which were probably houses, was necessary at Tikal. Such a program would provide some basis for an estimate of the city's population size and density—information critical for testing the conventional assumption that the Maya could not have sustained large concentrations of population because their subsistence practices were not adequate. Extensive excavation would also provide a sound basis for a reconstruction of the everyday life of the Maya, a people up till then known almost entirely through a study of ceremonial remains. Moreover, the excavation might shed light on the social organization of the Maya. For example, differences in house construction and in the quality and quantity of associated remains might suggest social class differences; or features of house distribution might reflect the existence of extended families or other types of kin groups. The excavation of both large and small structures could reveal the variations in architecture and associated artifacts and burials; such variations might reflect the social structure of the total population of Tikal.[3]

Surveying the Site

By the time the first excavations of small structures were undertaken, 6 km^2 surrounding the Great Plaza had already been extensively surveyed by mapping crews (see Figure 2.1). For this mapping, aerial photography was worthless because the tree canopy in this area is often 100 feet above the ground and obscures all but the tallest temples; many of the small ruins are practically invisible even to observers on the ground. The only effective way to explore the region is on foot. Once a ruin is found, it is not easy to mark its exact location. Even after 4 years of careful mapping, the limits of the site still had not been revealed. Ancient Tikal was far larger than the 6 km^2 surveyed till then. More time and money were required to continue surveying the area in order to define the city's boundaries. To simplify this problem, straight survey trails oriented toward the four cardinal directions, with the Great Plaza as the center point, were cut through the forest, measured, and staked by government surveyors. The distribution of ruins was plotted, using the trails as reference points, and the overall size of Tikal was calculated.[4]

The area selected for the first small-structure excavation was surveyed in 1957 while it was still covered by forest. A map was drafted, and 2 years later the first excavations were undertaken.[5] Six structures, two plazas, and

---

[3]Haviland, W. A. (2002). Settlement, society and demography at Tikal. In J. Sabloff (Ed.), *Tikal.* Santa Fe: School of American Research (in press).

[4]Puleston, D. E. (1983). *The settlement survey of Tikal.* Philadelphia: University Museum.

[5]Haviland, W. A., et al. (1985). *Excavations in small residential groups of Tikal: Groups 4F-1 and 4F-2.* Philadelphia: University Museum.

At Tikal, only the tallest temples are visible above the forest canopy. The two farthest temples are at either end of the Great Plaza, the civic and ceremonial heart of the city. (Those familiar with the original *Star Wars* movie will recognize this view.)

a platform were investigated. The original plan was to strip each of the structures to bedrock in order to obtain every bit of information possible. Three obstacles prevented this procedure, however. First was the discovery of new structures not visible before excavation; second, the structures turned out to be far more complex architecturally than anyone had expected; and, finally, the enormous quantity of artifacts found then had to be washed and catalogued, a time-consuming process. Consequently, not every structure was completely excavated, and some remained uninvestigated.

Evidence from the Excavation

Following this initial work, over 100 additional small structures were excavated in different parts of the site in order to ensure that a representative sample was investigated. Numerous test pits were sunk in various other small structure groups to supplement the information gained from more extensive excavations.

Excavation at Tikal revealed evidence of trade in nonperishable items. Granite, quartzite, hematite, pyrite, jade, slate, and obsidian all were imported, either as raw materials or finished products. Marine materials came from Caribbean and Pacific coastal areas. Tikal itself is located on a source of abundant flint, which may have been exported in the form of raw material and finished objects. The site also happens to be located between two river systems to the east and west, and so may have been on a major overland trade route between the two. There is indirect evidence that trade went on in perishable goods such as textiles, feathers, salt, and cacao. We can safely conclude that there were full-time traders among the Tikal Maya.

In the realm of technology, specialized woodworking, pottery, obsidian, and shell workshops have been found. The skillful stone carving displayed on stone monuments suggests that this was done by occupational specialists. The same is true of the fine artwork exhibited on ceramic

This painting from Cacaxtla in southern Mexico shows a deity with the typical backpack of a Maya merchant.

vessels. Those who painted these had to envision what their work would look like after their pale, relatively colorless slips had been fired. The complex Maya calendar required astronomers, and in order to control the large population, estimated to have been at least 50,000 people, there must have been some form of bureaucratic organization. We do know that the government was headed by a hereditary ruling dynasty, and that it had sufficient power to organize the construction and continuing maintenance of a massive system of defensive ditches and embankments on the northern and southern edges of the city (the longest of these ran for a distance of perhaps 19, if not 28 km). Although we do not have direct evidence, there are clues to the existence of textile workers, dental workers, makers of bark cloth "paper," scribes, masons, and other occupational specialists.

Carved monuments like this were commissioned by Tikal's rulers to commemorate important events in their reigns. Portrayed on this one is a king who ruled between A.D. 768 and A.D. 790 or a bit later. Such skilled stone carving could only have been accomplished by a specialist. (For a translation of the inscription on the monument's left side, see Figure 12.4.)

The religion of the Tikal Maya probably developed initially as a means to cope with the uncertainties of agriculture. When people are faced with problems unsolvable by technological or organizational means, they resort to manipulation of magic and the supernatural. Soils at Tikal are thin, and there is no water except that which can be collected in ponds. Rain is abundant in season, but its onset tends to be unreliable. Once the wet season arrives, there may be dry spells of varying duration that can seriously affect crop productivity. Or there may be too much rain, so that crops rot in the fields. Other risks include storm damage, locust plagues, and incursions of wild animals. To this day, the native inhabitants of the region display great concern about these very real risks involved in agriculture over which they have no direct control.

The Maya priesthood devoted much of its time to calendrical matters; the priests tried not only to placate the deities in times of drought but also to propitiate them in times of plenty. They determined the most auspicious time to plant crops and were concerned with other agricultural matters. The dependence of the population in and around Tikal upon their priesthood to manipulate supernatural beings and forces in their behalf, in order that their crops would not fail, tended to keep them in or near the city, although a slash-and-burn method of agriculture, which was probably the prevailing method early in Tikal's history, requires the constant shifting of plots and consequently tended to disperse the population over large areas.

As the population increased, land for agriculture became scarcer, and the Maya were forced to find new methods of food production that could sustain the dense population concentrated at Tikal. To slash-and-burn agriculture as their main form of subsistence, they added the planting and tending of fruit trees and other crops that could be grown around their houses in soils enriched by human waste (unlike houses at Teotihuacan, those at Tikal were not built close to one another). Along with increased reliance on household gardening went the construction of artificially raised fields in areas that were flooded each rainy season. In these fields, crops could be intensively cultivated year after year, as long as they were carefully maintained. Measures also were taken to maximize catchment of water for the dry season, by converting low areas into reservoirs and constructing channels to carry runoff from plazas and other architecture into these reservoirs. As these changes were taking place, a class of artisans, craftspeople, and other occupational specialists emerged to serve the needs first of religion, then of an elite consisting of the priesthood and a ruling dynasty. The arts flourished, and numerous temples, public buildings, and houses were built.

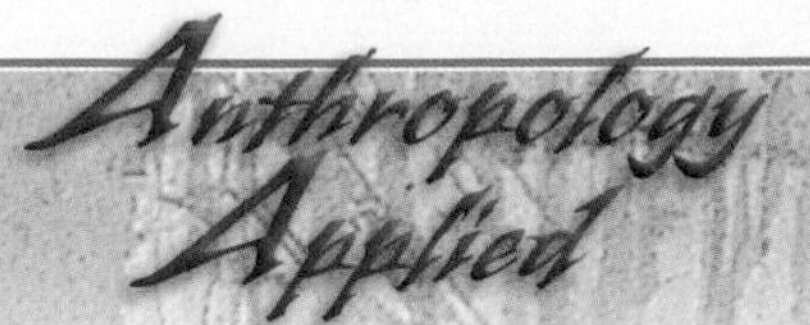

Economic Development and Tropical Forests

Prime targets for development in the world today, in the eyes of governments and private corporations alike, are vast tracts of tropical forests. On a global basis, forests are being rapidly cleared for lumber and fuel, as well as to make way for farms, ranches, mines, and other forms of economic development. The world's largest uninterrupted tracts are the forests of the Amazon and Orinoco watersheds of South America, which are being destroyed at about the rate of 4 percent a year. Just what the rate is for the world as a whole no one is quite sure, but it is clearly accelerating. And already there are signs of trouble, as extensive tracts of once-lush growth have been converted to semi-desert. Essential nutrients are lost, either through erosion (which increases by several orders of magnitude under deforestation) or by leaching too deeply, as soils are exposed to the direct force of the heavy tropical rains.

The problem is that developers, until recently, have lacked reliable models by which the long-term impact of their actions might be assessed. Such a model now exists, thanks to the efforts of archaeologists unraveling the mystery of how the ancient Maya, in a tropical rainforest setting, carried out large-scale urban construction and sustained huge numbers of people successfully for 2 millennia. The key to the Maya success was their implementation of sophisticated practices to reduce regionwide processes of nutrient loss, deterioration of soil structure, destabilization of water flows, soil erosion, and loss of productive components of their environment.* These included construction of terraces, canals, and raised fields, the fertility of which was maintained through mulching with water plants and the addition of organic wastes. Coupled with all this, crops were planted in such a way as to produce complex patterns of foliage distribution, canopy heights, and nutrient demands. Far different from "modern" monocrop agriculture, this reduced the impact on the soils of intensive farming, while making maximum use of nutrients and enhancing their cycling in the system.

In Mexico, where population growth has threatened the country's ability to provide sufficient food for its people, archaeologists and agriculturalists are already cooperating to apply our knowledge of ancient Maya techniques to the problems of modern food production in the tropics. Application of these techniques in other tropical forested countries, like Brazil, could do much to alleviate food shortages.

*Rice, D. S., & Rice, P. M. (1984). Lessons from the Maya. *Latin American Research Review, 19*(3), 24–28.

For several hundred years, Tikal was able to sustain its ever-growing population. Then the pressure for food and land reached a critical point, and population growth was halted. At the same time, warfare with other cities was becoming increasingly destructive. All of this is marked archaeologically by abandonment of houses on prime land in rural areas, by the advent of nutritional problems as evidenced by the bones from burials, and by the construction of the previously mentioned defensive ditches and embankments. In other words, a period of readjustment set in, which must have been directed by an already strong central authority. Activities then continued as before, but without further population growth for another 250 years or so.

CITIES AND CULTURAL CHANGE

If someone who grew up in a small village of Maine, Wyoming, or Mississippi were to move to Chicago, Detroit, or Los Angeles, that person would experience a number of marked changes in his or her way of life. The same sorts of changes in daily life would have been felt 5,000 years ago by a Neolithic village dweller upon moving into one of the world's first cities in Mesopotamia. Of course, the differences would be less extreme today. In the 20th century, every North American village, however small, is part of civilization; back when cities first developed, *they* were civilization, and the villages for the

HIGHWAY 1
Take a trip to the ancient Maya ruins of Tikal, and experience life in this large city over 2,000 years ago through this 360-degree virtual tour of the site. Learn about the cultural practices of this great ancient civilization through the artifacts and ruins.
www.destination360.com/tikal.htm

HIGHWAY 2
Visit the Teotihuacan home page to learn about this incredible pre-Aztec city. Stroll down the Avenue of the Dead and visit the pyramids of the Sun and the Moon.
http://archaeology.la.asu.edu/teo/

most part represented a continuation of Neolithic life. Four basic culture changes mark the transition from Neolithic village life to life in the first urban centers.

Agricultural Innovation

The first culture change characteristic of life in cities—hence, of civilization itself—occurred in farming methods. The ancient Sumerians, for example, built an extensive system of dikes, canals, and reservoirs to irrigate their farmlands. With such a system, they could control water resources at will; water could be held and then run off into the fields as necessary. Irrigation was an important factor affecting an increase of crop yields. Because farming could now be carried on independently of the seasons, more crops could be harvested in one year. On the other hand, this intensification of agriculture did not necessarily mean that people ate better than before. Under centralized governments, intensification was generally carried out with less regard for human health than when such governments did not exist.[6]

The ancient Maya who lived at Tikal developed systems of tree cultivation and constructed raised fields in seasonally flooded swamplands to supplement their earlier slash-and-burn farming. The resultant increase in crop yields provided for a higher population density. Increased crop yields, resulting from agricultural innovations such as those of the ancient Maya and Sumerians, were undoubtedly a factor contributing to the high population densities of all civilized societies.

This clay tablet map of farmland outside of the Mesopotamian city of Nippur dates to 1300 B.C. Shown are irrigation canals separating the various fields, each of which is identified with the name of the owner.

[6]Roosevelt, A. C. (1984). Population, health, and the evolution of subsistence: Conclusions from the conference. In M. N. Cohen & G. J. Armelagos (Eds.), *Paleopathology at the origins of agriculture* (p. 568). Orlando: Academic Press.

Diversification of Labor

The second culture change characteristic of civilization is diversification of labor. In a Neolithic village that possessed neither irrigation nor plow farming, the members of every family were primarily concerned with the raising of crops. The high crop yields made possible by new farming methods and the increased population meant that a sizable number of people were available to pursue nonagricultural activities on a full-time basis. In the early cities, some people still farmed (as at Tikal and Teotihuacan), but a substantial number of the inhabitants were skilled workers or craftspeople.

Ancient public records indicate there was a considerable variety of such skilled workers. For example, an early Mesopotamian document from the city of Lagash lists the artisans, craftspeople, and others paid from crop surpluses stored in the temple granaries. Among them were coppersmiths, silversmiths, sculptors, merchants, potters, tanners, engravers, butchers, carpenters, spinners, barbers, cabinetmakers, bakers, clerks, and brewers. At the ancient Maya city of Tikal we have evidence for traders, potters, woodworkers, obsidian workers, painters, scribes, and sculptors, and perhaps textile workers, dental workers, shell workers, and paper makers.

One technique of agricultural intensification used by the Maya reclaimed swampland by constructing raised fields surrounded by canals. Traces of these raised fields can still be seen, as shown here in Belize, at Pulltrous swamp.

With specialization came the expertise that led to the invention of new and novel ways of making and doing things. In the Old World, civilization ushered in what archaeologists often refer to as the **Bronze Age,** a period marked by the production of tools and ornaments of this metal. Metals were in great demand for the manufacture of farmers' and artisans' tools, as well as for weapons. Copper and tin—the raw

The earliest objects of bronze, such as this one, come from Ban Chiang, Thailand.

Bronze Age. In the Old World, the period marked by the production of tools and ornaments of bronze; began about 3000 B.C. in China and Southwest Asia and about 500 years earlier in Southeast Asia.

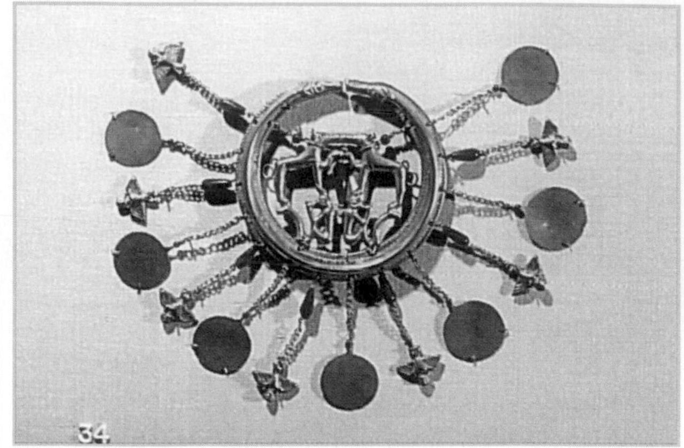

Bronze tools and weapons were more durable than their stone counterparts, which were more easily broken. The bronze sword (above) comes from Mycaenae, Greece, dating to about 1200 B.C. The ear pendant from Greece of about the same age is a fine example of the artistry that became possible with the introduction of bronze.

materials from which bronze is made—and eventually iron were smelted, separating them from their ores, then purified, and cast to make plows, swords, axes, and shields. In wars over border disputes or to extend a state's territory, stone knives, spears, and slings could not stand up against bronze spears, arrowheads, swords, or armor.

The native civilizations of the Americas also used metals—in South America, for tools as well as ceremonial and ornamental objects, but in Mesoamerica, mostly for ceremonial and ornamental objects. Why people like the Aztecs and Maya continued to rely on stone for their everyday tools has puzzled those who assume that metal is inherently superior. The answer, however, is simple: The ready availability of obsidian (a glass formed by volcanic activity), its extreme sharpness (many times sharper than the finest steel), and the ease with which it could be worked made it perfectly suited to their needs. With obsidian, these people fabricated tools with the sharpest cutting edges ever made.

In order to procure the raw materials needed for their technologies, extensive trade systems were developed by the early civilizations. The city of Teotihuacan, for example, controlled most of the obsidian trade in central Mexico. Trade agreements were maintained with distant peoples, not only to secure basic raw materials but to provide luxury items as well.

Boats gave greater access to trade centers; they could easily carry back to cities large loads of imports at less cost than if they had been brought back overland. A one-way trip from Egypt to the northern city of Byblos in Phoenicia (now Lebanon) took only four to eight days by rowboat. With a sailboat, it took even less.

Egyptian pharaohs sent expeditions to the Sinai Peninsula for copper; to Nubia for gold; to Arabia for spices and perfumes; to Asia for lapis lazuli (a blue semiprecious stone) and other jewels; to Lebanon for cedar, wine, and funerary oils; and to central Africa for ivory, ebony, ostrich feathers, leopard skins, cattle, and slaves.

With technological innovation, along with increased contact with foreign peoples through trade, came new knowledge. It was within the early civilizations that sciences such as geometry and astronomy were first developed. Geometry was used by the Egyptians for such purposes as measuring the area of a field or staking off an accurate right angle at the corner of a building.

Aztec spears tipped and edged with obsidian blades are shown in this 16th-century drawing of a battle with the Aztecs' Spanish conquerors. Though superior to steel for piercing, cutting, and slashing, the brittleness of obsidian placed the Aztecs at a disadvantage when faced with Spanish swords.

Paper making, invented in China 2,000 years ago, is an example of technological innovation by which farming societies evolved into civilizations.

Astronomy grew out of the need to know when to plant and harvest crops or to hold religious observances and to find exact bearings on voyages. Astronomy and mathematics were used to devise calendars. The Maya calculated that the solar year was 365 days (actually, it is 365 1/4 days), accurately predicted the appearances over time of the planet Venus as morning and evening "star," predicted eclipses, and tracked other astronomical events. As one scholar comments, "Maya science, in its representation of numbers, and its empirical base, is in many respects superior to the science of their European contemporaries."[7]

Central Government

The third culture change characteristic of civilization is the emergence of a governing elite, a strong central authority required to deal with the many problems arising within the new cities because of their size and complexity. The new governing elite saw to it that different interest groups, such as farmers, craft specialists, or money lenders, provided the services that were expected of them and did not infringe on one another's rights (to the extend that they had rights). It ensured that the city was safe from its enemies by constructing fortifications (such as those at Tikal) and raising an army. It levied taxes and appointed tax collectors so that construction workers, the army, and other public expenses could be paid. It saw to it that merchants, carpenters, or farmers who made legal claims received justice (however "justice" was defined). It guaranteed safety for the lives and property of ordinary people and assured that any harm done one person by another would be justly handled. In addition, surplus food had to be stored for times of scarcity, and public works such as extensive irrigation systems or fortifications had to be supervised by competent, disinterested individuals. The mechanisms of government served all these functions.

EVIDENCE OF CENTRALIZED AUTHORITY

Evidence of centralized authority in ancient civilizations comes from such sources as law codes, temple records, and royal chronicles. Excavation of the city structures themselves provides further evidence. For example, archaeologists believe that the cities of Mohenjo-Daro and Harappa in the Indus Valley, which flourished between 4,800 and 3,700 years ago, were governed by a centralized authority because they show definite signs of city planning. Both cities stretch out over a 3 mile distance; their main streets are laid out in a rectangular grid pattern; and both contain citywide drainage systems. Similar evidence for centralized planning comes from Teotihuacan where, in addition, the sudden relocation of people from the Basin of Mexico also attests to strong, centralized control.

[7]Frake, C. O. (1992). Lessons of the Mayan sky: A perspective from medieval Europe. In A. F. Aveni (Ed.), *The sky in Mayan literature* (p. 287). New York: Oxford University Press.

Construction of large-scale public works such as the Great Wall of China reflects the power of a centralized government to mobilize and supervise the labor necessary to carry out such monumental undertakings.

Monumental buildings and temples, palaces, and large sculptures are usually found in civilizations. The Maya city of Tikal contained over 300 major structures, including temples, ball courts, and "palaces" (residences of the aristocracy). The Pyramid of the Sun in the pre-Aztec city of Teotihuacan is 700 feet long and more than 200 feet high. Its interior is filled by more than 1 million cubic yards of sun-dried bricks. The tomb of the Egyptian pharaoh Khufu, known as the Great Pyramid, is 755 feet long and 481 feet high. It contains about 2,300,000 stone blocks, each with an average weight of 2.5 tons. The Greek historian Herodotus reports that it took 100,000 men 20 years to build this tomb. Such gigantic structures could be built only because the considerable labor force, engineering skills, and raw materials necessary for their construction could be harnessed by a powerful central authority.

Another indicator of the existence of centralized authority is writing, or some form of recorded information (Figure 12.3). With writing, central authorities could disseminate information and store, systematize, and deploy memory for political, religious, and economic purposes. In Mesopotamia, early governments found it useful to keep records of state affairs, such as accounts of their food surplus, tribute records, and other business receipts. The earliest documents appear to be just such records—lists of vegetables and animals bought and sold, tax lists, and storehouse inventories. Being able to record information was an extremely important invention, because governments could keep records of their assets instead of simply relying upon the memory of administrators.

Before 5,500 years ago, records consisted initially of "tokens," ceramic pieces with different shapes indicative of different commercial objects. Thus, a cone shape could represent a measure of grain, or a cylinder an animal. As the system developed, tokens represented different animals, processed foods such as oil, trussed ducks or bread, and manufactured or imported goods such as textiles and metal.[8] Ultimately, these tokens were replaced by clay tablets with impressed marks representing objects.

In the Mesopotamia city of Uruk, by 5,100 years ago, a new writing technique emerged, which used a reed stylus to make wedge-shaped markings on a tablet of damp clay. Originally, each marking stood for a word. Because most words in this language were monosyllabic, the markings came, in time, to stand for syllables. There were about 600 signs, half of them ideograms, the others functioning either as ideograms or as syllables.

In the New World, systems of writing came into use among various Mesoamerican peoples, but the most sophisticated was that of the Maya. Their hieroglyphic system had less to do with keeping track of state belongings than with "dynastic bombast." Maya lords glorified themselves by recording their dynastic genealogies, important

[8]Lawler, A. (2001). Writing gets a rewrite. *Science, 292,* 2,419.

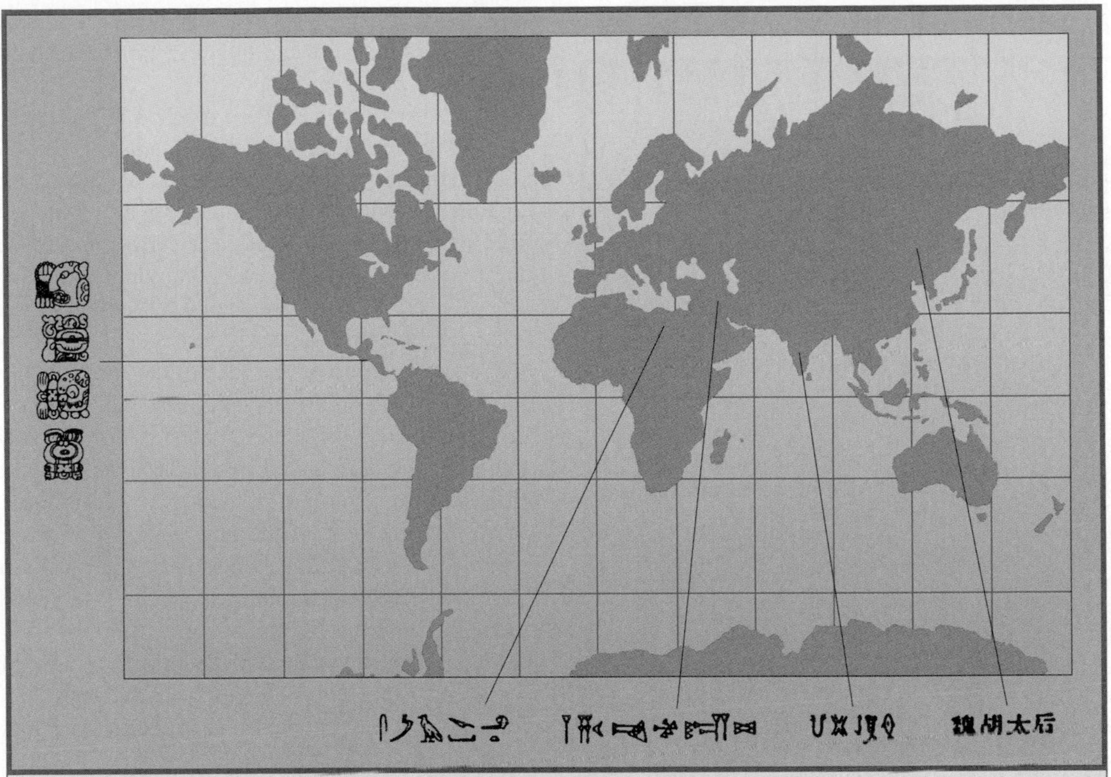

FIGURE 12.3

The impermanence of spoken words contrasts with the relative permanence of written records. In all of human history, writing has been independently invented no more than 5 times.

conquests, and royal marriages; by using grandiose titles to refer to themselves; and by associating their actions with important astrological events (Figure 12.4). Often, the latter involved complicated mathematical calculations. So important was the written word in reinforcing the power and authority of Maya kings that scribes were high-ranking members of royal courts. So closely tied to kings were they that, when a king was defeated in warfare, his scribes were captured, tortured, and then sacrificed. The torture was highly symbolic, involving finger mutilation that destroyed their ability to produce politically persuasive texts for any rival of the victor.

THE EARLIEST GOVERNMENTS

The government of the earliest cities was typically headed by a king and his special advisors. In addition, there were sometimes councils of lesser advisors. Formal laws were enacted, and courts sat in judgment over the claims of rival litigants or the criminal charges brought by the government against an individual.

Of the many ancient kings known, one stands out as truly remarkable for the efficient government organization and highly developed legal system that characterized his reign. This is Hammurabi, the Babylonian king who lived sometime between 1950 and 1700 B.C. He promulgated a set of laws for his kingdom, known as the Code of Hammurabi, which is notable for its thorough detail and standardization. It prescribes the correct form for legal procedures and determines penalties for perjury, false accusation, and injustice done by judges. It contains laws applying to property rights, loans and debts, family rights, and damages paid for malpractice by a physician. There are fixed rates to be charged in various trades and branches of commerce. The poor, women, children, and slaves are protected against injustice. The code was publicly displayed on huge stone slabs so that no one accused could plead ignorance. Even the poorest citizen was supposed to know his or her rights.

Some civilizations flourished under a ruler with extraordinary governing abilities, such as Hammurabi. Other civilizations possessed a widespread governing bureaucracy

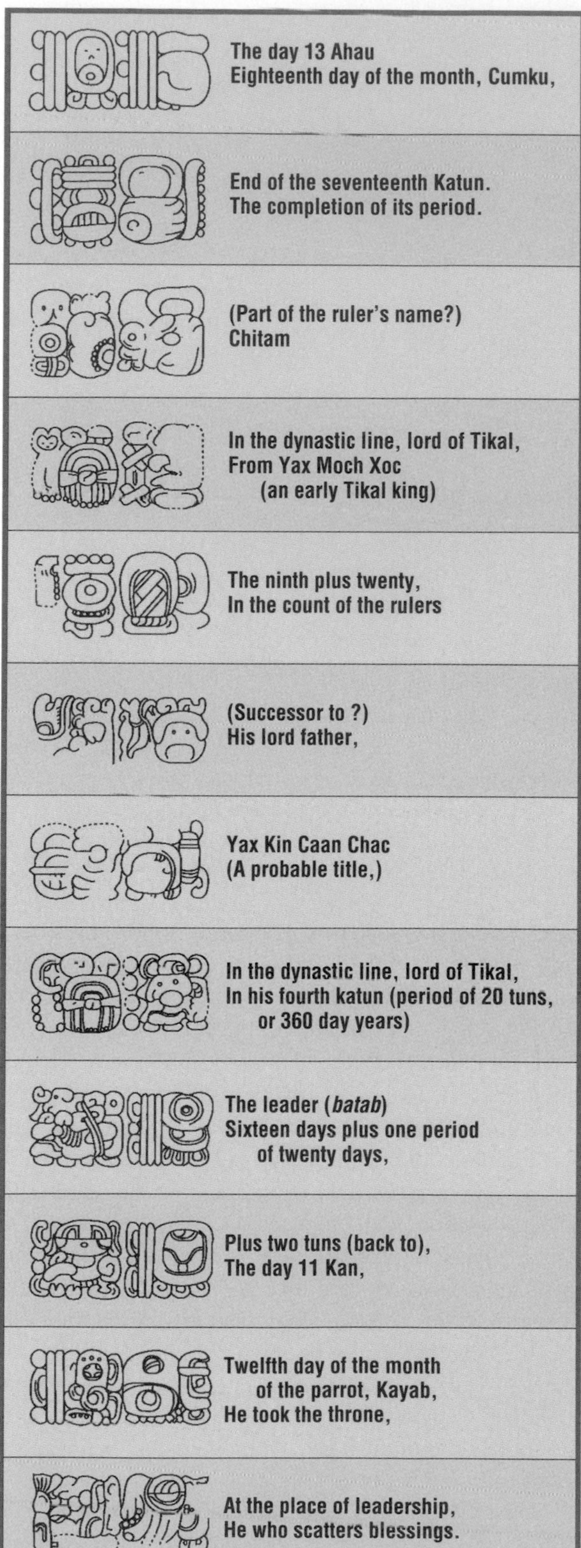

that was very efficient at every level. Teotihuacan was probably of this sort, but the government of the Inca civilization is better known.

The Inca empire of Peru reached its zenith 500 years ago, just before the arrival of the Spanish. In the mid-1400s A.D., the Inca kingdom probably did not extend more than 20 miles beyond the modern-day city of Cuzco, which was then its center. Within a 30-year period, in the late 1400s, the Inca kingdom enlarged a thousand times its original size. By A.D. 1525, it stretched 2,500 miles from north to south and 500 miles from east to west, making it at the time the greatest empire on the face of the earth. Its population numbered in the millions, composed of people of various ethnic groups. In the achievements of its governmental and political system, Inca civilization surpassed every other civilization of the New World and most of those of the Old World. At the head of the government was the emperor, regarded as semi-divine, followed by the royal family, the aristocracy, imperial administrators, the lower nobility, and the masses of artisans, craftspeople, and farmers.

The empire was divided into four administrative regions, further subdivided into provinces, and so on down to villages and families. Planting, irrigation, and harvesting were closely supervised by government agricultural and tax officials. Teams of professional relay runners could carry messages up to 250 miles in a single day over a network of roads and bridges that remains impressive even today. The Inca are unusual in that they had no writing that we know about; public records and historical chronicles were kept in the form of an ingenious system of colored beads, knots, and ropes.

Social Stratification

The rise of large, economically diversified populations presided over by centralized governing authorities brought with it the fourth culture change characteristic of civilization: social stratification, or the emergence of social classes. Thus, we note that symbols of special status and privilege appeared in the ancient cities of Mesopotamia,

FIGURE 12.4

THE TRANSLATION OF THE TEXT ON THE MONUMENT SHOWN ON P. 308 GIVES SOME INDICATION OF THE IMPORTANCE OF DYNASTIC GENEALOGY TO MAYA RULERS. THE "SCATTERING" MENTIONED MAY REFER TO BLOODLETTING AS PART OF THE CEREMONIES ASSOCIATED WITH THE END OF ONE 20-YEAR PERIOD, OR KATUN, AND THE BEGINNING OF THE NEXT.

and people were ranked according to the kind of work they did or the family into which they were born.

People who stood at or near the head of government were the earliest holders of high status. Although economic specialists of one sort or another—metal workers, tanners, traders, or the like—generally outranked farmers, such specialization did not necessarily bring with it high status. Rather, people engaged in economic activity were either of the lower class or outcasts.[9] The exception was those merchants who were in a position to buy their way into some kind of higher class. With time, the possession of wealth and the influence it could buy became in itself a requisite for high status.

EVIDENCE OF SOCIAL STRATIFICATION

How do archaeologists know that there were different social classes in ancient civilizations? One way they are revealed is by burial customs. Graves excavated at early Neolithic sites are mostly simple pits dug in the ground, containing few, if any, grave goods. Grave goods consist of things such as utensils, figurines, and personal possessions, which are placed in the grave in order that the dead person might use them in the afterlife. The lack of much variation between burials in terms of the wealth implied by grave goods in Neolithic sites indicates an essentially classless society. Graves excavated in civilizations, by contrast, vary widely in size, mode of burial, and the number and variety of grave goods. This indicates a stratified society—one divided into social classes. The graves of important persons contain not only a great variety of artifacts made from precious materials, but sometimes, as in some early Egyptian burials, even the remains of servants evidently killed to serve their master in the afterlife. The skeletons from the burials may also give evidence of stratification. At Tikal, skeletons from elaborate tombs indicate that the subjects of these tombs had longer life expectancy, ate better food, and enjoyed better health than the bulk of that city's population. In stratified societies, the elite usually live longer, eat better, and enjoy an easier life than other members of society.

As an example of what upper-class burials may look like, and what more they can tell us about the customs of the people placed in them, we may look at a spectacular tomb from one of the civilizations that preceded that of the Incas in Peru.

[9]Sjoberg, G. (1960). *The preindustrial city* (p. 325). New York: Free Press.

Finding the Tomb of a Moche Priestess[10]

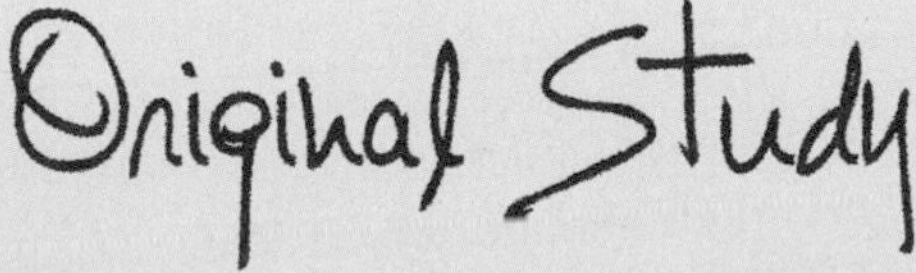

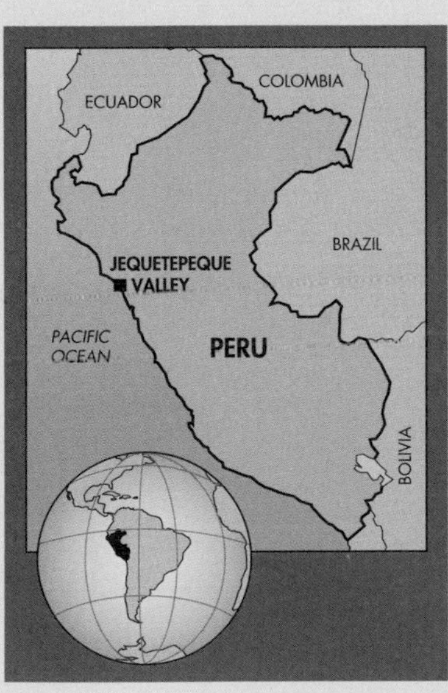

The Moche kingdom flourished on the north coast of Peru between A.D. 100 and 800. Although the Moche had no writing system, they left a vivid artistic record of their beliefs and activities on beautifully modeled and painted ceramic vessels. Because of the realism and detail of these depictions, we are able to reconstruct various aspects of Moche society such as religious ceremonies and mythology, as well as activities like hunting, weaving, and combat rarely preserved in the archaeological record.

During the past 20 years we have developed a major photographic archive of Moche art at the University of California, Los Angeles, which serves as an important resource for the study of their culture. Our goal has been to reconstruct aspects of Moche culture by combining systematic studies of their art with archaeological fieldwork in Peru. Our

[10]Donnan, C. B., & Castillo, L. J. (1992). Finding the tomb of a Moche priestess. *Archaeology, 45*(6), 38–42.

Original Study

analyses of sites, including residential compounds, palaces, temples, and cemeteries, and the artifacts associated with them have allowed us to document archaeologically some of the complex scenes illustrated in Moche art, and to understand aspects of their culture that are not portrayed in the art.

During the past 10 years our research has focused on the Jequetepeque Valley, located in the northern portion of the territory occupied by the Moche. In this region we have undertaken several lines of research, concentrating our efforts on the relationship between Moche ceremonial activities and socio-economic organization. In June 1991, UCLA began excavations at San José de Moro, a major ceremonial center in the lower Jequetepeque Valley. It was clear from its various ceramic styles that the site had a long history of occupation and thus would be ideal for answering questions about the cultural sequence of the region. Moreover, the quantity and variation in monumental construction at the site strongly suggested that it had served as a major ceremonial center through most of its occupation and thus could provide us with good insights about the nature of Moche ceremonial activity.

During our first field season we excavated three complex late-Moche tombs—each consisting of a room-sized burial chamber made of mud bricks. The tomb chambers had originally been roofed with large wooden beams. The principal occupant of each tomb was lying face up in an extended position, with the remains of complete llamas, humans, or both, at their feet. In two of the tombs the principal occupants were flanked by other individuals. Hundreds of ceramic vessels and metal objects, including ceremonial knives, lance points, sandals, cups, masks, and jewelry, had been placed in the tombs as offerings.

The most elaborate of the three tombs was that of a high-status adult female. It is the richest Moche female burial ever scientifically excavated and clearly demonstrates that in Moche society extraordinary wealth and power were not the exclusive domain of males. The tomb chamber was approximately 7-$^{1}/_{2}$ by 14 feet. The walls, which were made of mud brick, had niches—six on each side and four at the head of the tomb—in which ceramic vessels and parts of llamas had been placed. Additional ceramic vessels had been stacked on the floor of the tomb chamber.

Some of the artifacts associated with this burial provide clear evidence that the Moche were involved in long-distance trade and that their elite

A silver-copper alloy mask (left) was found near the priestess' skull. Her body (right) was covered with hammered metal arms and legs.

The Moche Sacrifice Ceremony

The Sacrifice Ceremony, an event at which prisoners of war are sacrificed and their blood ritually consumed, is a common iconographic theme in Moche art. One of the better-known representations of this ceremony appears on a stirrup spout bottle. The scene, center, shows four principal figures and attendants. Below them are bound captives having their throats slashed. During recent excavations at San José de Moro and at Sipán, the remains of several people who participated in this ceremony have been identified. Figure C, a priestess, was discovered at San José de Moro, while Figure A, a warrior-priest, and Figure B, a bird-warrior, were excavated at Sipán.

A goblet, recovered during the excavation of the priestess's tomb at San José de Moro, is decorated with a scene of anthropomorphic war clubs and shields drinking the blood of captives from tall goblets. A similar goblet is being passed between Figure A and Figure B in the drawing below.

Silver-copper alloy tassels worn by the principal occupant of the tomb allowed her to be identified as the priestess depicted in the Sacrifice Ceremony. The tassels are identical to those worn by Figure C in both the drawing and the Pañamarca mural, bottom.

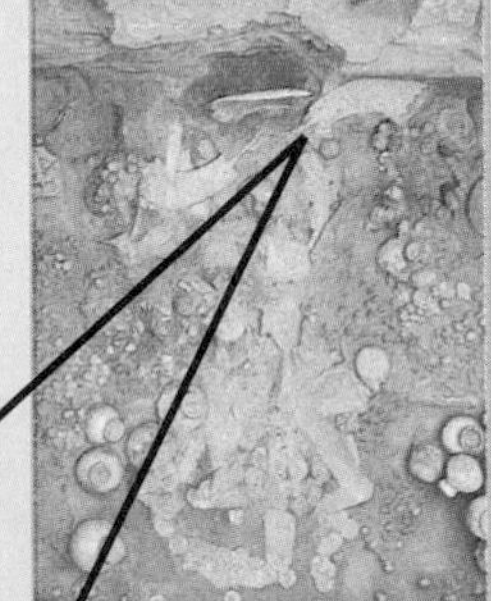

The Pañamarca mural, right, painted on an adobe wall at a Moche ceremonial center in the Nepeña Valley, shows Figure C accompanied by several attendants bearing goblets. Pictured too are three bound captives with their throats slashed and a ceramic basin containing cups. A similar basin, below, was found in the priestess's tomb.

Original Study

expended a great deal of effort to obtain precious materials. Included among the offerings were three imported ceramic vessels—a plate of Cajamarca style, which must have been brought to San José de Moro from the highland area located more than 70 miles to the east, and two exotic ceramic bottles of Nieveria style, a type of pottery that was made in the area of Lima, more than 350 miles to the south. Two other kinds of materials associated with the tomb provide further evidence of long-distance trade. Over the woman's chest and hands were *Spondylus princeps* shells that had been brought from Ecuador to the north, and around her neck were cylindrical beads of lapis lazuli that had been brought from Chile to the south.

The most remarkable aspect of this woman's tomb, however, was that the objects buried with her allow us to identify her as a specific priestess who is depicted in Moche art. This priestess was first identified in the Moche Archive at UCLA in 1975, at which time she was given the name "Figure C." Five years later, Anne Marie Hocquenghem and Patricia Lyon convincingly demonstrated that this individual was female. She was one of the principal participants in the "Sacrifice Ceremony," an event depicted in Moche art where prisoners of war were sacrificed and their blood ritually consumed in tall ceremonial goblets.

Figure C is always depicted with her hair in wrapped braids that hang across her chest, and wearing a long dresslike garment. Also characteristic of Figure C is her headdress, which is unique in having two prominent tassels. The tomb of the woman at San José de Moro contained an identical headdress with two huge tassels made of a silver copper alloy.

In one corner of the tomb was a large blackware ceramic basin containing cups and a tall goblet. An identical blackware basin with cups in it is shown associated with Figure C in a famous mural at the site of Pañamarca, a ceremonial center located in the Nepeña Valley. Furthermore, the tall goblet contained in the ceramic basin was of the type used in the Sacrifice Ceremony. It is decorated with a scene of anthropomorphized clubs and shields drinking blood from similar goblets. The tall goblet is a prominent feature in all depictions of the Sacrifice Ceremony, and it is often seen being presented by Figure C. Finding the tall goblet in her grave thus supports her identification as Figure C.

The tomb of Figure C at San José de Moro has profound implications for Moche studies. Excavations by Walter Alva at Sipán, located in a valley to the north of San José de Moro, have revealed the tombs of two other participants, Figure A and Figure B, in the Sacrifice Ceremony. The richest of these tombs is that of the Lord of Sipán, Figure A. He was buried with his characteristic crescent-shaped headdress, crescent-shaped nose ornament, large circular ear ornaments, and warrior's backflap, and was holding a rattle like that shown in representations of Figure A. The occupant of another tomb appears to be Figure B, a bird-warrior who is frequently shown as companion to Figure A. He was found wearing a headdress adorned with an owl. Although no grave of Figure C has yet been excavated at Sipán, it seems likely that someone who performed this role was also buried at that site.

How do the tombs at Sipán relate to the tomb of Figure C at San José de Moro? First, it should be noted that the two tombs at Sipán date to approximately A.D. 300, and those at San José de Moro at least 250 years later—sometime after A.D. 550. Clearly, the Sacrifice Ceremony had a long duration in Moche culture, with individuals consistently dressing in traditional garments and headdresses to perform the roles of specific members of the priesthood.

The Sacrifice Ceremony was also widespread geographically. The Pañamarca mural, which clearly depicts this ceremony, was found in the Nepeña Valley, in the southern part of the Moche kingdom. San José de Moro is more than 150 miles to the north of Pañamarca, and Sipán is another 40 miles further north. Moreover, in the 1960s rich tombs containing artifacts with Sacrifice Ceremony iconography were looted from the site of Loma Negra in the Piura Valley, more than 300 miles north of Pañamarca.

The four sites where evidence of the Sacrifice Ceremony has been found have certain characteristics in common. Each is located on an elevated area that rises naturally above the intensively cultivated valley floor and is near, but not immediately adjacent to, a river. Each was a major ceremonial complex, with multiple pyramids that for centuries served as staging areas for religious activities. Perhaps each of the other river valleys that made up the Moche kingdom also had a central ceremonial precinct where the Sacrifice Ceremony was enacted.

The fact that the Sacrifice Ceremony was so widespread in both time and space strongly implies that it was part of a state religion, with a priesthood in each part of the kingdom comprised of individuals who dressed in prescribed ritual attire. When members of the priesthood died, they were buried at the temple where the Sacrifice Ceremony took place, wearing their ceremonial paraphernalia and accompanied by the objects they had used to perform the ritual. Subsequently, other men and women were chosen to replace them, to dress like them, and to perform the same ceremonial role.

The careful excavation of the tomb of Figure C at San José de Moro has provided important new insights into the nature of Moche religious practices. As our excavations continue at this remarkable site, we expect to find additional archaeological evidence that will refine and improve upon these insights.

The End

In addition to burials, there are three other ways by which archaeologists may recognize the stratified nature of ancient civilizations:

1. The Size of Dwellings In early Neolithic sites, dwellings tended to be uniformly small in size. Even at Çatalhöyük, there was little difference in size between houses. In the oldest excavated cities, however, some dwellings were notably larger than others, well spaced, and located together in one district, whereas dwellings in other parts of the city were much smaller, sometimes little more than hovels. In the city of Eshnunna in Mesopotamia, archaeologists excavated houses that occupied an area of 200 meters situated on main thoroughfares and huts of but 50 meters located along narrow back alleys. The rooms in the larger houses often contained impressive artwork, such as friezes or murals. At Tikal, and other Maya cities, the elite lived in large, multiroomed, masonry houses, mostly in the city's center, whereas lower-class people lived in small, peripherally scattered houses of one or two rooms, built partly or wholly of pole and thatch materials.

2. Written Documents Preserved records of business transactions, royal chronicles, or law codes of a civilization reveal much about the social status of its inhabitants. Babylonian and Assyrian texts reveal three main social classes—aristocrats, commoners, and slaves. The members of each class had different rights and privileges. This stratification was clearly reflected by the law. If an aristocrat put out another's eye, then that person's eye was to be put out too; hence, the saying "an eye for an eye." If the aristocrat broke another's bone, then the first aristocrat's bone was to be broken in return. If the aristocrat put out the eye or broke the bone of a commoner, however, the punishment was to pay a mina of silver.[11]

Even in the absence of written information, people may record much about their society in other ways. As the Original Study demonstrates, the Moche recorded much information about their society in their art. The stratified nature of this ancient society is clearly revealed by the scenes painted on ceramic vessels.

3. Correspondence European documents describing the aboriginal cultures of the New World as seen by early European explorers and adventurers also offer evidence of social stratification. Letters written by the Spanish conquistadors about the Aztec empire indicate that they found a social order divided into three main classes: nobles, commoners, and serfs. The nobles operated outside the lineage system on the basis of land and serfs allotted them by the ruler from conquered peoples. The commoners were divided into lineages, on which they were dependent for land. Within each of these, individual status depended on the degree of descent from the founder; those more closely related to the lineage founder had higher status than those whose kinship was more distant. The third class in Aztec society consisted of serfs bound to the land and porters employed as carriers by

[11]Moseati, S. (1962). *The face of the ancient orient* (p. 90). New York: Doubleday.

This "palace," which housed members of Tikal's ruling dynasty, may be compared with the lower-class house in the photo below.

merchants. Lowest of this class were the slaves. Some had voluntarily sold themselves into bondage; others were captives taken in war.

Informative though accounts of other civilizations by Europeans may be, they are not without their problems. For example, the explorers, missionaries, and others did not always understand what they saw; moreover, they had their own interests (or those of their sponsors) to look out for, and were not above falsifying information to further those interests. These points are of major importance, given the tendency of Western peoples, with their tradition of literacy, to assume that written documents are reliable. In fact, they are not always reliable, and must be checked for accuracy against other sources of information. The same is true of ancient documents written by other people about themselves, for they, too, had their particular agendas. Ancient Maya inscriptions, for example, were often propagandistic in their intent, which was to impress people with particular rulers' importance.

THE MAKING OF CIVILIZATION

From Mesopotamia to China to the South American Andes, we witness the enduring achievements of the human intellect: magnificent palaces built high above ground; sculptures so perfect as to be unrivaled by those of contemporary artists; engineering projects so vast and daring as to awaken in us a sense of wonder. Looking back to the beginnings of written history, we can see a point at which humans transform themselves into "civilized" beings; they begin to live in cities and to expand the scope of their achievements at a rapid pace. How is it, then, that humans at a certain moment in history became consummate builders, harnessing mighty rivers so that they could irrigate crops, developing a system whereby their thoughts could be preserved in writing? The fascinating subject of the development of civilization has occupied the minds of philosophers and anthropologists alike for a long time. We do not yet have the answers, but a number of theories have been proposed.

Lower-class residents of Tikal lived in the same sort of houses in which most Maya live today.

Theories of Civilization's Emergence

Each of the theories sees the appearance of centralized government as the point at which there is no longer any question whether or not a civilization exists. So, the question they pose is: What brought about the appearance of a centralized government? Or, stated another way: What caused the transition from a small, egalitarian farming village to a large urban center in which population density, social inequality, and diversity of labor required a centralized government?

IRRIGATION SYSTEMS

One popular theory concerning the emergence of civilization was given its most forceful statement by Karl Wittfogel[12], and variants of this theory are still held by some anthropologists. Simply put, the irrigation or **hydraulic theory,** holds that Neolithic farmers in ancient Mesopotamia and Egypt, and later in the Americas, noticed that the river valleys that were periodically flooded contained better soils than those that were not; but they also noted that violent floods destroyed their planted fields and turned them into swamps. So the farmers built dikes and reservoirs to collect the floodwater and save it until it was needed. Then they released it into canals and ran it over the fields. At first, these dikes and canals, built by small groups of neighboring farmers, were very simple. The success of this measure led to larger, more complex irrigation systems, which eventually necessitated the emergence of a group of "specialists"—people whose sole responsibility was managing the irrigation system. The centralized effort to control the irrigation process blossomed into the first governing body and elite social class, and civilization was born.

There are several objections to this theory. One of them is that some of the earliest large-scale irrigation systems we know about anywhere in the world developed in highland New Guinea, where strong centralized governments never emerged. Conversely, actual field studies of ancient Mesopotamian irrigation systems reveal that by 4,000 years ago, by which time many cities had already flourished, irrigation was still carried out on a small scale, consisting of small canals and diversions of natural waterways. If there were state-managed irrigation, it is argued, such a system would have been far more extensive than excavations show it really was. Moreover, documents indicate that irrigation was regulated by officials of local temples and not by centralized government. The oldest irrigation system in the Americas is at Caral, in the coastal desert of Peru. By 4,600 years ago, a shallow channel had been cut to a river, where a simple headgate controlled the flow. The system was far simpler than later irrigation works in Peru, and one can argue here, as elsewhere in South America and Mesoamerica, that large-scale irrigation works were a consequence of civilization's development, rather than a cause.

TRADE NETWORKS

Some anthropologists argue that trade was a decisive factor in the development of civilizations. In regions of ecological diversity, so the argument goes, trade mechanisms are necessary to procure scarce resources. In Mexico, for example, maize was grown just about everywhere; but chilis were grown in the highlands, cotton and beans were planted at intermediate elevations, certain animals were found only in the river valleys, and salt was obtained along the coasts.

This theory holds that some form of centralized authority was necessary in order to organize trade for the procurement of these and other commodities. Once procured, some system was necessary in order to redistribute commodities throughout the population. Redistribution, like procurement, must have required a centralized authority, promoting the growth of a centralized government.

Although trade may have played an important role in the development of some civilizations, it did not invariably do so. For example, the native peoples of northeastern North America traded widely with one another for at least 6,000 years without developing civilizations comparable to those of Mexico or Peru. In the course of this trade, copper from deposits around Lake Superior wound up in such faraway places as New England, as did chert from Labrador and marine shells from the Gulf of Mexico. Wampum, made on the shores of Long Island

[12]Wittfogel, K. A. (1957). *Oriental despotism, a comparative study of total power.* New Haven, CT: Yale University Press.

Hydraulic theory. The theory that sees civilization's emergence as the result of the construction of elaborate irrigation systems, the functioning of which required full-time managers whose control blossomed into the first governing body and elite social class.

Sound, was carried westward, and obsidian from the Yellowstone region has been found in mounds in Ohio.[13]

ENVIRONMENTAL AND SOCIAL CIRCUMSCRIPTION

In a series of papers, Robert Carneiro[14] has advanced the theory that civilization develops where populations are hemmed in by such things as mountains, seas, or other human populations. As such populations grow, they have no space in which to expand, and so they begin to compete for increasingly scarce resources. Internally, this results in the development of social stratification, in which an elite controls important resources to which lower classes have limited access. Externally, this leads to warfare and conquest, which, to be successful, require elaborate organization under a centralized authority.

RELIGION

The three theories just summarized exemplify ecological approaches to explaining the development of civilization. Such theories emphasize the interrelation between people and what they do on the one hand and the environment in which they live on the other. Theories of the emergence of civilization have commonly taken some such approach. Although few anthropologists would deny the importance of the human-environment interrelationship, a growing number of them are dissatisfied with theories that do not take into account the beliefs and values that regulate the interaction between people and their environment.[15]

An example of a theory that does take into account the role of beliefs is one that seeks to explain the emergence of Maya civilization in Mesoamerica.[16] This theory holds that Maya civilization was the result of a process of urbanization that occurred at places like Tikal. In the case study on Tikal earlier in this chapter, it is suggested that Maya religion probably developed initially as a means of coping with the uncertainties of agriculture. In its early days, Tikal seems to have been an important religious center. Because of its religious importance, people sought to settle there, with the result that its population grew in size and density. A similar process may be seen at Çatalhöyük. As noted early in this chapter, this village was located so as to be near sources of lime-rich clay. This material was required to plaster the walls of houses, the medium for paintings and other art of apparently ritual significance. This seems to have been of such importance as to take precedence over convenient proximity to agricultural fields. Perhaps the inconvenience of having to travel so far to get to one's fields was a reason that Çatalhöyük never developed into a true city.

At Tikal, by contrast, the process went further. Because the concentration of a growing population was incompatible with the prevailing slash-and-burn agriculture, which tends to promote dispersed settlement, new subsistence techniques—such as raised fields—were developed. By chance, these were sufficiently productive to permit further population growth, and, by 1,500 years ago, Tikal had become an urban settlement of at least 50,000 people. By then, craft specialization had developed, at first in the service of religion but soon in the service of an emerging social elite as well. This social elite was concerned at first with calendrical ritual, but through the control of ritual it developed into the centralized governing elite that could control a population growing larger and more diversified in its interests.

Developing craft specialization itself served as another factor to pull people into Tikal, where their products were in demand. It also required further development of trade networks, if only to provide exotic raw materials. More long-distance trade contacts, of course, brought more contact with outside ideas, including some from as far afield as Teotihuacan. In other words, what we seem to have is a complex system with several factors—religious, economic, and political—acting to reinforce one another, with religion playing a central role in getting the system started in the first place.

A criticism that may be leveled at all of the above theories is that they fail to recognize the capacity of aggressive, charismatic leaders to shape the course of human history. Accordingly, anthropologists Joyce Marcus and Kent Flannery have developed what they call **action theory.**[17] This recognizes the systemic nature of

[13]Haviland, W. A., & Power, M. W. (1994). *The original Vermonters* (2nd ed., Chap. 3 & 4). Hanover, NH: University Press of New England.

[14]Carneiro, R. L. (1970). A theory of the origin of the state. *Science, 169,* 733–738.

[15]Adams, R. M. (2001). Scale and complexity in archaic states. *Latin American Antiquity, 11,* 188.

[16]Haviland, W. A. (1975). The ancient Maya and the evolution of urban society. *University of Colorado Museum of Anthropology, Miscellaneous Series,* no. 37.

[17]Marcus, J., & Flannery, K. V. (1996). *Zapotec civilization: How urban society evolved in Mexico's Oaxaca Valley.* New York: Thames & Hudson.

Action theory. The theory that self-serving actions by forceful leaders play a role in civilization's emergence.

At Çatalhöyük as at Tikal, religion seems to have been the initial impetus for nucleation. Here we see a reproduction of some wall paintings from Çatalhöyük. The site was located near the source of the material used for the wall plaster.

society and the impact of the environment in shaping social and cultural behavior but recognizes as well that forceful leaders in any society strive to advance their material or political positions through self-serving actions. In so doing, they may create change. Applying this to the Maya, for example, local leaders, who once relied on personal charisma for the economic and political support needed to sustain them in their positions, may have seized upon religion to solidify their grip on power. They did this by developing an ideology endowing them and their descendants with supernatural ancestry. Only they were seen as having the kind of access to the gods on which their followers depended. In this case, the nature of the existing system presented a situation in which certain individuals could monopolize power and emerge as divine kings, using their power to subjugate any rivals.

As the above example makes clear, the context in which a forceful leader operates is critical. In the case of the Maya, it was the combination of existing cultural and ecological factors that opened the way for emergence of political dynasties. Thus, explanations of civilization's emergence are likely to involve multiple causes, rather than just one. Furthermore, we may also have the cultural equivalent of what biologists call *convergence,* where somewhat similar forms come about in quite different ways. Consequently, a theory that accounts for the rise of civilization in one place may not account for its rise in another.

This mosaic death mask of greenstone, pyrite, and shell was worn by a king of the Maya city of Tikal who died about A.D. 527. Obviously the product of skilled craft work, such specialization developed first to serve the needs of religion, but soon served the needs of an emerging elite as well.

CIVILIZATION AND ITS DISCONTENTS

Living in the context of civilization ourselves, we are inclined to view its development as a great step upward on some sort of ladder of progress. Whatever benefits civilization has brought, though, the cultural changes it represents produced new sorts of problems. Among them is the problem of waste disposal. Actually, waste disposal probably began to be a problem in settled, farming communities even before the emergence of civilization. But as villages grew into towns and towns grew into cities, the problem became far more serious, as the buildup of garbage and sewage created optimum environments for such diseases as bubonic plague and typhoid. The latter is an intestinal disease caused by a *Salmonella* bacterium. In northern Europeans, mutation of a gene on Chromosome 7 that deletes 3 DNA bases (out of the gene's total of 250,000) makes carriers of this allele virtually immune to typhoid and other bacterial diarrheas.[18] Because of the mortality imposed by these diseases, selection favored spread of the allele among northern Europeans. But as with sickle-cell anemia, protection comes at a price. That price is cystic fibrosis, a usually fatal disease of the lungs and intestines contracted by those who are homozygous for the altered gene.

Unlike most ancient cities, Mohenjo-Daro, a 4,000-year-old metropolis in the Indus River Valley, had an extensive system of drains. Lack of adequate drains in cities contributed to poor public health.

Quite apart from sanitation problems and their attendant diseases, the rise of towns and cities brought with it a problem of acute, infectious diseases. In a small population, such diseases as chicken pox, influenza, measles, mumps, pertussis, polio, rubella, and smallpox will kill or immunize so high a proportion of the population that the virus cannot continue to propagate. Measles, for example, is likely to die out in any human population with fewer than half a million people.[19] Hence, such diseases, when introduced into small communities, spread immediately to the whole population and then die out. Their continued existence depends upon the presence of large population aggregates, such as towns and cities provide.

Another disease that became a serious problem in towns and cities (and is becoming so again in the 21st century) is tuberculosis. And here again it has triggered a genetic response not unlike what we have seen in response to malaria (sickle cell and other abnormal hemoglobins) and bacterial diarrheas (the cystic fibrosis gene). Among the Ashkenazi Jews of eastern Europe, a genetic variant that causes Tay-Sachs disease in homozygotes became comparatively common. Crammed into urban ghettos over several centuries, the Ashkenazim were especially exposed to tuberculosis, but those individuals heterozygous for the Tay-Sachs allele were protected from this disease.[20]

In essence, early cities tended to be disease-ridden places, with relatively high death rates. At Teotihuacan, for instance, very high infant and child mortality rates set a limit to the city's growth. Not until relatively recent times did public health measures reduce the risk of

---

[18]Ridley, M. (1999). *Genome, the autobiography of a species in 23 chapters* (p. 142). New York: HarperCollins.

[19]Diamond, J. (1997). *Guns, germs and steel* (p. 203). New York: Norton.

[20]Ridley, p. 191.

living in cities, and had it not been for a constant influx of rural peoples, they would have been hard pressed to maintain their population size, let alone increase it. Europe's urban population, for example, did not become self-sustaining until early in the 20th century.[21] One might wonder, then, what would have led people to go live in such unhealthy places? The answer is, they were attracted by the same sorts of things that lure people to cities today: They are vibrant, exciting places that also provide people with opportunities not available in rural communities. Of course, their experience in the cities did not always live up to advance expectations, any more than is true today.

In addition to health problems, early cities faced social problems strikingly similar to those found in modern North America. Dense population, class systems, and a strong centralized government created internal stress. The slaves and the poor saw that the wealthy had all the things that they themselves lacked. It was not just a question of luxury items; the poor did not have enough food nor space in which to live with comfort and dignity.

Evidence of warfare in early civilizations is common. Cities were fortified; documents list many battles, raids, and wars between groups; cylinder seals, paintings, and sculpture depict battle scenes, victorious kings, and captured prisoners of war. Increasing population and the accompanying scarcity of good farming land often led to boundary disputes and quarrels over land between civilized states or between so-called tribal peoples and a state. Open warfare often developed. People tended to crowd into walled cities for protection and to be near irrigation systems.

The class system also caused internal stress. As time went on, the rich became richer and the poor poorer. In early civilizations one's place in society was relatively fixed. Wealth was based on free labor from slaves. For this reason there was little or no impetus for social reform. Records from the Mesopotamian city of Lagash indicate that social unrest due to exploitation of the poor by the rich grew during this period. Members of the upper class received tracts of farmland some 20 times larger than those granted the lower class. An upper-class reformer, Urukaginal saw the danger and introduced changes to protect the poor from exploitation by the wealthy, thus preserving the stability of the city.

Signs of warfare are common in ancient civilizations. China's first emperor wanted his army to remain with him—in the form of 7,000 life-sized terra-cotta figures of warriors.

Given the problems associated with civilization, it is perhaps not surprising that a recurring phenomenon is their collapse. Nonetheless, the rise of cities and civilization laid the basis for modern life. It is discouraging to note that many of the problems associated with the first civilizations are still with us. Waste disposal, pollution-related health problems, crowding, social inequities, and warfare continue to be serious problems. Through the study of past civilizations, we now stand a chance of understanding why such problems persist. Such an understanding will be required if the problems are ever to be overcome. It would be nice if the next cultural revolution saw the human species transcending these problems. If this comes about, anthropology, through its comparative study of civilizations, will have played a key role.

[21]Diamond, p. 205.

CHAPTER SUMMARY

The world's first cities grew out of Neolithic villages between 6,000 and 4,500 years ago, first in Mesopotamia, then in Egypt and the Indus Valley. In China, the process was under way by 5,000 years ago. Somewhat later, and completely independently, similar changes took place in Mesoamerica and Peru. Four basic culture changes mark the transition from Neolithic village life to life in civilized urban centers. The first culture change is agricultural innovation as new farming methods were developed. For example, the ancient Sumerians built an irrigation system that enabled them to control their water resources and thus increase crop yields.

The second culture change is diversification of labor. With the growth of large populations in cities, some people could provide sufficient food for others to devote themselves fully to specialization as artisans and craftspeople. With specialization came the development of new technologies, leading to the beginnings of extensive trade systems. An outgrowth of technological innovation and increased contact with foreign people through trade was new knowledge; within the early civilizations sciences such as geometry and astronomy were first developed.

The third culture change that characterized urban life is the emergence of central government with authority to deal with the complex problems associated with cities. Evidence of a central governing authority comes from such sources as law codes, temple records, and royal chronicles. With the invention of writing, governments could keep records of their transactions and/or boast of their own power and glory. Further evidence of centralized government comes from monumental public structures and signs of centralized planning.

Typically, the first cities were headed by a king and his special advisors. The reign of the Babylonian King Hammurabi, sometime between 1950 and 1700 B.C., is well known for its efficient government organization and the standardization of its legal system. In the New World the Inca empire in Peru reached its culmination 500 years ago. With a population of several million people, the Inca state, headed by an emperor, possessed a widespread governing bureaucracy that functioned with great efficiency at every level.

The fourth culture change characteristic of civilization is social stratification, or the emergence of social classes. In the early cities of Mesopotamia, symbols of status and privilege appeared for the first time, and individuals were ranked according to the work they did or the position of their families. Archaeologists have been able to verify the existence of social classes in ancient civilizations in four ways: by studying burial customs, as well as skeletons, through grave excavations; by noting the size of dwellings in excavated cities; by examining preserved records in writing and art; and by studying the correspondence of Europeans who described the great civilizations that they destroyed in the New World.

A number of theories have been proposed to explain why civilizations developed. The hydraulic theory holds that the effort to build and control an irrigation system required a degree of social organization that eventually led to civilization. There are several objections to this theory, however. One might argue simply that sophisticated irrigation systems were a result of the development of civilization rather than a cause. Another theory suggests that in the multicrop economies of both the Old and New Worlds, some kind of system was needed to distribute the various food products throughout the population. Such a procedure would have required a centralized authority, leading to the emergence of a centralized government. A third theory holds that civilization develops where populations are circumscribed by environmental barriers or other societies. As such populations grow, competition for space and scarce resources leads to the development of centralized authority to control resources and organize warfare.

These theories all emphasize the interrelation of people and what they do on the one hand and the environment in which they live on the other. A theory that lays greater stress on the beliefs and values that regulate the interaction between people and their environment seeks to explain the emergence of Maya civilization in terms of the role religion may have played in keeping the Maya in and about cities like Tikal. Finally, action theory focuses attention on the actions of forceful leaders, whose efforts to promote their own interests may play a role in social change. Probably, several factors acted together, rather than singly, to bring about civilization's rise.

Sanitation problems in early cities, coupled with large numbers of people living in close proximity, created environments in which infectious diseases were rampant. Early urban centers also faced social problems strikingly similar to our own. Dense population, class systems, and a strong centralized government created internal stress. Warfare was common; cities were fortified, and armies served to protect the state. Nevertheless, a recurrent phenomenon in all civilizations has been their ultimate collapse.

CLASSIC READINGS

Diamond, J. (1997). *Guns, germs and steel.* New York: Norton.

Also recommended in the last chapter, this book has an excellent discussion of the relation among diseases, social complexity, and social change.

Marcus, J., & Flannery, K. V. (1996). *Zapote civilization: How urban society evolved in Mexico's Oaxaca Valley.* New York: Thames & Hudson.

With its lavish illustrations, this looks like a book for coffee table adornment, but it is in fact a thoughtful and serious work on the rise of a pristine civilization. In it, the authors present their action theory.

Meltzer, D., Fowler, D., & Sabloff, J. (Eds.). (1986). *American archaeology: Past and future.* Washington, DC: Smithsonian Institution Press.

This collection of articles contains one by Henry Wright, "The Evolution of Civilization," an excellent comparative consideration of the subject.

Pfeiffer, J. E. (1977). *The emergence of society.* New York: McGraw-Hill.

This is a comprehensive survey of the origins of food production and the world's first cities. In order to write the book, the author traveled to archaeological sites throughout the world and consulted with numerous investigators. The book is notable for its readability.

Redman, C. E. (1978). *The rise of civilization: From early farmers to urban society in the ancient Near East.* San Francisco: Freeman.

One of the best-documented examples of the rise of urban societies is that of Greater Mesopotamia in the Middle East. This clearly written textbook focuses on that development, presenting the data, discussing interpretations of those data, as well as problems.

Sabloff, J. A. (1997). *The cities of ancient Mexico* (Rev. ed.). New York: Thames & Hudson.

This well-written and lavishly illustrated book describes the major cities of the Olmecs, Zapotecs, Maya, Teotihuacanos, Toltecs, and Aztecs. Following the descriptions, Sabloff discusses the question of origins, the problems of archaeological reconstruction, and the basis on which he provides vignettes of life in the ancient cities. The book concludes with a gazetteer of 50 sites in Mesoamerica.

Sabloff, J. A., & Lamberg-Karlovsky, C. C. (Eds.). (1974). *The rise and fall of civilizations, modern archaeological approaches to ancient cultures.* Menlo Park, CA: Cummings.

The emphasis in this collection of articles is theoretical or methodological rather than purely descriptive. Special emphasis is on Mesopotamia and Mesoamerica, but papers are included on Peru, Egypt, the Indus Valley, China, and Europe.

CHAPTER 13

MODERN HUMAN DIVERSITY

One of the notable characteristics of the human species today is its great variability. Human diversity has long fascinated people, but unfortunately, it also has led to discrimination and even bloodshed.

CHAPTER PREVIEW

1 What Are the Causes of Physical Variability in Modern Animals?

In a species like *Homo sapiens,* there are various alleles for any given physical characteristic. When such a species is divided into geographically dispersed populations, forces such as drift and natural selection cause the store of genetic variability to be unevenly expressed. For example, alleles for dark skin are found in high frequency in human populations native to regions of heavy ultraviolet radiation, whereas alleles for light skin have a high incidence in populations native to regions of reduced ultraviolet radiation.

2 Is the Concept of Race Useful for Studying Human Physical Variation?

No. Because races are arbitrarily defined, it is impossible to agree on any specific classification. The problem is compounded by the tendency for "racial" characteristics to occur in gradations from one population to another without sharp breaks. Furthermore, because genes are assorted independently of one another, one characteristic may be distributed in a north-south gradient while another may occur in an east-west gradient. For these and other reasons, most anthropologists have actively worked to get rid of race as a biological category.

3 Are There Differences in Intelligence from One Population to Another?

No, although some populations receive lower average scores on IQ tests than others. Even so, many individuals in "lower-scoring" populations score higher than some in the "higher-scoring" populations. There is no agreement on what intelligence really is, but there is agreement that intelligence involves several different talents and abilities. Certainly, there are genes affecting these, but like other genes, they may be independently assorted, and their expression is affected significantly by environmental factors.

What a piece of work is man," said Hamlet. "How noble in reason, how infinite in faculties, in form and moving how express and admirable, in action how like an angel, in apprehension how like a god: the beauty of the world, the paragon of animals! And yet to me what is this quintessence of dust?"

What people are to one another is the province of anthropology: Physical anthropology reveals what we are; cultural anthropology reveals what we think we are. Our dreams of ourselves are as varied as our languages and our physical bodies. We are the same, but we differ. We speak English or French, our hair is curly or straight, our skin is lightly to heavily pigmented, and in height we range from short to tall. Human genetic variation generally is distributed in such a continuous range, with varying clusters of frequency. The significance we give our variations, the way we perceive them—in fact, whether we perceive them at all—is determined by our culture. For example, in many Polynesian countries, where skin color is not a determinant of social status, people really pay little attention to this physical characteristic; in the United States and South Africa, it is one of the first things people do notice.

VARIATION AND EVOLUTION

Many behavioral traits—reading, for instance—are learned or acquired by living in a society; other characteristics, such as blue eyes, are passed on physically by heredity. Environment affects both. A person growing up surrounded by books learns to read. If the culture insists that brown-eyed people watch TV and blue-eyed people read, the brown-eyed people may end up making videotapes while the blue-eyed people are writing books. These skills or tastes are acquired characteristics. Changes in such things within one population but not another are capable of making the two distinct in learned behavioral characteristics within relatively few generations.

PHYSICAL VARIABILITY

The physical characteristics of both populations and individuals, as we saw in Chapter 3, are a product of the interaction between genes and environments. Thus, one's genes predispose one to a particular skin color, for example, but the skin color one actually has is strongly affected by environmental factors such as the amount of solar radiation. In this case, phenotypic expression is strongly influenced by environment; in some others, such as one's A-B-O blood type, phenotypic expression closely reflects genotype.

For most characteristics, there are within the gene pool of *Homo sapiens* variant forms of genes, known as alleles. In the color of an eye, the shape of a hand, the texture of skin, many variations can occur. This kind of variability, found in many animal species, signifies a rich potential for new combinations of characteristics in future generations. Such a species is called **polymorphic** (meaning "many shapes"). Our blood types, determined by the alleles for Types A, B, and O blood, are an example of polymorphism, which in this case may appear in any of four distinct phenotypic forms. A polymorphic species faced with changing environmental conditions has within its gene pool the possibility of producing individuals with traits appropriate to its altered life. Many may not achieve reproductive success, but those whose physical characteristics enable them to do well in the new environment will usually reproduce, so that their genes will become more common in subsequent generations. Thus, humankind, being polymorphic, has been able to occupy a variety of environments.

A major expansion into new environments was under way by the time *Homo erectus* appeared on the scene (Chapter 8). Populations of this species were living in Africa, Southeast Asia, Europe, and China. Each of these places constitutes a different **faunal region,** which is to say that each possesses its own distinctive assemblage of animal life, not precisely like that of other regions. This differentiation of animal life is the result of selective pressures that, through the Pleistocene, differed from one region to another. For example, the conditions of life were quite different in China, which lies in the temperate zone, than they were in tropical Southeast Asia. Coupled with differing selective pressures were geographic features that restricted or prevented gene flow between populations of different faunal regions.

When a polymorphic species is divided into geographically dispersed populations, it usually is **polytypic** (many types); that is, the store of genetic variability is unevenly expressed. Genetic variants will be expressed

Polymorphic. A species with alternative forms (alleles) of particular genes. • **Faunal region.** A geographic region with its own distinctive assemblage of animal life, not precisely like that of other regions. • **Polytypic.** The expression of genetic variants in different frequencies in different populations of a species.

in different frequencies in different populations. For example, in the Old World, populations of *H. sapiens* living in the tropics have a higher frequency of alleles for dark skin color than do those living in more northerly regions. In blood type, *H. sapiens* is polymorphic, with four distinct groups (A, B, O, or AB). In the distribution of these types, the species is again polytypic. The frequency of the O allele is highest in American Indians, especially among some populations native to South America; the highest frequencies of the allele for Type A blood tend to be found among certain European populations (although the highest frequency of all is found among the Blackfoot and Blood Indians of North America); the highest frequencies of the B allele are found in some Asian populations (Figure 13.1). We would expect the earlier species, *H. erectus,* with populations in the four faunal regions of the Old World, to have been polytypic. This appears to have been the case, for the fossils from each of the four regions show some differences from those in the others. African *Homo erectus,* for example, had the tall linear body build often seen in some modern African populations, whereas Chinese *erectus,* like the modern Chinese, seems to have been shorter of stature. It seems, then, that the human species has been polytypic since at least the time of *H. erectus.*

THE MEANING OF RACE

Early anthropologists tried to explore the polytypic nature of the human species by systematically classifying *H. sapiens* into subspecies, or **races,** based on geographic location and phenotypic (physical) features such as skin color, body size, head shape, and hair texture. Such classifications were continually being challenged by the presence of individuals who did not fit the categories, such

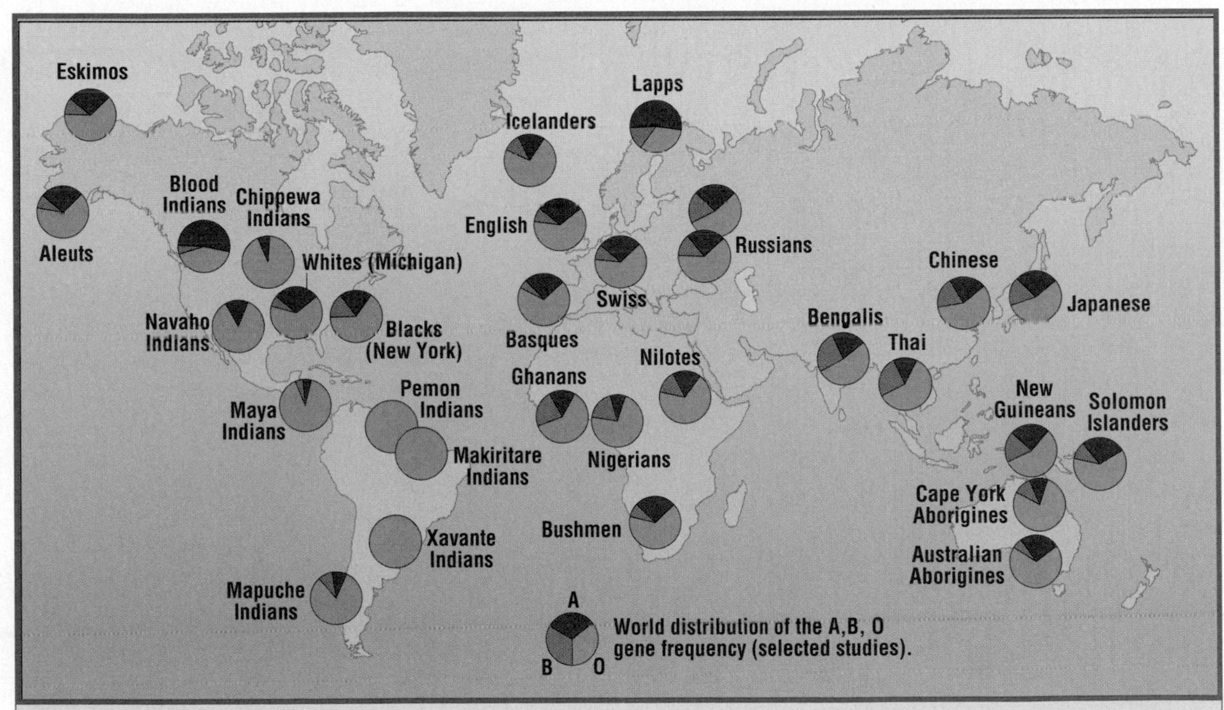

FIGURE 13.1

FREQUENCIES OF THE THREE ALLELES FOR THE A, B, AND O BLOOD GROUPS FOR SELECTED POPULATIONS AROUND THE WORLD DEMONSTRATE THE POLYTYPIC NATURE OF *H. SAPIENS*.

Race. In biology, a population of a species that differs in the frequency of the variants of some gene or genes from other populations of the same species.

as light-skinned Africans or dark-skinned "Caucasoids"; to get around the problem, it was assumed that these individuals were hybrids or the product of racial mixtures. Lack of concordance among traits—for example, the fact that long prominent noses are not only common among Europeans but have a high frequency in various East African populations as well—was usually explained away in a similar manner. The fact is, generalized references to human types such as "Asiatic" or "Mongoloid," "European" or "Caucasoid," and "African" or "Negroid" were at best mere statistical abstractions about populations in which certain physical features appeared in higher frequencies than in other populations; no example of "pure" racial types could be found. These categories turned out to be neither definitive nor particularly helpful. The visible traits were found to occur not in abrupt shifts from population to population but in a continuum that changed gradually, with few sharp breaks. To compound the problem, one trait might change gradually over a north-south gradient, whereas another might show a similar change from east to west. Human skin color, for instance, becomes progressively darker as one moves from northern Europe to central Africa, whereas blood Type B becomes progressively more common as one moves from western to eastern Europe.

Finally, there were many variations within each group, and those within groups were often greater than those between groups. In Africa, the skin color of someone from the Kalahari Desert might more closely resemble that of a person of East Indian extraction than the darkly pigmented Nilotic Sudanese who was supposed to be of the same race.

The Negroid was characterized as having dark skin, thick lips, a broad nose, and tightly curled hair; the Mongoloid, straight hair, a flat face, a flat nose, and spread nostrils; and the Caucasoid, pale skin, a narrow nose, and varied eye color and hair form. The classification then expanded to take in American Indians,

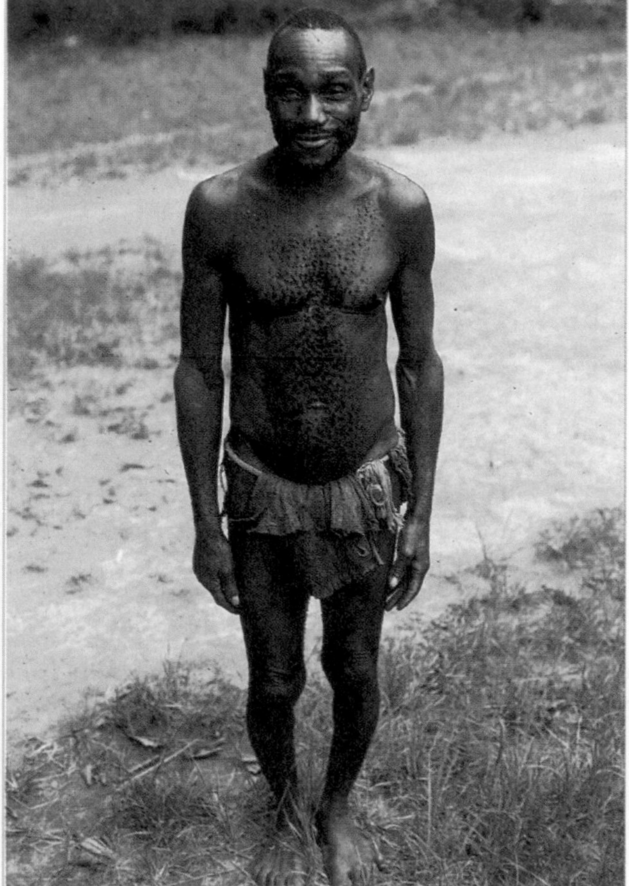

Among the tallest people in the world are the Tutsi (left), whereas among the smallest are the Efe (right). Both are from central Africa and illustrate the wide range of variation seen in a (supposedly) single racial category.

ASHLEY MONTAGU (1905–1999)

Born Israel Ehrenberg to a working-class immigrant Jewish family living in London's East End, Ashley Montagu (a name he adopted in the 1920s) went on to become a pioneering critic of the race concept and one of the best-known anthropologists of his time. An avid reader as a child, in 1922 he attended University College of London, where he studied anthropology and psychology. Among his professors were founders of the eugenics movement—a proposal to improve humanity by identifying those with supposedly undesirable hereditary characteristics and removing them from the breeding population. It was also at this time that he changed his name in response to the strong ethnic and class prejudice he experienced.

Also, in the 1920s, Montagu studied under the founders of British social anthropology at the London School of Economics. In 1927, however, he left for the United States, where he considered the society to be more congenial to social justice. At Columbia University, he studied under Franz Boas and other pioneers of North American anthropology, earning his doctorate in 1937 with a dissertation on knowledge of paternity among Australian aborigines.

Having felt the sting early on of ethnic and class prejudice himself, it is not surprising that Montagu became a strong critic of eugenics and other racist doctrines. As early as 1926, he focused on the mistake of viewing races as typological, bounded categories. This put him at odds with many of his old professors and colleagues but, as he put it, he learned early on "not to let the shadows of great men block out the light."* All his life, Montagu fought racism in his writing, in academic and public lectures, and in the courts.

Ashley Montagu wrote over 60 books and hundreds of articles, including a series in *Ladies Home Journal.* These ranged over subjects from primate anatomy to the importance of nurturance in human development, and even the history of human swearing. Of all his works, none is more important than his book *Man's Most Dangerous Myth: The Fallacy of Race.* Published in 1942, it took the lead in exposing, on purely scientific grounds, the fallacy of human races as biological entities. The book has since gone through six editions, the last in 1999. Although Montagu's once controversial ideas have since become mainstream, the book remains the most comprehensive treatment of its subject.

*Sperling, S. (2000). Ashley Montagu (1905–1999). *American Anthropologist, 102,* 584.

Australians, and Polynesians, but even the expanded system failed to account for dramatic differences in appearance among individuals, or even populations, in each racial category; for example, Europeans, Arabs, and East Indians were all lumped together as Caucasoids.

In an attempt to encompass such variations, schemes of racial classification proliferated. In 1926, J. Deniker classified 29 races according to texture of hair, presumably improving upon Roland B. Dixon's 1923 classification based on three indexes of body measures. Hair texture and body build were the characteristics used for another set of racial categories proposed in 1930. By 1947, Earnest Hooton had proposed three new composite races resulting from the interbreeding of "primary" races. Despite these classificatory attempts on the part of Western anthropologists, no definitive grouping of distinct, discontinuous biological groups was found for modern humanity.

While many anthropologists struggled with the problem of defining human races, others began to question the whole exercise. Most notable was Ashley Montagu, whose effective criticism of race as a valid biological concept began to influence people's thinking on the subject.

Also influential was a book, published in 1950, called *Races* by Carleton Coon, Stanley Garn, and Joseph Birdsell. Unlike Ashley Montagu, they did not reject the race concept, and like their predecessors, they too tried to classify modern humans into a number of racial groups, 30 in their case. They did, however, reject a trait-list approach. Instead, they recognized races as populations that owed certain common characteristics to environmental, primarily climatic, adaptation, which continued to change in response to evolutionary forces such as gene flow and altered selective pressures. Although this book certainly had its weaknesses—its continued assumption that races existed, for one—it did represent a significant departure from previous attempts at racial classification and was influential in paving the way for a sounder understanding of human variation.

RACE AS A BIOLOGICAL CONCEPT

To understand why the racial approach to human variation has been so unproductive, we must first understand the race concept in strictly biological terms. In biology, a race is defined as a population of a species that differs in the frequency of different variants of some gene or genes from other populations of the same species. Simple and straightforward though such a definition may seem, there are three very important things to note about it. First, it is arbitrary; there is no agreement on how many genetic differences it takes to make a race. For some who are interested in the topic, different frequencies in the variants of one gene are sufficient; for others, differences in frequencies involving several genes are necessary. Ultimately, it proved impossible to reach agreement on the number of genes and precisely which ones are the most important for defining races.

The arbitrariness of racial classification is well illustrated by the following Original Study.

Original Study

Race Without Color[1]

Science often violates simple common sense. Our eyes tell us that the Earth is flat, that the sun revolves around the Earth, and that we humans are not animals. But we now ignore that evidence of our senses. We have learned that our planet is in fact round and revolves around the sun, and that humans are slightly modified chimpanzees. The reality of human races is another commonsense "truth" destined to follow the flat Earth into oblivion.

What Could Be More Objective?

The commonsense view of races goes somewhat as follows. All native Swedes differ from all native Nigerians in appearance: There is no Swede whom you would mistake for a Nigerian, and vice versa. Swedes have lighter skin than Nigerians do. They also generally have blond or light brown hair, while Nigerians have very dark hair. Nigerians usually have more tightly coiled hair than Swedes do, dark eyes as opposed to eyes that are blue or gray, and fuller lips and broader noses.

In addition, other Europeans look much more like Swedes than like Nigerians, while other peoples of sub-Saharan Africa—except perhaps the Khoisan peoples of southern Africa—look much more like Nigerians than like Swedes. Yes, skin color does get darker in Europe toward the Mediterranean, but it is still lighter than the skin of sub-Saharan Africans. In Europe, very dark or curly hair becomes more common outside Scandinavia, but European hair is still not as tightly coiled as in Africa. Since it's easy then to distinguish almost any native European from any native sub-Saharan African, we recognize Europeans and sub-Saharan Africans as distinct races, which we name for their skin colors: whites and blacks, respectively.

As it turns out, this seemingly unassailable reasoning is not objective. There are many different, equally valid procedures for defining races, and those different procedures yield very different classifications. One such procedure would group Italians and Greeks with most African blacks. It would classify Xhosas—the South African 'black' group to which President Nelson Mandela belongs—with Swedes rather than Nigerians. Another equally valid procedure would place Swedes with Fulani (a Nigerian "black" group) and not with Italians, who would again be grouped with most other African blacks. Still another procedure would keep Swedes and Italians separate from all

[1]Diamond, J. (1994). Race without color. *Discover, 15*(11), 83–88.

African blacks but would throw the Swedes and Italians into the same race as New Guineans and American Indians. Faced with such differing classifications, many anthropologists today conclude that one cannot recognize any human races at all.

If we were just arguing about races of nonhuman animals, essentially the same uncertainties of classification would arise. But the debates would remain polite and would never attract attention outside the halls of academia. Classification of humans is different "only" in that it shapes our views of other peoples, fosters our subconscious differentiation between "us" and "them," and is invoked to justify political and socioeconomic discrimination. On this basis, many anthropologists therefore argue that even if one could classify humans into races, one should not.

To understand how such uncertainties in classification arise, let's steer clear of humans for a moment and instead focus on warblers and lions, about which we can easily remain dispassionate. Biologists begin by classifying living creatures into species. A species is a group of populations whose individual members would, if given the opportunity, interbreed with individuals of other populations of that group. But they would not interbreed with individuals of other species that are similarly defined. Thus all human populations, no matter how different they look, belong to the same species because they do interbreed and have interbred whenever they have encountered each other. Gorillas and humans, however, belong to two different species because—to the best of our knowledge—they have never interbred despite their coexisting in close proximity for millions of years.

We know that different populations classified together in the human species are visibly different. The same proves true for most other animal and plant species as well, whenever biologists look carefully. For example, consider one of the most familiar species of bird in North America, the yellow-rumped warbler. Breeding males of eastern and western North America can be distinguished at a glance by their throat color: white in the east, yellow in the west. Hence they are classified into two different races, or subspecies (alternative words with identical meanings), termed the myrtle and Audubon races, respectively. The white-throated eastern birds differ from the yellow-throated western birds in other characteristics as well, such as in voice and habitat preference. But where the two races meet, in western Canada, white-throated birds do indeed interbreed with yellow-throated birds. That's why we consider myrtle warblers and Audubon warblers as races of the same species rather than different species.

Racial classification of these birds is easy. Throat color, voice, and habitat preference all vary geographically in yellow-rumped warblers, but the variation of those three traits is "concordant"—that is, voice differences or habitat differences lead to the same racial classification as differences in throat color because the same populations that differ in throat color also differ in voice and habitat.

Racial classification of many other species, though, presents problems of concordance. For instance, a Pacific island bird species called the golden whistler varies from one island to the next. Some populations consist of big birds, some of small birds; some have black-winged males, others green-winged males; some have yellow-breasted females, others gray-breasted females; many other characteristics vary as well. But, unfortunately for humans like me who study these birds, those characteristics don't vary concordantly. Islands with green-winged males can have either yellow-breasted or gray-breasted females, and green-winged males are big on some islands but small on other islands. As a result, if you classified golden whistlers into races based on single traits, you would get entirely different classifications depending on which trait you chose.

Classification of these birds also presents problems of "hierarchy." Some of the golden whistler races recognized by ornithologists are wildly different from all the other races, but some are very similar to one another. They can therefore be grouped into a hierarchy of distinctness. You start by establishing the most distinct population as a race separate from all other populations. You then separate the most distinct of the remaining populations. You continue by grouping similar populations, and separating distinct populations or groups of populations as races or groups of races. The problem is that the extent to which you continue the racial classification is arbitrary, and it's a decision about which taxonomists disagree passionately. Some taxonomists, the "splitters," like to recognize

Original Study

many different races, partly for the egotistical motive of getting credit for having named a race. Other taxonomists, the "lumpers," prefer to recognize few races. Which type of taxonomist you are is a matter of personal preference.

How does that variability of traits by which we classify races come about in the first place? Some traits vary because of natural selection: That is, one form of the trait is advantageous for survival in one area, another form in a different area. For example, northern hares and weasels develop white fur in the winter, but southern ones retain brown fur year-round. The white winter fur is selected in the north for camouflage against the snow, while any animal unfortunate enough to turn white in the snowless southern states would stand out from afar against the brown ground and would be picked off by predators.

Other traits vary geographically because of sexual selection, meaning that those traits serve as arbitrary signals by which individuals of one sex attract mates of the opposite sex while intimidating rivals. Adult male lions, for instance, have a mane, but lionesses and young males don't. The adult male's mane signals to lionesses that he is sexually mature, and signals to young male rivals that he is a dangerous and experienced adversary. The length and color of a lion's mane vary among populations, being shorter and blacker in Indian lions than in African lions. Indian lions and lionesses evidently find short black manes sexy or intimidating; African lions don't.

Finally, some geographically variable traits have no known effect on survival and are invisible to rivals and to prospective sex partners. They merely reflect mutations that happened to arise and spread in one area. They could equally well have arisen and spread elsewhere—they just didn't.

Nothing that I've said about geographic variation in animals is likely to get me branded a racist. We don't attribute higher IQ or social status to black-winged whistlers than to green-winged whistlers. But now let's consider geographic variation in humans. We'll start with invisible traits, about which it's easy to remain dispassionate.

Many geographically variable human traits evolved by natural selection to adapt humans to particular climates or environments—just as the winter color of a hare or weasel did. Good examples are the mutations that people in tropical parts of the Old World evolved to help them survive malaria, the leading infectious disease of the Old World tropics. One such mutation is the sickle-cell gene, so-called because the red blood cells of people with that mutation tend to assume a sickle shape. People bearing the gene are more resistant to malaria than people without it. Not surprisingly, the gene is absent from northern Europe, where malaria is nonexistent, but it's common in tropical Africa, where malaria is widespread. Up to 40 percent of Africans in such areas carry the sickle-cell gene. It's also common in the malaria-ridden Arabian Peninsula and southern India, and rare or absent in the southernmost parts of South Africa, among the Xhosas, who live mostly beyond the tropical geographic range of malaria.

The geographic range of human malaria is much wider than the range of the sickle-cell gene. As it happens, other antimalarial genes take over the protective function of the sickle-cell gene in malarial Southeast Asia and New Guinea and in Italy, Greece, and other warm parts of the Mediterranean basin. Thus human races, if defined by antimalarial genes, would be very different from human races as traditionally defined by traits such as skin color. As classified by antimalarial genes (or their absence), Swedes are grouped with Xhosas but not with Italians or Greeks. Most other peoples usually viewed as African blacks are grouped with Arabia's "whites" and are kept separate from the "black" Xhosas.

Antimalarial genes exemplify the many features of our body chemistry that vary geographically under the influence of natural selection. Another such feature is the enzyme lactase, which enables us to digest the milk sugar lactose. Infant humans, like infants of almost all other mammal species, possess lactase and drink milk. Until about 6,000 years ago most humans, like all other mammal species, lost the lactase enzyme on reaching the age of weaning. The obvious reason is that it was unnecessary—no human or other mammal drank milk as an adult. Beginning around 4000 B.C., however, fresh milk obtained from domestic mammals became a major food for adults of a few human populations. Natural selection caused individuals in these populations to retain lactase into adulthood. Among such peoples are northern and central Europeans, Arabians, northern Indians, and several milk-drinking black African peoples, such as the Fulani of West Africa. Adult lactase is much less common in southern European populations and in most other African black populations, as well as in all populations of east Asians, aboriginal Australians, and American Indians.

Once again races defined by body chemistry don't match races defined by skin color. Swedes belong with Fulani in the "lactase-positive race," while most African "blacks," Japanese, and American Indians belong in the "lactase-negative race."

Not all the effects of natural selection are as invisible as lactase and sickle cells. Environmental pressures have also produced more noticeable differences among peoples, particularly in body shapes. Among the tallest and most long-limbed peoples in the world are the Nilotic peoples, such as the Dinkas, who live in the hot, dry areas of East Africa. At the opposite extreme in body shape are the Inuit, or Eskimo, who have compact bodies and relatively short arms and legs. The reasons have to do with heat loss. The greater the surface area of a warm body, the more body heat that's lost, since heat loss is directly proportional to surface area. For people of a given weight, a long-limbed, tall shape maximizes surface area, while a compact, short-limbed shape minimizes it. Dinkas and Inuit have opposite problems of heat balance: The former usually need desperately to get rid of body heat, while the latter need desperately to conserve it. Thus natural selection molded their body shapes oppositely, based on their contrasting climates.

Other visible traits that vary geographically among humans evolved by means of sexual selection. We all know that we find some individuals of the opposite sex more attractive than other individuals. We also know that in sizing up sex appeal, we pay more attention to certain parts of a prospective sex partner's body than to other parts. Men tend to be inordinately interested in women's breasts and much less concerned with women's toenails. Women, in turn, tend to be turned on by the shape of a man's buttocks or the details of a man's beard and body hair, if any, but not by the size of his feet.

But all those determinants of sex appeal vary geographically. Khoisan and Andaman Island women tend to have much larger buttocks than most other women. Nipple color and breast shape and size also vary geographically among women. European men are rather hairy by world standards, while Southeast Asian men tend to have very sparse beards and body hair.

What's the function of these traits that differ so markedly between men and women? They certainly don't aid survival: It's not the case that orange nipples help Khoisan women escape lions, while darker nipples help European women survive cold winters. Instead, these varying traits play a crucial role in sexual selection. Women with very large buttocks are a turn-on, or at least acceptable, to Khoisan and Andaman men but look freakish to many men from other parts of the world. Bearded and hairy men readily find mates in Europe but fare worse in Southeast Asia. The geographic variation of these traits, however, is as arbitrary as the geographic variation in the color of a lion's mane.

There is a third possible explanation for the function of geographically variable human traits, besides survival or sexual selection—namely, no function at all. A good example is provided by fingerprints, whose complex pattern of arches, loops, and whorls is determined genetically. Fingerprints also vary geographically: For example, Europeans' fingerprints tend to have many loops, while aboriginal Australians' fingerprints tend to have many whorls.

Fingerprints' patterns of loops, whorls, and arches are genetically determined. Grouping people on this basis would place most Europeans, sub-Saharan Africans, and East Asians together as "loops," Australian aborigines and the people of Mongolia together as "whorls," and central Europeans and the Bushmen of southern Africa together as "arches."

Original Study

If we classify human populations by their fingerprints, most Europeans and black Africans would sort out together in one race, Jews and some Indonesians in another, and aboriginal Australians in still another. But those geographic variations in fingerprint patterns possess no known function whatsoever. They play no role in survival: Whorls aren't especially suitable for grabbing kangaroos, nor do loops help bar mitzvah candidates hold on to the pointer for the Torah. They also play no role in sexual selection: While you've undoubtedly noticed whether your mate is bearded or has brown nipples, you surely haven't the faintest idea whether his or her fingerprints have more loops than whorls. Instead it's purely a matter of chance that whorls became common in aboriginal Australians, and loops among Jews. Our rhesus factor blood groups and numerous other human traits fall into the same category of genetic characteristics whose geographic variation serves no function.

The End

After arbitrariness, the second thing to note about the biological definition of race is that it does not mean that any one race has exclusive possession of any particular variant of any gene or genes. In human terms, the frequency of the allele for blood group O may be high in one population and low in another, but it is present in both. Races are genetically "open," meaning that gene flow takes place between them. Because they are genetically open, they are apt to be impermanent and subject to reamalgamation. Thus, one can easily see the fallacy of any attempt to identify pure races; if gene flow cannot take place between two populations, either directly or indirectly through intermediate populations, then they are not races but separate species.

The third thing to note about the biological definition of race is that individuals of one race will not necessarily be distinguishable from those of another. In fact, as we have just noted with respect to humans, the differences among individuals within a population are generally greater than the differences among populations. As

The "openness" of races to gene flow is illustrated by this picture of an Asian and African American couple with their children.

the science writer James Shreeve puts it, "most of what separates me genetically from a typical African or Eskimo also separates me from another average American of European ancestry."[2] This follows from the genetic "openness" of races; no one race has an exclusive claim to any particular gene or allele.

THE CONCEPT OF HUMAN RACES

As a device for understanding polytypic variation in humans, the biological race concept has serious drawbacks. One is that the category is arbitrary to begin with, which makes agreement on any given classification difficult, if not impossible. For example, if one researcher emphasizes skin color while another emphasizes blood group differences, they will not classify people in the same way. Perhaps if the human species were divided into a number of relatively discrete breeding populations, this wouldn't be such a problem, but even this is open to debate. What has happened, though, is that human populations have grown in the course of human evolution, and with this growth have come increased opportunities for contact and gene flow between populations. Since the advent of food production, the process has accelerated as higher birthrates and periodic food shortages (discussed in Chapter 11) have prompted the movement of farmers from their homelands to other places. In East Asia, for example, the development of farming, followed by the invention of bronze and a host of other technologies in China resulted in expansion of northern Chinese populations and displacement of southern Chinese peoples into Southeast Asia. This expansion effectively "swamped" the original populations of this region, except in a few out-of-the-way places like the Andaman Islands.[3] As a consequence of such movements, differences between human populations today are probably less clear-cut than back in the days of *H. erectus,* or even archaic *H. sapiens.*

Things are complicated even moreso because humans are complicated genetically. Thus, the genetic underpinnings of the phenotypic traits upon which traditional racial classifications are usually based are poorly understood. Compounding the problem, "race" exists as a cultural, as well as a biological, category. In various different ways, cultures define religious, linguistic, and ethnic groups as races, thereby confusing linguistic and cultural traits with physical traits. For example, in many Central and South American countries, people are commonly classified as "Indian," "Mestizo" (mixed), or "Ladino" (of Spanish descent). But despite the biological connotations of these terms, the criteria used for assigning individuals to these categories consist of things such as whether they wear shoes, sandals, or go barefoot; speak Spanish or some Indian language; live in a thatched hut or a European-style house; and so forth. Thus, an Indian—by speaking Spanish, wearing Western-style clothes, and living in a house in a

[2]Shreeve, J. (1994) Terms of estrangement. *Discover, 15*(11), 60.

[3]Diamond, J. (1996). Empire of uniformity. *Discover, 17*(3), 83–84.

The Andaman Islanders (left) are a remnant of the original inhabitants of Southeast Asia; the Vietnamese (right) are descendants of people from southern China who spread into the region after the invention of agriculture. In the process there was mixing of gene pools.

non-Indian neighborhood—ceases to be an Indian, no matter how many "Indian genes" he or she may possess.

This sort of confusion of nonbiological characteristics with what are spoken of as biological categories is by no means limited to Central and South American societies. To one degree or another, such confusion is found in most Western societies, including those of Europe and North America. Take, for example, the racial categories used by the U.S. Census Bureau: White, Black, American Indian, Asian, and Pacific Islander are large catchall categories that include diverse people. *Asian,* for example, includes such different people as Chinese and East Indians (to which Indians, at least, take exception), whereas *Eskimo* (a term these people, the Inuit, find offensive) and *Aleut* are far more restrictive. *Hispanic* is another problematic category, as it includes people who, in their countries of origin, might be classified as Indian, Mestizo, or Ladino. Addition of slots for native Hawaiians, Middle Easterners, and people who consider themselves multiracial does nothing to improve the situation. To compound the confusion, inclusion in one or another of these categories is usually based on self-identification. In short, what we are dealing with here are not biological categories at all, but rather social constructs.

To make matters even worse, this confusion of social with biological factors is frequently combined with attitudes that are then taken as excuses to exclude whole categories of people from certain roles or positions in society. In the United States, for example, the idea of race originated in the 18th century to refer to the diverse peoples—European settlers, conquered Indians, and Africans imported as slaves—that were brought together in colonial North America. This racial worldview assigned some groups to perpetual low status on the basis of their supposedly biological inferiority, whereas access to privilege, power, and wealth was reserved for favored groups of European descent.[4]

Different ways in which this discrimination plays out may be illustrated with two quite different examples. An old stereotype is that Blacks are born with rhythm, which somehow is thought to give them a natural affinity for jazz, soul music, rap, and related forms of musical expression. A corollary of this myth is that African Americans are unsuited "by nature" for symphonic music. Hence, until recently, one did not find an African American at the head of any major symphony orchestra in the United States, even though African American conductors such as James de Priest, Paul Freeman, and Dean Dixon made distinguished careers for themselves in Canada and Europe.

A particularly evil consequence of the racial worldview occurred when the Nazis declared the superiority of the "Aryan race" (which is really a linguistic grouping and not a race at all), and the inferiority of the Gypsy and Jewish "races" (really ethno-religious categories), and then used this distinction as an excuse to exclude Gypsies and Jews from life altogether. In all, 11 million people (Jews, Gypsies, Africans, homosexuals, and other supposedly inferior people) were deliberately put to death.

Tragically, such programs of extermination of one group by another continue to occur in many parts of the

[4]American Anthropological Association. (1998). Statement on "race." Available: *www.ameranthassn.org.*

Far from being a thing of the past, genocide continues to occur in the world today, as this picture taken in 1998 in the Yugoslav province of Kosovo vividly illustrates.

world today, including parts of South America, Africa, Europe, and Asia. Holocausts are by no means things of the past, nor are Gypsies and Jews their only victims. The well-meant vow "never again" contrasts with the reality of "frequently again."

Considering all the problems, confusion, and evil consequences, it is small wonder that there has been a lot of debate not just about how many human races there may be, but about what race is and is not. Often forgotten is the fact that a race, even if it can be defined biologically, is the result of the operation of evolutionary processes. Because it is these processes rather than racial categories themselves in which we are really interested, most anthropologists have abandoned the race concept as being of no particular utility in understanding human biological variation. Instead, they have found it more productive to study the distribution and significance of specific, genetically based characteristics, or else the characteristics of small breeding populations that are, after all, the smallest units in which evolutionary change occurs.

Some Physical Variables

Not only have attempts to classify people into races proved futile and counterproductive, it has also become apparent that the amount of genetic variation in humans is relatively low, compared to that of other primate species. Nonetheless, human biological variation is a fact of life, and physical anthropologists have learned a great deal about it. Much of it is related to climatic adaptation. For example, a correlation has been noted between body build and climate. Generally, people native to regions with cold climates tend to have greater body bulk (not to be equated with fat) relative to their extremities (arms and legs) than do people native to regions with hot climates, who tend to be long and slender. Interestingly, these differences show up as early as the time of *Homo erectus,* as already noted. Anthropologists generally argue that such differences of body build represent a climatic adaptation; certain body builds are better suited to particular living conditions than others. A person with larger body bulk and shorter extremities may suffer more from summer heat than someone whose extremities are long and whose body is slender. But they will conserve needed body heat under cold conditions. The reason is that a bulky body tends to conserve more heat than a less bulky one, because it has less surface relative to volume. People living in hot, open country, by contrast, benefit from a body build that can get rid of excess heat quickly so as to keep from overheating; for this, long extremities and a slender body, which increase surface area relative to volume, are advantageous.

Studies of body build and climatic adaptation are complicated by the intervening effects on physique of diet, because dietary differences will cause variation in body build. Another complicating factor is clothing. Thus, much of the way people adapt to cold is cultural, rather than biological. For example, Inuit peoples (the proper name for "Eskimos") live in a region where it is cold much of the year. To cope with this, they long ago developed efficient clothing to keep the body warm. Because of this, the Inuit are provided with what amount to artificial tropical environments inside their clothing. In spite of such considerations, it remains true that in

African Americans are disproportionately represented among professional basketball players in part because of the prevalence of tall, linear body shapes among them. This does not mean, however, that "Whites can't jump" or that the anatomy of Blacks necessarily makes them better basketball players. In fact, one reason there are so many African American basketball players has nothing to do with biology but is due rather to socioeconomic opportunities available to them in a society that still discriminates on the basis of skin color.

northerly regions of the world, bulky body builds predominate, whereas the reverse is true in the tropics.

Anthropologists have also studied such body features as nose and eye shape and hair textures in relation to climate. A wide flaring nose, for example, is common in populations living in tropical forests; here the air is warm and damp, and so the warming and humidifying functions of the nose are secondary. Longer, more prominent noses, common among cold dwellers, are helpful in humidifying and warming cold air before it reaches the lungs. They are also useful in cleaning and humidifying dry, dusty air in hot climates, which is why long prominent noses are not restricted to places like Europe. Coon, Garn, and Birdsell once proposed that the "Mongoloid face," common in populations native to East and Central Asia, as well as arctic North America, exhibits features adapted to life in very cold environments. The **epicanthic eye fold,** which minimizes eye exposure to the cold, a flat facial profile, and extensive fatty deposits may help to protect the face against frostbite. Although experimental studies have failed to sustain the frostbite hypothesis, it is true that a flat facial profile generally goes with a round head. A significant percentage of body heat may be lost from the head; however, a round head, having less surface area relative to volume, loses less heat than a longer, more elliptical head. As one would predict from this, long-headed populations are generally found in hotter climates; round-headed ones are more common in cold climates.

The epicanthic eye fold is common among people native to East Asia. Still, a comparison of this individual with those shown on p. 341 shows the absurdity of lumping all Asians in a single category.

Skin Color: A Case Study in Adaptation

In the United States, race is most commonly equated with skin color. Perhaps this is not surprising, because it is a highly visible trait. Skin color is subject to great variation, and there are at least four main factors associated with it: transparency or thickness of the skin, a copper-colored pigment called carotene, reflected color from the blood vessels (responsible for the rosy color of lightly pigmented people), and the amount of **melanin** found in a given area of skin. Exposure to sunlight increases the amount of melanin, a dark pigment, causing the skin to darken. Melanin is known to protect skin against damaging ultraviolet solar radiation;[5] consequently, darkly pigmented peoples are less susceptible to skin cancers and sunburn than are those whose skin has less melanin. They also seem to be less susceptible to photo-destruction of certain vitamins. Because the highest concentration of dark-skinned people tends to be found in the tropical regions of the world, it appears that natural selection has favored heavily pigmented skin as a protection against the strong solar radiation of equatorial latitudes, where ultraviolet radiation is most intense. Because skin cancers generally do not develop until later in life, they are unlikely to have interfered with the reproductive success of lightly pigmented

[5] Neer, R. M. (1975). The evolutionary significance of vitamin D, skin pigment, and ultraviolet light. *American Journal of Physical Anthropology, 43,* 409–416.

Epicanthic eye fold. A fold of skin at the inner corner of the eye that covers the true corner of the eye; common in Asiatic populations. • **Melanin.** The chemical responsible for dark skin pigmentation, which helps protect against damage from ultraviolet radiation.

individuals in the tropics, and so are unlikely to have been the agent of selection. On the other hand, severe sunburn, which is especially dangerous to infants, causes the body to overheat and interferes with its ability to sweat, by which it might rid itself of excess heat. Furthermore, it makes one susceptible to other kinds of infection. In addition to all this, decomposition of folate, an essential vitamin sensitive to heavy doses of ultraviolet radiation, can cause anemia, spontaneous abortion, and infertility.[6]

Although dark skin pigmentation has enjoyed a selective advantage in the tropics, the opposite is true in northern latitudes, where skins have generally been lightly pigmented. This lack of heavy amounts of melanin enables the weak ultraviolet radiation of northern latitudes to penetrate the skin and stimulate formation of vitamin D, necessary for calcium regulation. Dark pigmentation interferes with this process. Without access to external sources of vitamin D, once provided by cod liver oil but now more often provided in vitamin D-fortified milk, individuals incapable of synthesizing enough of this vitamin in their own bodies were selected against, for they contracted rickets, a disease that seriously deforms children's bones. At its worst, rickets prevents children from reaching reproductive age; at the least, it interferes with a woman's ability to give birth if she does reach reproductive age (Figure 13.2).

Given what we know about the adaptive significance of human skin color, and the fact that, until 800,000 years ago, hominines were exclusively creatures of the tropics, it is likely that lightly pigmented skins are a recent development in human history. Darkly pigmented skins likely are quite ancient. Consistent with this, the enzyme tyrosinase, which converts the amino acid tyrosine into the compound that forms melanin, is present in lightly pigmented peoples in sufficient quantity to make them very "black." The reason it does not is that they have genes that inactivate or inhibit it.[7] Human skin is more

[6]Branda, R. F., & Eatoil, J. W. (1978). Skin color and photolysis: An evolutionary hypothesis. *Science, 201,* 625–626.

[7]Wills, C. (1994). The skin we're in. *Discover, 15*(11), 79.

These photos of people from Spain, Scandinavia, Senegal, and Indonesia illustrate the range of variation in human skin color. Generally, the closer to the equator populations live, the darker the skin color.

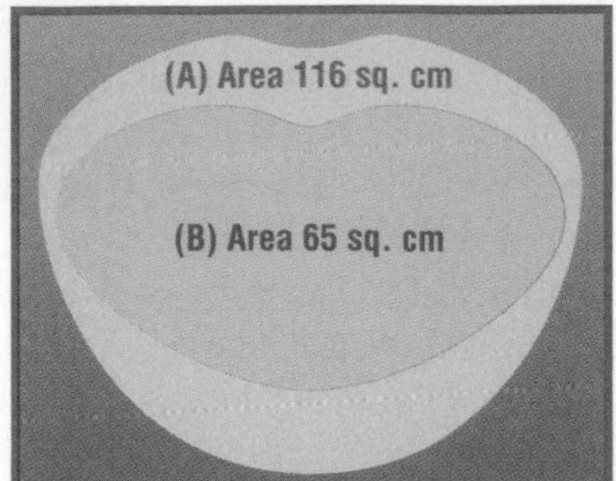

FIGURE 13.2
THE OUTLINE OF A NORMAL PELVIC INLET (A) COMPARED WITH THAT OF A WOMAN WITH RICKETS (B), WHICH WOULD INTERFERE WITH HER CAPACITY TO GIVE BIRTH. RICKETS IS CAUSED BY A DEFICIENCY OF VITAMIN D. IN THE ABSENCE OF ARTIFICIAL SOURCES OF THIS VITAMIN AMONG PEOPLE LIVING IN NORTHERN LATITUDES, LIGHTLY PIGMENTED PEOPLE ARE LEAST LIKELY TO CONTRACT RICKETS.

liberally endowed with sweat glands than is the skin of other mammals; in combination with our lack of heavy body hair, this makes for effective elimination of excess body heat in a hot climate. This would have been especially advantageous to early hominines on the savanna, who could have avoided confrontations with carnivorous animals by carrying out most of their activities in the heat of the day. For the most part, carnivores rest during this period, being active from dusk until early morning. Without much hair to cover early hominine bodies, selection would have favored dark skins; hence all humans appear to have had a "Black" ancestry, no matter how "White" some of them may be today.

One should not conclude that, because it is newer, lightly pigmented skin is better, or more highly evolved, than heavily pigmented skin. The latter is clearly more highly evolved to the conditions of life in the tropics, although with protective clothing, hats, and sunscreen lotions, lightly pigmented peoples can survive there. Conversely, the availability of supplementary sources of vitamin D allows heavily pigmented peoples to do quite well away from the tropics. In both cases, culture has rendered skin color differences largely irrelevant.

An interesting question is how long it took for light pigmentation to develop in populations living outside the tropics. We now know that the first people to reach Australia did so about 60,000 years ago. They came there from tropical Southeast Asia and, as we would expect, had darkly pigmented skin. In Australia, those populations that spread south of the tropics (where, as in northern latitudes, ultraviolet radiation is less intense) underwent some reduction of pigmentation. But for all that, their skin color is still far

Although Tasmania is as far south of the equator as Europe is north of it, native Tasmanians were more darkly pigmented. Although the ancestors of both Europeans and Tasmanians lived in tropical regions, populations did not arrive in Tasmania until a good deal later than they reached Europe. Consequently, Tasmanians have not been subject to selection for light pigmentation for as long as have Europeans.

darker than that of Europeans or East Asians (remember that most of today's Southeast Asian population spread there from southern China following the invention of farming—hence their relatively light pigmentation). The obvious conclusion is that 60,000 years is not enough to produce advanced depigmentation and that Europeans and East Asians lived outside the tropics for a far longer period.[8]

The inheritance of skin color is not well understood, except that several genes (rather than variants of a single gene), each with several alleles, must be involved. Nevertheless, its geographical distribution, with few

[8]Ferrie, H. (1997). An interview with C. Loring Brace. *Current Anthropology, 38,* 864.

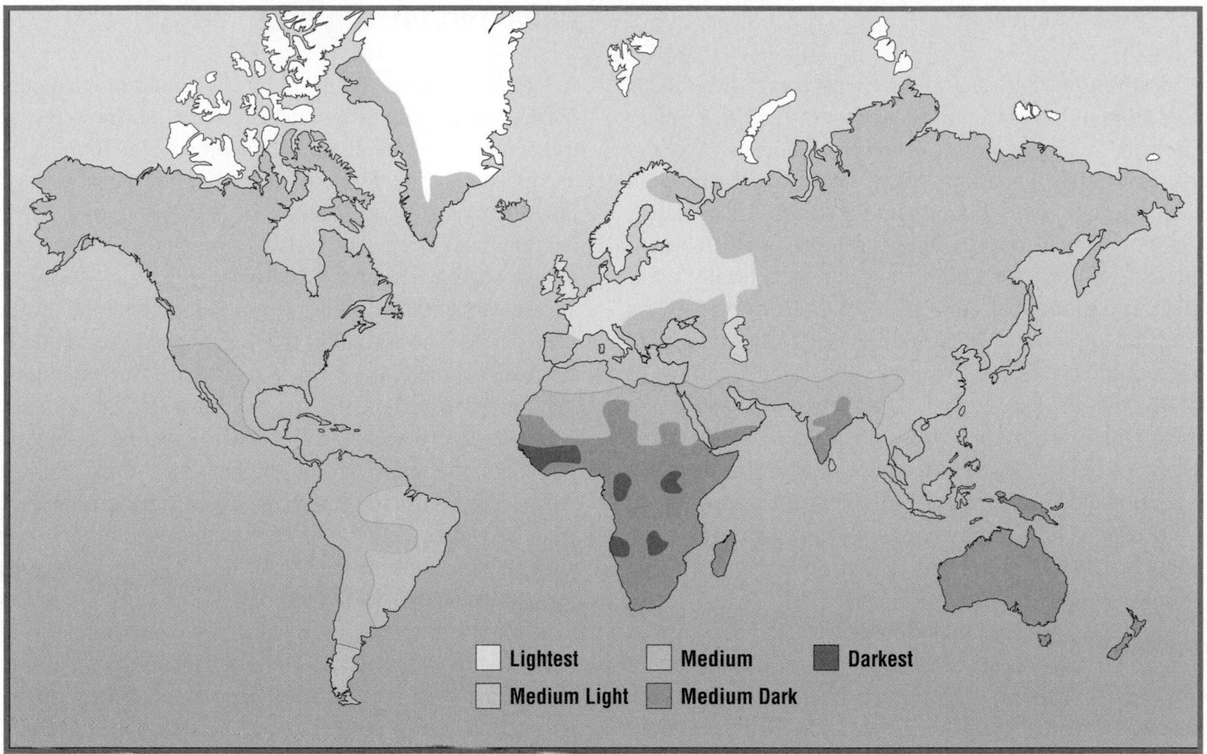

FIGURE 13.3

This map illustrates the distribution of dark and light human skin pigmentation before A.D. 1492. Medium-light skin color in Southeast Asia reflects the spread into that region of people from southern China, whereas the medium darkness of people native to southern Australia is a consequence of their tropical Southeast Asian ancestry. Lack of a dark skin pigmentation among tropical populations of native Americans reflects their ancestry in Northeast Asia a mere 20,000 years ago.

exceptions, tends to be continuous, like that of other human traits (Figure 13.3). The exceptions have to do with the movement of certain populations from their original homelands to other regions or the practice of selective mating, or both. For example, there have been repeated invasions of the Indian subcontinent by peoples from the north, who were then incorporated into the Hindu caste system. Still today, the higher the caste, the lighter its skin color. This skin color gradient is maintained by strict in-group marriage rules. In the United States, statistical studies have shown that there has been a similar trend among African Americans, with African American women of higher status choosing to marry lighter-skinned males, reflecting the culture's emphasis on the supposed superiority of people with light skin. It is quite possible that the Black Pride movement, which places positive value on features common among those of West African descent—such as dark skins, tightly curled hair, and broad, flat noses—is leading to a reversal of this cultural selection factor.

THE SOCIAL SIGNIFICANCE OF RACE: RACISM

Scientific facts, unfortunately, have been slow to change what people think about race. **Racism** can be viewed solely as a social problem, although at times it has been used by politicians as a purportedly scientific tool. It is an emotional phenomenon best explained in terms of collective psychology. Racial conflict results from long-suppressed resentments and hostilities. The racist responds to social stereotypes, not to known scientific facts.

Racism. A doctrine of racial superiority by which one group asserts its superiority over another.

Race and Behavior

The assumption that there are behavioral differences among human races remains an issue to which many people in contemporary society tenaciously cling. Throughout history, certain "races" have been attributed certain characteristics that assume a variety of names—national character, spirit, temperament—all of them vague and standing for a number of concepts totally unrelated to any biological concept of race. Common myths involve the "coldness" of Scandinavians or the "martial" character of Germanics or the "indolent" nature of Africans. These generalizations serve to characterize a people unjustly; German citizens do not necessarily advocate genocide, nor do Africans necessarily hate to work. The term *race* has a precise biological meaning, but in popular usage, as we have already seen, the term often acquires a meaning unrelated to that given by scientists, often with disastrous results.

To date, no innate behavioral characteristic can be attributed to any group of people that the nonscientist would most probably term a "race" that cannot be explained in terms of cultural practices. If the Chinese happen to exhibit exceptional visuo-spatial skills, it is probably because the business of learning to read Chinese characters requires a visuo-spatial kind of learning that is not needed to master Western alphabets.[9] If African Americans are not as well represented in managerial positions as their fellow citizens, it is because for a long time they were allowed neither the necessary training nor the opportunity (nor is the problem fully rectified today). The list could go on, and all such differences or characteristics can be explained in terms of culture.

Similarly, high crime rates among certain groups can be explained with reference to culture rather than biology. Individuals alienated and demoralized by poverty, injustice, and inequality of opportunity tend to display what the dominant members of society regard as antisocial behavior more frequently than those who are culturally well-integrated. For example, American Indians, when they have been equipped and allowed to compete on an equal footing with other North Americans, have not suffered from the high rate of alcoholism and criminal behavior exhibited by Indians living under conditions of poverty, whether on or off reservations.

[9]Chan, J. W. C., & Vernon, P. E. (1988). Individual differences among the peoples of China. In J. W. Berry (Ed.), *Human abilities in cultural context* (pp. 340–357). Cambridge, England: Cambridge University Press.

Race and Intelligence

A question frequently asked by those unfamiliar with the deficiencies of the race concept is whether some races are inherently more intelligent than others. Intelligence tests carried on in the United States by European American investigators among people of European and African descent have often shown that European Americans attain higher scores. During World War I, a series of IQ tests known as Alpha and Beta were regularly given to draftees. The results showed that the average score attained by European Americans was higher than that obtained by African Americans. Even though many African Americans scored higher than some European Americans, and some African Americans scored higher than most European Americans (African Americans from northern states, for instance, score better on average than southern Whites), many people took this as proof of the intellectual superiority of "White people." But all the tests really showed was that, on the average, European Americans outperformed African Americans in certain social situations. The tests did not measure "intelligence" per se, but the ability, conditioned by culture, of certain individuals to respond to certain socially conditioned problems. These tests had been conceived by European Americans for comparable middle-class European Americans. Although people of color coming from similar backgrounds generally did well (Chinese and Japanese Americans, for example, generally outperform Whites), African Americans as well as people of color coming from other backgrounds to meet the challenge of these tests were clearly at a disadvantage. It would be unrealistic to expect individuals unfamiliar with European American middle-class values and linguistic behavior to respond to a problem based on a familiarity with these.

Many large-scale intelligence tests continue to be administered in the United States. Notable among these are several series that attempt to hold environmental factors constant. Where this is done, African and European Americans tend to score equally well.[10] Nor is this surprising; because genes assort themselves independently of one another, there is no reason to suppose that whatever alleles may be associated with intelligence are likely to be concordant with the ones for skin pigmentation. Intelligence tests, however, have increasingly become the subject of controversy. There are many psychologists as well as anthropologists who are convinced that their use is overdone. Intelligence tests, they say, are of limited use, because they

[10]Sanday, P. R. (1975). On the causes of IQ differences between groups and implications for social policy. In M. F. A. Montagu (Ed.), *Race and IQ* (pp. 232–238). New York: Oxford.

are applicable only to particular cultural circumstances. Only when these circumstances are carefully met can any meaningful generalizations be derived from the use of tests.

Notwithstanding the foregoing, there continue to be some who insist that there are significant differences in intelligence among human populations. Recent proponents of this view are the psychologist Richard Herrnstein and Charles Murray, a social scientist who is a fellow of the American Enterprise Institute, a conservative think tank. Their argument, in a lengthy (and highly publicized) book entitled *The Bell Curve,* is that a well-documented 15-point difference in IQ exists between African and European Americans, with the latter scoring higher, though not quite as high as Asian Americans. Furthermore, they assert that these differences are mostly determined by genetic factors and are therefore immutable.

Herrnstein and Murray's book has been justly criticized on many grounds, including violation of basic rules of statistics and their practice of utilizing studies, no matter how flawed, that appear to support their thesis while ignoring or barely mentioning those that contradict it. But does this mean that they are wrong? On purely theoretical grounds, could we not suppose that, just as we see a spectrum of inherited variations in physical traits—skin color, hair texture, height, or whatever—might not there be similar variation in innate intellectual potential of different populations? It is likely that just as there are genes affecting the development of such things as blue eyes, curly hair, or heavily pigmented skin, there are others affecting the development of intelligence. Of course, even if genes affecting intelligence do exist, we would still need to ask why their distribution should be any more concordant with those for skin color than with ones that determine whether one has A, B, or O blood, normal or abnormal (antimalarial) hemoglobin, sufficient lactase to digest raw milk, or whatever.

A number of studies have appeared to indicate an appreciable degree of hereditary control of intelligence. First, there is a general tendency for those pairs of individuals who are most genetically similar (identical twins) to be most similar in intelligence, even when reared in different environments. Furthermore, the scores on IQ tests of biological parents and their children are correlated and tend to be similar, whereas foster parents and their foster children show less of this tendency. There are, however, enormous problems in attempting to separate genetic components from environmental contributors.[11] As biologists Richard Lewontin and Steven Rose with psychologist Leon Kamin observe, twin studies are plagued by a host of problems: inadequate sample sizes, biased subjective judgments, failure to make sure that "separated twins" really were raised separately, unrepresentative samples of adoptees to serve as controls, untested assumptions about similarity of environments. In fact, children reared by the same mother resemble her in IQ to the same degree, whether or not they share her genes.[12] Clearly, we do not know what the heritability of intelligence really is.[13]

Whatever the degree of heritability may be, it is clear that the effects of environment are important for intelligence. This should not surprise us, as even traits of high heritability are strongly influenced by environmental

[11]Andrews, L. B., & Nelkin, D. (1996). The bell curve: A statement. *Science, 271,* 13.

[12]Lewontin, R. C., Rose, S., & Kamin, L. J. (1984). *Not in our genes* (pp. 100, 113, 116). New York: Pantheon.

[13]Ibid., pp. 9, 121.

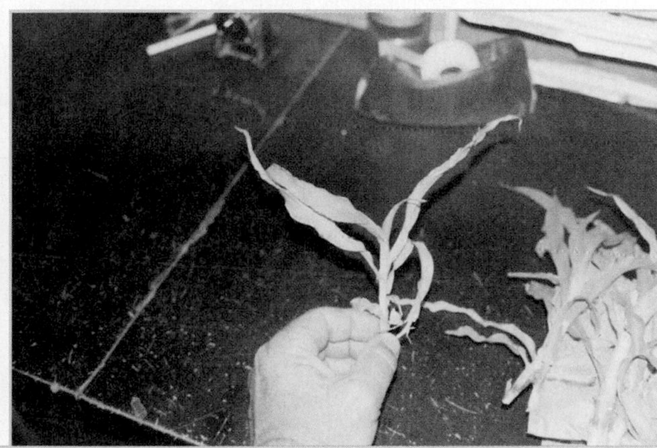

These photos show how important the environment is in the expression of genetic traits. The same strain of corn that flourishes in one set of circumstances may do quite poorly in another.

factors. Height in humans, for example, is genetically determined while being dependent both upon nutrition and health status (severe illness in childhood arrests growth, and renewed growth never makes up for this loss). With respect to intelligence, in the early 1900s, new immigrants to the United States, many of whom were Jews, scored lower on IQ tests than U.S.-born Whites. Today, the descendants of those Jewish immigrants score 10 points higher on average than Whites. In fact, as in most industrial countries, IQ scores of all groups in the United States have risen some 15 points in the last 40 years, some faster than others. The gap between African and European Americans, for example, is narrower today than in the past. Nor is this surprising, for there are studies showing impressive IQ scores for African American children from poor backgrounds who have been adopted into affluent and intellectual homes. It is now known that disadvantaged children adopted into affluent and stable families can boost their IQs by 20 points. It is also well known that IQ scores rise with the amount of schooling the test-takers have. More such cases could be cited, but these suffice to make the point: The assertion that IQ is fixed and immutable is clearly false. Just as millions of people routinely overcome deficiencies of vision that are far more heritable than *anyone* claims intelligence to be, so may enriched education increase intelligence.

Intelligence: What Is It?

A question that must now be asked is: What do we mean by the term *intelligence*? To some, the answer is: that which is measured by IQ tests. Unfortunately, there is no general agreement as to what abilities or talents actually make up what we call intelligence, even though there are some psychologists who insist that it is a single quantifiable thing. Many more psychologists have come to believe intelligence to be the product of the interaction of different sorts of cognitive abilities: verbal, mathematical-logical, spatial, linguistic, musical, bodily kinesthetic, social, and personal.[14] Each may be thought of as a particular kind of intelligence, unrelated to the others. This being so, they must be independently inherited (to the degree they are inherited), just as height, blood type, skin color, and so forth are independently inherited. Thus, the various abilities that constitute intelligence may be independently distributed as are, for example, the previously discussed skin color and blood type (compare Figures 13.3 and 13.4).

The next question is: If we are not exactly sure what IQ tests are measuring, how can we be sure of the valid-

[14]Jacoby, R., & Glauberman, N. (Eds.). (1995). *The Bell Curve debate* (pp. 7, 55–56, 59). New York: Random House.

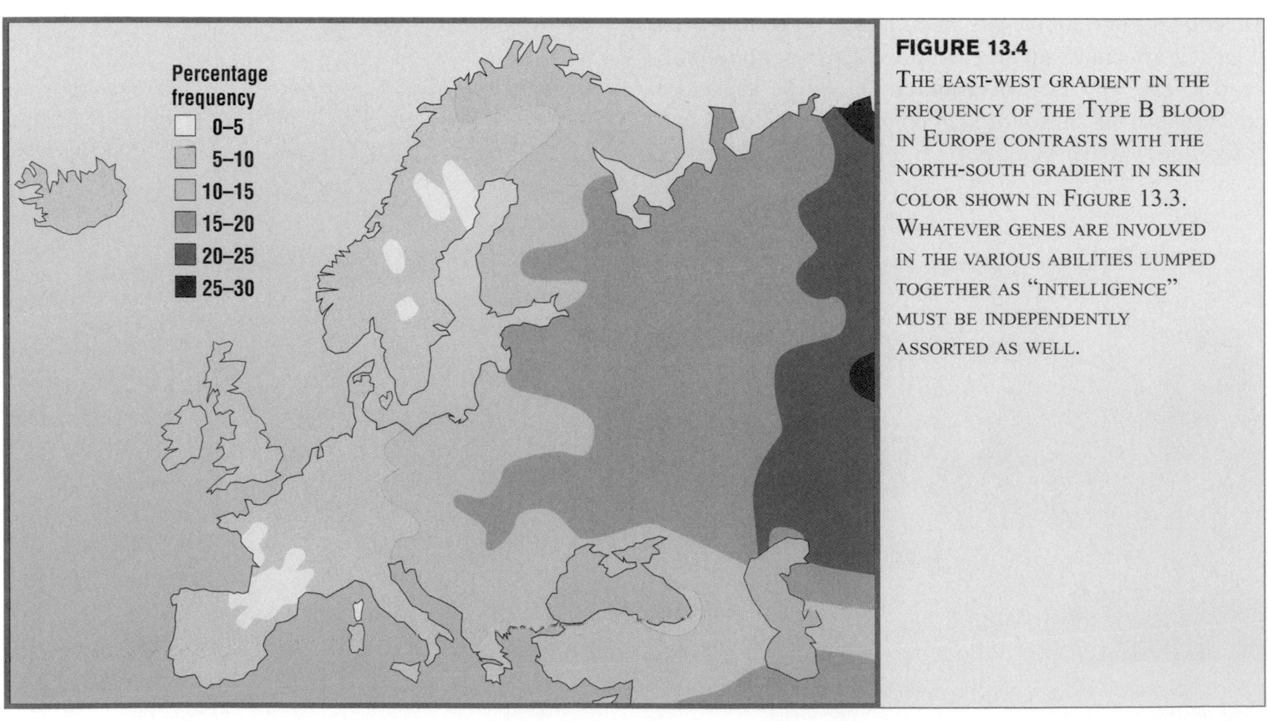

FIGURE 13.4

THE EAST-WEST GRADIENT IN THE FREQUENCY OF THE TYPE B BLOOD IN EUROPE CONTRASTS WITH THE NORTH-SOUTH GRADIENT IN SKIN COLOR SHOWN IN FIGURE 13.3. WHATEVER GENES ARE INVOLVED IN THE VARIOUS ABILITIES LUMPED TOGETHER AS "INTELLIGENCE" MUST BE INDEPENDENTLY ASSORTED AS WELL.

On one IQ test designed to be fair to both Black and White American students, they are asked to identify either of two famous scientists, Albert Einstein or George Washington Carver. Unfortunately, Carver is mostly a White person's Black hero, so a White is more likely to identify either than is a Black (see Mark Cohen, 1995, "Anthropology and Race: The Bell Curve Phenomenon," *General Anthropology 2*(1), p. 3).

ity of such tests—that is, can we be sure an IQ test measures what it is supposed to measure? The answer, of course, is that we cannot be sure. But, even at best, an IQ test measures performance (something that one does) rather than genetic disposition (something that lies within the individual). Reflected in one's performance are one's past experiences and present motivational state, as well as one's innate ability. In sum, it is fair to say that an IQ test is not a reliable measure of innate intelligence.

Attempts to prove the existence of significant differences in intelligence among human populations have been going on as long as people have been talking about race. But in spite of all, the hypothesis remains unproved. Nor is it ever likely to be proved, in view of what we saw in Chapter 10 as the major thrust in the evolution of the genus *Homo.* Over the past 2.5 million years, in all populations of this genus, the emphasis has been on cultural adaptation—actively inventing solutions to the problems of existence, rather than passively relying on biological adaptation. Thus, we would expect a comparable degree of intelligence in all present-day human populations. But even if this were not the case, it would mean only that dull and bright people are to be found in all human populations, though in different frequencies. Remember: Within-group variation is greater than between-group variation. Thus, geniuses can and do appear in any population, regardless of what that population's average intelligence may be. The fact of the matter is that the only way to be sure that individual human beings develop their innate abilities and skills, whatever they may be, to the fullest is to make sure they have access to the necessary resources and the opportunity to do so. This certainly cannot be accomplished if whole populations are assumed at the outset to be inferior.

This photo of African, Asian, Native American, and other winners of the Nobel Peace Prize was taken in 1998. It illustrates the point that individuals of exceptional ability can and do appear in any human population.

CONTINUING HUMAN BIOLOGICAL EVOLUTION

In the course of their evolution, humans in all parts of the world came to rely on cultural rather than biological adaptation for their survival. Nevertheless, as they spread beyond their tropical homeland into other parts of the world, they did develop considerable physical variation from one population to another. The forces responsible for this include genetic drift—especially at the margins of their range where small populations were easily isolated for varying amounts of time—and biological adaptation to differing climates.

Although much of this physical variation can still be seen in human populations today, the increasing effectiveness of cultural adaptation has often reduced its importance. For instance, the consumption of cod liver oil or vitamin D-fortified milk has canceled out the selective advantage of lightly pigmented skins in northern peoples. At the same time, culture has also imposed its own selective pressures, as we have seen in preceding chapters. Just as the invention of the spear-thrower was followed by a reduction in overall muscularity, or just as the transition to food production was followed by worsened health and mortality, so cultural practices today are affecting the human organism in important, often surprising, ways.

The probability of alterations in human biological makeup induced by culture raises a number of important questions. By trying to eliminate genetic variants for balanced polymorphic traits, such as the sickle-cell trait discussed in Chapter 3, are we also removing alleles that have survival value? Are we weakening the gene pool by allowing people with hereditary diseases and defects to reproduce? Are we reducing chances for genetic variation by trying to control population size?

We do not have answers to all of these questions. If we are able to wipe out sickle-cell anemia, we also may be able to wipe out malaria; thus, we would have eliminated the condition that made the sickle-cell trait advantageous. On the other hand, antimalarial campaigns have had no more than limited success, as the disease afflicts some 270 million people around the world. In 1997, 1.5 million to 2.7 million deaths were caused by malaria, making it the fifth largest infectious killer in the world. Moreover, as a consequence of global warming, the disease could spread (with a number of others) into more northerly regions. Although it is not certain, it is at least possible that over the next century, an average temperature increase of 3°C could result in 50 million to 80 million new malaria cases per year.[15] Nor is it strictly true that medical science is weakening the gene pool by letting those with disorders for which there may be a genetic predisposition, such as diabetes, reproduce. In the present environment, where medication is easily available, such people are as fit as anyone else. However, if such people are denied access to the needed medication, their biological fitness is lost and they die out. In fact, one's financial status affects one's access to medication, and so, however unintentional it may be, one's biological

[15]Stone, R. (1995). If the mercury soars, so may health hazards. *Science,* 267, 958.

fitness in North American society may be decided by one's financial status.

Examples of culture enabling individuals to reproduce even though they suffer from genetic disorders are familiar. Perhaps less familiar are the cases in which medical technology selects against some individuals by removing them from the reproducing population. One example can be seen in South Africa. About 1 percent of South Africans of Dutch descent have a gene that, in its dominant form, causes porphyria, a disorder that renders the skin of its victims sensitive to light and causes skin abrasions. If these Afrikaners remain in a rural environment, they suffer only minor skin abrasions as a result of their condition. However, the allele renders them very sensitive to modern medical treatment, such as they might receive in a large urban center like Johannesburg. If they are treated for some problem unrelated to porphyria, with barbiturates or similar drugs, they suffer acute attacks and very often die. In a relatively quiet rural environment where medical services are less readily accessible, the Afrikaners with this peculiar condition are able to live normal lives; it is only in an urban context, where they are more likely to receive medical attention, that they suffer physical impairment or loss of life.

Another example of culture acting as an agent of biological selection has to do with lactose tolerance: the ability to assimilate **lactose,** the primary constituent of fresh milk. This ability depends on the presence of a particular enzyme, **lactase,** in the small intestine. Failure to retain lactase into adulthood, although controlled by recessive alleles, is characteristic of mammals in general, as well as most human populations—especially Asian, native Australian, Native American, and many (but not all) African populations. Hence, only 10 to 30 percent of Americans of African descent and 0 to 30 percent of adult Asians retain lactase into adulthood and so are lactose tolerant.[16] By contrast, lactase retention and lactose tolerance are normal for over 80 percent of adults of northern European descent. Eastern Europeans, Arabs, and some East Africans are closer to northern Europeans in lactase retention than they are to Asians and other Africans. Generally speaking, a high retention of lactase is found in populations with a long tradition of fresh milk as an important dietary item. In such populations, selection has in the past favored those individuals with the dominant allele that confers the ability to assimilate lactose, selecting out those without this allele.

In developing countries, milk supplements are used in the treatment of acute protein-calorie malnutrition. Tube-fed diets of milk are used in connection with other medical procedures. Quite apart from medical practices, powdered milk has long been a staple of economic aid to other countries. Such practices in fact discriminate against the members of populations in which lactase is not commonly retained into adulthood. At the least, those individuals who are not lactose tolerant will be unable to

[16]Harrison, G. G. (1975). Primary adult lactase deficiency: A problem in anthropological genetics. *American Anthropologist, 77,* 815–819.

The routine use of antibiotics to prevent disease and reduce the amount of feed needed to fatten animals has produced lethal strains of bacteria (previously harmless to humans) that resist antibiotic treatment. One example is the emergence of enterococci as a threat to public health. These bacteria usually dwell peacefully in the human gut, but new strains have emerged that poison organs and cause the immune system to go haywire. Because of the bacteria's resistence to antibiotics, thousands of people die each year.

Lactose. The primary constituent of fresh milk. • **Lactase.** An enzyme in the small intestine that enables humans to assimilate lactose.

utilize the nutritive value of milk; frequently they will suffer diarrhea, abdominal cramping, and even bone degeneration, with serious results. In fact, the shipping of powdered milk to victims of South American earthquakes in the 1960s caused many deaths among them.

Among Europeans, the evolution of lactose tolerance is linked with evolution of a nonthrifty genotype.[17] Until about 6,000 years ago all humans were characterized by a **thrifty genotype.** This permitted efficient storage of fat to draw on in times of food shortage, and in times of scarcity conserved glucose (a simple sugar) for use in brain and red blood cells (as opposed to other tissues such as muscle), as well as nitrogen (vital for growth and health) through the body's diminished exertion. Regular access to lactose, a source of glucose, led to selection for the nonthrifty genotype as protection against adult-onset diabetes, or at least its onset relatively late in life (at a nonreproductive age). By contrast, populations that are lactose intolerant retain the thrifty genotype. As a consequence, when they are introduced to Western-style diets, characterized by abundance, particularly of foods high in sugar content, the incidence of diabetes skyrockets.

In recent years, there has been considerable concern about human activities that damage the earth's ozone layer. A major contributor to the ozone layer's deterioration has been the use of chlorofluorocarbons in aerosol sprays, refrigeration and air conditioning, and the manufacture of Styrofoam. Because the ozone layer screens out some of the sun's ultraviolet rays, its continued deterioration will expose humans to increased ultraviolet radiation. As we saw earlier in this chapter, some ultraviolet radiation is necessary for the production of vitamin D, but excessive amounts lead, among other things, to an increased incidence of skin cancers. Hence a rising incidence of skin cancers is not surprising, as the ozone layer continues to deteriorate.

Although a ban on the use of chlorofluorocarbons in aerosol sprays was imposed some years ago, the destruction of the ozone layer continued about twice as fast as scientists had predicted it would, even without the ban. Subsequently, an international treaty further limiting the use of chlorofluorocarbons was negotiated, but this ban has merely slowed, rather than halted, further deterioration. In fact, the ozone hole over Antarctica in October 1994 was the severest ever recorded in 35 years. Most immediately affected by the consequent increase in ultraviolet radiation are the world's lightly pigmented peoples, but ultimately, all will be affected.

Ozone depletion is merely one of a host of problems confronted by humans today that ultimately have an impact on human gene pools. In view of the consequences for human biology of such seemingly benign innovations as dairying or (as discussed in Chapter 11) farming, we may wonder about many recent practices—for example, the effects of increased exposure to radiation from increased use of x-rays and CT scans, nuclear accidents, increased production of radioactive wastes, and the like. To be sure, we are constantly reassured by various experts that we are protected by adequate safety regulations, but one is not reassured by discoveries, such as the one announced by the National Academy of Sciences in 1989, that what were accepted as safe levels of radiation were in fact too high; or the earlier discovery that the supposedly safe treatment of sinus disorders in the 1940s by massive doses of x-ray radiation produced a bumper crop of thyroid cancers in the late 1960s. But it is not just increased exposure to radiation that we confront but increased exposure to other known mutagenic agents, including a wide variety of chemicals, such as pesticides. Despite repeated assurances about their safety, there have been tens of thousands of cases of poisonings in the United States alone (probably more in so-called underdeveloped countries, where controls are even less effective than in the United States and where substances banned in the United States are routinely used), and thousands of cases of cancer related to the manufacture and use of pesticides. All this on top of the several million birds killed each year (many of which would otherwise have been happily gobbling down bugs and other pests), serious fish kills, honey bee kills (bees are needed for the efficient pollination of many crops), and the like. In all, pesticides alone (never mind other agricultural chemicals) are responsible for an estimated $8 *billion* worth of environmental and public health damage in the United States each year.[18]

Aside from pesticides, there are other dangerous substances, like the hormone-disrupting chemicals. In 1938, a synthetic estrogen known as DES was developed and subsequently prescribed for a variety of ailments ranging from acne to prostate cancer. Moreover, tons of it are routinely added to animal feeds. It was not until 1971, however, that the first indication that DES causes vaginal

[17]Allen, J. S., & Cheer, S. M. (1996). The non-thrifty genotype. *Current Anthropology, 37,* 831–842.

[18]Pimentel, D. (1991). Response. *Science, 252,* 358.

Thrifty genotype. Human genotype that permits efficient storage of fat to draw on in times of food shortage and conservation of glucose and nitrogen.

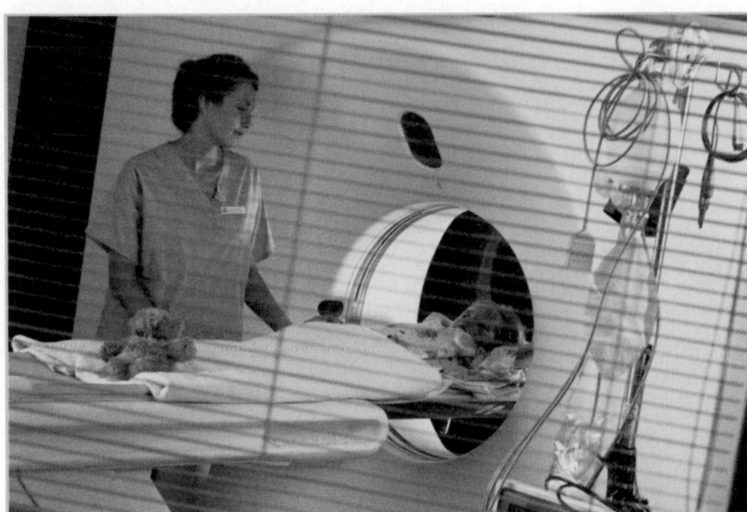

In 2001, the leading radiology journal in the United States published studies showing that children in this country receiving CT scans of the head and abdomen absorb 2 to 6 times the radiation needed to produce clear images. As a consequence, about 1,500 of them will die later of radiation-induced cancers.

cancer in young women came to light. Subsequent research has shown that DES causes problems with the male reproductive system and causes deformities of the female reproductive tract. DES mimics the natural hormone, binding with appropriate receptors in and on cells and thereby turns on biological activity associated with the hormone. As one group of scientists observes,

> The synthetic hormone has two troublesome traits. First, it triggers certain parts of the reproductive system more effectively than does estradiol, one of the body's own estrogens. . . . Even more important, it manages to circumvent a mechanism that protects the fetus from the developmentally disruptive effects of excessive estrogen exposure. Normally, special maternal and fetal blood proteins soak up almost all excess circulating estrogen. But they do not recognize DES. As a consequence, DES in the fetal blood supply remains biologically active.[19]

DES is not alone in its effects: At least 51 chemicals—many of them in common use—are now known to disrupt hormones, and even this could be the tip of the iceberg. Some of these chemicals mimic hormones in the manner of DES, whereas others interfere with other parts of the endocrine system, such as thyroid and testosterone metabolism. Included are such supposedly benign and inert substances as plastics widely used in laboratories and chemicals added to polystyrene and polyvinyl chloride (PVCs) to make them more stable and less breakable. These plastics are widely used in plumbing, food processing, and food packaging. Hormone disrupting chemicals are also found in many detergents and personal care products, contraceptive creams, the giant jugs used to bottle drinking water, and plastic linings in cans (about 85 percent of food cans in the United States are so lined).

In the spring of 2000 Dursban, the most widely used pesticide, was phased out of use in the United States. After some 30 years of use, it was found to be more dangerous than thought, and supposedly safe levels were found to be unsafe.

[19]Colburn, T., Dumanoski, D., & Myers, J. P. (1996). Hormonal sabotage. *Natural History,* (3), 45–46.

HIGHWAY 1

Read leading scientists critiques of Herrnstein and Murray's book, *The Bell Curve*. Learn more about the problems and biases built into race-based intelligence testing.
www.indiana.edu/~intell/bellcurve.html

HIGHWAY 2

Visit the American Anthropological Association Web site to read the discipline's statement on race. Also, see how professional anthropologists work to bring their intellectual framework into the realm of public policy through their response to Office of Management and Budget (OMB) Directive 15 on federal standards for the reporting of "racial" and "ethnic" statistics.
www.aaanet.org/stmts/racepp.htm

The implications of all these developments are sobering. We know that pathologies result from extremely low levels of exposure to harmful chemicals. Yet, besides those used domestically, millions of pounds are exported to the rest of the world (40 million pounds in 1991 alone).[20] It is quite possible that hormone disruptions are at least partially responsible for certain trends that have recently become causes for concern among scientists. These range from increasingly early onset of puberty in human females to dramatic declines in human sperm counts. With respect to the latter, some 61 separate studies confirm that sperm counts have dropped almost 50 percent from 1938 to 1990 (Figure 13.5). Most of these studies were carried out in the United States and Europe, but some from Africa, Asia, and South America show that this is essentially a worldwide phenomenon. If this trend continues, it will have profound results.

It is not that the experts who assure us of the safety of such things are deliberately misleading us. (Although there are cases of that too, one notorious example being the case of asbestos. As early as 1902 it was included in a list of dusts known to be hazardous. By 1933 it was well documented as a cause of lung cancer, yet in the 1960s, corporate executives denied ever hearing of the dangers.) For the most part, experts are convinced of the validity of what they say; the difficulty is that serious problems, such as those having to do with radiation or exposure to various chemicals, have a way of not being apparent until years, or even decades later. By then, of course, serious financial interests are at stake.

What is clear, then, is that cultural practices, probably as never before, are currently having an impact on human gene pools. Unquestionably, this impact is deleterious to those individuals who suffer the effects of negative selection, whose misery and death are the price paid for many of the material benefits of civilization we enjoy today. It remains to be seen just what the long-term effects on the human species as a whole will be. If the promise of genetic engineering offers hope of alleviating some of the misery and death that result from our own practices, it also raises the specter of removing genetic variants that might turn out to be of future adaptive value, or that might turn out to make us immediately susceptible to new problems that we don't even know about today.

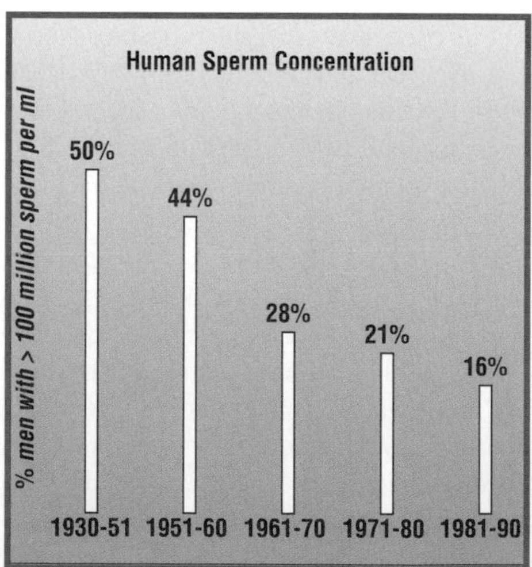

FIGURE 13.5
A DOCUMENTED DECLINE IN HUMAN MALE SPERM COUNTS WORLDWIDE MAY BE RELATED TO WIDESPREAD EXPOSURE TO HORMONE-DISRUPTING CHEMICALS.

[20] Ibid., 47.

Anthropology Applied

Studying the Emergence of New Diseases*

Ever since the Neolithic, humans have had to cope with a host of new diseases that got their start as a consequence of changes in human behavior. This has become a renewed source of concern following a recent resurgence of infectious diseases and appearance and spread of a host of new and lethal diseases. All told, more than 30 diseases new to medicine have emerged in the past 25 years, of which perhaps the best known is AIDS. This has now become number 4 among infectious killers of humans, with 5.8 million people infected in 1998 alone.† But there are others–like Ebola, which causes victims to hemorrhage to death, blood pouring from every orifice; hemorrhagic fevers like Dengue fever, Lassa fever, and Hantavirus; Invasive Streptococcus A, which consumes the victims' flesh; Legionnaire's disease; and Lyme disease. What has sparked the appearance and spread of these and other new diseases has been a considerable mystery, but one theory is that some are the result of human activities. In particular, the intrusion of people into new ecological settings, such as rain forests, along with construction of roads allows viruses and other infectious microbes to spread rapidly to large numbers of people. It is now generally accepted that the HIV virus responsible for AIDS transferred to humans from chimpanzees in the forests of the Democratic Republic of Congo as a consequence of hunting and butchering these animals for food. For the first 30 years, few people were affected; it was not until people began congregating in cities like Kinshasa that conditions were ripe for an epidemic.

To gain a better understanding of the interplay between ecological disturbance and the emergence of new diseases, anthropologist Carol Jenkins, whose specialty is medical anthropology, obtained a grant from the MacArthur Foundation in 1993. From her base at the Papua New Guinea Institute of Medical Research, she is following what happens to the health of local people in the wake of a massive logging operation, begun in 1993. From this should come a better understanding of how disease organisms spread from animal hosts to humans. Since most of the "new" viruses that have suddenly afflicted humans are in fact old ones that have been present in animals like monkeys (monkey pox), rodents (Hanta virus), deer (Lyme disease), and insects (West Nile virus), it appears that something new has enabled them to jump from their animal hosts to humans. A recent example comes from the Democratic Republic of Congo. Here civil war created a situation where villagers in the central part of the country were faced with starvation. Their response was to increase the hunting of animals, including monkeys, squirrels, and rats that carry a disease called monkey pox. Related to smallpox, the disease transfers easily to humans, resulting in the largest outbreak of this disease ever seen among humans. What makes this outbreak even more serious is an apparently new strain of the infection, enabling it to spread from person to person, instead of only from an animal host.‡

Large-scale habitat disturbance is an obvious candidate for such disease transfers, but this needs to be confirmed and the process understood. So far, it is hard to make more than a circumstantial case, by looking back after a disease outbreak. The work of Jenkins and her team is unique in that she was able to get baseline health data on local people before their environment was disturbed. Thus, she is in a position to follow events as they unfold.

It will be some time before conclusions can be drawn from Jenkins' study. Its importance is obvious; in an era of globalization, as air travel allows more and more tropical diseases to spread beyond the tropics, we need a fuller understanding of how viruses interact with their hosts if we are to devise effective preventive and therapeutic strategies to deal with them.

---

*Gibbons, A. (1993). Where are new diseases born? *Science, 261,* 680–681.

†Balter, M. (1998). On world AIDS day, a shadow looms over southern Africa. *Science, 282,* 1,790.

‡Cohen, J. (1997). Is an old virus up to new tricks? *Science, 277,* 312–313.

CHAPTER SUMMARY

In humans, most behavioral patterns are culturally learned or acquired. Other characteristics are determined by an interaction between genes and environment. The gene pools of populations contain various alternative alleles. When the environment changes, their gene pool confers the possibility for physical alteration to meet the change.

When a polymorphic species is separated into different faunal regions, it is usually polytypic; that is, populations differ in the frequency with which genetic variability is expressed. It appears that the human species has been polytypic at least since the time of *Homo erectus*. Gene flow, however, has prevented diversification into multiple species.

Early anthropologists classified *Homo sapiens* into subspecies, or races, based on geographic location and such phenotypic features as skin color, body size, head shape, and hair texture. The presence of atypical individuals and the nonconcordance of traits continually challenged these racial classifications. No examples of pure racial types could be found. The visible traits were found to occur in a worldwide continuum. No definite grouping of distinct, discontinuous biological groups has been found in modern humans.

A biological race is a population of a species that differs in the frequency of genetic variants from other populations of the same species. Three observations must be made concerning this biological definition: (1) It is arbitrary; (2) it does not mean that any one race has exclusive possession of any particular allele(s); and (3) individuals of one race will not necessarily be distinguishable from those of another. As a means for understanding human variation, the concept of race has several limitations. First, race is an arbitrary category, making agreement on any particular classification impossible; second, humans are so complex genetically that often the genetic basis of traits on which racial studies are based is itself poorly understood; and finally, race exists as a cultural as well as a biological category. Most anthropologists now view the race concept as useless for an understanding of human biological variation, preferring to study the distribution and significance of specific, genetically based characteristics, or else the characteristics of small breeding populations.

Physical anthropologists have determined that much of human physical variation appears related to climatic adaptation. People native to cold climates tend to have greater body bulk relative to their extremities than individuals who live in hot climates; the latter tend to be long and slender. Studies involving body build and climate are complicated by such other factors as the effects on physique of diet and of clothing.

In the United States, race is commonly thought of in terms of skin color. Subject to tremendous variation, skin color is a function of several factors: transparency or thickness of the skin, distribution of blood vessels, and amount of carotene and melanin in a given area of skin. Exposure to sunlight increases the amount of melanin, darkening the skin. Natural selection has favored heavily pigmented skin as protection against the strong solar radiation of equatorial latitudes. In northern latitudes, natural selection has favored relatively depigmented skins, which can utilize relatively weak solar radiation in the production of vitamin D. Selective mating, as well as geographic location, plays a part in skin color distribution.

Racism can be viewed solely as a social problem. It is an emotional phenomenon best explained in terms of collective psychology. The racist individual reacts on the basis of social stereotypes and not established scientific facts.

Notwithstanding the impossibility of defining biologically valid human races, many people have assumed that there are behavioral differences among human races. The innate behavioral characteristics attributed by these people to race can be explained in terms of enculturation rather than biology. Those intelligence tests that have been interpreted to indicate that European Americans are intellectually superior to African Americans are designed by European Americans for European Americans from similar backgrounds. It is not realistic to expect individuals who are not familiar with European American middle-class values to respond to items based on knowledge of these values. African and European Americans both, if they come from different types of backgrounds, are thus at a disadvantage. At present, it is not possible to separate the inherited components of intelligence from those that are culturally acquired. Furthermore, there is still no agreement on what intelligence really is, but it is made up probably of several different talents and abilities.

Although the human species has come to rely on cultural rather than biological adaptation for survival, human gene pools still continue to change in response to external factors. Many of these changes are brought about by cultural practices; for example, the shipment of powdered milk to human populations that are low in the frequency of the allele for lactase retention into adulthood may contribute to the death of large numbers of people. Those who survive are most likely to be those with the allele for lactase retention. Unquestionably, this kind of selection is deleterious to those individuals who are "selected out" in this way. Just what the long-term effects will be on the human species as a whole remains to be seen.

CLASSIC READINGS

Cohen, M. N. (1998). *Culture of intolerance: Chauvinism, class and racism in the United States.* New Haven, CT: Yale University Press.

This very readable book was written to counter political propaganda claiming that science affirms the need to shape the political order on the basis of inherent inequality and mutual disdain. In it, Cohen summarizes what scientific data *really* say about biological differences among humans; explores the depth, power, beauty, and potential value of cultural differences; shows how the cultural blinders of U.S. culture cause people in this country to misunderstand others as well as themselves; and looks at questionable assumptions in U.S. culture that promote intolerance and generate problems where none need exist.

Gould, S. J. (1996). *The mismeasure of man* (2nd ed.). New York: Norton.

This is an updating of a classic critique of supposedly scientific studies that attempt to rank all people on a linear scale of intrinsic and unalterable mental worth. The revision was prompted by what Gould refers to as the "latest cyclic episode of biodeterminism" represented by the publication of the widely discussed book, *The Bell Curve*.

Graves, J. L. (2001). *The emperor's new clothes: Biological theories of race at the millennium.* New Brunswick, NJ: Rutgers University Press.

Graves is a laboratory geneticist as well as an African American intellectual whose goal is to show the reader that there is no biological basis for separation of human beings into races and that the idea of race is a relatively recent social and political construction. His grasp of science is solid and up-to-date, and readers can benefit from the case he presents.

Jacoby, R., & Glauberman, N. (Eds.). (1995). *The Bell Curve debate.* New York: Random House.

This is a collection of articles by a wide variety of authors including biologists, anthropologists, psychologists, mathematicians, essayists, and others critically examining the claims and issues raised in the widely read and much discussed book, *The Bell Curve.* Included are pieces written to address many of the same issues as they were raised by earlier writers. For anyone who hopes to understand the race and intelligence debate, this book is a must.

Marks, J. (1995). *Human biodiversity: Genes, race and history.* Hawthorne, NY: Aldine de Gruyter.

In this book, Marks shows how genetics has undermined the fundamental assumptions of racial taxonomy. In addition to its presentation of the nature of human biodiversity, the book also deals with the history of cultural attitudes toward "race" and diversity.

PART V

Culture and Survival: Communicating, Raising Children, and Staying Alive

INTRODUCTION

All living creatures face a fundamental problem in common—that of survival. Simply put, unless they adapt themselves to some available environment, they cannot survive. Adaptation requires the development of behaviors that will help an organism use the environment to its advantage — to find food and sustenance, avoid hazards, and (if the species is to survive) reproduce its own kind. In turn, organisms need to have the biological equipment that allows development of appropriate patterns of behavior. For the hundreds of millions of years of life on earth, biological adaptation has been the primary means by which the problem of survival has been solved. This is accomplished as organisms of a particular kind, whose biological equipment is best suited to a particular way of life, produce more offspring than those whose equipment is not. In this way, advantageous characteristics become more common in succeeding generations, at the same time that less advantageous ones become less common.

One characteristic that ultimately did become common among mammals, to one degree or another, was the ability to learn new patterns of behavior to solve at least limited problems of existence. This problem-solving ability became particularly well developed among the last common ancestors of apes and humans, and by 2.5 million years ago (long after the human and ape lines of evolution had diverged), early members of the genus *Homo* began to rely increasingly on what their minds could invent rather than on what their bodies were capable of. Although the human species has not freed itself entirely, even today, from the forces of biological adaptation, it has come to rely primarily on culture — a body of learned traditions that, in essence, tells people how to live — as the medium through which the problems of human existence may be solved.

The consequences of this are profound. As the evolving genus *Homo* unconsciously came to rely more on cultural solutions to its problems as opposed to biological ones, its chances of survival improved. So it was that when members of this genus added scavenging to their subsistence practices some 2.5 million years ago, the resources available to them increased substantially. Moreover, the tools and techniques that made this new way of life possible made our ancient ancestors

less vulnerable to predators than they had been before. Thus, life became a bit easier, and with humans, as with other animals, this generally makes for easier reproduction. A slow but steady growth of human populations followed the development of scavenging and gathering.

Among most mammals, population growth frequently leads to the spillover of fringe populations into regions previously uninhabited by a species. There they find new environments, to which they must adapt or face extinction. This pattern of dispersal seems to have been followed by the evolving human species, for soon after the invention of scavenging and gathering, humans began to spread geographically, inhabiting new and even harsh environments. As they did so, they devised cultural rather than biological solutions to their new problems of existence. This is illustrated by human habitation of cold regions of the world, which was not dependent on the evolution of individuals capable of growing heavy coats of fur, as do other mammals that live in such places. Instead, our ancestors had the ability to devise forms of clothing and shelter that, coupled with the use of fire, enabled them to overcome the cold. Moreover, this "cold adaptation" could be rapidly changed in the face of different circumstances. The fact is that cultural equipment and techniques can be changed radically in less than a single generation. Biological change, by contrast, takes many generations to accomplish.

As the medium through which humans handle the problems of existence, culture is basic to human survival. It cannot do its job, though, unless it deals successfully with certain basic problems. Because culture is learned and not inherited biologically, its transmission from one person to another, and from one generation to the next, depends on an effective system of communication that must be far more complex than that of any other animal. Thus, a first requirement for any culture is providing a means of communication among individuals. All cultures do this through some form of language, one of the most distinctive of human possessions and the subject of Chapter 15.

In human societies each generation must learn its culture anew. The learning process itself is thus crucial to a culture's survival. A second requirement of culture, then, is the development of reliable means by which individuals learn the behavior expected of them as members of their community, and how children learn appears to be as important as what they learn. Since to a large extent adult personality is the product of life experiences, the ways children are raised and educated play a major part in the shaping of their later selves: The ability of individuals to function properly as adults depends, to a degree, upon how effectively their personalities have been shaped to fit their culture. As we see in Chapter 16, findings have emerged from anthropological investigations in these areas that have implications for human behavior that go beyond anthropology.

Important as effective communication and education are for the survival of a culture, they are of no avail unless the culture is able to satisfy the basic needs of the individuals who live by its rules. A third requirement of culture, therefore, is the ability to provide its members with food, water, and protection from the elements. Chapter 17 discusses the ways in which cultures handle people's basic needs and the ways societies adapt through culture to the environment. Since this leads to the production, distribution, and consumption of goods — the subject matter of economic anthropology — we conclude this section with a chapter (Chapter 18) on economic systems. ■

CHAPTER 14

THE NATURE OF CULTURE

The power of culture is illustrated by Cuban refugee Elian Gonzales and demonstrators against his return to Cuba. In this case, Elian was transformed into a symbol involving issues going far beyond his particular situation.

CHAPTER PREVIEW

1 What Is Culture?

Culture consists of the abstract values, beliefs, and perceptions of the world that lie behind people's behavior and that are reflected in their behavior. These are shared by members of a society, and when acted upon, they produce behavior that is intelligible to other members of that society. Cultures are learned, largely through the medium of language, rather than inherited biologically, and the parts of a culture function as an integrated whole.

2 How Is Culture Studied?

Anthropologists, like children, learn about a culture by experiencing it and talking about it with those who live by its rules. Of course, anthropologists have less time to learn, but they are more systematic in the way they learn. Through careful observation and discussion with informants who are particularly knowledgeable in the ways of their culture, the anthropologist abstracts a set of rules in order to explain how people behave in a particular society.

3 Why Do Cultures Exist?

People maintain cultures to deal with problems or matters that concern them. To survive, a culture must satisfy the basic needs of those who live by its rules, provide for its own continuity, and provide an orderly existence for the members of a society. In doing so, a culture must strike a balance between the self-interests of individuals and the needs of society as a whole. And finally, a culture must have the capacity to change in order to adapt to new circumstances or to altered perceptions of existing circumstances.

Students of anthropology are bound to find themselves studying a seemingly endless variety of human societies, each with its own distinctive system of politics, economics, and religion. Yet for all this variation, these societies have one thing in common. Each is a collection of people cooperating to ensure their collective survival and well-being. In order for this to work, some degree of predictable behavior is required of each individual within the society, for group living and cooperation are impossible unless individuals know how others are likely to behave in any given situation. In humans, it is culture that sets the limits of behavior and guides it along predictable paths.

THE CONCEPT OF CULTURE

The modern **culture** concept was first developed by anthropologists toward the end of the 19th century. The first really clear and comprehensive definition was that of the British anthropologist Sir Edward Burnett Tylor. Writing in 1871, Tylor defined culture as "that complex whole which includes knowledge, belief, art, law, morals, custom, and any other capabilities and habits acquired by man as a member of society." Since Tylor's time, definitions of culture have proliferated, so that by the early 1950s, North American anthropologists A. L. Kroeber and Clyde Kluckhohn were able to collect over a hundred definitions of culture from the literature. Recent definitions tend to distinguish more clearly between actual behavior on the one hand and the abstract values, beliefs, and perceptions of the world that lie behind that behavior on the other. To put it another way, culture is not observable behavior but rather the shared ideals, values, and beliefs that people use to interpret experience and generate behavior and that are reflected in their behavior.

CHARACTERISTICS OF CULTURE

Through the comparative study of many cultures, past and present, anthropologists have arrived at an understanding of the basic characteristics that all human cultures share. A careful study of these helps us to see the importance and the function of culture itself.

Culture Is Shared

Culture is a set of shared ideals, values, and standards of behavior; it is the common denominator that makes the actions of individuals intelligible to other members of their society and gives meaning to their lives. Because they share a common culture, people can predict how others are most likely to behave in a given circumstance and react accordingly. A group of people from different cultures, stranded over a period of time on a desert island, might appear to become a society of sorts. They would have a common interest—survival—and would develop techniques for living and working together. Each of the members of this group, however, would retain his or her own identity and cultural background, and the group would disintegrate without further ado as soon as its members were rescued from the island. The group would have been merely an aggregate in time and not a cultural entity. **Society** may be defined as a group of people who not only are dependent on each other for survival, but who share a common culture as well. The way in which these people depend upon each other can be seen in such things as their economic systems and their family relationships; moreover, members of a society are held together by a sense of common identity. The rule-governed relationships that hold a society together, with all their rights, duties, and obligations, are known as its **social structure.**

Culture and society are two closely related concepts, and anthropologists study both. Obviously, there can be no culture without a society, just as there can be no society without individuals. Conversely, there are no known human societies that do not exhibit culture. Some other species of animals, however, do lead a social existence. Ants and bees, for example, instinctively cooperate in a manner that clearly indicates a degree of social organization, yet this instinctual behavior is not a culture. One can, therefore, have a society (but not a *human* society) without a culture, even though one cannot have a culture without a society. Whether or not there exist animals other than humans that exhibit cultural behavior is a question that will be dealt with shortly.

While a culture is shared by members of a society, it is important to realize that all is not uniformity. For one thing, no one has the exact same version of his or her

Culture. The values, beliefs, and perceptions of the world shared by members of a society, that they use to interpret experience and generate behavior, and that are reflected in their behavior. • **Society.** A group of interdependent people who share a common culture. • **Social structure.** The rule-governed relationships of individuals and groups within a society that hold it together.

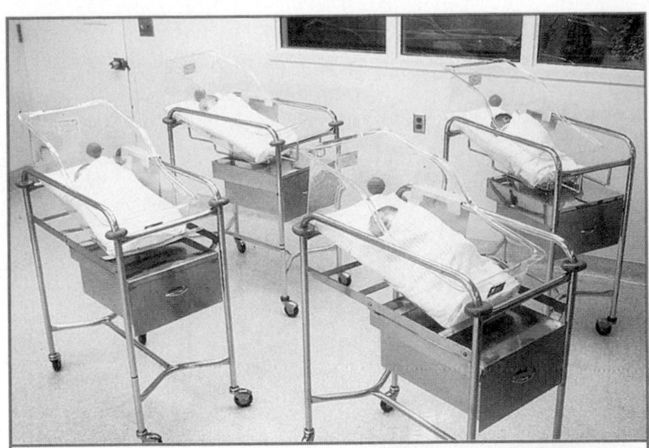

In the United States, European American culture requires that newborn infants be assigned a sexual identity of either male or female. Yet, significant numbers of infants are born each year whose genitalia do not conform to cultural expectations. Because only two genders are recognized, the usual reaction is surgery, to make the young bodies conform to cultural requirements. In most cases, male genitals are constructed, merely because they are easier.

culture. Beyond such individual variation, however, there is bound to be some further variation within a given culture. At the very least, in any human society, there is some difference between the roles of men and women. This stems from the fact that women give birth but men do not, and that there are obvious differences between male and female reproductive anatomy and physiology. What every culture does is to give meaning to these differences by explaining them and specifying what is to be done about them. Every culture as well specifies how the kinds of people resulting from the differences should relate to one another and to the world at large. Since each culture does this in its own way, there is tremendous variation from one society to another. Anthropologists use the term **gender** to refer to the cultural elaborations and meanings assigned to the biological differentiation between the sexes. Thus, though one's sex is biologically determined, one's sexual identity or gender is culturally constructed.

The distinction between sex, which is biological, and gender, which is cultural, is an important one. Presumably, gender differences are as old as human culture—about 2.5 million years—and arose from the biological differences between early human males and females. Back then, males were about twice the size of females, as they are today among such species as gorillas, orangutans, and baboons, all of which are closely related to humans. As humans evolved, however, the biological differences between the two sexes were radically reduced. Thus, apart from differences directly related to reproduction, whatever biological basis there once was for gender role differences has largely disappeared. Nevertheless, cultures have maintained some differentiation of gender roles ever since, although these are far greater in some societies than others. Paradoxically, gender differences were more extreme in late 19th and early 20th century Western (European and European derived) societies, when women were expected to submit unquestioningly to male authority, than they are among most historically known food-foraging peoples whose ways of life, though not unchanged, resemble those of the late Stone Age ancestors of Western peoples. Among food foragers, relations between men and women tend to be relatively egalitarian, and although they may not typically carry out the same tasks, such arrangements tend to be flexible. In other words, differences between the behavior of men and women in North American and Western societies today, which are thought by many to be rooted in human biology, are not so rooted at all. Rather, they appear to have been recently elaborated in the course of history.

In addition to cultural variation associated with gender, there will also be some related to differences in age. In any society, children are not expected to behave as adults, and the reverse is equally true. But then, who is a child and who is an adult? Again, although the age differences are "natural," cultures give their own meaning to the human life cycle. In North America, for example, individuals are not regarded as adults until the age of 18; in many others, adulthood begins earlier. Often, it is not tied so much to age as it is to passage through certain prescribed rituals. Besides age and gender variation, there may be variation between subgroups in societies. These may be occupational groups, where there is a complex division of labor, or social classes in a stratified society, or ethnic groups in some other societies (more will be said of these in subsequent chapters). When such groups exist within a society, each functioning by its own distinctive standards of behavior while at the same time sharing some standards in common, we speak of **subcultures.** The word *subculture,* it should be noted, carries no connotation of lesser status relative to the word *cultural.*

Gender. The elaborations and meanings assigned by cultures to the biological differentiation of the sexes. •
Subculture. A distinctive set of standards and behavior patterns by which a group within a larger society operates.

In all human societies, children's play is used both consciously and unconsciously to teach gender roles.

One example of a subculture in the United States can be seen in the Amish.[1] The old-order Amish originated in Central Europe during the Protestant revolutions sweeping Europe in the 16th century; today members of this order number about 60,000 and live mainly in Pennsylvania, Ohio, and Indiana. They are pacifistic, agrarian people, whose lives focus on their religious beliefs. They value simplicity, hard work, and a high degree of neighborly cooperation. They dress in a distinctive, plain garb, and even today rely on the horse for transportation as well as agricultural work. They mingle as little as possible with non-Amish.

The goal of Amish education is to teach reading, writing, and arithmetic and to instill Amish values in their children. They reject what they regard as "worldly" knowledge and the idea of schools producing good citizens for the state. The Amish insist that their children attend school near home and that teachers be committed to Amish values. Their nonconformity to many standards of the larger culture has caused frequent conflict with state authorities, as well as legal and personal harassment. The Amish have resisted all attempts to force their children to attend regular public schools. Some compromise has been necessary, and "vocational training" has been introduced beyond the elementary school level to fulfill state requirements. The Amish have succeeded in gaining control of their schools and maintaining their way of life, but they are a besieged community, more distrustful than ever of the dominant culture surrounding them.

The experience of the Amish is one example of the way a subculture may be dealt with by the larger culture within which it functions. Different as they are, the Amish actually practice many values that other citizens of the United States respect in the abstract: thrift, hard work, independence, a close family life. The degree of tolerance accorded to them is also due in part to the fact that the Amish are "white" Europeans; they are defined as being of the same race. Although the concept of race has been shown to have no biological validity when applied to humans, it still persists as a folk category.

American Indians are often seen as racially different, and their subcultures have been treated differently by Whites, who came as conquerors and who defined Indian values as "savage." This in spite of the fact that, as many Amish values are respected in the abstract by other "white" North Americans, so too do the latter share many values important in several Indian societies. These include honesty, social equality, strong family ties, strong sense of community, and freedom from oppressive authority. Indeed, many of the English colonists found these values to be so much more strongly honored among the so-called "savages" than in their own settlements that large numbers of them chose to join Indian communities. Nevertheless, for some 500 years, most Europeans and

[1] Hostetler, J., & Huntington, G. (1971). *Children in Amish society.* New York: Holt, Rinehart and Winston.

The Amish people have maintained a distinctive agrarian way of life in the midst of industrialized North American society. By maintaining their own schools to instill Amish values in their children, prohibiting mechanized vehicles and equipment, and dressing in their distinctive plain clothing, the Amish proclaim their own special identity.

their descendants in what is now the United States have generally accepted the notion that the Indian cultures were doomed to disappear; yet they still very much endure, even if in altered form.

Implicit in the discussion thus far is the fact that subcultures may develop in different ways. On the one hand, Amish subculture emerged as the product of the way these people have communicated and interacted in pursuit of their common goals within the wider society. On the other hand, many North American Indian subcultures were once independent cultures that were forcibly brought under the control of federal governments in the United States and Canada. Although all have undergone change as a result, many have remained different enough from European-American culture so that it is difficult to decide whether they remain as distinct cultures as opposed to subcultures. In this sense, *culture* and *subculture* represent opposite ends of a continuum, with no clear dividing line in the "gray area" between.

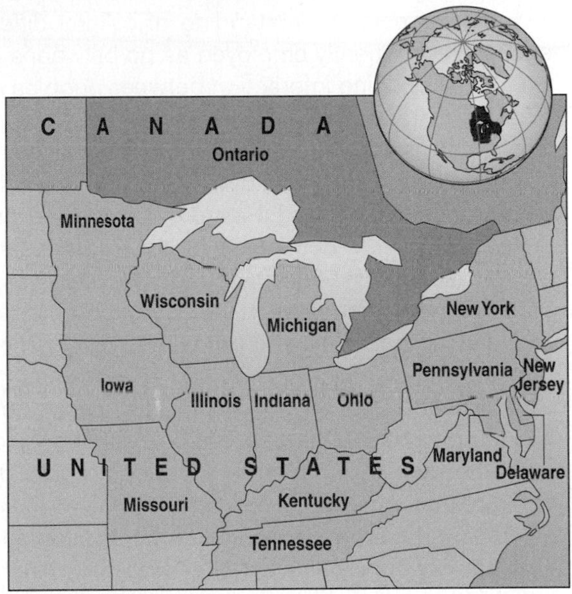

Raised here is the issue of so-called **pluralistic societies** in which cultural variation is especially marked and few standards, if any, are held in common. Pluralistic societies are, in effect, multicultural, and could not have existed before the first politically centralized states arose a mere 5,000 years ago. With the rise of the state, it became possible to bring about the political unification of two or more formerly independent societies, each with its own culture, thereby creating what amounts to a more complex order that transcends the theoretical one culture–one society linkage. Pluralistic societies, which are common in the world today (Figure 14.1), are characterized by a particular problem: The groups within them, by virtue of their high degree of cultural variation, are all essentially operating by different sets of rules. This can create problems, given the fact that social living demands predictable behavior. In a culturally pluralisitic society, it may become difficult for the members of any one subgroup to comprehend the different standards by which the

Pluralistic societies. Societies in which there exist a diversity of cultural patterns.

Anthropology Applied

New Houses for Apache Indians

The United States, in common with other industrialized countries of the world, has within it a number of more or less separate subcultures. Those who live by the standards of one particular subculture have their closest relationships with one another, receiving constant reassurance that their perceptions of the world are the only correct ones, and coming to take it for granted that the whole culture is as they see it. As a consequence, members of one subcultural group frequently have trouble understanding the needs and aspirations of other such groups. For this reason anthropologists, with their special understanding of cultural differences, are frequently employed as go-betweens in situations requiring interaction between peoples of differing cultural traditions.

As an example, George S. Esber, Jr., while still a graduate student in anthropology, was hired to work with architects and a band of Apache Indians in designing a new community for the Apaches.* Although architects began with an awareness that cross-cultural differences in the use of space exist, they had no idea of how to get relevant information from the Indians. For their part, the Apaches had no explicit awareness of their needs, for these were based on unconscious patterns of behavior. Moreover, the idea that patterns of behavior could be acted out unconsciously was an alien one to them.

Esber's task was to persuade the architects to hold back on their planning long enough for him to gather, through fieldwork and review of written records, the kind of data from which Apache housing needs could be abstracted. At the same time, he had to overcome Apache anxieties over an outsider coming into their midst to learn about matters as personal as their daily lives. With these things accomplished, Esber was able to identify and successfully communicate to the architects features of Apache life with important implications for community design. At the same time, discussions of findings with the Apaches themselves enhanced awareness of their own unique needs.

As a result of Esber's work, in 1981, the Apaches were able to move into houses that had been designed with *their* participation, for *their* specific needs. Among other things, account was taken of the Indians' need to ease into a social situation rather than to jump right in. Apache etiquette requires that all people be in full view of each other so each can assess from a distance the behavior of others in order to act appropriately with them. This requires a large, open living space. At the same time, hosts must be able to offer food to guests as a prelude to further social interaction. Thus, cooking and dining areas cannot be separated from living space. Nor can standard middle-class Anglo kitchen equipment be installed; the need for handling large quantities of food requires large pots and pans, for which extra-large sinks and cupboards are necessary. In such ways were the new houses made to accommodate long-standing native traditions.

* See Esber, G. (1987). Designing Apache houses with Apaches. In R. M. Wulff & S. J. Fiske (Eds.), *Anthropological praxis: Translating knowledge into action.* Boulder, CO: Westview.

others operate. At the least, this can lead to major misunderstandings, as in the following case reported in the *Wall Street Journal* of May 13, 1983:

> Salt Lake City—Police called it a cross-cultural misunderstanding. When the man showed up to buy the Shetland pony advertised for sale, the owner asked what he intended to do with the animal.
>
> "For my son's birthday," he replied, and the deal was closed.
>
> The buyer thereupon clubbed the pony to death with a two-by-four, dumped the carcass in his pickup truck and drove away. The horrified seller called the police, who tracked down the buyer. At his house they found a birthday party in progress. The pony was trussed and roasting in a luau pit.

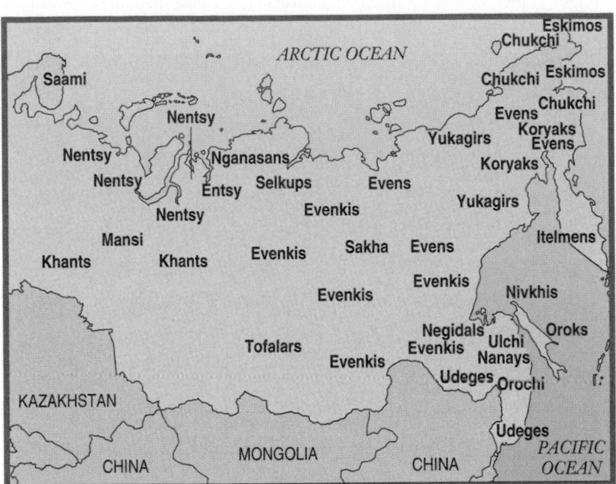

FIGURE 14.1

Shown here are a few of the ethnic groups of the Russian Federation. Contrary to popular belief, the ethnic conflicts that have broken out since the collapse of the Soviet Union stem not from a supposedly conflictive nature of ethnicity but from Stalin's policy of emphasizing ethnicity while preventing its expression and forcibly removing populations from their homelands to new localities.

We don't ride horses, we eat them, explained the buyer, a recent immigrant from Tonga.

The difficulty members of one subgroup within a pluralistic society may have understanding the standards by which members of others operate, unfortunately, can go far beyond mere misunderstanding, in which case violence and bloodshed may result. Many cases might be cited, but one that we shall look at in some detail in a later chapter (27) is Guatemala, where a government distrustful of its indigenous populations unleashed a reign of terror against them.

The difficulties of making pluralistic societies work is illustrated by the recent violence in Kosovo, once part of Yugoslavia. Here, Albanians watch Serbian houses burn.

In every culture, there are persons whose unusual behavior has earned them the labels "eccentric," "crazy," or "queer." Such persons are looked upon with disapproval by their society, and if their behavior becomes too peculiar, are sooner or later excluded from participating in the activities of the group. Such exclusion acts to keep what is defined as deviant behavior outside the group. On the other hand, what is regarded as deviant in one society may not be in another. In many Native American societies, for example, individuals were permitted to assume for life the role normally associated with people of the opposite sex. Thus, a man could dress as a woman and

In the United States, a man dressing as a woman has been regarded traditionally as abnormal behavior, but in some other cultures, such behavior is regarded as perfectly normal. Not only does culture define what is abnormal as well as normal, but also such definitions may change over time, as when women in the United States wear men's clothing without being regarded as at all odd.

engage in what were conventionally defined as "female" activities; conversely, women could achieve renown in activities normally in the masculine domain. In effect, four different gender identities were available: masculine men, feminine men, feminine women, and masculine women. Furthermore, masculine women and feminine men were not merely accepted, but were highly respected.

Because individuals who share a culture tend to marry within their society and thus to share certain physical characteristics, some people mistakenly believe that there is a direct relationship between culture and race. There are two problems with this, one of them being that racial categories lack biological validity. As noted in Chapter 1, the physical traits of humans do not covary; hence, a classification based upon differential skin color, for example, will be quite different from one based on some other characteristic. The second problem is that so-called racial characteristics represent biological adaptations to climate and have nothing to do with differences in intelligence or cultural capabilities. Some African Americans have argued that they have more in common with dark-skinned Africans than they do with light-skinned North Americans. Yet if they suddenly had to live in a traditional Bantu society, they would find themselves lacking the cultural knowledge to be successful members of this group. The culture they share with "white" North Americans is more significant than the physical traits they share with the "black" Africans.

Culture Is Learned

All culture is learned rather than biologically inherited, prompting anthropologist Ralph Linton to refer to it as humanity's "social heredity." One learns one's culture by growing up with it, and the process whereby culture is transmitted from one generation to the next is called **enculturation.**

Most animals eat and drink whenever the urge arises. Humans, however, are enculturated do most of their eating and drinking at certain culturally prescribed times and feel hungry as those times approach. These eating times vary from culture to culture, as does what is eaten, how it is prepared, and how it is eaten. To add complexity, food is used to do more than merely satisfy nutritional requirements. Differences in what and how people eat remind them of who they are in relation to others. When used to celebrate rituals and religious activities, as it often is, food "establishes relationships of give and take, of cooperation, of sharing, of an emotional bond that is universal."[2]

Through enculturation one learns the socially appropriate way of satisfying one's biologically determined needs. It is important to distinguish between the needs themselves, which are not learned, and the learned ways in which they are satisfied. Thus, a North American's idea of a comfortable way to sleep will vary greatly from that of a Japanese. The biological needs of humans are the same as those of other animals: besides food and sleep, they include shelter, companionship, self-defense, and sexual gratification. Each culture determines in its own way how these needs will be met.

Not all learned behavior is cultural. A pigeon may learn tricks, but this behavior is reflexive, the result of conditioning by repeated training, not the product of enculturation. On the other hand, learned behavior is exhibited to one degree or another by most, if not all, mammals. Several species may even be said to have culture, in that local populations share patterns of behavior that, just like humans, each generation learns from the one before and that differ from one population to another. Elizabeth Marshall Thomas, for example, has described a distinctive pattern of behavior among lions of southern Africa's Kalahari Desert that regulated interaction with the region's native people and that each generation passed onto the next.[3] She has shown as well how that culture changed over the past 30 years in response to new circumstances.

Among nonhuman primates, examples of cultural behavior are particularly evident. A chimpanzee, for example, will take a twig, strip it of all leaves, and smooth it down to fashion a tool for extracting termites from their nest. Such toolmaking, which juveniles learn from their elders, is unquestionably a form of cultural behavior once thought to be exclusively human. In Japan, macaques that learned the advantages of washing sweet potatoes before eating them passed the practice on to the next generation. And so it goes; what is interesting is that within any given primate species, the culture of one population often differs from that of others, just as it does among humans. Beyond this, we have discovered both in captivity and in

[2] Caroulis, J. (1996). Food for thought. *Pennsylvania Gazette,* 95 (3), 16.

[3] Thomas, E. M. (1994). *The tribe of the tiger* (pp. 109–186). New York: Simon and Schuster.

Enculturation. The process by which a society's culture is passed from one generation to the next and individuals become members of their society.

the wild that primates in general and apes in particular "possess a near-human intelligence generally, including the use of sounds in representational ways, a rich awareness of the aims and objectives of others, the ability to engage in tactical deception, and the ability to use symbols in communication with humans and each other."[4]

Given the degree of biological similarity between apes and humans (discussed in Chapter 4) it should come as no surprise to find that they are like us in other ways as well. In all respects the differences between apes and humans are differences of degree rather than kind (although the degree *does* make a difference). All of this knowledge has come as something of a shock, as it contradicts a belief deeply embedded in Western cultures: that there is supposed to be a deep and unbridgeable gap between humans and animals. It has not been easy to overcome this bias, and indeed, we still have not come to grips fully with the moral implications with respect to the way we treat primates in research laboratories.

Culture Is Based on Symbols

When anthropologist Leslie White observed that all human behavior originates in the use of symbols, he expressed an opinion shared by all anthropologists. Art, religion, and money involve the use of symbols. We are all familiar with the fervor and devotion that religion can elicit from a believer. A Christian cross, an Islamic crescent, a Jewish Star of David, or any object of worship may bring to mind centuries of struggle and persecution or may stand for a whole philosophy or creed. The most important symbolic aspect of culture is language—the substitution of words for objects.

Through language humans are able to transmit culture from one generation to another. In particular, language makes it possible to learn from cumulative, shared experience. Without it, one could not inform others about events to which they were not a party. We shall consider the important relationship between language and culture in greater detail in Chapter 15.

Culture Is Integrated

For purposes of comparison and analysis, anthropologists customarily break a culture down into many seemingly separate parts, even though such distinctions are arbitrary. Because cultures are systems, the anthropologist who examines one aspect invariably finds it necessary to examine others as well. As in any system, all aspects of a culture must be reasonably well integrated in order to function.

The integration of the economic, political, and social aspects of a culture can be illustrated by the Kapauku Papuans, a mountain people of western New Guinea studied in 1955 by the North American anthropologist Leopold Pospisil.[5] The Kapauku economy relies on plant cultivation, along with pig breeding, hunting, and fishing. Although plant cultivation provides most of the people's food, it is through pig breeding that men achieve political power and positions of legal authority.

Among the Kapauku, pig breeding is a complex business. Raising lots of pigs, obviously, requires lots of food to feed them. This consists primarily of sweet potatoes, grown in garden plots. Since Kapauku culture defines some essential gardening activities as women's work, they can be performed only by women. Furthermore, pigs must be cared for by women. So, to raise lots of pigs, a man has to have lots of women in the household. The way he gets them is by marrying them. In Kapauku society, multiple wives (polygyny) are not only permitted, they are highly desired. For each wife, however, a man must pay a bride price, and this can be expensive. Furthermore, wives have to be compensated for their care of pigs. Put simply, it takes pigs, by which wealth is measured, to get wives, without whom pigs cannot be raised in the first place. Needless to say, this requires considerable entrepreneurship. It is this ability that produces leaders in Kapauku society.

The interrelatedness of the various parts of Kapauku culture is even more complex than this. For example, one

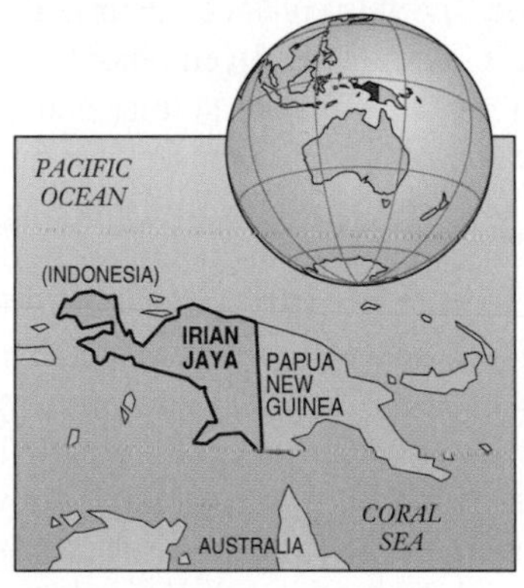

[4] Reynolds, V. (1994). Primates in the field, primates in the lab. *Anthropology Today,* 10 (2), 4.

[5] Pospisil, L. (1963). *The Kapauku Papuans of west New Guinea.* New York: Holt, Rinehart and Winston.

LESLIE A. WHITE (1900–1975)

Leslie White was a major theoretician in North American anthropology who saw culture as consisting of three essential components, which he referred to as techno-economic, social, and ideological. White defined the techno-economic aspect of a culture as the way members of the culture deal with their environment, and it is this aspect that then determines the social and ideological aspects of the culture. Although he acknowledged the importance of symbols, White considered the manner in which culture harnessed energy to be the most significant factor in its development. Hence, in his "culturological" approach, he saw culture (in this case, technology) determining culture, and extracultural phenomena were deemed irrelevant. In *The Evolution of Culture* (1959), White stated his basic law of evolution, that culture evolves in proportion to the amount of energy harnessed on the part of each individual, or to the increased efficiency with which that energy is put to work. In other words, culture develops in direct response to technological "progress." A problem with White's position is his equation of "evolution" with "progress," the latter being a concept invented by Europeans (and European Americans) in the 18th century to rationalize the transformation taking place in their societies with the advent of the industrial revolution. In this respect, his theories were heavily culture-bound. On the other hand, he did alert anthropologists to the importance that technological changes may have for the rest of culture.

condition conducive to polygyny is a surplus of adult women. In the Kapauku case, warfare is endemic, regarded as a necessary evil. By the rules of Kapauku warfare, men get killed but women do not. This system works to promote the kind of imbalance of sexes that facilitates polygyny. Polygyny also tends to work best if the several wives of a man come to live in his village, which is the case among the Kapauku, rather than the other way around. Thus, the men of a village are "blood" relatives of one another, and this enhances their ability to cooperate in warfare. Given all this, an emphasis on descent reckoned through men in Kapauku culture is not unexpected.

These examples by no means exhaust the interrelationships to be found in Kapauku culture. For example, both descent reckoning through men and near-constant warfare tend to promote male dominance, and so it is not surprising to find that positions of leadership in Kapauku society are held exclusively by men, who appropriate the products of women's labor in order to play their political "games." Assertions to the contrary notwithstanding, male dominance is by no means characteristic of all human societies. Rather, as in the Kapauku case, it arises only under particular sets of circumstances that, if changed, will alter the way in which men and women relate to one another.

From what has been said so far, one might suppose that the various parts of a culture must operate in perfect harmony at all times. The analogy would be that of a machine; all parts must be compatible and complementary or it won't run. Try putting diesel fuel in the tank of a car that runs on gasoline and you've got a problem; one part of the system is no longer compatible with the rest. To a degree, this is true of all cultures. A change in one part of a culture usually will affect other parts, sometimes in rather dramatic ways. This point, to which we will return later in this chapter, is of particular importance today as diverse agents seek to introduce changes of all sorts into societies all around the world.

At the same time that we must recognize that a degree of harmony is necessary in any properly functioning culture, we should not assume that complete harmony is required. Because no two individuals experience the enculturation process in precisely the same way, no two individuals perceive their culture in exactly the same way, and so there is always some potential for change in any culture. So we should speak, instead, of a strain to consistency in culture. So long as the parts are reasonably consistent, a culture will operate reasonably well. If, however, that strain to consistency breaks down, a situation of cultural crisis ensues.

A. R. RADCLIFFE-BROWN (1881–1955)

The British anthropologist A. R. Radcliffe-Brown was the originator of what has come to be known as the structural-functionalist school of thought. He and his followers maintained that each custom and belief of a society has a specific function that serves to perpetuate the structure of that society—its ordered arrangement of parts—so that the society's continued existence is possible. The job of the anthropologist, therefore, was to study the ways in which customs and beliefs function to solve the problem of maintaining the system. From such studies should emerge universal laws of human behavior.

The value of the structural-functionalist approach is that it caused anthropologists to analyze societies and their cultures as systems and to examine the interconnections between their various parts. It also gave a new dimension to comparative studies, as present-day societies were compared in terms of structural-functional similarities and differences rather than their presumed historical connections. Radcliffe-Brown's universal laws have not emerged, however, because human behavior is not the product of laws that operate in a mechanical, inflexible way. Unlike physics or chemistry (but like geology and evolutionary biology), anthropology is a historical science in which chance and historical contingency play important roles. To answer such questions as why particular customs arise in the first place, and how do cultures change, historical approaches are necessary.

STUDYING CULTURE IN THE FIELD

Armed, now, with some understanding of what culture is, the question arises, How does an anthropologist study culture in the field? Culture, being a set of rules or standards, cannot itself be directly observed; only actual behavior is observable. What the anthropologist must do is to abstract a set of rules from what is seen and heard in order to explain social behavior, much as a linguist, from the way people speak a language, tries to develop a set of rules to account for the ways those speakers combine sounds into meaningful phrases.

To pursue this further, consider the following discussion of exogamy—marriage outside one's own group—among the Trobriand Islanders, as described by Bronislaw Malinowski.

> If you were to inquire into the matter among the Trobrianders, you would find that . . . the natives show horror at the idea of violating the rules of exogamy and that they believe that sores, diseases, even death might follow clan incest. [But] from the viewpoint of the native libertine, *suvasova* (the breach of exogamy) is indeed a specially interesting and spicy form of erotic experience. Most of my informants would not only admit but did actually boast about having committed this offense.[6]

Malinowski himself determined that although such breaches did occur, they were much less frequent than gossip would have it. Had Malinowski relied solely on what the Trobrianders told him, his description of their culture would have been inaccurate. The same sort of discrepancy between cultural ideals and the way people really do behave can be found in any culture. In Chapter 1 we saw another example from contemporary North America in our discussion of the Garbage Project.

From these examples, it is obvious that an anthropologist must be cautious if a realistic description of a culture is to be given. To play it safe, data drawn in three different ways need to be considered. First, the people's own understanding of the rules they share—that is, their notion of the way their society *ought* to be—must be examined. Second, the extent to which people believe they

[6] Malinowski, B. (1922). *Argonauts of the western Pacific.* New York: Dutton.

Describing another culture is like trying to describe a new game. The people in this picture look as though they are playing baseball, but they are playing cricket. To describe cricket in the language of baseball would be at best a caricature of the game as the British know it. The problem in anthropology is how to describe another culture for an audience unfamiliar with it, so that the description is not a caricature.

are observing those rules—that is, how they think they actually do behave—needs to be looked at. Third, the behavior that can be directly observed should be considered—in the example of the Trobrianders, whether or not the rule of *suvasova* is actually violated. As we see here, and as we saw in our discussion of the Garbage Project, the way people think they *should* behave, the way in which they think they *do* behave, and the way in which they *actually* behave may be distinctly different. By carefully examining these elements, the anthropologist can draw up a set of rules that actually may explain the acceptable behavior within a culture. Of course, the anthropologist is only human. As discussed in Chapter 1, it is difficult to completely cast aside one's own personal feelings and biases, which have been shaped by one's own culture. Yet it is important to make every effort to do just this, for otherwise one may seriously misinterpret what one sees. As a case in point, we may see how the male bias of the Polish culture in which Malinowski had been raised caused him to miss important things in his pioneering study of the Trobriand Islanders. Unlike today, when anthropologists receive special training before going into the field, Malinowski early in the 20th century had received little formal preparation.

Original Study

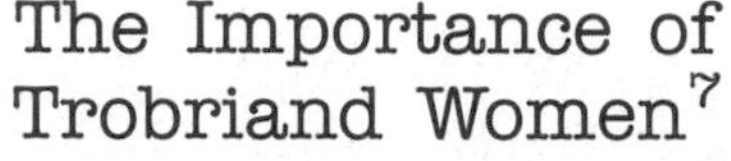

The Importance of Trobriand Women[7]

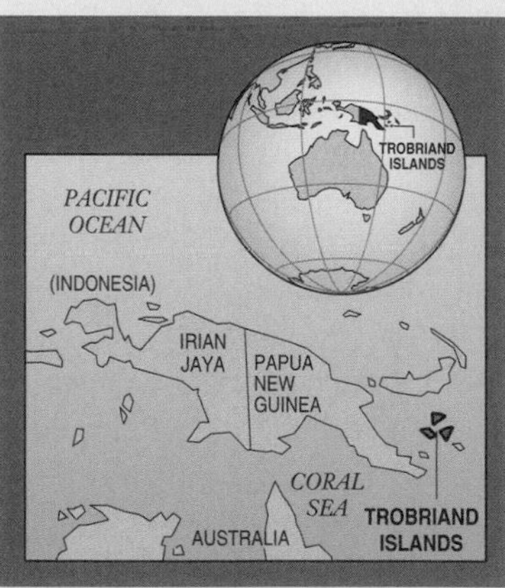

Walking into a village at the beginning of fieldwork is entering a world without cultural guideposts. The task of learning values that others live by is never easy. The rigors of fieldwork involve listening and watching, learning a new language of speech and actions, and most of all, letting go of one's own cultural assumptions in order to understand the meanings others give to work, power, death, family, and friends. As my fieldwork in the Trobriand Islands of Papua New Guinea was no exception, I wrestled doggedly with each of these problems. Doing research in the Trobriand Islands created one additional obstacle. I was working in the footsteps of a celebrated anthropological ancestor, Bronislaw Kasper Malinowski. . . .

In 1971, before my first trip to the Trobriands, I thought I understood many things about Trobriand customs and beliefs from having read Malinowski's exhaustive writings. Once there, however, I found that I had much more to discover about what I thought I already knew. For many months I worked with these discordant realities, always conscious of Malinowski's shadow, his words, his explanations. Although I found significant differences

[7] Weiner, A. B. (1988). *The Trobrianders of Papua New Guinea* (pp. 4–7). New York: Holt, Rinehart and Winston.

in areas of importance, I gradually came to understand how he reached certain conclusions. The answers we both received from informants were not so dissimilar, and I could actually trace how Malinowski had analyzed what his informants told him in a way that made sense and was scientifically significant—given what anthropologists generally then recognized about such societies. Sixty years separate our fieldwork, and any comparison of our studies illustrates not so much Malinowski's mistaken interpretations but the developments in anthropological knowledge and inquiry from his time to mine.

This important point has been forgotten by those anthropologists who today argue that ethnographic writing can never be more than a kind of fictional account of an author's experiences. Although Malinowski and I were in the Trobriands at vastly different historical moments and there also are many areas in which our analyses differ, a large part of what we learned in the field was similar. From the vantage point that time gives to me, I can illustrate how our differences, even those that are major, came to be. Taken together, our two studies profoundly exemplify the scientific basis that underlies the collection of ethnographic data. Like all such data, however, whether researched in a laboratory or a village, the more we learn about a subject, the more we can refine and revise earlier assumptions. This is the way all sciences create their own historical developments. Therefore, the lack of agreement between Malinowski's ethnography and mine must not be taken as an adversarial attack against an opponent. Nor should it be read as an example of the writing of ethnography as "fiction" or "partial truths." Each of our differences can be traced historically within the discipline of anthropology.

My most significant point of departure from Malinowski's analyses was the attention I gave to women's productive work. In my original research plans, women were not the central focus of study, but on the first day I took up residence in a village I was taken by them to watch a distribution of their own wealth—bundles of banana leaves and banana fiber skirts—which they exchanged with other women in commemoration of someone who had recently died. Watching that event forced me to take women's economic roles more seriously than I

In the Trobriand Islands, women's wealth consists of skirts and banana leaves, large quantities of which must be given away on the death of a relative.

Original Study

would have from reading Malinowski's studies. Although Malinowski noted the high status of Trobriand women, he attributed their importance to the fact that Trobrianders reckon descent through women, thereby giving them genealogical significance in a matrilineal society. Yet he never considered that this significance was underwritten by women's own wealth because he did not systematically investigate the women's productive activities. Although in his field notes he mentions Trobriand women making these seemingly useless banana bundles to be exchanged at a death, his published work only deals with men's wealth.

My taking seriously the importance of women's wealth not only brought women as the neglected half of society clearly into the ethnographic picture but also forced me to revise many of Malinowski's assumptions about Trobriand men. For example, Trobriand kinship as described by Malinowski has always been a subject of debate among anthropologists. For Malinowski, the basic relationships within a Trobriand family were guided by the matrilineal principle of "mother-right" and "father-love." A father was called "stranger" and had little authority over his own children. A woman's brother was the commanding figure and exercised control over his sister's sons because they were members of his matrilineage rather than their father's matrilineage.

According to Malinowski, this matrilineal drama was played out biologically by the Trobrianders' belief that a man has no role as genitor. A man's wife is thought to become pregnant when an ancestral spirit enters her body and causes conception. Even after a child is born, Malinowski reported, it is the woman's brother who presents a harvest of yams to his sister so that her child will be fed with food from its own matrilineage, rather than its father's matrilineage. In this way, Malinowski conceptualized matrilineality as an institution in which the father of a child, as a member of a **different** matrilineage, was excluded not only from participating in procreation but also from giving any objects of lasting value to his children, thus provisioning them only with love.

In my study of Trobriand women and men, a different configuration of matrilineal descent emerged. A Trobriand father is not a "stranger" in Malinowski's definition, nor is he a powerless figure as the third party to the relationship between a woman and her brother. The father is one of the most important persons in his child's life, and remains so even after his child grows up and marries. Even a father's procreative importance is incorporated into his child's growth and development. A Trobriand man gives his child many opportunities to gain things from his matrilineage, thereby adding to the available resources that he or she can draw upon. At the same time, this giving creates obligations on the part of a man's children toward him that last even beyond his death. Therefore, the roles that men and their children play in each other's lives are worked out through extensive cycles of exchanges, which define the strength of their relationships to each other and eventually benefit the other members of both their matrilineages. Central to these exchanges are women and their wealth.

That Malinowski never gave equal time to the women's side of things, given the deep significance of their role in societal and political life, is not surprising. Only recently have anthropologists begun to understand the importance of taking women's work seriously. In some cultures, such as the Middle East or among Australian aborigines, it is extremely difficult for ethnographers to cross the culturally bounded ritual worlds that separate women from men. In the past, however, both women and men ethnographers generally analyzed the societies they studied from a male perspective. The "women's point of view" was largely ignored in the study of gender roles, since anthropologists generally perceived women as living in the shadows of men—occupying the private rather than the public sectors of society, rearing children rather than engaging in economic or political pursuits.

The End

BRONISLAW MALINOWSKI (1884–1942)

Polish-born Bronislaw Malinowski argued that people everywhere share certain biological and psychological needs and that the ultimate function of all cultural institutions is to fulfill those needs. Everyone, for example, needs to feel secure in relation to the physical universe. Therefore, when science and technology are inadequate to explain certain natural phenomena—such as eclipses or earthquakes—people develop religion and magic to account for those phenomena and to establish a feeling of security. The nature of the institution, according to Malinowski, is determined by its function.

Malinowski outlined three fundamental levels of needs that he claimed had to be resolved by all cultures:

1. A culture must provide for biological needs, such as the need for food and procreation.
2. A culture must provide for instrumental needs, such as the need for law and education.
3. A culture must provide for integrative needs, such as religion and art.

If anthropologists could analyze the ways in which a culture fills these needs for its members, Malinowski believed that they could also deduce the origin of cultural traits. Although this belief was never justified, the quality of data called for by Malinowski's approach set new standards for ethnographic field work. He was the first to insist on the necessity to join in native life to really understand it. He himself showed the way with his work in the Trobriand Islands between 1915 and 1918. Never before had such in-depth work been done, nor had such insights been gained into the workings of another culture. Such was the quality of Malinowski's Trobriand research that, with it, ethnography can be said to have come of age as a scientific enterprise.

CULTURE AND ADAPTATION

In the course of their evolution humans, like all animals, have been continually faced with the problem of adapting to their environment. The term **adaptation** refers to a natural (rather than willful) process by which organisms achieve a beneficial adjustment to an available environment and the results of that process—the possession of characteristics that permit organisms to overcome the hazards and secure the resources they need in the particular environments in which they live. With the exception of humans, organisms have generally adapted as natural selection has provided them with advantageous anatomical and physiological characteristics. For example, a body covering of hair, coupled with certain other physiological mechanisms, protects mammals from extremes of temperature; specialized teeth help them to procure the kinds of food they need; and so on. Humans, however, have come to depend more and more on cultural adaptation. For example, biology has not provided them with built-in fur coats to protect them in cold climates, but it has provided them with the ability to make their own coats, build fires, and erect shelters to protect themselves against the cold. More than this, culture enables people to use a wide diversity of environments. By manipulating environments through cultural means, people have been able to move into the Arctic and the Sahara, and they have even set foot on the moon. Through culture the human species has secured not just its survival but its expansion as well.

This is not to say that everything that humans do they do *because* it is adaptive to a particular environment. For one thing, people don't just react to an environment as given; rather, they react to it as they perceive it, and

Adaptation. A process by which organisms achieve beneficial adjustment to an available environment and the results of that process—the characteristics of organisms that fit them to the particular set of conditions of the environment in which they are generally found.

What is adaptive at one time may not be at another. In the United States, the principal source of fruits, vegetables, and fiber is the Central Valley of California, where irrigation works have made the desert bloom. As happened in ancient Mesopotamia, evaporation concentrates salts in the water, but here pollution is made even worse by chemical fertilizers. These poisons are now accumulating in the soil and threaten to make the valley a desert again.

different groups of people may perceive the same environment in radically different ways. They also react to things other than the environment: their own biological natures, for one, and their beliefs, attitudes, and the consequences of their own behavior, for others. All of these things present them with problems, and people maintain cultures to deal with problems, or matters that concern them. To be sure, their cultures must produce behavior that is generally adaptive, or at least not maladaptive, but this is not the same as saying that cultural practices necessarily arise because they are adaptive in a given environment. The fact is, current utility of a custom is an unreliable guide to its origin.

A further complication is the relativity of any given adaptation: What is adaptive in one context may be seriously maladaptive in another. For example, the sanitation practices of food-foraging peoples—their toilet habits and methods of garbage disposal—are appropriate to contexts of low population levels and some degree of residential mobility. These same practices, however, become serious health hazards in the context of large, fully sedentary populations. Similarly, behavior that is adaptive in the short run may be maladaptive over the long run. Thus, the development of irrigation in ancient Mesopotamia (modern-day Iraq) made it possible over the short run to increase food production, but over the long run it favored the gradual accumulation of salts in the soils. This, in turn, contributed to the collapse of civilization there after 2000 B.C. Similarly, the "development" of prime farmland today in places like the eastern United States for purposes other than food production makes us increasingly dependent on food raised in marginal environments. High yields are presently possible through the application of expensive technology, but continuing loss of topsoil, increasing salinity of soils through evaporation of irrigation waters, and silting of irrigation works, not to mention impending shortages of water and fossil fuels, make continuing high yields over the long term unlikely.

Functions of Culture

From what has been said so far, it is clear that a culture cannot survive if it does not successfully deal with basic problems. A culture must provide for the production and distribution of goods and services considered necessary for life. It must provide for biological continuity through the reproduction of its members. It must enculturate new members so that they can become functioning adults. It must maintain order among its members, as well as between them and outsiders. It must motivate its members to survive and engage in those activities necessary for survival. On top of all of this, it must be able to change if it is to remain adaptive under changed conditions.

Culture and Change

All cultures change over time, although rarely as rapidly or as massively as many are doing today. Changes take place in response to such events as environmental crises, intrusion of outsiders, or modification of behavior and values within the culture. In North America, clothing fashions change frequently. Over the past century it became culturally permissible for men and women alike to bare more of their bodies not just in swimming but in dress as well. Along with this has come greater permissiveness about the body in photographs, movies, and television. Finally, in the latter half of the century, the sexual attitudes and practices of many North Americans became less restrictive. Obviously these changes are interrelated, reflecting an underlying change in attitudes toward cultural rules regarding the body in general and sex in particular.

Although cultures must have some flexibility to remain adaptive, culture change can also bring unexpected and often disastrous results. A case in point are the droughts that periodically afflict so many peoples living

HIGHWAY 1
Fieldwork site
http://www.truman.edu/academics/ss/faculty/tamakoshi

HIGHWAY 2
Debates on culture
http://www.wsu.edu:8001/vcwsu/commons/topics/culture/culture-index.html

in Africa just south of the Sahara Desert. Native to this region are some 14 million pastoral nomadic people whose lives are centered on cattle and other livestock, which are herded from place to place as required for pasturage and water. For thousands of years these people have been able to go about their business, efficiently utilizing vast areas of arid lands in ways that allowed them to survive severe droughts many times in the past. Unfortunately for them, their nomadic lifestyle, which makes it difficult to impose controls upon them and takes them across international boundaries at will, makes them a source of annoyance to the governments of the postcolonial states of the region. Seeing nomads as a challenge to their authority, these governments have gone all out to convert them into sedentary villagers. Overgrazing has resulted from this loss of mobility; moreover, the problem has been compounded by government efforts to involve the pastoralists in a market economy by encouraging them to raise many more animals than required for their own needs in order to have a surplus to sell. The resultant devastation, where there had previously been no significant overgrazing or erosion, now makes droughts far more disastrous than they would otherwise be and places the former nomads' very existence in jeopardy.

In the United States before 1950, matters pertaining to the human body were not considered suitable for polite conversation, so mention of President Roosevelt's paralyzed legs was scrupulously avoided in the 1930s and 1940s. By the 1980s, attitudes had changed so dramatically that the president's colon was discussed in great detail when he was hospitalized for cancer. By the 1990s even the presidential genitals were discussed in public.

CULTURE, SOCIETY, AND THE INDIVIDUAL

Ultimately, a society is no more than a union of individuals, all of whom have their own special needs and interests. If a society is to survive, it must succeed in balancing the self-interest of its members against the demands of the society as a whole. To accomplish this, a society offers rewards for adherence to its cultural standards. In most cases, these rewards assume the form of social acceptance. In contemporary North American society, a man who holds a good job, is faithful to his wife, and goes to church, for example, may be elected "Model Citizen" by his neighbors. To ensure the survival of the group, each person must learn to postpone certain immediate satisfactions. Yet the needs of the individual cannot be suppressed too far, lest levels of stress become too much to bear. Hence, a delicate balance always exists between an individual's personal interests and the demands made upon each person by the group.

Take, for example, the matter of sexuality, which, like anything that people do, is shaped by culture. Sexuality is important in any society, for it helps to strengthen cooperative bonds between men and women and ensures the perpetuation of the society itself. Yet sex can be disruptive to social living; if who has sexual access to whom is not clearly spelled out, competition for sexual privileges can destroy the cooperative bonds on which human survival depends. Uncontrolled sexual activity, too, can result in reproductive rates that cause a society's population to outstrip its resources. Hence, as it shapes sexual behavior, every culture must balance the needs of society against the need for sufficient individual gratification, lest frustration build up to the point of being disruptive in itself. Of course, cultures vary widely in the way they go about this, ranging all the way from the extremely restrictive approach of societies like those of Saudi Arabia or the North American Amish, which traditionally specified no sex out of wedlock, to practices among the Canela Indians in Brazil that guarantee that, sooner or later, everyone in a given village has had sex with just about everyone of the opposite sex. But permissive though the latter situation may sound, there are nonetheless strict rules as to how the system operates.[8]

In the United States, the rise of private militia groups reflects the frustration of people whose needs are poorly satisfied by the culture.

Not just in sex, but in all things, cultures must strike a balance between the needs of individuals and those of society. When those of society take precedence, then people experience excessive stress. Symptomatic of this are increased levels of mental illness and behavior regarded as antisocial: violence, crime, abuse of alcohol and other drugs, suicide, or simply alienation. If not corrected, the situation can result in cultural breakdown. But just as problems develop if the needs of society take precedence over those of the individual, so also do they develop if the balance is upset in the other direction.

EVALUATION OF CULTURE

We have knowledge of numerous highly diverse cultural solutions to the problems of human existence. The question often arises, Which is best? In the 19th century Europeans and European Americans (like, for instance, the Chinese and Japanese) had no doubts about the answer—they saw their civilization as the peak of human development. At the same time, though, anthropologists were intrigued to find that all cultures with which they had any familiarity saw themselves as the best of all possible worlds. Commonly, this was reflected in a name for the society that, roughly translated, meant "we human beings" as opposed to "you subhumans." We now know that any culture that is functioning adequately regards its ways as the only proper ones,

[8] Crocker, W. A. & Crocker, J. (1994). *The Canela, bonding through kinship, ritual and sex* (pp. 143–171). Fort Worth, TX: Harcourt Brace.

a view reflecting a phenomenon known as **ethnocentrism.** Hence, the 19th-century Europeans and European Americans were merely displaying their own ethnocentrism. Anthropologists have been actively engaged in the fight against ethnocentrism ever since they started to live among so-called savage peoples and discovered that they were no less human than anyone else. As a consequence, anthropologists began to examine each culture on its own terms, asking whether or not the culture satisfied the needs and expectations of the people themselves. If a people practiced human sacrifice, for example, they asked about the circumstances that made the taking of human life acceptable according to native values. The idea that one must suspend judgment on other peoples' practices in order to understand them in their own cultural terms is called **cultural relativism.** Only through such an approach can one gain an undistorted view of another peoples' ways, as well as insights into the practices of one's own society.

Take, for example, the 16th-century Aztec practice of sacrificing humans for ritual purposes. Few (if any) North Americans today would condone such practices, but by suspending judgment one can get beneath the surface and understand how it functioned to reassure the populace that the Aztec state was healthy and that the sun would remain in the heavens. Beyond this, one can understand how the death penalty functions in the same way in the United States today. Numerous studies by a variety of social scientists have clearly shown that the death penalty does not deter violent crime, any more than Aztec sacrifice really provided sustenance for the sun. In fact, cross-cultural studies show that homicide rates mostly decline after its abolition.[9] Just like Aztec human sacrifice, capital punishment is an institutionalized magical response to perceived disorder. As anthropologists Anthony Parades and Elizabeth D. Purdum point out, it "reassures many that society is not out of control after all, that the majesty of the law reigns and that God is indeed in his heaven."[10]

Essential though cultural relativism is as a research tool, it does not require suspension of judgment forever, nor that we must defend the right of any people to engage in any cultural practice, no matter how destructive. All that is necessary is that we avoid *premature* judgments until we have a full understanding of the culture in which we are interested. Then, and only then, may the anthropologist adopt a critical stance. As David Maybury-Lewis emphasizes, "one does not avoid making judgements, but rather postpones them in order to make informed judgements later."[11]

If anthropologists avoid the "anything goes" position of cultural relativism pushed to absurdity, they must nonetheless avoid the pitfall of judging the practices of other cultures in terms of ethnocentric criteria. A still useful formula for this was devised more than 40 years ago by anthropologist Walter Goldschmidt.[12] In his view the important question to ask is, How well does a given culture satisfy the physical and psychological needs of those whose behavior it guides? Specific indicators are to be found in the nutritional status and general physical and mental health of its population, the incidence of violence, crime and delinquency, the demographic structure, stability and tranquility of domestic life, and the group's relationship to its resource base. The culture of a people who experience high rates of malnutrition, violence, crime, delinquency, suicide, emotional disorders and despair, and environmental degradation may be said to be operating less well than that of another people who exhibit few such problems. In a well-working culture, people "can be proud, jealous, and pugnacious, and live a very satisfactory life without feeling *'angst,'* 'alienation,' 'anomie,' 'depression,' or any of the other pervasive ills of our own inhuman and civilized way of living."[13] It is when people feel helpless to effect their own lives in their own societies, when traditional ways of coping no longer seem to work, that the symptoms of cultural breakdown become prominent.

A culture is essentially a maintenance system to ensure the continued well-being of a group of people; therefore, it may be termed successful as long as it secures the survival of a society in a way that its members find to be reasonably fulfilling. What complicates matters is

[9] Ember, C. J., & Ember, M. (1996). What have we learned from cross-cultural research? *General Anthropology,* 2 (2), 5.

[10] Parades, J. A., & Purdum, E. D. (1990). "Bye, Bye Ted . . . " *Anthropology Today,* 6 (2), 9.

[11] Maybury-Lewis, D. H. P. (1993). A special sort of pleading. In W. A. Haviland & R. J. Gordon (Eds.), *Talking about people,* (*2nd.* ed.) (p.17). Mountain View, CA: Mayfield.

[12] Bodley, J. H. (1990). *Victims of progress* (3rd ed., p. 138). Mountain View, CA: Mayfield.

[13] Fox, R. (1968). *Encounter with anthropology* (p. 290). New York: Dell.

Ethnocentrism. The belief that the ways of one's own culture are the only proper ones. • **Cultural relativism.** The thesis that one must suspend judgement on other peoples' practices in order to understand them in their own cultural terms.

One sign that a culture is not adequately satisfying a people's needs and expectations is a high incidence of crime and delinquency. It is sobering to note that 25% of all imprisoned people in the world are in prisons in the United States, where numbers of prisoners have doubled in 10 years. School shootings have been on the rise, as have gated communities where those who can afford it can withdraw from the outside world.

that any society is made up of groups with different interests, raising the possibility that some people's interests may be served better than those of others. Therefore, a culture that is quite fulfilling for one group within a society may be less so for another. For this reason, the anthropologist must always ask: Whose needs, and whose survival, is best served by the culture in question? Only by looking at the overall situation can a reasonably objective judgment be made as to how well a culture is working.

CHAPTER SUMMARY

Culture, to the anthropologist, includes the ideals, values, and beliefs that are shared by members of a society, that they use to interpret experience and to generate behavior, and that are reflected in their behavior.

All cultures share certain basic characteristics; study of these sheds light on the nature and function of culture itself. Culture cannot exist without society: a structured group of people who are dependent on each other for survival. Society is held together by rule-governed relationships known as its social structure. Culture cannot exist without society, although it is possible to have society, as do creatures like ants and bees, without culture. All is not uniformity within a culture; one reason is that there is some difference between men's and women's roles in any human society. Anthropologists use the term *gender* to refer to the elaborations or meanings cultures assign to the biological differences between men and women. Age variation is also universal, and in some cultures there is other subcultural variation as well. A subculture shares certain overarching assumptions of the larger culture, while observing a set of rules that is distinctively different. One example of a subculture in the United States is that of the Amish. Pluralistic societies are those in which cultural variation is particularly marked. They are characterized by a number of groups operating under different sets of rules. In addition to being shared, all cultures are learned. Individual members of a society learn the accepted norms of social behavior through the process of enculturation. Another characteristic is that culture is based on symbols. It is transmitted through the communication of ideas, emotions, and desires expressed in language. Finally, culture is integrated, so that all aspects of a culture function as an integrated whole. In a properly functioning culture, though, total harmony of all elements is approximated rather than completely achieved.

The job of the anthropologist is to abstract a set of rules from what he or she observes in order to explain the social behavior of people. To arrive at a realistic description of a culture free from personal and cultural biases, the anthropologist must (1) examine a people's notion of the way their society ought to function; (2) determine how a people think they behave; and (3) compare these with how a people actually do behave. The anthropologist must also be as free as possible of the biases of his or her own culture. Cultural adaptation has enabled humans, in the course of evolution, to survive and expand in a variety of environments. Sometimes, though, what is adaptive in one set of circumstances, or over the short run, is maladaptive in another set of circumstances, or over the long run.

To survive, a culture must satisfy the basic biological needs of its members, provide for their continuity, and maintain order among its members as well as between its members and outsiders.

All cultures change over time, sometimes because the environment they must cope with has changed, sometimes as the result of the intrusion of outsiders, or because values within the culture have undergone modification. Although cultures must change to adapt to new circumstances, sometimes the unforeseen consequences of change are disastrous for a society.

A society must strike a balance between the self-interest of individuals and the needs of the group. If one or the other becomes paramount, the result may be cultural breakdown.

Ethnocentrism is the belief that one's own culture is superior to all others. To avoid making ethnocentric judgments, anthropologists adopt the approach of cultural relativism, which requires that each culture be examined in its own terms, according to its own standards. The least biased measure of a culture's success, however, employs criteria indicative of its effectiveness at securing the survival of a society in a way that its members see as being reasonably fulfilling.

CLASSIC READINGS

Brown, D. E. (1991). *Human universals.* New York: McGraw-Hill.

The message of this book is that we should not let our fascination with the diversity of cultural practices interfere with the study of human universals: those things that all cultures share in spite of their differences. Important though the differences are, the universals have special relevance for our understanding of the nature of all humanity and raise issues that transcend the boundaries of biological and social science, as well as the humanities.

Gamst, F. C., & Norbeck, E. (1976). *Ideas of culture: Sources and uses.* New York: Holt, Rinehart and Winston.

This is a book of selected writings, with editorial comments, about the culture concept. From these selections one can see how the concept has grown, as well as how it has given rise to narrow specializations within the field of anthropology.

Goodenough, W. H. (1970). *Description and comparison in cultural anthropology.* Chicago: Aldine.

The major question Goodenough addresses is how anthropologists are to avoid ethnocentric bias when studying culture. His approach relies on models of descriptive linguistics. A large part of the book is concerned with kinship and terminology, with a discussion of the problems of a universal definition of marriage and the family. This is a particularly lucid discussion of culture, its relation to society, and the problem of individual variance.

Hatch, E. (1983). *Culture and morality: The relativity of values in anthropology.* New York: Columbia University Press.

This book is about cultural relativism, often used as a cover term for the quite different concepts of relativity of knowledge, historical relativism, and ethical relativism. It traces the attempts of anthropologists to grapple with these concepts, beginning with the rise of the discipline in the 19th century.

Linton, R. (1963). *The study of man: An introduction.* New York: Appleton.

Linton wrote this book in 1936 with the intention of providing a general survey of the field of anthropology. His study of social structure is still illuminating today. This book is regarded as a classic and is an important source historically.

CHAPTER 15

LANGUAGE AND COMMUNICATION

Humans communicate in many ways, as this girl is doing through gesture. Our most distinctive form of communication, however, is language, which makes possible the richness of human culture.

CHAPTER PREVIEW

1 What Is Language?

Language is a system of sounds or gestures that, when put together according to certain rules, results in meanings that are intelligible to all speakers. Although humans rely primarily on language to communicate with one another, it is not their sole means of communication. Language is embedded in a gesture-call system that consists of paralanguage—extralinguistic noises that accompany language—and kinesics, or body motions that are used to convey messages.

2 How Is Language Related to Culture?

Without language, human culture as we know it could not exist. Languages are spoken by people, who are members of societies, that have their own distinctive cultures. Social variables, such as class, gender, and status of the speaker, will influence people's use of language. Moreover, people communicate what is meaningful to them, and what is or is not meaningful is defined by their particular culture. In fact, our use of language affects, and is affected by, our culture.

3 How Did Language Begin?

Many theories have been proposed to account for the origin of language, several of them quite farfetched. One theory held by anthropologists today is that human language began as a system of gestures with rudimentary syntax. As such, it represents an outgrowth of abilities possessed as well by the great apes. A key factor in its elaboration may have been the importance of planning ahead for future contingencies on the part of our ancient ancestors. Since speech, like gestures, is a product of muscular movements, spoken language may have emerged as the muscles of the mouth and vocal tract were favored, so that people could use their hands for other things as they talked and could communicate with others without having to be in full view to do so.

All normal humans have the ability to talk, and in many societies they may spend a considerable part of each day doing so. Indeed, **language** is so much a part of our lives that it permeates everything we do, and everything we do permeates language. There is no doubt that our ability to speak, whether through sounds or gestures (sign languages, such as the American Sign Language used by the hearing impaired, are fully developed languages in their own right), rests squarely upon our biological organization. We are "programmed" to speak, although only in a general sort of way. Beyond the cries of babies, which are not learned but which do communicate, humans must learn how to speak. We must be taught to speak a particular language, and any normal child from anywhere in the world readily learns whatever language is spoken where she or he happens to be reared.

Language is a system for the communication, in **symbols,** of any kind of information. In the sense that nonhuman animals also communicate certain kinds of information systematically, we may speak of animal language. "Symbol" in our definition, however, means any kind of sound or gesture to which cultural tradition has assigned meaning as standing for something, and not one that has a natural or self-evident meaning, which we call a **signal.** A tear is a signal of crying (absent hay fever or an eye infection), and crying is a signal of some kind of emotional or physical state; the word *crying,* however, is a symbol, a combination of sounds to which we have learned to assign the meaning of a particular action and which we can use to communicate that meaning whether or not anyone around us is actually crying.

At the moment language experts are not certain how much credit to give to animals, such as dolphins, or chimpanzees, for the ability to use symbols as well as signals, even though these animals and many others have been found to communicate in remarkable ways. Several apes have been taught American Sign Language. Even among vervet monkeys, at least 10 different calls are used for communication, nor are these mere indexes of degree of arousal or fear. As primatologist Allison Jolly notes:

This example of animal communication shows two albatrosses pressing their beaks together in a courtship display.

> They mean something in the outside world; they include which direction to look in or where to run. There is an audience effect: calls are given when there is someone appropriate to listen . . . monkey calls are far more than involuntary expressions of emotion.[1]

What are the implications of this for our understanding of the nature and evolution of language? No final answer will be evident until we have a better understanding of animal communication than now exists. What we can be sure of is that animal communication cannot be dismissed as a set of simple reflexes or fixed action patterns, even though debate continues over just how human and animal communication relate to one another.[2] The fact is that human culture, as we know it, is ultimately dependent on a system of communication far more complex than that of any other animal. The reason for this is the sheer amount of what must be learned by each individual from other individuals in order to control the knowledge and rules for behavior necessary for full participation in his or her society. Of course, learning can and does take place in the absence of language by observation and imitation, guided by a limited number of signs or symbols. All known cultures, however, are so rich in content that they require systems of communication that not only can give precise labels to various classes of phenomena but also permit people to think and talk about their own and oth-

[1] Jolly, A. (1991). Thinking like a vervet. *Science, 251,* 574.

[2] Armstrong, D. F., Stokoe, W. C., & Wilcox, S. E. (1993). Signs of the origin of syntax. *Current Anthropology, 34,* 349–368; Burling, R. (1993). Primate calls, human language, and nonverbal communication. *Current Anthropology, 34,* 25–53.

Language. A system of communication using sounds or gestures that are put together in meaningful ways according to a set of rules. • **Symbols.** Sounds or gestures that stand for meanings among a group of people. • **Signal.** A sound or gesture that has a natural or self-evident meaning.

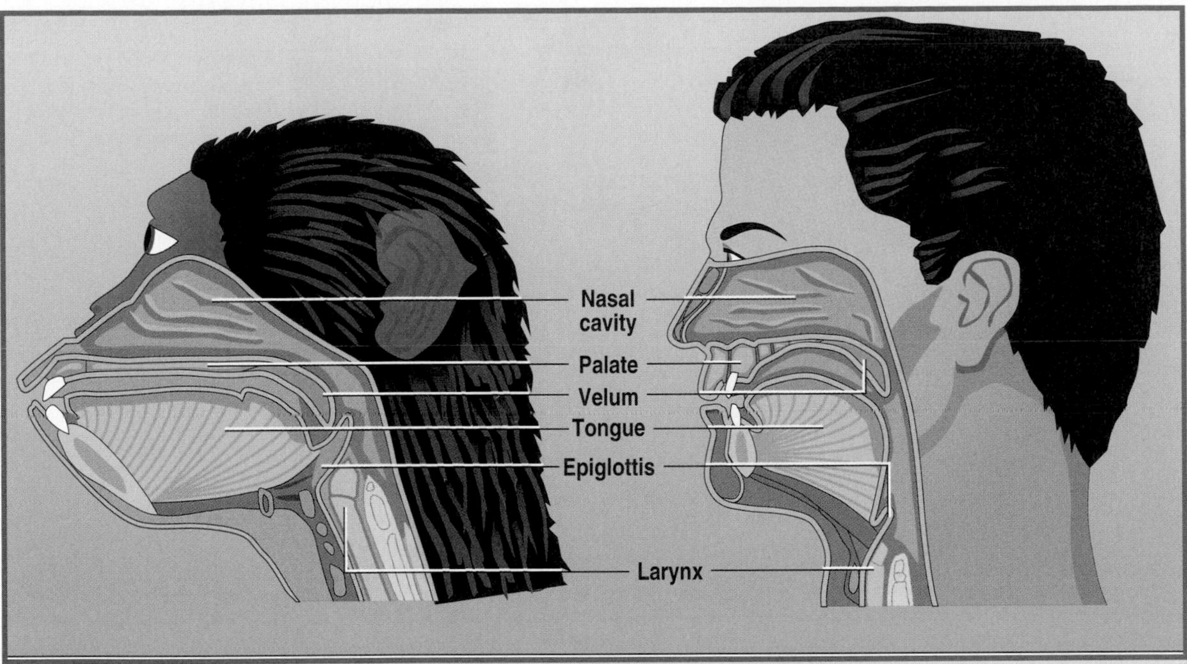

FIGURE 15.1
THE PRICE HUMANS PAY FOR SPOKEN LANGUAGE IS AN INCREASED RISK OF CHOKING TO DEATH, CAUSED BY A LOWER POSITION OF LARYNX AND EPIGLOTTIS.

ers' experiences, in the past and future as well as the present. The central and most highly developed human system of communication is language. So important to us is spoken language that we have paid a significant price for it: To be able to speak as we do, our vocal-respiratory tract has been modified in such a way as to greatly increase both our chances of choking to death and having impacted teeth, the latter condition generally being fatal until the 19th century (Figure 15.1). Knowledge of the workings of language, then, is essential to a full understanding of culture.

THE NATURE OF LANGUAGE

Any human language—English, Chinese, Swahili, or whatever—is obviously a means of transmitting information and sharing with others both cultural and individual experiences. Because we tend to take language for granted, it is perhaps not so obvious that language is also a system that enables us to translate our concerns, beliefs, and perceptions into symbols that can be understood and interpreted by others. In spoken language, this is done by taking a few sounds—no language uses more than about 50—and developing rules for putting them together in meaningful ways. Sign languages, such as American Sign Language, do the same thing, but with gestures rather than sounds. The many languages presently in existence all over the world—some 6,000 or so different ones—may well astound and mystify us by their great variety and complexity, but this should not blind us to the fact that all languages, as far back as we can trace them, are organized in the same basic way.

The roots of **linguistics**—the modern scientific study of language—go back a long way, to the works of ancient grammarians in India more than 2,000 years ago. With the European age of exploration and discovery in the 16th–18th centuries, the scientific study of language was given impetus by the accumulation of facts: the collection of sounds, words, and sentences from all sorts of different languages, chiefly those encountered in faraway places by European explorers, invaders, missionaries, and (ultimately) anthropologists. The great contribution of the

Linguistics. The modern scientific study of all aspects of language.

For linguists studying another language in the field, tape recorders and laptops have become indispensable tools.

19th century was the discovery of system, regularity, and relationships in the data and the tentative formulation of some laws and regular principles. In the 20th century, while we were still collecting data, we made considerable progress in the reasoning process, testing and working from new and improved theories. Insofar as theories and facts of language are verifiable by independent researchers looking at the same materials, there may now be said to be a science of linguistics.

The Sound and Shape of Language

How can an anthropologist, a missionary, a social worker, or anyone else approach and make sense of a language that has not yet been analyzed and described, or for which there are no immediately available materials? There are hundreds of such languages in the world; fortunately, effective methods have been developed to help with the task. It is a painstaking process to unravel a language, but it is ultimately rewarding and often even fascinating for its own sake.

For a spoken language, the process requires first a trained ear and a thorough understanding of the way speech sounds are produced. Otherwise, it will be extremely difficult to write out or make intelligent use of any data. To satisfy this preliminary requirement, most people need special training in **phonetics,** or the systematic study of the production, transmission, and reception of speech sounds.

PHONOLOGY

In order to analyze and describe any new language, an inventory of all of its sounds and an accurate way of writing them down are needed. Some sounds of other languages may be very much like the sounds of English, others (like the "clicks" in Bushman languages) may be sounds that English speakers have never consciously produced; but since all people have the same vocal equipment, we are all able, with practice, to reproduce all the sounds that anyone else makes. Once we have knowledge of all of the possible sounds in a language, we can study the patterns these sounds take as they are used to form words. From this, we discover the underlying rules that tell us which combinations of sounds are permissible in the language and which are not.

The first step in studying any particular language, once a number of utterances have been collected, is to isolate the **phonemes,** or the smallest classes of sound that make a difference in meaning. This isolation and analysis may be done by a process called the minimal-pair test: The linguist tries to find two short words that appear to be exactly alike except for one sound, such as *bit* and *pit* in English. If the substitution of *b* for *p* in this minimal pair makes a difference in meaning, as it does

Phonetics. The study of the production, transmission, and reception of speech sounds. • **Phonemes.** In linguistics, the smallest classes of sound that make a difference in meaning.

in English, then those two sounds have been identified as distinct phonemes of the language and will require two different symbols to record. If, however, the linguist finds two different pronunciations, as when "butter" is pronounced "budder," and then finds that there is no difference in their meaning for a native speaker, the sounds represented will be considered variants of the same phoneme. In such cases, for economy of representation only one of the two symbols will be used to record that sound wherever it is found. For greater accuracy and to avoid confusion with the various sounds of one's language, the symbols of a phonetic alphabet, such as was developed by Edward Sapir for the American Anthropological Association (Table 15.1), can be used to distinguish between the sounds of most languages in a way comprehensible to anyone who knows the system.

MORPHOLOGY

The process of making and studying an inventory of sounds may, of course, be a long task; concurrently, the linguist will begin to work out all groups or combinations of sounds that seem to have meaning. These are called **morphemes,** and they are the smallest units that have meaning in the language (unlike phonemes which, while making a difference in meaning, have no meaning by themselves). Morphemes may consist of words or parts of words. An anthropologist in the field can abstract morphemes and their meanings from speakers of a language by means of pointing or gesturing to elicit words and their meanings, but the ideal situation is to have an informant, someone who knows enough of a common second language, so that approximate translations can be made more efficiently and confidently. It is pointless to write down data without any suggestion of meaning for them. *Cat* and *dog* would, of course, turn out to be morphemes, or meaningful combinations of phonemes, in English. By pointing to two of either of them, the anthropologist could elicit *cats* and *dogs*. This indicates that there is another unit that carries meaning, an *-s,* that may be added to the original morpheme to mean "plural." When the anthropologist finds that this *-s* cannot occur in the language unattached, it will be identified as a **bound morpheme;** because *dog* and *cat* can occur unattached to anything, they are called **free morphemes.** Because the sound represented in writing as *s* is actually different in the two

TABLE 15.1 PHONETIC VOWEL SYMBOLS (SAPIR SYSTEMS)*

i (Fr. *fini*)	ü (Fr. *lune*)	*i*	*u̇* (Swed. *hus*)	*ï*	*u* (Ger. *gut*)
ι (Eng. *bit*)	ϋ (Ger. *Mütze*)	ι	υ̇	ϊ	υ (Eng. *put*)
e (Fr. *été*)	ö (Fr. *peu*)	–	ȯ	α (Eng. *but*)	o (Ger. *so*)
ε (Eng. *men*)	ɔ̈ (Ger. Götter)	–	ɔ̇	a (Ger. *Mann*)	ɔ (Ger. V*olk*)
–	ω̈ (Fr. peur)	–	ω̇	–	ω (Eng. *law*)
ä (Eng. *man*)	–	ȧ (Fr. *patte*)	–	–	–

* The symbol ∂ is used for an "indeterminate" vowel.

SOURCE: G. L. Trager. (1972). *Language and languages* (p. 304). San Francisco: Chandler Publishing Company.

Morphemes. In linguistics, the smallest units of sound that carry a meaning. • **Bound morpheme.** A sound that can occur in a language only in combination with other sounds, as s in English to signify the plural. • **Free morphemes.** Morphemes that can occur unattached in a language; for example, "dog" and "cat" are free morphemes in English.

HIGHWAY 1
Summer Institute of Linguistics home page
http://www.sil.org

HIGHWAY 2
Emuseum of the Anthropology Department at Minnesota State University, Mankato
http://www.anthro.mankato.msus.edu

HIGHWAY 3
Palomar College Anthropology Program: Language and Culture Tutorials
http://daphne.palomar.edu/anthro

words (*s* in *cats* and *z* in *dogs*), the anthropologist will conclude that the sounds *s* and *z* are two varieties of the same morpheme (even though they may be two different phonemes), occurring in different contexts but with no difference in meaning.

GRAMMAR AND SYNTAX

The next step is to see how morphemes are put together to form phrases or sentences. This process is known as identifying the syntactic units of the language, or the way morphemes are put together into larger chains or strings that have meaning. One way to do this is to use a method called **frame substitution.** By proceeding slowly at first and relying on pointing or gestures, the field worker can elicit such strings as *my cat, your cat,* or *her cat,* and *I see your cat, she sees my cat.* This begins to establish the rules or principles of phrase and sentence making, the **syntax** of the language. Further success of this sort of study depends greatly on individual ingenuity, tact, logic, and experience with language. A language may make extensive use of kinds of utterances that are not found at all in English, and which an English-speaking anthropologist may not, therefore, even think of asking for. Furthermore, certain speakers may pretend not to be able to say (or may truly not be able to say) certain things considered by their culture to be impolite, taboo, or inappropriate for mention to outsiders. It may even be unacceptable to point, in which case the field worker will have to devise roundabout ways of eliciting words for objects.

The **grammar** of the language will ultimately consist of all observations about its morphemes and syntax. Further work may include the establishment, by means of substitution frames, of all the **form classes** of the language: that is, the parts of speech or categories of words that work the same way in any sentence. For example, we may establish a category we call "nouns," defined as anything that will fit the substitution frame "I see a . . . " We simply make the frame, try out a number of words in it, and have a native speaker indicate "yes" or "no" for whether the words work. In English, the words *house* and *cat* will fit this frame and will be said to belong to the same form class, but the word *think* will not. Another

Frame substitution. A method used to identify the syntactic units of language. For example, a category called "nouns" may be established as anything that will fit the substitution frame "I see a . . . " • **Syntax.** In linguistics, the rules or principles of phrase and sentence making • **Grammar.** The entire formal structure of a language consisting of all observations about the morphemes and syntax. • **Form classes.** The parts of speech or categories of words that work the same way in any sentence.

Humans talk, while much communication among other primates is done through gestures. Still, humans have not abandoned gestural communication altogether, as we see here.

possible substitution frame for nouns might be "The . . . died," in which the word *cat* will fit, but not the word *house.* Thus, we can identify subclasses of our nouns: in this case, what we can call "animate" or "inanimate" subclasses. The same procedure may be followed for all the words of the language, using as many different frames as necessary, until we have a lexicon, or dictionary, that accurately describes the possible uses of all the words in the language.

One of the strengths of modern descriptive linguistics is the objectivity of its methods. The anthropologist who specializes in this will not approach a language with the idea that it must have nouns, verbs, prepositions, or any other of the form classes identifiable in English. She or he instead sees what turns up in the language and makes an attempt to describe it in terms of its own inner workings. For convenience, morphemes that behave approximately like English nouns and verbs may be labeled as such, but if it is thought that the terms are misleading, they may be called "x-words" and "y-words," or "form class A" and "form class B."

THE GESTURE-CALL SYSTEM

Efficient though languages are at naming and talking about things, all are deficient to some degree in communicating certain kinds of information that people need to know in order to understand what is being said. For this reason, human language is always embedded within a gesture-call system of a type that we share with monkeys and apes. The various sounds and gestures of this system serve to "key" speech, providing listeners with the appropriate frame for interpreting what a speaker is saying. Through it, we learn such things as the age and sex of the speaker, as well as his or her individual identity if it is someone we already know. Moreover, subtle messages about emotions and intentions are conveyed: Is the speaker happy, sad, enthusiastic, tired, or in some other emotional state? Is he or she requesting information, denying something, reporting factually, or lying? Very little of this information is conveyed by spoken language alone. In English, for example, at least 90 percent of emotional information is transmitted not by the words spoken but by "body language" and tone of voice. One (but not the only) reason why English has become the *lingua franca* of business is because of the ease with which deception can be carried out in its written form. Not all languages are as rich in mechanisms of evasion or impoverished in mechanisms for truth,[3] but none communicate people's emotions and intentions as effectively as the gesture-call system.

As something that we have inherited from our primate ancestors, many sounds and gestures of our gesture-call system are subject to greater genetic determination than language. This accounts for the universality of various cries and facial expressions, as well as for the great difficulty people have in bluffing or especially lying through gesture-calls. This is not to say the system is entirely immune to deliberate control, for it is not; merely that it is less subject to control than is spoken language.

---

[3] Elgin, S. H. (1994). I am not scowling fiercely as I write this. *Anthropology Newsletter, 35* (9), 44.

The importance of body language is shown by the role it played in the United States 2000 presidential election. George W. Bush's facial expression was taken as a sign of condescension and was a factor in his loss of the New Hampshire primary. Similarly, Al Gore's seemingly "wooden" body language played a role in his loss of the general election.

Kinesics

The gestural component of the gesture-call system consists of postures, facial expressions, and bodily motions that convey messages. The method for notating and analyzing this "body language" is known as **kinesics.** Kinesic messages may be communicated directly, as in the case of gestures. For example, in North America scratching one's scalp, biting one's lip, or knitting one's brows are ways of conveying doubt. A more complex example is afforded by the gender signals sent by North American men and women. Although there is some regional and class variation, women when standing generally bring their legs together, at times to the point that the upper legs cross, either in a full leg cross with feet still together, the outer sides of the feet parallel to one another, or in standing knee over knee. The pelvis is carried rolled slightly forward. The upper arms are held close to the body, and in movement, the entire body from neck to ankle is presented as a moving whole. Men, by contrast, hold their legs apart, with the upper legs at a 10 or 15 degree angle. Their pelvis is carried in a slightly rolled back position. The arms are held out at 10 to 15 degrees from the body, and they are moved independently of the body. Finally, a man may subtly wag his hips with a slight right and left presentation, with a movement involving a twist at the base of the rib cage and at the ankles.

Such gender markers should not be mistaken for invitations to sexual activity. Rather, they are conventions inscribed on the body through imitation and subtle training. In any culture, as little girls grow up, they imitate their mothers or other older women; little boys do the same with their fathers or other older men. In North American culture, by the time individuals become adults, they have acquired a host of gender markers that intrude into every moment of their lives, so much so that they are literally at a loss if they do not know the sex of someone with whom they must interact. This is easily verified, as the philosopher Marilyn Frye suggests:

Kinesics. A system of notating and analyzing postures, facial expressions, and body motions that convey messages.

To discover the differences in how you greet a woman and how you greet a man, for instance, just observe yourself, paying attention to the following sorts of things: frequency and duration of eye contact, frequency and type of touch, . . . physical distance maintained between bodies, how and whether you smile . . . , whether your body dips into a shadow curtsey or bow. That I have two repertories for handling introductions to people was vividly confirmed for me when a student introduced me to his friend, Pat, and I really could not tell what sex Pat was. For a moment I was stopped cold, completely incapable of action. I felt myself helplessly caught between two paths—the one I would take if Pat were female and the one I would take if Pat were male. Of course the paralysis does not last. One is rescued by one's ingenuity and good will: one can invent a way to behave as one says "How do you do?" to a human being. But the habitual ways are not for humans: they are one way for women and another for men.[4]

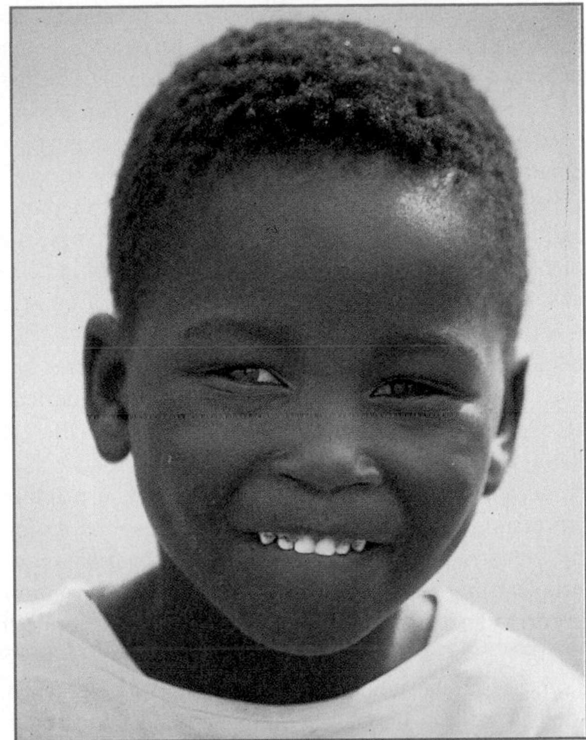

There is a great deal of similarity around the world in such basic expressions as smiling, laughing, crying, and anger, as one can see from the expressions of these children from Asia, Africa, and South America. Basic expressions such as these are part of the human inheritance from their primate ancestry.

[4] Frye, M. (1983). Sexism. In *The Politics of Reality* (p. 20). New York: The Crossing Press.

Often, gestural messages complement spoken messages, as by nodding the head while affirming something verbally. Other examples are punching the palm of the hand for emphasis, raising the head and brows when asking a question, or using the hands to illustrate what is being talked about. Such gestures may render abstract ideas in visible form, make what is being said more specific, or provide additional features of meaning. Like bound morphemes, they have meaning but don't stand alone, except in particular situations, such as a nodded response to a question.

Although little scientific notice was taken of "body language" prior to the 1950s, there has since been a great deal of research, particularly among North Americans. Cross-cultural research has shown, however, that there are many similarities around the world in such basic facial expressions as smiling, laughing, crying, and the facial expressions of anger. Such smirks, frowns, and so forth that we have inherited from our primate ancestry require little learning and are harder to "fake" than conventional gestures. There is great similarity, too, in the routine for greeting over a distance around the world. Europeans, Balinese, Papuans, Samoans, Bushmen, and at least some South American Indians all smile and nod, and if the individuals are especially friendly, they will raise their eyebrows with a rapid movement, keeping them raised for a fraction of a second. By doing so, they signal a readiness for contact. The Japanese, however, suppress the eyebrow flash, regarding it as indecent, which goes to show that there are important differences, as well as similarities, cross-culturally. This can be seen in gestural expressions for "yes" and "no." In North America, one nods the head for "yes" or shakes it for "no." The people of Sri Lanka, also, will nod to answer "yes" to a factual question, but if asked to do something, a slow sideways movement of the head means "yes." In Greece, the nodded head means "yes," but "no" is indicated by jerking the head back so as to lift the face; at the same time, the eyes are often closed and the eyebrows lifted. Body movements and gestures such as these, which vary cross-culturally and have to be learned, are known as conventional gestures.

Learned gestures different cultures assign different meanings to are known as conventional gestures. An example is this sign, which in North America means "OK." In Brazil, it is an obscene gesture.

Paralanguage

The second component of the gesture-call system is **paralanguage,** consisting of cries and other sounds that are not part of language but always accompany it. The importance of paralanguage is suggested by the comment, "It's not so much *what* was said as *how* it was said." Recent studies have shown, for example, that subliminal messages communicated by seemingly minor differences in phraseology, tempo, length of answers, and the like are far more important in courtroom proceedings than even the most perceptive trial lawyer may have realized. Among other things, how a witness gives testimony alters the reception it gets from jurors and bears on the witness' credibility where inconsistencies exist in testimony.[5]

VOICE QUALITIES

While it is not always easy to distinguish between the sounds of language and paralinguistic noises, two different kinds of the latter have been identified. The first has to do with **voice qualities,** which operate as the background characteristics of a speaker's voice. These involve pitch range (from low to high pitched); lip control (from closed to open); glottis control (sharp to smooth transitions in pitch); articulation control (forceful and relaxed speech); rhythm control (smooth or jerky setting off of portions of vocal activity); resonance (from resonant to thin); and tempo (an increase or decrease from the norm).

[5] O'Barr, W. M., & Conley, J. M. (1993). When a juror watches a lawyer. In W. A. Haviland and R. J. Gordon (Eds.), *Talking about people* (2nd. ed.)(pp. 42–45). Mountain View, CA: Mayfield.

Paralanguage. The extralinguistic noises that accompany language, for example, those of crying or laughing. •
Voice qualities. In paralanguage, the background characteristics of a speaker's voice.

Voice qualities are capable of communicating much about the state of being of the person who is speaking, quite apart from what is being said. An obvious example of this is slurred speech, which may indicate that the speaker is intoxicated. Or, if someone says rather languidly, coupled with a restricted pitch range, that she or he is delighted with something, it probably indicates that the person isn't delighted at all. The same thing said more rapidly, with increasing pitch, might indicate that the speaker really is genuinely excited about the matter. While the speaker's state of being is affected by his or her anatomical and physiological status, it is also markedly affected by the individual's overall self-image in the given situation. If a person is made to feel anxious by being crowded in some way, or by some aspects of the social situation, for example, this anxiety will probably be conveyed by certain voice qualities.

VOCALIZATIONS

The second kind of paralinguistic noises consists of **vocalizations.** Rather than being background characteristics, these are actual identifiable noises that, unlike voice qualities, are turned on and off at perceivable and relatively short intervals. They are, nonetheless, separate from language sounds. One category of vocalizations are **vocal characterizers:** the sounds of laughing or crying, yelling or whispering, yawning or belching, and the like. Many combine sounds with gestures. One "talks through" vocal characterizers, and they are generally indicative of the speaker's attitude. If one yawns while speaking to someone, for example, this may indicate an attitude of boredom on the part of the speaker. Breaking, an intermittent tensing and relaxing of the vocal musculature producing a tremulousness while speaking, may indicate great emotion on the part of the speaker.

Another category of vocalizations consists of **vocal qualifiers.** These are of briefer duration than vocal characterizers, being limited generally to the space of a single intonation, rather than over whole phrases. They modify utterances in terms of intensity—loud versus soft; pitch—high versus low; and extent—drawl versus clipping. These indicate the speaker's attitude to specific phrases such as "get out." The third category consists of **vocal segregates.** Sometimes called "*oh oh* expressions," these are somewhat like the actual sounds of language, but they don't appear in the kinds of sequences that can be called words. Examples of vocal segregates besides *oh oh* that are familiar to English-speaking peoples are such substitutes for language as *shh, uh-uh,* or *uh-huh.* Unlike such paralinguistic sounds as sobs, giggles, and screams, "*oh oh* expressions" are conventional, learned, and far more variable from culture to culture.

LINGUISTIC CHANGE

In our discussion of the sound and shape of language, we looked briefly at the internal organization of language—its phonology, morphology, syntax, and grammar. It is the descriptive approach to language that is concerned with registering and explaining all the features of any particular language at any one time in its history. The specialist in descriptive linguistics concentrates, for example, on the way modern French or Spanish function now, as if they were separate systems, consistent within themselves, without any reference to historical reasons for their development. Yet languages, like the rest of culture, have histories. The Latin *ille* ("that") is identifiable as the origin of both French *le* ("the") and Spanish *el* ("the"), even though the descriptive linguist treats *le* and *el* only as they function in the modern language, where the meaning "that" is no longer relevant and very few native speakers are aware that they are speaking modern derivatives of Latin. Specialists in historical linguistics, by contrast, investigate relationships between earlier and later forms of the same language, antecedents in older languages for developments in modern ones, and questions of relationships between older languages. Historical linguists, for example, attempt to identify and explain the development of early medieval spoken Latin into later medieval French and Spanish by investigating both natural change in the original language and the influence of contacts with invaders from the north. There is no conflict between historical and descriptive linguistics, the two approaches being recognized as interdependent. Even a modern language is constantly changing; consider, for example, the changed meaning of the word "gay" in English. Today it is used to refer to homosexual and lesbian persons. It's

Vocalizations. Identifiable paralinguistic noises that are turned on and off at perceivable and relatively short intervals. • **Vocal characterizers.** In paralanguage, sound productions such as laughing or crying that humans "speak through." • **Vocal qualifiers.** In paralanguage, sound productions of brief duration that modify utterances in terms of intensity. • **Vocal segregates.** In paralanguage, sound productions that are similar to the sounds of language, but do not appear in sequences that can properly be called words.

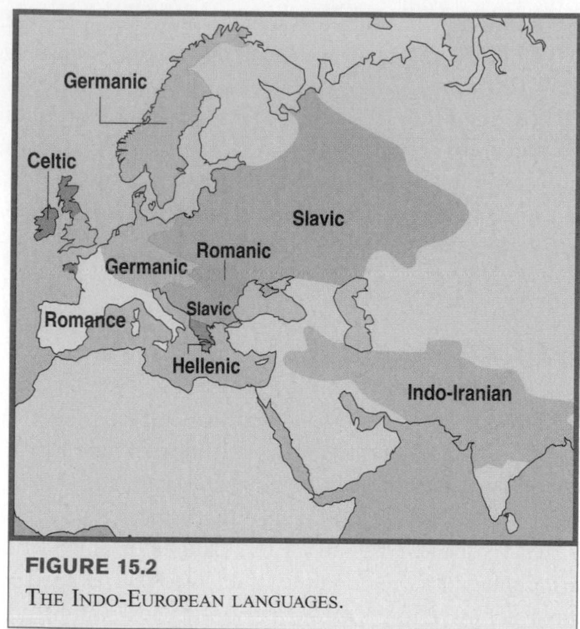

FIGURE 15.2
THE INDO-EUROPEAN LANGUAGES.

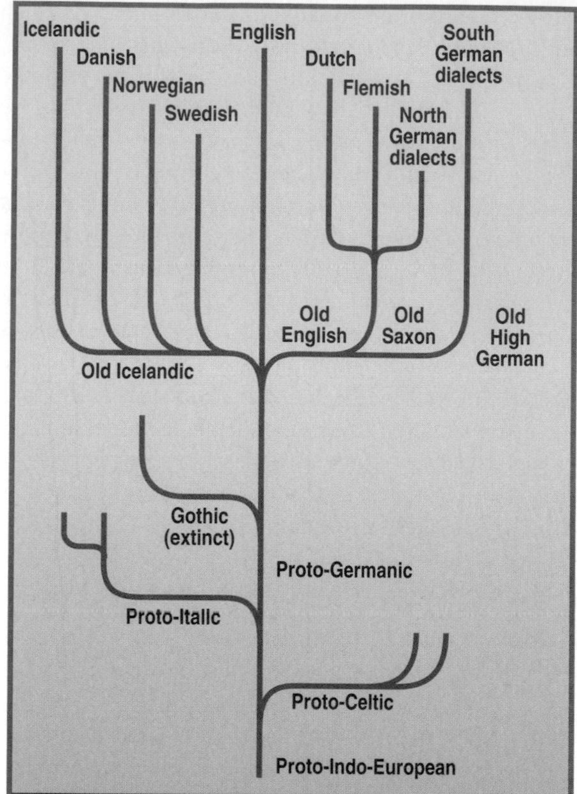

FIGURE 15.3
ENGLISH IS ONE OF A GROUP OF LANGUAGES IN THE GERMANIC SUBGROUP OF THE INDO-EUROPEAN FAMILY. THIS DIAGRAM SHOWS ITS RELATIONSHIP TO OTHER LANGUAGES IN THE SAME SUBGROUP. THE ROOT WAS PROTO-INDO-EUROPEAN, A LANGUAGE SPOKEN BY A PEOPLE WHO SPREAD WESTWARD OVER EUROPE, BRINGING WITH THEM BOTH THEIR CUSTOMS AND THEIR LANGUAGE.

meaning in the title of the 1942 play, *Our Hearts Were Young and Gay,* illustrates the word's different usage as recently as that time. Such changes take place according to principles that can be established only historically.

Historical linguists have achieved considerable success in working out the genealogical relationships between different languages, and these are reflected in schemes of classification. For example, English is one of approximately 140 languages classified in the Indo-European **language family** (Figure 15.2). This family is subdivided into some 11 subgroups, which reflect the fact that there has been a long period (6,000 years or so) of **linguistic divergence** from an ancient unified language (referred to as Proto-Indo-European) into separate "daughter" languages. English is one of several languages in the Germanic subgroup (Figure 15.3); all are more closely related to one another than they are to the languages of any other subgroup of the Indo-European family. So it is that, in spite of the differences between them, the languages of one subgroup show certain features in common when compared to those of another. As an illustration, the word for *father* in the Germanic languages always starts with an *f* or closely related *v* sound (Dutch *vader,* German *Vater,* Gothic *Fadar*). Among the Romance languages, by contrast, the comparable word always starts with a *p:* French *père,* Spanish and Italian *padre*, all derived from the Latin *pater*. The original Indo-European word for *father* was *p'tēr,* so in this case, the Romance languages have retained the earlier pronunciation, whereas the Germanic languages have diverged. Thus, many words that begin with *p* in the Romance languages, like Latin *piscis* and *pes*, become words like English *fish* and *foot* in the Germanic languages.

Historical linguists have been successful in describing the changes that have taken place as languages have diverged from more ancient parent languages. They have also developed means of estimating when certain migra-

Language family. A group of languages that are ultimately descended from a single ancestral language. • **Linguistic divergence.** The development of different languages from a single ancestral language.

tions, invasions, and contacts of peoples have taken place, on the basis of linguistic similarities and differences. The concept of linguistic divergence, for example, is used to guess at the time at which one group of speakers of a language separated from another group. A more complicated technique, known as **glottochronology,** was developed by Morris Swadesh and Sarah Gudscinsky in the early 1950s to try to date the divergence of related languages, such as Latin and Greek, from an earlier common language. The technique is based on the assumption that changes in a language's **core vocabulary**—pronouns, lower numerals, and names for parts of the body and natural objects—change at a more or less constant rate. By applying a logarithmic formula to two related core vocabularies, one should be able to determine how many years the languages have been separated. Although not as precise as this might suggest, glottochronology provides a useful way of estimating when languages may have separated.

While many of the changes that have taken place in the course of linguistic divergence are well known, their causes are not. One force for linguistic change is borrowing by one language from another, something that languages readily do when in a position to do so; but if borrowing were the sole force for change, linguistic differences would be expected to become less pronounced through time. Through the study of modern languages in their cultural settings one can begin to understand the forces for change. One such force is novelty, pure and simple. There seems to be a human tendency to admire the person who comes up with a new and clever idiom, a new and useful word, or a particularly stylish pronunciation, so long as these do not seriously interfere with communication. Indeed, in linguistic matters, complexity tends to be admired, while simplicity seems dull. Hence, about as fast as a language may be simplified, purged of needlessly complex constructions or phrases, new ones will arise.

Group membership also plays a role in linguistic change. Part of this is functional: Professions, sects, or other groups in a society often have need of special vocabularies to be able to communicate effectively about their special interests. Beyond this, special vocabularies may serve as labeling devices; those who use such vocabularies are set off as a group from those who do not. Here, we have the paradox of language acting to *prevent* communication, in this case between members of different groups. Such linguistic barriers serve to create a strong sense of group identity.

When a military officer speaks of "incontinent ordnance" and "collateral damage," a physician of "exsanguination," a dentist of the "oral cavity," or an anthropologist of "the structural implications of matrilateral cross-cousin marriage," they express, in part at least, their membership in a profession and their command of its language. For insiders, professional terminology reinforces their sense of belonging to a select "in-group"; to outsiders it often seems an unneeded and pretentious use of "bafflegab" where perfectly adequate and simple words would do as well. Whether needed or not, professional terminology does serve to differentiate language and to set the speech of one group apart from that of others. Therefore, it is a force for stylistic divergence.

Phonological differences between groups may be regarded in the same light as vocabulary differences. In a class-structured society, for example, members of the upper class may try to keep their pronunciation distinct from that of lower classes. An example of a different sort is afforded by coastal communities in the state of Maine, in particular, though it may be seen to varying degrees elsewhere along the New England coast. In the past, people in these communities developed a regional dialect with a style of pronunciation quite distinct from the styles of "people from away." More recently, as outsiders have moved into these coastal communities, either as summer people or as permanent residents, the traditional coastal style has come to identify those who adhere to traditional coastal values, as opposed to those who do not.

One other far-reaching force for linguistic change is **linguistic nationalism,** an attempt by whole countries to proclaim their independence by purging their vocabularies of "foreign" terms. This phenomenon is particularly characteristic of the former colonial countries of Africa and Asia today. It is by no means limited to those countries, however, as one can see by periodic French attempts to purge their language of such Americanisms as *le hamburger.* Also in the category of linguistic nationalism are revivals of languages long out of common use by ethnic minorities and sometimes even whole countries (an estimated 6000 languages have disappeared over the past 500

Glottochronology. In linguistics, a method of dating divergence in branches of language families. • **Core vocabulary.** In language, pronouns, lower numerals, and names for body parts and natural objects. • **Linguistic nationalism.** The attempt by ethnic minorities, and even countries to proclaim independence by purging their languages of foreign terms.

Anthropology Applied

Language Renewal Among the Northern Ute

On April 10, 1984, the Northern Ute Tribe became the first community of American Indians in the United States to affirm the right of its members to regain and maintain fluency in their ancestral language, as well as their right to use it as a means of communication throughout their lives. Like many other Native Americans, these people had experienced a decline in fluency in their native tongue, as they were forced to interact more and more intensively with outsiders who spoke only English. Once the on-reservation boarding school was closed in 1953, Ute children had to attend schools where teachers and most other students were ignorant of the Ute language. Outside the classroom as well, children and adults alike were increasingly bombarded by English as they sought employment off reservation, traded in non-Indian communities, or were exposed to television and other popular media. By the late 1960s, although Ute language fluency was still highly valued, many members of the community could no longer speak it.

Alarmed by this situation, the group of Ute parents and educators that supervises federally-funded tutorial services to Indian students decided that action needed to be taken, lest their native language be lost altogether. With the assistance of other community leaders, they launched discussions into what might be done about the situation, and invited anthropologist William L. Leap to join in these discussions. Previously, Leap had worked on language education with other tribes, and he was subsequently hired by the Utes to assist them in their efforts at linguistic renewal. One result of his work was the official statement of policy, by the tribe's governing body, noted above.

Leap began work for the Northern Utes in 1978, and his first task was to carry out a first-ever reservation-wide language survey. This found, among other things, that inability to speak Ute did not automatically imply loss of skill; evidently, many non-speakers retained a "passive fluency" in the language and could understand it, even though they couldn't speak it. Furthermore (and quite contrary to expectations), children who were still able to speak Ute had fewer problems with English in school than did non-speakers.

Over the next few years, Leap helped set up a Ute language renewal program within the tribe's Division of Education, wrote several grants to provide funding, led staff training workshops in linguistic transcription and grammatical analysis, provided technical assistance in designing a practical writing system for the language, and supervised data gathering sessions with already fluent speakers of the language. With the establishment in 1980 of an in-school program to provide developmental Ute and English instruction to Indian and other interested children, he became staff linguist. In this capacity he helped train the language teachers (all of whom were Ute, and none of whom had degrees in education); carried out research that resulted in numerous technical reports, publications and in-service workshops; helped prepare a practical Ute language handbook for home use so that parents and grandparents might enrich the children's language learning experience; prepared the preliminary text for the tribe's statement of policy on language, and helped persuade the governing body into acceptance of this. By 1984, not only did this policy become "official," but several (not just one) language development projects were in place on the reservation, all monitored and coordinated by a tribally sanctioned language and culture committee. Supported by both tribal and federal funds, these involved the participation of persons with varying degrees of familiarity with the language. Although literacy was not a goal, down-to-earth needs resulted in development of practical writing systems, and a number of people in fact became literate in Ute. One important reason for all this success was the involvement of the Ute people in all stages of development; not only did these projects originate in response to their own expressed needs, they were active participants in all discussions and made decisions at each stage of activities, participating not just as individuals, but as members of family, kin, community and band.

* See Leap, W. L. (1987). Tribally controlled culture change: The Northern Ute language renewal project. In Wulff, R. M., & Fiske, S. J. (Eds.), *Anthropological praxis: Translating knowledge into action.* Boulder CO: Westview.

Linguistic nationalism in East Timor. Following independence, a debate has begun over what the national language should be: Tetun, spoken by 90% of the population but not understood in the outside world; Portuguese (being taught in this language class), though tainted by colonialism; Indonesian, spoken by most youth, but a reminder of hated oppression; or English?

years). In the latter category is the successful revival of Hebrew as Israel's first language, though not without a bitter campaign against its competitor, Yiddish. In the former is the Ute's attempt to revive their language, as discussed in Anthropology Applied.

For ethnic minorities, the revival of lost languages or the maintenance of those not lost is important for their sense of identity and self worth. Furthermore, it serves as an effective barrier to penetration by outsiders, allowing people to pursue the livelihoods and interests they choose for themselves. By the same token, a prime means by which countries try to assert their dominance over minorities living within their borders is to suppress their languages. A good illustration of this was the policy pursued in the United States of taking Indian children away from their parents and putting them in boarding schools, where use of Indian languages was absolutely forbidden and punished with physical abuse and humiliation. Not until 1934 did the government begin to ease up on this harsh policy, but it was only as recently as 1990 that the Native American Languages Act was passed by Congress, encouraging Indians to use their own languages.

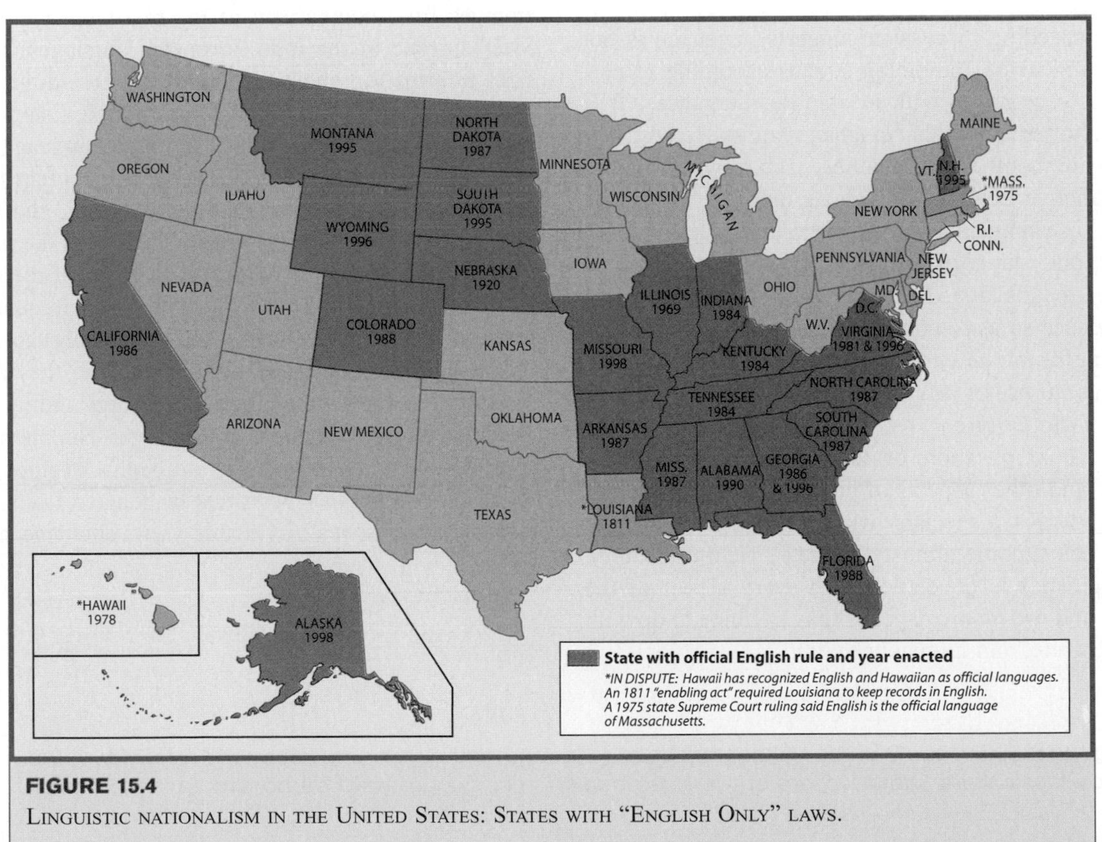

FIGURE 15.4

LINGUISTIC NATIONALISM IN THE UNITED STATES: STATES WITH "ENGLISH ONLY" LAWS.

In spite of such changes, the United States remains uneasy about linguistic diversity. This is reflected in a reluctance to learn foreign languages (in many human societies, it is not unusual for people to be fluent in two, three, or even four different languages, but to become so, it is important to begin learning them as children—not as high school or college students, as is traditional in the United States); more dramatically, it is illustrated by efforts to make "English only" national policy. Proponents of such a policy argue that multilingualism is divisive, and often cite the example of French separatism in Canada. What they do not cite are examples such as Bosnia-Herzegovina or Northern Ireland, both instances where speaking a single language has not prevented violent fighting between factions. Nor do they mention countries like Finland, where three languages are spoken, nor Switzerland where there are four, without people being at each other's throats. The fact is, where linguistic diversity is divisive, it is often *because* of official policies in favor of monolingualism.

LANGUAGE IN ITS CULTURAL SETTING

As the preceeding discussion suggests, language is not simply a matter of combining sounds according to certain rules to come up with meaningful utterances. It is important to remember that languages are spoken by people, who are members of societies, each of which has its own distinctive culture. Individuals tend to vary in the ways they use language, and social variables such as class, ethnicity, and status of the speaker will also influence their use of language. Moreover, people choose words and sentences so as to communicate meaning, and what is meaningful in one culture may not be in another. The fact is that our use of language affects, and is affected by, the rest of our culture.

The whole question of the relationships between language and other aspects of culture is the province of **ethnolinguistics,** a specialty within linguistic anthropology that has become almost a separate field of inquiry. Ethnolinguistics is concerned with every aspect of the structure and use of language that has anything to do with society, culture, and human behavior.

Language and Thought

An important ethnolinguistic concern of the 1930s and 1940s was the question of whether one's language might actually determine how one thinks, thereby shaping one's culture itself. The American anthropologist Edward Sapir had earlier formulated the problem, and his student, Benjamin Lee Whorf, drawing on his experience with the language of the Hopi Indians, developed a full-fledged theory of **linguistic relativity** (once called the Sapir-Whorf hypothesis). Whorf proposed that a language is not simply an encoding process for voicing our ideas and needs but is rather a shaping force. By providing habitual grooves of expression that predispose people to see the world in a certain way, language guides their thinking and behavior. Surprisingly, there was little follow-up to Whorf's original work, on the grounds that the problem was not amenable to any experimentation or proof. Recently, however, there has been a renewal of interest, and attempts are being made to develop means of testing the hypothesis.[6] To cite one example, speakers of Swedish and Finnish working at similar jobs in similar regions under similar laws and regulations show significantly different rates of on-the-job accidents. The rates are substantially lower among the Swedish speakers. What emerges from comparison of the two languages is that Swedish (one of the Indo-European languages) emphasizes information about movement in three-dimensional space. Finnish (a Ural-Altaic language, like Estonian and Hungarian, unrelated to Indo-European languages) emphasizes more static relations between coherent temporal entities. As a consequence, it seems that Finns organize the workplace in a way that favors the individual person over the temporal organization of the overall production process. This in turn leads to frequent disruptions in production, haste, and (ultimately) accidents.

Intriguing though such studies may be, they are not sufficient by themselves for a full understanding of the relation between language and thought. Supplementary approaches are necessary, and are being developed.

Another point of view is that language reflects, rather than determines, reality. In this view, language mirrors

[6] Lucy, J. A. (1997). Linguistic relativity. *Annual Review of Anthropology, 26,* 291–312.

Ethnolinguistics. The study of the relation between language and culture. • **Linguistic relativity.** The proposition that diverse interpretations of reality embodied in languages yield demonstrable influences on thought.

This tractor convoy of Albanian refugees in Kosovo, mistakenly bombed by NATO forces, is an example of "collateral damage."

cultural reality, and as the latter changes, so too will language. Some support for this is provided by studies of blue-green color terms. It has been shown that eye pigmentation acts to filter out the shorter wavelengths of solar radiation. Color vision is thus limited through a reduced sensitivity to blue and lack of distinction between the short visible wavelengths. The effect shows up in color-naming behavior, where green may be identified with blue, blue with black, or both green and blue with black. The severity of visual limitation, as well as the extent of lumping of color terms, depends on the density of eye pigmentation characteristic of the people in a given society.

These findings do not mean that language merely reflects reality, any more than thinking and behavior are wholly determined by language. The truth of the matter is more as anthropologist Peter Woolfson has put it:

> Reality should be the same for us all. Our nervous systems, however, are being bombarded by a continual flow of sensations of different kinds, intensities, and durations. It is obvious that all of these sensations do not reach our consciousness; some kind of filtering system reduces them to manageable propositions. The Whorfian hypothesis suggests that the filtering system is one's language. Our language, in effect, provides us with a special pair of glasses that heightens certain perceptions and dims others. Thus, while all sensations are received by the nervous system, only some are brought to the level of consciousness.[7]

Linguists have found that although language is generally flexible and adaptable, established terminologies do tend to perpetuate themselves, reflecting and revealing the social structure, common perceptions, and concerns of groups and people. For example, English is richly endowed with words having to do with war, the tactics of war, and the hierarchy of officers and fighting men. It is rich, too, in militaristic metaphors, as when we speak of "conquering" space, "fighting" the "battle" of the budget, carrying out a "war" on poverty, making a "killing" on the stock market, "shooting down" an argument, or "bombing" out on an exam, to mention just a few. An observer from an entirely different and perhaps warless culture could understand a great deal about the importance of warfare in our lives, as well as how we go about conducting it, simply from what we have found necessary to name and how we talk. Similarly, anthropologists have noted that the language of the Nuer, a nomadic people of

[7] Woolfson, P. (1972). Language, thought, and culture. In V. P. Clark, P. A. Escholz, & A. F. Rosa (Eds.), *Language* (p. 4). New York: St. Martin's.

So important are cattle to the Nuer of southern Sudan that they have more than 400 words to describe them.

southern Sudan, is rich in words and expressions having to do with cattle; not only are more than 400 words used to describe cattle, but Nuer boys actually take their names from them. Thus, by studying the language we can determine the importance of cattle to Nuer culture, attitudes to cattle, and the whole etiquette of human and cattle relationships. A people's language does not, however, prevent them from thinking in new and novel ways. If this leads to important changes in common perceptions and concerns, then language can be expected to change accordingly.

KINSHIP TERMS

In the same connection, anthropologists have paid considerable attention to the way people name their relatives in various societies, as we will see in Chapter 21. In English we have terms to identify brother, sister, mother, father, grandmother, grandfather, granddaughter, grandson, niece, nephew, mother-in-law, father-in-law, sister-in-law, and brother-in-law. Some people also distinguish first and second cousin and great-aunt and great-uncle. Is this the only possible system for naming relatives and identifying relationships? Obviously not. We could have separate terms, as some cultures do, for younger brother and older brother, for mother's sister and father's sister, and so on. What we can describe in English with a phrase, if pressed to do so, other languages make explicit from the outset, and vice versa: A number of languages use the same word to denote both a brother and a cousin, and a mother's sister may also be called by the same term as one's mother.

What do kinship terms reveal? From them, we can certainly gain a good idea of how families are structured, what relationships are considered especially important, and sometimes what attitudes toward relationships may prevail. Caution is required, however, in drawing conclusions from kinship terms. Just because we do not distinguish linguistically in English between our mother's parents and our father's parents (both are simply grandmother and grandfather), does that mean that we do not know which is which? Certainly not. Nevertheless, nonanthropologists, when confronted with a kinship system in which the same term is applied to father's brother as to father, frequently make the mistake of assuming that "these people don't know who their own father is."

Language and Gender

Throughout history, human beings have handled the relationship between men and women in many different ways, and here again language can be revealing. In English-speaking societies, for example, men and women use the language in different ways, revealing a deep-seated bias against women. For example, women frequently use the expression "I'm sorry" to indicate sympathy and concern rather than apology.

Unfortunately, men tend to accept it in the literal sense, as an apology, instead of its intended figurative sense. In so doing, whether purposeful or not, the woman is placed in a position of subordination. Similarly, words spoken by or about women imply, sometimes subtly and sometimes not, a lesser status. For example, behavior described as "forceful" in the case of a man might be described as "pushy" in a woman. Or, while a man may "pass out" (falling directly to the ground), a woman "faints" (as if giving way to weakness). While a man is "a fighter," a woman is "spunky," or "feisty," words suggestive of lesser power. In innumerable ways does the traditional inequality of men and women in North American society receive linguistic expression.

Social Dialects

In our previous discussion of linguistic change, phonological and vocabulary differences between groups were noted as important forces for linguistic change. Varying forms of a language that are similar enough to be mutually intelligible are known as **dialects,** and the study of dialects is a concern of **sociolinguistics.** Technically, all dialects are languages—there is nothing partial or sublinguistic about them—and the point at which two different dialects become distinctly different languages is roughly the point at which speakers of one are almost totally unable to communicate with speakers of the other. Boundaries may be psychological, geographical, social, or economic, and they are not always very clear. In the case of regional dialects, there is frequently a transitional territory, or perhaps a buffer zone, where features of both are found and understood, as between central and southern China. The fact is that if you learn the Chinese of Beijing, you cannot communicate with someone who comes from Canton or Hong Kong, although both languages—or dialects—are conventionally called Chinese.

A classic example of the kind of dialect that may set one group apart from others within a single society is one spoken by many inner-city African Americans. Technically known as "African American Vernacular English," it has often been referred to as "Black English" and (more recently) as "Ebonics."

Unfortunately, there is a widespread perception among upper- and middle-class whites and blacks alike that this dialect is somehow substandard or defective, which it is not. A basic principle of linguistics is that the selection of a prestige dialect—in this case, what we may call "Standard English" as opposed to "Ebonics"— is determined by accidental extralinguistic forces and is not dependent on indirect virtues of the dialects themselves. In fact, African-American Vernacular English is a highly structured mode of speech, capable of expressing anything its speakers care to express, often in extremely creative ways (as in "rapping"). Many of its distinctive features stem from retention of sound patterns, grammatical devices, and even words of the West African languages spoken by the ancestors of today's African Americans. Compared to the richness of Black English, the Standard English dialect lacks certain sounds, contains some sounds that are unnecessary for which others may serve just as well, doubles and drawls some of its vowel sounds in sequences that are unusual and difficult to imitate, lacks a method of forming an important tense (the habitual), requires more ways than necessary of indicating tense, plurality, and gender, and doesn't mark negatives in such a way as to make a strong negative statement.

Because their dialect differs so much from Standard English, and has been stigmatized so often, speakers of African American Vernacular English frequently find themselves at a disadvantage outside of their own communities. In schools, for example, African American children often have been seen by teachers as deficient in verbal skills and have even been diagnosed—quite wrongly—as "learning impaired." The great challenge for the schools is to find ways of teaching these children how to use Standard English in those situations where it is to their advantage to do so, without denigrating or affecting their ability to use the dialect of their own community. Unfortunately, the misunderstandings and prejudices of the general public are so great that a recent attempt by the school board of Oakland, California, to deal with the problem stirred up a firestorm of criticism. In the following Original Study, anthropologist Leila Monaghan and two colleagues discuss the controversy and the Oakland School Board's proposal.

Dialects. Varying forms of a language that reflect particular regions or social classes and that are similar enough to be mutually intelligible. • **Sociolinguistics.** The study of the structure and use of language as it relates to its social setting.

The Great Ebonics Controversy[8]

Original Study

Ebonics raised a storm of protest from around the country. The very names for this dialect reflect the diversity of views. What the Oakland school board refers to as Ebonics has also been known over time

[8] Monaghan, L., Hinton, L., & Kephart, R. (1997). Can't teach a dog to be a cat? The dialogue on ebonics. *Anthropology Newsletter, 38* (3), 1, 8, and 9.

Original Study

as Black English Vernacular (BEV), Black English (BE), African American Vernacular English (AAVE) and African American English (AAE). English used by African Americans ranges from distinctive styles of master orators like Martin Luther King and Jesse Jackson, through urban and rural vernaculars influenced by Southern roots and the language of recent Caribbean and African immigrants, to standard and local Englishes identical to those used by members of other communities. This diversity also makes us question how to designate what white Americans speak. In this piece we refer to Standard English (SE), which is strongly associated with written forms taught in school. There are, of course, numerous English vernacular forms, which have received less discussion.

Leanne Hinton (Linguistics, California-Berkeley)

The furor over Oakland's recently adopted resolution regarding Ebonics is based in large part on two issues: (1) there is a misunderstanding that the Oakland school system wants to teach BE in the schools; and (2) there is a sense of outrage among some that a stigmatized variety of English would be treated as a valid way of talking. When I attended the school board meeting at which the Ebonics resolution was adopted, all discussion in support of the resolution by board members, parents and teachers was centered around the importance of teaching SE to children. This resolution is not about teaching BE but about the best way to teach SE. The children whom the board is concerned about have learned BE at home, a linguistic variety that has many differences from SE. To teach SE the board has rightfully concluded that teachers need to understand BE to teach children the differences between these two linguistic varieties. It has also rightfully concluded that BE is not just some random form of "broken-down English" intrinsically inferior to SE but is a speech variety with its own long history, logical rules of grammar, discourse practices traceable to West African languages and a vibrant oral literature worthy of respect. BE has also been one of the major contributors of vocabulary to American English in general.

Whether Ebonics is a separate language in any technical sense is not what I think educators are concerned with here. What they are after is elevating the status of African American English (AAE). While from a linguistic point of view, these notions are being carried to an unscientific extreme, proponents of Ebonics are battling an even more unscientific set of extreme prejudices against AAE. The Oakland board is trying to promulgate a new set of political ideas about AAE as a legitimate form of speech, partly for the sake of African American pride but mainly for the sake of teaching SE in an emotionally positive way.

The notion that there is something just plain "bad" about nonstandard varieties of English is so deeply imbedded in the minds of many people that they tend to believe that children speak BE out of contrariness and need to be corrected by punishment. Educators have known better for a long time and don't want to be disrespectful of African American children's ways of speech, but that very respect has left them without a way of teaching SE. The method being embraced by the Oakland school board fills that void. By escaping the trap of thinking of nonstandard BE as a set of "errors" and instead treating it as it really is—a different system, not a wrong one—SE can be taught by helping children develop an awareness of the contrast between their two speech varieties and learning to use one without losing pride in the other.

Ron Kephart (Linguistic Anthropology and English, University of North Florida)

My take on the Ebonics issue has to do with being a linguistic anthropologist and having conducted research on reading in Creole English on Carriacou, Grenada. In both cases, one of the hardest problems seems to be making people understand what you are doing.

A major criticism of the Oakland proposal which I have heard is that teachers will be wasting time

The passions aroused by peoples' ideas about language are illustrated by the protests for and against the Oakland, California School Board's recognition of "Ebonics" for what it is: a rich and complex language spoken by many inner-city African Americans.

"teaching" AAVE when the kids should be learning SE. On Carriacou I often found it necessary to explain that I didn't have to "teach" children Creole; they were already native speakers when they got to school. I was giving them access to literacy through Creole and then attempting to test the extent this helped them acquire literacy in SE.

On Carriacou, "educational experts" claimed that taking children out of their SE classes and working with them in Creole would slow them down and confuse them. I found neither to be the case: working in Creole they continued to improve in reading SE as fast as others working entirely in SE and never seemed to confuse the two. (It helped, no doubt, that I wrote Creole with a broadly phonemic spelling system that made it look different.)

My research was interrupted by the coup and subsequent U.S. invasion of Grenada and Carriacou in 1983. As a result, I was unable to draw the strong conclusions I would have liked. Still, I showed that working on Creole did not slow down or confuse the children and was able to present some evidence that reading Creole helped their reading of SE. On a more qualitative note, they enjoyed it. Other teachers told me they had never seen children fight over who was going to read to the class. And they had rarely taken schoolbooks home to read before getting the little booklets in Creole we produced. Even children not in the Creole class asked for booklets.

Ultimately, this is a political issue. My experience on Grenada suggests that recognition of AAVE in Oakland can't hurt. Surely it can't hurt children to discover that what they bring with them to school—as a realization of the universal human potential for language and culture—is worthy of respect, worthy enough to be valued and used in their formal education. And it can't hurt teachers to learn this either. How much will it help? We have research from all over the world on the positive effects of native-language first-literacy acquisition and early schooling. Since it can't hurt, it seems worth finding out whether these results can be replicated in Oakland, and elsewhere, for AAVE.

We must also remain aware that simply gaining greater command of the standard language will not help unless society is willing to adjust its attitudes toward those involved. Otherwise, discrimination and exploitation will continue as before; racists will have one less justification to trot out, that's all. Perhaps this is where anthropologists and linguists have their most important work to do: raising public awareness and understanding of what linguistic, cultural, and biological differences mean and, most importantly, what they don't mean.

The End

Beneath all the rhetoric, what the Oakland School Board proposed is no different from what is being done, with considerable success, in several other countries. In Scotland, for example, Scots English is recognized in the schools as a valid and valued way of speaking, and is utilized in the teaching of Standard English. As a consequence, individuals become skilled at switching back and forth between the two dialects, depending on the situation in which one is speaking. Without being conscious of it, we all do the same sort of thing when

Martin Luther King Jr. Part of his effectiveness as a civil rights leader was his skill at code switching between Standard English and African American Vernacular English.

we switch from formality to informality in our speech, depending upon where we are and to whom we are talking. The process of changing from one level of language to another as the situation demands, whether from one language to another or from one dialect of a language to another, is known as **code switching,** and it has been the subject of a number of sociolinguistic studies.

THE ORIGINS OF LANGUAGE

A realization of the central importance of language for human culture leads inevitably to speculation about how language might have started in the first place. The question of the origin of language has long been a popular subject, and some reasonable and many not so reasonable ideas have been proposed: Exclamations became words, sounds in nature were imitated, or people simply got together and assigned sounds to objects and actions. The main trouble with past ideas is that there was so little in the way of evidence that attempts to explain language origins often amounted to little more than wild speculation. The result was a reaction against such speculation, exemplified by a ban imposed in 1866 by the Société de Linguistique de Paris against papers on linguistic origins. Now there is more evidence to work with—better knowledge of primate brains, new studies of primate communication, more information on the development of linguistic competence in children, more human fossils that can be used to tentatively reconstruct what ancient brains and vocal tracts were like, and a better understanding of early hominine ways of life. We still can't prove how and when human language developed, but we can speculate much less wildly than was once the case.

Attempts to teach other primates to talk like humans have not been successful. In one famous experiment in communication that went on for seven years, for example, the chimpanzee Viki learned to voice only a very few words, such as *up, mama,* and *papa.* This inability to speak is not the result of any obvious sensory or perceptual deficit, and apes can in fact produce many of the sounds used in speech. Evidently, their failure to speak has to do with either a lack of motor control mechanisms to produce articulation of speech or the virtually complete preoccupation of the vocal apparatus for expressing emotional states.

Better results have been achieved through nonvocal methods. Chimpanzees and gorillas in the wild make a variety of vocalizations, but these are often emotional rather than propositional. In this sense, they are equivalent to human paralanguage. Much of their communication takes place through use of specific gestures and postures. Indeed, some of these, such as grimacing, kissing, and embracing, are in virtually universal use today among humans as well as apes. Recognizing the importance of gestural communication to apes, psychologists Allen and Beatrice Gardner began teaching the American Sign Language, used by the deaf, to their young chimpanzee Washoe, the first of several who have since

Code switching. The process of changing from one level of language to another.

Owing to our common ancestry, some of the gestures humans use are shared with other primates.

learned to sign. With vocabularies of over 400 signs, chimps have shown themselves to be able to transfer each sign from its original referent to other appropriate objects and even pictures of objects. Their vocabularies include verbs, adjectives, and such words as *sorry* and *please;* furthermore, they can string signs together properly to produce original sentences, even inflecting their signs to indicate person, place, and instrument. More impressive still, Washoe was observed spontaneously teaching her adopted offspring Loulis how to sign by deliberately manipulating his hand. For 5 years, humans had refrained from signing when in sight of Loulis, over which time he learned no fewer than 50 signs. Today, Loulis and Washoe live with three other signing chimpanzees, all of whom are shown by remote videotaping to use signs to communicate among themselves when no humans are present.

Other chimpanzees have been taught to communicate by other means. One named Sarah learned to converse by means of pictographs—designs such as squares and triangles—on brightly colored plastic chips. Each pictograph stands for a noun or a verb. Sarah can also produce new sentences of her own. Another chimpanzee, Lana, learned to converse by means of a computer with a keyboard somewhat like that of a typewriter, but with symbols rather than letters. One of the most adept with this system is a bonobo named Kanzi who, rather than being taught by a human, learned it as an infant from its mother and soon went on to surpass her abilities.

Chimps have not been the only subjects of ape language experiments. Gorillas and orangutans have also been taught American Sign Language with results that replicate those obtained with chimps. As a consequence, there is now a growing consensus that all of the great apes can develop language skills at least to the level of a 2- to 3-year-old human.[9] Not only are comprehension skills similar, but so is acquisition order: What and where, what-to-do and who, as well as how questions are

[9] Miles, H. L. W. (1993). Language and the orang-utan: The old "person" of the forest. In P. Cavalieri & P. Singer (Eds.), *The great ape project* (p. 46). New York: St. Martin's Press.

acquired in that order by both apes and humans. Like humans, apes are capable of referring to events removed in time and space, a phenomenon known as **displacement** and one of the distinctive features of human language.

In view of apes' demonstrated abilities in the use of sign language, it is not surprising that a number of anthropologists, psychologists, and other linguists have shown new interest in an old hypothesis, that human language began as a gestural rather than vocal system. Certainly, the potential to communicate through gestures must have been as well developed among the earliest hominines as it is among today's apes, since they share it as a consequence of a common ancestry that predates the divergence of our own line of evolution. Moreover, the bipedalism of our earliest ancestors would have enabled them to use their hands more freely to gesture. Now, manual signing and gesturing are skilled activities in which hand preference plays a major role, and evidence for the pronounced "handedness" found only among humans is provided by the external configuration of the brain of *Homo habilis* as well as by the stone tools made by this hominine. Furthermore, among modern children learning American Sign Language, hand preference appears in signing *before* it does in object manipulation. Thus, not only is it likely that *Homo habilis* used gestures to communicate, but this may have played a role in the development of the manual dexterity involved in early stone tool making.

One of the most difficult problems for students dealing with the origin of language is the origin of syntax, which was necessary to enable our ancestors to articulate and communicate complex thought. Here, a look at the physical nature of gestures is helpful, for in fact, they can be construed not just as words but as sentences. This can be illustrated with the modern gesture meaning *seize:* The hand begins fully open or slightly bent, the elbow is slightly flexed and the upper arm rotates at the shoulder to bring the forearm and hand across the body until the moving hand closes around the upright forefinger of the other hand. What we have here is not just the word *seize* but a complete transitive sentence with a verb and a direct object, or in semantic terms, an agent, an action, and a patient.[10] In this case, there is a clear relation between the sign and what is signified, suggesting that syntax could have its origin in signs that mimic the things they stand for.

Another problem involves the shift from manual gestures to spoken language. Two things to keep in mind here are that: (1) the manual signs of a sign language are typically accompanied by facial gestures, and (2) just as a sign is the outcome of a particular motor act, so is speech the outcome of a series of motor acts, in this case concentrated in the mouth and throat. In other words, *all* language, signed or spoken, can be analyzed as gesture. Furthermore, research on hearing-impaired users of American Sign Language suggests that areas of the brain critical for speech may be critical to signing as well. Thus, continuity exists between gestural and spoken language, and the latter could have emerged from the former through increasing emphasis on finely controlled movements of the mouth and throat, a scenario consistent with the appearance of neurological structures underlying language in the earliest representatives of the genus *Homo* and steady enlargement of the human brain *before* the alteration of the vocal tract took place that allows us to speak the way we do.

The advantage of spoken over gestural language to a species increasingly dependent on tool use for survival is obvious. To talk with your hands, you must stop whatever else you are doing with them; speech does not interfere with that. Other benefits include being able to talk in the dark, past opaque objects, or among speakers whose attention is diverted. Just when the changeover to spoken language took place is not known, though all would agree that spoken languages are at least as old as anatomically modern *Homo sapiens.* There is, however, no anatomical evidence to support arguments that Neandertals and other representatives of archaic *H. sapiens* were incapable of speech. Perhaps its emergence began with *Homo erectus,* the first hominine to live in regions with cold climates. The ability to plan ahead for changes in seasonal conditions crucial to survival under such conditions would not have been possible without use of a grammatically structured language, whether it be gestural or vocal. Having the use of fire, we do know that *H. erectus* would not have had to cease all activity when darkness fell. We also know that the vocal tract and brain of *H. erectus* were intermediate between that of *H. sapi-*

[10] Armstrong, D. F., Stokoe, W. C., & Wilcox, S. E. (1994). Signs of the origin of syntax. *Current Anthropology, 35,* 355.

Displacement. The ability to refer to things and events removed in time and space.

Far from being "simple" or "primitive," the languages of non-literate people are often the opposite. For example, in World War II, the complexity of Navajo was such that, when used for a code by U.S. Marines in the Pacific, it defied all attempts by the Japanese to decipher it.

ens and earlier *Australopithecus.* It may be that the changeover from gestural to spoken language was a driving force in these evolutionary changes.

The once popular search for a truly primitive language spoken by a living people that might show the processes of language just beginning or developing has now been abandoned. The reason is that there is no such thing as a primitive language in the world today, or even in the recent past. So far, all human languages that have been described and studied, even among people with something approximating a Stone Age technology, are highly developed, complex, and capable of expressing infinite meanings. The truth is that people have been talking in this world for an extremely long time, and every known language, wherever it is, now has a long history and has developed subtleties and complexities that do not permit any label of "primitive." What a language may or may not express is not a measure of its age but of its speakers' way of life, reflecting what they want or need to share and communicate with others.

CHAPTER SUMMARY

Anthropologists need to understand the workings of language, because it is through language that people in every society are able to share their experiences, concerns, and beliefs, over the past and in the present, and to communicate these to the next generation. Language makes communication of infinite meanings possible by employing a few sounds or gestures that, when put together according to certain rules, result in meanings that are intelligible to all speakers.

Linguistics is the modern scientific study of all aspects of language by anthropologists, psychologists, and other specialists. Phonetics focuses on the production, transmission, and reception of speech sounds, or phonemes. Phonology studies the sound patterns of language in order to extract the rules that govern the way sounds are combined. Morphology is concerned with the smallest units of meaningful combinations of sounds—morphemes—in a language. Syntax refers to the principles according to which phrases and sentences are built. The entire formal structure of a language, consisting of all observations about its morphemes and syntax, constitutes the grammar of a language.

Human language is embedded in a gesture-call system inherited from our primate ancestors that serves to "key" speech, providing the appropriate frame for interpreting linguistic form. The gestural component of this system consists of body motions used to convey messages; the system of notating and recording these motions is known as kinesics. The call component is represented by paralanguage, consisting of extralinguistic noises involving various voice qualities and vocalizations.

Descriptive linguistics registers and explains the features of a language at a particular time in its history. Historical linguistics investigates relationships between earlier and later forms of the same language. A major concern of historical linguists is to identify the forces behind the changes that have taken place in languages in the course of linguistic divergence. Historical linguistics also provides a means of roughly dating certain migrations, invasions, and contacts of people.

Ethnolinguistics deals with language as it relates to society, the rest of culture, and human behavior. Some linguistic anthropologists, following Benjamin Lee Whorf, have proposed that language shapes the way people think and behave. Others have argued that language reflects reality. Although language is flexible and adaptable, a terminology once established tends to perpetuate itself and to reflect much about the speakers' beliefs and social relationships. Kinship terms, for example, help reveal how a family is structured, what relationships are considered close or distant, and what attitudes toward relationships are held. Similarly, gender language reveals how the men and women in a society relate to one another.

A social dialect is the language of a group of people within a larger one, all of whom may speak more or less the same language. Sociolinguists are concerned with whether dialect differences reflect cultural differences. They also study code switching—the process of changing from one level of language to another as the situation demands—for much the same reason.

One theory of language origins is that early hominines, by developing potentials exhibited also by apes and monkeys, with their hands freed by their bipedalism, began using gestures as a tool to communicate and implement intentions within a social setting. With the movement of *Homo erectus* out of the tropics, the need to plan for future needs in order to survive seasons of cold temperatures required the grammar and syntax necessary to communicate information about events removed in time and space. By the time archaic *Homo sapiens* appeared, emphasis on finely controlled movements of the mouth and throat had probably given rise to spoken language.

Once upon a time, scholars searched for a truly primitive language spoken by some living group that would reveal language in its very early state. This search has been abandoned. All languages that have been studied, including those of people with supposedly "primitive" cultures, are complex, sophisticated, and able to express a wide range of experiences. What a language is capable of expressing is anything its speakers wish to talk about, and has nothing to do with its age.

CLASSIC READINGS

Birdwhistell, R. L. (1970). *Kinesics and context: Essays in body motion communication.* Philadelphia: University of Pennsylvania Press.

Kinesics was first delineated as an area for anthropological research by Birdwhistell, so this book is particularly appropriate for those who wish to know more about the phenomenon.

Crane, L. B., Yeager, E., & Whitman, R. L. (1981). *An introduction to linguistics.* Boston: Little, Brown.

A book that gives balanced coverage to all subfields of linguistics, including topics traditionally ignored in textbooks.

Eastman, C. M. (1990). *Aspects of language and culture* (2nd ed.) Novato, CA: Chandler and Sharp.

The bulk of this book is devoted to the subjects of worldview, ethnography of communication, nonverbal behavior, animal communication, discourse pragmatics, conversational analysis, semiotics, and ethnicity. A single chapter deals with linguistics as a field tool.

Hickerson, N. P. (1980). *Linguistic anthropology.* New York: Holt, Rinehart and Winston.

A description and explanation of what anthropological linguistics is all about, written so as to be understood by beginning students.

Gardner, R. A., Gardner, B. T., & Van Cantfort, T. E., (Eds.) (1989). *Teaching sign language to chimpanzees.* Albany, NY: State University of New York Press.

In 10 jargon-free chapters, easily accessible to the interested layperson as well as professionals, the methods and results of the Gardners and their students are laid out in great detail. Psychologists and anthropologists who reviewed the book agree that it represents a milestone in ape language research, and as one put it, should be read by all interested in the evolution of human behavior.

Ruhlen, M. (1994). *The origin of language: Tracing the evolution of the mother tongue.* New York: John Wiley & Sons.

Scholarly in substance but written for a popular audience, this makes a good introduction to comparative linguistics for beginning anthropology students. With an evolutionary theme, it cuts through the difficult problems of our linguistic ancestors with plausible though still controversial results.

Trager, G. L. (1964). Paralanguage: A first approximation. In Dell Hymes (Ed.), *Language in culture and society* (pp. 274–279). New York: Harper & Row, 1964.

The author was the pioneer in paralinguistic research, and in this article he discusses what paralanguage is, why it should be studied, and how.

CHAPTER 16

GROWING UP HUMAN

Ethnographic research has revealed a wide range of approaches to the raising of children. These differences and their possible effects on adult personalities have long been of interest to anthropologists.

CHAPTER PREVIEW

1 What Is Enculturation?

Enculturation is the process by which culture is passed from one generation to the next, and through which individuals become members of their society. It begins soon after birth, as self-awareness—the ability to perceive oneself as an object in time and space and to judge one's own actions—starts to develop. For self-awareness to function, the individual must be provided with a behavioral environment. First, one learns about a world of objects other than self, and these always are perceived in terms specified by the culture he or she grows up in. Along with this, one is provided with spatial, temporal, and normative orientations.

2 What Is the Effect of Enculturation on Adult Personality?

Studies have shown that there is some kind of structural relationship between enculturation and personality development, although it is also clear that each individual begins with certain broad potentials and limitations that are genetically inherited. In some cultures particular child-rearing practices seem to promote the development of compliant personalities, while in others different practices seem to promote more independent, self-reliant personalities.

3 Are Different Personalities Characteristic of Different Cultures?

Although cultures vary a great deal in terms of the personality traits that are looked upon with admiration or disapproval, it is difficult to characterize cultures in terms of particular personalities. Of the several attempts made, the concept of modal personality is the most satisfactory. This recognizes that any human society has a range of individual personalities but some will be more "typical" than others.

4 Do Cultures Differ in What They Regard as Abnormal Personalities?

A normal personality may be thought of as one that approximates the modal personality of a particular culture. Since modal personalities may differ from one culture to another and since cultures may differ in the range of variation they will accept, it is clear that abnormal personality is a relative concept. A particular personality regarded as abnormal in one culture may not be so regarded in another.

In 1690 John Locke presented his *tabula rasa* theory in his book *An Essay Concerning Human Understanding.* This notion held that the newborn human was like a blank slate, and what the individual became in life was written on the slate by his or her life experiences. The implication is that all individuals are biologically identical at birth in their potential for personality development and that their adult personalities are exclusively the products of their postnatal experiences, which will differ from culture to culture. Stated in these terms, the theory is not acceptable, for we know now that each person is born with unique inherited tendencies that will help determine his or her adult personality. It is also known, however, that genetic inheritance sets certain broad potentials and limitations and that life experiences, particularly in the early years, are also important in the shaping of individual personalities. Since different cultures handle the raising and education of children in different ways, these practices and their effects on personalities are important subjects of anthropological inquiry. Such studies gave rise to the subfield of psychological anthropology, and are the subjects of the present chapter.

In the United States, the need for two paychecks to sustain desired standards of living means that large numbers of children spend time at home fending for themselves without adults present.

THE SELF AND THE BEHAVIORAL ENVIRONMENT

Since culture is created and learned rather than biologically inherited, all societies must somehow ensure that culture is adequately transmitted from one generation to the next. This process of transmission through which individuals become members of their society is known as **enculturation,** and it begins soon after birth. The first agents of enculturation in all societies are the members of the household into which a person is born. At first, the most important member of this household is the newborn's mother, but other members of the household soon come to play roles in the process. Just who these others are depends on how households are structured in the particular society (Chapter 20). In the United States, they ideally include the father or stepfather and the child's siblings. In other societies the father may have little contact with his children in their early years; indeed, there are societies where men do not even live with the mothers of their children. In such instances, brothers of the child's mother usually have important responsibilities toward their nieces and nephews. In many societies, grandparents, other wives of the father, brothers of the father, or sisters of the mother, not to mention their children, are also likely to be key players in the enculturation process.

As the young person matures, individuals outside the household are brought into the process. These usually include other kin, and certainly the individual's peers. The latter may be included informally in the form of play groups or formally in age associations, where children actually teach other children. In some societies, and that of the United States is a good example, professionals are brought into the process of enculturation to provide formal instruction. In many societies, however, children are pretty much allowed to learn through observation and participation, at their own speed.

The Self

Enculturation begins with the development of **self-awareness**—the ability to identify oneself as an object, to react to oneself, and to appraise or evaluate oneself. People do not have this ability at birth, even though it is

Enculturation. The process by which a society's culture is transmitted from one generation to the next, and through which individuals become members of their society. • **Self-awareness.** The ability to identify oneself as an object, to react to oneself, and to appraise oneself.

Self awareness is not restricted to humans. This chimpanzee knows that the individual in the mirror is himself and not some other chimp.

essential for existence in human societies. It is self-awareness that permits one to assume responsibility for one's conduct, to learn how to react to others, and to assume a variety of roles. An important aspect of self-awareness is the attachment of positive value to one's self. Without this, individuals cannot be motivated to act to their advantage rather than disadvantage; self-identification by itself is not sufficient for this.

Self-awareness does not come all at once. In modern North American society, for example, self and nonself are not clearly distinguished until about two years of age. This development of self-awareness in North American children, however, may lag somewhat behind other cultures. Self-awareness develops in concert with neuromotor development, which is known to proceed at a slower rate in infants from North America than in infants in many, perhaps even most, non-Western societies. The reasons for this slower rate are not yet clear, although the amount of human contact and stimulation that infants receive seems to play an important role. In the United States, for example, infants generally do not sleep with their parents, most often being put in rooms of their own. This is seen as an important step in making them into individuals, "owners" of themselves and their capacities, rather than part of some social whole. As a consequence, they are deprived of a steady stream of stimuli, including touch, smell, movement, and warmth, they would receive by cosleeping. It also deprives them of the opportunity for frequent nursing through the night.

In traditional societies, infants routinely sleep with their parents, or at least their mothers. What's more (again unlike practices in the United States), they are carried or held most other times, usually in an upright position. The mother typically responds to a cry or "fuss" literally within seconds, usually offering the infant her breast. Thus, among traditional Ju/'hoansi (of whom more in a moment) of southern Africa's Kalahari Desert, infants are nursed about four times an hour, for 1 or 2 minutes at a time. Overall, a 15-week-old Ju/'hoansi infant is in close contact with its mother about 70% of the time, as compared with 20% for home-reared infants in the United States. Moreover, their contacts are not usually limited to their mothers; they include numerous other adults and children of virtually all ages. In the United States and Canada, day-care centers now approximate these same conditions. The catch here is that their personnel must remain stable and (ideally) be recruited from the same neighborhood as the child if these centers are to have a positive effect on the cognitive and social development of the very young children enrolled in them. Unfortunately, these conditions commonly are not met. One reason is that low pay for caregivers virtually guarantees a high rate of personnel turnover.

In traditional societies around the world, infants are never left by themselves and so receive constant stimulation, an important element in their development. In the United States, by contrast, infants spend a great deal of time in isolation, without such stimulation.

From the above, it is obvious that infants in traditional societies are far more constantly exposed to a variety of stimuli than they are in North American (and most other industrialized) societies. This is important, for recent studies show that stimulation plays a key role in the "hard wiring" of the brain; the stimulation is necessary for development of the neural circuitry. Nor should the role of frequent nursing be overlooked, as studies show that the longer a child is breast-fed, the higher it will score on cognitive tests and the lower its risk of attention deficit hyperactivity disorder. Furthermore, breast-fed children have fewer allergies, fewer ear infections, less diarrhea, and are at less risk of sudden infant death syndrome.[1]

As a child develops self-awareness, *perception*—a kind of vague awareness of one's existence—precedes *conception,* or more specific knowledge of the interrelated needs, attitudes, concerns, and interests that define what one is. This involves a cultural definition of self, and in this definition language plays a crucial role. This is why in all cultures individuals become competent at using personal and possessive pronouns at an early age. Personal names, too, are important devices for self-identification in all cultures. Then, as infancy gives way to early childhood, the "I" or "me" is increasingly separated from the environment.

The Behavioral Environment

In order for self-awareness to emerge and function, basic orientations are necessary to structure the psychological field in which the self is prepared to act. Thus, each individual must learn about a world of objects other than

[1] Dettwyler, K. A. (1997, October). When to wean. *Natural History,* 49.

the self. The basis of this world of other-than-self is what we would think of as the physical environment of things. The physical environment, though, is organized culturally and mediated symbolically through language. Putting this another way, we might say that the world around us is perceived through cultural glasses. Culturally significant attributes of the environment are singled out for attention and labeled; those that are not may be ignored or lumped together in broad categories. Culture, however, also *explains* the perceived environment. This is important, for it provides the individual with an orderly, rather than chaotic, universe in which to act. Behind this lies a powerful psychological drive to reduce uncertainty, the product of a universal human need for a balanced and integrated perspective on the relevant universe. When confronted with ambiguity and uncertainty, people invariably strive to clarify and give structure to the situation; they do this, of course, in ways that their particular culture tells them are appropriate. Indeed, the less certainty, the greater individual suggestibility and persuadability tend to be. Thus, we should not be surprised to find that explanations of the universe are never entirely objective in nature, but are culturally constructed.

The behavioral environment in which the self acts involves more than *object orientation.* Action requires *spatial orientation,* or the ability to get from one object, or place, to another. In all societies, names and significant features of places are important means of discriminating and representing points of reference for spatial orientation. Individuals must know where they have been and will be in order to get from one place to another. They also need to maintain a sense of self-continuity, so that past actions are connected with those in the present and future. Hence, temporal orientation is also part of the behavioral environment. Just as the perceived environment is organized in cultural terms, so too are time and space.

The Ituri forest, in the geographical heart of Africa, is viewed in two very different ways by the people who live there. Mbuti foragers view it with affection; like a benevolent parent, it provides them with all they ask for: sustenance, protection, and security. Village-dwelling farmers, by contrast, view the forest with a mixture of fear, hostility, and mistrust—something they must constantly struggle to control.

For the Penobscot Indians, the river of the same name provided spatial orientation as well as an artery for canoe travel.

A final aspect of the behavioral environment is the *normative orientation*. Values, ideals, and standards, which are purely cultural in origin, are as much a part of the individual's behavioral environment as are trees, rivers, and mountains. Without them people would have nothing by which to judge either their own actions or those of others. In short, the self-appraisal aspect of self-awareness could not be made functional.

Like any aspect of culture, conceptions of the self vary considerably from one society to another. The Penobscot Indians, a people who at one time relied on fishing, hunting, and the gathering of wild plants (food foraging) for subsistence, and whose descendants still live today in the woodlands of northeastern North America, serve as an example.[2]

THE PENOBSCOT

When first encountered by Europeans, the Penobscot conceived of each individual as being made up of two parts—the body and a personal spirit. The latter, although dependent on the body, could have "out-of-body" experiences, disengaging itself from the body to travel about for short periods of time to perform overt acts and interact with other spirits. Such activity by one's personal spirit was thought to occur in dreams or in states of trance. As long as one's spirit returned to the body before the passage of too much time, the individual remained in good health; if, however, the spirit was prevented from returning to the body, then the individual sickened and died. Along with this dual nature of the self went a potential for every individual to work magic. Theoretically, it was possible to send one's personal spirit out to work mischief on others, just as it was possible for others to lure one's own spirit away from the body and take control of it, causing sickness and eventual death.

To many people today, the traditional Penobscot concept of self may seem strange. The British colonists of New England regarded such ideas as false and shot through with superstition, even though their own concept of self was every bit as supernaturalistic. To the Indians their concept made sense, for it adequately accounted for their experience, regardless of its truth in any objective sense. Furthermore, the Penobscot view of self is relevant for anyone who wishes to understand Penobscot behavior in the days when the British and French first tried to settle in North America. For one thing, it was responsible for an undercurrent of wariness of strangers, as well as the individual secretiveness that characterized Penobscot society at the time. This propensity for individual secretiveness made it difficult for a potentially malevolent stranger to gain control of an individual's personal spirit. Also, the belief that dreams are real experiences rather than expressions of unconscious desires could impose burdens of guilt and anxiety on individuals who dreamed of doing things not deemed proper. Finally, individuals indulged in acts that would strike many people today as quite mad. A case in point is a Penobscot Indian who spent the night literally fighting for his life with a fallen tree. To the Indian, this was a metamorphosed magician who was out to get him, and it would have been madness *not* to try to overcome his adversary.

[2] Speck, F. G. (1920). Penobscot shamanism. *Memoirs of the American Anthropological Association, 6,* 239–288.

The behavioral environment in which the Penobscot self operated consisted of a flat world, which these people thought to be surrounded on all sides by salt water. They could actually see the latter downstream, where the Penobscot River met the sea. The river itself was the spatial reference point and also was the main artery for canoe travel in the region. The largest of a number of watercourses, it flowed through forests abounding with game. Like humans, each animal also was composed of a body and a spirit. Along with the animals were various quasi-human supernatural beings that inhabited bodies of water and mountains or roamed freely through the forest. One of these, *Gluskabe,* created the all-important Penobscot River by overcoming a greedy giant frog that had monopolized the world's water supply. Gluskabe was also responsible for a number of other natural features of the world, often as a by-product of punishment for such transgressions of the moral code as that of the giant frog. Indeed, individuals had to be concerned about their behavior vis-à-vis both animals and these quasi-human beings or they, too, would come to various kinds of grief. Hence, these supernaturals not only "explained" many otherwise unexplainable natural phenomena to the Penobscot but were also important in structuring the Penobscot moral order. To the Penobscot, all of this was quite believable; the lone hunter, for example, off for extended periods in the forest, could hear in the night what sounded like the cry of *Pskedemus,* the swamp woman. And a Penobscot accepted as fact that his or her spirit routinely traveled about while the body slept, interacting with various of these supernatural beings.

Penobscot concepts of the self and behavioral environment have changed considerably since the 17th century, though no less so than those of the descendants of the Europeans who first came to New England. Both groups may now be said to hold more modern beliefs about the nature of their selves and the world they live in. Still, in both cases, aspects of the old beliefs remain. Associated with them were **patterns of affect**—how people *feel* about themselves and others—which differed considerably in Indian and European cultures. As Chinese-born anthropologist Francis Hsu pointed out, patterns of affect are likely to persist over thousands of years, even in the face of far-reaching changes in all other aspects of culture.[3] To illustrate, consider the following Original Study, written by Rhonda Kay Williamson while an undergraduate student of philosophy at Bryn Mawr College.

[3] Hsu, F. L. K. (1997). Role, affect, and anthropology. *American Anthropologist, 79,* 807.

Patterns of affect. How people feel about themselves and others.

Original Study

The Blessed Curse[4]

One morning not so long ago, a child was born. This birth, however, was no occasion for the customary celebration. Something was wrong: something very grave, very serious, very sinister. This child was born between sexes, an "intersexed" child. From the day of its birth, this child would be caught in a series of struggles involving virtually every aspect of its life. Things that required little thought under "ordinary" circumstances were, in this instance, extraordinarily difficult. Simple questions now had an air of complexity: "What is it, a girl or a boy?"; "What do we name it?"; "How shall we raise it?"; "Who (or what) is to blame for this?".

A Foot in Both Worlds

The child referred to in the introductory paragraph is myself. As I was born the great-granddaughter of a Cherokee woman, I was exposed to the Native

[4] Adapted from Williamson, R. K. (1995). The blessed curse: Spirituality and sexual difference as viewed by Euro-American and Native American cultures. *The College News, 17* (4).

Original Study

American view of people who were born intersexed, as I was, and individuals who exhibited transgendered characteristics. This view, unlike the Euro-American one, sees such individuals in a very positive and affirming light.

Yet my immediate family (mother, father, and brothers) were firmly fixed in the Christian Euro-American point of view. As a result, from a very early age I was presented with two different and conflicting views of myself. As might be expected, this resulted in a lot of confusion within me about what I was, how I came to be born the way I was, and what my intersexuality meant in terms of my spirituality as well as my place in society.

I remember, even as a small child, getting mixed messages about my own value and worth as a human being. My grandmother, in keeping with Native American ways, would tell me stories about my birth. She would tell me how she knew when I was born that I had a special place in life, given to me by God, the Great Spirit, and that I had been given "a great strength that girls never have, yet a gentle tenderness that boys never know" and that I was "too pretty and beautiful to be a boy only and too strong to be a girl only." She rejoiced at this "special gift" and taught me that it meant that the Great Spirit had "something important for me to do in this life." I remember how good I felt inside when she told me these things and how I soberly contemplated, even at the young age of five, that I must be diligent and try to learn and carry out the purpose designed just for me by the Great Spirit.

My parents, however, had a completely different view of my birth, of me as a human being, and of the origin of my intersexuality. My parents were so repulsed by it that they would never speak of it directly. They would just refer to it as "the work of Satan." To them, I was not at all blessed with a "special gift" from some "Great Spirit," but was "cursed and given over to the Devil" by God. I was treated with contempt by my father, and my mother wavered between contempt and distant indifference. I was taken from one charismatic church to another in order to have the "demon of mixed sex" cast out of me. At some of these "deliverance" services I was even given a napkin to cough out the demon into!

In the end, no demon ever popped out of me. Still I grew up believing that there was something inherent within me that caused God to hate me, that my intersexuality was a punishment for this something, a mark of condemnation.

There were periods in my life when I stayed at my grandmother's house for extensive amounts of time. During these stays, my fears would be allayed, for she would once again remind me that I was fortunate to have been given this special gift. She was distraught that my parents were treating me cruelly and pleaded with them to let me live with her, but they would not let me stay at her home permanently.

Nevertheless, they did let me spend a significant portion of my childhood with her. Had it not been for that, I might not have been able to survive the tremendous trials that awaited me in my walk through life.

Blessed Gift: The Native American View

It is now known that most, if not all, of the Native American societies had certain individuals which fell between the categories of "man" and "woman." The various nations had different names for this type of individual, but a term broadly used and recognized is "berdache," a term of French origin that designated a male, passive homosexual. [The preferred term today is "two-spirit."]

Some of these individuals were born physically intersexed. Others appeared to be anatomically normal males, who exhibited the character and the manners of women, and vice versa. The way native people treated such individuals reveals some interesting insights into Native American belief systems.

The Spirit

The extent to which Native Americans see spirituality is reflected in their belief that all things have a spirit: "Every object—plants, rocks, water, air, the moon, animals, humans, the earth itself—has a spirit. The spirit of one thing (including a human) is not superior to the spirit of any other.... The function of religion is not to try to condemn or to change what exists, but to accept the realities of the world and to appreciate their contributions to life. Everything that exists has a purpose."

This paradigm is the core of Native American thought and action. Because everything has a spirit, and no spirit is superior to that of another, there is no "above" or "below," no "superior" or "inferior," no "dominant" and "subordinate." These are only illusions which arise from unclear thinking. Thus, an intersexed child is not derided or viewed as a "freak of nature" in traditional Native American culture. Intersexuality (as well as masculinity in a female or effeminacy in a male) is seen as the manifestation of the spirit of the child, so an intersexed child is respected as much as a girl child or a boy child. It is the spirit of the child which determines what the gender of the child will ultimately be. According to a Lakota, Lame Deer, "the Great Spirit made them winktes [two-spirit] and we accepted them as such." In this sense, the child has no control over what her or his gender will be. It follows that where there is no choice, there can be no accountability on the part of the child. Indeed, the child who is given the spirit of a winkte is unable to resist becoming one.

"When an Omaha boy sees the Moon Being [Moon Being is a feminine Spirit] on his vision quest, the spirit holds in one hand a man's bow and arrow and in the other a woman's pack strap. 'When the youth tried to grasp the bow and arrows the Moon Being crossed [the boy's] hands very quickly, and if the youth was not very careful he seized the pack strap instead of the bow and arrows, thereby fixing his lot in later life. In such a case he could not help acting [like a] woman, speaking, dressing, and working just as...women...do.'"

Sacred Role

The Europeans were not only aghast, but amazed and dumbfounded as to why two-spirits were considered sacred. In the Native American view, because two-spirits were considered to have received their intersex spirit from the Great Spirit, and were different from the norm by the feminine/masculine combination of their nature, they were considered to be especially blessed by the Great Spirit. To be a two-spirit was considered to be a special gift from the Great Spirit.

The Curse: The Euro-American View

In contrast to the view of respect and admiration of physical intersexuality and transgendered behavior held by Native Americans, the Europeans who came to "Turtle Island" (the Cherokee name for North America) brought with them their world view, which was shaped primarily by their Judaeo-Christian beliefs. According to this religion, there had to be, by mandate of God, a complete dichotomy of the sexes. The Christian religion was also to be the basis by which Europeans claimed "divine right" to take from Native Americans both their home and their culture.

Will Roscoe, in **The Zuni Man-Woman,** reports (pp. 172–173): "Spanish oppression of 'homosexual' practices in the New World took brutal forms. In 1513, the explorer Balboa had some forty berdaches thrown to his dogs [to be eaten alive]—'a fine action by an honorable and Catholic Spaniard,' as one Spanish historian commented. In Peru, the Spaniards burned 'sodomites,' 'and in this way they frightened them in such a manner that they left this great sin.'"

It is abundantly clear that Christian Euro-Americans exerted every effort to destroy Native American culture: "In 1883, the U.S. Office of Indian Affairs issued a set of regulations that came to be known as the Code of Religious offenses" or Religious Crimes Code.... Indians who refused to adopt the habits of industry, or to engage in 'civilized pursuits or employments' were subject to arrest and punishment.... By interfering with native

Original Study

sexuality [and culture], the agents of assimilation effectively undermined the social fabric of entire tribes." (Ibid, p. 176).

The Role of Education

Any paradigm necessarily involves education. Here we have two paradigms which are based on completely opposed ideologies. The Native American view holds that each thing or person has its own spirit that is not condemned nor to be changed, but is respected and even encouraged. This paradigm has inherent in it an education wherein every part of the universe, every star, every tree, every creature, every grain of sand is considered to be sacred and holy.

Native Americans learned through stories told to the younger generation by the older generation. At first the stories seemed to have different themes when the telling of them (the education) began for the child, but in the end it became clear that the stories had an interdependence on one another. Over the years, a great Web of Life was woven. Each story, or strand in the Web, connected to another to make a beautiful weaving of the nature of all the world. No part of the Web was more important or less important than any other part. In sex and gender roles, man, woman, intersex, effeminate man and masculine woman were equally valid and necessary.

In contrast is the Christian, Euro-American paradigm within which there is **no** flexibility. There is one God and one way, only, to worship the Christian God (at least in theory). One wise Iroquois leader, Red Jacket, pointed out the fallacy of this theory in a speech to the Boston Missionary Society. In this speech he said: "Brother! You say there is but one way to worship and serve the Great Spirit. If there is but one religion, why do you white people differ so much about it? Why do you not all agree, as you can all read the book?"

The problem Christianity poses for any culture other than its own is the condemnation and destruction of it. It seeks to impose the moral and social ideology of one culture onto all the other cultures of the entire world. Moreover, the culture that it sets out to impose is an ancient one that was reported by a handful of men whose identity is not even known in many cases. Yet, the words from these unknown men are presented as "the divinely inspired word of God." Christianity is purportedly the most widespread religion in the world. Is this a wonder, though, when nearly all who have been opposed to its self-proclaimed manifest destiny ("Every knee shall bow and every tongue confess that Jesus Christ is Lord."—Revelation) have been all but obliterated in its founder's name?

A Personal Resolution

For me, the resolution to the dual message I was receiving was slow in coming, largely due to the fear and self-hatred instilled in me by Christianity. Eventually, though, the Spirit wins out. I came to adopt my Grandmother's teaching about my intersexuality. Through therapy, and a new, loving home environment, I was able to shed the constant fear of eternal punishment I felt for something I had no control over. After all, I did not create myself.

Because of my own experience, and drawing on the teaching of my grandmother, I am now able to see myself as a wondrous creation of the Great Spirit—but not only me. All creation is wondrous. There is a purpose for everyone in the gender spectrum. Each person's spirit is unique in her or his or her-his own way. It is only by living true to the nature that was bestowed upon us by the Great Spirit, in my view, that we are able to be at peace with ourselves and be in harmony with our neighbor. This, to me, is the Great Meaning and the Great Purpose... to be at peace with ourselves and to live in harmony with our neighbor.

The End

PERSONALITY

In the process of enculturation, we have seen that each individual is introduced to the concepts of self and the behavioral environment characteristic of his or her culture. The result is that a kind of cognitive or mental map of the operating world is built, in terms of which the individual will think and act. It is each person's "map" of how to run the "maze" of life. This cognitive map is an integrated, dynamic system of perceptual assemblages, including the self and its behavioral environment. When we speak of an individual's **personality,** we are generalizing about that individual's cognitive map over time. Hence, personalities are products of enculturation, as experienced by individuals, each with his or her distinctive genetic makeup. "Personality" does not lend itself to a formal definition, but for our purposes we may take it as the distinctive way a person thinks, feels, and behaves. The term is derived from the Latin word for *mask,* and as such relates to the idea of learning to play one's role in society. Gradually, the mask, as it is placed on the face, begins to shape the latter until there is little sense of the mask as a superimposed alien force. Instead it feels natural, as if one were born with it.

The Development of Personality

Although *what* one learns is important to personality development, most anthropologists assume that *how* one learns is no less important. Along with the psychoanalytic theorists, anthropologists view childhood experiences as strongly influencing adult personality. Indeed, many anthropologists have been strongly attracted by Freudian psychoanalytic theory, but with a critical eye. Psychoanalytic literature tends to be long on concepts, speculation, and clinical data, but short on less culture-bound studies. Anthropologists, for their part, are most interested in studies that seek to prove, modify, or at least shed light on the role of early childhood experiences in shaping personality. For example, the traditional ideal in Western societies has been for men to be tough, aggressive, assertive, dominant, self-reliant, and achievement oriented, whereas women have been expected to be passive, obedient, compliant, loyal, and caring. To many, these personality differences between the sexes seem so "natural" that they must be biologically grounded and therefore inescapable, unchangeable, and universal. But are they? Have anthropologists identified any psychological or personality characteristics that universally differentiate men and women?

As Margaret Mead's pioneering studies suggested, and subsequent cross-cultural studies have confirmed, whatever biological differences exist between men and women, they are extremely malleable; biology is not destiny. Among the Arapesh of New Guinea it is not just the women but the men, too, who are gentle and nonaggressive, while among the Mundugamor (also of New Guinea), both sexes are angry and aggressive. Although biological differences in male-female behavior cannot be entirely ruled out (although debate continues about the role biology plays), it is nonetheless clear that each culture has different expectations for male-female behavior. The criteria of differentiation in one may bear no relation to those in another and may in fact be poles apart. From this we may conclude that the political and economic dominance that men have traditionally exerted over women in Western societies is not inevitable and that other arrangements are possible.

To understand the importance of child-rearing practices for the development of gender-related personality characteristics, we may look briefly at how children grow up among the Ju/'hoansi (pronounced zhutwasi), a people native to the Kalahari Desert of Namibia and Botswana. The Ju/'hoansi are one of a number of people traditionally referred to as Bushmen, who once were widespread through much of southern Africa. In recent times, anthropologists have referred to these people as the San, thinking the word *Bushman* insulting. Unfortunately, San, a Nama word, is highly contemptuous. Moreover, anthropologists misunderstood the derivation of the word *Bushman,* which comes from the Dutch *Bossiesman,* meaning "bandit" or "outlaw." This designation the people earned for their refusal to knuckle under to colonial domination, and so to refer to them as Bushman honors their long and valiant, if costly, record of resistance to colonialization. But most important, Bushman is the term they themselves prefer as a generic word covering all groups.[5]

Traditionally food foragers, in the past 3 decades many Ju/'hoansi have adopted a more sedentary lifestyle, tending small herds of goats and planting gardens for their

[5] Gordon, R. J. (1992). *The bushman myth* (p. 6). Boulder, CO: Westview. Griffin, B. (1994). CHAGS 7. *Anthropology Newsletter, 35* (1), p. 13; Lewis-Williams, J. D., Dowson, T. A., & Deacon, J. (1993). Rock art and changing perceptions of Southern Africa's past: Ezeljagdspoort reviewed. *Antiquity, 67,* 273.

Personality. The distinctive way a person thinks, feels, and behaves.

livelihood.[6] Among those who forage for a living, dominance and aggressiveness are not tolerated in either sex, men are as mild-mannered as the women, and women are as energetic and self-reliant as the men. In the villages, by contrast, men and women exhibit personality characteristics approximating those traditionally thought of as typically masculine and feminine in Western societies. Among the food foragers, children of both sexes receive lengthy, intensive care from their mother, whose attention is not diverted by the birth of new offspring until after the passage of many years. This is not to say that they are constantly with their children, for they are not; when they go to collect wild plant foods in the bush, they do not always take their offspring with them. At such times, the children are supervised by their fathers or other community adults, one third to one half of whom are always found in camp on any given day. Because these include men as well as women, children are as much habituated to the male as to the female presence.

In traditional Ju/'hoansi society, fathers as well as mothers show great indulgence to children, who do not fear or respect men more than women.

Fathers, too, spend much time with their offspring, interacting with them in nonauthoritarian ways. Although they may correct their children's behavior, so may women who neither defer to male authority nor use the threat of paternal anger. Thus, among Ju/'hoansi foragers, no one grows up to respect or fear male authority any more than that of women. In fact, instead of being punished, a child who misbehaves will simply be carried away and interested in some other more inoffensive activity. Nor are boys or girls assigned tasks to do; both sexes do equally little work, instead spending much of their time in play groups that include members of both sexes of widely different ages. Thus, Ju/'hoansi children have few experiences that set one sex apart from another. Although older ones do amuse and monitor younger ones, this is done spontaneously rather than as an assigned chore, and the burden does not fall any more heavily on girls than boys.

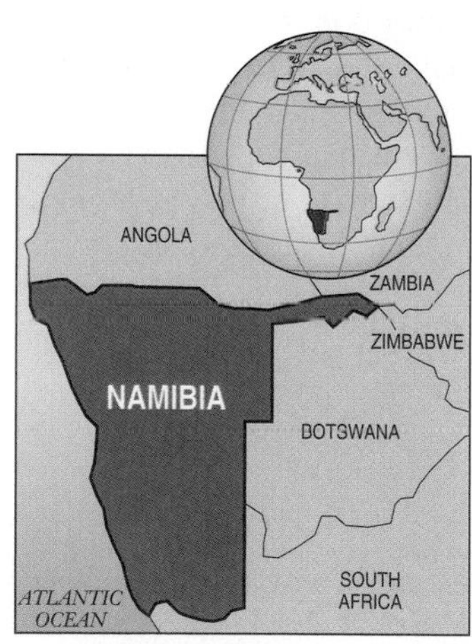

Among the sedentary villagers, women spend much of their time in and around the home preparing food and attending to other domestic chores, as well as tending the children. The work of men, by contrast, requires them to spend many hours outside the household. As a result, children are less habituated to their presence. This remoteness of the men, coupled with their more extensive knowledge of the outside world, tends to strengthen their influence within the household.

Within village households, sex role typing begins early as girls, as soon as they are old enough, are expected to attend to many of the needs of their younger siblings, thereby allowing the mother more time to attend to her other domestic tasks. This not only shapes but also limits the behavior of girls, who cannot range as widely or explore as freely and independently as they could without little brothers and sisters in tow. Indeed, they must stay close to home and be more careful, more obedient, and more sensitive to the wishes of others than they otherwise might be. Boys, by contrast, have little to do with the handling of infants, and when they are assigned work,

[6] Draper, P. (1975). !Kung women: Contrasts in sexual egalitarianism in foraging and sedentary contexts. In R. Reiter, (Ed.). *Toward an anthropology of women* (pp. 77–109). New York: Monthly Review Press.

MARGARET MEAD (1901–1978)

Although all of the natural and social sciences are able to look back and pay homage to certain "founding fathers," anthropologists take pride in the fact that they have a number of "founding mothers" to whom they pay homage. One is Margaret Mead, who was encouraged by her teacher Franz Boas to pursue a career in anthropology when most other academic disciplines rarely accepted women into their ranks. In 1925, she set out for Samoa to test the theory (then widely accepted) that the biological changes of adolescence could not be accomplished without a great deal of stress, both social and psychological. In her book *Coming of Age in Samoa: A Psychological Study of Primitive Youth for Western Civilization,* she concluded that adolescence does not have to be a time of stress and strain but cultural conditions may make it so. Published in 1928, this book is generally credited as marking the beginning of the field of culture and personality.

Pioneering works are never without their faults, and *Coming of Age* is no exception. For one, it is not clear that Mead's time in the field (9 months) was sufficient for her to understand fully the nuances of native speech and body language necessary to comprehend the innermost feelings of her informants. Furthermore, her sample of Samoan adolescents was a mere 50, half of whom had not yet passed puberty. That she exaggerated her findings is suggested by her dismissal as "deviant" of those girls who did not fit her ideal, and by inconsistencies with data collected elsewhere in Polynesia. But despite its faults, Mead's book stands as a landmark for several reasons: Not only was it a deliberate test of a Western psychological hypothesis, but it also showed psychologists the value of modifying intelligence tests to make them appropriate for the population under study. Furthermore, by emphasizing the lesson to be drawn for Mead's own society, it laid the groundwork for the popularization of anthropology and advanced the cause of applied anthropology.

it generally takes them away from the household. Thus, the space that girls occupy becomes restricted, and they are trained in behaviors that promote passivity and nurturance, whereas boys begin to become the distant, controlling figures they will be as adults.

From this comparison, we may begin to understand how a society's economy helps structure the way a child is brought up, and how this, in turn, influences the adult personality. It also shows that alternatives exist to the way that children are raised in Western societies and that by changing the conditions our children grow up in, we might make it significantly easier for men and women to interact on an equal basis than has been the case so far. Thus, child rearing emerges as not only an anthropological problem but a practical one as well.

DEPENDENCE TRAINING

Although Margaret Mead compared sex and temperament in three different societies in the early 1930s, most cross-cultural studies of the effects of child rearing on personality have been carried out more recently by John and Beatrice Whiting and Irving L. Child or their associates. Their work has demonstrated a number of apparent regularities. For example, it is possible to distinguish between two different patterns of child rearing at a broad level of generalization, which we may label for convenience "dependence training" and "independence training."[7]

[7] Wolf, E. (1966). *Peasants* (pp. 69–70). Englewood Cliffs, NJ: Prentice-Hall.

Dependence training promotes compliance in the performance of assigned tasks and favors keeping individuals within the group. This pattern is typically associated with extended families, which consist of several husband-wife-children units within the same household and which are most apt to be found in societies with an economy based on subsistence farming. Such families are important, for they provide the large labor force necessary to till the soil, tend whatever flocks are kept, and carry out other part-time economic pursuits considered necessary for existence. These large families, however, have built into them certain potentially disruptive tensions. For example, one of the adults typically makes the important family decisions, which must be followed by all other family members. In addition, the in-marrying spouses—husbands and/or wives—must subordinate themselves to the group's will, something that may not be easy for them.

Dependence training helps to keep these potential problems under control and involves both supportive and punitive aspects. On the supportive side, indulgence is shown to young children, particularly in the form of prolonged oral gratification. Nursing continues for several years and is virtually on demand. This may be interpreted as rewarding the child for seeking support within the family, the main agent in meeting the child's needs. Also on the supportive side, children at a relatively early age are assigned a number of child-care and domestic tasks, all of which make significant and obvious contributions to the family's welfare. Thus, family members all actively work to help and support one another. On the punitive side, behavior the adults interpret as aggressive or sexual is apt to be actively discouraged. Moreover, the adults tend to be quite insistent on overall obedience, which is seen as rendering the individual subordinate to the group. This combination of encouragement and discouragement ideally produces individuals who are obedient, supportive, noncompetitive, and generally responsible, who will stay within the fold and not do anything potentially disruptive. Indeed, their very definition of "self" comes from their being a part of a larger social whole rather than from their mere individual existence.

INDEPENDENCE TRAINING

By contrast, **independence training** emphasizes individual independence, self-reliance, and personal achievement. One becomes the owner of one's self and capacities. It is typically associated with societies in which nuclear families, consisting of a husband, wife, and their offspring, are independent rather than a part of some larger household group. Independence training is particularly characteristic of industrial and postindustrial societies such as that of the United States, where self-reliance and personal achievement, especially on the part of men, are important traits for survival. Again, this pattern of training involves both encouragement and discouragement. On the negative side, little emphasis is placed on prolonged oral gratification, and feeding is prompted more by schedule than demand. In the United States, for example, people like to establish a schedule as soon as possible, and it is not long before they start feeding infants baby food and even try to get them to feed themselves. Many parents are delighted if they can prop their infants up in the crib or playpen so that they can hold their own bottles. Moreover, as soon after birth as possible, children are given their own private space, away from their parents. As already noted, infants do not receive the amount of attention they so often do in nonindustrialized societies. In the United States a mother may be very affectionate with her 15-week-old infant during the 20 percent of the time she is in contact with it, but for the other 80 percent of the time the infant is more or less on its own. Collective responsibility is not encouraged in children; they are not given responsible tasks to perform until later in childhood, and these are generally few. Furthermore, the contribution of the tasks to the family's welfare is often not immediately apparent to the child, to whom the tasks appear arbitrary as a result. Indeed, children are often encouraged to perform tasks for play rather than as contributions to the family's welfare.

Displays of aggression and sexuality are encouraged, or at least tolerated to a greater degree than where dependence training is the rule. In schools, and even in the family, competition is emphasized. In the United States, we have gone to the extreme of turning the biological functions of infancy—eating, sleeping, crying, and elimination—into contests between parents and offspring. In our schools, considerable resources are devoted to competitive sports, but competition is fostered within the classroom as well: overtly, through such devices as spelling bees and competition for prizes, and covertly through such devices as grading on a curve. The latter practice, widely utilized especially for heavily enrolled

Dependence training. Child-rearing practices that foster compliance in the performance of assigned tasks and dependence on the domestic group, rather than reliance on oneself. • **Independence training.** Child-rearing practices that promote independence, self-reliance, and personal achievement on the part of the child.

The White Man's Bad Medicine, by American Indian artist Jerome Tiger (1941–1967). In the 1950s, in an effort to end its special relationship with the American Indians, the federal government terminated its establishment of, and aid to, some Indian reservations. This termination policy led many Indians to relocate to urban areas. Because they were a people whose definition of self springs from the group they were born into, separation from family and kin led many to severe depression and related problems.

courses on some college campuses, condemns some students to failure, irrespective of how well they actually do, if most of the class does better. This puts students in competition with one another, for they soon learn that their chances for a decent grade depend, as much as anything, on other class members not doing well themselves. If the stakes are high, students may devote considerable effort to placing obstacles in the way of classmates so that they are prevented from doing too well. Thus, by the time individuals have grown up in U.S. society, regardless of what one may think about it, they have received a clear message: Success is something that comes at someone else's expense. As anthropologist Colin Turnbull observed: "Even the team spirit, so loudly touted" in school athletics (or out of school in Little League baseball and the like), "is merely a more efficient way, through limited cooperation, to 'beat' a greater number of people more efficiently."[8]

In sum, independence training generally encourages individuals to seek help and attention rather than to give it, and to try to exert individual dominance. Such qualities are useful in societies with social structures that emphasize personal achievement and where individuals are expected to look out for their own interests.

[8] Turnbull, C. M. (1983). *The human cycle* (p. 74). New York: Simon & Schuster.

COMBINED DEPENDENCE/INDEPENDENCE TRAINING

In actuality, dependence and independence training represent extremes along a continuum, and particular situations may partake of elements of both. In food-foraging societies, for example, child-rearing practices combine elements of both. "Share and share alike" is the order of the day, so competitive behavior, which can interfere with the cooperation all else depends on, is discouraged. Thus, infants receive much in the way of positive, affectionate attention from adults, along with prolonged oral gratification. This, as well as low pressure for compliance and a lack of emphasis on competition, encourages individuals to be more supportive of one another than is often the case in modern industrial and postindustrial societies. At the same time, personal achievement and independence are encouraged, for those individuals most capable of self-reliance are apt to be the most successful in the food quest.

In the United States the argument is sometimes made (not by anthropologists) that "permissive" child rearing produces irresponsible adults. Yet the practices of food foragers seem to be about as "permissive" as they can get, and socially responsible adults are produced. The fact is, no particular system of child rearing is inherently better or worse than any other; what matters is whether the system is functional or dysfunctional in the context of a particular society. If compliant adults, who are accepting

In North American society, independence training pits individuals against one another through games and other forms of competition.

of authority, are required, then independence training will not work well in that society. Nor will dependence training serve very well a society whose adults are expected to be independent, self-reliant, and questioning of authority.

Sometimes, however, inconsistencies develop, and here we may look again at the situation in North America. As we have seen, independence training generally tends to be stressed in the United States, where people often speak in glowing terms of the worth of personal independence, the dignity of the individual, and so on. Their pronouncements, however, do not always suit their actions. In spite of the professed desire for personal independence and emphasis on competition, a strong underlying desire for compliance seems to exist. This is reflected, for example, in decisions handed down over the past few decades by the Supreme Court, which, as observers of the Court have noted, often have favored the rights of authority over those of individuals. It is reflected, too, by the fate of "whistle blowers" in both government and industry, who, if they don't lose their jobs, are at least shunted to one side and passed by when the rewards are handed out. They are not "team players." In business as well as in government, the rewards tend to be given to those who go along with the system, while criticism, no matter how constructive, is a risky business. In corporate and government bureaucracies, the ability to please, not shake up the system, is what is required for success. Yet, in spite of pressures for compliance, which would be most effectively served by dependence training, we continue to raise our children to be independent and then wonder why they so often refuse to behave in ways adults would have them behave.

GROUP PERSONALITY

From studies such as those reviewed here, it is clear that personality, child-rearing practices, and other aspects of culture are interrelated in some kind of nonrandom way. Whiting and Child argued that the child-rearing practices of a society originate in basic customs surrounding nourishment, shelter, and protection, and that these child-rearing practices in turn produce particular kinds of adult personalities.[9] The trouble is that correlations do not prove cause and effect. We still are left with the fact, however logical it may seem, that such a causal chain remains an unproven hypothesis.

The existence of a close, if not causal, relationship between child-rearing practices and personality, coupled with variation in child-rearing practices from one society to another, have led to a number of attempts to characterize whole societies in terms of particular kinds of personalities. Indeed, common sense suggests that personalities appropriate for one culture may be less appropriate for others. For example, an egocentric, aggressive personality would be out of place where cooperation and sharing are the keys to success. Or, in the context of traditional Penobscot Indian culture, examined briefly earlier in this chapter, an open and extroverted personality would seem inappropriate, given its inconsistency with the prevailing conception of the self.

Unfortunately, common sense, like conventional wisdom in general, isn't always the truth. A question worth asking is: Can we describe a group personality without falling into stereotyping? The answer appears to be a qualified yes; in an abstract way, we may speak of a generalized "cultural personality" for a society, so long as we do not expect to find a uniformity of personalities within that society. Put another way, each individual develops certain personality characteristics that, from common experience, resemble those of other people. Yet, because each individual is exposed to unique experiences as well, may react to common experiences in novel ways, and brings to these experiences a unique (except for the case of identical twins) genetic potential, each also acquires distinct personality traits. Because individual per-

[9] Whiting, J. W. M., & Child, I. L. (1953). *Child training and personality: A cross-cultural study.* New Haven, CT: Yale University Press.

HIGHWAY 1
Culture and learned behavior
http://www.wsu.edu:8001/vcwsu/commons/topics/culture/behaviors/index.html

HIGHWAY 2
Texas A&M Anthropology Department
http://www.tamu.edu/anthropology

sonalities differ, the organization of diversity is important to all cultures.

As an example of the fact that individual personalities in traditional societies are far from uniform, consider the case of the Yanomami, who live in the forests of northern Brazil and southern Venezuela. Among them, individual men appear to strive to achieve a reputation for fierceness and aggressiveness that they are willing to defend at the risk of serious personal injury and death. And yet there are men among the Yanomami who are quiet and somewhat retiring. In any gathering of these people, the quiet ones are all too easily overlooked by outsiders, when others are in the front row pushing and demanding attention.

Modal Personality

Obviously, any fruitful approach to the problem of group personality must recognize that each individual is unique to a degree in both inheritance and life experiences and must expect a range of personality types in any society. In addition, personality traits that may be regarded as appropriate in men may not be so regarded in women, and vice versa. Given all this, we may focus our attention on the **modal personality** of a group, defined as the personality typical of a culturally bounded population, as indicated by the central tendency of a defined frequency distribution. Modal personality is a statistical concept, and, as such, it opens up for investigation the questions of how societies organize diversity and how diversity relates to culture change. Such questions are easily overlooked if one associates one particular type of personality with one particular culture, as older approaches (like that of Ruth Benedict, described in the box on p. 431) tended to do. At the same time, modal personalities of different groups can be compared.

Data on modal personality are best gathered by means of psychological tests administered to a sample of the population in question. Those most often used include

Modal personality. The personality typical of a society as indicated by the central tendency of a defined frequency distribution.

Yanomami men display their fierceness. While flamboyant, belligerent personalities are especially compatible with the Yanomami ideal that men should be fierce, some are quiet and retiring.

the Rorschach, or "ink blot," test and the Thematic Apperception Test (TAT). The latter consists of pictures the individual tested is asked to explain, or tell what is going on.

Other sorts of projective tests have been used as well at one time or another; all have in common a purposeful ambiguity so that the individual tested has to structure the situation before responding. The idea is that one's personality is projected into the ambiguous situation. Along with such tests, observations recording the frequency of certain behaviors, the collection and analysis of life histories and dreams, and the analysis of oral literature are helpful in eliciting data on modal personality.

While having much to recommend it, the concept of modal personality as a means of dealing with group personality nevertheless presents certain difficulties. One is the complexity of the measurement techniques, which may be difficult to carry out in the field. For one, an adequate representative sample of subjects is necessary. The problem here is twofold: making sure the sample is genuinely representative and having the time and personnel necessary to administer the tests, conduct interviews, and so on, all of which can be lengthy proceedings. Also, the tests themselves constitute a problem, for those devised in one cultural setting may not be appropriate in another. This is more of a problem with the TAT than with some other tests, although different pictures have been devised for other cultures. Still, to minimize any hidden cultural bias, it is best not to rely on projective tests alone. In addition to all this, language differences may lead to misinterpretation. Furthermore, the field investigator may be in conflict with cultural values. A people like the Penobscot, whose concept of self we surveyed earlier, would not take kindly to revealing their dreams to strangers. Finally, what is being measured must be questioned. Just what, for example, is aggression? Does everyone define it the same way? Is it a legitimate entity, or does it involve other variables?

RUTH FULTON BENEDICT (1887–1947)

Ruth Benedict came late to anthropology; after her graduation from Vassar College, she taught high school English, published poetry, and tried her hand at social work. In anthropology, she developed the idea that culture was a projection of the personality of those who created it. In her most famous book *Patterns of Culture* (1934), she compared the cultures of three peoples—the Kwakiutl of western Canada, the Zuni of the southwestern United States, and the Dobuans of Melanesia. She held that each was comparable to a great work of art, with an internal coherence and consistency of its own. Seeing the Kwakiutl as egocentric, individualistic, and ecstatic in their rituals, she labeled their cultural configuration "Dionysian." The Zuni, whom she saw as living by the golden mean, wanting no part of excess or disruptive psychological states, and distrusting of individualism, she characterized as "Apollonian." The Dobuans, whose culture seemed to her magic-ridden, with everyone fearing and hating everyone else, she characterized as "paranoid."

Although *Patterns of Culture* still enjoys popularity in some nonanthropological circles, anthropologists have long since abandoned its approach as impressionistic and not susceptible to replication. To compound the problem, Benedict's characterizations of cultures are misleading (the supposedly "Apollonian" Zunis, for example, indulge in such seemingly "Dionysian" practices as sword swallowing and walking over hot coals), and the use of such value-laden terms as "paranoid" prejudices others against the culture so labeled. Nonetheless, the book did have an enormous and valuable influence by focusing attention on the problem of the interrelation between culture and personality and by popularizing the reality of cultural variation.

National Character

No discussion of group personality would be complete without considering national character, which popular thought all too often ascribes to the citizens of various countries. Henry Miller epitomizes this view when he says, "Madmen are logical—as are the French," suggesting that the French, in general, are overly rational. A Parisian, in contrast, might view North Americans as maudlin and unsophisticated. Similarly, we all have in mind some image, perhaps not well defined, of the "typical" citizen of Russia or Japan or England. Essentially, these are simply stereotypes. We might well ask, however, if these stereotypes have any basis in fact. In reality, does such a thing as national character exist?

Some anthropologists have thought that the answer, maybe, is yes. Accordingly, national character studies were begun that sought to discover basic personality traits shared by the majority of the peoples of modern countries. Along with these went an emphasis on child-rearing practices and education as the factors theoretically responsible for such characteristics. Margaret Mead, Ruth Benedict, Weston LaBarre, and Geoffrey Gorer conducted pioneering studies of national character using relatively small samples of informants. During World War II, techniques were developed for studying "culture at a distance" through the analysis of newspapers, books, photographs, and interviews with expatriates from the country in question. By investigating memories of childhood and cultural attitudes, and by examining graphic material for the appearance of recurrent themes and values, researchers attempted to portray national character.

THE JAPANESE

At the height of World War II, Geoffrey Gorer attempted to determine the underlying reasons for what he described as a contrast between the all-pervasive gentleness of family life in Japan, which has charmed nearly every visitor, and the overwhelming brutality and sadism of the Japanese at war. Strongly under the influence of Freud, Gorer sought his causes in the toilet-training practices of the Japanese, which he believed were severe and threatening. He suggested that because Japanese infants were forced to control their bowel movements before they had acquired the necessary muscular or neurological development, they grew up filled with repressed rage. As adults, the Japanese were able to express this rage in their ruthlessness in war.[10]

In the midst of war Gorer was not able to do fieldwork in Japan. After the war was over, though, the toilet-training hypothesis was tested, and it was found that the severity of Japanese toilet training was a myth. Children were not subject to threats of severe punishment. Nor were all Japanese soldiers brutal and sadistic in war; some were, but then so were some North Americans. Also, the participation of many Japanese in postwar peace movements in the Far East hardly conformed to the wartime image of brutality.

Gorer's study, along with others by Benedict and LaBarre, was most important not in revealing the importance of Japanese bowel control to the national character but in pointing out the dangers of generalizing from insufficient evidence and employing simplistic individual psychology to explain complex social phenomena.

OBJECTIONS TO NATIONAL CHARACTER STUDIES

Critics of national character theories have emphasized the tendency for such work to be based on unscientific and overgeneralized data. The concept of modal personality has a certain statistical validity, they argue, but to generalize the qualities of a complex country on the basis of such limited data is to lend insufficient recognition to the countless individuals who vary from the generalization. Further, such studies tend to be highly subjective; for example, the tendency during the late 1930s and 1940s for anthropologists to characterize the German people as aggressive paranoids was obviously a reflection of wartime hostilities rather than scientific objectivity. Finally, it has been pointed out that occupational and social status tend to cut across national boundaries. A French farmer may have less in common with a French factory worker than he does with a German farmer.

An alternative approach to national character—one that allows for the fact not all personalities will conform to cultural ideals—is that of anthropologist Francis Hsu. His approach was to study the **core values** of a country's culture and related personality traits. The Chinese, he suggested, value kin ties and cooperation above all else. To them, mutual dependence is the very essence of personal relationships and has been for thousands of years. Compliance and subordination of one's will to that of family and kin transcends all else, while self-reliance is neither promoted nor a source of pride. Following the 1949 revolution, Mao Tse-tung sought to expand the sphere of affect to the country as a whole, with himself as the "father" of all citizens.

Perhaps the core value held in highest esteem by North Americans of European descent is "rugged individualism," traditionally for men but in recent decades for women as well. Each individual is supposed to be able to achieve anything he or she likes, given a willingness to work hard enough. From their earliest years, individuals are subjected to relentless pressures to excel, and as we have already noted, competition and winning are seen as crucial to this. Undoubtedly, this contributes to the "restlessness" and "drivenness" of North American society, and to the degree that it motivates individuals to work hard and to go where the economy needs them, it fits well with the needs of an industrial and postindustrial society. Thus, while individuals in Chinese society are firmly bound into a larger group to which they have lifelong obligations, North Americans are isolated from all other kin save husband or wife, and even here commitment to marriage has lessened.[11] Many young couples live together without either marriage or future plans for marriage. When couples do marry, prenuptial agreements are made to protect their assets, and something like 50% of marriages do end in divorce. Even parents and children have no legal obligations to one another once the latter have

[10] Gorer, G. (1943). Themes in Japanese culture. *Transactions of the New York Academy of Sciences,* Series II, 5.

[11] This and most of the following observations on North American culture are drawn from Natadecha-Sponsal, P. (1993). The young, the rich and the famous: Individualism as an American cultural value. In P. R. DeVita & J. D. Armstrong (Eds.). *Distant mirrors: America as a foreign culture* (pp. 46–53). Belmont, CA: Wadsworth.

Core values. Those values especially promoted by a particular culture.

The core values of Chinese culture promote the integration of the individual into a larger group. By contrast, the core values of Anglo-American culture promote the separation of the individual from the group.

Unmarried couples cohabiting continues to rise

Year	Number
1960	439,000
1970	523,000
1980	1.6 million
1990	2.9 million
1998	4.2 million

FIGURE 16.1
NUMBER OF UNMARRIED COUPLES COHABITING IN THE UNITED STATES, BY YEAR.

reached the age of majority. Indeed, many North American parents seem to "lose" their children in their teenage years. As for relations with nonkin, these tend to remain at an abbreviated and superficial level.

NORMAL AND ABNORMAL PERSONALITY

The concept of modal personality holds that a range of personalities will exist in any society. The modal personality itself may be thought of as normal for that society but in fact may be shared by less than half the population. What of those personalities that differ from the norm? The Dobuans of New Guinea and Indians of the North American Great Plains furnish examples of normal and abnormal behavior strikingly different from that of North Americans of European descent.

The individual in Dobu the other villagers considered neurotic and thoroughly disoriented was a man who was naturally friendly and found activity an end in itself. He was a pleasant fellow who did not seek to overthrow his fellows or to punish them. He worked for anyone who asked him, and he was tireless in carrying out their commands. In any other Dobuan, this would have been scandalous behavior, but in him it was regarded as merely silly. The village treated him in a kindly fashion, not taking advantage of him nor making sport of or ridiculing him, but he was definitely regarded as one who stood outside the normal conventions of behavior.

To return to the subject of the Original Study earlier in this chapter, among North American Indians, a man, compelled by supernatural spirits, could assume women's attire and perform women's work; he could even marry another man, although not all men who assumed a woman's identity were homosexuals, nor did all homosexuals behave in this way (most Indian societies allowed individuals ways to engage in homosexual behavior without altering their gender status). Under this institution of the "two-spirit," a man could live in a dramatically different manner from most others of his sex; yet, although the two-spirit was rare among Indians, it was *not* looked upon as deviant behavior.[12] Quite the contrary, for the two-spirit was often sought out as a curer, artist, matchmaker, and companion of warriors because of the great spiritual power he was thought to possess.

Shown here is the famous Zuni Indian two-spirit named We'wha, who once had the experience of meeting President Grover Cleveland. For a man to assume a feminine identity was not regarded as abnormal by the Zuni; in fact, such individuals were regarded as special in that they bridged the gap between the purely feminine and purely masculine. European-Americans, by contrast, regarded such individuals with aversion.

In Western societies such as the United States, behavior like that of the Indian two-spirits has traditionally been regarded as abnormal. If a man dresses as a woman, it is still widely regarded as a cause for concern and is likely to lead to psychiatric intervention. Nor have jobs traditionally filled by women been seen as desirable for men. By contrast, women have more freedom to wear masculine-style clothing and to assume jobs traditionally held by men, even though to do so may cause others to brand them as somehow "unfeminine." Lying behind these views are traditional values (jobs customarily associated with men have been more highly valued then those associated with women) and a pattern of child rearing that creates problems of gender identity for both sexes, although of a different sort for each sex.

Nancy Chodorow, a sociologist with a strong background in anthropology,[13] has argued that in the United States, girls traditionally have been raised by women, usually their mothers, and most still are. Thus, feminine role models are constantly available and easily understandable. Very early, girls begin to do what women do and gradually and continuously acquire the identity deemed appropriate for their sex. Once they enter school, however, they learn that women are not all-powerful and prestigious, that it is men who generally run things and who are portrayed as the ones who have most advanced human progress. As a consequence, a girl finds that the feminine identity, which has become so easy for her, leaves much to be desired. Under the circumstances, she is bound to feel a certain resentment toward it.

[12] Although the European term "berdache" has been widely used in the literature, it carries a pejorative connotation and so has been abandoned for the term "two-spirit" favored by Native Americans. See Jacobs, S. E. (1994). Native American two-spirits. *Anthropology Newsletter, 35* (8), 7.

[13] She was a participant in the Harvard Chiapas Project directed by anthropologist Evon Z. Vogt.

The author's father as a little boy. In the United States, boys spent their earliest years in the company of women, and so were dressed like girls. Adoption of a masculine identity required rejection of an earlier feminine identity. Not until well into the 20th century did this change.

Boys have a different problem; like girls they too begin their lives in a feminine world. With adult men out of the house working, not only is a male model rarely present, but it is the mother who seems to be all-powerful. Under these conditions, boys begin to develop a feminine identity with its expected compliant personality. In keeping with all this, boys used to be even dressed as girls (dresses for little boys were not dropped from the Sears catalog until 1940) until the age thought proper to "graduate" into less feminine attire arrived. Once out of the house and in school, boys learn they must switch from a female to male identity; in a sense, they must renounce femininity and prove their maleness in a way that girls do not have to prove their femaleness. Generally speaking, the more distant a boy's father (or other male companion of his mother), the greater is the boy's insecurity in his male identity and the greater his compulsion to be seen as really masculine. To do this, he must strive all the harder to be aggressive and assert his dominance, particularly over women.

Nancy Chodorow sums up the consequences of this situation as follows:

> Sex-role ideology and socialization for these roles seem to ensure that neither boys nor girls can attain both stable identity and meaningful roles. The tragedy of woman's socialization is not that she is left unclear, as is the man, about her basic sexual identity. This identity is ascribed to her, and she does not need to prove to herself or to society that she has earned it or continues to have it. Her problem is that this identity is clearly devalued in the society in which she lives. This does not mean that women too should be required to compete for identity, to be assertive and to need to achieve—to "do" like men. Nor does it suggest that it is not crucial for everyone, men and women alike, to have a stable sexual identity. But until male "identity" does not depend upon men's proving themselves, their "doing" will be a reaction to insecurity, not a creative exercise of their humanity, and woman's "being," far from being an easy and positive acceptance of self, will be a resignation to inferiority. And as long as women must live through their children, and men do not genuinely contribute to socialization and provide easily accessible role models, women will continue to bring up sons whose sexual identity depends upon devaluing femininity inside and outside themselves, and daughters who must accept this devalued position and resign themselves to producing more men who will perpetuate the system that devalues them.[14]

This example shows how a culture itself actually may induce certain kinds of psychological conflicts with important consequences for the entire society. Although the conditions under which children are raised in the United States are changing, they have a long way to go before the conflicts just described become things of the past. Still, what has seemed to be "normal" in the past could become "abnormal" in the future.

It is also true that the abnormal may become normal. Anthropologist Emily Martin cites changing attitudes

---

[14] Chodorow, N. (1971). Being and doing: A cross-cultural examination of the socialization of males and females. In V. Gornick & B. K. Moran (Eds.). *Woman in sexist society* (p. 193). New York: Basic Books.

Anthropology Applied

Anthropologists and Mental Health

One consequence of "development" in the newly emerged states of Africa, Asia, and Central and South America is a rising incidence of mental disturbances among their people. Similarly, mental health problems abound among ethnic minorities living within industrialized countries. Unfortunately, orthodox approaches to mental health have not been successful at dealing with these problems for a number of reasons. For one, the various ethnic groups have different attitudes toward mental disorders than do medical practitioners (who are, after all, products of Western culture). For another, the diverse conditions different ethnic groups live under produce culturally patterned health conditions, including culture-bound syndromes not recognized by the orthodox medical profession. Among Puerto Ricans, for example, a widely held belief is that spirits are active in the world and that they influence human behavior. Thus, for someone with a psychiatric problem, it makes sense to go to a native spiritist for help rather than to a psychiatrist. In a Puerto Rican community, going to a spiritist is "normal." Not only does the client not understand the symbols of psychiatry, but to go to a psychiatrist implies that he or she is "crazy" and requires restraint or removal from the community.

Although practitioners of Western medicine have traditionally regarded spiritists and other folk healers as "ignorant," if not "charlatans," experimentation began in the 1950s with community-based treatment in which psychiatrists cooperated with traditional healers. Since then, this approach has gained widespread acceptance in many parts of the world, as when (in 1977) the World Health Organization advocated cooperation between health professionals and native specialists (including herbalists and midwives). As a consequence, many anthropologists have found work as cultural brokers, studying the cultural system of the client population and explaining this to the health professionals while also explaining the world of the psychiatrists to the folk healers and the client population.

To cite one example, as a part of the Miami Community Mental Health Program, a field team led by an anthropologist was established to work with the Puerto Rican community of Dade County.* Like other ethnic communities in the area, this one was characterized by low incomes, high rents, and a plethora of health (including mental health) problems, yet health facilities and social service agencies were underused. Working in the community, the team successfully built up support networks among the Puerto Ricans, involving extended families, churches, clubs, and spiritists. At the same time, they gathered information about the community, providing it to appropriate social service agencies. At the Dade County Hospital, team members acted as brokers between the psychiatric personnel and their Puerto Rican clients, and a training program was implemented for the mental health staff.

* See Willigan, J. V. (1986). *Applied anthropology* (pp. 128–129 and 133–139). South Hadley, MA: Bergin and Garvey.

toward manic-depression and attention deficit hyperactivity disorder (ADHD).[15] Usually regarded as dreaded liabilities, she suggests that, in North America, their "manic" and hyperactivity aspects are coming to be seen as assets in the quest for success. More and more, they are interpreted as indicative of "finely wired, exquisitely alert nervous systems" that make one constantly alert for signs of change, able to fly from one thing to another while pushing the limits of everything, and doing it all with an intense level of energy focused totally in the future. These are extolled as high virtues in the corporate world, and to be called "hyper" or "manic" is increasingly an expression of approval.

The standards that define normal behavior for any culture are determined by that culture itself. Take, for example, attitudes toward individuals who enter into altered states of consciousness. Among the Melemchi of Nepal, to effect a cure a healer must call the gods into his body

[15] Martin, E. (1999). Flexible survivors. *Anthropology News, 40* (6), 5–7.

Although the ability to enter trance is a consequence of having a normal human nervous system, some societies, such as that of the United States, define entering trance as abnormal, while many others accept it as normal. Among the Ju/'hoansi of Namibia, men enter trance in a dance, accompanied by the rhythmic clapping and singing of women. By entering trance, these men can summon supernatural power to heal, bring rain, and control animals.

to let them speak through him.[16] To do this, he must ride into their world. Through drumming and chanting, sometimes accompanied by use of hallucinogenic drugs and intoxicants, he enters an altered state of consciousness, or trance. This allows him to see and communicate with the gods. To outsiders, it appears the curer is hallucinating: seeing visions, smelling smells, hearing sounds, and experiencing bodily sensations that seem real, but are not seen, smelled, heard, or felt by others who are present but have not entered into trance. In modern North American society, behavior like that of the Melemchi curer is generally regarded as deviant, and the practice of entering altered states is apt to be seen as a sign of mental instability or even unlawful activity if it involves the use of hallucinogenic substances.

The negative attitude of North American culture to the contrary notwithstanding, there is nothing abnormal *per se* about the ability to enter trancelike states and experience a wide range of hallucinations. To the contrary, "The desire to alter consciousness periodically is an innate, normal drive analogous to hunger or the sexual drive."[17] There is even good evidence that chimpanzees, baboons, other monkeys, cats, dogs, and other animals hallucinate, and that the ability is a function of the mammalian, not just human, nervous system.[18] Thus, the ability to enter altered states and experience visions and other sensations appears to predate the appearance of *Homo sapiens,* and it is not surprising that the ability to enter trance is a human universal. Although some societies try to suppress the practice, the vast majority (like the Melemchi) accept trancing and shape it to their own ends. One study, for example, found that as many as 437 out of a sample of 488 historically known societies had some form of *institutionalized* altered states of consciousness.[19]

Is all this to suggest that "normalcy" is a meaningless concept when applied to personality? Within the

[16] Womack, M. (1994). Program 5: Psychological anthropology. *Faces of Culture.* Fountain Valley, CA: Coast Telecourses, Inc.

[17] Furst, P.T. (1976). *Hallucinogens and culture* (p.7). Novato, CA: Chandler and Sharp.

[18] Lewis-Williams, J. D., & Dowson, T. A. (1988). Signs of all times: Entoptic phenomena in Upper Paleolithic art. *Current Anthropology, 29,* 202.

[19] Lewis-Williams, J. D., & Dowson, T. D. (1993). On vision and power in the Neolithic: Evidence from the Decorated Monuments. *Current Anthropology, 34,* 55.

TABLE 16.1 ETHNIC PSYCHOSES AND OTHER CULTURE-BOUND PSYCHOLOGICAL DISORDERS

Name of Disorder	Culture	Description
Amok	Malaya (also observed in Java, Philippines, Africa, and Tierra del Fuego)	A disorder characterized by sudden, wild outbursts of homicidal aggression in which the afflicted person may kill or injure others. The rage disorder is usually found in males who are rather withdrawn, quiet, and inoffensive prior to the onset of the disorder. Stress, sleep deprivation, extreme heat, and alcohol are among the conditions thought to precipitate the disorder. Several stages have been observed: Typically in the first stage the person becomes more withdrawn; then a period of brooding follows in which a loss of reality contact is evident. Ideas of persecution and anger predominate. Finally, a phase of automatism, or *amok*, occurs, in which the person jumps up, yells, grabs a knife, and stabs people or objects within reach. Exhaustion and depression usually follow, with amnesia for the rage.
Anorexia nervosa	Western countries	A disorder occurring most frequently among young women in which a preoccupation with thinness produces a refusal to eat. This condition can result in death.
Latah	Malay	A fear reaction often occurring in middle-aged women of low intelligence who are subservient and self-effacing. The disorder is precipitated by the word *snake* or by tickling. It is characterized by *echolalia* (repetition of the words and sentences of others). The disturbed individual may also react with negativism and the compulsive use of obscene language.

context of a particular culture, the concept of normal personality is quite meaningful. A. I. Hallowell, a major figure in the development of psychological anthropology, somewhat ironically observed that it is normal to share the delusions traditionally accepted by one's society. Abnormality involves the development of a delusional system of which the culture does not approve. The individual who is disturbed because he or she cannot adequately measure up to the norms of society and be happy may be termed *neurotic*. When a person's delusional system is so different that it in no way reflects his or her society's norms, the individual may be termed *psychotic*.

Culturally induced conflicts not only can, if severe enough, produce psychosis but can determine the form of the psychosis as well. In a culture that encourages aggressiveness and suspicion, the insane person may be one who is passive and trusting. In a culture that encourages passivity and trust, the insane person may be the one who is aggressive and suspicious. Just as each society establishes its own norms, each individual is unique in his or her perceptions. Many anthropologists see the only meaningful criterion for personality evaluation as the correlation between personality and social conformity.

Although it is true that culture defines what is and is not normal behavior, the situation is complicated by findings suggesting that major categories of mental disorders may be universal types of human affliction. Take, for example, schizophrenia, probably the most common of all psychoses, and one that may be found in any culture, no matter how it may manifest itself. Individuals afflicted by schizophrenia experience distortions of reality that impair their ability to function adequately, so they withdraw from the social world into their own psychological shell, from which they do not emerge. Although environmental factors play a role, evidence exists that schizophrenia is caused by a biochemical disorder for which there is an inheritable tendency. One of its more severe forms is paranoid schizophrenia. Those suffering from it fear and mistrust most everyone; they hear voices that whisper

Name of Disorder	Culture	Description
Koro	Southeast Asia (particularly Malay Archipelago)	A fear reaction or anxiety in which the person fears that his penis will withdraw into his abdomen and he will die. This reaction may appear after sexual overindulgence or excessive masturbation. The anxiety is typically very intense and of sudden onset. The condition is "treated" by having the penis held firmly by the patient or by family members or friends. Often the penis is clamped to a wooden box.
Windigo	Algonkian Indians of Canada and northern United States	A fear reaction in which a hunter becomes anxious and agitated, convinced that he is bewitched. Fears center on his being turned into a cannibal by the power of a monster with an insatiable craving for human flesh.
Kitsunetsuki	Japan	A disorder in which victims believe that they are possessed by foxes and are said to change their facial expressions to resemble foxes. Entire families are often possessed and banned by the community.
Pibloktoq and other arctic hysterias	Circumpolar peoples from Lapland eastward across Siberia, northern Alaska, and Canada to Greenland	A disorder brought on by fright, which is followed by a short period of bizarre behavior; victim may tear clothes off, jump in water or fire, roll in snow, try to walk on the ceiling, throw things, thrash about, and "speak in tongues." Outburst followed by return to normal behavior.

Based on Carson, R. C., Butcher, J. N., & Coleman, J. C. (1990). (8th ed.) (p. 85). Glenview, IL: Scott Foresman.

dreadful things to them and they are convinced that someone is "out to get them." Acting on this conviction, they engage in bizarre sorts of behavior, which leads to their removal from society, usually to a mental institution.

A precise image of paranoid schizophrenia is one of the so-called **ethnic psychoses** known as *Windigo.* Such psychoses involve symptoms of mental disorder specific to particular ethnic groups (Table 16.1). Windigo psychosis is limited to northern Algonquian Indian groups such as the Cree, and Ojibwa. In their traditional belief systems, these northern Indians recognized the existence of cannibalistic monsters called Windigos. Individuals afflicted by the psychosis developed the delusion that, falling under control of these monsters, they themselves were being transformed into Windigos, with a craving for human flesh. As this happened, they saw people around them turning into various edible animals—fat, juicy beavers, for instance. Although no instances where sufferers of Windigo psychosis actually ate another human being are known, they nonetheless developed an acute fear of doing so. Furthermore, other members of their group genuinely feared that they might.

At first, Windigo psychosis seems quite different from Western clinical cases of paranoid schizophrenia, but a closer look suggests otherwise; the disorder was merely being expressed in ways compatible with traditional northern Algonquian culture. Ideas of persecution, instead of being directed toward other humans, are directed toward supernatural beings (the Windigo monsters); cannibalistic panic replaces homosexual panic;

Ethnic psychoses. Mental disorders specific to particular ethnic groups.

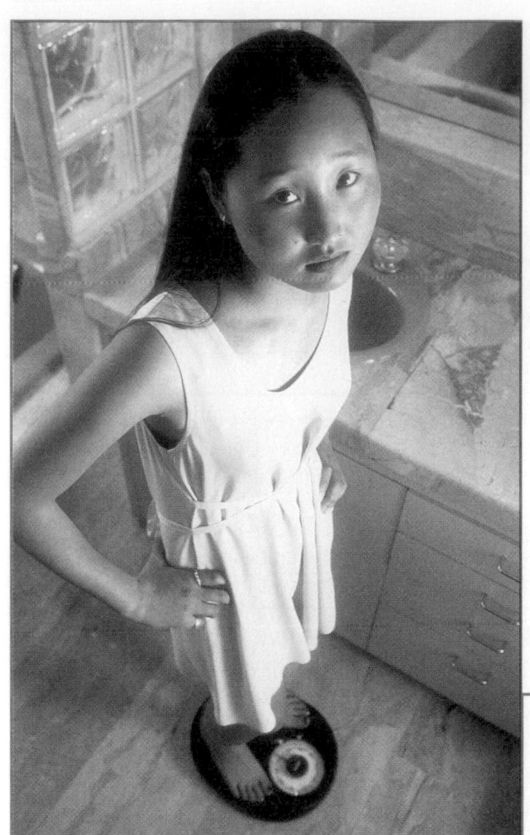

Anorexia nervosa, a psychological disorder most frequent among women in Western countries, can now be seen in some other industrializing countries such as Korea.

and the like. The northern Algonquian Indian, like the European-American, expresses his or her problem in terms compatible with the appropriate view of the self and its behavioral environment. The northern Algonquian, though, was removed from society not by being committed to a mental institution but by being killed.

Windigo behavior has seemed exotic and dramatic to the westerner. When all is said and done, however, the imagery and symbolism that a psychotic person has to draw upon is that which his or her culture has to offer, and in northern Algonquian culture, these involve myths in which cannibal giants figure prominently. By contrast, the delusions of Irish schizophrenics draw upon the images and symbols of Irish Catholicism, and feature Virgin and Savior motifs. Anglo-Americans, on the other hand, tend toward secular or electromagnetic persecution delusions. The underlying structure of the mental disorder is the same in all cases, but its expression is culturally specific.

CHAPTER SUMMARY

Enculturation, the process by which individuals become members of their society, begins soon after birth. Its first agents are the members of an individual's household, but later, other members of society become involved. For enculturation to proceed, individuals must possess self-awareness, or the ability to perceive themselves as objects in time and space and to judge their own actions. A major facet of self-awareness is a positive view of the self, for this is what motivates persons to act to their advantage rather than disadvantage.

Several requirements involving a person's behavioral environment need to be met in order for emerging self-awareness to function. The individual first needs to learn about a world of objects other than self; this environment is perceived in terms compatible with the values of his or her culture. Also required is a sense of both spatial and temporal orientation. Finally, the growing individual needs a normative orientation, or an understanding of the values, ideals, and standards that constitute the behavioral environment.

Personality is a product of enculturation and refers to the distinctive ways a person thinks, feels, and behaves. Along with psychoanalysts, most anthropologists believe adult personality is shaped by early childhood experiences. A prime goal of anthropologists has been to produce objective studies that test this theory. Cross-cultural studies of gender-related personality characteristics, for example, show that whatever biologically based personality differences exist between men and women, they are extremely malleable. A society's economy helps structure the way children are brought up, which in turn influences their adult personalities.

Anthropologists John and Beatrice Whiting and Irvin Child, on the basis of cross-cultural studies, have established the interrelation of personality, child-rearing practices, and other aspects of culture. For example, dependence training, usually associated with traditional farming societies, tries to ensure that members of society will willingly and routinely work for the benefit of the group, performing the jobs assigned to them. At the opposite extreme, independence training, typical of societies characterized by independent nuclear families, puts a premium on self-reliance and independent behavior. Although a society may emphasize one sort of behavior over the other, it may not emphasize it to the same degree in both sexes. The Whitings and Child believe that child-rearing practices have their roots in a society's customs for meeting the basic physical needs of its members; these practices, in turn, develop particular kinds of adult personalities.

Anthropologists early on began to work on the problem of whether it is possible to delineate a group personality without falling into stereotyping. Each culture chooses, from the vast array of possibilities, those traits that it sees as normative or ideal. Individuals who conform to these traits are rewarded; the rest are not. The modal personality of a group is the personality typical of a culturally bounded population, as indicated by the central tendency of a defined frequency distribution. As a statistical concept, it opens up for investigation how societies organize the diverse personalities of their members, some of which conform more than others to the modal "type."

National character studies have focused on the modal characteristics of modern countries. They have then attempted to determine the child-rearing practices and education that shape such a group personality. Investigators during World War II interviewed foreign-born nationals and analyzed other sources in an effort to depict national character. Many anthropologists believe national character theories are based on unscientific and overgeneralized data. Others have chosen to focus on the core values promoted in particular societies while recognizing that success in instilling these values in individuals may vary considerably.

What defines normal behavior in any culture is determined by the culture itself, and what may be acceptable, or even admirable, in one may not be in another. Abnormality involves developing personality traits not accepted by a culture. Culturally induced conflicts not only can produce psychological disturbance but can determine the form of the disturbance as well. Similarly, mental disorders that have a biological cause, like schizophrenia, will be expressed by symptoms specific to the culture of the afflicted individual.

CLASSIC READINGS

Barnouw, V. (1985). *Culture and personality* (4th ed.). Homewood, IL: Dorsey Press.

This is a revision of a well-respected text designed to introduce students to psychological anthropology.

Furst, P. T. (1976). *Hallucinogens and culture.* Novato, CA: Chandler and Sharp.

For those interested in altered states of consciousness, this book is the best place to start. This important cross-cultural study of mind-altering substances is thorough, yet easily read by those with no previous knowledge.

Suárez-Orozoco, M. M., Spindler, G., & Spindler, L. (1994). *The making of psychological anthropology II.* Fort Worth, TX: Harcourt Brace.

This collection of articles consists of firsthand accounts of the objectives, accomplishments, and failures of well-known specialists in psychological anthropology.

Wallace, A. F. C. (1970). *Culture and personality* (2nd ed.). New York: Random House.

The logical and methodological foundations of culture and personality as a science form the basis of this book. The study is guided by the assumptions that anthropology should develop a scientific theory about culture and that a theory pretending to explain or predict cultural phenomena must reckon with noncultural phenomena (such as personality) as well.

Whiting, J. W. M., & Child, I. (1953). *Child training and personality: A cross-cultural study.* New Haven, CT: Yale University Press.

How culture is integrated though the medium of personality processes is the main concern of this classic study. It covers the influence of both culture on personality and personality on culture. It is oriented toward testing general hypotheses about human behavior in any and all societies, rather than toward a detailed analysis of a particular society.

CHAPTER 17

PATTERNS OF SUBSISTENCE

Indonesians foraging for food at a dump. The basic business of culture is securing the survival of those who live by its rules, and so the study of subsistence is an important aspect of anthropological study.

CHAPTER PREVIEW

1 What Is Adaptation?

Adaptation refers to the process of interaction between changes an organism makes on its environment and changes the environment makes in the organism. This kind of two-way adjustment is necessary for the survival of all life forms, including human beings.

2 How Do Humans Adapt?

Humans adapt through the medium of culture, as they develop ways of doing things that are compatible with the resources they have available to them and within the limitations of the environment in which they live. In a particular region, people living in similar environments tend to borrow from one another customs that seem to work well in those environments. Once achieved, adaptations may be remarkably stable for long periods of time, even thousands of years.

3 What Sorts of Adaptations Have Humans Achieved Through the Ages?

Food foraging is the oldest and most universal type of human adaptation. To it we owe such important elements of social organization as the sexual division of labor, food sharing, and a home base as the center of daily activity and where food sharing is accomplished. Quite different adaptations, involving farming and animal husbandry, began to develop in some parts of the world between 9,000 and 11,000 years ago. Horticulture—the cultivation of domestic plants by means of simple hand tools—made possible more permanent settlements and a reorganization of the division of labor. Under pastoralism—reliance on herds of domestic grazing animals—nomadism continued, but new modes of interaction with other peoples were developed. Urbanism began to develop as early as 5,000 years ago in some places, as intensive agriculture produced sufficient food to support full-time specialists of various sorts. With this went a further transformation of the social fabric.

Several times today you will interrupt your activities to eat or drink. You may take this very much for granted, but if you went totally without food for as long as a day, you would begin to feel the symptoms of hunger: weakness, fatigue, headache. After a month of starvation, your body would probably never repair the damage. A mere week to 10 days without water would be enough to kill you.

All living beings, and people are no exception, must satisfy certain basic needs in order to stay alive. Among these needs are food, water, and shelter. Humans may not "live by bread alone," but nobody can live for long without any bread at all; and no creature could long survive if its relations with its environment were random and chaotic. Living beings must have regular access to a supply of food and water and a reliable means of obtaining and using it. A lion might die if all its prey disappeared, if its teeth and claws grew soft, or if its digestive system failed. Although people face these same sorts of problems, they have an overwhelming advantage over other creatures: People have culture. If our meat supply dwindles, we can turn to some vegetable, like the soybean, and process it to taste like meat. When our tools fail, we replace them or invent better ones. Even when our stomachs are incapable of digesting food, we can predigest food by boiling or pureeing. We are, however, subject to the same needs and pressures as all living creatures, and it is important to understand human behavior from this point of view. The crucial concept that underlies such a perspective is **adaptation,** that is, how humans manage to deal with the contingencies of daily life. Dealing with these contingencies is the basic business of all cultures. A people's cultural adaptation consists of a complex of ideas, activities, and technologies that allow them to stay alive.

ADAPTATION

The process of adaptation establishes a moving balance between the needs of a population and the potential of its environment. This process can be illustrated by the Tsembaga: New Guinea highlanders who support themselves chiefly through **horticulture**—the cultivation of

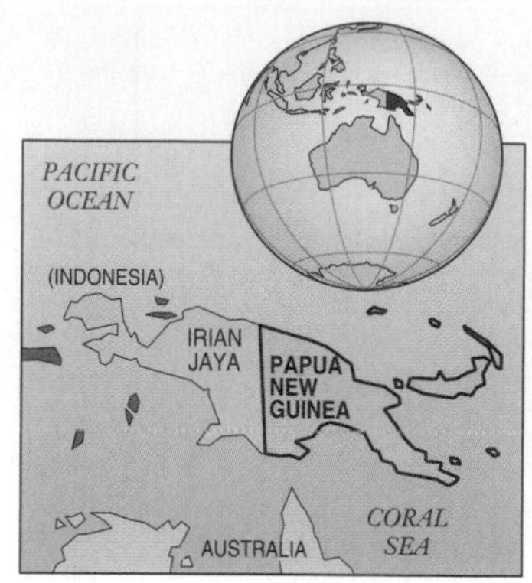

crops carried out with simple hand tools.[1] Although they also raise pigs, they eat them only under conditions of illness, injury, warfare, or celebration. At such times the pigs are sacrificed to ancestral spirits, and their flesh is ritually consumed by the people involved in the crisis. (This guarantees a supply of high-quality protein when it is most needed.)

Traditionally, the Tsembaga and their neighbors were bound together in a unique cycle of pig sacrifices that served to mark the end of hostilities between groups. Frequent hostilities were set off by a number of ecological pressures, with pigs playing a significant part. Since very few pigs normally were slaughtered and their food requirements were great, they could very quickly literally eat a local group out of house and home. The need to expand food production in order to support the prestigious but hungry pigs put a strain on the land best suited for farming. Therefore, when one group had driven another off its land, hostilities ended, and the new residents celebrated their victory with a pig festival. Many pigs were slaughtered, and the pork was widely shared among allied groups. Even without hostilities, festivals were held whenever the pig population became unmanageable, every 5 to 10 years, depending on the groups' success at farming. Thus, the cycle of fighting and feasting kept the balance among humans, land, and animals.

[1] Rappaport, R. A. (1969). Ritual regulation of environmental relations among a New Guinea people. In A. P. Vayda (Ed.), *Environment and cultural behavior* (pp. 181–201). Garden City, NY: Natural History Press.

Adaptation. The process organisms undergo to achieve a beneficial adjustment to an available environment and the result of that process—the characteristics of organisms that fit them to the particular environmental conditions in which they are found. • **Horticulture.** Cultivation of crops using hand tools such as digging sticks or hoes.

Human adaptations impact environments in various ways. In California, native food foragers regularly burned-over vast areas, thereby favoring the growth of oak trees (acorns were a staple food) and deer browse. Once "White" settlers stopped the practice, highly flammable brush and conifers flourished at the expense of oaks. As a consequence, disastrous outbreaks of wildfires periodically sweep through parts of the state, causing millions of dollars in property loss.

The term *adaptation* also refers to the process of interaction between changes an organism makes in its environment and changes the environment makes in the organism. The spread of the gene for sickle-cell anemia is a case in point. Long ago, in the tropics of central Africa, a genetic mutation appeared in human populations, causing the manufacture of red blood cells that take on a sickle shape under conditions of low oxygen pressure. Since persons who inherit a gene for this trait from each parent usually develop severe anemia and die in childhood, selective pressure was exerted against the spread of this gene in the local population. Then a new cultural practice, slash-and-burn horticulture, was introduced into this region, creating a change in the natural environment by removal—through cutting (slashing) and burning—of the natural vegetative cover. This was conducive to the breeding of mosquitos that carry the parasite causing falciparum malaria. When transmitted to humans, the parasites live in the red blood cells and cause a disease that is always debilitating and very often fatal. Individuals who inherited the gene for the sickle-cell trait from only one parent, however (receiving one "normal" gene from the other), turned out to have a natural defense against the parasite. The gene's presence caused only some of the cells to take on a sickle shape; when those cells circulated through the spleen, which routinely screens out all damaged or worn red blood cells, the infected cells and the parasites along with them were destroyed. Since these individuals did not succumb to malaria, they were favored by natural selection, and the sickling trait became more and more common in the population. Thus, as people's cultural practices changed their environment, their environment caused a biological change in them. Nor is this an isolated example; analogous forms of hereditary anemias that protect against malaria followed the spread of farming from Southwest and Southeast Asia as well.

Sickle-cell and similar anemias are a neat illustration of the relativity of any adaptation. In malarial areas, the genes responsible for these conditions are adaptive for

Though the Hopi and Navajo share the same environment, their cultures are quite different. Originally food foragers, Navajos became pastoral nomads, while the Hopi are village-dwelling farmers. Environments do not determine culture but do set certain potentials and limitations.

human populations, even though some individuals suffer as a result of their presence. In nonmalarial regions, however, they are highly maladaptive, for the genes confer no advantage at all on human populations living under such conditions. Yet, some individuals die as a result of their presence.

The Unit of Adaptation

The unit of adaptation includes both organisms and environment. Organisms, including human beings, exist as members of populations; populations, in turn, must have the flexibility to cope with variability and change within the environment. In biological terms, this means that different organisms within the population have somewhat differing genetic endowments. In cultural terms, it means that variation occurs among individual skills, knowledge, and personalities. Organisms and environments form interacting systems. People might as easily farm as fish, but we do not expect to find farmers north of the Arctic Circle or people who fish for a living in the Sahara Desert. In other words, although environments do not determine culture, they do present certain possibilities and limitations.

Consider the example of a lakeside people who live off fish. The fish in turn live off smaller organisms, and these in turn consume green plants; plants liberate minerals from water and mud, and, with energy from sunlight, transform them into proteins and carbohydrates. Dead plant and animal matter is decomposed by bacteria, returning chemicals to the soil and water. Some energy escapes from this system in the form of heat. Evaporation and rainfall constantly recirculate the water. People add chemicals to the system in the form of their wastes, and, if they are judicious, they may help to regulate the balance of animals and plants.

Some anthropologists have borrowed the ecologists' concept of **ecosystem.** An ecosystem is composed of both the physical environment and the organisms living within it. The system is bound by the activities of the organisms, as well as by such physical processes as erosion and evaporation.

Human ecologists are generally concerned with detailed microstudies of particular human ecosystems; they emphasize that all aspects of human culture must be considered, not just the most obvious technological ones. The Tsembaga's attitude toward pigs and the cycle of sacrifices have important economic and biological functions; outsiders may see them in this way, but the Tsembaga do not.

Ecosystem. A system, or a functioning whole, composed of both the physical environment and the organisms living within it.

A Comanche bison hunt as painted by artist George Catlin. Plains Indians such as the Cheyenne, Comanche, Crow, and Sioux developed similar cultures, as they had to adapt to similar environmental conditions (for a map of Native American culture areas, see Figure 17.1.)

They are motivated by their belief in the power and needs of their ancestral spirits. Although the pigs are consumed *by* the living, they are sacrificed *for* ancestors. Human ecosystems must often be interpreted in cultural terms.

Evolutionary Adaptation

Adaptation also must be understood from a historical point of view. For humans to fit into an ecosystem, like all organisms, they must have the potential to adjust to or become a part of it. The Comanche, whose history began in the harsh, arid country of southern Idaho, provide a good example.[2] In their original home they subsisted on wild plants, small animals, and occasionally larger game. Their material equipment was simple and limited to what their women and dogs could transport. The size of their groups was restricted, and what little social power could develop was in the hands of the shaman, who was a combination of medical curer and spiritual guide.

At some point in their nomadic history, the Comanche moved onto the Great Plains, where buffalo were abundant and the Indians' potential as hunters could be fully developed. As larger groups could be supported by the new food supply, the need arose for a more complex political organization. Hunting ability thus became a means to acquire political power.

Eventually the Comanche acquired horses and guns from "Whites," which greatly enhanced their hunting prowess, and the great hunting chiefs became powerful indeed. The Comanche became raiders in order to get horses, which they did not breed for themselves, and their hunting chiefs evolved into war chiefs. The once "poor" and peaceful hunter-gatherers of the Great Basin became wealthy and raiding became a way of life. In the late 18th and early 19th centuries they dominated the Southwest from the borders of New Spain (Mexico) in the south to those of New France (Louisiana) and the fledgling United States in the east and north. In moving from one environment to another, and in changing from one way of life to a second, the Comanche were able to capitalize on existing cultural capabilities to flourish in their new situation.

Sometimes societies that have developed independently find similar solutions to similar problems. For example, another group that moved out onto the Great Plains and took up a form of Plains Indian culture, similar in many ways to that of the Comanche, were the Cheyenne. Yet their cultural background was quite different; formerly, they were crop cultivators and wild rice gatherers in the woodlands of the Great Lakes area, with social, political, and religious institutions quite unlike

[2] Wallace, E., & Hoebel, E. A. (1952). *The Comanches.* Norman: University of Oklahoma Press.

those of the Comanche back in their ancestral homeland. This kind of development of similar cultural adaptations to similar environmental conditions by peoples whose ancestral cultures were quite different is called **convergent evolution.** Especially interesting is that the Cheyenne switch was from a crop cultivation to a food-foraging way of life. Contrary to Western notions of "progress," change in subsistence practices does not inevitably go from dependence on wild food to farming; it may go the other way as well.

Somewhat similar to the phenomenon of convergent evolution is **parallel evolution,** the difference being that similar adaptations are achieved by peoples whose ancestral cultures were already somewhat alike. For example, the development of farming in Southwest Asia and Mesoamerica took place independently, as people in both places, whose ways of life were already comparable, went on to become dependant on a narrow range of plant foods that depended upon human intervention for their protection and reproductive success.

Saying that a society is stable is not to say it is changeless. Descendants of people who maintained a stable way of life for 5000 years, Western Abenakis nevertheless incorporated new elements into their culture, including longhouses such as the one here. Today, 400 years after first contact with Europeans, Abenaki houses are like those of European Americans, but many traditional values and practices endure.

It is important to recognize that stability as well as change is involved in evolutionary adaptation and that once a satisfactory adaptation is achieved, too much in the way of change may cause it to break down. Thus, episodes of major change may be followed by long periods of relative stability. For example, by 3500 B.C., a way of life had evolved in northwestern New England and southern Quebec that was well attuned to the environmental conditions of the times.[3] Since those conditions remained more or less stable over the next 5,000 years or so, it is understandable that people's life ways remained so as well. This is not to say that change was entirely absent, for it was not. (*Stable* does not mean static.) Periodically, people refined and enhanced their way of life—for example, improving hunting methods by replacing spears used with spear throwers with bows and arrows; improving cooking by substituting pottery vessels for containers made from animal hide, wood, or bark; improving transport by replacing heavy and cumbersome dugouts with sturdy yet lightweight birchbark canoes; and supplementing the products of hunting, gathering, and fishing with limited cultivation of corn, beans, and squash. In spite of these changes, however, the native peoples of the region still retained the basic structure of their culture and tended toward a balance with their resource base well into the 17th century, when the culture had to adjust to pressures associated with European invasions of North America. Such long-term stability by no means implies "stagnation," "backwardness," or "failure to progress"; rather, it is indicative of success. Had this culture not effectively satisfied people's physical and psychological needs, it never would have endured as it did for thousands of years.

[3] Haviland, W. A., & Power, M. W. (1994). *The original Vermonters* (revised and expanded ed.). Hanover, NH: University Press of New England.

Culture Areas

The indigenous **culture area** of the Great Plains (Figure 17.1) was a geographic region where a number of societies with similar ways of life existed. Thirty-one politically independent peoples (of which the aforementioned Cheyenne and Comanche were but two) faced a common

Convergent evolution. In cultural evolution, the development of similar adaptations to similar environmental conditions by peoples whose ancestral cultures were quite different. • **Parallel evolution.** In cultural evolution, the development of similar adaptations to similar environmental conditions by peoples whose ancestral cultures were similar. • **Culture area.** A geographic region in which a number of different societies follow similar patterns of life.

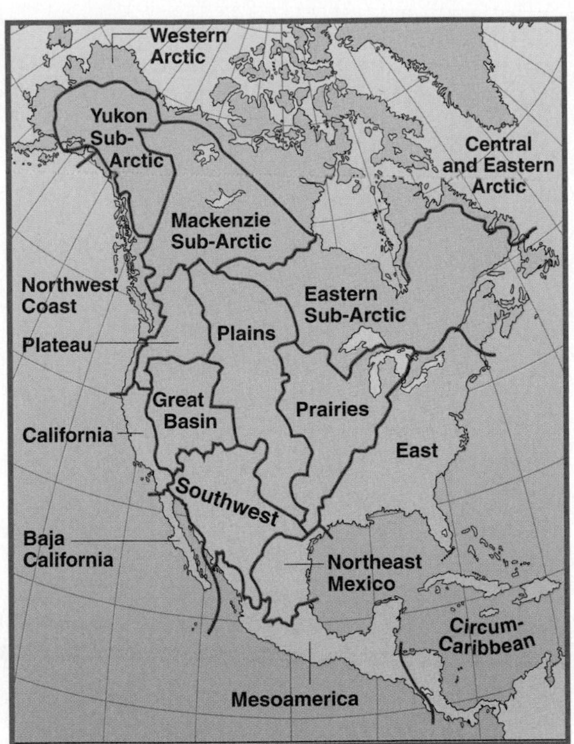

FIGURE 17.1

THE CULTURE-AREA CONCEPT WAS DEVELOPED BY NORTH AMERICAN ANTHROPOLOGISTS IN THE EARLY PART OF THE 20TH CENTURY. THIS MAP SHOWS THE CULTURE AREAS THAT HAVE BEEN DEFINED FOR NORTH AND CENTRAL AMERICA. WITHIN EACH, THERE IS AN OVERALL SIMILARITY OF NATIVE CULTURES, AS OPPOSED TO THE DIFFERENCES THAT DISTINGUISH THE CULTURES OF ONE AREA FROM THOSE OF ALL OTHERS.

environment, in which the buffalo was an obvious and practical source of food and materials for clothing and shelter. Living close by each other, they were able to share new inventions and discoveries. They reached a common and shared adaptation to a particular ecological zone.

The Indians of the Great Plains were, at the time of contact with Europeans, invariably buffalo hunters, dependent upon this animal for food, clothing, shelter, and bone tools. Each nation was organized into a number of warrior societies, and prestige came from hunting and fighting skills. Their villages were typically arranged in a distinctive circular pattern. Many religious rituals, such as the Sun Dance, were practiced throughout the Plains region.

Sometimes geographic regions are not uniform in climate and landscape, so new discoveries do not always spread from one group to another. Moreover, within a culture area, there are variations between local environments, and these favor variations in adaptation. The Great Basin of the western United States—an area embracing the states of Nevada and Utah, with adjacent portions of California, Oregon, Wyoming, and Idaho—is a case in point.[4] The Great Basin Shoshone Indians were divided into a northern and a western group, both primarily nomadic hunters and gatherers. In the north, a relative abundance of game animals provided for the maintenance of large populations, requiring a great deal of cooperation among local groups. The western Shoshone, by contrast, were almost entirely dependent upon the gathering of wild plants for their subsistence, and as these varied considerably in their seasonal and local availability, the western Shoshone were forced to cover vast distances in search of food. Under such conditions, it was most efficient to travel in groups of but a few families, only occasionally coming together with other groups, and not always with the same ones.

The Shoshone were not the only inhabitants of the Great Basin. To the south lived the closely related Paiutes. They, too, were hunter-gatherers living under the same environmental conditions as the Shoshone, but the Paiutes managed their food resources more actively by diverting small streams to irrigate wild crops. They did not plant and cultivate these, but they were able to secure higher yields than their northern neighbors. Hence, their populations were larger than those of the Shoshone, and they led a less nomadic existence.

To deal with variations within a given region, anthropologist Julian Steward proposed the concept of **culture type,** which refers to a collection of elements in a culture that generally occurs cross-culturally, and concerns a particular technology and its relationship with those environmental features that technology is equipped to deal with.

The example of the Great Plains shows how technology helps decide just which environmental features will be useful. The same grasslands that once supported buffalo hunters now support cattle ranchers and grain

[4] Steward, J. H. (1972). *Theory of culture change: The methodology of multilinear evolution.* Urbana: University of Illinois Press.

Culture type. The view of a culture in terms of the relation of its particular technology to the environment exploited by that technology.

JULIAN H. STEWARD (1902–1972)

North American anthropologist Julian H. Steward developed an approach he called **cultural ecology**—that is, the interaction of specific cultures with their environments. Initially, Steward was struck by a number of similarities in the development of urban civilizations in both Peru and Mesoamerica and noted that certain developments were paralleled in the ancient urban civilizations of the Old World. He identified the constants and abstracted from this his laws of cultural development. Steward proposed three fundamental procedures for cultural ecology:

1. The interrelationship of a culture's technology and its environment must be analyzed. How effectively does the culture take advantage of available resources to provide food and housing for its people?
2. The patterns of behavior associated with a culture's technology must be analyzed. How do members of the culture perform the work necessary for their survival?
3. The relation between those behavior patterns and the rest of the cultural system must be determined. How does the work people do to survive affect their attitudes and outlooks? How is their survival behavior linked to their social activities and their personal relationships?

farmers. The Indians were prevented from farming not for environmental reasons, nor for lack of knowledge about farming, since some of them, like the Cheyenne, had raised crops before they moved on to the Plains. They did not farm because the buffalo herds provided abundant food without farming, and because farming would have been difficult without deep wells, irrigation, and the steel-tipped plow that was needed to break up the compact prairie sod. The farming potential of the Great Plains was simply not a relevant feature of the environment, given the available resources and technology before Europeans arrived.

Culture Core

Environment and technology are not the only factors that determine a society's way of subsistence; social and political organization also affect the application of technology to the problem of staying alive. In order to understand the rise of irrigation agriculture in the great centers of ancient civilization, such as China, Mesopotamia, Mesoamerica and the Central Andes, it is important to note not only the technological and environmental factors that made the building of large-scale irrigation works possible but also the social and political organization that made it possible to mobilize the many workers necessary to build and maintain the systems. One must examine the monarchies and priesthoods that organized the work and decided where the water would be used and how the agricultural products of this collective venture would be distributed.

The cultural features that play a part in the society's way of making its living are called its **culture core.** This includes the society's productive techniques and knowledge of available resources. It encompasses the patterns of labor involved in applying those techniques to the local environment. For example, do people work every day for a fixed number of hours, or is most work concentrated during certain times of the year? The culture core configures other aspects of culture that bear on the production and distribution of food. Examples of the way ideology can indirectly affect subsistence can be seen in a number of cultures where religion may lead to failure to utilize both locally available and nutritionally valuable foods. One example is the taboo of the Tutchone, a people native to the Yukon territory of northwestern Canada, against eating otters, young ravens, or crows, even though their meat is perfectly edible. In their northern forest

Culture core. The features of a culture that play a part in matters relating to the society's way of making a living. • **Cultural ecology.** The study of the interaction of specific human cultures with their environment.

In Bali, gatherings for rituals at water temples allowed farmers to arrange schedules for flooding their rice paddies.

homeland, seasonal food shortages are always a threat, but even when faced with famine, the Tutchone adhere to their taboo. Instead of eating these animals, they resort to techniques such as finding an area previously used by mice and lighting a fire over it to melt the frozen soil, providing access to bare roots previously stored by the mice.[5]

A number of anthropologists, known as **ethnoscientists,** are actively attempting to understand the principles behind native idea systems and the ways those principles inform a people about their environment and keep them alive. On the Indonesian island of Bali, for example, ritual meetings were held regularly at water temples, located at the forks of rivers, to negotiate seasonal schedules for flooding the farmers' paddies. When the Indonesian government forced abandonment of this system in an effort to promote more productive growing techniques, disaster ensued. Without the water temple rituals, there was little coordination of irrigation, water shortages and pest infestation became the norm. Under the indigenous system, everyone got more rice with less variation in harvest, so there was no reason for people to be envious of their neighbors.[6] Because it worked better, the old system has been restored. The point of this example is that cultural beliefs, no matter how irrelevant they may seem to outsiders, are anything but irrelevant if one is to understand another society's subsistence practices.

[5] Legros, D. (1997). Comment. *Current Anthropology, 38,* 617.

[6] Fountain, H. (2000). Now the ancient ways are less mysterious. *New York Times,* January 30, News of the Week, p. 5.

THE FOOD-FORAGING WAY OF LIFE

At the present time, perhaps a quarter of a million people—less then 0.00005% of a world population of about 6 billion—support themselves chiefly through hunting, fishing, and the gathering of wild plant foods. Yet, before the domestication of plants and animals, which began a mere 10,000 years ago, all people supported themselves through some combination of wild plant collection, hunting, and fishing. Of all the people who have *ever* lived, most have been food foragers, and it was as food foragers that we became truly human, acquiring the basic habits of dealing with one another and with the world around us that still guide the behavior of individuals, communities, and nations. Thus, if we would know who we are and how we came to be, if we would understand the relationship between environment and culture, and if we want to comprehend the institutions of the food-producing societies that have arisen since the development of farming and animal husbandry, we should turn first to the oldest and most universal of fully human lifestyles, the food-foraging adaptation. The beginnings of this were examined in Chapter 4.

When food foragers had the world to themselves, as they did up to 10,000 years ago, they had their pick of the best environments. These long since have been appropriated by farming and, more recently, by industrial societies. Today, most food foragers are to be found only in the world's marginal areas—frozen Arctic tundra, deserts, and inaccessible forests. These habitats, although they may not support large or dense agricultural societies, provide a good living for food-foraging peoples.

Until recently it was assumed that a food-foraging life in these areas was difficult and that one had to work hard just to stay alive. Behind this view lies the Western notion of progress, which, although widely accepted as a fact of nature, is actually nothing more than a culturally conditioned bias. This predisposes us to see what is new as generally preferable to what is old, and to read human history as a more or less steady climb up an evolutionary ladder of progress. Thus, if food foraging as a way of life is much older than industrial civilization (as it is), the latter must be intrinsically better than the former. Hence, food-foraging societies are referred to as "primitive," "backward," or "undeveloped," labels economists, politicians, and other members of industrial or would-be industrial societies use to express their disapproval. In

Ethnoscientists. Anthropologists who seek to understand the principles behind native idea systems and the ways those principles inform a people about their environment and help them survive.

HIGHWAY 1
United Nations Food & Agriculture Organization
http://www.fao.org/gender

HIGHWAY 2
Women's World Summit Foundation
http://www.woman.ch

HIGHWAY 3
Mesa Community College Anthropology Program
http://www.mc.maricopa.edu/~reffland/anthropology

reality, food-foraging societies are very highly developed, but in ways quite different from industrial societies.

Detailed studies have revealed that life in food-foraging societies is far from being "solitary, poor, nasty, brutish, and short," as the philosopher Thomas Hobbes asserted about 350 years ago. Rather, food foragers' diets are well balanced and ample, and these people are less likely to experience severe famine than are farmers. While their material possessions are limited, so are their desires. On the other hand, they have plenty of leisure time for concentrating on family ties, social life, and spiritual development. The Ju/'hoansi, a Bushman people of southern Africa's Kalahari Desert (see Chapter 16)—scarcely what one would call a "lush" environment—obtain a diet in an average workweek of about 20 hours that surpasses internationally recommended levels of nutrients. If one adds to this the time spent making and repairing equipment, the total rises to just over 23 hours, while the equivalent of our "housework" adds another 19 hours. The grand total, just over 42 hours (44.5 for men, 40.1 for women), is still less than the time spent on the job (currently 41 hours for manufacturing jobs, just under 44 hours for "white-collar" jobs), on maintenance tasks, and housework in North America today.[7] Their lives are rich in human warmth and aesthetic experience, displaying a balance of work and love, ritual, and play that many of us might envy. Small wonder that some anthropologists have gone so far as to label this "the original affluent society." The Ju/'hoansi are not exceptional among food foragers today; one can only wonder about the level of affluence their ancient counterparts who lived in lusher environments achieved with more secure and plentiful supplies of food.

All modern food foragers have had some degree of interaction with neighbors whose ways of life often differ radically from their own. Bushman people such as the Ju/'hoansi, for example, have interacted for at least 2,000 years with Bantu-speaking farmers who kept cattle and sheep. Likewise, the food-foraging Mbuti of the Republic of Congo's Ituri rain forest live in a complex dependency relationship with their neighbors, Bantu- and Sudanic-speaking peoples who are farmers. They exchange meat and other products of the forest for farm produce and manufactured goods. During part of the year, they live in their patron's village and are incorporated into his kin group, even to the point of allowing him to initiate their sons.

Although some contemporary food foragers, such as the Mbuti, have continued to maintain traditional ways while adapting to neighbors and traders, various other groups have turned to this way of life after giving up other modes of subsistence. Some, like the Cheyenne of the Great Plains, were once crop cultivators, while others,

[7] Cashdan, E. (1989). Hunters and gatherers: Economic behavior in bands. In S. Plattner (Ed.). *Economic anthropology* (pp. 23–24). Stanford, CA: Stanford University Press.

Human groups (including food foragers) do not exist in isolation except occasionally, and even then not for long. The bicycle this Bushman of southern Africa is riding is indicative of his links with the wider world. For 2,000 years, Bushmen have been interacting regularly with farmers and pastoralists, and much of the ivory used for the pianos so widely sought in 19th-century North America came from the Bushmen.

such as some of the Bushmen of southern Africa, have at times been farmers and at others pastoral nomads. Nor are such transformations things of the past. In the 1980s, when a world economic recession led to the abandonment of many sheep stations in the Australian outback, a number of Aboriginal peoples returned to food foraging, thereby freeing themselves from a dependency on the government into which they had been forced.

An important point that emerges from the preceding discussion is this: People in the world today who subsist by hunting, fishing, and wild plant collection are not following an ancient way of life because they do not know any better; they are doing it either because they have been forced by circumstances into a situation where foraging is the best means of survival or because they simply prefer to live this way. In many cases, they find such satisfaction in living the way they do that, like the Hadza of northern Tanzania, they go to great lengths to avoid adopting other ways of life.[8] The fact is, foraging constitutes a rational response to particular ecological, economic, and sociopolitical realities. Moreover, for at least 2,000 years, a need has existed for specialized market hunters, fishers, and gatherers to supply commodities such as furs, hides, ivory, feathers, fish, pearls, honey, and bird's nests (for Chinese bird's nest soup) that have helped feed east-west trade since ancient times.[9] Like everyone else, food foragers are part of a larger world system.

Characteristics of the Food-Foraging Life

Food foragers are by definition people who do not farm or practice animal husbandry. Hence, they must seek to fit their places of residence to naturally available food sources. Thus, it is no wonder they move about a great deal. Such movement is not aimless wandering but is done within a fixed territory or home range. Some groups, such as the Ju/'hoansi, who depend on the reliable and highly drought-resistant Mongongo nut, may keep to fairly fixed annual routes and cover only a restricted territory. Others, such as the Great Basin Shoshone, must cover a wider territory; their course was determined by the local availability of the erratically productive pine nut. A crucial factor in this mobility is availability of water. The distance between the food supply and water must not be so great that more energy is required to fetch water than can be obtained from the food.

Another characteristic of the food-foraging adaptation is the small size of local groups, which usually include fewer than 100 people. Although no completely satisfactory explanation of group size has yet been of-

[8] Hawkes, K., O'Connell, J. F., & Blurton Jones, N. G. (1997). Hadza women's time allocation, offspring provisioning, and the evolution of long postmenopausal life spans. *Current Anthropology, 38,* 552.

[9] Stiles, D. (1992). The hunter–gatherer 'revisionist' debate. *Anthropology Today, 8* (2), 15.

Food foraging has by no means disappeared, even in industrial societies such as that of the United States. Some do it occasionally for pleasure, as the author is shown doing—gathering wild blueberries. Some, such as commercial fishers, forage full-time, as do many homeless people in order to survive.

fered, it seems certain that both ecological and social factors are involved. Among those suggested are the **carrying capacity** of the land, or the number of people whom the available resources can support at a given level of food-getting techniques, and the **density of social relations,** or roughly the number and intensity of interactions among camp members. More people means a higher social density, which, in turn, means more opportunities for conflict.

Both carrying capacity and social density are complex variables. Carrying capacity involves not only the immediate presence of food and water but also the tools and work necessary to secure them, as well as short- and long-term fluctuations in their availability. Social density involves not only the number of people and their interactions but also the circumstances and quality of those interactions as well as the mechanisms for regulating them. A mob of a hundred angry strangers has a different social density than the same number of neighbors enjoying themselves at a block party.

Among food-foraging populations, social density always seems in a state of flux as people spend more or less time away from camp and as they move to other camps, either on visits or more permanently. Among the Ju/'hoansi, for example, exhaustion of local food resources, conflict within the group, or the desire to visit friends or relatives living elsewhere cause people to leave one group for another. As Canadian anthropologist Richard Lee notes: "Ju love to go visiting, and the practice acts as a safety valve when tempers get frayed. In fact, the Ju usually move, not when their food is exhausted, but rather when only their patience is exhausted."[10] If a camp has so many children as to create a burden for the working adults, some young families may be encouraged to join others where fewer children live. Conversely, groups with few children may actively recruit families with young children in order to ensure the group's survival. Redistribution of people, then, is an important mechanism for regulating social density, as well as for assuring that the size and composition of local groups is suited to local variations in resources. Thus, cultural adaptations help transcend the limitations of the physical environment.

[10] Lee, R. (1993). *The Dobe Ju/'hoansi* (p. 65). Fort Worth: Harcourt Brace.

Carrying capacity. The number of people who can be supported by the available resources at a given level of technology. • **Density of social relations.** Roughly, the number and intensity of interactions among the members of a camp or other residential unit.

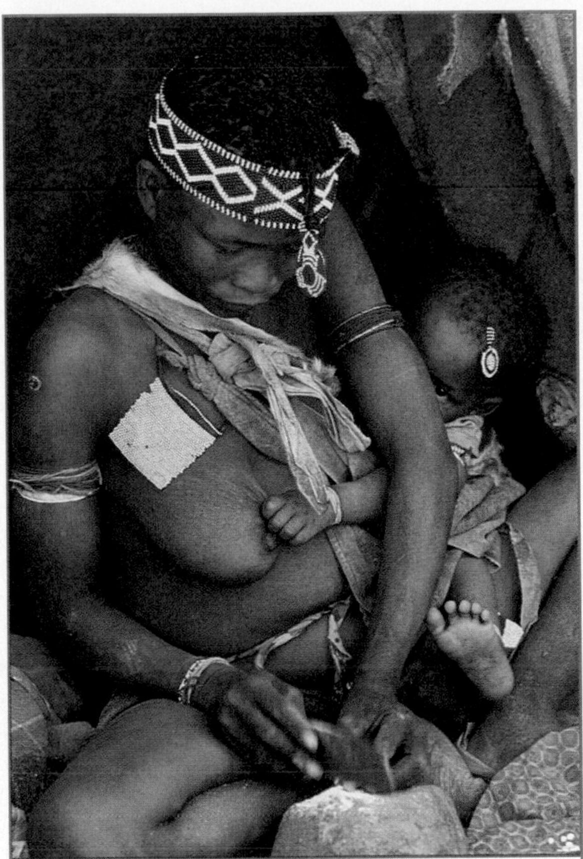

Frequent nursing of children over as many as four or five years acts to suppress ovulation among food foragers such as Bushmen. As a consequence, women give birth to relatively few offspring at widely spaced intervals.

In addition to seasonal or local adjustments, food foragers must make long-term adjustments to resources. Most food-foraging populations seem to stabilize at numbers well below the carrying capacity of their land. In fact, the home ranges of most food foragers could support from three to five times as many people as they typically do. In the long run, it may be more adaptive for a group to keep its numbers low rather than to expand indefinitely and risk destruction by a sudden and unexpected natural reduction in food resources. The population density of foraging groups surviving in marginal environments today rarely exceeds one person per square mile, a very low density, even though their resources could support greater numbers.

How food-foraging peoples regulate population size relates to two things: how much body fat they accumulate, and how they care for their children. Ovulation requires a certain minimum of body fat, and in traditional foraging societies, this is not achieved until early adulthood. Hence, female fertility peaks between the early and mid-twenties, and teenage pregnancies—at least, successful ones—are virtually unknown.[11] Once a child is born, its mother nurses it several times each hour, even at night, and this continues over a period of as many as 4 or 5 years. The constant stimulation of the mother's nipple suppresses the level of hormones that promote ovulation, making conception unlikely, especially if work keeps the mother physically active and she does not have a large store of body fat to draw on for energy.[12] By continuing to nurse for several years, women give birth only at widely spaced intervals. Thus, the total number of offspring remains low, but sufficient to maintain stable population size.

The Impact of Food Foraging on Human Society

Although much has been written on the theoretical importance of hunting for shaping the supposedly competitive and aggressive nature of the human species, most anthropologists are unconvinced by these arguments. To be sure, warlike behavior on the part of food-foraging people is known, but such behavior is a relatively recent phenomenon in response to pressure from expansionist states (see Chapter 23). In the absence of such pressures, food-foraging peoples are remarkably unaggressive and place more emphasis on peaceableness and cooperation than they do on competition. It does seem likely, however, that three crucial elements of human social organization developed with food foraging. The first of these is the division of labor by gender. Some form of this, however modified, has been observed in all human societies, and is probably as old as human culture (see Chapter 4). Western society is now moving away from such division, as we shall see in the next chapter, and one may ask what the implications are for future cooperative relationships between men and women. We will discuss this issue further in Chapters 19 and 20.

SUBSISTENCE AND GENDER

The hunting and butchering of large game as well as the processing of hard or tough raw materials are almost universally masculine occupations. Women's work, by contrast, usually consists of gathering and processing a

[11] Hrdy, S. B. (1999). Body fat and birth control. *Natural History, 108* (8), 88.

[12] Small, M. F. (1997). Making connections. *American Scientist, 85,* 503.

variety of vegetal foods, as well as other domestic chores. Historically, this pattern appears to have its origin in an earlier era, in which males, who were twice the size of females, got meat by scavenging from the carcasses of dead animals, butchered it with stone tools, and shared it with females (see Chapter 4). The latter, for their part, gathered wild plant foods, probably using digging sticks and carrying devices made of soft, perishable materials. As the hunting of live animals replaced scavenging as a source of meat and the biological differences between the sexes were reduced to minor proportions, the essence of the original division of labor was maintained nonetheless.

Among food foragers today, the work of women is no less arduous than that of men. Ju/'hoansi women, for example, may walk as many as 12 miles a day two or three times a week to gather food, carrying not only their children but also, on the return home, anywhere from 15 to 33 pounds of food. Still, they don't have to travel quite so far afield as do men on the hunt, nor is their work usually quite so dangerous. Finally, their tasks require less rapid mobility, do not need complete and undivided attention, and are readily resumed after interruption. All of this is compatible with those biological differences that remain between the sexes. Certainly women who are pregnant, or have infants to nurse, cannot as easily travel long distances in pursuit of game as can men. In addition to wide-ranging mobility, the successful hunter must also be able to mobilize rapidly high bursts of energy. Although some women can certainly run faster than some men, it is a fact that in general men can run faster than women, even when the latter are not pregnant or encumbered with infants. Because human females must be able to give birth to infants with relatively large heads, their pelvic structure differs from that of human males to a greater degree than it does among most other species of mammals. As a consequence, the human female is not as well equipped as is the human male for rapid and prolonged mobility.

To say that differing gender roles among food foragers are compatible with the biological differences between men and women is *not* to say that they are biologically determined. Among the Great Plains Indians of North America, for example, are numerous reported cases of women who gained fame as hunters and warriors, both regarded as men's activities. There is even one case of an Atsina girl captured by the Absaroke (Crow) who became one of their chiefs, so accomplished was she at what were considered to be masculine pursuits. Conversely, any young man who found masculine pursuits uncomfortable could assume the dress and demeanor of women, providing he had the necessary skills to achieve success in feminine activities. Although sexual preference might enter into the decision to assume a feminine identity, not all such individuals were homosexuals, nor did all homosexuals assume a woman's role. Clearly, sexual preference was of lesser importance than occupation and appearance. In fact, the division of labor by gender is often far less rigid among food foragers than it is in most other types of society. Thus, Ju/'hoansi men, willingly and without embarrassment, as the occasion demands, will gather wild plant foods, build huts, and collect water, even though all are regarded as women's work.

The nature of women's work in food-foraging societies is such that it can be done while taking care of children. They also can do it in company with other women, which helps alleviate somewhat the monotony of the work. In the past, the gender biases of their culture caused European and North American anthropologists to underestimate the contribution the food-gathering activities of women made to the survival of their group. We now know that modern food foragers may obtain up to 60 or 70% of their diets from plant foods, with perhaps some fish and shellfish provided by women (the exceptions tend to be food foragers living in the far north, where plant foods are not available for much of the year).

Although women in food-foraging societies may spend some time each day gathering plant food, men do not spend all or even the greatest part of their time hunting. The amount of energy expended in hunting, especially in hot climates, is often greater than the energy return from the kill. Too much time spent searching out game might actually be counterproductive. Energy itself is derived primarily from plant carbohydrates, and it is usually the female gatherer who brings in the bulk of the calories. A certain amount of meat in the diet, though, guarantees high-quality protein that is less easily obtained from plant sources, for meat contains exactly the right balance of all of the amino acids (the building blocks of protein) the human body requires. No one plant food does this, and in order to get by without meat, people must hit on exactly the right combination of plants to provide the essential amino acids in the correct proportions.

FOOD SHARING

A second key feature of human social organization associated with food foraging is the sharing of food between adults, something that is quite rare among nonhuman primates. It is easy enough to see why sharing takes place, with women supplying one kind of food and men another. Among the Ju/'hoansi, women have control over the food they collect and can share it with whomever they choose.

Food foragers like the Ju/'hoansi have a division of labor in which women gather and prepare "bush" food (here an ostrich egg omelette), but hunting is usually done by men.

Men, by contrast, are constrained by rules that specify how much meat is to be distributed and to whom. Thus, a hunter has little effective control over the meat he brings into camp. For the individual hunter, meat sharing is really a way of storing it for the future; his generosity, obligatory though it might be, gives him a claim on the future kills of other hunters. As a cultural trait, food sharing has the obvious survival value of distributing resources needed for subsistence.

Although carnivorous animals often share food, the few examples of food sharing among nonhuman primate adults mostly involve groups of male chimpanzees cooperating in a hunt and later sharing the spoils, frequently with adult females as well as juveniles. This suggests that the origins of food sharing and the division of labor are related to a shift in food habits from infrequent to more frequent meat eating. This seems to have occurred with the appearance of the earliest members of the genus *Homo* some 2.5 million years ago.

A final distinctive feature of the food-foraging economy is the importance of the camp as the center of daily activity and the place where food sharing actually occurs. Among nonhuman primates, and probably among human ancestors until they controlled the use of fire, activities tend to be divided between feeding areas and sleeping areas, and the latter tend to be shifted each evening. Historically known food-foraging people, however, live in camps of some permanence, ranging from the dry-season camps of the Ju/'hoansi that serve for the entire winter to the wet-season camps of the Hadza, oriented to berry picking and honey collection, that serve for a few weeks at most. Moreover, human camps are more than sleeping areas; people are in and out all day, eating, working, and socializing in camps to a greater extent than any other primates.

CULTURAL ADAPTATIONS AND MATERIAL TECHNOLOGY

The mobility of food-foraging groups may depend on the availability of water, as among the Ju/'hoansi; of pine nuts, as in the Shoshone example; or of game animals and other seasonal resources, as among the Hadza. Hunting styles and equipment may also play a role in determining population size and movement. Some Mbuti hunt big game with large nets. This requires the cooperation of 7 to 30 families; consequently, their camps are relatively large. On the other hand, the camps of those Mbuti who hunt with bow and arrow number from 3 to 6 families. Too many archers in the same locale means that each must travel a great distance daily to keep out of another's way. Only during midsummer do the archers collect into larger camps for religious ceremonies, matrimonial arrangements, and social exchange. At this time the bowmen turn to communal beat-hunts. Without nets they are less effective than their neighbors, and it is only when the net hunters are widely dispersed in the pursuit of honey (rather than meat) that the archers can come together.

EGALITARIAN SOCIETY

An important characteristic of the food-foraging society is its egalitarianism. Food foragers are usually highly mobile, and, lacking animal or mechanical transportation, they must be able to travel without many encumbrances, especially on food-getting expeditions. The average weight of an individual's personal belongings among the Ju/'hoansi, for example, is just under 25 pounds. The material goods of food foragers must be limited to the barest essentials, which include implements for hunting, gathering, fishing, building, and making tools, cooking utensils, traps, and nets. They have little chance to accumulate luxuries or surplus goods, and the fact that no one owns significantly more than another helps to limit status differences. Age and sex are usually the only sources of important status differences.

It is important to realize that status differences by themselves do not imply any necessary inequality, a point that is all too easily misunderstood, especially where relations between men and women are concerned. In traditional food-foraging societies, nothing necessitated special deference of women to men. To be sure, women may be excluded from some rituals males participate in, but the reverse is also true. Moreover, the fruits of women's labor are not controlled by men but by the women themselves. Nor do women sacrifice their autonomy even in societies in which male hunting, rather than female gathering, brings in the bulk of the food. Such was the case, for example, among the Innu Indians of Labrador. Theirs was a society in which the hunt was of overwhelming importance. For their part, women manufactured clothing and other necessities but provided much less of the food than is common among food foragers. Until recently, women as well as men could be shamans. Nevertheless, women were excluded from ritual feasts having to do with hunting, but then, so were men excluded from ritual feasts held by women. Basically, each gender carried out its own activities, with neither meddling in those of the other. Early missionaries to the Innu hunting bands lamented that men had no inclination to make their wives obey them and worked long and hard to convince the Indians that civilization required men to impose their authority on women. But after 300 years of trying, they still have achieved only limited success.

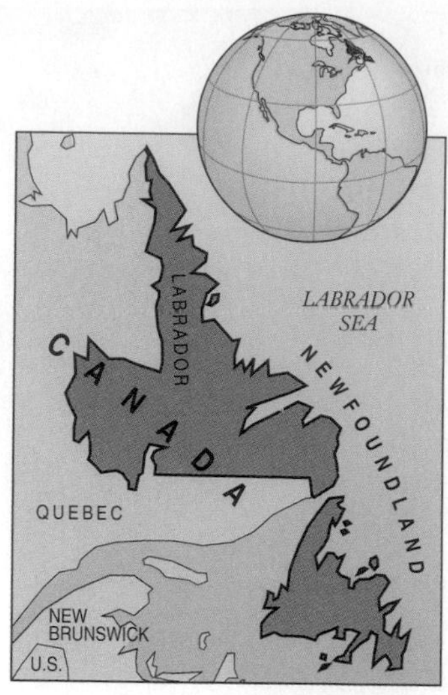

Food foragers make no attempt to accumulate surplus foodstuffs, often an important source of status in agrarian societies. This does not mean, however, they live constantly on the verge of starvation. Their environment is their natural storehouse, and, except in the coldest climates (where a surplus must be stored to see people through the lean season), or in times of acute ecological disaster, some food is always to be found in a group's territory. Because food resources are typically distributed equally throughout the group (share and share alike is the order of the day), no one achieves the wealth or status that hoarding might bring. In such a society, wealth is a sign of deviance rather than a desirable characteristic.

The food forager's concept of territory contributes as much to social equality as it does to the equal distribution of resources. Most groups have home ranges within which access to resources is open to all members: What is available to one is available to all. If a Mbuti hunter discovers a honey tree, he has first rights; but when he has taken his share, others have a turn. In the unlikely possibility that he does not take advantage of his discovery, others will. No individual within the community privately owns the tree; the system is first come, first served. Therefore, knowledge of the existence of food resources circulates quickly throughout the entire group.

Families move easily from one group to another, settling in any group where they have a previous kinship tie. (Although the idea of food foragers being patrilocal—that is, a wife moving to her husband's group—is still held by some, as discussed in Chapter 1, this represents a historic response to European exploration and colonization.) As noted earlier, the composition of groups among food foragers is always shifting. This loose attitude toward group membership promotes the widest access to resources while maintaining a balance between populations and resources.

The food-forager pattern of generalized exchange, or sharing without any expectation of a direct return, also serves the ends of resource distribution and social equality. A Ju/'hoansi man or woman spends as much as two thirds of his or her day visiting others or receiving guests; during this time, many exchanges of gifts take place. Refusing to share—hoarding—would be morally wrong. By sharing whatever is at hand, the Ju/'hoansi achieve social leveling and assure their right to share in the others' windfalls.

FOOD-PRODUCING SOCIETY

As we saw in Chapter 4, it was toolmaking that allowed humans to consume significant amounts of meat as well as plant foods. The next truly momentous event in human history was the domestication of plants and animals (Figure 17.2). The transition from food forager to food producer (the available evidence suggests this change began 9,000 to 11,000 years ago) has been termed revolutionary. By changing the way they provided for their subsistence, people changed the very nature of human society.

Just why this change came about is one of the important questions in anthropology. Since food production by and large requires more work than food foraging, is more monotonous, is often a less secure means of subsistence, and requires people to eat more of the foods that foragers eat only when they have no other choice, it is unlikely that people voluntarily became food producers. Initially, it appears that food production arose as a largely unintended by-product of existing food-management practices. By chance, these promoted the development of new varieties of particular plants and animals, which came to take on increasing importance for people's subsistence. Later on, many populations adopted farming out of necessity in situations where population growth outstripped people's ability to sustain themselves through food foraging. For them, food production became a subsistence option of last resort.

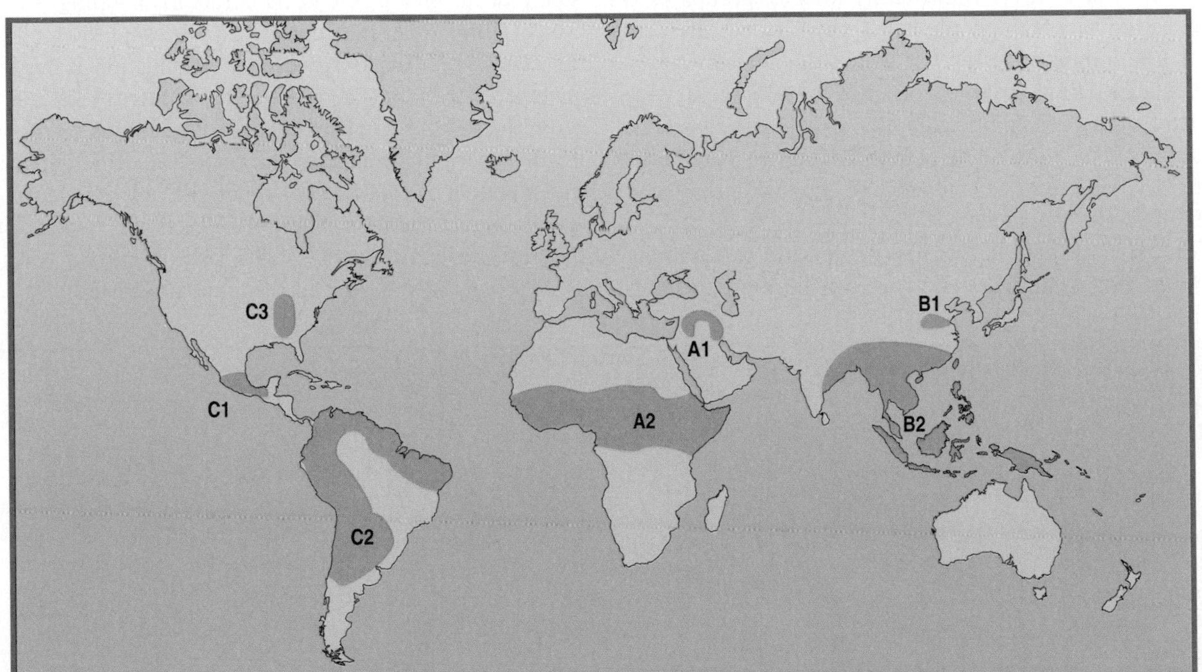

FIGURE 17.2
EARLY PLANT AND ANIMAL DOMESTICATION OCCURRED IN SUCH WIDELY SCATTERED PLACES AS SOUTHWEST ASIA (A1), CENTRAL AFRICA (A2), CHINA (B1), SOUTHEAST ASIA (B2), MESOAMERICA (C1), SOUTH AMERICA (C2), AND EASTERN NORTH AMERICA (C3).

The Settled Life of Farmers

While it supports larger and more sedentary populations than food foraging, farming generally requires longer and more monotonous work.

Whatever the causes, one of the most significant correlates of this new way of life was the development of permanent settlements, in which families of farmers lived together. As food foragers stay close to their food by moving around, farmers stay close to their food by staying near their gardens. The task of food production lent itself to a different kind of social organization; the hard work of some members of the group could provide food for all, thus freeing some people to devote their time to inventing and manufacturing the equipment needed for a new sedentary way of life. Harvesting and digging tools, pottery for storage and cooking, clothing made of woven textiles, and housing made of stone, wood, or sun-dried bricks were some of the results of this combination of new sedentary living conditions and altered division of labor.

The transition also brought important changes in social structure. At first, social relations were egalitarian and hardly different from those that prevailed among food foragers. As settlements grew, however, and large numbers of people began to share the same important resources, such as land and water, society became more elaborately structured. Multifamily kinship groups such as lineages, to which people belong by virtue of descent from a common ancestor but which do not commonly play a large part in the social order of food foragers, were probably the organizing units. As will be discussed in Chapter 21, they provide a convenient way to handle the distinctive problems of land use and ownership that arise in food-producing societies.

Humans adapted to this new settled life in a number of ways. For example, some societies became horticultural—small communities of gardeners working with simple hand tools and using neither irrigation nor the plow. Horticulturists typically cultivate several varieties of crops together in small gardens they have cleared by hand. Because these gardeners typically use a given garden plot for only a few years before abandoning it in favor of a new one, horticulture may be said to constitute an *extensive* form of agriculture. Production is for subsistence rather than to produce a surplus for sale; however, the politics of horticultural communities commonly involve periodic feasts, in the course of which substantial amounts of produce and other gifts are given away in order to gain prestige. Such prestige is the basis for the political power of leaders, who play important roles in production, exchange, and resource allocation.

This swidden plot in Chiapas, Mexico, shows what such gardens look like after slash has been burned but before the crops have begun to grow. Although it looks destructive, if properly carried out, swidden farming is an ecologically sound way of growing crops in the tropics.

One of the most widespread forms of horticulture, especially in the tropics, is slash-and-burn, or **swidden farming.** Unfortunately, widespread use of fire in connection with the clearing of vast tracts of Amazonian or Indonesian forest for cattle raising and other development schemes has led many people to see slash-and-burn farming in a negative light. In fact, it is an ecologically sophisticated and sustainable way of raising food, especially in the tropics, when carried out under the right conditions: low population densities and adequate amounts of land. Only when pursued in the absence of these conditions does the practice lead to environmental degradation and destruction. Properly carried out, swidden farming mimics the diversity of the natural ecosystem; moreover, growing several different crops together in the same field makes them less vulnerable to pests and plant diseases than growing single crops. Not only is the system ecologically sound, but it is far more energy efficient than farming as carried out in developed countries such as the United States, which requires the input of more energy than comes out of the system. By contrast, for every unit of energy expended, swidden farming produces between 10 and 20 units in return. A good example of how such a system works is provided by the Mekranoti Kayapo Indians of Brazil's Amazon forest.

Swidden farming. An extensive form of horticulture in which the natural vegetation is cut, the slash is subsequently burned, and crops then planted amongst the ashes.

Gardens of the Mekranoti Kayapo[13]

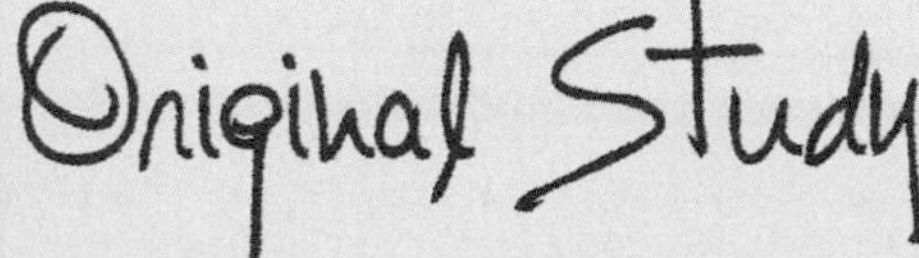

The planting of a Mekranoti garden always follows the same sequence. First, men clear the forest and then burn the debris. In the ashes, both men and women plant sweet potatoes, manioc, bananas, corn, pumpkins, papaya, sugar cane, pineapple, cotton, tobacco, and annatto, whose seeds yield achiote, the red dye used for painting ornaments and people's bodies. Since the Mekranoti don't bother with weeding, the forest gradually invades the garden. After the second year, only manioc, sweet potatoes, and bananas remain. And after three years or so there is usually nothing left but bananas. Except for a few tree species that require hundreds of years to grow, the area will look like the original forest twenty-five or thirty years later.

This gardening technique, known as slash-and-burn agriculture, is one of the most common in the world. The early European settlers in North America adopted the method from the surrounding Indians, although it had been used in an earlier period in Europe as well. At one time critics condemned the technique as wasteful and ecologically destructive, but today we know that, especially in the humid tropics, slash-and-burn agriculture may be one of the best gardening techniques possible.

Anthropologists were among the first to note the possibly disastrous consequences of U.S.-style agriculture in the tropics. Continuous high temperatures encourage the growth of the microorganisms that cause rot, so organic matter quickly

[13] Adapted from Werner, D. (1990). *Amazon journey* (pp. 105–112). Englewood Cliffs, NJ: Prentice Hall.

Original Study

breaks down into simple minerals. The heavy rains dissolve these valuable nutrients and carry them deep into the soils, out of the reach of plants. The tropical forest maintains its richness because the heavy foliage shades the earth, cooling it and inhibiting the growth of the decomposers. A good deal of the rain is captured by leaves before ever reaching the ground. When a tree falls in the forest, and begins to rot, other plants quickly absorb the nutrients that are released. With open-field agriculture, the sun heats the earth, the decomposers multiply, and the rains quickly leach the soils of their nutrients. In a few years a lush forest, if cleared for open one-crop agriculture, can be transformed into a barren wasteland.

Slash-and-burn agriculture is less of a problem than open-field agriculture. A few months after planting, banana and papaya trees shade the soil, just as the larger forest trees do. The mixing of different kinds of plants in the same area means that minerals can be absorbed as soon as they are released—corn picks up nutrients very fast, while manioc is slow. Also, the small and temporary clearings mean that the forest can quickly reinvade its lost territory.

Because decomposers need moisture as well as warmth, the long Mekranoti dry season could alter this whole picture of soil ecology. But soil samples from recently burned Mekranoti fields and the adjacent forest floor showed that, as in most of the humid tropics, the high fertility of the Indians' garden plots comes from the trees that are burned there, not from the soil, as in temperate climes.

Getting a good burn is a tricky operation. Perhaps for this reason its timing was left to the more experienced and knowledgeable members of the community. If the burn is too early, the rains will leach out the minerals in the ash before planting time. If too late, the debris will be too wet to burn properly. Then, insects and weeds that could plague the plants will not die and few minerals will be released into the soil. If the winds are too weak, the burn will not cover the entire plot. If they are too strong, the fire can get out of hand. In the past, the Mekranoti accidently burned down villages several times because of fires that spread too fast.

Ronaldo remembered an incident when a garden fire caught some of the houses in the village. Fearing the flames would spread from one rooftop to the next until the entire village circle was ablaze, the Indians ran inside their homes and gathered their belongings to set them in the center of the village plaza. In the past, this reaction made good sense. Constructions were simpler, and people had fewer belongings to lose. Since moves were frequent anyway, destroying a village in smoke was not very serious. A fire could even get rid of insect pests that infest villages after many years. But this time people were more concerned. Ronaldo finally persuaded some of the Indians to chop down some of the houses next to the burning structures and the village was saved.

Shortly after the burning of the garden plots and the clearing away of some of the charred debris, people began the long job of planting, which took up all of September and lasted into October. Tàkàkngo returned in time to help Kaxti and his wife with their garden. Although he could not walk well enough to work, Kaxti could accompany his wife, Nhàkkamro, to the garden and take care of their children, while she did most of the planting.

In the center of the circular garden plot the women dug holes and threw in a few pieces of sweet potatoes. After covering the tubers with dirt they usually asked a male—one of their husbands or anyone else who happened to be nearby—to stomp on the mound and make a ritual noise resembling a Bronx cheer. This magic would ensure a large crop, I was told. Forming a large ring around the sweet potatoes, the Indians rapidly thrust pieces of manioc stems into the ground, one after the other.

When grown, the manioc stems form a dense barrier to the sweet potato patch, and some of the plants must be cut down to gain entrance. Outside of the ring of manioc, the women plant yams, cotton, sugar cane, and annatto. Banana stalks and papaya trees, planted by simply throwing the seeds on the ground, form the outermost circle. The Indians also plant corn, pumpkins, watermelons, and pineapple throughout the garden. These grow rapidly and are harvested long before the manioc matures. The garden appears to change magically from corn and pumpkins to sweet potatoes and manioc without replanting.

Mekranoti gardens grew well. A few Indians complained now and then about a peccary that had eaten a watermelon they were looking forward to eating, or that had reduced their corn harvest. Capybara, large rodents usually found near the river banks, were known for their love of sugar cane, but in general the animals seemed to leave the crops alone. Even the leaf-cutting ants that are problems in other areas did not bother the Mekranoti. Occasionally a neighbor who had not planted a new garden would make off with a prized first-year crop, such as pumpkin, watermelon, or pineapple. But even these thefts were rare. In general, the Mekranoti could depend on harvesting whatever they planted.

Eventually, I wanted to calculate the productivity of Mekranoti gardens. Agronomists knew very little about slash-and-burn agriculture. They were accustomed to experiments in which a field was given over to one crop only, and in which the harvest happened all at once. Here, the plants were all mixed together, and people harvested piecemeal whenever they needed something. The manioc could stay in the ground, growing for several years before it was dug up.

I began measuring off areas of gardens to count how many manioc plants, ears of corn, or pumpkins were found there. The women thought it strange to see me struggling through the tangle of plants to measure off areas, 10 meters by 10 meters, placing string along the borders, and then counting what was inside. Sometimes I asked a woman to dig up all of the sweet potatoes within the marked-off area. The requests were bizarre, but the women cooperated just the same, holding on to the ends of the measuring tapes, or sending their children to help. For some plants, like bananas, I simply counted the number of clumps of stalks in the garden, and the number of banana bunches I could see growing in various clumps. By watching how long it took the bananas to grow, from the time I could see them until they were harvested, I could calculate a garden's total banana yield per year.

After returning from the field, I was able to combine the time allocation data with the garden productivities to get an idea of how hard the Mekranoti need to work to survive. The data showed that for every hour of gardening one Mekranoti adult produces almost 18,000 kilocalories of food. (As a basis for comparison, people in the United States consume approximately 3,000 kilocalories of food per day.) As insurance against bad years, and in case they receive visitors from other villages, they grow far more produce than they need. But even so, they don't need to work very hard to survive. A look at the average amount of time adults spend on different tasks every week shows just how easy going life in horticultural societies can be:

8.5 hours	Gardening
6.0 hours	Hunting
1.5 hours	Fishing
1.0 hour	Gathering wild foods
33.5 hours	All other jobs

Altogether, the Mekranoti need to work less than 51 hours a week, and this includes getting to and from work, cooking, repairing broken tools, and all of the other things we normally don't count as part of our work week.

The End

Technologically more complex than the horticulturists are intensive agriculturalists, whose practices usually result in far more modification of the landscape and the natural environment in general than do those of horticulturists. Employed are such techniques as irrigation, fertilizers, and the wooden or metal plow pulled by harnessed draft animals, or in the so-called developed countries of the world, tractors to produce food on larger plots of land. Such farmers are able to grow sufficient food to provide not just for their own needs but for those of various full-time specialists and nonproducing consumers as well. This surplus may be sold for cash, or it may be coerced out of the farmers through tribute, taxes, or rent paid to landowners. These landowners and other specialists typically reside in substantial towns or cities, where political power is centralized in the hands of a socially elite class of people. The distinction between horticulturist and intensive agriculturalist is not always an easy one to make. For example, the Hopi Indians of the North American Southwest, in addition to flood plain farming, also irrigate plots near springs, while using simple hand tools. Moreover, they produce for their own immediate needs, and live in towns without centralized political government.

As food producers, people have developed several major crop complexes: two adapted to seasonal uplands and two to tropical wetlands. In the dry uplands of Southwest Asia, for example, they time their agricultural activities with the rhythm of the changing seasons, cultivating wheat, barley, flax, rye, and millet. In the tropical wetlands of Southeast Asia, rice and tubers such as yams and taro are cultivated. In the Americas, people have adapted to environments similar to those of the Old World but have cultivated different plants. Maize, beans, squash, and the potato are typically grown in drier areas, whereas manioc is extensively grown in the tropical wetlands.

Pastoralism: The Bakhtiari

Before further discussion of agriculturalists, we should examine one of the more striking examples of human adaptation to the environment, that of the **pastoralist.** Pastoralists are people who view animal husbandry—the herding of grazing animals—as the proper way to make a living and consider movement of all or part of the society a normal and natural part of life. This cultural aspect is vitally important, for although some (but not all) pastoral nomads are dependent on nearby farmers for some of their supplies, and may even earn more from nonpastoral sources than from their own herds, the concept of nomadic pastoralism remains central to their identities. These societies are built around a pastoral economic specialization but imbued with values far beyond just doing a job. This distinguishes them from American ranchers, who likewise have a pastoral economic specialization but identify culturally with a larger society.[14] It also sets them apart from food foragers, migrant farm workers, corporate executives, or others who are nomadic but not pastoralists.

Pastoralism is an effective way of living—far more so than ranching—in places that are too dry, too cold, too steep, or too rocky for farming, such as the arid grasslands that stretch eastward from northern Africa through the Arabian Desert, across the plateau of Iran and into Turkestan and Mongolia. In Africa and Southwest Asia alone, more than 21 million people follow pastoral nomadic ways of life. One group living in this belt of arid lands is the Bakhtiari, a fiercely independent people who live in the south Zagros Mountains of western Iran, where

[14] Barfield, T. J. (1984). Introduction. *Cultural Survival Quarterly,* 8 (2).

Pastoral nomadism is an adaptation that works in many parts of the world that are too hot, too cold, or too dry for farming. In high elevations in Peru and Bolivia, the Incas and other native people relied on the herding of llamas and alpacas.

Pastoralist. Member of a society in which the herding of grazing animals is regarded as the ideal way of making a living, and in which movement of all or part of the society is considered a normal and natural way of life.

In East Africa, pastoral peoples are not dependent on farmers the way that pastoralists of the Middle East are.

they tend herds of goats and fat-tailed sheep.[15] Although some of the Bakhtiari own horses and most own donkeys, they are used only for transport; the animals these people's lives revolve around are the sheep and goat.

The harsh, bleak environment dominates the lives of the Bakhtiari: It determines when and where they move their flocks, the clothes they wear, the food they eat, and even their dispositions—they have been called "mountain bears" by Iranian townspeople. In the Zagros are snow-covered ridges that reach altitudes of 12,000 to 14,000 feet. Their steep, rocky trails and escarpments challenge the hardiest and ablest climbers; jagged peaks, deep chasms, and watercourses with thunderous torrents also make living and traveling hazardous.

The pastoral life of the Bakhtiari revolves around two seasonal migrations to find better grazing lands for the flocks. Twice a year the people move: in the fall from their summer quarters in the mountains and in the spring from their winter quarters in the lowlands. This pattern of strict seasonal movement is known as **transhumance.** In the fall, before the harsh winter comes to the mountains, the nomads load their tents and other belongings on donkeys and drive their flocks down to the warm plains that border Iraq in the west; grazing land here is excellent and well watered in the winter. In the spring, when the low-lying pastures dry up, the Bakhtiari return to the mountain valleys, where a new crop of grass is sprouting. For this trek, they split into five groups, each containing about 5,000 individuals and 50,000 animals.

The return trip north is the more dangerous because the mountain snows are melting and the gorges are full of turbulent, ice-cold water rushing down from the mountain peaks. This long trek is further burdened by the kids and lambs born in the spring, just before migration. Where the watercourses are not very deep, the nomads ford them. Deeper channels, including one river that is a half-mile wide, are crossed with the help of inflatable goatskin rafts, on which they place infants, the elderly and infirm, and lambs and kids; the rafts are then pushed by the men swimming alongside in the icy water. If they work from dawn to dusk, the nomads can get all of the people and animals across the river in 5 days. Not surprisingly, dozens of sheep are drowned each day at the river crossing.

In the mountain passes, where a biting wind numbs the skin and brings tears to the eyes, the Bakhtiari must make their way through slippery unmelted snow. Climbing the steep escarpments is dangerous, and the stronger men often must carry their own children and the newborn kids on their shoulders as they make their way over the ice and snow to the lush mountain valley that is their destination. During each migration the people may cover as many as 200 miles, and the trek can take weeks,

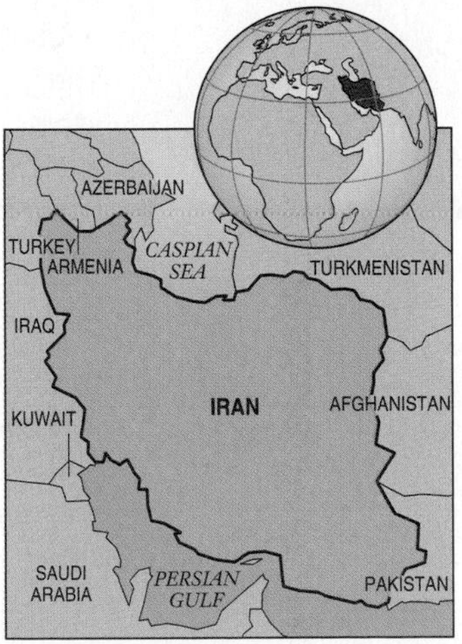

[15] Material on the Bakhtiari is drawn mainly from Barth, F. (1960). Nomadism in the mountain and plateau areas of south west Asia. *The problems of the arid zone* (pp. 341–355), UNESCO; Coon, C. S. (1958). *Caravan: The story of the Middle East* (2nd ed.) (Chapter 13). New York: Holt, Rinehart and Winston; Salzman, P. C. (1967). Political organization among nomadic peoples. *Proceedings of the American Philosophical Society, 111,* 115–131.

Transhumance. Pattern of strict seasonal movement between different environmental zones.

Anthropology Applied

Agricultural Development and the Anthropologist

As anthropologists have come to understand the traditional practices of indigenous peoples, the more they have been impressed by the soundness and sophistication of their knowledge. As this awareness has spread beyond the profession, a notion has grown popular among the public at large that indigenous groups invariably live in some sort of blissful oneness with their world. But as anthropologists know, traditional people are only human, and like all human beings, are capable of making mistakes. Yet, just as we have much to learn from their successes, so can we learn from their mistakes, as well as from how they cope with their mistakes.

Anthropologist Ann Kendall is doing just this in the Patacacha Valley in the Andes Mountains of southern Peru.* Kendall is director of the Cusichaca trust in Ballbroughton, England, a rural development project that revives ancient farming practices. Working with botanist Alex Chepstow-Lusty of Cambridge University, they have recovered evidence of intensive farming in the Patacacha Valley, beginning about 4,000 years ago. Unfortunately, the widespread clearing to establish and maintain farm plots, coupled with minimal terracing of hillsides, led to a great deal of soil loss through erosion. By 1,900 years ago degradation of soils, coupled with the onset of a cooler climate, led to a dramatic reduction in farming. Then, about 1,000 years ago, there was a sudden cessation of erosion as farming was revived, this time with soil-sparing techniques. These involved construction of a complex irrigation canal 5.8 km long to distribute water to hillside plots, along with extensive terraces to prevent erosion. To build these, soil was laboriously carried up from the valley floor and river beds. Finally, alder trees were extensively planted, both to stabilize the soil and to provide firewood as well as building materials.

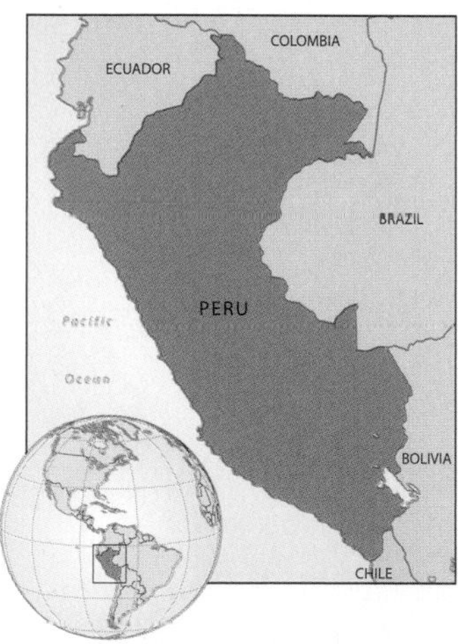

So successful was this new system of farming that the number of people living in the valley quadrupled to modern levels of about 4,000. Unfortunately, when the Spanish took over Peru, the terraces and trees here and elsewhere were allowed to deteriorate. Now, the Cusichaca trust is funding a project to excavate and rebuild the Patacancha Valley terraces using the old methods. Since 1995, local families have reconstructed the canal and replanted 160 hectares of old terraces with potatoes, corn, and wheat. They have found that the terraces produce well while requiring less fertilizer than other plots.

* Krajick, K. (1998). Green farming by the Incas? *Science, 281,* 323.

In Mongolia, pastoral production has increased dramatically following the fall of communism. Today, some 2.2 million people herd 2 million animals, and 79% of the land is under pasture—the largest common grazing land in the world.

because the flocks travel slowly and require constant attention. The nomads have fixed routes and a somewhat definite itinerary; they know about where they should be and when they should be there. On the drive the men and boys herd the sheep and goats, while the women and children along with tents and other equipment ride the donkeys.

When they reach their destination, the Bakhtiari live in black tents of goat-hair cloth woven by the women. The tents have sloping tops and vertical sides held up by wooden poles. Inside, the furnishings are sparse: Rugs woven by the women or heavy felt pads cover the floor. Against one side of the tent are blankets; containers made of goatskin, copper utensils, clay jugs, and bags of grain line the opposite side. Bakhtiari tents provide an excellent example of adaptation to a changing environment. The goat-hair cloth retains heat and repels water during the winter and keeps out heat during the summer. These portable homes are easy to erect, take down, and transport.

Sheep and goats are central to Bakhtiari subsistence: They provide milk, cheese, butter, meat, hides, and wool. The latter is woven into clothes, tents, storage bags, and other essentials by the women or sold in towns. The people also engage in very limited horticulture; they own lands that contain orchards, producing fruit that is consumed by the nomads or sold to townspeople. The division of labor is according to gender. The men, who take great pride in their marksmanship and horsemanship, engage in a limited amount of hunting on horseback, but their chief task is the tending of the flocks. The women cook, sew, weave, care for the children, and carry fuel and water.

The Bakhtiari have their own system of justice, including laws and a penal code. They are governed by tribal leaders, or *khans,* men who are elected or inherit their office. Because men own and control the livestock, women lack control of the economy and are relegated to the domestic sphere. This prominence of men in both economic and political affairs is common among pastoral nomads; theirs is very much a man's world. Thus, women typically occupy subordinate positions vis-à-vis men, even though elderly women eventually may gain a good deal of power. Most of the Bakhtiari *khans* grew wealthy when oil was discovered in their homeland around the start of the 20th century, and many of them are well educated, having attended Iranian or foreign universities. Despite this, and although some of them own houses in cities, the *khans* spend much of their lives among their people.

Intensive Agriculture and Nonindustrial Cities

With the intensification of agriculture, some farming villages grew into towns and even cities (Figure 17.3). In them, individuals who had previously been engaged in farming were freed to specialize in other activities. Thus, craft specialists such as carpenters, blacksmiths, sculptors, basketmakers, and stonecutters contribute to the vibrant, diversified life of the city.

Unlike horticulturists and pastoralists, city dwellers are only indirectly concerned with adapting to their natural environment. Far more important is the need to adapt to living and getting along with their fellow urbanites. To an important degree, this is true as well for the farmers who provide the city dwellers with their food. Under the political control of an urban elite, much of what the farmers do is governed by economic forces over which they have little, if any, control. Urbanization brings with it a new social order: Marked inequality develops as society becomes stratified and people are ranked according to their gender, the kind of work they do, or the family they are born into. As social institutions cease to operate in simple, face-to-face groups of relatives, friends, and acquaintances, they become more formal and bureaucratic, with specialized political institutions.

With urbanization came a sharp increase in the tempo of human cultural evolution. Writing was invented, trade intensified and expanded, the wheel and the sail were invented, and metallurgy and other crafts were developed. In many early cities, monumental buildings, such as royal palaces and temples, were built by thousands of men,

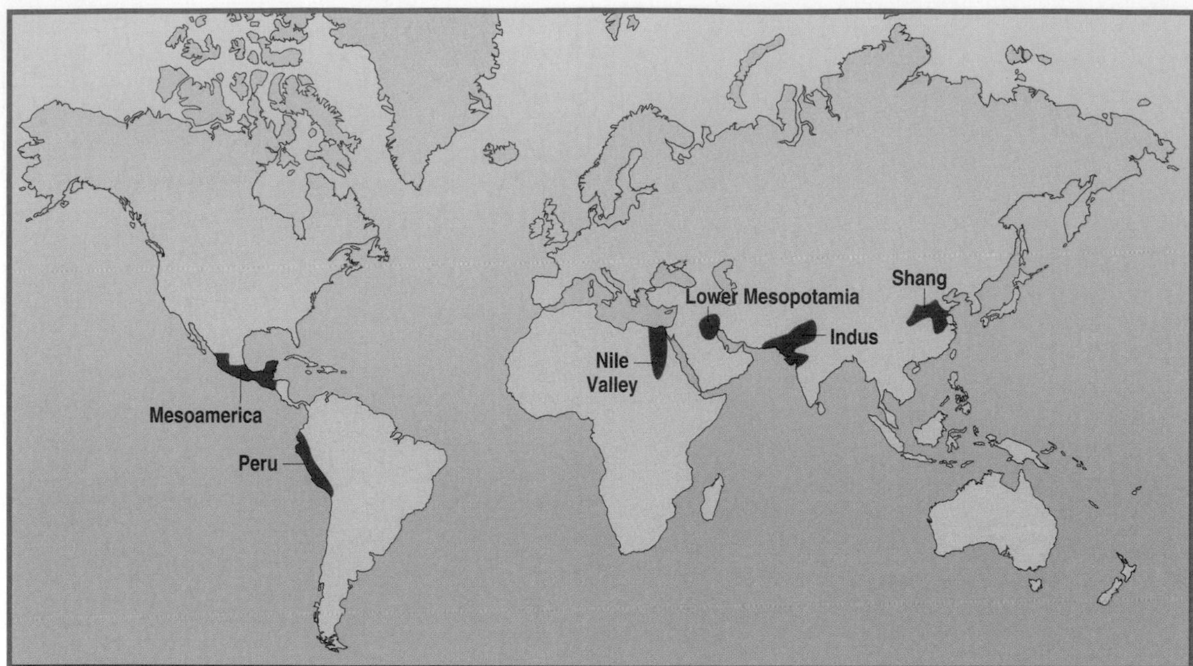

FIGURE 17.3
LOCATIONS OF MAJOR EARLY CIVILIZATIONS. THOSE OF NORTH AND SOUTH AMERICA DEVELOPED WHOLLY INDEPENDENTLY OF THOSE IN AFRICA AND ASIA. CHINESE CIVILIZATION MAY HAVE DEVELOPED INDEPENDENTLY OF SOUTHWEST ASIAN (INCLUDING THE NILE AND INDUS) CIVILIZATION.

often slaves taken in war; these feats of engineering still amaze modern architects and engineers. The inhabitants of these buildings—the ruling class composed of nobles and priests—formed a central government that dictated social and religious rules; in turn, the rules were carried out by the merchants, soldiers, artisans, farmers, and other citizens.

AZTEC CITY LIFE

The Aztec empire, which flourished in Mexico in the 16th century, is a good example of a highly developed urban society among non-Western peoples.[16] The capital city of the empire, Tenochtitlán (modern-day Mexico City), was located in a fertile valley 7,000 feet above sea level. Its population, along with that of its sister city, Tlatelolco, was about 200,000 in 1519, when the Spanish conqueror Hernan Cortes first saw it. This makes it five times more populous than the city of London at the same time. The Aztec metropolis sat on an island in the middle of a lake, which has since been drained and filled, and two aqueducts brought in fresh water from springs on the mainland. A 10-mile dike rimmed the eastern end of the city to prevent nearby salty waters from entering the lake around Tenochtitlán.

As in the early cities of Southwest Asia, the foundation of Aztec society was intensive agriculture. Corn was the principal crop. Each family, allotted a plot of land by its lineage, cultivated any of a number of crops, including beans, squash, gourds, peppers, tomatoes, cotton, and tobacco. Unlike Old World societies, however, only a few animals were domesticated; these included dogs and turkeys (both for eating). Many (but not all) crops were grown in plots around Tenochtitlán that were artificially constructed in the shallow waters of the surrounding lake. Canals between these *chinampas,* or raised fields, not only facilitated transport but were also a source of water plants used for heavy mulching. In addition, muck rich in fish feces was periodically dredged from the canals

[16] Most of the following information is taken from Berdan, F. F. (1982). *The Aztecs of central Mexico.* New York: Holt, Rinehart and Winston.

One form of intensive agriculture, the *chinampa,* was perfected in ancient Mexico. This picture is of a modern *chinampa* garden on the Gulf Coast of Mexico.

and spread over the gardens to maintain their fertility. Because they were incredibly productive as well as sustainable, *chinampas* are still in use today at Xochimilco, on the outskirts of Mexico City.

Aztec agricultural success provided for an increasingly large population and the diversification of labor. Skilled artisans, such as sculptors, silversmiths, stone workers, potters, weavers, feather workers, and painters could make good livings by pursuing these crafts exclusively. Since religion was central to the operation of the Aztec social order, these craftspeople were continuously engaged in the manufacture of religious artifacts, clothing, and decorations for buildings and temples. Other nonagricultural specialists included some of the warriors, the traveling merchants or *pochteca,* the priests, and the government bureaucracy of nobles.

As specialization increased, both among individuals and cities of the Aztec empire, the market became an extremely important economic and social institution. In addition to the daily markets in each city, larger markets were held in the various cities at different times of year. Buyers and sellers traveled to these from the far reaches of the empire. The market at Tlatelolco, Tenochtitlán's sister city, was so huge that the Spanish compared it to those of Rome and Constantinople. At the Aztec markets barter was the primary means of exchange. At times, however, cacao beans and cotton cloaks were used as currency. In addition to its obvious economic use, the market served

Model of the center of Tenochtitlán, the Aztec capital city.

social functions: People went there not only to buy or to sell but also to meet other people and to hear the latest news. A law actually required that each person go to market at least once within a specified number of days; this ensured that the citizenry was kept informed of all important news. The other major economic institution, trade networks between the Aztec capital and other cities, brought goods such as chocolate, vanilla beans, and pineapples into Tenochtitlán.

The Aztec social order was stratified into three main classes: nobles, commoners, and serfs. The nobles, among whom gender inequality was most marked, operated outside the lineage system on the basis of land and serfs the ruler allotted them from conquered peoples. The commoners were grouped into lineages, on which they were dependent for land. Within each of these, individual status depended on the degree of descent from the founder: Those more closely related to the lineage founder had higher status than those whose kinship was more distant. The third class in Aztec society consisted of serfs bound to the land and porters employed as carriers by merchants. Lowest of this class were the slaves. Some voluntarily had sold themselves into bondage; others were captives taken in war.

The Aztecs were governed by a semidivine king, chosen from among candidates of royal lineage by a council of nobles, priests, and leaders. Although the king was an absolute monarch, the councilors advised him on affairs of state. A vast number of government officials oversaw various functions, such as maintenance of the tax system and the courts of justice, management of government storehouses, and control of military training.

The typical Aztec city was rectangular and reflected the way the land was divided among the lineages. In the center was a large plaza containing the temple and the house of the city's ruler. At Tenochtitlán, with a total area of about 20 square miles, a huge temple and two lavish palaces stood in the central plaza, also called the Sacred Precinct. Surrounding this area were other ceremonial buildings belonging to each lineage.

As in a modern city, housing in Tenochtitlán ranged from squalid to magnificent. On the outskirts of the city, on *chinampas,* were the farmers' huts, built of wooden posts, thatched straw, and wattle plastered with mud. In the city proper were the houses of the more affluent—graceful, multiroomed, single- and two-story stone and mortar buildings, each surrounding a flower-filled patio and built on a stone platform for protection against floods. It is estimated that there were about 60,000 houses in Tenochtitlán. The focal points of the city were the *teocallis,* or pyramidal temples, where religious ceremonies, including human sacrifice, were held. The 100-foot-high double temple dedicated to the war god and the rain god was made of stone and featured a steep staircase leading

The modern industrial city is a very recent human development, although its roots lie in the so-called preindustrial city. The widespread belief that preindustrial cities are things of the past and that industrial cities are things of the future is based upon culture-bound assumptions rather than established facts.

to a platform with an altar, a chamber containing shrines, and an antechamber for the priests.

The palace of the emperor Moctezuma boasted numerous rooms for attendants and concubines, a menagerie, hanging gardens, and a swimming pool. Since Tenochtitlán sat in the middle of a lake, it was unfortified and connected to the mainland by three causeways. Communication among different parts of the city was easy, and people could travel either by land or by water. A series of canals, with footpaths beside them, ran throughout the city. The Spaniards who came to the Aztec capital reported that thousands of canoes plied the canals, carrying passengers and cargo around the city; these Europeans were so impressed by the communication network that they called Tenochtitlán the Venice of the New World. This, however, did not prevent its destruction by the Spanish invaders.

NONINDUSTRIAL CITIES IN THE MODERN WORLD

Tenochtitlán is a good example of the kind of urban settlement characteristic of most ancient, nonindustrial civilizations. Commonly termed **preindustrial cities,** they are apt to be thought of as part of the past, or as little more than stages in some sort of inevitable progression toward the kinds of industrial cities found today in places like Europe and North America. This essentially ethnocentric view obscures the fact that "preindustrial" cities are far from uncommon in the world today—especially in the so-called underdeveloped countries of the world. Furthermore, industrial cities have not yet come close to demonstrating they have the long-term viability shown by nonindustrial cities, which in some parts of the world have been around for not just hundreds but thousands of years.

Preindustrial cities. The kinds of urban settlements that are characteristic of nonindustrial civilizations.

CHAPTER SUMMARY

To meet their requirements for food, water, and shelter, people must adjust their behavior to suit their environment. This adjustment, which involves both change and stability, is a part of adaptation. Adaptation means a moving balance exists between a society's needs and its environmental potential. Adaptation also refers to the interaction between an organism—be it a human or some other animal—and its environment, with each causing changes in the other. Adaptation is a continuing process, and it is essential for survival. An ecosystem is bound by the activities of organisms and by physical forces such as erosion. Human ecosystems must be considered in terms of all aspects of culture.

To fit into an ecosystem an organism must be able to adapt or become a part of it. Once such a fit is achieved, stability may serve the organism's interest more than change, until the system is upset in some way.

A culture area is a region in which different societies follow similar patterns of life. Since geographic regions are not always uniform in climate and topography, new discoveries do not always spread to every group. Environmental variation also favors variation in technology, since needs may be quite different from area to area.

Julian Steward used the concept of culture type to explain variations within geographical regions. In this view a culture is considered in terms of a particular technology and of the particular environmental features that technology is best suited for.

The social and political organization of a society are other factors that influence how technology can be used to ensure survival. Those features of a culture that play a part in the way the society makes a living are its culture core. Anthropologists can trace direct relationships between types of culture cores and types of environments.

The food-foraging way of life, the oldest and most universal type of human adaptation, requires that people move their residence according to changing food sources. For as yet unknown ecological and social factors, local group size is kept small. One explanation contends that small sizes fit the land's capacity to sustain the groups.

Another states that the fewer the people, the less the chance of social conflict. The primary mechanisms for regulation of population size among food foragers are absence of sufficient reserves of fat in females before early adulthood, and frequent stimulation of their nipples, which prevents ovulation, as infants nurse several times an hour for several years.

Three important elements of human social organization probably developed along with scavenging and hunting for meat. These are a division of labor by gender, food sharing, and the camp as the center of daily activity and the place where food sharing takes place.

A characteristic of food-foraging societies is their egalitarianism. Since this way of life requires mobility, people accumulate only the material goods necessary for survival, so that status differences are limited to those based on age and sex. Status differences associated with sex, however, do not imply subordination of women to men. Food resources are distributed equally throughout the groups; thus no individual can achieve the wealth or status that hoarding might bring.

The reason for the transition from food foraging to food production, which began about 11,000 to 9,000 years ago, was likely the unforeseen result of increased management of wild food resources. One correlate of the food-producing revolution was the development of permanent settlements as people practiced horticulture using simple hand tools. One common form of horticulture is slash-and-burn, or swidden farming. Intensive agriculture, a more complex activity, requires irrigation, fertilizers, and draft animals. Pastoralism is a means of subsistence that relies on raising herds of domesticated animals, such as cattle, sheep, and goats. Pastoralists are usually nomads, moving to different pastures as required for grass and water.

Cities developed as intensified agricultural techniques created a surplus, freeing individuals to specialize full-time in other activities. Social structure becomes increasingly stratified with the development of cities, and people are ranked according to gender, the work they do, and the family they are born into. Social relationships grow more formal and centralized political institutions are formed.

One should not conclude that the sequence from food foraging, through horticultural/pastoral, to intensive agricultural nonindustrial urban and then industrial societies is inevitable, even though these did appear in that order. Where older adaptations continue to prevail, it is because conditions are such that they continue to work so well and provide such satisfaction that the people who maintain them prefer them to the alternatives of which they are aware. It is not because of any "backwardness" or ignorance. Modern food-foraging, horticultural, pastoral, nonindustrial, and industrial urban societies are all highly evolved adaptations, each in its own particular way.

CLASSIC READINGS

Bates, D. G. and Plog, F. (1991). *Human adaptive strategies.* New York: McGraw-Hill.

This book takes an ecological approach to understanding human cultural diversity. A chapter each is devoted to hunting and gathering, horticultural, pastoral, intensive agricultural, and industrial societies, with a final chapter devoted to change and development. Theoretical issues are made easy to grasp through use of readable ethnographic cases.

Lustig-Arecco, V. (1975). *Technology: Strategies for survival.* New York: Holt, Rinehart and Winston.

Although the early anthropologists devoted a good deal of attention to technology, the subject fell into neglect early in the 20th century. This is one of the few more recent studies of the subject. The author's particular interest is the technoeconomic adaptation of hunters, pastoralists, and farmers.

Mintz, S. W. (1996). *Tasting food, tasting freedom: Excursions into eating, culture and the past.* Boston: Beacon Press.

As the popular saying goes, "We are what we eat," for what we eat says much about who we are. In this book, Mintz explores how humans take the most basic of biological functions—eating—and invest it with all sorts of social meaning.

Schrire, C. (Ed.). (1984). *Past and present in hunter gatherer studies.* Orlando, FL: Academic Press.

This collection of papers demolishes many a myth (including several held by anthropologists) about food-foraging societies. Especially recommended is the editor's introduction, "Wild Surmises on Savage Thoughts."

Vayda, A., (Ed.). (1969). *Environment and cultural behavior: Ecological studies in cultural anthropology.* Garden City, NY: Natural History Press.

The focus of the studies collected here is the interrelationship between cultural behavior and environmental phenomena. The writers attempt to make cultural behavior intelligible by relating it to the material world in which it develops. This volume includes articles concerning population, divination, ritual, warfare, food production, climate, and diseases.

CHAPTER 18

ECONOMIC SYSTEMS

A fundamental characteristic of the market in non-Western societies is that it always means a literal marketplace, where actual goods are exchanged. At this market in Guatemala, people exchange items they have produced for things they need but can only get from others.

CHAPTER PREVIEW

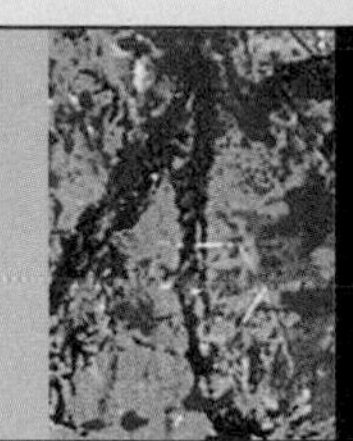

1 How Do Anthropologists Study Economic Systems?

Anthropologists study the means by which goods are produced, distributed, and consumed in the context of the total culture of particular societies. Although they have borrowed theories and concepts from economists, most anthropologists feel that principles derived from the study of Western market economies have limited applicability to economic systems where people do not produce and exchange goods for profit.

2 How Do the Economies of Nonindustrial Peoples Work?

In non-Western, nonindustrial societies there is always a division of labor by age and sex, with some additional craft specialization. Land and other valuable resources are usually controlled by groups of relatives, such as bands or lineages, and individual ownership is rare. Production takes place in the quantity and at the time required, and most goods are consumed by the group that produces them. Leveling mechanisms ensure that no one accumulates significantly more goods than anyone else.

3 How and Why Are Goods Exchanged in Nonindustrial Societies?

Nonindustrial peoples exchange goods through the processes of reciprocity, redistribution, and market exchange. Reciprocity involves the exchange of goods and services of roughly equivalent value, and it is often undertaken for ritual purposes or in order to gain prestige. Redistribution requires some sort of government and/or religious elite to collect and then reallocate resources, in the form of either goods or services. Market exchange, which in nonindustrial societies means going to a specific place for direct exchange of goods, also serves as entertainment and as a means of exchanging important information. The latter are frequently primary motivating forces bringing people into the marketplace.

An economic system may be defined as a means of producing, distributing, and consuming goods. Since a people, in pursuing a particular means of subsistence, necessarily produces, distributes, and consumes things, it is obvious that our earlier discussion of subsistence patterns (Chapter 17) involved economic matters. Yet economic systems encompass much more than we have so far covered. This chapter will look at aspects of economic systems—specifically systems of production, exchange, and redistribution—that require more discussion than possible in the last chapter.

ECONOMIC ANTHROPOLOGY

It is in the study of the economies of traditional small-scale societies that we are perhaps most apt to fall prey to interpreting anthropological data in terms of our own technologies, our own values of work and property, and our own determination of what is rational. Take, for example, the following statement from just one respected textbook in economics: "In all societies, the prevailing reality of life has been the inadequacy of output to fill the wants and needs of the people."[1] This ethnocentric assertion fails to realize that in many societies people's wants are maintained at levels that can be fully and continuously satisfied, and without jeopardizing the environment. In such societies, goods are produced in the quantity and at the time required, and to do more than this makes no sense at all. Thus, no matter how hard people may work when hard work is called for, at other times they will have available hours, days, or even weeks on end to devote to "unproductive" (in the economic sense) activities. To Western observers, such people are apt to appear lazy (Figure 18.1); "instead of disciplined workers, they are reluctant and untrained laborers."[2] If the people happen to be hunters and gatherers, even the hard work is likely to be misinterpreted. In Western culture hunting is defined as a "sport"; hence, the men in food-foraging societies are often perceived as spending virtually all of their time in "recreational pursuits," while the women are seen as working themselves to the bone.

The point to be made here is that to understand how the schedule of wants or demands of a given society is balanced against the supply of goods and services available, it is necessary to introduce a noneconomic variable—the anthropological variable of culture. In any given economic system, economic processes cannot be interpreted without culturally defining the demands and understanding the conventions that dictate how and when they are satisfied. The fact is, the economic sphere of behavior is *not* separate from the social, religious, and political spheres, and thus not completely free to follow its own purely economic logic. To be sure, economic behavior and institutions can be analyzed in purely economic terms, but to do so is to ignore crucial noneconomic considerations, which do, after all, have an impact on the way things are in real life.

As a case in point, we may look briefly at yam production among the Trobriand Islanders, who inhabit a group of coral islands in the southern Pacific that lie north of New Guinea's eastern end.[3] Trobriand men spend a great deal of their time and energy raising yams, not for themselves or their own households, but to give to others, normally their sisters and married daughters. The purpose of this yam production is not to provision the households that receive them, because most of what people eat they grow for themselves in gardens where they plant taro, sweet potatoes, tapioca, greens, beans, and squash, as well as breadfruit and banana trees. The reason a man gives yams to a woman is to show his support for her husband and to enhance his own influence.

Once received by the woman, they are loaded into her husband's yam house, symbolizing his worth as a man of power and influence in his community. Some of these yams he may use to purchase a variety of things, including arm shells, shell necklaces and earrings, betel nuts, pigs, chickens, and locally produced goods such as wooden bowls, combs, floor mats, lime pots, and even magic spells. Some he must use to discharge obligations, as in the presentation of yams to the relatives of his daughter's husband when she marries or making the required payments following the death of a member of his lineage (an organized group of relatives descended, in this case, through women, from a common ancestor). Finally, any man who aspires to high status and power is expected to show his worth by organizing a yam competition, in the course of which he gives away huge quantities of yams to invited guests. As anthropologist Annette Weiner explains: "A yam house, then, is like a bank account; when full, a man is wealthy and powerful. Until yams are

[1] Heilbroner, R. L., & Thurow, L. C. (1981). *The economic problem* (6th ed.) (p. 327). Englewood Cliffs, NJ: Prentice-Hall.

[2] Ibid., p. 609.

[3] Weiner, A. B. (1988). *The Trobrianders of Papua New Guinea.* New York: Holt, Rinehart and Winston.

The Chief Registrar of Natives, N.A.D. Form No 54/________
NAIROBI.

COMPLAINT OF DESERTION OF REGISTERED NATIVE

Native's Certificate No. ________________ Name ________________

The above native deserted from my employ________________
(date)

He was engaged ________________ on ________________days verbal contract
(date)
________________months written contract

at ____
(place) *(Contract No.)*

I wish to prosecute him for this offence and hereby agree to appear as a witness or to produce evidence if and when called upon.

____
Signature of Employer

Address ________________
____

Date ________________

FIGURE 18.1

PEOPLE WITH INDUSTRIAL ECONOMIES FREQUENTLY MISUNDERSTAND THE WORK ETHIC IN SO-CALLED TRIBAL SOCIETIES. THUS THE BRITISH IN COLONIAL KENYA THOUGHT IT NECESSARY TO TEACH NATIVES "THE DIGNITY OF LABOR" AND MADE IT A CRIME FOR A TRIBAL PERSON TO QUIT WORK WITHOUT AUTHORIZATION.

cooked or they rot, they may circulate as limited currency. That is why, once harvested, the usage of yams for daily food is avoided as much as possible."[4]

By giving yams to his sister or daughter, a man not only expresses his confidence in the woman's husband, but he also makes the latter indebted to him. Although the recipient rewards the gardener and his helpers by throwing a feast, at which they are fed cooked yams, taro, and—what everyone especially looks forward to—ample pieces of pork, this in no way pays off the debt. Nor does the gift of a stone ax blade (another valuable in the Trobriand system), which may reward an especially good harvest. The debt can only be repaid in women's wealth, which consists of bundles of banana leaves and skirts made of the same material dyed red.

Although the bundles are of no utilitarian value, extensive labor is invested in their production, and large quantities of them, along with skirts, are regarded as essential for paying off all the members of other lineages who were close to a recently deceased relative in life and who assisted with the funeral. Also, the wealth and vitality of the dead person's lineage is measured by the quality and quantity of the bundles and skirts so distributed. Because a man has received yams from his wife's brother, he is obligated to provide his wife with yams for purchasing the necessary bundles and skirts, beyond those she has produced, to help with payments following the death of a member of her lineage. Because deaths are unpredictable, and can occur at any time, a man must have yams available for his wife when she needs them. This, and the fact she may require all of his yams, acts as an effective check on a man's wealth.

Like people the world over, the Trobriand Islanders assign meanings to objects that make those objects worth far more than their cost in labor or materials. Yams, for example, establish long-term relationships that lead to other advantages, such as access to land, protection, assistance, and other kinds of wealth. Thus, yam exchanges are as much social and political transactions, as they are economic ones. Banana leaf bundles and skirts, for their part, are symbolic of the political state of lineages and of their immortality. In their distribution, which is related to rituals associated with death, we see how men in

[4] Ibid., p. 86.

In Seattle, people protest the policies of the World Trade Organization. While the field of economics is about markets, anthropology is about people.

Trobriand Island men devote a great deal of time and energy to raising yams, not for themselves but to give to others. These yams, which have been raised by men related through marriage to a chief, are about to be loaded into the chief's yam house.

Trobriand society are ultimately dependent on women and their valuables. So important are these matters to the Trobrianders that even in the face of Western money, education, religion, and law, these people remain as committed today as in the past to yam cultivation and the production of women's wealth. Looked at in terms of Western economics, these activities appear to make little sense, but viewed in terms of Trobriand values and concerns, they make a great deal of sense.

RESOURCES

In every society customs and rules govern the kinds of work done, who does the work, who controls the resources and tools, and how the work is accomplished. Raw materials, labor, and technology are the productive resources that a social group may use to produce desired goods and services. The rules surrounding the use of these are embedded in the culture and determine the way the economy operates.

Patterns of Labor

Every human society has always had a division of labor by both gender and age categories; such division is an elaboration of patterns found among all monkeys and apes. Division by gender increases the chances that the learning of necessary skills will be more efficient, since only half the adult repertoire needs to be learned by any one individual. Division by age provides sufficient time for developing those skills.

DIVISION OF LABOR BY GENDER

Anthropologists have studied extensively the division of labor by gender in societies of all sorts, and we discussed some aspects of it in Chapters 4 and 17. Whether men or women do a particular job varies from group to group, but much work has been set apart as the work of either one or the other. For example, we have seen that the tasks most often regarded as "women's work" tend to be those that can be carried out near home and that are easily resumed after interruption. The tasks most often regarded as "men's work" tend to be those requiring physical strength, rapid mobilization of high bursts of energy, frequent travel at some distance from home, and assumption of high levels of risk and danger. However, plenty of exceptions occur, as in those societies where women regularly carry burdensome loads or put in long hours of hard work cultivating crops in the fields. In some societies, women perform almost three quarters of all work, and there are even societies where women serve as warriors. In the 19th-century kingdom of Dahomey, in West Africa, thousands of women served in the armed forces of the Dahomean king and in the eyes of some observers were better fighters than their male counterparts. Also, references to women warriors in ancient Ireland exist, archaeological evidence indicates their presence among the Vikings, and among the Abkhasians of Georgia women were trained in weaponry until quite recently. Clearly, the division of labor by gender cannot be explained simply as a consequence of sex differences, whether they be of male strength and expendibility, or female reproductive biology.

Instead of looking for biological imperatives to explain the division of labor by gender, a more productive strategy is to examine the kinds of work men and women do in the context of specific societies to see how it relates to other cultural and historical factors. Researchers find three configurations, one featuring flexibility and integration of men and women, another rigid segregation by gender, and a third featuring elements of the other two.[5] The flexible/integrated pattern is exemplified by people such as the Ju/'hoansi (whose practices we examined in Chapters 16 and 17) and is seen most often among food foragers and subsistence farmers. In such societies, men and women perform up to 35 percent of activities with approximately equal participation, while those tasks deemed appropriate for one gender may be performed by the other, without loss of face, as the situation warrants. Where these practices prevail, boys and girls grow up in much the same way, learn to value cooperation over competition, and become equally habituated to adult men and women, who interact with one another on a relatively equal basis.

Societies segregated by gender rigidly define almost all work as either masculine or feminine, so men and women rarely engage in joint efforts of any kind. In such societies, it is inconceivable that someone would even think of doing something considered the work of the opposite sex! This pattern is frequently seen in pastoral nomadic, intensive agricultural, and industrial societies, where men's work keeps them outside the home for much of the time. Thus, boys and girls alike are raised primarily by women, who encourage compliance in their

[5] Sanday, P. R. (1981). *Female power and male dominance: On the origins of sexual inequality* (pp. 79–80). Cambridge: Cambridge University Press.

Often, work that is considered inappropriate for men (or women) in one society is performed by them in another. Here, a Uigir man in China sews, and a woman in Bhutan carries concrete for bridge construction.

In nonindustrial societies, households produce much of what they consume. Among the Maya, men work in the fields to produce foods for the household; women prepare the food and take care of other chores that can be performed in or near the house.

charges. At some point, however, boys must undergo a role reversal to become like men, who are supposed to be tough, aggressive, and competitive. To do this, they must prove their masculinity in ways women do not to prove their feminine identity. Commonly, this involves assertions of male superiority, and hence authority, over women. Historically, societies segregated by gender often have imposed their control on those featuring integration, upsetting the egalitarian nature of the latter.

In the third, sometimes called the dual sex configuration, men and women carry out their work separately, as in societies segregated by gender, but the relationship between them is one of balanced complementarity rather than inequality. Although competition is a prevailing ethic, each gender manages its own affairs, and the interests of both men and women are represented at all levels. Thus, as in integrated societies, neither gender exerts dominance over the other. The "dual sex" orientation may be seen among certain American Indian peoples whose economies were based upon subsistence farming, as well as among several West African kingdoms, including that of the aforementioned Dahomeans.

AGE DIVISION OF LABOR

Division of labor according to age is also typical of human societies. Among the Ju/'hoansi of the Kalahari desert, for example, children are not expected to contribute significantly to subsistence until they reach their late teens. Indeed, until they possess adult levels of strength and endurance, many "bush foods"—edible tubers, for example—are not readily accessible to them. The Ju/'hoansi equivalent of "retirement" comes somewhere around the age of 60. Elderly people, while they will usually do some foraging for themselves, are not expected to contribute much food. However, older men and women alike play an essential role in spiritual matters; freed from food taboos and other restrictions that apply to younger adults, they may handle ritual substances considered dangerous to those still involved with hunting or having children. By virtue of their old age, they also remember things that happened far in the past. Thus, they are repositories of accumulated wisdom—the "libraries" of a nonliterate people—and are able to suggest solutions to problems younger adults have never before had to face. Thus, they are far from being unproductive members of society.

In some food-foraging societies, women do continue to make a significant contribution to provisioning in their older years. Among the Hadza of Tanzania, their contribution is critical to their daughters, whose foraging abilities are significantly impaired when they have new infants to nurse. This is because lactation is energetically expensive, while at the same time holding, carrying, and nursing an infant interfere with the mother's foraging efficiency. Those most immediately affected by this are a woman's weaned children not yet old enough to forage effectively for themselves. The problem is overcome, however, by the foraging efforts of grandmothers, whose time spent collecting food is greatest when their infant grandchildren are youngest and their weaned grandchildren receive the least food from their mothers.[6]

In many traditional farming societies, not just older people but children as well may make a greater contribution to the economy in terms of work and responsibility than is common in industrial North America. For instance, in Maya communities in southern Mexico and Guatemala, young children not only look after their younger brothers and sisters but help with housework as well. Girls begin to make a substantial contribution to the work of the household by age 7 or 8 and by age 11 are constantly busy grinding corn, making *tortillas*, fetching wood and water, sweeping the house, and so forth. Boys have less to do but are given small tasks, such as bringing in the chickens or playing with a baby; by age 12, however, they are carrying toasted *tortillas* to the men out working in the fields, and returning with loads of corn.[7]

Similar situations are not unknown in industrial societies. In Naples, Italy, children play a significant role in the economy. At a very young age, girls begin to take on responsibilities for housework, freeing the labor of their mothers and older sisters so they may earn money for the household. Nor is it long before they are apprenticed out to neighbors and kin, from whom they learn the skills that enable them, by age 14, to enter a small factory or workshop. The wages earned are typically turned over to the girls' mothers. Boys, too, are also apprenticed out at an early age, though they may achieve more freedom from adult control by becoming involved in various street activities not available to girls.[8]

The use of child labor has become a matter of increasing concern as large capitalist corporations rely more and more on the low-cost manufacture of goods in the world's poorer countries. Although reliable figures are hard to come by, it is estimated that there are some 15 million bonded child laborers in south Asia alone, including some as young as 4 years old. Each year, the United States imports at least $100 million worth of products manufactured by poorly paid children, ranging from rugs and carpets to clothing and soccer balls.[9] Early in his presidency, Bill Clinton signed into law legislation that would prevent importation of products made by children who are forced into wage labor, but how effectively it can be enforced still remains to be seen.

This Thai girl exemplifies the use of child labor in many parts of the world, often by large corporations. Even in Western countries, child labor plays a major economic role.

COOPERATION

Cooperative work groups can be found everywhere foraging as well as food-producing and in nonindustrial as well as industrial societies. Often, if the effort involves the whole community, a festive spirit permeates the work. Jomo Kenyatta, the Kikuyu tribesman educated in a British mission school who studied anthropology at Cambridge University and became the first president of

[6] Hawkes, K., O'Connell, J. F., & Blurton Jones, N. G. (1997). Hadza women's time allocation, offspring, provisioning, and the evolution of long postmenopausal life spans. *Current Anthropology, 38,* 551–577.

[7] Vogt, E. Z. (1990). *The Zinacantecos of Mexico, a modern Maya way of life* (2nd ed.) (pp. 83–87). Fort Worth, TX: Holt, Rinehart and Winston.

[8] Goddard, V. (1993). Child labor in Naples. In W. A. Haviland & R. J. Gordon (Eds.). *Talking about people* (pp. 105–109). Mountain View, CA: Mayfield.

[9] It's the law: Child labor protection. *Peace and Justice News,* November/December 1997, 11.

Jomo Kenyatta, Kenya's first president, took the concept of cooperation from the local level and applied it to the state. His national slogan *Harambee* meant "Pull Together."

independent Kenya, described the time of enjoyment after a day's labor in his country:

> If a stranger happens to pass by, he will have no idea that these people who are singing and dancing have completed their day's work. This is why most Europeans have erred by not realizing that the African in his own environment does not count hours or work by the movement of the clock, but works with good spirit and enthusiasm to complete the tasks before him.[10]

In some parts of East Africa, work parties begin with the display of a pot of millet beer to be consumed after the tasks have been finished. Yet, the beer is not payment for the work; indeed, the labor involved is worth far more than the beer consumed. Rather, the beverage is more of a symbol, whereas recompense comes as individuals sooner or later participate in work parties for others.

Among the Ju/'hoansi, women's work is frequently highly social. About three times a week, they go out to gather wild plant foods away from the camp. Although they may do this alone, they more often go out in groups, talking loudly all the while. This not only turns what might otherwise seem a monotonous task into a social occasion, it also causes large animals—potential sources of danger—to move elsewhere.

In most human societies, the basic unit within which cooperation takes place is the household. It is both a unit of production and consumption; only in industrial societies have these two things been separated. The Maya farmer, for example, unlike his North American counterpart (but like peasant and subsistence farmers everywhere), is not so much running a commercial enterprise as he is a household. He is motivated by a desire to provide for the welfare of his own family; each family, as an economic unit, works as a group for its own good. Cooperative work may be undertaken outside the household, however, for other reasons, though not always voluntarily. It may be part of fulfilling duties to in-laws, or it may be performed for political officials or priests by command. Thus, institutions of family, kinship, religion, and the state all may act as organizing elements that define the nature and condition of each worker's cooperative obligations.

As anthropologist Magdala Hurtado points out, the spatial separation of work from household requires especially cruel trade-offs. Working outside the home and caring for children full-time are equally beneficial to her and her offspring. The problem is that inflexible work hours and commuting make them mutually exclusive.[11]

CRAFT SPECIALIZATION

In foraging and traditional crop-cultivating societies, where division of labor occurs along lines of age and gender, each person has knowledge and competence in all aspects of work appropriate to his or her age and gender. In contemporary industrial societies, by contrast, a greater diversity of more specialized tasks to be performed exists, and no individual even can begin to know of all those appropriate for his or her age and gender. Yet even in nonindustrial societies there is some specialization of craft. This is often minimal in food-foraging societies, but even here the arrow points of one man may be in some demand because of his particular skill at making them. Among people who produce their own food, specialization is more apt to occur. In the Trobriand Islands, for example, if a man wanted stone to make ax blades, he had to travel some distance to a particular island where the appropriate kind of stone was quarried;

[10] Herskovits, M. (1952). *Economic anthropology: A study in comparative economics* (2nd ed.)(p.103). New York: Knopf.

[11] Hurtado, A. M. (2000). Origins of trade-offs in maternal care. *Science, 287,* 434.

The separation of wage work from the household presents women with a cruel tradeoff: caring for children versus earning an income. For some women, the rise of the Internet may restore work to the home.

clay pots, on the other hand, were made by people living on yet another island.

One example of specialization is afforded by the Afar people of the desolate Danakil Depression of northeastern Ethiopia. Afar men are miners of salt, which since ancient times has been widely traded in East Africa. It is mined from the crust of an extensive salt plain, and to get to it is a risky and difficult business. L. M. Nesbitt, the first European to successfully cross the depression, called it "the hell-hole of creation."[12] The heat is extreme during the day, with shade temperatures between 140°F and 156°F not unusual. Shade is not found on the salt plain, however, unless a shelter of salt blocks is built. Nor is there food or water for man or beast. To add to the difficulty, until recently the Muslim Afars and the Christian Tigrians, highlanders who also mine salt, were sworn enemies.

Successful mining, then, requires specialized skill at planning and organization, as well as physical strength and the will to work under the most trying conditions.[13] Pack animals to carry the salt have to be fed in advance, for carrying sufficient fodder for them interferes with their ability to carry out salt. Food and water must be carried for the miners, who usually number 30 to 40 per group. Travel is planned to take place at night to avoid the intense heat of day. In the past, measures to protect against attack had to be taken. Finally, timing is critical; a party has to return to sources of food and water before their own supplies are too long exhausted and before their animals are unable to continue farther.

Control of Land and Water

All societies have regulations that determine the way valuable natural resources and particular tracts of land and water will be allocated. Food foragers must determine who can hunt game and gather plants and where these activities take place. Similar problems are faced by those who fish on large bodies of water. Horticulturists must decide how their farmland is to be acquired, worked, and passed on. Pastoralists require a system that determines rights to watering places and grazing land, as well as the right of access to land over which they move their herds. Full-time or intensive agriculturalists must have some means of determining title to land and access to water supplies for irrigation. In industrialized Western societies, a system of private ownership of land and rights to natural resources generally prevails. Although elaborate laws have been enacted to regulate the buying, owning, and selling of land and water resources, if individuals wish to reallocate valuable farmland, for instance, to some other purpose, they generally can.

In traditional societies, land is often controlled by kinship groups such as the lineage (discussed in Chapter 21) or band rather than by individuals. For example, among the Ju/'hoansi, each band of anywhere from 10 to 30 people lives on roughly 250 square miles of land, which they consider to be their territory—their own country. These territories are defined not in terms of boundaries but in terms of water holes that are located within them. The land is said to be "owned" by those who have lived the longest in the band, usually a group of brothers and sisters or cousins. Their concept of ownership, however, is not something easily translated in modern Western terms. Within their traditional worldview, no part of their homeland can be sold for money or traded away for goods. However, their permission must be asked by outsiders to enter the territory. To refuse such permission, though, would be unthinkable.

The practice of defining territories on the basis of core features, be they water holes (as among the Ju/'hoansi), distinctive features of the landscape where ancestral spirits are thought to dwell (as among Australian Aborigines), watercourses (as among Indians of the

[12] Nesbitt, L. M. (1935). *Hell-hole of creation.* New York: Knopf.

[13] Mesghinua, H. M. (1966). Salt mining in Enderta. *Journal of Ethiopian Studies, 4* (2); O'Mahoney, K. (1970). The salt trade. *Journal of Ethiopian Studies, 8* (2).

northeastern United States), or whatever, is typical of food foragers. Territorial boundaries are left typically rather vaguely defined. To avoid friction, they may designate part of their territory as a buffer zone between them and their neighbors. The adaptive value of this is quite obvious—the size of band territories, as well as the size of the bands, can adjust to keep in balance with availability of resources in any given place. Such adjustment would be more difficult under a system of individual ownership of clearly bounded land.

Among some West African farmers, a tributary system of land ownership prevails: All land is said to belong to the head chief. He allocates it to various subchiefs, who in turn distribute it to lineages; lineage leaders then assign individual plots to each farmer. Just as in medieval Europe, these African people owe allegiance to the subchiefs (or nobles) and the principal chief (or king). The people who work the land must pay tribute in the form of products or special services such as fighting for the king when necessary.

These people do not really own the land; rather, it is a form of lease. Yet as long as the land is kept in use, rights to such use will pass to their heirs. No user, however, can give away, sell, or otherwise dispose of a plot of land without approval from the elder of the lineage. When an individual no longer uses the allocated land, it reverts to the lineage head, who reallocates it to some other member of the lineage. The important operative principle here is that the system extends the individual's right to use land for an indefinite period, but the land is not "owned" outright. This serves to maintain the integrity of valuable farmland as such, preventing its loss through subdivision and conversion to other uses.

Technology

All societies have some means of creating and allocating the tools and other artifacts used to produce goods and that are passed on to succeeding generations. The number and kinds of tools a society uses—which, together with knowledge about how to make and use them constitute its **technology**—are related to the lifestyles of its members. Food foragers and pastoral nomads, who are frequently on the move, are apt to have fewer and simpler tools than the more sedentary farmer, in part because a great number of complex tools would interfere with their mobility.

Food foragers make and use a variety of tools, many of which are ingenious in their effectiveness. Some of these they make for their individual use, but codes of generosity are such that a person may not refuse to give or loan what is requested. Thus, tools may be given or loaned to others in exchange for the products resulting from their use. For example, a Ju/'hoansi who gives his arrow to another hunter has a right to a share in any animals the hunter kills. Game is considered to "belong" to the man whose arrow killed it, even when he is not present on the hunt.

Among horticulturists, the ax, digging stick, or hoe are the primary tools. Since these are relatively easy to produce, every person can make them. Although the maker has first rights to their use, when that person is not using them, any family member may ask to use them and usually is granted permission to do so. Refusal would cause people to treat the tool owner with scorn for this singular lack of concern for others. If a relative helps raise the crop traded for a particular tool, that relative becomes part owner of the implement, and it may not be traded or given away without his or her permission.

In permanently settled communities, which farming makes possible, tools and other productive goods are more complex, more difficult, and costlier to make. Where this happens, individual ownership in them usually is more absolute, as are the conditions under which persons may borrow and use such equipment. It is easy to replace a knife lost by a relative during palm cultivation but much more difficult to replace an iron plow or a diesel-fueled harvesting machine. Rights to the ownership of complex tools are more rigidly applied; generally the person who has funded the purchase of a complex piece of machinery is considered the sole owner and may decide how and by whom it will be used.

Leveling Mechanisms

In spite of the increased opportunities that exist in permanently settled farming communities for people to accumulate belongings, limits on property acquisition may be as prominent in them as among nomadic peoples. In such communities, social obligations compel people to divest themselves of wealth, and no one is permitted to accumulate too much more than others. Greater wealth

Technology. Tools and other material equipment, together with the knowledge of how to make and use them.

Among the Ju/'hoansi, game "belongs" to the man whose arrow killed it. But because arrows are freely loaned or given, the man who "owns" the kill may not even have been present on the hunt.

simply brings greater obligation to give. Anthropologists refer to such obligations as **leveling mechanisms.**

Leveling mechanisms are found in communities where property must not be allowed to threaten a more-or-less egalitarian social order, as in many Maya villages and towns in the highlands of Mexico and Guatemala. In these communities, *cargo systems* function to siphon off any excess wealth people may accumulate. A cargo system is a civil-religious hierarchy that, on a revolving basis, combines most of a community's civic and ceremonial offices. All offices are open to all men, and eventually virtually every man has at least one term in office, each term lasting for 1 year. The scale is pyramidal, which means that more offices exist at the lower levels, with progressively fewer toward the top. For example, a community of about 8,000 people may have four levels of offices, with 32 on the lowest level, 12 on the next one up, 6 on the next, and 2 at the apex. Positions at the lowest level include those for the performance of various menial chores, such as sweeping and carrying messages. The higher offices are councilmen, judges, mayors, and ceremonial positions. All positions are regarded as burdens for which the holders are not paid. Instead, the officeholder is expected to pay for the food, liquor, music, fireworks, or whatever is required for community festivals or for banquets associated with the transmission of office. For some cargos, the cost is as much as a man can earn in 4 years! After holding a cargo position, a man usually returns to normal life for a period, during which he may accumulate sufficient resources to campaign for a higher office. Each male citizen of the community is socially obligated to serve in the system at least once, and social pressure to do so is such that it drives individuals who have once again accumulated excess wealth to apply for higher offices in order to raise their social status. Ideally, while some individuals gain appreciably more prestige than others in their community, no one has appreciably more wealth in a material sense than anyone else. In actuality, the ideal is not always achieved, in which case service in the cargo system functions to legitimize wealth differences, thereby preventing disruptive envy.

In addition to equalizing (or legitimizing) wealth, the cargo system accomplishes other results. Through its system of offices, it ensures that necessary services within the community are performed. It also keeps goods in circulation rather than sitting around gathering dust. Moreover, members are pressured into investing their resources in their own community rather than elsewhere. Likewise, the costs of holding office require participants to produce and sell a surplus or seek work outside the community in order to secure sufficient funds, thereby benefiting outside interests. To the degree that outsiders can control the goods and wages cargo holders require, the basic system's function may be subverted to serve as a means of drawing wealth and labor *out* of the community.

Leveling Mechanism. A societal obligation compelling a family to distribute goods so that no one accumulates more wealth than anyone else.

HIGHWAY 1
SUNY, Plattsburgh: "Global Problems and the Culture of Capitalism"
http://www.faculty.plattsburgh.edu/richard.robbins/legacy

HIGHWAY 2
Online exhibits at Peabody Museum of Archaeology & Ethnology
http:www.peabody.harvard.edu/exhibitions.html

HIGHWAY 3
Anthropology at about.com: Search for Kula Ring
http://www.anthropology.about.com/science/anthropology

DISTRIBUTION AND EXCHANGE

The money economy of industrial societies involves a two-step process between labor and consumption. The money received for labor must be translated into something else before it is directly consumable. In societies with no such medium of exchange, the rewards for labor are usually direct. The workers in a family group consume what they harvest; they eat what the hunter or gatherer brings home and they use the tools they themselves make. But even where there is no formal medium of exchange, some distribution of goods takes place. Karl Polanyi, an economist, classified the cultural systems of distributing material goods into three modes: reciprocity, redistribution, and market exchange.[14]

[14] Polanyi, K. (1968). The economy as instituted process. In E. E. LeClair Jr., & H. K. Schneider (Eds.). *Economic anthropology: Readings in theory and analysis* (pp. 127–138). New York: Holt, Rinehart and Winston.

Reciprocity

Reciprocity refers to a transaction between two parties whereby goods and services of roughly equivalent value are exchanged. This may involve gift giving, but in non-Western societies pure selflessness in gift giving is as rare as it is in the United States or any other Western society. The overriding motive is to fulfill social obligations and perhaps to gain a bit of prestige in the process. It might be best compared in North American society to someone who gives a party. He or she may go to great lengths to impress others by the excellence of the food and drink served, not to mention the quality of wit and conversation of those in attendance. The expectation is that, sooner or later, he or she will be invited to similar parties by some, although perhaps not all, of the guests.

Social customs dictate the nature and occasion of exchange. When an animal is killed by a group of Aboriginal hunters in Australia, the meat is divided among the hunters' families and other relatives. Each person in the camp gets a share, the size depending on the nature of

Reciprocity. The exchange of goods and services, of approximately equal value, between two parties.

Ju/'hoansi cutting up meat, which will be shared by others in the camp. The food distribution practices of such food foragers are an example of generalized reciprocity.

the person's kinship tie to the hunters. The least desirable parts may be kept by the hunters themselves. When a kangaroo is killed, for example, the left hind leg goes to the brother of the hunter, the tail to his father's brother's son, the loins and the fat to his father-in-law, the ribs to his mother-in-law, the forelegs to his father's younger sister, the head to his wife, and the entrails and the blood to the hunter. If arguments were to arise over the apportionment, it would be because the principles of distribution were not followed properly. The hunter and his family seem to fare badly in this arrangement, but they have their turn when another man makes a kill. The giving and receiving is obligatory, as is the particularity of the distribution. Such sharing of food reinforces community bonds and ensures that everyone eats. It also might be viewed as a way of saving perishable goods. By giving away part of his kill, the hunter gets a social IOU for a similar amount of food in the future. It is a little bit like putting money in a time-deposit savings account.

The food-distribution practices just described for Aboriginal Australian hunters constitute an example of **generalized reciprocity.** This may be defined as exchange in which the value of what is given is not calculated, nor is the time of repayment specified. Gift giving, in the unselfish sense, also falls in this category. So, too, does the act of a kindhearted soul who stops to help a stranded motorist or someone else in distress and refuses payment with the admonition: "Pass it on to the next person in need." Most generalized reciprocity, though, occurs among close kin or people who otherwise have very close ties with one another. Typically, participants will deny that the exchanges are economic, and will couch them explicitly in terms of kinship and friendship obligations.

Balanced reciprocity differs in that it is not part of a long-term process. The giving and receiving, as well as the time involved, are more specific; one has a direct obligation to reciprocate promptly in equal value in order for the social relationship to continue. Examples of balanced reciprocity in North American society include such practices as trading baseball cards or buying drinks when one's turn comes at a gathering of friends or associates. Examples from a non-Western society include those related by anthropologist Robert Lowie in his classic

Generalized reciprocity. A mode of exchange in which the value of the gift is not calculated, nor is the time of repayment specified. • **Balanced reciprocity.** A mode of exchange in which the giving and the receiving are specific as to the value of the goods and the time of their delivery.

account of the Absaroke (Crow) Indians.[15] A woman skilled in the tanning of buffalo hides might offer her services to a neighbor who needed a new cover for her tepee. It took an expert to design a tepee cover, which required from 14 to 20 skins. The designer might need as many as 20 collaborators, whom she instructed in the sewing together of the skins and whom the tepee owner might remunerate with a feast. The designer herself would be given some kind of property by the tepee owner. In another example from the Absaroke, Lowie reports that if a married woman brought her brother a present of food, he might reciprocate with a present of 10 arrows for her husband, which rated as the equivalent of a horse.

Giving, receiving, and sharing as so far described constitute a form of social security or insurance. A family contributes to others when they have the means and can count on receiving from others in time of need. A leveling mechanism is at work in the process of generalized or balanced reciprocity, promoting an egalitarian distribution of wealth over the long run.

Negative reciprocity is a third form of exchange, in which the giver tries to get the better of the deal. The parties involved have opposing interests, usually are members of different communities, and are not closely related. The ultimate form of negative reciprocity is to take something by force. Less extreme forms involve guile and deception, or at the least, hard bargaining. In the United States, an example would be the stereotype of the car salesman who claims a car was "driven by a little old lady to church" when in fact it was not and is likely to develop problems soon after it leaves the sales lot. Among the Navajo Indians of the southwestern United States, according to anthropologist Clyde Kluckhohn, "to deceive when trading with foreign peoples is morally accepted."[16]

BARTER AND TRADE

Exchanges that occur within a group of people generally take the form of generalized or balanced reciprocity. When they occur between two groups, a potential for hostility and competition is apt to exist. Therefore, such exchanges may well be in the form of negative reciprocity, unless some sort of arrangement has been made to ensure at least an approach to balance. *Barter* is one form of negative reciprocity by which scarce items from one group are exchanged for desirable goods from another group. Relative value is calculated, and despite an outward show of indifference, sharp trading is more the rule, when compared to the more balanced nature of exchanges within a group.

An arrangement that combined elements of balanced reciprocity as well as barter existed between the Kota, in India, and three neighboring peoples who traded their surplus goods and certain services with the Kota. The Kota were the musicians and artisans for the region. They exchanged their iron tools with the other three groups and provided the music essential for ceremonial occasions. The Toda furnished to the Kota ghee (a kind of butter) for certain ceremonies and buffalo for funerals; relations between the two peoples were amicable. The Badaga were agricultural and traded their grain for music and tools. Between the Kota and Badaga there was a feeling of great competition, which sometimes led to one-sided trading practices; usually the Kota procured the advantage. The forest-dwelling Kurumba, who were renowned as sorcerers, had honey, canes, and occasionally fruits to offer, but their main contribution was protection against the supernatural. The Kota feared the Kurumba, and the Kurumba took advantage of this in their trade dealings, so that they always got more than they gave. Thus, great latent hostility existed between these two peoples.

Silent trade is a specialized form of barter in which no verbal communication takes place. In fact, it may involve no actual face-to-face contact at all. Such cases have often characterized the dealings between food-foraging peoples and their food-producing neighbors, as the former have supplied over the past 2,000 or so years various commodities in demand in the world economy. A classic description of such trade follows:

> The forest people creep through the lianas to the trading place, and leave a neat pile of jungle products, such as wax, camphor, monkeys' gall bladders, birds' nests for Chinese soup. They creep back a certain distance, and wait in a safe place. The partners to the exchange, who are usually agriculturalists with a more elaborate and extensive set of material possessions but who cannot be bothered stumbling through the jungle after

[15] Lowie, R. (1956). *Crow Indians* (p. 75). New York: Holt, Rinehart and Winston. (Original edition, 1935.)

[16] Kluckhohn, C. (1972). Quoted in Sahlins, M. (1972). *Stone Age economics* (p. 200). Chicago: Aldine.

Negative reciprocity. A form of exchange in which the giver tries to get the better of the exchange. • **Silent trade.** A form of barter in which no verbal communication takes place.

Political fund-raising in the United States involves elements of both balance and negative reciprocity. Large contributors expect that their "generosity" will buy influence with a candidate, resulting in considerations and benefits of equal value. The recipient of the contribution, however, may seek to do as little as possible in return, but not so little as to jeopardize future contributions.

wax when they have someone else to do it for them, discover the little pile, and lay down beside it what they consider its equivalent in metal cutting tools, cheap cloth, bananas, and the like. They too discreetly retire. The shy folk then reappear, inspect the two piles, and if they are satisfied, take the second one away. Then the opposite group comes back and takes pile number one, and the exchange is completed. If the forest people are dissatisfied, they can retire once more, and if the other people want to increase their offering they may, time and again, until everyone is happy.[17]

To speculate about the reasons for silent trade, in some situations it may be silent for lack of a common language. More often silent trade may serve to control situations of distrust so as to keep relations peaceful. In a very real sense, good relations are maintained by preventing relations. Another possibility that does not exclude the others is that it makes exchange possible where problems of status might make verbal communication unthinkable. In any event, it provides for the exchange of goods between groups in spite of potential barriers.

The Kula Ring

Although we tend to think of trade as something undertaken for purely practical purposes in order to gain access to desired goods and services, not all trade is motivated by economic considerations. A classic case of this is the Kula ring (also referred to as the Kula), a Trobriand inter-island trading system whereby prestige items are ceremoniously exchanged. Malinowski first described

[17] Coon, C. S. (1948). *A reader in general anthropology* (p. 594). New York: Holt, Rinehart and Winston.

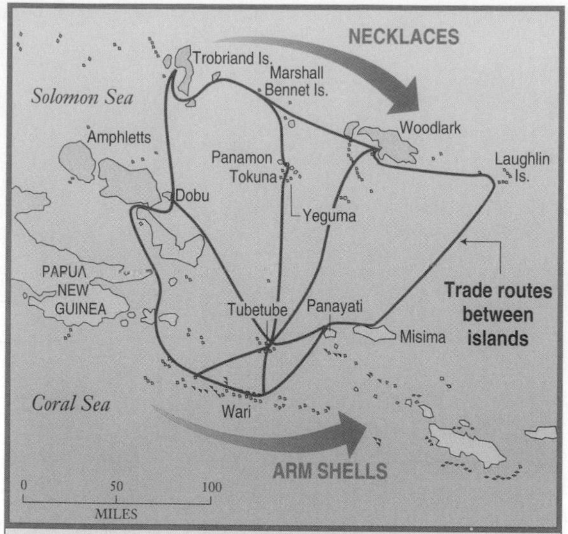

FIGURE 18.2
THE CEREMONIAL TRADING OF NECKLACES AND ARM SHELLS IN THE KULA RING ENCOURAGES TRADE THROUGHOUT MELANESIA.

the Kula in 1920, but it is still going strong today.[18] From their coral atolls, men periodically set sail in their canoes to exchange shell valuables with their Kula partners, who live on distant islands. These voyages take men away from their homes for weeks, even months, at a time and may expose them to various hardships along the way. The valuables are red shell necklaces that always circulate in a clockwise direction, and ornate white arm shells that move in the opposite direction (Figure 18.2). These objects are ranked according to their size, their color, how finely polished they are, and their particular histories. Such is the fame of some that, when they appear in a village, they create a sensation. No one man holds these valuables for very long—at most, perhaps 10 years. Holding on to an arm shell or necklace too long risks disrupting the "path" it must follow as it is passed from one partner to another.

Although men on Kula voyages may use the opportunity to trade for other things, this is not the reason for such voyages, nor is the Kula even necessary for trade to occur. In fact, overseas trade is regularly undertaken without the exchange of shell valuables. Instead, Trobriand men seek to create history through their Kula exchanges. By circulating armbands and necklaces that accumulate the histories of their travels and names of those who have possessed them, men proclaim their individual fame and talent, gaining considerable influence for themselves in the process. Although the idea is to match the size and value of one shell for another, men draw on all their negotiating skills, material resources, and magical expertise to gain access to the strongest partners and most valuable shells; thus, an element of negative reciprocity arises, as a man may divert shells from their proper "paths," or entice others to compete for whatever necklaces and armbands he may have to offer. But when all is said and done, success is limited, for although a man may keep a shell for 5 or 10 years, sooner or later it must be passed on to others.

The Kula is a most elaborate complex of ceremony, political relationships, economic exchange, travel, magic, and social integration. To see it only in its economic aspects is to misunderstand it completely. The Kula demonstrates once more how inseparable economic matters are from the rest of culture and shows that economics is not a realm unto itself. This is just as true in modern industrial societies as it is in traditional Trobriand society; when the United States stopped trading with Cuba, Haiti, Iran, Iraq, and Serbia, for instance, it was for political rather than economic reasons. Indeed, economic embar-

This photo shows Kula valuables.

[18] Weiner, A. B. (1988). *The Trobrianders of Papua New Guinea* (pp. 139–157). New York: Holt, Rinehart and Winston.

In the United States, the progressive income tax acts to redistribute wealth from more-to-less wealthy people. Here, presidential candidate George W. Bush explains his tax-cut proposal to a group at a political rally. Because it promotes accumulation by the already wealthy, this, too, would act to redistribute wealth, as taxes invariably do.

goes have become popular as political weapons wielded by both governments and special interest groups. On a less political note, consider how retail activity in the United States peaks in December for a combination of religious and social, rather than purely economic, reasons.

Redistribution

In societies with a sufficient surplus to support some sort of government, income flows into the public coffers in the form of gifts, taxes, and the spoils of war, following which it is distributed again. The chief, king, or whoever the agent of redistribution may be has three motives in disposing of this income: The first is to maintain a position of superiority through a display of wealth; the second is to assure those who support the agent an adequate standard of living; and the third is to establish alliances outside the agent's territory.

The administration of the ancient Inca empire in the Andes highlands of South America was one of the most efficient the world has ever known, both in the collection of taxes and methods of control.[19] A census was kept of the population and resources. Tributes in goods and, more important, in services were levied. Each craft specialist had to produce a specific quota of goods from materials supplied by overseers. Forced labor was used for some agricultural work or work in the mines. Forced labor was also employed in a program of public works that included a remarkable system of roads and bridges throughout the mountainous terrain, aqueducts that guaranteed a supply of water, and storehouses that held surplus food for times of famine. Careful accounts were kept of income and expenditures. A governmental bureaucracy had the responsibility for ensuring production was maintained and commodities were distributed according to the regulations set forth by the ruling powers.

Through the activities of the government, **redistribution** took place. The ruling class lived in great luxury, but goods were redistributed to the common people as necessary. Redistribution is a pattern of distribution in which the exchange is not between individuals or between groups, but, rather, a proportion of the products of labor is funneled into one source and is parceled out again as directed by a central administration. Commonly, it involves an element of coercion. Taxes are a form of redistribution in the United States. People pay taxes to the government, some of which support the government itself while the rest are redistributed either in cash, such as welfare payments and government loans or subsidies to business, or in the form of services, such as food and drug inspection, construction of highways, support of the

[19] Mason, J. A. (1957). *The ancient civilizations of Peru.* Baltimore, MD: Penguin.

Redistribution. A form of exchange in which goods flow into a central place, where they are sorted, counted, and reallocated.

The giving of gifts at a potlatch on the Northwest Coast of North America. Among these Native Americans, one gains prestige by giving away valuables at the potlatch.

military, and the like. With the growth of the federal deficit after 1980, more and more wealth in the United States was increasingly redistributed from middle-income taxpayers to wealthy holders of government securities. For redistribution to be possible, a society must have a centralized system of political organization, as well as an economic surplus beyond people's immediate needs.

Distribution of Wealth

In societies where people devote most of their time to subsistence activities, gradations of wealth are small, kept that way through leveling mechanisms and systems of reciprocity that serve to distribute in a fairly equitable fashion what little wealth exists. Display for social prestige, what economist Thorstein Veblen called **conspicuous consumption,** is a strong motivating force for the distribution of wealth in societies where a substantial surplus is produced. It has, of course, long been recognized that conspicuous consumption plays a prominent role in Western societies as individuals compete with one another for prestige. Indeed, many North Americans spend much of their lives trying to impress others, and this requires the display of items symbolic of prestigious positions in life. This all fits very nicely into an economy based on consumer wants:

> In an expanding economy based on consumer wants, every effort must be made to place the standard of living in the center of public and private consideration, and every effort must therefore be lent to remove material and psychological impediments to consumption. Hence, rather than feelings of restraint, feelings of letting-go must be in the ascendant, and the institutions supporting restraint must recede into the background and give way to their opposite.[20]

A form of conspicuous consumption also occurs in some foraging and crop-cultivating societies, as illustrated by the potlatches given by Indians on the Northwest Coast of North America, or the lavish feasts given by Big Men in many societies of Papua New Guinea. In both cases, food and various other items of wealth, laboriously accumulated over several preceding months, are publically given away to others. Western observers are apt to see such grandiose displays as wasteful in the extreme, one reason why the Canadian government sought for many decades to suppress potlatches. To the people involved, however, these giveaways accomplish important social and political goals, as the following analysis demonstrates.

[20] Henry, J. (1974). A theory for an anthropological analysis of American culture. In J. G. Jorgensen & M. Truzzi (Eds.). *Anthropology and American life* (p. 14). Englewood Cliffs, NJ: Prentice-Hall.

Conspicuous consumption. A term coined by Thorstein Veblen to describe the display of wealth for social prestige.

Prestige Economics in Papua New Guinea[21]

Original Study

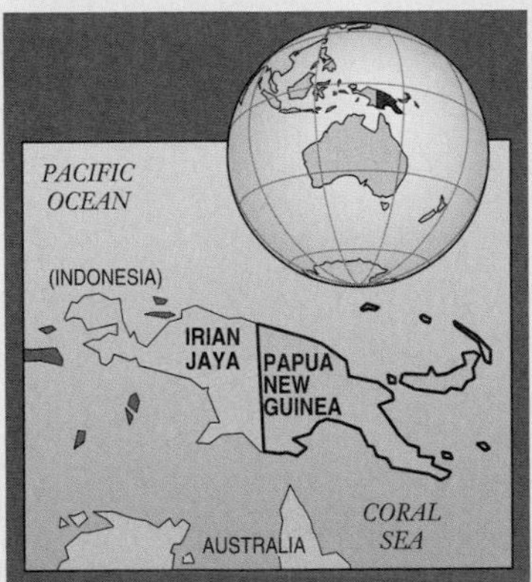

The average Enga patrilineage group [people who trace their descent back through men to a particular male ancestor] numbers about 33 and . . . [constitutes a] . . . close knit extended family. . . . At the next level, however, is the Enga subclan, a [larger order patrilineal descent] group numbering about 90 members that owns a sacred dance ground and a sacred grove of trees. Members of a subclan are required to pool wealth for bride payments whenever any of their members marries and in support of one of their members who is striving to become a Big Man. A subclan is in competition with other subclans for prestige, which affects its members' ability to obtain wives and their desirability as partners in regional alliances. An individual householder is motivated to contribute to his subclan's political and economic activities, therefore, because his immediate family's self-interest is intimately bound with that of the subclan.

The Enga subclan is a unit approximately the size of the largest corporate kin groups in societies occupying the less densely populated highland fringe of New Guinea, such as the Tsembaga [see Chapter 6]. But the Enga are organized into a still higher level grouping [also based on patrilineal descent], the clan, which averages about 350 members and is the ultimate owner and defender of the territory of the clan, from which all clan members ultimately derive their subsistence. Clans own carefully defined territories and defend them both in battle and on ceremonial occasions. They are led by Big Men who speak for their clans in interclan relations and who work within their clans to mobilize the separate households for military, political, and ceremonial action.

Like the subclan, the clan is an arena for dramatic public activities. The clan owns a main dance ground and an ancestral cult house. At these ceremonial centers, public gatherings take place that emphasize the unity of the group as against other clans. Sackschewsky . . . sees this as an essential tactic to overcome the fierce independence of Enga households, where "each man makes his own decisions." Such familistic independence creates problems for Big Men, who encourage interfamily unity in the effort to enhance the strength of their own clans in a fiercely competitive and dangerous social environment.

Let us imagine the problems faced by the members of an Enga clan. They are trying to make an adequate subsistence from small amounts of intensely utilized land. Surrounding them is a world of enemies ready to drive them from their land and seize it at the first sign of weakness. They must attempt to neutralize this external threat by several means: (1) by maintaining a large, unified group, they show strength in numbers, making others afraid to attack them; (2) by collaborating in the accumulation of food and wealth to be generously given away at ceremonies, they make themselves attractive as feasting partners; and (3) by being strong and wealthy, they become attractive as allies for defensive purposes, turning their neighbors either into friends or into outnumbered enemies. These three goals can be achieved only if each member of a clan is willing to fight on behalf of other members, to avoid fighting within the clan (even though it is with his clan members that a man is most directly in competition for

[21] Johnson, A. (1989). Horticulturists: Economic behavior in tribes. In S. Plattner (Ed.). *Economic anthropology* (pp. 63–67). Stanford, CA: Stanford University Press.

Original Study

land, since they are his most immediate neighbors), and to give up a share of his precious household accumulation of food and wealth objects in order that his Big Man may host an impressive feast.

This dependence of the household on the economic and political success of the clan is the basis of the Big Man's power. A Big Man is a local leader who motivates his followers to act in concert. He does not hold office and has no ultimate institutional power, so he must lead by pleading and bullyragging. His personal characteristics make him a leader . . . : He is usually a good speaker, convincing to his listeners; he has an excellent memory for kinship relations and for past transactions in societies where there is no writing; he is a peacemaker whenever possible, arranging compensatory payments and fines in order to avoid direct violent retribution from groups who feel they have been injured; and, when all else fails, he leads his followers into battle.

Of great importance in this system is the exchange of brides between patrilineal groups, for which payments of food, especially pigs, and wealth objects are required. An individual's political position—which affects his access to land, pigs, and other necessities—depends on alliances formed via his own marriage and those of his close kin. A Big Man, skilled as a negotiator and extremely knowledgeable about the delicate web of alliances created across the generations by a myriad of previous marriages and wealth payments, can help a group to marry well and maintain its competitive edge. By arranging his own marriages, of course, the Big Man can not only increase the number of alliances in which he is personally involved, but he can also bring more women, which is to say, more production of sweet potatoes and pigs, under his control. Hence, as he strengthens his group, he does not neglect his own personal power, as measured by his control of women, pigs, and wealth objects. His efforts both public and personal come together most visibly when he succeeds in hosting a feast.

Among the most dramatic economic institutions on earth, the Melanesian feasts have fascinated economic anthropologists. The Big Man works for months, painfully acquiring food and wealth from his reluctant followers, only to present them in spectacular accumulations—as **gifts** to his allies. But the generosity has an edge, as the Kawelka Big Man Ongka put it: "I have won. I have knocked you down by giving so much. . . . " And the Big Man expects that his turn will come to be hosted by his allies, when they will be morally bound to return his gift with an equivalent or larger one. The "conspicuous consumption" and underlying competitiveness of these displays of generosity have been regarded as so similar to philanthropy in our own economy as to seem to close the gap between "primitive" and "modern" economies.

But the Big Man feast must be understood in context. Similar to the famous potlatch of the Northwest Coast of North America, these feasts do not exist merely as arenas for grandiose men to flaunt their ambition. As analyzed for the Northwest Coast, the competitive feast is the most dramatic event in a complex of interactions that maintain what Newman . . . calls "the intergroup collectivity." We must remember that, beyond the Enga clan, there is no group that can guarantee the rights of the individual, in the sense that the modern state does for us. Beyond the clan are only allies, strangers, and enemies. Many of them covet the desirable lands of other clans, and, if they sense weakness, they will strike. Small groups—weak in numbers and vulnerable to attack—must seek to swell their numbers and to attract allies in other clans. Thus an individual family's access to the means of subsistence depends on the success of its clan in the political arena, ultimately in the size of fighting force that can be mounted from within the clan and recruited from allied clans.

In the absence of courts and constitutions regulating intergroup relations, the Big Men assume central importance. It is they who maintain and advertise their group's attractiveness as allies (hence the bragging and showmanship that accompany Big Man feasts), who mediate disputes to avoid the dangerous extremity of homicidal violence, who remember old alliances and initiate new ones. Despite the public competitiveness between Big Men as they attempt to humiliate one another with generosity, over time they develop relationships of a predictable, even trustworthy, nature with other Big Men, lending intergroup stability in an unstable world.

A good example of this stabilizing effect is seen in the **Te** cycle, a series of competitive exchanges that link many Central Enga clans. Starting at one end of the chain, initiatory gifts of pigs, salt, and other valuables are given as individual exchanges from one partner to the next down the chain of clans. Big Men do not have to be directly involved, since such individual exchanges follow personal lines of alliance. But because the gifts are flowing in one direction down the chain of clans, after a time the giving clans begin to demand repayment. As this signal passes through the system, individuals amass pigs for larger feasts at the opposite, or receiving end, of the chain. These larger interclan ceremonies are full of oratory and display that serve to advertise the size and wealth of individual clans. Over a period of months a series of large gifting ceremonies move back up the chain of clans toward the beginning. The emphasis on prestige in these ceremonies is certainly gratifying to the participants, but it serves larger purposes: to maintain peace by substituting competitive feasting for open warfare, to establish and reinforce alliances, and to advertise a clan's attractiveness as an ally and fearsomeness as an enemy.

The central points to note from this example are the following:

1. The high population density of the Enga . . . implies two related developments: First, there is little wild forest left and virtually no supply of wild foods for the diet; and, second, the best horticultural land is fully occupied and in permanent use. These two primary consequences of population growth have further implications.
2. One is an intensive mode of food production that does not rely so much on regeneration of natural soil fertility through fallowing as upon mounding and the addition of green manure to soils. Because of the Enga's reliance on pigs, these fields must support not only the human population but also that of the pigs, who consume as much garden produce as humans do. The labor costs of pigs therefore include both producing their food and building fences to control their predation of gardens. Although the Enga populations are able to provide their basic nutritional needs in this manner, other highland groups with similar economies do show some signs of malnutrition, suggesting that overall production is not much more than adequate.
3. Furthermore, with land scarce, warfare shows a clear emphasis on territorial expansion and displacement. In response to this basic threat to their livelihood, families participate, albeit somewhat reluctantly, in the political activities of the lineage and clan. Although these activities often appear belligerent and can lead to warfare by deflecting hostilities outside the clan or local alliance of clans, it remains true that they have the primary function of preventing violence and stabilizing access to land.

The three major paths for creating alliances are marriage exchanges, sharing of food at feasts (commensality), and an intricate web of debt and credit established through exchanges of food and wealth objects. All of these together constitute the prestige economies for which such groups are famous. Crucial junctures in the prestige economy are occupied by Big Men, who earn their status by personally managing the complex alliances that provide a degree of security to otherwise vulnerable groups of closely related kin.

The End

For these Big Man feasts, a surplus is created for the express purpose of gaining prestige—hence the term **prestige economy**—through a display of wealth and generous giving of gifts. But, unlike conspicuous consumption in Western societies, the emphasis is not on the accumulation of goods that then become unavailable to others. Instead, the emphasis is on giving away, or at least getting rid of one's wealth goods. Thus, these feasts serve as a leveling mechanism, preventing some individuals from accumulating too much wealth at the expense of other members of society.

A packer from Kozmo.com prepares an order. With the advent of online shopping, people can buy and sell even though goods are not physically present.

Market Exchange

To an economist, **market exchange** has to do with the buying and selling of goods and services, with prices set by powers of supply and demand. Loyalties and values are not supposed to play a role, but they often do. Just where the buying and selling takes place is largely irrelevant, so we must distinguish between market *exchange* and the market *place.* Although some of our market transactions do take place in a specific identifiable location—much of the trade in cotton, for example, takes place in the New Orleans Cotton Exchange—it is also quite possible for a North American to buy and sell goods without ever being on the same side of the continent as the other party. When people talk about a market in today's world, the particular place where something is sold is often not important at all. For example, think of the way people speak of a "market" for certain types of automobiles, or for mouthwash.

Until well into the 20th century, market exchange typically was carried out in specific places, as it still is in much of the non-Western world, and even numerous centuries-old European towns and cities. In peasant or agrarian societies, marketplaces overseen by a centralized political authority provide the opportunity for farmers living in rural regions to exchange some of their livestock and produce for needed items manufactured in factories or the workshops of craft specialists living (usually) in towns and cities. Thus, some sort of complex division of labor as well as centralized political organization is necessary for the appearance of markets. In the marketplace land, labor, and occupations are not bought and sold as they are through the Western market economy. In other words, what happens in these marketplaces has little to do with the price of land, the amount paid for labor, or the cost of services. The market is local, specific, and contained. Prices are apt to be set on the basis of face-to-face bargaining (buy cheap and sell dear is the order of the day) rather than by faceless "market forces" wholly removed from the transaction itself. Nor need some form of money be involved; instead, goods may be directly exchanged through some form of reciprocity between the specific individuals involved.

In non-Western societies, marketplaces have much of the excitement of a fair; they are vibrant places where one's senses are assaulted by a host of colorful sights, sounds, and smells. Indeed, many of the large urban and suburban malls built in the United States and other industrialized countries over the past few decades have tried to recreate, though in a more contrived manner, some of the interest and excitement of more traditional marketplaces. In the latter, noneconomic activities may even overshadow the economic. Social relationships are as important there as they

Prestige economy. Creation of a surplus for the express purpose of gaining prestige through a public display of wealth that is given away as gifts. • **Market exchange.** The buying and selling of goods and services, with prices set by powers of supply and demand.

In many non-Western societies, the market is an important focus of social as well as economic activity, as typified by this market in Toubokru, Ivory Coast.

are anywhere else. As anthropologist Stuart Plattner observes, the marketplace is where friendships are made, love affairs begun, and marriages arranged.[22] Dancers and musicians may perform, and the end of the day may be marked by drinking, dancing, and fighting. At the market, too, people gather to hear news. In ancient Mexico, under the Aztecs, people were required by law to go to market at specific intervals to keep informed about current events. Government officials held court and settled judicial disputes at the market. Thus, the market is a gathering place where people renew friendships, see relatives, gossip, and keep up with the world, while procuring needed goods they cannot produce for themselves.

Although there have been marketplaces without money of any sort, money does facilitate trade. **Money** may be defined as something used to make payments for other goods and services as well as to measure their value. Its critical attributes are durability, portability, divisibility, recognizability, and fungibility (ability to substitute any item of money for any other monetary item of the same value, as when four quarters are substituted for a dollar bill). The wide range of things that have been used as money in one or another society includes salt, shells, stones, beads, feathers, fur, bones, teeth, and of course metals, from iron to gold and silver. Among the Aztecs of Mexico, both cacao beans and cotton cloaks served as money. The beans could be used to purchase merchandise and labor, though usually as a supplement to barter; if the value of the items exchanged was not equal, cacao beans could be used to make up the difference. Cotton cloaks represented a higher denomination in the monetary system, with 65 to 300 beans equivalent to one cloak, depending on the latter's quality. Cloaks could be used to obtain credit, to purchase land, as restitution for theft, and to ransom slaves, whose value in any case was measured in terms of cloaks. Interestingly, counterfeiting was not unknown to the Aztecs—unscrupulous people sometimes carefully peeled back the outer skin of cacao beans, removed the contents, and then substituted packed earth!

Ancient Lydian money: the world's first coins. Lydia was located in Anatolia, which is now Turkey.

[22] Plattner, S. (1989). Markets and market places. In S. Plattner (Ed.). *Economic anthropology* (p. 171). Stanford, CA: Stanford University Press.

Money. Anything used to make payments for other things (goods or labor) as well as to measure their value; may be special purpose or multipurpose.

Among the Tiv of West Africa, brass rods might be exchanged for cattle, with the seller then using the rods to purchase slaves (the economic value of the cattle being converted into the rods and then reconverted into slaves). In both the Aztec and Tiv cases, the money in question is (or was) only used for special purposes. To a Tiv, the idea of exchanging a brass rod for subsistence foods is repugnant, and most market exchanges involve direct barter. Special-purpose monies usually have more moral restrictions on their use than do general-purpose monies, which can be used to purchase just about anything. Even the latter category, however, has limits. For example, in the United States it is considered immoral, as well as illegal, to exchange money for sexual and political favors, even though infractions of these constraints occur.

The United States, as part of a reaction to the increasingly "face-to-faceless" nature of the modern economic system, is having something of a revival and proliferation of "flea markets" (Figure 18.3), where anyone, for a small fee, may display and sell handicrafts, secondhand items, farm produce, and paintings in a face-to-face setting. There is excitement in the search for bargains and an opportunity for haggling. A carnival atmosphere prevails, with eating, laughing, and conversation, and items even may be bartered without any cash passing hands. These flea markets, fairs, festivals, and farmers' markets are similar to the marketplaces of non-Western societies.

Flea markets also raise the issue of the distinction between the informal and formal sectors of the market economy. The **informal economy** may be defined as the system by which producers of goods and services provide marketable commodities that for various reasons escape government control (enumeration, regulation, or other type of public monitoring or auditing). Such enterprises may encompass just about anything: market gardening, making and selling beer or other alcoholic beverages, doing repair or construction work, begging, selling things on the street, performing ritual services, lending money, dealing drugs, picking pockets, and gambling, to mention just a few. These sorts of "off-the-books" or "black market" activities have been known for a long time but generally have been dismissed by econ-

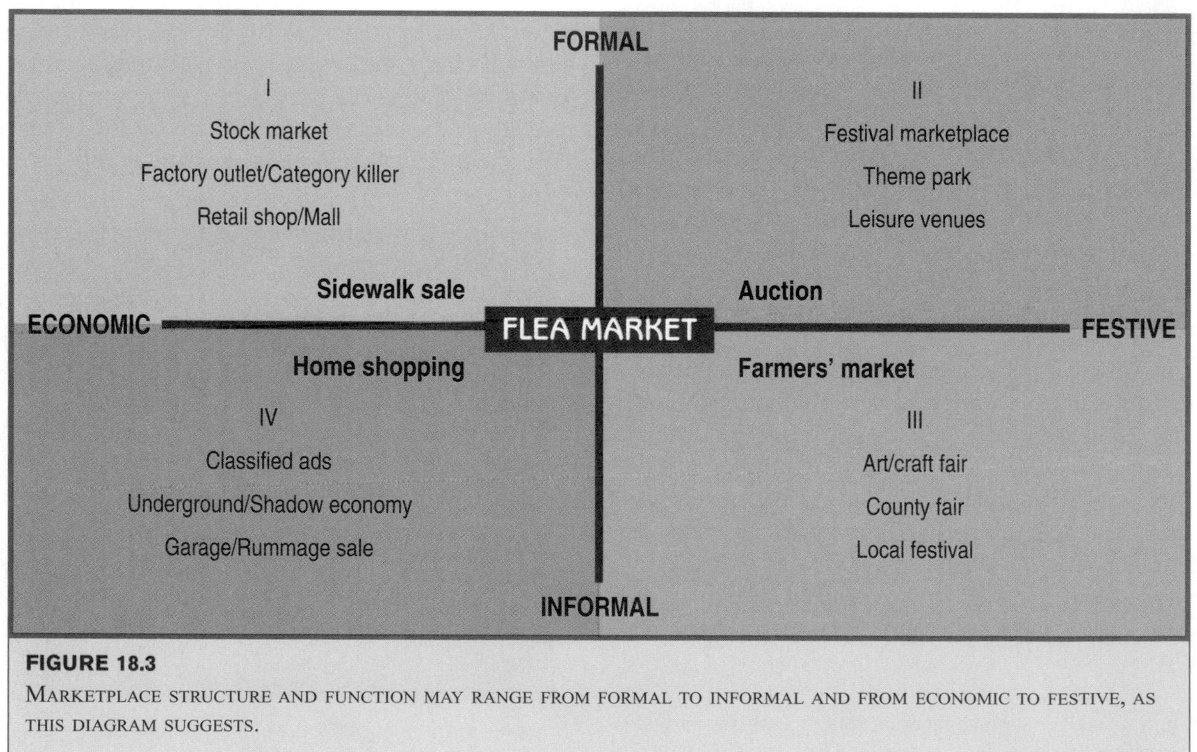

FIGURE 18.3
MARKETPLACE STRUCTURE AND FUNCTION MAY RANGE FROM FORMAL TO INFORMAL AND FROM ECONOMIC TO FESTIVE, AS THIS DIAGRAM SUGGESTS.

Informal economy. The production of marketable commodities that for various reasons escape enumeration, regulation, or any other sort of public monitoring or auditing.

omists as marginal and therefore more of an annoyance than anything of importance. It is also difficult for them to track; yet, in many countries of the world, the informal economy is, in fact, more important than the formal economy. In many places, large numbers of under- and unemployed people who have only limited access to the formal sector in effect improvise as best they can various means of "getting by" on scant resources. Meanwhile, more affluent members of society may evade various regulations in order to maximize returns and/or to vent their frustrations at their perceived loss of self-determination in the face of increasing government regulation.

ECONOMICS, CULTURE, AND THE WORLD OF BUSINESS

At the start of this chapter, we noted that when studying the economies of foraging, pastoral, and traditional farming peoples we perhaps are most apt to fall prey to our own ethnocentric biases. The misunderstandings that result from our failure to overcome these biases are of major importance to us in the modern world in at least two ways. For one, they encourage development schemes for countries that, by Western economic standards, are regarded as "underdeveloped" (a comfortably ethnocentric term), schemes that all too often result in poverty, poor health, discontent, and a host of other ills. In northeastern Brazil, for example, development of large-scale plantations to grow sisal for export to the United States took over numerous small farms where peasants grew food in order to feed themselves. With this change, peasants were forced into the ranks of the unemployed. Because the farmers were unable to earn enough money to satisfy their minimal nutritional needs, the incidence of malnutrition rose dramatically. Similarly, development projects in Africa, designed to bring about changes in local hydrology, vegetation, and settlement patterns—and even programs aimed at reducing certain diseases—have frequently led directly to *increased* disease rates.[23] Fortunately, there is now a growing awareness on the part of development officials that future projects are unlikely to succeed without the expertise that anthropologically trained people can bring to bear.

Achieving an understanding of the economic systems of other peoples that is not limited by the logic, hopes, and expectations of one's own culture has also become important for corporate executives in today's world. At least, recognition of how embedded such systems are within the cultures of which the systems are parts could avoid problems of the sort experienced by Gerber, when this corporation started selling baby foods in Africa. As in the United States, Gerber's labels featured a picture of a smiling baby. Only later did company officials learn that, in Africa, companies routinely put pictures on their labels of the product inside, since many people can't read. Along the same line, Frank Perdue's line in ads for Perdue chickens, "It takes a strong man to make a tender chicken" was translated into Spanish as "It takes an aroused man to make a chicken affectionate."[24] Anthropologists Edward and Mildred Hall describe another case of the same sort:

Steve Barnett, who earned his Ph.D. in anthropology from the University of Chicago, was for several years head of a consulting firm that served several large corporations. He is now a vice pesident at Citibank in Long Island City, New York, where he studies long-term cultural trends in patterns of consumption worldwide.

> José Ybarra and Sir Edmund Jones are at the same party and it is important for them to establish a cordial relationship for business reasons. Each is trying to be warm and friendly, yet they will part with mutual distrust and their business transaction will probably fall through. José, in Latin fashion, moved closer and closer to Sir Edmund as

---

[23] Bodley, J. H. (1990). *Victims of progress* (3rd ed.)(p. 141). Mountain View, CA: Mayfield.

[24] Anonymous (1999). Madison Avenue relevance. *Anthropology Newsletter, 40* (4):32.

These Kikyuyu women in highland Kenya exemplify the fact that in Africa much of the farming is women's work. Failure to accept this is responsible for the failure of many development schemes, since outside experts design projects that usually assume the men are the farmers.

they spoke, and this movement was miscommunicated as pushiness to Sir Edmund, who kept backing away from this intimacy, and this was miscommunicated to José as coldness.[25]

When the so-called underdeveloped countries of Africa, Asia, and Central and South America are involved, the chances for cross-cultural misunderstandings increase dramatically. The executives of major corporations realize their dependency on these countries for raw materials, they are increasingly inclined to manufacture their products in them, and they see their best potential for market expansion as lying outside North America and Europe. That is why business recruiters on college campuses in the United States are on the lookout for job candidates with the kind of understanding of the world anthropology provides.

[25] Hall, E. T., & Hall, M. R. (1986). The sounds of silence. In E. Angeloni (Ed.). *Anthropology 86/87* (p. 65). Guilford CT: Dushkin.

Anthropology Applied

Anthropology and the World of Business

When people hear of anthropologists working for, and sometimes running, private-sector businesses ranging from major financial institutions to consulting firms for major corporations, their reaction is usually one of surprise. In the public mind, anthropologists are supposed to work in exotic, faraway places like remote islands, deep forests, hostile deserts, or arctic wastes—not in the world of business. After all, when anthropology gains the attention of the media, is it not on account of the "discovery" of a "last surviving Stone Age tribe," the uncovering of some ancient "lost city," or the recovery of bones of some remote human ancestor, usually in some out-of-the-way part of the world?

Not only have anthropologists found niches for themselves in the world of business, but since 1972, the number of them going into business has grown fivefold. The reason for their success is that they have skills to offer the corporate world that other social and behavioral scientists do not. As anthropologist Dureen Hughes, who has spent the years since receiving her Ph.D. (in 1994) doing international consulting for a large computer firm, explains:

> An anthropology degree brings a unique value to various fields in corporate America. Especially valuable to corporate consulting is the training in research methods, specifically nonjudgmental participant observation. This research method translates directly into successful corporate consulting. People like it. People do not like psychology methods (patient-therapist mode), nor do they like sociology methods (survey based). High-end corporate consulting often means going into a situation ignorant of what is really going on. Often your original plans have to be scrapped altogether, and you have to devise new ones on the fly. It's not so different from doing initial anthropological research in an unfamiliar culture: the research methods, essentially nonjudgmental attitude of cultural relativism and ethical dedication to doing no harm to one's informants and their "culture" all prove very attractive, and extremely useful in high-end consulting engagements.
>
> An anthropology degree also brings knowledge of applied anthropology. Initially in high-end consulting engagements, you have to find out through participant observation what is going on, who is involved, what's the problem and what they are trying to accomplish.
>
> The next step is to help them formulate a solution. It's high-end problem solving, planning the steps toward the solution, then making sure that plan is fully agreed to and executed. People with anthropology degrees can bring knowledge of how to craft an acceptable solution and implement that solution to increase the probability of good outcome.*

* Hughes, D. (1999). Mandatory marketing. *Anthropology News, 40* (7), 4.

CHAPTER SUMMARY

An economic system is the means by which goods are produced, distributed, and consumed. Studying the economics of nonliterate, nonindustrial societies can be undertaken only in the context of the total culture of each society. Each society solves the problem of subsisting by allocating raw materials, land, labor, and technology and by distributing goods according to its own priorities.

The work people do is a major productive resource, and the allotment of work is always governed by rules according to gender and age. Only a few broad generalizations can be made covering the kinds of work performed by men and women. Instead of looking for biological imperatives to explain the division of labor by gender, a more productive strategy is to examine the kinds of work men and women do in the context of specific societies to see how it relates to other cultural and historical factors. The cooperation of many people working together is a typical feature of both nonindustrial and industrial societies. Specialization of craft is important even in societies with very simple technologies.

All societies regulate the allocation of land and other valuable resources. In nonindustrial societies, individual ownership of land is rare; generally land is controlled by kinship groups, such as the lineage or band. This system provides flexibility of land use, since the size of the bands and their territories can be adjusted according to availability of resources in any particular place. The technology of a people, in the form of the tools they use and associated knowledge, is related to their mode of subsistence.

In food-foraging societies, codes of generosity promote free access to tools, even though individuals may have made these for their own use. Settled farming communities offer greater opportunities to accumulate material belongings, and inequalities of wealth may develop. In many such communities, though, a relatively egalitarian social order may be maintained through leveling mechanisms.

Nonindustrial people consume most of what they produce themselves, but they do exchange goods. The processes of distribution may be distinguished as reciprocity, redistribution, and market exchange. Reciprocity is a transaction between individuals or groups, involving the exchange of goods and services of roughly equivalent value. Usually it is prescribed by ritual and ceremony.

Barter and trade take place between groups. Trading exchanges have elements of reciprocity but involve a greater calculation of the relative value of goods exchanged. Barter is one form of negative reciprocity, whereby scarce goods from one group are exchanged for desirable goods from another group. Silent trade, which need not involve face-to-face contact, is a specialized form of barter with no verbal communication. It allows control of the potential dangers of negative reciprocity. A classic example of exchange between groups that partakes of both reciprocity and sharp trading is the Kula ring of the Trobriand Islanders.

Strong, centralized political organization is necessary for redistribution to occur. The government assesses each citizen a tax or tribute, uses the proceeds to support the governmental and religious elite, and redistributes the rest, usually in the form of public services. The collection of taxes and delivery of government services and subsidies in the United States is a form of redistribution.

Display for social prestige is a motivating force in societies that produce some surplus of goods. In the United States, goods accumulated for display generally remain in the hands of those who accumulated them, whereas in other societies they are generally given away; the prestige comes from publicly divesting oneself of valuables.

Exchange in the marketplace serves to distribute goods in a region. In nonindustrial societies, the marketplace is usually a specific site where produce, livestock, and material items the people produce are exchanged. It also functions as a social gathering place and a news medium. Although market exchanges may take place without money through bartering and other forms of reciprocity, some form of money at least for special transactions makes market exchange more efficient.

In market economies, the informal sector may become more important than the formal sector as large numbers of under- and unemployed people with marginal access to the formal economy seek to survive. The informal economy consists of those economic activities that escape official scrutiny and regulation.

The anthropological approach to economics has taken on new importance in today's world of international development and commerce. Without it, development schemes for so-called "under-developed" countries are prone to failure, and international trade is handicapped as a result of cross-cultural misunderstandings.

CLASSIC READINGS

Dalton, G. (1971). *Traditional tribal and peasant economies: An introductory survey of economic anthropology.* Reading, MA: Addison-Wesley.

This is just what the title says it is, by a major specialist in economic anthropology.

Leclair, E. E., Jr., & Schneider, H. K. (Eds.). (1968) *Economic anthropology: Readings in theory and analysis.* New York: Holt, Rinehart and Winston.

This book is a selection of significant writings in economic anthropology from the preceding 50 years. In the first section are theoretical papers covering major points of view, and in the second are case materials selected to show the practical application of the various theoretical positions.

Nash, M. (1966). *Primitive and peasant economic systems.* San Francisco: Chandler.

Heavily theoretical, this book studies the problems of economic anthropology, especially the dynamics of social and economic change, in terms of "primitive" and peasant economic systems. It draws on the author's fieldwork in Guatemala, Mexico, and Burma.

Plattner, S. (Ed.) (1989). *Economic anthropology.* Stanford, CA: Stanford University Press.

This is the first comprehensive text in economic anthropology to appear since the 1970s. Twelve scholars in the field contributed chapters on a variety of issues ranging from economic behavior in foraging, horticultural, "preindustrial" state, peasant, and industrial societies; to sex-roles, common-property resources, informal economics in industrial societies, and mass-marketing in urban areas.

PART VI

The Formation of Groups: Solving the Problem of Cooperation

INTRODUCTION

One of the really important things to come from anthropological study is how fundamental cooperation is to human survival. Through cooperation, humans handle even the most basic problems of existence — the need for food and protection not just from the elements but from predatory animals and even one another. To some extent, this is true not only for humans but for other primates. But what really sets humans apart from other primates is some form of regular cooperation between adults in subsistence activities. At the least, this takes the form of a division of labor by gender as seen among food-foraging peoples. Such cooperation is not usual among nonhuman primates; adult chimpanzees, for example, may cooperate to get meat and share it when they get it, but they don't get meat very often, and they don't normally share other kinds of food the way humans regularly do.

Just as cooperation is basic to human nature, the organization of groups is basic to cooperation. Humans form many kinds of groups, each geared toward solving different kinds of problems people must cope with. Social groups are important to humans also because they give identity and support to their members. The basic building block of human societies is the household, where economic production, consumption, inheritance, child rearing, and shelter are organized. Usually, the core of the household consists of some form of family, a group of relatives that stems from the parent-child bond and the interdependence of men and women. Although it may be structured in many different ways, the family always provides for economic cooperation between men and women while furnishing the kind of setting required for child rearing. Another problem all human societies face is the need to regulate sexual activity, and this is one job of marriage. Given the inevitable connection between sexual activity and the production of children, who then must be nurtured, a close interconnection between marriage and family is to be expected.

Many different marriage and family patterns exist the world over, but all societies have some form of marriage and most have some form of family organization. As shown in Chapters 19 and 20, the forms of family and marriage organization are to a large extent shaped by the specific kinds of problems people must solve in particular situations.

Solutions to some organizational challenges are beyond the scope of family and household. These include defense, allocation of resources, and provision of labor for tasks too large for single households. Nonindustrial societies frequently meet these challenges through kinship groups, discussed in Chapter 21. These large, cohesive groups of individuals base their loyalty to one another on descent from a common ancestor or their relationship to a living individual. In cases where a great number of people are linked by kinship, these groups serve the important function of precisely defining the social roles of their members. In this way they reduce the potential for tension that might arise from an individual's sudden and unexpected behavior. They also provide their members with material security and moral support through ritual activities.

Other important forms of human social groups are the subjects of Chapter 22. Where kinship ties do not provide for all of a society's organizational needs, grouping by age and sex are forces that may be used to create social groups. In North America, as well as in many non-Western countries, today and in the past, the organization of persons by age is common. In many cases, too, social groups based on the common interests of their members serve a vital function. In developing countries, they may help ease the transition of rural individuals into urban settings. Finally, groups based on social rank—social classes—are characteristic of the world's civilizations, past and present.

Class structure involves inequalities between classes and is the means one group may use to dominate large numbers of other people. To the extent social class membership cuts across lines of kinship, residence, age, or other group membership, it may work to counteract tendencies for a society to fragment into discrete special-interest groups. Paradoxically, it does so in a divisive way, in that class distinctions systematically deprive people of equal access to important resources. Thus, class conflict has been a recurrent phenomenon in class-structured societies, in spite of the existence of political and religious institutions that function to maintain the status quo. ■

CHAPTER 19

SEX AND MARRIAGE

In the United States, people like to think of marriage in terms of love and starting a family, but as this scene from the television show "Who Wants to Marry a Multi-millionaire?" illustrates, economic concerns enter in as well, as they do in all cultures.

CHAPTER PREVIEW

1

What Is Marriage?

A non-ethnocentric definition of marriage is a relationship between one or more men (male or female) and one or more women (female or male) who are recognized by society as having a continuing claim to the right of sexual access to one another. Because gender is culturally defined, the "man" may be a female, or the "woman" a male. Although in many societies, husbands and wives live together as members of the same household, this is not true in all societies. And though most marriages around the world tend to involve a single spouse, most societies permit, and regard as most desirable, marriage of an individual to multiple spouses.

What Is the Difference Between Marriage and Mating?

All animals, including humans, mate—that is, most form a sexual bond with individuals of the opposite sex. In some species, the bond lasts for life, but in some others, it lasts no longer than a single sex act. Thus, some animals mate with a single individual, while others mate with several. Only marriage, however, is backed by social, legal, and economic forces. Consequently, while mating is biological, marriage is cultural.

Why Is Marriage Universal?

A problem universal to all human societies is the need to regulate sexual relations so that competition over sexual access does not introduce a disruptive, combative influence into society. Because the problem marriage deals with is universal, it follows that it should be universal. The specific form marriage takes is related to who has rights to offspring that normally result from sexual intercourse, as well as how property is distributed.

Among the Trobriand Islanders, whose yam exchanges and Kula voyages we examined in Chapter 18, children who have reached the age of 7 or 8 years begin playing erotic games with each other and imitating adult seductive attitudes. Within another 4 or 5 years they begin to pursue sexual partners in earnest, changing partners often, experimenting sexually first with one, and then another. By the time they are in their midteens, meetings between lovers take up most of the night, and affairs between them are apt to last for several months. Ultimately, lovers begin to meet the same partner again and again, rejecting the advances of others. When the couple is ready, they appear together one morning outside the young man's house as a way of announcing their intention to be married.

For young Trobrianders, attracting sexual partners is an important business, and they spend a great deal of time making themselves look as attractive and seductive as possible. Youthful conversations during the day are loaded with sexual innuendos, and magical spells as well as small gifts are employed to entice a prospective sex partner to the beach at night or to the house in which boys sleep apart from their parents. Because girls, too, sleep apart from their parents, youths and adolescents have considerable freedom in arranging their love affairs. Boys and girls play this game as equals, with neither sex having an advantage over the other.

As anthropologist Annette Weiner points out, all of this sexual activity is not a frivolous, adolescent pastime. Attracting lovers:

> is the first step toward entering the adult world of strategies, where the line between influencing others while not allowing others to gain control of

To attract lovers, young Trobriand Islanders must look as attractive and seductive as possible. The young men shown here have decorated themselves with Johnson's Baby Powder, while the young girl's beauty has been enhanced by decorations given by her father.

> oneself must be carefully learned. . . . Sexual liaisons give adolescents the time and occasion to experiment with all the possibilities and problems that adults face in creating relationships with those who are not relatives. Individual wills may clash, and the achievement of one's desire takes patience, hard work, and determination. The adolescent world of lovemaking has its own dangers and disillusionments. Young people, to the degree they are capable, must learn to be both careful and fearless.[1]

Until the latter part of the 20th century, the Trobriand attitude toward adolescent sexuality was in marked contrast to that of North American society. In the United States, individuals were not supposed to have sexual relations outside of wedlock. Since then, practices in the United States have converged toward those of the Trobriands, even though the traditional ideal of premarital abstinence has not been abandoned entirely. Premarital sexual activity in North American society still cannot be conducted with quite the openness and approval that characterizes the Trobriand situation. As a consequence, it is not subject to the kind of social pressures from the community at large that prepare traditional Trobriand youths for the adult world after marriage.

Unlike chimpanzees and other female apes that signal their fertility through highly visible swelling of their skin, the human female gives no such signal. Thus, males do not know when females are fertile, an inducement for them to hang around for successful reproduction.

CONTROL OF SEXUAL RELATIONS

One distinctively human characteristic is the ability for the human female, like the human male, to engage in sexual relations at any time she wants to or whenever her culture deems it appropriate. Although this ability to perform at any time when provided with the appropriate cue is not unusual for male mammals in general, it is not usual for females. Among most primate species, females whose offspring are weaned but who have not yet become pregnant again are likely to engage in sexual activity around the time of ovulation (approximately once a month), at which time they advertise their availability through highly visible physical signs. Otherwise, they are little interested in such activity. It is among the species most closely related to us, especially bonobos, that exceptions are found. Among both chimpanzees and bonobos, genital swelling indicates ovulation, and sexual activity usually occurs. Such swelling continues, however, even after conception, and so does sex. What sets bonobos apart is that sex may occur even when the female is not swollen; moreover, it takes place between individuals in virtually all combinations of ages and sex. Humans differ, in that female fertility is not signaled by any visible display. Otherwise, they are similar to bonobos in their willingness to engage in sex at any time, or even when the female is pregnant. In some human societies, intercourse during pregnancy is thought to promote the growth of the fetus. Among Trobriand Islanders, for example, a child's identity is thought to come from its mother, but it is the father's job to build up and nurture the child, which he begins to do before birth through frequent intercourse with its mother.

Nor is homosexual behavior at all uncommon among humans. In many societies, as we saw in Chapter 16, it is not looked upon as unnatural, and in some societies homosexual acts are part of rituals required of all boys to become adult men.[2] Certain New Guinea societies, for example, see the transmission of semen from older to younger boys, through oral sex, as vital for building up the strength needed to protect against the supposedly debilitating effects of adult heterosexual intercourse.[3] Even in the United States, with its long-standing hostility toward homosexuality, the phenomenon is far from

[1] Weiner, A. B. (1988). *The Trobrianders of Papua New Guinea* (p. 71). New York: Holt, Rinehart and Winston.

[2] Kirkpatrick, R. C. (2000). The evolution of human homosexual behavior. *Current Anthropology, 41,* 385.

[3] Herdt, G. H. (1993). Semen transactions in Sambia culture. In D. N. Suggs & A. W. Mirade (Eds.). *Culture and human sexuality* (pp. 298–327). Pacific Grove, CA: Brooks/Cole.

Homosexuality, in one form or another, is a widespread phenomenon in human societies. One of the few cultures that has tried to condemn it is the United States where, paradoxically, the immensely popular game of football is loaded with homosexual symbolism.

Attempts by males to dominate females may introduce a competitive, combative element into social relations. Among gorillas, male silverbacks maintain absolute breeding rights over females in their group. All other adult males must acknowledge this dominance or leave the group and attempt to lure females from other groups.

uncommon. It is found in diverse contexts ranging from supposedly celibate clergy to populations in both men's and women's prisons; from lifelong loving relationships between consenting partners to athletic hazing rituals. Even that most popular athletic pastime, American football, is loaded with unequivocal homosexual symbolism and allowed body contact between men, ranging from body blocks and tackles to pats on teammates' bottoms. Indeed, the whole point of the game is for groups of males to assert their masculinity by "penetrating" the "endzones" of rivals.[4]

As much of the above discussion suggests, homosexuality among humans is no more mutually exclusive of heterosexuality than it is among bonobos. But among humans it is always given cultural meaning and subject to social rules, as is *all* sexual behavior. That said, the rules and meanings are subject to great variability from one society to another. On the basis of clues from the behavior of other primates, anthropologists have speculated about the evolutionary significance of the human female's capacity for sexual arousal at any time. The best current explanation is that it arose as a side effect of persistent bipedal locomotion in early hominines.[5] The energetic requirements of this form of locomotion are such that endurance is impossible without a significantly greater hormone output than other primates have. These hormones catalyze the steady release of muscular energy required for endurance; consequently, they make us the "sexiest" of all primates. This is not to say that either men or women are simply at the mercy of their hormones where sex is concerned, for in the human species both males and females have voluntary control over sex. People engage in it when it suits them to do so and when it is deemed appropriate.

Although developed as an accidental by-product of something else, a common phenomenon in evolution, the ability of females as well as males to engage in sex at any time would have been advantageous to early hominines to the extent that it acted, not alone but with other factors, to tie members of both sexes more firmly to the social groups so crucial to their survival. However, while sexual activity can reinforce group ties, it can also be disruptive. This stems from the common primate characteristic of male dominance. On average, males are bigger

[4] Dundes, A. (1996). Into the endzone for a touchdown: A psychoanalytical consideration of American football. In W. A. Haviland & R. J. Gordon (Eds.). *Talking about people: Readings in contemporary anthropology* (2nd ed.) (p. 68). Mountain View, CA: Mayfield.

[5] Spuhler, J. N. (1979). Continuities and discontinuities in anthropoid-hominid behavioral evolution: Bipedal locomotion and sexual reception. In N. A. Chagnon & W. Irons (Eds.). *Evolutionary biology and human social behavior* (pp. 454–461). North Scituate, MA: Duxbury Press.

Anthropology Applied

Anthropology and AIDS

An irony of human life is that sexual activity, necessary for perpetuation of the species as well as a source of pleasure and fulfillment, also can be a source of danger. The problem lies in sexually transmitted diseases, which in recent years have been spreading and increasing in variety. Among these is acquired immune deficiency syndrome, or AIDS, although intravenous drug use and blood transfusions also contributed to its spread. Recent reports specify that 16,000 new cases of AIDS arise in the world *every day!* (See Figure 19.1.) What follows is A. M. Williams's account of what she and other anthropologists have to contribute to our understanding and control of this disease.

> After a decade and a half, it is clear that AIDS is a pandemic experienced in significant ways at local levels. The World Health Organization (WHO) estimates 36 million people are infected with HIV (the virus present in most people with AIDS) worldwide. While HIV and AIDS have hit areas of sub-Saharan Africa and Southeast Asia hardest, as of November 2000, there was a cumulative total of 920,000 AIDS cases in the United States. Where I work in San Francisco, California, a city of less than 800,000 people, there have been 24,509 AIDS cases and 16,838 deaths from AIDS reported since 1980. Of these cases, 22,161 are among gay and bisexual men in the city.*

* *Centers for Disease Control semi-annual AIDS report (through June 1996)*. 1997. Centers For Disease Control. Atlanta, Georgia, and *AIDS monthly surveillance summary (through July 1997)*. 1997. San Francisco Department of Public Health AIDS Office, Seroepidemiology and Surveillance Branch. San Francisco, CA. The earliest tracking of HIV and AIDS were problematic, and many people today still do not know their HIV status. Therefore, the cases reported in San Francisco or anywhere in the world must be understood to be undercounted.

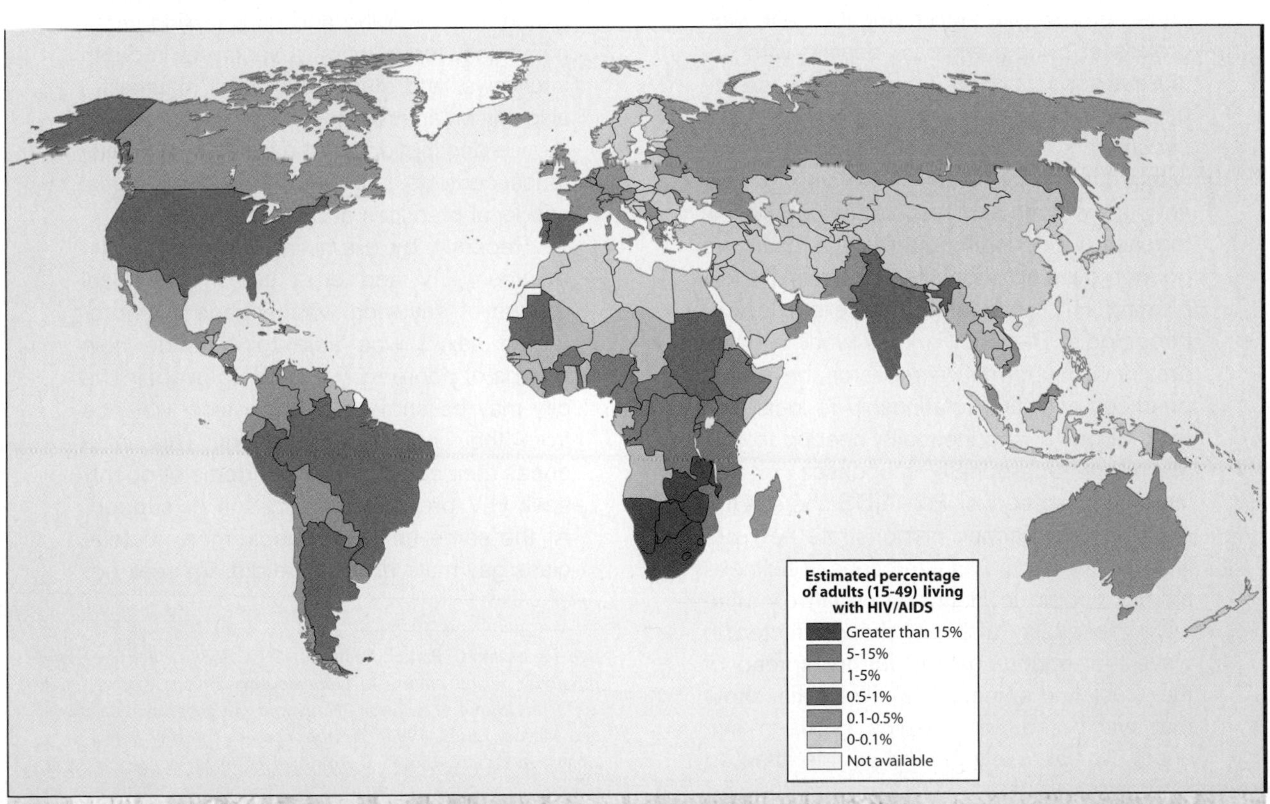

To grasp the proportions of the pandemic, public health perspectives, epidemiological models, biomedical information, and psychological interpretations are used to help figure out who is infected, who will become infected, and where these infections are most likely to occur. However, anthropology takes a different approach, one that helps to clarify the dynamic relationship between people, who are infected or at risk for infection, and their social, cultural, political and economic surroundings. Such research is important because it can provide rich explanations of why people become infected or progress rapidly in HIV disease. This in turn can assist all manner of institutions in addressing a wide variety of local issues for those who need their services and support. Moreover, anthropological analyses often help describe the dynamic links between individual practices, social and cultural systems, and larger structural forces, all of which may combine in ways that encourage the problems of HIV.

Working alone or as part of teams to collect and analyze data, most anthropologists enter into an extended engagement with groups of people who are dealing with numerous aspects of HIV and AIDS. Since anthropology begins from the premise that circumstances and phenomena are complex within different populations, we employ a variety of methods and theoretical frameworks to reach our understandings. As a result, we do not develop monolithic models for explaining HIV and AIDS. For example, anthropologist Richard Parker's work in Brazil provided the formative research on sexual practices and their relationship to local systems of power and inequality needed to create more appropriate responses to the increasing spread of HIV/AIDS there. Others, like Paul Farmer, demonstrate how political economy and constructions of sickness among people in Haiti can negatively influence the quality of life of those infected in ways that encourage the further spread of the virus. And some, like Emily Martin, show that within the relationships between science, clinical research, and people affected by HIV and AIDS there emerge new concepts of body and AIDS that can reveal dynamics about society and the authoritative role of experts in shaping public awareness.†

These anthropological studies and many others contribute to a very broad research and theoretical literature on HIV and AIDS, which can be drawn upon by community-based organizations, policy makers, and other researchers. However, some anthropologists like myself work more directly with groups and organizations on problems posed by primary prevention (preventing HIV transmission) and secondary prevention (slowing the disease's progression). Here anthropology is well-suited for both formative research and conducting evaluations of programs and services. As the anthropologist on a multi-disciplinary research team at the Center for AIDS Prevention Studies, University of California San Francisco, I work directly with local gay male populations and such local AIDS organizations as the San Francisco AIDS Foundation and the STOP AIDS Project. While the team uses many strategies of inquiry, I specifically employ anthropological methods of investigation such as living and participating in the community, conducting a variety of in-depth interviews, and studying archival materials. I also rely on anthropological perspectives that require descriptions of the links between historical contexts, larger structural phenomena, and local practices and understandings.

Recently, by examining the relationship between HIV and drug use in two local groups of gay men who engage in unprotected sex, I was able to describe how groups of poorer gay male drug users in the city may be subjected to physical violence from their homophobic peers. This influences their ability to use condoms or openly seek HIV prevention education or support. At the same time, groups of more middle-class gay male drug users did not seek ed-

† See for example, Parker, Richard. 1991. *Bodies, pleasures, and passions: Sexual culture in contemporary Brazil;* Farmer, Paul. 1992. *AIDS and accusation: Haiti and the geography of blame*; and Martin, Emily. 1994. *Flexible bodies: Tracking immunity in American culture—From the days of polio to the age of AIDS.*

ucation or support because their social location and values encouraged them to believe that they did not need these resources because they had everything under control.‡ With a greater clarity regarding local social and cultural barriers to HIV prevention, some local HIV prevention program designers rapidly developed more culturally appropriate prevention programs for these groups of men. Because HIV and AIDS are a dynamic part of lived experiences, learning about how people conceptualize and shape their ideas and practices around the virus, selfhood, sex practices, collective life, and institutions is important. And when these concepts become part of a foundation for HIV/AIDS programs, the services are better able to respond to people's needs since the programs make better sense within the contexts of people's lived realities.

As we head into the next century, biotechnology's advances are beginning to reconfigure the HIV/AIDS pandemic. While this is good news, it also means the meanings of HIV and AIDS become more complex and difficult to navigate. Moreover while new pharmaceutical therapies are providing hope for many enfranchised people in the West, infection rates climb and many more people remain unable to access these treatments. For most of us, culturally specific education and services will still be the most effective means to prevent infection or stem disease progression in many communities. In this light, the variety of perspectives offered by anthropology becomes even more crucial. This is because the foundations of these prevention efforts and services need to be developed with considerable understanding of how HIV and AIDS are constructed and shaped in a dynamic relationship with local complexities and concerns.

‡ See Williams, A. M. *Sex, drugs and HIV: A Sociocultural analysis of two groups of gay and bisexual male substance users who practice unprotected sex.* Unpublished manuscript.

and more muscular than females, although this differentiation has become drastically reduced in modern *Homo sapiens* compared to the earliest hominines. Among other primates, the males' larger size allows them to try to dominate females when the latter are at the height of their sexuality. This can be seen among baboons, gorillas, and, though less obviously, chimpanzees. (Significantly, the size difference between male and female chimpanzees is not as great as among baboons or gorillas, but it is still substantially greater than among modern humans.) With early hominine females potentially ready for sexual intercourse at any time, dominant males may have attempted to monopolize females; an added inducement could have been the prowess of the female at food gathering. (In food-foraging societies, women usually provide the bulk of the food through their gathering activities.) In any event, a tendency to monopolize females would introduce the kind of competitive, combative element into hominine groupings seen among many other primate species—an element that cannot be allowed to disrupt harmonious social relationships. The solution to this problem is to bring sexual activity under cultural control. Thus, just as a culture tells people what, when, and how they should eat, so does it tell them when, where, how, and with whom they should have sex.

Rules of Sexual Access

We find that everywhere societies have cultural rules that seek to regulate sexual relations. In the United States and Canada, the traditional ideal was that all sexual activity outside of wedlock was taboo. One was supposed to establish a family through marriage, by which a person established a continuing claim to the right of sexual access to another person. Actually very few known societies—only about 5 percent—prohibit all sexual involvement outside of marriage, and as already noted, even North American society, too, has become less restrictive. Among other peoples, as we have already seen, practices are often quite different. As a further example, we may look at the Nayar peoples of India.[6]

The Nayar constitute a landowning, warrior caste (rather than an independent society) from southwest India. Among them, estates are held by corporations of sorts, which are made up of kinsmen related in the female line. These kinsmen all live together in a large household, with

[6] My interpretation of the Nayar follows W. H. Goodenough. (1970). *Description and comparison in cultural anthropology* (pp. 6–11). Chicago: Aldine.

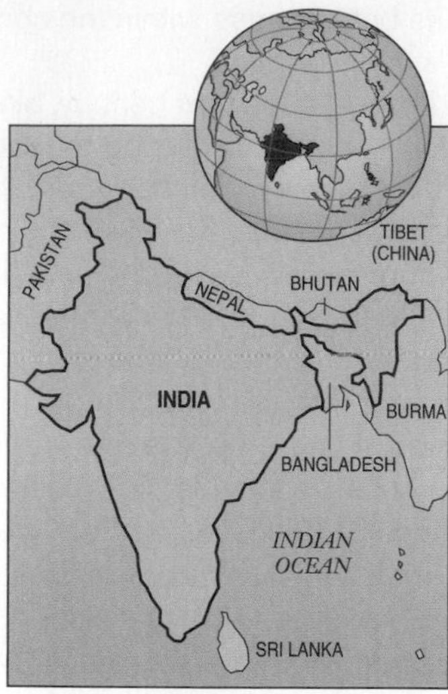

the eldest male serving as manager. In the past, military training for young males started around the age of 7, and from this time through much of their young adulthood as warfare required, they were away from their homes.

Three Nayar transactions are of interest here. The first occurs shortly before a girl undergoes her first menstruation. It involves a ceremony that joins together in a temporary union the girl with a young man. This union, which may or may not involve sexual relations, lasts for a few days and then breaks up. Neither individual has any further obligation, although the woman and her future children probably will mourn for the man when he dies. This transaction establishes the girl's eligibility for sexual activity with men approved by her household. With this, she is officially an adult.

The second transaction takes place when a girl enters into a continuing sexual liaison with an approved man. This is a formal relationship that requires the man to present her with gifts three times each year until the relationship is terminated. In return, the man may spend the nights with her. In spite of continuing sexual privileges, however, the man has no obligation to support his sex partner economically, nor is her home regarded as his home. In fact, she may have such an arrangement with more than one man at the same time. Regardless of how many men are involved with one woman, this second Nayar transaction, their version of marriage, clearly specifies who has sexual rights to whom so as to avoid conflict. We may define **marriage** as a relationship between one or more men (male or female) and one or more women (female or male) recognized by society as having a continuing claim to the right of sexual access to one another.[7] Thus defined, marriage is universal, presumably because the problems with which it deals are universal. As the Nayar case demonstrates, however, marriage need not have anything to do with starting a new family or even establishing a cooperative economic relationship between people of opposite gender.

The qualification in our definition of marriage—that the man may actually be a female, or the woman may actually be a male—may seem awkward, but it is an important one. It stems from the fact gender does not automatically follow from biological sex but is culturally defined (as discussed in Chapters 14 and 16). Thus we find that, in many societies, same-sex marriages are regarded as appropriate and normal in particular circumstances, even though opposite-sex marriages are far more common. We shall return to this point later in the chapter.

In the absence of effective birth-control devices, the usual outcome of sexual activity between individuals of opposite sex is that, sooner or later, the woman becomes pregnant. When this happens among the Nayar, some man (who may or may not be the biological father) must formally acknowledge paternity. He does this by making gifts to the woman and the midwife. Though he may continue to take much interest in the child, he has no further obligations, for the child's education and support are the responsibility of the child's mother's brothers, with whom the child and its mother live. This third transaction establishes the child's legitimacy. In this sense, it is the counterpart of the registration of birth in North American culture that spells out motherhood and fatherhood. In Western societies generally, the father is supposed to be the mother's husband, but he doesn't have to be. In the United States, the child of an unwed mother may be spoken of as "illegitimate," yet its citizenship rights, as well as those of inheritance, are not denied. Nor does legitimacy require the father to be married to the mother. In numerous other societies—for example, among the Pueblo peoples (such as the Hopi) of the North American Southwest—fatherhood is utterly irrelevant to the

[7] This definition of marriage is adapted from Bell, D. (1997). Defining marriage and legitimacy, and Jain, R. K. (1997). Comment. *Current Anthropology, 38,* 241 and 248.

Marriage. A relationship between one or more men (male or female) and one or more women (female or male) who are recognized by society as having a continuing claim to the right of sexual access to one another.

In the United States, gay or lesbian couples who wish to marry have met with considerable resistance, in spite of the fact that there is nothing unnatural, in any scientific sense, about such unions. In a number of other societies, same-sex marriages are regarded as perfectly appropriate.

child's legitimacy. In their societies legitimacy comes automatically from one's mother, regardless of whether or not she is married.

Before we leave the Nayar, it is important to note that there is nothing in their society comparable to the family as known in North America. The group that forms the household does not include **affinal kin,** or those individuals joined by a **conjugal bond** established by marriage. As will be shown in Chapter 20, a household doesn't have to be a family as we know it. Among the Nayar the household is composed wholly of what we often call "blood" relatives, technically known as **consanguineal kin.** Sexual relations are with those who are not consanguineal kin, and thus live in other households. This brings us to another human universal, the incest taboo.

The Incest Taboo

A cultural rule that has long fascinated anthropologists as well as other students of human behavior is the **incest taboo.** This prohibits sexual relations at least between parents and children of opposite sex, and usually siblings as well. Once thought to be universal, save for a few exceptions involving siblings, it became something of a challenge for anthropologists to explain both the taboo's supposed universality and why incest commonly should be regarded as such loathsome behavior.

Many explanations have been given. Of those that have gained some popularity at one time or another, the simplest and least satisfactory is based on "human nature"—that is, some instinctive horror of incest. It has been documented that human beings raised together have less sexual attraction for one another, but by itself this "familiarity breeds contempt" argument may simply substitute the result for the cause. The incest taboo ensures that children and their parents, who are constantly in intimate contact, avoid regarding one another as sexual objects. Besides this, if an instinctive horror of incest exists, we would be hard pressed to account for the far from rare violations of the incest taboo, such as occur in North American society (an estimated 10 to 14% of children under 18 years of age in the United States have been involved in incestuous relations[8]), or for cases of institutionalized incest, such as that which required the head of the Inca empire in Peru to marry his own sister.

Various psychological explanations of the incest taboo have been advanced at one time or another. Sigmund Freud tried to account for it in his psychoanalytic theory of the unconscious. According to him, the son desires the mother (familiarity breeds attempt), creating a rivalry with the father. (Freud called this the Oedipus complex.) The son must suppress these feelings or earn the wrath of the father, who is far more powerful than he. Similarly, the attraction of the daughter to the father (the Electra complex) places her in rivalry with her mother. From this, we might expect a same-sex bias in the case of intrafamily homicides—mother versus daughter or son versus father—but in fact no such bias exists. Some

[8] Whelehan, P. (1985). Review of incest, a biosocial view. *American Anthropologist, 87,* 678.

Affinal kin. Relatives by marriage. • **Conjugal bond.** The bond between two individuals who are married. • **Consanguineal kin.** Relatives by birth; so-called "blood" relatives. • **Incest taboo.** The prohibition of sexual relations between specified individuals, usually parent-child and sibling relations at a minimum.

HIGHWAY 1
Palomar College Anthropology Program: Sex and Marriage Tutorials
http://daphne.palomar.edu/anthro

HIGHWAY 2
Female Genital Mutilation Research
http://www.hollyfield.org

HIGHWAY 3
Search for matchmakers in various cultures
http://home.about.com/index.htm

psychologists have argued that young children can be emotionally scarred by sexual experiences, which they may interpret as violent and frightening acts of aggression. The incest taboo thus protects children against sexual advances by older members of the family. A closely related theory is that the incest taboo helps prevent girls who are socially and emotionally too young for motherhood from becoming pregnant.

Early students of genetics argued that the incest taboo precluded the harmful effects of inbreeding. While this is so, it is also true that, as with domestic animals, inbreeding can increase desired characteristics as well as detrimental ones. Furthermore, undesirable effects will show up sooner than without inbreeding, so whatever genes are responsible for them are quickly eliminated from the population. However, a preference for a genetically different mate does tend to maintain a higher level of genetic diversity within a population, and in evolution this generally works to a species' advantage. Without genetic diversity a species cannot adapt biologically to a changed environment when and if this becomes necessary.

A truly convincing explanation of the incest taboo has yet to be advanced. Certainly, there are persistent hints that it may be a cultural elaboration of an underlying biological tendency toward avoidance of inbreeding. Studies of animal behavior have shown such a tendency to be common among relatively large, long-lived, slow-to-mature, and intelligent species. Humans qualify for membership in this group on all counts. So do a number of other primates, including those most closely related to humans—bonobos and chimpanzees. Although they exhibit few sexual inhibitions, these apes do tend to avoid inbreeding between siblings and between females and their male offspring. This suggests that the tendency for human children to look for sexual partners outside the group they have been raised in is not just the result of a cultural taboo. Studies that might seem to support this show that children raised together on an Israeli kibbutz (a communalistic rural village), although not required or even encouraged to do so, almost invariably marry outside their group. In this case, however, appearances seem to be deceiving. There is hardly a kibbutz, for example, without a report of heterosexual relationships between adolescents who have grown up together since infancy.[9] As for actual marriage, most Israeli youths leave the kibbutz in their late teens for obligatory service in the armed forces.This takes them away from the kibbutz precisely when they are most ready to consider marriage. Consequently, those most available as potential spouses are from other parts of the country.

An even greater challenge to the "biological avoidance" theory, however, is raised by detailed census records made in Roman Egypt that conclusively demonstrate that brother-sister marriages were not only common but also preferred by ordinary members of the farming class.[10] Moreover, anthropologist Nancy

[9] Leavitt, G. C. (1990). Sociobiological explanations of incest avoidance: A critical review of evidential claims. *American Anthropologist, 92,* 973.

[10] Ibid., p. 982.

Although children rasied together on an Israeli kibbutz rarely marry one another, it is not because of any instinctive desire to avoid mating with people who are close. Rather, they marry outside their group because service in the military takes them out of their kibbutz, where they meet new people, precisely when they are most likely to begin thinking about marriage.

Thornhill found that, in a sample of 129 societies, only 57 had specific rules against parent-child or sibling incest (so much for the universality of the incest taboo!). Twice that number, 114, had explicit rules to control activity with cousins, in-laws, or both.[11]

If indeed a biological basis for inbreeding avoidance exists among humans, it clearly is far from completely effective in its operation. Nor is its mechanism understood. Moreover, it still leaves us with such questions as these: Why do some societies have an explicit taboo while others do not? And why do some societies not only condone certain kinds of incest but even favor them?

Endogamy and Exogamy

Whatever its cause, the utility of the incest taboo can be seen by examining its effects on social structure. Closely related to prohibitions against incest are rules against **endogamy,** or marriage within a particular group of individuals (cousins and in-laws, for example). If the group is defined as one's immediate family alone, then societies generally prohibit or at least discourage endogamy, thereby promoting **exogamy,** or marriage outside the group. Yet, a society that practices exogamy at one level may practice endogamy at another. Among the Trobriand Islanders, for example, each individual has to marry outside of his or her own clan and lineage (exogamy). However, since eligible sex partners are to be found within one's own community, village endogamy, though not obligatory, is commonly practiced. Interestingly, a wide variety exists among societies as to which relatives are or are not covered by rules of exogamy. For example, the Catholic Church has long had a prohibition on marriages to first cousins, and such marriages are illegal in 31 of the United States. They are not illegal in the 19 other states, nor in Europe. Furthermore, in numerous other societies, first cousins are preferred spouses. Despite myths to the contrary, there is no great risk to the children of first-cousin marriage.[12]

In the 19th century, Sir Edward Tylor advanced the proposition that alternatives to inbreeding were either "marrying out or being killed out."[13] Our ancestors, he

[11] Thornhill, N. (1993). Quoted in W. A. Haviland & R. J. Gordon (Eds.). *Talking about people* (p. 127). Mountain View, CA: Mayfield.

[12] Ottenheimer, M. (1996). *Forbidden relatives* (p.116–133). Champaign, IL: University of Illinois Press.

[13] Quoted in R. M. Keesing. (1976). *Cultural anthropology: A contemporary perspective* (p. 286). New York: Holt, Rinehart and Winston.

Endogamy. Marriage within a particular group or category of individuals. • **Exogamy.** Marriage outside the group.

CLAUDE LÉVI-STRAUSS (B.1908)

Claude Lévi-Strauss is the leading exponent of French structuralism, which sees culture as a surface representation of underlying mental structures that have been affected by a group's physical and social environment as well as its history. Thus, cultures may vary considerably, even though the structure of the human thought processes responsible for them is the same for all people everywhere.

Human thought processes are structured, according to Lévi-Strauss, into contrastive pairs of polar opposites, such as light versus dark, good versus evil, nature versus culture, and raw versus cooked. The ultimate contrastive pair is that of "self" versus "others," which is necessary for true symbolic communication to occur and upon which culture depends. Communication is a reciprocal exchange, which is extended to include goods and marital partners. Hence, the incest taboo stems from this fundamental contrastive pair of "self" versus "others." From this universal taboo are built the many and varied marriage rules ethnographers have described.

suggested, discovered the advantage of intermarriage to create bonds of friendship. French anthropologist Claude Lévi-Strauss elaborated on this idea. He saw exogamy as the basis of a distinction between early hominine life in isolated endogamous groups and the life of *Homo sapiens* in a supportive society with an accumulating culture. Alliances with other groups, established and strengthened by marriage ties, make possible a sharing of culture. Building on Lévi-Strauss's work, anthropologist Yehudi Cohen suggests that exogamy was an important means of promoting trade between groups, thereby ensuring access to needed goods and resources not otherwise available. Noting that incest taboos necessitating exogamy are generally most widely extended in the least complex of human societies but do not extend beyond parents and siblings in industrialized societies, he argues that as formal governments and other institutions have come to control trade, the need for extended taboos has been removed. Indeed, he suggests that this may have reached the point where the incest taboo is becoming obsolete altogether.

In a roundabout way, exogamy also helps to explain some exceptions to the incest taboo, such as that of obligatory brother and sister marriage within the royal families of ancient Egypt, the Inca empire, and Hawaii. Members of these royal families were considered semidivine, and their very sacredness kept them from marrying mere mortals. The brother and sister married so as *not* to share their godliness, thereby maintaining the "purity" of the royal line, not to mention control of royal property. By the same token, in Roman Egypt, where property was inherited by women as well as men, and where the relationship between land and people was particularly tight, brother-sister marriages among the farming class acted to prevent fragmentation of a family's holdings.

The Distinction Between Marriage and Mating

Having defined marriage in terms of sexual access, we must make clear the distinction between systems of marriage and mating. All animals, including humans, mate—some for life and some not, some with a single individual of the opposite sex, and some with several. Mates are secured and held solely through individual effort, as opposed to marriage, which is a right conferred by society. Only marriage is backed by legal, economic, and social forces. Even among the Nayar, where marriage seems to involve little else than a sexual relationship, a woman's husband is legally obligated to provide her with gifts at specified intervals. Nor may a woman legally have sex with a man she is not married to. Thus, while mating is biological, marriage is cultural.

The distinction between marriage and mating may be seen by looking, briefly, at practices in contemporary

North American society, where **monogamy**—the taking of a single spouse—is the only legally recognized form of marriage. Not only are other forms not legally sanctioned, but also systems of inheritance, whereby property and wealth are transferred from one generation to the next, are predicated upon the institution of monogamous marriage. Mating patterns, by contrast, are frequently *not* monogamous. Not only is adultery far from rare in the United States and Canada, but it has become acceptable for individuals of opposite sex—particularly young people who have not yet married—to live together outside of wedlock. None of these arrangements, however, are legally sanctioned. Frequently, even married couples who do not engage in sexual activity outside of wedlock mate with more than one individual of the opposite sex; this follows from the fact that more than 50% of first marriages in the United States end in divorce, and most divorced people ultimately remarry.

Among primates in general, monogamous mating patterns are not common. Although some smaller species of South American monkeys, a few island-dwelling populations of leaf-eating Old World monkeys, and all of the smaller apes (gibbons and siamangs) do mate for life with a single individual of opposite sex, none of these are closely related to human beings, nor do "monogamous" primates ever display the degree of anatomical differences between males and females characteristic of our closest primate relatives or that were characteristic of our own ancient ancestors. Thus it is not likely that the human species began its career as one with monogamous mating patterns. Certainly, one cannot say the human species is, by nature, monogamous in its mating behavior, as some have tried to assert.

Marriage and the Family

Although, as we saw in our discussion of the Nayar, marriage need not involve establishment of a new family, it can easily serve this purpose, in addition to its main function of indicating who has continuing sexual access to whom. Consequently, new families are established through marriage in most human societies. Therefore, some mention of family organization—otherwise discussed in Chapter 20—is necessary before we proceed further with discussion of marriage. If we were to define the family in familiar terms, as requiring fathers, mothers, and children, then we would have to say people like the Nayar (who, as we shall see in Chapter 20, do not constitute a unique case) do not have families. We can, however, define the **family** in a less ethnocentric way as a group composed of a woman and her dependent children and at least one adult male joined through marriage or blood relationship.[14] (The subject of nontraditional families will be dealt with in Chapter 20.) The Nayar form **consanguine** families, consisting of women, their dependent offspring, and the women's brothers. In such societies, men and women get married but do not live together as members of one household. Rather, they spend their lives in the households they grew up in, with the men "commuting" for sexual activity with their wives. Economic cooperation between men and women occurs between sisters and brothers rather than husbands and wives.

Conjugal, as opposed to consanguine families, are formed on the basis of marital ties between husband and wife. Minimally, a conjugal family consists of a married couple with their dependent children, otherwise known as the **nuclear family;** other forms of conjugal families are *polygynous* and *polyandrous* families, which may be thought of as aggregates of nuclear families with one spouse in common. A polygynous family includes the multiple wives of a single husband, while a polyandrous family includes the multiple husbands of a single wife. Both are often lumped together under the heading of polygamous families.

FORMS OF MARRIAGE

Monogamy is the form of marriage North Americans are most familiar with. It is also the most common, but for economic rather than moral reasons. In many polygynous societies, a man must be fairly wealthy to be able to afford **polygyny,** or marriage to more than one wife. Among the Kapauku of western New Guinea, the ideal is to have as many wives as possible, and a woman actually urges

---

[14] Goodenough, W. H. (1970). *Description and comparison in cultural anthropology* (p. 19). Chicago, Aldine.

Monogamy. Marriage in which an individual has a single spouse. • **Family.** A residential kin group composed of a woman, her dependent children, and at least one adult male joined through marriage or blood relationship. • **Consanguine family.** A family consisting of related women, their brothers, and the offspring of the women. • **Nuclear family.** A family unit consisting of husband, wife, and dependent children. • **Polygyny.** Marriage of a man to two or more women at the same time; a form of polygamy.

her husband to spend money on acquiring additional wives.[15] She even has the legal right to divorce him if she can prove that he has money for bride-prices and refuses to remarry. As we saw in Chapter 14, wives are desirable because they work in the gardens and care for pigs, by which wealth is measured, but not all men are wealthy enough to afford bride-prices for multiple wives.

Among the Turkana, a pastoral nomadic people of northern Kenya, the number of animals at a family's disposal is directly related to the number of adult women available to care for them. The more wives a man has, the more women there are to look after the livestock and the more substantial the family's holdings can be. Thus, it is not uncommon for a man's existing wife to actively search for another woman to marry her husband. Again, however, a substantial bride-price is involved in marriage, and only men of wealth and prominence can afford large numbers of wives.

Although monogamy may be the commonest form of marriage around the world, it is not the most preferred. That distinction goes to polygyny, which is favored by about 80 to 85% of the world's societies. Even in the United States, somewhere between 20,000 and 60,000 people in the Rocky Mountain states live in households made up of a man with two or more wives.[16] Most consider themselves Mormons, even though the official Mormon church does not approve of the practices. A growing minority, however, call themselves "Christian polygamists," citing the Old Testament of the Judeo-Christian Bible as justifying their practice.[17] In spite of its illegality, regional law enforcement officials have adopted a "live and let live" attitude toward polygyny in their region. Nor are those involved in such marriages uneducated. One woman—a lawyer and one of nine cowives—expresses her attitude as follows:

> I see it as the ideal way for a woman to have a career and children. In our family, the women can help each other care for the children. Women in monogamous relationships don't have that luxury. As I see it, if this life style didn't already exist, it would have to be invented to accommodate career women.[18]

[15] Pospisil, L. (1963). *The Kapauku Papuans of West New Guinea.* New York: Holt, Rinehart and Winston.

[16] Egan, T. (1999, February 28). The persistence of polygamy. *New York Times Magazine,* 52.

[17] Wolfson, H. (2000, January 22). Polygamists make the Christian connection. *Burlington Free Press,* 2c.

[18] Johnson, D. (1996). Polygamists emerge from secrecy, seeking not just peace but respect. In W. A. Haviland & R. J. Gordon, (Eds.). *Talking about people* (2nd ed.) (pp. 129–131). Mountain View, CA: Mayfield.

Polygyny is particularly common in societies that support themselves by growing crops and where women do the bulk of the farmwork. Under these conditions, women are valued both as workers and as childbearers. Because the labor of wives in polygynous households generates wealth and little support is required from husbands, the wives have a strong bargaining position within the household. Often, they have considerable freedom of movement and some economic independence from sale of crops. Commonly, each wife within the household lives with her children in her own dwelling, apart from her cowives and husband, who occupy other houses within some sort of larger household compound (note that the terms *house* and *household* need not be synonymous; a household may consist of several houses together, as here). Because of this residential autonomy, fathers are usually remote from their sons, who grow up among women. As noted in Chapter 16, this is the sort of setting conducive to development of aggressiveness in adult males, who must prove their masculinity. As a consequence, a high value is often placed on military glory, and one reason for going to war is to capture women, who may then become a warrior's cowives. This wealth-increasing pattern is found in its fullest elaboration in sub-Saharan Africa, though it is known elsewhere as well (the Kapauku are another case). Moreover, it is still intact in the world today, because its wealth-generating properties at the household level make it an economically productive system.[19]

In societies practicing wealth-generating polygyny, most men and women do enter into polygynous marriages, although some are able to do so earlier in life than others. This is made possible by a female-biased sex ratio and/or a mean age at marriage for females significantly below that for males. (This creates a cohort of women looking for husbands that is larger than the cohort of men looking for wives.) By contrast, in societies where men are more heavily involved in productive work, generally only a small minority of marriages are polygynous. Under these circumstances, women are more dependant on men for support, so they are valued as childbearers more than for the work they do. This is commonly the case in pastoral nomadic societies where men are the primary owners and tenders of livestock. This makes women especially vulnerable if they prove incapable of bearing children, which is one reason a man may seek another wife. Another reason for a man to take on

[19] White, D. R. (1988). Rethinking polygyny: Co-Wives, codes and cultural systems. *Current Anthropology, 29,* 529–572.

A Christian polygamist poses with his three wives and children in front of their dormitory-style home in Utah.

secondary wives is to demonstrate his high position in society. But where men do most of the productive work, they must work exceptionally hard to support more than one wife, and few actually do so. Usually, it is the exceptional hunter, or male shaman ("medicine man") in a food-foraging society or a particularly wealthy man in an agricultural or pastoral society who is most apt to practice polygyny. When he does, it is usually of the *sororal* type, with the cowives being sisters. Having lived their lives together before marriage, the sisters continue to do so with their husband, instead of occupying separate dwellings of their own.

Although monogamy and polygyny are the most common forms of marriage in the world today, other forms do occur, however rarely. **Polyandry,** the marriage of one woman to two or more men simultaneously, is known in only a few societies, perhaps in part because a man's life expectancy is shorter than a woman's and male infant mortality is high, so a surplus of men in a society is unlikely. Where sex ratios are balanced, as in Ladakh, many women are likely to remain unmarried. Another reason for polyandry's rarity is that it limits a man's descendants more than any other pattern. Among the Nayar, however, polyandry maximizes female fertility, ensuring production of children for her descent group. Fewer than a dozen societies are known to have favored this form of marriage, but they involve people as widely separated from one another as the eastern Inuit (Eskimos), Marquesan Islanders of Polynesia, and Tibetans. In Tibet, where inheritance is in the male line and arable land is limited, the marriage of brothers to a single woman averts the danger of constantly subdividing farmlands among all the sons of any one landholder. Unlike monogamy, it also restrains population growth, thereby avoiding increased pressures on resources. Finally, it provides the household with an adequate pool of male labor. With their tripartite economy of farming, herding, and trading, trifraternal polyandry is highly valued by Tibetans, as it allows the three brothers who are cohusbands to pursue all three options at once.[20]

Group marriage, in which several men and women have sexual access to one another, also occurs but rarely. Even in recent communal groups among young people seeking alternatives to modern marriage forms, group marriage seems to be a transitory phenomenon, despite the publicity it sometimes has received.

[20] Levine, N. E., & Silk, J. B. (1997). Why polyandry fails. *Current Anthropology, 38,* 375–398.

Polyandry. Marriage of a woman to two or more men at one time; a form of polygamy. • **Group marriage.** Marriage in which several men and women have sexual access to one another.

The Levirate and the Sororate

If a husband dies, leaving a wife and children, it is often the custom that the wife marry one of the brothers of the dead man. This custom, called the **levirate,** not only provides social security for the widow and her children but also is a way for the husband's family to maintain their rights over her sexuality and her future children: It acts to preserve relationships previously established. When a man marries the sister of his dead wife, it is called the **sororate;** in essence, a family of "wife givers" supplies one of "wife takers" with another spouse to take the dead one's place. In societies that have the levirate and sororate, the relationship between the two families is maintained even after the spouse's death; and in such societies, an adequate supply of brothers and sisters is generally ensured by the structure of the kinship system (discussed in Chapter 21), whereby individuals North Americans would call "cousins" are classified as brothers and sisters.

North American celebrities Jane Fonda and Ted Turner. Their marriage, like 50% of those in the United States, ended in divorce. Even so, most divorced individuals remarry, making serial monogamy very common.

Serial Monogamy

A form of marriage increasingly common in North America today is **serial monogamy,** whereby the man or the woman marries a series of partners in succession. Currently, more than 50% of first marriages end in divorce, and some experts project that two thirds of recent marriages will not last.[21] Upon dissolution of a marriage, the children more often than not remain with the mother. This pattern is similar to one sociologists and anthropologists first described among West Indians and lower-class urban African Americans in the United States. Early in life, women begin to bear children by men who are not married to them. To support themselves and their children, the women must look for work outside of the household, but to do so they must seek help from other kin, most commonly their mother. As a consequence, households are frequently headed by women (on average, about 32% are so headed in the West Indies). After a number of years, however, an unmarried woman usually does marry a man, who may or may not be the father of some or all of her children. Under conditions of poverty, where this pattern has been common, women are driven to seek this male support, owing to the difficulties of supporting themselves and their children while fulfilling their domestic obligations.

In the United States, with the rise of live-in premarital arrangements between couples, the increasing necessity for women to seek work outside the home, and rising divorce rates, a similar pattern is becoming more common among middle-class whites. In 90% of divorce cases, it is the women who assume responsibility for any children; furthermore, of all children born in the United States today, fully 25% are born out of wedlock. Frequently isolated from kin or other assistance, women in single-parent households (which now outnumber nuclear family households) commonly find it difficult to cope. Within a year following divorce, the standard of living for women drops some 73% whereas that of men *increases* by about 42%.[22] To be sure, fathers of children are usually expected to provide child support, but in 50%

[21] Stacey, J. (1990). *Brave new families* (pp. 15; 286, n. 46). New York: Basic Books.

[22] Weitzman, L. J. (1985). *The divorce revolution: The unexpected social and economic consequences for women and children in America* (p. 338). New York: The Free Press.

Levirate. A marriage custom according to which a widow marries a brother of her dead husband (a man marries his dead brother's widow). • **Sororate.** A marriage custom according to which a widower marries his dead wife's sister (a woman marries her deceased sister's husband). • **Serial monogamy.** A marriage form in which a man or a woman marries or lives with a series of partners in succession.

of the cases of children born out of wedlock, paternity cannot be established. Furthermore, failure of fathers to live up to their obligations is far from rare. One solution for unmarried women is to marry (often, to remarry) to get the assistance of another adult.

In some countries, such as Norway and the Netherlands, a like pattern has emerged for different reasons. In Norway, for example, something like 60% of children are born to single mothers. This is not a function of poverty, but of wealth (from natural gas in the North Sea). In this very affluent society, the traditional economic role of the husband as provider has been taken over by generous state support.

Choice of Spouse

The Western egalitarian ideal that an individual should be free to marry whomever he or she chooses is an unusual arrangement, certainly not universally embraced. However desirable such an ideal may be in the abstract, it is fraught with difficulties and certainly contributes to the apparent instability of marital relationships in modern North American society. Part of the problem is the great emphasis the culture places on the importance of youth and glamour—especially of women—for romantic love. Female youth and beauty are perhaps most glaringly exploited by the women's wear, cosmetics, and beauty parlor industries, but movies, television, and the recorded-music business generally do not lag far behind, nor do advertisements for cigarettes, hard and soft drinks, beer, automobiles, and a host of other products that make liberal use of young, glamorous women. As anthropologist Jules Henry once observed, "even men's wear and toiletries could not be marketed as efficiently without an adoring, pretty woman (well under thirty-five years of age) looking at a man wearing a stylish shirt or sniffing at a man wearing a deodorant."[23] By no means are all North Americans taken in by this, but it does tend to nudge people in such a way that marriages may all too easily be based on trivial and transient characteristics. In no other part of the world are such chances taken with something as momentous as marriage.

In many societies, marriage and the establishment of a family are considered far too important to be left to the whims of young people. The marriage of two individuals who are expected to spend their whole lives together and raise their children together is incidental to the more serious matter of making allies of two families through the marriage bond. Marriage involves a transfer of rights between families, including rights to property and rights over children, as well as sexual rights. Thus, marriages tend to be arranged for the economic and political advantage of the family unit.

Arranged marriages, needless to say, are not commonplace in North American society, but they do occur. Among ethnic minorities, they may serve to preserve traditional values that people fear might otherwise be lost. Among families of wealth and power, marriages may be arranged by segregating their children in private schools and carefully steering them toward "proper" marriages. A careful reading of announced engagements in the society pages of the *New York Times* provides clear evidence of such family alliances. The following Original Study illustrates how marriages may be arranged in societies where such practices are commonplace.

[23] Henry, J. (1966). The metaphysic of youth, beauty, and romantic love. In S. Farber & R. Wilson (Eds.). *The challenge to women.* New York: Basic Books.

The United States' obsession with a particular ideal of feminine beauty is now spreading to other parts of the world, as illustrated by this Venezuelan runner-up for the title in a Miss Universe contest.

Marriage is a means of creating alliances between groups of people. Since such alliances have important economic and political implications, the decision cannot be left in the hands of the two young and inexperienced people. At the left is shown an Indian bride, whose marriage has been arranged between her parents and those of the groom. The picture on the right was taken at the wedding of Prince Charles and Lady Diana in England.

Original Study

Arranging Marriage in India[24]

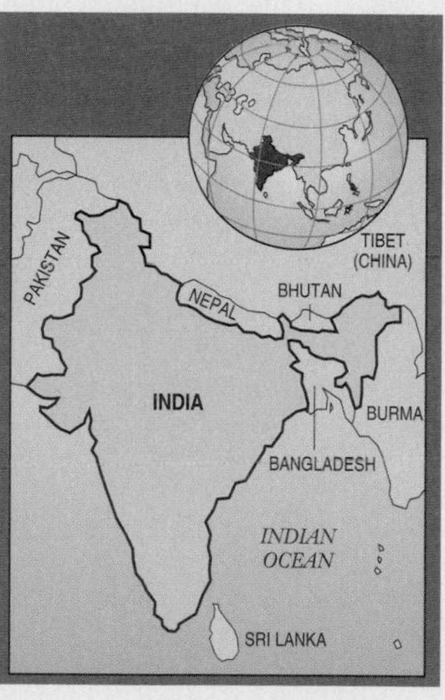

Six years [after my first field trip] I returned to India to again do fieldwork, this time among the middle class in Bombay, a modern, sophisticated city. From the experience of my earlier visit, I decided to include a study of arranged marriages in my project. By this time I had met many Indian couples whose marriages had been arranged and who seemed very happy. Particularly in contrast to the fate of many of my married friends in the United States who were already in the process of divorce the positive aspects of arranged marriages appeared to me to outweigh the negatives. In fact, I thought I might even participate in arranging a marriage myself. I had been fairly successful in the United States in "fixing up" many of my friends, and I was confident that my matchmaking skills could be easily applied to this new situation, once I learned the basic rules. "After all," I thought, "how complicated can it be? People want pretty much the same things in a marriage whether it is in India or America."

An opportunity presented itself almost immediately. A friend from my previous Indian trip was in the process of arranging for the marriage of her eldest son. In India there is a perceived shortage of "good boys," and since my friend's family was eminently respectable and the boy himself personable, well educated, and nice looking, I was sure that by the end of my year's fieldwork, we would have found a match.

The basic rule seems to be that a family's reputation is most important. It is understood that

[24] Nanda, S. (1992). Arranging a marriage in India. In P. R. De Vita (Ed.). *The naked anthropologist* (pp. 139–143). Belmont, CA: Wadsworth.

matches would be arranged only within the same caste and general social class, although some crossing of subcastes is permissible if the class positions of the bride's and groom's families are similar. Although dowry is now prohibited by law in India, extensive gift exchanges took place with every marriage. Even when the boy's family do not "make demands," every girl's family nevertheless feels the obligation to give the traditional gifts, to the girl, to the boy, and to the boy's family. Particularly when the couple would be living in the joint family—that is, with the boy's parents and his married brothers and their families, as well as with unmarried siblings—which is still very common even among the urban, upper-middle class in India, the girl's parents are anxious to establish smooth relations between their family and that of the boy. Offering the proper gifts, even when not called "dowry," is often an important factor in influencing the relationship between the bride's and groom's families and perhaps, also, the treatment of the bride in her new home.

In a society where divorce is still a scandal and where, in fact, the divorce rate is exceedingly low, an arranged marriage is the beginning of a lifetime relationship not just between the bride and groom but between their families as well. Thus, while a girl's looks are important, her character is even more so, for she is being judged as a prospective daughter-in-law as much as a prospective bride. Where she would be living in a joint family, as was the case with my friend, the girl's ability to get along harmoniously in a family is perhaps the single most important quality in assessing her suitability.

My friend is a highly esteemed wife, mother, and daughter-in-law. She is religious, soft-spoken, modest, and deferential. She rarely gossips and never quarrels, two qualities highly desirable in a woman. A family that has the reputation for gossip and conflict among its womenfolk will not find it easy to get good wives for their sons. Parents will not want to send their daughter to a house in which there is conflict.

My friend's family were originally from North India. They had lived in Bombay, where her husband owned a business, for forty years. The family had delayed in seeking a match for their eldest son because he had been an Air Force pilot for several years, stationed in such remote places that it had seemed fruitless to try to find a girl who would be willing to accompany him. In their social class, a military career, despite its economic security, has little prestige and is considered a drawback in finding a suitable bride. Many families would not allow their daughters to marry a man in an occupation so potentially dangerous and which requires so much moving around.

The son had recently left the military and joined his father's business. Since he was a college graduate, modern, and well traveled, from such a good family, and, I thought, quite handsome, it seemed to me that he, or rather his family, was in a position to pick and choose. I said as much to my friend.

While she agreed that there were many advantages on their side, she also said, "We must keep in mind that my son is both short and dark; these are drawbacks in finding the right match." While the boy's height had not escaped my notice, "dark" seemed to me inaccurate; I would have called him "wheat" colored perhaps, and in any case, I did not realize that color would be a consideration. I discovered, however, that while a boy's skin color is a less important consideration than a girl's, it is still a factor.

An important source of contacts in trying to arrange her son's marriage was my friend's social club in Bombay. Many of the women had daughters of the right age, and some had already expressed an interest in my friend's son. I was most enthusiastic about the possibilities of one particular family who had five daughters, all of whom were pretty, demure, and well educated. Their mother had told my friend, "You can have your pick for your son, whichever one of my daughters appeals to you most."

I saw a match in sight. "Surely," I said to my friend, "we will find one there. Let's go visit and make our choice." But my friend held back; she did not seem to share my enthusiasm, for reasons I could not then fathom.

When I kept pressing for an explanation of her reluctance, she admitted, "See, Serena, here is the problem. The family has so many daughters, how will they be able to provide nicely for any of them? We are not making any demands, but still, with so many daughters to marry off, one wonders whether she will even be able to make a proper

Original Study

wedding. Since this is our eldest son, it's best if we marry him to a girl who is the only daughter, then the wedding will truly be a gala affair." I argued that surely the quality of the girls themselves made up for any deficiency in the elaborateness of the wedding. My friend admitted this point but still seemed reluctant to proceed.

"Is there something else," I asked her, "some factor I have missed?" "Well," she finally said, "there is one other thing. They have one daughter already married and living in Bombay. The mother is always complaining to me that the girl's in-laws don't let her visit her own family often enough. So it makes me wonder, will she be that kind of mother who always wants her daughter at her own home? This will prevent the girl from adjusting to our house. It is not a good thing." And so, this family of five daughters was dropped as a possibility.

Somewhat disappointed, I nevertheless respected my friend's reasoning and geared up for the next prospect. This was also the daughter of a woman in my friend's social club. There was clear interest in this family and I could see why. The family's reputation was excellent; in fact, they came from a subcaste slightly higher than my friend's own. The girl, who was an only daughter, was pretty and well educated and had a brother studying in the United States. Yet, after expressing an interest to me in this family, all talk of them suddenly died down and the search began elsewhere.

"What happened to that girl as a prospect?" I asked one day. "You never mention her anymore. She is so pretty and so educated, what did you find wrong?"

"She is too educated. We've decided against it. My husband's father saw the girl on the bus the other day and thought her forward. A girl who 'roams about' the city by herself is not the girl for our family." My disappointment this time was even greater, as I thought the son would have liked the girl very much. But then I thought, my friend is right, a girl who is going to live in a joint family cannot be too independent or she will make life miserable for everyone. I also learned that if the family of the girl has even a slightly higher social status than the family of the boy, the bride may think herself too good for them, and this too will cause problems. Later my friend admitted to me that this had been an important factor in her decision not to pursue the match.

The next candidate was the daughter of a client of my friend's husband. When the client learned that the family was looking for a match for their son, he said, "Look no further, we have a daughter." This man then invited my friends to dinner to see the girl. He had already seen their son at the office and decided that "he liked the boy." We all went together for tea, rather than dinner—it was less of a commitment—and while we were there, the girl's mother showed us around the house. The girl was studying for her exams and was briefly introduced to us.

After we left, I was anxious to hear my friend's opinion. While her husband liked the family very much and was impressed with his client's business accomplishments and reputation, the wife didn't like the girl's looks. "She is short, no doubt, which is an important plus point, but she is also fat and wears glasses." My friend obviously thought she could do better for her son and asked her husband to make his excuses to his client by saying that they had decided to postpone the boy's marriage indefinitely.

By this time almost six months had passed and I was becoming impatient. What I had thought would be an easy matter to arrange was turning out to be quite complicated. I began to believe that between my friend's desire for a girl who was modest enough to fit into her joint family, yet attractive and educated enough to be an acceptable partner for her son, she would not find anyone suitable. My friend laughed at my impatience: "Don't be so much in a hurry," she said. "You Americans want everything done so quickly. You get married quickly and then just as quickly get divorced. Here we take marriage more seriously. We must take all the factors into account. It is not enough for us to learn by our mistakes. This is too serious a business. If a mistake is made we have not only ruined the life of our son or daughter, but we have spoiled the reputation of our family as well. And that will make it much harder for their brothers and sisters to get married. So we must be very careful."

What she said was true and I promised myself to be more patient, though it was not easy. I had really hoped and expected that the match would be made before my year in India was up. But it was not to be. When I left India my friend seemed no further along in finding a suitable match for her son than when I had arrived.

Two years later, I returned to India and still my friend had not found a girl for her son. By this time, he was close to thirty, and I think she was a little worried. Since she knew I had friends all over India, and I was going to be there for a year, she asked me to "help her in this work" and keep an eye out for someone suitable. I was flattered that my judgment was respected, but knowing now how complicated the process was, I had lost my earlier confidence as a matchmaker. Nevertheless, I promised that I would try.

It was almost at the end of my year's stay in India that I met a family with a marriageable daughter whom I felt might be a good possibility for my friend's son. The girl's father was related to a good friend of mine and by coincidence came from the same village as my friend's husband. This new family had a successful business in a medium-sized city in central India and were from the same subcaste as my friend. The daughter was pretty and chic; in fact, she had studied fashion design in college. Her parents would not allow her to go off by herself to any of the major cities in India where she could make a career, but they had compromised with her wish to work by allowing her to run a small dress-making boutique from their home. In spite of her desire to have a career, the daughter was both modest and home-loving and had had a traditional, sheltered upbringing. She had only one other sister, already married, and a brother who was in his father's business.

I mentioned the possibility of a match with my friend's son. The girl's parents were most interested. Although their daughter was not eager to marry just yet, the idea of living in Bombay—a sophisticated, extremely fashion-conscious city where she could continue her education in clothing design—was a great inducement. I gave the girl's father my friend's address and suggested that when they went to Bombay on some business or whatever, they look up the boy's family.

Returning to Bombay on my way to New York, I told my friend of this newly discovered possibility. She seemed to feel there was potential but, in spite of my urging, would not make any moves herself. She rather preferred to wait for the girl's family to call upon them. I hoped something would come of this introduction, though by now I had learned to rein in my optimism.

A year later I received a letter from my friend. The family had indeed come to visit Bombay, and their daughter and my friend's daughter, who were near in age, had become very good friends. During that year, the two girls had frequently visited each other. I thought things looked promising.

Last week I received an invitation to a wedding: My friend's son and the girl were getting married. Since I had found the match, my presence was particularly requested at the wedding. I was thrilled. Success at last! As I prepared to leave for India, I began thinking, "Now, my friend's younger son, who do I know who has a nice girl for him . . . ?"

The End

Cousin Marriage

In some societies, preferred marriages are a man marrying his father's brother's daughter. This is known as **patrilateral parallel-cousin marriage** (Figure 19.2; a parallel cousin is the child of a father's brother or a mother's sister). Although not obligatory, such marriages have been favored historically among Arabs, the ancient Israelites, and also in ancient Greece. All of these societies are (or were) hierarchial in nature—that is, some people have more property than others—and although male dominance and descent are emphasized, property of interest to men is inherited by daughters as well as sons. Thus, when a man marries his father's brother's daughter (or, from the woman's point of view, she marries her father's brother's son), property is retained within the single male line of descent. In these societies, generally speaking, the greater the property, the more this form of parallel-cousin marriage is apt to occur.

Patrilateral parallel-cousin marriage. Marriage of a man to his father's brother's daughter, or a woman to her father's brother's son (i.e., to a parallel cousin on the paternal side).

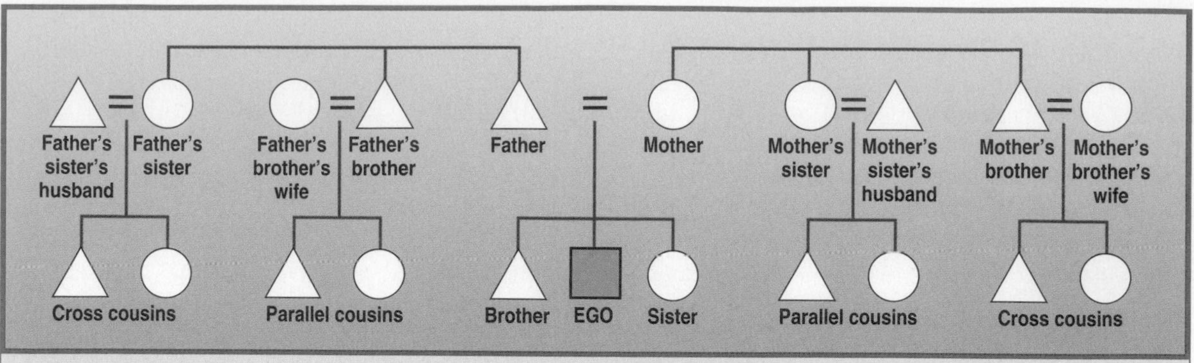

FIGURE 19.2

ANTHROPOLOGISTS USE DIAGRAMS OF THIS SORT TO ILLUSTRATE KINSHIP RELATIONSHIPS. SHOWN IN THIS ONE IS THE DISTINCTION BETWEEN CROSS AND PARALLEL COUSINS. IN SUCH DIAGRAMS, MALES ARE ALWAYS SHOWN AS TRIANGLES, FEMALES AS CIRCLES, MARITAL TIES BY AN =, SIBLING RELATIONSHIPS AS A HORIZONTAL LINE, AND PARENT-CHILD RELATIONSHIPS AS A VERTICAL LINE. TERMS ARE GIVEN FROM THE PERSPECTIVE OF THE INDIVIDUAL LABELED *EGO,* WHO CAN BE FEMALE OR MALE.

Matrilateral cross-cousin marriage (Figure 19.2)—that is, of a man to his mother's brother's daughter, or a woman to her father's sister's son (a cross cousin is the child of a mother's brother or a father's sister)—is a preferred form of marriage in a variety of societies ranging from food foragers (Australian Aborigines, for example) to intensive agriculturists (such as various peoples of South India). Among food-foraging peoples, who inherit relatively little in the way of property, such marriages help establish and maintain ties of solidarity between social groups. In agricultural societies, however, the transmission of property is an important determinant. In societies that trace descent exclusively in the female line, for instance, property and other important rights usually pass from a man to his sister's son; under cross-cousin marriage, the sister's son is also the man's daughter's husband.

Marriage Exchanges

In the Trobriand Islands, when a young couple decides to get married, they sit in public on the veranda of the young man's adolescent retreat, where all may see them. Here they remain until the bride's mother brings the couple cooked yams, which they then eat together, making their marriage official. A day later the bride is presented with three long skirts by the husband's sister, a symbol of the fact that the sexual freedom of adolescence is now over for the newly wed woman. This is followed by a large presentation of uncooked yams by the bride's father and her mother's brother, who represent both her father's and her own lineages.

Meanwhile, the groom's father and mother's brother—representing his father's and his own lineages—collect such valuables as stone ax blades, clay pots, money, and the occasional Kula shell (see Chapter 18) to present to the young wife's maternal kin and father. After the first year of the marriage, during which the bride's mother continues to provide the couple's meals of cooked yams, each of the young husband's relatives who provided valuables for his father and mother's brother to present to the bride's relatives will receive yams from her maternal relatives and father. All of this gift giving back and forth between the husband's and wife's lineages, as well as those of their fathers, serve to bind the four parties together in a way that people respect, and honor the marriage, and that create obligations on the part of the woman's kin to take care of her husband in the future.

As among the Trobriand Islanders, marriages in many human societies are formalized by some sort of economic exchange. Among the Trobrianders, this takes the form of a gift exchange, as just described. Far more common is

Matrilateral cross-cousin marriage. Marriage of a woman to her father's sister's son, or a man to his mother's brother's daughter (her cross-cousin on the paternal side, his cross-cousin on the maternal side).

On the day her marriage is announced, the Trobriand bride must give up the provocative miniskirts she has worn until then in favor of longer skirts, the first of which the groom's sister provides. This announces that her days of sexual freedom are gone.

bride-price, sometimes called bride wealth. This involves payments of money or other valuables to a bride's parents or other close kin. This usually happens in societies where the bride will become a member of the household where her husband grew up; this household will benefit from her labor as well as from the offspring she produces. Thus, her family must be compensated for their loss.

Not only is bride-price *not* a simple "buying and selling" of women, but also the bride's parents may use the money to buy jewelery or household furnishings for her or to finance an elaborate and costly wedding celebration. It also contributes to the stability of the marriage, because it usually must be refunded if the couple separates. Other forms of compensation are an exchange of women between families—"My son will marry your daughter if your son will marry my daughter"—or **bride service,** a period of time during which the groom works for the bride's family.

In a number of societies more or less restricted to the western, southern, and eastern margins of Eurasia, where the economy is based on intensive agriculture, women often bring a **dowry** with them at marriage. A form of dowry in the United States is the custom of the bride's family paying the wedding expenses. In effect, a dowry is a woman's share of parental property that, instead of passing to her upon her parents' death, is distributed to her at the time of her marriage. This does not mean that she retains control of this property after marriage. In a number of European countries, for example, a woman's property falls exclusively under her husband's control.

In many African societies, bride-price takes the form of cattle, which are paid by the groom's family to the bride's family.

Bride-price. Compensation the groom or his family pays to the bride's family upon marriage. •
Bride service. A designated period of time after marriage when the groom works for the bride's family. •
Dowry. Payment of a woman's inheritance at the time of her marriage, either to her or to her husband.

In some societies when a woman marries, she receives her share of the family inheritance (her dowry), which she brings to her new family (unlike bride-price, which passes from the groom's family to the bride's family). Shown here are Slovakian women carrying the objects of a woman's dowry.

Having benefited by what she has brought to the marriage, however, he is obligated to look out for her future well-being, even after his death. Thus, one of the functions of dowry is to ensure a woman's support in widowhood (or after divorce), an important consideration in a society where men carry out the bulk of productive work and women are valued for their reproductive potential rather than for the work they do. In such societies, women incapable of bearing children are especially vulnerable, but the dowry they bring with them at marriage helps protect them against desertion. Another function of dowry is to reflect the economic status of the woman in societies where differences in wealth are important. Thus, the property that a woman brings with her at marriage demonstrates that the man is marrying a woman whose standing is on a par with his own. It also permits women, with the aid of their parents and kin, to compete through dowry for desirable (that is, wealthy) husbands.

Same-Sex Marriage

As we saw earlier in this chapter, although marriage is defined in terms of a continuing sexual relationship between a man and woman, the cultural nature of gender is such that someone whose sex is female may be defined as a "man," or a male as a "woman." Thus, marriages between individuals of the same sex may be regarded as proper and normal. Such marriages provide a way of dealing with problems for which opposite-sex marriage offers no satisfactory solution. This is the case with woman/woman marriage, a practice sanctioned in many societies of sub-Saharan Africa, although in none does it involve more than a small minority of all women.

Although details differ from one society to another, woman/woman marriages among the Nandi of western Kenya may be taken as reasonably representative of such practices in Africa.[25] The Nandi are a pastoral people who also do considerable farming. Control of most significant property and the primary means of production—livestock and land—is exclusively in the hands of men, and may only be transmitted to their male heirs, usually their sons. Since polygyny is the preferred form of marriage, a man's property is normally divided equally among his wives for their sons to inherit. Within the household, each wife has

[25] The following is based on Obler, R. S. (1982). Is the female husband a man? Woman/woman marriage among the Nandi of Kenya. *Ethnology, 19,* 69–88.

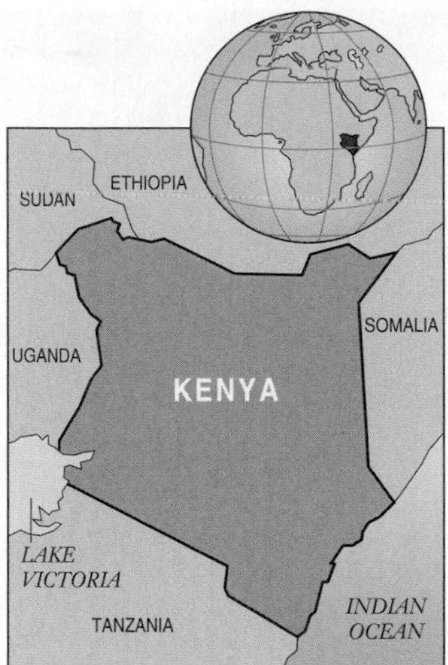

her own house in which she lives with her children, but all are under the authority of the woman's husband, who is a remote and aloof figure within the household. In such situations, the position of a woman who bears no sons is difficult; not only does she not help perpetuate her husband's male line—a major concern among the Nandi—but also she has no one to inherit the proper share of her husband's property.

To get around these problems, a woman of advanced age who bore no sons may become a female husband by marrying a young woman. The purpose of this arrangement is for the young wife to provide the male heirs her female husband could not. To accomplish this, the woman's wife enters into a sexual relationship with a man other than her female husband's male husband; usually it is one of his male relatives. No other obligations exist between this woman and her male sex partner, and her female husband is recognized as the social and legal father of any children born under these conditions.

In keeping with her role as female husband, this woman is expected to abandon her female gender identity and, ideally, dress and behave as a man. In practice, the ideal is not completely achieved, for the habits of a lifetime are difficult to reverse. Generally, it is in the context of domestic activities, which are most highly symbolic of female identity, that female husbands most completely assume a male identity.

The individuals who are parties to woman/woman marriages enjoy several advantages. By assuming male identity, a barren or sonless woman raises her status considerably and even achieves near equality with men, who otherwise occupy a far more favored position in Nandi society than women. A woman who marries a female husband is usually one who is unable to make a good marriage, often because she (the female husband's wife) has lost face as a consequence of premarital pregnancy. By marrying a female husband, she too raises her status and also secures legitimacy for her children. Moreover, a female husband is usually less harsh and demanding, spends more time with her, and allows her a greater say in decision making than a male husband does. The one thing she may not do is engage in sexual activity with her marriage partner; in fact, female husbands are expected to abandon sexual activity altogether, even with their male husbands to whom they remain married even though the women now have their own wives.

In Europe, where both men and women inherit family wealth, the "marriage" of women to the Church as nuns passed wealth that might otherwise have gone to husbands and offspring to the Church instead.

Recently, the issue of same-sex marriage has become a matter for debate in the United States. In several states,

William Lippert, the only openly gay member of the Vermont House of Representatives, embraces his partner upon passage of a bill legalizing civil unions.

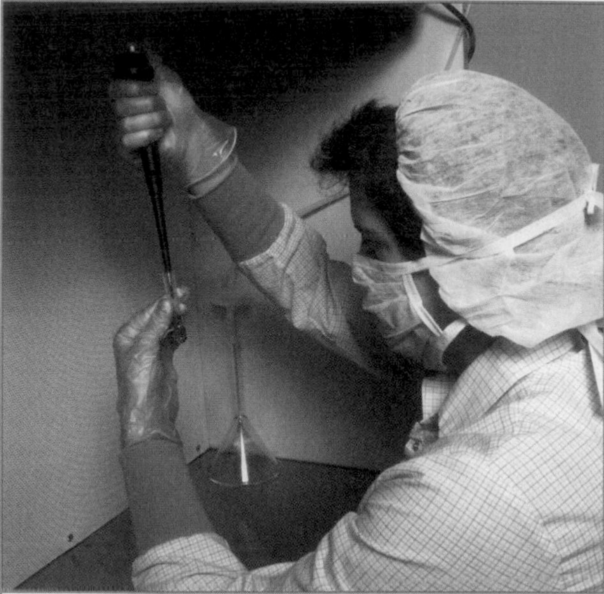
Shown here is a nurse creating a human embryo. No longer is biological sex the only way to beget children, opening the way to a whole industry and transformation of children into consumer goods.

resolutions or laws have been passed forbidding such marriages. In Vermont, however, the legislature has just passed, and the governor has signed, a bill that permits same-sex partners to enjoy the benefits of marriage. The arguments most commonly marshaled by opponents of same-sex unions are, first, that marriage has always been between males and females, but as we have just seen, this is not true. Same-sex marriages have been documented not only for a number of societies in Africa but in other parts of the world as well. As among the Nandi, they provide acceptable positions in society for individuals who might otherwise be marginalized.

A second argument against same-sex unions is that they legitimize marriages between gays and lesbians, whose sexual orientations have been widely regarded in the United States as unnatural. But again, as evidence discussed in this and Chapter 16 shows, neither cross-cultural studies, nor those of other animals, suggest that homosexual behavior is at all unnatural. A third argument, that the function of marriage is to produce children, is also flawed. At best, it is a partial truth, as marriage involves economic, political, and legal considerations as well. There is also the fact that in many societies, there is a separation between the sexual and reproductive attributes of women; two such cases are the Nandi and the Nayar. The irony here is that no societies have achieved greater separation of these elements than the United States and other Western countries, with their development of new reproductive technologies.

DIVORCE

Like marriage, divorce in non-Western societies is a matter of great concern to the couple's families. Since marriage is less often a religious than an economic matter, divorce arrangements can be made for a variety of reasons and with varying degrees of difficulty.

Among the Gusii of Kenya, sterility or impotence were grounds for a divorce. Among the Chenchu of Hyderabad and certain aboriginal peoples in northern Canada, divorce was discouraged after children were born; couples usually were urged by their families to adjust their differences. By contrast, in the southwestern United States, a Hopi Indian woman in Arizona might divorce her husband at any time merely by placing his belongings outside the door to indicate he was no longer welcome. Divorce was fairly common among the Yahgan, who lived at the southernmost tip of South America, and was seen as justified if the husband was considered cruel or failed as a provider.

Divorce in these societies seems familiar and even sensible, and in one way or another, the children are taken care of. An adult unmarried woman is almost unheard of in most non-Western societies; a divorced woman soon remarries. In many societies, economic considerations are often the strongest motivation to marry. On the island of New Guinea, a man does not marry because of sexual needs, which he can readily satisfy out of wedlock, but because he needs a woman to make pots and cook his meals, to fabricate nets and weed his plantings. A man without a wife among the Australian aborigines is in an unsatisfactory position, since he has no one to supply him regularly with food or firewood.

Although divorce rates may be high in some non-Western societies, notably matrilineal societies such as that of the Hopi, they have become so high in Western societies as to cause many North Americans to worry about the future of marriage and the family in the contemporary world. Between A.D. 1000 and 1800, divorce was next to impossible, but few marriages lasted more than about 10 or 20 years, owing low life expectancy.[26] With a lower rate of separation by death has come a higher rate by legal action. Undoubtedly, the causes of divorce in the United States are many and varied. Among them are the trivial and transient characteristics we have already mentioned that marriages may all too easily be based upon. Beyond this, marriage in the United States is supposed to involve an enduring, supportive, and intimate bond between a man and woman, full of affection and love. In this relationship, people are supposed to find escape from the pressures of the competitive workaday world, as well as from the legal and social constraints that so affect their behavior outside the family. Yet in a society where people are brought up to seek individual gratification, where this often is seen to come through competition at someone else's expense (see Chapter 16), and where women traditionally have been expected to be submissive to men, it should not come as a surprise to find that the reality of marriage does not always live up to the ideal. Harsh treatment and neglect of spouses—usually of wives by husbands—in the United States is neither new nor rare; furthermore, people are more tolerant of violence directed against spouses and children than they are against outsiders. It is still true today, as anthropologists Collier, Rosaldo, and Yanagisako observed in 1982: "A smaller percentage of homicides involving family members are prosecuted than those involving strangers. We are faced with the irony that in our society the place where nurturance and noncontingent [unconditional] affection are supposed to be located is simultaneously the place where violence is most tolerated."[27] What has happened in recent years is that people have become less inclined toward moral censure of those—women especially—who seek escape from unsatisfactory marriages. No longer are people as willing to "stick it out at all costs" no matter how intolerable the situation may be. Thus, divorce is increasingly exercised as a sensible reaction to marriages that do not work.

[26] Stone, L. (1998). *Kinship and gender: An introduction* (p. 235). Boulder, CO: Westview.

[27] Collier, J., Rosaldo, M. Z., & Yanagisako, S. (1982). Is there a family? New anthropological views. In B. Thorne & M. Yalom (Eds.). *Rethinking the family: Some feminist problems* (p. 36). New York: Longman.

CHAPTER SUMMARY

Among primates, the human female is unusual in her ability to engage in sexual activity whenever she wants to or whenever her culture tells her it is appropriate, irrespective of whether or not she is fertile. Although such activity may reinforce social bonds between individuals, competition for sexual access can also be disruptive, so every society has rules that govern such access. The near universality of the incest taboo, which forbids sexual relations between parents and their children, and usually between siblings, long has interested anthropologists, but a truly convincing explanation of the taboo has yet to be advanced. Related to incest are the practices of endogamy and exogamy. Endogamy is marriage within a group of individuals; exogamy is marriage outside the group. If the group is limited to the immediate family, almost all societies can be said to prohibit endogamy and practice exogamy. Likewise, societies that practice exogamy at one level may practice endogamy at another. Community endogamy, for example, is a relatively common practice. In a few societies, royal families are known to have practiced endogamy rather than exogamy among siblings to preserve intact the purity of the royal line and its property.

Although defined in terms of a continuing sexual relationship between a man and woman, marriage should not be confused with mating. Although mating occurs within marriage, it often occurs outside of it as well. Unlike mating, marriage is backed by social, legal, and economic forces. In some societies, new families are formed through marriage, but this is not true for all societies.

Monogamy, or the taking of a single spouse, is the most common form of marriage, primarily for economic reasons. A man must have a certain amount of wealth to be able to afford polygyny, or marriage to more than one wife at the same time. Yet in societies where women do most of the productive work, polygyny may serve as a means of generating wealth for a household. Although few marriages in a given society may be polygynous, it is regarded as an appropriate, and even preferred, form of marriage in the majority of the world's societies. Since few communities have a surplus of men, polyandry, or the custom of a woman having several husbands, is uncommon. Also rare is group marriage, in which several men and several women have sexual access to one another. The levirate ensures the security of a woman by providing that a widow marry her husband's brother; the sororate provides that a widower marry his wife's sister. Serial monogamy is a form of marriage in which a man or woman marries a series of partners. In recent decades, this pattern has become increasingly common among middle-class North Americans as individuals divorce and remarry.

In the United States and many of the other industrialized countries of the West, marriages run the risk of being based on an ideal of romantic love that emphasizes youthful beauty. In no other parts of the world would marriages based on such trivial and transitory characteristics be expected to work. In non-Western societies economic considerations are of major concern in arranging marriages. Love follows rather than precedes marriage. The family arranges marriages in societies in which it is the most powerful social institution. Marriage serves to bind two families as allies.

Preferred marriage partners in many societies are particular cross cousins (mother's brother's daughter if a man; father's sister's son if a woman) or, less commonly, parallel cousins on the paternal side (father's brother's son or daughter). Cross-cousin marriage is a means of establishing and maintaining solidarity between groups. Marriage to a paternal parallel cousin serves to retain property and a woman's offspring within a single male line of descent.

In many human societies, marriages are formalized by some sort of economic exchange. Sometimes, this takes the form of reciprocal gift exchange between the bride's and groom's relatives. More common is bride-price, the payment of money or other valuables from the groom's to the bride's kin; this is characteristic of societies where the women both work and bear children for the husband's family. An alternative arrangement is for families to exchange daughters. Bride service occurs when the groom is expected to work for a period for the bride's family. A dowry is the payment of a woman's inheritance at the time of marriage to her or her husband; its purpose is to ensure support for women in societies where men do most of the productive work and women are valued for their reproductive potential alone.

In some societies, marriage arrangements exist between individuals of the same sex. An example is woman/woman marriage as practiced in many African societies. Such marriages provide a socially approved way to deal with problems for which marriages between individuals of opposite sex offer no satisfactory solution.

Divorce is possible in all societies, though reasons for divorce as well as its frequency vary widely from one society to another. In the United States, factors contributing to the breakup of marriages include the trivial and transitory characteristics many marriages are based on and the difficulty of establishing a supportive, intimate bond in a society in which people are brought up to seek individual gratification, often through competition at someone else's expense, and in which women have traditionally been expected to be submissive to men.

CLASSIC READINGS

duToit, B. M. (1991). *Human sexuality: Cross cultural readings.* New York: McGraw Hill.

Of the numerous texts that deal with most aspects of human sexuality, this is one of the few that gives adequate recognition to the fact most peoples in the world do things differently from North Americans. This reader deals cross-culturally with such topics as menstrual cycle, pair bonding, sexuality, pregnancy and childbirth, childhood, puberty, birth control, sexually transmitted diseases, sex roles, and the climacteric.

Goody, J. (1976). *Production and reproduction: A comparative study of the domestic domain.* Cambridge: Cambridge University Press.

This book is especially good in its discussion of the interrelationship between marriage, property, and inheritance. Although cross-cultural in its approach, readers will be fascinated by the many insights into the history of marriage in the Western world.

Ottenheimer, M. (1996). *Forbidden relatives.* Champaign, IL: University of Illinois Press.

This book examines the laws against cousin marriage in the United States. It describes their distribution and explains why some states have such laws and others do not. It also contrasts these laws with the absence of such laws in any other country in the western world and tells the reasons for this difference. Noting that there is no empirical evidence to support such anti-cousin marriage legislation, this book argues that it is based on a myth and analyzes the cultural historical context for the prohibition of such marriages by law.

Stone, L. (2000). *Kinship and gender: An introduction* (2nd ed.). Boulder, CO: Westview.

With a focus on gender, Stone considers all the cross-cultural variations in marriage practices in the broader context of kinship studies. A particular strength is the inclusion of specific case studies to illustrate general principles. The book ends with a thought-provoking discussion of new reproductive technologies and their repercussions for both kinship and gender.

Suggs, D. N., & Miracle, A. W. (Eds.) (1993). *Culture and human sexuality: A reader.* Pacific Grove, CA: Brooks/Cole.

This collection of articles covers a wide range of topics including evolution, gender, family, life cycle, incest, religion, sexual orientation, and disease-related issues. Illustrated are the variety of sexual expression around the world and the role of culture in the patterning of sexual ideas and activities.

CHAPTER 20

FAMILY AND HOUSEHOLD

A Bedouin family group in Iraq. One of the basic functions of the family is raising children.

CHAPTER PREVIEW

1

What Is the Family?

Although the word *family* means different things to different people, in anthropological terms it is a group composed of a woman, her dependent children, and at least one adult man joined through marriage or blood relationship. The family may take many forms, ranging all the way from a single married couple with their children, as in North American society, to a large group composed of several brothers and sisters with the sisters' children, as in southwest India among the Nayar. The particular form taken by the family is related to particular social, historical, and ecological circumstances.

2

What Is the Difference Between Family and Household?

Households are task-oriented residential units within which economic production, consumption, inheritance, child rearing, and shelter are organized and implemented. In the vast majority of human societies, households either consist of families or their core members constitute families, even though some household members may not be relatives of the family around which it is built. In some societies, although households are present, families are not. Furthermore, in some societies where families are present, they may be less important in people's thinking than the households of which they are parts.

What Are Some of the Problems of Family and Household Organization?

Although families and households exist to solve in various ways problems all peoples must deal with, the different forms they may take are all accompanied by their own characteristic problems. Where families and households are small and relatively independent, as they are in North American society, their members may be isolated from the aid and support of kin and must fend for themselves in many situations. By contrast, families that include several adults within the same large household must find ways to control various kinds of tensions that invariably exist among their members.

The family, long regarded by North Americans as a critically necessary core social institution, today has become a matter of controversy and discussion. Women going outside the home to take income-producing jobs rather than staying home with children, couples, sometimes of the same sex, living together without the formality of marriage, high divorce rates, and increasing numbers of households headed by a single parent have raised questions about the functions of the family in North American society and its ability to survive in a period of rapid social change. Evidence of widespread interest in these questions can be seen in the convening, in 1980, of a White House Conference on Families. Since then, scarcely a political campaign for national office has passed without frequent reference to what candidates like to call "traditional family values."

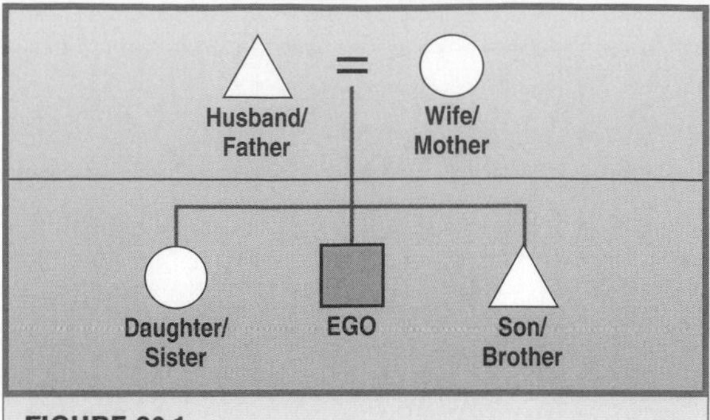

FIGURE 20.1

THIS DIAGRAM SHOWS THE RELATIONSHIPS IN A NUCLEAR FAMILY, SUCH AS THOSE FOUND IN NORTH AMERICAN SOCIETY.

Does the family, as most North Americans think of it, offer the best environment for bringing up children? Does it impose an inferior status on the woman, confined and isolated in the home performing household and child-raising chores? Does the man, locked into an authoritarian role, suffer unduly in his personal development from bearing the primary responsibility for support of the family? Do adequate substitutes exist for people who have no family to care for them, such as old people and orphans? If the family as people in the United States think of it is found wanting, what are the alternatives?

Historical and cross-cultural studies of the family offer as many different family patterns as the fertile human imagination can invent. The one regarded as "normal" or "natural" by most North Americans—a discrete and independent living unit consisting of the nuclear family (Figure 20.1)—is in fact no more normal or natural than any other and cannot be used as the standard for measuring other forms. Neither universal nor even common among human societies, the independent nuclear family emerged only recently in human history. Its roots go back to a series of regulations imposed by the Roman Catholic Church in the 4th century A.D. that prohibited close marriages, discouraged adoption, and condemned polygyny, concubinage, divorce, and remarriage (all of which previously had been perfectly respectable, as the Old Testament of the Bible, among other sources, makes clear). Not only did these prohibitions strengthen the conjugal tie between one man and one woman, at the expense of consanguineal or "blood" ties, but it also ensured that large numbers of people would be left with no male heirs. It is a biological fact that 20% of all couples will have only daughters, and another 20% will have no children at all. By eliminating polygyny, concubinage, divorce, and remarriage, and by discouraging adoption, the church removed the means by which people overcame these odds and made sure that they would have male heirs. In the absence of such heirs, property was commonly transferred from families to the Roman Catholic Church, which rapidly became the largest landowner in most European countries, a position it has retained to this day. By insinuating itself into the very fabric of domestic life, heirship, and marriage, the Church gained tremendous control over the grass roots of society, enriching itself in the process.[1]

The nuclear family, consisting of a married couple and dependent offspring, is held up as the ideal in the United States.

With the industrialization of Europe and North America, the nuclear family became further isolated from other kin. One reason for this is that industrial economies re-

[1] Goody, J. (1983). *The development of the family and marriage in Europe* (pp. 44–46). Cambridge: Cambridge University Press.

quire a mobile labor force; people must be prepared to move to where the jobs are, something that is most easily done without excess kin in tow. Another reason is that the family came to be seen as a kind of refuge from a public world that people saw as threatening to their sense of privacy and self-determination.[2] Within the family, relationships were supposed to be enduring and noncontingent, entailing love and affection, based upon cooperation, and governed by feeling and morality. Outside the family, where people sold their work and negotiated contracts, relationships increasingly were seen as competitive, temporary, and contingent upon performance, requiring buttressing by law and legal sanction. Such views were held most widely in the late 19th and early 20th centuries, and in the United States independent nuclear family households reached their highest frequency around 1950, when 60% of all households conformed to this model.[3]

In North America, families are widely believed to be places of refuge from the rough-and-tumble outside world. Yet, domestic violence is far from rare, and women and children are its usual victims.

The Holy Family of Christianity. Mary's husband Joseph was her father's brother's son and was himself the product of a leviratic marriage. Even though both kinds of marriage were considered proper in the early days of Christianity, they were not allowed by the Church after the 4th century.

Since then, things have changed, and a mere 26% of U.S. households now conform to the independent nuclear family ideal. More are now headed by divorced, separated, and never-married individuals. This situation has arisen as increasingly large numbers of people find more intimacy and emotional support in relationships outside the family and are less inclined to tolerate the harsh treatment and neglect of children and spouses, especially wives, that all too commonly occur within families. (In the United States, 28% of women have experienced domestic violence, and 10 women are killed by their batterers every day.[4])

The family as it has emerged in Europe, Canada, and the United States, then, is the product of particular historical and social circumstances; where these have differed, so have family forms. Thus, how men and women in other societies live together must be studied not as bizarre and exotic forms of human behavior but as logical outcomes of people's experience living in particular times, places, and social situations.

FAMILY AND SOCIETY

Although many North Americans continue to think of families as standing in opposition to the rest of society, the truth is that they are affected by, and in turn affect, the values and structure of the society in which they are embedded. For a closer look at this, we may take a closer look at the rise and fall of nuclear families in the United States.

[2] Collier, J., Rosaldo, M. Z., & Yanagisako, S. (1982). Is there a family? New anthropological views. In B. Thorne and M. Yalom (Eds.). *Rethinking the family: Some feminist questions* (pp. 34–35). New York: Longman.

[3] Stacey, J. (1990). *Brave new families* (pp. 5, 10). New York: Basic Books.

[4] Seager, J. (1997). *The state of women in the world atlas* (2nd ed.) (p. 26). New York: Penguin.

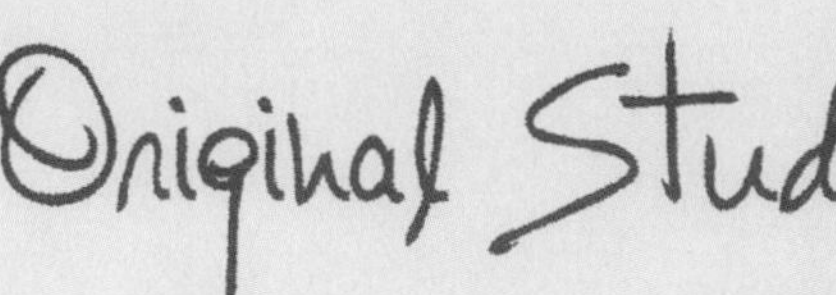

The Ever-Changing Family in North America[5]

The colonists lived in households, each typically consisting of a nuclear family; wealthier households contained servants as well. In addition, many less wealthy families sent their children to wealthier families to work as servants or to learn a trade, a practice also common in Europe. Some people had come to the New World as indentured servants, agreeing to serve a master's household in return for the cost of passage out of Europe. Thus many households contained large numbers of people who were not kin to one another. It was these households, rather than their own "biological" families as such, that were important in people's daily lives. Biological children were treated much like servants, especially if they were of the same or similar age.

The households themselves did not contain separate, private spaces for married couples or for parents and their children. As Coontz [in her book on the history of American families] writes: "The central room or hall was where work, meals, play, religious instruction, and often sleep took place. . . . Even genteel families put several people to a room and several people to a bed. Most household members sat together on benches for meals and prayers, rather than in separate chairs. There was thus little concept of a private family set apart from the world of work, servants, and neighbors." Households were closely linked to one another, and highly interdependent on one another for cooperation and economic exchanges. People freely intruded into one another's households, and the affairs of all were carefully monitored and regulated by village and church officials. What we would consider very private business today was then considered the business of neighbors and the whole community. This point is strikingly illustrated by Coontz:

> The assumption that household affairs were the business of all community members is seen in Nancy Cott's study of divorce records, which show that neighbors nonchalantly entered what modern people would consider the most private areas of life. Mary Angel and Abagail Galloway, for example, testified that they had caught sight through an open window of Adam Air "in the Act of Copulation" with Pamela Brichford. They walked into the house "and after observing them some time . . . asked him if he was not Ashamed to act so when he had a Wife at home."

The contrast to the private, bounded nuclear family of later North American life is obvious. The family of colonial times was not separated out, nor was "the home" seen as a retreat from the strain of the outside world. Indeed, since the colonial household was a center of economic production (in terms of, for example, agriculture and farm management, cloth production and trade), there was little division between the public and domestic spheres of life. In the household, both women and men played active roles in production. Aside from food processing and preparation, wives wove cloth, traded with neighbors, managed servants, and helped to keep accounts.

Each household was under the authority of its male property owner. Wives were under the authority of husbands, but so were children, servants, apprentices, and anyone else attached to the man's household. In fact, colonial society itself was altogether hierarchical, such that lower males were subservient to higher ones to the same extent that wives were to husbands. Women did not need to grapple with reasons for their lack of equal status, since equal status was not even a social value for men. This was a society that viewed its parts as interdependent and so required a hierarchy for its organization. Women were clearly subordinate, but a colonial woman's subordination was viewed as a social necessity—one of many unequal relations required by society—not as a unique female condition caused by her biology.

[5] Adapted from Stone, L. (1998). *Kinship and gender: An introduction* (pp. 248–250, 255–256). Boulder, CO: Westview.

Many of us associate colonial society with rather strict rules governing sex. And, indeed, there were laws against fornication and adultery in all the colonies (though these laws seem to have reverted to the Roman definition as adultery sex between a man and a married woman, excluding sex between a married man and an unmarried woman). Adultery was often severely punished, with public flogging or even death. Dancing and certain forms of dress were also widely forbidden. Still, sex was openly and frankly discussed, offenses were openly described and punished, and sexual matters were not hidden away from children. Moreover, wives were expected to be affectionate companions to husbands.

Initially, marriages followed the general European pattern of dowry (both direct and indirect) and parental control. In some places, such as the South (U.S.) and New France (Quebec), cousin marriage was practiced in order to consolidate land and transmit wealth in family lines; and thus, as in Europe, the dowry and endogamy promoted the solidification of classes.

The patriarchal colonial family faded away as population expansion, migration, new waves of immigrants, urbanization, and other economic and political changes occurred in North America. In general terms there was a trend toward increasing **privacy** of the nuclear family. However, this trend took hold much more slowly in rural and working class families, and its effects were gradual among all classes. Nevertheless, families maintained important ties with wider kin for support and help, especially during periods of war, economic disruption, and urbanization over the next few centuries.

Important changes in family life and gender correlated with industrialization in the late eighteenth and early nineteenth centuries. New industries needed workers and managers, often at work sites away from the home. Whereas the household had formerly been a unit of production and consumption, it was now a unit of consumption only. Hence the split between the home (private, domestic) and the workplace (public, productive) was born. Among poor and working class people, both women and men went out to work, though women were pushed into lower-paying jobs with less hope of advancement—as is still generally true for North American women today. Among the middle and upper classes, industrialization meant the withdrawal of women from production. Their roles became confined to the home, to childrearing, to domesticity. Indeed, among the middle classes, a nonworking wife was important for the social image and self-esteem of males, who believed it was their duty to provide for and protect wives and children. It was with a sense of shame that a middle-class married woman went to work because she **had** to, owing to widowhood, sudden unemployment in the husband, or some other financial difficulty.

This shift of production from the home to the workplace had an impact on North American family life and gender that cannot be overstated. Many writers have drawn attention to the links between the industrial capitalist economy that prevailed at the time and the perpetuation of patriarchal social relations in America and Europe. Removed from production, wives become economically dependent on husbands and in this condition are easily subordinated to them. Males, now expected to support wives and children, "become bound to their work and often endure difficult conditions out of fear of losing their jobs and falling short of their society's and their own expectations."

Some look back to the post World War II period as the Golden Age of the American Family, a time when what some refer to as the 1950s "Leave it to Beaver" family prevailed. A thoroughly middle-class phenomenon, this was a nuclear family that had moved to the suburbs, where it eventually owned its own home. The father-husband went off to work and functioned as the "breadwinner." The fulltime wife-mother stayed at home, absorbed in domestic efficiency, wife-companionship, and childrearing. According to this particular ideal, the father, though busy at work, had an active family life too. The family was very private, and its members spent quality time together; all were happy and had a lot of good, clean middle-class fun.

But Coontz suggests that this 1950s family is largely a myth; it represents nostalgia for a re-created past, not a solid American tradition. For one thing, she contends, this ideal family was never a reality for the majority of North Americans and

Original Study

certainly not for groups such as the blacks and the poor. Some families maintained a facade of this ideal on the outside, but inside were wracked by alcoholic parents and abusive relationships. And women of this time were excluded from so many fields and suffered so many financial restrictions (e.g., not being allowed to take out credit cards in their own names) that "there were not many permissible alternatives to baking brownies [or] experimenting with new canned soups."

Many women were not happy with their isolated, domestic roles or their full economic dependence on their husbands. Of the same period Rothman writes that the wife-companion became lonely in suburbia and saw that her identity was encompassed by that of her husband and children. Everything she did was for others, not herself.

Even for those few North Americans who had anything like the ideal 1950s family, this outcome, according to Coontz, was a historical fluke. It is true that, with the end of the war and relief at its end, the age of marriage dropped, fertility rose, divorce declined, and the middle class moved to the suburbs. But the 1950s family with its nonworking wives and affordable homes emerged only because of North America's brief postwar prosperity. Within a short span of time the American dream was no longer affordable and middle-class women went out to work.

Indeed, women's participation in the labor force increased then and has been increasing ever since. Today a majority of working-age women and of women with young children are in the work force. This increase among working women was as much a function of economic necessity as a response to the doldrums of housework.

The End

FUNCTIONS OF THE FAMILY

Among humans, reliance on group living for survival is a basic characteristic. They have inherited this from their primate ancestors, though they have developed it in their own distinctively human ways. Even among monkeys and apes, group living requires the participation of adults of both sexes. Among species that, like us, have taken up life on the ground, as well as among species most closely related to us, adult males are normally much larger and stronger than females, and their teeth are usually more efficient for fighting. Thus, they are essential for the group's defense. Moreover, the close and prolonged relationship between infants and their mothers, without which the infants cannot survive, renders the adult primate female less well suited than the males to handle defense.

Nurturance of Children

Taking care of the young is primarily the job of the adult primate female. Primate babies are born relatively helpless and remain dependent upon their mothers for a longer time than any other animals (a chimpanzee, for example, cannot survive without its mother until it reaches age 4 or even 5). Not only is this dependence for food and physical care, but also, as numerous studies have shown, primate infants deprived of maternal attention will not grow and develop normally, if they survive at all. The protective presence of adult males shields the mothers from both danger and harassment from other group members, allowing them to give their infants the attention they require.

Among humans, the division of labor by gender has been developed beyond the sexual division of other primates. Until the recent advent of substitutes for human breast milk, human females more often than not were occupied much of their adult lives with child rearing. And human infants need no less active "mothering" than do the young of other primates. For one thing, they are even more helpless at birth, and for another, the period of infant dependency is longer in humans. Besides all this, studies have shown that human infants, no less than other primates, need more than just food and physical care if they are to develop normally. But among humans, unlike other primates, the infant's biological mother does not have to provide all this "mothering." Not only may other women provide the child with much of the attention it needs, but so may men. In many societies children are handled as much by men as by women, and in some societies men are more nurturing to children than are women.

A female baboon with her infant and male friend. Baboon males are protective of their female friends, even though they are not always the fathers of their friends' infants. Thus shielded from danger and harassment from other troop members, females can give their infants the attention they require to survive.

Economic Cooperation

In all human societies, even though women may be the primary providers of child care, women have other responsibilities as well. Although several of the economic activities they traditionally have engaged in have been compatible with their child-rearing role and have not placed their offspring at risk, this cannot be said of all their activities. Consider how the common combination of child care with food preparation, especially if cooking is done over an open fire, creates a potentially hazardous situation for children. With the mother (or other caregiver) distracted by some other task, the child may all too easily receive a severe burn or bad cut, with serious consequences. What can be said is that the economic activities of women generally have complemented those of men, even though, in some societies, individuals may perform tasks normally assigned to the opposite sex, as the occasion dictates. Thus, men and women could share the results of their labors on a regular basis, as was discussed in Chapters 17 and 18.

An effective way both to facilitate economic cooperation between men and women and to provide for a close bond between mother and child at the same time is through the establishment of residential groups that include adults of both sexes. The differing nature of male and female roles, as these are defined by different cultures, requires a child to have an adult of the same sex available to serve as a proper model for the appropriate adult role. The presence of adult men and women in the same residential group provides for this. As defined in Chapter 19, a family is a residential group composed of a woman, her dependent children, and at least one man joined through marriage or consanguineal ("blood") relationship. Again (see Chapter 19), as gender roles are culturally defined, another female may fill the man's role.

Well suited though the family may be for these tasks, we should not suppose it is the only unit capable of providing such conditions, or even the best one. In fact, other arrangements that are no less effective are possible, one example being the Israeli kibbutz, where paired teams of male and female specialists raise groups of children. In many food-foraging societies (the Ju/'hoansi and Mbuti, discussed in Chapters 16 and 17, are good examples), all adult members of a community share in the responsibilities of child care. Thus, when parents go off to hunt or to collect plants and herbs, they may leave their children behind, secure in the knowledge they will be looked after by whatever adults remain in the camp. Yet another arrangement may be seen among the Mundurucu, a horticultural people of South America's Amazon forest. Their children live in houses with their mothers, apart from all men until the age of 13, whereupon the boys leave their mothers' houses to go live with the village men. Because Mundurucu men and women do not live together as members of discrete residential units, it cannot be said that they have families.

One alternative to the family as a child-rearing unit is the Israeli kibbutz. Here, children of a kibbutz are shown in a supervised session of creative play.

FAMILY AND HOUSEHOLD

Although it is often stated that some form of family is present in all human societies, the Mundurucu case just cited demonstrates this is not so. In Mundurucu villages, the men all live together in one house with all boys over the age of 13; women live with others of their sex as well as younger boys in two or three houses grouped around the men's house. As among the Nayar (discussed in Chapter 19), married men and women are members of separate households, meeting periodically for sexual activity.

Although the family is not universally present in human societies, the **household,** defined as the basic residential unit where economic production, consumption, inheritance, child rearing, and shelter are organized and implemented, is universally present. Among the Mundurucu, the men's house constitutes one household, and the women's houses constitute others. Although, in this case as in many, each house is in effect a household, a number of societies have households made up of two or more houses together, as we shall see later in this chapter.

In many human societies, most households in fact constitute families, although other sorts of households may be present as well (single-parent households, for example, in the United States and many Caribbean countries). Often, a household may consist of a family along with some more distant relatives of family members. Or coresidents may be unrelated, such as the service personnel in an elaborate royal household, apprentices in the household of craft specialists, or low-status clients in the household of rich and powerful patrons. In such societies, even though people may think in terms of households rather than families, the households are built around the latter. Thus, even though the family is not universal, in the vast majority of human societies, the family is the basic core of the household.

Household. The basic residential unit in which economic production, consumption, inheritance, child rearing, and shelter are organized and carried out; may or may not be synonymous with family.

A celebration at the palace in the Yoruba city of Oyo, Nigeria. As is usual in societies where royal households are found, that of the Yoruba includes many individuals not related to the ruler, as well as the royal family.

FORM OF THE FAMILY

As suggested earlier in this chapter, the family may take any one of a number of forms in response to particular social, historical, and ecological circumstances. At the outset, a distinction must be made between **conjugal families,** which are formed on the basis of marital ties, and consanguineal families, which are not. As defined in Chapter 19, consanguineal families consist of related women, their brothers, and the women's offspring. Such families are not common; the classic case is the Nayar household group. The Nayar are not unique, however, and consanguineal families are found elsewhere—for example, among the Musuo of southwestern China or the Tory Islanders, a Roman Catholic, Gaelic-speaking fisherfolk living off the coast of Ireland. The Tory Islanders, who do not marry until they are in their late 20s or early 30s, look at it this way: "Oh well, you get married at that age, it's too late to break up arrangements that you have already known for a long time. . . . You know, I have my sisters and brothers to look after, why should I leave home to go live with a husband? After all, he's got his sisters and his brothers looking after him."[6] Because the community numbers but a few hundred people, husbands and wives are within easy commuting distance of one another.

The Nuclear Family

The form of conjugal family familiar to most North Americans is the independent nuclear family, which in spite of its precipitous decline is still widely regarded as the ideal in the United States and Canada. In these countries it is not considered desirable for young people to live with their parents beyond a certain age, nor is it considered a moral responsibility for a couple to take their aged parents into their home when the old people no longer can care for themselves. Retirement communities and nursing homes provide these services, and to take aged parents into one's home is commonly regarded as not only an economic burden but also a threat to the household's privacy and independence.

The nuclear family is also apt to be prominent in societies such as the Inuit that live in harsh environments. In the winter the Inuit husband and wife, with their children, roam the vast Arctic wilderness in their quest for food. The husband hunts and makes shelters. The wife cooks, is responsible for the children, and makes the

[6] Fox, R. (1981, December 3). Interview for Coast Telecourses, Inc., Los Angeles.

Conjugal Family. A family consisting of one (or more) man (who may be a female) married to one (or more) woman (who may be a male), and their offspring.

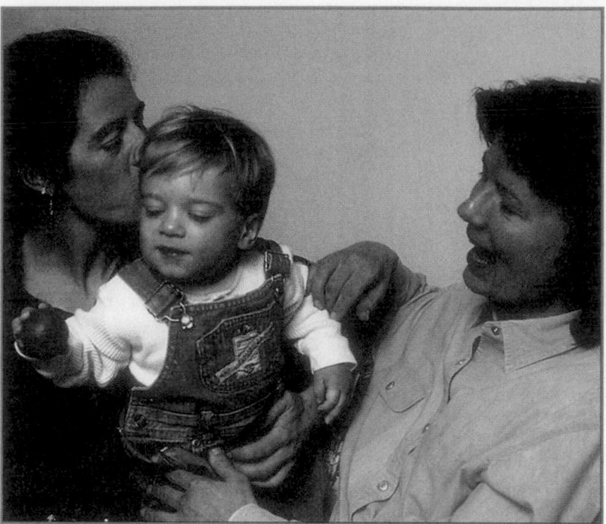

In the United States, one alternative to the traditional nuclear family is the gay or lesbian family which, through adoption or the new reproductive technologies, may include children.

clothing and keeps it in good repair. One of her chores is to chew her husband's boots to soften the leather for the next day so that he can resume his quest for game. The wife and her children could not survive without the husband, and life for a man is unimaginable without a wife.

Certain parallels can be drawn between the nuclear family in industrial societies and families living under especially harsh environmental conditions. In both cases, the family is an independent unit that must be prepared to fend for itself; this creates for individual members a strong dependence on one another. Minimal help is available from outside in the event of emergencies or catastrophes. When their usefulness ends, the elderly are cared for only if it is feasible. In the event of the mother or father's death, life becomes precarious for the child. Yet this form of family is well adapted to a life that requires a high degree of geographical mobility. For the Inuit, this mobility permits the hunt for food; for other North Americans, the hunt for jobs and improved social status requires a mobile form of family unit.

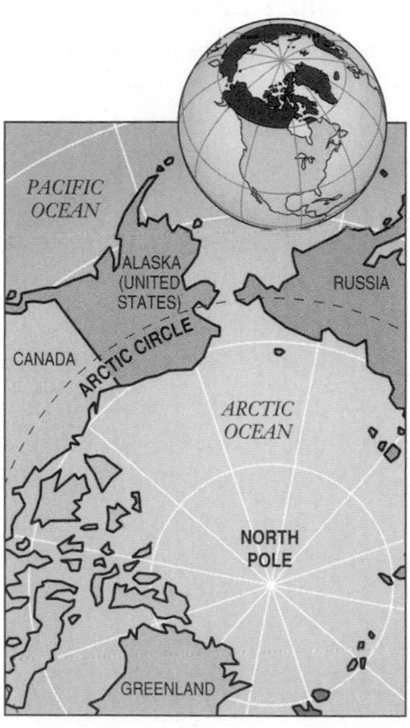

Not even among the Inuit, however, is the nuclear family as separated from other kin as it has become among most non-native North Americans. When Inuit families are off by themselves, it is regarded as a matter of temporary expediency; most of the time, they are found in groups of at least a few families together, with members of one family having relatives in all of the others.[7] Thus families cooperate with one another on a daily basis, sharing food and other resources, looking out for each other's children, and sometimes even eating together. The sense of shared responsibility for one another's children and for the general welfare in Inuit multifamily groups contrasts with families in the United States, which are basically "on their own." Here the state has assigned sole responsibility to the family for child care and the welfare of family members, with relatively little assistance from outside.[8] To be sure, families can and often do help one another out, but they are under no obligation to do so. In fact, once children reach the age of majority (18), parents have no further legal obligation to them, nor do the children to their parents. When families do have difficulty fulfilling their assigned functions—as is increasingly the case—even though it be through no fault of their own, less support is available to them from the community at large than in most of the world's "stateless" societies, including that of the Inuit.

---

[7] Graburn, N. H. H. (1969). *Eskimos without igloos: Social and economic development in Sugluk* (pp. 56–58). Boston: Little Brown.

[8] Collier, R., Rosaldo, M. Z., & Yanagisako, S. (1982). Is there a family? Some new anthropological views. In B. Thorne and M. Yalom (Eds.). *Rethinking the family: Some feminist problems* (pp. 28–29). New York: Longman.

Among the Inuit, nuclear families such as the one shown here are the norm, although they are not as isolated from other kin as are nuclear families in the United States.

HIGHWAY 1
Interactive anthropology tutorial site
http://www.umanitoba.ca/anthropology/tutor

The Extended Family

In North America, nuclear families have not always had the degree of independence that they came to have with the rise of industrialism. In an earlier, more agrarian era, the small nuclear family sometimes was part of a larger **extended family.** This kind of family, in part conjugal and in part consanguine, might include grandparents, mother and father, brothers and sisters, perhaps an uncle and aunt, and a stray cousin or two. All these people, some related "by blood" and some by marriage, lived and worked together. Because members of the younger generation brought their spouses (husbands or wives) to live in the family, extended families, like consanguine families, had continuity through time. As older members died off, new members were born into the family.

Extended family. A collection of nuclear families, related by ties of blood, that live together in one household.

In the United States, such families have survived until recently in some communities, as along the Maine coast.[9] There they developed in response to a unique economy featuring a mix of farming and seafaring, coupled with an ideal of self-sufficiency. Because family farms were incapable of providing self-sufficiency, seafaring was taken up as an economic alternative. Seagoing commerce, however, was periodically afflicted by depression, so family farming remained important as a cushion against economic hard times. The need for a sufficient labor pool to tend the farm, while at the same time furnishing officers, crew, or (frequently) both for locally owned vessels, was satisfied by the practice of a newly married couple settling on the farm of either the bride's or the groom's parents. Thus, most people spent their lives cooperating on a day-to-day basis in economic activities with close relatives, all of whom lived together (even if in separate houses) on the same farm.

The Maya of Guatemala and southern Mexico also live in extended family households.[10] In many of their communities, sons bring their wives to live in houses built on the edges of a small open plaza, on one edge of which their father's house already stands (Figure 20.2). Numerous household activities are carried out on this plaza; here women may weave, men may receive guests, and children play together. The head of the family is the sons' father, who makes most of the important decisions. All members of the family work together for the common good and deal with outsiders as a single unit.

Extended families living together in single households were and often still are important social units among the Hopi Indians of Arizona.[11] Ideally, the head of the household is an old woman; her married daughters, their husbands, and their children live with her. The women of the household own land, but the men (usually their husbands) till it. When extra help is needed during the harvest, for example, other male relatives, or friends, or persons local religious organizations designate form work groups and turn the hard work into a festive occasion. The women perform household tasks, such as processing food or making pottery, together.

The 1960s saw a number of attempts on the part of young people in the United States to reinvent a form of extended family living. Their families (often called communes) were groups of unrelated nuclear families that held property in common and lived together. It is further noteworthy that the lifestyle of these modern families often emphasized the kinds of cooperative ties found in the rural North American extended family of old, which provided a labor pool for the many tasks required for economic survival. In some of them the members even reverted to traditional gender roles; the women took care of the child rearing and household chores, while the men took care of those tasks preformed outside of the household itself.

Residence Patterns

Where some form of conjugal or extended family is the norm, family exogamy requires that either the husband or wife, if not both, must move to a new household upon marriage. There are five common patterns of residence that a newly married couple may adopt, the prime determinant being ecological circumstances, although other factors enter in as well. Thus, postmarital residence arrangements, far from being arbitrary, are adaptive in nature. One option is **patrilocal residence;** as just described for the Maya, a woman goes to live with her husband in the household in which he grew up. Favoring this arrangement is a predominant role for men in subsistence, particularly if they own property that can be accumulated, if polygyny is customary, if warfare is prominent enough to make cooperation among men especially important, and if an elaborate political organization exists in which men wield authority. These conditions are most often found together in societies that rely on animal husbandry and/or intensive agriculture for their subsistence. Where patrilocal residence is customary, the bride often must move to a different band or community. In such cases, her parents' family is not only losing the services of a useful family member, but they are losing her potential offspring as well. Hence, some kind of compensation to her family, most commonly bride-price, is usual.

[9] Haviland, W. A. (1973). Farming, seafaring and bilocal residence on the coast of Maine. *Man in the Northeast, 6,* 31–44.

[10] Vogt, E. Z. (1990). *The Zinacantecos of Mexico, A modern Maya way of life* (2nd ed.)(pp. 30–34). Fort Worth, TX: Holt, Rinehart and Winston.

[11] Forde, C. D. (1950). *Habitat, economy and society* (pp. 225–245). New York: Dutton.

Patrilocal residence. A residence pattern in which a married couple lives in the locality associated with the husband's father's relatives.

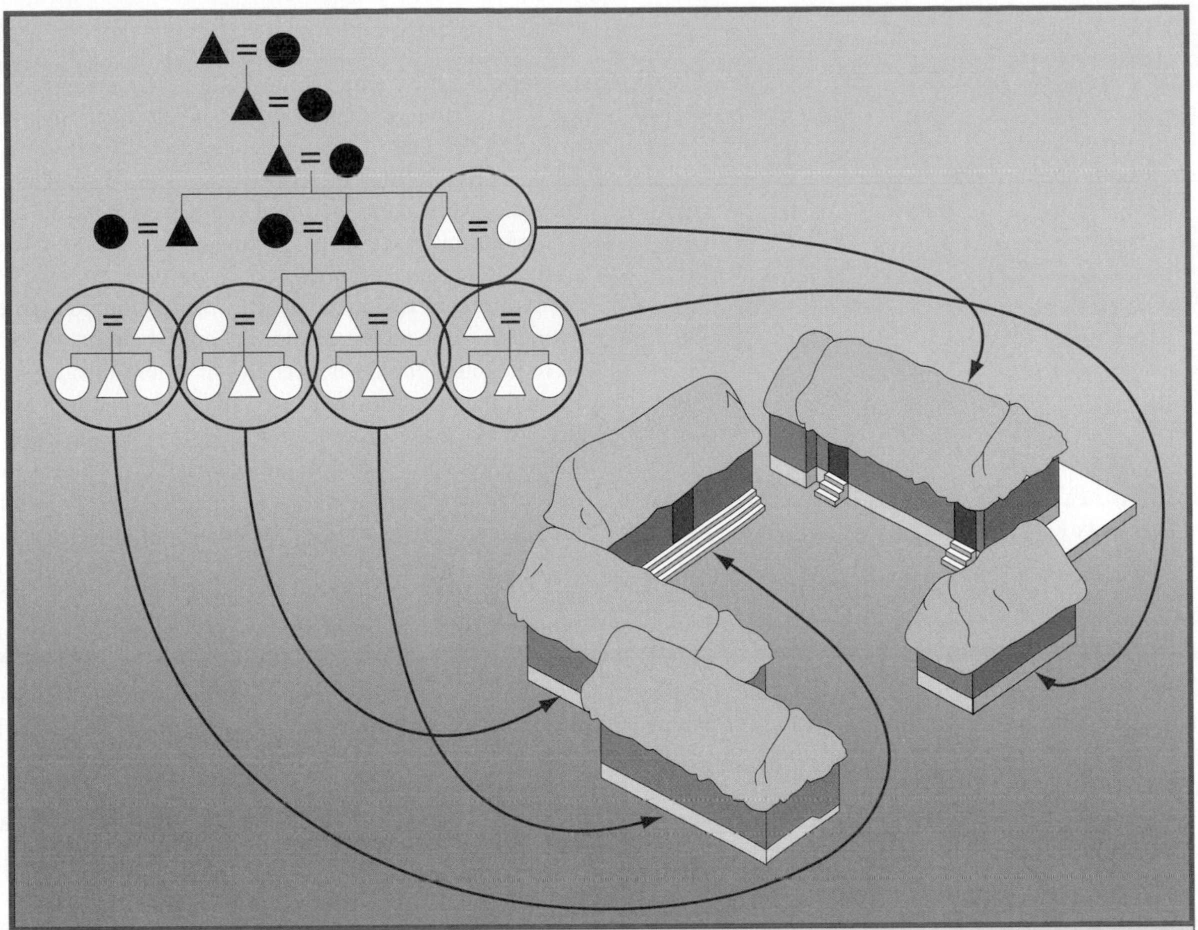

FIGURE 20.2

THIS DIAGRAM SHOWS THE LIVING ARRANGEMENTS AND RELATIONSHIPS IN A PATRILOCAL EXTENDED FAMILY. DECEASED HOUSEHOLD MEMBERS ARE BLACKED OUT.

Members of modern Maya extended families carry out various activities on the household plaza; here, for example, women weave and family members interact with outsiders.

This old photo shows members of a Hopi Indian matrilocal extended family in front of their house. Traditionally, women who were sisters and daughters lived with their husbands in adjacent rooms of a single tenement.

Matrilocal residence, where the man leaves the family he grew up in to go live with his wife in her parents' household, is a likely result if ecological circumstances make the role of the woman predominant in subsistence. It is found most often in horticultural societies, where political organization is relatively uncentralized and where cooperation among women is important. The Hopi Indians provide one example; although it is the men who do the farming, the women control access to land and "own" the harvest. Indeed, men are not even allowed in the granaries. Under matrilocal residence, men usually do not move very far from the family they were raised in, so they are available to help out there from time to time. Therefore, marriage usually does not involve compensation to the groom's family.

Ambilocal residence is adaptive in situations where economic cooperation of more people than are available in the nuclear family is needed but where resources are limited in some way. Because the couple can join either the bride's or the groom's family, family membership is flexible, and the two can live where the resources look best or where their labor is most needed. This was once the situation on the peninsulas and islands along the coast of Maine, where, as already noted, extended family households were based upon ambilocal residence. The same residential pattern is particularly common among food-foraging peoples, as among the Mbuti of Africa's Ituri forest. Typically, a Mbuti marries someone from another band, so that one spouse always has in-laws who live elsewhere. Thus, if foraging is bad in their part of the forest, the couple has somewhere else to go where food may be more readily available. Ambilocality greatly enhances the Mbutis' opportunity to find food. It also

Although Hopi society is matrilocal, It is men's labor that provides the food. In the past, however, it is probable that women were the farmers, with men taking over the task as irrigation became more important.

Matrilocal residence. A residence pattern in which a married couple lives in the locality associated with the wife's relatives. • **Ambilocal residence.** A pattern in which a married couple may choose either matrilocal or patrilocal residence.

provides a place to go if a dispute breaks out with someone in the band where the couple is currently living. Consequently, Mbuti camps are constantly changing their composition as people split off to go live with their in-laws, while others are joining from other groups. For a people like food foragers, who find their food in nature and who maintain an egalitarian social order, ambilocal residence can be a crucial factor in both survival and conflict resolution.

Under **neolocal residence,** a married couple forms a household in a separate location. This occurs where the independence of the nuclear family is emphasized. In industrial societies such as the United States, where most economic activity occurs outside rather than inside the family and where it is important for individuals to be able to move where jobs can be found, neolocal residence is better suited than any of the other patterns. **Avunculocal residence,** in which a married couple goes to live with the groom's mother's brother (Figure 20.3) is favored by the same factors that promote patrilocal residence, but only in societies where descent through women is deemed crucial for the transmission of important rights and property. Such is the case among the people of the Trobriand Islands, where each individual is a member from birth of a group of relatives who trace their descent back through their mother, their mother's mother, and so on to the one woman all others are descended from. Each of these descent groups holds property, consisting of hamlet sites, bush and garden lands, and, in some cases, beach fronts, to which members have rights of access. These properties are controlled each generation by a male chief or other leader who inherits

Food foragers, such as the aboriginal Australians shown here in their ceremonial dress, often have been described as practicing patrilocal residence. Rather than being an ancient practice, this appears to be a response to an upsurge in violence associated with European colonial expansion. Earlier foragers were more flexible in their living arrangements.

these rights and obligations, but because descent is traced exclusively through women, a man cannot inherit these from his father. Thus, succession to positions of leadership passes from a man to his sister's son. For this reason, a man who is in line to take control of his descent group's assets will take his wife to live with the one he will succeed—his mother's brother. This enables him to observe how the older man takes care of his hamlet's affairs, as well as to learn the oral traditions and magic he will need to be an effective leader.

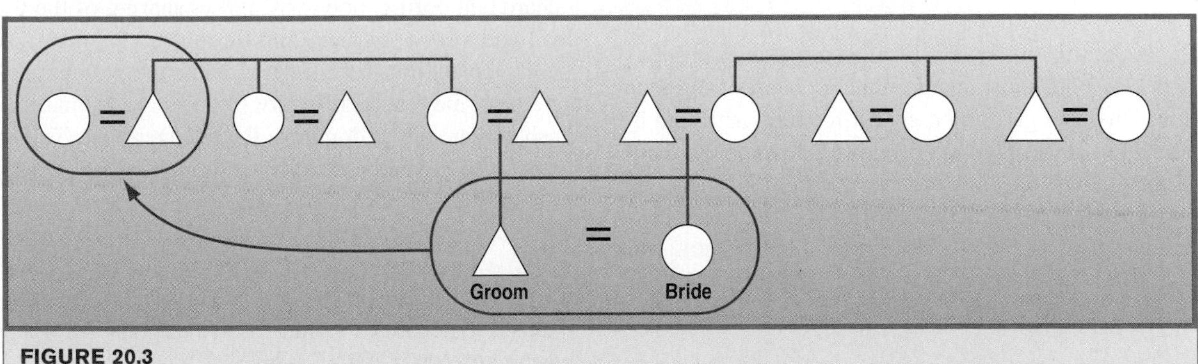

FIGURE 20.3
UNDER AVUNCULOCAL RESIDENCE, A NEWLY MARRIED COUPLE GOES TO LIVE WITH THE HUSBAND'S MOTHER'S BROTHER.

Neolocal residence. A pattern in which a married couple may establish their household in a location apart from either the husband's or the wife's relatives. • **Avunculocal residence.** Residence of a married couple with the husband's mother's brother.

This Trobriand Island chief, shown in front of his house, will be succeeded by his sister's son. Hence, men who will become chiefs live avunculocally.

Although Trobriand leaders and chiefs live avunculocally, most married couples in this society live patrilocally. This allows sons to fulfill their obligations to their fathers, who helped build up and nurture them when they were small; in return, the sons will inherit personal property such as clay pots and valuable stone ax blades from their fathers. This also gives men access to land controlled by their fathers' descent groups in addition to their own land, enabling them to improve their own economic and political position in Trobriand society. In short, here, as in any human society, practical considerations play a central role in determining where people will live following marriage.

PROBLEMS OF FAMILY AND HOUSEHOLD ORGANIZATION

Effective though the family may be at organizing economic production, consumption, inheritance, and child rearing, at the household level relationships within the family inevitably involve a certain amount of conflict and tension. This does not mean that they may not also involve a great deal of support and affection. Nevertheless, at least the potential for conflict is always there and must be dealt with lest families become dysfunctional. Different forms of families are associated with different sorts of tensions, and the means employed to manage these tensions differ accordingly.

Polygamous Families

A major source of tension within polygamous families is the potential for conflict that exists between the multiple spouses of the individual they are married to. For example, under polygyny (the most common form of polygamy), the several wives of a man must be able to get along with a minimum of bickering and jealousy. One way to handle this is through sororal polygyny, or marriage to women who are sisters. Presumably, women who have grown up together can get along as cowives of a man more easily than can women who grew up in different households and have never had to live together before. Another mechanism is to provide each wife with a separate apartment or house within a family compound and perhaps require the husband to adhere to a system of rotation for sleeping purposes. The latter at least prevents the husband from playing obvious favorites among his wives. Although polygyny can be difficult for the women involved, this is not always the case (recall the comments of the women in polygynous marriages in the Rocky Mountains discussed in the previous chapter). In some polygynous societies, women enjoy considerable economic autonomy, and in societies where women's work is hard and boring, polygyny allows sharing of the workload and alleviating boredom through sociability.

In polyandrous families, two distinctive structural characteristics may cause difficulty. One is that a woman's older husbands are apt to dominate the younger ones. The other is that, under conditions of fraternal polyandry (where cohusbands are brothers), the most common kind, youngest brothers are likely to be considerably younger than their wives, whose reproductive years are limited. Hence, a young husband's chances of reproducing successfully are reduced, compared to older husbands. Not surprisingly, when polyandrous families in Tibet break up, it is usually the younger husbands who depart. Moreover, larger family groups are more prone to discord than smaller ones.[12]

[12] Levine, N. E., & Silk, J. B. (1997). Why polyandry fails. *Current Anthropology, 38,* 385–387.

A Bakhtiari man, his wives, and his children. In polygamous families, tensions may arise between cowives, or (in case of polygyny), the man and his wives.

Some young North Americans have attempted to re-create the extended family in the formation of communes. These attempts sometimes run into trouble as members cope with stress associated with extended family organization they are unprepared for.

Extended Families

Extended families too, no matter how well they may work, have their own potential areas of stress. Decision making in such families usually rests with an older individual, and other family members must defer to the elder's decisions. Among a group of siblings, an older one usually has the authority. Other difficulties confront in-marrying spouses, who must adjust their ways to conform to the expectations of the family they have joined. To combat these problems, cultures rely on various techniques to promote harmony, including such things as dependence training and the concept of "face" or "honor." Dependence training, discussed in Chapter 16, is typically associated with extended family organization, and raises people who are more inclined to be compliant and accept their lot in life than are individuals raised to be independent. One of the many problems faced by young people in North American society who have experimented with extended family living is that they generally have been raised to be independent, making it hard to defer to other's wishes when they disagree.

The concept of "face" may constitute a particularly potent check on the power of senior members of extended families. Among pastoral nomads of North Africa, for example, young men can escape from ill treatment by a father or older brother by leaving the patrilocal extended family to join the family of his maternal relatives, in-laws, or even an unrelated family willing to take him in.[13] Because men lose face if their sons or brothers flee in this way, they are generally at pains to control their behavior in order to prevent this from happening. Women, who are the in-marrying spouses, also may return to their natal families if they are mistreated in their husband's family. A woman who does this exposes her husband and his family to scolding by her kin, again causing loss of face.

---

[13] Abu-Lughod, L.(1988). *Veiled sentiments: Honor and poetry in a Bedouin society* (pp. 99–103). Berkeley, CA: University of California Press.

Effective though such techniques may be in societies that stress the importance of the group over the individual, and where loss of face is to be avoided at almost any cost, not all conflict may be avoided. When all else fails to restore harmony, siblings may be forced to demand their share of family assets in order to set up separate households, and in this way new families arise. Divorce, too, may be possible, although how easily this may be accomplished varies considerably from one society to another. In societies that practice matrilocal residence, divorce rates tend to be high, reflecting the ease with which unsatisfactory marriages may be terminated. In some (not all) societies with patrilocal residence, by contrast, divorce may be all but impossible, at least for women (the in-marrying spouses). This was the case in traditional China, for example, where women were raised to be cast out of their families.[14] When they married, they exchanged their dependence on fathers and brothers for absolute dependence on husbands and, later in life, sons. Without divorce as an option, to protect themselves against ill treatment, women went to great lengths to develop the strongest bond possible between themselves and their sons so that the latter would rise to their mother's defense when necessary. So single-minded were many women toward developing such relationships with their sons that they often made life miserable for their daughters-in-law, who were seen as competitors for their sons' affections.

Nuclear Families

Just as extended families have built into them particular sources of stress and tensions, so too do nuclear families, especially in modern industrial societies where nuclear family households have lost one of their chief reasons for being: their economic function as basic units of production. Instead of staying within the fold, working with and for each other, one or both adults must seek work for wages outside of the family. Furthermore, that work may keep them away for prolonged periods. If both spouses are employed (as is increasingly the case, since couples find it ever more difficult to maintain their desired standard of living on one income), the requirement for workers to go where their jobs take them may pull the husband and wife in different directions. On top of all this, neolocal residence tends to isolate husbands and wives from both sets of kin. Because clearly established patterns of responsibility no longer exist between husbands and wives, couples must work these out for themselves. Two factors make this difficult, one being the women's traditional dependence on men that for so long has been a feature of Western society. In spite of recent progress toward greater equality between men and women, all too often the partners to a marriage do not come to it as equals. The other problem is the great emphasis North American society places on the pursuit of individual gratification through competition, often at someone else's expense. The problem is especially acute if the husband and wife grew up in households with widely divergent outlooks on life and ways of doing things. Furthermore, their separation from kin means no is one on hand to help stabilize the new marriage; for that matter, intervention of kin is commonly regarded as interference.

Separation from kin also means that a young mother-to-be must face pregnancy and childbirth without the direct aid and support of female kin she already has a relationship with and who have been through pregnancy and childbirth themselves. Instead, for advice and guidance she must turn to physicians (who are more often men than women), books, and friends and neighbors who themselves are often inexperienced. The problem continues through motherhood, in the absence of experienced women within the family as well as a clear model for child rearing. So reliance on physicians, books, and mostly inexperienced friends for advice and support continues. The problems are exacerbated because families differ widely in how they deal with their children. In the competitive society of the United States, the children themselves recognize this and often use such differences against their parents to their own ends.

Women who have devoted themselves entirely to raising children confront a further problem: What to do when the children are gone? One answer to this, of course, is to pursue an outside career, but this, too, may present problems. She may have a husband with traditional values who thinks "a woman's place is in the home." Or it may be difficult to begin a career in middle age. To begin a career earlier, though, may involve difficult choices: Should she have her career at the expense of having children, or should she have both simultaneously? If the latter, she is not likely to find kin available to look after the children, as would be possible in an extended family, so arrangements must be made with people who are not kin. And, of course, all of these thorny decisions must be made without the aid and support of kin.

---

[14] Wolf, M. (1972). *Women and the family in rural Taiwan* (pp. 32–35). Stanford, CA: Stanford University Press.

Anthropology Applied: Dealing With Infant Mortality

In 1979 Dr. Margaret Boone, an anthropologist who now works as a social science analyst with the Program Evaluation and Methodology Division of the United States government's General Accounting Office, began a residency on the staff of Washington D.C.'s only public hospital. Her task was to gain an understanding of the sociocultural basis of poor maternal and infant health among inner-city blacks–something about which little was known at the time–and to communicate that understanding to the relevant public and private agencies, as well as to a wider public. As Dr. Boone put it:

> The problem was death–the highest infant death rate in the United States. In Washington, D.C., babies were dying in their first years of life at the highest rate for any large American city, and nobody could figure out why.*

In Washington, as in the rest of the United States, infant mortality has become a major health problem for African Americans because of the large and increasing number of disadvantaged "black" women; their infants die at almost twice the rate of "white" infants. In the hospital in which Boone worked, the population served was overwhelmingly poor and African American.

For the next year and a half, Boone worked intensively reviewing medical, birth, and death records; carrying out statistical analyses; and interviewing women whose infants had died, as well as nurses, physicians, social workers, and administrators. As she herself points out, no matter how important the records review and statistical analyses were (and they were important), her basic understanding of reproduction in the inner-city black community came from the daily experience working in the "community center" for birth and death, which was the hospital–classic anthropological participant observation.

What Boone found out was that infant death and miscarriage are associated with absence of prenatal care, smoking, the consumption of alcohol, psychological distress during pregnancy and hospitalization, evidence of violence, ineffective contraception, rapid childbearing in the teens (average age at first pregnancy was 18), and the use of several harmful drugs together (contrary to everyone's expectations, heroin abuse was less important a factor than alcohol abuse, and drug abuse in general was no higher among women whose infants died than among those whose infants did not). Cultural factors found to be important include a belief in a birth for every death, a high value placed on children, a value on gestation without necessarily any causal or sequential understanding of the children it will produce, a lack of planning ability, distrust of both men and women, and a separation of men's roles from the process of family formation (indeed, three quarters of the women in Boone's study were unmarried at the time of delivery). Of course, some of these factors were already known to be related to infant mortality, but many were not.

As a consequence of Boone's work, there have been important changes in policies and programs relating to infant mortality. It is now widely recognized that the problem goes beyond mere medicine, and that medical solutions have gone about as far as they can go. Only by dealing with the social and cultural factors connected to poor health of inner city African Americans will further progress be made, and new service delivery systems are slowly emerging to reflect this fact.

---

* Boone, E.S. (1987). Practicing sociomedicine: Redefining the problem of infant mortality in Washington, D.C. In R. M. Wulff & S. J. Fiske (Eds.). *Anthropological praxis: Translating knowledge into action* (p. 56). Boulder, CO: Westview Press.

Louise Woodward, the *au pair* found guilty in 1997 by a Massachusetts jury of causing the death of the child in her care. Her case illustrates the danger inherent in the separation between child and parent in the United States that inevitably results as adults pursue careers or other interests.

In the United States, single mothers who are heads of households are often placed in no-win situations: If they work to support the household, they are seen as unfit mothers; if they stay home with the children, they are labeled "deadbeats."

The impermanence of the nuclear family itself may constitute a problem, in the form of anxieties over old age. Once the children are gone, who will care for the parents in their old age? In North American society, no *requirement* exists for their children to do so. The problem does not arise in an extended family, where one is cared for from womb to tomb.

Female-Headed Households

In North America, increasing numbers of people live as members of what are often called *non-traditional families*. These include single-parent households, some of which are the result of the death of a marriage partner. Others are a consequence of divorce, as adults escape from dysfunctional nuclear families. Yet others are the result of increased sexual activity outside of wedlock. In the United States, the percentage of households made up of married couples with children dropped from 45% in the early 1970s to 26% in 1998. Over the same period, the percentage of children living with single parents rose from 4.7% to 18.2%.[15] In the vast majority of cases, as we saw in Chapter 19, children remain with their mother, who then faces the problem of having to provide for them as well as for herself. In divorce cases, fathers are usually required to pay child support, but they are not always able or willing to do this, and when they are the amount is often not sufficient to pay for all the necessary food, clothes, and medical care, let alone the cost of child carc so that the woman can seek or continue income-producing work to support herself. One of the problems here is that support payments determined in court are based not so much on the needs of the woman and her children as on her "earning potential," which, if she has been true to middle-class values by staying at home rather than going out to earn money, is seen as low given that she has not brought income into the family. What is ignored, of

[15] Irvine, M. (1999, November 24). Mom-and-Pop houses grow rare. *Burlington Free Press.*

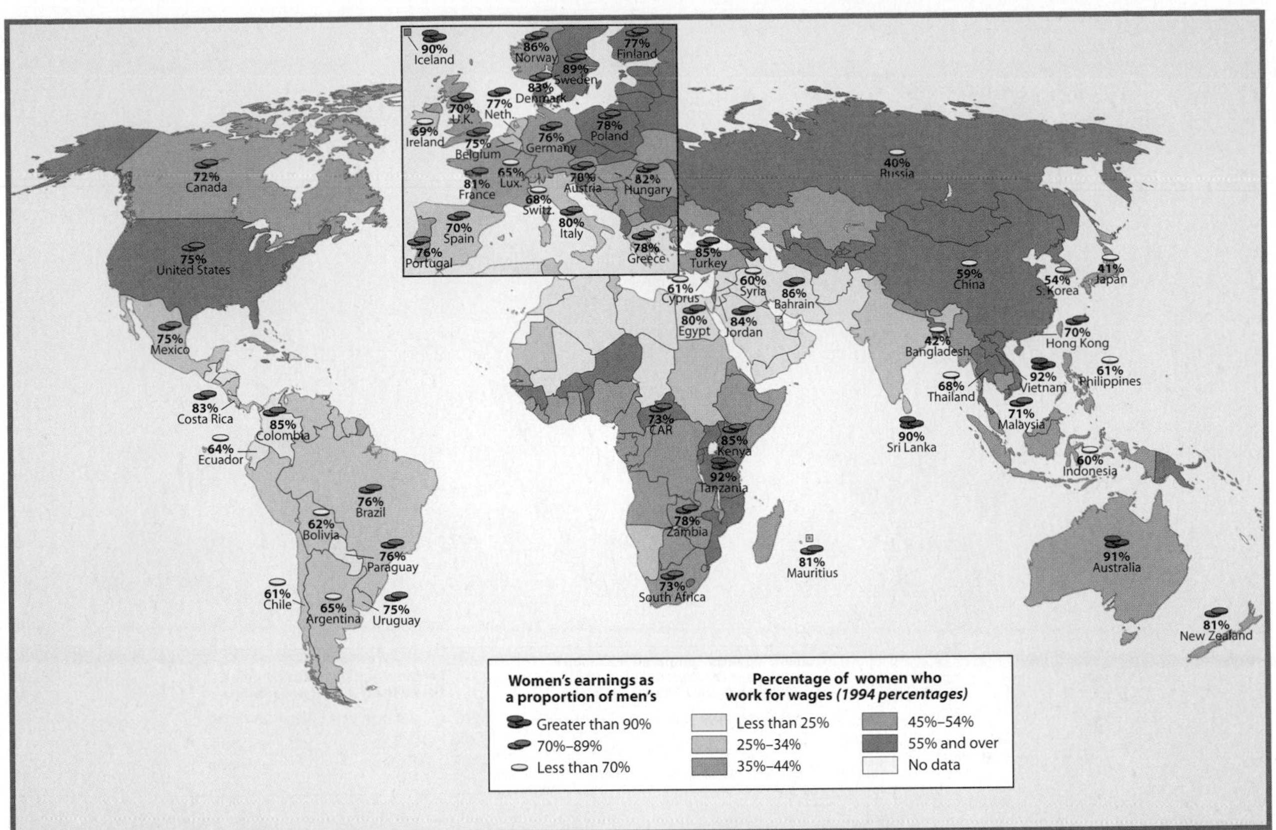

FIGURE 20.4

INCREASING NUMBERS OF WOMEN WORK FOR WAGES, BUT MOST ARE PAID LESS THAN MEN. JOBS DEFINED SPECIFICALLY AS WOMEN'S WORK TYPICALLY ARE OF LOW STATUS AND PAY LOW WAGES.

course, is the fact that her unpaid work at home contributed to her husband's ability to pursue a financially rewarding career, but since she is not paid for her work at home, no value is set on it.

As also in the case of working women who remain with their husbands, kin may not be available to look after the single mother's children, so outside help must be sought and (usually) paid for, thereupon making it even more difficult for the mother to support herself adequately. To compound the problem, women frequently lack the skills necessary to secure more than menial and low-paying jobs, not having acquired such skills earlier in order to raise children. Even when they do have skills, it is still a fact women are not paid as much as are men who hold the same jobs (Figure 20.4).

Not surprisingly, as the number of female-headed households has increased, so has the number of women (and, of course, their children) who live below the poverty line (Figure 20.5). More than one third of all female-headed households in the United States now fall into this category, and one quarter of all children are poor. Moreover, these women and children are the ones most severely affected by cutbacks in social welfare programs made since 1980. Even before then, the purchasing power of women was declining, and ever since, the programs that most assisted women and children have suffered the deepest cuts. One reason for this is a flawed assumption that is nonetheless entrenched in public policy: that the poverty seen in so many female-headed households is caused by the supposedly deviant nature of such households. This deviation is allegedly caused in part by women wanting to go outside the home to earn money instead of finding husbands to support them so that they can stay home and bring up the children, as

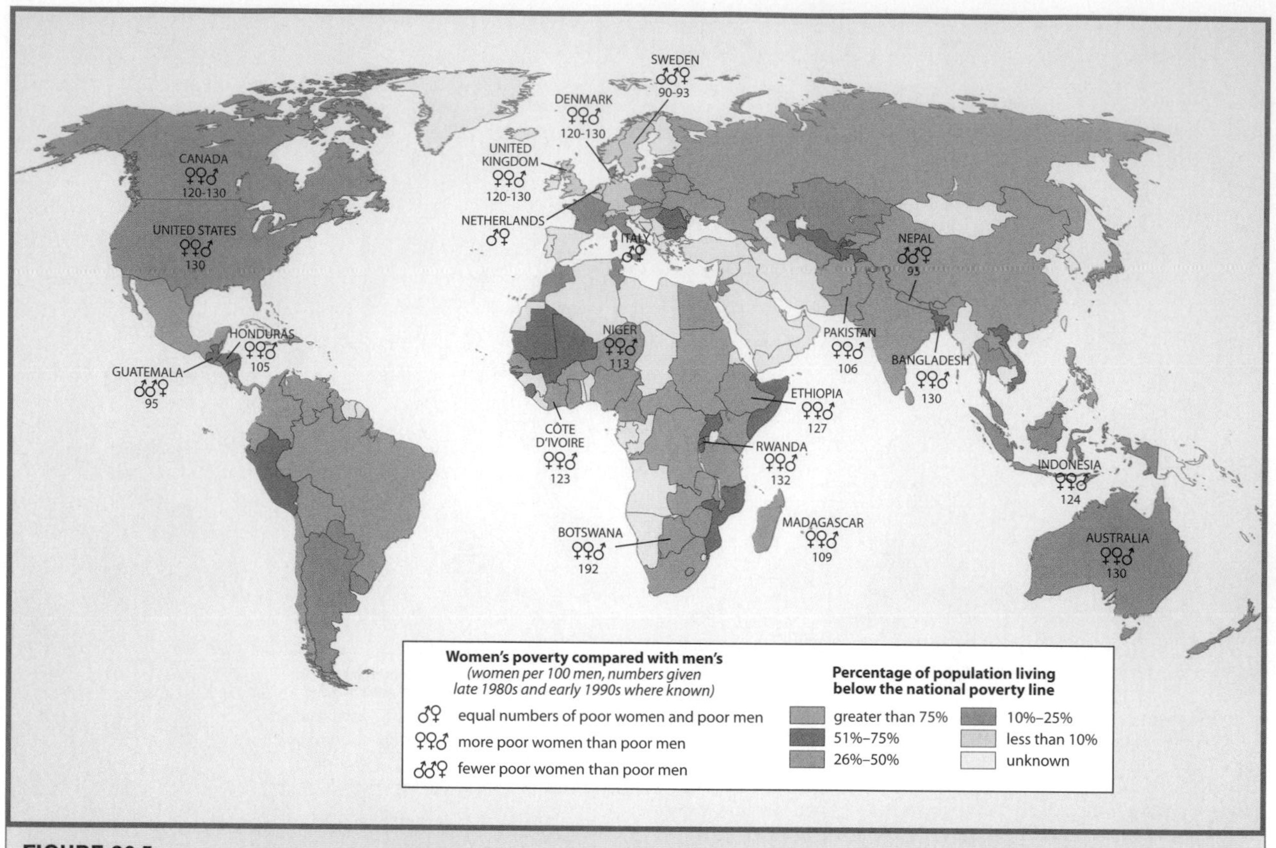

FIGURE 20.5

WOMEN (AND THEIR CHILDREN) ARE THE GREATEST AND FASTEST GROWING SHARE OF THE WORLD'S POOR. MORE THAN MEN, THEY LACK THE RESOURCES TO CLIMB OUT OF POVERTY.

women are "supposed" to do. In fact, women have participated in the labor force throughout United States history, whereas only a limited proportion of the population ever possessed the resources to be "proper," nonworking "ladies."[16] Far from deviant, female-headed households are in fact a rational response to economic constraints in a society that defines gender roles in such a way as to put women at a disadvantage.

Single-parent households headed by women are neither new nor restricted to industrialized societies such as the United States. They have been known and studied for a long time in the countries of the Caribbean basin, where men historically have been exploited as a cheap source of labor on plantations. Under such conditions, men have no power and few economic rewards; hence they are tenuously attached at best to any particular household. These are held together by women, who as producers of subsistence foods provide the means of economic survival for households. Similar female-headed households are becoming increasingly common in other "underdeveloped" countries, too, as development projects increasingly restrict the ability of women to earn a living wage (reasons for this are discussed in Chapters 26 and 27).

Thus, women constitute the majority of the poor, the underprivileged, and the economically and socially disadvantaged in most of the world's societies, just as is becoming true in the United States. In "underdeveloped" countries, the situation has been made worse by "reforms" the International Monetary Fund (IMF) requires

[16] Mullings, L. (1989). Gender and the application of anthropological knowledge to public policy in the United States. In S. Morgen (Ed.). *Gender and anthropology* (pp. 362–365). Washington: American Anthropological Association.

to renegotiate payment of foreign debts. Cutbacks in government education, health, and social programs for debt service have their most direct (and negative) impact on women and children, while further development designed to increase foreign exchange (for debt repayment and the financing of further industrialization) also comes at the expense of women and children. Meanwhile, the prices people must pay for basic necessities of life increase (to cut down on unfavorable trade balances). If a women is *lucky,* the wage she earns to buy bread for herself and her children remains constant, even if low, while the price she must pay for that bread continues to rise.

At the start of this chapter we posed a number of questions relating to the effectiveness North America families in meeting human needs. From what we have just discussed, it is obvious that neolocal nuclear families impose considerable anxiety and stress upon individuals in such families. Deprived of the security and multiplicity of emotional ties found in polygamous, extended, or consanguineal families, these nuclear families find that if something goes wrong, it is potentially more devastating to the individuals involved. Yet it is also obvious that alternative forms of family and household organization come complete with their distinctive stresses and strains. To the question of which alternative is preferable, we must answer that it depends on what problems one wishes to overcome and what price one is willing to pay.

In the United States, it is clear the problems inherent in the "traditional" nuclear family have contributed to a marked decline in the percentage of households occupied by such families. Furthermore, the conditions that gave rise to these families in the first place have changed. So far, no single family structure or ideology has arisen to supplant the nuclear family, nor can we predict which (if any) of the alternatives will gain preeminence in the future. The only certainty is that family and household arrangements, not just in the United States but throughout the world, will continue to evolve, as they always have, as the conditions they are sensitive to change.

CHAPTER SUMMARY

Dependence on group living for survival is a basic human characteristic. Nurturing children traditionally has been the adult female's job, although men also may play a role, and in some societies men are even more involved with their children than are women. In addition to at least some child care, women also carry out other economic tasks that complement those of men. The presence of adults of both sexes in a residential group is advantageous, in that it provides the child with adult models of the same sex, from whom they can learn the gender-appropriate roles as defined in that society.

A definition of the family that avoids Western ethnocentrism sees it as a group composed of a woman and her dependent children, with at least one adult man joined through marriage or blood relationship. In most human societies, families either constitute households or households are built around families. Although families are not universally present in human societies, households are. Households are defined as the basic residential units where economic production, consumption, inheritance, child rearing, and shelter are organized and implemented.

Far from being stable, unchanging entities, families and households may take any one of a number of forms in response to particular social, historical, and ecological circumstances. Conjugal families are those formed on the basis of marital ties. The smallest conjugal unit of mother, father, and their dependent children is called the nuclear family. Contrasting with the conjugal is the consanguineal family, consisting of women, their dependent children, and their brothers. The nuclear family, which became the ideal in the United States and Canada, is also found in societies that live in harsh environments, as do the Inuit. In industrial societies as well as societies in particularly harsh environments, the nuclear family must be able to look after itself. The result is that individual members are strongly dependent on very few people. This form of family is well suited to the mobility required both in food-foraging groups and in industrial societies where job changes are frequent. Among food foragers, however, the nuclear family is not as isolated from other kin as in modern industrial society.

Characteristic of many nonindustrial societies is the large extended, or conjugal-consanguineal, family. Ideally, some of an extended family's members are related by blood, others are related by marriage, and all live and work together as members of a single household. Conjugal or extended families are based upon five basic residence patterns: patrilocal, matrilocal, ambilocal, neolocal, and avunculocal.

Different forms of family organization are accompanied by their distinctive problems. Polygamous families have the potential for conflict among the several spouses of the individual to whom they are married. One way to ameliorate this problem is through sororal polygyny or fraternal polyandry. Under polyandry, an added difficulty for younger husbands is reduced opportunity for reproduction. In extended families, the allocation of authority may be the source of stress, as decisions are made by an older individual whose views may not coincide with those of the younger family members. In-marrying spouses in particular may have trouble complying with the demands of the family they must now live in.

In neolocal nuclear families, individuals are removed from the direct aid and support of kin, so husbands and wives must work out their own solutions to the problems of living together and having children. The problems are especially difficult in North American society, owing to the inequality that still persists between men and women, the great emphasis placed on individualism and competition, and an absence of clearly understood patterns of responsibility between husbands and wives, as well as a clear model for child rearing.

In North America, a rational alternative to the independent nuclear family, one which is now more common, is the single-parent household, usually headed by a woman. Female-headed households are also common in underdeveloped countries. Because the women in such households are hard pressed to provide adequately for themselves as well as for their children, more and more women than ever in the United States and abroad find themselves sinking ever more deeply into poverty.

CLASSIC READINGS

Fox, R. (1968). *Kinship and marriage in an anthropological perspective.* Baltimore: Penguin.

Fox's book is a good introduction to older, orthodox theories about the family.

Goody, J. (1983). *Development of the family and marriage in Europe*. Cambridge: Cambridge University Press.

This historical study shows how the nature of the family changed in Europe in response to regulations the Catholic Church introduced to weaken the power of kin groups and gain access to property. It explains how European patterns of kinship and marriage came to differ from those of the ancient circum-Mediterranean world and from those that succeeded them in the Middle East and North Africa.

Netting, R. M., Wilk, R. R., & Arnold, E. J. (Eds.) (1984). *Households: Comparative and historical studies of the domestic group*. Berkeley, CA: University of California Press.

This collection of essays by 20 anthropologists and historians focuses on how and why households vary within and between societies and over time within single societies.

Stacey, J. (1990) *Brave new families*. New York: Basic Books.

Written by a sociologist, this book (subtitled *Stories of domestic conflict in late twentieth century America*) takes an anthropological approach to understanding the changes affecting family structure in the United States. Her conclusion is that "the family" is *not* here to stay, nor should we wish otherwise. For all the difficulties attendant on "the family's demise," alternative arrangements offer hopeful possibilities for the future.

Thorne, B., & Yalom, M. (Eds.) (1982). *Rethinking the family: Some feminist questions*. New York: Longman.

As anthropologists have paid more attention to how institutions and practices work from a woman's perspective, they have had to reexamine existing assumptions about families in human societies. The 12 original essays in this volume, by scholars in economics, history, law, literature, philosophy, psychology, and sociology, as well as anthropology, examine such topics as the idea of the monolithic family, the sexual division of labor and inequality, motherhood, parenting, and mental illness and relations between family, class, and state. Especially recommended is the essay: "Is There a Family? New Anthropological Views."

CHAPTER 21

KINSHIP AND DESCENT

In the Indian pueblos of the North American southwest, as among many peoples around the world, clans and other kin groups are important units of social organization. This family, from one of the southwestern pueblos, is part of a larger clan based on descent traced exclusively through women from a founding ancestor.

CHAPTER PREVIEW

1 What Are Descent Groups?

A descent group is a kind of kinship group in which being a lineal descendant of a particular real or mythical ancestor is a criterion of membership. Descent may be reckoned exclusively through men, exclusively through women, or through either at the discretion of the individual. In some cases, two different means of reckoning descent are used at the same time, to assign individuals to different groups for different purposes.

2 What Functions Do Descent Groups Serve?

Descent groups of various kinds—lineages, clans, phratries, and moieties—are convenient devices for solving a number of problems that commonly confront human societies: how to maintain the integrity of resources that can not be divided without being destroyed; provide work forces for tasks that require a labor pool larger than households can provide; and allow members of one independent local group to claim support and protection from members of another. Not all societies have descent groups; in many food-foraging and industrial societies, some of these problems are often handled by the kindred, a group of people with a living blood relative in common. The kindred, however, does not endure beyond a single generation, as does the descent group, nor is its membership as clearly and explicitly defined. Hence, it is generally a weaker unit than the descent group.

3 How Do Descent Groups Evolve?

Descent groups arise from extended family organization, so long as there are problems of organization that such groups help to solve. This is most apt to happen in food-producing as opposed to food-foraging societies. First to develop are localized lineages, followed by larger, dispersed groups such as clans and phratries. With the passage of time kinship terminology itself is affected by and adjusts to the kinds of descent or other kinship groups that are important in a society.

All societies have found some form of family and/or household organization a convenient way to deal with problems all human groups face: how to facilitate economic cooperation between the sexes, how to provide a proper setting for child rearing, and how to regulate sexual activity. Efficient and flexible though family and household organization may be in rising to challenges connected with such problems, the fact is that many societies confront problems that are beyond the coping ability of family and household organization. For one, members of one sovereign local group often need some means of claiming support and protection from individuals in another group. This can be important for defense against natural or human-made disasters; if people have the right of entry into local groups other than their own, they can secure protection or critical resources when their own group cannot provide them. For another, a group frequently needs to share rights to some means of production that cannot be divided without its destruction. This is often the case in horticultural societies, where division of land is impractical beyond a certain point. The problem can be avoided if land ownership is vested in a corporate group that exists in perpetuity. Finally, people often need some means of providing cooperative workforces for tasks that require more participants than households alone can provide.

Many ways to deal with these sorts of problems exist. One is through a formal political system, with personnel to make and enforce laws, keep the peace, allocate resources, and perform other regulatory and societal functions. A more common way in nonindustrial societies—especially horticultural and pastoral societies—is by means of kinship groups.

DESCENT GROUPS

A common way of organizing a society along kinship lines is by creating what anthropologists call descent groups. A **descent group** is any publicly recognized social entity requiring lineal descent from a particular real

On this altar, King Yax-Pac of the ancient Maya city of Copan portrays himself and his predecessors, thereby tracing his descent back to the founder of the dynasty. In many human societies, such genealogical connections are used to define each individual's rights, privileges, and obligations.

Descent group. Any publicly recognized social entity requiring lineal descent from a particular real or mythical ancestor for membership.

or mythical ancestor for membership. Members of a descent group trace their connections back to a common ancestor through a chain of parent-child links. This feature may explain why descent groups are found in so many human societies. They appear to stem from the parent-child bond, which is built upon as the basis for a structured social group. This is a convenient thing to seize upon, and the addition of a few nonburdensome obligations and taboos acts as a kind of glue to help hold the group together.

To operate most efficiently, descent group membership ought to be clearly defined. Otherwise, membership overlaps and it is not always clear where one's primary loyalty belongs. Membership can be restricted in a number of ways. It can be based on where people live; for example, if your parents live patrilocally, affiliation with your father's descent group might be automatic. Another way is through choice; each individual might be presented with a number of options. This, though, introduces a possibility of competition and conflict as groups vie for members, a potential source of problems. The most common way to restrict membership is by making sex jurally (legally) relevant. Instead of tracing membership back to the common ancestor, sometimes through men and sometimes through women, one does it exclusively through one sex. In this way, each individual is automatically assigned from the moment of birth to his or her mother's or father's group, and to that group only.

Unilineal Descent

Unilineal descent (sometimes called unilateral descent) establishes descent group membership exclusively through the male or the female line. In non-Western societies, unilineal descent groups are quite common. The individual is assigned at birth to membership in a specific descent group, which may be traced either by **matrilineal descent,** through the female line, or by **patrilineal descent,** through the male line, depending on the culture. In patrilineal societies the males are far more important than the females, for they are considered responsible for the group's continued existence. In matrilineal societies, this responsibility falls on the female members of the group, whose importance is thereby enhanced.

A close relation between the descent system and a society's economy seems to exist. Generally, patrilineal descent predominates where male labor is considered of prime importance, as among pastoralists and intensive agriculturalists. Matrilineal descent predominates mainly among horticulturists in societies where women's work in subsistence is especially important. Numerous matrilineal societies are found in south Asia, one of the cradles of food production in the Old World. These include societies in India, Sri Lanka, Indonesia, Tibet, and South China. They are also prominent in parts of aboriginal North America and parts of Africa.

HIGHWAY 1
Emuseum of the Anthropology Department at Minnesota State University: Kinship Tutorial
http://anthro.mankato.msus.edu

HIGHWAY 2
Palomar College Anthropology Program: Kinship Tutorial
http://daphne.palomar.edu/anthro

Unilineal descent. Descent that establishes group membership exclusively through either the mother's or the father's line. • **Matrilineal descent.** Descent traced exclusively through the female line to establish group membership. • **Patrilineal descent.** Descent traced exclusively through the male line to establish group membership.

It is now recognized that in all societies, the kin of both mother and father are important components of the social structure. Just because descent may be reckoned patrilineally, for example, does not mean that matrilineal relatives are necessarily unimportant. It simply means that, for purposes of *group membership,* the mother's relatives are excluded. Similarly, under matrilineal descent, the father's relatives are excluded for purposes of group membership. By way of example, we have already seen in the two preceding chapters how important paternal relatives are among the matrilineal Trobriand Islanders. Although children belong to their mother's descent groups, fathers play an important role in nurturing and building them up. Upon marriage, the bride's and groom's paternal relatives contribute to the exchange of gifts, and, throughout life, a man may expect his paternal kin to help him improve his economic and political position in society. Eventually, sons may expect to inherit personal property from their fathers.

PATRILINEAL DESCENT AND ORGANIZATION

Patrilineal descent (sometimes called agnatic or male descent) is the more widespread of the two systems of unilineal descent. The male members of a patrilineal descent group trace through other males their descent from a common ancestor (Figure 21.1). Brothers and sisters belong to the descent group of their father's father, their father, their father's siblings, and their father's brother's children. A man's son and daughter also trace their descent back through the male line to their common ancestor. In the typical patrilineal group, authority over the children rests with the father or his elder brother. A woman belongs to the same descent group as her father and his brothers, but her children cannot trace their descent through them. A person's paternal aunt's children, for example, trace their descent through the patrilineal group of her husband.

TRADITIONAL CHINA: A PATRILINEAL SOCIETY

Until the communist takeover in 1949, rural Chinese society was strongly patrilineal. Since then, considerable changes have occurred, although vestiges of the old system persist to varying degrees in different regions. Traditionally, the basic unit for economic cooperation was the large extended family, typically including aged parents, and their sons, their sons' wives and their sons' children[1]. Residence, therefore, was patrilocal, as defined in Chapter 20. As in most patrilocal societies, children grew up in a household dominated by their father and his male relatives. The father was a source of discipline from whom a child would maintain a respectful social distance. Often, the father's brother and his sons were members of the same household. Thus,

[1] Most of the following is from Hsiaotung, F. (1939). *Peasant life in China*. London: Kegan, Paul, Trench and Truber.

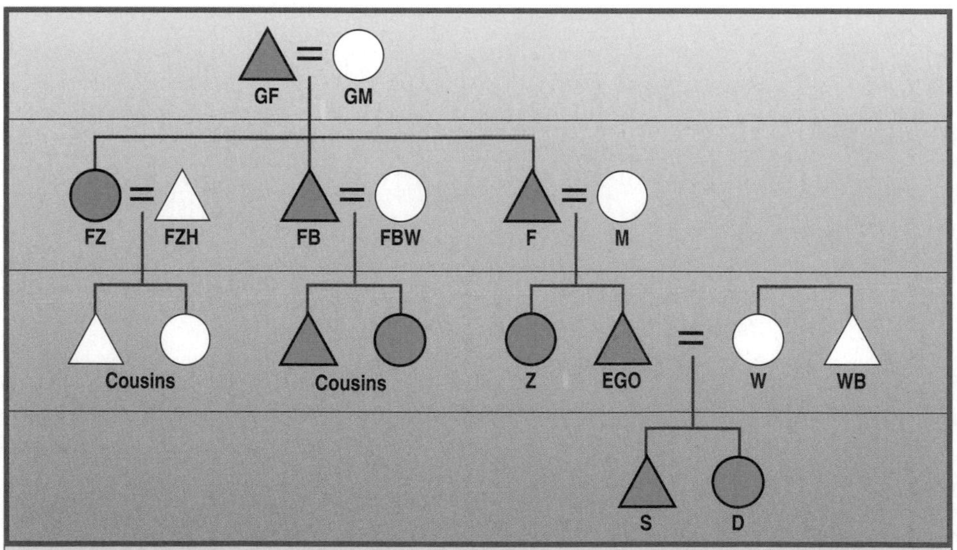

FIGURE 21.1

HOW PATRILINEAL DESCENT IS TRACED. ONLY THE INDIVIDUALS SYMBOLIZED BY A FILLED-IN CIRCLE OR TRIANGLE ARE IN THE SAME DESCENT GROUP AS EGO. THE ABBREVIATION *F* STANDS FOR FATHER, *B* FOR BROTHER, *H* FOR HUSBAND, *S* FOR SON, *M* FOR MOTHER, *Z* FOR SISTER, *D* FOR DAUGHTER, AND *W* FOR WIFE.

one's paternal uncle was rather like a second father and was treated with obedience and respect, while his sons were like one's brothers. Accordingly, the kinship term applied to one's own father was extended to the father's brother, as the term for a brother was extended to the father's brother's sons. When families became too large and unwieldy, as frequently happened, one or more sons would move elsewhere to establish separate households; when a son did so, however, the tie to the household in which he was born remained strong.

Important though family membership was for each individual, it was the *tsu* that was regarded as the primary social unit. Each *tsu* consisted of men who traced their ancestry back through the male line to a common ancestor, usually within about five generations. Although a woman belonged to her father's *tsu,* for all practical purposes she was absorbed by that of her husband, whom she went to live with after marriage. Nonetheless, members of her natal (birth) *tsu* retained some interest in her after her departure. Her mother, for example, would assist her in the birth of her children, and her brother or some other male relative would look after her interests, perhaps even intervening if her husband or other members of his family treated her badly.

The function of the *tsu* was to assist its members economically and to gather on ceremonial occasions such as weddings and funerals or to make offerings to the ancestors. Recently deceased ancestors, up to about three generations back, were given offerings of food and paper money on the anniversaries of their births and deaths,

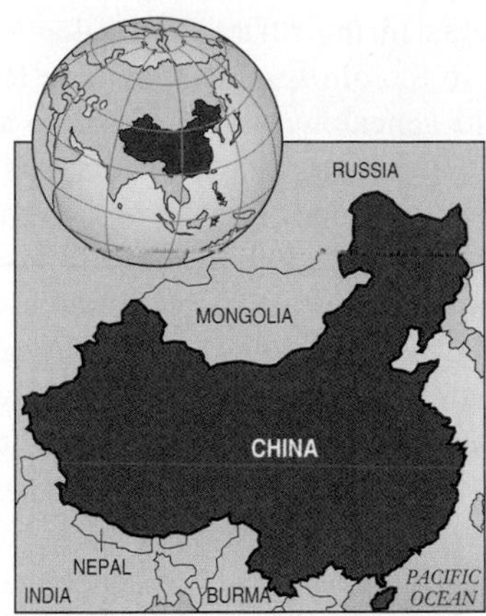

while more distant ancestors were collectively worshipped five times a year. Each *tsu* maintained its own shrine for storage of ancestral tablets on which the names of all members were recorded. In addition to its economic and ritual functions, the *tsu* also functioned as a legal body, passing judgment on misbehaving members.

Just as families periodically split up into new ones, so would the larger descent groups periodically splinter along the lines of their main family branches. Causes included disputes among brothers over management of land holdings and suspicion of unfair division of profits. When such separation occurred, a representative of the new *tsu* would return periodically to the ancestral temple in order to pay respect to the ancestors and record recent

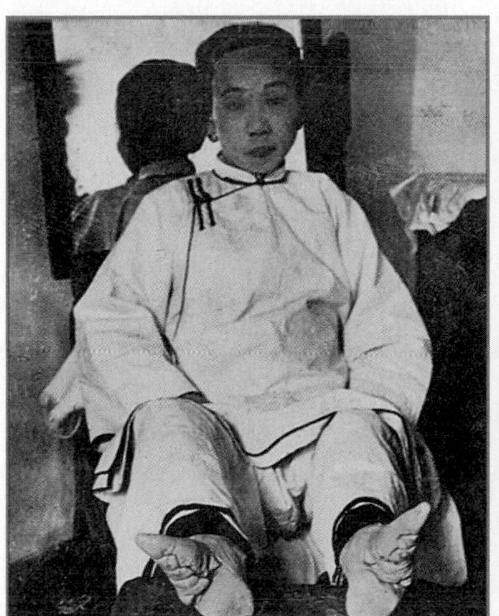

In patrilineal and other societies that promote the dominance of men over women, this practice sometimes goes to the extreme of inflicting physical, as well as social, disabilities on women. In the 19th century, Chinese women had their feet tightly bound, while in North America women often were tightly corseted. The result in both cases was actual physical impairment.

births and deaths in the official genealogy. Ultimately, though the tie to the old *tsu* still would be recognized, a copy of the old genealogy would be made and brought home to the younger *tsu,* and then only its births and deaths would be recorded. In this way, over many centuries, a whole hierarchy of descent groups developed, with all persons having the same surname considering themselves to be members of a great patrilineal clan. With this went surname exogamy, which is still widely practiced today even though clan members no longer carry on ceremonial activities together.

The patrilineal system permeated all of rural Chinese social relations. Children owed obedience and respect to their fathers and older patrilineal relatives in life and had to marry whomever their parents chose for them. It was the duty of sons to care for their parents when they became old and helpless, and even after death sons had ceremonial obligations to them. Inheritance passed from fathers to sons, with an extra share going to the eldest, since he ordinarily made the greatest contribution to the household and had the greatest responsibility toward his parents after their deaths. Women, by contrast, had no claims on their families' heritable property. Once married, a woman was in effect cast off by her own patrilineal kin (even though they might continue to take an interest in her) in order to produce children for her husband's family and *tsu.*

As the preceding suggests, a patrilineal society is very much a man's world; no matter how valued women may be, they inevitably find themselves in a difficult position. Far from resigning themselves to a subordinate position, however, they actively manipulate the system to their own advantage as best they can. To learn how they may do so, let us look more closely at the way women relate to one another in traditional Chinese society.

Original Study

Coping as a Woman in a Man's World[2]

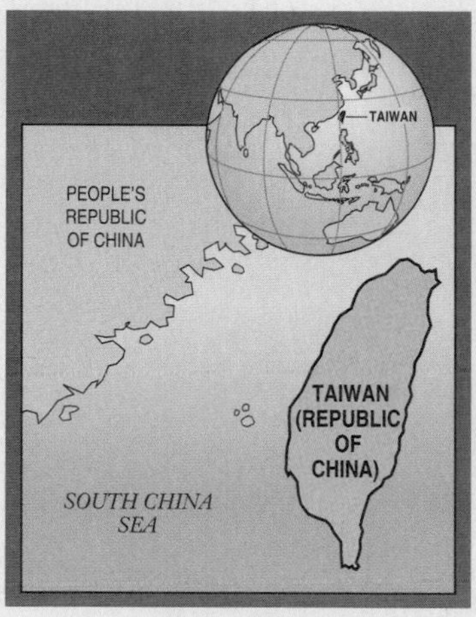

Women in rural Taiwan do not live their lives in the walled courtyards of their husbands' households. If they did, they might be as powerless as their stereotype. It is in their relations in the outside world (and for women in rural Taiwan that world consists almost entirely of the village) that women develop sufficient backing to maintain some independence under their powerful mothers-in-law. A successful venture into the men's world is no small feat when one recalls that the men of a village were born there and are often related to one another, whereas the women are unlikely to have either the ties of childhood or the ties of kinship to unite them. All the same, shared interests, and common problems of women are reflected in every village in a loosely knit society that can when needed be called on to exercise considerable influence.

Women carry on as many of their activities as possible outside the house. They wash clothes on the riverbank, clean and pare vegetables at a communal pump, mend under a tree that is a known meeting place, and stop to rest on a bench or group of stones with other women. There is a continual moving back and forth between kitchens, and conversations are carried on from open doorways through the long, hot afternoons of summer. The shy young girl who enters the village as a bride is examined as frankly and suspiciously by the women as an animal that is up for sale. If she is deferential to her elders, does not criticize or compare her new world unfavorably with the one she has left, the older residents will gradually accept her presence on the edge of their conversations and stop changing the topic to general subjects when she brings the family laundry to scrub on the rocks near them. As the young bride meets other girls in her position, she makes allies for the future, but she must also develop relationships with the older women. She learns to use considerable discretion in making and receiving confidences,

[2] Wolf, M. (1972). *Women and the family in rural Taiwan* (pp. 37–41). Stanford, CA: Stanford University Press.

for a girl who gossips freely about the affairs of her husband's household may find herself always on the outside of the group, or worse yet, accused of snobbery. I described in **The House of Lim** the plight of Lim Chui-ieng, who had little village backing in her troubles with her husband and his family as a result of her arrogance toward the women's community. In Peihotien the young wife of the storekeeper's son suffered a similar lack of support. Warned by her husband's parents not to be too "easy" with the other villagers lest they try to buy things on credit, she obeyed to the point of being considered unfriendly by the women of the village. When she began to have serious troubles with her husband and eventually his family, there was no one in the village she could turn to for solace, advice, and most important, peacemaking.

Once a young bride has established herself as a member of the women's community, she has also established for herself a certain amount of protection. If the members of her husband's family step beyond the limits of propriety in their treatment of her—such as refusing to allow her to return to her natal home for her brother's wedding or beating her without serious justification—she can complain to a woman friend, preferably older, while they are washing vegetables at the communal pump. The story will quickly spread to the other women, and one of them will take it upon herself to check the facts with another member of the girl's household. For a few days the matter will be thoroughly discussed whenever a few women gather. In a young wife's first few years in the community, she can expect to have her mother-in-law's side of any disagreement given fuller weight than her own—her mother-in-law has, after all, been a part of the community a lot longer. However, the discussion itself will serve to curb many offenses. Even if the older woman knows that public opinion is falling to her side, she will be somewhat more judicious about refusing her daughter-in-law's next request. Still, the daughter-in-law who hopes to make use of the village forum to depose her mother-in-law or at least gain herself special privilege will discover just how important the prerogatives of age and length of residence are. Although the women can serve as a powerful protective force for their defenseless younger members, they are also a very conservative force in the village.

Taiwanese women can and do make use of their collective power to lose face for their menfolk in order to influence decisions that are ostensibly not theirs to make. Although young women may have little or no influence over their husbands and would not dare express an unsolicited opinion (and perhaps not even a solicited one) to their fathers-in-law, older women who have raised their sons properly retain considerable influence over their sons' actions, even in activities exclusive to men. Further, older women who have displayed years of good judgement are regularly consulted by their husbands about major as well as minor economic and social projects. But even men who think themselves free to ignore the opinions of their women are never free of their own concept, face. It is much easier to lose face than to have face. We once asked a male friend in Peihotien just what "having face" amounted to. He replied, "When no one is talking about a family, you can say it has face." This is precisely where women wield their power. When a man behaves in a way that they consider wrong, they talk about him—not only among themselves, but to their sons and husbands. No one "tells him how to mind his own business," but it becomes abundantly clear that he is losing face and by continuing in this manner may bring shame to the family of his ancestors and descendants. Few men will risk that.

The rules that a Taiwanese man must learn and obey to be a successful member of his society are well developed, clear, and relatively easy to stay within. A Taiwanese woman must also learn the rules, but if she is to be a successful woman, she must learn not to stay within them, but to appear to stay within them; to manipulate them, but not to appear to be manipulating them; to teach them to her children, but not to depend on her children for her protection. A truly successful Taiwanese woman is a rugged individualist who has learned to depend largely on herself while appearing to lean on her father, her husband, and her son. The contrast between the terrified young bride and the loud, confident, often lewd old woman who has outlived her mother-in-law and her husband reflects the tests met and passed by not strictly following the rules and by making purposeful use of those who must. The Chinese male's conception of women as "narrow-hearted" and socially inept may well be his vague recognition of this facet of women's power and technique.

The End

MATRILINEAL DESCENT AND ORGANIZATION

In one respect, matrilineal descent is the opposite of patrilineal: It is reckoned through the female line (Figure 21.2). The matrilineal pattern differs from the patrilineal, however, in that descent does not automatically confer authority. Thus, although patrilineal societies are patriarchal, matrilineal societies are not matriarchal. Although descent passes through the female line and women may have considerable power, they do not hold exclusive authority in the descent group: They share it with men. These are the brothers, rather than the husbands, of the women through whom descent is reckoned. Apparently, the adaptive purpose of matrilineal systems is to provide continuous female solidarity within the female work group. Matrilineal systems are usually found in horticultural societies in which women perform much of the productive work. Because women's labor as crop cultivators is regarded as so important to the society, matrilineal descent prevails.

In a matrilineal system, brothers and sisters belong to the descent group of the mother, the mother's mother, the mother's siblings, and the mother's sisters' children. Males belong to the same descent group as their mother and sister, but their children cannot trace their descent through them. For example, the children of a man's maternal uncle are considered members of the uncle's wife's matrilineal descent group. Similarly, a man's children belong to his wife's, but not his, descent group.

Although not true of all matrilineal systems, a common feature is the weakness of the tie between husband and wife. The wife's brother, and not the husband/father, distributes goods, organizes work, settles disputes, administers inheritance and succession rules, and supervises rituals. The husband does not have legal authority in his household, but in that of his sister. Furthermore, his property and status are inherited by his sister's son rather than his son. Thus, brothers and sisters maintain lifelong ties with one another, whereas marital ties are easily severed. In matrilineal societies, unsatisfactory marriages are more easily ended than in patrilineal societies.

THE HOPI: A MATRILINEAL SOCIETY

In northeastern Arizona are the villages, or pueblos, of the Hopi Indians, a farming people whose ancestors have lived in the region for at least 2,000 years. Their society is divided into a number of named clans based strictly on matrilineal descent.[3] Each individual is assigned from birth to his or her mother's clan, and so important is this

[3] Most of the following is from Connelly, J. C. (1979). Hopi social organization. In A. Ortiz (Ed.). *Handbook of North American Indians,* Vol. 9, *Southwest* (pp. 539–553). Washington: Smithsonian Institution.

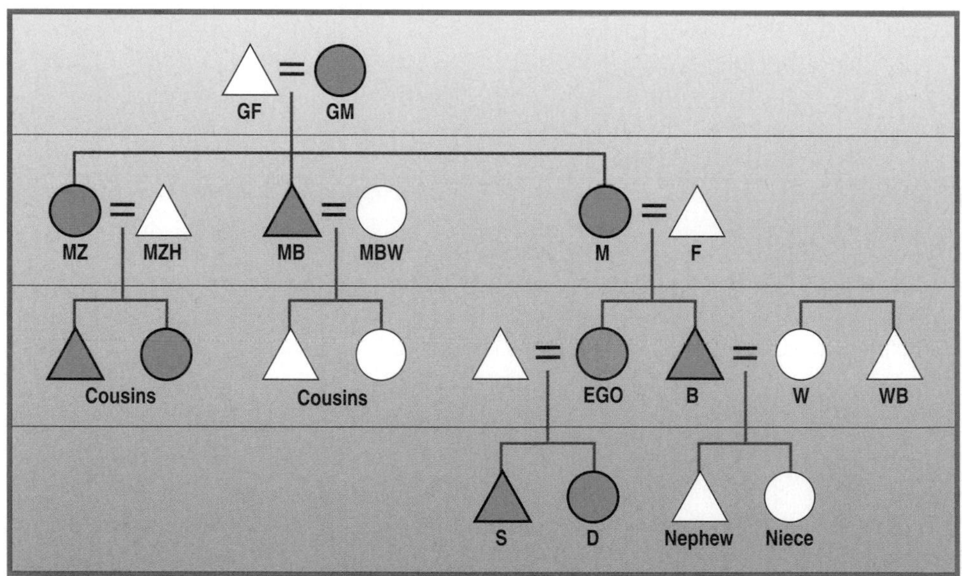

FIGURE 21.2

This diagram, which traces descent matrilineally, can be compared with that in Figure 21.1, showing patrilineal descent. The two patterns are virtually mirror images. Note that a man cannot transmit descent to his own children.

The Masuo of southwest China are strongly matrilineal. The women in the family shown here are blood relatives of one another, and the men are their brothers. As among the Nayar (Chapter 19), husbands live apart from their wives, in the households of their sisters.

affiliation that, in a very real sense, a person has no identity apart from it. Two or more clans together constitute larger, supraclan units, or phratries, of which nine exist in Hopi society. Within each of these, member clans are expected to support one another and to observe strict exogamy. Because members of all nine phratries can be found living in any given pueblo, marriage partners usually can be found in one's home community. This same dispersal of membership provides individuals with rights of entry into villages other than their own.

Although clans are the major units in Hopi thinking, the functional units consist of subclans, or lineages, and there are several in each village. Each is headed by a senior woman—usually the eldest, although it is her brother or mother's brother who keeps the sacred "medicine bundle" (objects of spiritual power considered essential for peoples' well being) and plays an active role in running lineage affairs. The woman, however, is no mere figurehead; she may act as mediator to help resolve disputes among group members, nor does she yield any authority to her brother or uncle. Although these men have the right to offer her advice and criticism, they are equally obligated to listen to what she has to say. Most female authority, however, is exerted within the household, and here men clearly take second place. These households consist of the women of the lineage with their husbands and unmarried sons, all of whom used to live in sets of adjacent rooms in single large tenements. Nowadays, nuclear families often live (frequently with a maternal relative or two) in separate houses, but pickup trucks enable related households to maintain close contacts and to cooperate as before.

Lineages function as landholding corporations, allocating land for the support of member households. These

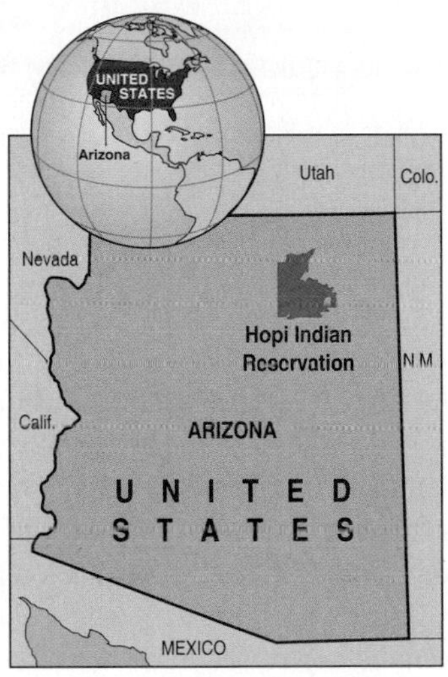

lands are farmed by "outsiders," the husbands of the women whose lineage owns the land, and the harvest belongs to these women. Thus, Hopi men spend their lives laboring for alien lineages (their wives'), and in return they are given food and shelter (by their wives). Although sons learn from their fathers how to farm, a man has no real authority over his son (the two belong to different lineages). Thus, when parents have difficulty with an unruly child, the mother's brother is called upon to mete out discipline. Male loyalties are therefore divided between their wives' households on the one hand and their sisters' on the other. If, at any time, a man is perceived as being an unsatisfactory husband, his wife merely has to place his belongings outside the door, and the marriage is over.

Many of the things that Hopi women do are done in the company of other women; thus, they have ample opportunity to discuss issues of importance to them.

In addition to their economic and legal functions, lineages play a role in Hopi ceremonial activities. Although membership in the associations that actually perform ceremonies is open to all who have the proper qualifications, clans own and manage all the associations, and in each village, a leading lineage acts as its clan's representative. This lineage owns a special house where the clan's religious paraphernalia are stored and cared for by the "clan mother." Together with her brother, the clan's "Big Uncle," she helps manage ceremonial activity. Although men control most of the associations that do the actual performing, women still have vital roles to play. For example, they provide the cornmeal, symbolic of natural and spiritual life that is a necessary ingredient in virtually all ceremonies.

Prior to the the United States government's imposition in 1936 of a different system, each Hopi pueblo was politically autonomous, with its own chief and village council. Here again, however, descent group organization made itself felt, for the council was made up of men who inherited their positions through their clans. Moreover, the powers of the chief and his council were limited; the chief's major job was to maintain harmony between his village and the spiritual world, and whatever authority he and his council wielded was directed at coordination of community effort, not enforcement of official decrees. Decisions were made on a consensual basis, and women's views had to be considered, as well as those of men. Once again, although men held positions of authority, women had considerable control over their decisions in a behind-the-scenes way. These men, after all, lived in households women controlled, and their position within them depended largely on how well they got along with the senior women. Outside the household, women's refusal to play their part in the performance of ceremonies gave them veto power. Small wonder, then, that Hopi men readily admit that "women usually get their way."[4]

Double Descent

Double descent, or double unilineal descent, whereby descent is reckoned both patrilineally and matrilineally at the same time, is very rare. In this system descent is matrilineal for some purposes and patrilineal for others. Generally, where double descent is reckoned, the matrilineal and patrilineal groups take action in different spheres of society.

For example, among the Yakö of eastern Nigeria, property is divided into both patrilineal possessions and matrilineal possessions.[5] The patrilineage owns perpetual productive resources, such as land, whereas the matrilineage owns consumable property, such as livestock. The legally weaker matriline is somewhat more important in religious matters than the patriline. Through double descent, a Yakö might inherit grazing lands from the father's patrilineal group and certain ritual privileges from the mother's matrilineal group.

[4] Schlegel, A. (1977). Male and female in Hopi thought and action. In A. Schlegel (Ed.). *Sexual stratification* (p. 254). New York: Columbia University Press.

[5] Forde, C. D. (1968). Double descent among the Yakö. In P. Bohannan & J. Middleton (Eds.). *Kinship and social organization* (pp. 179–191). Garden City, NY: Natural History Press.

Double descent. A system tracing descent matrilineally for some purposes and patrilineally for others.

Ambilineal Descent

As previously noted, unilineal descent does not mean that relatives outside one's own descent line are ignored or forgotten. As a consequence, some tension or conflict may exist between descent group interests on the one hand and other kinship-based sentiments on the other.[6] Still, unilineal descent does provide an easy way of restricting descent group membership so as to minimize problems of divided loyalty and the like. A number of societies, many of them in the Pacific and in Southeast Asia, accomplish the same thing in other ways, though perhaps not quite so neatly. The resultant descent groups are known as ambilineal, nonunilineal, or cognatic. **Ambilineal descent** provides a measure of flexibility not normally found under unilineal descent; each individual has the option of affiliating with either the mother's or the father's descent group. In many of these societies, an individual is allowed to belong to only one group at any one time, regardless of how many groups he or she may be eligible to join. Thus, the society may be divided into the same sorts of discrete and separate groups of kin as in a patrilineal or matrilineal society. Other cognatic societies, however, such as the Samoans of the South Pacific or some of those of the Pacific Northwest Coast of North America, allow overlapping membership in a number of descent groups. As anthropologist George Murdock observed, too great a range of individual choice interferes with the orderly functioning of any kin-ordered society:

> An individual's plural membership almost inevitably becomes segregated into one primary membership, which is strongly activated by residence, and one or more secondary memberships in which participation is only partial or occasional.[7]

AMBILINEAL DESCENT AMONG NEW YORK CITY JEWS

For an example of ambilineal organization we might easily turn to a traditional non-Western society, as we have for patrilineal and matrilineal organization. Instead, we shall turn to contemporary North American society to dispel the common (but false) notion that descent groups are necessarily incompatible in structure and function with the demands of modern industrial society. In fact, large corporate descent groups that hold assets in common and exist with some permanence are to be found in New York City, as well as in every large city in the United States where a substantial Jewish population of eastern European background is to be found.[8] Moreover, these descent groups are not survivals of an old eastern European descent-based organization. Rather, they represent a social innovation designed to restructure and preserve the traditionally close affective family ties of the old eastern European Jewish culture in the face of continuing immigration to the United States, subsequent dispersal from New York City, and the development of significant social and even temperamental differences among their descendants. The earliest of these descent groups did not develop until the end of the first decade of the 1900s, some 40 years after the immigration of eastern European Jews began in earnest. Although some groups have disbanded, they generally have remained alive and vital right down to the present day.

The original Jewish descent groups in New York City are known as *family circles.* The potential members of a family circle consist of all living descendants, with their spouses, of an ancestral pair. In actuality, not all who are eligible actually join, so an element of voluntarism exists. But eligibility is explicitly determined by descent, using both male and female links, without set order, to establish the connection with the ancestral pair. Thus, individuals are normally eligible for membership in more than one group or "circle." To activate a membership, one simply pays the required dues, attends meetings, and participates in the group's affairs. Individuals can, and frequently do, belong at the same time to two or three groups for which they are eligible. Each family circle bears a name, usually including the surname of the male ancestor; each has elected officers; and each meets regularly throughout the year rather than just once or twice. At the least, the family circle as a corporation holds funds in common, and some hold title to burial plots for members. Originally, they functioned as mutual-aid societies, as well as for the purpose of maintaining family solidarity.

[6] Stone, L. (1998). *Kinship and gender* (p. 73). Boulder, CO: Westview.

[7] Murdock, G. P. (1960). Cognatic forms of social organization. In G. P. Murdock, *Social structure in Southeast Asia* (p. 11). Chicago: Quadrangle Books.

[8] Mitchell, W. E. (1978). *Mishpokhe: A study of New York City Jewish family clubs.* The Hague: Mouton.

Ambilineal descent. Descent in which the individual may affiliate with either the mother's or the father's descent group.

Close family ties have always been important in eastern European Jewish culture. To maintain such ties in the United States, the descendants of eastern European Jews developed ambilineal descent groups.

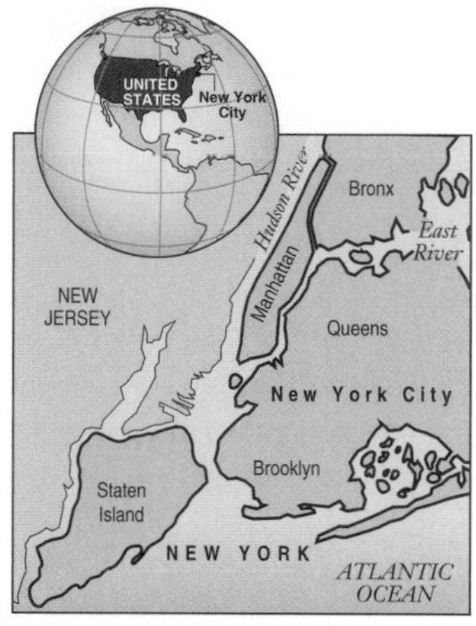

Now, as the mutual-aid functions have been taken over by outside agencies, the promotion of solidarity has become their primary goal. It will be interesting to see if reduced government funding for these agencies leads to a resurgence of the mutual-aid function of family circles.

In the years just prior to World War II, an interesting variant of the ambilineal descent group developed among younger-generation descendants of east European Jewish immigrants. Being more assimilated into North American culture, some of them sought to separate themselves somewhat from members of older generations, who were perceived as a bit old-fashioned. Yet, they still wished to maintain the traditional Jewish ethic of family solidarity. The result was the *cousins club,* which consists of a group of first cousins who share a common ancestry, their spouses, and their descendants. Excluded are parents and grandparents of the cousins, with their older views and lifestyles. Ambilineal descent remains the primary organizing principle, but it has been modified by a generational principle. Otherwise, cousins clubs are organized and function in many of the same ways as family circles.

FORMS AND FUNCTIONS OF DESCENT GROUPS

Descent groups with restricted membership, regardless of how descent is reckoned, are usually more than mere groups of relatives providing emotional support and a sense of belonging; in nonindustrial societies they are tightly organized working units providing security and services in what can be a difficult, uncertain life. The tasks descent groups perform are manifold. Besides acting as economic units providing mutual aid to their members, they may act to support the aged and infirm and help with marriages and deaths. Often, they play a role in determining who an individual may or may not marry. The descent group also may act as a repository of religious traditions. Ancestor worship, for example, is often a powerful force acting to reinforce group solidarity.

Lineage

A **lineage** (such as those of the Hopi or the *tsu* of China) is a corporate descent group composed of consanguineal kin who trace descent genealogically through known links

Lineage. A corporate descent group whose members trace their genealogical links to a common ancestor.

Anthropologist Peggy Reeves Sanday with members of a matrilineal clan among the Minangkabau of Sumatra gathered for a house-raising ceremony. The one adult male is the brother of the senior female leader (the woman on Sanday's left); he is the clan's male leader. Absence of other men reflects the predominance of women in this society.

back to a common ancestor. The term is usually employed where a form of unilineal descent is the rule, but some ambilineal groups are similar, such as the Jewish family circles just discussed.

The lineage is ancestor oriented; membership in the group is recognized only if relationship to a common ancestor can be traced and proved. In many societies an individual has no legal or political status except as a lineage member. Since "citizenship" is derived from lineage membership and legal status depends on it, political and religious power are derived from it as well. Important religious and magical powers, such as those associated with the cults of gods and ancestors, may also be bound to the lineage.

The lineage, like General Motors or IBM, is a corporate group. Because it endures after the deaths of members with new members continually born into it, it has a continuing existence that enables it to act like a corporation, as in owning property, organizing productive activities, distributing goods and labor power, assigning status, and regulating relations with other groups. The lineage is a strong, effective base of social organization.

A common feature of lineages is exogamy. This means that lineage members must find their marriage partners in other lineages. One advantage of lineage exogamy is that potential sexual competition within the group is curbed, promoting the group's solidarity. Lineage exogamy also means that each marriage is more than a union between two individuals; it amounts as well to a new alliance between lineages. This helps to maintain them as components of larger social systems. Finally, lineage exogamy maintains open communication within a society, promoting the diffusion of knowledge from one lineage to another.

Clan

In the course of time, as generation succeeds generation and new members are born into the lineage, its membership may become too large to be manageable, or too much for the lineage's resources to support. When this happens, as we have seen with the Chinese *tsu,* **fission** occurs; that is, the original lineage splits into new, smaller lineages.

Fission. The splitting of a descent group into two or more new descent groups.

When this happens, usually the members of the new lineages continue to recognize their ultimate relationship to one another. The result of this process is the appearance of a larger kind of descent group, the **clan.** The term clan, and its close relative, the term sib, have been used differently by different anthropologists, and a certain amount of confusion exists about their meaning. The clan (or sib) is now generally defined as a noncorporate descent group whose members assume descent from a common ancestor (who may be real or fictive) but are unable to trace the precise genealogical links back to that ancestor. This stems from the great genealogical depth of the clan, whose founding ancestor lived so far in the past that the links must be assumed rather than known in detail. A clan differs from a lineage in another respect: It lacks the residential unity generally—though not invariably—characteristic of a lineage's core members. As with the lineage, descent may be patrilineal, matrilineal, or ambilineal.

Because clan membership is dispersed rather than localized, it usually does not hold tangible property corporately. Instead, it tends to be more a unit for ceremonial and political matters. Only on special occasions will the membership gather together for specific purposes. Clans, however, may handle important integrative functions. Like lineages, they may regulate marriage through exogamy. Because of their dispersed membership, they give individuals the right of entry into local groups other than their own. Members usually are expected to give protection and hospitality to others in the clan. Hence, these can be expected in any local group that includes people who belong to a single clan.

Clans, lacking the residential unity of lineages, frequently depend on symbols—of animals, plants, natural forces, colors and special objects—to provide members with solidarity and a ready means of identification. These symbols, called totems, often are associated with the clan's mythical origin and reinforce for clan members an awareness of their common descent. The word totem comes from the Ojibwa American Indian word *ototeman,* meaning "he is a relative of mine." **Totemism** was defined by the British anthropologist A. R. Radcliffe-Brown as a set of "customs and beliefs by which there is set up a special system of relations between the society and the plants, animals, and other natural objects that are important in the social life."[9] Hopi Indian matriclans, for example, bear such totemic names as Bear, Bluebird, Butterfly, Lizard, Spider, and Snake.

Totemism is a changing concept that varies from clan to clan. A kind of watered-down totemism may be found even in modern North American society, where baseball and football teams are given the names of such powerful wild animals as bears, tigers, and wildcats. This extends to the Democratic Party's donkey and the Republican Party's elephant, to the Elks, the Lions, and other fraternal and social organizations. These animal emblems, or mascots, however, do not involve notions of descent and strong sense of kinship that they have for clans, nor are they linked with the various ritual observances associated with clan totems.

Phratries and Moieties

Other kinds of descent group are phratries and moieties (Figure 21.3). A **phratry,** such as those of the Hopi we have already discussed, is a unilineal descent group composed of at least two clans that supposedly share a common ancestry, whether or not they really do. Like individuals in the clan, phratry members cannot trace

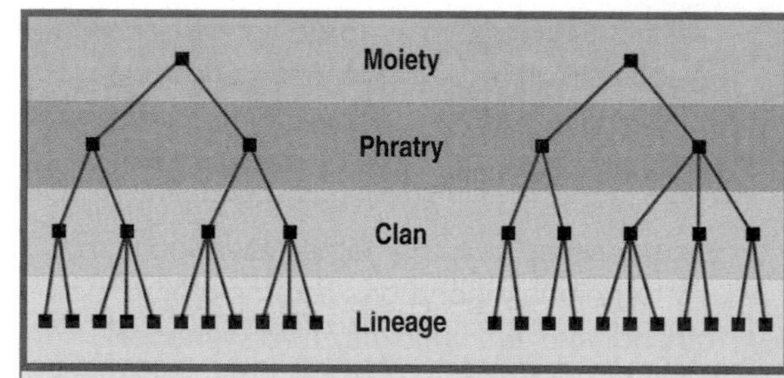

FIGURE 21.3
THIS DIAGRAM SHOWS HOW LINEAGES, CLANS, PHRATRIES, AND MOIETIES FORM AN ORGANIZATIONAL HIERARCHY. EACH MOIETY IS SUBDIVIDED INTO PHRATRIES, EACH PHRATRY IS SUBDIVIDED INTO CLANS, AND EACH CLAN IS SUBDIVIDED INTO LINEAGES.

[9] Radcliffe-Brown, A. R. (1931). Social organization of Australian tribes. *Oceania Monographs, 1,* 29.

Clan. A noncorporate descent group whose members claim descent from a common ancestor without actually knowing the genealogical links to that ancestor. • **Totemism.** The belief that people are related to particular animals, plants, or natural objects by virtue of descent from common ancestral spirits. • **Phratry.** A unilineal descent group composed of two or more clans that claim to be of common ancestry. If only two such groups exist, each is a moiety.

Anthropology Applied

Resolving a Native American Tribal Membership Dispute

In autumn 1998, the tribal chief of the Aroostook Band of Micmacs in Maine contacted anthropologist Harald Prins to help establish and implement a mechanism to resolve a bitter tribal membership dispute. The conflict centered on the fact that several hundred individuals had been accepted as tribal members without proper certification of their Micmac ancestry and historical ties to the region. With the formal status of so many members in question, the tribal administration could not properly determine who was entitled to benefit from the federal programs and special funding and services earmarked for Native Americans. Moreover, Micmac traditionalists (whose Indian status had been officially confirmed by the federal government) argued that their tribal organization was being taken over by "non-Indians." After some hostile confrontations between both factions, the controversy undermined the Band's functioning as a self-governing tribal community and even threatened its continued existence. In order to solve the conflict, some tribal elders requested a formal investigation into tribal membership. In response, the chief called Prins, who already had a history of working with the Band.

The Sanipass-Lafford family cluster in Chapman, Maine, represents a traditional Mi'kmaq residential kin group. Such extended families typically include grandchildren and bilaterally related family members such as in-laws, uncles, and aunts. Taken from the Sanipass family album, this picture shows a handful of members in the mid-1980s: Marline Sanipass Morey with two of her nephews and uncles.

The Micmacs had earlier employed the Dutch anthropologist (and his partner Bunny McBride) in 1981. Fresh from fieldwork in the Argentine pampas in South America and frustrated by an anthropology that had little practical use for the people being studied, he welcomed the opportunity to engage in advocacy anthropology in northern Maine. At the time, these Micmacs were members of an off-reservation Indian organization that also represented other widely scattered Native families in the region. Living in the backlands hugging the Canadian border, most of them resided in shacks or run-down apartments. Crushed by destitution and often suffering from poor health, many were alcoholics. Few had more than an eighth-grade education and almost all felt victimized by racial discrimination. Inspired by the civil rights movement, a small group of Micmacs had become politically mobilized. Reclaiming traditional rights to hunt, trap, and fish in the region, they even demanded return of lost territory.

Appointed Director of Research and Development, Prins quickly realized the difficulty of the task. A year earlier, in 1980, Maine's other three Indian tribal groups (Penobscot, Passamaquoddy, and Maliseet) had negotiated a land claims settlement with the U.S. government and the state of Maine, winning federal recognition and money to buy back about 300,000 acres of land. Micmacs had been left out because no one had done the historical and ethnographic research needed to ensure their inclusion.

With the assistance of McBride and others, Prins helped the region's Micmacs reorganize based on their ethnic identity. Newly incorporated as the Aroostook Band of Micmacs, the tribal community set up new headquarters in Presque Isle. As staff anthropologist, Prins sought funding for the organization and worked closely with Micmac leaders to define political strategies. He also helped generate broad popular support for the effort, in part through making a documentary film about the community, entitled *Our Lives in Our Hands* (1986). Most important, he gathered detailed documentation to address government requirements for federal recognition. American Indian groups seeking this official status in the U.S. must present an elaborate document that includes: (1) Historical and genealogical records of its existence as a distinct community from ancient times to the present, (2) Evidence that the group has maintained political influence over its members on a continual basis, (3) Proof that its members are descendants of a tribe historically inhabiting the area.

Aroostook Micmacs faced many obstacles in meeting these requirements. Several years of research yielded the data needed to counter these problems. For instance, Prins helped unearth important genealogical records showing that most Micmac adults in the region were at least "half-blood" (having two of their grandparents officially recorded as Indians). He also demonstrated that the loosely-structured Micmac community, with its informal system of political leadership, matched that of traditional hunting bands in their ancestral homeland. And, finding historical evidence that Micmacs were no strangers to northern Maine, he showed that the region fell within the aboriginal range of their ancestors who were historically allied with Maine's other tribes. Based on this evidence, Aroostook Micmacs effectively argued that they would have been able to claim aboriginal title to jointly used lands in the region and should not have been left out of the earlier settlement. They convinced the state's Congressional delegation in Washington, D.C., to introduce a special bill to acknowledge their tribal status and settle their land claims. When formal hearings were held in 1990, Prins testified as expert witness for the Micmacs in the U.S. Senate. The following year, the *Aroostook Band of Micmacs Settlement Act* became federal law. By then, the anthropologist had left the tribal community and became a university professor. At the time of federal recognition, almost 500 Micmacs formed part of the Aroostook Band. Because of their newly-acquired official status as an Indian tribe in the United States, these Micmacs were entitled to financial assistance (health, housing, education and child welfare) and loan guarantees for economic development available to all federally-recognized tribes. Moreover, having settled their land claim in northern Maine, they had also received special funding to buy a 5,000-acre territorial base in the region. Soon, they received millions of dollars in services and direct funding. In the course of time, the Band purchased a small reservation near Presque Isle, which now holds a Micmac community with a few dozen family homes, as well as a new tribal administration center and a new health clinic.

Flush with federal funding and rapidly expanding its activities, the Aroostook Band of Micmacs was soon overwhelmed by complex bureaucratic regulations now governing their existence. Without formally established ground rules determining who can actually apply for membership in the Band, and overlooking federally-imposed regulations, several successive tribal administrations somewhat casually added about 700 new names to its tribal rolls. Among them were many Micmacs hailing from across the Canadian border, whereas U.S. federal law stipulates that only U.S. citizens may be added. Others never provided documentary evidence of their Micmac ancestry or had no ties to the region. Most importantly, however, the successive tribal administrations had forgotten about the federal law stipulating that new members had to be officially approved by the U.S. Secretary of Interior who controls the Bureau of Indian Affairs. By 1997, the Aroostook Band population had ballooned to almost 1200 members. Meanwhile, Micmac traditionalists viewed many of the newcomers with growing suspicion and questioned their legitimacy as authentic Micmacs. Gradually, the growing conflict between factions escalated and even threatened to destroy the Band as an organization. In order to solve the problem, the tribal chief invited Prins as an impartial scholar long familiar with the community to evaluate critically the membership claims of more than half the tribe. In early 1999, he traveled to northern Maine and over the next few months, with the support of a local assistant, he helped answer questions about ancestry research, offered guidance to archival documentation, and, most importantly, evaluated information submitted by hundreds of individuals whose membership on the tribal rolls was in question.

Several months later, having reviewed the historical and genealogical documentation and helped many dozens track down elusive data, Prins offered his final report to the Micmac community. After traditional prayers, sweetgrass burning, drumming, and a traditional meal of salmon and moose, he was formally introduced by the tribal leadership and presented his findings: based on the official criteria, in addition to about 100 lineal descendants of the original members, just over 150 newcomers met the minimal required qualifications for membership; the remainder would have to be stripped from the tribal rolls. After singing, drumming, and closing prayers, the Micmac gathering dispersed.

* Harald Prins, now a tenured Professor of Anthropology at Kansas State University, currently serves as a Mi'kmaq aboriginal rights expert witness for the Miawpukek First Nation in the Supreme Court of Newfoundland. For further information, see also his case study *The Mi'kmaq: Resistance, accommodation, and cultural survival* (Harcourt Brace, 1996).

precisely their descent links to a common ancestor, though they firmly believe such an ancestor existed.

If the entire society is divided into only two major descent groups, whether they are equivalent to clans or phratries or involve an even more all-inclusive level, each group is called a **moiety** (after the French word for "half"). Members of the moiety believe themselves to share a common ancestor but cannot prove it through definite genealogical links. As a rule, the feelings of kinship among members of lineages and clans are stronger than those of members of phratries and moieties. This may be due to the larger size and more diffuse nature of the latter groups.

Like lineages and clans, phratries and moieties are often exogamous, and so are bound together by marriages between their members. And like clans, they provide members rights of access to other communities, as among the Hopi. In a community that does not include one's clan members, one's phratry members are still there to turn to for hospitality. Finally, moieties may perform reciprocal services for one another, as among the Mohawks and other Iroquoian nations of what is now New York State. Among them, individuals turn to members of the opposite moiety for the necessary rituals when a member of their own moiety dies. Such interdependence between moieties, again, serves to maintain the integrity of the entire society.

Bilateral Kinship and the Kindred

Important though descent groups are in many societies, they are not found in all societies, nor are they the only kinds of extended kinship groups to be found. Bilateral kinship (sometimes erroneously referred to as bilateral descent), a characteristic of Western society as well as a number of food-foraging societies, affiliates a person with close "blood" relatives (but not in-laws) through both sexes; in other words, the individual traces descent through both parents, all four grandparents, and so forth, recognizing multiple ancestors. Theoretically, one is associated equally with all consanguineal relatives on both the mother's and father's sides of the family. Thus, this principle relates an individual lineally to all eight great-grandparents and laterally to all third and fourth cousins. Since such a huge group is too big to be socially practical, it is usually reduced to a small circle of paternal and maternal relatives, called the **kindred.** The kindred may be defined as a group of people closely related to one living individual through both parents. Since the kindred is laterally rather than lineally organized—that is, ego, or the focal person from whom the degree of each relationship is reckoned, is the center of the group (Figure 21.4)—it is not a true descent group.

North Americans are all familiar with the kindred; those who belong are simply called relatives. It includes those consanguineal relatives on both sides of the family who are seen on important occasions, such as family reunions and funerals. Most people in the United States can identify the members of their kindred up to grandparents and first, if not always second, cousins. The limits of the kindred, however, are variable and indefinite; no one ever can be absolutely certain which relatives to invite to every important function and which to exclude. Inevitably, situations arise that require some debate about whether or not to invite particular, usually distant, relatives. Kindreds are thus not clearly bounded and lack the distinctiveness

Moiety. Each group that results from a division of a society into two halves on the basis of descent. •
Kindred. A group of consanguineal kin linked by their relationship to one living individual; includes both maternal and paternal kin.

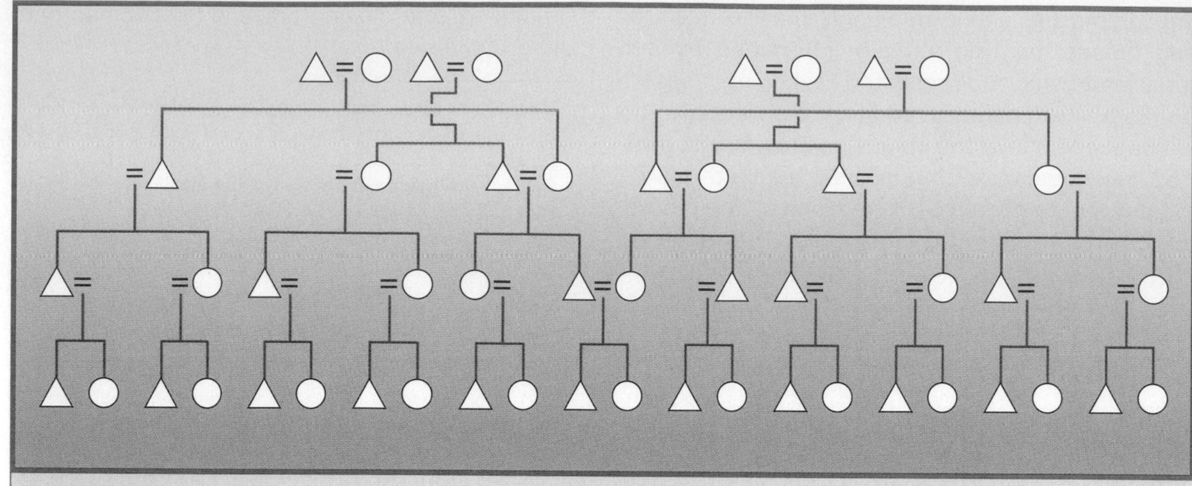

FIGURE 21.4

THE KINSHIP PATTERN OF THE KINDRED. THESE PEOPLE ARE RELATED NOT TO A COMMON ANCESTOR BUT, RATHER, TO A LIVING RELATIVE, HERE THE SISTER AND BROTHER SHOWN AT THE CENTER OF THE BOTTOM ROW.

of the unilineal or ambilineal descent group. (They are also temporary, lasting only as long as the functions they are assembled for.)

Because of its bilateral structure, a kindred is never the same for any two persons except siblings (brothers and sisters). Thus, no two people (except siblings) belong to the same kindred. The kindred of ego's first cousin on the father's side, for example, includes not only the father's sister (or brother), as does ego's, but the father's sister's (or brother's) spouse, as well as consanguineal relatives of the latter. As for the kindreds of ego's parents, these will range lineally to grandparents and laterally to cousins too distant for ego to know, and the same is true of ego's aunts and uncles. Thus, the kindred is not composed of people with an ancestor in common but with a living relative in common—ego. Furthermore, as ego goes through life, the kindreds he or she is affiliated with will change. When young, individuals belong to the kindreds of their parents; ultimately, they belong to the kindreds of their sons and daughters as well as their nieces and nephews. Because of its vagueness, temporary nature, and changing affiliation, the kindred cannot function as a group except in relation to ego. Unlike descent groups, it is not self-perpetuating—it ceases with ego's death. It has no constant leader, nor can it easily hold, administer, or pass on property. In most cases, it cannot organize work, nor can it easily administer justice or assign status. It can, however, be turned to for aid. In non-Western societies, for example, raiding or trading parties may be composed of kindreds. The group comes together to perform some particular function, shares the results, and then disbands. It also can act as a ceremonial group for rites of passage: initiation ceremonies and the like. In traditional European societies, kindreds acted to raise bail, compensate a victim's family, or take revenge for the murder or injury of someone in one's own kindred. Finally, kindreds also can regulate marriage through exogamy.

Kindreds are frequently found in industrial societies such as that of the United States, where mobility weakens contact with relatives. Individuality is emphasized in such societies, and strong kinship organization is usually not as important as it is among non-Western peoples. Even so, bilateral kindreds also may be found in societies where kinship ties are important, and in some instances, they even occur alongside descent groups.

Evolution of the Descent Group

Just as different types of families occur in different societies, so do different kinds of nonfamilial kin groups. Descent groups, for example, are not a common feature of food-foraging societies, where marriage acts as the social mechanism for integrating individuals within communities. In horticultural, pastoral, or many intensive agricultural societies, however, the descent group usually provides the structural framework upon which the fabric of the society rests.

It is generally agreed that lineages arise from extended family organization, so long as organizational problems exist that such groups help solve. All that is required, re-

Members of the groom's personal kindred shown here are his father, mother, two brothers, aunt, and niece.

ally, is that as members of existing extended families find it necessary to split off and establish new households elsewhere, they not move too far away; that the core members of such related families (men in patrilocal, women in matrilocal, members of both sexes in ambilocal extended families) explicitly acknowledge their descent from a common ancestor; and that they continue to participate in common activities in an organized way. As this process proceeds, lineages will develop, and these may with time give rise to clans and ultimately phratries.

Another way that clans may arise is as legal fictions to integrate otherwise autonomous units. The six Iroquois Indian nations of what now is New York State, for example, developed clans by simply behaving as if lineages of the same name in different villages were related. Thus, their members became fictitious "brothers" and "sisters." By this device, members of, say, a Turtle clan in one village could travel to another and be welcomed in and hosted by members of another Turtle clan. In this way, the "Six Nations" achieved a wider unity than had previously existed.

As larger, dispersed descent groups develop, the conditions that gave rise to extended families and lineages may change. For example, economic diversity and the availability of alternative occupations for individuals may conflict with the residential unity of extended families and (usually) lineages. Or, lineages may lose their economic bases if developing political institutions take control of resources. In such circumstances, lineages would be expected to disappear as important organizational units. Clans, however, might survive, if they continue to provide an important integrative function. In this sense, the Jewish family circles and cousins clubs discussed

Clans among the Iroquois of New York State were a legal fiction that allowed people to travel between villages of the "Six Nations." This portrait, done in 1910, shows a member of the Mohawk Nation. Behind him stands a bear, which represents his clan.

earlier have become essentially clanlike in their function. This helps explain their continued strength and vitality in the United States today: They perform an integrative function among kin who are geographically dispersed as well as socially diverse but in a way that does not conflict with the mobility characteristic of North American society.

In societies where small domestic units—nuclear families or single-parent households—are of primary importance, bilateral kinship and kindred organization are apt to result. This can be seen in modern industrial societies, in newly emerging societies in the "underdeveloped" world, and many food-foraging societies throughout the world.

KINSHIP TERMINOLOGY AND KINSHIP GROUPS

Any system of organizing people who are relatives into different kinds of groups, whether descent based or ego oriented, is bound to have an important effect upon the ways in which relatives are labeled in any given society. The fact is, the kinship terminologies of other peoples are far from being what Western people all too often interpret as arbitrary and even capricious ways of labeling relatives. Rather, they reflect the positions individuals occupy within their society. In particular, kinship terminology is affected by, and adjusts to, the kinds of kinship groups that exist in a society. However, other factors also are at work in each system of kinship terminology that help differentiate one kin from another. These factors may be sex, generational differences, or genealogical differences. In the various systems of kinship terminology, any one of these factors may be emphasized at the expense of others, and sometimes they are qualified by distinguishing younger from older individuals in a particular category, or by emphasizing the sex of the person referring to a particular relative. But regardless of the factors emphasized, all kinship terminologies accomplish two important tasks. First, they classify similar kinds of persons into single specific categories; second, they separate different kinds of persons into distinct categories. Generally, two or more kin are merged under the same term when the individuals share similar status, which emphasizes these similarities.

Six different systems of kinship terminology result from the application of the above principles just mentioned: the Eskimo, Hawaiian, Iroquois, Crow, Omaha, and Sudanese or descriptive systems, each identified according to the way cousins are classified.

Eskimo System

The **Eskimo system,** comparatively rare among all the world's systems, is the one used by Anglo-Americans, as well as by a number of food-foraging peoples (including the Inuit, once called Eskimos; hence the name). The Eskimo or lineal system emphasizes the nuclear family by specifically identifying mother, father, brother, and sister while lumping together all other relatives into a few gross categories (Figure 21.5). For example, the father is

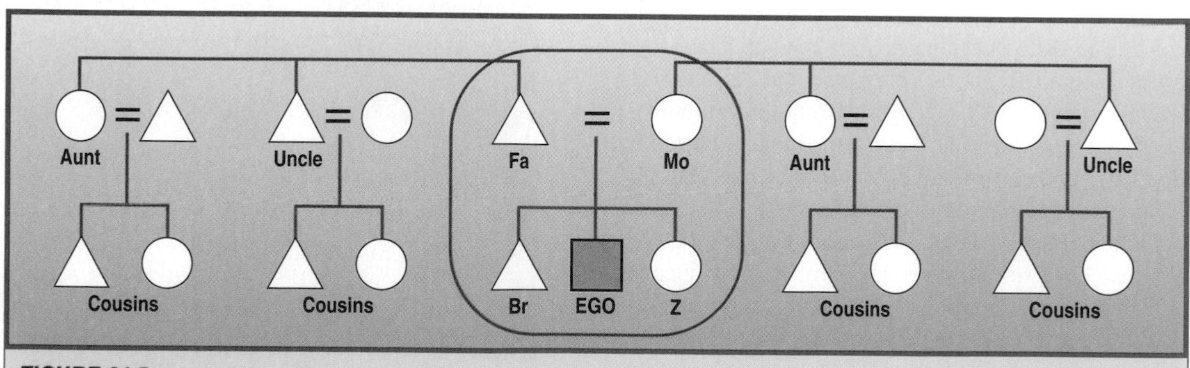

FIGURE 21.5
THE ESKIMO SYSTEM OF KINSHIP TERMINOLOGY EMPHASIZES THE NUCLEAR FAMILY (SURROUNDED BY THE RED LINE). EGO'S FATHER AND MOTHER ARE DISTINGUISHED FROM EGO'S AUNTS AND UNCLES, AND SIBLINGS FROM COUSINS.

Eskimo system. System of kinship terminology, also called lineal system, that emphasizes the nuclear family by specifically identifying the mother, father, brother, and sister, while lumping together all other relatives into broad categories such as **uncle, aunt,** and **cousin.**

distinguished from the father's brother (uncle); but the father's brother is not distinguished from the mother's brother (both are called uncle). The mother's sister and father's sister are treated similarly, both called aunt. In addition, all the sons and daughters of aunts and uncles are called cousin, thereby making a generational distinction but without indicating the side of the family they belong to or even their sex.

Unlike other terminologies, the Eskimo system provides separate and distinct terms for the nuclear family member. This is probably because the Eskimo system is generally found in bilateral societies where the dominant kin group is the kindred, in which only immediate family members are important in day-to-day affairs. This is especially true of modern North American society, where the family is independent, living apart from, and not directly involved with, other kin except on ceremonial occasions. Thus, people in the United States distinguish between their closest kin (parents and siblings), but lump together (as aunts, uncles, cousins) other kin on both sides of the family.

Hawaiian System

The **Hawaiian system** of kinship terminology, common (as its name implies) in Hawaii and other Malayo-Polynesian-speaking areas but found elsewhere as well, is the least complex system, in that it uses the fewest terms. The Hawaiian system is also called the generational system, since all relatives of the same generation and sex are referred to by the same term (Figure 21.6). For example, in one's parents' generation, the term used to refer to one's father is used as well for the father's brother and mother's brother. Similarly, one's mother, her sister, and one's father's sister are all lumped together under a single term. In ego's generation, male and female cousins are distinguished by sex and are equated with brothers and sisters.

The Hawaiian system reflects the absence of strong unilineal descent and is usually associated with ambilineal descent. Because ambilineal rules allow individuals the option of tracing their ancestry back through either side of the family and members on both the father's and the mother's side are viewed as more-or-less equal, a certain degree of similarity is created among the father's and the mother's siblings. Thus, they are all simultaneously recognized as being similar relations and are merged together under a single term appropriate for their sex. In like manner, the children of the mother's and father's siblings are related to ego in the same way brother and sister are. Thus, they are ruled out as potential marriage partners.

Iroquois System

In the **Iroquois system** of kinship terminology, the father and father's brother are referred to by a single term, as are the mother and mother's sister; however, the

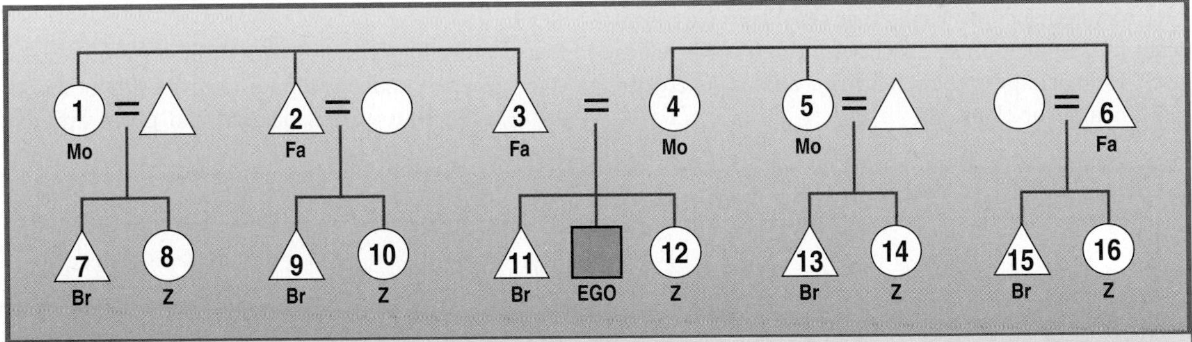

FIGURE 21.6

THE HAWAIIAN KINSHIP SYSTEM. THE MEN NUMBERED 2 AND 6 ARE CALLED BY THE SAME TERM AS FATHER (3) BY EGO; THE WOMEN NUMBERED 1 AND 5 ARE CALLED BY THE SAME TERM AS MOTHER (4). ALL COUSINS OF EGO'S OWN GENERATION (7–16) ARE CONSIDERED BROTHERS AND SISTERS.

Hawaiian system. Kinship reckoning in which all relatives of the same sex and generation are referred to by the same term. • **Iroquois system.** Kinship terminology wherein a father and father's brother are given a single term, as are a mother and mother's sister, but a father's sister and mother's brother are given separate terms. Parallel cousins are classified with brothers and sisters, while cross cousins are classified separately, but (unlike Crow and Omaha kinship) not equated with relatives of some other generation.

LEWIS HENRY MORGAN (1818–1881)

This major theoretician of 19th-century North American anthropology has been regarded as the founder of kinship studies. In *Systems of Consanguinity and Affinity of the Human Family* (1871), he classified and compared the kinship systems of peoples around the world in an attempt to prove the Asiatic origin of American Indians. In doing so, he developed the idea that the human family had evolved through a series of evolutionary stages, from primitive promiscuity on the one hand to the monogamous, patriarchal family on the other. Although subsequent work showed Morgan to be wrong about this and a number of other things, his work showed the potential value of studying the distribution of different kinship systems in order to frame hypotheses of a developmental or historical nature and, by noting the connection between terminology and behavior, showed the value of kinship for sociological study. Besides his contributions to kinship and evolutionary studies, he produced an ethnography of the Iroquois, which still stands as a major source of information.

father's sister and mother's brother are given separate terms (Figure 21.7). In one's own generation, brothers, sisters, and parallel cousins (offspring of parental siblings of the same sex, that is, the children of the mother's sister or father's brother) of the same sex are referred to by the same terms, which is logical enough considering that they are the offspring of people who are classified in the same category as ego's actual mother and father. Cross cousins (offspring of parental siblings of opposite sex, that is, the children of the mother's brother or father's sister) are distinguished by terms that set them apart from all other kin. In fact, cross cousins are often preferred as spouses, for marriage to them reaffirms alliances between related lineages or clans.

Iroquois terminology, named for the Iroquoian Indians of northeastern North America who employ such terminology, is in fact very widespread and is usually found with unilineal descent groups. It was, for example, the terminology in use until recently in rural Chinese society.

Crow System

In the preceding systems of terminology some relatives were grouped under common terms, while others of the same generation were separated and given different la-

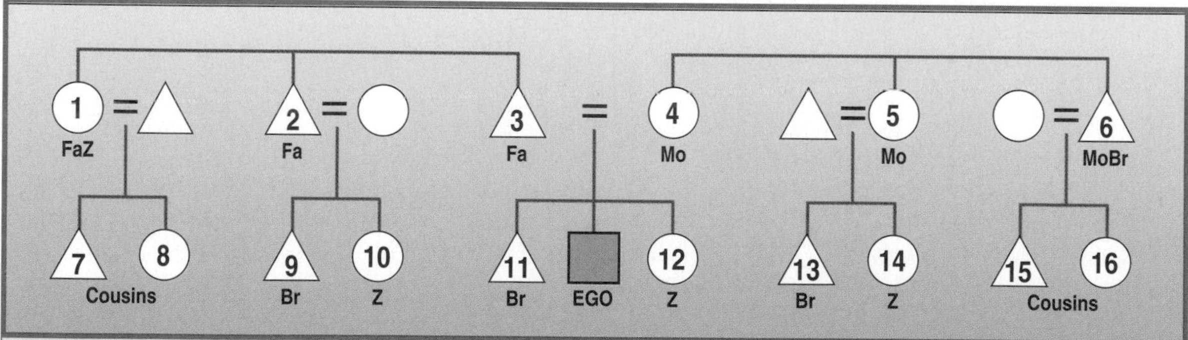

FIGURE 21.7

ACCORDING TO THE IROQUOIS SYSTEM OF KINSHIP TERMINOLOGY, THE FATHER'S BROTHER (2) IS CALLED BY THE SAME TERM AS THE FATHER (3); THE MOTHER'S SISTER (5) IS CALLED BY THE SAME TERM AS THE MOTHER (4); BUT THE PEOPLE NUMBERED 1 AND 6 HAVE SEPARATE TERMS FOR THEMSELVES. THOSE PEOPLE NUMBERED 9–14 ARE ALL CONSIDERED SIBLINGS, BUT 7, 8, 15, AND 16 ARE COUSINS.

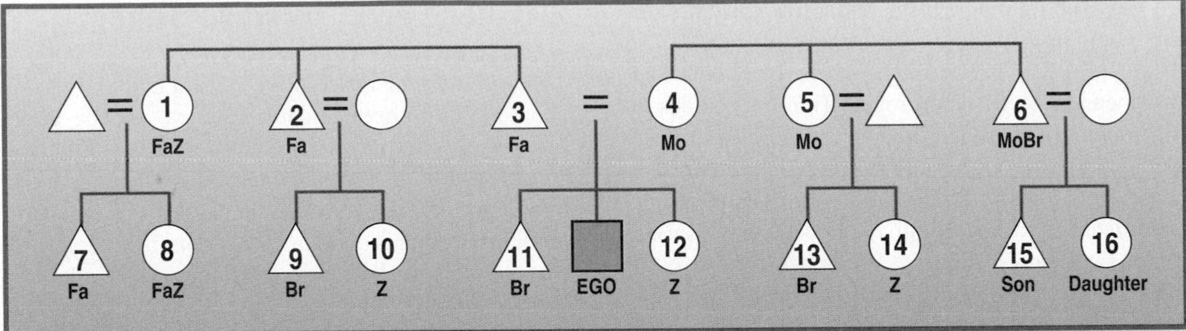

FIGURE 21.8

THE CROW SYSTEM IS THE OBVERSE OF THE OMAHA SYSTEM, SHOWN IN FIGURE 21.9. THOSE NUMBERED 4 AND 5 ARE MERGED UNDER A SINGLE TERM, AS ARE 2 AND 3. EGO'S PARALLEL COUSINS (9, 10, 13, 14) ARE CONSIDERED SIBLINGS, WHILE THE MOTHER'S BROTHER'S CHILDREN ARE EQUATED WITH THE CHILDREN OF A MALE EGO AND HIS BROTHER.

bels or terms. In the Crow system, another variable enters the picture: The system ignores the distinction that occurs between generations among certain kin.

The **Crow system** (named for the Crow Indians, more properly the Apsaroke, of Montana), found in many parts of the world, happens to be the one used by the Hopi Indians, who were discussed earlier in this chapter. Associated with strong matrilineal descent organization, it groups differently the relations on the father's side and mother's side (Figure 21.8). Cross cousins on the father's side are equated with relatives on the parental generation while those on the mother's side are equated with ego's children's generation. Otherwise, the system is much like Iroquois terminology.

In matrilineal societies with Crow kinship, sisters remain close to one another throughout their lives. Such a people are the Hopi, in whose traditional housing sisters lived in adjacent rooms. Under these circumstances, very little differentiates a mother and her sister or siblings and the children of the mother's sister. The mother's brother and his children, however, live elsewhere.

Crow system. Kinship classification usually associated with matrilineal descent in which a father's sister and father's sister's daughter are called by the same term, a mother and mother's sister are merged under another, and a father and father's brother are lumped in a third. Parallel cousins are equated with brothers and sisters.

To those unfamiliar with it, the Crow system seems terribly complex and illogical. Why does it exist? In societies such as that of the Hopi, where individual identity is dependent on descent group affiliation and descent is matrilineal, it makes sense to merge the father's sister, her daughter, and even her mother together under a single term, regardless of generation. These are women whose descent is traced through the lineage that sired ego, just as a male ego's children, along with those of his mother's brother, were sired by men of ego's lineage. Thus, it is perfectly logical for ego to equate his maternal cross cousins with his own children's generation.

Omaha System

The **Omaha system** (named for the Omaha Indians of Nebraska) is the patrilineal equivalent of the matrilineal Crow system. Thus, a mother and her sister are designated by a single term, a father and his brother are merged together under another, and parallel cousins are merged with brothers and sisters (Figure 21.9). Cross cousins on the maternal side are raised a generation, while those on the paternal side are equated with ego's children's generation. Thus, children born of women from one patrilineage for the men of another patrilineage are lowered by one generation.

Sudanese or Descriptive System

The **Sudanese or descriptive system** is found among the peoples of southern Sudan in Africa—hence the name Sudanese. Otherwise, it is found among few of the world's societies, although it has come to replace Iroquois terminology among rural Chinese. In this system, the mother's brother is distinguished from the father's brother, who is distinguished from the father; the mother's sister is distinguished from the mother, as well as from the father's sister. Each cousin is distinguished from all others, as well as from siblings. It is therefore more precise than any of the other systems (including that used by Anglo-Americans), which may be one reason it is so rare. In few societies are all one's aunts, uncles, cousins, and siblings treated differently from one another.

If systems of kinship reckoning other than one's own seem strange and complex, consider the implications of an event that took place in 1978: the production of the world's first "test-tube" baby, in a petri dish outside the womb, without sexual intercourse. Since then, thousands of babies have been created in this way, and all sorts of new reproductive techniques have "taken off." It is now possible, for example, for a woman to give birth to her genetic uncle; does that make her his niece or his mother? If a child is conceived from a donor egg, implanted in another woman's womb to be raised by yet another

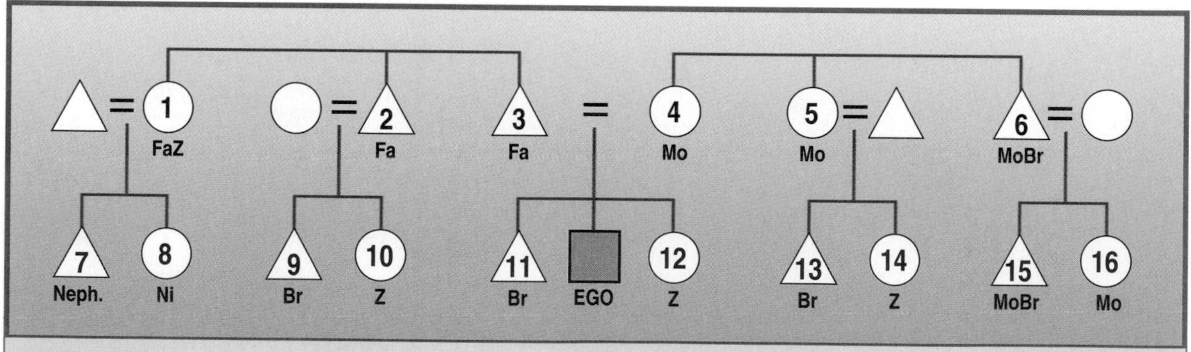

FIGURE 21.9

In the Omaha system, 2 is called by the same term as father (3); 5 is called by the same term as mother (4); but 1 and 6 have separate terms. In EGO's generation 9–14 are all considered siblings, but 7 and 8 are equated with the generation of EGO's children, while 15 and 16 are equated with the generation of EGO's parents.

Omaha system. The patrilineal equivalent of the Crow system; the line of a mother's patrilineal kin are equated across generations. • **Sudanese or descriptive system.** System of kinship terminology whereby a father, father's brother, and mother's brother are distinguished from one another as are a mother, mother's sister, and father's sister; cross and parallel cousins are distinguished from each other as well as from siblings.

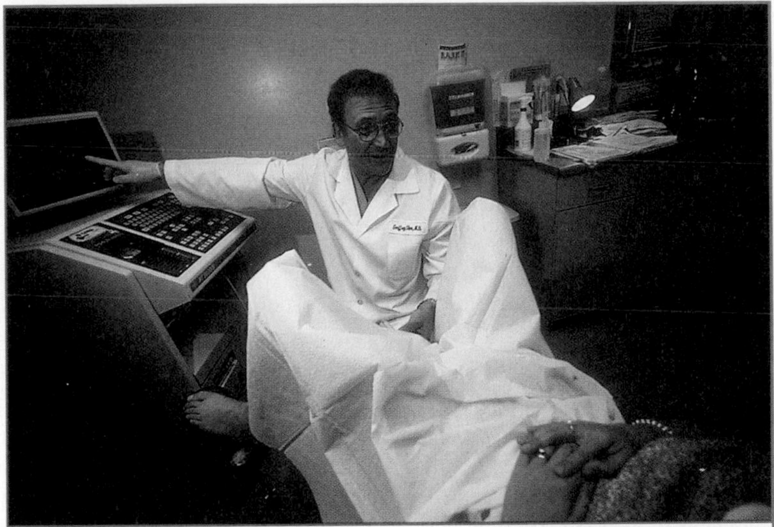

Here, the pregnancy of a woman in whom another woman's egg has been implanted is monitored. The development of new reproductive technologies has profound implications for notions of kinship, at the same time allowing the commodification of children.

woman, who is its mother? To complicate matters even further, the egg may have been fertilized by sperm from a donor not married to, or in a sexual relationship with, any of these women. Indeed, it has been suggested that we need at least ten different terms to cover the concepts of "mother" and "father" in Western societies:[10]

1. Genetic mother
2. Carrying mother
3. Nurturing mother
4. Complete mother
5. Genetic/carrying mother
6. Genetic/nurturing mother
7. Carrying/nurturing mother
8. Genetic father
9. Nurturing father
10. Complete father

While we cannot predict what the future will bring, it seems evident that the new reproductive technologies will have an important impact on traditional notions of gender and kinship.

[10] Stone, L. (1998). *Kinship and gender* (p. 272). Boulder, CO: Westview.

CHAPTER SUMMARY

In nonindustrial societies, kinship groups commonly deal with problems families and households cannot handle alone; problems such as those involving defense, allocation of property, and the pooling of other resources. As societies become larger and more complex, formal political systems take over many of these matters.

A common form of kinship group is the descent group, which has as its criterion of membership descent from a common ancestor through a series of parent-child links. Unilineal descent establishes kin group membership exclusively through the male or female line. Matrilineal descent is traced through the female line; patrilineal, through the male.

The descent system is closely tied to a society's economic base. Generally, patrilineal descent predominates where males, and matrilineal where females, do much of the productive work. Anthropologists now recognize that in all societies the kin of both mother and father are important elements in the social structure, regardless of how descent group membership is defined.

The male members of a patrilineage trace their descent from a common male ancestor. A female belongs to the same descent group as her father and his brother, but her children cannot trace their descent through them. Typically, authority over the children lies with the father or his elder brother. The requirement for younger men to defer to older men and for women to defer to men, as well as to the women of a household they marry into, are common sources of tension in a patrilineal society.

In one respect, matrilineal is the opposite of patrilineal descent, with descent being traced through the female line. Unlike the patrilineal pattern, which confers authority on men, matrilineal descent does not necessarily confer public authority on women, although they usually have more of a say in decision making than they do in patrilineal societies. The matrilineal system is common in societies where women perform much of the productive work. This system may be a source of family tension, since the husband's authority lies not in his own household but in that of his sister. This, and the ease with which unsatisfactory marriages may be ended, often results in higher divorce rates in matrilineal than in patrilineal societies.

Double descent is matrilineal for some purposes and patrilineal for others. Ambilineal descent provides a measure of flexibility in that an individual has the option of affiliating with either the mother's or father's descent group.

Descent groups are often highly structured economic units that provide aid and security to their members. They also may be repositories of religious tradition, with group solidarity enhanced by worship of a common ancestor. A lineage is a corporate descent group made up of consanguineal kin who can trace their genealogical links to a common ancestor. Since lineages are commonly exogamous, sexual competition within the group is largely avoided. In addition, marriage of a group member represents an alliance of two lineages. Lineage exogamy also serves to maintain open communication within a society and fosters the exchange of information among lineages.

Fission is the splitting of a large lineage group into new, smaller ones, with the original lineage becoming a clan. Clan members claim descent from a common ancestor but without actually knowing the genealogical links to that ancestor. Unlike lineages, clan residence is usually dispersed rather than localized. In the absence of residential unity, clan identification is often reinforced by totems, usually symbols from nature that remind members of their common ancestry. A phratry or moiety is a unilineal descent group of two or more clans that supposedly share a common ancestry. If there are but two such groups, they are called moieties.

In bilateral societies, such as industrial, modernizing, and many food-foraging societies, individuals are affiliated equally with all relatives on both the mother's and father's sides. Such a large group is socially impractical and is usually reduced to a small circle of paternal and maternal relatives called the kindred. A kindred is never the same for any two persons except siblings.

Different types of descent systems appear in different societies. In those where the nuclear family is paramount, bilateral kinship and kindred organization are likely to prevail.

In any society cultural rules dictate the way kinship relationships are defined. Factors such as sex and generational or genealogical differences help distinguish one kin from another. The Hawaiian system is the simplest system of kinship terminology. All relatives of the same generation and sex are referred to by the same term. The Eskimo system, used by Anglo-Americans, emphasizes the nuclear family and merges all other relatives in a given generation into a few large, generally undifferentiated categories. In the Iroquois system, a single term is used for father and his brother and another for a mother and her sister. Parallel cousins are equated with brothers and sisters but distinguished from cross cousins. The same is true in the Omaha and Crow systems, except they equate cross cousins with relatives of other generations. The relatively rare Sudanese or descriptive system treats all aunts, uncles, cousins, and siblings as different from one another.

With the advent of new reproductive technologies that separate conception from birth and eggs from wombs, traditional notions of kinship and gender are becoming strained. The end results of this remain to be seen, but some sort of change seems inevitable.

CLASSIC READINGS

Fox, R. (1968). *Kinship and marriage in an anthropological perspective.* Baltimore: Penguin.

An excellent introduction to the concepts of kinship and marriage, this book outlines some of the methods of analysis used in the anthropological treatment of kinship and marriage. It updates Radcliffe-Brown's *African Systems of Kinship and Marriage* and features a perspective focused on kinship groups and social organization.

Goodenough, W. H. (1970). *Description and comparison in cultural anthropology.* Chicago: Aldine.

This is an important contribution to the study of social organization that confronts the problem of describing kinship organization—kindred and clan, sibling and cousin—in such a way that meaningful cross-cultural comparisons can be made.

Keesing, R. M. (1975). *Kin groups and social structure.* New York: Holt, Rinehart and Winston.

This is a high-level introduction to kinship theory suitable for advanced undergraduate students. A strong point of the work is the attention given to nonunilineal, as well as unilineal, systems.

Schusky, E. L. (1983). *Manual for kinship analysis* (2nd ed.). Lanham, MD: University Press of America.

This useful book discusses the elements of kinship, diagraming, systems classification, and descent with specific examples.

Stone, L. (2000). *Kinship and gender: An introduction* (2nd ed.). Boulder, CO: Westview.

Anthropological interest in kinship languished somewhat in the 1980s, but has since undergone a strong revival. Part of this renewed interest relates to new reproductive technologies and their implications for kinship. This book provides coverage of the field of kinship at the introductory level, while exploring the repercussions of the new reproduction technologies on both kinship and gender.

CHAPTER 22

GROUPING BY SEX, AGE, COMMON INTEREST, AND CLASS

These teenage girls with their instruments exemplify the phenomenon of grouping by sex, age, and common interest, some of the means by which people may be organized into groups without recourse to kinship or descent.

CHAPTER PREVIEW

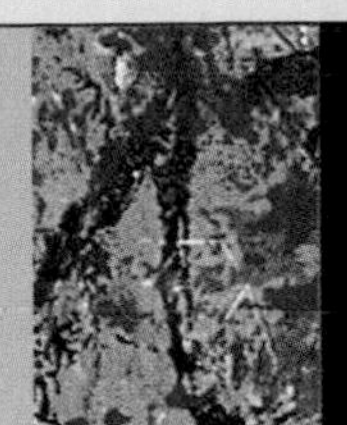

1 What Principles, Besides Kinship and Marriage, Do People Use to Organize Societies?

People group themselves by sex, age, common interest, and position within a ranked hierarchy (class stratification) to deal with problems not conveniently handled by marriage, the family and/or household, descent group, or kindred.

2 What Is Age Grading?

Age grading—the formation of groups on an age basis—is a widely used means of organizing people in societies, including those of Europe and North America. In industrial societies, or nonindustrial societies with relatively large populations, age grades may be broken down into age sets—groups of people of approximately the same age who move as groups through the series of age grades.

3 What Are Common-Interest Associations?

Common-interest associations, formed to deal with specific problems, acquire members as individuals act to join them. Such acts may range all the way from fully voluntary to compulsory. Common-interest associations have been a feature of human societies since the advent of the first farming villages several thousand years ago, but have become especially prominent in modern industrial or industrializing societies.

4 What Is Social Stratification?

Stratification is the division of society into two or more classes of people that do not share equally in basic resources, influence, or prestige. Such class structure is characteristic of all of the world's societies having large and heterogeneous populations with centralized political control. Among others, these include the ancient civilizations of southern and eastern Asia, Mesoamerica, the Central Andes, and also modern industrial societies, including the United States.

Social organization based on kinship and marriage has received an extraordinary amount of attention from anthropologists, and the subject usually is quite prominent in anthropological writing. There are several reasons for this: In one way or another, kinship and marriage operate as organizing principles in all societies, and in the small stateless societies so often studied by anthropologists, they are usually the most important organizational principles. There is, too, a certain fascination in the almost mathematical way kinship systems at least appear to work. To the unwary, all this attention to kinship and marriage may convey the impression that these are the only principles of social organization that really count. Yet it is obvious from viewing modern industrial societies that other principles of social organization not only exist but also may be quite important. Those principles that we will examine in this chapter are grouping by gender, age, common interest, and class (stratification).

GROUPING BY GENDER

As shown in preceding chapters, some division of labor along gender lines is characteristic of all human societies. Although in some—the Ju/'hoansi for example (Chapter 17)—many tasks men and women undertake may be shared, and people may perform work normally assigned to the opposite sex without loss of face, in others, men and women are rigidly segregated in what they do. For instance, among the Mohawk, Oneida, Onondaga, Cayuga, Seneca, and Tuscarora Indians of New York—the famous Six Nations of the Iroquois—society was divided into two parts consisting of sedentary women on the one hand and highly mobile men on the other. Living in villages were the women, who were "blood" relatives of one another and whose job was to grow the corn, beans, and squash on which all Iroquois relied for subsistence. Although houses and the palisades that protected villages were built by men, who also helped women clear their fields, the most important of men's work was pursued at some distance from their villages. This consisted of hunting, fishing, trading, warring, and diplomacy. As a consequence, men were mostly transients in the villages, being present for only brief periods.

Although masculine activities were considered to be more prestigious than those of women, the latter were explicitly acknowledged by all as the sustainers of life. Moreover, women headed the longhouses (dwellings occupied by matrilocal extended families), descent and inheritance passed through women, and ceremonial life centered on women's activities. Although men held all leadership positions outside households, on the councils of the villages, tribes, and the league of Six Nations, the women of their clans were the ones who nominated them for these positions and held veto power over them. Thus, male leadership was balanced by female authority. Overall, the phrase "separate but equal" accurately describes relations between the sexes in Six Nations Iroquois society, with members of neither sex being dominant nor submissive to the other. Related to this seems to have been a low incidence of rape; outside observers in the 19th century widely commented upon its apparent absence within Iroquois communities. Even in warfare, sexual violation of female captives was virtually unheard of; as General James Clinton observed in 1779: "Bad as

Among the Iroquois of New York, society was divided into sedentary women and highly mobile men, whose work was carried out away from the village. Many still follow this pattern today, as men leave their villages for extended periods to do much of the high steel work in the cities of North America.

In the United States, women were long expected to submit to male authority, but in recent decades, there has been a major effort to achieve more egalitarian gender relations. That the change is not complete is illustrated by the Southern Baptist Convention's official policy that women should submit gracefully to men.

the savages are, they never violate the chastity of any women of their prisoners."[1]

Although Iroquoian men often were absent from the village, when present they ate and slept with women. Among the Mundurucu of the Amazon, discussed briefly in Chapter 20, men not only work apart from women but eat and sleep separately as well. All men from age 13 on live in a large house of their own, while women with their young children occupy two or three houses grouped around that of the men. For all intents and purposes, men associate with men, and women with women. The relation between the sexes is not harmonious but rather one of opposition. According to Mundurucu belief, sex roles were once reversed: Women ruled over men and controlled the sacred trumpets that are the symbols of power and represent the generative capacities of women. But because women could not hunt, they could not supply the meat demanded by the ancient spirits contained within the trumpets, enabling the men to take the trumpets from the women, establishing their dominance in the process. Ever since, the trumpets have been kept carefully guarded and hidden in the men's house, and no woman can see them under penalty of gang rape. Thus, Mundurucu men express fear and envy toward women whom they seek to control by force. For their part, the women neither like nor accept a submissive status, and even though men occupy all formal positions of political and religious leadership, women are autonomous in the economic realm.

In spite of important differences, there are nonetheless interesting similarities between Mundurucu beliefs and those of traditional European (including European-American) cultures. The idea of rule by men replacing an earlier state of matriarchy (rule by women), for example, was held by many 19th-century intellectuals. Moreover, the idea that men may use force to control women is deeply embedded in both Judaic and Christian traditions (and even today, in spite of changing attitudes, one out of three women in the United States is sexually assaulted at some time in her life). A major difference between Mundurucu and traditional European societies is that, in the latter, women often have not had control of their own economic activities. This is now changing, but women in North America and other Western countries still have some distance to go before they achieve economic parity with men.

AGE GROUPING

Age grouping is so familiar and so important that it and sex sometimes have been called the only universal factors that determine a person's positions in society. In North America today, one's first friends generally are children one's own age. Together they are sent off to school, where together they remain until their late teens. At specified ages they finally are allowed to do things reserved for adults, such as driving a car, voting, and

[1] Littlewood, R. (1997). Military rape. *Anthropology Today, 13* (2), 14.

Age grading in modern North America is exemplified by the educational system, which specifies that children at 4 or 5 years should begin kindergarten.

drinking alcoholic beverages, and are required to go off to war if called upon to do so. Ultimately, North Americans retire from their jobs at a specified age and, more and more, live out the final years of their lives in "retirement communities," segregated from the rest of society. As North Americans age, they are labeled "teenagers," "middle-aged," and "senior citizens," whether they like it or not and for no other reason than their age.

The pervasiveness of age grouping in North American society is further illustrated by its effects on the Jewish descent groups discussed in Chapter 10. Until well into the 1930s, these always took on a more-or-less conventional ambilineal structure, which united relatives of all generations from the very old to the very young, with no age restrictions. By the late 1930s, however, young generations of Jews of eastern European background were becoming assimilated into North American culture to such a degree that some of them began to form new descent groups that deliberately excluded any kin of the parental and grandparental generations. In these new cousins clubs, as they are called, descendants of the cousins are eligible for membership, but not until they reach legal majority or are married, whichever comes first. Here again, these new descent groups contrast with the older family circles, which allowed activation of membership at any age, no matter how young.

Age classification also plays a significant role in non-Western societies, which at least make a distinction between immature, mature, and older people whose physical powers are waning. Old age often has profound significance, bringing with it the period of greatest respect (for women it may mean the first social equality with men); rarely are the elderly shunted aside or abandoned. Even the Inuit, who are often cited as a people who quite literally abandon their aged relatives, do so only in truly desperate circumstances, when the group's physical survival is at stake. In all nonliterate societies, the elders are the repositories of accumulated wisdom; they are the "living libraries" for their people. In keeping with this, and their freedom from many subsistence activities, they play a major role in passing on cultural traditions to their grandchildren. For a nonliterate society to cast them aside would be analogous to closing down all the schools, archives, and libraries in a modern industrial state.

In the United States people rely on the written word, rather than on their elders, for long-term memory. Moreover, people have become so accustomed to rapid change that they tend to assume that the experiences of their grandparents and others of their generation are hardly relevant to them in "today's world." Indeed, retirement from earning a living implies that one has nothing further to offer society and should stay out of the way of those who are younger. "The symbolism of the traditional gold watch [once a customary retirement gift] is all too plain: you should have made your money by now, and your time has run out. The watch will merely tick off the hours that remain between the end of adulthood and death."[2] Elder status is made even more problematic because they now constitute so large (and growing) a part of the overall population. Consequently, achievement of old age seems less of an accomplishment than it once did and so commands less respect. Furthermore, the elderly begin to be seen as not just unproductive but as a serious economic burden. The ultimate irony is that in the United States all of the ingenuity of modern science is used to keep alive the bodies of individuals who, in virtually every other way, society has shunted aside.

In the institutionalization of age, cultural rather than biological factors are of prime importance in determining social status. All human societies recognize a number of life stages; precisely how they are defined varies from one culture to another. Out of this recognition they establish patterns of activity, attitudes, prohibitions, and obligations. In some instances, these are designed to help the transition from one age to another, to teach needed skills, or to lend economic assistance. Often they are taken as the basis for the formation of organized groups.

[2] Turnbull, C. M. (1983). *The human cycle* (p. 229). New York: Simon & Schuster.

Institutions of Age Grouping

An organized class of people with membership on the basis of age is known as an **age grade.** Theoretically speaking, membership in an age grade ought to be automatic: One reaches the appropriate age, and so is included, without question, in the particular age grade. Just such situations exist, for example, among the East African Tiriki, whose system we will examine shortly. Sometimes, though, individuals must buy their way into the age grade they are eligible for. This was the case among some of the Indians of North America's plains, who required boys to purchase the appropriate costumes, dances, and songs for age-grade membership. In societies where entrance fees are expensive, not all people eligible for membership in a particular age grade may actually be able to join.

Entry into and transfer out of age grades may be accomplished individually, either by a biological distinction, such as puberty, or by a socially recognized status, such as marriage or childbirth. Whereas age-grade members may have much in common, may engage in similar activities, may cooperate with one another, and may share the same orientation and aspirations, their membership may not be entirely parallel with physiological age. A specific time is often ritually established for moving from a younger to an older grade—the Jewish Bar Mitzvah ceremony is a good example. Although members of senior groups commonly expect deference from and acknowledge certain responsibilities to their juniors, this does not necessarily mean that one grade is seen as better, or worse, or even more important than another. There can be standardized competition (opposition) between age grades, such as that traditionally between first-year students and sophomores on U.S. college campuses. Individuals can, comparably, accept the realities of being a teenager without feeling the need to "prove" anything. In some societies, age grades are subdivided into **age sets** (sometimes referred to as age classes). An age set is a group of persons initiated into an age grade who move through the system together. For example, among the Tiriki of East Africa, the age group consisting of those initiated into an age grade over a 15-year period amounts to an age set. Age sets, unlike age grades, do not cease to exist after a specified number of years; the members of an age set usually remain closely associated throughout their lives, or at least through much of their lives.

There has been some argument among anthropologists over the relative strength, cohesiveness, and stability that go into an age grouping. The age-set notion implies strong feelings of loyalty and mutual support. Because such groups may possess property, songs, shield designs, and rituals and are internally organized for collective decision making and leadership, a distinction is called for between them and simple age grades. One also may distinguish between transitory age grades—which initially concern younger men (sometimes women too) but become less important and disintegrate as the members grow older—and the comprehensive systems that affect people through the whole of their lives.

Age Grouping in African Societies

Although age is a criterion for group membership in many parts of the world, its most varied and elaborate use is found in Africa, south of the Sahara. An example may be seen among the Tiriki, one of several pastoral nomadic groups living in Kenya.[3] In this society, each boy born over a 15-year period becomes a member of a particular age set then open for membership. Seven such named age sets exist, only one of which is open for membership at a time; when membership in one is closed, the next one is open for a 15-year period and so on until the passage of 105 years (7 times 15), when the first set once again takes in new "recruits."

Members of Tiriki age sets remain together for life as they move through four age grades: Advancement occurs at 15-year intervals at the same time one age set closes and another opens for membership. Each age grade has its particular duties and responsibilities. The first, or "Warrior" age grade, traditionally served as guardians of the country, and members gained renown through fighting. Since colonial times, however, this traditional function has been lost with cessation of warfare, and members of this age grade now find excitement and adventure by leaving their community for extended employment or study elsewhere.

[3] Sangree, W. H. (1965). The Bantu Tiriki of Western Kenya. In J. L. Gibbs, Jr. (Ed.). *Peoples of Africa* (pp. 69–72). New York: Holt, Rinehart and Winston.

Age grade. An organized category of people based on age; every individual passes through a series of such categories over his or her lifetime. • **Age sets.** Groups of persons simultaneously initiated into age grades at the same time and who move through the series of categories together.

In many societies it is common for children of the same age to play, eat, and learn together, such as these Maasai boys, who are gathering for the first time to receive instruction for their initiation into an age grade.

The next age grade, the "Elder Warriors," traditionally had few specialized tasks but learned skills they would need later on by assuming an increasing share of administrative activities. For example, they would chair the postfuneral gatherings held to settle property claims after someone's death. Elder Warriors also served as envoys between elders of different communities. Nowadays, Elder Warriors hold nearly all of the administrative and executive roles opened up by the creation and growth of a centralized Tiriki administrative bureaucracy.

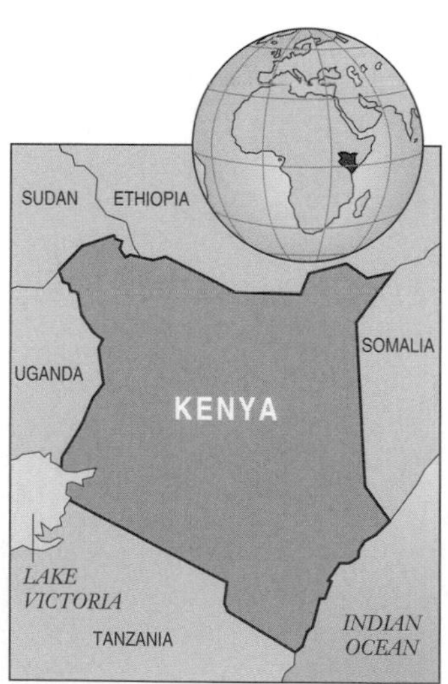

"Judicial Elders," the third age grade, traditionally handled most tasks connected with the administration and settlement of local disputes. Today, they still serve as the local judiciary body. Members of the "Ritual Elders," the senior age grade, presided over the priestly functions of ancestral shrine observances on the household level, at subclan meetings, at semiannual community appeals, and at rites of initiation into the various age grades. They also were credited with access to special magical powers. With the decline of ancestor worship over the past several decades, many of these traditional functions have been lost and no new ones have arisen to take their places. Nonetheless, Ritual Elders continue to hold the most important positions in the initiation ceremonies, and their power as sorcerers and expungers of witchcraft are still recognized.

COMMON-INTEREST ASSOCIATIONS

The proliferation of **common-interest associations** is a phenomenon intimately associated with the rise of urban, industrialized societies in which individuals are commonly separated from their kin. To compensate, as anthropologist Meredith Small observes:

Common-interest associations. Associations not based on age, kinship, marriage, or territory but result from an act of joining.

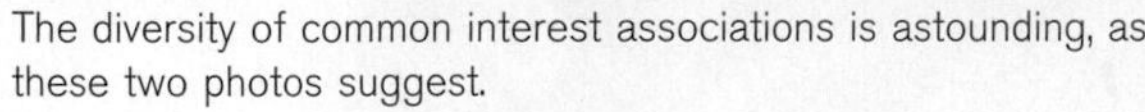

The diversity of common interest associations is astounding, as these two photos suggest.

> . . . we often imprint lines of kinship on friends and colleagues, transferring familial expectations onto those with whom we share time but not blood or genes or vows, so that we can have the experience of an extended family. Young people join gangs, older people join clubs, and even babies are put into play groups. Pushed by a culture that favors independence and self reliance, the social animal in us nonetheless seeks connections, even if they are bloodless and fragile.[4]

Moreover, common-interest associations help with such problems as learning to cope with life in a new and bewildering environment, or learning a new language or mannerisms necessary for the change from village to city, or one country to another. Because common-interest associations are by nature quite flexible, they have often been turned to, both in cities and in traditional villages, as a way of filling these needs. Common-interest associations are not, however, restricted to modernizing societies alone. They also are found in many traditional societies, and there is reason to believe they arose with the emergence of the first horticultural villages. Furthermore, associations in traditional societies may be just as complex and highly organized as those of countries such as the United States and Canada.

Common-interest associations have often been referred to in the anthropological literature as voluntary associations, but this term is misleading. The act of joining may range from fully voluntary to one required by law. For example, in the United States, under the draft laws individuals often became members of the armed forces without choosing to join. It is not really compulsory to join a labor union, but unless one does, one cannot work in a union shop. What the term *voluntary association* really refers to are those associations not based on sex, age, kinship, marriage, or territory that result from an act of joining. The act often may be voluntary, but it does not have to be.

Kinds of Common-Interest Associations

The diversity of common-interest associations is astonishing. In the United States, they include such diverse entities as women's clubs of all sorts, street gangs, private militias, Kiwanis, Rotary Clubs, Parent Teacher Associations, churches and other religious organizations, political parties, labor unions, environmental organizations, human rights organizations such as Amnesty International—the list could go on and on. Their goals may include the pursuit of friendship, recreation, and promotion of certain values, as well as governing and the pursuit or defense of economic interests. Associations also have served to preserve traditional songs, history, language, and

[4] Small, M. F. (2000). Kinship envy. *Natural History, 109* (2), 88.

Non-governmental organizations such as the International Indian Treaty Council are common-interest associations that have arisen to promote the rights of indigenous peoples. Shown here are Antonio Gonzales of the Council and Chief Gideon James of Venetie, Alaska, testifying at the 54th session of the UN Commission on Human Rights at Geneva in 1998.

moral beliefs among various ethnic minorities; the Tribal Unions of West Africa, for example, continue to serve this purpose. Similar organizations, often operating secretly, have kept traditions alive among North American Indians, who are undergoing a resurgence of ethnic pride despite generations of schooling designed to stamp out their cultural identity. Another significant force in the formation of associations may be a supernatural experience common to all members; the Crow Indian Tobacco Society, the secret associations of the Kwakiutl Indians of British Columbia with cycles of rituals known only to initiates, and the Kachina associations of the Hopi Indians are well-known examples. Among other traditional forms of association are military, occupational, political, and entertainment groups that parallel such familiar organizations as the American Legion, labor unions, block associations, college fraternities and sororities, not to mention co-ops of every kind.

In nonindustrial societies, such organizations are frequently exclusive, but a prevailing characteristic is their concern for the general well-being of an entire village or group of villages. The rain that falls as a result of the work of Hopi rainmakers nourishes the crops of members and nonmembers alike.

MEN'S AND WOMEN'S ASSOCIATIONS

For a long time, women's contributions to common-interest associations were dismissed by scholars as less developed than men's. The reason was that men's associations attracted more notice around the world than did women's. Heinrich Schurtz's theory, published in 1902, that underlying the differentiation between kinship and associational groups is a profound difference in the psychology of the sexes, was widely accepted for years. Schurtz regarded women as unsocial beings who preferred to remain in kinship groups based on sexual relations and the reproductive function rather than forming units based on commonly held interests. Men, by contrast, were said to view sexual relations as isolated episodes, an attitude that fostered the purely social factor that makes "birds of a feather flock together."

In the 1960s, scholars of both sexes began to recognize the culture-bound nature of this kind of thinking. In some societies women have not formed associations to the extent men have because the demands of raising a family and their daily activities have not permitted it and because men have not always allowed them to do so. Given the plethora of women's clubs of all kinds in the United States for several generations, however, one wonders how this belief in women as unsocial beings survived as long as it did. Earlier in U.S. history, of course, in rural areas where women were stuck at home with no near neighbors, they had little chance to participate in common-interest associations. Moreover, some functions of men's associations–such as military duties–often are culturally defined as purely for men or repugnant to women. In a number of the world's traditional societies, however, the opportunities for female sociability are so great that there may be

Common-interest associations are not limited to modern industrial societies. This 1832 picture shows a Mandan Indian Bull Dance. The Bulls were one of several common-interest groups concerned with both social and military affairs.

little need for women's associations. Among the Indians of northeastern North America (including the Six Nations Iroquois discussed earlier), the men spent extended periods off in the woods hunting, either by themselves or with a single companion. The women, by contrast, spent most of their time in and around their village, in close, everyday contact with all the other women of the community. Not only did they have many people to talk to, but also they always had someone available to help with whatever tasks required assistance.

Still, as cross-cultural research makes clear, women do play important roles in associations of their own as well as in those in which men predominate. Among the Apsaroke (Crow) Indians, women participated even in the secret Tobacco Society, in addition to their own exclusive groups. Throughout Africa women's social clubs complement the men's and are concerned with educating women, with crafts, and with charitable activities. In Sierra Leone, where once-simple dancing societies have developed under urban conditions into complex organizations with a set of new objectives, the dancing *compin* is made up of young women as well as men who together perform plays based on traditional music and dancing and raise money for various mutual-benefit causes.

Women's rights organizations, consciousness-raising groups, and professional organizations for women are examples of some of the associations arising directly or indirectly out of today's social climate. These groups cover the entire range of association formation, from simple friendship and support groups to political, guildlike, and economic (the publication of magazines, groups designed to influence advertising) associations on a national scale. If an unresolved point does exist in the matter of women's participation, it is in determining why women are excluded from associations in some societies, while in others their participation is essentially equal to that of men.

Associations in the Postindustrial World

In spite of the recent diversity and vitality of common-interest associations, some have noted a recent decline in participation in all sorts of these groups, at least in North America. Those who have observed this trend see it is part of a more general drop in civic participation. People are spending less time socializing with others in bars, at dinner parties, having friends over, and so on. One can only speculate on the causes, but they likely include further isolation of individuals as they spend more and more of their free time with home entertainment. For example, in the United States, adults spend an average of 4 hours each day in front of their TV. Then, too, the frequency with which people move interferes with their ability to establish more than superficial friendship with others. Add to this the fact that North Americans work longer hours on average than people in almost all industrialized countries, leaving less time for socialization. In this connection, some have noted a 10% drop in civic participation for every 10 minutes of commuting time. Finally, there is the rise of the Internet; as people spend more and more time "online," they can stay in touch without having to leave home. In effect, the cyberworld has seen an explosion of what are, in effect, "virtual" common-interest associations, all of which have their own particular rules on matters such as what members may or may not post and how they should behave online. In short, common-interest associations may not be showing a decline so much as a transformation. As an example of this transformation, the following Original Study explores the use of the Internet by Native American and other indigenous peoples.

Original Study

Digital Revolution: Indigenous Peoples in Cyberia[5]

The current Digital Revolution is changing the world we all live in, and many indigenous communities are taking active part in this global transformation. Linking even the most remote corners of the world by fiberoptic cables, radars, and communication satellites orbiting the planet, modern cybertechnology enables anyone with access to Internet-connected computers to instantly communicate and exchange information. Lured by the promises and opportunities of the World Wide Web (WWW), hundreds of North American Indian tribes (or First Nations) have already put up their own web sites. With the help of powerful search engines such as Inktomi (named after the Spider trickster of Lakota Indian myth), it is not difficult to navigate through cyberspace and discover the virtual home of one or another tribal community in Canada, the United States, New Zealand, or elsewhere in the world.

The idea of the Internet started in 1962. Initially developed for US military purposes during the Cold War, it quickly expanded to academic institutions. As soon as a special networking protocol was developed ten years later, widely dispersed computer networks were "internetted." From then on, electronically-linked machines could instantly communicate and exchange information. Soon, commercial services began to offer access to the Internet, resulting in an explosive growth rate in cyberspace development. Essential graphical browser software to design and put up Web sites was developed in 1992. Precisely 500 years after Columbus' "discovery" of the Americas, another "New World" had emerged—the WWW.

Immediately, technologically more advanced institutions, media organizations, and commercial companies rushed to post their own sites on the WWW. Within the first year, the Web expanded from a handful to several thousand sites. With the growth rate doubling every six months, there are now several million. Although most Internet users reside in wealthy industrialized countries, hundreds of millions across the globe now participate in this electronic communication revolution.

Allowing instant gathering and spreading of almost unlimited information, the Internet serves as a mega-bulletin board without the filtering mechanisms of mainstream media. As such, it renders it difficult for governments and corporate print and broadcast media to be gatekeepers of information. Widely recognized as an effective collaboration tool for local, regional, national, and global

[5] Prins, H. E. L. (2000). *Digital revolution: Indigenous peoples in Cyberia.* Manuscript © by author, Department of Anthropology, Kansas State University.

political organizations, cultural institutions, businesses, and so on, the Internet has also been adopted as an effective communications medium by many tribal communities. Quickly recognizing its strategic potential for global networking, information sharing, marketing, and political action, as well as other functions, a myriad of indigenous organizations and enterprises have become active on the Internet and have posted their own web sites. Particularly attractive to them is that this new medium enables them to creatively represent themselves on their own terms and according to their own aesthetic preferences to the entire world.

As early as May 1994, even before the U.S. President's Office in the White House made its presence known on the WWW, the Oneida Indian Nation, one of the six Iroquois tribes still residing in upstate New York, had posted its own web site, **oneida-nation.net**. Emblazoned on its homepage is its official seal, depicting the Iroquois Confederacy wampum belt superimposed on a green pine tree with an eagle perched atop, all on a field of red. The site offers numerous hyperlinks to very well designed and artfully illustrated sites, some enhanced with sound. It reports news and events, and offers basic information about Iroquois cultural history, clans, wampum belts, and treaties. In addition to web pages devoted to the Oneida cultural center, it contains links to pages dealing with the controversial Oneida Indian landclaim (including e-mail address for comments and questions). There are also links to the tribally-owned Shenandoah Golf and Country Club, as well as to its multimillion dollar Turning Stone Casino Resort. Further, it provides useful information links to government resources, other indigenous Web sites, and hosts a special communication section for a number of smaller eastern tribes in the United States that do not yet have their own Internet capabilities.

In Canada, the first tribal group to launch its own web site was the Blackfoot Confederacy in Alberta, organized as the Treaty 7 First Nation Reserves Interband Council (in September 1995). These Blackfeet Indians mark their virtual headquarters (**www.treaty7.org**) with a logo of its own "coat of arms"—a shield with five eagle feathers dangling down, a stylized thunderbird doubling as a mountain range, a yellow sun at the top, and a crossed spear and stone tomahawk at the center. Using their own resources, the Blackfeet also took the initiative to establish Canada's first Native Internet server, which provides thirteen direct links, plus many indirect, to a host of other Indian Web sites. Capitalizing on their modern electronic communications skills, they also offer multimedia development services through a special computing and Internet services department. These services include video digitizing, editing, and titling, as well as photo/document scanning and editing, video, audio, graphics design and animation production in 2D and 3D, as well as CD-ROM production.

Today, taking an excursion through virtual "Indian Country," one may even opt for a guided cybertour, choosing from a dozen or so indigenous "Web rings." For instance, the Seminole Tribe in Florida runs the **Indian Webring**, while the Lac d'Oreille Ojibway own the **Native People's Ring**. One of the most heavily trafficked indigenous Web rings is **The Native Trail**, which interconnects about 600 Canadian Native and Native-related sites. Some of these Web rings, including The Native Trail, offer cybermaps to a wide range of clearly marked and hyperlinked indigenous Web sites. These sites are not only of value to widely-dispersed tribal members, but, for various reasons, must also appeal to outside visitors. Typically identifiable as "Indian," these sites are often beautifully designed with stereotypical images such as eagles, buffalo skulls, feathers, calumets (ceremonial pipes), tipis, war bonnets, petroglyphs (rock etchings), or wild animal tracks. But, there are also more culture-specific motifs. For instance, quite a few Mi'kmaq web sites are marked by the eight-pointed star, or **kagwet**; well known from traditional porcupine quillwork designs, this symbol is said to represent a place of happiness.

Especially since 1997, the Internet has made deep inroads on other tribal peoples scattered throughout the world. Many thousands of modern tribespeople, often living far away from their home villages, log on frequently to stay in touch with each other, trying to stay informed about their relatives and friends, and letting each other know about gossip, political news, and special celebrations. Through the Internet, they seek to maintain a sense of cultural belonging in spite of the enor-

Original Study

mous geographic distances that may separate them from their home villages.

Although indigenous peoples are proportionally under-represented in cyberspace—for obvious reasons such as economic poverty, technological inexperience, linguistic isolation, political repression and/or cultural resistance—the Internet has vastly extended traditional networks of information and communication. Greatly enhancing the visibility of otherwise marginal communities and individuals, it also provides them with new opportunities to market traditional arts and crafts to a far-flung clientele. And although the super information highway is not without its dangers, it enables even very small and isolated communities to expand their sphere of influence and mobilize political support in their struggles for cultural survival. In addition to maintaining contact with their own communities, indigenous peoples also use the Internet to connect with other widely dispersed tribal groups in the world. Today, it is not unusual for a Mi'kmaq in Newfoundland to go on the Internet and communicate with individuals belonging to other remote groups such as the Maori in New Zealand, Saami in Norway, Kuna in Panama, or Navajo in Arizona. Together with the rest of us, they have pioneered across the new cultural frontier and are now surfing daily through Cyberia.

The End

With new computer technology has come the rise of "virtual," online common interest associations. Here, an Hispanic woman uses a chat room on America Online.

SOCIAL STRATIFICATION

The study of social stratification involves the examination of distinctions that, when we think about them, impress us as unfair and even outrageous, but social stratification is a common and powerful phenomenon in some of the world's societies. Civilizations, in particular, with their large and heterogeneous populations, are invariably stratified. Basically, a **stratified society** is one that is divided into two or more categories of people ranked high and low relative to one another. When the people in one such social layer or stratum are compared with those in another, marked differences in privileges, rewards, restrictions, and obligations become apparent. Members of low-ranked strata will tend to have fewer privileges and less power than those in higher ranked strata. In addition, they tend not to be rewarded to the same degree and are denied equal access to basic resources. Their restrictions and obligations, too, are usually more onerous, although members of high-ranked

Stratified society. The division of society into two or more categories of people who do not share equally in the basic resources that support life, influence, and prestige.

strata will usually have their own distinctive restrictions and obligations to attend to. In short, social stratification amounts to institutionalized inequality. Without ranking—high versus low—no stratification exists; social differences without this do not constitute stratification.

Stratified societies stand in sharp contrast to **egalitarian societies.** As we saw in Chapter 17, societies of food-foraging peoples are characteristically egalitarian, although there are some exceptions. Such societies have as many valued positions as people capable of filling them. Hence, individuals depend mostly on their own abilities for their positions in society. A poor hunter may become a good hunter if he has the ability; he is not excluded from such a prestigious position because he comes from a group of poor hunters. Poor hunters do not constitute a social stratum. Furthermore, they have as much right to their society's resources as any other of its members. No one can deny a poor hunter a fair share of food, the right to be heard when important decisions are to be made, or anything else to which a man is entitled.

Despite their close association, the clothing worn by these two individuals and the way they interact clearly indicate they are of different social classes.

Class and Caste

A **social class** may be defined as a category of individuals of equal or nearly equal prestige according to the system of evaluation. The qualification "nearly equal" is important, for a certain amount of inequality may occur even within a given class. If this is so, to an outside observer low-ranking individuals in an upper class may not seem much different from the highest ranking members of a lower class. Yet marked differences exist when the classes are compared as wholes with one another. The point here is that class distinctions are not clear-cut and obvious in societies such as those of North America that have a continuous range of differential privileges, for example, from virtually none to several. Such a continuum can be divided into classes in a variety of ways. If fine distinctions are made, then many classes may be recognized. If, however, only a few gross distinctions are made, then only a few classes will be recognized. Thus, some speak of North American society as divided into three classes: lower, middle, and upper. Others speak of several classes: lower lower, middle lower, upper lower, lower middle, and so forth.

A caste is a particular kind of social class in which membership is fairly fixed or impermeable. Castes are strongly endogamous, and offspring are automatically members of their parents' caste. The classic case is the caste system of India. Coupled with strict endogamy and membership by descent in Indian castes is an association of particular castes with specific occupations and customs, such as food habits and styles of dress, along with rituals involving notions of purity and impurity. The literally thousands of castes, or *jatis,* are organized into a hierarchy of four named categories, or *varnas,* at the top of which are the priests or *Brahmins,* the bearers of universal order and values and of highest ritual purity. Below them are the powerful—though less pure—warriors. Dominant at the local level, besides fulfilling warrior

Egalitarian societies. Social systems that have as many valued positions as persons capable of filling them. • **Social class.** A category of individuals who enjoy equal or nearly equal prestige according to the system of evaluation. • **Caste.** A special form of social class in which membership is determined by birth and remains fixed for life.

Anthropology Applied

Anthropologists and Social Impact Assessment

A kind of policy research anthropologists frequently do is a social-impact assessment, which entails collection of data about a community or neighborhood for planners of development projects. Such an assessment seeks to determine a project's effect by determining how and upon whom its impact will fall and whether the impact is likely to be positive or negative. In the United States, any project requiring a federal permit or license, or using federal funds, by law must be preceded by a social impact assessment as part of the environmental review process. Examples of such projects include highway construction, urban renewal, water diversion schemes, and land reclamation. Often, projects of these sorts are sited so that their impact falls most heavily on neighborhoods or communities inhabited by people in low socioeconomic strata, sometimes because the projects are seen as ways of improving the lives of poor people and sometimes because the poor people are seen as having less political power to block proposals that others conceive as (sometimes rightly, sometimes wrongly) in "the public interest."

As an illustration of this kind of work, anthropologist Sue Ellen Jacobs was hired to do a social impact assessment of a water diversion project in New Mexico planned by the Bureau of Land Reclamation in cooperation with the Bureau of Indian Affairs. This project proposed construction of a diversion dam and an extensive canal system for irrigation on the Rio Grande. Affected by this would be 22 communities inhabited primarily by Spanish Americans, as well as two Indian Pueblos. In the region, unemployment was high (19.1% in June 1970), and the project was seen as a way to promote a perceived trend to urbanism (which theoretically would be associated with industrial development), while bringing new land into production for intensive agriculture.

What the planners failed to take into account was that both the Hispanic and Indian populations were heavily committed to farming for household consumption, with some surpluses raised for the market, using a system of irrigation canals established as many as 300 years ago. These canals are maintained by elected supervisors who know the communities as well as the requirements of the land and crops, water laws, and ditch management skills. Such individuals can allocate water equitably in times of scarcity and can prevent and resolve conflict in the realm of water and land use, as well as in community life beyond the ditches. Under the proposed project, this system was to be given up in favor of one in which fewer people would control larger tracts of land and water allocation would be in the hands of a government technocrat. One of the strongest measures of local government would be lost.

Not surprisingly, Jacobs discovered widespread community opposition to this project, and her report helped convince Congress that any positive impact was far outweighed by negative effects.

> One of the major objections to the construction of the project is that it would result in the obliteration of the three-hundred-year-old irrigation system structures. Project planners did not seem to recognize the antiquity and cultural significance of the traditional irrigation system. These were referred to as "temporary diversion structures." The fact that the old dams associated with the ditches were attached to local descent groups was simply not recognized by the official documents.*

Other negative effects of the project, besides loss of local control, would be problems associated with population growth and relocation, loss of fishing and other river-related resources, and new health hazards, including increased threat of drowning, insects breeding, and airborne dust. Finally, physical transformation of the communities' life space was seen likely to result in changes in the context of the informal processes of enculturation that take place within the communities.

* Van Willigen, J. (1986). *Applied anthropology* (p. 169). South Hadley, MA: Bergain and Garvey.

functions, they control all village lands. Furnishing services to the landowners, and owning the tools of their trade, are two lower-ranking, landless caste groups of artisans and laborers. At the bottom of the system, owning neither land nor the tools of their trade, are the outcasts, or "untouchables." Considered the most impure of all people, India's untouchables constitute a large pool of labor at the beck and call of those controlling economic and political affairs, the land-holding warrior caste.

Although some argue that the term "caste" should be restricted to the Indian situation, others find this much too narrow a usage, since caste-like situations are known elsewhere in the world. In South Africa, for example, although the situation is now changing, Blacks traditionally were relegated to a low-ranking stratum in society, until recently were barred by law from marrying non-Blacks, and could not hold property except to a limited degree in specified "black homelands." Most Blacks still perform menial jobs for Whites, but even the small cadre of "middle-class" Blacks that existed were until recently prohibited from living where Whites do, or even swimming in the same water or holding the hand of someone who is White. All of this brings to mind the concepts of ritual purity and pollution so basic to the Indian caste system. In South Africa, Whites feared pollution of their purity through improper contact with Blacks. In India and South Africa, untouchables and Blacks comprised categories of landless or near-landless people who served as a body of mobile laborers always available for exploitation by those in political control. A similar mobile labor force of landless men at the state's disposal emerged in China as many as 2,200 years ago (caste, in India, is at least as old). Paradoxically, at the very same time that South Africa is trying to change its system, a similar caste-like underclass has emerged in the United States, as automation has reduced the need for unskilled workers and downsizing has taken place. This underclass accounts for about 20% of the total United States' population, and its members consist of unemployed, unemployable, or drastically underemployed people who own little, if any, property and who live "out on the streets" or—at best—in urban or rural slums. Lacking both economic and political power, they have no access to the kinds of educational facilities that would enable them or their children to improve their lot. Under conditions of significant unemployment, this new underclass has served the economy by ensuring a significant incidence of permanent unemployment, thereby making the employed feel less secure in their jobs. As a consequence, the employed were apt to be less demanding of wages and benefits from their employers. Now, with outright unemployment at historically low levels, the underclass (as in China, India, and South Africa) provides a pool of cheap labor.

India, South Africa, China, and the United States—all very different countries, in different parts of the world, with different ideologies—and yet a similar phenomenon has emerged in each. Is there something about the structure of socially stratified states that sooner or later produces some sort of exploitable, impoverished outcast group? The answer to this is clearly unknown, but the question is deserving of the attention of anthropologists and other social scientists.

The basis of social class structure is role differentiation. Some role differentiation, of course, exists in any society, at least along the lines of sex and age. Furthermore, any necessary role will always be valued to some degree. In a food-foraging society, the role of "good hunter" will be valued. The fact that one man may already play that role does not, however, prevent another man from playing it, too, in an egalitarian society. Therefore, role differentiation by itself is not sufficient for stratification. Two more ingredients are necessary: formalized

Outcast groups such as India's untouchables are a common feature of stratified societies; in the United States, for example, 20–23% of the population belongs to a caste-like underclass.

HIGHWAY 1
Info on India's caste system
http://www.inet.uni2.dk/~tvinddns/DmM/in2t4.htm

HIGHWAY 2
Service and common interest groups
http://dmoz.org/society/organizations/fraternal

evaluation of roles involving attitudes such as like/dislike or admiration/revulsion, and restricted access to the more highly valued roles. Obviously, the greater the diversity of roles in a society, the more complex evaluation and restriction can become. Since great role diversity is most characteristic of civilizations, it is not surprising they provide the greatest opportunities for stratification. Furthermore, the large size and heterogeneity of populations in civilizations create a need for classification of people into a manageable number of social categories. Small wonder, then, that social stratification is one of the defining characteristics of a true civilization.

Social classes are manifest in several ways. One is through **verbal evaluation**—what people say about others in their own society. For this, anything can be singled out for attention and spoken of favorably or unfavorably: political, military, religious, economic, or professional roles; wealth and property; kinship; personal qualities (skin color, for example); community activity; linguistic dialect; and a host of other traits. Cultures do this differently, and what may be spoken of favorably in one may be spoken of unfavorably in another and ignored in a third. Furthermore, cultural values may change, so that something regarded favorably at one time may not be at another. This is one reason why a researcher may be misled by verbal evaluation, for what people say may not correspond completely with social reality. As an example, the official language of Egypt is Classical Arabic, the language of the Qur'an (the most holy of Islamic texts). Though it is highly valued, no one in Egypt uses this language in daily interaction; rather, it is used for official documents or on formal occasions. Those most proficient in it are not of the upper class but, rather, of the lower middle classes. These are the people educated in the public schools (where Classical Arabic is the language of schooling) and who hold jobs in the government bureaucracy (which requires the most use of Classical Arabic). Upper-class Egyptians, by contrast, go to private schools, where they learn the foreign languages essential for success in diplomacy and (in the global economy) business and industry.[6]

Social classes also are manifest through patterns of association: not just who interacts with whom but how and in what context. In Western society, informal, friendly relations take place mostly within one's own class. Relations with members of other classes tend to be less informal and occur in the context of specific situations. For example, a corporate executive and a janitor normally are members of different social classes. They may have frequent contact with one another, but it occurs in the setting of the corporate offices and usually requires certain stereotyped behavior patterns.

A third way social classes are manifest is through **symbolic indicators.** Included here are activities and possessions indicative of class. For example, in North American society, occupation (a garbage collector has

[6] Haeri, N. (1997). The reproduction of symbolic capital: Language, state and class in Egypt. *Current Anthropology, 38,* 795–816.

Verbal evaluation. The way people in a stratified society evaluate others in their society. • **Symbolic indicators.** In a stratified society, activities and possessions indicative of social class.

different class status than a physician); wealth (rich people—see Figure 22.1—generally are in a higher social class than poor people); dress (we have all heard the expression "white collar" versus "blue collar"); form of recreation (upper-class people are expected to play golf rather than shoot pool down at the pool hall—but they can shoot pool at home or in a club); residential location (upper-class people do not ordinarily live in slums); kind of car; and so on. The fact is all sorts of status symbols are indicative of class position, including such measures as how many bathrooms a person's house has. At the same time, symbolic indicators may be cruder reflections of class position than verbal indicators or patterns of association. One reason is that access to wealth may not be wholly restricted to upper classes, enabling individuals to buy symbols suggestive of upper-class status whether or not this really is their status. To take an extreme example, the head of an organized crime ring may display more of the symbols of high-class status than may some members of old, established upper-class families. For that matter, someone from an upper class deliberately may choose a simpler lifestyle than is customary. Instead of driving a Mercedes, he or she may drive a beat-up Volkswagen.

Symbolic indicators involve factors of lifestyle, but differences in life chances may also signal differences in class standing. Life is apt to be less hard for members of an upper class as opposed to a lower class. This shows up in a tendency for lower infant mortality and longer life expectancy for the upper class. There is also a tendency for greater physical stature and robustness among upper-class people, the result of better diet and protection from serious illness in their juvenile years.

Mobility

All stratified societies offer at least some **mobility,** and this helps to ease the strains inherent in any system of inequality. Even the Indian caste system, with its guiding ideology that pretends that all arrangements within it are static, has a surprising amount of flexibility and mobility, not all of it associated with the recent changes

Symbolic indicators of class or caste include factors of lifestyle, such as the kind of housing one lives in.

Mobility. The ability to change one's class position.

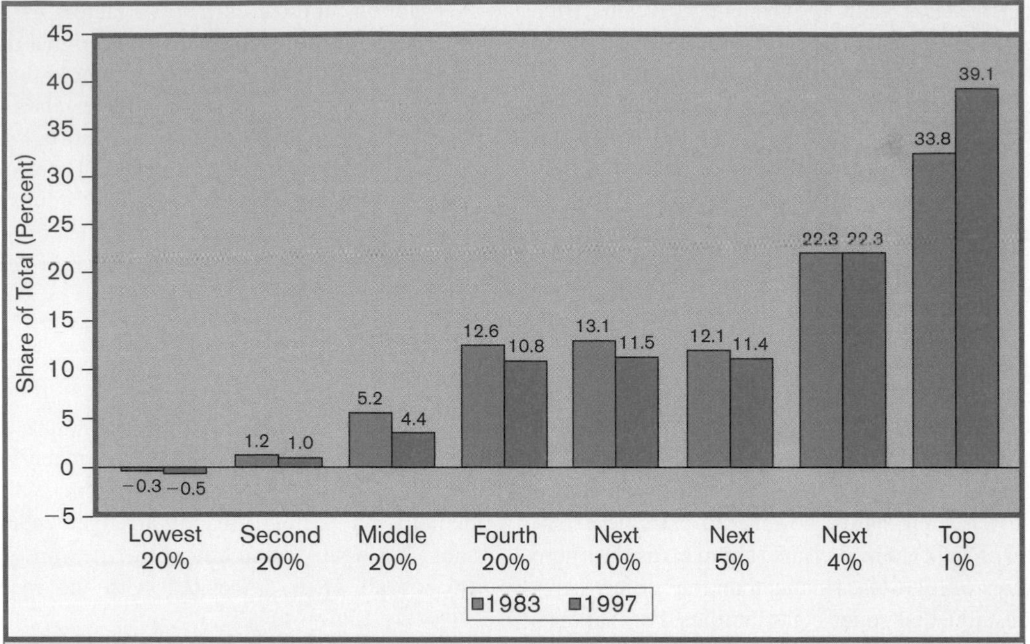

FIGURE 22.1

WEALTH INEQUALITY HAS GROWN IN THE 1990S. AS OF 1997 (THE LATEST YEAR FOR WHICH DATA IS AVAILABLE), THE TOP 1% OF U.S. HOUSEHOLDS CONTROLLED 39.1% OF ALL WEALTH. WHEN COMPARING THE CHANGES IN WEALTH DISTRIBUTION OVER THE 1983–97 PERIOD, THE LARGE SHIFT IN WEALTH PRIMARILY BENEFITED THE TOP 1% (RISING FROM 33.8% TO 39.1% OF ALL WEALTH). IN COMPARISON, THE BOTTOM 95% OF THE WEALTH DISTRIBUTION EXPERIENCED FLAT OR FALLING GROWTH IN WEALTH OVER THE SAME PERIOD.

"modernization" has brought to India. As a rather dramatic case in point, in the state of Rajasthan, those who own and control most land and who are wealthy and politically powerful are not of the warrior caste, as one would expect, but of the lowest caste. Their tenants and laborers, by contrast, are Brahmins. Thus, the group that is ritually superior to all others finds itself in the same social position as untouchables, whereas the landowners who are the Brahmins' ritual inferiors are superior in all other ways. Meanwhile, a group of leatherworkers in the untouchable category, who have gained political power in India's new democracy, are trying to better their position by claiming they are Brahmins who were tricked in the past into doing defiling work. Although individuals cannot move up or down the caste hierarchy, whole groups can do so depending on claims they can make for higher status and on how well they can manipulate others into acknowledging their claims. Interestingly, the people at the bottom of India's caste system traditionally have not questioned the validity of the system itself so much as their particular position within it.

With their limited mobility, caste-structured societies exemplify **closed-class societies.** Those that permit a great deal of mobility are referred to as **open-class societies.** Even here, however, mobility is apt to be more limited than one might suppose. In the United States, in spite of its "rags-to-riches" ideology, most mobility involves a move up or down only a notch, although if this continues in a family over several generations, it may add up to a major change. Generally, the culture makes much of those relatively rare examples of great upward mobility consistent with its cultural values and does its best to ignore, or at least downplay, the numerous cases of little or no upward, not to mention downward, mobility.

The degree of mobility in a stratified society is related to the prevailing kind of family organization. In societies where the extended family is the usual form, mobility is apt to be difficult, because each individual is strongly tied to the large family group. Hence, for a person to move up to a higher social class, his or her family must move up as well. Mobility is easier for

Closed-class societies. Stratified societies that severely restrict social mobility. • **Open-class societies.** Stratified societies that permit a great deal of social mobility.

In the United States, the ability to "move up" in the system of stratification is increasingly dependent upon access to higher education.

independent nuclear families where the individual is closely tied to fewer persons. Moreover, under neolocal residence, individuals normally leave their family of birth. So it is, then, that through careful marriage, occupational success, and by disassociating themselves from the lower-class family they grew up in, all of which are made possible by residential mobility, individuals can more easily "move up" in society.

Gender Stratification

Closely associated with class and caste stratification is the related phenomenon of gender stratification. For instance, in our earlier discussion of sex as an organizing principle, we saw that in some (but not all) societies, men and women may be regarded as unequal, with the former outranking the latter. Generally speaking, sexual inequality is characteristic of societies stratified in other ways as well; thus women have historically occupied a position of inferiority to men in the class-structured societies of the Western world. Nevertheless, sexual inequality sometimes may be seen in societies not otherwise stratified; in such instances, men and women are always physically as well as conceptually separated from one another. Yet, as the Iroquoian case cited earlier in this chapter demonstrates, not all societies in which men and women are separated exhibit gender stratification.

The rise of gender stratification often seems to be associated with the development of strongly centralized states. For example, among the Maya of Mesoamerica the basic social unit in the past as today was the complementary gender pair. On the household level, men raise the crops and bring in the other raw materials, which the women transform into food, textiles, and other cultural objects. The same complementarity existed in public ritual and politics, but in the last century B.C. at the Maya city of Tikal, things began to change. With the development of strong dynastic rule by men, women began to be excluded from favored places for burial, their graves were not as richly stocked with material items as were those of important men, they all but disappeared from public art, and they were rarely mentioned in inscriptions. When women were portrayed or mentioned, it was because of their relationship to a particular male ruler. Clearly, women came to hold a lesser place in Maya society than did men, although gender stratification was not nearly as marked at the grass roots of society as it was among the elite. When the Tikal state collapsed, as it did in the 9th century A.D., the relationship of equality between men and women returned to what it had been 8 or 9 centuries before.[7]

[7] Haviland, W. A. (1997). The rise and fall of sexual inequality: Death and gender at Tikal, Guatemala. *Ancient Mesoamerica, 8,* 1–12.

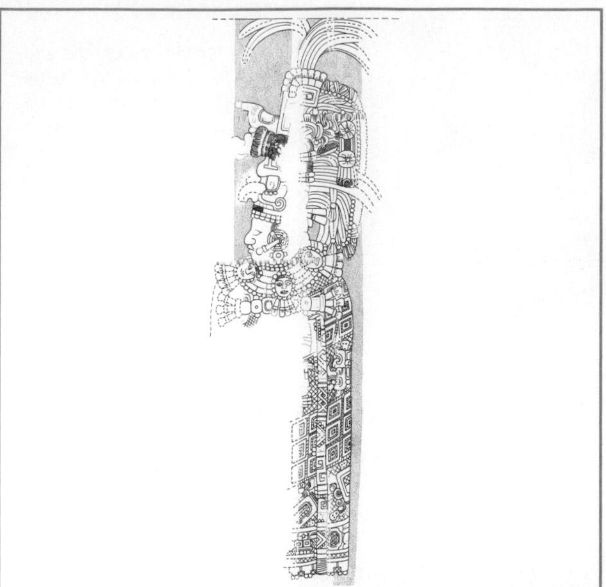

At the ancient Maya city of Tikal, in Central America, one reflection of gender stratification is the rarity of the portrayals of women, compared to men, in the city's public art. The woman shown in this drawing was portrayed on a wooden lintel only because of her relationship to the king who commissioned the temple of which the lintel is a part.

Development of Stratification

Because social stratification of any kind generally makes life oppressive for large segments of a population, the lower classes are usually placated through religion, which promises them a better existence in the hereafter. If they have this to look forward to, they are more likely to accept an existing disadvantaged position. In India, for example, belief in reincarnation and the existence of an incorruptible supernatural power that assigns people to a particular caste position as a reward or punishment for the deeds and misdeeds of past lives justifies one's position in this life. If, however, individuals perform the duties appropriate to their caste in this lifetime, then they can expect to be reborn into a higher caste in a future existence. Truly exemplary performance of their duties may even release them from the cycle of rebirth, to be reunited with the divinity from which all existence springs. In the minds of orthodox Hindus, then, one's caste position is something earned (an achieved status) rather than the accident of birth (ascribed) it appears to outside observers. Thus, although the caste system explicitly recognizes (and accepts as legitimate) inequality between people, it is underlain by an implicit assumption of ultimate equality. This contrasts with the situation in the United States, where the equality of all people is proclaimed even while various groups clearly are treated as unequal.

When considering the origin of social stratification, we must reckon with such common tendencies as the desire for prestige, either for oneself or one's group. Although the impulse need not result inevitably in the ranking of individuals or groups relative to one another, it sometimes may. Among the Iroquois and Hopi Indians and the Sherente and Ugandan peoples, the superiority of some kinship lineages over others is recognized in electing chiefs, performing sacred rituals, and other special tasks, whether or not membership entails any economic advantages.

This sort of situation could easily develop into full-fledged stratification. Just such a development may have taken place among the Maya of Mesoamerica.[8] These people began as horticulturists with a relatively egalitarian, kinship-based organization. In the last centuries B.C., elaborate rituals developed for dealing with the very serious problems of agriculture, such as uncertain rains, vulnerability of crops to a variety of pests, and periodic devastation from hurricanes. As this development took place, a full-time priesthood arose, along with some craft specialization in the service of religion. Out of the priesthood developed, in the last century B.C., the hereditary ruling dynasties mentioned earlier. In this developmental process, certain lineages seem to have monopolized the important civic and ceremonial positions, and so came to be ranked above other lineages, forming the basis of an upper class.

Just as lineages may come to be ranked differentially relative to one another, so may ethnic groups. In South Africa, for example, Europeans came as conquerors, establishing a social order by which they could maintain their favored position. In the United States, the importation of African slaves produced a severely disadvantaged caste-like group at the bottom of the social order. Not only was it nearly impossible for such individuals to rise above this group, but also downward mobility into it was possible, owing to the belief that "a single drop of Black blood" was enough to define one as Black (a belief similar to South African concepts of purity and pollution).

---

[8] Haviland, W. A. (1975). The ancient Maya and the evolution of urban society. *University of Colorado Museum of Anthropology Miscellaneous Series, 37;* and Haviland, W. A., & Moholy-Nagy, H. (1992). Distinguishing the high and mighty from the hoi polloi at Tikal, Guatemala. In A. F. Chase & D. Z. Chase (Eds.). *Mesoamerican elites: An archaeological assessment*. Norman, OK: University of Oklahoma Press.

The high status of the two Maya kings shown in this painting from a pottery vessel is revealed by their jewelry, elaborate headdress, and the fact they sit on thrones. Among these people, stratification arose as certain lineages monopolized important offices.

In the United States, it has taken a long time for African Americans to move up in the class system, though the legacy persists, as they are still disproportionately represented in the lower ranks of society. Even without conquest and/or slavery, ethnic differences often are a factor in the definition of social classes and castes, as not only African Americans but also members of other North American minorities have experienced through the racial stereotyping that leads to social and economic disadvantages.

Sometimes, rather than providing the basis for stratification, ethnicity comes to serve as a metaphor for what began as nothing more than distinctions of class. A dramatic example of this can be found in the African state of Rwanda, where what began simply as class distinctions were misinterpreted by Belgian colonial authorities as differences in ethnicity. Ultimately, they were magnified to the point that the whole country erupted in a bloodbath, illustrating how class systems have built into them the seeds of their own destruction. In Rwanda, this happened through an intersection of class differences with the interests of particular common-interest associations.[9]

Before it became a colony, Rwanda was inhabited by a single people who spoke the same language, shared the same culture and religion, and who lived in the same places. The society was, however, divided into three caste-like strata differentiated by occupation and political status. At the top were the Tutsis, below them were the Hutu, and below them the Twa. Although mobility was difficult, there was some movement between classes.

[9] My discussion of Rwanda is based on de Waal, A. (1994). Genocide in Rwanda. *Anthropology Today, 10* (3), 1 2.

In South Africa, stratification emerged as conquerors excluded the conquered from positions of importance and restricted their access to basic resources. Shown here is the Black township outside the capital of Namibia, until recently ruled from South Africa.

When German and Belgian colonists arrived, they misinterpreted this situation in the light of their own prejudices. The aristocratic Tutsi they saw as a distinct people racially related to the populations in the Middle East. The Hutu peasants were regarded as purely African, while the Twa were seen as a remnant of a primitive aboriginal people. They then proceeded to impose a rigid system of tribute and exploitation, disrupting the existing reciprocity in Hutu-Tutsi relations that had diluted the latter's dominance. As is common in stratified societies, Tutsis tended to be taller than those in the lower classes. However, these differences were highly exaggerated by colonial authorities; in fact, it is rarely possible to tell whether an individual is a Tutsi, Hutu, or Twa from his or her height. Rather, such identification depends upon knowledge of the individual's ancestry and his or her possession of an identity card specifying group membership. This system, a legacy of Belgian rule, was established by law in 1926. Those with 10 or more cows were classified as Tutsi; those with fewer as Hutu, with a small residue as Twa.

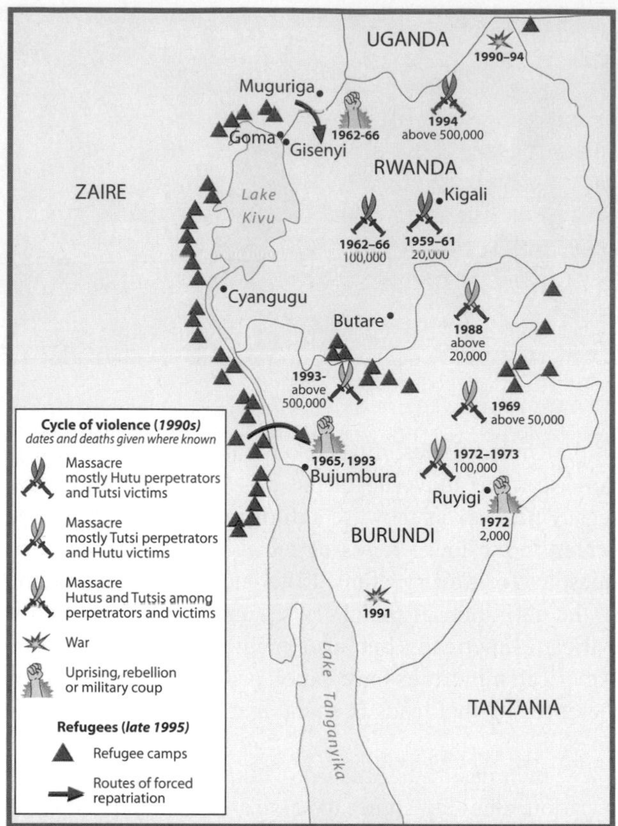

FIGURE 22.2

CONFLICT BETWEEN TUTSIS AND HUTUS IN RWANDA AND NEIGHBORING BURUNDI.

With the three original classes redefined as distinct ethnic groups and codified in law, the stage was set for the genocide that erupted after Rwanda gained independence. This was perpetuated by members of two political parties (common-interest groups), who at first directed violence at members of opposition parties, journalists, and human rights activists, whether Hutu or Tutsi. As the killing spread to rural areas, it became a program of genocide aimed specifically at the Tutsi. Carried out at first by the army, the presidential guard, and paramilitary death squads, the Hutu-controlled government, through use of the media, was able to mobilize much of the civilian population to carry out the killings. In 1991, one man from every 10 houses was armed, following which several hundreds of thousands of Tutsis were murdered by their neighbors, their schoolteachers, their local shopkeepers. Because the situation was misdiagnosed by the international community as spontaneous ethnic violence, the killers were allowed to carry out their slaughter undisturbed, until an uneasy peace was imposed in the mid 1990s (Figure 22.2).

Although the cost is great—social classes do, after all, make life oppressive for large numbers of people—classes may nevertheless perform an integrative function in society. By cutting across some or all lines of kinship, residence, occupation, and age group, depending on the particular society, they counteract potential tendencies for society to fragment into discrete entities. In India diverse national groups were incorporated into the larger society by certification of their leaders as warriors and by marriage of their women to Brahmins. The problem is that stratification, by its very nature, provides a means by which one, usually small, group of people may dominate and make life miserable for large numbers of others, as in the just cited case of Rwanda, or as in South Africa where 4.5 million Whites dominated 25 million non-Whites. In India a succession of conquerors was able to move into the caste hierarchy near its top as warriors.

In any system of stratification, those who dominate proclaim their supposedly "superior" status, which they try to convert into respect, or at least acquiescence on the

In the United States, "racial profiling" is one of the means by which those who control society try to keep others "in their place."

part of the lower classes. As anthropologist Laura Nader points out: "Systems of thought develop over time and reflect the interests of certain classes or groups in the society who manage to universalize their beliefs and values."[10] One sees this, for example, in religious ideologies that assert that the social order is divinely fixed and therefore not to be questioned. Thus, they hope that members of the lower classes will thereby "know their place" and not contest their domination by the "chosen elite." If, however, this domination is contested, the elite usually control the power of the state, which they use to protect their privileged position.

[10] Nader, L. (1997). Controlling processes: Tracing the dynamic components of power. *Current Anthropology, 38,* 271.

CHAPTER SUMMARY

Grouping by sex separates men and women to varying degrees in different societies; in some, they may be together much of the time, while in others they may spend much of their time apart, even to the extreme of eating and sleeping separately. Although men perceive women to be their inferiors in some sexually segregated societies, in others men perceive women as equals.

Age grouping is another form of association that may augment or replace kinship grouping. An age grade is a category of persons, usually of the same sex, organized by age. Age grades in some societies are subdivided into age sets, which include individuals who are initiated into an age grade at the same time who move together through a series of life stages. A specific time is often ritually established for moving from a younger to an older age grade.

The most varied use of age grouping is found in African societies south of the Sahara. Among the Tiriki of East Africa, for example, seven named age sets pass through four successive age grades. Each age set embraces a 15-year span and so opens to accept new initiates every 105 years. In principle, the system resembles our college classes, where, say, the "Class of 2004" (an age set) will move through the four age grades: first year, sophomore, junior, senior.

Common-interest associations are linked with rapid social change and urbanization. They have increasingly assumed the roles formerly played by kinship or age groups. In urban areas they help new arrivals cope with the changes demanded by the move from the village, previous city, or country to the new city. Common-interest associations also are seen in traditional societies, and their roots probably are to be found in the first horticultural villages. Membership may range from voluntary to legally compulsory.

For a long time social scientists mistakenly viewed women's common-interest associations as less developed than men's, largely because of culture-bound assumptions. A question that remains to be resolved is why women are barred from associations in some societies, while in others they participate on an equal basis with men.

Recently, participation in conventional common-interest associations has shown a decline, as individuals have less time for civic participation generally and spend more of their free time in their homes. Compensating for this is the rise of the Internet and "virtual" (online) associations.

A stratified society is divided into two or more categories of people who do not share equally in basic resources, influence, or prestige. This form contrasts with the egalitarian society, which has as many valued positions as persons capable of filling them. Societies may be stratified in various ways, such as by gender, age, social class, or caste. Members of a class enjoy equal or nearly equal access to basic resources and prestige (according to the way the latter is defined). Class differences are not always clear-cut and obvious. Where fine distinctions are made in privileges, the result is a multiplicity of classes. In societies where only gross distinctions are made, only a few social classes may be recognized.

Caste is a special form of social class in which membership is determined by birth and fixed for life. Endogamy is particularly marked within castes, and children automatically belong to their parents' caste. Social class structure is based on role differentiation, although this by itself is not sufficient for stratification. Also necessary are formalized positive and negative attitudes toward roles, and restricted access to the more valued ones.

Social classes are given expression in several ways. One is through verbal evaluation, or what people say about other people in their society. Another is through patterns of association—who interacts with whom, how, and in what context. Social classes are also manifest through symbolic indicators: activities and possessions indicative of class position. Finally, they are reflected by differences in life chances, as high-status people generally live longer and in better health than people of low status.

Mobility is present to a greater or lesser extent in all stratified societies. Open-class societies are those with the easiest mobility. In most cases, however, the move is limited to one rung up or down the social ladder. The degree of mobility is related to factors such as access to higher education or the type of family organization that prevails in a society. Where the extended family is the norm, mobility tends to be severely limited. The independent nuclear family makes mobility easier.

Social stratification can be based on many criteria, such as wealth, legal status, birth, personal qualities, and ideology. A rigidly stratified society with limited mobility normally makes life particularly oppressive for large segments of a population.

CLASSIC READINGS

Bernardi, B. (1985). *Age class systems: Social institutions and policies based on age.* New York: Cambridge University Press.

This is a cross-cultural analysis of age as a device for organizing society and seeing to the distribution and rotation of power.

Bradfield, R. M. (1973). *A natural history of associations.* New York: International Universities Press.

This two-volume work is the first major anthropological study of common-interest associations since 1902. It attempts to provide a comprehensive theory of the origin of associations and their role in kin-based societies.

Hammond, D. (1972). *Associations.* Reading, MA: Addison-Wesley Modular Publications, 14.

This is a brief, first-rate review of anthropological thinking and of the literature on common-interest associations and age groups.

Lenski, G. E. (1966). *Power and privilege: A theory of social stratification.* New York: McGraw-Hill.

Who gets what and why is explained by the distributive process and systems of social stratification in industrial countries: the United States, Russia, Sweden, and Britain. Using a broadly comparative approach, the author makes heavy use of anthropological and historical material, as well as the usual sociological materials on modern industrial societies. The basic approach is theoretical and analytical; the book builds on certain postulates about the nature of humans and society, seeking to develop in a systematic manner an explanation of a variety of patterns of stratification. The theory presented is a synthesis of the two dominant theoretical traditions of the past and present, currently represented in both Marxist and functionalist theory.

Price, T. D., & Feinman, G. M. (Eds.) (1995). *Foundations of social inequality.* New York: Plenam.

This book is a collection of essays by various contributors that examines the emergence of social inequality.

Sanday, P. R. (1981). *Female power and male dominance: On the origins of sexual inequality.* Cambridge: Cambridge University Press.

In this cross-cultural study, Professor Sanday reveals the various ways that male-female relations are organized in human societies and demonstrates that male dominance is not inherent in those relations. Rather, it appears to emerge in situations of stress as a result of such things as chronic food shortages, migration, and colonial domination.

PART VII

The Search for Order: Solving the Problem of Disorder

INTRODUCTION

An irony of human life is that something as fundamental to our existence as cooperation should contain within it the seeds of its own destruction. It is nonetheless true that the groups that people form to fulfill important organizational needs do not just facilitate cooperation among the members of those groups, but they also create conditions that may lead to the disruption of society. A case in point is the gang violence seen in many North American cities. The attitude that "my group is better than your group" is not confined to any one of the world's cultures and it not infrequently takes the form of a sense of rivalry between groups: descent group against descent group, men against women, age grade against age grade, social class against social class, and so forth. This does not mean that such rivalry has to be disruptive; indeed, it may function to ensure that the members of groups perform their jobs well so as not to "lose face" or be subject to ridicule. Rivalry, however, can become a serious problem if it erupts into violence.

The fact is, social living inevitably entails a certain amount of friction—not just between groups but between individual members of groups as well. Thus, any society can count on a degree of disruptive behavior by some of its members at one time or other. Yet, no one can know precisely when such outbursts will occur

or what form they will take. Not only does this uncertainty go against the predictability social life demands, but it also goes against the deep-seated psychological need each individual has for structure and certainty, which we discussed in Chapter 16. Therefore, every society must have means by which conflicts can be resolved and breakdown of the social order prevented. Control of people's behavior and political systems, which have as their primary function the maintenance of the social order, is the subject of Chapter 23.

Religion and politics may seem like strange bedfellows, but both fulfill the same goal: to protect society against the unexpected and unwanted. Effective though a culture may be in equipping, organizing, and controlling a society to provide for its members' needs, certain problems always defy existing technological or organizational solutions. The response of every culture is to devise a set of beliefs, with a set of rituals to express them, aimed at solving these problems through manipulation of supernatural beings and powers. In short, what we think of as "religion" and "magic" serve to transform the uncertainties of life into certainties. In addition, they may serve as powerful integrative forces through commonly held values, beliefs, and practices. Also important is rationalization of the existing social order in such a way that it becomes a moral order as well. Thus, there is a link between "religion" and "magic" on the one hand and political organization and social control on the other. Culture and the supernatural, then, is an appropriate subject for discussion in Chapter 24 of this section on the search for order.

Like "religion" and "magic," the arts also contribute to human well-being and help give shape and significance to life. Indeed, the relationship between art and religion goes deeper than this, for much of what we call art has been created in the service of "religion": myths to explain ritual practices, objects to portray important deities, music and dances for ceremonial use, pictorial art to record supernatural experiences and/or to serve as objects of supernatural power in their own right, and the like. In a very real sense, music, dance, or any other form of art, like magic, exploits psychological susceptibilities so as to enchant other people and cause them to perceive social reality in a way favorable to the interests of the enchanter. And, like "religion," art of any kind expresses the human search for order, in that the artist gives form to some essentially formless raw material. Accordingly, a chapter on the arts follows that on culture and the supernatural, concluding this section. ■

CHAPTER 23

POLITICAL ORGANIZATION AND SOCIAL CONTROL

Political organization in human societies takes many forms, of which the state is but one. One reason states generally do not last very long is that they are often controlled by members of one nationality who try to repress (or even exterminate) other nationalities within the state. This is what Europeans have tried to do in the Americas over the 500 years since Columbus. Here, members of Indian nations march to protest the 500th anniversary of the Portuguese arrival in Brazil, while armed police stand by.

CHAPTER PREVIEW

1 What Is Political Organization?

Political organization refers to the means by which a society maintains order internally and manages its affairs with other societies externally. It may be relatively uncentralized and informal, as in bands and tribes, or more centralized and formal, as in chiefdoms and states.

2 How Is Order Maintained Within a Society?

Social controls may be internalized—"built into" individuals—or externalized, in the form of sanctions. Built-in controls rely on deterrents such as personal shame and fear of supernatural punishment; negative sanctions rely on actions other members of society take toward specifically approved or disapproved behavior. Positive sanctions encourage approved behavior, while negative sanctions discourage disapproved behavior. Negative sanctions are called laws if they are formalized and enforced by an authorized political agency. Consequently, we may say that laws are sanctions, but not all sanctions are laws. Similarly, societies do not maintain order through law alone.

3 How Is Order Maintained Between Societies?

Just as the threatened or actual use of force may be employed to maintain order within a society, it also may be used to manage affairs among bands, lineages, clans, or whatever the largest autonomous political units may be. Not all societies, however, rely on physical force, because some do not practice warfare as we know it. Such societies generally have views of themselves and their place in the world quite different from those characteristic of centrally organized states.

4 How Do Political Systems Obtain People's Allegiance?

No form of political organization can function without the loyalty and support of those it governs. To a greater or lesser extent, political organizations the world over seek to legitimize their power through recourse to supernatural powers. In uncentralized systems people freely give loyalty and cooperation because everyone participates in making decisions. Centralized systems, by contrast, rely more heavily on force and coercion, although in the long run these may lessen the system's effectiveness.

Louis XIV proclaimed, "I am the state." With this sweeping statement, the king declared absolute rule over France; he held himself to be the law, the lawmaker, the court, the judge, jailer, and executioner—in short, the seat of all political power in France.

Louis XIV took a great deal of responsibility on his royal shoulders; had he actually performed each of these functions, he would have done the work of thousands of people, the number required to keep the machinery of a large political organization such as a state running at full steam. As a form of political organization, the 17th-century French state was not much different from those that exist in modern times. All large states require elaborate centralized structures, with hierarchies of executives, legislators, and judges who initiate, pass, and enforce laws that affect large numbers of people.

Such complex structures, however, have not always existed: Few European states are much older than the United States, and many are much younger. Even today some societies depend on far less formal means of organization. In some societies, flexible and informal kinship systems with leaders who lack real power prevail. Problems, such as homicide and theft, are perceived as serious "family quarrels" rather than affairs that affect the entire community. Between these two polarities of political organization lies a world of variety, including societies with chiefs, Big Men, or charismatic leaders and segmented tribal societies with multicentric authority systems. Such disparity prompts this question: What is political organization?

The term *political organization* refers to the way power—the ability to control others' behavior—is distributed and embedded in society, whether in organizing a giraffe hunt or raising an army. In other words, political organization has to do with the way power is used to coordinate and regulate behavior so that order is maintained. Government, on the other hand, consists of an administrative system having specialized personnel that may or may not form a part of the political organization, depending on the society's complexity. Some form of political organization exists in all societies, but it is not always a government.

KINDS OF POLITICAL SYSTEMS

Political organization is the means through which a society maintains social order and reduces social disorder. It assumes a variety of forms among the peoples of the world, but scholars have simplified this complex subject by identifying four basic kinds of political systems: bands, tribes, chiefdoms, and states. The first two are uncentralized systems; the latter two are centralized.

Uncentralized Political Systems

Until recently, many non-Western peoples have had neither chiefs with established rights and duties nor any fixed form of government, as those who live in modern states understand the term. Instead, marriage and kinship form the principal means of social organization among such peoples. The economies of these societies are primarily of a subsistence type, and populations are typically quite small. Leaders do not have real power to force compliance with the society's customs or rules, but if individual members do not conform, they may become targets of scorn and gossip or even be banished. Important decisions are usually made in a collective manner by agreement among adults, often including women as well as men; dissenting members may decide to act with the majority, or they may choose to adopt some other course of action, if they are willing to risk the social consequences. This form of political organization provides great flexibility, which in many situations offers an adaptive advantage.

BAND ORGANIZATION

The **band** is a small group of politically independent, though related, households and is the least complicated form of political organization. Bands usually are found among food foragers and other nomadic societies where people organize into politically autonomous extended-family groups that usually camp together, although the members of such families frequently may split into smaller groups for periods to forage for food or visit other relatives. Bands are thus kin groups, composed of men and/or women who are related (or are assumed to be) with their spouses and unmarried children. Bands may be characterized as associations of related families who occupy a common (often vaguely defined) territory and who live there together, so long as environmental and subsistence circumstances are favorable. The band is probably the oldest form of political organization, since all humans were once food foragers and remained so until the development of farming and pastoralism over the past 10,000 years.

Since bands are small, numbering at most a few hundred people, no real need exists for formal, centralized political systems. In egalitarian groups, where everyone

Band. A small group of related households occupying a particular region that gather periodically on an **ad hoc** basis but that do not yield their sovereignty to the larger collective.

TABLE 23.1 TYPES OF POLITICAL ORGANIZATION

	Band	Tribe	Chiefdom	State
Membership				
Number of people	dozens	hundreds	thousands	tens of thousands and up
Settlement pattern	mobile	fixed: 1 or more villages	fixed: 1 or more villages	fixed: many villages and cities
Basis of relationships	kin	descent groups	rank and residence	class and residence
Ethnicities and languages	1	1	1	1 or more
Government				
Decision making, leadership	"egalitarian"	"egalitarian" or Big-Man	centralized, hereditary	centralized
Bureaucracy	none	none	none, or 1 or 2 levels	many levels
Monopoly of force and information	no	no	yes	yes
Conflict resolution	informal	informal	centralized	laws, judges
Hierarchy of settlement	no	no	no → paramount village or town	capital
Economy				
Food production	no	no → yes	yes → intensive	intensive
Division of labor	no	no	no → yes	yes
Exchanges	reciprocal	reciprocal	redistributive ("tribute")	redistributive ("taxes")
Control of land	band	descent group	chief	various
Society				
Stratified	no	no	ranked by kin	yes, not by kin
Slavery	no	no	small-scale	large-scale
Luxury goods for elite	no	no	yes	yes
Public architecture	no	no	no → yes	yes
Indigenous literacy	no	no	no	often

A horizontal arrow indicates that the attribute varies between less and more complex societies of that type.

is related to—and knows on a personal basis—everyone else with whom dealings are required and where most everyone values "getting along," the potential for conflicts to develop is quite low. Many of those that do arise are settled informally through gossip, ridicule, direct negotiation, or mediation. In the latter instances, the emphasis is on achieving a solution considered just by most parties concerned rather than conforming to some abstract law or rule. Where all else fails, disgruntled individuals have the option of leaving the band to go live in another where they may have relatives.

Decisions affecting a band are made with the participation of all its adult members, with an emphasis on achieving consensus rather than a simple majority. Leaders become such by virtue of their abilities and serve in that capacity only so long as they retain the confidence

Toma, a Ju/'hoansi headman known to many North Americans through the documentary film *The Hunters.*

of the community. Thus, they have neither a guaranteed hold on their position for a specified length of time nor the power to force people to abide by their decisions. People will follow them only as long as they consider it to be in their best interests, and a leader who exceeds what people are willing to accept quickly loses followers.

An example of the informal nature of leadership in the band is found among the Ju/'hoansi Bushmen of the Kalahari Desert, whom we met in Chapters 16 and 17. Each Ju/'hoansi band is composed of a group of families who live together, linked to one another and to the headman or, less often, headwoman through kinship. Although each band has rights to the territory it occupies and the resources within it, two or more bands may range over the same territory. The head, called the *kxau,* or "owner," is the focal point for the band's claims on the territory. The headman or headwoman does not really own the land or resources but symbolically personifies the rights of band members to them. If the head leaves a territory to live elsewhere, he or she ceases to be the band's head, and people turn to someone else to lead them.

The head coordinates the Ju/'hoansi band's movements when resources are no longer adequate for subsistence in a particular territory. This leader's chief duty is to plan when and where the group will move; when the move begins, his or her position is at the head of the line. The leader chooses the site for the new settlement and has the first choice of a spot for his or her own fire. There are no other rewards or duties. For example, a headman does not organize hunting parties, trading expeditions, the making of artifacts, or gift giving; nor does he make marriage arrangements. Instead, individuals initiate their own activities. The headman or headwoman is not a judge and does not punish other band members. Wrongdoers are judged and held accountable by public opinion, usually expressed by gossip among band members. A prime technique for resolving disputes, or even avoiding them in the first place, is mobility. Those unable to get along with others of their group simply move to another group where kinship ties give them rights of entry.

TRIBAL ORGANIZATION

The second type of uncentralized or multicentric authority system is the **tribe,** a word that, unfortunately, is used in different ways by different people. Among the general public, it is used commonly to label any people who are not organized into states, regardless of whether or not they constitute what anthropologists would call bands, tribes, or chiefdoms. Sometimes, the term is even applied to non-Western peoples who in fact had strongly centralized states (the Aztecs, for example), a practice no more warranted than calling the Chinese people a tribe. Historically,

Tribe. A group of nominally independent communities occupying a specific region that share a common language and culture and that are integrated by some unifying factor.

Shown here is a meeting of the Navajo Tribal Council, a nontraditional governing body created in response to requirements set by the U.S. government in order for the Navajo to exercise national sovereignty.

Europeans coined the term to contrast people whom they regarded as inferior with supposedly superior, "civilized" Europeans. The word is still often used in a derogatory way, as when political unrest in many parts of the world is blamed on "tribalism," which it is not (usually, the strife is the direct consequence of the creation of multinational states that make it possible for a governing elite of one nationality to exploit others for their own benefit).[1] To complicate matters, the term *tribe* also has a distinct legal meaning in the United States; it refers to a centralized political organization imposed upon American Indian communities that traditionally were organized in a variety of ways—some as bands, some as tribes (in the anthropological sense), and some as chiefdoms.

So what, then, do anthropologists have in mind when they speak of tribal organization? To them, a tribal system involves separate bands or villages integrated by factors such as clans that unite people in separate communities or age grades or associations that crosscut kinship or territorial boundaries. In such cases people sacrifice a degree of household autonomy to some larger-order group in return for greater security against enemy attacks or starvation. Typically, though not invariably, a tribe has an economy based on some form of crop cultivation or herding. Since these production methods usually yield more food than those of the food-foraging band, tribal membership is usually larger than band membership. Compared to bands, where population densities are usually less than 1 person per square mile, tribal population densities generally exceed 1 person per square mile, and may be as high as 250 per square mile. Greater population density in tribes than in bands brings a new set of problems to be solved as opportunities for bickering, begging, adultery, and theft increase markedly, especially among people living in sedentary villages.

Each tribe consists of one or more small, autonomous local communities, which may then form alliances with one another for various purposes. As in the band, political organization in the tribe is informal and temporary. Whenever a situation requiring political integration of all or several groups within the tribe arises—perhaps for defense, to carry out a raid, to pool resources in times of scarcity, or to capitalize on a windfall that must be distributed quickly lest it spoil—they join to deal with the situation in a cooperative manner. When the problem is satisfactorily solved, each group then returns to its autonomous state.

Leadership among tribes is also informal. The Navajo Indians, for example, did not think of government as something fixed and all-powerful, and leadership was not vested in a central authority. A local leader was a man respected for his age, integrity, and wisdom. His advice

---

[1] Whitehead, N. L., & Ferguson, R. B. (1993, November 10). Deceptive stereotypes about tribal warfare (p. A48). *Chronicle of Higher Education.* Van Den Berghe, P. L. (1992). The modern state: Nation builder or nation killer? *International Journal of Group Tensions, 92* (3), 199–200.

therefore was sought frequently, but he had no formal means of control and could not force any decision on those who asked for his help. Group decisions were made by public consensus, although the most influential man usually played a key role in reaching a decision. Among the social mechanisms that induced members to abide by group decisions were withdrawal of cooperation, gossip, criticism, and the belief that antisocial actions caused disease.

Another example of tribal leadership is the Melanesian Big Man. Such men are leaders of localized descent groups or of a territorial group. The Big Man combines a small amount of interest in his tribe's welfare with a great deal of cunning and calculation for his own personal gain. His authority is personal; he does not come to office in any formal sense, nor is he elected. His status is the result of acts that raise him above most other tribe members and attract to him a number of loyal followers.

Typical of this form of political organization are the Kapauku of west New Guinea. Among them, the Big Man is called the *tonowi,* or "rich one." To achieve this status, one must be male, wealthy, generous, and eloquent; physical bravery and skills in dealing with the supernatural also are frequent characteristics of a *tonowi,* but they are not essential. The *tonowi* functions as the headman of the village unit.

Kapauku culture places a high value on wealth, so it is not surprising that a wealthy man is considered successful and admirable. Yet the possession of wealth must be coupled with the trait of generosity, which in this society means not gift giving but willingness to make loans. Wealthy men who refuse to lend money to other villagers may be ostracized, ridiculed, and, in extreme cases, actually executed by a group of warriors. This social pressure ensures that economic wealth is rarely hoarded but is distributed throughout the group.

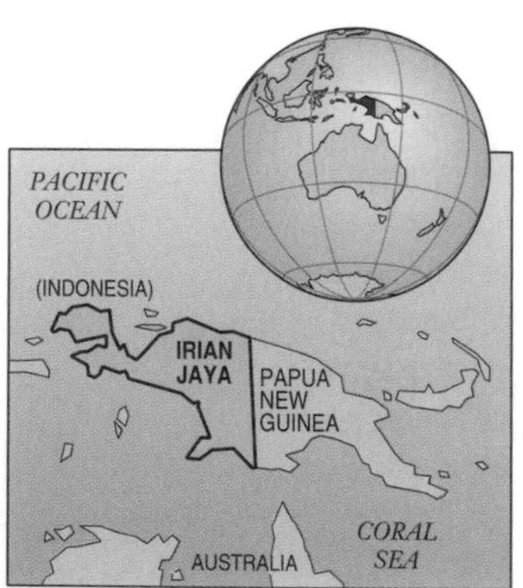

Through the loans he makes the *tonowi* acquires his political power. Other villagers comply with his requests because they are in his debt (often without paying interest), and they do not want to have to repay their loans. Those who have not yet borrowed from the *tonowi* may wish to do so in the future, and so they, too, want to keep his goodwill.

Other sources of support for the *tonowi* are apprentices he has taken into his household for training. They are fed, housed, given a chance to learn the *tonowi*'s business wisdom, and given a loan to get a wife when they leave; in return, they act as messengers and bodyguards. Even after they leave his household, these men are tied to the *tonowi* by bonds of affection and gratitude. Political support also comes from the *tonowi*'s kinsmen, whose relationship brings with it varying obligations.

The *tonowi* functions as a leader in a wide variety of situations. He represents his group in dealing with outsiders and other villages; he acts as negotiator and/or

This Big Man from New Guinea is wearing his "official" regalia.

judge when disputes break out among his followers. Leopold Pospisil, who studied the Kapauku notes:

> The multiple functions of a *tonowi* are not limited to the political and legal fields only. His word also carries weight in economic and social matters. He is especially influential in determining proper dates for pig feasts and pig markets, in inducing specific individuals to become co-sponsors at feasts, in sponsoring communal dance expeditions to other villages, and in initiating large projects, such as extensive drainage ditches and main fences or bridges, the completion of which requires a joint effort of the whole community.[2]

The *tonowi*'s wealth comes from his success at pig breeding (as we discussed in Chapter 14), for pigs are the focus of the entire Kapauku economy. Like all kinds of cultivation and domestication, raising pigs requires a combination of strength, skill, and luck. It is not uncommon for a *tonowi* to lose his fortune rapidly due to bad management or bad luck with his pigs. Thus the Kapauku political structure shifts frequently; as one man loses wealth and consequently power, another gains it and becomes a *tonowi*. These changes confer a degree of flexibility on the political organization and prevent any one *tonowi* from holding political power for too long.

KINSHIP ORGANIZATION

In many tribal societies (as among the Kapauku) the organizing unit and seat of political authority is the clan, an association of people who believe themselves to share a common ancestry. Within the clan, elders or headmen regulate members' affairs and represent their clan in relations with other clans. As a group, the elders of all the clans may form a council that acts within the community or for the community in dealings with outsiders. Because clan members usually do not all live together in one community, clan organization facilitates joint action with members of related communities when necessary.

Another form of tribal kinship bond that provides political organization is the **segmentary lineage system.** This system is similar in operation to the clan, but it is less extensive and is relatively rare. The best known examples are East African societies such as the Somali and the Dinka or Nuer of the Sudan: pastoral nomads who are highly mobile and widely scattered over large territories. Unlike other East African pastoralists (the Maasai, for example), they lack the age-grading organization that cuts across descent group membership.

The economy of the segmentary tribe is generally just above subsistence level. Production is small-scale, and the labor pool is just large enough to provide necessities. Since each lineage in the tribe produces the same goods, none depends on another for goods or services. Political organization among segmentary lineage societies is usually informal: They have neither political offices nor chiefs, although older tribal members may exercise some personal authority. In his classic study of segmentary lineage organization, Marshall Sahlins describes how this works among the Nuer.[3] According to Sahlins, segmentation is the normal process of tribal growth. It is also the social means of temporary unification of a fragmented tribal society to join in particular action. The segmentary lineage may be viewed as a substitute for the fixed political structure that a tribe cannot maintain.

Among the Nuer, who number some 200,000 people living in the swampland and savanna of Sudan, at least

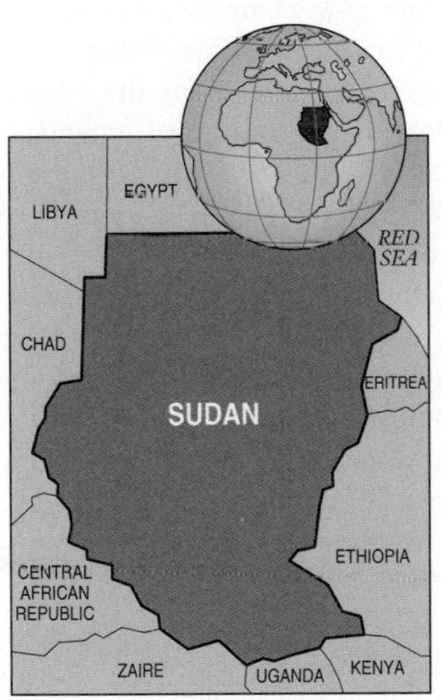

[2] Pospisil, L. (1963) *The Kapauku Papuans of West New Guinea* (pp. 51–52). New York: Holt, Rinehart and Winston.

[3] Sahlins, M. (1961). The segmentary lineage: An organization of predatory expansion. *American Anthropologist, 63,* 322–343.

Segmentary lineage system. A form of political organization in which a larger group is broken up into clans that are further divided into lineages.

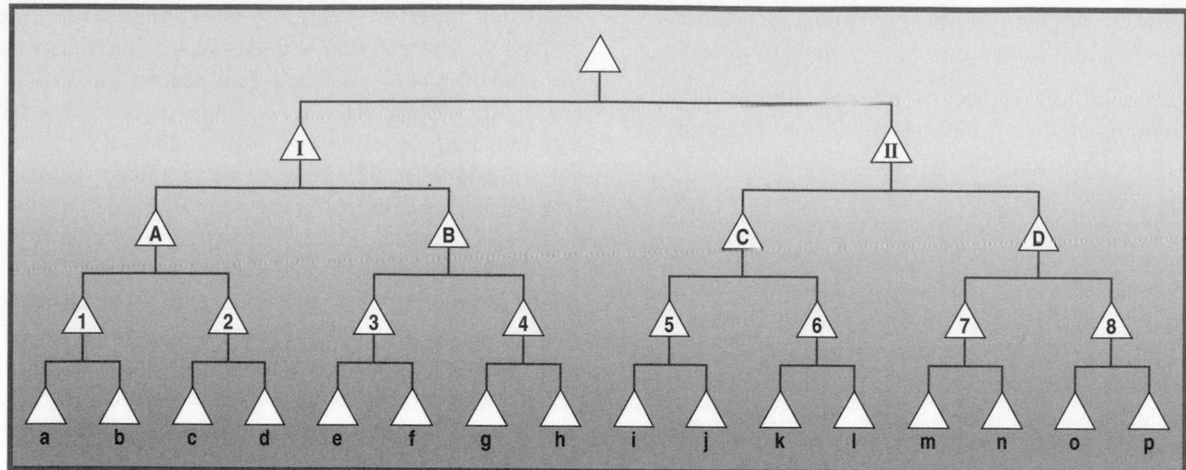

FIGURE 23.1

SEGMENTARY LINEAGE ORGANIZATION: a AND b REPRESENT MINIMAL LINEAGES OF 1; 1 AND 2 REPRESENT MINOR LINEAGES OF A; A AND B REPRESENT MAJOR LINEAGES OF I; AND I AND II REPRESENT MAXIMAL LINEAGES OF A SINGLE CLAN. IN A SERIOUS DISPUTE BETWEEN (SAY) A AND E, MEMBERS OF B, C, AND D WILL JOIN FORCES AGAINST E BECAUSE THEY ARE MORE CLOSELY RELATED TO A THAN ANY ARE TO E.

20 clans exist. Each is patrilineal and segmented into maximal lineages; each of these is in turn segmented into major lineages, which are segmented into minor lineages, which in turn are segmented into minimal lineages. The minimal lineage is a group descended from one great-grandfather or great-great-grandfather (Figure 23.1).

The lineage segments among the Nuer are all equal, and no real leadership or political organization at all exists above the level of the autonomous minimal or primary segments. The entire superstructure of the lineage is nothing more than an alliance, active only during conflicts between any of the minimal segments. In any serious dispute between members of different minimal lineage segments, members of all other segments take the side of the contestant to whom they are most closely related, and the issue is then joined between the higher-order lineages involved. Such a system of political organization is known as *complementary* or *balanced opposition.*

Disputes among the Nuer are frequent, as they are among others with similar organization, and under the segmentary lineage system, they can lead to widespread feuds. This possible source of social disruption is minimized by the actions of the "leopard-skin chief," not really a chief but a holder of a ritual office of conciliation. The leopard-skin chief has no political power and is viewed as standing outside the lineage network. All he can do is try to persuade feuding lineages to accept payment in "blood cattle" rather than taking another life. His mediation gives each side the chance to back down gracefully before too many people are killed; but if the participants are for some reason unwilling to compromise, the leopard-skin chief has no authority to enforce a settlement.

AGE-GRADE ORGANIZATION

Age-grade systems provide a tribal society with a means of political integration beyond the kin group. Under this system, youths are initiated into an age grade, following which they pass as sets from one age grade to another at appropriate ages. Age grades and sets cut across territorial and kin groupings and thus may be important means of political organization. This was the case with the Tiriki of East Africa, whose age grades and sets we examined in Chapter 22. Among them, the warrior age grade guarded the country, while judicial elders resolved disputes. Between these two age grades were elder warriors, who were in a sense understudies to the judicial elders. The oldest age grade, the ritual elders, advised on matters involving the well-being of all the Tiriki people. Thus, the tribe's political affairs were in the hands of the age grades and their officers. East African pastoralists, with age-grading like the Tiriki generally experience less feuding than do those with segmentary lineage organization.

ASSOCIATION ORGANIZATION

Common-interest associations that function as politically integrative systems within tribes are found in many parts of the world, including Africa, Melanesia, and India. A

Among the Nuer, the leopard-skin chief tries to settle disputes between lineages.

good example of association organization functioned during the 19th century among the Plains Indians of the United States, such as the Cheyenne, whom we will talk about again later in this chapter. The basic Cheyenne territorial and political unit was the band, but seven military societies, or warriors' clubs, were common to the entire tribe; the clubs functioned in several areas. A boy might be invited to join one of these societies when he achieved warrior status, whereupon he became familiar with the society's particular insignia, songs, and rituals. In addition to their military functions, the warriors' societies also had ceremonial and social functions.

The Cheyenne warriors' routine daily tasks consisted of overseeing movements in the camp, protecting a moving column, and enforcing rules against individual hunting when the whole tribe was on a buffalo hunt. In addition, each warrior society had its own repertoire of dances the members performed on special ceremonial occasions. Since each Cheyenne band had identical military societies bearing identical names, the societies served to integrate the entire tribe for military and political purposes.[4]

Centralized Political Systems

In bands and tribes, political authority is uncentralized, and each group is economically and politically autonomous. Political organization is vested in kinship, age, and common-interest groups. Populations are small and relatively homogeneous, with people engaged for the most part in the same sorts of activities throughout their lives. As a society's social life becomes more complex, however, as population rises and technology becomes more complex, and as specialization of labor and trade networks produce surpluses of goods, the opportunity for some individuals or groups to exercise control increases. In such societies, political authority and power are concentrated in a single individual—the chief—or in a body of individuals—the state. The state is a form of organization found in societies where each individual must interact on a regular basis with large numbers of people with diversified interests who are neither kin nor close acquaintances.

CHIEFDOMS

A **chiefdom** is a regional polity in which two or more local groups are organized under a single ruling individual—the chief—who is at the head of a ranked hierarchy of people. An individual's status in such a polity is determined by the closeness of his or her relationship to the chief. Those closest are officially superior and receive deferential treatment from those in lower ranks.

The office of the chief is usually for life and often hereditary, passing from a man to his own or his sister's son, depending on whether descent is reckoned patrilineally or matrilineally. Unlike the headmen in bands and lineages, the chief is generally a true authority figure, and his authority serves to unite his people in all affairs and at all times. For example, a chief can distribute land among his community members and recruit people into his military service. Chiefdoms have a recognized hierarchy consisting of major and minor

4 Hoebel, E. A. (1960). *The Cheyennes: Indians of the Great Plains.* New York: Holt, Rinehart and Winston.

Chiefdom. A regional polity in which two or more local groups are organized under a single chief, who is at the head of a ranked hierarchy of people.

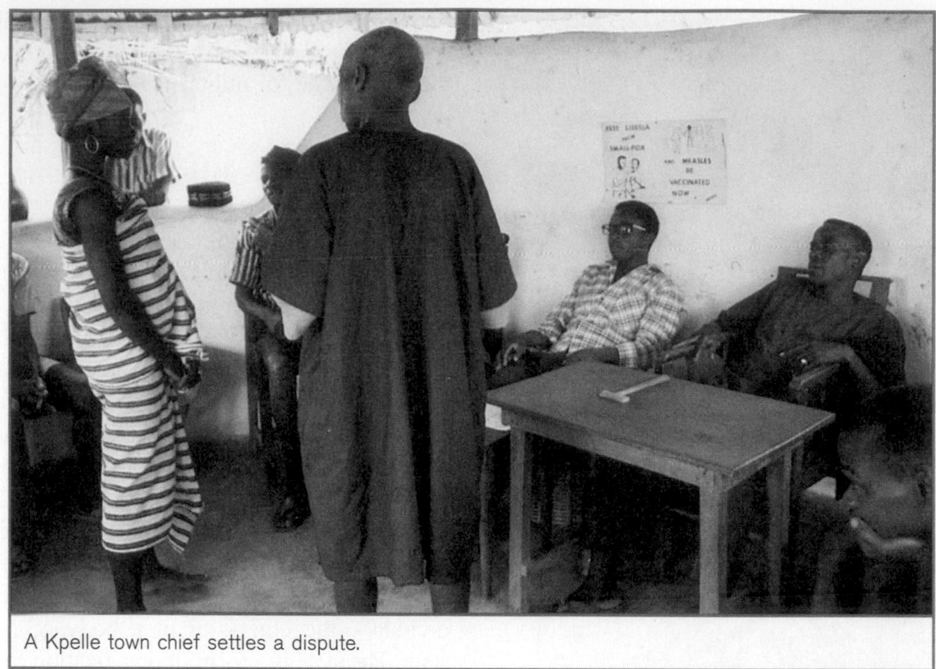

A Kpelle town chief settles a dispute.

authorities who control major and minor subdivisions. Such an arrangement is, in effect, a chain of command, linking leaders at every level. It serves to bind groups in the heartland to the chief's headquarters, be it a mud and dung hut or a marble palace.

The chief controls the economic activities of his people. Chiefdoms involve typically redistributive systems; the chief has control over surplus goods and perhaps even over the community's labor force. Thus, he may demand a quota of rice from farmers, which he will redistribute to the entire community. Similarly, he may recruit laborers to build irrigation works, a palace, or a temple.

The chief may also amass a great amount of personal wealth and pass it on to his heirs. Land, cattle, and luxury goods produced by specialists can be collected by the chief and become part of his power base. Moreover, high-ranking families of the chiefdom may engage in the same practice and use their possessions as evidence of status.

An example of this form of political organization may be seen among the Kpelle of Liberia in West Africa.[5] Among them is a class of paramount chiefs, each of whom presides over one of the Kpelle chiefdoms (each of which is now a district of the Liberian state). The paramount chiefs' traditional tasks are hearing disputes, preserving order, seeing to the upkeep of trails, and maintaining "medicines." In addition, they are now salaried officials of the Liberian government, mediating between it and their own people. Other rewards a paramount chief receives include a commission on taxes collected within his chiefdom, a commission for laborers furnished for the rubber plantations, a portion of court fees collected, a stipulated amount of rice from each household, and gifts from people who come to request favors and intercessions. In keeping with his exalted station in life, a paramount chief has at his disposal uniformed messengers, a literate clerk, and the symbols of wealth: many wives, embroidered gowns, and freedom from manual labor.

[5] Gibbs, J. L., Jr. (1965). The Kpelle of Liberia. In J. L. Gibbs, Jr. (Ed.). *Peoples of Africa* (pp. 216–218). New York: Holt, Rinehart and Winston.

In a ranked hierarchy beneath each Kpelle paramount chief are several lesser chiefs: one for each district within the chiefdom, one for each town within a district, and one for each quarter of all but the smallest towns. Each acts as a kind of lieutenant for his chief of the next higher rank and also serves as a liaison between him and those of lower rank. Unlike paramount or district chiefs, who are comparatively remote, town and quarter chiefs are readily accessible to people at the local level.

Traditionally chiefdoms in all parts of the world have been highly unstable. This happens as lesser chiefs try to take power from higher ranking chiefs or as paramount chiefs vie with one another for supreme power. In precolonial Hawaii, for example, war was the way to gain territory and maintain power; great chiefs set out to conquer one another in an effort to become paramount chief of all the islands. When one chief conquered another, the loser and all his nobles were dispossessed of all property and were lucky if they escaped alive. The new chief then appointed his own supporters to positions of political power. As a consequence, there was very little continuity of governmental or religious administration.

Use of force by the state controlled by one nationality against members of other nationalities within their boundaries is exemplified by this photo of Serbian police beating an Albanian in the capital of Kosovo.

STATE SYSTEMS

The **state,** the most formal of political organizations, is (like stratification) one of the hallmarks of civilization. In the state, political power is centralized in a government, which may legitimately use physical force to regulate the affairs of its citizens, as well as its relations with other states. As anthropologist Bruce Knauft observes:

> It is likely . . . that coercion and violence as systematic means of organizational constraint developed especially with the increasing socioeconomic complexity and potential for political hierarchy afforded by substantial food surplus and food production.[6]

Associated with increased food production is increased population. Together, these lead to a filling in of the landscape, improvements such as irrigation and terracing, carefully managed rotation cycles, intensive competition for clearly demarcated lands, and rural populations large enough to support market systems and a specialized urban sector. Under such conditions, corporate groups that stress exclusive membership proliferate, ethnic differentiation and ethnocentrism become more pronounced, and the potential for social conflict increases dramatically. Given these circumstances, state institutions, which minimally involve a bureaucracy, a military, and (usually) an official religion, provide a means for numerous and diverse groups to function together as an integrated whole.

Although their guiding ideology pretends that they are permanent and stable, the truth is, since their first appearance some 5,000 years ago, states have been anything but permanent. Whatever stability they have achieved has been short term at best; over the long term, they show a clear tendency toward instability and transience. Nowhere have states even begun to show the staying power exhibited by more uncentralized political systems, the longest lasting social forms invented by humans.

An important distinction to make at this point is between **nation** and state. Today, there are roughly almost 200 states in the world, and most did not exist before the end of World War II. By contrast, probably about 5,000

[6] Knauft, B. M. (1991). Violence and sociality in human evolution. *Current Anthropology, 32,* 391.

State. In anthropology, a centralized political system that may legitimately use force to maintain social order. • **Nation.** Communities of people who see themselves as "one people" on the basis of common ancestry, history, society, institutions, ideology, language, territory, and (often) religion.

nations exist in the world today. "What makes each a nation is that its people share a language, culture, territorial base, and political organization and history."[7] Today, states commonly have living within their boundaries people of more than one nation; for example, the Yanomami are but one of many nations within the state of Brazil (other Yanomami live within the state of Venezuela). Rarely do state and nation coincide, as they do, for example, in Iceland, Japan, Somalia, and Swaziland. By contrast, some 73% of the world's states are multinational.[8]

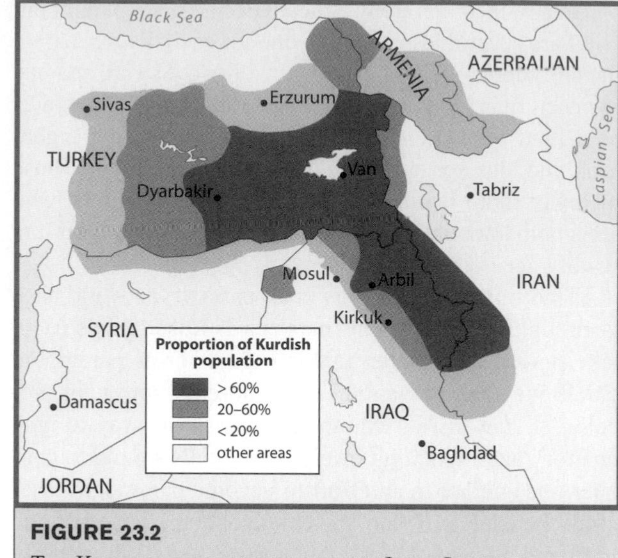

FIGURE 23.2

THE KURDS, MOST OF WHOM LIVE IN IRAN, IRAQ, AND TURKEY, ARE AN EXAMPLE OF A STATELESS NATION.

An important aspect of the state is its delegation of authority to maintain order within and outside its borders. Police, foreign ministries, war ministries, and other bureaucracies function to control and punish disruptive acts of crime, terror, and rebellion. By such agencies the state asserts authority impersonally and in a consistent, predictable manner.

Western forms of government, like that of the United States (in reality a megastate), of course, are state governments, and their organization and workings are undoubtedly familiar to most everyone. An example of a not-so-familiar state is that of the Swazi of Swaziland (one of the world's few true nation-states), a Bantu-speaking people who live in southeast Africa.[9] They are primarily farmers, but cattle raising is more highly valued than farming: the ritual, wealth, and power of their authority system are all intricately linked with cattle. In addition to farming and cattle raising, there is some specialization of labor; certain people become specialists in ritual, smithing, wood carving, and pottery. Their goods and services are traded, although the Swazi do not have elaborate markets.

The traditional Swazi authority system was characterized by a highly developed dual monarchy (now a thing of the past), a hereditary aristocracy, and elaborate kinship rituals, as well as by statewide age sets. The king and his mother were the central figures of all national activity, linking all the people of the Swazi state: They presided over higher courts, summoned national gatherings, controlled age classes, allocated land, disbursed national wealth, took precedence in ritual, and helped organize important social events.

Advising the king were the senior princes, who were usually his uncles and half-brothers. Between the king and the princes were two specially created *tinsila,* or "blood brothers," who were chosen from certain common clans. These men were his shields, protecting him from evildoers and serving him in intimate personal situations. In addition, the king was guided by two *tindvuna,* or counselors, one civil and one military. The people of the state made their opinions known through two councils: the *liqoqo,* or privy council (dissolved in 1986), composed of senior princes, and the *libanda,* or council of state,

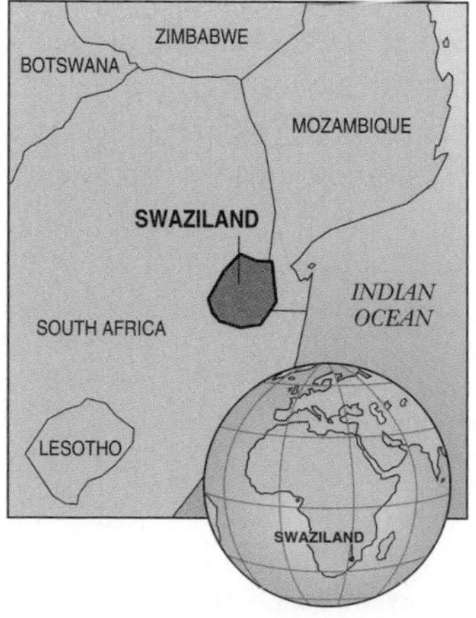

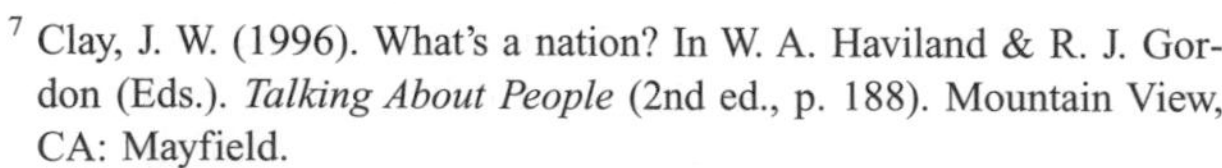

[7] Clay, J. W. (1996). What's a nation? In W. A. Haviland & R. J. Gordon (Eds.). *Talking About People* (2nd ed., p. 188). Mountain View, CA: Mayfield.

[8] Van Den Berghe, P. L. (1992). The modern state: Nation builder or nation killer? *International Journal of Group Tensions, 92* (3), 193.

[9] Kuper, H. (1965). The Swazi of Swaziland. In J. L. Gibbs, Jr. (Ed.). *Peoples of Africa* (pp. 475–512). New York: Holt, Rinehart and Winston.

composed of chiefs and headmen and open to all adult males of the state. The *liqoqo* could advise the king, make decisions, and carry them out. For example, they could rule on questions about land, education, traditional ritual, court procedure, and transport.

Swazi government extended from the smallest local unit—the homestead—upward to the central administration. The head of a homestead had legal and administrative powers; he was responsible for the crimes of those under him, controlled their property, and spoke for them before his superiors. On the district level, political organization was similar to that of the central government. The relationship between a district chief, however, and his subjects was personal and familiar; he knew all the families in his district. The main check on any autocratic tendencies he might have exhibited rested in his subjects' ability to transfer their allegiance to a more responsive chief. Swazi officials held their positions for life and were dismissed only for treason or witchcraft. Incompetence, drunkenness, and stupidity were frowned upon, but they were not considered to be sufficient grounds for dismissal.

Political Leadership and Gender

Irrespective of cultural configuration, or type of political organization, it is a fact that women rarely hold important positions of political leadership. Furthermore, when they do occupy publicly recognized offices, their power and authority rarely exceed those of men. Nevertheless, exceptions occur, as in the Philippines, Sri Lanka, India, Pakistan, Israel, Norway, the Netherlands, Ireland, Great Britain, and Guyana, where women are, or have recently served as, heads of government. Historically, one might cite the occasional woman chiefs mentioned in early accounts of New England Indians, the last native monarch of Hawaii, and powerful queens such as Elizabeth I of England or Catherine the Great of Russia. When women do hold high office, it is often because of their relationship to men. Thus, a queen is either the wife of a reigning monarch or else the daughter of a king who died without a male heir to succeed him. Moreover, women in focal positions frequently must adopt many of the characteristics of temperament normally deemed appropriate for men in their societies. For instance, in her role as prime minister, Margaret Thatcher of Great Britain displayed the toughness and assertiveness that, in Western societies, have long been considered desirable masculine qualities rather than the nurturance and compliance that Westerners traditionally have expected of women.

In spite of all this, in a number of societies, women regularly enjoy as much political power as men. In band societies, it is common for them to have as much of a say in public affairs as men, even though the latter more often than not are the nominal leaders of their groups. Among the Iroquois nations of New York State (discussed in Chapter 22), all leadership positions above the household and clan level were, without exception, filled by men. Thus they held all positions on the village and tribal councils, as well as on the great council of the league of Six Nations. However, they were completely beholden to women, for only the latter could nominate men to high office. Moreover, women actively lobbied the men on the councils and could remove someone from office whenever it suited them.

As this case makes clear, low visibility of women in politics does not necessarily exclude them from the realm of social control, nor does it mean that men have more power in political affairs. Sometimes, though, women may play more visible roles, as in the dual-sex systems of West Africa. Among the Igbo of Nigeria, in each

This Seneca chief, Cornplanter, participated in three treaties with the United States in the late 18th century. Although Iroquois chiefs were always men, they served strictly at the pleasure of women, whose position in society was equal to that of men.

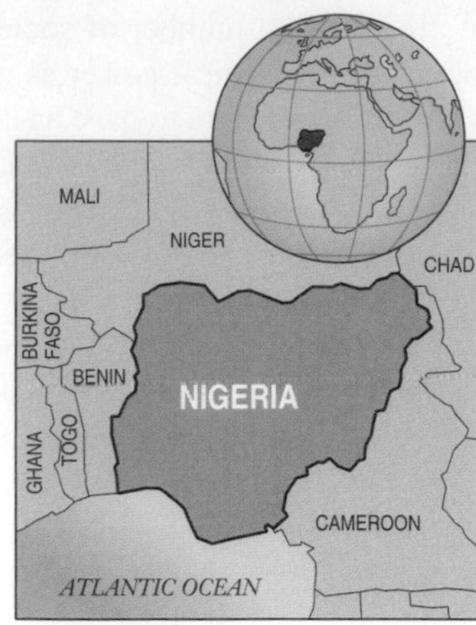

political unit, separate political institutions for men and women give each sex their own autonomous spheres of authority, as well as an area of shared responsibility.[10] At the head of each was a male *obi,* considered thc head of government though in fact he presided over the male community, and a female *omu,* the acknowledged mother of the whole community but in practice concerned with the female section of the community. Unlike a queen (though both she and the *obi* were crowned), the *omu* was neither the obi's wife nor the previous obi's daughter.

Just as the *obi* had a council of dignitaries to advise him and act as a check against any arbitrary exercise of power, the *omu* was served by a council of women in equal number to the *obi*'s male councilors. The duties of the *omu* and her councilors involved such tasks as establishing rules and regulations for the community market (marketing was a woman's activity) and hearing cases involving women brought to her from throughout the town or village. If such cases also involved men, then she and her council would cooperate with the *obi* and his council. Widows also went to the *omu* for the final rites required to end their period of mourning for dead husbands. Since the *omu* represented all women, she had to be responsive to her constituency and would seek their approval and cooperation in all major decisions.

In addition to the *omu* and her council, the Igbo women's government included a representative body of women chosen from each quarter or section of the village or town on the basis of their ability to think clearly and speak well. In addition, acting at the village or lineage level were political pressure groups of women who acted to stop quarrels and prevent wars. These were of two types: women born into a community, most of whom lived elsewhere since villages were exogamous and residence was patrilocal, and women who had married into their community. Their duties included helping companion wives in times of illness and stress and meting out discipline to lazy or recalcitrant husbands.

In the Igbo system, then, women managed their own affairs, and their interests were represented at all levels of government. Moreover, they had the right to enforce their decisions and rules with sanctions similar to those employed by men. Included were strikes, boycotts, and "sitting on a man" or woman. Political scientist Judith Van Allen describes the latter:

> To "sit on" or "make war on" a man involved gathering at his compound, sometimes late at night, dancing, singing scurrilous songs which detailed the women's grievances against him and often called his manhood into question, banging on his hut with the pestles women used for pounding yams, and perhaps demolishing his hut or plastering it with mud and roughing him up a bit. A man might be sanctioned in this way for mistreating his wife, for violating the women's market rules, or for letting his cows eat the women's crops. The women would stay at his hut throughout the day, and late into the night if necessary, until he repented and promised to mend his ways. . . . Although this could hardly have been a pleasant experience for the offending man, it was considered legitimate and no man would consider intervening.[11]

Given the high visibility of women in the Igbo political system, it may come as a surprise to learn that when the British imposed colonial rule upon these people, they failed to recognize the autonomy and power those women possessed. The reason is the British were blinded by their Victorian values, which then were at their height. To them, a woman's mind was not strong enough for such supposedly masculine subjects as science, business, and politics; her place was clearly in the home. Hence, they considered it inconceivable that women might play important roles in politics. As a consequence, the British introduced "reforms" that destroyed women's traditional forms of autonomy and power without providing alternative forms in exchange. Far from enhancing women's status, as Western people like to think their influence does, in this case,

[10] Okonjo, K. (1976). The dual-sex political system in operation: Igbo women and community politics in midwestern Nigeria. In N. Hafkin & E. Bay (Eds.). *Women in Africa*. Stanford, CA: Stanford University Press.

[11] Van Allen, J. (1979). Sitting on a man: Colonialism and the lost political institutions of Igbo women. In S. Tiffany (Ed.). *Women in Society* (p. 169). St. Albans, VT: Eden Press.

women lost their equality and became subordinate to men. Nor is the Igbo situation unusual in this regard. Historically, in state-organized societies, women usually have been subordinate to men. Hence, when states impose their control on societies where men and women are equal to one another, the situation almost invariably changes so that women become subordinate to men.

POLITICAL ORGANIZATION AND THE MAINTENANCE OF ORDER

Whatever form a society's political organization may take, and whatever else it may do, it is always involved in one way or another with maintaining social order. Always it seeks to ensure that people behave in acceptable ways and defines the proper action to take when they do not. In chiefdoms and states, some sort of authority has the power to regulate the affairs of society. In bands and tribes, however, people behave generally as they are expected to, without the direct intervention of any centralized political authority. To a large degree, gossip, criticism, fear of supernatural forces, and the like serve as effective deterrents to antisocial behavior.

As an example of how such seemingly informal considerations serve to keep people in line, we may look at the Wape people of Papua New Guinea, who believe the spirits of deceased ancestors roam lineage lands, protecting them from trespassers and helping their hunting descendants by driving game their way.[12] These ancestral spirits also punish those who have wronged them or their descendants by preventing hunters from finding game or causing them to miss their shots, thereby depriving people of much needed meat. Nowadays, the Wape hunt with shotguns, which the community purchases for the use of one man, whose job it is to hunt for all the others. The cartridges used in the hunt, however, are invariably supplied by individual community members. Not always is the gunman successful; if he shoots and misses, it is because the owner of the fired shell, or some close relative, has quarrelled or wronged another person whose deceased relative is securing revenge by causing the hunter to miss. Or, if the gunman cannot even find game, it is because vengeful ancestors have chased the animals away. As a proxy hunter for the villagers, the gunman is potentially subject to sanctions by ancestral spirits in response to collective wrongs by those for whom he hunts.

For the Wape, then, successful hunting depends upon avoiding quarrels and maintaining tranquility within the community so as not to antagonize anybody's deceased ancestor. Unfortunately, complete peace and tranquility are impossible to achieve in any human community, and the Wape are no exception. Thus, when hunting is poor, the gunman must discover what quarrels and wrongs have occurred within his village to identify the proper ancestral spirits to appeal to for renewed success. Usually, this is done in a special meeting where confessions of wrongdoing may be forthcoming. If not, questioning accusations are bandied about until resolution occurs, but even with no resolution, the meeting must end amicably to prevent new antagonisms. Thus, everyone's behavior comes under public scrutiny, reminding everyone of what is expected of them and encouraging everyone to avoid acts that will cast them in an unfavorable light.

Internalized Controls

The Wape concern about ancestral spirits is a good example of internalized, or cultural, controls—beliefs that are so thoroughly ingrained that each person becomes personally responsible for his or her own conduct. **Cultural control** may be thought of as internalized control by the mind, as opposed to **social control**, which involves external enforcement. Examples of cultural control can also be found in North American society; for instance, people refrain from committing incest not so much from fear of legal punishment as from a sense of deep disgust at the thought of the act and the shame they would feel in performing it. Obviously, not all members of North American society feel this disgust, or there would not be the high incidence of incest that occurs, especially between fathers and daughters, but, then, no deterrent to misbehavior is ever 100% effective. Cultural controls are embedded in our consciousness, and rely on such deterrents as fear of supernatural punishment—ancestral spirits sabotaging the hunting, for example—and magical retaliation. Like the devout Christian who avoids sinning for fear of hell, the individual expects some sort of punishment, even though no one in the community may be aware of the wrongdoing.

[12] Mitchell, W. E. (1973, December). A new weapon stirs up old ghosts. *Natural History Magazine*, 77–84.

Cultural control. Control through beliefs and values deeply internalized in the minds of individuals. • **Social control.** Control over groups through open coercion.

HIGHWAY 1
Introduction to Social Organization
http://www.maricopa.edu/academic/cult_sci/anthro/lost-tribes/soc_pol.tml

HIGHWAY 2
Association for Political & Legal Anthropology
http://www.aaanet.org/apla/indexf.htm

HIGHWAY 3
Information on politics, activism, and current issues
http://dmoz.org/society/

Externalized Controls

Because internalized controls are not wholly sufficient even in bands and tribes, every society develops beliefs and customs designed to encourage conformity to social norms. These institutions are referred to as **sanctions;** they are externalized controls, and involve varying mixes of cultural and social control. According to Radcliffe-Brown, "A sanction is a reaction on the part of a society or of a considerable number of its members to a mode of behavior which is thereby approved (positive sanctions) or disapproved (negative sanctions)."[13] Sanctions may also be either formal or informal and may vary significantly within a given society.

Sanctions operate within social groups of all sizes. Moreover, they need not be enacted into law in order to play a significant role in regulating people's behavior: "They include not only the organized sanctions of the law but also the gossip of neighbors or the customs regulating norms of production that are spontaneously generated among workers on the factory floor. In small scale communities . . . informal sanctions may become more drastic than the penalties provided for in the legal code."[14] If, however, a sanction is to be effective, it cannot be arbitrary. Quite the opposite: Sanctions must be consistently applied, and their existence must be known generally by the society's members.

Social sanctions may be categorized as either positive or negative. Positive sanctions consist of incentives to conformity such as awards, titles, and recognition by one's neighbors. Negative sanctions consist of threats such as imprisonment, fines, corporal punishment, or ostracism from the community for violation of social norms. One example of a negative sanction discussed earlier is the Igbo practice of "sitting on a man." If some individuals are not convinced of the advantages of social conformity, they are still more likely obey society's rules than to accept the consequences of not doing so.

Sanctions may also be categorized as either formal or informal, depending on whether or not a legal statute is involved. In the United States, the man who wears tennis shorts to a church service may be subject to a variety of informal sanctions, ranging from disapproving glances from the clergy to the chuckling of other parishioners. If,

[13] Radcliffe-Brown, A. R. (1952). *Structure and function in primitive society* (p. 205). New York: Free Press.

[14] Epstein, A. L. (1968). Sanctions. *International Encyclopedia of Social Sciences* (Vol. 14, p. 3).

Sanctions. Externalized social controls designed to encourage conformity to social norms.

Kim Dae Jung of South Korea, who in 2000 was awarded the Nobel Peace Prize. Such awards are examples of positive sanctions, by which societies promote approved behavior.

however, he were to show up without any trousers at all, he would be subject to the formal negative sanction of arrest for indecent exposure. Only in the second instance would he have been guilty of breaking the **law.**

Formal sanctions, such as laws, are always organized, because they attempt to precisely and explicitly regulate people's behavior. Other examples of organized sanctions include, on the positive side, military decorations and monetary rewards. On the negative side are loss of face, exclusion from social life and its privileges, seizure of property, imprisonment, and even bodily mutilation or death.

Informal sanctions emphasize cultural control and are diffuse in nature, involving spontaneous expressions of approval or disapproval by members of the group or community. They are, nonetheless, very effective in enforcing a large number of seemingly unimportant customs. Because most people want to be accepted, they are willing to acquiesce to the rules that govern dress, eating, and conversation, even in the absence of actual laws.

To show how informal sanctions work, we will examine them in the context of power relationships among the Bedouins of Egypt's western desert. The example is especially interesting, for it shows how sanctions not only act to control people's behavior but also act to keep individuals in their place in a heirarchical society.

Negative sanctions may involve some form of regulated combat, seen here as armed dancers near Mount Hagen in New Guinea demand redress for murder.

Law. Formal negative sanctions.

Original Study

Limits on Power in Bedouin Society[15]

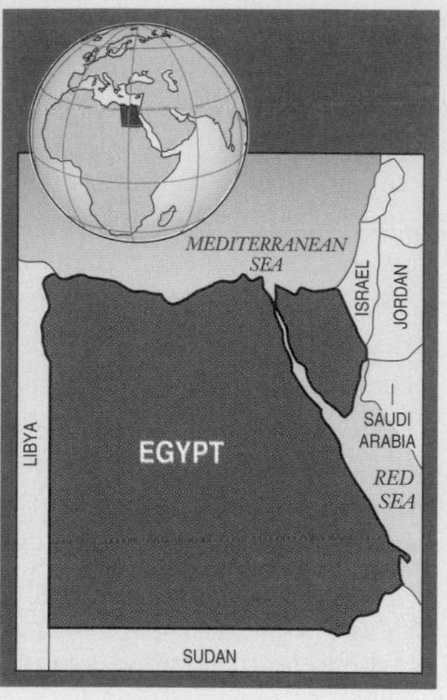

Where individuals value their independence and believe in equality, those who exercise authority over others enjoy a precarious status. In Bedouin society, social precedence or power depends not on force but on demonstration of the moral virtues that win respect from others. Persons in positions of power are said to have social standing (**gíma**), which is recognized by the respect paid them. To win the respect of others, in particular dependents, such persons must adhere to the ideals of honor, provide for and protect their dependents, and be fair, taking no undue advantage of their positions. They must assert their authority gingerly lest it so compromise their dependents' autonomy that it provoke rebellion and be exposed as a sham.

Because those in authority are expected to treat their dependents, even children, with some respect, they must draw as little attention as possible to the inequality of their relationships. Euphemisms that obscure the nature of such relationships abound. For example, Sa`ádi [free tribes] individuals do not like to call Mrábit [client tribes] associates Mrábtín in their presence. My host corrected me once when I referred to his shepherds by the technical word for shepherd, saying, "We prefer to call them 'people of the sheep' [**hal il-ghanam**]. It sounds nicer." The use of fictive kin terms serves the same function of masking relations of inequality, as for example in the case of patrons and clients.

Those in authority are also expected to respect their dependents' dignity by minimizing open assertion of their power over them. Because the provider's position requires dependents, he risks losing his power base if he alienates them. When a superior publicly orders, insults, or beats a dependent, he invites the rebellion that would undermine his position. Such moments are fraught with tension, as the dependent might feel the need to respond to a public humiliation to preserve his dignity or honor. Indeed, refusal to comply with an unreasonable order, or an order given in a compromising way, reflects well on the dependent and undercuts the authority of the person who gave it.

Tyranny is never tolerated for long. Most dependents wield sanctions that check the power of their providers. Anyone can appeal to a mediator to intervene on his or her behalf, and more radical solutions are open to all but young children. Clients can simply leave an unreasonable patron and attach themselves to a new one. Young men can always escape the tyranny of a father or paternal uncle by leaving to join maternal relatives or, if they have them, affines, or even to become clients to some other family. For the last twenty years or so, young men could go to Libya to find work.

Younger brothers commonly get out from under difficult elder brothers by splitting off from them, demanding their share of the patrimony and setting up separate households. The dynamic is clear in the case of four brothers who constituted the core of the camp in which I lived. Two had split off and lived in separate households. Another two still shared property, herds, and expenses. While I was there, tensions began to develop. Although the elder brother was more important in the community at large, and the younger brother was slightly irresponsible and less intelligent, for the most part they worked various enterprises jointly and without friction. The younger brother deferred to his older brother and usually executed his decisions.

---

[15] Abu-Lughod, L. (1986). *Veiled sentiments: Honor and poetry in a Bedouin society* (pp. 99–103). Berkeley, CA: University of California Press.

But one day the tensions surfaced. The elder brother came home at midday in a bad mood only to find that no one had prepared him lunch. He went to one of his wives and scolded her for not having prepared any lunch, asserting that his children had complained that they were hungry. He accused her of trying to starve his children and threatened to beat her. His younger brother tried to intervene, but the elder brother then turned on him, calling him names. Accusing him of being lazy (because he had failed to follow through on a promise involving the care of the sheep that day), he then asked why the younger brother let his wife get away with sitting in her room when there was plenty of work to be done around the household. Then he went off toward his other wife carrying a big stick and yelling.

The younger brother was furious and set off to get their mother. The matriarch, accompanied by another of her sons, arrived and conferred at length with the quarreling men. The younger son wished to split off from his elder brother's household; the other brother scolded him for being so sensitive about a few words, reminding him that this was his elder brother, from whom even a beating should not matter. His mother disapproved of splitting up the households. Eventually everyone calmed down. But it is likely that a few more incidents such as that will eventually lead the younger brother to demand a separate household.

Even a woman can resist a tyrannical husband by leaving for her natal home "angry" (**mughtáóa**). This is the approved response to abuse, and it forces the husband or his representatives to face the scolding of the woman's kin and, sometimes, to appease her with gifts. Women have less recourse against tyrannical fathers or guardians, but various informal means to resist the imposition of unwanted decisions do exist. As a last resort there is always suicide, and I heard of a number of both young men and women who committed suicide in desperate resistance to their fathers' decisions, especially regarding marriage. One old woman's tale illustrates the extent to which force can be resisted, even by women. Náfla reminisced:

> My first marriage was to my paternal cousin [**ibn 'amm**]. He was from the same camp. One day the men came over to our tent. I saw the tent full of men and wondered why. I heard they were coming to ask for my hand [**yukhultú fiyya**]. I went and stood at the edge of the tent and called out, "If you're planning to do anything, stop. I don't want it." Well, they went ahead anyway, and every day I would cry and say that I did not want to marry him. I was young, perhaps fourteen. When they began drumming and singing, everyone assured me that it was in celebration of another cousin's wedding, so I sang and danced along with them. This went on for days. Then on the day of the wedding my aunt and another relative caught me in the tent and suddenly closed it and took out the washbasin. They wanted to bathe me. I screamed. I screamed and screamed; every time they held a pitcher of water to wash me with, I knocked it out of their hands.
>
> His relatives came with camels and dragged me into the litter and took me to his tent. I screamed and screamed when he came into the tent in the afternoon [for the defloration]. Then at night, I hid among the blankets. Look as they might, they couldn't find me. My father was furious. After a few days he insisted I had to stay in my tent with my husband. As soon as he left, I ran off and hid behind the tent in which the groom's sister stayed. I made her promise not to tell anyone I was there and slept there.
>
> But they made me go back. That night, my father stood guard nearby with his gun. Every time I started to leave the tent, he would take a puff on his cigarette so I could see that he was still there. Finally I rolled myself up in the straw mat. When the groom came, he looked and looked but could not find me.
>
> Finally I went back to my family's household. I pretended to be possessed. I tensed my body, rolled my eyes, and everyone rushed about, brought me incense and prayed for me. They brought the healer [or holyman, **fǵih**], who blamed the unwanted marriage. Then they decided that perhaps I

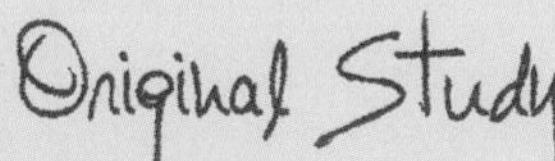

was too young and that I should not be forced to return to my husband. I came out of the seizure, and they were so grateful that they forced my husband's family to grant a divorce. My family returned the bride-price, and I stayed at home.

Náfla could not oppose her father's decision directly, but she was nevertheless able to resist his will through indirect means. Like other options for resistance by dependents unfairly treated, abused, or humiliated publicly, her rebellion served as a check on her father's and, perhaps, more important, her paternal uncle's power.

Supernatural sanctions, which seem to be associated with the weak and with dependents, provide the final check on abuse of authority. Supernatural retribution is believed to follow when the saintly lineages of Mrábtín are mistreated, their curses causing death or the downfall of the offender's lineage. In one Bedouin tale, when a woman denied food to two young girls, she fell ill, and blood appeared on food she cooked—a punishment for mistreating the helpless. Possession, as Náfla's tale illustrates, may also be a form of resistance . . . .

All these sanctions serve to check the abuse of power by eminent persons who have the resources to be autonomous and to control those who are dependent upon them. At the same time, moreover, figures of authority are vulnerable to their dependents because their positions rest on the respect these people are willing to give them.

The End

Another agent of control in societies, whether or not they possess centralized political systems, may be witchcraft. An individual naturally would hesitate to offend a neighbor, when that neighbor might retaliate by resorting to black magic. Similarly, individuals may not wish to be accused of practicing witchcraft, and so they behave with greater circumspection. Among the Azande of the Sudan, people who think they have been bewitched may consult an oracle, who, after performing the appropriate mystical rites, then may establish or confirm the identity of the offending witch.[16] Confronted with this evidence, the "witch" will usually agree to cooperate in order to avoid any additional trouble. Should the victim die, the relatives of the deceased may choose to make magic against the witch, ultimately accepting the death of some villager both as evidence of guilt and of the efficacy of their magic. For the Azande, witchcraft provides not only a sanction against antisocial behavior but also a means of dealing with natural hostilities and death. No one wishes to be thought of as a witch, and surely no one wishes to be victimized by one. By institutionalizing their emotional responses, the Azande successfully maintain social order. (For more on witchcraft, see Chapter 24.)

[16] Evans-Pritchard, E. E. (1937). *Witchcraft, oracles and magic among the Azande.* London: Oxford University Press.

SOCIAL CONTROL THROUGH LAW

Among the Inuit of northern Canada, all offenses are considered to involve disputes between individuals; thus, they must be settled between the disputants themselves. One way they may do so is through a song duel, in which they heap insults upon one another in songs specially composed for the occasion. Although society does not intervene, its interests are represented by spectators, whose applause determines the outcome. If, however, social harmony cannot be restored—and that, rather than assigning and punishing guilt, is the goal—one or the other disputant may move to another band. Among the Inuit, the alternative to peaceful settlement is to leave the group. Ultimately, there is no binding legal authority.

In Western society, by contrast, someone who commits an offense against another person may become subject to a series of complex legal proceedings. In criminal cases the primary concern is to assign and punish guilt rather than to help out the victim. The offender will be arrested by the police; tried before a judge and, perhaps, a jury; and, depending on the severity of the crime, may be fined, imprisoned, or even executed. Rarely does the victim receive restitution or compensation. Throughout this chain of events, the accused party is dealt with by (presumably) disinterested police, judges, jurors, and jailers, who may have

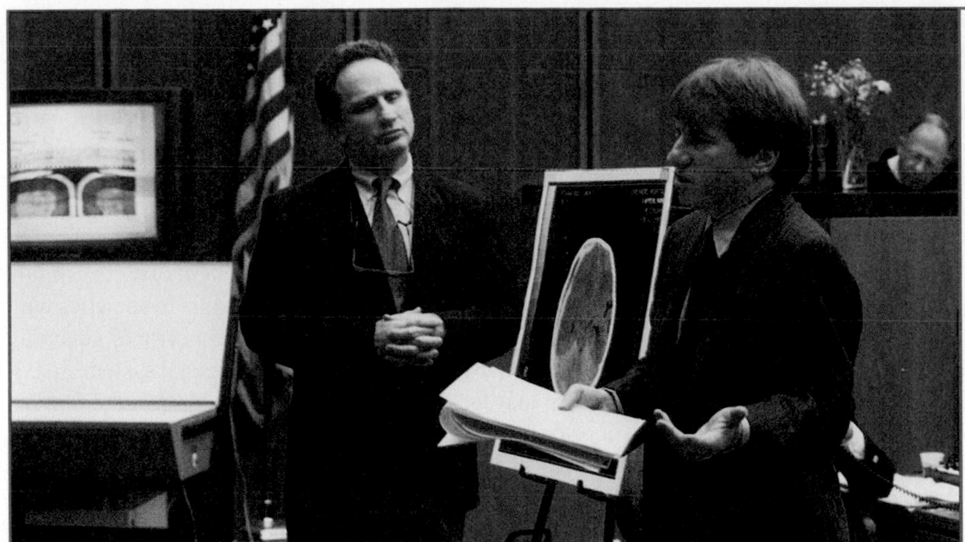

In Western society, someone who commits an offense against someone else is subject to a series of complex proceedings, in which the emphasis is on assigning and punishing guilt. In non-Western societies, by contrast, the emphasis is often on finding a solution that both parties can live with.

no personal acquaintance whatsoever with the plaintiff or the defendant. How strange this all seems from the standpoint of traditional Inuit culture! Clearly, the two systems operate under distinctly different assumptions.

Definition of Law

Once two Inuit settle a dispute by engaging in a song contest, the affair is considered closed; no further action is expected. Would we choose to describe the outcome of such a contest as a legal decision? If every law is a sanction but not every sanction is a law, how are we to distinguish between social sanctions in general and those to which we apply the label law?

The definition of *law* has been a lively point of contention among anthropologists in the 20th century. In 1926, Malinowski argued that the rules of law are distinguished from the rules of custom in that "they are regarded as the obligation of one person and the rightful claim of another, sanctioned not by mere psychological motive, but by a definite social machinery of binding force based . . . upon mutual dependence."[17] In other words, laws exemplify social control because they employ overt coercion. An example of one rule of custom in contemporary North American society might be the dictate that guests at a dinner party should repay the person who gave the party with entertainment in the future. A host or hostess who does not receive a return invitation may feel cheated of something thought to be owed but has no legal claim against the ungrateful guest for the $22.67 spent on food. If, however, an individual was cheated of the same sum by the grocer when shopping, the law could be invoked. Although Malinowski's definition introduced several important elements of law, his failure to distinguish adequately between legal and nonlegal sanctions left the problem of formulating a workable definition of *law* in the hands of later anthropologists.

An important pioneer in the anthropological study of law was E. Adamson Hoebel, according to whom "a social norm is legal if its neglect or infraction is regularly met, in threat or in fact, by the application of physical force by an individual or group possessing the socially recognized privilege of so acting."[18] In stressing the legitimate use of physical coercion, Hoebel de-emphasized the traditional association of law with a centralized court system. Although judge and jury are fundamental features of Western jurisprudence, they are not the universal backbone of human law. Some anthropologists have proposed that a precise definition of *law* is an impossible—and perhaps even undesirable—undertaking. When we speak of "the law," are we not inclined to fall back on our familiar Western conception of rules enacted by an authorized legislative body and enforced by the judicial mechanisms of the state? Can any concept of law be applied to such societies as the Nuer or the Inuit, for whom the notion of a centralized judiciary is virtually meaningless? How shall we categorize duels, song contests, and other socially condoned forms of self-help that seem to meet some but not all of the criteria of law?

---

[17] Malinowski, B. (1951). *Crime and custom in savage society* (p. 55). London: Routledge.

[18] Hoebel, E. A. (1954). *The law of primitive man: A study in comparative legal dynamics* (p.28). Cambridge, MA: Harvard University Press.

Ultimately, it is always of greatest value to consider each case within its cultural context. After all, law reflects a society's basic postulates, so to understand any society's laws, one must understand the underlying values and assumptions. Nonetheless, a working definition of law is useful for purposes of discussion and cross-cultural comparison, and for this, *law* is adequately characterized as formal negative sanctions.

Functions of Law

In his 1954 book, *The Law of Primitive Man,* Hoebel writes of a time when the notion that private property should be generously shared was a fundamental precept of Cheyenne Indian life. Subsequently, however, some men assumed the privilege of borrowing other men's horses without bothering to obtain permission. When Wolf Lies Down complained of such unauthorized borrowing to the members of the Elk Soldier Society, the Elk Soldiers not only had his horse returned to him but also secured an award for damages from the offender. The Elk Soldiers then announced that, to avoid such difficulties in the future, horses no longer could be borrowed without permission. Furthermore, they declared their intention to retrieve any such property and administer a whipping to anyone who resisted their efforts to return improperly borrowed goods.

The case of Wolf Lies Down and the Elk Soldier Society clearly illustrates three basic functions of law. First, it defines relationships among society's members, determining proper behavior under specified circumstances. Knowledge of the law permits each person to know his or her rights and duties in respect to every other member of society. Second, law allocates the authority to employ coercion in the enforcement of sanctions. In societies with centralized political systems, such authority is generally vested in the government and its judiciary system. In societies that lack centralized political control, the authority to employ force may be allocated directly to the injured party. Third, law functions to redefine social relations and to ensure social flexibility. As new situations arise, law must determine whether old rules and assumptions retain their validity and to what extent they must be altered. Law, if it is to operate efficiently, must allow room for change.

In practice, law is rarely the smooth and well-integrated system described here. In any given society, various legal sanctions may apply at various levels. Because the people in a society are usually members of numerous subgroups, they are subject to the various dictates of these diverse groups. Each individual Kapauku is simultaneously a

Law, if it is to operate effectively, must allow room for change. Here, supporters of Vermont's new law allowing same sex couples to enter into civil unions demonstrate in front of the state house in the fall of 2000.

member of a family, a household, a sublineage, and a confederacy and is subject to all the rules and regulations of each. In some cases it may be impossible for an individual to submit to contradictory legal indications:

> In one of the confederacy's lineages, incestuous relations between members of the same clan were punished by execution of the culprits, and in another by severe beating, in the third constituent lineage such a relationship was not punishable and . . . was not regarded as incest at all. In one of the sublineages, it became even a preferred type of marriage.[19]

Furthermore, the power to employ sanctions may vary from level to level within a given society. The head of a Kapauku household may punish a household member by slapping or beating, but the authority to confiscate property is vested exclusively in the headman of the lineage. Analogous distinctions exist in the United States among municipal, state, and federal jurisdictions. The complexity of legal jurisdiction within each society makes any easy generalization about law difficult.

Crime

As we have observed, an important function of negative sanctions, legal or otherwise, is to discourage the breach of social norms. A person contemplating theft is aware of the possibility of being caught and punished. Yet, even in the face of severe sanctions, individuals in every society sometimes violate the norms and subject themselves to the consequences of their behavior. What is the nature of crime in non-Western societies?

Western society makes a clear distinction between offenses against the state and offenses against an individual. *Black's Law Dictionary* tells us:

> The distinction between a crime and a tort or civil injury is that the former is a breach and violation of the public right and of duties due to the whole community considered as such, and in its social and aggregate capacity; whereas the latter is an infringement or privation of the civil rights of individuals merely.[20]

Thus, a reckless driver who crashes into another car may be guilty of a crime by endangering public safety. The same driver may also be guilty of a tort in causing damages to the other car, and the other driver can sue for their cost.

Many non-Western societies, however, have no conception of a central state. Consequently, all offenses are viewed as against individuals, rendering the distinction between crime and tort of no value. Indeed, a dispute between individuals may seriously disrupt the social order, especially in small groups where the number of disputants, though small in absolute numbers, may be a large percentage of the total population. Although the Inuit traditionally have no effective domestic or economic unit beyond the family, a dispute between two people will interfere with the ability of members of separate families to come to one another's aid when necessary and is consequently a matter of wider social concern. The goal of judicial proceedings in most cases is to restore social harmony instead of punishing an offender. When distinguishing between offenses of concern to the community as a whole and those of concern only to a few individuals, we may refer to offenses as collective or personal, rather than distinguishing between criminal and civil law. In this way we may avoid values and assumptions that are irrelevant to a discussion of non-Western systems of law.

Basically, disputes are settled in either of two ways. First, disputing parties may, through argument and compromise, voluntarily arrive at a mutually satisfactory agreement. This form of settlement is referred to as **negotiation** or, if it involves the assistance of an unbiased third party, **mediation.** In bands and tribes a third-party mediator has no coercive power and thus cannot force disputants to abide by such a decision, but as a person who commands great personal respect, the mediator frequently may effect a settlement through these judgments.

Second, in chiefdoms and states, an authorized third party may issue a binding decision the disputing parties will be compelled to respect. This process is referred to as **adjudication.** The difference between mediation and adjudication is basically a difference in authorization. In a dispute settled by adjudication, the disputing parties

[19] Pospisil, L. (1971). *Anthropology of law: A comparative theory* (p. 36). New York: Harper & Row.

[20] Black, H. C. (1968). *Black's Law Dictionary.* St. Paul, MN: West.

Negotiation. The use of direct argument and compromise by the parties to a dispute to arrive voluntarily at a mutually satisfactory agreement. • **Mediation.** Settlement of a dispute through negotiation assisted by an unbiased third party. • **Adjudication.** Mediation with an unbiased third party making the ultimate decision.

In the United States, a distinction is made between offenses against the state and those against individuals. When O. J. Simpson was tried for the murder of his wife and her friend Ronald Goldman in criminal court, he was found not guilty on the basis of reasonable doubt, but in the subsequent civil trial, was found liable for the wrongful death of both.

present their positions as compellingly as they can, but they do not participate in the ultimate decision making.

Although the adjudication process is not universally characteristic, every society employs some form of negotiation to settle disputes. Often negotiation acts as a prerequisite or an alternative to adjudication. For example, in the resolution of U.S. labor disputes, striking workers may first negotiate with management, often with the mediation of a third party. If the state decides the strike constitutes a threat to the public welfare, the disputing parties may be forced to submit to adjudication. In this case, the responsibility for resolving the dispute is transferred to a presumably impartial judge.

The judge's work is difficult and complex. Not only must the evidence presented be sifted through, but also the judge must consider a wide range of norms, values, and earlier rulings to arrive at a decision intended to be considered just not only by the disputing parties but by the public and other judges as well.

In the United States, over the past three decades there has been significant movement away from the courts in favor of outside negotiation and mediation to resolve a wide variety of disputes. Many jurists see this as a means to clear overloaded court dockets so as to concentrate on more important cases. A correlate of this move is a change in ideology, elevating order and harmony to positive values and replacing open coercion (seen as "undemocratic") with control through persuasion. In the abstract, this seems like a good idea and suggests a return to a system of cultural control characteristic of band and tribal societies. However, a crucial difference exists. In tribal and band societies, consensus is less likely to be coercive, because all concerned individuals can negotiate and mediate on relatively equal terms. The United States, by contrast, has great disparities in power, and evidence indicates that it is the stronger parties that prefer mediation and negotiation. As anthropologist Laura Nader points out, there is now less emphasis on justice and concern with causes of disputes than on smoothing things over in ways that tend to be pacifying and restrictive; an emphasis that produces order of a repressive sort.[21]

[21] Nader, L. (1997). Controlling processes: Tracing the dynamic components of power. *Current Anthropology, 38,* 714–715.

Anthropology Applied

Dispute Resolution and the Anthropologist

In an era in which the peaceful resolution of disputes is increasingly valued, the field of dispute management is one of growing anthropological involvement (and employment). One practioner is William L. Ury, an independent negotiations specialist who earned his Ph.D. at Harvard University. His 1982 dissertation was titled *Talk Out or Walk Out: The Role and Control of Conflict in a Kentucky Coal Mine*.

At Harvard, Ury cofounded—with Roger Fisher of the law school—the Program on Negotiation. Together, the two also authored what has become the negotiator's "bible": *Getting to Yes: Negotiating Agreement Without Giving In* (published in 1981, it has been translated into 21 languages). In 1980, Ury helped the United States and the Soviet Union replace their obsolete "hot line" with fully equipped nuclear crisis centers in each capital.

Ury now runs regular workshops on dealing with difficult people and situations. Among those who have enlisted his services is the Ford Motor Company, whose 6,000 top executives worldwide have taken his seminars. As one put it: "His influence on the company is incalculable. He inoculated a whole culture with a new way of looking at things."* Now, he specializes in ethnic and secessionist disputes, including those between "white" and "black" South Africans, Serbs and Croats, Turks and Kurds. One of his toughest jobs was to mediate a peace (since broken) between the Russians and Chechans, a task that brought together other adversaries from the former Soviet Union as well: Tatars, Crimeans, Moldovans, and Georgians.

In a recent book, *Getting Past No: Negotiating Your Way from Confrontation,* Ury praises the perspective of Japan's "home-run king" who viewed opposing pitchers not as enemies trying to do him in but as partners offering repeated opportunities to hit another ball out of the park. In dealing with the Chechans, one of his techniques was to have them imagine the speech Russian president Boris Yeltsin could give that would help his people accept the Chechans' goal. The Russians were asked to do the same: What kind of speech could the Chechan president give that would persuade his followers to remain in the Russian Federation? What Ury and others are doing is helping create a culture of negotiation in a world where adversarial, win-lose attitudes are out of step with the increasingly interdependent relations between people. But as the collapse of the Chechan-Russian agreement shows, the task is far from easy.

*Stewart, D. (1997). Expanding the pie before you divvy it up. *Smithsonian,* 28, 82.

In many politically centralized societies, incorruptible supernatural, or at least nonhuman, powers are thought to make judgments through a trial by ordeal. Among the Kpelle of Liberia, for example, when guilt is in doubt an ordeal operator licensed by the government may apply a hot knife to a suspect's leg. If the leg is burned, the suspect is guilty; if not, innocence is assumed. But the operator does not merely heat the knife and apply it. After massaging the suspect's legs and determining the knife is hot enough, the operator then strokes his own leg with it without being burned, demonstrating that the innocent will escape injury. The knife is then applied to the suspect. Up to this point—consciously or unconsciously—the operator has read the suspect's nonverbal cues: gestures, the degree of muscular tension, amount of perspiration, and so forth. From this the operator can judge whether or not the accused is showing so much anxiety as to indicate probable guilt; in effect, a psychological stress evaluation has been made. As the knife is applied, it is manipulated to either burn or not burn the suspect, once this judgment has been made. The operator does this manipulation easily by controlling how long

Two means of psychological evaluation: a Kpelle trial by ordeal and a Western polygraph ("lie detector").

the knife is in the fire, as well as the pressure and angle at which it is pressed against the leg.[22]

Similar to this is the use of the lie detector (polygraph) in the United States, although the guiding ideology is scientific rather than supernaturalistic. Nevertheless, an incorruptible nonhuman agency is thought to establish who is lying and who is not, whereas in reality the polygraph operator cannot just "read" the needles of the machine. He or she must judge whether or not they are registering a high level of anxiety brought on by the testing situation, as opposed to the stress of guilt. Thus, the polygraph operator has much in common with the Kpelle ordeal operator.

POLITICAL ORGANIZATION AND EXTERNAL AFFAIRS

Although the regulation of internal affairs is an important function of any political system, it is by no means the sole function. Another is the management of external or international affairs—relations not just between states but between different bands, lineages, clans, or whatever the largest autonomous political unit may be. And just as the threatened or actual use of force may be used to maintain order within a society, it also may be used in the conduct of external affairs.

[22] Gibbs, J. L., Jr. (1983). Interview, *Faces of Culture: Program 18.* Fountain Valley, CA: Coast Telecourses.

War

One of the state's responsibilities is the organization and execution of war. Throughout the past few thousand years of history, people have engaged in a seemingly endless chain of wars and intergroup hostilities. Why do wars occur? Are humans naturally aggressive, as some have argued? Those who take this position point to aggressive group behavior exhibited by chimpanzees in Tanzania. Here, observers saw one group systematically destroy another, whose territory they took over. As well, they cite the behavior of people such as the Yanomami, who live on either side of the border between Brazil and Venezuela. Portrayed as living in a chronic state of war, they are cited as exemplifying the way all humans once behaved.

Critics of these arguments point out that "warlike" behavior among chimpanzees and their close relatives, bonobos, has not been widely observed.[23] As for the Yanomami, not all agree that they are as fierce as portrayed, nor can we assume that all people once lived the way they do. Like all people, the Yanomami have a history, and their present activities undoubtedly reflect a particular historical context, one that, in the 20th century, has included increasing levels of disruption and violence caused by increasing pressures as outsiders have penetrated the Amazon and Orinoco rain forests in which the Yanomami live.[24] In other words,

[23] Power, M. G. (1995). Gombe revisited: Are chimpanzees violent and heirarchical in the "free" state? *General Anthropology, 2* (1), 5–9.

[24] Mann, C. C. (2000). Misconduct alleged in Yanomamo studies. *Science,* 289: 2253.

Often depicted as "warlike by nature," the Yanomami may be no such thing; rather, Yanomami warfare is likely a recent phenomenon related to outside pressures originating in the Brazilian and Venezuelan states.

warfare among humans, as well as aggressive group behavior among apes, may be situation specific rather than an unavoidable expression of some sort of biological predisposition. This is not to say that violence was unknown among ancient humans, as some have argued. The occasional discovery of stone spear points embedded in human skeletons, such as that of a nearly 9,000-year-old man found in Kennewick, Washington, or even older ones from the Grimaldi caves in Italy proves otherwise. Nevertheless, it is clear that war is not a universal phenomenon, for in various parts of the world there are societies that do not practice warfare as we know it. Examples include people as diverse as the Bushmen of southern Africa, the Arapesh of New Guinea, and the Jain of India. Among societies that do practice warfare, levels of violence may differ dramatically. Of warfare in New Guinea, for example, anthropologist Robert Gordon notes that:

> It's slightly more "civilized" than the violence of warfare which we practice insofar as it's strictly between two groups. And as an outsider, you can go up and interview people and talk to them while they're fighting and the arrows will miss you. It's quite safe and you can take photographs. Now, of course, the problem with modern warfare is precisely that it kills indiscriminately and you can't do much research on it, but at the same time, you can learn a lot talking to these people about the dynamics of how violence escalates into full-blown warfare.[25]

We have ample reason to suppose that war has become a problem only in the last 10,000 years, since the invention of food-production techniques, and especially since the invention of centralized states. It has reached crisis proportions in the past 200 years, with the invention of modern weaponry and increased direction of violence against civilian populations. In contemporary warfare, we have reached the point where casualties not just of civilians but also of *children* far outnumber those of soldiers. Thus, war is not so much an age-old problem as it is a relatively recent one.

Among food foragers, with their uncentralized political systems, although violence emerges sporadically, warfare was all but unknown until recent times. Because territorial boundaries and membership among food-foraging bands are usually fluid and loosely defined, a man who hunts with one band today may hunt with a neighboring band tomorrow. Warfare is further rendered impractical by the systematic interchange of marriage partners among food-foraging groups—it is likely that someone in each band will have a sister, a brother, or a

[25] Gordon, R. J. (1981, December). [Interview] Los Angeles: Coast Telecourses.

cousin in a neighboring band. Moreover, absence of a food surplus does not permit prolonged combat. Where populations are small, food surpluses absent, property ownership minimal, and no state organization exists, the likelihood of organized violence by one group against another is minimal.[26]

Although peaceful farmers exist, despite the traditional view of the farmer as a gentle tiller of the soil, it is among such people, along with pastoralists, that warfare becomes prominent. One reason may be that food-producing peoples are far more prone to population growth than are food foragers, whose numbers are generally maintained well below carrying capacity. This population growth, if unchecked, can lead to resource depletion, one solution to which may be seizure of some other people's resources. In addition, the commitment to a fixed piece of land inherent in farming makes such societies somewhat less fluid in their membership than those of food-foragers. Instead of marrying distantly, farmers marry locally, depriving them of long-distance kin networks. In rigidly matrilocal or patrilocal societies, each new generation is bound to the same territory, no matter how small it may be or how large the group trying to live within it.

The availability of empty land may not serve as a sufficient detriment to the outbreak of war. Among slash-and-burn horticulturists, for example, competition for land cleared of old growth forest frequently leads to hostility and armed conflict. The centralization of political control and the possession of valuable property among farming people provide many more stimuli for warfare. It is among such peoples, especially those organized into states, that the violence of warfare is most apt to result in indiscriminate killing. This development has reached its peak in modern states. Indeed, much (but not all) of the warfare that has been observed in recent stateless societies (so-called tribal warfare) has been induced by states as a reaction to colonial expansion.[27]

Another difference between food-gathering and food-producing populations lies in their different **worldviews.** As a general rule, food foragers tend to conceive of themselves as a part of the natural world and in some sort of balance with it. This is reflected in their attitudes toward the animals they kill. Western Abenaki hunters, for example, thought that animals, like humans, were composed of both a body and a personal spirit. Although Abenakis hunted and killed animals to sustain their own lives, they clearly recognized that animals were entitled to proper respect. Thus, when beaver, muskrat, or waterfowl were killed, the hunters could not just toss their bones into the nearest garbage pit. Proper respect required that their bones be returned to the water, with a request that the species be continued. Such attitudes may be referred to as parts of a naturalistic worldview.

The Abenaki's sense of oneness with nature contrasts sharply with the kind of worldview prevalent among farmers and pastoralists, who do not find their food in nature but impose their dominance upon nature to produce food for themselves. The attitude that nature exists only for humans' use may be referred to as an exploitative worldview. With such an outlook, it is a small step from dominating the rest of nature to dominating other societies for the benefit of one's own. The exploitative worldview, prevalent among food-producing peoples, is an important contributor to intersocietal warfare.

A comparison between the Western Abenakis and their Iroquoian neighbors to the west is instructive. Among the Abenakis warfare was essentially a defensive activity. Though they grew crops, plant cultivation merely supplemented the main business of food foraging, on which the Western Abenakis relied. Having a naturalistic worldview, they believed they could not operate in someone else's territory, since they did not control the necessary supernatural powers. Furthermore, operating far below carrying capacity, they had no need to prey upon the resources of others. The Iroquois, by contrast, relied on slash-and-burn horticulture and engaged in predatory warfare. Evidence indicates significant environmental degradation around their settlements, suggesting overutilization of resources. Although the Iroquois went to war to replace men lost in previous battles, the main motive was to achieve dominance by making their victims acknowledge Iroquoian superiority. The relation between victim and victor, however, was not outright subordination. Imposed payment of tribute purchased "protection" from the Iroquois, no doubt helping to offset the depletion of resources near the village of the would-be protectors. The price of protection went further than this,

[26] Knauft, B. (1991).Violence and sociality in human evolution. *Current Anthropology, 32,* 391–409.

[27] Whitehead, N. L. & Ferguson, R. B. (1993, November). Deceptive stereotypes about tribal warfare. *Chronicle of Higher Education,* A48.

Worldviews. The conceptions, explicit and implicit, an individual or society has of the limits and workings of its world.

Shown here are U.S. soldiers in Kosovo, where they are part of a NATO peacekeeping force. Since World War II, no state has gone to war as often as the United States.

though; it included constant and public ceremonial deference to the Iroquois, free passage for their war parties through the subordinate group's country, and the contribution of young men to Iroquoian war parties.

A comparison between the Iroquois and Europeans is also instructive. Sometime in the 16th century (if not earlier), five Iroquoian nations—the Mohawks, Oneidas, Onondagas, Cayugas, and Senecas—determined to end warfare among themselves by the simple device of directing their predatory activities against outsiders rather than each other. In this way the famous League of the Iroquois came into being. Similarly, in the year 1095, Pope Urban II launched the Crusades with a speech urging the Christian nobles of Europe to end their ceaseless wars against each other by directing their hostilities outward against the Islamic Turks and Arabs. In that same speech he also alluded to the economic benefits to be realized by seizing the resources of the infidels. Although rationalized as a "holy war," the Crusades clearly were motivated by more than religious ideology.

Although the Europeans never achieved more than limited, temporary success at "liberating" the Holy Land, some of them did benefit from the booty obtained in battle, lending credence to the idea that people could live better than they had before by locating and seizing the resources of others. Thus, the state formation that took place in Europe in the centuries after A.D. 1000 was followed by colonial expansion into other parts of the world. Proceeding in concert with this growth and outward expansion was the development of the technology and organization of warfare.

The idea that warfare is an acceptable way to bring about economic benefits is still a part of the European cultural tradition, as the following from a quite serious letter, that appeared in New Hampshire's largest daily newspaper a few years ago, illustrates: "If a war is necessary to stabilize the economy, then we shall have a war. It affects the everyday lives of most of us so little that we need hardly acknowledge the fact that it is going on. Surely the sacrifice of a son, husband or father by a hundred or so of our citizens every week is not that overwhelming. They will forget their losses in time."[28]

Certainly, we would like to think that this kind of attitude is not widespread in the United States, and perhaps it is not, but we do not know this for a fact. Nor do we really know the extent to which it is or is not held by members of those segments of U.S. society that tend to influence the setting of public policy. These are

[28] Quoted in MacNeil, R. (1982). *The right place at the right time* (p. 263). Boston: Little, Brown.

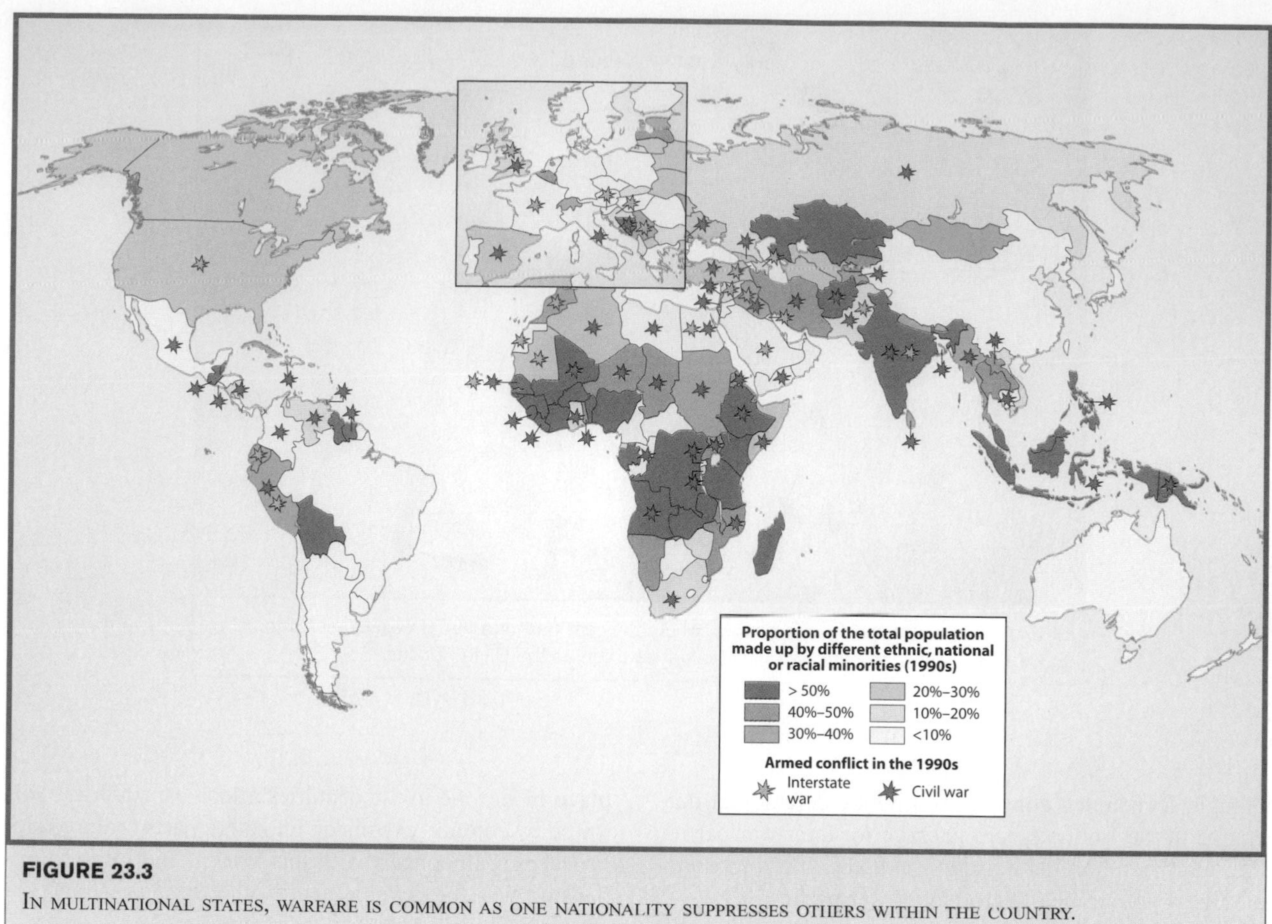

FIGURE 23.3

IN MULTINATIONAL STATES, WARFARE IS COMMON AS ONE NATIONALITY SUPPRESSES OTHERS WITHIN THE COUNTRY.

obviously important questions, and we need to find out more about them.

As the above examples show, the causes of warfare are complex; economic, political, and ideological factors are all involved. With the emergence of states (not just in Europe but in other parts of the world as well) has come a dramatic increase in the scale of warfare. Perhaps this is not surprising, given the state's acceptance of force as a legitimate tool for regulating human affairs and its ability to organize large numbers of people. In the modern world, we are as far (and probably further) from the elimination of war as humanity ever has been, a fact reflected in the 120-odd shooting wars at the end of the 20th century. Moreover, value systems seem to be as crucial as any element to the continued existence of warfare.

POLITICAL SYSTEMS AND THE QUESTION OF LEGITIMACY

Whatever form a society's political system may take and however it may go about its business, it always must find some way to obtain the people's allegiance. In uncentralized systems, where every adult participates in all decision making, loyalty and cooperation are freely given, since each person is considered a part of the political system. As the group grows larger, however, and the organization becomes more formal, the problem of obtaining and keeping public support becomes greater.

In centralized political systems, increased reliance is placed upon coercion as a means of social control. This, however, tends to lessen the effectiveness of a political system. For example, the personnel needed to apply force often must be large and may itself grow to be a political power. The emphasis on force also may create resentment from those to whom it is applied, which lessens cooperation. Thus, police states are generally short-lived; most societies choose less extreme forms of social coercion. In the United States, this is reflected in the increasing emphasis placed on cultural, as opposed to social, control.

Also basic to the political process is the concept of legitimacy, or the right of political leaders to rule. Like force, legitimacy is a form of support for a political system; unlike force, legitimacy is based on the values a particular society holds. For example, among the Kapauku the legitimacy of the *tonowi*'s power comes from his wealth; the kings of Hawaii, and of England and France before their revolutions, were thought to have a divine right to rule; and the head of the Dahomey state of West Africa acquired legitimacy through his age, as he was always the oldest living male.

Legitimacy grants the right to hold, use, and allocate power. Power based on legitimacy, a form of cultural control, may be distinguished from power based solely on force, actual or threatened (social control): Obedience to the former results from the belief that obedience is "right"; compliance to power based on force results from fear of being deprived of liberty, physical well-being, life, or material property. Thus, power based on legitimacy is symbolic and depends not upon any intrinsic value but upon the positive expectations of those who recognize and accede to it. If the expectations are not met regularly (if the head of state fails to deliver "economic prosperity" or the leader is continuously unsuccessful in preventing or dealing with calamities), the legitimacy of the recognized power figure erodes or may collapse altogether.

RELIGION AND POLITICS

Religion is intricately connected with politics. Religious beliefs may influence laws: Acts that people believe to be sinful, such as sodomy and incest, are often illegal as well. Frequently it is religion that legitimizes the political order.

In both industrial and nonindustrial societies, belief in the supernatural is important and is reflected in people's governments. One place where the effect of religion on politics was well exemplified was in medieval Europe:

In the United States, in spite of an official separation of church and state, the president is always sworn in over a Christian Bible.

holy wars were fought over the smallest matter; labor was mobilized to build immense cathedrals in honor of the Virgin and other saints; kings and queens ruled by "divine right," and (in the West) pledged allegiance to the pope, and asked his blessing in all important ventures, were they marital or martial. In the pre-Columbian Americas the Aztec state was a religious state, with a divine king, that thrived in spite of more-or-less constant warfare carried out to procure captives for human sacrifices to assuage or please the gods. In Peru the Inca emperor proclaimed absolute authority based on the proposition that he was descended from the sun god. Modern Iran was proclaimed an "Islamic republic" and its first head of state was the most holy of all Shiite Muslim holy men. In the United States the Declaration of Independence, which is an expression of the country's social and political values, stresses a belief in a supreme being. The document states that "all men are created [by God] equal," a tenet that gave rise to American democracy because it implied that all people should participate in governing themselves. The fact that the president of the United States takes the oath of office by swearing on the Bible is another instance of the use of religion to legitimize political power, as is the phrase "one nation, under God" in the Pledge of Allegiance. On U.S. coins is the phrase "In God We Trust," many meetings of government bodies begin with a prayer or invocation, and the phrase "so help me God" is routinely used in legal proceedings. In spite of an official separation of church and state, religious legitimization of government lingers on.

CHAPTER SUMMARY

Political organization and control are about the ways power is distributed and embedded in society. Through political organization, societies maintain social order, manage public affairs, and reduce social disorder. No group can live together without persuading or coercing its members to conform to agreed-upon rules of conduct. To properly understand a society's political organization, one needs to view it in the light of its ecological, social, and ideological context.

Four basic types of political systems may be identified. In order of complexity, these range from uncentralized bands and tribes to centralized chiefdoms and states. The band, characteristic of food-foraging and some other mobile societies, is an association of politically independent but related families or households occupying a common territory. Political organization in bands is democratic, and informal control is exerted by public opinion in the form of gossip and ridicule. Band leaders are older men, or sometimes women, whose personal authority lasts only as long as members believe they are leading well and making the right decisions.

The tribe is composed of separate bands or other social units tied together by such unifying factors as descent groups, age grading, or common interest. With an economy usually based on crop cultivation or herding, the tribe's population is larger than that of the band, although family units within the tribe are still relatively autonomous and egalitarian. As in the band, political organization is transitory, and leaders have no coercive means of maintaining authority.

Many tribal societies vest political authority in the clan, an association of people who consider themselves descended from a common ancestor. A group of elders or headmen or headwomen regulate the affairs of members and represent their group in relations with other clans. Another variant of authority in tribes in Melanesia is the Big Man, who builds up his wealth and political power until he must be reckoned with as a leader. The segmentary lineage system, similar in operation to the clan, is a rare form of tribal organization based on kinship bonds.

Tribal age-grade systems cut across territorial and kin groupings. Leadership is vested in men in the group who were initiated into the age grade at the same time and passed as a set from one age grade to another until reaching the proper age to become elders. Common-interest associations wield political authority in some tribes. A boy joins one club or another when he reaches warrior status. These organizations administer tribal affairs.

As societies include larger numbers of people and become more heterogeneous socially, politically, and economically, leadership becomes more centralized. Chiefdoms are ranked societies in which every member has a position in the hierarchy. Status is determined by the individual's position in a descent group and distance of relationship to the chief. Power is concentrated in a single chief whose true authority serves to unite his community in all matters. The chief may accumulate great personal wealth, which enhances his power base and which he may pass on to his heirs.

The most centralized of political organizations is the state. It has a central power that legitimately can use force to administer a rigid code of laws and to maintain order, even beyond its borders. A large bureaucracy functions to uphold the central power's authority. The state is found only in societies with numerous diverse groups. Typically, it is a stratified society where economic functions and wealth are distributed unequally. Although thought of as being stable and permanent, it is, in fact, inherently unstable and transitory. States differ from nations, which are communities of people who see themselves as "one people" with a common culture, but who may or may not have a centralized form of political organization.

Historically women have rarely held important positions of political leadership, and when they have, it has sometimes been for lack of a qualified man to hold the position. Nonetheless, in a number of societies, women have enjoyed political equality with men, as among the Iroquoian tribes of New York State. Among them, all men held office at the pleasure of women, who not only appointed them but could remove them as well. Among the Igbo of midwestern Nigeria, women held positions in an administrative hierarchy that paralleled and balanced that of the men. Under centralized political systems, women are most apt to be subordinate to men, and when states impose their control on societies marked by sexual egalitarianism, the relationship changes so that men dominate women.

Two kinds of control exist: internalized and externalized. Internalized controls are self-imposed by individuals. These are purely cultural in nature, as they are built into the people's minds. They rely on such deterrents as personal shame, fear of divine punishment, and magical retaliation. Although bands and tribes rely heavily upon them, internalized controls are generally insufficient by themselves. Every society develops externalized controls, called sanctions, that mix cultural and social control. The latter involves overt coercion. Positive sanctions, in the form of rewards or recognition by one's neighbors, is the position a society, or a number of its members, takes toward approved behavior; negative sanctions, such as threat of imprisonment, fines, corporal punishment, or "loss of face," reflect societal reactions to disapproved behavior.

Sanctions also may be classified as either formal, including actual laws, or informal, involving norms. Formal sanctions are organized and reward or punish behavior through a prescribed social procedure. Informal sanctions are diffuse, involving immediate reactions of approval or disapproval by individual community members to a compatriot's behavior. Other important agents of social control are witchcraft beliefs and religious sanctions.

Sanctions serve to assure conformity to group norms, including actual law, and to maintain each social faction in a community in its "proper" place. An adequate working definition of law is that it consists of formal negative sanctions.

Law serves several basic functions. First, it defines relationships among a society's members and thereby dictates proper behavior under different circumstances. Second, law allocates authority to employ coercion to enforce sanctions. In centralized political systems, this authority rests with the government and court system. Uncentralized societies may give this authority directly to the injured party. Third, law redefines social relations and aids its own efficient operation by ensuring it allows change.

Western societies clearly distinguish offenses against the state, called crimes, from offenses against an individual, called torts. Uncentralized societies may view all offenses as against individuals. One way to understand the nature of law is to analyze individual dispute cases against their own cultural background. A dispute may be settled in two ways: negotiation and adjudication. All societies use negotiation to settle individual disputes. In negotiation the parties to the dispute reach an agreement themselves, with or without the help of a third party. In adjudication, not found in some societies, an authorized third party issues a binding decision. The disputing parties present their petitions, but play no part in the decision making.

In addition to regulating internal affairs, political systems also attempt to regulate external affairs, or relations between politically autonomous units. In doing so they may resort to the threat or use of force.

War is not a universal phenomenon, since there are societies that do not practice warfare as we know it. Usually, these are stateless societies that have some kind of naturalistic worldview, an attitude that until recently had become nearly extinguished in modern industrial societies.

A major problem any form of political organization faces is obtaining and maintaining people's loyalty and support. Reliance on force and coercion usually tends in the long run to lessen a political system's effectiveness. A basic instrument of political implementation is legitimacy, or the right of political leaders to exercise authority. Power based on legitimacy stems from the belief of a society's members that obedience is "right," and therefore from the positive expectations of those who obey. It may be distinguished from compliance based on force, which stems from fear and thus from negative expectations.

Religion is so intricately woven into the life of the people in both industrial and nonindustrial countries that its presence is inevitably felt in the political sphere. To a greater or lesser extent, most governments the world over use religion to legitimize political power.

CLASSIC READINGS

Cohen, R., & Middleton, J. (Eds.) (1967). *Comparative political systems.* Garden City, NY: Natural History Press.

The editors have selected some 20 studies in the politics of nonindustrial societies by such well-known scholars as Lévi-Strauss, S. F. Nadel, Marshall Sahlins, and S. N. Eisenstadt.

Fried, M. (1967). *The evolution of political society: An essay in political anthropology.* New York: Random House.

The author attempts to trace the evolution of political society through a study of simple, egalitarian societies. The character of the state and how this organizational form takes shape are considered in terms of pristine and secondary states, the latter formed because preexisting states supplied the stimuli or models for organization.

Gordon, R. J., & Meggitt, M. J. (1985). *Law and order in the New Guinea highlands.* Hanover, NH: University Press of New England.

This ethnographic study of the resurgence of tribal fighting among the Mae-Enga addresses two issues of major importance in today's world: the changing nature of law and order in "underdeveloped" countries and the nature of violence in human societies.

Johnson, A. W., & Earle, T. (1987). *The evolution of human societies, from foraging group to agrarian state.* Stanford CA: Stanford University Press.

Although written as a synthesis of economic and ecological anthropology, this is also a book on the evolution of political organization in human societies. Proceeding from family-level organization up through state organization, the authors discuss nine levels, illustrating each with specific case studies, and specify the conditions that give rise to each level.

Nader, L. (Ed.) (1980). *No access to law: Alternatives to the American judicial system.* New York: Academic Press.

This is an eye-opening study of how consumer complaints are resolved in U.S. society. After 10 years of study, Nader found repeated and documented offenses by business that cannot be handled by present complaint mechanisms, either in or out of court. The high cost exacted includes a terrible sense of apathy and loss of faith in the system.

Whitehead, N., & Ferguson, R. B. (Eds.) (1992). *War in the tribal zone.* Santa Fe: School of American Research Press.

The central point of this book is that both the transformation and intensification of war, as well as the formation of tribes, result from complex interaction in the "tribal zone" that begins where centralized authority makes contact with stateless people it does not rule. In such zones, newly introduced plants, animals, diseases, and technologies often spread widely, even before colonizers appear. These and other changes disrupt existing social and political relationships, fostering new alliances and creating new kinds of conflicts.

CHAPTER 24

CULTURE AND THE SUPERNATURAL

People relate to the supernatural through ritual, and trance, dance, music, and sacrifice are frequently part of the ritual. Shown here are Haitians in Miami, celebrating the Gede spirits who oversee cemeteries.

CHAPTER PREVIEW

1

What Is Religion?

Religion may be regarded as organized beliefs in the supernatural that guide humans in their attempts to make sense of the world and deal with problems they view as important, but defy solution through application of known technology or techniques of organization. To overcome these limitations, people appeal to, or seek to influence and even manipulate supernatural beings and powers.

2

What Are Religion's Identifying Features?

Religion consists of various beliefs and rituals—prayers, songs, dances, offerings, and sacrifices—that people use to interpret, appeal to, and manipulate supernatural beings and powers to their advantage. These beings and powers may consist of gods and goddesses, ancestral and other spirits, or impersonal powers, either by themselves or in various combinations. In all societies certain individuals are especially skilled at dealing with these beings and powers and assist other members of society in their ritual activities. A body of myths rationalizes or "explains" the system in a manner consistent with people's experience in the world in which they live.

What Functions Does Religion Serve?

Whether or not a particular religion accomplishes what people believe it does, all religions serve a number of important psychological and social functions. They reduce anxiety by explaining the unknown and making it understandable, as well as provide comfort with the belief supernatural aid is available in times of crisis. They sanction a wide range of human conduct by providing notions of right and wrong, setting precedents for acceptable behavior, and transferring the burden of decision making from individuals to supernatural powers. Through ritual, religion may be used to enhance the learning of oral traditions. Finally, religion plays an important role in maintaining social solidarity.

According to their origin myth, the Tewa-speaking Pueblo Indians of New Mexico emerged from a lake far to the north of where they now live. Once on dry land, they divided into two groups, the Summer People and the Winter People, and migrated south along the Rio Grande. During their travels they made 12 stops before finally reuniting into a single community.

For the Tewa all existence is divided into six categories, three human and three supernatural. Each of the human categories, which are arranged in a hierarchy, is matched by a spiritual category so that when people die, they immediately pass into their proper spiritual role. Not only are the supernatural categories identified with human categories, they also correspond to divisions in the natural world.

To those of other religious persuasions, such beliefs may seem, at best, irrational and arbitrary, but in fact they are neither. The late Alfonso Ortiz, an anthropologist who was also a Tewa, showed that his native religion is not only logical and socially functional but also the very model of Tewa society.[1] These people have a society that is divided into two independent moieties, each with its own economy, rituals, and authority. The individual is introduced into one of these moieties (which in this case are *not* based on kinship), and his or her membership is regularly reinforced through a series of life-cycle rituals that correspond to the stops on the mythical journey down the Rio Grande. The rites of birth and death are shared by the whole community; other rites differ in the two moieties. The highest status of the human hierarchy belongs to the priests, who also help integrate this divided society; they mediate not only between the human and spiritual world but between the two moieties as well.

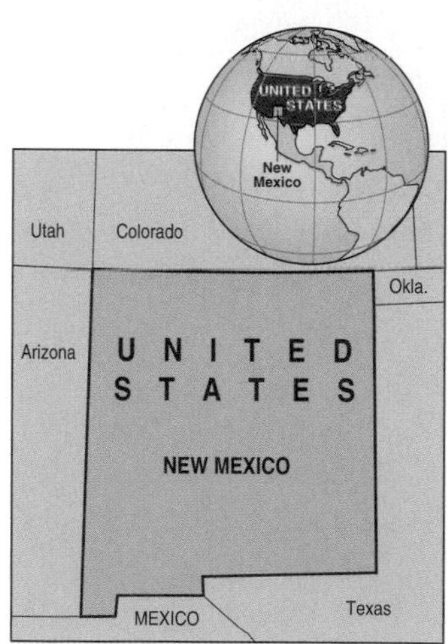

[1] Ortiz, A. (1969). *The Tewa world* (p. 43). Chicago: University of Chicago Press.

Tewa religion enters into virtually every aspect of Tewa life and society. It is the basis of the simultaneously dualistic and unified worldview of the individual Tewa. It provides numerous points of mediation so that the two moieties can continue to exist together as a single community. It sanctifies the community by linking its origin with the realm of the supernatural, and it offers divine sanction to *rites of passage* that soften life's major transitions. By providing an afterworld that is the mirror image of human society, it answers the question of death in a manner that reinforces social structure. In short, Tewa religion, by weaving all elements of Tewa experience into a single pattern, gives a solid foundation to the stability and continuity of Tewa society.

Religion is viewed most simply as organized belief in the supernatural, and all fulfill numerous social and psychological needs. Some of these—the need to confront and explain death, for example—appear to be universal; indeed, we know of no group of people anywhere on the face of the earth who, at any time over the past 100,000 years, have been without religion. Not even in Albania and the Soviet Union, where atheism was the state dogma, did religion disappear. Unbound by time, religion gives meaning to individual and group life, drawing power from "the time of the gods in the Beginning," and offering continuity of existence beyond death. It can provide the path by which people transcend their arduous earthly existence and attain, if only momentarily, spiritual selfhood. The social functions of religion are no less important than the psychological ones. A traditional religion reinforces group norms, provides moral sanctions for individual conduct, and furnishes the substratum of common purpose and values upon which the well-being of the community depends.

In the 19th century, the European intellectual tradition gave rise to the idea that science would ultimately destroy religion by showing people the irrationality of their myths and rituals. Indeed, many still believe that as scientific explanations replace those of religion, the latter will wither on the vine. Yet an opposite tendency has occurred; although traditional, mainline religions have shown some decline, fundamentalist religions are having a strong resurgence. Examples include Islamic fundamentalism in countries such as Afghanistan, Algeria, and Iran; Jewish fundamentalism in Israel; and Hindu fundamentalism in India. Christian fundamentalism is represented in the dramatic growth of evangelical denominations in the United States (Table 24.1). Often, these take a strong antiscience position. Other religions continue to grow in North Amer-

TABLE 24.1	INCREASE OR DECREASE OF SELECTED CHRISTIAN DENOMINATIONS FOR THE PAST 30 YEARS AS A PROPORTION OF THE U.S. POPULATION
Episcopal	−44%
Methodist	−38
Roman Catholic	−3
Southern Baptist	+8
Mormon	+96
Jehovah's Witnesses	+119
Assemblies of God	+211
Church of God in Christ	+863

SOURCE: Shorto, R. (1997, December 7). Belief by the numbers. *New York Times Magazine,* 60.

ica as well, including Islam (at least 3.5 million in the United States, comparable to the number of Presbyterians), Buddhism (750,000 in the United States), Hinduism (800,000 in the United States, up from about 70,000 in 1977), not to mention various "New Age" options such as Wicca (at least 100,000, possibly 1,000,000, practitioners in the United States).[2]

Science, far from destroying religion, may have contributed to the creation of a veritable religious boom. In the United States, the latter is worth billions of tax-free dollars each year, and some religious leaders even go so far as to flaunt luxurious life styles as proof that they enjoy God's favor. Science has fostered this religious boom by removing many traditional psychological props while creating, in its technological applications, a host of new problems: threat of nuclear catastrophe; health threats from pollution; unease about the consequences of new developments in biotechnology such as the cloning of animals, production of new strains of genetically engineered organisms, ability to store human sperm and eggs for future fertilization, and manipulation of human DNA; fear of loss of economic security as machines replace workers; and suffering loneliness in a society that isolates us from our kin and that places obstacles in the way of establishing deep and lasting friendships—to list but a few issues people now must deal with. In the face of these new anxieties, religion offers social and psychological support.

The continuing strength of religion in the face of Western rationalism clearly reveals that it is a powerful and dynamic force in society. Although anthropologists are not qualified to pass judgment on the metaphysical truth of any particular religion, they can show how each embodies a number of "truths" about humans and society.

Far from causing the death of religion, the growth of scientific knowledge, by producing new anxieties and raising new questions about human existence, may have contributed to the continuing practice of religion in modern life. North Americans continue to participate in traditional religions, such as Judaism (top), as well as imported sects, such as the new Vrindaban (middle) and evangelism (bottom).

[2] Ferla, R. L. (2000, February 13). Like magic, witchcraft charms teenagers. *New York Times,* Section 9, 1 & 2; Shorto, R. (1997, December 7). Belief by the numbers. *New York Times Magazine,* 60.

New developments in biotechnology, such as gene transfer from one species into another (these green mice owe their color to a gene transferred from a jellyfish), have been a source of new anxieties. Answers to these anxieties are often sought in religion.

THE ANTHROPOLOGICAL APPROACH TO RELIGION

Anthropologist Anthony F. C. Wallace defined **religion** as "a set of rituals, rationalized by myth, which mobilizes supernatural powers for the purpose of achieving or preventing transformations of state in man and nature."[3] Behind this definition lies a recognition that people, when they cannot "fix" through technological or organizational means serious problems that cause them anxiety, try to do so through manipulation of supernatural beings and powers. This requires ritual, which can be seen as the primary expression of religion, or "religion in action." Its major functions are to reduce anxiety and keep confidence high, necessary to keep people in some sort of shape to cope with reality. It is this that gives religion survival value.

[3] Wallace, A. F. C. (1966) *Religion: An anthropological view.* New York: Random House.

Religion, then, may be regarded as organized beliefs in the supernatural and the associated ritual by which people try to interpret and control aspects of the universe otherwise beyond their control. Since no known culture, including those of modern industrial societies, has achieved complete certainty in controlling existing or future conditions and circumstances, religion is a part of all known cultures. However, considerable variability exists here. At one end of the human spectrum are food-foraging peoples, whose technological ability to manipulate their environment is limited and who tend to see themselves more as part, rather than masters, of nature. This is what we referred to in Chapter 23 as a naturalistic worldview. Among food foragers religion is apt to be inseparable from the rest of daily life. It also mirrors and confirms the egalitarian nature of social relations in their societies, in that individuals do not plead for aid to high-ranking deities the way members of stratified societies do. At the other end of the human spectrum is Western civilization, with its ideological commitment to overcoming problems through technological and organizational skills. Here religion is less a part of daily activities and is restricted to more specific occasions. Moreover, with its hierarchy of supernatural beings—for instance, God, the angels, and (in some denominations) the saints of Christianity—it reflects and confirms the stratified nature of the society in which it is embedded.

Even so, there is variation within society. Religious activity may be less prominent in the lives of social elites, who may see themselves as more in control of their own destinies, than it is in the lives of peasants or members of lower classes. Among the latter, religion may afford some compensation for a dependent position in society. Yet religion is still important to elite members of society, in that it rationalizes the system in such a way that less advantaged people are not as likely to question the existing social order as they might otherwise be. After all, with hope for a better existence after death, one may be more willing to put up with a disadvantaged position in life. Thus, religious beliefs serve to influence and perpetuate conceptions, if not actual relations, between different classes of people.

THE PRACTICE OF RELIGION

Much of religion's value comes from the activities called for by its prescriptions and rules. Participation in religious ceremonies may bring a sense of personal lift—a wave of re-

Religion. Organized beliefs in the supernatural that rationalize rituals aimed at interpreting and controlling aspects of the universe otherwise beyond human control.

The huge public participation in the funeral of former Canadian Prime Minister Pierre Elliot Trudeau, as in all collective rituals, created a sense of communion that encouraged belief in shared values.

assurance, security, and even ecstasy—or a feeling of closeness to fellow participants. Although the beliefs and ceremonial practices of religions vary considerably, even rituals that may seem to us most bizarrely exotic can be shown to serve the same basic social and psychological functions.

Supernatural Beings and Powers

A hallmark of religion is belief in supernatural beings and forces. In attempting to control by religious means what cannot be controlled in other ways, humans turn to prayer, sacrifice, and other religious rituals. These presuppose a world of supernatural beings who have an interest in human affairs and to whom one may turn for aid. For convenience we may divide these beings into three categories: major deities (gods and goddesses), ancestral spirits, and other sorts of spirit beings. Although the variety of deities and spirits recognized by the world's cultures is tremendous, certain generalizations about them are possible.

GODS AND GODDESSES

Gods and goddesses are the great and more remote beings. They are usually seen as controlling the universe,

HIGHWAY 1
Sacred Sites
http://www.sacredsites.com

HIGHWAY 2
Anthropology of Religion
http://www.as.au.edu/ant/faculty/murphy/419/419www.htm

or, if several are recognized (known as **polytheism**), each has charge of a particular part of the universe. Such was the case of the gods and goddesses of ancient Greece: Zeus was lord of the sky, Poseidon was ruler of the sea, and Hades was lord of the underworld and ruler of the dead. In addition to these three brothers were a host of other deities, female as well as male, each similarly concerned with specific aspects of life and the universe. **Pantheons,** or collections of gods and goddesses such as those of the Greeks, are common in non-Western states as well. Since states commonly have grown through conquest, their pantheons often have expanded as local deities of conquered peoples were incorporated into the official state pantheon. Although creators of the present world may be included, this is not always the case; the Greeks, to cite but one example, did not include them. Another frequent though not invariable feature of pantheons is the presence of a supreme deity, who may be all but totally ignored by humans. The Aztecs of Mexico, for instance, recognized a supreme pair to whom they paid little attention. After all, being so remote, they were unlikely to be interested in human affairs. The sensible practice, then, was to focus attention on less remote deities who therefore were more directly concerned with human matters.

Whether or not a people recognize gods, goddesses, or both has to do with how men and women relate to one another in everyday life. Generally speaking, societies that subordinate women to men define the godhead in exclusively masculine terms. Such societies are mainly those with economies based upon the herding of animals or intensive agriculture carried out by men, who as fathers are distant and controlling figures to their children.

Goddesses, by contrast, are apt to be most prominent in societies where women make a major contribution to the economy, enjoy relative equality with men, and where men are more involved in their children's lives. Such societies are most often those that depend upon farming, much or all of which is done by women. As an illustration, the early Israelites, like other pastoral nomadic tribes of the Middle East, described their god in masculine, authoritarian terms. By contrast, goddesses played central roles in religious ritual and the popular consciousness of the region's agricultural peoples. Associated with these

The patriarchal nature of Western society is expressed in its theology, in which a masculine God gives life to the first man, as depicted here on the ceiling of the Sistine Chapel. Only after this is the first woman created from the first man.

Polytheism. Belief in several gods and/or goddesses (as contrasted with monotheism—belief in one god or goddess). • **Pantheon.** The several gods and goddesses of a people.

goddesses were concepts of light, love, fertility and procreation. Around 1300 B.C., the Israelite tribes entered the land of Canaan and began to practice agriculture, requiring them to establish a new kind of relationship with the soil. As they became dependent upon rainfall and on the rotation of seasons for crops and concerned about fertility (as the Canaanites already were), they adopted many of the Canaanite goddess cults. Although diametrically opposed to the original Israelite cult, belief in the Canaanite goddesses catered to the human desire for security by seeking to control the forces of fertility in the interest of people's well-being.

Later on, when the Israelite tribes sought national unity in the face of a military threat by the Philistines and when they strengthened their identity as a "chosen people," the goddess cults lost out to followers of the old masculine tribal god. This ancient masculine-authoritarian concept of god has been perpetuated down to the present, not just in the Judaic tradition but also by Christians and Muslims, whose religions stem from the old Israelite religion. As a consequence, this masculine-authoritarian model has played an important role in perpetuating a relationship between men and women in which the latter traditionally have been expected to submit to the "rule" of men at every level of Jewish, Christian, and Islamic society.

ANCESTRAL SPIRITS

A belief in ancestral spirits is consistent with the widespread notion that human beings are made up of two parts, a body and some kind of vital spirit. For example, the Penobscot Indians, whom we met in Chapter 16, maintained that each person had a vital spirit that could detach itself and travel about apart from the body, while the latter remained inert. Given such a concept, the idea of the spirit being freed from the body by death and having an existence thereafter seems quite logical.

Where a belief in ancestral spirits exists, these beings frequently are seen as retaining an active interest and even membership in society. In Chapter 23, for instance, we saw how deceased ancestors of the Wape acted to provide or withhold meat from their living descendants. Like living persons, ancestral spirits may be benevolent or malevolent, but no one is ever quite sure what their behavior will be. The same feeling of uncertainty—"How will they react to what I have done?"—may be displayed toward ancestral spirits and tends to be displayed toward people of a senior generation who hold authority over individuals. Beyond this, ancestral spirits closely resemble living humans in their appetites, feelings, emotions, and behavior. Thus, they reflect and reinforce social reality.

A belief in ancestral spirits of one sort or another is found in many parts of the world, especially among people with unilineal descent systems. In several such African societies, the concept is highly elaborated. Here one frequently finds ancestral spirits behaving just like humans. They are able to feel hot, cold, and pain, and they may be capable of dying a second death by drowning or burning. They even may participate in family and lineage affairs, and seats will be provided for them, even though the spirits are invisible. If they are annoyed, they may send sickness or even death. Eventually, they are reborn as new members of their lineage, and, in societies that hold such beliefs, adults need to observe infants closely to determine just who has been reborn.

Deceased ancestors were also important in the patrilineal society of traditional China. For the gift of life, a boy was forever indebted to his parents, owing them obedience, deference, and a comfortable old age. Even after their death, he had to provide for them in the spirit world, offering food, money, and incense to them on the anniversaries of their births and deaths. In addition, people collectively worshiped all lineage ancestors periodically throughout the year. Even the birth of sons was regarded as an obligation to the ancestors, because this ensured the latter's needs would continue to be attended to even after their own sons' death. To satisfy ancestors' needs for descendants (and a man's own need to be respectable in a culture that demanded he satisfy his ancestors' needs), a man would go so far as to marry a girl who had been adopted into his family as an infant so she could be raised as a dutiful wife for him, even when this arrangement went against the wishes of both parties. Furthermore, a man readily would force his daughter to marry a man against her will. In fact, a female child was raised to be cast out by her natal family yet might not find acceptance in her husband's family for years. Not until after death, when her soul was carried in a tablet and placed in the shrine of her husband's family, was she an official member of it. As a consequence, once a son was born to her, a woman worked long and hard to establish the strongest possible tie between herself and her son to ensure she would be looked after in life.

Strong beliefs in ancestral spirits are particularly appropriate in a society of descent-based groups with their associated ancestor orientation. More than this, though, these beliefs provide a strong sense of continuity that links the past, present, and future.

SIR EDWARD B. TYLOR (1832–1917)

The concept of animism was first brought to the attention of anthropologists by the British scholar Sir Edward B. Tylor.

Though not university educated himself, Tylor was the first person to hold a chair in anthropology at a British university, with his appointment first as lecturer, then reader, and finally (in 1895) as professor at Oxford. His interest in anthropology developed from travels that took him as a young man to the United States (where he visited an Indian pueblo), Cuba, and Mexico, where he was especially impressed by the achievements of the ancient Aztec and the more recent blend of Indian and Spanish culture.

Tylor's numerous publications ranged over such diverse topics as the possible historical connection between the games of pachisi and patolli (played in India and ancient Mexico); the origin of games of Cat's Cradle; and the structural connections between postmarital residence, descent, and certain other customs such as in-law avoidance and the couvade (the confinement of a child's father following birth). Tylor also formulated the first widely accepted definition of culture (see Chapter 14). The considerable attention he paid to religious concepts and practices in his writings stemmed from a lifelong commitment to combat the idea, still widely held in his time, that so-called savage people had degenerated more than civilized people from an original state of grace. To Tylor, who was raised as a Quaker, "savages" were intellectuals just like anyone else, grappling with their problems but handicapped (as was Tylor in his intellectual life) by limited information.

ANIMISM

One of the most widespread beliefs about supernatural beings is **animism,** which sees nature as animated by all sorts of spirits. In reality, the term masks a wide range of variation. Animals and plants, like humans, all may have their individual spirits, as may springs, mountains, or other natural features. So too may stones, weapons, ornaments, and so on. In addition, the woods may be full of a variety of unattached or free-ranging spirits. The various spirits involved are a highly diverse lot. Generally speaking, though, they are less remote from people than gods and goddesses and are more involved in daily affairs. They may be benevolent, malevolent, or just plain neutral. They also may be awesome, terrifying, lovable, or even mischievous. Since they may be pleased or irritated by human actions, people are obliged to be concerned about them.

Animism is typical of those who see themselves as being a part of nature rather than superior to it. This takes in most food foragers, as well as those food-producing peoples who acknowledge little qualitative difference between a human life and that of any living entity, including trees, plants, or even such things as rivers and mountains. In such societies, gods and goddesses are relatively unimportant, but the woods are full of all sorts of spirits. (For a good example, see the discussion of the Penobscot behavioral environment in Chapter 16.) Gods and goddesses, if they exist at all, may be seen as having created the world and perhaps making it fit to live in; but it is spirits individuals turn to for curing, who help or hinder the shaman, and whom the ordinary hunter may meet when off in the woods.

ANIMATISM

Although supernatural power is often thought of as being vested in supernatural beings, it doesn't have to be. The Melanesians, for example, think of *mana* as a force inherent in all objects. It is not in itself physical, but it can reveal itself physically. A warrior's success in fighting is not attributed to his own strength but to the *mana* contained in an amulet that hangs around his neck. Similarly, a farmer may know a great deal about horticulture, soil conditioning, and the correct time for sowing and harvesting but nevertheless depend upon *mana* for a suc-

Animism. A belief in spirit beings thought to animate nature.

Native Indians carved these faces into a rock along the Connecticut River to depict spirit beings they saw here while in states of trance.

cessful crop, often building a simple altar to this power at the end of the field. If the crop is good, it is a sign that the farmer has in some way appropriated the necessary *mana*. Far from being a personalized force, *mana* is abstract in the extreme, a power or potency lying always just beyond reach of the senses. As R. H. Codrington described it, "Virtue, prestige, authority, good fortune, influence, sanctity, luck are all words which, under certain conditions, give something near the meaning. . . . *Mana* sometimes means a more than natural virtue or power attaching to some person or thing."[4] This concept of impersonal potency, or energy, also was widespread among North American Indians. The Iroquois called it *orenda;* to the Sioux it was *wakonda;* to the Algonquians, *manitu.* Nevertheless, though found on every continent, the concept is not necessarily universal.

R. R. Marett called this concept of impersonal power or potency **animatism.** The two concepts, animatism (which is inanimate) and animism (a belief in spirit beings), are not mutually exclusive. They are often found in the same culture, as in Melanesia, and also in the Indian societies mentioned above.

People trying to comprehend beliefs in the supernatural beings and powers that others recognize frequently ask how such beliefs are maintained. In part, the answer is through manifestations of power. Given a belief in animatism and/or the powers of supernatural beings, one is predisposed to see what appear to be results of the application of such powers. For example, if a Melanesian warrior is convinced of his power because he possesses the necessary *mana* and he is successful, he is likely to interpret this success as proof of the power of *mana*. "After all, I would have lost had I not possessed it, wouldn't I?" Beyond this, because of his confidence in his *mana,* he may be willing to take more chances in his fighting, and this indeed could mean the difference between success or failure.

Failures, of course, do occur, but they can be explained. Perhaps one's prayer was not answered because a deity or spirit was still angry about some past insult. Or perhaps our Melanesian warrior lost his battle—the obvious explanation is that he was not as successful in bringing *mana* to bear as he thought, or else his opponent had more of it. In any case, humans generally emphasize successes over failures, and long after many of the latter have been forgotten, tales probably still will be told of striking cases of the workings of supernatural powers.

[4] Quoted by G. Leinhardt (1960). Religion. In H. Shapiro (Ed.). *Man, culture, and society* (p. 368). London: Oxford University Press.

Animatism. A belief that the world is animated by impersonal supernatural powers.

Another feature that tends to perpetuate beliefs in supernatural beings is that the beings have attributes with which people are familiar. Allowing for the fact that supernatural beings are in a sense larger than life, they generally are conceived of as living the way people do and as having the same sorts of interests. For example, the Penobscot Indians believed in a quasi-human culture hero, a giant magician called Gluskabe. Like ordinary mortals, Gluskabe traveled about in a canoe, used snowshoes, lived in a wigwam, and made stone arrowheads. The gods and goddesses of the ancient Greeks had all the familiar human lusts and jealousies. Such features serve to make supernatural beings believable.

The role of mythology in maintaining beliefs should not be overlooked. *Myths,* which are discussed in some detail in Chapter 25, are explanatory narratives that rationalize religious beliefs and practices. To European Americans, the word *myth* immediately conjures up the idea of a story about imaginary events, but the people responsible for a particular myth usually do not see it that way. To them myths are true stories, analogous to historical documents in modern North American culture. Even so, myths exist even in literate societies, as in the case of the two Judaic and Christian accounts of creation contained in the Bible's Book of Genesis. Myths invariably are full of accounts of the doings of various supernatural beings and thus serve to reinforce beliefs in them.

As the contribution of women to the economy has become increasingly important, some Christian denominations have allowed women to enter the ministry.

Religious Specialists

PRIESTS AND PRIESTESSES

All human societies include individuals whose task it is to guide and supplement the religious practices of others. Such individuals are highly skilled at contacting and influencing supernatural beings and manipulating supernatural forces. Often their qualification for this is that they have undergone special training. In addition, they may display certain distinctive personality traits that particularly suit them for their responsibilities. Societies with the resources to support full-time occupational specialists give the role of guiding religious practices and influencing the supernatural to the **priest** or **priestess.** He or she is the socially initiated, ceremonially inducted member of a recognized religious organization, with a rank and function that belongs to him or her as the holder of a position others have held before. The sources of power are the society and the institution within which the priest or priestess functions. The priest, if not the priestess, is a familiar figure in Western societies; he is the priest, minister, pastor, rector, rabbi, or whatever the official title may be in an organized religion. With their god defined historically in masculine, authoritarian terms, it is not surprising that, in the Judaic, Christian, and Islamic religions, the most important positions traditionally have been filled by men. Only in societies where women make a major contribution to the economy and that recognize goddesses as well as gods are female religious specialists likely to be found.

SHAMANS

Societies that lack full-time occupational specialization have existed far longer than those with such specialization, and the former have always included individuals with special powers and skills that enable them to make contact with and manipulate supernatural beings and forces. These powers and skills have come to them through some personal experience, usually in solitude. In an altered state of consciousness, they receive some sort of vision that empowers them to heal the sick, change the weather, control the movements of animals, and foretell

Priest or Priestess. A full-time religious specialist.

the future. As they perfect these and related skills, they assume the role of **shaman.**

In the United States millions of people learned something about shamans through the popular autobiography of Black Elk, a traditional Lakota Indian Holy Man, and Carlos Castaneda's largely fictional accounts of his experiences with Don Juan, the Yaqui Indian shaman. Numerous books and other publications on shamanism have appeared over the past three decades, and some European Americans have gone into practice as shamans, a development that has triggered considerable resentment among American Indians ("They stole our land, now they are stealing our religion."). In addition to so-called New Age enthusiasts, among whom shamanism is particularly popular, the faith healers and many other evangelists among fundamentalist Christians share most of the characteristics of shamanism.

Typically, one becomes a shaman by passing through stages commonly set forth in many myths. These stages may be thought to involve torture and violent dismemberment of the body; scraping away of the flesh until the body is reduced to a skeleton; substitution of the internal organs of the body and renewal of the blood; a period spent in a nether region, or land of the dead, during which the shaman is taught by the souls of dead shamans and other spirit beings; and an ascent to a sky realm. Among the Penobscot Indians, for example, any person could become a shaman, since no ecclesiastical organization provided rules and regulations to guide religious consciousness. The search for shamanistic visions was pursued by most adult Penobscot males, who would go off alone and, through meditation, sensory deprivation, and hyperventilation induce an altered state of consciousness in which they would receive a vision.

Not all were successful, but failure carried no social stigma. Those who did achieve success experienced a sense of disembodiment in which they established a special relationship with a particular animal that appeared in their vision. This became the shaman's animal helper—a common element in shamanism—who thereafter would assist the shaman in performance of his tasks.

Because shamanism is rooted in altered states of consciousness, and because the human nervous system that produces these states is a human universal, those involved experience similarly structured visual, auditory, somatic, olfactory, and gustatory (taste) hallucinations (for more on altered states see Chapters 16 and 25). The widespread occurrence of shamanism and the remarkable similarities between shamanic traditions wherever found are consequences of this universal neurological inheritance. At the same time, the meanings ascribed to sensations experienced in altered states and made of their content are culturally determined; hence, in spite of their overall similarities, local traditions always vary in their details.

As this photo of a "New Age" shaman shows, shamanism is by no means absent in modern industrial societies.

The shaman is essentially a religious entrepreneur who acts on behalf of some human client, often to bring about a cure or foretell some future event. To do so, the shaman intervenes to influence or impose his or her will on supernatural powers. The shaman can be contrasted with the priest or priestess, whose "clients" are the deities. Priests and priestesses frequently tell people what to do; the shaman tells supernaturals what to do. In return for services rendered, the shaman may collect a fee—fresh meat, yams, or a favorite possession. In some cases, the added prestige, authority, and social power attached to the shaman's status are reward enough.

When a shaman acts on behalf of a client, he or she may put on something of a show—one that heightens

Shaman. A part-time religious specialist whose special power to contact and manipulate supernatural beings and forces in an altered state of consciousness comes to him or her through some personal experience.

the basic drama with a sense of danger. Typically, the shaman enters a trancelike state, in which he or she experiences the sensation of traveling to the spirit world and seeing and interacting with spirit beings. The shaman tries to impose his or her will upon these spirits, an inherently dangerous contest, considering the superhuman powers spirits usually are thought to possess. One example of this is afforded by the trance dances of the Ju/'hoansi Bushmen of Africa's Kalahari Desert. Among these people shamans constitute, on average, about half the men and a third of the older women in any group. The most common reasons for their going into trance are to bring rain, control animals, and—as in the present example—to heal the sick (always an important activity of shamans, wherever they are found).

Original Study

Healing Among the Ju/'hoansi of the Kalahari[5]

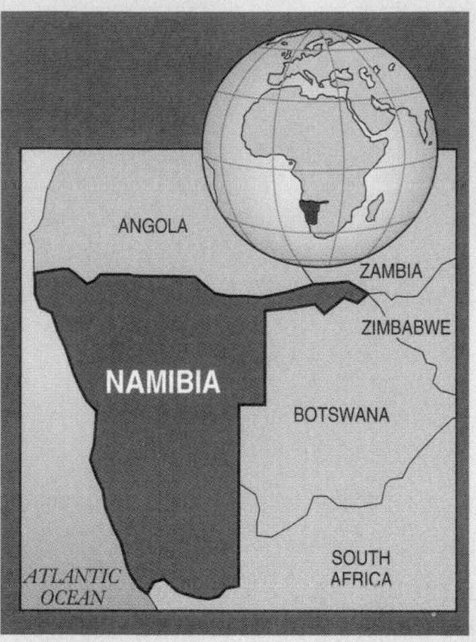

One way the spirits affect humans is by shooting them with invisible arrows carrying disease, death, or misfortune. If the arrows can be warded off, illness will not take hold. If illness has already penetrated, the arrows must be removed to enable the sick person to recover. An ancestral spirit may exercise this power against the living if a person is not being treated well by others. If people argue with her frequently, if her husband shows how little he values her by carrying on blatant affairs, or if people refuse to cooperate or share with her, the spirit may conclude that no one cares whether or not she remains alive and may "take her into the sky."

Interceding with the spirits and drawing out their invisible arrows is the task of [Ju/'hoansi] healers, men and women who possess the powerful healing force called **n/um** [the Ju/'hoansi equivalent of **mana**]. N/um generally remains dormant in a healer until an effort is made to activate it. Although an occasional healer can accomplish this through solo singing or instrumental playing, the usual way of activating n/um is through the medicinal curing ceremony or trance dance. To the sound of undulating melodies sung by women, healers dance around and around the fire, sometimes for hours. The music, the strenuous dancing, the smoke, the heat of the fire, and the healers' intense concentration cause their n/um to heat up. When it comes to a boil, trance is achieved.

At this moment the n/um becomes available as a powerful healing force, to serve the entire community. In trance, a healer lays hands on and rit-

Ju/'hoansi healers, when entering trance, are assisted by others among the trance dancers.

[5] Shostak, M. (1983). *Nisa: The life and words of a !Kung woman* (pp. 291–293). New York: Vintage.

ually cures everyone sitting around the fire. His hands flutter lightly beside each person's head or chest or wherever illness is evident; his body trembles; his breathing becomes deep and coarse; and he becomes coated with a thick sweat—also considered to be imbued with power. Whatever "badness" is discovered in the person is drawn into the healer's own body and met by the n/um coursing up his spinal column. The healer gives a mounting cry that culminates in a soul-wrenching shriek as the illness is catapulted out of his body and into the air.

While in trance, many healers see various gods and spirits sitting just outside the circle of firelight, enjoying the spectacle of the dance. Sometimes the spirits are recognizable—departed relatives and friends—at other times they are "just people." Whoever these beings are, healers in trance usually blame them for whatever misfortune is being experienced by the community. They are barraged by hurled objects, shouted at, and aggressively warned not to take any of the living back with them to the village of the spirits.

To cure a very serious illness, the most experienced healers may be called upon, for only they have enough knowledge to undertake the dangerous spiritual exploration that may be necessary to effect a cure. When they are in a trance, their souls are said to leave their bodies and to travel to the spirit world to discover the cause of the illness or the problem. An ancestral spirit or a god is usually found responsible and asked to reconsider. If the healer is persuasive and the spirit agrees, the sick person recovers. If the spirit is elusive or unsympathetic, a cure is not achieved. The healer may go to the principal god, but even this does not always work. As one healer put it, "Sometimes, when you speak with God, he says, 'I want this person to die and won't help you make him better.' At other times, God helps; the next morning, someone who has been lying on the ground, seriously ill, gets up and walks again."

These journeys are considered dangerous because while the healer's soul is absent his body is in half-death. Akin to loss of consciousness, this state has been observed and verified by medical and scientific investigators. The power of other healers' n/um is all that is thought to protect the healer in this state from actual death. He receives lavish attention and care—his body is vigorously massaged, his skin is rubbed with sweat, and hands are laid on him. Only when consciousness returns—the signal that his soul has been reunited with his body—do the other healers cease their efforts.

The End

In many human societies trancing is accompanied by sleight-of-hand tricks and ventriloquism. Among Arctic peoples, for example, a shaman may summon spirits in the dark and produce all sorts of flapping noises and strange voices to impress the audiences. Some Western observers regard this kind of trickery as evidence of the fraudulent nature of shamanism, but is this so? The truth is that shamans know perfectly well they are pulling the wool over people's eyes with their tricks. Yet virtually everyone who has studied them agrees shamans really believe in their power to deal with supernatural powers and spirits. The proof lies in their experience when in trance. It is their power that gives them the right as well as the ability to manipulate people in minor technical matters. In short, the shaman regards his or her ability to perform extraordinary tricks as further proof of superior powers.

The importance of shamanism in a society should not be underestimated. For individual members, it promotes, through the drama of performance, a feeling of ecstasy and release of tension. It provides psychological assurance, through prevailing upon supernatural powers and spirits otherwise beyond human control, of such things as invulnerability from attack, success at love, or the return of health. In fact, a frequent reason for a shamanistic performance is to cure illness. Although the treatment may not be medically effective, the state of mind induced in the patient may be critical to his or her recovery.

What shamanism provides for society is a focal point of attention. This is not without danger to the shaman. Someone with so much skill and power has the ability to work evil as well as good and so is potentially dangerous. The group may interpret too much nonsuccess on the part of a shaman as evidence of malpractice and may drive out or even kill the shaman. Likewise, the shaman may help maintain social control through an ability to detect and punish evildoers.

The benefits of shamanism for the shaman are that it provides prestige and perhaps even wealth. It may also be therapeutic, in that it provides an approved outlet for the outbreaks of what otherwise might seem an unstable personality. An individual who is psychologically unstable (and not all shamans are) actually may get better by becoming intensely involved with the problems of others. In this respect, shamanism is a bit like self-analysis. Finally, shamanism is a good outlet for the self-expression of those who might be described as endowed with an "artistic temperament."

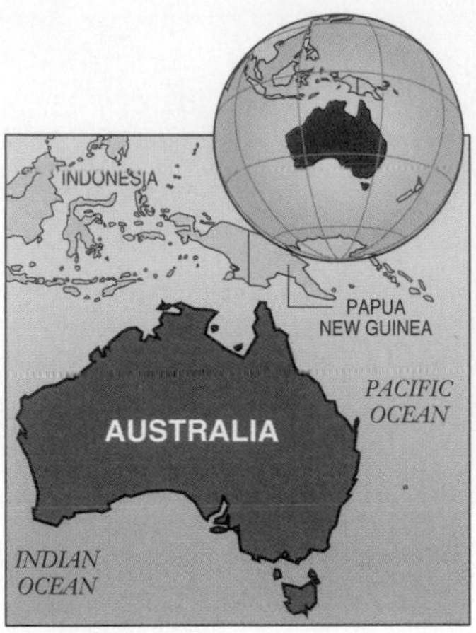

Rituals and Ceremonies

Although not all rituals are religious in nature (graduation ceremonies in North America, for example), those that are play a crucial role in religious activity. Religious ritual is the means through which persons relate to the supernatural; it is religion in action. Not only is ritual a means for reinforcing a group's social bonds and for relieving tensions, but it is also one way many important events are celebrated and crises, such as death, made less socially disruptive and less difficult for individuals to bear. Anthropologists have classified several different types of ritual, among them **rites of passage,** which pertain to stages in an individual's life cycle, and **rites of intensification,** which take place during a crisis in the life of the group, serving to bind individuals together.

RITES OF PASSAGE

In one of anthropology's classic works, Arnold Van Gennep analyzed the rites of passage that help individuals through the crucial crises of their lives, such as birth, puberty, marriage, parenthood, advancement to a higher class, occupational specialization, and death.[6] He found it useful to divide ceremonies for all of these life crises into three stages: **separation, transition,** and **incorporation.** The individual first would be ritually removed from the society as a whole, then isolated for a period, and finally incorporated back into society in his or her new status.

INDONESIA
PAPUA NEW GUINEA
PACIFIC OCEAN
AUSTRALIA
INDIAN OCEAN

Van Gennep described the male initiation rites of Australian Aborigines. When the elders decide the time for initiation, the boys are taken from the village (separation), while the women cry and make a ritual show of resistance. At a place distant from the camp, groups of men from many villages gather. The elders sing and dance, while the initiates act as though they are dead. The climax of this part of the ritual is a bodily operation, such as circumcision or the knocking out of a tooth. Anthropologist A. P. Elkin comments:

> This is partly a continuation of the drama of death. The tooth-knocking, circumcision or other symbolical act "killed" the novice; after this he does not return to the general camp and normally may not be seen by any woman. He is dead to the ordinary life of the tribe.[7]

In this transitional stage, the novice may be shown secret ceremonies and receive some instruction, but the most significant element is his complete removal from society. In the course of these Australian puberty rites, the initiate must learn the lore that all adult men are expected to know; he is given, in effect, a "cram course." The trauma of the occasion is a pedagogical technique that ensures he will learn and remember everything; in a nonliterate society the perpetuation of cultural traditions requires no less, and so effective teaching methods are necessary.

[6] Van Gennep, A. (1960). *The rites of passage*. Chicago: University of Chicago Press.

[7] Elkin, A. P. (1964). *The Australian Aborigines*. Garden City, NY: Doubleday/Anchor Books.

Rites of passage. Rituals, often religious in nature, marking important stages in the lives of individuals, such as birth, marriage, and death. • **Rites of intensification.** Religious rituals enacted during a group's real or potential crisis. • **Separation.** In rites of passage, the ritual removal of the individual from society. • **Transition.** In rites of passage, isolation of the individual following separation and prior to incorporation into society. • **Incorporation.** In rites of passage, reincorporation of the individual into society in his or her new status.

On his return to society (incorporation) the novice is welcomed with ceremonies, as though he had returned from the dead. This alerts the society at large to the individual's new status—that people can expect him to act in certain ways and in return they must act in the appropriate ways toward him. The individual's new rights and duties are thus clearly defined. He is spared, for example, the problems of a teenager in North America, a time when an individual is neither adult nor child but a person whose status is ill defined.

In the Australian case just cited, boys are prepared not just for adulthood but also for *manhood*. In their society, for example, courage and endurance are considered important masculine virtues, and the pain of tooth-knocking and circumcision help instill these in initiates. In a similar way, female initiation rites help prepare Mende girls in West Africa for womanhood. After they have begun to menstruate, the girls are removed from society to spend weeks, or even months, in seclusion. There they discard the clothes of childhood, smear their bodies with white clay, and dress in brief skirts and many strands of beads. Shortly after entering this transitional stage, they undergo surgery that excises their clitoris and part of the labia minora, something they believe enhances their procreative potential. Until their incorporation back into society, they are trained in the moral and practical responsibilities of potential childbearers by experienced women in the Sande association, an organization to which the initiates will belong once their training has ended. This training is not all harsh, however, for it is accompanied by a good deal of singing, dancing, and storytelling, and the initiates are very well fed. Thus, they acquire both a positive image of womanhood and a strong sense of sisterhood. Once their training is complete, a medicine made by brewing leaves in water is used for a ritual washing, removing the magical protection that has shielded them during the period of their confinement.

Mende women emerge from their initiation, then, as women in knowledgeable control of their sexuality, eligible for marriage and childbearing. The pain and danger of the surgery, endured in the context of intense social support from other women, serves as a metaphor for childbirth, which may well take place in the same place of seclusion, again with the support of Sande women. It also has been suggested that, symbolically, the clitoridectomy (excision of the clitoris, the feminine version of the male penis), removed sexual ambiguity.[8] Once it is done, a woman *knows* she is "all woman." Thus we have symbolic expression of gender as something important in people's cultural lives.

[8] MacCormack, C. P. (1977). Biological events and cultural control. *Signs, 3,* 98.

In the case just cited, the anthropological commitment to cultural relativism permits an understanding of the practice of clitoridectomy in the Mende female initiation rites. But as discussed earlier in this book (see Chapter 14), cultural relativism does not preclude the anthropologist from criticizing a given practice. In this case, removal of the clitoris (like male circumcision) is a form of genital mutilation, and a particularly dangerous one at that. Some form of genital mutilation, ranging from removal of the clitoris to removal of the entire external female genitalia, including the partial closing of the vaginal opening (surgically opened, or even torn open, for intercourse and closed again after giving birth until the male again desires intercourse), affects an estimated 80 million women in the world today, and is particularly widespread in Africa, where it occurs in 28 countries (At least 2 million girls are at risk each year). The custom is found also among some groups outside Africa: in Oman, Yemen, the United Arab Emirates (but not Iran, Iraq, Jordan, Libya, or Saudi Arabia); among some Muslims in Malaya and Indonesia; and an estimated 27,000 women in New York State.[9] As this list suggests, female genital mutilation is not required by Islamic religion; neither the Qu'ran nor the Bible makes any mention of cutting women to please God. Where the custom is practiced by Muslims (as well as the occasional Christian and Jewish group), it functions as a means for men to control women's sexuality (unlike among the Mende).

The consequences for women are extreme. One Somali woman who underwent the procedure as a child poses the questions:

> What about the girl back in the bush, walking miles and miles to water her goats, while she's in such pain from her period that she can barely stand up straight? Or the wife who will be sewn back up with a needle and thread like a piece of cloth as soon as she gives birth, so her vagina will remain tight for her husband? Or the woman nine months pregnant hunting for food to feed her other eleven starving children? Or what happens to the new wife whose first baby is to be born?"[10]

Quite apart from the pain and the effect of the operation on a woman's future sexual satisfaction, significant

[9] Armstrong, S. (1991). Female circumcision: Fighting a cruel tradition. *New Scientist,* p. 42; Dirie, W., & Miller, C. (1998). *Desert flower: The extraordinary journey of a desert nomad* (pp. 218, 219). New York: William Morrow.

[10] Dirie, W., & Miller, C. (1998). *Desert flower: The extraordinary journey of a desert nomad* (pp. 213). New York: William Morrow.

Waris Dirie, a Somali woman who underwent genital mutilation at age 6, holds the book in which she recounts her experience.

numbers of young women die from excessive bleeding, shock, infection, damage to the urethra or anus, tetanus, bladder infections, septicemia, HIV, hepatitis B, or (later on) when giving birth as scar tissue tears. Not surprisingly, the practice has been widely condemned as a human rights violation in recent years, and committees to end such practices have been set up in 22 African countries.

RITES OF INTENSIFICATION

Rites of intensification are rituals that mark occasions of crisis in the life of the group rather than an individual. Whatever the precise nature of the crisis—a severe lack of rain that threatens crops, the sudden appearance of an enemy war party, the onset of an epidemic, or some other event that disturbs everyone—mass ceremonies are performed to allay the danger to the group. This unites people in a common effort so that fear and confusion yield to collective action and a degree of optimism. The balance in the relations of all concerned, which has been upset, is restored to normal, and the community's values are celebrated and affirmed.

While an individual's death might be regarded as the ultimate crisis in that person's life, it is, as well, a crisis for the entire group, particularly if the group is small. A member of the community has been removed, so its composition has been seriously altered. The survivors, therefore, must readjust and restore balance. They also need to reconcile themselves to the loss of someone to whom they were emotionally tied. Funerary ceremonies, then, can be regarded as rites of intensification that permit the living to express in nondisruptive ways their upset over the death while providing for social readjustment. A frequent feature of such ceremonies is an ambivalence toward the dead person. For example, one of the parts of the funerary rites of certain Melanesians was the eating of the dead person's flesh. This ritual cannibalism, witnessed by anthropologist Bronislaw Malinowski, was performed with "extreme repugnance and dread and usually followed by a violent vomiting fit. At the same time it is felt to be a supreme act of reverence, love and devotion."[11] This custom and the emotions accompanying it clearly reveal an ambiguous attitude toward death: On the one hand, there is the survivors' desire to maintain the tie to the dead person, and, on the other hand, they feel disgust and fear at the transformation wrought by death. According to Malinowski, funeral ceremonies provide an approved collective means for individuals to express these feelings while maintaining social cohesiveness and preventing disruption of society.

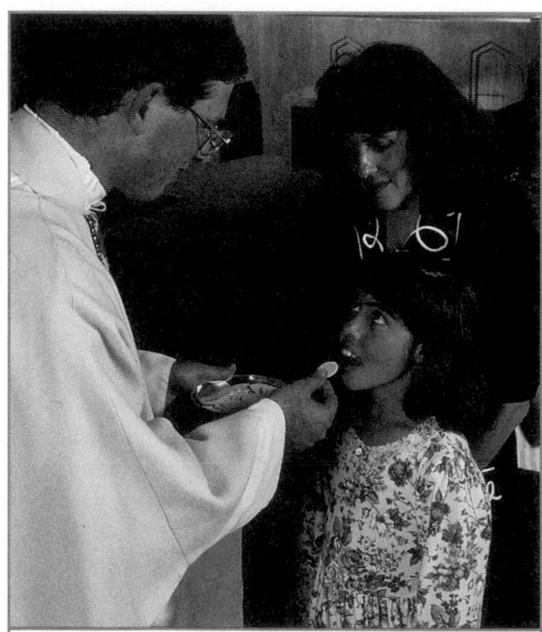

Ritual cannibalism appears in various societies in diverse forms. In Christianity, it is symbolic rather than actual, although some Christians believe the communion water actually becomes the body of Christ.

[11] Malinowski, B. (1954). *Magic, science and religion* (p. 50). Garden City, NY: Doubleday.

The performance of rites of intensification does not have to be limited to times of overt crisis. In regions where the seasons differ enough that human activities must change accordingly, they will take the form of annual ceremonies. These are particularly common among horticultural and agricultural people, with their planting, first-fruit, and harvest ceremonies. These are critical times in the lives of people in such societies, and the ceremonies express a reverent attitude toward nature's forces of generation and fertility upon which people's very existence depends. If all goes well, as it often does at such times, participation in a festive situation reinforces group involvement. It also serves as a kind of dress rehearsal for serious crisis situations; it promotes a habit of reliance on supernatural forces through ritual activity, which can be activated easily under stressful circumstances when it is important not to give way to fear and despair.

RELIGION, MAGIC, AND WITCHCRAFT

Among the most fascinating of ritual practices is application of the belief that supernatural powers can be compelled to act in certain ways for good or evil purposes by recourse to certain specified formulas. This is a classical anthropological notion of magic. Many societies have magical rituals to ensure good crops, the replenishment of game, the fertility of domestic animals, and the avoidance or cure of illness in humans.

Although many Western peoples today, seeking to objectify and demythologize their world, have often tried to suppress the existence of magic mysteries in their own consciousness, they continue to be fascinated by them. Not only are books and films about demonic possession and witchcraft avidly devoured and discussed, but horoscope columns are a regular feature of daily newspapers in the United States. While it may raise few eyebrows that Abraham Lincoln's wife invited psychics to the White House, it caused a considerable stir when it was learned that President Reagan's wife regularly consulted an astrologer. As for psychics or spirit mediums, they are consulted by growing numbers of people in the United States today. In 1996, a Gallup poll found that 20% of the respondents believed the dead could contact the living, and another 22% thought it might be possible. Anthropologist Lauren Kendall notes that "Many witches, wizards, druids, Cabalists, and shamans . . . practice modern magic in contemporary England and the United States, where their ranks are comfortably reckoned in the tens of thousands." Furthermore, "The usual magician is ordinary, generally middle class, and often highly intelligent—a noticeable number of them have something to do with computers."[12] Although it is certainly true that non-Western and peasant peoples tend to endow their world quite freely with magical properties, so do many highly educated Western peoples.

In the 19th century Sir James George Frazer, author of one of the most widely read anthropological books of all time, *The Golden Bough,* made a strong distinction between religion and magic. Religion he saw as "a propitiation or conciliation of powers superior to man which are believed to direct and control the course of nature and human life."[13] Magic, by contrast, he saw as an attempt to manipulate certain perceived "laws" of nature. The magician never doubts the same causes always will produce the same effects. Thus, Frazer saw magic as a sort of pseudoscience, differing from modern science only in its misconception of the nature of the particular laws that govern the succession of events.

Useful though Frazer's characterization of magic has been, anthropologists no longer accept his distinction between it and religion. Far from being separate, magical procedures frequently are part of religious rituals, and both magic and religion deal directly with the supernatural. In fact, Frazer's distinction seems to be no more than

Nancy Reagan, whose advice was important to her husband the president, consulted regularly with an astrologer while in the White House.

[12] Kendall, L. (1990, October). In the company of witches. *Natural History, 92.*

[13] Frazer, J. G. (1931). Magic and religion. In V. F. Calverton (Ed.). *The making of man: An outline of anthropology* (p. 693). New York: Modern Library.

What these two pictures have in common is that both are examples of institutionalized magical responses to concerns many harbor in their societies. In death-penalty states, executing criminals does no more to deter violent crimes than Aztec human sacrifices did to keep the sun in the sky.

a bias of Western culture, which regards magic as quite separate from religion.

Frazer did make a useful distinction between two fundamental principles of magic. The first principle, that "like produces like," he called **imitative magic** (sometimes called *sympathetic magic*). In Burma, for example, a rejected lover might engage a sorcerer to make an image of his would-be love. If this image were tossed into water, to the accompaniment of certain charms, the hapless girl would go mad. Thus, the girl would suffer a fate similar to that of her image.

Frazer's second principle was called **contagious magic**—the idea being that things or persons once in contact can influence one another after the contact is broken. The most common example of contagious magic is the permanent relationship between an individual and any part of his or her body, such as hair, fingernails, or teeth. Frazer cites the Basutos of Lesotho in southern Africa, who were careful to conceal their extracted teeth, because these might fall into the hands of certain mythical beings who could harm the owners of the teeth by working magic on them. Related to this is the custom, in Western societies, of treasuring things that have been touched by special people. Such things range from a saint's relics to possessions of other admired or idolized individuals.

Witchcraft

In Salem, Massachusetts, 200 suspected witches were arrested in 1692; of these, 19 were hanged and 1 was hounded to death. Despite the awarding of damages to descendants of some of the victims 19 years later, not until 1957 were the last of the Salem witches exonerated by the Massachusetts legislature. **Witchcraft** is an explanation of events based on the belief that certain individuals possess an innate psychic power capable of causing harm, including sickness and death. Although many North Americans suppose it to be something that belongs to a less enlightened past, in fact, witchcraft is alive and well in the United States today. Indeed, starting in the 1960s, witchcraft began to undergo something of a boom in this country. North Americans are by no means alone in this; for example, as the Ibibio of Nigeria have become increasingly exposed to modern education and scientific training, their reliance on witchcraft as an explanation for misfortune has increased.[14] Furthermore, it is often the younger, more educated members of Ibibio society who

[14] Offiong, D. (1985). Witchcraft among the Ibibio of Nigeria. In A. C. Lehmann & J. E. Myers (Eds.), *Magic, witchcraft and religion* (pp. 152–165). Palo Alto, CA: Mayfield.

Imitative magic. Magic based on the principle that like produces like. Sometimes called sympathetic magic. • **Contagious magic.** Magic based on the principle that things once in contact can influence one another after separation. • **Witchcraft.** An explanation of events based on the belief that certain individuals possess an innate psychic power capable of causing harm, including sickness and death.

The treasuring of objects once touched by special people is well represented in modern industrial societies. Here we see Princess Diana's fifth evening gown being auctioned at Christie's in June of 1997.

accuse others of bewitching them. Frequently, the accused are older, more traditional members of society; thus, we have an expression of the intergenerational hostility that often exists in fast-changing traditional societies.

IBIBIO WITCHCRAFT

Among the Ibibio, as among most traditional peoples of sub-Saharan Africa, witchcraft beliefs are highly developed and long standing. A rat that eats up a person's crops is not really a rat but a witch that changed into one; if a young and enterprising man cannot get a job or fails an exam, he has been bewitched; if someone's money is wasted away or if the person becomes sick, is bitten by a snake, or is struck by lightning, the reason is always the same—witchcraft. Indeed, virtually all misfortune, illness, or death are attributed to the malevolent activity of witches. The modern Ibibio's knowledge of such facts as the role microorganisms play in disease has little impact; after all, it says nothing about why these were sent to the afflicted individual. Although Ibibio religious beliefs provide alternative explanations for misfortune, they carry negative connotations and do not elicit nearly as much sympathy from others. Thus, if evil befalls a person, witchcraft is a far more satisfying explanation than something such as offspring disobedience or violation of some taboo.

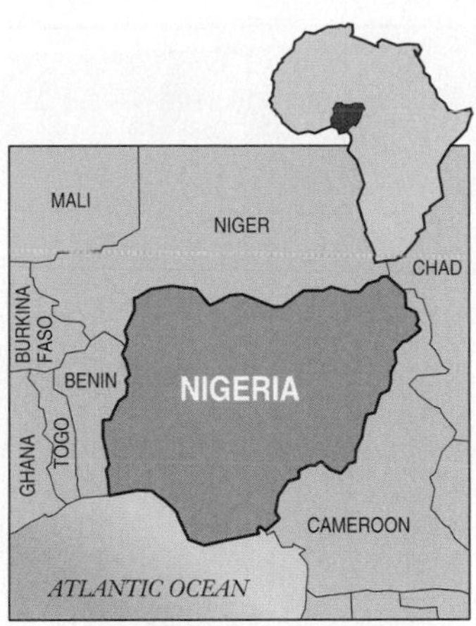

Who are these Ibibio witches? They are thought to be men or women who have within them a special substance acquired from another established witch. This substance is made up of red, white, and black threads, needles, and other ingredients, and one gets it by swallowing it. From it comes a special power that causes harm, up to and including death, regardless of whether its possessor intends to cause harm or not. The power is purely psychic, and witches do not perform rites nor make use of "bad medicine." It gives them the ability to transform into animals and to travel any distance at incredible speed to get at their victims, whom they may torture or kill by transferring the victim's soul into an animal, which is then eaten.

To identify a witch, an Ibibio looks for any person whose behavior is odd, out of the ordinary. Specifically, any combination of the following may cause someone to be labeled a witch: not being fond of greeting people; living alone in a place apart from others; charging too high a price for something; enjoying adultery or committing incest; walking about at night; not showing sufficient grief upon the death of a relative or other member of the community; taking improper care of one's parents, children, or wives; and hardheartedness. Witches are apt to look and act mean and to be socially disruptive people in the sense that their behavior too far exceeds the range of variance considered acceptable.

Neither the Ibibio in particular nor Africans in general are alone in attributing most harmful happenings to witchcraft. Similar beliefs can be found in any human society, including—as already noted—that of the United States. As among the Ibibio, the powers (however they may be gained) are generally considered innate and uncontrollable; they result in activities that are the antithesis of proper behavior, and persons displaying undesirable personality characteristics (however these may be defined) are generally the ones accused of being witches.

In North America, interest in and practice of witchcraft have grown significantly over the past 30 years, often among highly educated segments of society. Contrary to popular belief, witchcraft (sometimes called Wicca) is *not* concerned exclusively, or even primarily, with working evil.

The Ibibio make a distinction between sorcerers, whose acts are especially diabolical and destructive, and benign witches, whose witchcraft is relatively harmless, even though their powers are thought to be greater than those of their malevolent counterparts. This exemplifies a common distinction between what Lucy Mair, a British anthropologist, has dubbed "nightmare witches" and "everyday witches."[15] The nightmare witch is the very embodiment of a society's conception of evil, a being that flouts the rules of sexual behavior and disregards every other standard of decency. Nightmare witches, being almost literally the product of dreams and repressed fantasies, have much in common wherever they appear: The modern Navajo and the ancient Roman, for example, like the Ibibio, conceived of witches that could "shape change," that is, turn themselves into animals and gather to feast on their victims. Everyday witches are often the community's nonconformists, who are morose, who eat alone, who are arrogant and unfriendly, but who otherwise cause little trouble. Such witches may be dangerous when offended and retaliate by causing sickness, death, crop failure, cattle disease, or any number of lesser ills; people thought to be witches are usually treated very courteously.

The Functions of Witchcraft

Why witchcraft? We might better ask, why not? As Mair aptly observed, in a world where there are few proven techniques for dealing with everyday crises, especially sickness, a belief in witches is not foolish; it is indispensable. No one wants to resign oneself to illness, and if the malady is caused by a witch's curse, then magical countermeasures should cure it. Not only does the idea of personalized evil answer the problem of unmerited suffering, but it also provides an explanation for many happenings for which no cause can be discovered. Witchcraft, then, cannot be refuted. Even if we could convince a person that his or her illness was due to natural causes, the victim would still ask, as the Ibibio do, Why me? Why now? Such a view leaves no room for pure chance; everything must be assigned a cause or meaning. Witchcraft provides the explanation and, in so doing, also provides both the basis and the means for taking counteraction.

Nor is witchcraft always harmful; even during the Spanish Inquisition, church officials recognized a benevolent variety. The positive functions of even malevolent witchcraft may be seen in many African societies where people believe sickness and death are caused by witches. The ensuing search for the perpetrator of the misfortune becomes, in effect, a communal probe into social behavior.

A witch-hunt is, in fact, a systematic investigation, through a public hearing, into all social relationships involving the victim of the sickness or death. Was a husband or wife unfaithful or a son lacking in the performance of his duties? Were an individual's friends uncooperative, or was the victim guilty of any of these wrongs? Accusations are reciprocal, and before long just about every unsocial or hostile act that has occurred in that society since the last outbreak of witchcraft (sickness or death) is brought into the open.[16]

Through such periodic public scrutiny of everyone's behavior, people are reminded of what their society regards as both strengths and weaknesses of character. This encourages individuals to suppress as best they can those personality traits that are looked upon with disapproval, for if they do not, they at some time may be accused of being a witch. A belief in witchcraft thus serves a function of social control.

[15] Mair, L. (1969). *Witchcraft* (p. 37). New York: McGraw-Hill.

[16] Turnbull, C. M. (1983). *The human cycle* (p. 181). New York: Simon & Schuster.

Anthropology Applied

Reconciling Modern Medicine with Traditional Beliefs in Swaziland

Although the biomedical germ theory is generally accepted in Western societies today, this is not the case in many other societies around the world. In southern Africa's Swaziland, for example, all types of illnesses are generally thought to be caused by sorcery or by loss of ancestral protection. Even where the effectiveness of Western medicine is recognized, the ultimate question remains: Why was the disease sent in the first place? Thus, for the treatment of disease, the Swazi have traditionally relied upon herbalists, diviner mediums through whom ancestor spirits are thought to work, and Christian faith healers. Unfortunately, such individuals have usually been regarded as quacks and charlatans by the medical establishment, even though the herbal medicines used by traditional healers are effective in several ways, and the reassurance provided patient and family alike through rituals that reduce stress and anxiety plays an important role in the patient's recovery. In a country where there is 1 traditional healer for every 110 people, but only 1 physician for every 10,000, the potential benefit of cooperation between physicians and healers seems self-evident. Nevertheless, it was unrecognized until proposed by anthropologist Edward C. Green.*

Green, who is now senior research associate with a private firm, went to Swaziland in 1981 as a researcher for a Rural Water-Borne Disease Control Project, funded by the United States Agency for International Development. Assigned the task of finding out about knowledge, attitudes, and practices related to water and sanitation, and aware of the serious deficiencies of conventional surveys that rely on precoded questionnaires (see Chapter 1), Green used instead the traditional anthropological techniques of open-ended interviews with key informants, along with participant observation. The key informants were traditional healers, patients, and rural health motivators (individuals communities chose to receive eight weeks of training in preventive health care in regional clinics). Without such work, Green would have found it impossible to design and interpret a reliable survey instrument, but the added payoff was that Green learned a great deal about Swazi theories of disease and its treatment.

Disposed at the outset to recognize the positive value of many traditional practices, Green could also see how cooperation with physicians might be achieved. For example, traditional healers already recognized the utility of Western medicines for treatment of diseases not indigenous to Africa, and traditional medicines were routinely given to children through inhalation and a kind of vaccination. Thus, nontraditional medicines and vaccinations might be accepted, if presented in traditional terms.

Realizing the suspicion existing on both sides, Green and his Swazi associate Lydia Makhubu (a chemist who had studied the properties of native medicines) recommended to the Minister of Health a cooperative project focused on a problem of concern to health professionals and native healers alike: infant diarrheal diseases. These had recently become a health problem of high concern to the general public; healers wanted a means to prevent such diseases, and a means of treatment existed—oral rehydration therapy—that was compatible with traditional treatments for diarrhea (herbal preparations taken orally over a period of time). Packets of oral rehydration salts, along with instructions, were provided healers in a pilot project, with positive results. This helped convince health professionals of the benefits of cooperation, while the healers saw the distribution of packets to them as a gesture of trust and cooperation on the part of the Ministry of Health.

Since then, further steps toward cooperation have been taken. All of this demonstrates the importance of finding how to work in ways compatible with existing belief systems. Directly challenging traditional beliefs, as all too often happens, does little more than create stress, confusion and resentment among people.

---

* Green, E. C. (1987). The planning of health education strategies in Swaziland, and The Integration of modern and traditional health sectors in Swaziland. In R. M. Wulff & S. J. Fiske (Eds.). *Anthropological praxis: Translating knowledge into action* (pp. 15–25 and 87–97). Boulder, CO: Westview.

PSYCHOLOGICAL FUNCTIONS OF WITCHCRAFT AMONG THE NAVAJO

Widely known among American Indians are the Navajo, who possess a highly developed concept of witchcraft. Several types of witchcraft are distinguished. *Witchery* encompasses the practices of witches, who are said to meet at night to practice cannibalism and kill people at a distance. *Sorcery* is distinguished from witchery only by the methods used by the sorcerer, who casts spells on individuals using the victim's fingernails, hair, or discarded clothing. *Wizardry* is not distinguished so much by its effects as by its manner of working: Wizards kill by injecting a cursed substance, such as a tooth from a corpse, into the victim's body.

Whether or not a particular illness results from Navajo witchcraft is determined by **divination,** a magical procedure that reveals the witch's identity. Once a person is charged with witchcraft, he or she is publicly interrogated—in the past, possibly even tortured until there is a confession. It is believed the witch's own curse will turn against the witch once this happens, so it is expected that the witch will die within a year. Some confessed witches have been allowed to live in exile.

According to Clyde Kluckhohn, Navajo witchcraft serves to channel anxieties, tensions, and frustrations caused by the pressures from Anglo Americans.[17] The rigid rules of proper behavior among the Navajo allow little means for expression of hostility, except through accusations of witchcraft. Such accusations funnel pent-up negative emotions against individuals without upsetting the wider society. Another function of witchcraft accusations is that they permit direct expression of hostile feelings against people toward whom one ordinarily would be unable to express anger or enmity. On a more positive note, individuals strive to behave in ways that will prevent their being accused of witchcraft. Since excessive wealth is believed to result from witchcraft, individuals are encouraged to redistribute their assets among friends and relatives, thereby leveling economic differences. Similarly, because Navajos believe elders, if neglected, will turn into witches, people are strongly motivated to take care of aged relatives. And because leaders are thought to be witches, people are understandably reluctant to go against their wishes, less they suffer supernatural retribution.

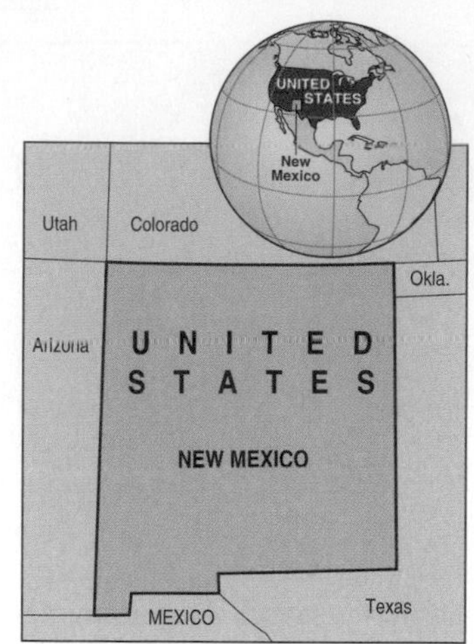

Analyses such as these demonstrate that witchcraft, in spite of its often negative image, frequently functions in a very positive way to manage tensions within a society. Nonetheless, events may get out of hand, particularly in crisis situations, when widespread accusations may cause great suffering. This certainly was the case in the Salem witch trials, but even those pale in comparison to the something like half a million individuals executed as witches in Europe from the 15th through 17th centuries. This was a time of profound change in European society, marked by a good deal of political and religious conflict. At such times, it is all too easy to search out scapegoats on whom to place the blame for what people believe are undesirable changes.

THE FUNCTIONS OF RELIGION

Just as belief in witchcraft may serve a variety of psychological and social functions, so too do religious beliefs and practices in general. Here we may summarize these functions in a somewhat more systematic way. One psychological function is to provide an orderly model of the universe; its importance for orderly human behavior is discussed in Chapter 16. Beyond this, by explaining the unknown and making it understandable, religion reduces the fears and anxieties of individuals. As we have seen, the explanations typically assume the existence of various sorts of supernatural beings and powers, which people may potentially appeal to or manipulate. This being so, a means is provided for dealing with crises: Divine aid is, theoretically, available when all else fails.

A social function of religion is to advocate a wide range of conduct. In this context, religion plays a role in

[17] Kluckhohn, C. (1944). Navajo witchcraft. *Papers of the Peabody Museum of American Archaeology and Ethnology, 22,* (2).

Divination. A magical procedure for determining the cause of a particular event, such as illness, or foretelling the future.

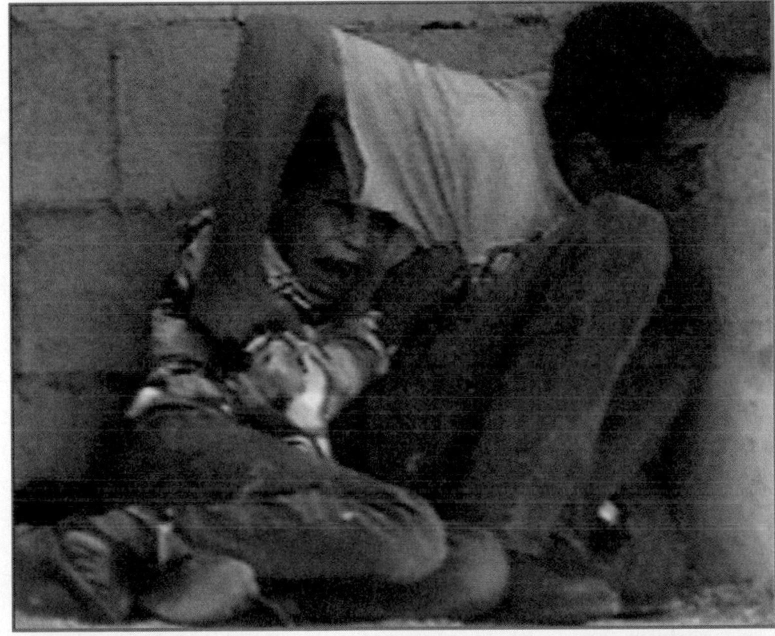

Members of the same religion may engage in, as well as suffer, persecution. In the former Yugoslavia (top), Roman Catholic Croats and Eastern Orthodox Serbs fought each other, while both fought Islamic Bosnians. This 13-year-old Arab boy (middle, taken from video) was killed by Israelis while cowering behind his father. In the Middle East (bottom), at the same time that Jews are the victims of violence from Islamic fundamentalists, fundamentalist Jews have directed violence against Muslims.

social control, which, as we saw in Chapter 23, does not rely on law alone. This is done through notions of right and wrong, good and evil. Right actions earn the approval of whatever supernatural powers are recognized by a particular culture. Wrong actions may cause revenge or punishment through supernatural agencies. In short, by deliberately *raising* people's feelings of guilt and anxiety about their actions, religion helps keep them in line.

Religion does more than this, though; it sets guidelines for acceptable behavior. We have noted already the connection between myths and religion. Usually, myths are full of tales of various supernatural beings that in various ways illustrate the society's ethical code in action. So it is that Gluskabe, the Penobscot culture hero, is portrayed in Penobscot traditions as tricking and punishing those who mock others, lie, are greedy, or go in for extremes of behavior. Moreover, the specific situations serve as guidelines for human behavior in similar circumstances. The Old and New Testaments of the Bible are rich in the same sort of material as is the Qu'ran. Related to this, by the models religion presents and the morals it espouses, religion serves to justify and perpetuate a particular social order. Thus, in the Jewish, Christian, and Islamic traditions, a masculine-authoritarian godhead along with a creation story that portrays a woman as responsible for a fall from grace serves to justify a social order in which men exercise control over women.

A psychological function also is tied up in all this. A society's moral code, since it is considered divinely fixed, lifts the burden of responsibility for conduct from the shoulders of the society's individual members, at least in important situations. It can be a tremendous relief to individuals to know that the responsibility for the way things are rests with the gods rather than with themselves.

Another social function of religion is its role in the maintenance of social solidarity. In our discussion of shamans, we saw how such individuals provide focal points of interest, thus supplying one ingredient of assistance for maintaining group unity. In addition, common participation in rituals, coupled with a basic uniformity of beliefs, helps to bind people together and reinforce their identification with their group. Particularly effective may be their participation together in rituals, when the atmosphere is charged with emotion. The ecstatic feelings people may experience in such circumstances serve as a positive reinforcement in that they feel good as a result. Here, once again, we find religion providing psychological assurance while providing for the needs of society.

One other area in which religion serves a social function is education. In our discussion of rites of passage, we noted that Australian aboriginal puberty rituals served as a kind of cram course in traditional lore. By providing a memorable occasion, initiation rites can serve to enhance learning and so help ensure the perpetuation of a nonliterate culture. And as we saw in the female initiation rites among the Mende, they can serve to ensure that individuals have the knowledge they will need to fulfill their adult roles in society. Education also may be served by rites of intensification. Frequently, such rites involve dramas that portray matters of cultural importance. For example, among a food-foraging people dances may imitate the movement of game and techniques of hunting. Among farmers a fixed round of ceremonies may emphasize the steps necessary for good crops. This all helps preserve knowledge important to a people's material well-being.

RELIGION AND CULTURAL CHANGE

Although the subject of culture change is taken up in a later chapter, no anthropological consideration of religion is complete without some mention of *revitalization movements*. In 1931, at Buka in the Solomon Islands (in the Pacific Ocean), a native religious movement suddenly emerged, its prophets predicting that a deluge would soon engulf all Whites. This would be followed by the arrival of a ship laden with Western industrial commodities. The believers were to construct a storehouse for the goods and to prepare themselves to repulse the colonial police. Because the ship would arrive only after the natives had used up all their own supplies, they ceased working in the fields. Although the leaders of the movement were arrested, the cult continued for some years.

This was not an isolated event. Such "cargo cults"—and many other movements promising resurrection of the dead, destruction or enslavement of Whites, and the coming of utopian riches—have sporadically appeared throughout Melanesia ever since the beginning of this century. Since these cults are widely separated in space and time, their similarities are apparently the result of similarities in social conditions. In these areas the traditional cultures of the indigenous peoples have been uprooted. Europeans, or European-influenced natives, hold all political and economic power. Natives are employed in unloading and distributing Western-made goods, but have no practical knowledge of how to attain these goods. When cold reality offers no hope from the daily frustrations of cultural deterioration and economic deprivation, religion offers the solution.

Shown here are members of the Unarias Academy of Science, a "New Age" revitalization movement that believes in the future arrival of wise space beings who will inspire a new spiritual awareness in human beings.

Revitalization Movements

From the 1890 Ghost Dance of many North American Indians to the Mau Mau of Kenya to the "cargo cults" of Melanesia, extreme and sometimes violent religious reactions to European domination are so common that anthropologists have sought to formulate their underlying causes and general characteristics. Yet **revitalization movements,** as they are now called, are by no means restricted to the colonial world, and in the United States alone hundreds of such movements have sprung up. Among the more widely known are Mormonism, which began in the 19th century; the more recent Unification Church of the Reverend Sun Myung Moon; the Branch Davidians whose "prophet" was David Koresh; and the Heaven's Gate cult led by Marshall Herf Applewhite and Bonnie Lu Trousdale Nettles. As these four examples suggest, revitalization movements show a great deal of diversity, and some have been much more successful than others.

A revitalization movement is a deliberate effort by members of a society to construct a more satisfying culture. The emphasis in this definition is on the reformation not just of the religious sphere of activity but also of the entire cultural system. Such a drastic solution is attempted when a group's anxiety and frustration have become so intense that the only way to reduce the stress is to overturn the entire social system and replace it with a new one.

Anthropologist Anthony Wallace outlined a sequence common to all expressions of the revitalization process.[18] First is the normal state of society, in which stress is not too great and sufficient cultural means of satisfying needs exist. Under certain conditions, such as domination by a more powerful group or severe economic depression, stress and frustration are steadily amplified; this ushers in the second phase, or period of increased individual stress. If there are no significant adaptive changes, a period of cultural distortion follows, in which stress becomes so chronic that socially approved methods of releasing tension begin to break down. This steady deterioration of the culture may be checked by a period of revitalization, during which a dynamic cult or religious movement grips a sizable portion of the population. Often the movement will be so out of touch with existing circumstances that it is doomed to failure from the beginning. This was the case with the Heaven's Gate cult, which mixed bits and pieces of apocalyptic Christian beliefs predicting destruction of the world at the end of the millennium with folk myths of contemporary North American culture, UFOlogy in particular. Its followers self-destructed from suicide out of a conviction their spiritual essences would reunite with extraterrestrial higher bodies in a spaceship that awaited them behind the tail of the Hale-Bopp comet to take them "home." A similar case of self-destruction took place among the Branch Davidians, where hostility toward government authorities caused the latter to assault the cult's compound. In reaction, cult members committed mass suicide by deliberately immolating themselves in their headquarters.

More rarely, a movement may tap long-dormant adaptive forces underlying a culture, and an enduring religion may result. Such was the case with Mormonism. Though heavily persecuted at first and hounded from place to place, Mormons adapted to the point that their religion thrives in the United States today. Indeed, revitalization movements lie at the root of all known religions, Judaism, Christianity, and Islam included. We shall return to revitalization movements in Chapter 26.

[18] Wallace, A. F. C. (1970). *Culture and personality* (2nd ed.) (pp. 191–196). New York: Random House.

Revitalization movements. Social movements, often of a religious nature, with the purpose of totally reforming a society.

In the United States, Mormonism is an example of a revitalization movement that is enormously successful in gaining acceptance in the wider society. By contrast, the Branch Davidians so antagonized elements of mainstream society that a confrontation occurred, ending with the mass immolation of many cult members.

CHAPTER SUMMARY

Religion is a part of all cultures. It consists of beliefs and behavior patterns by which people try to control the area of the universe that is otherwise beyond their control. Among food-foraging peoples religion is a basic ingredient of everyday life. As societies become more complex, religion may become less a part of daily activities and tends to be restricted to particular occasions.

Religion is characterized by a belief in supernatural beings and forces. Through prayer, sacrifice, and other rituals, people appeal to the supernatural for aid. Supernatural beings may be grouped into three categories: major deities (gods and goddesses), ancestral spirits, and other sorts of spirit beings. Gods and goddesses are great but remote beings. They are usually thought to control the universe or a specific part of it. Whether or not people recognize gods, goddesses, or both has to do with how men and women relate to one another in everyday life. Animism is a belief in spirit beings, other than ancestors, who are believed to animate all of nature. These spirit beings are closer to humans than gods and goddesses and are intimately concerned with human activities. Animism is typical of peoples who see themselves as a part of nature rather than as superior to it. A belief in ancestral spirits is based on the idea that human beings are made up of a body and soul. At death the spirit is freed from the body and continues to participate in human affairs. Belief in ancestral spirits is particularly characteristic of descent-based groups with their associated ancestor orientation. Animatism may be found with animism in the same culture. Animatism is a force or power directed to a successful outcome, which may make itself manifest in any object.

Beliefs in supernatural beings and powers are maintained, first, through what are interpreted as manifestations of power. Second, they are perpetuated because supernatural beings possess attributes familiar to people. Finally, myths serve to rationalize religious beliefs and practices.

All human societies have specialists—priests and priestesses and/or shamans—to guide religious practices and to intervene with the supernatural world. Shamans are individuals skilled at contacting and manipulating supernatural beings and powers through altered states of consciousness. Their performances promote a release of tension among individuals in a society. The shaman provides a focal point of attention for society and can help to maintain social control. The benefits of shamanism for the shaman are prestige, sometimes wealth, and an outlet for artistic self-expression.

Religious rituals are religion in action. Through ritual acts, social bonds are reinforced. Times of life crises are occasions for ritual. Arnold Van Gennep divided such rites of passage into rites of separation, transition, and incorporation. Rites of intensification are rituals to mark occasions of crisis in the life of the group rather than the individual. They serve to unite people, allay fear of the crisis, and prompt collective action. Funerary ceremonies are rites of intensification that provide for social readjustment after loss of the deceased. Rites of intensification may also involve annual ceremonies to seek favorable conditions surrounding critical activities such as planting and harvesting.

Ritual practices of Western and non-Western peoples alike may express the belief that supernatural powers can be made to act in certain ways through use of certain prescribed formulas. This is the classic anthropological notion of magic. Sir James Frazer differentiated two principles of magic—"like produces like," or imitative magic, and the law of contagion.

Witchcraft functions as an effective way for people to explain away personal misfortune without having to shoulder any of the blame themselves. Even malevolent witchcraft may function positively in the realm of social control. It may also provide an outlet for feelings of hostility and frustration without disturbing the norms of the larger group.

Religion (including magic and witchcraft) serves several important social functions. First, it sanctions a wide range of conduct by providing notions of right and wrong. Second, it sets standards for acceptable behavior and helps perpetuate an existing social order. Third, it serves to lift the burden of decision making from individuals and places responsibility with the gods. Fourth, it plays a large role in maintaining social solidarity. Finally, religion serves education. Ritual ceremonies enhance learning of traditional lore and thus help to ensure continuation of a nonliterate culture.

Domination by Western society has been the cause of revitalization movements in non-Western societies. In the islands of Melanesia, these take the form of cargo cults that have appeared spontaneously at different times since the beginning of the 20th century. Anthony Wallace has interpreted revitalization movements as attempts, sometimes successful, to change the society. Regardless of the society they appear in, revitalization movements all follow a common sequence, and all religions stem from such movements.

CLASSIC READINGS

Kalwet, H. (1988). *Dreamtime and inner space: The world of the shaman*. New York: Random House.

Written by an ethnopsychologist, this book surveys the practices and paranormal experiences of healers and shamans from Africa, the Americas, Asia, and Australia.

Lehmann, A. C., & Myers, J. E. (Eds.). (1993). *Magic, witchcraft and religion: An anthropological study of the supernatural* (3rd ed.). Mountain View, CA: Mayfield.

This anthology of readings is cross-cultural in scope, covering traditional as well as nontraditional themes. Well represented are both "tribal" and "modern" religions. It is a good source for discovering the relevance and vitality of anthropological approaches to the supernatural.

Malinowski, B. (1954). *Magic, science and religion, and other essays.* Garden City, NY: Doubleday/Anchor Books.

The articles collected here provide a discussion of the Trobriand Islanders as illustrative of conceptual and theoretical knowledge of humankind. The author covers such diversified topics as religion, life, death, character of "primitive" cults, magic, faith, and myth.

Norbeck, E. (1974). *Religion in human life: Anthropological views.* New York: Holt, Rinehart and Winston.

The author presents a comprehensive view of religion based on twin themes: the description of religious events, rituals, and states of mind and the nature of anthropological aims, views, procedures, and interpretations.

Wallace, A. F. C. (1966). *Religion: An anthropological view.* New York: Random House.

This is a classic textbook treatment of religion by an anthropologist who has specialized in the study of revitalization movements.

CHAPTER 25

THE ARTS

An irresistible human urge to embellish lies at the root of art and leads us to decorate almost every sort of object, including our own bodies. Using what is probably one of the earliest forms of art, people all over the world embellish their bodies through various combinations of painting, tattooing, scarification, piercing, ornamentation, and even reshaping.

CHAPTER PREVIEW

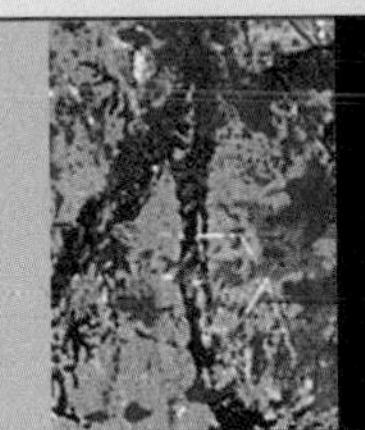

1 What Is Art?

Although difficult to define, art may be taken as the creative use of the human imagination to interpret, express, and enjoy life. Although the idea of art serving nonuseful, nonpractical purposes seems firmly entrenched in the thinking of modern Western peoples, in other cultures art usually serves what are regarded as important, practical purposes.

2 Why Do Anthropologists Study Art?

Anthropologists have found that art reflects a people's cultural values and concerns. This is especially true of the verbal arts—myths, legends, and tales. From these the anthropologist may learn how a people order their universe and may discover much about a people's history as well. Also, music and the visual arts may provide insights into a people's worldview and, through distributional studies, may provide information about a people's history.

3 What Are the Functions of the Arts?

Aside from adding beauty and pleasure to everyday life, the various arts serve a number of functions. Myths, for example, set standards for orderly behavior, and the verbal arts generally transmit and preserve a culture's customs and values. Songs, too, may do this within the restrictions imposed by musical form. And any art form, to the degree that it is characteristic of a particular society, may contribute to the cohesiveness or solidarity of that society.

In the United States, the arts often are seen as something of a luxury, something to be engaged in apart from more productive pursuits for one's personal enjoyment, to provide pleasure for others, or both. This attitude becomes apparent whenever public funds are in short supply; on the local level, for example, in battles over school budgets, art programs often are the first to be cut. Unlike sports, which usually are supported more than the arts because they are perceived as providing skills thought to be essential to success in a competitive world, the arts are seen as nonessential; pleasurable and worthwhile but expensive, with little practical payoff. On the national level, fiscal conservatives seek to cut back funds for the arts, on the premise that they lack the practical importance of defense, economic, or other governmental activities. Indeed, artists and their supporters are seen as something of an elite, subsidized at the expense of hard-working "practical" people. Yet one might ask, why has the National Endowment for the Arts so often been the center of hot political controversy? If art really is such an unimportant, diversionary activity, why have politicians so often devoted great time and energy to often bitter fights to control the kind of art that is accessible to the public?

The fact is that artistic expression is far from unimportant, and is as basic to human beings as talking. Just as speech is used to communicate feelings and to make statements, so too is artistic expression. Moreover, it is not merely a special category of persons called "artists" who do this; for example, all human beings adorn their bodies in certain ways and by doing so make a statement about who they are, both as individuals and as members of social groups of various sorts. Similarly, all people tell stories, in which they express their values, their hopes, and their concerns, in the process revealing much about themselves and the nature of the world as they see it. In short, all peoples engage in artistic expression as they use their imagination creatively to interpret, understand, celebrate, and even enjoy life. What's more, they have been doing this for at least 40,000 years, if not longer. Far from being a luxury to be afforded or appreciated by a minority of aesthetes or escapists, art is a necessary kind of activity in which every normal human being participates.

The power of art is illustrated by the reaction to exhibition of Chris Ofilis's *The Holy Virgin Mary* in New York's Brooklyn Museum in 1999. The uproar was caused by its use of elephant dung, and the city's mayor was so outraged he tried to withdraw funding from the museum.

This picture of a 6-month-old child at a piano suggests the importance of music for developing brains; recent studies show that exposure to music early in life significantly enhances learning.

The idea of art serving nonuseful, nonpractical purposes seems firmly entrenched in the thinking of many contemporary Western peoples. Today, for example, the objects from the tomb of the young Egyptian king Tutankhamen are on display in a museum, where they may be seen and admired as the exquisite works of art that they are. They were made, however, to be hidden away from human eyes, where they were to guarantee the eternal life of the king and protect him from evil forces that might enter his body and gain control over it. Or we may listen to the singing of a sea chantey purely for aesthetic pleasure, as a form of entertainment. In fact, in the days of sail, sea chanteys served very useful and practical purposes. They set the appropriate rhythm for the performance of specific shipboard tasks, and the same qualities that make them pleasurable to listen to today served to relieve the boredom of those tasks. Such links between art and other aspects are common in human societies around the world. Only in the West—and only recently at that—has *fine art* become established as a distinct category of art for art's sake; less accessible to members of the society at large than to wealthy collectors who commission and purchase artworks for their personal enjoyment in the privacy of their homes. Yet, folk art continues to thrive. Because art, like any aspect of culture, is inextricably intertwined with everything else people do, it affords us glimpses into other aspects of people's lives, including their values and worldview.

To people today, the making of exquisite objects of gold and precious stones to place in a tomb might seem like throwing them away. Yet, something of the same sort happens when a Navajo Indian creates an intricate sand painting as part of a ritual act, only to destroy it once the ritual is over. Johann Sebastian Bach did something similar when, some 300 years ago, he composed his cantatas to be used for church services. They were "throwaway" music, meant to be discarded after the services for which they were written. That many of them are still performed

Much of the world's art is created for functional rather than aesthetic purposes. Shown here, counterclockwise, are examples of art used to cure sickness (a Navajo sand painting), to express cultural identity (the Mardi Gras costume of one of New Orleans' "Black Indians"), and for political purposes (graffiti from Katatura, Namibia).

today is something of an accident, for Bach did not compose them for posterity. In many human societies creating art is often of greater importance than the final product itself.

Whether a particular work of art is intended to be appreciated purely as such or (as in the examples just noted) to serve some practical purpose, it will in every case require the same special combination of the symbolic representation of form and the expression of feeling that constitute the creative imagination. Since the creative use of the human ability to symbolize is universal and both expresses and is shaped by cultural values and concerns, it is an important subject for anthropological study.

As an activity or kind of behavior that contributes to human well-being and that helps give shape and significance to life, art is related to, yet differentiated from, religion. As British anthropologist Raymond Firth observed: "Religion is an art of making sense out of experience, and like any other art, say, poetry, it must be taken symbolically, not literally."[1] Nor is it easy to say, for example, precisely where art stops and religion begins in an elaborate ceremony involving ornamentation, masks, costumes, songs, dances, and effigies. Furthermore music, dance, and other arts may be used, like magic, to "enchant"—to take advantage of the emotional or psychological predispositions of another person or group so as to cause them to perceive reality in a way favorable to the interests of the "enchanter." Indeed, the arts may be used to manipulate a seemingly inexhaustible list of human passions, including desire, terror, wonder, cupidity, fantasy, and vanity.[2] Marketing specialists, of course, are well aware of this, which is why they routinely employ certain music and pictorial images in their advertising.

The effectiveness of this Coca Cola ad in the Mexican state of Chiapas lies in the use of these particular colors. To Maya Indians, red is the color of sacred blood and symbolizes the dawn and birth; green, the color of jade, symbolizes life-giving rain and the heavens, precious water, and fertility.

THE ANTHROPOLOGICAL STUDY OF ART

In approaching art as a cultural phenomenon, anthropologists have the pleasant task of cataloging, photographing, recording, and describing all possible forms of imaginative activity in any particular culture. An enormous variety of forms and modes of artistic expression exists in the world. Because people everywhere continue to create and develop in new directions, no point of diminishing returns is foreseeable in the interesting process of collecting and describing the world's ornaments, body decorations, variations in clothing, blanket and rug designs, pottery and basket styles, architectural embellishments, monuments, ceremonial masks, legends, work songs, dances, and other art forms. The collecting process, however, eventually must lead to some kind of analysis and generalizations about relationships between art and the rest of culture.

A good way to begin a study of the relationships between art and the rest of culture is to examine critically some of the generalizations that have already been made about specific arts. Since it is impossible to cover all forms of art in the space of a single chapter, we shall concentrate on just a few: verbal arts, music, and pictorial art. We will start with the verbal arts, for we have already touched upon them in earlier discussions of religion (Chapter 24) and worldview (Chapters 16 and 23).

---

[1] Herdt, G. H. (1993). Semen transactions in Sambia culture. In D. N. Suggs & A. D. Mirade (Eds.). *Culture and human sexuality* (p. 319). Pacific Grove, CA: Brooks/Cole.

[2] Gell, A. (1988). Technology and magic. *Anthropology Today, 4* (2), 7; Lewis-Williams, J. D. (1997). Agency, art and altered consciousness: A motif in French (Quercy) upper paleolithic parietal art. *Antiquity, 71,* 810–830.

Anthropology Applied: Protecting Cultural Heritages

In these last years of the 20th century, the time is long past when the anthropologist could go out and describe small band and tribal groups in out-of-the-way places that (supposedly) had not been "contaminated" by contact with Western people. Not only do few such groups exist in the world today, but also those that do remain face strong pressures to abandon their traditional ways in the name of "progress." All too often, band and tribal peoples are made to forfeit their indigenous identity and are pressed into a mold that allows them neither the opportunity nor the motivation to rise above the lowest rung of the social ladder. From an autonomous people able to provide for their own needs, with pride and a strong sense of their own identity as a people, they are transformed into a deprived underclass with neither pride nor a sense of their own identity, often despised by more fortunate members of some multinational state in which they live.

The basic rights of groups of people to be themselves and not to be deprived of their own distinctive cultural identities is and should be our paramount consideration and will be dealt with in the final two chapters of this book. However, anthropologists have additional reasons to be concerned about the disappearance of the societies and cultures they have studied traditionally. For one thing, the need for information about them has become steadily more apparent. If we are ever to have a realistic understanding of that elusive thing called human nature, we need reliable data on all humans. More is involved than this, though; once a traditional society is gone, it is lost to humanity, unless an adequate record of it exists. When a culture is lost without any record of it, humanity is the poorer for the loss. Hence, anthropologists have in a sense rescued many such societies from oblivion. This not only helps to preserve the human heritage, but it also may be important to an ethnic group that, having become westernized, wishes to rediscover and reassert its traditional cultural identity. Better yet, of course, is to find ways to prevent the loss of cultural traditions in the first place.

To the Pomo Indians of California, the art of basket making has been important for their sense of who they are since before the coming of European settlers. Recognized for their skilled techniques and aesthetic artistry, Pomo baskets—some of the finest in the world—are prized by museums and private collectors alike. Nevertheless, the art of Pomo basket making was threatened in the 1970s by the impending construction of the Warm Springs Dam–Lake Sonoma Project to the north of San Francisco. The effect of this project would be to wipe out virtually all existing habitat for a particular species of sedge essential for the weaving of Pomo baskets.

Pomo Indian basketmakers

Accordingly, a coalition of archaeologists, Native Americans, and others with objections to the project brought suit in federal district court. As it happened, the U.S. Army Corps of Engineers had recently hired anthropologist Richard N. Lerner for its San Francisco District Office to advise on sociocultural factors associated with water resources programs in northwestern California. One of Lerner's first tasks, therefore, was to undertake studies of the problem and to find ways to overcome it.*

After comprehensive archaeological, ethnographic, and other studies were completed in 1976, Lerner succeeded in having the Pomo basketry materials recognized by the National Register of Historic Places as "historic property," requiring the Corps of Engineers to find ways to mitigate the adverse impact dam construction would have. The result was a complex ethnobotanical project developed and implemented by Lerner. Working in concert with Pomo Indians as well as botanists, Lerner relocated 48,000 sedge plants onto nearly 3 acres of suitable lands downstream from the dam. By the fall of 1983, the sedge was doing well enough to be harvested and proved to be of excellent quality. Since this initial harvest, groups of weavers have returned each year, and the art of Pomo Indian basket making appears to be safe for the time being.

*Lerner, R. N. (1987). Preserving plants for Pomos. In R. M. Wulff & S. J. Fiske (Eds.). *Anthropological praxis: Translating knowledge into action* (pp. 212–222). Boulder CO: Westview.

VERBAL ARTS

The term **folklore** was coined in the 19th century to denote the unwritten stories, beliefs, and customs of European peasantry, as opposed to the traditions of the literate elite. The subsequent study of folklore, **folkloristics,** has become a discipline allied to but somewhat independent of anthropology, working on cross-cultural comparisons of themes, motifs, genres, and structures from a literary as well as ethnological point of view. Many linguists and anthropologists prefer to speak of a culture's oral traditions and verbal arts rather than its folklore and folktales, recognizing that creative verbal expression takes many forms and that the implied distinction between folk and "fine" art is a projection of the recent attitude of European (and European-derived) cultures onto others.

The verbal arts include narratives, dramas, poetry, incantations, proverbs, riddles, word games, and even naming procedures, compliments, and insults, when these take structured and special forms. Narrative seems to be one of the easiest kinds of the verbal arts to record or collect. Perhaps because they also are the most publishable, with popular appeal in North American culture, they have received the most study and attention. Generally, narratives have been divided into three basic and recurring categories: myth, legend, and tale.

Myth

The word *myth,* in popular usage, refers to something that is widely believed to be true, but probably is not. Actually, a true **myth** is basically religious, in that it provides a rationale for religious beliefs and practices. Its subject matter concerns the fundamentals of human existence: where we and everything in our world came from, why we are here, and where we are going. As was noted in Chapter 24, a myth has an explanatory function; it depicts and describes an orderly universe, which sets the stage for orderly behavior. A typical origin myth, traditional with the western Abenaki of northwestern New England and southern Quebec, goes as follows:

> In the beginning, *Tabaldak,* "The Owner," created all living things but one—the spirit being who was to accomplish the final transformation of the earth. Man and woman *Tabaldak* made out of a piece of stone, but he didn't like the result, their hearts being cold and hard. This being so, he broke them

Folklore. A 19th-century term first used to refer to the traditional oral stories and sayings of the European peasant, and later extended to those traditions preserved orally in all societies. • **Folkloristics.** The study of folklore (as linguistics is the study of language). • **Myth.** A sacred narrative explaining how the world came to be in its present form.

up, and their remains today can be seen in the many stones that litter the landscape of the Abenaki homeland. But *Tabaldak* tried again, this time using living wood, and from this came all later Abenakis. Like the trees from which the wood came, these people were rooted in the earth and (like trees when blown by the wind) could dance gracefully. The one living thing not created by *Tabaldak* was *Odzihózo,* "He Makes Himself from Something." This being seems to have created himself out of dust, but since he was a transformer, rather than creator, he wasn't able to accomplish it all at once. At first, he managed only his head, body, and arms; the legs came later, growing slowly as legs do on a tadpole. Not waiting until his legs were grown, he set out to transform the shape of the earth. He dragged his body about with his hands, gouging channels that became the rivers. To make the mountains, he piled dirt up with his hands. Once his legs grew, *Odzihózo's* task was made easier; by merely extending his legs, he made the tributaries of the main streams.

Odzihózo, then, was the Abenaki transformer who laid out the river channels and lake basins and shaped the hills and mountains. Just how long he took is a subject which Abenakis have discussed for as long as any can remember. Once he was finished, he surveyed his handiwork and found it was good. The last work he made was Lake Champlain and this he found especially good. He liked it so well that he climbed onto a rock in Burlington Bay and changed himself into stone so that he could sit there and enjoy his masterpiece through the ages. He still likes it, because he is still there and he is still given offerings of tobacco as Abenakis pass this way. The Abenaki call the rock *Odzihózo,* since it is the Transformer himself.[3]

Such a myth, insofar as it is believed, accepted, and perpetuated in a culture, may be said to express a part of the worldview of a people: the unexpressed but implicit conceptions of their place in nature and of the limits and workings of their world. (This concept we discussed in Chapters 16 and 23.) Extrapolating from the details of the Abenaki myth, we might arrive at the conclusion that these people recognize a kinship among all living things; after all, they were all part of the same creation, and humans even were made from living wood. Moreover, an attempt to make them of nonliving stone was not satisfactory. This idea of a closeness between all living things led the Abenaki to show special respect to the animals they hunted in order to sustain their own lives. For example, after killing a beaver, muskrat, or waterfowl, one could not unceremoniously toss its bones into the nearest garbage pit. Proper respect required that the bones be returned to the water, with a request to continue its kind. Similarly, before eating meat, the Abenaki placed an offering of grease on the fire to thank *Tabaldak.* More generally, waste was to be

[3] Haviland, W. A., & Power, M. W. (1994). *The Original Vermonters: Native inhabitants, past and present* (rev. and expanded ed.) (p. 193). Hanover, NH: University Press of New England.

To the Abenaki, these rocks in a northern New England blueberry field are the remains of the first man and woman, who were broken up by the Creator as their hearts were cold and hard.

avoided so as not to offend the animals. Failure to respect their rights would result in an unwillingness to sacrifice their lives that people might live.

By transforming himself into stone in order to enjoy his work for all eternity, *Odzihózo* may be seen as setting an example for people; they should see the beauty in things as they are and not seek to alter what is already good. To question the goodness of existing reality would be to call into question the judgment of a powerful deity. A characteristic of explanatory myths, such as this one, is that the unknown is simplified and explained in terms of the known. This myth, in terms of human experience, accounts for the existence of rivers, mountains, lakes, and other features of the landscape, as well as of humans and all other living things. It also sanctions particular attitudes and behaviors. It is a product of creative imagination, and it is a work of art, as well as a potentially religious statement.

One aspect of mythology that has attracted a good deal of interest over the years is the similarity of certain themes in the stories of peoples living in separate parts of the world. One of these themes is the myth of matriarchy, or one-time rule by women. In a number of societies, stories tell about a time when women ruled over men. Eventually, so these stories go, men were forced to rise up and assert their dominance over women to combat their tyranny or incompetence (or both). In the 19th century, a number of European scholars interpreted such myths as evidence for an early stage of matriarchy in the evolution of human culture, an idea some feminists recently have revived. Although a number of societies are known where the two sexes relate to one another as equals (Western Abenaki society was one), never have anthropologists found one where women rule over or dominate men. The interesting thing about myths of matriarchy is that they generally are found in societies where men dominate women, even though the latter have considerable autonomy.[4] Under such conditions, male dominance is insecure, and a rationale is needed to justify it. Thus, myths of men overthrowing women and taking control reflect an existing paradoxical relationship between the two sexes.

The analysis and interpretation of myths have been carried to great lengths, becoming a field of study almost unto itself. It is certain that myth making is an extremely important kind of human creativity, and the study of the myth-making process and its results can give valuable clues to the way people perceive and think about their world. The dangers and problems of interpretation, however, are great. Several questions arise: Are myths literally believed or perhaps accepted symbolically or emotionally as a different kind of truth? To what extent do myths actually determine or reflect human behavior? Can an outsider discover the meaning that a myth has in its own culture? How do we account for contradictory myths (such as the two accounts of creation in the Bible's Book of Genesis) in the same culture? New myths arise and old ones die. Is it then the myth's content or the structure that is important? All of these questions deserve, and are currently receiving, serious consideration.

Legend

Less problematical, but perhaps more complex than myth, is the legend. **Legends** are stories told as true, set in the postcreation world. An example of a modern "urban legend" in the United States is one that was often told by Ronald Reagan when he was president, about an African American woman on welfare in Chicago. Supposedly, her ability to collect something like 103 welfare checks under different names enabled her to live lavishly. Although proven to be false, the story was told as if true (by the president even after he was informed that it was not true) as all legends are. This particular legend illustrates a number of features all such narratives share: They cannot be attributed to any known author; they always exist in multiple versions, but, in spite of variation, they are told with sufficient detail to be plausible; and they tell us something about the societies in which they are found. In this case, we learn something about the existence of racism in U.S. society (the story is told by Whites, who identify the woman as an African American), social policy (the existence of government policies to help the poor), and attitudes toward the poor (distrust, if not dislike).

As this illustration shows, legends (no more than myths) are not confined to nonliterate, nonindustrialized societies. Commonly, legends consist of pseudohistorical narratives that account for the deeds of heroes, the movements of peoples, and the establishment of local customs, typically with a mixture of realism and the supernatural or extraordinary. As stories, they are not necessarily believed or disbelieved, but they usually serve to

[4] Sanday, P. R. (1981). *Female power and male dominance: On the origins of sexual inequality* (p. 181). Cambridge: Cambridge University Press.

Legends. Stories told as true, set in the postcreation world.

entertain, as well as to instruct and to inspire or bolster pride in family, community, or nation.

To a degree, in literate societies (such as the United States), the function of legends has been taken over by history. Yet much of what passes for history, to paraphrase one historian, consists of the legends we develop to make ourselves feel better about who we are.[5] The trouble is that history does not always tell people what they want to hear about themselves, or, conversely, it tells them things that they would prefer not to hear. By projecting their culture's hopes and expectations onto the record of the past, they seize upon and even exaggerate some past events while ignoring or giving scant attention to others. Although this often takes place unconsciously, so strong is the motivation to transform history into legend that states often have gone so far as to deliberately rewrite it, as when the Aztecs in the reign of their 15th-century king Itzcoatl rewrote their history in a way more flattering to their position of dominance in ancient Mexico. An example from of the United States may be seen in the way conventional histories of New England were written. King Philip's War, an uprising of New England Indians in 1675, is portrayed as a treacherous uprising (rather than the desperate bid for survival in the face of English provocation that it was), following which Indians disappeared from the region (in spite of clear evidence to the contrary).[6] In modern times, the Soviet Union was particularly well-known for similar practices. Historians, when attempting to separate fact from fiction, frequently incur the wrath of people who will not willingly abandon what they wish to believe is true, whether or not it really is. This may be seen in recent debates in the United States over the "proper" teaching of history.

Long legends, sometimes in poetry or in rhythmic prose, and even basic melody, are known as **epics.** In parts of West and central Africa people held remarkably elaborate and formalized recitations of extremely long legends, lasting several hours and even days. These long narratives have been described as veritable encyclopedias of a culture's most diverse aspects, with direct and indirect statements about history, institutions, relationships, values, and ideas. Epics are typically found in nonliterate societies with a form of state political organization; they serve to transmit and preserve a culture's legal and political precedents and practices.

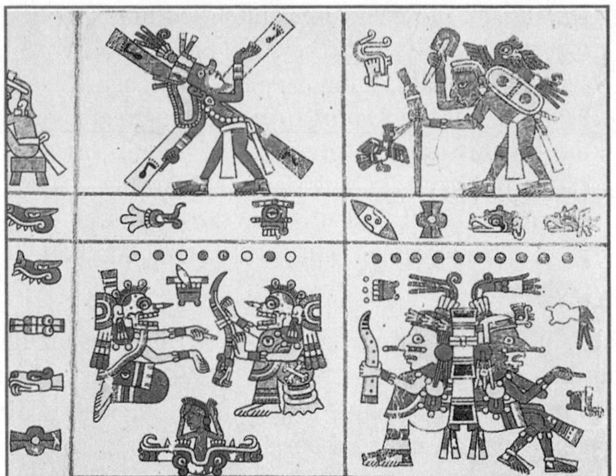

Part of an ancient Aztec manuscript. In the reign of King Itzcoatl, the Aztecs rewrote their history in a way to better glorify their past. In politically centralized states, such rewriting of history is a common practice.

Legends may incorporate mythological details, especially when they make an appeal to the supernatural, and are therefore not always clearly distinct from myth. The Mwindo epic of the Nyanga people follows Mwindo through the earth, the atmosphere, the underworld, and the remote sky and gives a comprehensive picture of the Nyanga people's view of the organization and limits of their world. Legends may also incorporate proverbs and incidental tales and thus be related to other forms of verbal art as well. A recitation of the Kambili epic of the Mende, for example, has been said to include as many as 150 proverbs.

An example of a short legend that instructs, traditional with the Western Abenakis of northwestern New England and southern Quebec, follows.

> This is a story of a lonesome little boy who used to wander down to the riverbank at Odanak [a village on the St. Francis River in Quebec] or downhill toward the two swamps. He used to hear someone call his name but when he got to the swamp pond, there was no one to be seen or heard. But when he went back, he heard his name called again. As he was sitting by the marshy bank

[5] Stoler, M. (1982). To tell the truth. *Vermont Visions, 82* (3), 3.

[6] Calloway, C. (1997). Introduction: Surviving the dark ages. In C. G. Calloway (Ed.). *After King Philip's war: Presence and persistence in Indian New England* (pp. 1–28). Hanover, NH: University Press of New England.

Epics. Long oral narratives, sometimes in poetry or rhythmic prose, recounting the glorious events in the life of a real or legendary person.

> waiting, an old man came and asked him why he was waiting. When the boy told him, the old man said that the same thing happened long ago. What he heard was the Swamp Creature and pointed out the big tussocks of grass where it hid; having called out it would sink down behind them. The old man said: "It just wants to drown you. If you go out there you will sink in the mud. You better go home!"[7]

The moral of this story is quite simple: Swamps are dangerous places; stay away from them. When told well, the story is a lot more effective in keeping children away from swamps then just telling them, "Don't go near swamps."

For the anthropologist, a major significance of the secular and apparently realistic portions of legends, whether long or short, is the clues they provide to what constitutes a culture's approved or ideal ethical behavior. The subject matter of legends is essentially problem solving and mentoring, and the content is likely to include combat, warfare, confrontations, and physical and psychological trials of many kinds. Certain questions may be answered explicitly or implicitly. In what circumstances, if any, does the culture permit homicide? What kinds of behavior are considered brave or cowardly? What is the etiquette of combat or warfare? Does the culture honor or recognize a concept of altruism or self-sacrifice? Here again, however, there are pitfalls in the process of interpreting art in relation to life. It is always possible that certain kinds of behavior are acceptable or even admirable, with the distance or objectivity afforded by art, but are not at all so approved in daily life. In European American culture, murderers, charlatans, and rakes sometimes have become popular heroes and the subjects of legends; North Americans would object, however, to an outsider's inference that they necessarily approved or wanted to emulate the morality of Billy the Kid or Jesse James.

Tale

The term **tale** is a nonspecific label for a third category of creative narratives, those purely secular, nonhistorical, and recognized as fiction for entertainment, though they may draw a moral or teach a practical lesson, as well. Consider this brief summary of a tale from Ghana, in West Africa, known as "Father, Son, and Donkey":

> A father and his son farmed their corn, sold it, and spent part of the profit on a donkey. When the hot season came, they harvested their yams and prepared to take them to storage, using their donkey. The father mounted the donkey and they all three proceeded on their way until they met some people. "What? You lazy man!" the people said to the father. "You let your young son walk barefoot on this hot ground while you ride on a donkey? For shame!" The father yielded his place to the son, and they proceeded until they came to an old woman. "What? You useless boy!" said the old woman. "You ride on the donkey and let your poor father walk barefoot on this hot ground? For shame!" The son dismounted, and both father and son walked on the road, leading the donkey behind them until they came to an old man. "What? You foolish people!" said the old man. "You have a donkey and you walk barefoot on the hot ground instead of riding?" And so it goes. Listen: when you are doing something and other people come along, just keep on doing what you like.

This is precisely the kind of tale that is of special interest in traditional folklore studies. It is an internationally popular "numbskull" tale; versions of it have been recorded in India, the Middle East, the Balkans, Italy, Spain, England, and the United States, as well as in West Africa. It is classified or catalogued as exhibiting a basic **motif** or story situation—father and son trying to please everyone—one of the many thousands that have been found to recur in world folktales. Despite variations in detail, every version has about the same basic structure in the sequence of events, sometimes called the *syntax* of the tale: A peasant father and son work together, a beast of burden is purchased, the three set out on a short excursion, the father rides and is criticized, the son rides and is criticized, both walk and are criticized, and a conclusion is drawn.

Tales of this sort (not to mention myths and legends) that are found to have wide geographical distribution raise the question: Where did they originate? Did the story arise only once and then pass from one culture to another (*diffusion*)? Or did the stories arise independently (*independent invention*) in response to like causes in similar settings, or perhaps as a consequence of inherited mental

[7] Day, G. M. (1972). Quoted in the film *Prehistoric life in the Champlain Valley,* by Thomas C. Vogelman and others. Burlington, VT: Department of Anthropology, University of Vermont.

Tale. A creative narrative recognized as fiction for entertainment. • **Motif.** A story situation in a folktale.

preferences and images deeply embedded in the evolutionary construction of the human brain? Or is it merely that there are logical limits to the structure of stories, so that, by coincidence, different cultures are bound to come up with similar motifs and syntax?[8] A surprisingly large number of motifs in European and African tales are traceable to ancient sources in India, evidence of diffusion of tales in neighboring areas. Of course, purely local tales exist, as well as tales with wide distributions. Within any particular culture, anthropologists usually can categorize local types of tales: animal, human experience, trickster, dilemma, ghost, moral, scatological, nonsense tales, and so on. In West Africa there is a remarkable prevalence of animal stories, for example, with such creatures as the spider, the rabbit, and the hyena as the protagonists. Many were carried to the slave-holding areas of the Americas; the Uncle Remus stories about Brer Rabbit, Brer Fox, and other animals may be a survival of this tradition.

The significance of tales for the anthropologist rests partly in this matter of their distribution. They provide evidence of either cultural contacts or cultural isolation and of limits of influence and cultural cohesion. Debated for decades now, for example, has been the extent to which the cultures of West Africa were transmitted to the southeast United States. As far as folktales are concerned, one school of folklorists always has found and insisted on European origins; another school, somewhat more recently, points to African prototypes. Anthropologists are interested, however, in more than these questions of distribution. Like legends, tales very often illustrate local solutions to universal human ethical problems, and in some sense they state a moral philosophy. Anthropologists see that whether the tale of the father, the son, and the donkey originated in West Africa or arrived there from Europe or the Middle East, the very fact it is told in West Africa suggests that it states something valid for that culture. The tale's lesson of a necessary degree of self-confidence in the face of arbitrary social criticism is therefore something that can be read into the culture's values and beliefs.

Other Verbal Arts

Myths, legends, and tales, prominent as they are in anthropological studies, in many cultures turn out to be no more important than the other verbal arts. In the culture of the Awlad 'Ali Bedouins of Egypt's western desert, for

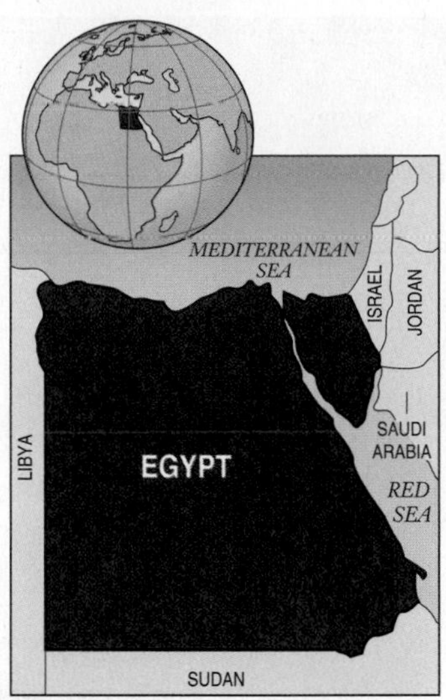

example, poetry is a lively and active verbal art, especially as a vehicle for personal expression and private communication. These people use two forms of poetry, one being the elaborately structured and heroic poems men chant or recite only on ceremonial occasions and in specific public contexts. The other is the *ghinnáwa,* or "little songs" that punctuate everyday conversations. Simple in structure, these deal with personal matters and feelings more appropriate to informal social situations, and older men regard them as the unimportant productions of women and youths. Despite this official devaluation in the male-dominated Bedouin society, however, they play a vital part in people's daily lives. In their "little songs" individuals are shielded from the consequences of making statements and expressing sentiments that contravene the moral system. Paradoxically, sharing these "immoral" sentiments only with intimates and veiling them in impersonal traditional formulas, those who recite them demonstrate that they have a certain control, which actually enhances their moral standing.

As is often true of folklore in general, the "little songs" of the Awlad 'Ali provide a culturally appropriate outlet for otherwise taboo thoughts or opinions. Disaster jokes are an example of this in contemporary North American society. As anthropologist Lila Abu-Lughod points out:

> What may be peculiar to Awlad 'Ali is that their discourse of rebellion is both culturally elaborated and sanctioned. Although poetry refers to personal life, it is not individual, spontaneous, idiosyncratic, or unofficial but public, conventional, and formulaic—a highly developed art. More

[8] Gould, S. J. (2000). The narthex of San Marco and the pangenetic paradigm. *Natural History, 109* (6), 29.

The "little songs" of the Awlad 'Ali Bedouins punctuate conversations carried out while the people perform everyday chores, such as making bread, as these young women are doing. Through these "little songs," they can express what otherwise are taboo topics.

important, this poetic discourse of defiance is not condemned, or even just tolerated, as well it might be given all the constraints of time and place and form that bind it. Poetry is a privileged discourse in Awlad 'Ali society. Like other Arabs, and perhaps like many oral cultures, the Bedouins cherish poetry and other verbal arts. . . . They are drawn to *ghinnáwas*, and at the same time they consider them risqué, against religion, and slightly improper. . . . This ambivalence about poetry is significant, and it makes sense only in terms of the cultural meaning of opposition. Because ordinary discourse is informed by the values of honor and modesty, the moral correlates of the ideology that upholds the Awlad 'Ali social and political system, we would expect the antistructural poetic discourse with its contradictory messages, to be informed by an opposing set of values. This is not the case. Poetry as a discourse of defiance of the system symbolizes freedom—the ultimate value of the system and the essential entailment of the honor code.[9]

[9] Abu-Lughod, L. (1986). *Veiled sentiments* (p. 252). Berkeley, CA: University of California Press.

In all cultures the words of songs constitute a kind of poetry. Poetry and stories recited with gesture, movement, and props become drama. Drama combined with dance, music, and spectacle becomes a public celebration. The more we look at the individual arts, the clearer it becomes that they often are interrelated and interdependent. The verbal arts are, in fact, simply differing manifestations of the same creative imagination that produces music and the other arts.

THE ART OF MUSIC

The study of music in specific cultural settings, beginning in the 19th century with the collection of folksongs, has developed into a specialized field, called **ethnomusicology.** Like the study of folktales for their own sake, ethnomusicology is both related to and somewhat independent of anthropology. Nevertheless, it is possible to sort out several concepts that are of interest in general anthropology from the field's various concerns.

To begin, we may ask: How does a culture conceive of music? What is considered of primary importance when distinguishing music from other modes of expression? What is music to one person is mere noise to an-

Ethnomusicology. The study of a society's music in terms of its cultural setting.

FREDERICA DE LAGUNA (b. 1906)

A concern with the arts of non-Western people has always been an important part of anthropology, and the work of anthropologist Frederica de Laguna is representative. Educated at Bryn Mawr College and Columbia University, where she was awarded her Ph.D., she made her first trip into the field with a Danish expedition to Greenland in 1929. A year later, she began work in southeastern Alaska, a region to which she has returned repeatedly since. Her first work here was archaeological, and she was the pioneer in southeastern Alaskan prehistory. But as her interest in native people grew, she became more and more involved with ethnographic work as well. She found out that to understand the past, one had to know what it led to, just as to understand the present native people, one had to know their past.

After many seasons of work in different localities, de Laguna began in 1949 a project to trace the beginnings of the way of life of the Tlingit Indians of Yakutat through a combination of archaeological and ethnographic research. This resulted in a monumental three-volume work, published in 1972, *Under Mount St. Elias.* It amounted to no less than a holistic picture of Tlingit culture through their eyes. Since songs and stories are important parts of any nonliterate culture, much space was devoted to their transcriptions just as they were related and performed by elders now long dead (one whole volume is devoted to the words and music of songs). The importance of this work goes far beyond anthropology and has been of enormous importance to the Tlingit themselves.

When de Laguna began to work at Yakutat, the children were being sent to government boarding schools, where they were told nothing of their own culture and were harshly punished for even speaking their own language. The aim was to stamp out native culture to facilitate assimilation into "mainstream American" culture. Thus, as the elders died out, many traditions were being lost. But with the publication of *Under Mount St. Elias* (copies of which were avidly snapped up by the Tlingit), as well as "Freddy" de Laguna's continuing participation in the community, the people were able to regain much that they were in danger of losing. As de Laguna says, songs and stories are for giving back, and so it was that in 1997 the Tlingit of Yakutat honored her for what she gave back to them. As they themselves acknowledge, the new vigor shown by Tlingit culture and their renewed pride in who they are, owes much to their "Grandmother Freddy's" work.

other. Music is a form of communication that includes a nonverbal component. The information transmitted is often abstract emotion rather than concrete ideas, and is experienced in a variety of ways by different listeners. This, and music's communication of something that is verbally incommunicable, makes it very difficult to discuss music. In fact, not even a single definition of music can be agreed upon, because different peoples may include or exclude different ideas within that category. Ethnomusicologists must often rely upon a working definition as the basis for their investigations and often distinguish between "music" and that which is "musical." The way to approach an unfamiliar kind of musical expression is to define it either in indigenous terms or in orthodox musicological terms such as melody, rhythm, and form.

Much of the historical development of ethnomusicology has been based upon musicology, which is primarily the study of European music. One problem has been the tendency to discuss music in terms of elements considered important in European music (tonality, rhythm, melody, etc.), when these may be of little importance to the practitioner. European music is defined, primarily, in terms of the presence of melody and rhythm. Melody is a function of tonality, and rhythm is an organizing concept involving tempo, stress, and measured repetition. Although these can be addressed in non-European musics, they may not be the defining characteristics of a performance.

Early investigators of non-European song were struck by the apparent simplicity of *pentatonic* (five-tone) scales and a seemingly endless repetition of phrases. They often did not give sufficient credit to the formal function of repetition in such music, confusing repetition with lack of invention. A great deal of complex, sophisticated, non-European music was dismissed as "primitive" and formless and typically treated as trivial. Repetition, nevertheless, is a fact of music, including European music, and a basic formal principle.

In general, human music is said to differ from natural music—the songs of birds, wolves, and whales, for example—by being almost everywhere perceived in terms of a repertory of tones at fixed or regular intervals: in other words, a scale. Scale systems and their modifications comprise what is known as **tonality** in music. Humans make closed systems out of a formless range of possible sounds by dividing the distance between a tone and its first *overtone* or sympathetic vibration (which always has exactly twice as many vibrations as the basic tone) into a series of measured steps. In the Western or European system, the distance between the basic tone and the first overtone is called the *octave*; it consists of seven steps—five *whole* tones and two *semitones*. The whole tones are further divided into semitones for a total working scale of 12 tones. Interestingly, some birds pitch their songs to the same scale as Western music,[10] perhaps influencing the way these people developed their scale. Ambient sound is a central component of natural habitats, and it has been observed that this is similar to a modern orchestra. The voice of each creature has its own frequency, amplitude, timbre, and duration, and occupies a unique niche among the other "musicians." This "animal orchestra" which sends a clear acoustic message, represents a unique sound grouping for any given biome.[11] Perhaps this is one reason why something that sounds natural to one people sounds unnatural to another. In any event, Western people learn at an early age to recognize

[10] Gray, P. M., Krause, B., Atema, J., Payne, R., Krumhansl, C., & Baptista, L. (2001). The music of nature and the nature of music. *Science,* 291, 52.

[11] Gray, P. M., Krause, B., Atema, J., Payne, R., Krumhansl, C., & Baptista, L. (2001). The music of nature and the nature of music. *Science,* 291, 53.

TABLE25.1 **TWO DIFFERENT WAYS OF DIVIDING THE OCTAVE INTO SEVEN STEPS**

Pipe Scale	Just Scale
A′	A′
10/9	16/15
G	G#
27/25	9/8
F	F#
10/9	10/9
E	E
10/9	9/8
D	D
27/25	16/15
C	C#
10/9	10/9
B	B
9/8	9/8
A	A

The conventional scale of Western music is represented graphically on the right, that used by bagpipers on the left. Neither is a variation of the other. All the notes are out of tune, but only slightly so; once heard often enough, they sound just fine.

Tonality. In music, scale systems and their modifications.

and imitate the arbitrary 12 tone scale and its conventions, and it comes to sound natural (Table 25.1). Yet the overtone series, on which it is partially based, is the only part of it that can be considered a wholly natural phenomenon.

One of the most common alternatives to the semitonal system is the pentatonic system, which, as noted, divides the scale into five nearly equidistant tones. Such scales may be found all over the world, including in much European folk music. In Java people use scales of both five and seven equal steps, which have no relation to the intervals Europeans and European Americans hear as "natural." Arabic and Persian music have smaller units of a third of a tone with scales of 17 and 24 steps in the octave. Even quarter-tone scales are used in India with subtleties of shading that are nearly indistinguishable to a Western ear. Small wonder, then, that even when Westerners can hear what sounds like melody and rhythm in these systems, the total result may sound peculiar to them, or "out of tune." Anthropologists need a very practiced ear to learn to appreciate—perhaps even to tolerate—some of the music they hear, and only some of the most skilled folksong collectors have attempted to notate and analyze the music of nonsemitonal systems.

As another organizing factor in music, whether regular or irregular, rhythm may be more important than tonality. One reason for this may be our constant exposure to natural rhythms, such as our own heartbeat and rhythms of breathing and walking, not to mention surrounding rhythms such as dripping water or lapping waves. Even before we are born, we are exposed to our mother's heartbeat and rhythms of her movements, and as infants experience rhythmic touching, petting, stroking, and rocking.[12]

Traditional European music is most often measured into recurrent patterns of two, three, and four beats, with combinations of weak and strong beats to mark the division and form patterns. Non-European music is likely to move in patterns of 5, 7, or 11 beats, with complex arrangements of internal beats and sometimes polyrhythms: one instrument or singer going in a pattern of 3 beats, for example, while another is in a pattern of 5 or 7. Polyrhythms are frequent in the drum music of West Africa, which shows remarkable precision in the overlapping of rhythmic lines. Non-European music also may contain shifting rhythms: a pattern of three beats, for example, followed by a pattern of two or five beats with little or no regular recurrence or repetition of any one pattern, though the patterns are fixed and identifiable as units.

Even among food-foraging peoples, music plays an important role. Shown here is a native Australian playing a digeridoo.

Although anthropologists do not necessarily have to untangle these complicated technical matters, they will want to know enough to be aware of the degree of skill involved in a performance. This allows a measure of the extent to which people in a culture have learned to practice and respond to this often important creative activity. Moreover, the distribution of musical forms and instruments can reveal much about cultural contact or isolation.

Functions of Music

Even without concern for technical matters, anthropologists can productively investigate the function of music in a society. First, music-making seems to be a part of all cultures. Bone flutes and whistles as much as 40,000 years old, that resemble today's recorders, have been found by archaeologists, nor have historically known food-foraging peoples been without their music. In the Kalahari Desert for example, a Ju/'hoansi hunter off by himself would play a tune for himself on his bow simply to help while away the time (long before anyone thought of beating swords into plowshares some genius discovered—when and where we do not know—that bows could be used not just to kill but to make music as well). In northern New England Abenaki shamans used cedar flutes to call game, lure enemies, and attract women. In addition, a drum over which two rawhide strings were

[12] Dissanayake, E. (2000). Birth of the arts. *Natural History, 109* (10), 89.

A widespread technique used by shamans is persistent drumming, as rhythmic and audio driving are effective ways to induce trance.

stretched to produce a buzzing sound, thought to represent singing, gave the shaman the power to communicate with the spirit world.

Music is also a powerful identifier. Many marginalized groups have used music for purposes of self-identification, bringing the group together and in many cases contraposing their own forms against the onslaught of a dominant culture or voicing social and political commentary. Examples of this include so-called punk groups such as the Dead Kennedys and rap groups such as Public Enemy or L.L.Cool J, as well as ethnic groups sponsoring musical festivals. Potlatches and powwows, among other occasions, allow various Native American groups to reaffirm and celebrate their ethnic identity, among other functions. Music plays an important part at these gatherings, thus becoming closely bound to the group identity, both from without and from within the group. It should be understood, too, that these associations of music with groups are not dependent upon words alone but also upon particular tonal, rhythmic, and instrumental conventions. For example, Scottish gatherings would not be "Scottish" without the sound of the Highland bagpipes and the fiddle.

This power of music to shape identity has been recognized everywhere, with varying consequences. The English recognized the power of the bagpipes for creating a strong sense of identity among the Highland regiments of the British army and encouraged it within certain bounds, even while suppressing piping in Scotland itself under the Disarming Act. Over time, the British military piping tradition was assimilated into the Scottish piping tradition, and so was accepted and spread by Scottish pipers. As a result, much of the supposedly Scottish piping one hears today consists of marches written within the conventions of the musical tradition of England, though shaped to fit the physical constraints of the instrument. Less often heard is the "classical" music known as pibroch, or *ceol mor.* The latter, however, has been undergoing a series of revivals over the past century and is now often associated with rising nationalist sentiments.

Although much music performed by Scottish pipers is of English origin, it has been so thoroughly absorbed that most people think of it as purely Scottish.

The English adoption of the highland bagpipe into Scottish regiments is an instance of those in authority employing music to further a political agenda. So too in Spain, former dictator Francisco Franco (who came to power in the 1930s) established community choruses in even the smallest towns to promote the singing of patriotic songs. Similarly, in Ireland Comhaltas Ceoltoiri Eireann has promoted the collection and performance of traditional Irish music; in Brittany and Galicia music is

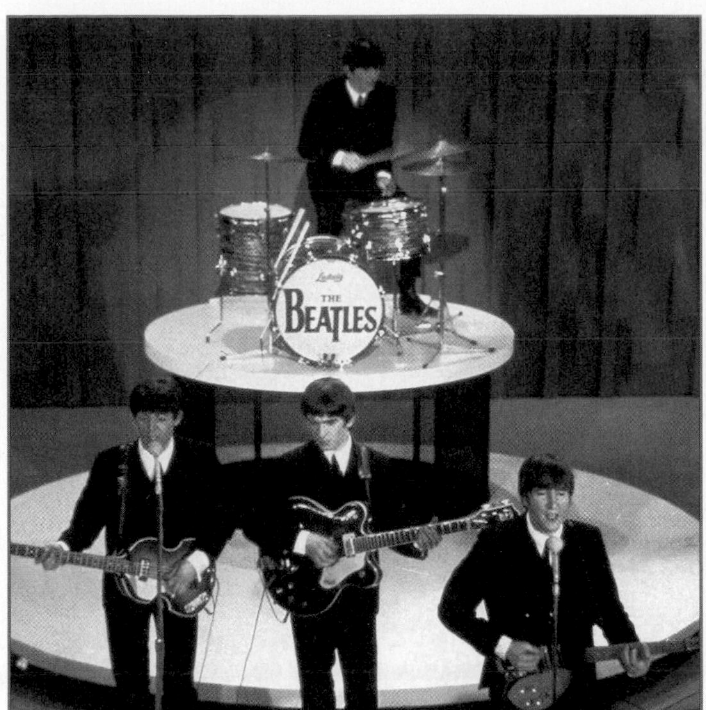

The Beatles were a British group that transformed the music of such African American musicians as Chuck Berry and made it international.

playing an important role in attempts to revive the spirits of the indigenous Celtic cultures in these regions of France and Spain; and the list goes on. But however played, or for whatever reason, music (like all art) is a creative skill that one can cultivate and be proud of, whether from a sense of accomplishment or the sheer pleasure of performing; and it is a form of social behavior through which there is a communication or sharing of feelings and life experience with other humans. Still, because each human's creativity is constrained by the traditions of his or her particular culture, each society's art is distinctive and helps to define its members' sense of identity.

The social function of music is perhaps most obvious in song, since these contain verbal text. This is probably why many earlier studies concentrated upon them. Songs, like other verbal forms, often express a group's values, beliefs, and concerns, but they do so with an increased formalism resulting from adherence to the restrictions of systematic "rules," or conventions, of pitch, rhythm, timbre, and musical genre.

Songs serve many purposes, entertainment being only one of these. Work songs long have played an important part in manual labor, serving to coordinate efforts in heavy or dangerous labor, such as weighing anchor and furling sail on board ships, to coordinate ax or hammer strokes, and to pass time and relieve tedium as with oyster shucking songs. Songs also have been used to soothe babies to sleep, to charm animals into giving more milk or to keep witchcraft at bay, to advertise goods, and much more. Songs may also serve social and political purposes, spreading particular ideas swiftly and effectively by giving them a special form involving poetic language and rhythm and by attaching a pleasing and appropriate tune, be it solemn or light.

In the United States numerous examples exist of marginalized social and ethnic groups attempting to gain a larger audience and more compassion for their plight through song. Perhaps no better example exists than African Americans, whose ancestors were brought to the New World as slaves. Out of their experience emerged spirituals and, ultimately gospel, jazz, blues, rock and roll, and rap. These forms all found their way into the North American mainstream and White performers such as Elvis Presley and Benny Goodman (the latter with integrated bands—unusual in the 1930s) presented their own versions of this music to White audiences. Even composers of so-called serious music ranging from Bernstein to Gershwin to Dvorák to Poulenc were influenced by the music of African Americans. In short, music of a marginalized group of former slaves eventually captivated the entire world, even while the descendants of those slaves have had to struggle continually to escape their subordinate status.

In the 1950s and 1960s performers such as Joan Baez and Pete Seeger gained great visibility when supporting

HIGHWAY 1
Problems with imitation Hopi arts and crafts
http://www.hanksville.org/sand/intellect/art.html

HIGHWAY 2
Maori body art
http://maori.culture.co.nz

HIGHWAY 3
Ancient human artwork
http://www.culture.fr./culture/arcnat/lascaux/fr

civil and human rights causes. Indeed, both performers' celebrity status led to the broader dissemination of their social and political beliefs. Such celebrity status comes from skill in performing and communicating with the intended audience. So powerful a force was music in the civil rights and peace movements of the time that Seeger was targeted by Senator Joseph McCarthy and his investigating committee, becoming one of many performers blacklisted by the entertainment industry.

In Australia, traditional Aboriginal songs have taken on a new legal function, as they are being introduced into court as evidence of early settlement patterns. This helps the native peoples to claim more extensive land ownership, thus allowing them greater authority to use the land, as well as to negotiate and profit from the sale of natural resources. This had been impossible before. The British, upon their annexation of Australia, declared the land ownerless (Terra Nullius). Although the Aborigines had preserved their records of ownership in song and story, these were not admissible in the British courts. In the early 1970s, however, the Aboriginal peoples exposed the injustice of the situation and the Australian government began responding in a more favorable, if still limited, fashion, granting the claims of traditional ownership to groups in the Northern Territory. In 1992 the legitimacy of the concept of Terra Nullius was overturned, and native claims are now being presented in the other territories as well. These newer claimants are granted equal partnership with developers and others. Sacred sites are being recognized, and profits are being shared with the traditional owners. Proof of native ownership includes recordings of traditional songs indicative of traditional settlement, travel patterns, and land use.[13]

Music gives a concrete form, made memorable and attractive with melody and rhythm, to basic human ideas. Whether a song's content is didactic, satirical, inspirational, religious, political, or purely emotional, the important thing is that the formless has been given form and that feelings hard to express in words alone are communicated in a symbolic and memorable way that can be repeated and shared. The group is consequently united and has the sense that their shared experience, whatever it may be, has shape and meaning. This, in turn, shapes and gives meaning to the community.

PICTORAL ART

To many Europeans and European Americans, the first thing that springs to mind in connection with the word *art* is some sort of picture, be it a painting, drawing, sketch, or whatever. And indeed, in many parts of the

[13] Koch, G. (1997). Songs, land rights and archives in Australia. *Cultural Survival Quarterly,* 20 (4).

This stylized painting on a ceremonial shirt represents a bear. Though the art of the Northwest Coast Indians often portrays actual animals, they are not depicted in a naturalistic style. To identify them, one must be familiar with the conventions of this art.

world, people have been making pictures in one way or another for a very long time—etching them in bone, engraving them in rock, painting them on cave walls and rock surfaces, carving and painting them on wood, gourds, pots, or painting them on textiles, bark, bark cloth, animal hide, or even their own bodies. As with musical art, some form of pictorial art is a part of every historically known human culture.

As a type of symbolic expression, pictorial art may be representational, imitating closely the forms of nature, or abstract, drawing from natural forms but representing only their basic patterns or arrangements. Actually, the two categories are not mutually exclusive, for even the most naturalistic portrayal is partly abstract to the extent it generalizes from nature and abstracts patterns of ideal beauty, ugliness, or typical expressions of emotion. But between the most naturalistic and the most schematic or symbolic abstract art lies a continuum. In some of the Indian art of North America's Northwest Coast, for example, animal figures may be so highly stylized as to be difficult for an outsider to identify. Although the art appears abstract, the artist has drawn on nature, even though he or she has exaggerated and deliberately transformed some of its shapes to express a particular feeling toward them. Because artists do these exaggerations and transformations according to the aesthetic principles of Northwest Coast Indian culture, their meanings are understood not just by the artist but by other members of the community as well.

Southern African Rock Art

The rock art of southern Africa, which has been described and studied in considerable detail, especially over the past three decades, is a rich non-Western tradition that helps illustrate different ways of approaching the study of art. This rock art is one of the world's oldest traditions, extending unbroken from at least 27,000 years ago until a mere 100 years ago. It came to an end only with the destruction of the Bushman people responsible for it at the hands of European colonizers. Those (such as the Ju/'hoansi) who have survived in places such as Namibia and Botswana did not themselves produce rock art but do share the same general belief system the rock art expresses.

Bushman rock art consists of both paintings and engravings on the faces of rock outcrops as well as on the walls of rock shelters. Depicted are a variety of animals as well as humans in highly sophisticated ways, sometimes in static poses but often in highly animated scenes. Associated with these figures are a variety of abstract signs including dots, zigzags, nested curves, and the like. Until fairly recently, the significance of these latter was not understood by non-Bushmen; equally puzzling was the frequent presence of new pictures painted or engraved directly over existing ones.

In spite of its puzzling aspects, southern African rock art has long been considered worthy of being viewed and admired. The paintings, especially, are generally seen as quite beautiful, and a source of pleasure to look at. Consequently, it is not surprising that the earliest study of the art took the aesthetic approach, one also well developed in the study of European and other Western art. Thus, the art could be studied for its use of pigments: charcoal and specularite for black; silica, china clay, and gypsum for white; and ferric oxide for red and reddish-brown hues. These were mixed with fat, blood, and perhaps water and

Bushman rock paintings and engravings from southern Africa often depict animals thought to possess great supernatural power. Shamans appear as well: In the painted example at the top, we see rain shamans with swallowtails acting in the spirit realm to protect people from the dangers of storms. Like modern Bushman shamans, several of these hold paired dance sticks. The idea of shamans transforming into birds, as well as being greatly elongated (note one figure's long, undulating body above the lower row of shamans), is based on sensations experienced in trance. Other undulating lines and dots in the picture are entoptic phenomena.

applied to the rough rock with great skill. The effectiveness of line and the way shading is used to mold the contours of animal bodies elicits admiration, as does the rendering of all sorts of realistic details. One of the more popular animals depicted was the eland, a large ox-like antelope, shown with such details as the tuft of red hair on its forehead, the black line running along its back, the darkening of its snout, its cloven hoofs, the folds of skin on its shoulders, and the twist of its horns.

Similar anatomical details of humans are shown, including the details of dress, headgear, and body ornamentation, including leather bands and ostrich eggshell beads. Nevertheless, human figures appear more as caricatures rather than as literal depictions; features such as fatness and thinness may be exaggerated, and the figures are sometimes elongated, often in positions suggestive of flying across the rock face. Sometimes, too, the feet take on the appearance of a swallowtail or a fish's tail. Even more puzzling are figures that appear to be part human-part animal (therianthropes).

Another obvious approach to studying Bushman rock art, the narrative, focuses on *what* it depicts, supplementing the focus of the aesthetic approach on *how* things are

Leonardo da Vinci's *The Last Supper.*

depicted. Certainly, aspects of Bushman life are shown, as in several hunting scenes depicting men with bows, arrows, quivers, and hunting bags. Some depictions show nets used in the hunt and also fish traps. Women are also portrayed—identifiable by their primary sexual characteristics and the stone-weighted digging sticks they carry, but they are rarely shown gathering food. Considering the importance of food gathered by women in the Bushman diet, this seems rather odd. Of course, it might merely reflect the importance Bushmen attach to the hunt, but the fact is that hunting scenes are not at all common, either. Furthermore, the animals shown in the art are *not* representative of the meat eaten; animals commonly depicted (such as the eland) are not commonly eaten. Thus, a narrative approach can lead to a distorted view of Bushman life.

Other scenes portrayed in the art clearly relate to the trance dance, still the most important ritual today among Bushmen (see the Original Study in Chapter 24). This is clearly indicated by the numbers of people shown and the arrangement of hand-clapping women surrounding dancing men, whose bodies are bent forward in the distinctive posture caused by the cramping of abdominal muscles as they go into trance, whose noses are shown bleeding (common today when Bushmen trance), whose arms are stretched behind their backs (modern Bushmen do this to gather more of the supernatural potency—*n/um*), who are wearing dance rattles, and who carry fly whisks (used to extract invisible arrows of sickness). As it turns out, we have here a significant clue to what the art is really all about, though we can not discern this from the narrative and aesthetic approaches alone. For this we need the third, or *interpretive* approach.

The distinction between the aesthetic, narrative, and interpretive approaches becomes clear if we pause for a moment to consider a famous work of Western art, Leonardo da Vinci's painting *The Last Supper.*[14] A non-Christian viewing this mural will see what appear to be 13 ordinary men at a table, apparently enjoying an ordinary meal. Although one of the men appears a bit clumsy, knocking over the salt, and clutches a bag of money, nothing else here indicates the scene to be anything out of the ordinary. Aesthetically, our non-Christian observer may admire the way the composition fits the space available, the way the attitudes of the men are depicted, and the way the artist conveys a sense of movement. As narrative, the painting may be seen as a record of customs, table manners, dress, and architecture. But to know the real meaning of this picture, the viewer must be aware that, in Western culture, spilling the salt is a symbol of impending disaster and that money symbolizes the root of all evil. But even this is not enough; for a full understanding of this work of art, one must know something of the beliefs of Christianity. To move to the interpretive level, then, requires knowledge of the symbols and beliefs of the people responsible for the art.

[14] This example is drawn from Lewis-Williams, J. D. (1990). *Discovering Southern African rock art* (p. 9). Cape Town and Johannesburg: David Philip.

The zigzags and curves in two of these pictures, drawn by migraine sufferers, are classic entoptic phenomena seen in early stages of trance. The "tunnel" with lattice walls in the third picture is representative of those seen when passing from the second to third stage of trance.

Applying the interpretive approach to southern African rock art requires knowledge of two things: Bushman ethnography and the nature of trance. With respect to the latter, a clear understanding comes from a combination of ethnographic data and data gained experimentally in laboratories. Because all human beings have essentially the same nervous system, whether they be urban dwellers from the United States, food foragers from southern Africa, horticulturalists from the Amazon forest, or whoever, they all progress through the same three stages when going into trance. In the first stage, the nervous system generates a variety of luminous, pulsating, revolving, and constantly shifting geometric patterns known as **entoptic phenomena** (anyone who has suffered from migraine headaches is familiar with these). Typical imagery includes grids, parallel lines, zigzags, dots, nested curves, and filigrees, often in a spiral pattern.

As one goes into deeper trance, the brain tries to "make sense" of these abstract forms, just as it does of sensations received when in an unaltered state of consciousness. This process is known as **construal,** and here differences in culture and experience come into play. Commonly, a Bushman in trance will construe a grid pattern as markings on the skin of a giraffe, nested curves as a honeycomb (honey is a Bushman delicacy, and the auditory sensation of buzzing that often accompanies trance promotes the illusion), and

Entoptic phenomena. Bright, pulsating geometric forms that are generated by the central nervous system and "seen" in states of trance. • **Construal.** In the second stage of trance, the process by which the brain tries to "make sense" of entoptic images.

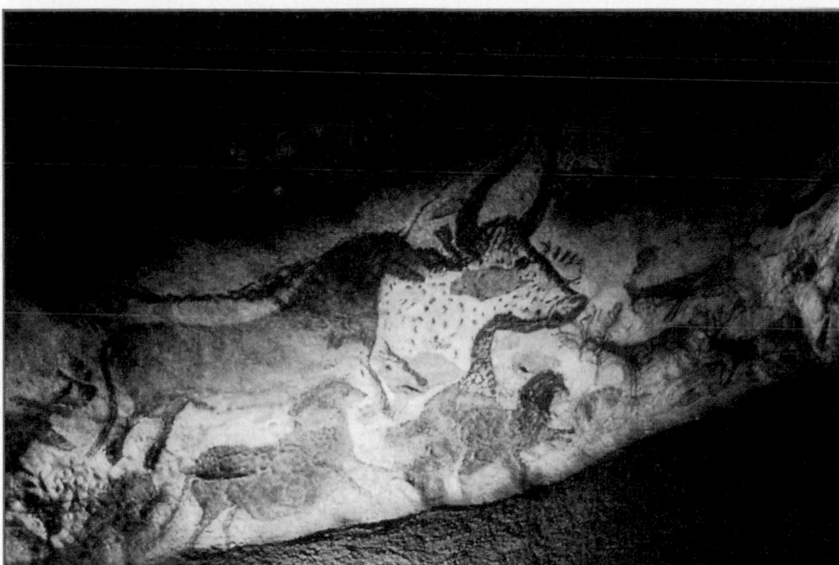

This late Stone Age painting from the Peche Merle cave in France incorporates dot entoptics over and near the body of a bull, one indication the artist was painting something seen in a state of trance. An association of rock art with trance experience has been noted in many parts of the world.

dots as *nu/m,* the potency seen only by shamans in trance. Obviously, we would not expect an Inuit or someone from Los Angeles to construe these patterns in the same way.

In the third and deepest trance stage, subjects cease to be observers of their hallucinations but seem to become part of them. As this happens, they feel themselves passing into a rotating tunnel or vortex with lattice-like sides and on which appear images of animals, humans, and monsters of various sorts. In the process, the entoptic forms of the earlier stages become integrated into these **iconic images,** as they are called. The entoptics may be hard to discern apart from the main image, although sometimes they appear as a kind of background. Iconic images are culture specific; individuals see what their culture disposes them to see; often, these images are things having high emotional content. In the case of Bushmen, they often see the eland, an animal thought to be imbued with specially strong potency, particularly for rain making. Given this, one of the things shamans try to do in trance is to "capture" elands—"rain animals"— for purposes of making rain.

From all of this, we begin to understand why elands are so prominent in the rock art. Moreover, it reveals the significance of the zigzags, dots, grids, and so forth that are so often a part of the compositions. It also leads to an understanding of other puzzling features of the art. For example, the third trance stage includes such sensations as being stretched out or elongated, weightlessness as in flight or in the water, and difficulty breathing as when under water. Hence we find depictions in the art of humans who appear to be abnormally long, as well as individuals who appear to be swimming or flying. Another well-documented trance phenomenon is the sense of being transformed into some sort of animal. Such sensations are triggered in the deepest stage of trance if the individual sees or thinks of an animal, and the sensation accounts for the part human–part animal therianthropes in the art. Finally, the superpositioning of one work of art over another becomes comprehensible; not only are the visions seen in trance commonly superimposed on one another as they rotate and move, but if the trancer stares at a painting or engraving of an earlier vision, the new one will appear as if projected on the old.

The interpretive approach makes clear, then, that the rock art of southern Africa—even in the case of compositions that otherwise might appear to be scenes of everyday life—is intimately connected with the practices and beliefs of shamanism. After shamans came out of trance and reflected on their visions, they then proceeded to paint or engrave their recollections of them on the rock faces. But these were more than records of important visions; they had their own innate power, owing to their supposed supernatural origin. This being so, when the need arose for a new trance experience, it might be held where the old vision was recorded to draw power from it.

With the fuller understanding the interpretive approach provides, we now may look at the broader significance of what the Bushmen tried to achieve through their art. For this, we turn to the writings of the two South African anthropologists who are the leading authorities on the rock art.

Iconic images. Hallucinations of people, animals, and monsters, "seen" in the deepest stage of trance.

Original Study

Bushman Rock Art and Political Power[15]

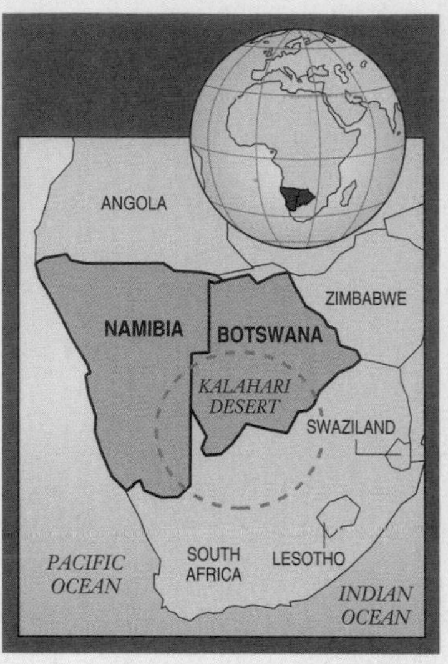

Whatever may be said about Bushman rock art, its images are not the "banal, meaningless artefacts" into which exhibits can so easily transform them. "Meaning" is, of course, an elusive concept. Like all art, the Bushman images did not have a single, one-to-one "meaning" that they unequivocally transmitted from maker to viewer. "Meaning" was historically and complexly constituted; Bushman viewers shared with the makers of the art in the construction of "meaning." Similarly, modern viewers who engage the images will inevitably bring with them their own contribution to their "meaning." If all the original viewers did not "read" the images identically, each viewer having had his or her own socially constituted perspective, how much less likely is it that modern viewers will share identical responses? None the less, some general observations on the art's "meaning" and its role in Bushman communities can be made in the hope that they will challenge the current trivialising stereotypes.

The "ideas which most deeply moved the Bushman mind" were rooted in what our reading of the nineteenth-century accounts suggests was a three-tiered, though not strictly demarcated, view of the cosmos: the level of daily life, the realm above and the realm below. These levels were mediated by shamans. Amongst the Kalahari groups of the 1950s and 1960s, about half of the men and a third of the women were shamans. Entering an altered state of consciousness during a communal dance or in more solitary circumstances, these shamans were believed to activate a supernatural potency so that they could move between the cosmological levels as they performed such diverse tasks as curing the sick, making rain and controlling animals.

The making of rock art was associated with these shamanistic practices in ways not fully understood. The images comprise: representations of animals that were believed to possess supernatural potency, privileged views of communal dances that show not only what ordinary people saw but also elements, such as potency, that were seen by shamans only; conflicts in the spiritual realm between benign shamans and shamans of illness; rain-animals that shamans killed so that their blood and milk would fall as rain; therianthropic figures showing the blending of a shaman with a power-animal; geometric images derived from entoptic phenomena (bright pulsating forms "seen" in certain altered states of consciousness); and a range of other fantastic experiences.

The images were not, however, simply records of religious experiences. There is reason to believe that at least some of them were reservoirs of potency that could be tapped by trancing shamans. They were not just pictures, but powerful things in themselves that could be implicated in effecting alterations in the shamans' states of consciousness, that is, in facilitating the mediation of the cosmological realms.

Even this brief outline shows that the art can be presented as a challenge to the popular belief that the making of art was, for the Bushmen, an idle pastime. The artists' manipulation of metaphors and symbols was far more complex and subtle than many modern viewers realize. The painted and engraved images explore unknown and unsuspected realms in often idiosyncratic ways. In the past the images were active; today they are made static by being separated from their highly charged ritual, social and conceptual contexts.

---

[15] Adapted from Dowson, T. A., & Lewis-Williams, J. D. (1993, November). Myths, museums, and southern African rock art. *South African Historical Journal, 29*, pp. 52–56.

The activity of the images, however, extended beyond the generation of religious experience to the negotiation of political power. Especially in the last two hundred years of the Bushmen's occupation of the south-eastern part of the subcontinent, major and escalating changes were talking place. For many hundreds of years the Bushmen had interacted in various and changing ways with Bantu-speaking agropastoralists, but these, for the most part amicable, exchanges were disrupted by colonial expansion. New social relations began to develop. Shamans, who were already being paid with cattle and a share of the crops by the agropastoralists for whom they made rain, found that they had access to new resources. As the colonists shot out the game and the Bushman territories became more and more restricted, relations with the agropastoralists increased in importance, and political and economic struggles developed between competing shamans and between shamans and ordinary people. The "egalitarian" values that militated against development of political power by shamans were eroded.

Rock painting was implicated in these changes. To illustrate the artistic dynamics of, largely, the nineteenth century, we mention three types of painting. One type shows groups of people, some of whom are identifiable by various features as shamans, in which no one is larger or more elaborately painted than another. A second type shows groups of people in which two or three shaman figures are more elaborately and individually depicted. The third type shows an elaborately painted central shaman with sometimes, facial features, surrounded by "lesser" figures. The historical record from parts of the Kalahari combines with these three types of paintings to suggest that the art became a site of struggle. As social circumstances changed, shamans translated their supernatural potency into political power and vied with one another for control of resources that were, in the final decades, increasingly derived from rain-making for agropastoralists.

The artists who made these types of paintings were not merely painting historical events, chronicling social changes. Such an understanding would be related to the close-to-nature stereotype—simple people painting what was happening around them. Rather, the making of each painting was a socio-political intervention that negotiated the artist's (or artists') political status. The art did not simply reflect social relations: in some instances it transformed those relations; in other instances it worked to reproduce them. Each painting was more than an image of the way things were, or even of the way artists wished they would become. Because the images were themselves charged with the supernatural potency that mediated the levels of the cosmos and made shamanistic activity possible, they exercised a coercive, persuasive influence that was founded in their factuality.

In specific and diverse historical circumstances, the artists invoked this coercive function in their responses to the colonial invasion. Unlike the agropastoralists, the colonists were not intended to be among the viewers of the art, but their threatening presence implicated them in the social production of the art none the less. As the shamans had, for centuries, battled in the spiritual realm with marauding shamans of illness, who often took feline forms, so, the art suggests, did they battle in the spiritual realm with the colonists. The shamans tried to deploy their powers in such a way as to thwart the advance of the colonists. As we know, their efforts were fruitless; the colonists' rifles were, in the end, invincible. At times prosecuting a policy of calculated genocide, at other times mounting ad hoc but nevertheless vicious "retaliatory" commandos, the colonists all but wiped out the Bushman communities south of the Orange River. Many Bushmen, it is true, intermarried with agropastoralists and others went to live with them, but, all in all, the unpalatable truth of the matter is that genocide was the finality.

The End

Although southern African rock art is all too often dismissively labeled as "primitive" or "simple," the discussion here shows that it is anything but. Neither the art itself or the belief system in which it was embedded can be described as remotely "simple." Understanding such art requires a good deal more than simple staring at a picture, but the effort is well worth making.

CHAPTER SUMMARY

Although hard to explain, art is usefully regarded as the creative use of the human imagination to interpret, express, and enjoy life. It stems from the uniquely human ability to use symbols to give shape and significance to the physical world for more than just a utilitarian purpose. Anthropologists are concerned with art as a reflection of the cultural values and concerns of people.

Oral traditions denote a culture's unwritten stories, beliefs, and customs. Verbal arts include narrative, drama, poetry, incantations, proverbs, riddles, and word games. Narratives, which have received the most study, have been divided into three categories: myths, legends, and tales.

Myths are basically sacred narratives that explain how the world came to be as it is. By describing an orderly universe, myths function to set standards for orderly behavior. Legends are stories told as if true that often recount the exploits of heroes, the movements of people, and the establishment of local customs. Epics, which are long legends in poetry or prose, typically are found in nonliterate societies with a form of state political organization. They serve to transmit and preserve a culture's legal and political practices. In literate states, history has taken over these functions to one degree or another. Anthropologists are interested in legends because they provide clues about what constitutes model ethical behavior in a culture. Tales are fictional, secular, and nonhistorical narratives that instruct as they entertain. Anthropological interest in tales centers in part on the fact that their distribution provides evidence of cultural contacts or cultural isolation.

The study of music in specific cultural settings has developed into the specialized field of ethnomusicology. Almost everywhere human music is perceived in terms of a scale. Scale systems and their modifications comprise tonality in music. Tonality determines the possibilities and limits of melody and harmony. Rhythm is an organizing factor in music. Traditional European music is measured into recurrent patterns of two, three, and four beats.

The social function of music is most obvious in song. Like tales, songs may express a group's concerns, but with greater formalism because of the restrictions imposed by closed systems of tonality, rhythm, and musical form. Music also serves as a powerful way for a social or ethnic group to assert its distinctive identity. As well, it may be used to advance particular political, economic, and social agendas, or for any one of a number of other purposes.

Pictorial art may be regarded as either representational or abstract, though in truth these categories represent polar ends of a continuum. The rock art of southern Africa illustrates three ways the study of art may be approached. The aesthetic and narrative approaches focus on *how* and *what* things are depicted. By themselves they reveal little about what the art is all about and may convey a distorted view of the people responsible for it. Only the interpretive approach can reveal the meaning of another people's art. This approach requires a rich body of ethnography and often other sets of data to draw on. The effort is worthwhile, as it may reveal the art to be far more complex than one might otherwise expect. Applied to southern African rock art, it shows how paintings and engravings were actually part of Bushman strategy for negotiating changing power relations as colonists invaded their lands.

CLASSIC READINGS

Dundes, A. (1980). *Interpreting folk lore*. Bloomington: Indiana University.

A collection of articles that assess the materials folklorists have amassed and classified, this book seeks to broaden and refine traditional assumptions about the proper subject matter and methods of folklore.

Hannah, J. L. (1988). *Dance, sex and gender*. Chicago: University of Chicago Press.

Like other art forms, dances are social acts that contribute to the continuation and emergence of culture. One of the oldest—if not the oldest—art forms, dance shares the same instrument, the human body, with sexuality. This book, written for a broad nonspecialist audience, explicitly examines sexuality and the construction of gender identities as they are played out in the production and visual imagery of dance.

Hatcher, E. P. (1985). *Art as culture: An Introduction to the anthropology of art*. New York: University Press of America.

This handy, clearly written book does a nice job of relating the visual arts to other aspects of culture. Topics include "The Technological Means," "The Psychological Perspective," "Social Contexts and Social Functions," "Art as Communication," and "The Time Dimension." Numerous line drawings help the reader understand the varied forms of art in non-Western societies.

Layton, R. (1991). *The anthropology of art* (2nd ed.) Cambridge, Eng.: Cambridge University Press.

This readable introduction to the diversity of non-Western art deals with questions of aesthetic appreciation, the use of art, and the big question: What *is* art?

Merriam, A. P. (1964). *The anthropology of music.* Chicago: Northwestern University Press.

This book focuses upon music as a complex of behavior that resonates throughout all of culture: social organization, aesthetic activity, economics, and religion.

Otten, C. M. (1971). *Anthropology and art: Readings in cross-cultural aesthetics.* Garden City, NY: Natural History Press.

This is a collection of articles by anthropologists and art historians with emphasis on the functional relationships between art and culture.

PART VIII

Change and the Future: Solving the Problem of Adjusting to Changed Conditions

INTRODUCTION

Understanding the processes of change, the subject of Chapter 26, is one of the most important and fundamental of anthropological goals. Unfortunately, the task is made difficult by the cultural biases of most modern North Americans, which predispose them to see change as a progressive process leading in a predictable and determined way to where they are now, and even on beyond into a future to which they lead the rest of humanity. So pervasive is this notion of progress that it motivates the thinking of many North Americans in ways of which they are hardly aware. Among other ideas, it often leads them to view cultures not like their own as "backward" and "underdeveloped." Of course, they are no such thing; as we saw in Chapter 17, no culture is static, and cultures may be very highly developed in quite different ways.

A simple analogy with the world of nature is helpful here. In the course of evolution, simple bacteria appeared long before vertebrate animals, and land vertebrates such as mammals are relative latecomers indeed. Yet, bacteria abound in the world today, not as relics of the past but as organisms highly adapted to situations for which mammals are totally unsuited. Just because mammals got here late does not mean that a dog is "better" or "more progressive" than bacteria.

Belief in "progress" and its inevitability has important implications for North Americans as well as others. For people in the United States, it means that change has become necessary for its own sake, for whatever exists today is, by definition, not as good as what will come tomorrow. Whatever is old is, by virtue of that fact alone, inadequate and should be abandoned, no matter how well it seems to be working. Toward others, the logic runs like this: If the old must inevitably give way to the new, then societies North Americans perceive as "old" or "out of the past" also must give way to the new. Since the U.S. way of life is a recent development in human history, it must represent the new. "Old" societies therefore must become like that of the United States, or else it is their fate to disappear altogether. This reasoning amounts to a charter for massive intervention into the lives of others, whether they want this or not; the outcome, more often than not, is the destabilization and even destruction of other societies in the world.

A conscious attempt to identify and eliminate the biases of North American culture allows us to see change in a very different way. It allows us to recognize that although people can change their ways in response to particular problems, much change occurs accidentally. The fact is that the historical record is quirky and full of random events. And although it is true that without change cultures could never adapt to altered conditions, we also must recognize that too much large-scale, continuing change may place a culture in jeopardy. It conflicts with the social need for predictability, discussed in Chapter 14; individuals' needs for regularity and structure, discussed in Chapter 16; and a population's need for an adaptive "fit" with its environment, discussed in Chapter 17.

The more anthropologists study change and learn about the various ways people solve their problems of existence, the more aware they become of a great paradox of culture. The basic business of culture is to solve problems, but, in doing so, new problems inevitably are created that demand solutions. Throughout this book we have seen examples of this—the problems of forming groups in order to cooperate in solving the problems of staying alive, the problem of overcoming the stresses and strains on individuals as a consequence of their group memberships, and the structural problems inherent in division of society into a number of smaller groups, to mention a few. It is apparent every solution to a problem has its price, but as long as culture can keep at least a step ahead of the problems, all is reasonably well.

When we see all the problems faced by the human species today (Chapter 27), most of them the result of cultural practices, we may wonder if we have passed some critical threshold where culture has begun to fall a step behind the problems. This does not mean the future necessarily has to be bleak for the generations that follow, but it would be irresponsible to project a rosy science-fiction-type of future as inevitable, at least on the basis of present evidence.

To prevent a bleak future, humans will have to rise to the challenge of changing their behavior and ideas to conquer the large problems that threaten to annihilate them: overpopulation and unequal access to basic resources with their concomitant starvation, poverty, and squalor; environmental pollution and poisoning; and the culture of discontent and bitterness that arises from the widening economic gap separating industrialized from nonindustrialized countries and the "haves" from the "have nots" within countries. ■

CHAPTER 26

CULTURAL CHANGE

The ability to change has always been important to human cultures. Probably at no time has the pace of change equaled that of today, as traditional peoples all over the world are pressured, directly or indirectly, by the industrialized countries of the world to "change their ways." These Yanomami children can no longer play in many rivers in their homeland, as these have been polluted by mercury from gold mining operations.

CHAPTER PREVIEW

1 Why Do Cultures Change?

All cultures change at one time or another for a variety of reasons. Although people deliberately may change their ways in response to some perceived problem, much change is accidental, including the unforeseen outcome of existing events. Or contact with other peoples may introduce "foreign" ideas, leading to changes in existing values and behavior. This may even involve the massive imposition of foreign ways through conquest of one group by another. Through change, cultures can adapt to altered conditions; however, not all change is adaptive.

2 How Do Cultures Change?

The mechanisms of change are innovation, diffusion, cultural loss, and acculturation. Innovation occurs when someone within a society discovers something new that is then accepted by other society members. Diffusion is the borrowing of something from another group, and cultural loss is the abandonment of an existing practice or trait, with or without replacement. Acculturation is the massive change that comes about with the sort of intensive, firsthand contact that has occurred under colonialism.

3 What Is Modernization?

Modernization is an ethnocentric term used to refer to a global process of change by which traditional, nonindustrial societies seek to acquire characteristics of industrially "advanced" societies. Although modernization generally has been assumed to be a good thing, and there have been some successes, it frequently has led to the development of a new "culture of discontent," a level of aspirations far exceeding the bounds of an individual's local opportunities. Sometimes it leads to the destruction of cherished customs and values people had no desire to abandon.

Culture is the medium through which the human species solves the problems of existence, as these are perceived by members of the species. Various cultural institutions, such as kinship and marriage, political and economic organization, and religion, mesh together to form an integrated cultural system. Because systems generally work to maintain stability, cultures are often fairly stable and remain so unless either the conditions to which they are adapted or human perceptions of those conditions change. Archaeological studies reveal how elements of a culture may persist for long periods. In Chapter 17, for example, we saw how the culture of the native inhabitants of northwestern New England and southern Quebec remained relatively stable over thousands of years.

Although stability may be a striking feature of many cultures, none are ever changeless, as the cultures of food foragers, subsistence farmers, or pastoralists are all too often assumed to be. In a stable society, change may occur gently and gradually, without altering in any fundamental way the culture's underlying logic. Sometimes, though, the pace of change may increase dramatically, causing a radical cultural alteration in a relatively short period. The modern world is full of examples as diverse as the disintegration of the Soviet Union, or what is happening to the native peoples of the Amazon forest as the Brazilian state presses ahead to "develop" this vast region.

The causes of change are many and include the unexpected outcome of existing activities. To cite an example from U.S. history, the settlement of what we now call New England by English-speaking people had nothing to do with their culture being "better" or "more advanced" than those of the region's native Algonquian-speaking inhabitants (one might argue it was just the reverse, as at the time, New England's Indians had higher quality diets, enjoyed better health, and experienced less violence in their lives than did most Europeans[1]). Rather, the new settlement was the outcome of a series of unrelated events that happened to coincide at a critical time. In Britain, economic and political developments that drove large numbers of farmers off the land, occurring at a time of population growth, forced an outward migration of people; it was purely chance that this happened shortly after the European discovery of the Americas.

Even at that, attempts to establish British colonies in New England ended in failure until an epidemic of unprecedented scope resulted in the sudden death of about 90% of the native inhabitants of coastal New England. This epidemic did not happen because the British could not settle unless the land were cleared of its original occupants but, rather, because the Indians had been in regular contact with European fishermen and fur traders—whose activities were independent of British attempts at colonization—from whom they contracted the disease. For centuries, up to this time, Europeans had been living under conditions that were ideal for the incubation and spread of all sorts of infectious diseases, which periodically killed off up to 80% of local populations. Since those who survived had a higher resistance to the diseases than those who succumbed, such resistance became more common in European populations over time. Indians, by contrast, lacked all resistance to these diseases. To be sure, the consequences were inevitable, once direct contact between these people occurred; nonetheless, differential immunity did not occur for the purpose of clearing the coast of New England for British settlement. And even once those settlements were established, it is unlikely the colonists could have dispossessed the remaining natives from their land had they not come equipped with the political and military techniques for dominating other peoples, tactics previously used by England to impose its control upon the Scots, Irish, and Welsh.

In sum, had not a number of otherwise unrelated phenomena come together by chance at just the right time, English might very well not be the language spoken by most North Americans today.

Not just the unexpected outcome of existing activities but other sorts of accidents, too, may bring about changes if people perceive them as useful. Of course, people also may respond deliberately to altered conditions, thereby correcting the perceived problem that made the cultural modification seem necessary. Change may also be forced upon one group by another, as happened in colonial New England and as is happening in so much of the world today in the course of especially intense contact between two societies. Progress and adaptation, on the other hand, are *not* causes of change; the latter is a consequence of it that happens to work well for a population, and the former is a judgment of those consequences in terms of the group's cultural values. Progress is however it is defined.

---

[1] Stannard, D. E. (1992). *American holocaust* (pp. 57–67). Oxford: Oxford University Press.

MECHANISMS OF CHANGE

Innovation

The ultimate source of all change is innovation: any new practice, tool, or principle that gains widespread acceptance within a group. Those that involve the chance discovery of a new principle we refer to as **primary innovations**; those that result from deliberate applications of known principles are **secondary innovations.** The latter correspond most closely to Western culture's model of change as predictable and determined, while the former involves accidents of one sort or another.

An example of a primary innovation is the discovery that the firing of clay makes it permanently hard. Presumably, accidental firing of clay occurred frequently in ancient cooking fires. An accidental occurrence is of no account, however, unless someone perceives an application of it. This perception first took place about 25,000 years ago, when people began making figurines of fired clay. Pottery vessels were not made, however, nor did the practice of making objects of fired clay reach Southwest Asia; at least if it did, it failed to take root. Not until some time between 7000 and 6500 B.C. did people living in Southwest Asia recognize a significant application of fired clay, when they began using it to make cheap, durable, and easy-to-produce containers and cooking vessels.

As nearly as we can reconstruct it, the development of the earliest known pottery vessels came about in the following way.[2] By 7000 B.C., cooking areas in Southwest Asia included clay-lined basins built into the floor, clay ovens, and hearths, making the accidental firing of clay inevitable. Moreover, people were already familiar with the working of clay, which they used to build houses, line storage pits, and model figurines. For containers, however, they still relied upon baskets, and bags made of animal hides.

Once the significance of fired clay—the primary innovation—was perceived, then the application of known

[2] Amiran, R. (1965). The Beginnings of pottery-making in the Near East. In F. R. Matson (Ed.), *Ceramics and man* (pp. 240–247). Viking Fund Publications in Anthropology, 41.

A Hopi woman firing pottery vessels. The discovery that firing clay vessels makes them indestructible (unless they are dropped or otherwise smashed) probably came about when clay-lined basins next to cooking fires in the Middle East were accidentally fired.

Primary Innovation. The chance discovery of some new principle. • **Secondary innovation.** Something new that results from the deliberate application of known principles.

techniques to it—secondary innovation—became possible. Clay could be modeled in the familiar way, but now into the known shapes of baskets, bags, and stone bowls and then fired, either in an open fire or in the same facilities used for cooking food. In fact, the earliest known southwest Asian pottery imitates leather and stone containers, and the decoration consists of motifs transferred from basketry, even though they were ill suited to the new medium. Eventually, potters developed shapes and decorative techniques more suited to the new technology.

Since men are seldom (if ever) the potters in traditional societies unless the craft has become something of a commercial operation, women probably made the first pottery. The vessels that they produced were initially handmade, and the earliest kilns were the same ovens used for cooking. As people became more adept at making pottery, there were further technological refinements. To aid in production, the clay could be modeled on a mat or other surface, which the woman could move as work progressed. Hence, she could sit in one place while she worked, without having to get up to move around the clay. A further refinement was to mount the movable surface on a vertical rotating shaft—an application of a known principle used for drills—creating the potter's wheel and permitting mass production. Kilns, too, were improved for better heat circulation by separating the firing chamber from the fire itself. By chance, these improved kilns produced enough heat to smelt ores such as copper, tin, gold, silver, and lead. Presumably, this discovery was made by accident—another primary innovation—and the stage was set for the eventual development of the forced-draft furnace out of the earlier pottery kiln.

The accidents responsible for primary innovations are not generated by environmental change or some other "need," nor are they preferentially oriented in an adaptive direction (see Figure 26.1). They are, however, given structure by the cultural context. Thus, the outcome of the discovery of fired clay by mobile food foragers 25,000 years ago was very different from what it was when discovered later by more sedentary farmers in Southwest Asia, where it set off a veritable chain reaction as one invention led to another. Indeed, given certain sets of cultural goals, values, and knowledge, particular innovations are almost bound to be made, as illustrated by penicillin. This antibiotic was discovered in 1928 when a mold blew in through the window of Sir Alexander Fleming's lab and landed on a microbial colony of staphylococcus, which it then dissolved. Fleming recognized the importance of this accident, because he was sensitive to the need for more than antiseptics and immunization, the mainstays of medicine at the time, to fight infection. Of course, he was not alone in his awareness, nor was this accident at all unusual. Physicians who studied medicine in the early part of the 20th century had stories about having to scrub down laboratories when their studies in bacteriology were brought to a halt by molds that persisted in contaminating cultures and killing off the bacteria. To them, it was an annoyance; to Fleming, it was a "magic bullet" to fight infection. Un-

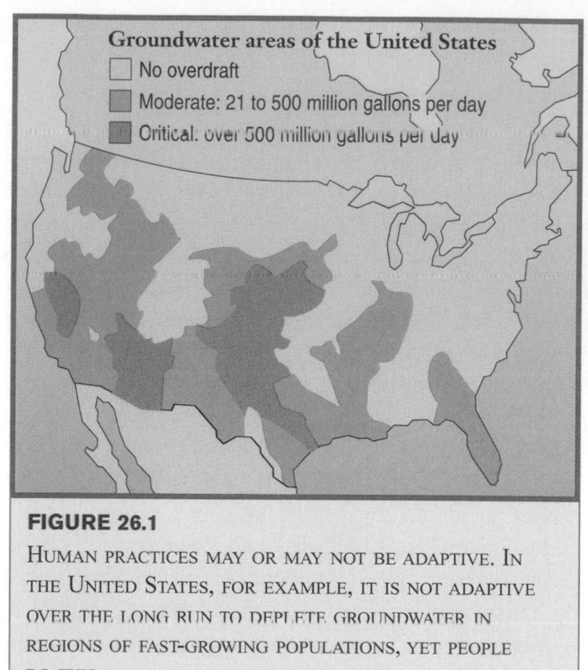

FIGURE 26.1
HUMAN PRACTICES MAY OR MAY NOT BE ADAPTIVE. IN THE UNITED STATES, FOR EXAMPLE, IT IS NOT ADAPTIVE OVER THE LONG RUN TO DEPLETE GROUNDWATER IN REGIONS OF FAST-GROWING POPULATIONS, YET PEOPLE DO THIS.

Things invented for one purpose may come to serve other, quite unrelated purposes. In Great Britain, researchers from the University of Liverpool found men using their mobile phones as display pieces to advertise to women their status and desirability as potential mates.

der the circumstances, however, had he not made the discovery, someone else would have before long.

Although a culture's internal dynamics may encourage certain innovative tendencies, they may discourage others, or even remain neutral with respect to yet others. Indeed, Copernicus's discovery of the rotation of the planets around the sun and Mendel's discovery of the basic laws of heredity are instances of genuine creative insights out of step with the established needs, values, and goals of their times and places. In fact, Mendel's work remained obscure until 16 years after his death, when three scientists working independently rediscovered, all in the same year (1900), the same laws of heredity. Thus, in the context of turn-of-the-century Western culture, Mendel's laws were bound to be discovered, even had Mendel himself not hit upon them earlier.

Although an innovation must be reasonably consistent with a society's needs, values, and goals if it is to be accepted, this is not sufficient to assure its acceptance. Force of habit tends to be an obstacle to acceptance; people will generally tend to stick with what they are used to rather than adopt something new that will require some adjustment on their part. An example of this can be seen in the continued use of the QWERTY keyboard for typewriters and computers (named from the starting arrangement of letters). Devised in 1874, the arrangement minimized jamming of type bars and was combined with other desirable mechanical features to become the first commercially successful typewriter. Yet, the QWERTY keyboard has a number of serious drawbacks. The more typing one can do in the "home row" (second from bottom) of keys, the faster one can type, with the fewest errors and least strain on the fingers. But with QWERTY, only 32% of strokes are done on the home row, versus 52% on the upper row and 16% on the (hardest) bottom row. What's more, it requires overuse of the weaker (left) hand, and the weakest (fifth) finger.

In 1932, after extensive study, August Dvorak developed a keyboard that avoids the defects of QWERTY (Figure 26.2). Tests consistently show that the Dvorak keyboard

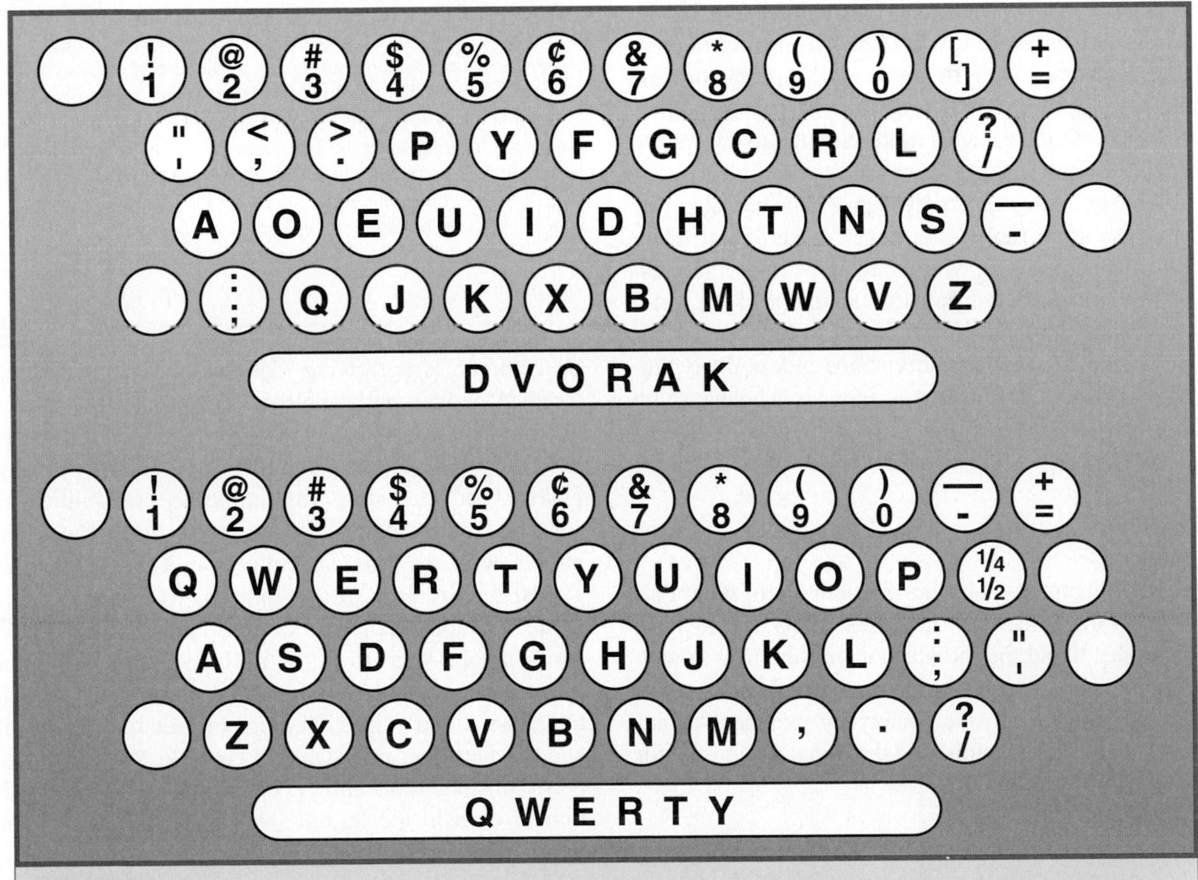

FIGURE 26.2

DVORAK AND QWERTY KEYBOARDS, COMPARED. THOUGH SUPERIOR TO THE LATTER IN VIRTUALLY EVERY WAY, DVORAK HAS NOT BEEN ADOPTED OWING TO THE HEAD START ENJOYED BY QWERTY.

Once one's reflexes become adjusted to doing something one way, it becomes difficult to do it differently. Thus, when a North American or European goes to Great Britain, learning to drive on the "wrong" side of the road is difficult.

The way people creatively shape things borrowed from other cultures to make them distinctively their own is illustrated by the way people in Zambia reconfigure used clothing imported from the United States. This photo of teenage boys in Lusaka was taken in 1995. Their outfits from secondhand clothing consist of headgear, made from sleeves of leather jackets, and bomber jackets under which one is wearing an untucked shirt. Their trousers have pleats around the hips and straight wide legs. They are wearing leather shoes.

can be learned in one third the time. Once they learn it, typists increase their accuracy by 68% and their speed by 74%, and they experience significantly less fatigue. So why has not Dvorak replaced QWERTY? The answer is commitment. Because QWERTY had a head start, by the time Dvorak came along manufacturers, typists, teachers, salespeople, and office managers were committed to the old keyboard; it was what they were used to.[3]

Obviously, being markedly better than the thing or idea an innovation replaces is not necessarily sufficient to ensure its acceptance. Much may depend on the prestige of the innovator and potential adopters. If the innovator's prestige is high, this will help gain acceptance for the innovation. If it is low, acceptance is less likely, unless the innovator can attract a sponsor who has high prestige.

Diffusion

When the Pilgrims established their colony of New Plymouth in North America, they very likely would have starved to death had the Indians not showed them how to grow the native American crop, corn. The borrowing of cultural elements from one society by members of another is known as **diffusion,** and the donor society is, for all intents and purposes, the "inventor" of that element. So common is borrowing that the late Ralph Linton, a North American anthropologist, suggested that borrowing accounts for as much as 90% of any culture's content. People are creative about their borrowing, however, picking and choosing from multiple possibilities and sources. Usually their selections are limited to those compatible with the existing culture. In Guatemala in the 1960s, for example, Maya Indians, who then (as now) made up more than half of that country's population, would adopt Western ways if the value of what they adopted was self-evident and did not conflict with traditional ways and values. The use of metal hoes, shovels, and machetes became standard early on, for they are superior to stone tools and yet compatible with the cultivation of corn in the traditional way by men using hand tools.

[3] Diamond, J. (1997). The curse of QWERTY. *Discover, 18* (4), 34–42.

Diffusion. The spread of customs or practices from one culture to another.

Yet certain other "modern" practices that might seem advantageous to the Maya were resisted if they were perceived as running counter to Indian tradition. Thus, a young man in one community who tried his hand at truck gardening, using chemical fertilizers and pesticides to grow cash crops with market value only in the city—vegetables never eaten by the Maya—could not secure a "good" woman for a wife (a "good" woman being one who has never had sex with another man and is skilled at domestic chores, not lazy, and willing to attend to her husband's needs). After he abandoned his unorthodox ways, however, his community accepted him as a "real" man, no longer different from the rest of them and therefore conspicuous (a "real" man is one who will work steadily to provide his household with what they need to live by farming and making charcoal in the traditional ways). Before long, he was well married.[4]

Although the tendency toward borrowing is so great it led Robert Lowie to comment, "Culture is a thing of shreds and patches," the borrowed traits usually undergo sufficient modifications to make this wry comment more colorful than accurate. Moreover, existing cultural traits may be modified to accommodate a borrowed one. An awareness of the extent of borrowing can be eye opening. Take, for example, the numerous things European Americans have borrowed from American Indians. Domestic plants developed ("invented") by the Indians—"Irish" potatoes, avocados, corn, beans, squash, tomatoes, peanuts, manioc, chili peppers, chocolate, and sweet potatoes, to name a few, furnish a major portion of the world's food supply. In fact, American Indians remain the developers of the world's largest array of nutritious foods and the primary contributors to the world's varied cuisine.[5] Among drugs and stimulants, tobacco is the best known (Figure 26.3), but others include coca in cocaine, ephedra in ephedrine, datura in pain relievers, and cascara in laxatives. Early on, European physicians recognized that Indians had the world's most sophisticated pharmacy, and Indians used all but a handful of drugs known today made from plants native to the Americas. More than 200 plants and herbs they used for medicinal purposes have at one time or another been included in

[4] Reina, R. E. (1966). *The law of the saints* (pp. 65–68). Indianapolis: Bobbs-Merrill.

[5] Weatherford, J. (1988). *Indian givers: How the Indians of the Americas transformed the New World* (p. 115). New York: Ballantine.

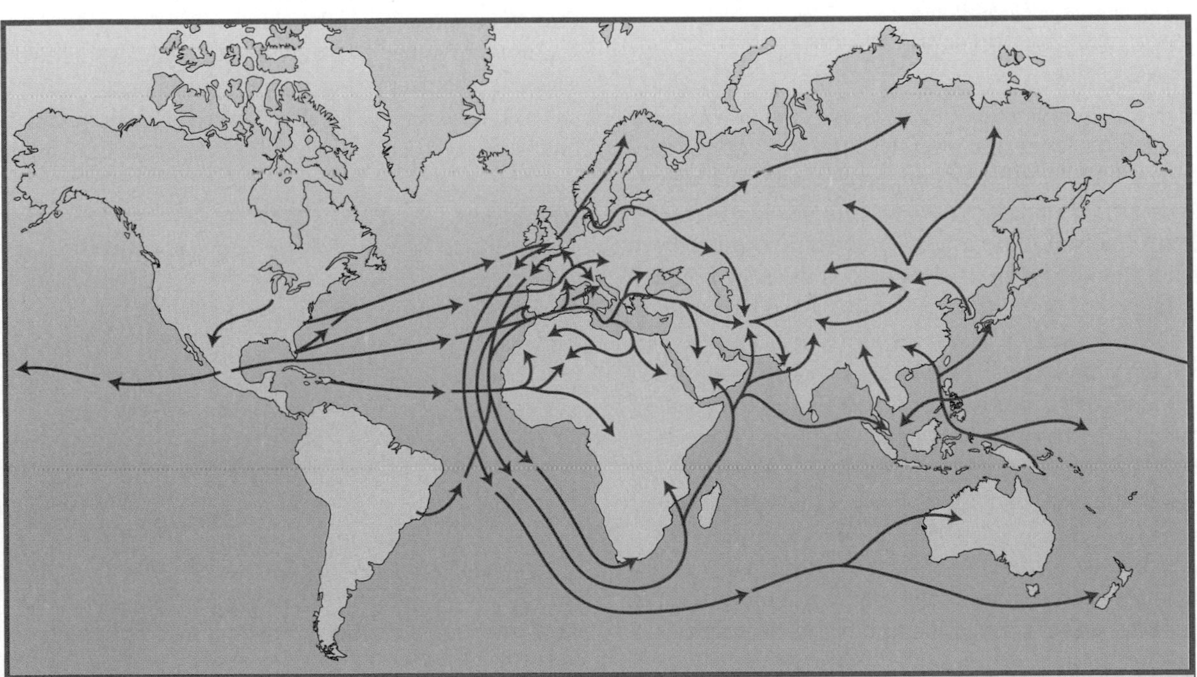

FIGURE 26.3

THE DIFFUSION OF TOBACCO. HAVING SPREAD FROM THE TROPICS OF THE WESTERN HEMISPHERE TO MUCH OF THE REST OF NORTH AND SOUTH AMERICA, IT RAPIDLY SPREAD AFTER 1492 TO THE REST OF THE WORLD.

While cultural change may have unanticipated consequences, so may resistance to change. The United States' reluctance to adopt the metric system led to a crash of a spacecraft on Mars. Unbeknownst to each other, one set of engineers was using the metric system, while another used the old English system.

the *Pharmacopeia of the United States* or in the *National Formulary.* Varieties of cotton developed by Indians supply much of the world's clothing needs, while the woolen poncho, the parka, and moccasins are universally familiar items. Not only has Anglo-American literature been permanently shaped by such works as the New England poet Henry W. Longfellow's *Hiawatha* and novelist James Fenimore Cooper's *Leatherstocking Tales,* but also American Indian music has contributed to world music such ultramodern devices as unusual intervals, arbitrary scales, conflicting rhythms, and hypnotic monotony. These borrowings are so thoroughly integrated into modern North American culture that few people are aware of their source.

Despite the obvious importance of diffusion, accepting an innovation from another culture probably faces more obstacles than accepting one that is "homegrown." In addition to the same obstacles that stand in the way of homegrown inventions is the fact that a borrowed one is, by its very nature, foreign. In the United States, for example, this is one reason why people have been so reluctant to abandon completely the awkward and cumbersome old English system of weights and measures for the far more logical metric system, which has been adopted by just about everyone else on the face of the earth. (The only holdouts besides the United States are South Yemen and Liberia.) Hence, the ethnocentrism of the potential borrowing culture may act as a barrier to acceptance.

Cultural Loss

Most often people tend to think of change as an accumulation of innovations; adding new things to those already there. They think so because this seems so much a part of the way they live. A little reflection, however, leads to the realization that frequently the acceptance of a new innovation leads to the loss of an older one. This sort of replacement is not just a feature of Western civilization. For example, in ancient times, chariots and carts were in widespread use in the Middle East, but by the 6th century A.D., wheeled vehicles had virtually disappeared from Morocco to Afghanistan. They were replaced by camels, not because of some reversion to the past by the region's inhabitants but because camels, used as pack animals, worked better. By the 6th century Roman roads had deteriorated, but camels, as long as they were not used as draft animals, were not bound to them. Not only that, their longevity, endurance, and ability to ford rivers and traverse rough ground without people having to build roads in the first place made pack camels admirably suited for the region. Finally, they were economical of labor: A wagon required a man for every two draft animals,

New inventions may result in unexpected cultural change, as microwave ovens have contributed to the demise of family meals in the United States.

whereas a single person can manage from three to six pack camels. Stephen Jay Gould comments:

> We are initially surprised . . . because wheels have come to symbolize in our culture . . . intelligent exploitation and technological progress. Once invented, their superiority cannot be gainsaid or superseded. Indeed, "reinventing the wheel" has become our standard metaphor for deriding the repetition of such obvious truths. In an earlier era of triumphant social Darwinism, wheels stood as an ineluctable stage of human progress. The "inferior" cultures of Africa slid to defeat; their conquerors rolled to victory. The "advanced" cultures of Mexico and Peru might have repulsed Cortés and Pizarro if only a clever artisan had thought of turning a calendar stone into a cartwheel. The notion that carts could ever be replaced by pack animals strikes us not only as backward but almost sacrilegious.
>
> The success of camels reemphasizes a fundamental theme. . . . Adaptation, be it biological or cultural, represents a better fit to specific, local environments, not an inevitable stage in a ladder of progress. Wheels were a formidable invention, and their uses are manifold (potters and millers did not abandon them, even when cartwrights were eclipsed). But camels may work better in some circumstances. Wheels, like wings, fins, and brains, are exquisite devices for certain purposes, not signs of intrinsic superiority.[6]

Often overlooked is another facet of losing of apparently useful traits: loss without replacement. An example of this is the absence of boats among the inhabitants of the Canary Islands, an archipelago isolated in the stormy seas off the coast of West Africa. The ancestors of these people must have had boats, for without them they could never have transported themselves and their domestic livestock to the islands in the first place. Later, without boats, they had no way to communicate between islands. The cause of this loss of something useful was the islands' lack of stone suitable for making polished stone axes, which in turn limited the islanders' carpentry.[7]

[6] Gould, S. J. (1983). *Hens' teeth and horses' toes* (p. 159). New York: Norton.

[7] Coon, C. S. (1954). *The story of man* (p. 174). New York: Knopf.

REPRESSIVE CHANGE

Innovation, diffusion, and cultural loss all may take place among peoples who are free to decide for themselves what changes they will or will not accept. Not always, however, are people left free to make their own choices; frequently, changes they would not willingly make themselves have been forced upon them by some other group, usually in the course of conquest and colonialism. A direct outcome in many cases is a phenomenon anthropologists call acculturation.

Acculturation

Acculturation occurs when groups having different cultures come into intensive firsthand contact, with subsequent massive changes in the original cultural patterns of one or both groups. It always involves an element of force, either directly, as in conquests, or indirectly, as in the implicit or explicit threat that force will be used if people refuse to make the changes those in the other group expect them to make. Other variables include degree of cultural difference; circumstances, intensity, frequency, and hostility of contact; relative status of the agents of contact; who is dominant and who is submissive; and whether the nature of the flow is reciprocal or nonreciprocal. It must be emphasized that acculturation and diffusion are not equivalent terms; one culture can borrow from another without being in the least acculturated.

In the course of acculturation, any one of a number of things may happen. Merger or fusion occurs when two cultures lose their separate identities and form a single culture, as expressed by the "melting pot" ideology of Anglo-American culture in the United States. Sometimes, though, one of the cultures loses its autonomy but retains its identity as a subculture in the form of a caste, class, or ethnic group; this is typical of conquest or slavery situations, and the United States has examples in spite of its melting-pot ideology. One need look no farther afield than the nearest Indian reservation. Today, in virtually all parts of the world, people are faced with the tragedy of forced removal from their traditional homelands, as entire communities are uprooted to make way for hydroelectric projects, grazing lands for cattle, mining operations, or highway construction. In Brazil's rush to develop the Amazon basin, for instance, whole villages have been relocated

Acculturation. Major culture changes that people are forced to make as a consequence of intensive, firsthand contact between societies.

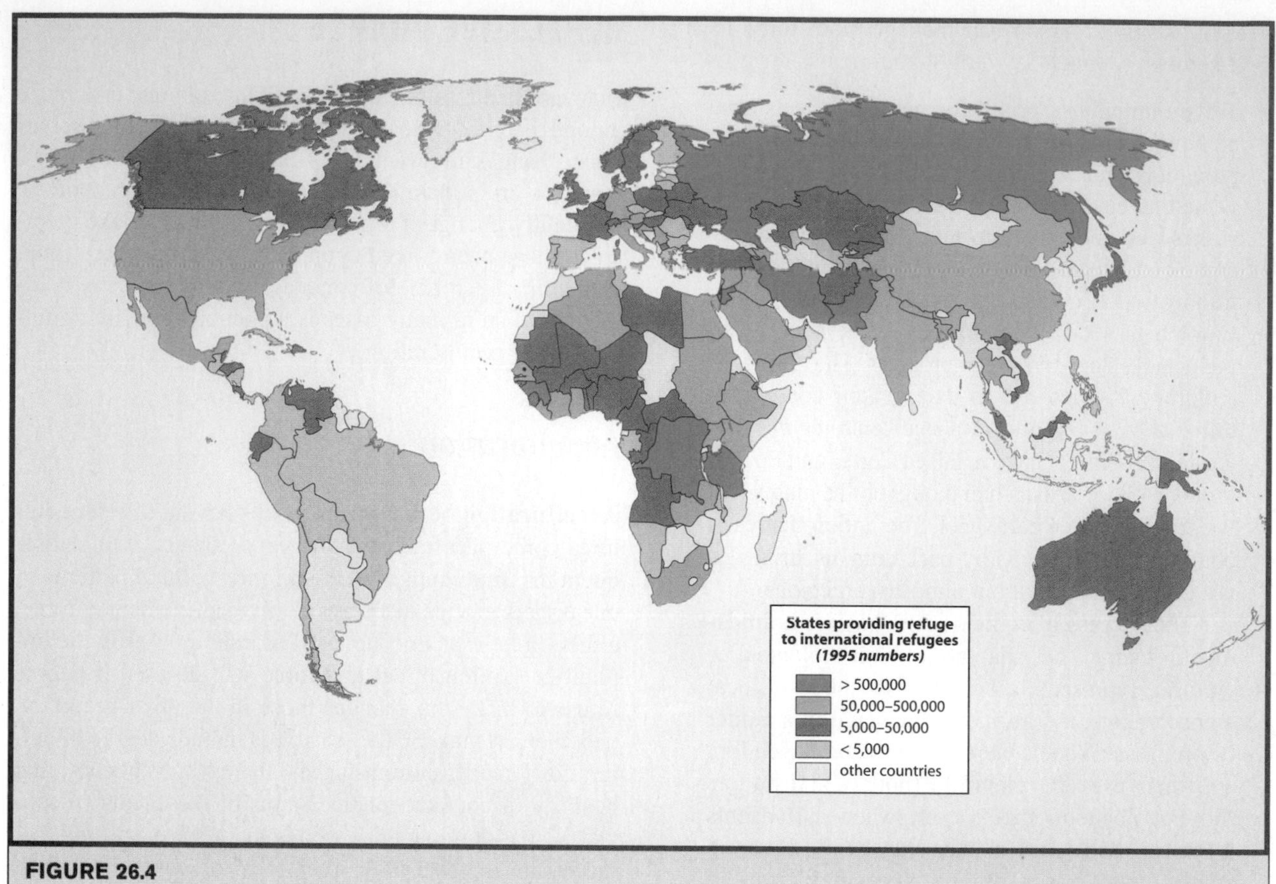

FIGURE 26.4

INCREASING REFUGEE POPULATIONS, A CONSEQUENCE OF CONFLICT BETWEEN NATIONALITIES LIVING IN MULTINATIONAL STATES, HAVE BECOME A BURDEN AND SOURCE OF INSTABILITY IN THE STATES TO WHICH THEY HAVE FLED.

to "national parks," where resources are inadequate for so many people, and where former enemies are often forced to live in close proximity.

Extinction is the phenomenon in which so many carriers of a culture die that those who survive become refugees, living among peoples of other cultures. Examples of this may be seen in many parts of the world today (Figure 26.4); the closest examples are to be found in many parts of South America, again as in Brazil's Amazon basin. One particularly well-documented case occurred in 1968, when hired killers tried to wipe out several Indian groups, including the Cinta-Larga. For this they used arsenic, dynamite, and machine guns from light planes; in the case of the Cinta-Largas, the killers chose a time when an important native ceremony was taking place to attack a village seen as an obstacle to development. Violence continues to be used in Brazil as a means of dealing with native people. For example, as a conservative estimate, at least 1,500 Yanomami died in the 1980s, often as victims of deliberate massacres, as cattle ranchers and miners poured into northern Brazil. By 1990, 70% of the Yanomami's land in Brazil had been unconstitutionally expropriated; their fish supplies were poisoned by mercury contamination of rivers; and malaria, venereal disease, and tuberculosis were running rampant. The Yanomami were dying at the rate of 10% a year, and their fertility had dropped to near zero. Many villages were left with no children or old people, and the survivors awaited their fate with a profound terror of extinction.[8]

The usual Brazilian attitude to such situations is illustrated by the reaction of their government when two Kayapó Indians and an anthropologist traveled to the United States, where they spoke with members of sev-

[8] Turner, T. (1991). Major shift in Brazilian Yanomami policy. *Anthropology Newsletter, 32* (5), 1, 46.

In Namibia, Bushmen from the Kalahari Desert were collected in settlements like Tsumkwe, shown here. Deprived of the means to secure their own necessities in life, such people commonly lapse into apathy and depression.

eral congressional committees, as well as officials of the Department of State, the Treasury, and the World Bank, about the destruction of their land and way of life caused by internationally financed development projects. All three were charged with violating Brazil's Foreign Sedition Act. Fortunately, international expressions of outrage at these and other atrocities have brought positive changes on the part of Brazilian authorities, but whether the recommendations of these authorities will be sufficient, or will even be acted upon fully, remains to be seen. We will return to this problem later in this chapter.

Genocide

The Brazilian Indian case just cited raises the issue of **genocide**—the extermination of one group of people by another, often deliberately and in the name of "progress." Genocide is not new in the world, as we need look no farther than North American history to see. In 1637, for example, a deliberate attempt was made to destroy the Pequot Indians by setting afire their village at Mystic, Connecticut, and then shooting down all those—primarily women and children—who sought to escape from being burned alive. To try to ensure that even their very memory would be stamped out, colonial authorities forbade even the mention of the Pequots' name. Several other massacres of Indian peoples occurred thereafter, up until the last one at Wounded Knee, South Dakota, in 1890.

Genocide. The extermination of one people by another, often in the name of "progress," either as a deliberate act or as the accidental outcome of activities carried out by one people with little regard for their impact on others.

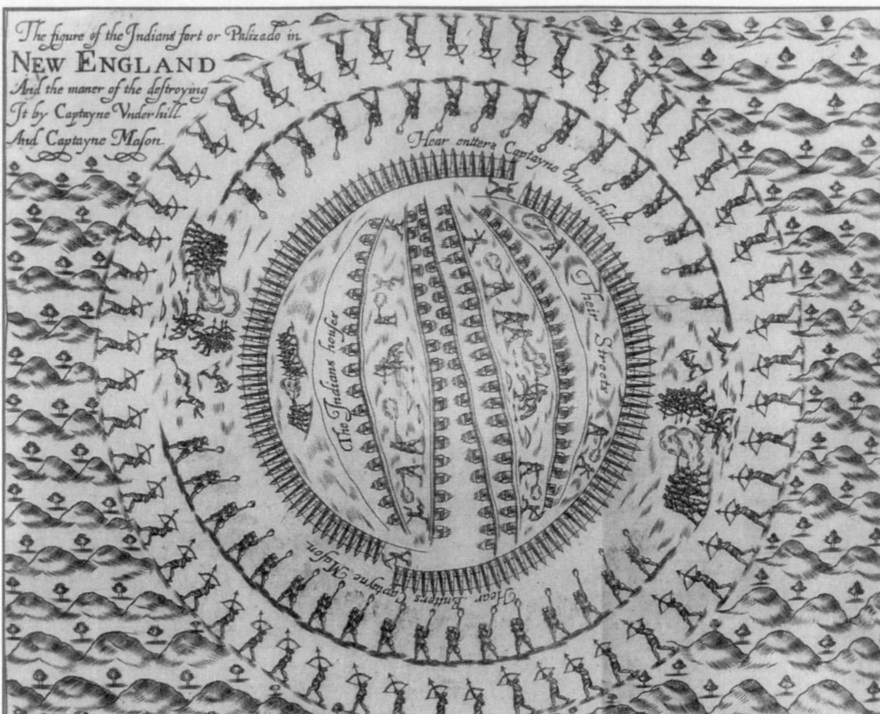

Genocide is not new in the world; this 1638 illustration shows English colonists with their Narragansett allies (the outer ring of bowmen) shooting down Pequot Indian women, children, and unarmed men attempting to flee their homes, which have been set afire.

Of course, such acts were by no means restricted to North America; one of the most famous 19th-century acts of genocide was the extermination of the aboriginal inhabitants of Tasmania, a large island just south of Australia. In this case, the use of military force failed to achieve the complete elimination of the Tasmanians, but what the military could not achieve, a missionary could. George Augustus Robinson was able to round up the surviving natives, and at his mission station the deadly combination of psychological depression and European diseases brought about the demise of the last full-blooded Tasmanians in time for Robinson to retire to England a moderately wealthy man.

The most widely known act of genocide in recent history was the attempt of the Nazi Germans to wipe out European Jews and Roma (gypsies) in the name of racial superiority. Unfortunately, the common practice of referring to this as "*the* holocaust"—as if it were something unique, or at least exceptional—tends to blind us to the fact that this thoroughly monstrous act is simply one more example of an all-too-common phenomenon. From 1945 to 1987, a minimum of 6.8 million, but perhaps as many as 16.3 million, people were victims of internal (within state) genocide, as compared to the 3.34 million people who have died in wars between different countries from 1945 to 1980.[9] Moreover, genocide has continued since then, as in 1988 when the Iraqi government began to use poison gas against Kurdish villagers, or (as we will see in Chapter 27) in Guatemala where, in the early 1980s, government-sponsored terrorism against indigenous communities reached its height, or in the 1990s in Rwanda (as discussed in Chapter 22), or in more recent cases of violence between Albanians and Serbs in Kosovo.

If such ugly practices are ever to be ended, we must gain a better understanding of them than currently exists. Anthropologists are actively engaged in this, carrying out cross-cultural as well as individual case studies. One finding to emerge is the regularity with which religious, economic, and political interests are allied in cases of genocide. In Tasmania, for example, British wool growers wanted Aborigines off the land so that they could have it for their sheep. The government advanced their interests through its military campaigns against the natives, but it was Robinson's missionary work that finally secured Tasmania for the wool interests. In the 1960s and

[9] Van Den Berghe, P. (1992). The modern state: Nation builder or nation killer? *International Journal of Group Tensions, 22* (3), 198.

HIGHWAY 1
Palomar College Anthropology Program: Culture Change Tutorial
http://daphne.palomar.edu/anthro

HIGHWAY 2
Cultural Survival
http://www.cs.org

Two examples (out of many) of attempted genocide in the 20th century: Hitler's Germany against Jews and gypsies in the 1930s and the 1940s; and Hutus against Tutsis in Rwanda, as in this 1997 massacre.

1970s, the Ju/'hoansi living in Namibia found themselves in a situation remarkably similar to that experienced earlier by the Tasmanians; a combination of religious (Dutch Reformed church), political (Namibia's Department of Nature Conservation), and economic (agricultural/pastoral and touristic) interests forced the people's confinement to a reserve where disease and apathy caused death rates to outstrip birthrates. Other such cases might be cited, but the latter one is important, for it clearly illustrates that genocide is not always a deliberate act. It also occurs as the unforseen outcome of activities carried out with little regard for their impact on other peoples. For the people whose lives are snuffed out, however, it makes no difference whether the genocide is deliberate or not; for them, the outcome is the same.

Directed Change

The most extreme cases of acculturation usually occur as a result of military conquest or massive invasion and breaking up of traditional political structures by dominant newcomers who know or care nothing about the culture they control. The indigenous people, unable to resist effectively changes imposed on them and obstructed in carrying out many of their traditional social, religious, and economic activities, may be forced into new activities that tend to isolate individuals and tear apart the integration of their societies. Such a people are the Ju/'hoansi of Namibia, who were rounded up in the early 1960s and confined to a reserve where they could not possibly provide for their own needs. In this situation, the government provided them with rations insufficient to meet their nutritional needs. In poor health and prevented from developing meaningful alternatives to traditional activities, the people became argumentative and depressed, and, as already noted, their death rate came to exceed birthrates. After a visit to the reserve in 1980, anthropologist Robert J. Gordon commented: "I had never been in a place where one could literally smell death and decay, as in Tsumkwe."[10] In the 1980s, however, the Ju/'hoansi began to take matters into their own hands, returning to water holes in their traditional homeland, where, assisted by anthropologists and others concerned with their welfare, they are trying to sustain themselves by raising livestock. Whether this will succeed or not remains to be seen, as there are still many obstacles to success.

One by-product of colonial dealings with indigenous peoples has been the growth of **applied anthropology,** or practical anthropology, and the use of anthropological techniques and knowledge for certain "pragmatic" ends. For example, British anthropology has often been considered the "handmaiden" of that country's colonial policy, for it typically provided information needed to maintain effective colonial rule. In the United States, the Bureau of American Ethnology was founded toward the end of the 19th century to gather reliable data the government might use to formulate Indian policies. At the time, North American anthropologists were convinced of the practicality of their discipline, and many who did ethnographic work among Indians devoted a great deal of time, energy, and even money to assisting their informants, whose interests were frequently threatened from outside.

In the 20th century, the scope of applied anthropology broadened. Early on, the applied work of Franz Boas, who almost single-handedly trained a generation of anthropologists in the United States, was instrumental in reforming the country's immigration policies. In the 1930s, anthropologists with clearly pragmatic objectives did a number of studies in industrial and other institutional settings in the United States. With World War II came the first efforts at colonial administration beyond U.S. borders, especially in the Pacific, by officers trained in anthropology. The rapid recovery of Japan was due in no small measure to the influence of anthropologists in structuring the U.S. occupation. Anthropologists continue to play an active role today in administering U.S. trust territories in the Pacific. The past 30 years, too, have seen the growth of action anthropology, or advocacy, on behalf of indigenous societies and ethnic minorities.

Today, applied anthropologists are in growing demand in the field of international development because of their specialized knowledge of social structure, value systems, and the functional interrelatedness of cultures targeted for development. The role of applied anthropologists, however, is far from easy; as anthropologists, they are bound to respect other peoples' dignity and cultural integrity, yet they are asked for advice on how to change certain aspects of those cultures. If the request comes from the people themselves, that is one thing, but more often than not, the request comes from some outsiders. Supposedly, the

[10] Gordon, R. J. (1992). *The Bushman myth: The making of a Namibian underclass* (p. 3). Boulder, CO: Westview.

Applied anthropology. The use of anthropological knowledge and techniques for the purpose of solving "practical" problems, often for a specific "client."

Anthropology Applied

Development Anthropology and Dams*

Over his career of 35 years of scholarly and applied work, Michael M. Horowitz, president and executive director of the Institute for Development Anthropology (IDA) and professor of anthropology at the State University of New York at Binghamton, has made pioneering contributions to the development of applied anthropology and to anthropology's role in public policy and service.

Horowitz was one of the founders and has been the principal leader of the Institute for Development Anthropology from 1976 to date. His tireless dedication has been critical in institutionalizing anthropology as an applied science in international development organizations such as the World Bank, the Food and Agriculture Organization (FAO), USAID, and nongovernmental organizations such as Oxfam. Horowitz has mentored several generations of young scholars and professionals, particularly encouraging young people from developing countries as well as domestic institutions to contribute to programs for sustainable development.

Horowitz's work with pastoralists and with floodplain dwellers has had enormous positive impact in the well-being of small producers and small holders in the developing world. His work on dam displacement and the needs and uses of downstream residents transformed the way resettlement and integration after dam development is carried out. Rigorous anthropological research conducted in Senegal resulted in decisions by the Senegalese government to permanently institute a controlled flood on the Senegal River, downstream from the Manataali Dam. Horowitz and his team demonstrated through long-term field research that economic, environmental, and sociocultural benefits of seasonal flooding would benefit nearly a million small producers.

This work and its recognition by funding agencies, NGOs and national governments was a breakthrough in the concepts of resettlement and river management. As a result of Horowitz's contributions, river basin development policy is an area where anthropologists are now playing a major role worldwide. His leadership with the Senegal River Basin Monitoring Activity (SRMBA) team from 1986 to 1991 continues to bear fruit 10 years later. The impact of this research has been monumental, and not only has the government of Senegal supported the SRBMA model, but Horowitz has been asked to apply it to other river basins around the world. Prior to the IDA team, no hydropower dam had ever been managed with a controlled flood. IDA has been asked to explore the utility of the SRBMA model to the lower Zambezi River in Mozambique and currently on the Mekong in southeast Asia, the last free-flowing river in Asia.

* Adapted from Young, W. (Ed.) (2000). Kimball Award Winner. *Anthropology News, 41* (8), 29.

proposed change is for the good of the targeted population, yet those people do not always see it that way. Just how far applied anthropologists should go in advising how people—especially ones without the power to resist—can be manipulated to embrace changes proposed for them is a serious ethical question.

Despite such difficulties, applied anthropology is flourishing today as never before. As the several Anthropology Applied boxes placed throughout this book illustrate, anthropologists now practice their profession in many different nonacademic settings, both at home and abroad, in a wide variety of ways.

FRANZ BOAS (1858–1942)

Born in Germany, where he studied physics and geography, Franz Boas came to the United States to live in 1888. His interest in anthropology began a few years earlier with a research trip to Baffin Island, where he met his first so-called "primitives," the Inuit. Thereafter, he and his students came to dominate anthropology in North America for the first three decades of the 20th century. Through meticulous and detailed fieldwork, which set new standards for excellence, Boas and his students exposed the shortcomings of the grandiose, culture-bound schemes of cultural evolution earlier social theorists had proposed. His insistence that each culture must be understood according to its own standards and values, rather than those of the outside investigator, represented a major breakthrough in the dominant worldview of his time. (The photo shows Boas posing as a Kwakiutl *hanatsa* dancer for a National Museum diorama, 1895).

REACTIONS TO REPRESSIVE CHANGE

The reactions of indigenous peoples to the changes outsiders have thrust upon them have varied considerably. Some have responded by moving to the nearest available forest, desert, or other remote places in hopes of being left alone. In Brazil, a number of communities once located near the coast took this option a few hundred years ago and were successful until the great push to develop the Amazon forest began in the 1960s. Others, like many Indians of North America, took up arms to fight back but were ultimately forced to sign treaties and surrender much of their ancestral lands, after which they were reduced to an impoverished underclass in their own land. Today, they continue to fight to retain their identities as distinct peoples through nonmilitary means, and seek to regain control over natural resources on their lands.

When people are able to hold on to some of their traditions in the face of powerful outside domination, the result may be **syncretism.** This is a blending of indigenous and foreign elements into a new system, and a fine illustration of it is the game of cricket as played by the Trobriand Islanders, some of whose practices we looked at in Chapters 18, 19, and 20.

Under British rule, the Trobrianders were introduced by missionaries to the rather staid British game of cricket to replace the erotic dancing and open sexuality that normally followed the yam harvests. Traditionally, this was when chiefs sought to spread their fame by hosting nights of dancing, providing food for the hundreds of young married people who participated. For two months or so, there would be night after night of provocative dancing, accompanied by chanting and shouting full of sexual innuendo, each night ending as couples disappeared off into the bush together. Since no chief wished to be outdone by any other (to be outdone reflected on the strength of one's magic), all of this dancing had a strong competitive element, and fighting sometimes erupted. To the British missionaries, cricket seemed a good way to end all of this in a way that would encourage conformity to "civilized" comportment in dress, religion, and "sportsmanship." The Trobrianders, however, were determined to "rubbish" (throw out) the British game and turned it into the same kind of distinctly Trobriand event their dance competitions had once been.

The Trobrianders made cricket their own by adding battle dress and battle magic and by incorporating erotic dancing into the festivities. Instead of inviting dancers each night, chiefs now arrange games of cricket. Pitching has been modified from the British style to one closer to their old way of throwing a spear. Following the game, they hold massive feasts, where wealth is displayed to enhance their prestige. Cricket, in its altered form, has been made to serve traditional systems of prestige and ex-

Syncretism. In acculturation, the blending of indigenous and foreign traits to form a new system.

In the past few decades, Western countries have sent technological "missionaries" to teach people in other places new ways of doing old tasks. Unless they have had anthropological training, however, such "missionaries" are apt to be unaware of the side effects their new ways will have.

American Indians have fought back against foreign domination in many ways. The Mashuntucket Pequots in Connecticut have created a "state of the art" museum, financed from the proceeds of their Foxwoods Casino, to keep alive and celebrate their history.

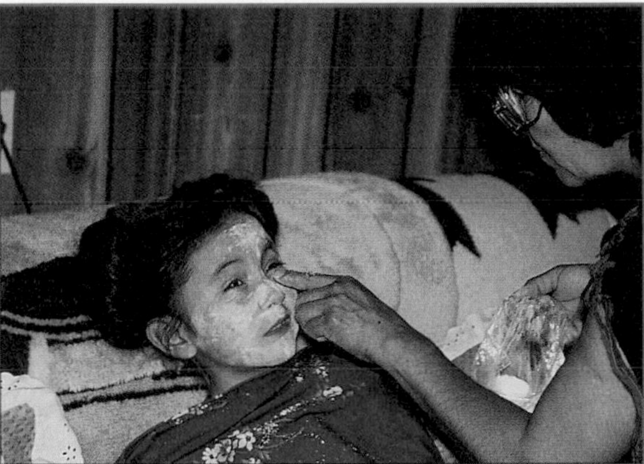

An example of syncretism. Although the Hopi Indians have adopted a number of items from European Americans (note the glasses and electrical outlet), such "borrowed" things are combined with traditional ones, as in the ritual use of cornmeal, here being applied to a young girl as required by ancient tradition.

change. Neither "primitive" nor passively accepted in its original form, Trobriand cricket was thoughtfully and creatively adapted into a sophisticated activity reflecting the importance of basic indigenous cultural premises. Exuberance and pride are displayed by everyone associated with the game, and the players are as much concerned with conveying the full meaning of who they are as with scoring well. From the sensual dressing in preparation for the game to the team chanting of songs full of sexual metaphors to erotic chorus-line dancing between the innings, it is clear that each player is playing for his own importance, for the fame of his team, and for the hundreds of attractive young women who usually watch the game.

Revitalization Movements

Another common reaction to repressive change is revitalization, a cultural process already touched upon in Chapter 24. Revitalization may be looked upon as a deliberate attempt by some members of a society to construct a more satisfactory culture by the rapid acceptance of a pattern of multiple innovations. Once primary ties of culture, social relationships, and activities are broken and meaningless activity is imposed by outside forces, individuals and groups characteristically react with fantasy, withdrawal, and escape.

Examples of revitalization movements have been common in the history of the United States whenever significant segments of the population have found their conditions in life to be at odds with the values of "the American Dream." For example, in the 19th century, periodic depression and the disillusionment of the decades after the Civil War produced a host of revitalization movements, the most successful being that of the Mormons. In the 20th century, movements repeatedly sprang up in the slums of major cities, as well as in depressed rural areas such as Appalachia. By the 1960s, a number of movements were becoming less inward looking and more "activist," a good example being the rise of the Black Muslim movement. The 1960s also saw the rise of revitalization movements among the young of middle-class and even upper-class families. In their case, the professed cultural values of peace, equality, and individual freedom were seen to be at odds with the reality of persistent war, poverty, and constraints on individual action imposed by a variety of impersonal institutions. Their reactions to these realities was expressed by their use of drugs; in their outlandish or "freaky" clothes, hairstyles, music, and speech; and in their behavior toward authority and authority figures. Whether or not all of these movements were sparked by individuals who experienced personal supernatural experiences, they do show overall similarities.

By the 1980s such movements were becoming prominent even among older, more affluent segments of society, as in the rise of the so-called religious right. In these cases, the reaction is not so much against a perceived failure of the American Dream as it is against perceived threats to that dream by dissenters and activists within their society, by foreign governments, by new ideas that challenge other ideas they prefer to believe, and by the sheer complexity of modern life.

Revitalization movements that attempt to revive traditional ways of the past are not restricted to "underdeveloped" countries; in the United States, the Reverend Pat Robertson is a leader in such a movement.

Clearly, when value systems get out of step with existing realities, for whatever reason, a condition of cultural crisis is likely to build up that may breed some forms of reactive movement. Not all suppressed, conquered, or colonized people eventually rebel against established authority, although why they do not is still a debated issue. When they do, however, cultural resistance may take one of several forms, all of which are varieties of revitalization movements. A culture may seek to speed up the acculturation process to share more fully in the supposed benefits of the dominant cultures. Melanesian cargo cults of the post–World War II era generally have been of this sort, although earlier ones stressed a revival of traditional ways. Sometimes, a movement tries to reconstitute a destroyed but not yet forgotten way of life, as did many Plains Indians with the Ghost Dance in the 19th century and as do movements on the "religious right" today. Sometimes, a suppressed pariah group, which has long suffered in an inferior social standing and which has its own special subcultural ideology, attempts to create a new social order; the most familiar examples of this to Western peoples are prophetic Judaism and early Christianity. If the movement's aim is directed from within at the ideological systems and the attendant social and political structure of a cultural system, it is then called **revolutionary.**

Revolutionary. A revitalization movement from within, directed primarily at the ideological system and the attendant social structure of a culture.

REBELLION AND REVOLUTION

When the scale of discontent within a society reaches a certain level, the possibilities for rebellion and revolution—such as the Iranian Revolution, the Taliban Revolution in Afghanistan, the Sandinista Revolution in Nicaragua, or the Zapatista Maya Indian uprising in Mexico—are high.

The question of why revolutions erupt, as well as why they frequently fail to live up to the expectations of the people initiating them, is a problem. It is clear, however, that the colonial policies of countries such as Britain, France, Spain, Portugal, and the United States during the 19th and early 20th centuries have created a worldwide situation in which revolution is nearly inevitable. Despite the political independence most colonies have gained since World War II, more powerful countries continue to exploit many of these "underdeveloped" countries for their natural resources and cheap labor, causing a deep resentment of rulers beholden to foreign powers. Further discontent has been caused as governing elites in newly independent states try to assert their control over peoples living within their boundaries who, by virtue of a common ancestry, possession of distinct cultures, persistent occupation of their own territories, and traditions of self-determination, identify themselves as distinct nations and refuse to recognize the legitimacy of what they regard as a foreign government. Thus, in many a former colony, large numbers of people have taken up arms to resist annexation and absorption by imposed state governments controlled by people of other nationalities. As they attempt to make their multiethnic states into unified nations, ruling elites of one nationality set about stripping the peoples of other nations within their states of their lands, resources, and sense of cultural identity as a distinct people. The phenomenon is so common that it led anthropologist Pierre Van Den Berghe to label what modern states refer to as "nation building" as, in fact, "nation killing."[11] One of the most important facts of our time is that the vast majority of the distinct peoples of the world have never consented to rule by the governments of states within which they find themselves living.[12] In many a newly emerged country, such peoples feel they have no other option than to fight.

State-sponsored terrorism is a technique frequently used by heads of state, such as Augusto Pinochet of Chile, to control their citizens.

In many countries of the world, governments controlled by people of one nation frequently use repression to control people of other nations within the state. This frequently results in internal warfare as in the case of East Timor, whose people recently gained their independence from Indonesia.

From an examination of various revolutions of the past, the following conditions have been offered as precipitators of rebellion and revolution:

[11] Van Den Berghe, P. (1992). The modern state: Nation builder or nation killer? *International Journal of Group Tensions, 22* (3), pp. 191–207.

[12] Nietschmann, B. (1987). The third world war. *Cultural Survival Quarterly, 11* (3), 3.

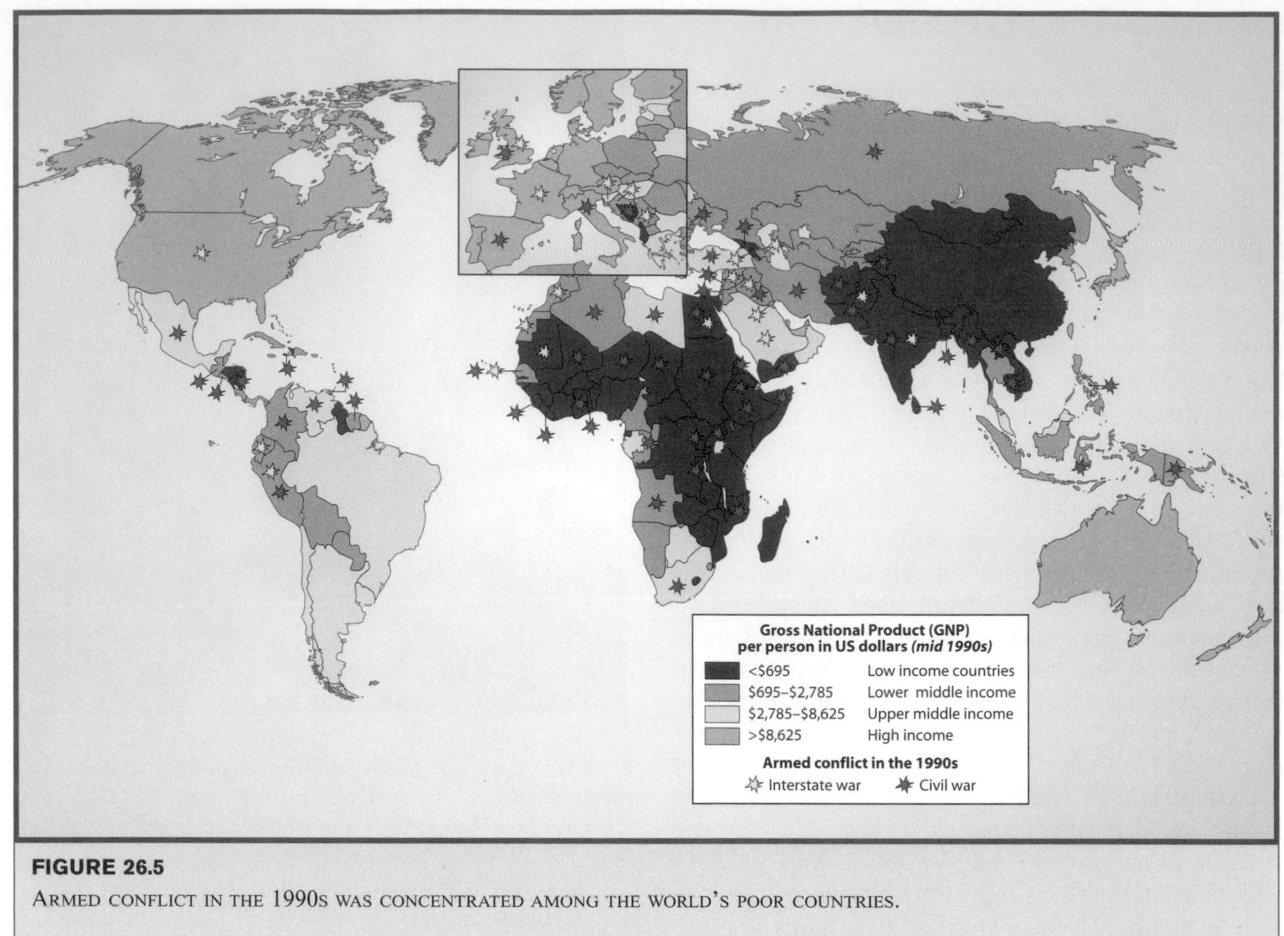

FIGURE 26.5

ARMED CONFLICT IN THE 1990S WAS CONCENTRATED AMONG THE WORLD'S POOR COUNTRIES.

1. Loss of prestige of established authority, often from the failure of foreign policy, financial difficulties, dismissals of popular ministers, or alteration of popular policies.
2. Threat to recent economic improvement. In France and Russia, sections of the population (professional classes and urban workers) whose economic fortunes previously had taken an upward swing were radicalized by unexpected setbacks, such as steeply rising food prices and unemployment.
3. Indecisiveness of government, as exemplified by lack of consistent policy; such governments appear to be controlled by, rather than in control of, events.
4. Loss of support of the intellectual class. Such a loss deprived the prerevolutionary governments of France and Russia of philosophical support, thus leading to their lack of popularity with the literate public.
5. A leader or group of leaders with charisma, or popular appeal, enough to mobilize a substantial part of the population against the establishment.

Apart from resistance to internal authority, such as in the Chinese, French, and Russian revolutions, many revolutions in modern times have been struggles against an authority imposed by outsiders. Such resistance usually takes the form of independence movements that wage campaigns of armed defiance against colonial powers. The Algerian struggle for independence from France is a relevant example. Of the 120 or so armed conflicts in the world today, 98% are in the economically poor countries of Africa, Asia, Central and South America, almost all of which were at one time under European colonial domination (Figure 26.5). Of these wars, 75% are between the state and one or more peoples within the state's borders who are seeking to maintain or regain control of their persons, communities, lands, and resources in the face of what they regard as subjugation by a foreign power.[13]

Not all revolts are truly revolutionary in their consequences. According to South African anthropologist Max Gluckman, rebellions

> ". . . throw the rascals out" and substitute another set, but there is no attempt to alter either the cultural ideology or the form of the social structure. In political revolution, attempts are made to seize the offices of power in order to change social structure, belief systems, and their symbolic representations. Political revolutions are usually turbulent, violent, and not long-lasting. A successful revolution soon moves to re-establish a stable, though changed, social structure; yet it has far-reaching political, social and sometimes economic and cultural consequences.[14]

Not always are revolutions successful about accomplishing what they set out to do. One of the stated goals of the Chinese revolution, for example, was to liberate women from the oppression of a strongly patriarchal society in which a woman owed lifelong obedience to some male relative or other—first her father, later her husband and, after his death, her oldest son. Although some change was made, the transformation overall has been frustrated by the cultural lens through which the revolutionaries viewed their work. A tradition of deeply rooted patriarchy extending back at least 22 centuries is not easily overcome and has unconsciously influenced many of the decisions made by communist China's leaders since 1949. In rural China today, as in the past, a woman's life is still usually determined by her relationship to some man, be it her father, husband, or son, rather than by her own efforts or failures. What's more, women are being told more and more that their primary roles are as wives and mothers. When they do work outside the house, it is generally at jobs with low pay, low status, and no benefits. Indeed, the 1990s saw a major outbreak of the abduction and sale of women from rural areas as brides and workers. Their no-wage labor for their husbands' household or low-wage labor outside (which goes back to the household) has been essential to China's economic expansion, which relies on the allocation of labor by the heads of patrilineal households.[15] Thus, despite whatever freedom women may achieve for a while, they become totally dependent in their old age on their sons.

This situation shows that the undermining of revolutionary goals, if it occurs, is not necessarily by political opponents. Rather, it may be a consequence of the revolutionaries' own cultural background. In rural China, as

[13] Nietschmann, B. (1987). The third world war. *Cultural Survival Quarterly, 11* (3), 7.

[14] Hoebel, E. A. (1972). *Anthropology: The study of man* (4th ed.)(p. 667). New York: McGraw-Hill.

[15] Gates, H. (1996). Buying brides in China—again. *Anthropology Today, 12* (4), 10.

In China, women's labor has become critical to economic expansion. Much of this labor is controlled by male heads of families, who act as agents of the state in allocating labor.

long as women marry out and their labor is controlled by male heads of families, women always will be seen as something of a commodity.

It should be understood that revolution is a relatively recent phenomenon, occurring only during the past 5,000 years or so. The reason is that political rebellion requires a centralized political authority (chiefdom or state) to rebel against, and states (if not chiefdoms) did not exist before 5,000 years ago. Obviously, then, in societies organized as tribes and bands, without central authority, there could be no rebellion or political revolution.

MODERNIZATION

One of the most frequently used terms to describe social and cultural changes as they are occurring today is **modernization.** This is most clearly defined as an all-encompassing and global process of cultural and socioeconomic change, whereby societies seek to acquire some of the characteristics common to Western industrial societies. A close look at this definition, reveals that "becoming modern" is imagined as "becoming like us" ("us" being the United States and other industrial societies), with the very clear implication that not being like us is to be antiquated and obsolete. Not only is this ethnocentric, but it also fosters the notion that these other societies must be *changed* to be more like us, regardless of other considerations. It is unfortunate that the term *modernization* continues to be so widely used. Since we seem to be stuck with it, the best we can do at the moment is to recognize its problematic one-sidedness, even as we continue to use it.

The process of modernization may be best understood as consisting of four subprocesses, of which one is *technological development.* In the course of modernization, traditional knowledge and techniques give way to the application of scientific knowledge and techniques borrowed mainly from the industrialized West. Another subprocess is *agricultural development,* represented by a shift in emphasis from subsistence farming to commercial farming. Instead of raising crops and livestock for their own use, people turn with increasing frequency to the production of cash crops, with greater reliance on a cash economy and on global markets for selling farm products and purchasing goods. A third subprocess is *industrialization,* with a greater emphasis placed on material forms of energy—especially fossil fuels—to drive machines. Human and animal power become less important, as do handicrafts in general. The fourth subprocess is *urbanization,* marked particularly by population movements from rural settlements into cities. Although all four subprocesses are interrelated, there is no fixed order of appearance.

As modernization proceeds, other changes are likely to follow. In the political realm, political parties and some sort of electoral apparatus frequently appear, along with the development of an administrative bureaucracy. In formal education, institutional learning opportunities expand, literacy increases, and an indigenous educated elite develops. Religion becomes less important in many areas of thought and behavior as traditional beliefs and practices are undermined. Many traditional rights and duties connected with kinship are altered, if not eliminated, especially where distant relatives are concerned. Finally, where social stratification is a factor, mobility increases as ascribed status becomes less important and personal achievement counts for more.

Two other features of modernization go hand in hand with those already noted. One, **structural differentiation,** is the division of single traditional roles, which embrace two or more functions, into two or more separate roles, each with one particular specialized function. This represents a kind of fragmentation of society, which must be counteracted by new **integrative mechanisms** if the society is not to fall apart into a number of discrete units. These new mechanisms take such forms as formal governmental structures, official state ideologies, political parties, legal codes, labor and trade unions, as well as other common-interest associations. All of these crosscut other societal divisions and thus serve to oppose differentiating forces. These two forces, however, are not

Modernization. The process of cultural and socioeconomic change, whereby developing societies acquire some of the characteristics of Western industrialized societies. • **Structural differentiation.** The division of single traditional roles, which embrace two or more functions (for example, political, economic, and religious) into two or more roles, each with a single specialized function. • **Integrative mechanisms.** Cultural mechanisms that oppose forces for differentiation in a society; in modernizing societies, they include formal governmental structures, official state ideologies, political parties, legal codes, labor and trade unions, and other common-interest associations.

Structural differentiation. Whereas most items for daily use were once made at home, such as butter (*left*), almost everything we use today is the product of specialized production, as is the butter we buy in the food store.

the only ones in opposition in a situation of modernization; to them must be added a third, the force of **tradition.** This opposes the new forces of both differentiation and integration. Yet the conflict does not have to be total. Traditional ways on occasion may facilitate modernization. For example, traditional kinship ties may assist rural people as they move into cities if they have relatives already there to turn to for aid. One's relatives, too, may provide the financing necessary for business success.

One aspect of modernization, the technological explosion, has made it possible to transport human beings and ideas from one place to another with astounding speed and in great numbers. Formerly independent cultural systems have been brought into contact with others. Cultural differences between New York and Pukapuka are declining, while differences between fisherfolk and physicists are increasing. No one knows whether this implies a net gain or net loss in cultural diversity, but the worldwide spread of anything, whether it is DDT (an insecticide banned in the United States as too toxic) or a new idea, should be viewed with at least caution. That human beings and human cultural systems are different is the most exciting thing about them, yet the destruction of diversity is implicit in the worldwide spread of blue jeans, Coca-Cola, rock-and-roll, socialism, capitalism, or anything else. When a song is forgotten or a ceremony ceases to be performed, a part of the human heritage is destroyed forever.

An examination of two traditional cultures that have felt the impact of modernization or other cultural changes will help to pinpoint some of the problems such cultures have met. The cultures are the Skolt Lapps, a division of the Saami people whose homeland straddles the Arctic Circle in Norway, Sweden, Finland, and Russia, and the Shuar Indians of Ecuador.

Tradition. In a modernizing society, old cultural practices, which may oppose new forces of differentiation and integration.

Skolt Lapps and the Snowmobile Revolution

The Skolt Lapps, whose homeland is in northern Finland, traditionally supported themselves by fishing and herding reindeer.[16] Although they depended on the outside world for certain material goods, the resources crucial for their system were present locally and were for all practical purposes available to all. No one was denied access to critical resources, and little social and economic differentiation existed among the people. Theirs was basically an egalitarian society.

Of particular importance to the Skolt Lapps was reindeer herding. Indeed, herd management is central to their definition of themselves as a people. These animals were a source of meat for home consumption or for sale to procure outside goods. They were also a source of hides for shoes and clothing, sinews for sewing, and antlers and bones for making various objects. Finally, reindeer were used to pull sleds in the winter and as pack animals when there was no snow on the ground. Understandably, the animals were the objects of much attention. The herds were not large, but without a great deal of attention, productivity suffered. Hence, most winter activities centered on reindeer. Men, operating on skis, were closely associated with their herds, intensively from November to January and periodically from January to April.

In the early 1960s these reindeer herders speedily adopted snowmobiles on the premise the new machines would make herding physically easier and economically more advantageous. The first machine arrived in Finland in 1962; by 1971 there were 70 operating machines owned by the Skolt Lapps and non-Lapps in the same area. Although men on skis still carry out some herding activity, their importance and prestige are now diminished. As early as 1967 only four people were still using reindeer sleds for winter travel; most had gotten rid of draft animals. Those who had not converted to snowmobiles felt disadvantaged compared to the rest.

A Saami man separating his reindeer from those of other herds.

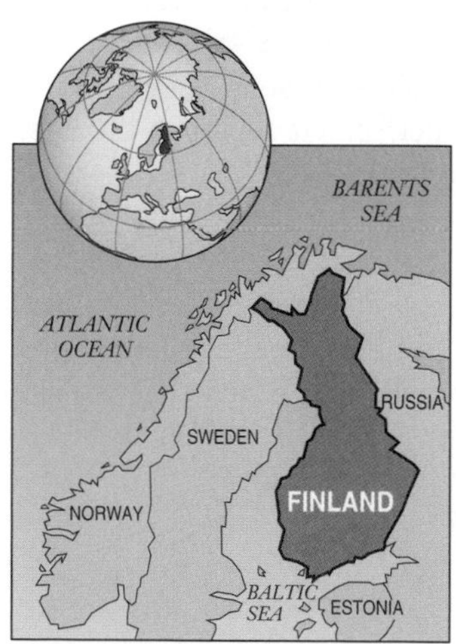

The consequences of this mechanization were extraordinary and far reaching. The need for snowmobiles, parts and equipment to maintain them, and a steady supply of gasoline created a dependency on the outside world unlike anything that had previously existed. As snowmobile technology replaced traditional skills, the ability of the Lapps to determine their own survival without dependence on outsiders, should this be necessary, was lost. Snowmobiles are also expensive, costing several thousand dollars in the Arctic. Maintenance and gasoline expenses must be added to this initial cost. Accordingly, a sharp rise in the need for cash occurred. To get this, men must go outside the Lapp community for wage work more than just occasionally, as had once been the case, or else rely on such sources as government pensions or welfare.

The argument may be made that dependency and the need for cash are prices worth paying for an improved system of reindeer herding; but has it improved? In truth, snowmobiles contributed in a significant way to a disastrous decline in reindeer herding. By 1971 the average size of the family herd had declined from 50 to 12. Not only is this too small a number to be economically viable, but also it is too small to maintain at all. The reason is that the animals in such small herds will take the first opportunity to run off to join another larger one. The old close, prolonged, and largely peaceful relationship between herdsman and beast has changed to a noisy, traumatic relationship. Now, when men appear, it is to come speeding

[16] Pelto, P. J. (1973). *The snowmobile revolution: Technology and social change in the Arctic.* Menlo Park, CA: Cummings.

out of the woods on snarling, smelly machines that invariably chase animals, often for long distances. Instead of helping the animals in their winter food quest, helping females with their calves, and protecting them from predators, men appear either to slaughter or castrate them. Naturally enough, the reindeer have become wary. The result has been actual de-domestication, with reindeer scattering and running off to more inaccessible areas, given the slightest chance. Moreover, there are indications that snowmobile harassment has adversely effected the number of viable calves added to the herds. This is a classic illustration of the fact change is not always adaptive.

The cost of mechanized herding—and the decline of the herds—has led many Lapps to abandon herding altogether. Now, the majority of males are no longer herders at all. This constitutes a serious economic problem, since few economic alternatives are available. The problem is compounded by the fact that participation in a cash-credit economy means that most people, employed or not, have payments to make. This is more than just an economic problem, for in the traditional culture of this people, being a herder of reindeer is the very essence of manhood. Hence, today's nonherders are not only poor in a way that they could not be in previous times, but they are in a sense inadequate as "men" quite apart from this.

This economic differentiation with its reevaluation of roles has led to the development of a stratified society out of the older egalitarian one. Differences have arisen in terms of wealth and, with this, in lifestyles. It is difficult to break into reindeer herding now, for one needs a substantial cash outlay. And herding now requires skills and knowledge that were not a part of traditional culture. Not everyone has these, and those without them are dependent on others if they are to participate. Hence, access to critical resources is now restricted, where once it had been open to all.

The Shuar Solution

Although the Skolt Lapps have not escaped many negative aspects of modernization, the choice to modernize or not was essentially theirs. The Shuar (sometimes called Jivaro) Indians, by contrast, deliberately avoided modernization until they felt that they had no other option if they were to fend off the same outside forces that elsewhere in the Amazon Basin have destroyed whole societies. Threatened with the loss of their land base as more and more Ecuadoran colonists intruded into their territory, the Shuar in 1964 founded a fully independent corporate body, the Shuar Federation, to take control over their own future. Recognized by Ecuador's government, albeit grudgingly, the federation is officially dedicated to promotion of the social, economic, and moral advancement of its members and to coordination of development with official governmental agencies. Since its founding, the federation has secured title to more than 96,000 hectares of communal land; has established a cattle herd of more than 15,000 head as the people's primary source of income; has taken control of their own education, using their own language and mostly Shuar teachers; and has established their own bilingual broadcasting station and a bilingual newspaper. Obviously, all this has required enormous changes by the Shuar, but they have been able to maintain a variety of distinctive cultural markers, including their language, communal land tenure, cooperative production and distribution, a basically egalitarian economy, and kin-based communities that retain maximum autonomy. Thus, for all the changes, they feel they are still Shuar, and quite distinct from other Ecuadorans.[17]

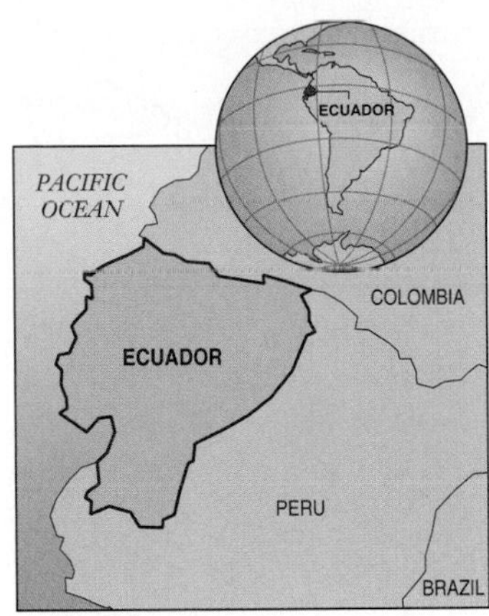

The Shuar case shows that Amazonian Indian nations are capable of taking control of their own destinies even in the face of intense outside pressures, *if* allowed to do so. Unfortunately, until recently, few have had that option. Prior to European invasions of the Amazonian rainforest, more than 700 distinct indigenous nations inhabited this vast region. By 1900 in Brazil, the number was down to 270, and today something like 180 remain.[18] Many of these survivors find themselves in situations not unlike that of the Yanomami, described earlier in this chapter. Nevertheless, many of these peoples are showing a new resourcefulness in resisting the outside forces of destruction arrayed against them. That these forces are formidable is illustrated in the following account by an anthropologist who lives in Brazil and has done fieldwork in the Amazon since 1976.

[17] Bodley, J. H. (1990). *Victims of progress* (3rd ed.) (pp. 160–162). Mountain View, CA: Mayfield.

[18] *Cultural Survival Quarterly, 15* (4), (1991) 38.

Original Study

Violence on Indian Day in Brazil 1997[19]

Sunday evening, April 20, 1997, the Brazilian television network Rede Globo on its weekly program Fantástico, carried the tragic story of a Pataxó Indian of Bahia who had been brutally murdered. The Pataxó are the same indigenous people whom Pedro Álvares Cabral encountered in his "discovery" of Brazil in 1500.

According to the news story, the 44 year old Pataxó leader, Gildino Jesus dos Santos, had gone to Brasilia with a number of his people to discuss their land claims with government officials, to participate in the demonstrations and festivities held in commemoration of Indian Day in Brazil, and to welcome thousands of landless poor, or Sem Terra, from all over Brazil—a historic moment in Brazilian struggles to institute agrarian reform. According to other Pataxós lodged in a FUNAI boarding house [FUNAI is the Brazilian Indian service], Gildino came back late from the festivities and was barred entrance to the boarding house by military police. He wandered around the area for awhile and decided to sleep on a bus stop bench. An eyewitness report declared that a car with five youths approached, poured flammable liquid over the body of the sleeping Indian and set fire to him. It was later determined that the youths thought the Pataxó was another of the numerous **mendingo** or street beggars that wander the streets in all the major cities of Brazil. Every month at least one mendingo is killed in this fashion just for the "fun" of seeing the beggar run in panic and attempt to extinguish the fire before it completely burns him.

In the case of the Gildno dos Santos, 95% of his body was severely burned and he died the next day in the hospital where he had been taken by one of the few witnesses to the crime. Five youths between the ages of 16 and 19 years old were taken prisoner. All are from upper middle class families (one the son of a colonel, two others the sons of judges). The crime is punishable by a sentence of between 13 and 30 years of imprisonment. But will there be punishment? Certainly, the moment is propitious for an exemplary punishment since Brazilians are reeling from the recent shock of scenes of police brutality in Diadema, Saõ Paulo, and Cidade de Deus, Rio de Janeiro. But, this threatens to be another horrible death statistic involving the Indians in Brazil.

When I was asked to prepare an article . . . in commemoration of **Cultural Survival**'s 25th anniversary—for me an honor considering **Cultural Survival** has focused on Brazil from its beginning—I initially intended to write about the political victories and "conquests" by the Indigenous movement in Brazil, as demonstrated in an exemplary fashion by the Federation of Indigenous Organizations of the Rio Negro (FOIRN) in the Northwest Amazon. Victories which mark significant advances for the approximately 20,000 Indians of various linguistic families in the region, with the demarcation of a large and continuous land reserve and the participation of indigenous leadership in key positions of municipal government. I intended to focus on this area because it is where I have conducted anthropological and historical research since 1976 and I have been in contact with the Federation over the past 12 years since I returned to live in Brazil. A remarkable situation has changed from complete subordination and dependence on external agents of contact (the missionaries and military, principally) 20 years ago, to

[19] Wright, R. M. (1997). Violence on Indian day in Brazil 1997: Symbol of the past and future. *Cultural Survival Quarterly, 21* (2), 47–49.

Statue "celebrating" gold miner in the main square of Boa Vista in Brazil. Gold miners and others who have invaded Indian lands have caused massive death and devastation. In 1993, when a group of Indians succeeded in evicting a rancher from their land, a man phoned one radio show, identified himself as a professional "hit man" and offered to kill the local Bishop (who supported the Indians), cut off his head, and display it in the miner's pan.

an effervescence of local indigenous political associations (over 20), coordinated by a region-wide indigenous confederation. Cultural traditions long suppressed by the missionaries to the point where indigenous people were "embarrassed" with their identity, have evolved in the form of a brilliant leader, Baniwa Gersen Luciano Santos, whose intellectual contribution to the indigenous movement in Amazonia in general will surely have long-term consequences.

The Northwest Amazon has become a critical testing ground in Brazil for important questions revolving around sustainable development and how these models are to be translated into practice. Are such models viable alternatives in the Northwest Amazon context, or is there still an enormous distance between NGOs [nongovernment organizations] and academic discourses about such models and the specific and immediate needs of native peoples? What are the effects of NGO involvement in local-level politics on Indian/white relations and the indigenous cultural revitalization movement in general in this area? The immediate problem, which the incident in Brasilia on Indian Day revealed in all its horror, is not the new models, but the old problems and the old wounds which have never had sufficient time to heal. Racism and impunity, the two principal villains, constantly tear away at the heart of victories. For those who have short memories and may have forgotten what these two villains have done in recent years, it may be well worth a quick review of other incidents and their outcomes.

Every year the Indigenous Missionary Council (CIMI, a branch of the Brazilian Catholic Church most directly involved in indigenous affairs) publishes a report on violence against the indigenous population in Brazil. The statistics show that not

Original Study

only is there an increase in violence year by year, but also in the kinds of aggression committed against indigenous peoples: murders of leaders, massacres, epidemic diseases caused by neglect of official health agencies, illegal detentions, and police brutality. One can only be shocked by the repeated acts of violence against Indians throughout the country. Yet how are these cases represented and reported in the national media and how are they dealt with by authorities? Are there patterns in the violence that characterize Indian/White relations?

Violence Against Indigenous People in Brazil

The most common pattern characterizing violence against indigenous people in Brazil is impunity. Violence against the indigenous people in Brazil is horrible and lamentable, but it is ultimately beyond control. In case after case, the same scenario is revealed in which violent acts against Indians are never brought to justice. Conflicts and tensions, particularly over land and resource rights, build up over the years, and coupled with the inertia of FUNAI, explode in traumatic massacres or murders. Investigations are immediately initiated and the accused are apprehended; in this initial phase, international pressure has played an important role. The second phase includes a long period of procrastination which takes the steam out of the initial urgency of the case. Next, the accused stall for time to manipulate the proceedings while the investigations drag on. When, or if the case is finally brought to the courts, there is never sufficient evidence to incriminate the accused who are then absolved or given light sentences. The consequence of this scenario is the reproduction of violence in interethnic relations.

For example, a well-known Guaraní leader, Marçal Tupã-y, was murdered in 1983 by the hired gunmen of a local rancher that disputed the lands of Marçal's people. An entire decade passed before the perpetrator of the crime—known to everyone in the region—was brought to trial in a local court. In the end, the rancher was absolved of the crime for "lack of evidence." Another example is the 1988 massacre of Ticuna Indians of the upper Solimões that left 14 dead, 23 wounded, and 10 "disappeared." The massacre was perpetrated by 14 gunmen hired by a local lumber businessman in order to "settle" a land claim. This claim had dragged on for years because both federal authorities and local interests wished to suppress the movement. Despite the immediate national and international attention, today, nearly a decade later, news of the process has virtually disappeared from the press and the process of judicial procrastination has not gotten further than determining the jurisdiction for the trial—if there is to be one.

There is yet another scenario in which, through the manipulation of discourse about violence by the mass media, actual victims are transformed into perpetrators of violence against themselves or "blaming the victim," in which actual physical violence is compounded with symbolic violence against the victims. The case of the Yanomami in Brazil and Venezuela is certainly the most dramatic instance of this process.

In this case, structural amnesia and impunity have not been worse because the eyes of the world have focused on the Yanomami situation for so long. This has not immunized the Yanomami from physical violence (the 1993 massacre of 17 Yanomami of the village of Haxlmu), or from racist attacks such as those which characterized the articles published by Janer Cristaldo, an unknown journalist, in the Folha de São Paulo, two years ago. Cristaldo, in his initial article titled "Behind the Scenes of the Lano-Bluff," not only questioned the evidence of the massacre, but also systematically diverted the focus of the issue by claiming that numerous aggressions by indigenous peoples against the white man had never been brought to justice. Basing his characterization of the Yanomami on the "Fierce People" image popularized by Napoleon Chagnon, Cristaldo argued that Yanomami culture is itself "marked by violence" and that the international outrage over the Haxlmu massacre was nothing more than a conspiracy organized by anthropologists and indigenous defense organizations. He characterized the Yanomami as fodder for a supposed campaign to internationalize Amazonia. "[e]ither the Armed Forces beware of this conspiracy by anthropologists," he warned, "or soon we will have the blue helmets [referring to UN intervention] in Amazonia." In this discourse, Brazilians are the victims while the Yanomami and their supporters are the aggressor.

"Sensationalizing" Violence

Numerous other cases could be analyzed to illustrate the kinds of structural violence that characterize Indian/White relations in Brazil today and the ways mass media has represented interethnic violence. In many cases, it is clear that media discourse serves the interests of local, regional and national power structures. It is also clear that the explanation of such violence is not sufficient to account for the incidents of brutality against individuals or whole groups of people. Indigenous peoples have shown that they are able to resist, adapt, and change, often in extraordinarily creative ways, to demands imposed on them from outside. Brazilian society, however, has repeatedly demonstrated that it is incapable of overcoming two of its deepest internal conflicts: racism and impunity. Governments continue to demonstrate their inability to implement viable political and economic models that could enable ethnic and social minorities to co-exist and live in dignity in a plural society.

As always, on Indian Day in Brazil, a kind of macabre ritual takes place. The mass media talk about the "inevitable extinction" of indigenous peoples as if they were a disappearing species. Ecologists and anthropologists reaffirm the vitality of socio-diversity and the necessity of indigenous peoples for the future survival of the planet. Brazilian consciousness, in relation to Indians and minorities in general, needs to change, not the Indians who have shown that they are not merely "survivors" or "remnants" of a once great past, but fully capable of forging viable models for their future.

At noon on Monday, April 21st, Tiradentes Day (Tiradentes is a Brazilian national hero), Brasilia declared three days of mourning for the Pataxó Indian who died. A requiem for the old models of Brazilian society as well?

The End

Modernization and the "Underdeveloped" World

The examples just examined show how modernization has affected indigenous peoples in otherwise "modern" states. Elsewhere in the so-called underdeveloped world, whole countries are in the throes of modernization. Throughout Africa, Asia, and South and Central America we are witnessing the widespread removal of economic activities—or at least their control—from the family–community setting; the altered structure of the family in the face of the changing labor market; the increased reliance of young children on parents alone for affection, instead of on the extended family; the decline of general parental authority; schools replacing the family as the primary educational unit; the discovery of a generation gap; and many other changes. The difficulty is that it all happens so fast traditional societies are unable to deal with it gradually. Changes that took generations to accomplish in Europe and North America are attempted within the span of a single generation in developing countries. In the process they frequently face the erosion of a number of dearly held values they had no intention of giving up.

Commonly, the burden of modernization falls most heavily on women. For example, the commercialization of agriculture often involves land reforms that overlook or ignore women's traditional land rights. This reduces their control of and access to resources at the same time that mechanization of food production and processing drastically reduces their opportunities for employment. As a consequence, they are confined more and more to traditional domestic tasks, which, as commercial production becomes peoples' dominant concern, are increasingly downgraded in value. Moreover, the domestic work load tends to increase, because men are less available to help out, while tasks such as fuel gathering and water collection are made more difficult as common land and resources come to be privately owned, and as woodlands are reserved for commercial exploitation. To top it all off, the growing of nonfood crops such as cotton and sisal or luxury crops such as tea, coffee, and cacao (source of chocolate) for the world market makes households vulnerable to wide price fluctuations. As a result, people cannot afford the high-quality diet subsistence farming provided and become malnourished. In short, with modernization, women frequently find themselves in an increasingly inferior position. As their work load increases, the value assigned the work they do declines, as does their relative educational status, not to mention their health and nutrition.

Modernization: Must It Always Be Painful?

Although most anthropologists see the change that is affecting traditional non-Western peoples caught up in the modern technological world as an ordeal, the more common attitude in the industrial West has been that it is a good thing—that however disagreeable the "medicine" may be, it is worth it for the "backward" people to become just like "us" (i.e., the people of Europe and Anglo North America). This view of modernization, unfortunately, is based more on the hopes and expectations of Western culture than it is on reality. Western peoples certainly would like to see the non-Western world attain the high levels of development seen in Europe and North America, as many Japanese, South Koreans, Taiwanese, and some other Asians, in fact, have done. Overlooked is the stark fact that the standard of living in the Western world is based on a rate of consumption of nonrenewable resources whereby far less than 50% of the world's population uses a good deal more than 50% of these resources. By the early 1970s, for example, the people of the United States—less than 5% (approximately) of the world's population—were consuming over 50% of all of the world's resources. Figures like this suggest it is not realistic to expect most peoples of the world to achieve a standard of living comparable to that of the

An urban slum near Juarez, Mexico. All over the world, people are fleeing to the cities for a "better life," only to experience disease and poverty in such slums.

Western world in the near future, if at all. At the very least, the countries of the Western world would have to cut drastically their consumption of resources. So far, they have shown no willingness to do this, and if they did, their living standards would have to change.

Yet more non-Western people than ever, quite understandably, aspire to a standard of living such as Western countries now enjoy, even though the gap between the rich and poor people of the world is widening rather than narrowing. Every year, some 25 million people slide below the poverty level.[20] This has led to the development of what anthropologist Paul Magnarella called a new "culture of discontent," a level of aspirations far exceeding the bounds of local opportunities. No longer satisfied with traditional values, and often unable to sustain themselves in the rural backlands, people all over the world are moving to the large cities to find a "better life," all too often to live out their days in poor, congested, and diseased slums in an attempt to achieve what is usually beyond their reach. Unfortunately, despite all sorts of rosy predictions about a better future, this wretched reality remains.

[20] Kurth, P. (1998, October 14). Capitol crimes. *Seven Days,* 7.

CHAPTER SUMMARY

Although cultures may be remarkably stable, culture change is characteristic of all cultures to a greater or lesser degree. Change is often caused by accidents, including the unexpected outcome of existing events. Another cause is people's deliberate attempt to solve some perceived problem. Finally, change may be forced upon one group in the course of especially intense contact between two societies. Adaptation and progress are consequences rather than causes of change, although not all changes are necessarily adaptive. Progress is however a culture defines it.

The mechanisms involved in cultural change are innovation, diffusion, cultural loss, and acculturation. The ultimate source of change is through innovation: some new practice, tool, or principle. Other individuals adopt the innovation, and it becomes socially shared. Primary innovations are chance discoveries of new principles—for example, the discovery that the firing of clay makes the material permanently hard. Secondary innovations are improvements made by applying known principles—for example, modeling the clay to be fired by known techniques into familiar objects. Primary innovations may prompt rapid culture change and stimulate other inventions. An innovation's chance of being accepted depends partly, but not entirely, on its perceived superiority to the method or object it replaces. Its acceptance is also connected with the prestige of the innovator and recipient groups. Diffusion is the borrowing of a cultural element from one society by another. Cultural loss involves the abandonment of some trait or practice with or without replacement. Anthropologists have given considerable attention to acculturation. It stems from intensive firsthand contact of groups with different cultures and produces major changes in the cultural patterns of one or both groups. The actual or threatened use of force is always a factor in acculturation.

Applied anthropology arose as anthropologists sought to provide colonial administrators with a better understanding of native cultures, often to control them better, sometimes to avoid serious disruption of them. Later, anthropologists tried to help indigenous people cope with outside threats to their interests. A serious ethical issue for applied anthropologists is how far they should go in trying to change the ways of other peoples.

Reactions of indigenous peoples to changes forced upon them vary considerably. Some have retreated to inaccessible places in hopes of being left alone, while some others have lapsed into apathy. Some, like the Trobriand Islanders, have reasserted their traditional culture's values by modifying foreign practices to conform to indigenous values, a phenomenon known as syncretism. If a culture's values get widely out of step with reality, revitalization movements may appear. Some revitalization movements try to speed up the acculturation process to get more of the benefits expected from the dominant culture. Others try to reconstitute a gone but not forgotten way of life. In other cases, a pariah group may try to introduce a new social order based on its idealogy. Revolutionary movements try to reform the culture from within. Rebellion differs from revolution, in that the aim is merely to replace one set of officeholders with another.

Modernization refers to a global process of cultural and socioeconomic change whereby developing societies seek to acquire characteristics of industrially "advanced" Western societies. The process consists of four subprocesses: technological development, agricultural development, industrialization, and urbanization. Other changes follow in the areas of political organization, education, religion, and social organization. Two other accompaniments of modernization are structural differentiation and new forces of social integration. An example of modernization is found in the Skolt Lapps of Finland, whose traditional reindeer-herding economy was all but destroyed when snowmobiles were adopted to make herding easier. In Ecuador, the Shuar Indians modernized to escape the destruction visited upon many other Amazonian peoples. So far they have been successful, and others are mobilizing their resources in attempts to achieve similar success. Nevertheless, formidable forces are still arrayed against such cultures, and on a worldwide basis, it is probably fair to say that modernization has led to a deterioration rather than improvement of peoples' quality of life.

CLASSIC READINGS

Barnett, H. G. (1953). *Innovation: The basis of cultural change.* New York: McGraw-Hill.

This is the standard work on the subject, widely quoted by virtually everyone who writes about change.

Bodley, J. H. (1990). *Victims of progress* (3rd ed.). Mountain View, CA: Mayfield.

Few North Americans are aware of the devastation unleashed upon indigenous peoples in the name of "progress," nor are they aware this continues on an unprecedented scale today or of the extent their own society's institutions contribute to it. For most, this book will be a real eye opener.

Gordon, R. J. (1992) *The Bushman myth: The making of a Namibian underclass.* Boulder, CO: Westview.

This is a remarkably enlightening study of how both Bushman culture and European myths about the Bushman have changed over the past 150 years. Not only does it demolish myths ranging from the "Bushmen as Vermin" stereotype of the colonial era to the childlike innocence of the film *The Gods Must Be Crazy,* but also it shows how these people have been part of the world system since before their first "discovery" by Europeans. To see how they have managed their interactions with outsiders and how outsiders have manipulated images of the Bushmen for their own economic, political, and social interests is enlightening.

Magnarella, P. J. (1974). *Tradition and change in a Turkish town.* New York: Wiley.

This book, one of the best anthropological community studies of the Middle East, still is an excellent introduction to the phenomenon known as modernization. It has none of the facile generalizations about modernization that one so often finds, and the author's view of the phenomenon, which is well documented, is quite different from what is all too often promoted by optimistic developers and politicians.

Stannard, D. E. (1992). *American holocaust.* Oxford: Oxford University Press.

Stannard deals with 500 years of culture change in the Americas arising from contact between European and native cultures. In doing so, he focuses on genocide, relates it to "the holocaust" of World War II, and demonstrates how deeply rooted the phenomenon is in Western culture and Christianity.

CHAPTER 27

ANTHROPOLOGY AND THE FUTURE

If humanity is to have a future, it will have to solve the political and economic problems that are responsible for a worldwide flood of refugees. What drives this is the increasing economic disparity between the industrialized countries of Europe and North America on the one hand and most of the other countries of the world, and the political turmoil caused by states controlled by people of one nationality who try to repress attempts by people of other nationalities to retain and assert their own identities and traditions.

CHAPTER PREVIEW

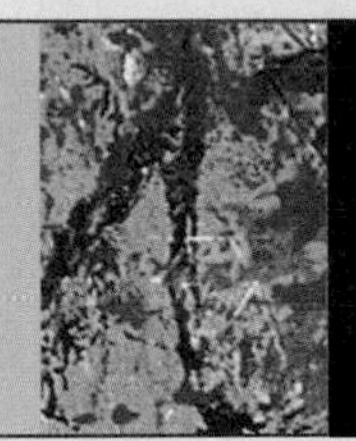

1 What Can Anthropologists Tell Us of the Future?

Anthropologists cannot accurately predict future cultural forms any more than biologists can predict future life forms or geologists future land forms. They can, though, identify certain patterns and trends of which we might otherwise be unaware and can anticipate some of the consequences these might have if they continue. They also can shed light on problems others may already have identified by showing how these relate to each other as well as to cultural facts of which "experts" in other disciplines are often unaware. This ability to consider problems in their wider context is an anthropological specialty, and it is essential if these problems are ever to be solved.

2 What Are Some Present-Day Trends in Cultural Evolution?

One major trend in present-day cultural evolution is toward worldwide adoption of the products, technology, and practices of the Western industrialized world. This apparent gravitation toward a homogenized, global culture is, however, opposed by another very strong trend for ethnic groups all over the world to reassert their own distinctive cultural identities. A third trend, of which we are just becoming aware, is that the problems certain cultural practices create seem to be overwhelming the capacity of human societies to find solutions to such problems.

3 What Problems Will Have to Be Solved If the Human Species Is to Have a Future?

If our species is to have a future, human cultures will have to find solutions to problems posed by slowed population growth, food and other resource shortages, pollution, and a growing culture of discontent. One difficulty is that, up to now, people have tended to see these problems as if they were isolated and unrelated. Thus, attempts to deal with one problem, such as food shortages, are often at cross-purposes with other problems, such as an inequitable world market for the distribution of basic resources. Unless humanity has a more realistic understanding of the "global society" than presently exists, it cannot solve the problems whose solutions are crucial for its future.

Anthropology is often described by those who know little about it as an exotic and retrospective discipline. The most common stereotype is that anthropologists devote all of their attention to the interpretation of the past and the description of present-day "tribal" remnants. Yet as we saw in Chapter 1, as well as in the Anthropology Applied box for Chapter 17, not even archaeologists, the anthropologists most prone to looking into the past, limit their interests to ancient times, nor are ethnologists uninterested in their own cultures. Thus, throughout this book we constantly have made comparisons between "us" and "others." Moreover, anthropologists have a special concern with the future and the changes it may bring. Like many members of Western industrialized societies, they wonder what the "postindustrial" society now taking shape will hold. They also wonder what changes the coming years will bring to non-Western traditional cultures. As we saw in the preceding chapter, when traditional peoples are thrown into intense contact with Western industrialized peoples, their cultures rapidly change, often for the worse, becoming both less supportive and less adaptive. Since Western people show no inclination to leave traditional non-Western people alone, we may ask: How can these threatened cultures adapt to the future?

THE CULTURAL FUTURE OF HUMANITY

Whatever the biological future of the human species, culture remains the mechanism by which people solve their problems of existence. Yet some anthropologists have noted with concern—and interpret as a trend—that the problems of human existence seem to be outstripping any culture's ability to find solutions. The main problem seems to be that in solving existing problems, culture inevitably poses new ones. To paraphrase anthropologist Jules Henry, although cultures are "for" people, they are also "against" them.[1] As we shall see, this dilemma is now posing serious new challenges for human beings. What can anthropologists tell us about future cultures?

Anthropologists—like geologists and evolutionary biologists—are historical scientists; as such, they can identify and understand the processes that have shaped the past and will shape the future. They cannot, however, tell us precisely what these processes will produce in the way of future cultures, any more than biologists can predict future life forms, or geologists future land forms. The cultural future of humanity, though, certainly will be affected in important ways by decisions that we humans are making today. This being so, if those decisions are to be made intelligently, it behooves us to have a clear understanding of the way things are in the world today. It is here that anthropologists have something vital to offer.

To comprehend anthropology's role in understanding and solving problems in times to come, we must look at certain flaws frequently seen in the enormous body of future-oriented literature that has appeared over the past few decades, not to mention the efforts to plan for the future that have become commonplace at regional, national, and international levels. For one thing, rarely do futurist writers or planners look more than about 50 years ahead, and the trends they project, more often than not, are those of recent history. This predisposes people to think that a trend that seems fine today will always be so and that it may be projected indefinitely into the future. The danger inherent in this is neatly captured in anthropologist George Cowgill's comment: "It is worth recalling the story of the person who leaped from a very tall building and on being asked how things were going as he passed the 20th floor replied 'Fine, so far.'"[2]

Another flaw is a tendency to treat subjects in isolation, without reference to pertinent trends outside an expert's field of competence. For example, agricultural planning is often predicated upon the assumption that a certain amount of water is available for irrigation, whether or not urban planners or others have designs upon that same water. Thus—as in the southwestern United States, where more of the Colorado River's water has been allocated than actually exists—people may be counting on resources in the future that will not, in fact, be available. One would suppose that this would be a cause for concern, but as two well-known futurists put it, "If you find inconsistencies the model is better off without them."[3] These same two authorities, in editing a volume aimed at refuting the somewhat pessimistic projections of *Global 2000* (the first attempt at a coordinated analysis of global resources on the part of the U.S. government), deliberately avoided going into population growth and its implications, because they knew that to do so would lead their contributing authors to disagree with one another.[4] This brings us to yet another common flaw: A tendency to project the hopes and expectations of one's own culture into the fu-

---

[1] Henry, J. (1965). *Culture against man* (p. 12). New York: Vintage Books.

[2] Cowgill, G. L. (1980). Letter, *Science, 210*, 1305.

[3] Holden, C. (1983). Simon and Kahn versus *Global 2000. Science, 221*, 342.

[4] Holden, C. (1983). Simon and Kahn versus *Global 2000. Science, 221*, 343.

ture interferes with the scientific objectivity necessary to address the problem.

Against this background, anthropology's contribution to our view of the future is clear. With their holistic perspective, anthropologists are specialists at seeing how parts fit together into a larger whole. With their long-term historical perspective, they can see short-term trends in longer term perspective. With more than 100 years of cross-cultural research behind them, anthropologists can recognize culture-bound assertions when they encounter them; and, finally, they are familiar with alternative ways of dealing with a wide variety of problems.

Global Culture

A popular belief since the end of World War II has been that the future world will see the development of a single homogeneous world culture. The idea that such a global culture is emerging is based largely on the observation that developments in communication, transportation, and trade so link the peoples of the world that they are increasingly wearing the same kinds of clothes, eating the same kinds of food, reading the same kinds of newspapers, watching the same kinds of television programs, communicating directly with one another via the Internet, satellites, and World Wide Web, and so on. The continuation of such trends, so this thinking goes, should lead North Americans who travel in the year 2100 to Tierra del Fuego, China, or New Guinea to find the inhabitants living in a manner identical or similar to theirs. But is this so?

Certainly striking is the extent to which such items as Western-style clothing, computers, Coca-Cola, and bicycles have spread to virtually all parts of the world, and many countries—Japan, for example—have gone a long way toward becoming "Westernized." Moreover, if one looks back over the past 5,000 years of human history, one will see that political units have tended to become larger and more all-encompassing while becoming fewer in number. A logical outcome if this continued into the future would be a further reduction of autonomous political units to a single one encompassing the entire world. In fact, by extrapolating from this past trend into the future, some anthropologists even predicted that the world will become politically integrated, perhaps by the 23rd century but no later than the year 4850.[5]

[5] Ember, C. R., & Ember, M. (1985). *Cultural anthropology* (4th ed.) (p. 230). Englewood Cliffs, NJ: Prentice-Hall.

The worldwide spread of such products as Pepsi is taken by some as a sign that a homogeneous world culture is developing.

One problem with such a prediction is that it ignores the one thing all large states, past and present, irrespective of other differences between them, have in common: a tendency to come apart. Not only have the great empires of the past, without exception, broken up into numbers of smaller independent states, but also countries in virtually all parts of the world today are showing a tendency to fragment. The most dramatic illustrations of this in recent years have been the breakup of the Soviet Union into several smaller independent states, the similar break up of Yugoslavia, and the separation of East Timor from Indonesia. It can also be seen in separatist movements such as that of French-speaking peoples in Canada; Basque and Catalonian nationalist movements in Spain; Scottish, Irish, and Welsh nationalism in Britain; Tibetan nationalism in China; Kurdish nationalism in Turkey, Iran, and Iraq; Sikh separatism in India; Tamil separatism in Sri Lanka; Igbo separatism in Nigeria; Eritrean and Tigrean secession movements in Ethiopia; Namibian nationalism; and so on—this list is far from exhaustive. Nor is the United States immune, as can be seen from Puerto Rican independence movements and Native American attempts to secure greater political sovereignty.

These examples all involve peoples who consider themselves to be members of distinct nations by virtue of birth and cultural and territorial heritage, over whom peoples of some other ethnic background have tried to assert control. An estimated 5,000 such national groups exist in the world today, as opposed to a mere 190 recognized states (up from fewer than 50 in the 1940s).[6] Although some of these national groups are quite small in population and area—100 or so people living on a few acres—some are quite large. The Karen people of Burma (Figure 27.1), for example, number some 4.5 to 5 million, making them larger than 48% of United Nations member states.

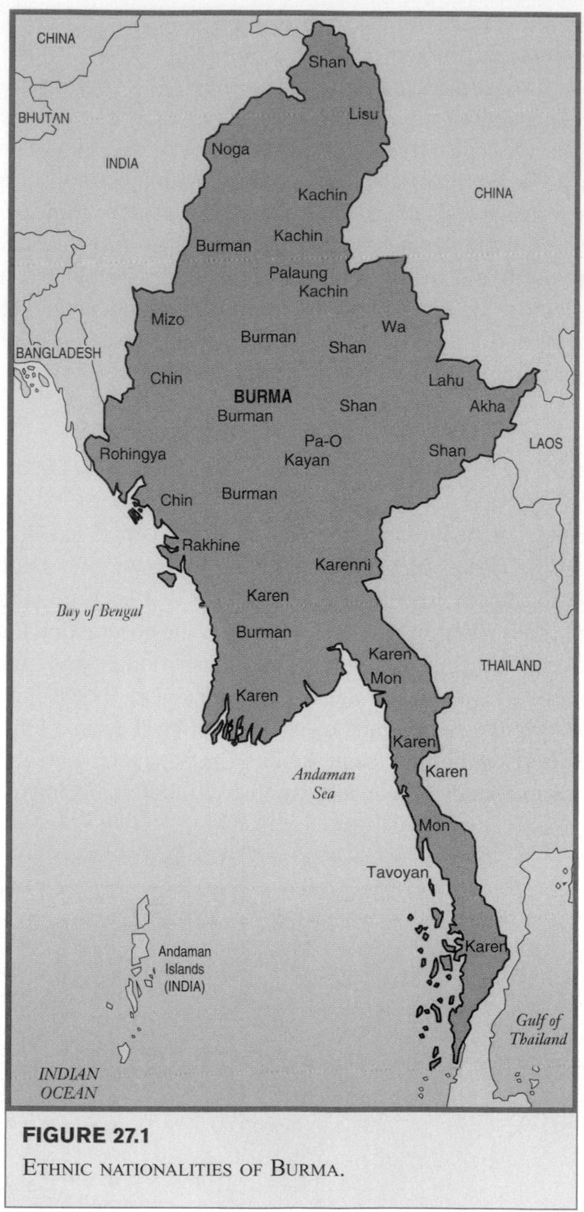

FIGURE 27.1
ETHNIC NATIONALITIES OF BURMA.

Reactions of these peoples to attempts at annexation and absorption by imposed state regimes other peoples control range all the way from East Timor's successful fight for independence from Indonesia (or the Chechen's so-far unsuccessful fight for independence from Russia) to the nonviolence of Scottish and Welsh nationalism. Many struggles for independence have been going on for years, such is the case of Karen resistance to the Burmese invasion of their territory in 1948; the takeover of Kurdistan by Iraq, Iran, and Turkey in 1925; and the even earlier Russian takeover of Chechnya. Even in relatively nonviolent cases the stresses and strains are obviously there. Similar stresses and strains may develop even in the absence of ethnic differences when regional interests within a large country become increasingly competitive. Again, hints of this may be seen in the United States: for example, in arguments over access to Colorado River water, in attempts by oil- and gas-producing states to get the most out of their resources at the expense of other states ("Let the Bastards Freeze in the Dark" proclaimed bumper stickers in oil- and gas-producing states during the Arab oil embargo of the 1970s), or in the refusal in some states to curb smokestack emissions that cause acid rain, which is destroying resources and endangering the

[6] *Cultural Survival Quarterly, 15* (4), 38. (1991).

The 1997 confrontation between Republic of Texas separatists and law enforcement officials is symptomatic of the stresses and strains that exist in United States society.

health of people in "downwind" states (not to mention other countries, Canada in particular).

Expansionist attempts by existing states to annex all or parts of other states also seem to be running into difficulty, as in the Iraqi attempt to take over Kuwait. It is just possible that we are reaching a point where the old tendency for political units to increase in size while decreasing in number is being canceled out by the tendency for such units to fragment into a greater number of smaller ones. At the present time, the integration of Europe seems to be the only notable exception to this political fragmentation.

The Rise of the Multinational Corporations

The resistance of the world to political integration seems to be offset to some extent by the rise of multinational corporations. Because these cut across the boundaries between states, they are a force for global integration despite the political differences that divide people. Situations such as this are well known to anthropologists, as illustrated by this description of Zuni Indian integrative mechanisms:

> Four or five different planes of systemization crosscut each other and thus preserve for the whole society an integrity that would speedily be lost if the planes merged and thereby inclined to encourage segregation and fission. The clans, the fraternities, the priesthoods, the kivas, in a measure the gaming parties, are all dividing agencies. If they coincided, the rifts in the social structure would be deep; by countering each other they cause segmentations which produce an almost marvelous complexity, but can never break apart the national entity.[7]

Multinational corporations are not new in the world (the Dutch East India Company is a good example from the 17th century), but they became common only in the latter half of the 20th century. Now, they have become a major force in the world. These modern-day giants are actually clusters of corporations of diverse nationality joined together by ties of common ownership and responsive to a common management strategy. Usually tightly controlled by a head office in one country, these multinationals organize and integrate production across the boundaries of different countries for interests formulated in corporate boardrooms, irrespective of whether or not these are consistent with the interests of people in the countries where they operate. In a sense they are products of the technological revolution, for without sophisticated data-processing equipment and electronic communication, the multinationals could not keep adequate track of their worldwide operations.

Though typically thought of as responding impersonally to outside market forces, large corporations are in fact controlled by powerful economic elites who benefit directly from their operations. For example, in 1994, just 10 individuals helped direct 37 North American companies whose combined assets of $2 *trillion* rival those of many national governments (Figure 27.2), and represented nearly 10% of all corporate assets in U.S. "for profit" businesses. Yet, the world's largest individual stockholders and most powerful directors, unlike political leaders, are known to few people (a mere 447 individuals own $1.1 trillion, equivalent to the income of the bottom 52% of the people in the world). For that matter, most people cannot even name the five largest multinational corporations.[8]

So great is the power of multinationals that they increasingly thwart the wishes of governments. Because the information these corporations process is kept from flowing in a meaningful way to the population at large, or even to lower levels within the organization, it becomes difficult

[7] Kroeber, A. L. (1970). Quoted in Dozier, E. *The Pueblo Indians of North America* (p. 19). New York: Holt, Rinehart and Winston.

[8] Bodley, J. H. (1997). Comment. *Current Anthropology, 38*, 725; Pyburn. K. A. (2000). Altered states: Archaeologists under siege in academe. In S. J. Bender & G. S. Smith (Eds.). *Teaching archaeology in the twenty-first century* (p. 122). Washington: Society for American Archaeology.

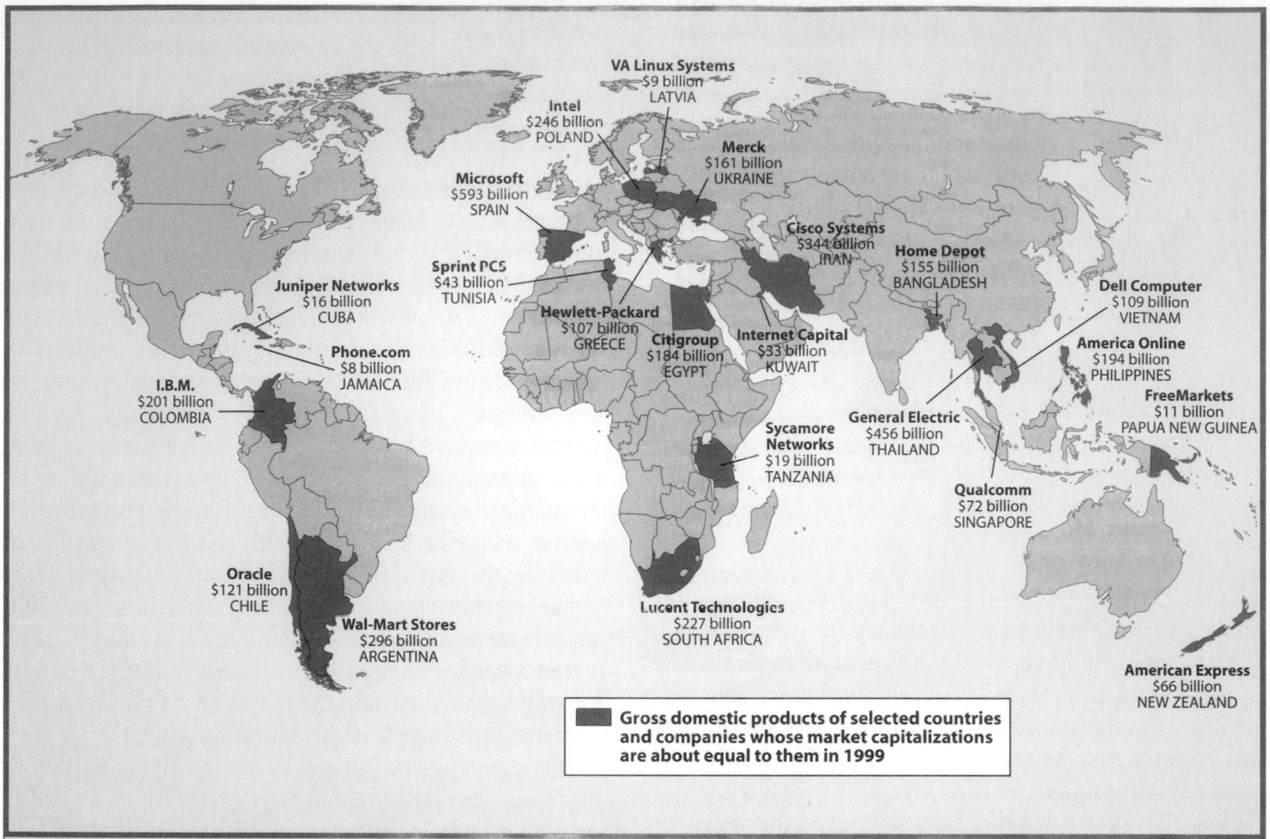
VA Linux Systems
$9 billion
LATVIA
Intel
$246 billion
POLAND
Merck
$161 billion
UKRAINE
Microsoft
$593 billion
SPAIN
Cisco Systems
$344 billion
IRAN
Home Depot
$155 billion
BANGLADESH
Sprint PCS
$43 billion
TUNISIA
Juniper Networks
$16 billion
CUBA
Dell Computer
$109 billion
VIETNAM
Hewlett-Packard
$107 billion
GREECE
Citigroup
$184 billion
EGYPT
Internet Capital
$33 billion
KUWAIT
Phone.com
$8 billion
JAMAICA
America Online
$194 billion
PHILIPPINES
I.B.M.
$201 billion
COLOMBIA
FreeMarkets
$11 billion
PAPUA NEW GUINEA
General Electric
$456 billion
THAILAND
Sycamore Networks
$19 billion
TANZANIA
Qualcomm
$72 billion
SINGAPORE
Oracle
$121 billion
CHILE
Lucent Technologies
$227 billion
SOUTH AFRICA
Wal-Mart Stores
$296 billion
ARGENTINA
American Express
$66 billion
NEW ZEALAND
Gross domestic products of selected countries and companies whose market capitalizations are about equal to them in 1999

FIGURE 27.2
THE WEALTH OF STATES AND CORPORATIONS.

for governments to get the information they need for informed policy decisions. Consider how long it took for the U.S. Congress to extract the information it needed from tobacco companies to decide what to do about tobacco legislation. Nor is this an isolated case. Beyond this, though, the multinationals have shown they can overrule foreign-policy decisions, as when they got around a U.S. embargo on pipeline equipment for the Soviet Union in the 1980s. While some might see this as a hopeful augury for the transcendence of national vices and rivalries, it raises the unsettling issue of whether or not the global order should be determined by corporations interested only in financial profits.

If the ability of multinational corporations to ignore the wishes of sovereign governments is cause for concern, so is their ability to act in concert with such governments. Here, in fact, is where their worst excesses have occurred. In Brazil, for example, where the situation is hardly unique but is especially well documented, a partnership emerged, after a military coup in 1964, between a government anxious to

Cheap raw Materials is bad Ag Policy
WTO
WE DEMAND PUBLIC VOICE
NO POLICE BRUTALITY
WTO CUTS JOBS & FORESTS STOP IT!
From Italian protesters Venice
LABOR SAYS... WTO Ends
LABOR SAYS... WTO End
ONE JUSTICE

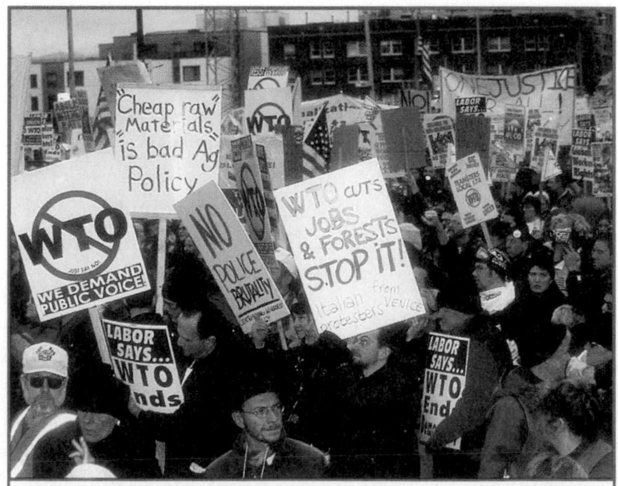

These protests at a 1999 meeting of the World Trade Organization were triggered by a conviction that it represents corporate interests, rather than the interests of people at large.

Brazil's Grand Carajas iron ore mine is an example of the kind of project states favor in their drive to develop. Not only does this introduce ecologically unsound technologies, but it also commonly has devastating effects on the indigenous people whose land is seized.

proceed as rapidly as possible with "development" of the Amazon rain forest; a number of multinational corporations such as ALCOA, Borden, Union Carbide, Swift-Armour, and Volkswagen, to mention only a very few; and several international lending institutions, such as the Export-Import Bank, the Inter-American Development Bank, and the World Bank.[9] To realize their goals, these allies introduced inappropriate technology and ecologically unsound practices into the region, converting vast areas into semidesert.

Far more shocking, however, has been the practice of uprooting whole human societies because they are seen as obstacles to economic growth. Literally overnight, people are deprived of the means to provide for their own needs and forcibly removed to places where they do not choose to live. Little distinction is made here between indigenous peoples and neo-Brazilian peasants who were brought into the region in the first place by a government eager to alleviate acute land shortages in the country's impoverished northeast. Bad as this is for these Brazilian peasants, the amount of disease, death, and human suffering unleashed upon the native Indians can only be described as massive. In the process, whole peoples have been (and are still being) destroyed with a thoroughness not achieved even by Stalin during his "Great Terror" in the Soviet Union of the 1930s or the Nazis in World War II. Were it not so well documented, it would be beyond belief. This is "culture against people" with a vengeance.

The power of multinational corporations creates problems on the domestic as well as on the international scene. Anthropologist Jules Henry, in a classic study of life in the United States, observed that working for any large corporation—multinational or not—tends to generate "hostility, instability, and fear of being obsolete and unprotected. For most people their job was what they had to do rather than what they wanted to do, . . . taking a job, therefore, meant giving up part of their selves."[10]

The power of corporations extends far beyond governments and workers. Their control of television and other media, not to mention the advertising industry, gives them enormous power over the lives of millions of "ordinary" people in ways they little suspect. The following is a case in point.

[9] Davis, S. H. (1982). *Victims of the miracle*. Cambridge: Cambridge University Press.

[10] Henry, J. (1965). *Culture against man* (p. 127.). New York: Vintage Books.

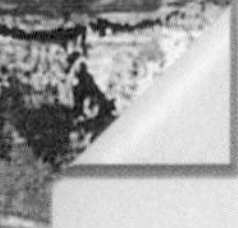

Original Study

Standardizing the Body: The Question of Choice[11]

The question of choice is central to the story of how medicine and business generate controlling processes in the shaping of women's bodies. Michel Foucault [in **Madness and Civilization**] demonstrates how changes in the concept of madness led to changes in diagnosis and treatment of the insane and of social attitudes toward them. He describes how changing perceptions of madness in parts of Western Europe from the Middle Ages to the end of the 19th century led to the separation of "mad" persons from the rest of society, their classification as deviants, and finally their subjection to social control. He focuses on the cultural controls that led to the social controls; ideas about madness led to asylums for the mad. A similar incremental process is central to discussions of the commodification of a woman's body.

Images of the body appear natural within their specific cultural milieus. For example, feminist researchers have analyzed the practice of breast implantation in the United States from the vantage point of the cultural milieu, and in the Sudan, female circumcision and infibulation [the most extreme form of female genital mutilation] serve to accentuate a feminine appearance. Thus, Sudanese and other African women, North American women, and others experience body mutilation as part of engendering rites. However, many writers differentiate infibulation from breast implantation by arguing that North American women **choose** to have breast implants whereas in Africa women are presumably subject to indoctrination (and besides, young girls are too young to choose). One of the most heated debates arising from the public health concern over breast implants is whether the recipients are freely situated—that is, whether their decision is voluntary or whether control is disguised as free will.

An informed response to the free-choice argument requires knowing how the beauty-industrial complex works. It requires sensitive fieldwork in multiple sites and an understanding of emergent idea systems in incremental change. Linda Coco builds upon the insights revealed by Howard Zinn's **The Twentieth Century: A People's History**. Zinn cites a 1930s magazine article which begins with the statement, "The average American woman has sixteen square feet of skin." This is followed by an itemized list of the annual beauty needs of every woman. Sixty years later the beauty-industrial complex is a multibillion-dollar industry that segments the female body and manufactures commodities of and for the body.

As Coco shows, some women get caught in the official beauty ideology, and in the case of silicone-gel breast implants some hundreds of thousands of women have been ensnared. But who gets caught and when is important to an understanding of the ecology of power. The average age of a woman having breast implantation is 36 years, and she has an average of two children. She is the beauty industry's insecure consumer recast as a patient. She is somehow deviant; her social illness is deformity or hypertrophy (small breasts). Coco quotes a past president of the American Society of Plastic and Reconstructive Surgery (ASPRS): "There is substantial and enlarging medical knowledge to the effect that these deformities [small breasts] are really a disease which result in the patient's feelings of inadequacies, lack of self-confidence, distortion of body image, and a total lack of well-being due to a lack of self-perceived femininity. . . . Enlargement . . . is therefore . . . necessary to ensure the quality of life for the [female] patient." In other words, cosmetic surgery is necessary to the patient's psychological health.

The plastic surgeon regards the construction of the official breast as art, the aim being to reform the female body according to the ideals of classic Western art. One surgeon pioneering procedures for correcting deformity took as his ideal female figure that of ancient Greek statues, which he carefully measured, noticing the exact size and shape of the breasts, their vertical location between

[11] Adapted from Nader, L. (1997). Controlling processes: Tracing the dynamics of power. *Current Anthropology, 38*, 715–717.

the third and seventh ribs, the horizontal between the line of the sternal ["breast bone"] border and the anterior axillary line, and so forth. In Coco's analysis the exercise of the plastic surgeon's techno-art recreates a particular static, official breast shape and applies this creation ostensibly to relieve women's mental suffering. The surgeon becomes a psychological healer as well as an artist.

Along with art and psychology, there is, of course, the business of organized plastic surgery, which responds to the demands and opportunities of market economics (Figure 27.3). By the late 1970s and early 1980s there was a glut of plastic surgeons. The ASPRS began to operate like a commercial enterprise instead of a medical society, saturating the media with ads and even providing low-cost financing. The discourse became a sales pitch. Women "seek" breast implants to keep their husbands or their jobs, to attract men, or to become socially acceptable. Coco calls this "patriarchal capitalism" and questions whether this is free choice or "mind colonization."

Understanding "choice" led Coco to an examination of the power both in the doctor-patient relationship and in the control of information. By various means certain women—the insecure consumers—are led to trust and believe in modern medical technology. What is most important in being "caught" is their internalization of the social message [cultural control]. Coco's conclusion that North American women are subtly indoctrinated to recognize and desire a certain kind of beauty presents an interesting possibility. Women "were told by the media, plastic surgeons, women's magazines, other women, and the business world that they could enhance their lives by enhancing their bust lines. . . . the social imperative for appearance was personalized, psychologized, and normalized." Social surveys indicate that, to the extent that women internalize the social imperative, they feel they are making the decision on their own.

Not surprisingly, women whose surgery resulted in medical complications often came to recognize the external processes of coercive persuasion that had led them to seek implants. In some ways, they resembled former cult members who had been deprogrammed: their disillusionment caused them to question the system that had encouraged them to make the decision in the first place. The result was a gradual building of protest against the industry, expressed in networks, newsletters, support groups, workshops, and seminars. As have some former cult members, women have brought suit, testified before lawmakers, and challenged in other ways some of the largest corporations and insurance companies in the land. The choice of implants, they learn, is part of a matrix of controlling processes in which women are subjects. Given the right circumstances it could happen to anyone. In the Sudan, the young girl is told that circumcision and infibulation are done for her and not to her. In the United States the mutilation of natural breasts is also done for the recreation of femininity. Although power is exercised differently in these two cases, Coco notes the sim-

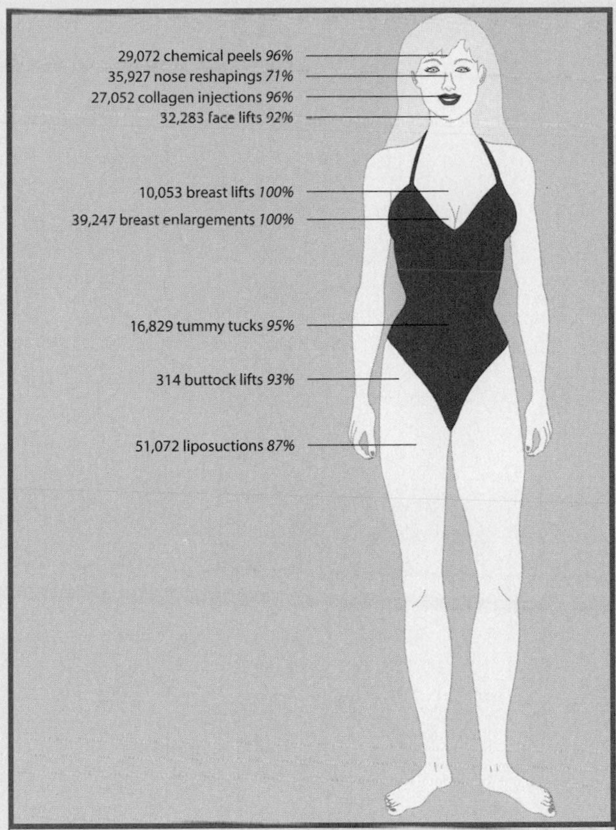

FIGURE 27.3
Cosmetic Surgery in the United States (1994) Number of operations in one year and percentage who were women.

Original Study

ilarity: "The operation on the female breast in [North] America holds much of the same social symbolism and expression of cultural mandate as does infibulation in Sudan. Thus, the question of why women choose breast augmentation becomes moot."

Breast implantation is now spreading elsewhere, most notably to China. Will it become a functional equivalent to foot-binding in China as part of the competition between patriarchies East and West? Whatever the answer, many social thinkers agree that people are always more vulnerable to intense persuasion during periods of historical dislocation—a break with structures and symbols familiar to the life cycle—in which the media can bring us images and ideas originating in past, contemporary, or even imaginary worlds.

Feminist researchers have sought to crack controlling paradigms such as those that define women's capacities and those that construct a standardized body shape and determine what is beautiful in women. **Our Bodies, Ourselves** (Boston Women's Health Book Collective) introduced women to their own bodies as a site for the exercise of power. Works such as Lakoff and Sherr's **Face Value: The Politics of Beauty** and Naomi Wolf's **The Beauty Myth: How Images of Beauty Are Used Against Women** are attempts to free the mind from the beauty constructions of cosmetic industries and fashion magazines. Others have written about how the one model of Western beauty is affecting members of ethnic groups who aspire to look the way advertisements say they should. Choice is an illusion, since the restructuring of taste is inextricably linked to shifts in the organization of consumption.

The End

Consumers have other problems with big business. After a 10-year intensive study of relations between producers and consumers of products and services, anthropologist Laura Nader found repeated and documented offenses by business that cannot be handled by present complaint mechanisms, either in or out of court. Viable alternatives to a failed judicial system do not seem to be emerging. Face-to-faceless relations between producers and consumers, among whom there is a grossly unequal distribution of power, exact a high cost: a terrible sense of apathy, even a loss of faith in the system itself.

These problems are exacerbated and new ones arise in the "sprawling, anonymous, networks" that are the multinational corporations.[12] Not only are corporate decisions made in boardrooms far removed from where other corporate operations take place, but also, given corporations' dependence on ever more sophisticated data-processing systems to keep their operations running smoothly, many decisions can be and are being made by computers programmed for given contingencies and strategies. As anthropologist Alvin Wolfe has observed, "A social actor has been created which is much less under the control of men than we expected it to be, much less so than many even think it to be."[13] In the face of such seemingly mindless systems for making decisions in the corporate interest, employees become ever more fearful that, if they ask too much of the corporation, it simply may shift its operations to another part of the globe where it can find cheaper, more submissive personnel, as has happened with some frequency to labor forces. Indeed, whole communities become fearful that if they do not acquiesce to corporate interests, local operations may be closed down.

In their never-ending search for cheap labor, multinational corporations have returned to a practice once seen in the textile mills of 19th century new England, but on a larger scale. More than ever before, they have come to favor women for low-skilled assembly jobs. In so-called "underdeveloped" countries, as subsistence farm-

[12] Pitt, D. (1977). Comment. *Current Anthropology, 18*, 628.

[13] Wolfe, A. W. (1977). The supranational organization of production: An evolutionary perspective. *Current Anthropology. 18*, 619.

The power of corporations over individuals is illustrated by their ability to get consumers to pay, by purchasing goods such as this T-shirt, to advertise corporate products.

ing gives way to mechanical agriculture for production of crops for export, women are less able to contribute to their families' survival. Together with devaluation of the worth of domestic work, this places pressure on women to seek jobs outside the household to contribute to its support. Since most women in these countries do not have the time or resources to get an education or to develop special job skills, only low-paying jobs are open to them. Corporate officials, for their part, assume female workers are strictly temporary, and high turnover means that wages can be kept low. Unmarried women are especially favored for employment, for it is assumed that they are free from family responsibilities until they marry, whereupon they will leave the labor force. Thus, the increasing importance of the multinationals in developing countries is contributing to the emergence of a prominent gender-segregated division of labor. On top of their housework, women hold low-paying jobs that require little skill; altogether, they may work as many as 15 hours a day. Higher paying jobs, or at least those that require special skills, are generally held by men, whose workday may be shorter since they do not have additional domestic tasks to perform. Men who lack special skills—and many do—are often doomed to lives of unemployment.

In sum, multinational corporations have become a major force in the world today, drawing people more firmly than ever before into a truly global system of relationships. Although this brings with it potential benefits, it is also clear that it poses serious new problems that now must be addressed.

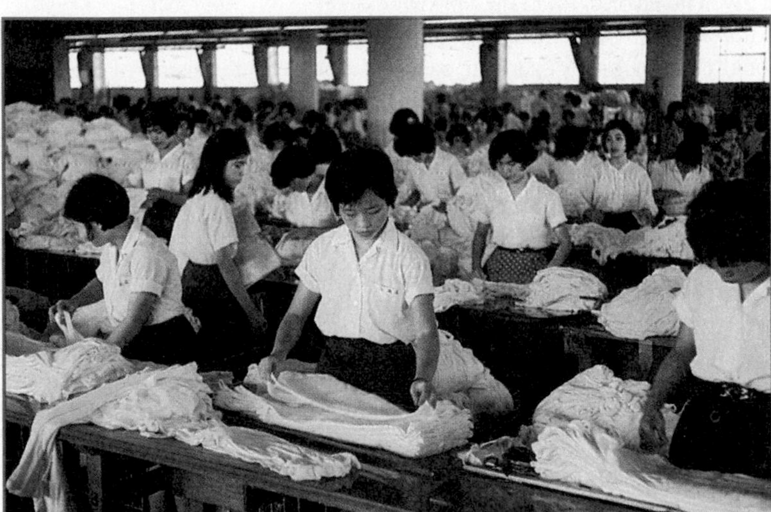
In so-called "underdeveloped" countries, women have become a source of cheap labor for large corporations, as subsistence farming has given way to mechanized agriculture. Unable to contribute to their families' well-being in any other way, they have no choice but to take on menial jobs for low wages.

Global Culture: A Good Idea or Not?

In the abstract, the idea of a single culture for all the world's people has had a degree of popular appeal, in that it might offer fewer chances for the kinds of misunderstandings to develop that, so often in the past few hundred years, have led to wars. Many anthropologists question this, though, in the face of evidence that traditional ways of thinking of oneself and the rest of the world may persist, even in the face of massive changes in other aspects of culture. Indeed, one might argue that the chances for misunderstandings actually increase; an example of this is the Original Study in Chapter 16.

Some have argued that perhaps a generalized world culture would be desirable in the future, because some cultures of today may be too specialized to survive in a changed environment. Examples of this situation are sometimes said to abound in modern anthropology. When a traditional culture that is highly adapted to a specific environment—such as that of the Indians of Brazil, who are well adapted to life in a tropical rain forest—meets European-derived culture and the social environment changes suddenly and drastically, the traditional culture often collapses. The reason for this, it is argued, is that its traditions and its political and social organizations are not at all adapted to "modern" ways. Here we have, once again, the ethnocentric notion (discussed in Chapter 26) that "old" cultures are destined to give way to the new. Since this is regarded as inevitable, actions are taken that by their very nature virtually guarantee the traditional cultures will not survive; it is a classic case of the self-fulfilling prophecy.

Increasingly, indigenous peoples around the world are organizing to defend their own interests against both developers and governments. Here, Aymara and Quechua Indians protest efforts that began more than 500 years ago with Columbus to stamp out native American peoples and cultures, all in the name of progress.

A problem with this argument is that, far from being unable to adapt, traditional societies in such places as Brazil's Amazon forest usually have been given no chance to work out their own adaptations. It is *not* any laws of nature that cause the collapse of traditional cultures but rather the political choices of the powerful, their willingness to invade lands already occupied by indigenous people, to overpower them, and their unwillingness to live and let live. That Amazonian Indians can adapt themselves to the modern world if allowed to do so, without losing their distinctive ethnic and cultural identity, is demonstrated by the Shuar case in Ecuador, noted in the preceding chapter. In Brazil, however, the pressures to "develop" the Amazon are so great that whole groups of people are swept aside so that multinational corporations and agribusiness can pursue their own particular interests. People do not have much chance to work out their own adaptations to the modern world if they are transported en masse from their homelands and deprived literally overnight of their means of survival so that more acreage can be devoted to the raising of beef cattle. Few neo-Brazilians get to eat any of this meat, for the bulk of it is shipped to Europe; nor do many of the profits stay in Brazil, since the major ranches are owned and operated by corporations based elsewhere. In spite of the designation of large tracts of land as Indian reservations since the mid 1990s, the process continues, nonetheless.

There is an important issue at stake in such situations, for what has happened is that some of the world's people with the power to do so have defined others—indeed, whole societies—as obsolete. This is surely a dangerous precedent, which if allowed to stand, means that any of the world's people may at some time in the future be declared obsolete by others who think they have the power to back it up.

Ethnic Resurgence

Despite the worldwide adoption of such products as Coca-Cola and the "Big Mac," and despite pressure for traditional cultures to disappear, it is clear that cultural differences are still very much with us in the world today. In fact, a tendency for peoples around the world to resist modernization, and in many cases retreat from it, is strengthening. Diverse manifestations of this to which we have already alluded are the separatist movements around the world, the dramatic revival of pastoral nomadism in Mongolia, the success so far of the Shuar in retaining their own ethnic and cultural identity, and the increasing political activism of Brazilian Indians—indeed, of native peoples throughout the world.

During the 1970s the world's indigenous peoples began to organize self-determination movements, culminating in the formation of the World Council of Indigenous Peoples in 1975. This group now has official status as a nongovernmental organization of the United Nations, which allows it to present the cases of indigenous people before the world community. Leaders of this movement see their own societies as community based, egalitarian, and close to nature, and are intent upon maintaining them that way. In 1993, representatives of some 124 indigenous groups and organizations agreed to a draft Declaration of the Rights of Indigenous Peoples. Currently under consideration for adoption by the United Nations General Assembly, it urges respect for indigenous cultural heritages, calls for recognition of indigenous land titles and rights of self-determination, and demands an end to all forms of oppression and discrimination as a principle of international law.

European Americans often have difficulty adjusting to the fact that not everyone wants to be just like they are. In the United States, children are taught to believe that "the American way of life" is one to which all other peoples aspire (and how arrogant they are to appropriate the label "Americans" strictly to themselves!), but it isn't only people such as the Shuar who resist becoming "just like us." In the world today whole countries, having striven to emulate Western ways, have become disenchanted and suddenly backed off. One striking case of such a retreat from modernity is the Taliban movement in Afghanistan. With their rise to power, attempts to modernize were abandoned in favor of a radical attempt to return to an Islamic republic out of a past "golden age" (mythical though the latter is). A somewhat similar, though far less radical, retreat from modernity took place in the United States, which, in the 1980s and again in 1994, elected politicians dedicated to a return to certain supposed "traditional values" from its past. To note just one other parallel between the two situations, in the United States, the analogue to the control of the Afghan government by Islamic fundamentalist religious leaders was the strong association of Christian fundamentalists with the Republican Party.[14]

[14] Marsella, J. (1982). Pulling it together: Discussion and comments. In S. Pastner & W. A. Haviland (Eds.). *Confronting the Creationists* (pp. 79–80). *Northeastern Anthropological Association, Occasional Proceedings*, 1.

Sometimes, resistance to modernization takes the form of a fundamentalist reaction, as it is today in Afghanistan and Algeria. This photo is of an FIS (Islamic Salvation Front) rally in Algiers.

Cultural Pluralism

Since a single homogenous world culture is not necessarily the wave of the future, what is? Some see **cultural pluralism,** in which more than one culture exists in a given society, as the future condition of humanity. Cultural pluralism is the social and political interaction of people with different ways of living and thinking within the same society or multinational state. Ideally, it implies a rejection of bigotry, bias, and racism in favor of respect for the differing cultural traditions of other citizens. In reality, it has rarely worked out that way.

Elements of pluralism are to be found in the United States, in spite of its "melting-pot" idelogy. For example, in New York City neighborhoods of Puerto Ricans, with their own distinctive cultural traditions and values, exist side by side with Chinese, Italian, and other New Yorkers. Besides living in their own *barrio*, the Puerto Ricans have their own language, music, religion, and food. This particular pluralism, however, may be temporary, a stage in the process of integration into what is sometimes referred to as "standard American culture." Thus, the Puerto Ricans, in four or five generations, like many Italians, Irish, and eastern European Jews before them, may also become (North) Americanized to the point where their lifestyle will be indistinguishable from others around them. Yet, there are many Puerto Ricans, African and Asian Americans, American Indians, Hispanics, and others who have strongly resisted abandoning their distinctive cultural identities. Whether this marks the beginning of a trend away from the melting-pot philosophy and toward real pluralism, however, remains to be seen.

Some familiar examples of cultural pluralism may be seen in Switzerland, where Italian, German, and French cultures exist side by side; in Belgium, where the French Walloons and the Dutch Flemish have somewhat different cultural heritages; and in Canada, where French- and English-speaking Canadians live in a pluralistic society (but where equal recognition of most native people is still problematic). In none of these cases, though, are the cultural differences (save those of native people in Canada) of the magnitude seen in many a non-Western pluralistic society. As an example of one such society—and its attendant problems—we may look at the Central American country of Guatemala.

Changing attitudes toward the rights of Canada's native people led to the creation of Nunavit, a province roughly the size of Western Europe, to be governed by the Inuit. Here, an Inuit elder lights a traditional "qulluliq" at the dedication of Nunavit's legislature on March 30, 1999.

GUATEMALAN CULTURAL PLURALISM

Guatemala, like many other pluralistic countries, came into being through conquest. In Guatemala's case the conquest was about as violent and brutal as it could be, given the technology of the time (the 1500s), as a rough gang of Spanish adventurers led by a man known even then for his cruelty and inhuman treatment of foes defeated people whose civilization was far older than Spain's. The conquerors' aim was quite simply to extract as much wealth as they could, primarily for themselves but also for Spain, by seizing the riches of those they conquered and by putting the native population to work extracting the gold and silver they expected to find. Although the treasures to be had did not live up to the conquerors' expectations (no rich deposits of ore were found), their main

Cultural pluralism. Social and political interaction of people with different ways of living and thinking within the same society.

interest in their new possession continued to be whatever they could extract from it that could be turned into wealth for themselves. For the nearly 500 years since, their *Ladino* descendants have continued to be motivated by the same interests, even after independence from Spain.

Following its conquest, Guatemala never experienced substantial immigration from Spain, or anywhere else in Europe. The conquerors and their descendants, for their part, wished to restrict the spoils of victory as much as possible to themselves, even though those spoils did not live up to advance expectations. In fact, the country had little to attract outsiders. Thus, Indians have always outnumbered non-Indians in Guatemala, and continue to do so today. Nonetheless, Indians never have been allowed to hold any important political power; the apparatus of state, with its instruments of force (the police and army) remained firmly in the hands of the *Ladino* (non-Indian) minority. This enabled them to continue exacting tribute and forced labor from Indian communities.

In the 19th century Guatemala's *Ladino* population saw coffee and cotton exports as new sources of wealth for themselves. For this, they took over huge amounts of Indian lands to create their plantations, thereby depriving Indians of sufficient land for their own needs (Figure 27.4). Consequently, the latter had no option but to work for the plantation owners on their enlarged holdings at wages cheap beyond belief. Any reluctance on the part of these native laborers was dealt with by brute force.

In the 1940s democratic reforms were begun in Guatemala. Although Indians played no role in bringing them about, they benefitted from them; for the first time in over 400 years native peoples could at least hold municipal offices in their own communities. In the 1950s the Roman Catholic Church began to promote agricultural, consumer, and credit cooperatives in rural areas (which, in Guatemala, are predominantly Indian).

With the U.S. engineered military coup of 1954, this brief interlude, when the government recognized Indians

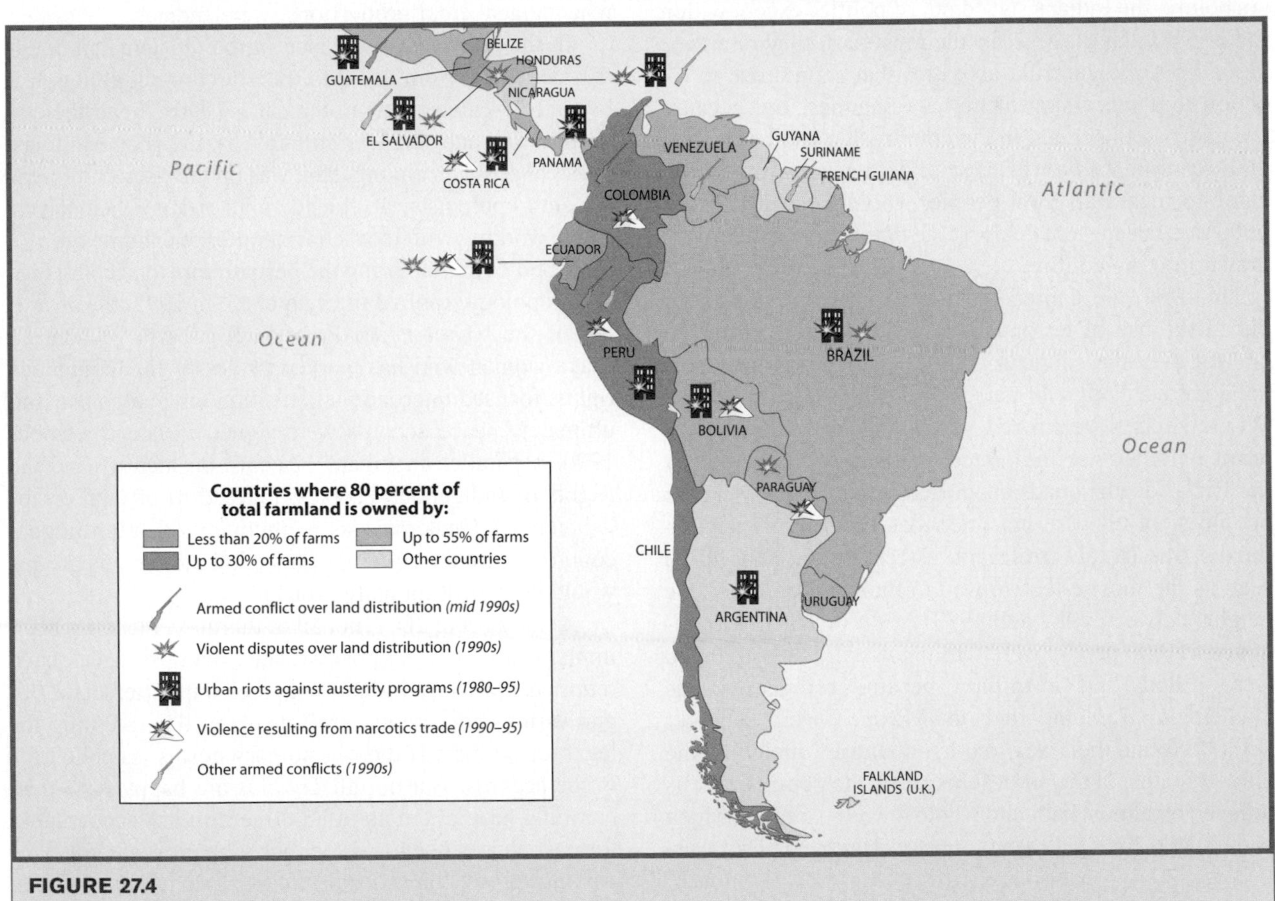

FIGURE 27.4
LAND OWNERSHIP IN CENTRAL AND SOUTH AMERICA.

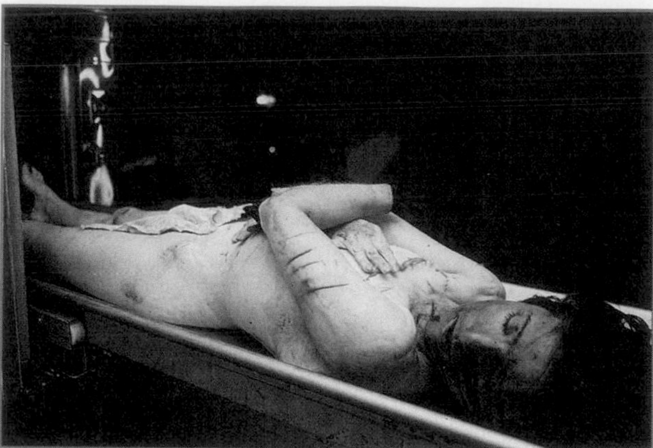

In Guatemala, the military and other groups sanctioned by the government used violence to maintain the control of one nationality (*ladino*) over others (Maya). As the illustration from a 1552 Spanish source shows, this has an eerie similarity to the way Spaniards treated the native Maya of Guatemala 450 years ago. Although the violence has subsided, it has not ended completely.

had social, economic, and cultural rights, came to an end. As before, the Indians stayed out of politics except within their own villages. And, for the most part, they remained aloof from the guerrilla activities that soon arose in reaction to a succession of military regimes. But because the guerrillas operated in the countryside and because of 400 years of *Ladino* distrust of Indians, these regimes came to regard all rural people, who are mostly Indian, with ever deeper suspicion. Inevitably, the latter were drawn into the conflict.

In 1966, the United States Advisory Mission introduced the use of terror tactics to maintain government control over the countryside.[15] By 1978, this had escalated into a "reign of terror" known as *La Violencia*: Whole villages were razed, inhabitants killed, and bodies burnt or otherwise multilated by either the army or by unofficial death squads supported by the army. Whether people were or were not guerrillas or guerrilla sympathizers was largely irrelevant, as repression came to be seen as the most effective way to maintain order. At the height (between 1981 and 1983) of *La Violencia* an estimated 15,000 people were "disappeared," at least 90,000 were killed, half a million became refugees inside Guatemala, 150,000 fled to Mexico, while another 200,000 found their way to other countries, including the United States. In the hardest hit areas, the population was reduced by almost half, and whole towns—some of which had existed for 1,000 years—were destroyed. The overwhelming majority of victims of this violence, which reached genocidal proportions, were Indians.

In the late 1980s, violence in the Guatemalan countryside lapsed from acute to merely chronic, although it began to escalate anew in the early 1990s. Nevertheless, despite this and the fear still felt by the Maya Indians, political activism among them was on the rise. And forensic anthropologists, at considerable risk to themselves, began working with local communities to exhume the victims' bodies to help bring the perpetrators to account (see Anthropology Applied in Chapter 1). In 1992, the awarding of the Nobel Peace Prize to Rigoberta Menchú, a Maya woman who has worked tirelessly for indigenous rights, focused international attention on Guatemala, and ultimately peace accords were signed in late December 1996. A parallel document, "Accord on Identity and the Rights of Indigenous Peoples," agreed to official establishment of Guatemala as a multicultural, multilingual country where the cultural rights of all indigenous groups would be constitutionally protected.

At the start of 2001, not all of this agreement has been implemented. On the positive side, many refugees have returned, and Maya Indians with their supporters have begun various educational projects, as well as pressing for legal recognition of their customary norms, as called for in the accords. But not all *Ladinos* are happy with this. Not only have attempts to hold the military accountable for past abuses been resisted, but robberies, assaults (including torture), and death threats against human rights groups, journalists, and nongovernmental organizations were on the increase in the year 2000. Moreover, in the neighboring Mexican state of Chiapas, there has been

[15] Zur, J. (1994). The psychological impact of impunity. *Anthropology Today, 10* (3), 16.

Forensic anthropologists in Guatemala exhume victims of a state-sponsored massacre from a mass grave.

continuing violence by large landowners, condoned by local government officials, against native Maya supporters of the indigenous Zapatista revolutionaries and their campaign for indigenous rights. All of this is reminiscent of the previous violence in Guatemala.

Meanwhile, in Guatemala, the *Ladino* elite is talking more about the need to forge a true national identity in their country, but will this be done in a manner consistent with the "Accord on Identity and the Rights of Indigenous Peoples"? We can of course remain hopeful, but we cannot escape the fact that, historically, what has been called nation building, in all parts of the world, in most cases involves attempts to destroy the cultures of peoples belonging to nations other than those who control the government.[16] Even in the 1980s, states were borrowing more money to fight peoples within their boundaries than for all other programs combined. Nearly all state debt in Africa and nearly half of all other debt in "underdeveloped" countries comes from the cost of weapons purchased by states to fight people claimed to be citizens by those very same states.[17] Nor was the situation in the 1990s any better.

Of all the world's states, Switzerland is one of the very few where pluralism really has worked out to the satisfaction of all parties to the arrangement, perhaps because despite linguistic differences, their are few other cultural differences between them. In Northern Ireland, by contrast, having an Irish background in common did not prevent violence and bloodshed. The more divergent cultural traditions are, the more difficult it is to make pluralism work.

---

[16] Van Den Berghe, P. (1992). The modern state: Nation builder or nation killer? *International Journal of Group Tensions, 22* (3), 194–198.

[17] *Cultural Survival Quarterly, 15* (4), 38 (1991).

HIGHWAY 1
Great Green Web game
http://www.ucsusa.org/game/index.html

HIGHWAY 2
Initiative on Conflict Resolution and Ethnicity
http://www.incore.ulst.ac.uk/cds/countries/index.html

HIGHWAY 3
University of Michigan's Center for the Ethnography of Everyday Life
http://www.ethno.isr.umich.edu

Although a peace agreement in Guatemala has greatly reduced violence against that country's Maya population, anti-Maya violence is on the increase in the neighboring Mexican state of Chiapas. Shown here are coffins with victims of the December 1997 massacre.

Given this dismal situation, can anything be done about it? As anthropologists David Maybury-Lewis and Pierre Van Den Berghe point out, we tend to idealize the peace and social order maintained by the unitary state and to exaggerate the danger to this vision presented by allowance of cultural distinctiveness and/or local autonomy to peoples of other nationalities.[18] The sooner we recognize these tendencies, the better off we will be. After all, states as political constructs are human products of cultural imagination, and nothing prevents us from imagining in ways more tolerant of pluralism. Obviously, this will take a good deal of work, but at least the recognition exists that such things as *group* rights exist. Even though it often fails to act on it, the United Nations General Assembly in its Covenant of Human Rights, passed in 1966, states unequivocally that: "In those states in which ethnic, religious or linguistic minorities exist, persons belonging to such minorities shall not be denied the rights, in community with the other members of their group, to enjoy their own culture, to profess and practice their own religion or to use their own language."[19] Besides education, one of the things that can help make this acknowledged right a reality is the advocacy work on behalf of indigenous peoples engaged in by substantial numbers of anthropologists (see the Anthropology Applied box in this chapter).

Ethnocentrism

The major problem associated with cultural pluralism has to do with ethnocentrism, a concept introduced in Chapter 14. To function effectively, a society must embrace the idea that its ways are the only proper ones, irrespective of how other cultures do things. This provides individuals with a sense of ethnic pride in and loyalty to their cultural traditions, from which they derive psychological support, and which binds them firmly to their group. In societies where one's self-identification derives from the group, ethnocentrism is essential to a sense of personal worth. The problem with ethnocentrism is that it all too easily can be taken as a charter for condemning other

[18] Maybury-Lewis, D. (1993). A new world dilemma: The Indian question in the Americas. *Symbols, 22*; Van Den Berghe, P. (1992). The modern state: Nation builder or nation killer? *International Journal of Group Tensions*, *22* (3), 191–192.

[19] Quoted in Bodley, J. H. (1990). *Victims of progress* (3rd ed., p. 99). Mountain View, CA: Mayfield.

These pictures show a Chechen woman in front of her home that has been destroyed by a Russian rocket and federal marshals at Wounded Knee, South Dakota, where U.S. troops laid siege to the Sioux Indian town in 1973. Both exemplify the willingness of states one nationality controls to use their armies against people of other nationalities within their borders to promote the state's interests over those of the other nationality.

cultures as inferior, and as such exploiting them for the benefit of one's own, even though—as we saw in Chapter 23—this does not have to be the choice. When it is, however, unrest, hostility, and violence commonly result.

In a typical expression of ethnocentrism, President James Monroe, in 1817, said this of Native American rights:

> The hunter state can exist only in the vast uncultivated deserts. It yields to the . . . greater force of civilized population; and of right, it ought to yeild, for the earth was given to mankind to support the greater number of which it is capable; and no tribe or people have a right to withhold from the wants of others, more than is necessary for their support and comfort.[20]

This attitude is, of course, alive and well in the world today, and governments frequently use the idea that no group has the right to stand in the way of "the greater good for the greater number" to justify the development of resources in regions occupied by subsistence farmers, pastoral nomads, or food foragers—irrespective of the wishes of those peoples. But is it truly the greater good for the greater number? A look at the world as it exists today as a kind of global society, with all the world's peoples bound by interdependency, raises serious questions.

Global Apartheid

Apartheid, the official governmental policy of the Republic of South Africa prior to the mid-1990s, consisted of programs or measures that aimed to maintain "racial" segregation. Structurally, it served to perpetuate the dominance of a small White minority over a large non-White majority through the social, economic, political, military, and cultural constitution of society. Non-Whites were denied effective participation in political affairs, were restricted in where they could live and what they could do, and were denied the right to travel freely. Whites, by contrast, controlled the government, including, of course, the military and police. Although there were 4.7 non-Whites for every White, being White and belonging to the upper stratum of society tended to go together. The richest 20% of South Africa took 58% of the country's income and enjoyed a high standard of living, while the poorest 40% of the population received but 6.2% of the national product. Even with the end of apartheid and White control of the government, the figures are not much different today.

What has the Republic of South Africa to do with a global society? Structurally, global society is an extreme version of South Africa's society, even though there are no explicit "race laws" connected with global apartheid.[21] In the world society about two thirds of the population is non-White and one-third White. In the world as a whole, being White and belonging to the upper stratum tend to go together, although some exceptions exist. Certainly, wealthy non-Whites exist in countries such as Japan and Kuwait, at the same time that poor Whites also exist. Although the Whites in this upper stratum have not been a homogeneous group, being divided until recently into communist and non-communist peoples, neither was the

[20] Quoted in Forbes, J. D. (1964). *The Indian in America's past* (p. 103). Englewood Cliffs, NJ: Prentice-Hall.

[21] The concept of global apartheid is drawn from G. Kohler (1996), Global apartheid. Reprinted in W. A. Haviland & R. J. Gordon, (Eds.). *Talking about people: Readings in contemporary cultural anthropology* (2nd ed., pp. 262–268). Mountain View, CA: Mayfield.

Anthropology Applied

Advocacy for the Rights of Indigenous Peoples

Anthropologists are increasingly concerned about the rapid disappearance of the world's remaining indigenous peoples for a number of reasons, foremost among them the basic issue of human rights. The world today is rushing to develop those parts of the planet Earth that have so far escaped industrialization, or the extraction of resources regarded as vital to the well-being of "developed" economies. These development efforts are planned, financed, and carried out both by governments and businesses (generally the huge multinational corporations), as well as by international lending institutions. Unfortunately, the rights of native peoples generally have not been incorporated into the programs and concerns of these organizations, even where laws exist that are supposed to protect the rights of such peoples.

For example, the typical pattern for development of Brazil's Amazon basin has been for the government to build roads, along which it settles poor people from other parts of the country. This brings them into conflict with Indians already living there, who begin to die off in large numbers from diseases contracted from the new settlers. Before long, the neo-Brazilian settlers learn that the soils are not suited for their kind of farming; meanwhile, outside logging, mining, and agribusiness interests exert pressure to get them off the land. Ultimately, the neo-Brazilians wind up living in disease-ridden slums, while the Indians are decimated by the diseases and violence unleashed upon them by the outsiders. Those who survive are usually relocated to places where resources are inadequate to support them.

In an attempt to do what they can to help indigenous peoples gain title to their lands and avoid exploitation by outsiders, anthropologists in various countries have formed advocacy groups. The major one in the United States is Cultural Survival, Inc., based in Cambridge, Massachusetts. This organization's interest is not in preserving indigenous cultures in some sort of romantic, pristine condition, so that they will be there to study or to serve as "living museum exhibits," as it were. Rather, it is to provide the information and support to help endangered groups to assess their situation, maintain or even strengthen their sense of self, and adapt to the changing circumstances. It does not regard assimilation of these groups into the mainstream societies of states as necessarily desirable; rather, they should be allowed the freedom to make their own decisions about how they wish to live. Instead of designing projects and then imposing them on endangered societies, Cultural Survival prefers to respond to the requests and desires of groups that see a problem and the need to address it. Cultural Survival can suggest ways to help and can activate extensive networks of anthropologists, of other indigenous peoples who already have faced similar problems, and of those government officials whose support can be critical to success.

Most Cultural Survival project funds or assists have been focused on securing the land rights of indigenous peoples and organizing native federations. It has also identified and funded a number of locally designed experiments in sustainable development, such as the Turkmen Weaving Project, which helps Afghan refugees to make profitable income from traditional rug weaving; the Ikwe Marketing Collective through which Minnesota Indians market wild rice and crafts; or Cultural Survival Enterprises, which has developed and expanded markets for such products as the nuts used in the popular Rain Forest Crunch (itself a creation of Cultural Survival). Of major importance was the success of Cultural Survival in getting the World Bank, in 1982, to adopt the policy that the rights and autonomy of tribal peoples and minorities be *guaranteed* in any project in which the bank is involved. Despite such successes, however, much remains to be done to secure the survival of indigenous peoples in all parts of the world.

upper stratum of South African society, where friction has always existed between the English, who controlled business and industry, and the Afrikaners (Whites of Dutch descent), who controlled the government and military. In the world today, the poorest 80% of the population make do with 14% of the world's goods and services, the poorest 20% with a mere 1.3%. Meanwhile, the richest 20% of the population enjoys 86% of all goods and services. Indeed, the world's 225 richest individuals have a combined wealth equal to the annual income of the poorest 47% of the entire world's population.[22] Life expectancy, as in South Africa, is poorest among non-Whites. Most of the world's weapons of mass destruction are still owned by Whites—the United States, Russia, France, and Britain—even after India and Pakistan became nuclear powers. As in South Africa, death and suffering from war and violence are distributed unequally; in the world, the poorest 70% of the population suffer over 90% of violent death in all categories.

One could go on, but enough has been said to make the point: The parallels between the current world situation and that of apartheid in South Africa are striking. To be sure, a number of non-White countries, such as South Korea, Taiwan, Malaysia, Thailand, and Indonesia, showed dramatic economic growth prior to 1997. Unfortunately, the economic crash then experienced by these countries interrupted this "progress," and recovery has been uneven. The price poor countries have had to pay to gain help from the industrialized (mostly White) countries of the world is to conform to requirements imposed by institutions, such as the International Monetary Fund, controlled by these countries (Figure 27.5). Moreover, it has become much easier for interests in the United States

[22] Kurth, P. (1998, October 14). Capital crimes. *Seven Days*, p. 7.

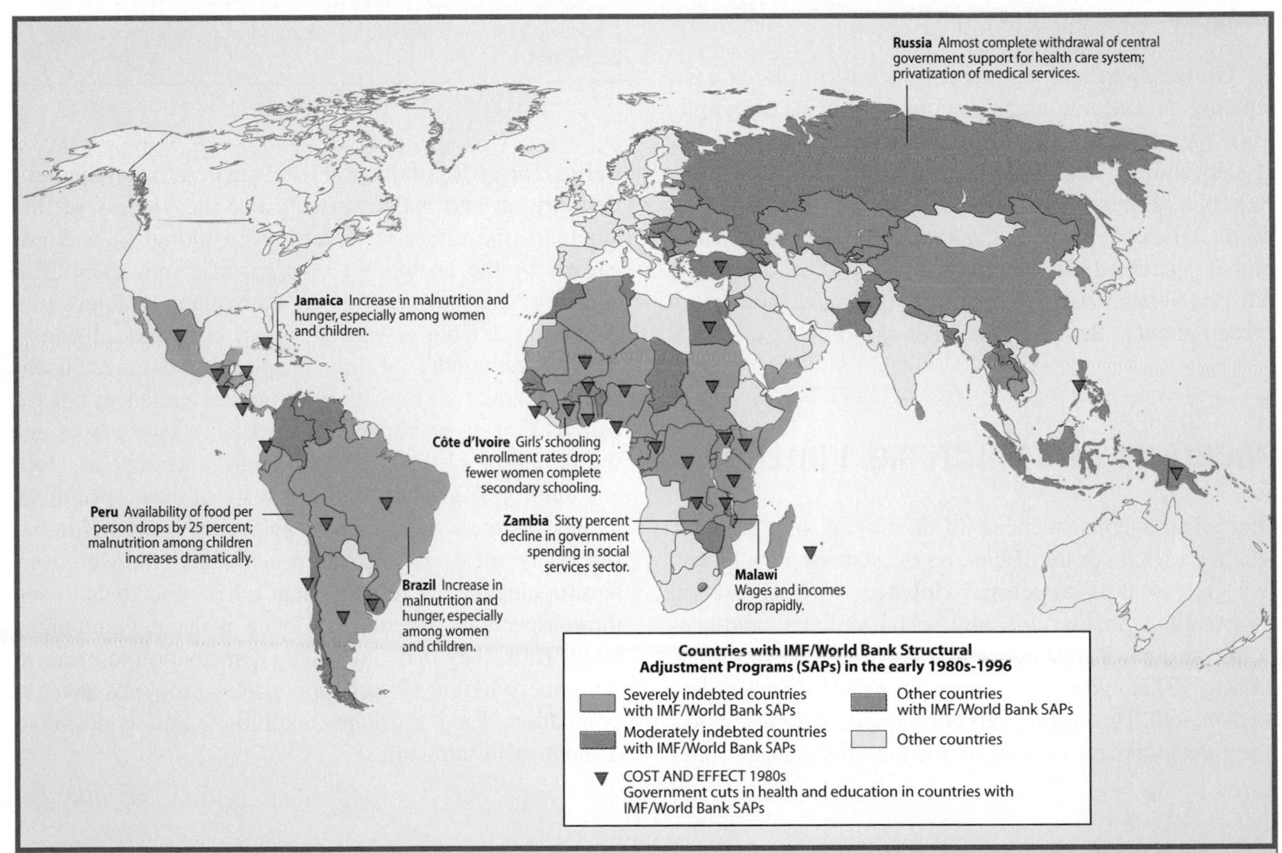

FIGURE 27.5

IMF and World Bank loans come with conditions of varying severity, known as Structural Adjustment Programs (SAPs). These programs require governments to reduce state subsidies and social spending, and to increase economic growth through privatization and international trade.

and other industrialized countries to buy up enterprises in countries in trouble. In financial bailouts in Latin America, for example, the borrowers were hurt far more than the lenders in wealthy countries, and more recent Asian bailouts seem headed in the same direction.[23]

We may sum up global apartheid as a de facto structure of world society that combines socioeconomic and racial antagonisms and that has these characteristics:

1. A minority of largely White people occupies the pole of affluence, while a majority composed mostly of people of color occupies the pole of poverty.
2. Social integration of the two groups is made extremely difficult by barriers of skin color, economic position, political boundaries, and other factors.
3. Economic development of the two groups is interdependent.
4. The affluent, largely White minority possesses a disproportionately large share of the world society's political, economic, and military power.

Global apartheid is thus a structure of extreme inequality in cultural, racial, social, political, economic, military, and legal terms, as was South African apartheid.

Around the world, condemnation of apartheid in the Republic of South Africa was close to universal, and even South Africa itself eventually abolished the system. Since global apartheid is even more severe than the South African version was, we ought to be much more concerned about it than we have been up to now.

This picture of a flood in Bangladesh exemplifies the structural violence that will result from global warming. As sea levels rise, flooding of low-lying areas will become more extensive and frequent.

PROBLEMS OF STRUCTURAL VIOLENCE

One of the consequences of a system of apartheid, whether official or unofficial, on the state or global level, is a great deal of **structural violence:** violence exerted by situations, institutions, and social, political, and economic structures. For example, in south Asian countries, 25% to 50% of all children born are characterized by low birth weight. This has serious consequences for the child's brain development as well as for the child's health later in life. The cause of the problem is maternal and fetal undernutrition and malnutrition.[24] For the victims of this situation, the effect is violent, even though it was not caused by the hostile act of a specific individual. The source of the violence was an anonymous structure (the economy), and this is what structural violence is all about.

The remainder of this chapter leaves insufficient space to cover all aspects of structural violence, but we can look at some aspects of particular concern to anthropologists. They are of concern to other scholars, too, and anthropologists draw on the work of these specialists as well as their own, thereby fulfilling their traditional role as synthesizers (discussed in Chapter 1). Moreover, anthropologists are less apt than other specialists to see these aspects of structural violence as discrete and unrelated. Thus, they may have a key contribution to make to our understanding of such modern-day problems as overpopulation, food shortages, pollution, and widespread discontent in the world.

[23] Avoiding the next crisis. (1998, January 12) *Washington Post National Weekly Edition*, p. 26.

[24] Swaminathan, M. S. (2000). Science in response to basic human needs. *Science*, *287*, 425.

Structural violence. Violence exerted by situations, institutions, and social, political, and economic structures.

World Hunger

As frequently dramatized by events in various parts of Africa, a major source of structural violence in the world today is a failure to provide food for all of its people. Not only is Africa losing the capacity to feed itself, but also 52 countries worldwide by 1980 were producing less food per capita than they were 10 years previously, and in 42 countries available food supplies were not adequate to supply the caloric requirements of their populations.[25] One factor that has contributed to this food crisis is a dramatic growth in the world's population. Population growth is more than a simple addition of people. If it were just that, the addition of 20 people a year to a population of 1,000 would double that population in 50 years; but because the added people beget more people, the doubling time is actually much less than 50 years. Hence, it took the whole of human existence for the world's population to reach 1 billion people, which it had by 1750. By 1950, world population had reached almost 2.5 billion, representing an annual growth rate of about 0.8%. By the year 2000, it had increased to 6 billion (Figure 27.6). India and China alone have more than 1 billion inhabitants each.

The obvious question arising from the burgeoning world population is, can we produce enough food to feed all of those people? The majority opinion among agricultural specialists is that we can do so, but how far into the future we can is open to question. In the 1960s a major effort was launched to expand food production in the poor countries of the world by introducing new high-yield strains of grains. Yet despite some dramatic gains from this "green revolution"—India, for example, was able to double its wheat crop in six years and was on the verge

[25] Bodley, J. H. (1985). *Anthropology and contemporary human problems* (2nd ed., p. 114). Palo Alto, CA: Mayfield.

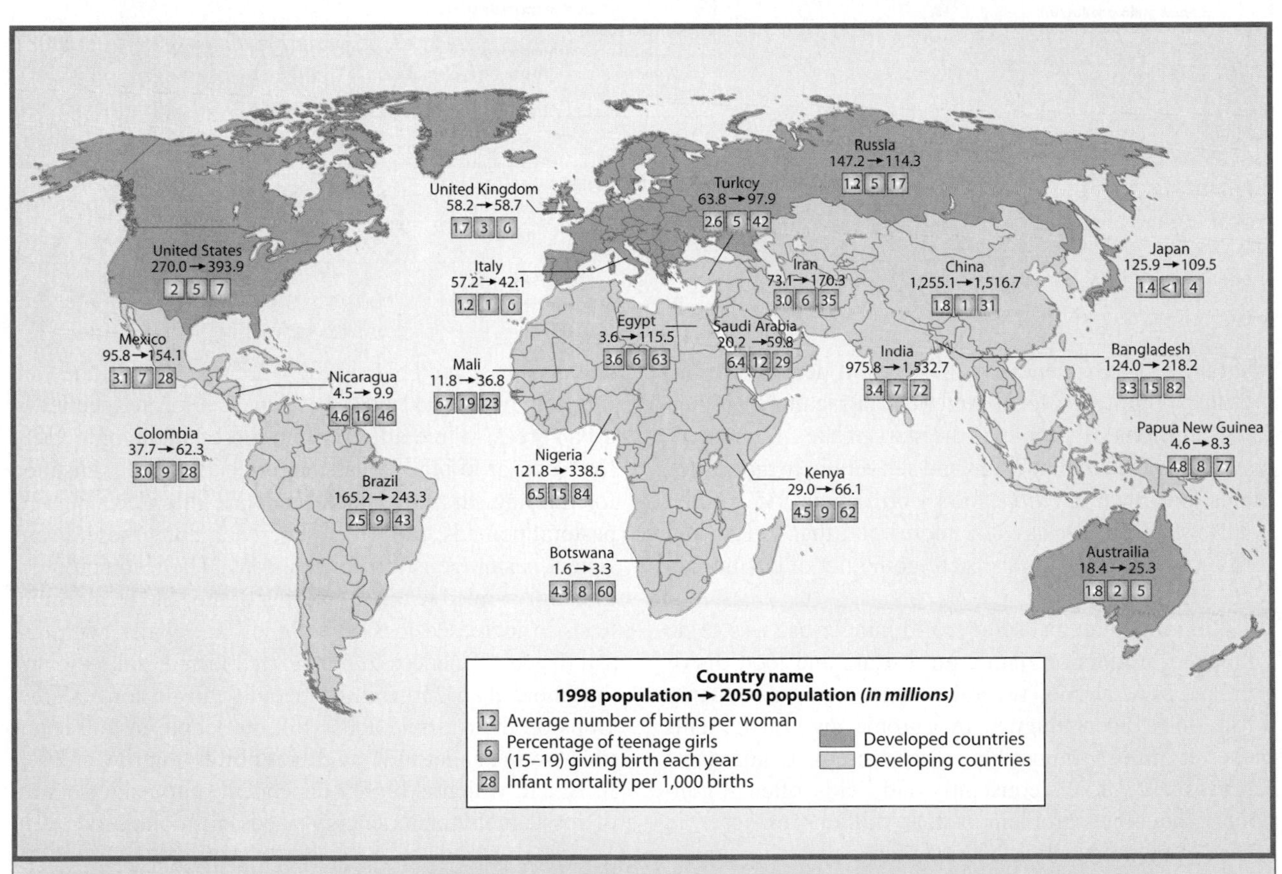

FIGURE 27.6
POPULATION PROJECTIONS INTO THE 21ST CENTURY.

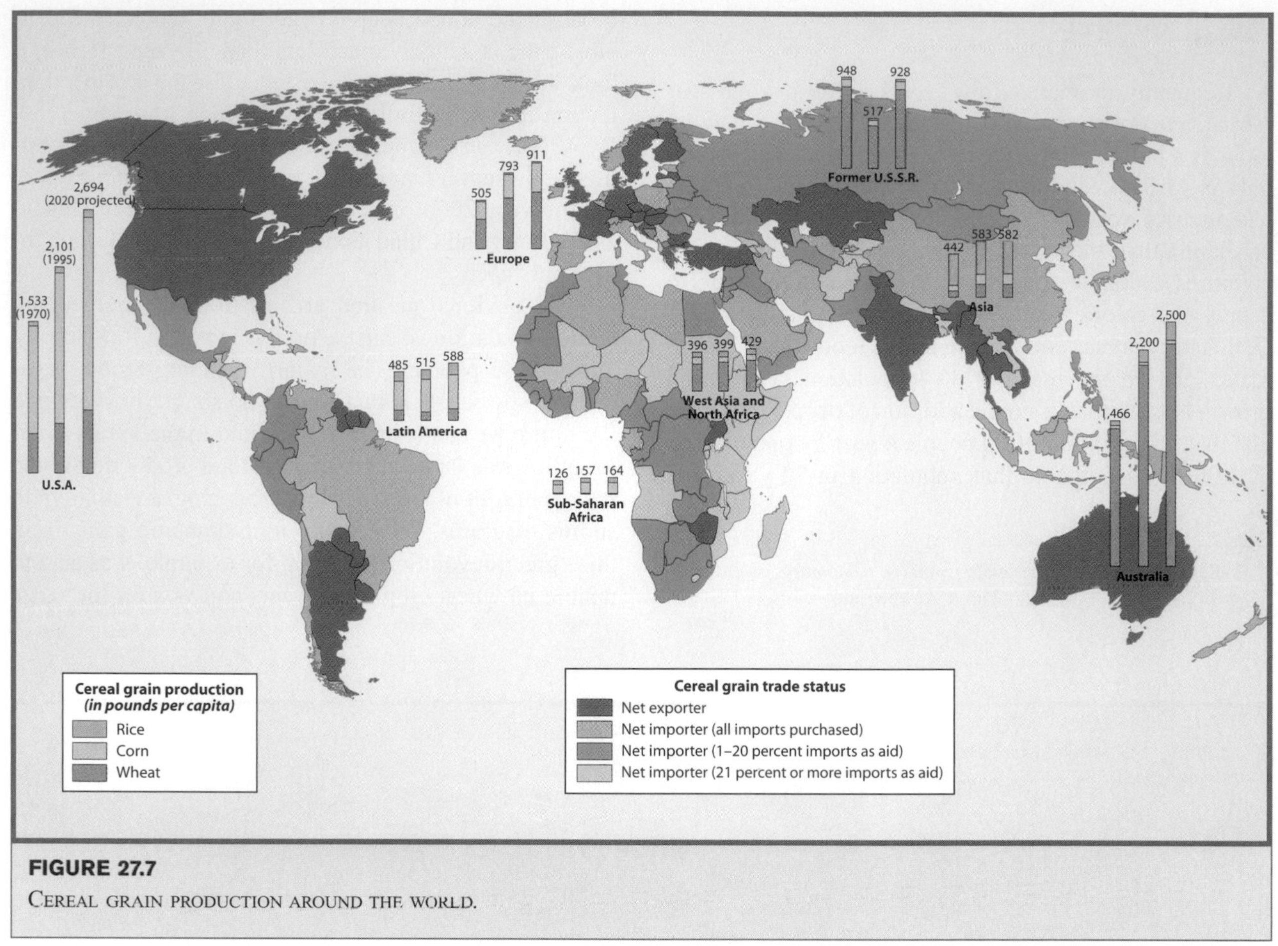

FIGURE 27.7
CEREAL GRAIN PRODUCTION AROUND THE WORLD.

of grain self-sufficiency by 1970—and despite the impressive output of North American agriculture (Figure 27.7), millions of people at the start of the 21st century continue to face malnutrition and starvation. In the United States, meanwhile, *edible* food worth about $85 million is thrown out every day (far more food than is sent out for famine relief), and farms are going out of business in record numbers.

The immediate cause of world hunger has less to do with food production than with warfare and food distribution. For example, several countries of sub-Saharan Africa have been plagued by chronic civil strife. This makes it almost impossible to raise crops as hoards of refugees and soldiers constantly raid fields, often at gunpoint. The other problem is that millions of acres in Africa, Asia, and Latin America once devoted to subsistence farming have been given over to the raising of cash crops for export, to satisfy appetites in the "developed" countries of the world for foods such as coffee, tea, chocolate, bananas, and beef. Those who used to farm the land for their own food needs have been relocated, either to urban areas, where all too often there is no employment for them, or to other areas that are ecologically unsuited for farming. In Africa such lands are often occupied by pastoral nomads; as farmers encroach upon these, insufficient pasturage is left for livestock. The resultant overgrazing, coupled with the clearing of the land for farming, leads to increased loss of both soil and water, with disastrous consequences to nomad and farmer alike. So it is that more than 250 million people can no longer grow crops on their farms, and 1 billion people in 100 countries are in danger of losing their ability to grow crops.[26] In Brazil, which is highly dependent on outside sources of fossil fuels for its energy needs, millions of acres in

[26] Godfrey, T. (2000, December 27). Biotech threatening biodiversity. *Burlington Free Press*, p. 10A.

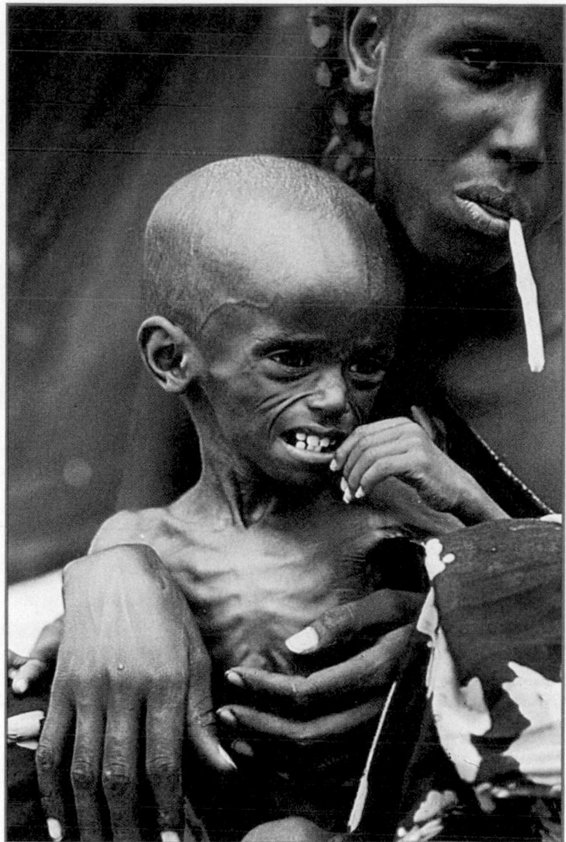

Hunger stalks much of the world as a result of a world food system geared to satisfy an affluent minority in the world's developed nations.

the northeast were taken over for production of sugar used to make alcohol to fuel the vehicles in Rio. The people who were displaced by this were given small holdings in the Amazonian rain forest, where they now are being uprooted to make way for huge ranches on which beef is raised for export.

One strategy urged upon so-called "underdeveloped" countries, especially by government officials and development advisors from the United States, is to adopt the practices that have made North American agriculture so incredibly productive. On the face of it, this seems like a good idea, but it overlooks the fact it requires investment in expensive seeds and chemicals that neither small farmers nor poor countries can afford. Intensive agriculture on the U.S. model requires enormous inputs of chemical fertilizers, pesticides, and herbicides, not to mention fossil fuels needed to run all the mechanized equipment. Even where high production lowers costs, the price is often beyond the reach of poor farmers. It also has other problems: Farming United States style is energy inefficient. For every calorie produced, at least 8—some say as many as 20—calories go into its production and distribution.[27] By contrast, an Asian wet-rice farmer using traditional methods produces 300 calories for each 1 expended. North American agriculture is wasteful of other resources as well: About 30 pounds of fertile topsoil are ruined for every pound of food produced.[28] In the midwestern United States, about 50 percent of the topsoil has been lost over the past 100 years. Meanwhile, toxic substances from chemical nutrients and pesticides pile up in unexpected places, poisoning ground and surface waters, killing fish, birds, and other useful forms of life, upsetting natural ecological cycles, and causing major public-health problems. Despite its spectacular short-term success, serious questions arise about whether such a profligate food production system can be sustained over the long run, even in North America.

Pollution

It is ironic that a life-sustaining activity such as farming should constitute a health hazard, but that is precisely what it becomes when agricultural chemicals poison soils and waters and food additives (over 2,500 are or have been in use) expose people to substances that all too often turn out to be harmful. This, though, is but a part of a larger problem of environmental pollution. Industrial activities are producing highly toxic waste at unprecedented rates, and emissions from factories are poisoning the air. For example, smokestack gases are clearly implicated in "acid rain," which is causing damage to lakes and forests all over northeastern North America. Air containing water vapor with a high acid content is, of course, harmful to the lungs, but the health hazard is greater than this. As surface and ground waters become more acidic, the solubility of lead, cadmium, mercury, and aluminum, all of them toxic, increases sharply. The increase of dissolved aluminum, in particular, is becoming truly massive, and aluminum contamination is high enough on 17% of the world's farmland to be toxic to plants. Moreover, aluminum has been found to be associated with senile dementia as well as Alzheimer's and Parkinson's diseases. Today, these rank as major health problems in the United

[27] Bodley, J. H. (1985). *Anthropology and contemporary human problems* (2nd ed., p. 128). Palo Alto, CA: Mayfield.

[28] Chasin, B. H., & Franke, R. W. (1983). U.S. farming: A world model? *Global Reporter, 1* (2), 10.

Spraying chemicals on crops, as here in California's Central Valley, trades short-term benefits for long-term pollution and health problems.

States. Finally, toxic substances find their way into the world's oceans where they create a health hazard for consumers of seafood. Today, the Inuit are seriously affected by toxins in their bodies from eating fish and sea mammals that have fed in contaminated waters.

Added to this is the problem of global warming—the greenhouse effect—caused primarily by the burning of fossil fuels. Although much is unknown about the extent of global warming, scientists now overwhelmingly agree it is real and that its long-term effects will be harmful. Unfortunately, the response from energy interests has been similar to the campaign carried out for so long by tobacco companies to convince the public that smoking was not hazardous. The energy interests have launched massive public relations campaigns to persuade the public that global warming is not real; as a consequence, it becomes difficult to do anything about it.

As with world hunger, the structural violence from pollution tends to be greatest in the poorer countries of the world, where chemicals banned in countries like the United States are still widely used. Moreover, the industrial countries have taken advantage of lax environmental regulations in "underdeveloped" states to get rid of hazardous wastes. For instance, the president of Benin a decade ago signed a contract with a European waste company to dump toxic and low-grade radioactive waste on the lands of his political opposition.[29] In the United

In opposition to overwhelming scientific opinion, energy interests continue to assert that global warming has not been demonstrated. Given the ties of the current United States president and vice president to the oil industry, it is not surprising that candidate George Bush, in an interview with *Science* (North America's foremost scientific journal), lent his support to the doubters.

States, both government and industry have tried to persuade Indians on reservations experiencing severe economic depression that the solution to their problems lies in allowing disposal of nuclear and other hazardous waste on their lands.

Meanwhile, as manufacturing shifts from the developed to the developing countries of the world, a trend also encouraged by extremely cheap labor as well as fewer safety and environmental regulations, lethal accidents such as the one that occurred in 1988 at Chernobyl, Ukraine, may be expected to increase. Here, a faulty reactor at a nuclear power plant released radiation, causing numerous deaths, relocation of 126,000 people, increased thyroid cancer, and damaged immune systems even 10 years later, increased birth defects, and economic privation for people living as far away (the Arctic Circle) as the Saami, whose reindeer herds were contaminated by radioactive fallout. Indeed, development itself seems to be a health hazard; it is well known that indigenous peoples in Africa, the Pacific Islands, South America, and elsewhere are relatively free from diabetes, obesity, hypertension, and a variety of circulatory diseases until they adopt the ways of the developed countries. Then rates of these "diseases of development" escalate dramatically.

Modern humanity knows the causes of pollution and realizes it is a danger to future survival. Why, then, does not humanity control this evil by which it fouls its own

[29] *Cultural Survival Quarterly*, *15* (4), 5 (1991).

The popularity of sports utility vehicles (SUVs) in North America illustrates how consumers in affluent countries contribute to environmental destruction in the world's poorer countries. In Brazil, chainsaws are used to destroy vast tracts of forest in order to procure wood for production of charcoal. This is required to make the pig iron used in the strongest steel to make SUVs. In addition to the environmental devastation, oppressed labor is used to burn the charcoal.

nest? At least part of the answer lies in philosophical and theological traditions. As we saw in Chapter 23, Western industrialized societies accept the biblical assertion (found in the Qu'ran as well) they have dominion over the earth with all that grows and lives on it, which it is their duty to subdue. These societies are the biggest contributors to global pollution. One North American, for example, consumes hundreds of times the resources of a single African, with all that implies with respect to waste disposal and environmental degradation. Moreover, each person in North America adds, on average, 20 tons of carbon dioxide (a greenhouse gas) a year to the atmosphere. In "underdeveloped" countries, less than 3 tons per person are emitted.[30]

The exploitative worldview, characteristic of all civilizations, extends to all natural resources (Figure 27.8). Only when problems have reached crisis proportions, such as the destruction of the earth's protective ozone layer, have Western peoples protected or replaced what their greed and acquisitiveness have prompted them to take from the environment. In recent years, recognizing the seriousness of the environmental crisis people are creating for themselves, various bodies have passed laws against or restricted such activities as hunting whales out of existence, dumping toxic wastes into streams and rivers, and poisoning the air with harmful fumes. However, most such laws apply to the more affluent countries of the world—the very ones where levels of consumption drive the forces of exploitation responsible for environmental degradation in the poor countries of the world.

A large part of the problem in this and similar situations is people's reluctance to perceive as disadvantageous practices that previously seemed to work well. Frequently, practices carried out on one particular scale or that were suited to a particular context become unsuitable when carried out on another scale or in another context. Because they are trained to look at customs in their broader context, anthropologists would seem to have an important role to play in convincing people that solutions to many problems require changed behavior.

Indigenous peoples, too, may help show us the way. Though they, too, can make mistakes (see the Anthropology Applied box in Chapter 17), they are apt to stand in awe of natural forces, bestowing on them a special place in their religious system. For example, many people believe that rushing rapids, storms, the mountains, and the jungles possess awesome powers. This is also true of fire, which both warms and destroys. For farmers, the sun, rain, and thunder are important to their existence and are often considered divine. Such worldviews are not foolproof checks to the kind of environmental manipulation that causes severe pollution, but they certainly act as powerful restraining influences.

Riot police patrol as the prime minister of France addresses the opening of an international conference on global warming in September 2000. Though it is known that the industrialized countries are the greatest contributors to greenhouse gasses, and that the consequences of global warming will be extremely harmful, governments have yet to take effective steps to deal with the problem.

[30] Broecker, W. S. (1992, April). Global warming on trial. *Natural History*, 14.

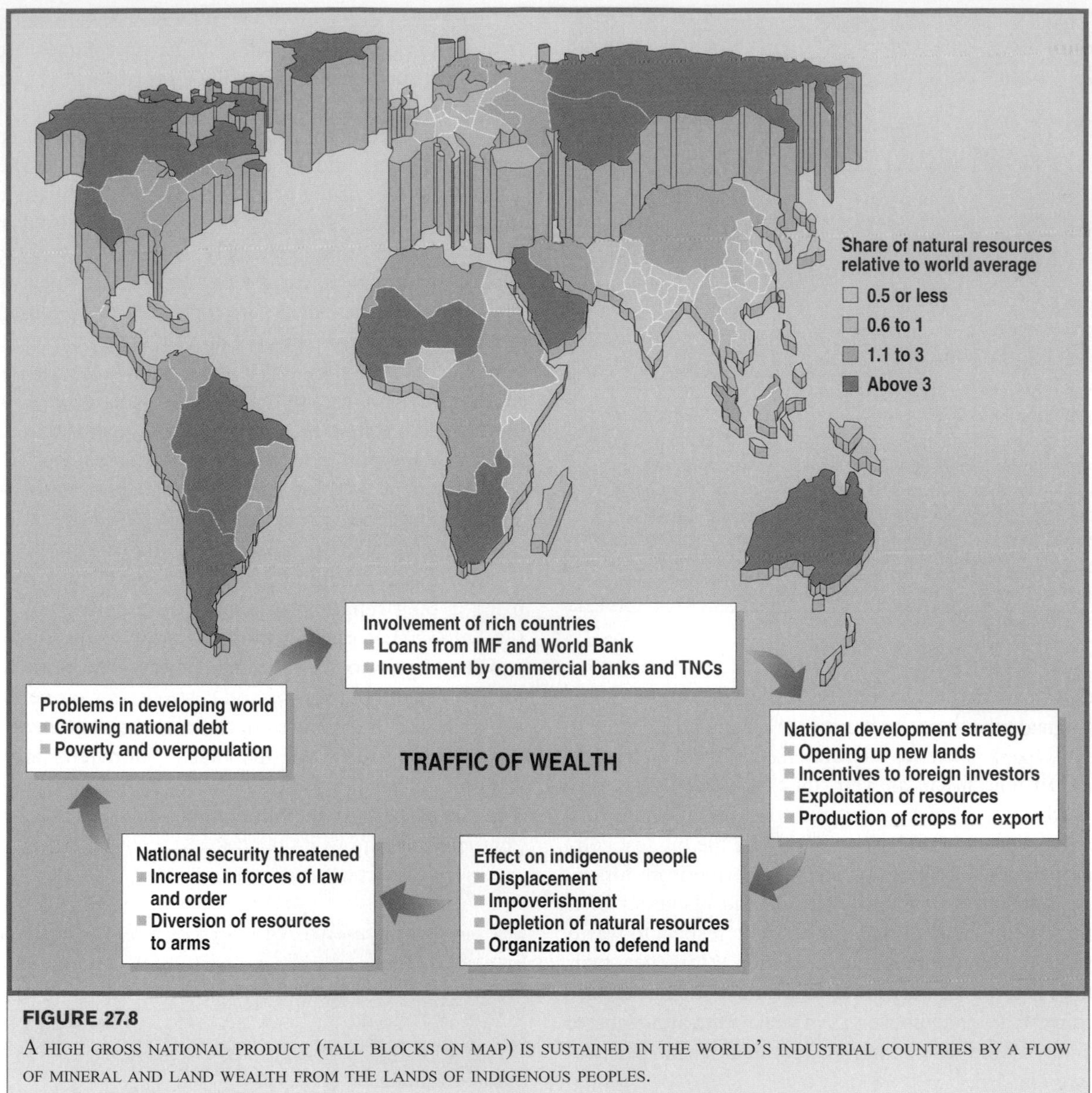

FIGURE 27.8

A HIGH GROSS NATIONAL PRODUCT (TALL BLOCKS ON MAP) IS SUSTAINED IN THE WORLD'S INDUSTRIAL COUNTRIES BY A FLOW OF MINERAL AND LAND WEALTH FROM THE LANDS OF INDIGENOUS PEOPLES.

Population Control

Although the problems discussed so far may not be caused by population growth, they are certainly made worse by it. One reason is that it increases the scale of the problems; thus, the waste a small population generates is far easier to deal with than what a large one generates. Another reason is that population growth often nullifies efforts made to solve the problems, as when increased food production is offset by increased numbers of people to be fed. Although solving the population growth problem does not by itself make the other problems go away, it is unlikely those other problems can be solved unless population growth is arrested.

As our earlier look at population demonstrated, the number of people in the world has increased enormously since the beginning of the industrial age. Prior to 1976, there was no sign of a significant decline in birthrates, with the exception of European and North American populations, where birthrates had dropped below death rates (a balance between the two is required for **replacement reproduction**). The reason that poor people, in particular, tended to have so many children is simple: Children are their main resource. They provide a needed labor pool to work farms, and they are the only source of security for the elderly; hence, having many offspring makes sense (especially if infant mortality rates are high). Historically, people were apt to limit the size of their families only when they became wealthy enough that their money replaced children as their main resource; at that point, children actually *cost* them money. Given this, we can see why birthrates remained high for so long in the world's poorer countries. To those who live in poverty, children are seen as the only hope.

Since 1976 the situation has changed, as birthrates in virtually every industrialized country have dropped below replacement levels (birth and death rates balance out at about 2.1 children per woman). Other encouraging signs are steep declines in the birthrates in countries such as China, one of 19 "underdeveloped" countries where birthrates have actually dropped *below* replacement levels. In Africa, as well as much of south Asia and much of Central and South America (again, the world's poorer countries), birthrates have also declined, but far less dramatically (see Figure 27.6). Examples include Bangladesh, where the rate has fallen from 6.2 to 3.4 (in just 10 years); Tunisia, where the rate has fallen from 7.2 to 2.9; and Mexico, which has moved 80% of the way to replacement level.[31]

Still, despite such improvements, fertility rates remain above replacement, so continual population growth makes it difficult for these countries even to maintain their present per capita share of food and other resources. Even if they could achieve immediate replacement reproduction, their populations would continue to grow for the next 50 years before the age distribution flattened out and zero growth could be achieved. The reason is that even though each woman has fewer children, there are more women having them. This population momentum is exacerbated as life expectancy is improved. Current projections are that global population will peak around 2050 at about 9.37 billion people.

In the modern world, children are not only exploited as a source of cheap labor, but also as soldiers, as in the case of this 12-year-old Liberian boy.

The problem's severity becomes clear when it is realized that the present world population of more than 6 billion people can be sustained only by using up nonrenewable resources, which is like living off income-producing capital. It works for a time, but once the capital is gone, so is the possibility of even having an income to live on.

Desirable though it may be to halt population growth, programs to do so, and their consequences, pose many new problems. These are well illustrated by China's much publicized policy to promote one-child families. Although this has slowed the growth rate of China's population (birthrates are now below replacement level), it has given rise to some serious new problems. One difficulty stems from a basic contradiction to another policy, to raise agricultural productivity by granting more economic autonomy to rural households and the continued existence of families, which (as in old China) are strongly patriarchal. Within such families, men are responsible for farmwork, perpetuation of the male line of descent is considered essential to everyone's well-being, and postmarital residence is strictly patrilocal. Under these circumstances, the birth of male children is considered essential; without them, the household will not have the workforce it needs and will suffer economically. Furthermore, the parents will have no one to support them

[31] Bongaarts, J. (1998). Demographic consequences of declining fertility. *Science, 282*, 419; Wattenberg, B. J. (1997, November 23). The population explosion is over. *New York Times Magazine*, 60.

Replacement reproduction. When birth rates and death rates are in equilibrium; people produce only enough offspring to replace themselves when they die.

As birthrates fall around the world, there will be a rise in the percentage of the elderly, with an attendant rise in health care costs.

once they are too old for physical labor. Daughters are of little use to them, as they will marry out of the household and can offer little aid to their parents. Since married couples are supposed to have only one child, the birth of a daughter is greeted with dismay, for if the couple tries again for a boy, local officials of the state will exert tremendous pressures for the woman to have an abortion and for her or her husband to undergo sterilization.

Not surprisingly, in the face of all this, female infanticide is on the rise in China, and women who bear daughters are often physically and mentally abused by their husbands and mothers-in-law, sometimes to the point of committing suicide. (Although the state teaches that men determine the baby's sex, most rural Chinese believe that the woman is still responsible for the outcome of a birth, perhaps through her diet and behavior.) Women pay in other ways with their bodies; when a second pregnancy occurs, the woman must have the abortion, and usually she is the one sterilized (surgical intervention in men in their prime is discouraged, owing to the importance of their labor in agriculture). This leaves the man free to coerce his daughter-bearing wife into a divorce so that he can try again for a son with a new wife, leaving the old one of no use to anyone and with no son to care for her in old age. One means of preventing a married woman's unauthorized pregnancy is by placement of an intrauterine device (IUD) in her womb. This cannot be removed without official permission, which is hard to get even in the face of compelling medical reasons, since removal is contrary to official Chinese policy. Nor is an attached cord for removal provided, all of which have led to proliferation of back-alley practitioners who remove IUDs with improvised hooks, often leading to infection and death.

If women in rural areas are seen to be of little value, the same is not true where manufacture of goods is an option. For this, female labor is in some demand, and as a consequence, abduction of young women from rural communities has risen dramatically. Although firm figures are hard to get, an estimate for 1993 is that 100,000 women and children were kidnapped in that year.[32] Such women are commonly sold as brides to men in families who then control their labor, either sending them out to bring wages to the family or putting them to work without wages in family enterprises.

The problem of who will care for the elders in their old age is not just a problem for the Chinese but also will be a problem for any society whose birthrates are below replacement level. The inevitable consequence is that the number of old people "explodes" relative to the number of productive people of younger age. Already the United States is beginning to worry about this. Care of the elderly is expensive, but fewer young exist to assume the costs. Where will the money come from? As yet, nobody knows.

---

[32] Gates, H. (1996). Buying brides in China–again. *Anthropology Today*, *12* (4), 9.

The Culture of Discontent

Despite the difficulties, stabilization of the world's population appears to be a necessary step if the future's problems are ever to be solved. Without this, whatever else is done, the world's inability to provide enough food seems inevitable. Up until about 1950, growth in the world's food supply came almost entirely from expanding the amount of land under cultivation. Since then, it has come increasingly from high-energy inputs of chemical fertilizers that new high-yield varieties of crops depend upon, of pesticides and herbicides, and of fuel to run tractors and other mechanical equipment, including irrigation pumps. The source of almost all this energy is oil, yet, although the demand for food is projected to rise until at least the middle of the 21st century, oil supplies are diminishing and becoming more expensive. Surely, these trends will continue.

Insufficient food supplies are bound to result in increased structural violence in the form of higher death rates in the world's "underdeveloped" countries. This surely will have an impact on the "developed" countries, with their relatively stable populations and high living standards. It is hard to imagine how such countries could exist peacefully side by side with others experiencing high death rates and abysmally low living standards. (In 1993, 1.3 billion people lived on less than $1 per day and another 3 billion lived on less than $2 per day; the situation today is no better.[33]) Already, the combination of overpopulation and poverty is causing a rising tide of migration from the impoverished to the more affluent countries of Europe and North America, with a consequent rise of intolerance, antiforeign feeling, and general social unrest.

Necessary though birth control may be for solving problems of the future, there is no reason to suppose that it will be sufficient by itself. The result would be only to stabilize conditions as they are. The problem is twofold. For the past several years, the world's poor countries have been sold on the idea they should enjoy a standard of living comparable to that of the rich countries. Yet, the resources necessary to maintain such a standard of living are running out. As we saw in the last chapter, this situation has led to the creation of a culture of discontent, whereby people's aspirations far exceed their opportunities. The problem involves not just population growth outstripping food supplies, but it is also one of unequal access to decent jobs, housing, sanitation, health care, and adequate police and fire protection. And it is one of steady deterioration of the natural environment as a result of increasing industrialization and overuse of the land.

Some dramatic changes in cultural values and motivations, as well as in social institutions, are required. The emphasis on individual self-interest, materialism, and conspicuous production, acquisition, and consumption, characteristic of the world's affluent countries, needs to be abandoned in favor of a more human self-image and social ethic. These can be created from values still found in many of the world's non-Western cultures. Such values include a worldview that sees humanity as part of the natural world rather than superior to it. Included, too, is a sense of social responsibility that recognizes that no individual, people, or state has the right to expropriate resources at the expense of others. Finally, an awareness is needed of how important supportive ties are for individuals, such as seen in kinship or other associations in the world's traditional societies. Is humanity up to the challenge? Who knows, but it appears significant changes are bound to come, one way or another.

---

[33] Swaminathan, M. S. (2000). Science in response to basic human needs. *Science*, *287*, 425.

CHAPTER SUMMARY

Since future forms of culture will be shaped by decisions humans have yet to make, they cannot be predicted with any accuracy. Thus, instead of trying to foretell the future, a number of anthropologists are attempting to gain a better understanding of the existing world situation so that decisions may be made intelligently. Anthropologists are especially well suited for this, owing to their experience at seeing things in context, their long-term historical perspective, their ability to recognize culture-bound biases, and their familiarity with cultural alternatives.

However humanity changes biologically, culture remains the chief means by which humans try to solve their problems of existence. Some anthropologists are concerned that there is a trend for the problems to outstrip any culture's ability to find solutions. Rapid developments in communication, transportation, and world trade, some believe, will link people together to the point that a single world culture will result. Their thinking is that such a homogenized superculture would offer fewer chances for conflict between peoples than in the past. Most anthropologists are skeptical of such an argument, in view of the recent tendency for ethnic groups to reassert their own distinctive identities and in view of the persistence of traditional ways of thinking about oneself and others, even in the face of massive changes in other aspects of culture. Anthropologists also are concerned about peoples' tendency to treat many of the world's traditional societies as obsolete when they appear to stand in the way of "development."

Another alternative is for humanity to move in the direction of cultural pluralism, where more than one culture exists in a society. To work, cultural pluralism must reject bigotry, bias, and racism. Some anthropologists maintain that pluralistic arrangements are the only feasible means for achieving global equilibrium and peace. A problem associated with cultural pluralism is ethnocentrism. All too often, in the name of "nation building," it has led one group to impose its control on others. Common consequences are prolonged, violent, and bloody political upheavals, including genocide.

Viewing the world today reveals a picture strikingly similar to South Africa's former system of apartheid. This global apartheid serves to maintain the dominance of a largely White minority over a mostly non-White majority through the social, economic, political, military, and cultural constitution of the current "global society."

One consequence of any apartheid system is a great deal of structural violence exerted by situations, institutions, and social, political, and economic structures. Such violence involves phenomena including overpopulation and food shortages, which anthropologists are actively working to understand and help alleviate. One challenge the world over is to provide food resources to keep pace with the burgeoning population. The immediate problem, though, is not so much one of producing enough food as it is political turmoil and a food-distribution system geared to the satisfaction of appetites in the world's richest countries at the expense of those living in poorer countries.

Pollution has become a direct threat to humanity. Western peoples have protected their environments only when some crisis forced them to do so, and even at that their rates of consumption continue to drive environmental degradation in other countries. Western societies have felt no long-term responsibilities toward the earth or its resources and could learn much from those non-Western peoples who see themselves as integral parts of the earth.

Meeting the problems of structural violence that beset the human species today probably can be done only if we continue to reduce the birthrate. Effective birth-control methods are now available. Whether or not these methods are used on a vast enough scale depends on their availability and acceptance. Many of the world's developing countries have policies aimed at controlling population growth, but these sometimes conflict with other policies, and in any case give rise to new kinds of problems. Even if replacement reproduction were immediately achieved, populations would continue to grow for another 50 years.

Solving the problems of the global society depends also on lessening the gap between the living standards of impoverished and developed countries. This calls for dramatic changes in the values of Western societies, with their materialistic consumer orientation. All people need to see themselves as a part of nature rather than as superior to it. Also needed are a social responsibility that recognizes that no people has a right to expropriate important resources at the expense of others and an awareness of how important supportive ties are between individuals.

CLASSIC READINGS

Bodley, J. H. (1985). *Anthropology and contemporary human problems* (2nd ed.). Palo Alto, CA: Mayfield.

Anthropologist Bodley examines some of the most serious problems in the world today: overconsumption, resource depletion, hunger and starvation, overpopulation, violence and war.

Bodley, J. H. (1990). *Victims of progress* (3rd. ed.). Mountain View, CA: Mayfield.

This book explores the impact of industrial civilization on the world's indigenous peoples and how the latter are organizing to protect themselves.

Davis, S. H. (1982). *Victims of the miracle*. Cambridge: Cambridge University Press.

An anthropologist looks at Brazil's efforts to develop the Amazon region, the motivations behind those efforts, and their impact on indigenous peoples. Davis pays special attention to the role played by multinational corporations, how they relate to the Brazilian government, and who benefits from it all.

Maybury-Lewis, D. (ed.) (1984). *The prospects for plural societies* (1982 Proceedings of the American Ethnological Society). American Ethnological Society.

In 1982, a group of anthropologists met to discuss one of the most crucial issues of our time, the prospects for multiethnic societies. What emerged as the "villain" of the conference was the state—not just particular countries but states as a kind of political structure and the hold they have over modern thought and political action. Maybury-Lewis confronts this issue in the concluding essay, which by itself makes this volume worth obtaining.

Miller, S. (ed.) (1993). *State of the peoples: A global human rights report on societies in danger*. Boston: Beacon Press.

This important publication from *Cultural Survival* systematically reports on the situation of indigenous people throughout the world, region by region. Also included are "expert" articles on critical issues affecting such diverse peoples as Bosnians and Bushmen, all sorts of useful maps and charts, and suggested solutions to many challenges facing indigenous peoples. A "must read" for anyone who is in any way concerned with the "New World Disorder."

GLOSSARY

"Absolute" or chronometric dates: In archaeology and paleoanthropology, dates for archaeological materials based on solar years, centuries, or other units of absolute time.

Acculturation: Major culture changes that people are forced to make as a consequence of intensive, firsthand contact between societies.

Acheulean tradition: The toolmaking tradition of Homo erectus in Africa, Europe, and Southwest Asia in which handaxes were developed from the earlier Oldowan chopper.

Action theory: The theory that self-serving actions by forceful leaders play a role in civilization's emergence.

Adaptation: A process by which organisms achieve a beneficial adjustment to an available environment; also the results of that process the characteristics of organisms that fit them to the particular set of conditions of the environment in which they are generally found.

Adaptive radiation: Rapid diversification of an evolving population as it adapts to a variety of available niches.

Adjudication: Mediation with an unbiased third party making the ultimate decision.

Affinal kin: Relatives by marriage.

Age grade: An organized category of people based on age; every individual passes through a series of such categories over his or her lifetime.

Age sets: Groups of persons simultaneously initiated into age grades at the same time and who move through the series of categories together.

Alleles: Alternate forms of a single gene.

Altered fossils: Remains of plants and animals that lived in the past that have been altered, as by the replacement of organic material by calcium carbonate or silica.

Ambilineal descent: Descent in which the individual may affiliate with either the mother's or the father's descent group.

Ambilocal residence: A pattern in which a married couple may choose either matrilocal or patrilocal residence.

Amino acid racemization dating: In archaeology and paleoanthropology, a technique for chronometric dating that measures the ratio of right- to left-handed amino acids.

Analogies: In biology, structures that are superficially similar; the result of convergent evolution.

Animatism: A belief that the world is animated by impersonal supernatural powers.

Animism: A belief in spirit beings thought to animate nature.

Anthropology: The study of humankind, in all times and places.

Anthropomorphism: The ascription of human attributes to nonhuman beings.

Applied anthropology: The use of anthropological knowledge and methods to solve practical problems, often for a specific client.

Arboreal: Tree-dwelling.

Archaeology: The study of material remains, usually from the past, to describe and explain human behavior.

Archaic cultures: Term used to refer to Mesolithic cultures in the Americas.

Ardipithecus ramidus: Probable early hominine; lived about 5.8 to 4.4 million years ago.

Artifact: Any object fashioned or altered by humans.

Aurignacian tradition: Toolmaking tradition in Europe and western Asia at the beginning of the Upper Paleolithic.

Australopithecus: The first well-known hominine; lived between 4.2 and 1 million years ago. Characterized by bipedal locomotion when on the ground, but with an apelike brain; includes at least five species: *afarensis, africanus, anamensis, boisei,* and *robustus.*

Avunculocal residence: Residence of a married couple with the husband's mother's brother.

Balanced reciprocity: A mode of exchange in which the giving and the receiving are specific as to the value of the goods and the time of their delivery.

Band: A small group of related households occupying a particular region that gather periodically on an ad hoc basis but that do not yield their sovereignty to the larger collective.

Baton method: The technique of stone tool manufacture performed by striking the raw material with a bone or antler "baton" to remove flakes.

Blade technique: A technique of stone tool manufacture by which long, parallel-sided flakes are struck off the edges of a specially prepared core.

Bound morpheme: A sound that can occur in a language only in combination with other sounds, as s in English to signify the plural.

Brachiate: To use the arms to move from branch to branch, with the body hanging suspended beneath the arms.

Bride-price: Compensation the groom or his family pays to the bride's family upon marriage.

Bride service: A designated period of time after marriage when the groom works for the bride's family.

Bronze Age: In the Old World, the period marked by the production of tools and ornaments of bronze; began about 3000 b.c. in China and Southwest Asia and about 500 years earlier in Southeast Asia.

Carrying capacity: The number of people who can be supported by the available resources at a given level of technology.

Caste: A special form of social class in which membership is determined by birth and remains fixed for life.

Catarrhini: A haplorhine infraorder that includes Old World monkeys, apes, and humans.

Chiefdom: A regional polity in which two or more local groups are organized under a single chief, who is at the head of a ranked hierarchy of people.

Chromosome: In the cell nucleus, long strands of DNA combined with a protein that can be seen under the microscope.

Civilization: In anthropology a type of society marked by the presence of cities, social classes, and the state.

Clan: A noncorporate descent group whose members claim descent from a common ancestor without actually knowing the genealogical links to that ancestor.

Clavicle: The collarbone.

Closed-class societies: Stratified societies that severely restrict social mobility.

Code switching: The process of changing from one level of language to another.

Codon: Three-base sequence of a gene that specifies production of an amino acid.

Cognitive capacity: A broad concept including intelligence, educability, concept formation, self-awareness, self-evaluation, attention span, sensitivity in discrimination, and creativity.

Cold-blooded: Animals whose body temperature rises or falls according to the temperature of the surrounding environment.

Common-interest associations: Associations not based on age, kinship, marriage, or territory but result from an act of joining.

Conjugal bond: The bond between two individuals who are married.

Conjugal family: A family consisting of one (or more) man (who may be a female) married to one (or more) woman (who may be a male), and their offspring.

Consanguine family: A family consisting of related women, their brothers, and the offspring of the women.

Consanguineal kin: Relatives by birth; so-called "blood" relatives.

Conspicuous consumption: A term coined by Thorstein Veblen to describe the display of wealth for social prestige.

Construal: In the second stage of trance, the process by which the brain tries to "make sense" of entoptic images.

Contagious magic: Magic based on the principle that things once in contact can influence one another after separation.

Convergence: A process by which unrelated populations develop similarities to one another.

Convergent evolution: In cultural evolution, the development of similar adaptations to similar environmental conditions by peoples whose ancestral cultures were quite different.

Core values: Those values especially promoted by a particular culture.

Core vocabulary: In language, pronouns, lower numerals, and names for body parts and natural objects.

Cranium: The brain case of the skull.

Cro-Magnons: Europeans of the Upper Paleolithic after about 36,000 years ago.

Crow system: Kinship classification usually associated with matrilineal descent in which a father's sister and father's sister's daughter are called by the same term, a mother and mother's sister are merged under another, and a father and father's brother are lumped in a third. Parallel cousins are equated with brothers and sisters.

Cultural anthropology: The branch of anthropology that focuses on humans as a culture-making species.

Cultural control: Control through beliefs and values deeply internalized in the minds of individuals.

Cultural ecology: The study of the interaction of specific human cultures with their environment.

Cultural pluralism: Social and political interaction of people with different ways of living and thinking within the same society.

Cultural relativism: The thesis that one must suspend judgement on other peoples' practices in order to understand them in their own cultural terms.

Culture: The values, beliefs, and perceptions of the world shared by members of a society, that they use to interpret experience and generate behavior, and that are reflected in their behavior.

Culture area: A geographic region in which a number of different societies follow similar patterns of life.

Culture-bound: Theories about the world and reality based on the assumptions and values of one's own culture.

Culture core: The features of a culture that play a part in matters relating to the society's way of making a living.

Culture type: The view of a culture in terms of the relation of its particular technology to the environment exploited by that technology.

Datum point: The starting, or reference, point for a grid system.

Dendrochronology: In archaeology, a method of chronometric dating based on the number of rings of growth found in a tree trunk.

Density of social relations: Roughly, the number and intensity of interactions among the members of a camp or other residential unit.

Dependence training: Child-rearing practices that foster compliance in the performance of assigned tasks and dependence on the domestic group, rather than reliance on oneself.

Descent group: Any publicly recognized social entity requiring lineal descent from a particular real or mythical ancestor for membership.

Dialects: Varying forms of a language that reflect particular regions or social classes and that are similar enough to be mutually intelligible.

Diffusion: The spread of customs or practices from one culture to another.

Displacement: The ability to refer to things and events removed in time and space.

Divergent or branching evolution: An evolutionary process in which an ancestral population gives rise to two or more descendant populations that differ from one another.

Divination: A magical procedure for determining the cause of a particular event, such as illness, or foretelling the future.

DNA: The genetic material, deoxyribonucleic acid; a complex molecule with information to direct the synthesis of proteins. DNA molecules have the unique property of being able to produce exact copies of themselves.

Domestication: An evolutionary process whereby humans modify, either intentionally or unintentionally, the genetic makeup of a population of plants or animals, sometimes to the extent that members of the population are unable to survive and/or reproduce without human assistance.

Double descent: A system tracing descent matrilineally for some purposes and patrilineally for others.

Dowry: Payment of a woman's inheritance at the time of her marriage, either to her or to her husband.

Ecological niche: A species' way of life considered in the context of its environment, including other species found in that environment.

Ecosystem: A system, or a functioning whole, composed of both the physical environment and the organisms living within it.

Egalitarian societies: Social systems that have as many valued positions as persons capable of filling them.

Electron spin resonance: In archaeology and paleoanthropology, a technique for chronometric dating that measures the number of trapped electrons in bone or shell.

Enculturation: The process by which a society's culture is passed from one generation to the next and individuals become members of their society.

Endocast: A cast of the inside of a skull; helps determine the size and shape of the brain.

Endogamy: Marriage within a particular group or category of individuals.

Entoptic phenomena: Bright pulsating forms that are generated by the central nervous system and seen in states of trance.

Enzyme: Proteins that initiate and direct chemical reactions in an organism.

Epicanthic eye fold: A fold of skin at the inner corner of the eye that covers the true corner of the eye; common in Asiatic populations.

Epics: Long oral narratives, sometimes in poetry or rhythmic prose, recounting the glorious events in the life of a real or legendary person.

Eskimo system: System of kinship terminology, also called lineal system, that emphasizes the nuclear family by specifically identifying the mother, father, brother, and sister, while lumping together all other relatives into broad categories such as uncle, aunt, and cousin.

Estrus: In primate females, the time of sexual receptivity during which ovulation takes place.

Ethnic psychoses: Mental disorders specific to particular ethnic groups.

Ethnocentrism: The belief that the ways of one's own culture are the only proper ones.

Ethnography: The systematic description of a particular culture based on firsthand observation.

Ethnohistory: The study of cultures of the recent past through oral histories; accounts left by explorers, missionaries, and traders; and analysis of such records as land titles, birth and death records, and other archival materials.

Ethnolinguistics: The study of the relation between language and culture.

Ethnologist: An anthropologist who studies cultures from a comparative or historical point of view, utilizing ethnographic accounts.

Ethnomusicology: The study of a society's music in terms of its cultural setting.

Ethnoscientists: Anthropologists who seek to understand the principles behind native idea systems and the ways those principles inform a people about their environment and help them survive.

Evolution: Descent with modification.

Exogamy: Marriage outside the group.

Extended family: A collection of nuclear families, related by ties of blood, that live together in one household.

Fact: An observation verified by several observers skilled in the necessary techniques of observation.

Family: A residential kin group composed of a woman, her dependent children, and at least one adult male joined through marriage or blood relationship.

Faunal region: A geographic region with its own distinctive assemblage of animal life, not precisely like that of other regions.

Fission: The splitting of a descent group into two or more new descent groups.

Flotation: An archeological technique employed to recover very tiny objects by immersion of soil samples in water to separate heavy from light particles.

Fluorine test: In archaeology or paleoanthropology, a technique for relative dating based on the fact that the amount of fluorine in bones is proportional to their age.

Folklore: A 19th-century term first used to refer to the traditional oral stories and sayings of the European peasant, and later extended to those traditions preserved orally in all societies.

Folkloristics: The study of folklore (as linguistics is the study of language).

Foramen magnum: A large opening in the skull through which the spinal cord passes and connects to the brain.

Forensic anthropology: Field of applied physical anthropology that specializes in the identification of human skeletal remains for legal purposes.

Form classes: The parts of speech or categories of words that work the same way in any sentence.

Fossil: The preserved remains of plants and animals that lived in the past.

Fossil locality: In paleoanthropology, a place where fossils are found.

Fovea centralis: A shallow pit in the retina of the eye that enables an animal to focus on an object while maintaining visual contact with its surroundings.

Frame substitution: A method used to identify the syntactic units of language. For example, a category called "nouns" may be established as anything that will fit the substitution frame "I see a . . . "

Free morphemes: Morphemes that can occur unattached in a language; for example, "dog" and "cat" are free morphemes in English.

Gender: The elaborations and meanings assigned by cultures to the biological differentiation of the sexes.

Gene flow: The introduction of alleles from the gene pool of one population into that of another.

Gene pool: The genetic variants available to a population.

Genera; genus: In the system of plant and animal classification, a group of like species.

Generalized reciprocity: A mode of exchange in which the value of the gift is not calculated, nor is the time of repayment specified.

Genes: Portions of DNA molecules that direct the synthesis of proteins. DNA molecules have the unique property of being able to produce exact copies of themselves.

Genetic code: The sequence of DNA bases that specifies production of a particular amino acid.

Genetic drift: Chance fluctuations of allele frequencies in the gene pool of a population.

Genocide: The extermination of one people by another, often in the name of "progress," either as a deliberate act or as the accidental outcome of activities carried out by one people with little regard for their impact on others.

Genome: The complete sequence of DNA for a species.

Genotype: The actual genetic makeup of an organism.

Genus *Homo:* Hominine genus characterized by expansion of brain, reduction of jaws, and reliance on cultural adaptation; includes at least three species: *habilis, erectus,* and *sapiens.*

Glottochronology: In linguistics, a method of dating divergence in branches of language families.

Gracile Australopithecines: Smaller, more lightly built members of the genus Australopithecus.

Grammar: The entire formal structure of a language consisting of all observations about the morphemes and syntax.

Grid system: A system for recording data from an archaeological excavation.

Group marriage: Marriage in which several men and women have sexual access to one another.

Haplorhini: A primate suborder that includes tarsiers, monkeys, apes, and humans.

Hardy-Weinberg principle: Demonstrates algebraically that the percentage of individuals that are homozygous for the dominant allele, homozygous for the recessive allele, and heterozygous should remain constant from one generation to the next, provided that certain specified conditions are met.

Hawaiian system: Kinship reckoning in which all relatives of the same sex and generation are referred to by the same term.

Hemoglobin: The protein that carries oxygen in the red blood cells.

Heterozygous: Refers to a chromosome pair that bears different alleles for a single gene.

Holistic perspective: A fundamental principle of anthropology, that the various parts of culture must be viewed in the broadest possible context in order to understand their interconnections and interdependence.

Home range: The area within which a group of primates usually moves.

Hominid: Hominoid family to which humans alone used to be assigned; now includes African apes and humans, with the latter assigned to the subfamily Homininae.

Hominine: Member of the Homininae, the subfamily of hominids to which humans belong.

Hominoid: A catarrhine primate superfamily that includes apes and humans.

Homo habilis: Earliest representative of the genus *Homo;* lived between 2.4 and 1.6 million years ago. Characterized by expansion and reorganization of the brain, compared to *Australopithecus.*

Homologies: In biology, structures possessed by two different organisms that arise in similar fashion and pass through similar stages during embryonic development.

Homozygous: Refers to a chromosome pair that bears identical alleles for a single gene.

Horticulture: Cultivation of crops using hand tools such as digging sticks or hoes.

Household: The basic residential unit in which economic production, consumption, inheritance, child rearing, and shelter are organized and carried out; may or may not be synonymous with family.

Hydraulic theory: The theory that sees civilization's emergence as the result of the construction of elaborate irrigation systems, the functioning of which required full-time managers whose control blossomed into the first governing body and elite social class.

Hypoglossal canal. The opening in the skull through which the tongue-controlling hypoglossal nerve passes.

Hypothesis: A tentative explanation of the relation between certain phenomena.

Iconic images: Hallucinations of people, animals, and monsters, "seen" in the deepest stage of trance.

Imitative magic: Magic based on the principle that like produces like. Sometimes called sympathetic magic.

Incest taboo: The prohibition of sexual relations between specified individuals, usually parent-child and sibling relations at a minimum.

Incorporation: In rites of passage, reincorporation of the individual into society in his or her new status.

Independence training: Child-rearing practices that promote independence, self-reliance, and personal achievement on the part of the child.

Informal economy: The production of marketable commodities that for various reasons escape enumeration, regulation, or any other sort of public monitoring or auditing.

Informants: Members of a society in which the ethnographer works who help interpret what she or he sees taking place.

Integrative mechanisms: Cultural mechanisms that oppose forces for differentiation in a society; in modernizing societies, they include formal governmental structures, official state ideologies, political parties, legal codes, labor and trade unions, and other common-interest associations.

Intensive agriculture: Intensive farming of large plots of land, employing fertilizers, plows, and/or extensive irrigation.

Interspecies gene transfer: Transfer of DNA as when retroviruses insert DNA into the cells of one species from another.

Iroquois system: Kinship terminology wherein a father and father's brother are given a single term, as are a mother and mother's sister, but a father's sister and mother's brother are given separate terms. Parallel cousins are classified with brothers and sisters, while cross cousins are classified separately, but (unlike Crow and Omaha kinship) not equated with relatives of some other generation.

Isolating mechanisms: Factors that separate breeding populations, thereby preventing gene flow, creating divergent subspecies and ultimately (if maintained) divergent species.

Kenyanthropus platyops: Hominine contemporary with early Australopithecines; not certainly a separate species.

Kindred: A group of consanguineal kin linked by their relationship to one living individual; includes both maternal and paternal kin.

Kinesics: A system of notating and analyzing postures, facial expressions, and body motions that convey messages.

Lactase: An enzyme in the small intestine that enables humans to assimilate lactose.

Lactose: The primary constituent of fresh milk.

Language family: A group of languages that are ultimately descended from a single ancestral language.

Language: A system of communication using sounds or gestures that are put together in meaningful ways according to a set of rules.

Law: Formal negative sanctions.

Law of competitive exclusion: When two closely related species compete for the same niche, one will out-compete the other, bringing about the latter's extinction.

Law of dominance and recessiveness: Certain alleles are able to mask the presence of others.

Law of independent assortment: Genes controlling different traits are inherited independently of one another.

Law of segregation: Variants of genes for a particular trait retain their separate identities through the generations.

Legends: Stories told as true, set in the postcreation world.

Lemuriformes: A strepsirhine infraorder that includes lemurs and lorises.

Levalloisian technique: Toolmaking technique by which three or four long triangular flakes were detached from a specially prepared core. Developed by humans transitional from *Homo erectus* to *Homo sapiens*.

Leveling mechanism: A societal obligation compelling a family to distribute goods so that no one accumulates more wealth than anyone else.

Levirate: A marriage custom according to which a widow marries a brother of her dead husband (a man marries his dead brother's widow).

Lineage: A corporate descent group whose members trace their genealogical links to a common ancestor.

Linear evolution: A sustained directional shift in a population's average characteristics.

Linguistic anthropology: The branch of cultural anthropology that studies human language.

Linguistic divergence: The development of different languages from a single ancestral language.

Linguistic nationalism: The attempt by ethnic minorities, and even countries to proclaim independence by purging their languages of foreign terms.

Linguistic relativity: The proposition that diverse interpretations of reality embodied in languages yield demonstrable influences on thought.

Linguistics: The modern scientific study of all aspects of language.

Lower Paleolithic: The first part of the Old Stone Age; its beginning is marked by the appearance 2.6 million years ago of Oldowan tools.

Maritime Archaic culture: An Archaic culture of northeastern North America, centered on the Gulf of St. Lawrence, that emphasized the utilization of marine resources.

Market exchange: The buying and selling of goods and services, with prices set by powers of supply and demand.

Marriage: A relationship between one or more men (male or female) and one or more women (female or male) who are recognized by society as having a continuing claim to the right of sexual access to one another.

Matrilateral cross-cousin marriage: Marriage of a woman to her father's sister's son, or a man to his mother's brother's daughter (her cross-cousin on the paternal side, his cross-cousin on the maternal side).

Matrilineal descent: Descent traced exclusively through the female line to establish group membership.

Matrilocal residence: A residence pattern in which a married couple lives in the locality associated with the wife's relatives.

Mediation: Settlement of a dispute through negotiation assisted by an unbiased third party.

Meiosis: A kind of cell division that produces the sex cells, each of which has half the number of chromosomes, and hence genes, as the parent cell.

Melanin: The chemical responsible for dark skin pigmentation, which helps protect against damage from ultraviolet radiation.

Mesolithic: The Middle Stone Age of Europe and Southwest Asia; began about 12,000 years ago.

Microlith: A small blade of flint or similar stone, several of which were hafted together in wooden handles to make tools; widespread in the Mesolithic.

Middle Paleolithic: The middle part of the Old Stone Age characterized by the emergence of archaic *H. sapiens* and the development of the Mousterian tradition of toolmaking.

Mitosis: A kind of cell division that produces new cells having exactly the same number of chromosome pairs, and hence genes, as the parent cell.

Mobility: The ability to change one's class position.

Modal personality: The personality typical of a society as indicated by the central tendency of a defined frequency distribution.

Modernization: The process of cultural and socioeconomic change, whereby developing societies acquire some of the characteristics of Western industrialized societies.

Moiety: Each group that results from a division of a society into two halves on the basis of descent.

Money: Anything used to make payments for other things (goods or labor) as well as to measure their value; may be special purpose or multipurpose.

Monogamy: Marriage in which an individual has a single spouse.

Morphemes: In linguistics, the smallest units of sound that carry a meaning.

Motif: A story situation in a folktale.

Mousterian tradition: Toolmaking tradition of the Neandertals and their contemporaries of Europe, western Asia, and northern Africa, featuring flake tools that are lighter and smaller than earlier Levalloisian flake tools.

Mutation: Chance alteration of a gene that produces a new allele.

Myth: A sacred narrative explaining how the world came to be in its present form.

Nation: Communities of people who see themselves as "one people" on the basis of common ancestry, history, society, institutions, ideology, language, territory, and (often) religion.

Natufian culture: A Mesolithic culture of Israel, Lebanon, and western Syria, between about 12,500 and 10,200 years ago.

Natural selection: The evolutionary process through which factors in the environment exert pressure that favors some individuals over others to produce the next generation.

Neandertals: Representatives of "archaic" *Homo sapiens* in Europe and western Asia, living from about 130,000 years ago to about 35,000 years ago.

Negative reciprocity: A form of exchange in which the giver tries to get the better of the exchange.

Negotiation: The use of direct argument and compromise by the parties to a dispute to arrive voluntarily at a mutually satisfactory agreement.

Neolithic period: The New Stone Age; began about 11,000 years ago in Southwest Asia.

Neolocal residence: A pattern in which a married couple may establish their household in a location apart from either the husband's or the wife's relatives.

Notochord: A rodlike structure of cartilage that, in vertebrates, is replaced by the vertebral column.

Nuclear family: A family unit consisting of husband, wife, and dependent children.

Oldowan tool tradition: The earliest identifiable stone tools.

Omaha system: The patrilineal equivalent of the Crow system; the line of a mother's patrilineal kin are equated across generations.

Open-class societies: Stratified societies that permit a great deal of social mobility.

Orrorin tugenensis: Possible hominine; lived 6 million years ago.

Paleoanthropologist: An anthropologist who studies human evolution from fossil remains.

Paleoindian: The earliest inhabitants of North America.

Paleolithic: The Old Stone Age, characterized by manufacture and use of chipped stone tools.

Palynology: In archaeology and paleoanthropology, a method of relative dating based on changes in fossil pollen over time.

Pantheon: The several gods and goddesses of a people.

Paralanguage: The extralinguistic noises that accompany language, for example, those of crying or laughing.

Parallel evolution: In cultural evolution, the development of similar adaptations to similar environmental conditions by peoples whose ancestral cultures were similar.

Participant observation: In ethnography, the technique of learning a people's culture through direct participation in their everyday life over an extended period of time.

Pastoralist: Member of a society in which the herding of grazing animals is regarded as the ideal way of making a living, and in which movement of all or part of the society is considered a normal and natural way of life.

Patrilateral parallel-cousin marriage: Marriage of a man to his father's brother's daughter, or a woman to her father's brother's son (i.e., to a parallel cousin on the paternal side).

Patrilineal descent: Descent traced exclusively through the male line to establish group membership.

Patrilocal residence: A residence pattern in which a married couple lives in the locality associated with the husband's father's relatives.

Patterns of affect: How people feel about themselves and others.

Pentadactyly: Possessing five digits (fingers and toes).

Percussion method: A technique of stone tool manufacture performed by striking the raw material with a hammerstone or by striking raw material against a stone anvil to remove flakes.

Personality: The distinctive way a person thinks, feels, and behaves.

Phenotype: The physical appearance of an organism that may or may not reflect a particular genotype because the latter may or may not include recessive alleles.

Phonemes: In linguistics, the smallest classes of sound that make a difference in meaning.

Phonetics: The study of the production, transmission, and reception of speech sounds.

Phratry: A unilineal descent group composed of two or more clans that claim to be of common ancestry. If only two such groups exist, each is a moiety.

Physical anthropology: The systematic study of humans as biological organisms.

Platyrrhini: A haplorhine infraorder that includes the New World monkeys.

Pluralistic societies: Societies in which there exist a diversity of cultural patterns.

Polyandry: Marriage of a woman to two or more men at one time; a form of polygamy.

Polygenetic inheritance: When two or more genes work together to effect a single phenotypic character.

Polygyny: Marriage of a man to two or more women at the same time; a form of polygamy.

Polymorphic: A species with alternative forms (alleles) of particular genes.

Polytheism: Belief in several gods and/or goddesses (as contrasted with monotheism—belief in one god or goddess).

Polytypic: The expression of genetic variants in different frequencies in different populations of a species.

Population: In biology, a group of similar individuals that can and do interbreed.

Potassium-argon analysis: In archaeology and paleoanthropology, a technique for chronometric dating that measures the ratio of radioactive potassium to argon in volcanic debris associated with human remains.

Prehensile: Having the ability to grasp.

Prehistoric: A conventional term used to refer to the period of time before the appearance of written records. Does not deny the existence of history, merely of written history.

Preindustrial cities: The kinds of urban settlements that are characteristic of nonindustrial civilizations.

Pressure flaking: A technique of stone tool manufacture in which a bone, antler, or wooden tool is used to press, rather than strike off, small flakes from a piece of flint or similar stone.: Burins. Stone tools with chisel-like edges used for working bone and antler.

Prestige economy: Creation of a surplus for the express purpose of gaining prestige through a public display of wealth that is given away as gifts.

Priest or Priestess: A full-time religious specialist.

Primary innovation: The chance discovery of some new principle.

Primates: The group of mammals that includes lemurs, lorises, tarsiers, monkeys, apes, and humans.

Race: In biology, a population of a species that differs in the frequency of the variants of some gene or genes from other populations of the same species.

Racism: A doctrine of racial superiority by which one group asserts its superiority over another.

Radiocarbon analysis: In archaeology and paleoanthropology, a technique for chronometric dating based on measuring the amount of radioactive carbon (C-14) left in organic materials found in archaeological sites.

Reciprocity: The exchange of goods and services, of approximately equal value, between two parties.

Redistribution: A form of exchange in which goods flow into a central place, where they are sorted, counted, and reallocated.

Relative dating: In archaeology and paleoanthropology, designating an event, object, or fossil as being older or younger than another.

Religion: Organized beliefs in the supernatural that rationalize rituals aimed at interpreting and controlling aspects of the universe otherwise beyond human control.

Replacement reproduction: When birth rates and death rates are in equilibrium; people produce only enough offspring to replace themselves when they die.

Revitalization movements: Social movements, often of a religious nature, with the purpose of totally reforming a society.

Revolutionary: A revitalization movement from within, directed primarily at the ideological system and the attendant social structure of a culture.

Ribosomes: Structures in the cell where translation occurs.

Rites of intensification: Religious rituals enacted during a group's real or potential crisis.

Rites of passage: Rituals, often religious in nature, marking important stages in the lives of individuals, such as birth, marriage, and death.

RNA: Ribonucleic acid; similar to DNA but with uracil substituted for the base thymine. Carries instructions from DNA to produce amino acids for protein building.

Robust Australopithecines: Slightly larger and more robust than gracile members of genus *Australopithecus,* with larger, more powerful jaws.

Sagittal crest: A crest running from front to back on the top of the skull in the midline.

Sanctions: Externalized social controls designed to encourage conformity to social norms.

Scapula: The shoulder blade.

Secondary innovation: Something new that results from the deliberate application of known principles.

Segmentary lineage system: A form of political organization in which a larger group is broken up into clans that are further divided into lineages.

Self-awareness: The ability to identify oneself as an object, to react to oneself, and to appraise oneself.

Separation: In rites of passage, the ritual removal of the individual from society.

Serial monogamy: A marriage form in which a man or a woman marries or lives with a series of partners in succession.

Sexual dimorphism: Within a single species, the presence of marked anatomical differences between males and females.

Shaman: A part-time religious specialist whose special power to contact and manipulate supernatural beings and forces in an altered state of consciousness comes to him or her through some personal experience.

Sickle-cell anemia: An inherited form of anemia caused by the red blood cells assuming a sickled shape.

Signal: A sound or gesture that has a natural or self-evident meaning.

Silent trade: A form of barter in which no verbal communication takes place.

Site: In archaeology, a place containing remains of previous human activity.

Social class: A category of individuals who enjoy equal or nearly equal prestige according to the system of evaluation.

Social control: Control over groups through open coercion.

Social structure: The rule-governed relationships of individuals and groups within a society that hold it together.

Society: A group of interdependent people who share a common culture.

Sociolinguistics: The study of the structure and use of language as it relates to its social setting.

Soil marks: Stains that show up on the surface of recently plowed fields that reveal an archaeological site.

Sororate: A marriage custom according to which a widower marries his dead wife's sister (a woman marries her deceased sister's husband).

Species: In biology, a population or group of populations that is capable of interbreeding but that is reproductively isolated from other such populations.

Stabilizing selection: Natural selection as it acts to promote stability, rather than change, in a population's gene pool.

State: In anthropology, a centralized political system that may legitimately use force to maintain social order.

Stereoscopic vision: Three-dimensional vision.

Stratified society: The division of society into two or more categories of people who do not share equally in the basic resources that support life, influence, and prestige.

Stratified: Layered; said of archaeological sites where the remains lie in layers, one upon another.

Stratigraphy: In archaeology and paleoanthropology, the most reliable method of relative dating by means of strata.

Strepsirhini: A primate suborder that includes the single infraorder Lemuriformes.

Structural differentiation: The division of single traditional roles, which embrace two or more functions (for example, political, economic, and religious) into two or more roles, each with a single specialized function.

Structural violence: Violence exerted by situations, institutions, and social, political, and economic structures.

Subculture: A distinctive set of standards and behavior patterns by which a group within a larger society operates.

Sudanese or descriptive system: System of kinship terminology whereby a father, father's brother, and mother's brother are distinguished from one another as are a mother, mother's sister, and father's sister; cross and parallel cousins are distinguished from each other as well as from siblings.

Swidden farming: An extensive form of horticulture in which the natural vegetation is cut, the slash is subsequently burned, and crops then planted amongst the ashes.

Symbolic indicators: In a stratified society, activities and possessions indicative of social class.

Symbols: Sounds or gestures that stand for meanings among a group of people.

Syncretism: In acculturation, the blending of indigenous and foreign traits to form a new system.

Syntax: In linguistics, the rules or principles of phrase and sentence making

Tale: A creative narrative recognized as fiction for entertainment.

Tarsii: A haplorhine infraorder that includes tarsiers.

Technology: The knowledge that people employ to make and use objects.

Theory: In science, an explanation of natural phenomena, supported by a reliable body of data.

Thrifty genotype: Human genotype that permits efficient storage of fat to draw on in times of food shortage and conservation of glucose and nitrogen.

Tonality: In music, scale systems and their modifications.

Tool: An object used to facilitate some task or activity. Although toolmaking involves intentional modification of the material of which it is made, tool use may involve objects either modified for some particular purpose or completely unmodified.

Totemism: The belief that people are related to particular animals, plants, or natural objects by virtue of descent from common ancestral spirits.

Tradition: In a modernizing society, old cultural practices, which may oppose new forces of differentiation and integration.

Transcription: Process of conversion of instructions from DNA into RNA.

Transhumance: Among pastoralists, the grazing of sheep and goats in low steppe lands in the winter and then moving to high pastures on the plateaus in the summer.

Transition: In rites of passage, isolation of the individual following separation and prior to incorporation into society.

Translation: Process of conversion of RNA instructions into proteins.

Tribe: A group of nominally independent communities occupying a specific region that share a common language and culture and that are integrated by some unifying factor.

Unaltered fossil: Remains of plants and animals that lived in the past and that have not been altered in any significant way.

Unconscious selection: The preservation of valued variants of a plant or animal species and the destruction of less valued ones, with no thought as to the long-range consequences.

Unilineal descent: Descent that establishes group membership exclusively through either the mother's or the father's line.

Upper Paleolithic: The last part of the Old Stone Age, characterized by the emergence of more modern-looking hominines and an emphasis on the blade technique of toolmaking.

Vegeculture: The cultivation of domesticated root crops, such as yams and taro.

Verbal evaluation: The way people in a stratified society evaluate others in their society.

Vocal characterizers: In paralanguage, sound productions such as laughing or crying that humans "spcak through."

Vocalizations: Identifiable paralinguistic noises that are turned on and off at perceivable and relatively short intervals.

Vocal qualifiers: In paralanguage, sound productions of brief duration that modify utterances in terms of intensity.

Vocal segregates: In paralanguage, sound productions that are similar to the sounds of language, but do not appear in sequences that can properly be called words.

Voice qualities: In paralanguage, the background characteristics of a speaker's voice.

Warm-blooded: Animals that maintain a relatively constant body temperature.

Witchcraft: An explanation of events based on the belief that certain individuals possess an innate psychic power capable of causing harm, including sickness and death.

Worldviews: The conceptions, explicit and implicit, an individual or society has of the limits and workings of its world.

BIBLIOGRAPHY

Aberle, D. F., Bronfenbrenner, U., Hess, E. H., Miller, D. R., Schneider, D. H., & Spuhler, J. N. (1963). The incest taboo and the mating patterns of animals. *American Anthropologist, 65,* 253–265.

Abu-Lughod, L. (1986). *Veiled sentiments: Honor and poetry in a Bedouin society.* Berkeley: University of California Press.

Adams, R. E. W. (1977). *Prehistoric Mesoamerica.* Boston: Little, Brown.

Adams, R. M. (1966). The evolution of urban society. Chicago: Aldine.

Adams, R. (2001). Scale and complexity in archaic states. *American Antiquity, 11,* 188.

AIDS monthly surveillance summary (through July 1997). (1997). San Francisco.

Al-Issa, I., & Dennis, W. (Eds.). (1970). *Cross-cultural studies of behavior.* New York: Holt, Rinehart & Winston.

Alland, A., Jr. (1970). *Adaptation in cultural evolution: An approach to medical anthropology.* New York: Columbia University Press.

Alland, A., Jr. (1971). *Human diversity.* New York: Columbia University Press.

Allen, J. S., & Cheer, S. M. (1996). The non-thrifty genotype. *Current Anthropology, 37,* 831–842.

Allen, S. L. (1984). Media anthropology: Building a public perspective. *Anthropology Newsletter, 25,* 6.

Amábile-Cuevas, C. F., & Chicurel, M. E. (1993). Horizontal gene transfer. *American Scientist, 81,* 332–341.

Ambrose, S. H. (2001). Paleolithic technology and human evolution. *Science, 291.*

American Anthropological Association. (1998). Code of ethics of the American Anthropological Association. *Anthropology Newsletter, 39*(6), 19–20.

American Anthropological Association. (1998). Statement on "race." Available: *www.ameranthassn.org.*

Amiran, R. (1965). The beginnings of pottery-making in the Near East. In F. R. Matson (Ed.), *Ceramics and man* (pp. 240–247). Viking Fund Publications in Anthropology, No. 41.

Anderson, C. M. (1989). Neanderthal pelvis and gestational length. *American Anthropologist, 91,* 327–340.

Andrews, L. B., & Nelkin, D. (1996). The bell curve: A statement. *Science, 271,* 13.

Ankel-Simons, F., Fleagle, J. G., & Chatrath, P. S. (1998). Femoral anatomy of *Aegypto-pithecus zeuxis,* an early Oligocene anthropoid. *American Journal of Physical Anthropology, 106,* 413–424.

Appenzeller, T. (1998). Art: Evolution or revolution? *Science, 282,* 1,451–1,454.

Arensberg, C. M. (1961). The community as object and sample. *American Anthropologist, 63,* 241–264.

Armstrong, D. F., Stokoe, W. C., & Wilcox, S. E. (1993). Signs of the origin of syntax. *Current Anthropology,* 34, 349–368.

Armstrong, S. (1991, February 2). Female circumcision: Fighting a cruel tradition. *New Scientist,* 42–47.

Ashmore, W. (Ed.). (1981). *Lowland Maya settlement patterns.* Albuquerque: University of New Mexico Press.

Avoiding the next crisis. (1998, January 12). *Washington Post National Weekly Edition,* p. 26.

Balandier, G. (1971). *Political anthropology.* New York: Pantheon

Balter, M. (1998). On world AIDS day, a shadow looms over southern Africa. *Science, 282,* 1,790.

Balter, M. (1998). Why settle down? The mystery of communities. *Science, 282,* 1,442–1,444.

Balter, M. (1999). A long season puts Çatalhöyük in context. *Science, 286,* 890–891.

Balter, M. (2001). Did plaster hold Neolithic society together? *Science, 294,* 2,278–2,281.

Balter, M. (2001). Fossil tangles roots of human family tree. *Science, 291,* 2,289–2,291.

Balter, M. (2001). In search of the first Europeans. *Science, 291,* 1,724.

Balter, M. (2001). Scientists spar over claims of earliest human ancestor. *Science, 291,* 1,460–1,461.

Balter, M. (2002). From a modern human's brow—or doodling? *Science, 295,* 247–249.

Banton, M. (1968). Voluntary association: Anthropological aspects. In *International encyclopedia of the social sciences* (Vol. 16, pp. 357–362). New York: Macmillan.

Barber, B. (1957). *Social stratification.* New York: Harcourt.

Barfield, T. J. (1984). Introduction. *Cultural Survival Quarterly, 8,* 2.

Barham, L. S. (1998). Possible early pigment use in South-Central Africa. *Current Anthropology, 39,* 703–710.

Barnett, H. (1953). *Innovation: The basis of cultural change.* New York: McGraw-Hill.

Barnouw, V. (1985). *Culture and personality* (4th ed.). Homewood, IL: Dorsey Press.

Barr, R. G. (1997, October). The crying game. *Natural History, 47.*

Barth, F. (1961). *Nomads of South Persia: The Basseri tribe of the Khamseh Confederacy.* Boston: Little, Brown (Series in Anthropology).

Barth, F. (1962). Nomadism in the mountain and plateau areas of South West Asia. *The Problems of the Arid Zone* (pp. 341–355). Paris: UNESCO.

Barton, R. F. (1919). Ifugao law. Berkeley: *University of California Publications in American Archaeology and Ethnology,* Vol. XV.

Bar-Yosef, O. (1986). The walls of Jericho: An alternative interpretation. *Current Anthropology, 27,* 157–162.

Bar-Yosef, O., Vandermeesch, B., Arensburg, B., Belfer-Cohen, A., Goldberg, P., Laville, H., Meignen, L., Rak, Y., Speth, J. D., Tchernov, E., Tillier, A-M., & Weiner, S.

(1992). The excavations in Kebara Cave, Mt. Carmel. *Current Anthropology, 33,* 497–550.

Bascom, W. (1969). *The Yoruba of Southwestern Nigeria.* New York: Holt, Rinehart & Winston.

Bates, D. G., & Plog, F. (1991). *Human adaptive strategies.* New York: McGraw-Hill.

Beals, A. R. (1972). *Gopalpur: A South Indian village.* New York: Holt, Rinehart &Winston.

Beattie, J. (1964). *Other cultures: Aims, methods and achievements.* New York: Free Press.

Bednarik, R. G. (1995). Concept-mediated marking in the Lower Paleolithic. *Current Anthropology, 36,* 605–634.

Behrensmeyer, A. K., Todd, N. E., Potts, R., & McBrinn, G. E. (1997). Late Pliocene faunal turnover in the Turkana basin, Kenya and Ethiopia. *Science, 278,* 1,589–1,594.

Beidelman, T. O. (Ed.). (1971). *The transition of culture: Essays to E. E. Evans-Pritchard.* London: Tavistock.

Bell, D. (1997). Defining marriage and legitimacy. *Current Anthropology, 38,* 241.

Belshaw, C. S. (1958). The significance of modern cults in Melanesian development. In W. Lessa & E. Z. Vogt (Eds.), *Reader in comparative religion: An anthropological approach.* New York: Harper & Row.

Benedict, R. (1959). *Patterns of culture.* New York: New American Library.

Bennett, J. W. (1964). Myth, theory and value in cultural anthropology. In E. W. Caint & G. T. Bowles (Eds.), *Fact and theory in social science.* Syracuse, NY: Syracuse University Press.

Berdan, F. F. (1982). *The Aztecs of Central Mexico.* New York: Holt, Rinehart & Winston.

Bermúdez de Castro, J. M., Arsuaga, J. L., Cabonell, E., Rosas, A., Martinez, I., & Mosquera, M. (1997). A Hominid from the lower Pleistocene of Atapuerca, Spain: Possible ancestor to Neandertals and modern humans. *Science, 276,* 1,392–1,395.

Bernal, I. (1969). *The Olmec world.* Berkeley: University of California Press.

Bernard, H. R., & Sibley, W. E. (1975). *Anthropology and jobs.* Washington, DC: American Anthropological Association.

Bernardi, B. (1985). *Age class systems: Social institutions and policies based on age.* New York: Cambridge University Press.

Berra, T. M. (1990). *Evolution and the myth of creationism.* Stanford, CA: Stanford University Press.

Berreman, G. D. (1962). *Behind many masks: Ethnography and impression management in a Himalayan village.* Ithaca, NY: Society for Applied Anthropology (Monograph No. 4).

Berreman, G. D. (1968). Caste: The concept of caste. In *International Encyclopedia of the Social Sciences* (Vol. 2, pp. 333–338). New York: Macmillan.

Bicchieri, M. G. (Ed.). (1972). *Hunters and gatherers today: A socioeconomic study of eleven such cultures in the twentieth century.* New York: Holt, Rinehart & Winston.

Binford, L. R. (1972). *An archaeological perspective.* New York: Seminar Press.

Binford, L. R., & Chuan, K. H. (1985). Taphonomy at a distance: Zhoukoudian, the cave home of Beijing man? *Current Anthropology, 26,* 413–442.

Birdwhistell, R. (1970). *Kinesics and context: Essays in body motion communication.* Philadelphia: University of Pennsylvania Press.

Black, H. C. (1968). *Black's law dictionary.* St. Paul, MN: West.

Blumer, M. A., & Byrne, R. (1991). The ecological genetics and domestication and the origins of agriculture. *Current Anthropology, 32,* 23–54.

Boas, F. (1962). *Primitive art.* Gloucester, MA: Peter Smith.

Boas, F. (1966). *Race, language and culture.* New York: Free Press.

Bodley, J. H. (1985). *Anthropology and contemporary human problems* (2nd ed.). Palo Alto, CA: Mayfield.

Bodley, J. H. (1990). *Victims of progress* (3rd ed.). Mountain View, CA: Mayfield.

Bodley, J. H. (1997). Comment. *Current Anthropology, 38,* 725.

Boehm, C. (2000). The evolution of moral communities. School of American Research, *2000 Annual Report,* p. 7.

Bohannan, P. (Ed.). (1967). *Law and warfare: Studies in the anthropology of conflict.* Garden City, NY: Natural History Press.

Bohannan, P., & Dalton, G. (Eds.) (1962). *Markets in Africa.* Evanston, IL: Northwestern University Press.

Bohannan, P., & Middleton, J. (Eds.). (1968). *Kinship and social organization.* Garden City, NY: Natural History Press (American Museum Source Books in Anthropology).

Bohannan, P., & Middleton, J. (Eds.). (1968). *Marriage, family, and residence.* Garden City, NY: Natural History Press (American Museum Source Books in Anthropology).

Bolinger, D. (1968). *Aspects of language.* New York: Harcourt.

Boone, E. S. (1987). Practicing sociomedicine: Redefining the problem of infant mortality in Washington, D.C. In R. M. Wulff & S. J. Fiske (Eds.), *Anthropological praxis: Translating knowledge into action* (p. 56). Boulder, CO: Westview Press.

Bordes, F. (1972). *A tale of two caves.* New York: Harper & Row.

Bornstein, M. H. (1975). The influence of visual perception on culture. *American Anthropologist, 77*(4), 774–798.

Brace, C. L. (1981). Tales of the phylogenetic woods: The evolution and significance of phylogenetic trees. *American Journal of Physical Anthropology, 56,* 411–429.

Brace, C. L. (1997). Cro-Magnons "Я" us? *Anthropology Newsletter, 38*(8), 1, 4.

Brace, C. L. (2000). *Evolution in an anthropological view.* Walnut Creek, CA: Altamira.

Brace, C. L., Nelson, H., & Korn, N. (1979). *Atlas of human evolution* (2nd ed.). New York: Holt, Rinehart & Winston.

Brace, C. L., Ryan, A. S., & Smith, B. (1981). Comment. *Current Anthropology, 22*(4), 426–430.

Bradfield, R. (1973). *A natural history of associations.* New York: International Universities Press.

Braidwood, R. J. (1960). The agricultural revolution. *Scientific American, 203,* 130–141.

Braidwood, R. J. (1975). *Prehistoric men* (8th ed.). Glenview, IL: Scott, Foresman.

Brain, C. K. (1968). Who killed the Swartkrans ape-men? *South African Museums Association Bulletin, 9,* 127–139.

Brain, C. K. (1969). The contribution of Namib Desert Hottentots to an understanding of Australopithecine bone accumulations. *Scientific Papers of the Namib Desert Research Station,* 13.

Branda, R. F. & Eatoil, J. W. (1978). Skin color and photolysis: An evolutionary hypothesis. *Science, 201,* 625–626.

Brew, J. O. (1968). *One hundred years of anthropology.* Cambridge, MA: Harvard University Press.

Broecker, W. S. (1992, April). Global warming on trial. *Natural History, 14.*

Brothwell, D. R., & Higgs, E. (Eds.). (1969). *Science in archaeology* (Rev. ed.). London: Thames & Hudson.

Brown, B., Walker, A., Ward, C. V., & Leakey, R. E. (1993). New *Australopithecus boisei* calvaria from East Lake Turkana, Kenya. *American Journal of Physical Anthropology, 91,* 137–159.

Brown, D. E. (1991). *Human universals.* New York: McGraw-Hill.

Brues, A. M. (1977). *People and races.* New York: Macmillan.

Bull, J. J., & Wichman, H. A. (1998). A revolution in evolution. *Science, 281,* 1,959.

Burling, R. (1969). Linguistics and ethnographic description. *American Anthropologist, 71,* 817–827.

Burling, R. (1970). *Man's many voices: Language in its cultural context.* New York: Holt, Rinehart & Winston.

Burling, R. (1993). Primate calls, human language, and nonverbal communication. *Current Anthropology, 34,* 25–53.

Butzer, K. (1971). *Environment and anthropology: An ecological approach to prehistory* (2nd ed.). Chicago: Aldine.

Byers, D. S. (Ed.). (1967). *The prehistory of the Tehuacan Valley: Vol. 1. Environment and Subsistence.* Austin: University of Texas Press.

Cachel, S. (1997). Dietary shifts and the European Upper Paleolithic transition. *Current Anthropology, 38,* 590.

Calloway, C. (1997). Introduction: Surviving the Dark Ages. In C. G. Calloway (Ed.), *After King Philip's War: Presence and persistence in Indian New England* (pp. 1–28). Hanover, NH: University Press of New England.

Campbell, B. G., & Loy, J. D. (1995). *Humankind emerging* (7th ed.). New York: HarperCollins.

Carmack, R. (1983). Indians and the Guatemalan revolution. *Cultural Survival Quarterly, 7*(3), 52–54.

Carneiro, R. L. (1970). A theory of the origin of the state. *Science, 169,* 733–738.

Caroulis, J. (1996). Food for thought. *Pennsylvania Gazette, 95*(3), 16.

Carpenter, E. (1973). *Eskimo realities.* New York: Holt, Rinehart & Winston.

Carroll, J. B. (Ed.). (1956). *Language, thought and reality: Selected writings of Benjamin Lee Whorf.* New York: Wiley.

Cartmill, M. (1998). The gift of gab. *Discover 19*(11), 64.

Cashdan, E. (1989). Hunters and gatherers: Economic behavior in bands. In S. Plattner (Ed.), *Economic anthropology* (pp. 21–48). Stanford, CA: Stanford University Press.

Cavalli-Sforza, L. L. (1977). *Elements of human genetics.* Menlo Park, CA: W. A. Benjamin.

Cavallo, J. A. (1990, February). Cat in the human cradle. *Natural History,* 54–60.

Centers for Disease Control. (1997). *Centers for Disease Control semi-annual AIDS report* (through June 1996). Atlanta, GA.

Chagnon, N. A. (1988). *Yanomamo: The fierce people* (3rd ed.) New York: Holt, Rinehart & Winston.

Chagnon, N. A., & Irons, W. (Eds.). (1979). *Evolutionary biology and human social behavior.* North Scituate, MA: Duxbury Press.

Chambers, R. (1983). *Rural development: Putting the last first.* New York: Longman.

Chan, J. W. C., & Vernon, P. E. (1988). Individual differences among the peoples of China. In J. W. Berry (Ed.), *Human abilities in cultural context* (pp. 340–357). Cambridge, England: Cambridge University Press.

Chang, K. C. (Ed.). (1968). *Settlement archaeology.* Palo Alto, CA: National Press.

Chapple, E. D. (1970). *Cultural and biological man: Explorations in behavioral anthropology.* New York: Holt, Rinehart & Winston.

Chasin, B. H., & Franke, R. W. (1983). U.S. farming: A world model? *Global Reporter, 1*(2), 10.

Chicurel, M. (2001). Can organisms speed their own evolution? *Science, 292,* 1,824–1,827.

Childe, V. G. (1951, orig. 1936). *Man makes himself.* New York: New American Library.

Childe, V. G. (1954). *What happened in history.* Baltimore: Penguin.

Chodorow, N. (1971). Being and doing: A cross-cultural examination of the socialization of males and females. In V. Gornick & B. K. Moran (Eds.), *Woman in sexist society.* New York: Basic Books.

Ciochon, R. L., & Fleagle, J. G. (1987). Ramapithecus and human origins. In R. L. Ciochon & J. G. Fleagle (Eds.), *Primate evolution and human origins.* Hawthorne, NY: Aldine de Gruyter.

Ciochon, R. L., & Fleagle, J. G. (Eds.). (1987). *Primate evolution and human origins.* Hawthorne, NY: Aldine de Gruyter.

Ciochon, R. L., & Fleagle, J. G. (1993). *The human evolution source book.* Englewood Cliffs, NJ: Prentice-Hall.

Clark, E. E. (1966). *Indian legends of the Pacific Northwest.* Berkley: University of California Press.

Clark, G. (1967). *The Stone Age hunters.* New York: McGraw-Hill.

Clark, G. (1972). *Starr Carr: A case study in bioarchaeology.* Reading, MA: Addison-Wesley.

Clark, G. A. (1997). Neandertal genetics. *Science, 277,* 1,024.

Clark, J. G. D. (1962). *Prehistoric Europe: The economic basis.* Stanford, CA: Stanford University Press.

Clark, W. E. L. (1960). *The antecedents of man.* Chicago: Quadrangle Books.

Clark, W. E. L. (1966). *History of the primates* (5th ed.). Chicago: University of Chicago Press.

Clark, W. E. L. (1967). *Man-apes or ape-men? The story of discoveries in Africa.* New York: Holt, Rinehart & Winston.

Clarke, R. J., & Tobias, P. V. (1995). Sterkfontein member 2 foot bones of the oldest South African hominid. *Science, 269,* 521–524.

Clay, J. W. (1987). Genocide in the Age of Enlightenment. *Cultural Survival Quarterly, 12*(3).

Clay, J. W. (1996). What's a nation? In W. A. Haviland & R. J. Gordon (Eds.), *Talking about people* (2nd ed., pp. 188–189). Mountain View, CA: Mayfield.

Clough, S. B., & Cole, C. W. (1952). *Economic history of Europe* (3rd ed.). Lexington, MA: Heath.

Codere, H. (1950). *Fighting with property.* Seattle: University of Washington Press (American Ethnological Society, Monograph 18).

Coe, S. D. (1994). *America's first cuisines.* Austin: University of Texas Press.

Coe, W. R. (1967). *Tikal: A handbook of the ancient Maya ruins.* Philadelphia: University of Pennsylvania Museum.

Coe, W. R., & Haviland, W. A. (1982). *Introduction to the archaeology of Tikal.* Philadelphia: University Museum.

Cohen, J. (1997). Is an old virus up to new tricks? *Science, 277,* 312–313.

Cohen, M. N. (1977). *The food crisis in prehistory.* New Haven, CT: Yale University Press.

Cohen, M. N. (1995). Anthropology and race: The bell curve phenomenon. *General Anthropology, 2*(1), 1–4.

Cohen, M., & Armelagos, G. (Eds.). (1984). *Paleopathology at the origins of agriculture.* Orlando: Academic Press.

Cohen, M. N., & Armelagos, G. J. (1984). Paleopathology at the origins of agriculture: Editors' summation. In M. N. Cohen & G. J. Armelagos (Eds.), *Paleopathology at the origins of agriculture.* Orlando: Academic Press.

Cohen, M. L. (1967). Variations in complexity among Chinese family groups: The impact of modernization. *Transactions of the New York Academy of Sciences, 295,* 638–647.

Cohen, M. L. (1968). A case study of Chinese family economy and development. *Journal of Asian and African Studies, 3,* 161–180.

Cohen, R., & Middleton, J. (Eds.). (1967). *Comparative political systems.* Garden City, NY: Natural History Press.

Cohen, Y. (1968). *Man in adaptation: The cultural present.* Chicago: Aldine.

Colburn, T., Dumanoski, D., & Myers, J. P. (1996, March). Hormonal sabotage. *Natural History,* 45–46.

Cole, S. (1975). *Leakey's luck: The life of Louis Seymour Bazett Leakey. 1903–1972.* New York: Harcourt Brace Jovanovich.

Collier, J., Rosaldo, M. Z., & Yanagisako, S. (1982). Is there a family? New anthropological views. In B. Thorne & M. Yalom (Eds.), *Rethinking the family: Some feminist questions* (pp. 25–39). New York: Longman.

Collier, J. F., & Yanagisako, S. J. (Eds.). (1987). *Gender and kinship: Essays toward a unified analysis.* Stanford, CA: Stanford University Press.

Connelly, J. C. (1979). Hopi social organization. In A. Ortiz (Ed.), *Handbook of North American Indians, Vol. 9, Southwest* (pp. 539–553). Washington, DC: Smithsonian Institution.

Connor, M. (1996). The archaeology of contemporary mass graves. *SAA Bulletin, 14*(4), 6 & 31.

Conroy, G. C. (1997). *Reconstructing human origins: A modern synthesis.* New York: Norton.

Constable, G., & the Editors of Time-Life. (1973). *The Neanderthals.* New York: Time-Life.

Cook, S. F. (1972). *Prehistoric demography.* Reading, MA: Addison-Wesley.

Coon, C. S. (1957). *The seven caves.* New York: Knopf.

Coon, C. S. (1958). *Caravan: The story of the Middle East* (2nd ed.). New York: Holt, Rinehart & Winston.

Coon, C. S. (1971). *The hunting peoples.* Boston: Little, Brown.

Coon, C. S., Garn, S. N., & Birdsell, J. (1950). *Races: A study of the problems of race formation in man.* Springfield, IL: Charles C Thomas.

Cooper, A., Poinar, H. N., Pääbo, S., Radovci, C. J., Debénath, A., Caparros, M., Barroso-Ruiz, C., Bertranpetit, J., Nielsen-March, C., Hedges, R. E. M., & Sykes, B. (1997). Neanderthal genetics. *Science, 277,* 1,021–1,024.

Coppens, Y., Howell, F. C., Isaac, G. L., & Leakey, R. E. F. (Eds.). (1976). *Earliest man and environments in the Lake Rudolf Basin: Stratigraphy, paleoecology, and evolution.* Chicago: University of Chicago Press.

Cornwell, T. (1995, November 10). Skeleton staff. *Times Higher Education,* p. 20.

Corruccini, R. S. (1992). Metrical reconsideration of the Skhul IV and IX and Border Cave I crania in the context of modern human origins. *American Journal of Physical Anthropology, 87,* 433–445.

Cottrell, F. (1965). *Energy and society: The relation between energy, social changes and economic development.* New York: McGraw-Hill.

Cottrell, L. (1963). *The lost pharaohs.* New York: Grosset & Dunlap.

Courlander, H. (1971). *The fourth world of the Hopis.* New York: Crown.

Cowgill, G. L. (1980). Letter. *Science, 210,* 1,305.

Cowgill, G. L. (1997). State and society at Teotihuacan, Mexico. *Annual Review of Anthropology, 26,* 129–161.

Cox, O. C. (1959). *Caste, class and race: A study in dynamics.* New York: Monthly Review Press.

Crane, L. B., Yeager, E., & Whitman, R. L. (1981). *An introduction to linguistics.* Boston: Little, Brown.

Crocker, W. A., & Crocker, J. (1994). *The canela, bonding through kinship, ritual and sex.* Fort Worth, TX: Harcourt Brace.

Culbert, T. P. (Ed.). (1973). *The Classic Maya collapse.* Albuquerque: University of New Mexico Press.

Culotta, E. (1992). A new take on anthropoid origins. *Science, 256,* 1,516–1,517.

Culotta, E. (1995). Asian hominids grow older. *Science, 270,* 1,116–1,117.

Culotta, E. (1995). New finds rekindle debate over anthropoid origins. *Science, 268,* 1,851.

Culotta, E. (1995). New hominid crowds the field. *Science, 269,* 918.

Culotta, E., & Koshland, D. E., Jr. (1994). DNA repair works its way to the top. *Science, 266,* 1,926.

Cultural Survival Quarterly. (1991). *15*(4), 5, 38.

Dalton, G. (Ed.). (1967). *Tribal and peasant economics: Readings in economic anthropology.* Garden City, NY: Natural History Press.

Dalton, G. (1971). *Traditional tribal and peasant economics: An introductory survey of economic anthropology.* Reading, MA:Addison-Wesley.

Daniel, G. (1970). *The first civilizations: The archaeology of their origins.* New York: Apollo Editions.

Daniel, G. (1975). *A hundred and fifty years of archaeology* (2nd ed.). London: Duckworth.

Darwin, C. (1936; orig. 1871). *The descent of man and selection in relation to sex.* New York: Random House (Modern Library).

Darwin, C. (1967; orig. 1859). *On the origin of species.* New York: Atheneum.

Davenport, W. (1959). Linear descent and descent groups. *American Anthropologist, 61,* 557–573.

Davis, S. H. (1982). *Victims of the miracle.* Cambridge England: Cambridge University Press.

Day, G. M. (1972). Quoted in Vogelman, T. C. (Director), and Department of Anthropology (Producer). *Prehistoric life in the Champlain Valley* [Film]. Burlington: University of Vermont.

Death and disorder in Guatemala. (1983). *Cultural Survival Quarterly, 7*(1).

Dettinger, K. A. (1997, October). When to wean. *Natural History, 49.*

de Laguna, F. (1977). *Voyage to Greenland: A personal initiation into anthropology.* New York: Norton.

de Laguna, G. A. (1966). *On existence and the human world.* New Haven, CT: Yale University Press.

de Pelliam, A., & Burton, F. D. (1976). More on predatory behavior in nonhuman primates. *Current Anthropology, 17* (3).

de Waal, A. (1994). Genocide in Rwanda. *Anthropology Today, 10* (3), 1–2.

de Waal, F. (1996). *Good natured: The origins of right and wrong in humans and other animals.* Cambridge, MA: Harvard University Press.

de Waal, F. (2001). *The ape and the sushi master.* New York: Basic Books

de Waal, F. (2001). Sing the song of evolution. *Natural History, 110*(8), 76–77.

de Waal, F., Kano, T., & Parish, A. R. (1998). Comments. *Current Anthropology, 39,* 407–408, 410–411, 413–414.

Dean, M. C., Beynon, A. D., Thackeray, J. F., & Macho, G. A. (1993). Histological reconstruction of dental development and age at death of a juvenile *Paranthropus robustus* specimen, SK 63, from Swartkrans, South Africa. *American Journal of Physical Anthropology, 91,* 401–419.

DeBeer, Sir G. R. (1964). *Atlas of evolution.* London: Nelson.

Deetz, J. (1967). *Invitation to archaeology.* New York: Doubleday.

Deevy, E. S., Jr. (1960). The human population. *Scientific American, 203,* 194–204.

Devereux, G. (1963). Institutionalized homosexuality of the Mohave Indians. In H. M. Ruitenbeck (Ed.), *The problem of homosexuality in modern society.* New York: Dutton.

DeVore, I. (Ed.). (1965). *Primate behavior: Field studies of monkeys and apes.* New York: Holt, Rinehart & Winston.

Diamond, J. (1994). How Africa became black. *Discover, 15*(2); 72–81.

Diamond, J. (1994). Race without color. *Discover, 15*(11), 83–89.

Diamond, J. (1996). Empire of uniformity. *Discover, 17*(3), 78–85.

Diamond, J. (1997). The curse of QWERTY. *Discover, 18*(4), 34–42.

Diamond, J. (1997). *Guns, germs, and steel.* New York: Norton.

Diamond, J. (1998). Ants, crops, and history. *Science, 281,* 1,974–1,975.

Dixon, J. E., Cann, J. R., & Renfrew, C. (1968). Obsidian and the origins of trade. *Scientific American, 218,* 38–46.

Dobyns, H. F., Doughty, P. L., & Lasswell, H. D. (Eds.). (1971). *Peasants, power, and applied social change.* London: Sage.

Dobzhansky, T. (1962). *Mankind evolving.* New Haven, CT: Yale University Press.

Doist, R. (1997). Molecular evolution and scientific inquiry, misperceived. *American Scientist, 85,* 475.

Donnan, C. B., & Castillo, L. J. (1992). Finding the tomb of a Moche priestess. *Archaeology, 45* (6), 38–42.

Douglas, M. (1958). Raffia cloth distribution in the Lele economy. *Africa, 28,* 109–122.

Dowson, T. A., & Lewis-Williams, J. D. (1993). Myths, museums, and southern African rock art. *South African Historical Journal, 29,* 44–60.

Dozier, E. (1970). *The Pueblo Indians of North America.* New York: Holt, Rinehart & Winston.

Draper, P. (1975). !Kung women: Contrasts in sexual egalitarianism in foraging and sedentary contexts. In R. Reiter (Ed.), *Toward an anthropology of women* (pp. 77–109). New York: Monthly Review Press.

Driver, H. (1964). *Indians of North America.* Chicago: University of Chicago Press.

Dubois, C. (1944). *The people of Alor.* Minneapolis: University of Minnesota Press.

Dubos, R. (1968). *So human an animal.* New York: Scribner.

Duncan, A. S., Kappelman, J., & Shapiro, L. J. (1994). Metatasophalangeal joint function and positional behavior in *Australopithecus afarensis. American Journal of Physical Anthropology, 93,* 67–81.

Dundes, A. (1980). *Interpreting folklore.* Bloomington: Indiana University Press.

Durant, J. C. (2000, April 23). Everybody into the gene pool. *New York Times Book Review,* pp. 11–12.

Durkheim, E. (1964). *The division of labor in society.* New York: Free Press.

Durkheim, E. (1965). *The elementary forms of the religious life.* New York: Free Press.

duToit, B. M. (1991). *Human sexuality: Cross cultural readings.* New York: McGraw-Hill.

Eastman, C. M. (1990). *Aspects of language and culture* (2nd ed.). Novato, CA: Chandler & Sharp.

Edey, M., & the Editors of Time-Life. (1972). *The missing link.* New York: Time-Life.

Edey, M. A., & Johannson, D. (1989). *Blueprints: Solving the mystery of evolution.* Boston: Little, Brown.

Edmonson, M. S. (1971). *Lore: An introduction to the science of folklore.* New York: Holt, Rinehart & Winston.

Edwards, S. W. (1978). Nonutilitarian activities on the Lower Paleolithic: A look at the two kinds of evidence. *Current Anthropology, 19*(1), 135–137.

Eggan, F. (1954). Social anthropology and the method of controlled comparison. *American Anthropologist, 56,* 743–763.

Eiseley, L. (1958). *Darwin's century: Evolution and the men who discovered it.* New York: Doubleday.

Eisenstadt, S. N. (1956). *From generation to generation: Age groups and social structure.* New York: Free Press.

Elgin, S. H. (1994). I am not scowling fiercely as I write this. *Anthropology Newsletter, 35*(9), 44.

Elkin, A. P. (1964). *The Australian aborigines.* Garden City, NY: DoubleDay/Anchor Books.

Ellison, P. T. (1990). Human ovarian function and reproductive ecology: New hypotheses. *American Anthropologist, 92,* 933–952.

Ember, C. R., & Ember, M. (1985). *Cultural anthropology* (4th ed.). Englewood Cliffs, NJ: Prentice-Hall.

Ember, C. R., & Ember, M. (1996). What have we learned from cross-cultural research? *General Anthropology, 2* (2), 5.

Epstein, A. (1968). Sanctions. In *International encyclopedia of the social sciences* (Vol. 14, p. 3). New York: Macmillan.

Erasmus, C. J. (1950). Patolli, Pachisi, and the limitation of possibilities. *Southwestern Journal of Anthropology, 6,* 369–381.

Erasmus, C. J., & Smith, W. (1967). Cultural anthropology in the United States since 1900. *Southwestern Journal of Anthropology, 23,* 11–40.

Ervin-Tripp, S. (1973). *Language acquisition and communicative choice.* Stanford, CA: Stanford University Press.

Esber, G. S., Jr. (1987). Designing Apache houses with Apaches. In R. M. Wulff & S. J. Fiske (Eds.), *Anthropological praxis: Translating knowledge into action* (pp. 187–196). Boulder, CO: Westview Press.

Evans, W. (1968). *Communication in the animal world.* New York: Crowell.

Evans-Pritchard, E. E. (1937). *Witchcraft, oracles, and magic among the Azande.* London: Oxford University Press.

Evans-Pritchard, E. E. (1968). *The Nuer: A description of the modes of livelihood and political institutions of a Nilotic people.* London: Oxford University Press.

Fagan, B. M. (1995). The quest for the past. In L. L. Hasten (Ed.), *Annual editions 95/96, archaeology* (p. 10). Guilford, CT: Dushkin.

Fagan, B. M. (1998). *People of the earth* (9th ed.). New York: Longman.

Falk, D. (1975). Comparative anatomy of the larynx in man and the chimpanzee: Implications for language in Neanderthal. *American Journal of Physical Anthropology, 43*(1), 123–132.

Falk, D. (1989). Ape-like endocast of "Ape Man Taung." *American Journal of Physical Anthropology, 80,* 335–339.

Falk, D. (1993). A good brain is hard to cool. *Natural History, 102* (8), 65.

Falk, D. (1993). Hominid paleoneurology. In R. L. Ciochon & J. G. Fleagle (Eds.), *The human evolution source book.* Englewood Cliffs, NJ: Prentice-Hall.

Farmer, P. (1992). *AIDS and accusation: Haiti and the geography of blame.* Berkeley: University of California Press.

Farsoun, S. K. (1970). Family structures and society in modern Lebanon. In L. E. Sweet (Ed.), *Peoples and cultures of the Middle East* (Vol. 2). Garden City, NY: Natural History Press.

Feder, K. L. (1999). *Frauds, myths, and mysteries* (3rd ed.). Mountain View, CA: Mayfield.

Federoff, N. E., & Nowak, R. M. (1997). Man and his dog. *Science, 278,* 305.

Fedigan, L. M. (1986).The changing role of women in models of human evolution. *Annual Review of Anthropology, 15,* 25–56.

Ferber, D. (2000). Superbugs on the hoof? *Science, 288,* 792–794.

Ferguson, T. J. (1996). *Archaeology for and by Native Americans.* Paper presented at the 95th Annual Meeting, American Anthropological Association.

Fernandez-Carriba, S., & Loeches, A. (2001). Fruit smearing by captive chimpanzees: A newly observed food-processing behavior. *Current Anthropology, 42,* 143–147.

Ferrie, H. (1997). An interview with C. Loring Brace. *Current Anthropology, 38,* 851–869.

Firth, R. (1952). *Elements of social organization.* London: Watts.

Firth, R. (1957). *Man and culture: An evaluation of Bronislaw Malinowski.* London: Routledge.

Firth, R. (1963). *We the Tikopia.* Boston: Beacon Press.

Firth, R. (Ed.). (1967). *Themes in economic anthropology.* London: Tavistock.

Fishman, J. (1994). Putting a new spin on the human birth. *Science, 264,* 1,082–1,083.

Flannery, K. V. (1973). The origins of agriculture. In B. J. Siegel, A. R. Beals, & Stephen A. Tyler (Eds.), *Annual Review of Anthropology* (Vol. 2, pp. 271–310). Palo Alto, CA: Annual Reviews.

Flannery, K. V. (Ed.). (1976). *The Mesoamerican village.* New York: Seminar Press.

Fleagle, J. G. (1992, December). *Early anthropoid evolution* Paper presented at the 91st Annual Meeting of the American Anthropological Association.

Folger, T. (1993). The naked and the bipedal. *Discover, 14* (11), 34–35.

Forbes, J. D. (1964). *The Indian in America's past.* Englewood Cliffs, NJ: Prentice-Hall.

Forde, C. D. (1953). *Habitat, economy, and society.* New York: Dutton.

Forde, C. D. (1955). The Nupe. In D. Forde (Ed.), *Peoples of the Niger-Benue confluence*. London: International African Institute (Ethnographic Survey of Africa. Western Africa, part 10).

Forde, C. D. (1968). Double descent among the Yako. In P. Bohannan & J. Middleton (Eds.), *Kinship and social organization* (pp. 179–191). Garden City, NY: Natural History Press.

Fortes, M. (1950). Kinship and marriage among the Ashanti. In A. R. Radcliffe-Brown & C. Daryll Forde (Eds.), *African systems of kinship and marriage.* London: Oxford University Press.

Fortes, M. (1969). *Kinship and the social order: The legacy of Lewis Henry Morgan.* Chicago: Aldine.

Fortes, M., & Evans-Prichard, E. E. (Eds.). (1962; orig. 1940). *African political systems.* London: Oxford University Press.

Fossey, D. (1983). *Gorillas in the mist.* Burlington, MA: Houghton Mifflin.

Foster, G. M. (1955). Peasant society and the image of the limited good. *American Anthropologist, 67,* 293–315.

Fox, R. (1967). *Kinship and marriage in an anthropological perspective.* Baltimore: Penguin.

Fox, R. (1968). *Encounter with anthropology.* New York: Dell.

Frake, C. O. (1992). Lessons of the Mayan sky. In A. F. Aveni (Ed.), *The sky in Mayan literature* (pp. 274–291). New York: Oxford University Press.

France, D. L., & Horn, A. D. (1992). *Lab manual and workbook for physical anthropology* (2nd ed.). New York: West.

Frankfort, H. (1968). *The birth of civilization in the Near East.* New York: Barnes & Noble.

Fraser, D. (1962). *Primitive art.* New York: Doubleday.

Fraser, D. (Ed.). (1966). *The many faces of primitive art: A critical anthology.* Englewood Cliffs, NJ: Prentice-Hall.

Frayer, D. W. (1981). Body size, weapon use, and natural selection in the European Upper Paleolithic and Mesolithic. *American Anthropologist, 83,* 57–73.

Frazer, Sir J. G. (1961 reissue). *The new golden bough.* New York: Doubleday, Anchor Books.

Freeman, J. D. (1960). The Iban of western Borneo. In G. P. Murdock (Ed.), *Social structure in Southeast Asia.* Chicago: Quadrangle Books.

Freeman, L. G. (1992). *Ambrona and Torralba: New evidence and interpretation.* Paper presented at 91st Annual Meeting of the American Anthropological Association, San Francisco.

Fried, M. 1960. On the evolution of social stratification and the state. In S. Diamond (Ed.), *Culture in history: Essays in honor of Paul Radin.* New York: Columbia University Press.

Fried, M. (1967). *The evolution of political society: An essay in political anthropology.* New York: Random House.

Fried, M. (1972). *The study of anthropology.* New York: Crowell.

Fried, M., Harris, M., & Murphy, R. (1968). *War: The anthropology of armed conflict and aggression.* Garden City, NY: Natural History Press.

Friedl, E. (1975). *Women and men: An anthropologist's view.* New York: Holt, Rinehart & Winston.

Fritz, G. J. (1994). Are the first American farmers getting younger? *Current Anthropology, 35,* 305–309.

Frye, M. (1983). Sexism. In *The politics of reality* (pp. 17–40). New York: Crossing Press.

Furst, P. T. (1976). *Hallucinogens and culture* (p. 7). Novato, CA: Chandler and Sharp.

Gabunia, L., Vekua, A., Lordkipanidze, D., Swisher III, C. C., Ferring, R., Justus, A., Nioradze, M., Tvalchrelidze, M., Anton, S. C., Bosinski, G., Joris, O., de Lumley, M.-A., Majsuradze, G., & Mouskhelishvili, G. (2000). Earliest Pleistocene hominid cranial remains from Dmanisi, Republic of Georgia: Taxonomy, geological setting, and age. *Science, 288,* 1,019–1,025.

Gamble, C. (1986). *The Paleolithic settlement of Europe.* Cambridge, England: Cambridge University Press.

Gardner, R. A., Gardner, B. T., & Van Cantfort, T. E. (Eds.). (1989). *Teaching sign language to chimpanzees.* Albany: State University of New York Press.

Gamst, F. C., & Norbeck, E. (1976). *Ideas of culture: Sources and uses.* New York: Holt, Rinehart & Winston.

Garn, S. M. (1970). *Human races* (3rd ed.). Springfield, IL: Charles C Thomas.

Gates, H. (1996). Buying brides in China—again. *Anthropology Today, 12*(4), 10.

Gebo, D. L., Dagosto, D., Beard, K.C., & Tao, Q. (2001). Middle Eocene primate tarsals from China: Implications for haplorhine evolution. *American Journal of Physical Anthropology, 116,* 83–107.

Gebo, D. L., MacLatchy, L., Kityo, R., Deino, A., Kingston, J., & Pilbeam, D. (1997). A hominoid genus from the early Miocene of Uganda. *Science, 276,* 401–404.

Geertz, C. (1963). *Agricultural involution: The process of ecological change in Indonesia.* Berkeley: University of California Press.

Geertz, C. (1965). The impact of the concept of culture on the concept of man. In J. R. Platt (Ed.), *New views of man.* Chicago: University of Chicago Press.

Geertz, C. (1984). Distinguished lecture: Anti-relativism. *American Anthropologist, 86,* 263–278.

Gelb, I. J. (1952). *A study of writing.* London: Routledge.

Gell, A. (1988). Technology and magic. *Anthropology Today, 4*(2), 6–9.

Gellner, E. (1969). *Saints of the atlas.* Chicago: University of Chicago Press (The Nature of Human Society Series).

Gennep, A. Van (1960). *The rites of passage.* Chicago: University of Chicago Press.

Gibbons, A. (1992). Mitochondrial Eve: Wounded, but not yet dead. *Science, 257,* 873–875.

Gibbons, A. (1993). Where are new diseases born? *Science, 261,* 680–681.

Gibbons, A. (1996). Did Neandertals lose an evolutionary "arms" race? *Science, 272,* 1,586–1,587.

Gibbons, A. (1997). Ideas on human origins evolve at anthropology gathering. *Science, 276,* 535–536.

Gibbons, A. (1997). A new face for human ancestors. *Science, 276,* 1,331–1,333.

Gibbons, A. (1998). Ancient island tools suggest *Homo erectus* was a seafarer. *Science, 279,* 1,635–1,637.

Gibbons, A. (2001). The riddle of coexistence. *Science, 291,* 1,726.

Gibbons, A. (2001). Studying humans—and their cousins and parasites. *Science, 292,* 627–629.

Gibbons, A., & Culotta, E. (1997). Miocene primates go ape. *Science, 276,* 355–356.

Gibbs, J. L., Jr. (1965). The Kpelle of Liberia. In J. L. Gibbs (Ed.), *Peoples of Africa* (pp. 197–240). New York: Holt, Rinehart & Winston.

Glausiusz, J. (1995). Hidden benefits. *Discover, 16*(3), 30–31.

Glausiusz, J. (1995). Micro gets macro. *Discover, 16*(11), 40.

Gleason, H. A., Jr. (1966). *An introduction to descriptive linguistics* (Rev. ed.). New York: Holt, Rinehart & Winston.

Glob, P. (1969). *The bog people.* London: Faber & Faber.

Gluckman, M. (1955). *The judicial process among the Barotse of Northern Rhodesia.* New York: Free Press.

Goddard, V. (1993). Child labor in Naples. In W. A. Haviland & R. J. Gordon (Eds.), *Talking about people* (pp. 105–109). Mountain View, CA: Mayfield.

Godlier, M. (1971). Salt currency and the circulation of commodities among the Baruya of New Guinea. In G. Dalton (Ed.), *Studies in economic anthropology.* Washington, DC: American Anthropological Association (Anthropological Studies No. 7).

Golden, M., Birns, B., Bridger, W., & Moss, A. (1971). Social-class differentiation in cognitive development among black preschool children. *Child Development, 42,* 37–45.

Goodall, J. (1986). *The chimpanzees of Gombe: Patterns of behavior.* Cambridge, MA: Belknap Press.

Goodall, J. (1990). *Through a window: My thirty years with the chimpanzees of Gombe.* Boston: Houghton Mifflin.

Goode, W. (1963). *World revolution and family patterns.* New York: Free Press.

Goodenough, W. (1956). Residence rules. *Southwestern Journal of Anthropology, 12,* 22–37.

Goodenough, W. (1961). Comment on cultural evolution. *Daedalus, 90,* 521–528.

Goodenough, W. (Ed.). (1964). *Explorations in cultural anthropology: Essays in honor of George Murdock.* New York: McGraw-Hill.

Goodenough, W. (1965). Rethinking status. And Role: Toward a general model of the cultural organization of social relationships. In M. Benton (Ed.), *The relevance of models for social anthropology.* New York: Praeger (ASA Monographs l).

Goodenough, W. (1970). *Description and comparison in cultural anthropology.* Chicago: Aldine.

Goodenough, W. (1990). Evolution of the human capacity for beliefs. *American Anthropologist, 92,* 597–612.

Goodman, M., Bartez, W. J., Hayasaka, K., Stanhope, M. J., Slightom, J., & Czelusniak, J. (1994). Molecular evidence on primate phylogeny from DNA sequences. *American Journal of Physical Anthropology, 94,* 3–24.

Goodman, M. E. (1967). *The individual and culture.* Homewood, IL: Dorsey Press.

Goody, J. (Ed.). (1972). *Developmental cycle in domestic groups.* New York: Cambridge University Press (Papers in Social Anthropology, No. 1).

Goody, J. (1969). *Comparative studies in kinship.* Stanford, CA: Stanford University Press.

Goody, J. (1976). *Production and reproduction: A comparative study of the domestic domain.* Cambridge, MA: Cambridge University Press.

Goody, J. (1983). *The development of the family and marriage in Europe.* Cambridge, MA: Cambridge University Press.

Gordon, R. (1981, December). [Interview for Coast Telecourses, Inc.]. Los Angeles.

Gordon, R. (1990). The field researcher as a deviant: A Namibian case study. In P. Hugo (Ed.), *Truth be in the field: Social science research in southern Africa.* Pretoria: University of South Africa.

Gordon, R. J. (1992). *The Bushman myth: The making of a Namibian underclass.* Boulder, CO: Westview.

Gordon, R. J., & Megitt, M. J. (1985). *Law and order in the New Guinea highlands.* Hanover, NH: University Press of New England.

Gorer, G. (1943). Themes in Japanese culture. *Transactions of the New York Academy of Sciences,* Series 11, 5.

Gorman, E. M. (1989). The AIDS epidemic in San Francisco: Epidemiological and anthropological perspectives. In A. Podolefsky & P. J. Brown (Eds.), *Applying anthropology, An introductory reader.* Mountain View, CA: Mayfield.

Gornick, V., & Moran, B. K. (Eds.). (1971). *Woman in sexist society.* New York: Basic Books.

Gould, S. J. (1983). *Hen's teeth and horses' toes.* New York: Norton.

Gould, S. J. (1985). *The flamingo's smile: Reflections in natural history.* New York: Norton.

Gould, S. J. (1986). Of kiwi eggs and the Liberty Bell. *Natural History, 95,* 20–29.

Gould, S. J. (1989). *Wonderful life.* New York: Norton.

Gould, S. J. (1991). *Bully for brontosaurus.* New York: Norton.

Gould, S. J. (1996). *Full house: The spread of excellence from Plato to Darwin.* New York: Harmony Books.

Gould, S. J. (1996). *The mismeasure of man* (Rev. ed.). New York: Norton.

Gould, S. J. (1997). *Questioning the millennium.* New York: Crown.

Gould, S. J. (2000). What does the dreaded "E" word mean, anyway? *Natural History, 109*(1), 28–44.

Graburn, N. H. (1969). *Eskimos without igloos: Social and economic development in Sugluk.* Boston: Little, Brown.

Graburn, N. H. (1971). *Readings in kinship and social structure.* New York: Harper & Row.

Graham, S. B. (1979). Biology and human social behavior: A response to van den Berghe and Barash. *American Anthropologist, 81*(2), 357–360.

Graves, J. L. (2001). *The emperor's new clothes: Biological theories of race at the millennium.* New Brunswick, NJ: Rutgers University Press.

Graves, P. (1991). New models and metaphors for the Neanderthal debate. *Current Anthropology, 32*(5), 513–543.

Green, E. C. (1987). The planning of health education strategies in Swaziland. In R. M. Wulff & S. J. Fiske (Eds.), *Anthropological praxis: Translating knowledge into action* (pp. 15–25). Boulder, CO: Westview.

Greenberg, J. H. (1968). *Anthropological linguistics: An introduction.* New York: Random House.

Greenfield, L. O. (1979). On the adaptive pattern of *Ramapithecus. American Journal of Physical Anthropology, 50,* 527–547.

Greenfield, L. O. (1980). A late divergence hypothesis. *American Journal of Physical Anthropology, 52,* 351–366.

Griffin, B. (1994). CHAGS7. *Anthropology Newsletter, 35* (1), 12–14.

Grine, F. E. (1993). Australopithecine taxonomy and phylogeny: Historical background and recent interpretation. In R. L. Ciochon & J. G. Fleagle (Eds.), *The human evolution source book,* Englewood Cliffs, NJ: Prentice-Hall.

Grün, R., & Thorne, A. (1997). Dating the Ngandong humans. *Science, 276,* 1,575.

Gulliver, P. (1968). Age differentiation. In *International encyclopedia of the social sciences* (Vol. 1, pp. 157–162). New York: Macmillan.

Gutin, J. A. (1995). Do Kenya tools root birth of modern thought in Africa? *Science, 270,* 1,118–1,119.

Haeri, N. (1997). The reproduction of symbolic capital: Language, state and class in Egypt. *Current Anthropology, 38,* 795–816.

Hafkin, N., & Bay, E. (Eds.). (1976). *Women in Africa.* Stanford, CA: Stanford University Press.

Hall, E. T., & Hall, M. R. (1986). The sounds of silence. In E. Angeloni (Ed.), *Anthropology 86/87* (pp. 65–70). Guilford, CT: Dushkin.

Hall, K. R. L., & DeVore, I. (1965). Baboon social behavior. In I. DeVore (Ed.), *Primate behavior.* New York: Holt, Rinehart & Winston.

Hallowell, A. I. (1955). *Culture and experience.* Philadelphia: University of Pennsylvania Press.

Halverson, J. (1989). Review of *Altimira revisited and other essays on early art. American Antiquity, 54,* 883.

Hamblin, D. J., & the Editors of Time-Life. (1973). *The first cities.* New York: Time-Life.

Hamburg, D. A., & McGown, E. R. (Eds.). (1979). *The great apes.* Menlo Park, CA: Cummings.

Hammond, D. (1972). *Associations.* Reading, MA: Addison-Wesley.

Hannah, J. L. (1988). *Dance, sex and gender.* Chicago: University of Chicago Press.

Harlow, H. F. (1962). Social deprivation in monkeys. *Scientific American, 206,* 1–10.

Harpending, J. H. & Harpending, H. C. (1995). Ancient differences in population can mimic a recent African origin of modern humans. *Current Anthropology, 36,* 667–674.

Harris, M. (1965). The cultural ecology of India's sacred cattle. *Current Anthropology, 7,* 51–66.

Harris, M. (1968). *The rise of anthropological theory: A history of theories of culture.* New York: Crowell.

Harrison, G. G. (1975). Primary adult lactase deficiency: A problem in anthropological genetics. *American Anthropologist, 77,* 812–835.

Hart, C. W., Pilling, A. R., & Goodale, J. (1988). *Tiwi of North Australia* (3rd ed.). New York: Holt, Rinehart & Winston.

Hartwig, W. C., & Doneski, K. (1998). Evolution of the Hominid hand and toolmaking behavior. *American Journal of Physical Anthropology, 106,* 401–402.

Hatch, E. (1983). *Culture and morality: The relativity of values in anthropology.* New York: Columbia University Press.

Hatcher, E. P. (1985). *Art as culture, an introduction to the anthropology of art.* New York: University Press of America.

Haviland, W. (1970). Tikal, Guatemala and Mesoamerican urbanism. *World Archaeology, 2,* 186–198.

Haviland, W. A. (1972). A new look at Classic Maya social organization at Tikal. *Ceramica de Cultura Maya, 8,* 1–16.

Haviland, W. A. (1974). Farming, seafaring and bilocal residence on the coast of Maine. *Man in the Northeast, 6,* 31–44.

Haviland, W. A. (1975). The ancient Maya and the evolution of urban society. *University of Northern Colorado Museum of Anthropology, Miscellaneous Series,* 37.

Haviland, W. A. (1983). *Human evolution and prehistory* (2nd ed.). New York: Holt, Rinehart & Winston.

Haviland, W. A. (1991). *Star wars at Tikal, or did Caracol do what the glyphs say they did?* Paper presented at the 90th Annual Meeting of the American Anthropological Association.

Haviland, W. A. (1997). Cleansing young minds, or what should we be doing in introductory anthropology? In C. P. Kottak, J. J. White, R. H. Furlow, & P. C. Rice

(Eds.), *The teaching of anthropology: Problems, issues and decisions* (p. 35). Mountain View, CA: Mayfield.

Haviland, W. A. (1997). The rise and fall of sexual inequality: Death and gender at Tikal, Guatemala. *Ancient Mesoamerica, 8,* 1–12.

Haviland, W. A. (2002). Settlement, society and demography at Tikal. In J. Sabloff (Ed.), *Tikal.* Santa Fe, NM: School of American Research (in press).

Haviland, W. A., et al. (1985). *Excavations in small residential groups of Tikal: Groups 4F-1 and 4F-2.* Philadelphia: University Museum.

Haviland, W. A., & Moholy-Nagy, H. (1992). Distinguishing the high and mighty from the hoi polloi at Tikal, Guatemala. In A. F. Chase & D. Z. Chase (Eds.), *Mesoamerican elites: An archaeological assessment.* Norman: Oklahoma University Press.

Haviland, W. A., & Power, M. W. (1994). *The original Vermonters: Native inhabitants, past and present* (Rev. and exp. ed.). Hanover, NH: University Press of New England.

Hawkes, K., O'Connell, J. F., & Blurton-Jones, N. G. (1997). Hadza women's time allocation, offspring, provisioning, and the evolution of long postmenopausal life spans. *Current Anthropology, 38,* 551–577.

Hawkins, G. S. (1965). *Stonehenge decoded.* New York: Doubleday.

Hays, H. R. (1965). *From ape to angel: An informal history of social anthropology.* New York: Knopf.

Heichel, G. (1976). Agricultural production and energy resources. *American Scientist, 64.*

Heilbroner, R. L. (1972). *The making of economic society* (4th ed.). Englewood Cliffs, NJ: Prentice-Hall.

Heilbroner, R. L., & Thurow, L. C. (1981). *The economic problem* (6th ed.). Englewood Cliffs, NJ: Prentice-Hall.

Helm, J. (1962). The ecological approach in anthropology. *American Journal of Sociology, 67,* 630–649.

Henry, J. (1965). *Culture against man.* New York: Vintage Books.

Henry, J. (1966). The metaphysic of youth, beauty, and romantic love. In S. Farber & R. Wilson (Eds.), *The challenge of women.* New York: Basic Books.

Henry, J. (1974). A theory for an anthropological analysis of American culture. In J. G. Jorgensen & M. Truzzi (Eds.), *Anthropology and American life.* Englewood Cliffs, NJ: Prentice-Hall.

Herskovits, M. J. (1952). *Economic anthropology: A study in comparative economics* (2nd ed.). New York: Knopf.

Herskovits, M. J. (1964). *Cultural dynamics.* New York: Knopf.

Hewes, G. W. (1973). Primate communication and the gestural origin of language. *Current Anthropology, 14,* 5–24.

Hickerson, N. P. (1980). *Linguistic anthropology.* New York: Holt, Rinehart & Winston.

Hodgen, M. (1964). *Early anthropology in the sixteenth and seventeenth centuries.* Philadelphia: University of Pennsylvania Press.

Hoebel, E. A. (1954). *The law of primitive man: A study in comparative legal dynamics.* Cambridge, MA: Harvard University Press.

Hoebel, E. A. (1960). *The Cheyennes: Indians of the Great Plains.* New York: Holt, Rinehart & Winston.

Hoebel, E. A. (1972). *Anthropology: The study of man* (4th ed.). New York: McGraw-Hill.

Hogbin, I. (1964). *A Guadalcanal society.* New York: Holt, Rinehart & Winston.

Holden, C. (1983). Simon and Kahn versus *Global 2000. Science, 221,* 342.

Holden, C. (1996). Missing link for miocene apes. *Science, 271,* 151.

Holden, C. (1998). No last word on language origins. *Science, 282,* 1,455–1,458.

Holden, C. (1999). A new look into Neandertal's noses. *Science, 285,* 31–33.

Hole, F. (1966). Investigating the origins of Mesopotamian civilization. *Science, 153,* 605–611.

Hole, F., & Heizer, R. F. (1969). *An introduction to prehistoric archeology.* New York: Holt, Rinehart & Winston.

Holloway, R. L. (1980). The O. H. 7 (Olduvai Gorge, Tanzania) hominid partial brain endocast revisited. *American Journal of Physical Anthropology, 53,* 267–274.

Holloway, R. L. (1981). The Indonesian *Homo erectus* brain endocast revisited. *American Journal of Physical Anthropology, 55,* 503–521.

Holloway, R. L. (1981). Volumetric and asymmetry determinations on recent hominid endocasts: Spy I and II, Djebel Jhroud 1, and the Salb *Homo erectus* specimens, with some notes on Neanderthal brain size. *American Journal of Physical Anthropology, 55,* 385–393.

Hostetler, J., & Huntington, G. (1971). *Children in Amish society.* New York: Holt, Rinehart & Winston.

Houle, A. (1999). The origin of platyrrhines: An evaluation of the Antarctic scenario and the floating island model. *American Journal of Physical Anthropology, 109,* 541–559.

Howell, F. C. (1970). *Early man.* New York: Time-Life.

Hsiaotung, F. (1939). *Peasant life in China.* London: Kegan, Paul, Trench, & Truber.

Hsu, F. L. (1961). *Psychological anthropology: Approaches to culture and personality.* Homewood, IL: Dorsey Press.

Hsu, F. L. (1997). Role, affect, and anthropology. *American Anthropologist, 79,* 805–808.

Hsu, F. L. K. (1979). The cultural problems of the cultural anthropologist. *American Anthropologist, 81,* 517–532.

Hubert, H., & Mauss, M. (1964). *Sacrifice.* Chicago: University of Chicago Press.

Hunt, R. C. (Ed.). (1967). *Personalities and cultures: Readings in psychological anthropology.* Garden City, NY: Natural History Press.

Hymes, D. (1964). *Language in culture and society: A reader in linguistics and anthropology.* New York: Harper & Row.

Hymes, D. (Ed.). (1972). *Reinventing anthropology.* New York: Pantheon.

Ingmanson, E. J. (1998). Comment. *Current Anthropology, 39,* 409–410.

Inkeles, A., Hanfmann, E., & Beier, H. (1961). Modal personality and adjustment to the Soviet socio-political system. In B. Kaplan (Ed.), *Studying personality cross-culturally.* New York: Harper & Row.

Inkeles, A., & Levinson, D. J. (1954). National character: The study of modal personality and socio-cultural systems. In G. Lindzey (Ed.), *Handbook of social psychology.* Reading, MA: Addison-Wesley.

Ireland, E. (1991). Neither warriors nor victims, the Wauja peacefully organize to defend their land. *Cultural Survival Quarterly, 15*(1), 54–59.

It's the law: Child labor protection. (1997, November/December). *Peace and Justice News,* 11.

Jacobs, S. E. (1994). Native American Two-spirits. *Anthropology Newsletter, 35*(8), 7.

Jacoby, R., & Glauberman, N. (Eds.). (1995). *The bell curve.* New York: Random House.

Jennings, F. (1976). *The invasion of America.* New York: Norton.

Jennings, J. D. (1974). *Prehistory of North America* (2nd ed.). New York: McGraw-Hill.

Johanson, D., & Shreeve, J. (1989). *Lucy's child: The discovery of a human ancestor.* New York: Avon.

Johanson, D. C., & Edey, M. (1981). *Lucy, the beginnings of humankind.* New York: Simon & Schuster.

Johanson, D. C., & White, T. D. (1979). A systematic assessment of early African hominids. *Science, 203,* 321–330.

John, V. (1971). Whose is the failure? In C. L. Brace, G. R. Gamble, & J. T. Bond (Eds.), *Race and intelligence.* Washington, DC: American Anthropological Association (Anthropological Studies No. 8).

Johnson, A. (1989). Horticulturalists: Economic behavior in tribes. In S. Plattner (Ed.), *Economic anthropology* (pp. 49–77). Stanford, CA: Stanford University Press.

Johnson, A. W., & Earle, T. (1987). *The evolution of human societies, from foraging group to agrarian state.* Stanford, CA: Stanford University Press.

Johnson, D. (1996). Polygamists emerge from secrecy, seeking not just peace but respect. In W. A. Haviland & R. J. Gordon (Eds.), *Talking about people* (2nd ed., pp. 129–131). Mountain View, CA: Mayfield.

Jolly, A. (1985). The evolution of primate behavior. *American Scientist, 73*(3), 230–239.

Jolly, A. (1985). *The evolution of primate behavior* (2nd ed.). New York: Macmillan.

Jolly, A. (1985). Thinking like a Vervet. *Science, 251,* 574.

Jolly, C. J. (1970). The seed eaters: A new model of hominid differentiation based on a baboon analogy. *Man, 5,* 5–26.

Jolly, C. J., & Plog, F. (1986). *Physical anthropology and archaeology* (4th ed.). New York: Knopf.

Jones, S., Martin, R., & Pilbeam, D. (Eds.). (1992). *The Cambridge encyclopedia of human evolution.* New York: Cambridge University Press.

Jopling, C. F. (1971). *Art and aesthetics in primitive societies: A critical anthology.* New York: Dutton.

Jorgensen, J. (1972). *The sun dance religion.* Chicago: University of Chicago Press.

Joukowsky, M. A. (1980). *A complete field manual of archeology: Tools and techniques of field work for archaeologists.* Englewood Cliffs, NJ: Prentice-Hall.

Joyce, C. (1991). *Witnesses from the grave: The stories bones tell.* Boston: Little, Brown.

Kahn, H., & Wiener, A. J. (1967). *The year 2000.* New York: Macmillan.

Kaiser, J. (1994). A new theory of insect wing origins takes off. *Science, 266,* 363.

Kalwet, H. (1988). *Dreamtime and inner space: The world of the shaman.* New York: Random House.

Kaplan, D. (1972). *Culture theory.* Englewood Cliffs, NJ: Prentice-Hall (Foundations of Modern Anthropology).

Karavani, I., & Smith, F. H. (2000). More on the Neanderthal problem: The Vindija case. *Current Anthropology, 41,* 838–840.

Kardiner, A. (1939). *The individual and his society: The psycho-dynamics of primitive social organization.* New York: Columbia University Press.

Kardiner, A., & Preble, E. (1961). *They studied men.* New York: Mentor.

Kay, R. F. (1981). The nut-crackers—A new theory of the adaptations of the Ramapithecinae. *American Journal of Physical Anthropology, 55,* 141–151.

Kay, R. F., Fleagle, J. F., & Simons, E. L. (1981). A revision of the Oligocene apes of the Fayum Province, Egypt. *American Journal of Physical Anthropology, 55,* 293–322.

Kay, R. F., Ross, C., & Williams, B. A. (1997). Anthropoid origins. *Science, 275,* 797–804.

Kay, R. F., Theweissen, J. G. M., & Yoder, A. D. (1992). Cranial anatomy of *Ignacius graybullianus* and the affinities of the plesiadapiformes. *American Journal of Physical Anthropology, 89*(4), 477–498.

Keesing, R. M. (1975). *Kin groups and social structure.* New York: Holt, Rinehart & Winston.

Kendall, L. (1990, October). In the company of witches. *Natural History,* 92–95.

Kenyon, K. (1957). *Digging up Jericho.* London: Ben.

Kerri, J. N. (1976). Studying voluntary associations as adaptive mechanisms: A review of anthropological perspectives. *Current Anthropology, 17*(1).

Kessler, E. (1975). *Women.* New York: Holt, Rinehart & Winston.

Kirkpatrick, R. C. (2000). The evolution of human homosexual behavior. *Current Anthropology, 41,* 385–413.

Kleinman, A. (1982). The failure of western medicine. In D. Hunter & P. Whitten (Eds.), *Anthropology: Contemporary perspectives.* Boston: Little, Brown.

Kluckhohn, C. (1970). *Mirror for man.* Greenwich, CT: Fawcett.

Kluckhohn, C. (1994). Navajo witchcraft. *Papers of the Peabody Museum of American Archaeology and Ethnology, 22*(2).

Knauft, B. (1991). Violence and sociality in human evolution. *Current Anthropology, 32,* 391–409.

Koch, G. (1997). Songs, land rights and archives in Australia. *Cultural Survival Quarterly, 20*(4).

Kohler, G. (1996). Global apartheid. Reprinted in W. A. Haviland & R. J. Gordon (Eds.), *Talking about people: Readings in contemporary cultural anthropology* (2nd ed., pp. 262–268). Mountain View, CA: Mayfield.

Koufos, G. (1993). Mandible of Ouranopithecus macedoniensis (hominidae: primates) from a new late Miocene locality in Macedonia (Greece). *American Journal of Physical Anthropology, 91,* 225–234.

Krader, L. (1968). *Formation of the state.* Englewood Cliffs, NJ: Prentice-Hall (Foundation of Modern Anthropology).

Kramer, P. A. (1998). The costs of human locomotion: Maternal investment in child transport. *American Journal of Physical Anthropology, 107*, 71–85.

Kroeber, A. (1958). Totem and taboo: An ethnologic psychoanalysis. In W. Lessa & E. Z. Vogt (Eds.), *Reader in comparative religion: An anthropological approach.* New York: Harper & Row.

Kroeber, A. L. (1939). Cultural and natural areas of native North America. *American archaeology and ethnology* (Vol. 38). Berkeley: University of California Press.

Kroeber, A. L. (1963). *Anthropology: Cultural processes and patterns.* New York: Harcourt.

Kroeber, A. L., & Kluckhohn, C. (1952). *Culture: A critical review of concepts and definitions.* Cambridge, MA: Harvard University Press (Papers of the Peabody Museum of American Archaeology and Ethnology, 47).

Kuhn, T. (1968). *The structure of scientific revolutions.* Chicago: University of Chicago Press (International Encyclopedia of Unified Science, 2[27]).

Kummer, H. (1971). *Primate societies: Group techniques of ecological adaptation.* Chicago: Aldine.

Kunzig, R. (1999). A tale of two obsessed archaeologists, one ancient city and nagging doubts about whether science can ever hope to reveal the past. *Discover, 20*(5), 84–92.

Kuper, H. (1965). The Swazi of Swaziland. In J. L. Gibbs (Ed.), *Peoples of Africa* (pp. 479–511). New York: Holt, Rinehart & Winston.

Kurath, G. P. (1960). Panorama of dance ethnology. *Current Anthropology, 1,* 233–254.

Kushner, G. (1969). *Anthropology of complex societies.* Stanford, CA: Stanford University Press.

La Barre, W. (1945). Some observations of character structure in the Orient: The Japanese. *Psychiatry,* 8.

Lancaster, J. B. (1975). *Primate behavior and the emergence of human culture.* New York: Holt, Rinehart & Winston.

Landes, R. (1982). Comment. *Current Anthropology, 23,* 401.

Lanning, E. P. (1967). *Peru before the Incas.* Englewood Cliffs, NJ: Prentice-Hall.

Lanternari, V. (1963). *The religions of the oppressed.* New York: Mentor.

Lasker, G. W., & Tyzzer, R. (1982). *Physical anthropology* (3rd ed.) New York: Holt, Rinehart & Winston.

Laughlin, W. S., & Osborne, R. H. (Eds.). (1967). *Human variation and origins.* San Francisco: Freeman.

Laurel, K. (1990). In the company of witches. *Natural History*, 92.

Lawler, A. (2001). Writing gets a rewrite. *Science, 292,* 2,419.

Layton, R. (1991). *The anthropology of art* (2nd ed.). Cambridge, England: Cambridge University Press.

Leach, E. (1961). *Rethinking anthropology.* London: Athione Press.

Leach, E. (1962). The determinants of differential cross-cousin marriage. *Man, 62,* 238.

Leach, E. (1962). On certain unconsidered aspects of double descent systems. *Man, 214,* 13–34.

Leach, E. (1965). *Political systems of highland Burma.* Boston: Beacon Press.

Leach, E. (1982). *Social anthropology.* Glasgow: Fontana Paperbacks.

Leacock, E. (1981). *Myths of male dominance: Collected articles on women cross culturally.* New York: Monthly Review Press.

Leacock, E. (1981). Women's status in egalitarian society: Implications for social evolution. In *Myths of male dominance: Collected articles on women cross culturally.* New York: Monthly Review Press.

Leakey, L. S. B. (1965). *Olduvai Gorge, 1951–1961* (Vol. 1). London: Cambridge University Press.

Leakey, L. S. B. (1967). Development of aggression as a factor in early man and prehuman evolution. In C. Clements & D. Lundsley (Eds.), *Aggression and defense.* Los Angeles: University of California Press.

Leakey, M. D. (1971). *Olduvai Gorge: Excavations in Beds I and II. 1960–1963.* London and New York: Cambridge University Press.

Leap, W. L. (1987). Tribally controlled culture change: The Northern Ute language revival project. In R. M. Wulff & S. J. Fiske (Eds.), *Anthropological praxis: Translating knowledge into action* (pp. 197–211). Boulder, CO: Westview.

Leavitt, G. C. (1990). Sociobiological explanations of incest avoidance: A critical review of evidential claims. *American Anthropologist, 92,* 971–993.

Le Clair, E., & Schneider, H. K. (Eds.). (1968). *Economic anthropology: Readings in theory and analysis.* New York: Holt, Rinehart & Winston.

Lee, R. (1993). *The Dobe Ju/boansi.* Ft. Worth, TX: Harcourt Brace.

Lee, R. B., & DeVore, I. (Eds.). (1968). *Man the hunter.* Chicago: Aldine.

Leeds, A., & Vayda, A. P. (Eds.). (1965). *Man, culture and animals: The role of animals in human ecological adjustments.* Washington, DC: American Association for the Advancement of Science.

Lees, R. (1953). The basis of glottochronology. *Language, 29,* 113–127.

Legros, D. (1997). Comment. *Current Anthropology, 38,* 617.

LeGros Clark, W. E. (1966). *History of the primates* (5th ed.). Chicago: University of Chicago Press.

Lehmann, A. C., & Myers, J. E. (Eds.). (1993). *Magic, witchcraft and religion: An anthropological study of the supernatural* (3rd ed.). Mountain View, CA: Mayfield.

Lehmann, W. P. (1973). *Historical linguistics, an introduction* (2nd ed.). New York: Holt, Rinehart & Winston.

Leigh, S. R., & Park, P. B. (1998). Evolution of human growth prolongation. *American Journal of Physical Anthropology, 107,* 331–350.

Leinhardt, G. (1964). *Social anthropology.* London: Oxford University Press.

Leinhardt, G. (1971). Religion. In H. Shapiro (Ed.), *Man, culture and society* (2nd ed.). London: Oxford University Press.

LeMay, M. (1975). The language capability of Neanderthal man. *American Journal of Physical Anthropology, 43*(1), 9–14.

Lenski, G. (1966). *Power and privilege: A theory of social stratification.* New York: McGraw-Hill.

Leonard, W. R., & Hegman, M. (1987). Evolution of P_3 morphology in *Australopithecus afarensis. American Journal of Physical Anthropology, 73,* 41–63.

Lerner, R. N. (1987). Preserving plants for Pomos. In R. M. Wulff & S. J. Fiske (Eds.), *Anthropological praxis: Translating knowledge into action* (pp. 212–222). Boulder, CO: Westview.

Leroi-Gourhan, A. (1968). The evolution of Paleolithic art. *Scientific American, 218,* 58ff.

Lestel, D. (1998). How chimpanzees have domesticated humans. *Anthropology Today, 14*(3), 12–15.

Lett, J. (1987). *The human enterprise: A critical introduction to anthropological theory.* Boulder, CO: Westview.

Levanthes, L. E. (1987). The mysteries of the bog. *National Geographic, 171,* 397–420.

Levine, N. E., & Silk, J. B. (1997). Why polyandry fails. *Current Anthropology, 38,* 375–398.

Levine, R. (1973). *Culture, behavior and personality.* Chicago: Aldine.

Levine, R. P. (1968). *Genetics.* New York: Holt, Rinehart & Winston.

Lev-Yadun, S., Gopher, A., & Abbo, Shahal. (2000). The cradle of agriculture. *Science, 288,* 1,602–1,603.

Lewin, R. (1983). Is the orangutan a living fossil? *Science, 222,* 1,223.

Lewin, R. (1985). Tooth enamel tells a complex story. *Science, 228,* 707.

Lewin, R. (1986). New fossil upsets human family. *Science, 233,* 720–721.

Lewin, R. (1987). Debate over emergence of human tooth pattern. *Science, 235,* 749.

Lewin, R. (1987). The earliest "humans" were more like apes. *Science, 236,* 1,062–1,063.

Lewin, R. (1987). Four legs bad, two legs good. *Science, 235,* 969.

Lewin, R. (1987). Why is ape tool use so confusing? *Science, 236,* 776–777.

Lewin, R. (1988). Molecular clocks turn a quarter century. *Science, 235,* 969–971.

Lewin, R. (1993). Paleolithic paint job. *Discover, 14*(7), 64–70.

Lewis, I. M. (1965). Problems in the comparative study of unilineal descent. In M. Banton (Ed.), *The relevance of models for social organization* (A.S.A. Monograph No. 1). London: Tavistock.

Lewis, I. M. (1976). *Social anthropology in perspective.* Harmondsworth, England: Penguin.

Lewis-Williams, J. D. (1990). *Discovering southern African rock art.* Cape Town and Johannesburg: David Philip.

Lewis-Williams, J. D., & Dowson, T. A. (1988). Signs of all times: Entoptic phenomena in Upper Paleolithic art. *Current Anthropology, 29,* 201–245.

Lewis-Williams, J. D., & Dowson, T. A. (1993). On vision and power in the Neolithic: Evidence from the decorated monuments. *Current Anthropology, 34,* 55–65.

Lewis-Williams, J. D., Dowson, T. A., & Deacon, J. (1993). Rock art and changing perceptions of Southern Africa's past: Ezeljagdspoort reviewed. *Antiquity, 67,* 273–291.

Lewontin, R. C., Rose, S., & Kamin, L. J. (1984). *Not in our genes.* New York: Pantheon.

Linton, R. (1964, orig. 1936). *The study of man: An introduction.* New York: Appleton.

Little, K. (1964). The role of voluntary associations in West African urbanization. In P. van den Berghe (Ed.), *Africa: Social problems of change and conflict.* San Francisco: Chandler.

Livingstone, F. B. (1973). The distribution of abnormal hemoglobin genes and their significance for human evolution. In C. Loring Brace & J. Metress (Eds.), *Man in evolutionary perspective.* New York: Wiley.

Lorenzo, C., Carretero, J. M., Arsuaga, J. L., Gracia, A., & Martinez, I. (1998). Intrapopulational body size variation and cranial capacity variation in middle Pleistocene humans: The Sima de los Huesos sample (Sierra de Atapuerca, Spain). *American Journal of Physical Anthropology, 106,* 19–33.

Louckey, J., & Carlsen, R. (1991). Massacre in Santiago Atitlán. *Cultural Survival Quarterly, 15*(3), 70.

Lounsbury, F. (1964). The structural analysis of kinship semantics. In H. G. Lunt (Ed.), *Proceedings of the Ninth International Congress of Linguists.* The Hague: Mouton.

Lovejoy, C. O. (1981). Origin of man. *Science, 211* (4,480), 341–350.

Lowenstein, J. M. (1992, December). Genetic surprises. *Discover, 13,* 82–88.

Lowie, R. H. (1948). *Social organization.* New York: Holt, Rinehart & Winston.

Lowie, R. H. (1956, orig. 1935). *Crow Indians.* New York: Holt, Rinehart & Winston.

Lowie, R. H. (1966). *Culture and ethnology.* New York: Basic Books.

Lustig-Arecco, V. (1975). *Technology strategies for survival.* New York: Holt, Rinehart & Winston.

MacCormack, C. P. (1977). Biological events and cultural control. *Signs, 3,* 93–100.

MacLarnon, A. M., & Hewitt, G. P. (1999). The evolution of human speech: The role of enhanced breathing control. *American Journal of Physical Anthropology, 109,* 341–363.

MacNeish, R. S. (1992). *The origins of agriculture and settled life.* Norman: University of Oklahoma Press.

MacNiel, R. (1982). *The right place at the right time.* Boston: Little, Brown.

Magnarella, P. J. (1974). *Tradition and change in a Turkish town.* New York: Wiley.

Mair, L. (1969). *Witchcraft.* New York: McGraw-Hill.

Mair, L. (1971). *Marriage.* Baltimore: Penguin.

Malefijt, A. de W. (1969). *Religion and culture: An introduction to anthropology of religion.* London: Macmillan.

Malefijt, A. de W. (1974). *Images of man.* New York: Knopf.

Malinowski, B. (1922). *Argonauts of the western Pacific.* New York: Dutton.

Malinowski, B. (1945). *The dynamics of culture change.* New Haven, CT: Yale University Press.

Malinowski, B. (1951). *Crime and custom in savage society.* London: Routledge.

Malinowski, B. (1954). *Magic, science and religion.* Garden City, NY: Doubleday/Anchor Books.

Marano, L. (1982). Windigo psychosis: The anatomy of an emic-etic confusion. *Current Anthropology, 23,* 385–412.

Marcus, J., & Flannery, K. V. (1996). *Zapotec civilization: How urban society evolved in Mexico's Oaxaca Valley.* New York: Thames & Hudson.

Marks, J. (1995). *Human biodiversity: Genes, race and history.* Hawthorne, NY: Aldine.

Marsella, J. (1982). Pulling it together: Discussion and comments. In S. Pastner & W. A. Haviland (Eds.), *Confronting the creationists.* Northeastern Anthropological Association, Occasional Proceedings, No. 1, 77–80.

Marshack, A. (1972). *The roots of civilization: A study in prehistoric cognition; The origins of art, symbol and notation.* New York: McGraw-Hill.

Marshack, A. (1976). Some implications of the paleolithic symbolic evidence for the origin of language. *Current Anthropology, 17*(2), 274–282.

Marshack, A. (1989). Evolution of the human capacity: The symbolic evidence. *Yearbook of physical anthropology* (Vol. 32, pp. 1–34). New York: Alan R. Liss.

Marshall, E. (2001). Preclovis sites fight for acceptance. *Science, 291,* 1,732.

Marshall, L. (1961). Sharing, talking and giving: Relief of social tensions among !Kung bushmen. *Africa, 31,* 231–249.

Marshall, M. (1990). Two tales from the Trukese taproom. In P. R. DeVita (Ed.), *The humbled anthropologist* (pp. 12–17). Belmont, CA: Wadsworth.

Martin, E. (1994). *Flexible bodies: Tracking immunity in American culture—from the days of polio to the age of AIDS.* Boston: Beacon Press.

Mason, J. A. (1957). *The ancient civilizations of Peru.* Baltimore: Penguin.

Matson, F. R. (Ed.). (1965). *Ceramics and man.* New York: Viking Fund Publications in Anthropology, No. 41.

Maybury-Lewis, D. (1960). Parallel descent and the Apinaye anomaly. *Southwestern Journal of Anthropology, 16,* 191–216.

Maybury-Lewis, D. (1984). *The prospects for plural societies.* 1982 Proceedings of the American Ethnological Society.

Maybury-Lewis, D. (1993, Fall). A new world dilemma: The Indian question in the Americas. *Symbols,* 17–23.

Maybury-Lewis, D. H. P. (1993). A special sort of pleading. In W. A. Haviland & R. J. Gordon (Eds.), *Talking about people* (pp. 16–24). Mountain View, CA: Mayfield.

McCorriston, J., & Hole, F. (1991). The ecology of seasonal stress and the origins of agriculture in the Near East. *American Anthropologist, 93,* 46–69.

McFee, M. (1972). *Modern Blackfeet: Montanans on a reservation.* New York: Holt, Rinehart & Winston.

McGrew, W. C. (2000). Dental care in chimps. *Science, 288,* 1,747.

McHale, J. (1969). *The future of the future.* New York: Braziller.

McHenry, H. (1975). Fossils and the mosaic nature of human evolution. *Science, 190,* 524–431.

McHenry, H. M. (1992). Body size and proportions in early hominids. American *Journal of Physical Anthropology, 87,* 407–431.

McKenna, J. (1997, October). Bedtime story. *Natural History,* 50.

Mead, M. (1928). *Coming of age in Samoa.* New York: Morrow.

Mead, M. (1963). *Sex and temperament in three primitive societies* (3rd ed.). New York: Morrow.

Mead, M. (1970). *Culture and commitment.* Garden City, NY: Natural History Press.

Meadows, D. H., Meadows, D. L., Randers J., & Behrens III, W. W. (1974). *The limits to growth.* New York: Universe Books.

Melaart, J. (1967). *Catal Hüyük: A Neolithic town in Anatolia.* London: Thames & Hudson.

Mellars, P. (1989). Major issues in the emergence of modern humans. *Current Anthropology, 30,* 349–385.

Meltzer, D., Fowler, D., & Sabloff, J. (Eds.). (1986). *American archaeology: Past & future.* Washington, DC: Smithsonian Institution Press.

Merrell, D. J. (1962). *Evolution and genetics: The modern theory of genetics.* New York: Holt, Rinehart & Winston.

Merriam, A. P. (1964). *The anthropology of music.* Chicago: Northwestern University Press.

Mesghinua, H. M. (1966). Salt mining in Enderta. *Journal of Ethiopian Studies, 4* (2).

Michaels, J. W. (1973). *Dating methods in archaeology.* New York: Seminar Press.

Middleton, J. (Ed.). (1970). *From child to adult: Studies in the anthropology of education.* Garden City, NY: Natural History Press (American Museum Source Books in Anthropology).

Miles, H. L. W. (1993). Language and the orangutan: The old "person" of the forest. In P. Cavalieri & P. Singer (Eds.), *The great ape project* (pp. 42–57). New York: St. Martin's Press.

Miller, J. M. A. (2000). Craniofacial variation in *Homo habilis:* An analysis of the evidence for multiple species. *American Journal of Physical Anthropology, 112,* 103–128.

Millon, R. (1973). *Urbanization of Teotihuacán, Mexico: Vol. 1, Part 1. The Teotihuacán Map.* Austin: University of Texas Press.

Mintz, S. (1996). A taste of history. In W. A. Haviland & R. J. Gordon (Eds.), *Talking about people* (2nd ed., pp. 79–82). Mountain View, CA: Mayfield.

Mintz, S. (2002). A taste of history. In W. A. Haviland & R. J. Gordon (Eds.), *Talking about people* (3rd ed., pp. 87–90). New York: McGraw-Hill.

Minugh-Purvis, N. (1992). The inhabitants of Ice Age Europe. *Expedition, 34*(3), 23–36.

Mitchell, W. E. (1973, December). A new weapon stirs up old ghosts. *Natural History Magazine,* 77–84.

Mitchell, W. E. (1978). *Mishpokhe: A study of New York City Jewish family clubs.* The Hague: Mouton.

Moffat, A. S. (2002). New fossils and a glimpse of evolution. *Science, 295,* 613–615.

Molnar, S. (1992). *Human variation: Races, types and ethnic groups* (3rd ed.). Englewood Cliffs, NJ: Prentice-Hall.

Montagu, A. (1964). *The concept of race.* London: Macmillan.

Montagu, A. (1964). *Man's most dangerous myth: The fallacy of race* (4th ed.) New York: World Publishing.

Montagu, A. (1975). *Race and IQ.* New York: Oxford University Press.

Moore, J. (1998). Comment. *Current Anthropology, 39,* 412.

Morgan, L. H. (1877). *Ancient society.* New York: World Publishing.

Moscati, S. (1962). *The face of the ancient orient.* New York: Doubleday.

Mullings, L. (1989). Gender and the application of anthropological knowledge to public policy in the United States. In S. Morgan (Ed.), *Gender and anthropology* (pp. 360–381). Washington: American Anthropological Association.

Murdock, G. (1960). Cognatic forms of social organization. In G. P. Murdock (Ed.), *Social structure in Southeast Asia* (pp. 1–14). Chicago: Quadrangle Books.

Murdock, G. P. (1965). *Social structure.* New York: Free Press.

Murdock, G. P. (1971). How culture changes. In H. L. Shapiro (Ed.), *Man, culture and society* (2nd ed.) New York: Oxford University Press.

Murphy, R. (1971). *The dialectics of social life: Alarms and excursions in anthropological theory.* New York: Basic Books.

Murphy, R., & Kasdan, L. (1959). The structure of parallel cousin marriage. *American Anthropologist, 61,* 17–29.

Murray, G. F. (1989). The domestication of wood in Haiti: A case study in applied evolution. In A. Podolefsky & P. J. Brown (Eds.), *Applying anthropology, an introductory reader.* Mountain View, CA: Mayfield.

Mydens, S. (2001, August 12). He's not hairy, he's my brother. *New York Times,* Sect. 4, p. 5.

Myrdal, G. (1974). Challenge to affluence: The emergence of an "under-class." In J. G. Jorgensen & M. Truzzi (Eds.), *Anthropology and American life.* Englewood Cliffs, NJ: Prentice-Hall.

Nader, L. (Ed.). (1965). The ethnography of law. *American Anthropologist,* Part II, *67*(6).

Nader, L. (Ed.). (1969). *Law in culture and society.* Chicago: Aldine.

Nader, L. (Ed.). (1980). *No access to law: Alternatives to the American judicial system.* New York: Academic Press.

Nader, L. (1981, December). [Interview for Coast Telecourses, Inc.]. Los Angeles.

Nader, L. (1997). Controlling processes: Tracing the dynamic components of power. *Current Anthropology, 38,* 714–715.

Nance, C. R. (1997). Review of Haviland's *Cultural anthropology* (p. 2).

Nanda, S. (1992). Arranging a marriage in India. In P. R. De Vita (Ed.), *The naked anthropologist* (pp. 139–143). Belmont, CA: Wadsworth.

Naroll, R. (1973). Holocultural theory tests. In R. Naroll & F. Naroll (Eds.), *Main currents in cultural anthropology.* New York: Appleton.

Nash, M. (1966). *Primitive and peasant economic systems.* San Francisco: Chandler.

Natadecha-Sponsal, P. (1993). The young, the rich and the famous: Individualism as an American cultural value. In P. R. DeVita & J. D. Armstrong (Eds.), *Distant mirrors: America as a foreign culture* (pp. 46–53). Belmont, CA: Wadsworth.

Needham, R. (Ed.). (1971). *Rethinking kinship and marriage.* London: Tavistock.

Needham, R. (1972). *Belief, language and experience.* Chicago: University of Chicago Press.

Neer, R. M. (1975). The evolutionary significance of Vitamin D, skin pigment and ultraviolet light. *American Journal of Physical Anthropology, 43,* 409–416.

Nesbitt, L. M. (1935). *Hell-hole of creation.* New York: Knopf.

Netting, R. M., Wilk, R. R., & Arnould, E. J. (Eds.). (1984). *Households: Comparative and historical studies of the domestic group.* Berkeley: University of California Press.

Nettl, B. (1956). *Music in primitive culture.* Cambridge, MA: Harvard University Press.

Newman, P. L. (1965). *Knowing the Gururumba.* New York: Holt, Rinehart & Winston.

Nietschmann, B. (1987). The third world war. *Cultural Survival Quarterly, 11*(3), 1–16.

Norbeck, E. (1974). *Religion in human life: Anthropological views.* New York: Holt, Rinehart & Winston.

Norbeck, E., Price-Williams, D., & McCord, W. (Eds.). (1968). *The study of personality: An interdisciplinary appraisal.* New York: Holt, Rinehart & Winston.

Normile, D. (1998). Habitat seen as playing larger role in shaping behavior. *Science, 279,* 1,454–1,455.

Normile, D. (2001). Gene expression differs in human and chimp brains. *Science, 292,* 44–45.

Nunney, L. (1998). Are we selfish, are we nice, or are we nice because we are selfish? *Science, 281,* 1,619.

Nye, E. I., & Berardo, F. M. (1975). *The family: Its structure and interaction.* New York: Macmillan.

Oakley, K. P. (1964). *Man the tool-maker.* Chicago: University of Chicago Press.

O'Barr, W. M., & Conley, J. M. (1993). When a juror watches a lawyer. In W. A. Haviland & R. J. Gordon (Eds.), *Talking about people* (2nd ed., pp. 44–47). Mountain View, CA: Mayfield.

Oboler, R. S. (1980). Is the female husband a man? Woman/woman marriage among the Nandi of Kenya. *Ethnology, 19,* 69–88.

Offiong, D. (1985). Witchcraft among the Ibibio of Nigeria. In A. C. Lehmann & J. E. Myers (Eds.), *Magic, witchcraft and religion* (pp. 152–165). Palo Alto, CA. Mayfield.

Okonjo, K. (1976). The dual-sex political system in operation: Igbo women and community politics in midwestern Nigeria. In N. Hafkin & E. Bay (Eds.), *Women in Africa* (pp. 45–58). Stanford, CA: Stanford University Press.

Oliwenstein, L. (1995). New footsteps into walking debate. *Science, 269,* 476.

Olszewki, D. I. (1991). Comment. *Current Anthropology, 32,* 43.

O'Mahoney, K. (1970). The salt trade. *Journal of Ethiopian Studies, 8*(2).

Ortiz, A. (1969). *The Tewa world.* Chicago: University of Chicago Press.

Oswalt, W. H. (1970). *Understanding our culture.* New York: Holt, Rinehart & Winston.

Oswalt, W. H. (1972). *Habitat and technology.* New York: Holt, Rinehart & Winston.

Oswalt, W. H. (1972). *Other peoples other customs: World ethnography and its history.* New York: Holt, Rinehart & Winston.

Otte, M. (2000). On the suggested bone flute from Slovenia. *Current Anthropology, 41,* 271–272.

Otten, C. M. (1971). *Anthropology and art: Readings in cross-cultural aesthetics.* Garden City, NY: Natural History Press.

Ottenberg, P. (1965). The Afikpo Ibo of eastern Nigeria. In J. L. Gibbs (Ed.), *Peoples of Africa.* New York: Holt, Rinehart & Winston.

Otterbein, K. F. (1971). *The evolution of war.* New Haven, CT: HRAF Press.

Parades, J. A., & Purdum, E. J. (1990). Bye bye Ted. . . . *Anthropology Today, 6* (2), 9–11.

Parés, J. M., Perez-Gonzalez, A., Weil, A. B., & Arsuaga, J. L. (2000). On the age of hominid fossils at the Sima de los Huesos, Sierra de Atapuerca, Spain: Paleomagnetic evidence. *American Journal of Physical Anthropology, 111,* 451–461.

Parish, A. R. (1998). Comment. *Current Anthropology, 39,* 413–414.

Parker, R. G. (1991). *Bodies, pleasures, and passions: Sexual culture in contemporary Brazil.* Boston: Beacon Press.

Parker, S., & Parker, H. (1979). The myth of male superiority: Rise and demise. *American Anthropologist, 81*(2), 289–309.

Parnell, R. (1999). Gorilla exposé. *Natural History, 108*(8), 38–43.

Partridge, W. (Ed.). (1984). *Training manual in development anthropology.* Washington, DC: American Anthropological Association.

Pastner, S., & Haviland, W. A. (Eds.). (1982). Confronting the creationists. *Northeastern Anthropological Association Occasional Proceedings,* I.

Patterson, F., & Linden, E. (1981). *The education of Koko.* New York: Holt, Rinehart & Winston.

Patterson, T. C. (1981). *Archeology: The evolution of ancient societies.* Englewood Cliffs, NJ: Prentice-Hall.

Peacock, J. L. (1986). *The anthropological lens: Harsh light, soft focus.* New York: Cambridge University Press.

Pelliam, A. de, & Burton, F. D. (1976). More on predatory behavior in nonhuman primates. *Current Anthropology, 17*(3), 512–513.

Pelto, P. J. (1973). *The snowmobile revolution: Technology and social change in the Arctic.* Menlo Park, CA: Cummings.

Penniman, T. K. (1965). *A hundred years of anthropology.* London: Duckworth.

Peters, C. R. (1979). Toward an ecological model of African Plio-Pleistocene hominid adaptations. *American Anthropologist, 81*(2), 261–278.

Peterson, F. L. (1962). *Ancient Mexico, An introduction to the pre-Hispanic cultures.* New York: Capricorn Books.

Pfeiffer, J. E. (1977). *The emergence of society.* New York: McGraw-Hill.

Pfeiffer, J. E. (1978). *The emergence of man.* New York: Harper & Row.

Pfeiffer, J. E. (1985). *The creative explosion.* Ithaca, NY: Cornell University Press.

Pickering, T. R., White, T. D., & Toth, N. (2000). Cutmarks on a Plio-Pleistocene Hominid from Sterkfontein, South Africa. *American Journal of Physical Anthropology, 111,* 579–584.

Piddocke, S. (1965). The potlatch system of the southern Kwakiutl: A new perspective. *Southwestern Journal of Anthropology, 21,* 244–264.

Piggott, S. (1965). Ancient Europe. Chicago: Aldine.

Pilbeam D. (1986). *Human origins.* David Skamp Distinguished Lecture in Anthropology, Indiana University.

Pilbeam, D. (1987). Rethinking human origins. In *Primate evolution and human origins.* Hawthorne, NY: Aldine de Gruytar.

Pilbeam, D., & Gould, S. J. (1974). Size and scaling in human evolution. *Science, 186,* 892–901.

Pimentel, D. (1991). Response. *Science, 252,* 358.

Pimentel, D., Hurd, L. E., Bellotti, A. C., Forster, M. J., Oka, I. N., Sholes, O. D., & Whitman, R. J. (1973). Food production and the energy crisis. *Science, 182.*

Piperno, D. R. (2001). On maize and the sunflower. *Science, 292,* 2,260–2,261.

Piperno, D. R., & Fritz, G. J. (1994). On the emergence of agriculture in the new world. *Current Anthropology, 35,* 637–643.

Pitt, D. (1977). Comment. *Current Anthropology, 18,* 628.

Plattner, S. (1989). Markets and market places. In S. Plattner (Ed.), *Economic anthropology.* Stanford, CA: Stanford University Press.

Podolefsky, A., & Brown, P. J. (Eds.). (1989). *Applying anthropology, an introductory reader.* Mountain View, CA: Mayfield.

Polanyi, K. (1968). The economy as instituted process. In E. E. LeClair, Jr. & H. K. Schneider (Eds.), *Economic anthropology: Readings in theory and analysis* (pp. 122–167). New York: Holt, Rinehart & Winston.

Pope, G. (1989, October). Bamboo and human evolution. *Natural History, 98,* 48–57.

Pope, G. G. (1992). Craniofacial evidence for the origin of modern humans in China. *Yearbook of Physical Anthropology, 35,* 243–298.

Pospisil, L. (1963). *The Kapauku Papuans of West New Guinea.* New York: Holt, Rinehart & Winston.

Pospisil, L. (1971). *Anthropology of law: A comparative theory.* New York: Harper & Row.

Powdermaker, H. (1966). *Stranger and friend: The way of an anthropologist.* New York: Norton.

Power, M. G. (1995). Gombe revisited: Are chimpanzees violent and hierarchical in the free state? *General Anthropology, 2*(1), 5–9.

Premack, A. J., & Premack, D. (1972). Teaching language to an ape. *Scientific American, 277*(4), 92–99.

Price, T. D., & Feinman, G. M. (Eds.). (1995). *Foundations of social inequality.* New York: Plenam.

Price-Williams, D. R. (Ed.). (1970). *Cross-cultural studies: Selected readings.* Baltimore, Penguin (Penguin Modern Psychology Readings).

Prideaux, T., & the Editors of Time-Life. (1973). *Cro-Magnon man.* New York: Time-Life.

Pringle, H. (1997). Ice Age communities may be earliest known net hunters. *Science, 277,* 1,203–1,204.

Pringle, H. (1998). The slow birth of agriculture. *Science, 282,* 1,446–1,450.

Prins, A. H. (1953). *East African class systems.* Gronigen, the Netherlands: J. B. Walters.

Prins, H. (1996). *The Mi'kmaq: Resistance, accommodation, and cultural survival.* Fort Worth, TX: Harcourt Brace.

Puleston, D. E. (1983). *The settlement survey of Tikal.* Philadelphia: University Museum.

Radcliffe-Brown, A. (1952). *Structure and function in primitive society.* New York: Free Press.

Radcliffe-Brown, A. R. (1931). Social organization of Australian tribes. *Oceania Monographs,* No. 1. Melbourne: Macmillan.

Radcliffe-Brown, A. R., & Forde, C. D. (Eds.). (1950). *African systems of kinship and marriage.* London: Oxford University Press.

Rappaport, R. (1984). *Pigs for the ancestors* (Enlarged ed.). New Haven, CT: Yale University Press.

Rappaport, R. A. (1969). Ritual regulation of environmental relations among a New Guinea people. In A. P. Vayda (Ed.), *Environment and cultural behavior* (pp. 181–201). Garden City, NY: Natural History Press.

Rappaport, R. A. (1994). Commentary. *Anthropology Newsletters, 35*(6), 76.

Rathje, W. L. (1974). The garbage project: A new way of looking at the problems of archaeology. *Archaeology, 27,* 236–241.

Rathje, W. L. (1993). Rubbish! In W. A. Haviland & R. J. Gordon (Eds.), *Talking about people: Readings in contemporary cultural anthropology.* Mountain View, CA: Mayfield.

Read, C. E. (1973). *The role of faunal analysis in reconstructing human behavior: A Mousterian example.* Paper presented at the meetings of the California Academy of Sciences, Long Beach.

Read-Martin, C. E., & Read, D. W. (1975). Australopithecine scavenging and human evolution: An approach from faunal analysis. *Current Anthropology, 16*(3), 359–368.

Recer, P. (1998, February 16). Apes shown to communicate in the wild. *Burlington Free Press,* p. 12A.

Redfield, R., Linton, R., & Herskovits, M. J. (1936). Memorandum of the study of acculturation. *American Anthropologist, 38,* 149–152.

Redman, C. L. (1978). *The rise of civilization: From early farmers to urban society in the ancient Near East.* San Francisco: Freeman.

Reid, J. J., Schiffer, M. B., & Rathje, W. L. (1975). Behavioral archaeology: Four strategies. *American Anthropologist, 77,* 864–869.

Reina, R. (1966). *The law of the saints.* Indianapolis: Bobbs-Merrill.

Reiter, R. (Ed.). (1975). *Toward an anthropology of women.* New York: Monthly Review Press.

Relethford, J. H. (2001). Absence of regional affinities of Neandertal DNA with living humans does not reject multiregional evolution. *American Journal of Physical Anthropology, 115,* 95–98.

Relethford, J. H., & Harpending, H. C. (1994). Craniometric variation, genetic theory, and modern human origins. *American Journal of Physical Anthropology, 95,* 249–270.

Renfrew, C. (1973). *Before civilization: The radiocarbon revolution and prehistoric Europe.* London: Jonathan Cape.

Reynolds, V. (1994). Primates in the field, primates in the lab. *Anthropology Today, 10*(2), 3–5.

Rice, D. S., & Prudence, M. (1984). Lessons from the Maya. *Latin American Research Review, 19*(3), 7–34.

Rice, P. (2000). Paleoanthropology 2000—part 1. *General Anthropology, 7*(1), 11.

Richmond, B. G., Fleagle, J. K., & Swisher III, C. C. (1998). First Hominoid elbow from the miocene of Ethiopia and the evolution of the Catarrhine elbow. *American Journal of Physical Anthropology, 105,* 257–277.

Ridley, M. (1999). *Genome, the autobiography of a species in 23 chapters.* New York: HarperCollins.

Rightmire, G. P. (1990). *The evolution of* Homo erectus: *Comparative anatomical studies of an extinct human species.* Cambridge, England: Cambridge University Press.

Rightmire, G. P. (1998). Evidence from facial morphology for similarity of Asian and African representatives of *Homo erectus. American Journal of Physical Anthropology, 106,* 61–85.

Rindos, D. (1984). *The origins of agriculture: An evolutionary perspective.* Orlando: Academic Press.

Rodman, H. (1968). Class culture. *International encyclopedia of the social sciences* (Vol. 15, pp. 332–337). New York: Macmillan.

Rogers, J. (1994). Levels of the genealogical hierarchy and the problem of hominoid phylogeny. *American Journal of Physical Anthropology, 94,* 81–88.

Romer, A. S. (1945). *Vertebrate paleontology.* Chicago: University of Chicago Press.

Roosevelt, A. C. (1984). Population, health, and the evolution of subsistence: Conclusions from the conference. In M. N. Cohen & G. J. Armelagos (Eds.), *Paleopathology at the origins of agriculture.* Orlando: Academic Press.

Rosas, A. (2001). Occurrence of Neandertal features from the Atapunerea-SH site. *American Journal of Physical Anthropology, 114,* 74–91.

Rosas, A., & Bermudez de Castro, J. M. (1998). On the taxonomic affinities of the Dmanisi mandible (Georgia). *American Journal of Physical Anthropology, 107,* 145–162.

Roscoe, P. B. (1995). The perils of "positivism" in cultural anthropology. *American Anthropologist, 97,* 497.

Rowe, T. (1988). New issues for phylogenetics. *Science, 239,* 1,183–1,184.

Ruhlen, M. (1994). *The origin of language: Tracing the evolution of the mother tongue.* New York: Wiley.

Ruvdo, M. (1994). Molecular evolutionary processes and conflicting gene trees: The hominoid case. *American Journal of Physical Anthropology, 94,* 89–113.

Sabloff, J., & Lambert-Karlovsky, C. C. (1973). *Ancient civilization and trade.* Albuquerque: University of New Mexico Press.

Sabloff, J. A. (1989). *The cities of ancient Mexico.* New York: Thomas & Hudson.

Sabloff, J. A., & Lambert-Karlovsky, C. C. (Eds.). (1974). *The rise and fall of civilizations, modern archaeological approaches to ancient cultures.* Menlo Park, CA: Cummings.

Sahlins, M. (1961). The segmentary lineage: An organization of predatory expansion. *American Anthropologist, 63,* 322–343.

Sahlins, M. (1968). *Tribesmen.* Englewood Cliffs, NJ: Prentice-Hall (Foundations of Modern Anthropology).

Sahlins, M. (1972). *Stone age economics.* Chicago: Aldine.

Salthe, S. N. (1972). *Evolutionary biology.* New York: Holt, Rinehart & Winston.

Salzman, P. C. (1967). Political organization among nomadic peoples. *Proceedings of the American Philosophical Society, 3,* 115–131.

Sanday, P. R. (1975). On the causes of IQ differences between groups and implications for social policy. In A. Montagu (Ed.), *Race and IQ.* London: Oxford.

Sanday, P. R. (1981). *Female power and male dominance: On the origins of sexual inequality.* Cambridge, England: Cambridge University Press.

Sangree, W. H. (1965). The Bantu Tiriki of western Kenya. In J. L. Gibbs (Ed.), *Peoples of Africa.* New York: Holt, Rinehart & Winston.

Sanjek, R. (Ed.) (1990). *Fieldnotes: The making of anthropology.* Ithaca, NY: Cornell University Press.

Sapir, E. (1921). *Language.* New York: Harcourt.

Savage, J. M. (1969). *Evolution* (3rd ed.). New York: Holt, Rinehart & Winston.

Scaglion, R. (1987). Contemporary law development in Papua New Guinea. In R. M. Wulff & S. J. Fiske (Eds.), *Anthropological praxis: Translating knowledge into action.* Boulder, CO: Westview.

Scarr-Salapatek, S. (1971). Unknowns in the IQ equation. *Science, 174,* 1,223–1,228.

Schaller, G. B. (1971). *The year of the gorilla.* New York: Ballantine.

Scheflen, A. E. (1972). *Body language and the social order.* Englewood Cliffs, NJ: Prentice-Hall.

Schepartz, L. A. (1993). Language and human origins. *Yearbook of Physical Anthropology, 36,* 91–126.

Scheper-Hughes, N. (1979). *Saints, scholars and schizophrenics.* Berkeley: University of California Press.

Schlegel, A. (1977). Male and female in Hopi thought and action. In A. Schlegel (Ed.), *Sexual stratification* (pp. 245–269). New York: Columbia University Press.

Schrire, C. (Ed.). (1984). *Past and present in hunter-gatherer studies.* Orlando: Academic Press.

Schurtz, H. (1902). *Alterklassen und Männerbünde.* Berlin: Reimer.

Schusky, E. L. (1975). *Variation in kinship.* New York: Holt, Rinehart & Winston.

Schusky, E. L. (1983). *Manual for kinship analysis* (2nd ed.). Lanham, MD: University Press of America.

Schwartländer, B., Garnett, G., Walker, N., & Anderson, R. (2000). AIDS in a new millennium. *Science, 289,* 64–67.

Schwartz, J. H. (1984). Hominoid evolution: A review and a reassessment. *Current Anthropology, 25*(5), 655–672.

Selim, J. (2002). Out of left field. *Discover, 23*(1), 30–31.

Sellen, D.W., & Mace, R. (1997). Fertility and mode of substance: A phylogenetic analysis. *Current Anthropology, 38,* 878–889.

Semenov, S. A. (1964). *Prehistoric technology.* New York: Barnes & Noble.

Sen, G., & Grown, C. (1987). *Development, crisis, and alternative visions: Third World women's perspectives.* New York: Monthly Review Press.

Seymour, D. Z. (1986). Black children, black speech. In P. Escholz, A. Rosa, & V. Clark (Eds.), *Language awareness* (4th ed.). New York: St. Martin's Press.

Shapiro, H. (Ed.). (1971). *Man, culture and society* (2nd ed.). New York: Oxford University Press.

Sharer, R. J., & W. Ashmore. (1993). *Archaeology: Discovering our past* (2nd ed.). Palo Alto, CA: Mayfield.

Sharp, L. (1952). Steel axes for Stone Age Australians. In E. H. Spicer (Ed.), *Human problems in technological change.* New York: Russell Sage.

Shaw, D. G. (1984). A light at the end of the tunnel: Anthropological contributions toward global competence. *Anthropology Newsletter, 25,* 16.

Shearer, R. R., & Gould, S. J. (1999). Of two minds and one nature. *Science, 286,* 1,093.

Sheets, P. (1993). Dawn of a New Stone Age in eye surgery. In R. J. Sharer & W. Ashmore, *Archaeology: Discovering our past* (2nd ed.). Palo Alto, CA: Mayfield.

Shimkin, D. B., Tax, S., & Morrison, J. W. (Eds.). (1978). *Anthropology for the future.* Urbana: Department of Anthropology, University of Illinois, Research Report No. 4.

Shinnie, M. (1970). *Ancient African kingdoms.* New York: New American Library.

Shipman, P. (1981). *Life history of a fossil: An introduction to taphonomy and paleoecology.* Cambridge, MA: Harvard University Press.

Shorto, R. (1997, December 7). Belief by the numbers. *New York Times Magazine,* p. 60.

Shostak, M. (1983). *Nisa: The life and worlds of a !Kung woman.* New York: Vintage.

Shreeve, J. (1994). "Lucy," crucial early human ancestor, finally gets a head. *Science, 264,* 34–35.

Shreeve, J. (1994). Terms of estrangement. *Discover, 15*(11), 56–63.

Shreeve, J. (1995). *The Neandertal enigma.* New York: Willliam Morrow.

Shuey, A. M. (1966). *The testing of Negro intelligence.* New York: Social Science Press.

Sillen, A. & Brain, C. K. (1990). Old flame. *Natural History, 4,* 6–10.

Simons, E. L. (1972). *Primate evolution.* New York: Macmillan.

Simons, E. L. (1989). Human origins. *Science, 245,* 1,343–1,350.

Simons, E. L. (1995). Skulls and anterior teeth of *Catopithecus* (primates: anthropoidea) from the Eocene and anthropoid origins. *Science, 268,* 1,885–1,888.

Simons, E. L., Rasmussen, D. T., & Gebo, D. L. (1987). A new species of Propliopithecus from the Fayum, Egypt. *American Journal of Physical Anthropology, 73,* 139–147.

Simpson, G. G. (1949). *The meaning of evolution.* New Haven, CT: Yale University Press.

Sjoberg, G. (1960). *The preindustrial city.* New York: Free Press.

Skelton, R. R., McHenry, H. M., & Drawhorn, G. M. (1986). Phylogenetic analysis of early hominids. *Current Anthropology, 27,* 21–43.

Slobin, D. I. (1971). *Psycholinguistics.* Glenview, IL: Scott, Foresman.

Small, M. F. (1997). Making connections. *American Scientist, 85,* 503.

Smith, A. H., & Fisher, J. L. (1970). *Anthropology.* Englewood Cliffs, NJ: Prentice-Hall.

Smith, B. D. (1977). Archaeological inference and inductive confirmation. *American Anthropologist, 79*(3), 598–617.

Smith, B. H. (1994). Patterns of dental development in *Homo, Australopithecus, Pan,* and *gorilla. American Journal of Physical Anthropology, 94,* 307–325.

Smith, F. H., & Raynard, G. C. (1980). Evolution of the supraorbital region in Upper Pleistocene fossil hominids from South-Central Europe. *American Journal of Physical Anthropology, 53,* 589–610.

Smith, P. E. L. (1976). *Food production and its consequences* (2nd ed.). Menlo Park, CA: Cummings.

Smith, R. (1970). Social stratification in the Caribbean. In L. Plotnicov & A. Tudin (Eds.), *Essays in comparative social stratification.* Pittsburgh: University of Pittsburgh Press.

Smuts, B. (1987). What are friends for? *Natural History, 96* (2), 36–44.

Snowden, C. T. (1990). Language capabilities of nonhuman animals. *Yearbook of Physical Anthropology, 33,* 215–243.

Solis, R. S., Haas, J., & Creamer, W. (2001). Dating Caral, a preceramic site in the Supe valley on the central coast of Peru. *Science, 292,* 723–726.

Solomon, R. (2001, February 20). Genome's riddle. *New York Times,* p. D3.

Speck, F. G. (1920). Penobscot shamanism. *Memoirs of the American Anthropological Association, 6,* 239–288.

Speck, F. G. (1935). Penobscot tales and religious beliefs. *Journal of American Folk-Lore, 48* (187), 1–107.

Speck, F. G. (1970). *Penobscot man: The life history of a forest tribe in Maine.* New York: Octagon Books.

Spencer, F., & Smith, F. H. (1981). The significance of Ales Hrdlicka's "Neanderthal phase of man": A historical and current assessment. *American Journal of Physical Anthropology, 56,* 435–459.

Spencer, H. (1896). *Principles of sociology.* New York: Appleton.

Spiro, M. E. (1966). Religion: Problems of definition and explanation. In M. Banton (Ed.), *Anthropological approaches to the study of religion* (A.S.A. Monographs). London: Tavistock.

Spitz, R. A. (1949). Hospitalism. *The psychoanalytic study of the child* (Vol. 1). New York: International Universities Press.

Spradley, J. P. (1979). *The ethnographic interview.* New York: Holt, Rinehart & Winston.

Spradley, J. P. (1980). *Participant observation.* New York: Holt, Rinehart & Winston.

Spuhler, J. N. (1979). Continuities and discontinuities in anthropoid-hominid behavioral evolution: Bipedal locomotion and sexual reception. In N. A. Chagnon & W. Irons (Eds.), *Evolutionary biology and human social behavior* (pp. 454–461). North Scituate, MA: Duxbury Press.

Squires, S. (1997). The market research and product industry discovers anthropology. *Anthropology Newsletter, 38*(4), 31.

Stacey, J. (1990). *Brave new families.* New York: Basic Books.

Stahl, A. B. (1984). Hominid dietary selection before fire. *Current Anthropology, 25,* 151–168.

Stanford, C. G. (1998). The social behavior of chimpanzees and bonobos: Empirical evidence and shifting assumptions. *Current Anthropology, 39,* 399–420.

Stanley, S. M. (1979). *Macroevolution.* San Francisco: Freeman.

Stannard, D. E. (1992). *American holocaust.* Oxford: Oxford University Press.

Stanner, W. E. (1968). Radcliffe-Brown, A. R. *International encyclopedia of the social sciences* (Vol. 13). New York: Macmillan.

Steward, J. H. (1972). *Theory of culture change: The methodology of multilinear evolution.* Urbana: University of Illinois Press.

Stewart, D. (1997). Expanding the pie before you divvy it up. *Smithsonian, 28,* 82.

Stiles, D. (1979). Early Acheulian and developed Oldowan. *Current Anthropology, 20*(1), 126–129.

Stiles, D. (1992). The hunter-gatherer "revisionist" debate. *Anthropology Today, 8*(2), 13–17.

Stiner, M. C., Munro, N. D., Surovell, T. A., Tchernov, E., & Bar-Yosef, O. (1999). Paleolithic population growth pulses evidenced by small annual exploitation. *Science, 283,* 190–194.

Stirton, R. A. (1967). *Time, life, and man.* New York: Wiley.

Stocker, T. (1987, spring). A technological mystery resolved. *Invention and Technology,* 64.

Stocking, G. W., Jr. (1968). *Race, culture and evolution: Essays in the history of anthropology.* New York: Free Press.

Stoler, M. (1982). To tell the truth. *Vermont Visions, 82*(3), 3.

Stone, R. (1995). If the mercury soars, so may health hazards. *Science, 267,* 958.

Straughan, B. (1996). The secrets of ancient Tiwanaku are benefiting today's Bolivia. In W. A. Haviland & R. J. Gordon (Eds.), *Talking about people* (2nd ed., pp. 76–78). Mountain View, CA: Mayfield.

Straus, W. L., & Cave, A. J. E. (1957). Pathology and the posture of Neanderthal man. *Quarterly Review of Biology,* 32.

Stringer, C. B., & McKie, R. (1996). *African exodus: The origins of modern humanity.* London: Jonathan Cape.

Suarez-Orozoco, M. M., Spindler, G., & Spindler, L. (1994). *The making of psychological anthropology, II.* Fort Worth, TX: Harcourt Brace.

Susman, R. L. (1988). Hand of *Paranthropus robustus* from Member 1, Swartkrans: Fossil evidence for tool behavior. *Science, 240,* 781–784.

Swadesh, M. (1959). Linguistics as an instrument of prehistory. *Southwestern Journal of Anthropology, 15,* 20–35.

Swartz, M. J., Turner, V. W., & Tuden, A. (1966). *Political Anthropology.* Chicago: Aldine.

Swisher III, C. C., Curtis, G. H., Jacob, T., Getty, A. G., Suprijo, A., & Widiasmoro. (1994). Age of the earliest known hominids in Java, Indonesia. *Science, 263,* 1,118–1,121.

Tague, R. G. (1992). Sexual dimorphism in the human bony pelvis, with a consideration of the Neanderthal pelvis from Kebara Cave, Israel. *American Journal of Physical Anthropology, 88,* 1–21.

Tannen, D. (1990). *You just don't understand: Women and men in conversation.* New York: William Morrow.

Tardieu, C. (1998). Short adolescence in early hominids: Infantile and adolescent growth of the human femur. *American Journal of Physical Anthropology, 107,* 163–178.

Tax, S. (1953). *Penny capitalism: A Guatemalan Indian economy.* Smithsonian Institution, Institute of Social Anthropology, Pub. No. 16. Washington, DC: GPO.

Tax, S. (Ed.). (1962). *Anthropology today: Selections.* Chicago: University of Chicago Press.

Tax, S., Stanley, S., et al. (1975). In honor of Sol Tax. *Current Anthropology, 16,* 507–540.

Templeton, A. R. (1994). "Eve": Hypothesis compatability versus hypothesis testing. *American Anthropologist, 96,* 144–147.

The first Americans, ca. 20,000 B.C. (1998). *Discover, 19*(6), 24.

Thomas, D. H. (1974). *Predicting the past.* New York: Holt, Rinehart & Winston.

Thomas, D. H. (1998). *Archaeology* (3rd ed.). Fort Worth, TX: Harcourt Brace.

Thomas, E. M. (1994). *The tribe of the tiger.* New York: Simon & Schuster.

Thomas, W. L. (Ed.). (1956). *Man's role in changing the face of the earth.* Chicago: University of Chicago Press.

Thompson, S. (1960). *The folktale.* New York: Holt, Rinehart & Winston.

Thomson, K. S. (1997). Natural selection and evolution's smoking gun. *American Scientist, 85,* 516–518.

Thorne, A. G., & Wolpoff, M. D. H. (1981). Regional continuity in Australasian Pleistocene hominid evolution. *American Journal of Physical Anthropology, 55,* 337–349.

Thorne, B., & Yalom, M. (Eds.). (1982). *Rethinking the family: Some feminist questions.* New York: Longman.

Thornhill, N. (1993). Quoted in W. A. Haviland & R. J. Gordon (Eds.), *Talking about people* (p. 127). Mountain View, CA: Mayfield.

Tiffany, S. (Ed.). (1979). *Women in Africa.* St. Albans, VT: Eden Press.

Tobias, P. V. (1980). The natural history of the heliocoidal occlusal plane and its evolution in early Homo. *American Journal of Physical Anthropology, 53,* 173–187.

Tobias, P. V., & von Konigswald, G. H. R. (1964). A comparison between the Olduvai hominines and those of Java and some implications for hominid phylogeny. *Nature, 204,* 515–518.

Togue, R. G. (1992). Sexual dimorphism in the human bony pelvis, with a consideration of the Neanderthal pelvis from Kebara Cave, Israel. *American Journal of Physical Anthropology, 88,* 1–21.

Trager, G. L. (1964). Paralanguage: A first approximation. In D. Hymes (Ed.), *Language in culture and society.* New York: Harper & Row.

Trinkaus, E. (1986). The Neanderthals and modern human origins. *Annual Review of Anthropology, 15,* 197.

Trinkaus, E., & Shipman, P. (1992). *The Neandertals: Changing the image of mankind.* New York: Alfred A. Knopf.

Tuden, A. (1970). Slavery and stratification among the Ila of central Africa. In A. Tuden & L. Plotnicov (Eds.), *Social stratification in Africa.* New York: Free Press.

Tumin, M. M. (1967). *Social stratification: The forms and functions of inequality.* Englewood Cliffs, NJ: Prentice-Hall (Foundations of Modern Sociology).

Turnbull, C. M. (1961). *The forest people.* New York: Simon & Schuster.

Turnbull, C. M. (1983). *The human cycle.* New York: Simon & Schuster.

Turnbull, C. (1983). *Mbuti Pygmies: Change and adaptation.* New York: Holt, Rinehart & Winston.

Turner, T. (1991). Major shift in Brazilian Yanomami policy. *Anthropology Newsletter, 32*(5), 1 & 46.

Turner, V. W. (1957). *Schism and continuity in an African society.* Manchester, England: University Press.

Turner, V. W. (1969). *The ritual process.* Chicago: Aldine.

Tylor, E. B. (1871). *Primitive culture: Researches into the development of mythology, philosophy, religion, language, art and customs.* London: Murray.

Tylor, Sir E. B. (1931). Animism. In V. F. Calverton (Ed.), *The making of man: An outline of anthropology.* New York: Modern Library.

Ucko, P. J., & Rosenfeld, A. (1967). *Paleolithic cave art.* New York: McGraw-Hill.

Ucko, P. J., Tringham, R., & Dimbleby, G. W. (Eds.). (1972). *Man, settlement and urbanism.* London: Duckworth.

Valentine, C. A. (1968). *Culture and poverty.* Chicago: University of Chicago Press.

Van Allen, J. (1979). Sitting on a man: Colonialism and the lost political institutions of Igbo women. In S. Tiffany (Ed.), *Women in society* (pp. 163–187). St. Albans, VT: Eden Press.

Van Den Berghe, P. (1992). The modern state: Nation builder or nation killer? *International Journal of Group Tensions, 22*(3), 191–207.

Van Gennep, A. (1960). *The rites of passage.* Chicago: University of Chicago Press.

Vansina, J. (1965). *Oral tradition: A study in historical methodology* (H. M. Wright, Trans.). Chicago: Aldine.

Van Willigen, J. (1986). *Applied anthropology.* South Hadley, MA: Bergin & Garvey.

Vayda, A. (Ed.). (1969). *Environment and cultural behavior: Ecological studies in cultural anthropology.* Garden City, NY: Natural History Press.

Vayda, A. P. (1961). Expansion and warfare among swidden agriculturalists. *American Anthropologist, 63,* 346–358.

Vincent, J. (1979). On the special division of labor, population, and the origins of agriculture. *Current Anthropology, 20*(2), 422–425.

Vogelman, T. C., et al. (1972). *Prehistoric life in the Champlain Valley* (Film). Burlington, VT: Department of Anthropology, University of Vermont.

Voget, F. W. (1960). Man and culture: An essay in changing anthropological interpretation. *American Anthropologist, 62,* 943–965.

Voget, F. W. (1975). *A history of ethnology.* New York, Holt, Rinehart & Winston.

Vogt, E. Z. (1990). *The Zinacantecos of Mexico, a modern way of life* (2nd ed.). New York: Holt, Rinehart & Winston.

Wagner, P. L. (1960). *A history of ethnology.* New York: Holt, Rinehart & Winston.

Wallace, A. F. C. (1956). Revitalization movements. *American Anthropologist, 58,* 264–281.

Wallace, A. F. C. (1965). The problem of the psychological validity of componential analysis. *American Anthropologist, Special Publication* (Part 2), *67*(5), 229–248.

Wallace, A. F. C. (1966). *Religion: An anthropological view.* New York: Random House.

Wallace, A. F. C. (1970). *Culture and personality* (2nd ed.). New York: Random House.

Wallace, E., & Hoebel, E. A. (1952). *The Comanches.* Norman: University of Oklahoma Press.

Ward, C. V., Walker, A., Teaford, M. F., & Odhiambo, I. (1993). Partial skeleton of *Proconsul nyanzae* from Mfangano Island, Kenya. *American Journal of Physical Anthropology, 90,* 77–111.

Wardhaugh, R. (1972). *Introduction to linguistics.* New York: McGraw-Hill.

Wattenberg, B. J. (1997, November 23). The population explosion is over. *New York Times Magazine,* p. 60.

Washburn, S. L., & Moore, R. (1980). *Ape into human: A study of human evolution* (2nd ed.). Boston: Little, Brown.

Weatherford, J. (1988). *Indian givers: How the Indians of the Americas transformed the world.* New York: Fawcett Columbine.

Weaver, M. P. (1972). *The Aztecs, Maya and their predecessors.* New York: Seminar Press.

Weiner, A. B. (1977). Review of Trobriand cricket: An ingenious response to colonialism. *American Anthropologist, 79,* 506.

Weiner, A. B. (1988). The Trobrianders of Papua New Guinea. New York: Holt, Rinehart & Winston.

Weiner, J. S. (1955). *The Piltdown forgery.* Oxford: Oxford University Press.

Weiner, M. (1966). *Modernization: The dynamics of growth.* New York: Basic Books.

Weiss, M. L., & Mann, A. E. (1990). *Human biology and behavior* (5th ed.). Boston: Little, Brown.

Weitzman, L. J. (1985). *The divorce revolution: The unexpected social and economic consequences for women and children in America.* New York: Free Press.

Werner, D. (1990). *Amazon journey.* Englewood Cliffs, NJ: Prentice-Hall.

Wernick, R., & the Editors of Time-Life. (1973). *The monument builders.* New York: Time-Life.

Westermarck, E. A. (1926). *A short history of marriage.* New York: Macmillan.

Wheeler, P. (1993). Human ancestors walked tall, stayed cool. *Natural History, 102*(8), 65–66.

Whelehan, P. (1985). Review of *Incest, A Biosocial View. American Anthropologist, 87,* 677–678.

White, D. R. (1988). Rethinking polygyny: Co-wives, codes and cultural systems. *Current Anthropology, 29,* 529–572.

White, E., Brown, D., & the Editors of Time-Life. (1973). *The first men.* New York: Time-Life.

White, L. (1949). *The science of culture: A study of man and civilization.* New York: Farrar, Strauss.

White, L. (1959). *The evolution of culture: The development of civilization to the fall of Rome.* New York: McGraw-Hill.

White, P. (1976). *The past is human* (2nd ed.). New York: Maplinger.

White, R. (1992). The earliest images: Ice Age "art" in Europe. *Expedition, 34*(3), 37–51.

White, T. D. (1979). Evolutionary implications of Pliocene hominid footprints. *Science, 208,* 175–176.

Whitehead, N., & Ferguson, R. B. (Eds.). (1992). *War in the tribal zone.* Santa Fe, NM: School of American Research Press.

Whitehead, N. L., & Ferguson, R. B. (1993, November 10). Deceptive stereotypes about tribal warfare. *Chronicle of Higher Education,* p. A48.

Whiting, B. B. (Ed.). (1963). *Six cultures: Studies of child rearing.* New York: Wiley.

Whiting, J. W. M., & Child, I. L. (1953). *Child training and personality: A cross-cultural study.* New Haven, CT: Yale University Press.

Whiting, J. W. M., Sodergem, J. A., & Stigler, S. M. (1982). Winter temperature as a constraint to the migration of preindustrial peoples. *American Anthropologist, 84,* 289.

Whitten, A., & Boesch, C. (2001). Cultures of chimpanzees. *Scientific American, 284*(1), 63–67.

Willey, G. R. (1966). *An introduction to American archaeology: Vol. 1. North America.* Englewood Cliffs, NJ: Prentice-Hall.

Willey, G. R. (1971). *An introduction to American archaeology; Vol. 2: South America.* Englewood Cliffs, NJ: Prentice-Hall.

Williams, A. M. (1996). *Sex, drugs and HIV: A sociocultural analysis of two groups of gay and bisexual male substance users who practice unprotected sex.* Unpublished manuscript.

Williamson, R. K. (1995). The blessed curse: Spirituality and sexual difference as viewed by Euro-American and Native American cultures. *The College News, 17*(4).

Willigan, J. V. (1986). *Applied anthropology* (pp. 128–129, 133–139). South Hadley, MA: Bergin & Garvey.

Wills, C. (1994). The skin we're in. *Discover, 15*(11), 77–81.

Wilson, A. K., & Sarich, V. M. (1969). A molecular time scale for human evolution. *Proceedings of the National Academy of Science, 63,* 1,089–1,093.

Wingert, P. (1965). *Primitive art: Its tradition and styles.* New York: World.

Wirsing, R. L. (1985). The health of traditional societies and the effects of acculturation. *Current Anthropology, 26*(3), 303–322.

Wittfogel, K. A. (1957). *Oriental despotism, a comparative study of total power.* New Haven, CT: Yale University Press.

Wolf, E. (1959). *Sons of the shaking earth.* Chicago: University of Chicago Press.

Wolf, E. (1966). *Peasants.* Englewood Cliffs, NJ: Prentice-Hall.

Wolf, E. (1982). *Europe and the people without history.* Berkeley: University of California Press.

Wolf, M. (1972). *Women and the family in rural Taiwan.* Stanford, CA: Stanford University Press.

Wolf, M. (1985). *Revolution postponed: Women in contemporary China.* Stanford, CA: Stanford University Press.

Wolfe, A. W. (1977). The supranational organization of production: An evolutionary perspective. *Current Anthropology, 18,* 165–635.

Wolpoff, M. H. (1971). Interstitial wear. *American Journal of Physical Anthropology, 34,* 205–227.

Wolpoff, M. H. (1977). Review of earliest man in the Lake Rudolf Basin. *American Anthropologist, 79,* 708–711.

Wolpoff, M. H. (1982). *Ramapithecus* and hominid origins. *Current Anthropology, 23,* 501–522.

Wolpoff, M. H. (1993). Evolution in *Homo erectus:* The question of stasis. In R. L. Ciochon & J. G. Fleagle (Eds.), *The human evolution source book.* Englewood Cliffs, NJ: Prentice-Hall.

Wolpoff, M. H. (1993). Multiregional evolution: The fossil alternative to Eden. In R. L. Ciochon & J. G. Fleagle (Eds.), *The human evolution source book.* Englewood Cliffs, NJ: Prentice-Hall.

Wolpoff, M. (1996). *Australopithecus:* A new look at an old ancestor. *General Anthropology, 3*(1), 2.

Wolpoff, M. H. (1999). Review of Neandertals and modern humans in western Asia. *American Journal of Physical Anthropology, 109,* 416–423.

Wolpoff, M., & Caspari, R. (1997). *Race and human evolution.* New York: Simon & Schuster.

Wolpoff, M. H., Hawks, J., Frayer, D. W., & Hunley, K. (2001). Modern human ancestry at the peripheries: A test of the replacement theory. *Science, 291,* 293–297.

Womack, M. (1994). Program 5: Psychological anthropology. *Faces of culture.* Fountain Valley, CA: Coast Telecourses, Inc.

Wong, K. (1998, January). Ancestral quandary: Neanderthals not our ancestors? Not so fast. *Scientific American,* 30–32.

Wood, B., & Aiello, L. C. (1998). Taxonomic and functional implications of mandibular scaling in early Hominines. *American Journal of Physical Anthropology, 105,* 523–538.

Wood, B., & Collard, M. (1999). The human genus. *Science, 284,* 68.

Wood, B., Wood, C., & Konigsberg, L. (1994). *Paranthropus boisei:* An example of evolutionary stasis? *American Journal of Physical Anthropology, 95,* 117–136.

Woodward, V. (1992). *Human heredity and society.* St. Paul, MN: West.

Woolfson, P. (1972). Language, thought, and culture. In V. P. Clark, P. A. Escholz, & A. F. Rosa (Eds.), *Language.* New York: St. Martin's Press.

World Bank. (1982). *Tribal peoples and economic development.* Washington, DC: World Bank.

Wright, R. (1984). Towards a new Indian policy in Brazil. *Cultural Survival Quarterly, 8*(1).

Wright, R. M. (1997). Violence on Indian day in Brazil 1997: Symbol of the past and future. *Cultural Survival Quarterly, 21*(2), 47–49.

Wulff, R. M., & Fiske, S. J. (1987). *Anthropological praxis: Translating knowledge into action.* Boulder, CO: Westview.

Zeder, M. A., & Hesse, B. (2000). The initial domestication of goats *(Capra hircus)* in the Zagros mountains 10,000 years ago. *Science, 287,* 2,254–2,257.

Zilhão, J. (2000). Fate of the Neandertals. *Archaeology, 53*(4), 30.

Zimmer, C. (1999). New date for the dawn of dream time. *Science, 284,* 1,243–1,246.

Zimmer, C. (2001). *Evolution: The triumph of an idea.* New York: HarperCollins.

Zohary, D., & Hopf, M. (1993). *Domestication of plants in the Old World* (2nd ed.). Oxford: Clarenden Press.

Zur, J. (1994). The psychological impact of impunity. *Anthropology Today, 10*(3), 12–17.

PHOTO CREDITS

2 © Ancient Art & Architecture Collection; **3** © James Stanfield / NGS Image Collection; **4** © Giraudon / Art Resource, NY; **7** (top) The Granger Collection, New York; **7** (bottom) Smithsonian Institution Photo No. 56196; **8** Courtesy of Vice-Chancellor Mamphela Ramphele, © Shawn Benjamin; **9** AP / Wide World Photos; **11** (left) © Rhoda Sidney / PhotoEdit; **11** (right) © Laura Dwight / PhotoEdit; **12** © Roger Ressmeyer / Corbis; **13** Photographs furnished by the U.S. General Services Administration; **15** Peggy O'Neill-Vivanco; **20** © Mark Richards / PhotoEdit; **21** (top) © Bettmann / Corbis; **21** (middle) The Granger Collection, New York; **21** (bottom) Culver Pictures; **24** © Bettmann / Corbis; **27** AP / Wide World Photos; **28** Gordon Gahan / NGS Image Collection; **28** (top left) Wartenberg / Picture Press / Corbis; **28** (bottom) Alden Pellett / The Image Works; **29** © Paula Bronstein / Getty Images; **32** © Sisse Brimberg / NGS Image Collection; **35** AP / Wide World Photos; 37 Courtesy of Glenn Sheehan and Anne Jensen; **39** © 1985 David L. Brill; 40 Courtesy of Institute for Exploration; **41** © Mike Andrews / Ancient Art & Architecture Collection; **42** © James B. Petersen, Dept. of Anthropology, University of Vermont; **43** © G. Gorgoni / Leo de Wys, Inc.; **46** (both) © William A. Haviland; **47** Reprinted with permission from Kuttruff et al, Science 281, 73 (1998) fig. 1. Copyright 1998 American Association for the Advancement of Science; **48** From *Tikal, A Handbook of the Ancient Maya Ruins* by William R. Coe. University of Pennsylvania Museum, Philadelphia 1967; **49** © Andrew Lawler / Science Magazine; **51** University of Pennsylvania Museum; **54** © Kenneth Garrett / NGS Image Collection; **58** © UNEP-Topham / The Image Works; **61** (top left) © Anthro-Photo; **61** (top right) © Michael J. Doolittle / The Image Works; **61** (bottom left) © Cleo Freelana Photos / PhotoEdit, **61** (bottom right) © Colin Milkins, Oxford Scientific Films / Animals, Animals; **62** © Layne Kennedy / Corbis; **63** © Bettmann / Corbis; **68** (top) © Photo Researchers, Inc.; **68 b** © SuperStock; **70** © Biophoto Associates / Photo Researchers, Inc.; **73** © Meckes / Ottawa / Photo Researchers, Inc.; **75** (top) © 1999 Don Couch Photography; **75** (bottom) © The Image Works; **76** AP/Wide World Photos; **77** (top left) © George Obremski / The Image Bank; **77** (top right) © Steve Elmore; **77** (bottom) © Lawrence Manning / Woodfin Camp and Associates; **79** (both) © E. R. Degginger/Color-Pic, Inc.; **80** (both) © E. R. Degginger/Color-Pic, Inc.; **82** Otorohanga Zoological Society; **86** © 1997 Tom Brakefield / The Image Works; **87** © Bojan Brecelj / Corbis; **88** © 1998 Jim Leachman; **90** © Bettmann / Corbis; **92** © James Moore / Anthro-Photo; **96** (both) © 1998 Jim Leachman; **97** (top) © Reuters / Getty Images; **100** (left) AP / Wide World Photos; **100** (right) © David Agee / Anthro-Photo; **101** © Michael Dick / Animals, Animals; **102** (top) © E. R. Degginger / Color-Pic, Inc.; **102** (bottom) © Peter Drowne / Color-Pic, Inc.; **103** (left) © Miriam Silverstein / Animals, Animals; **103** (right) © David Watts / Anthro-Photo; **105** © Irven DeVore / Anthro-Photo; **106** (both) © Anita de Laguna Haviland; **107** (top) © Bromhall / Animals Animals; **107** (bottom) © Amy Parish / Anthro-Photo; **111** © Bromhall / Animals Animals; **114** © David Bygott / Kibuyu Partners; **118** Illustration by Nancy J. Perkins; **121** (top) © 1999 Don Couch Photography; **121** (bottom left) © David Bygott / Kibuyu Partners; **121** (bottom right) © Donna Day / Corbis; **124** © O. Louis Mazzatenta / NGS Image Collection; **126** © Anita de Laguna Haviland; **127** © Martin Harvey; **129** © E. L. Simons / Duke Primate Center; **130** © Ollie Ellison / Duke University; **131** © 1985 David L. Brill; **137** © 1985 David L. Brill; artifact credit, Peabody Museum, Harvard University; **138** © Anup and Manoj Shah; **140** © National Museums of Kenya; **141** Irven DeVore/Anthro-Photo; **144** © 1998 David L. Brill \ Brill Atlanta; **146** AP/Wide World Photos; 148 1985 David L. Brill by permission of Owen Lovejoy; **151** © William H. Kimbel, Ph.D., Institute of Human Origins; **152** © Tim White, Department of Anthropology, University of California at Berkeley; **154** (left) Lee R. Burger, PURE, University of Witwatersrand; **154** (right) © Des Bartlett / NGS Image Collection; **155** © Melville Bell Grosvenor / National Geographic Society; **156** © National Museums of Kenya; **157** (top) © 1985 David L. Brill; artifact credits, (left) A. africanus, Transvaal Museum, Pretoria, (right) A. boisei, National Museum of Tanzania, Dar es Salaam; **157** (bottom) © 1994 Tim O. White / David L. Brill, Atlanta; **158** 2000 © Philippe Plailly / Eurelios; **159** © Dr. Fred Spoor / National Museums of Kenya; **160** Photo by Dr. Rose Sevcik. Courtesy of The Language Research Center, Georgia State University; **161** © John Giustina; **166** © Michael Nichols / NGS Image Collection; **168** © John-Marshall Mantel / Corbis; **169** © Archivo Iconografico, S.A. / Corbis; **170** National Museums of Kenya; **176** (left) © National Museums of Kenya; **176** (right) © Kenneth Garrett / NGS Image Collection; **179** all David L. Brill, copyright © The National Geographic Society; **180 t** © William A. Haviland; **180** (bottom) © J & B Photo/Animals, Animals; **182** © E. R. Degginger/Color-Pic, Inc.; **185** © Andy Freeberg 1991 Discover Magazine; **186** © Sue Savage-Rumbaugh / Language Research Center; **187** © Anita de Laguna Haviland; **188** (top) © David Bygott / Anthro-Photo; **188** (bottom left and right) © 1993 Mary Ann Fittipaldi; **192** © Russell L. Ciochon, University of Iowa; **194** (top) Negative No. A11. Courtesy Department of Library Sciences, American Museum of Natural History; **194** (bottom) Courtesy of Dr. Phillip V. Tobias, South Africa; **196** © Russell Ciochon, University of Iowa; **197** (top) National Museums of Kenya; **197** (bottom left) Transparency No. 626. Courtesy Department of Library Sciences, American Museum of Natural History; **197** (bottom right) © 1985 David L. Brill; artifact credit, National Museum of Kenya, Niarobi; 198 © Antoine Devouard/REA/Corbis SABA; **199** Kenneth Garrett/NGS Image Collection; **201** National Museum of Kenya; **203** (right) © R. Potts and W. Huang, Human Origins Program; **203** (left) © R. Potts, Smithsonian Institution; **207** (top) © R. Potts, Smithsonian Institution; **207** (bottom) © 1985

David L. Brill; **208** Geoffrey G. Pope, Anthropology Department, The William Paterson College of New Jersey; **210** © 1985 David L. Brill; **211** (both) © Kenneth Garrett / NGS Image Collection; **212** © Alexander Marshack; **216** © 1995 David L. Brill\Atlanta, original housed in the British Museum; **219** (top) © Javier Trueba/Madrid Scientific Films; **219** (bottom left) © 1985 David L. Brill; artifact credit, National Museum of Ethiopia, Addis Ababa; **219** (bottom right) Zhou Guoxing, Beijing Natural History Museum; **222** ©1985 David L. Brill; **223** (top) Paul Jaronski, UM Photo Services. Karen Diane Harvey, Sculptor; **223** (bottom) Professor Wu Xinzhi, Bejing, China; **224** © Milford H. Wolpoff; **225** © Photo Researchers; **226** © Ralph S. Solecki; **228** (both) © Alexander Marshack, New York University; **229** Neandertal flute / University of Liege. Courtesy of Marcel Otte; **231** Negative No. 335658. Courtesy Department of Library Sciences, American Museum of Natural History; **233** Courtesy of Dr. B. Vandermeersch. Item from Israel Antiquities Authority; **234** L. W. T. Lawrence, The South African Museum; **235** © Sally McBrearty; **240** Cliché Philippe Morel, Ministère de la Culture et de la Communication; **242** © 1985 David L. Brill; artifact credit, Musce De L'Homme, Paris; **244** © McBrearty / Anthro-Photo; **246** (both) © William A. Haviland/UVM Photo Service; **250** © Alexander Marshack, 1997; **251** (both) © Anita de Laguna Haviland; **252** (top left) Negative No. K15806. Courtesy Department of Library Services, American Museum of Natural History; **252** (right) Negative No. K15872. Courtesy Department of Library Services, American Museum of Natural History; **252** (bottom left) Negative No. K15823. Courtesy Department of Library Services, American Museum of Natural History; **253** © Jean Vertut; **255** © Randall White; **256** © Claudio Vazquez; **257** © Göran Burenhult; **259** (top) Peabody Museum; **259** (bottom) Joe Ben Wheat Photo, University of Colorado Museum, Boulder; **260** Courtesy of Anthropos Institute, Brno; **261** Jose Zilhao © Instituto Portugues Arqueologia; **262** (left) Professor Wu Xinzhi, Bejing, China; **262** (right) Drawing from Up From The Ape by Earnest A. Hooton, Copyright © 1931, 1946 by The MacMillan Company, New York; **266** AFP Photo Steven Jaffe © AFP / Corbis; **267** University of Pennsylvania Museum Image #T35-882; **268** Paul Conklin/PhotoEdit; **271** © William A. Haviland; **273** W. Fitzhugh; **274** © William A. Haviland; **275** (top left, top right) © Dr. W. van Zeist, Biologisch-Archaeologisch Institut, Rijksuniversiteit Gronigen; **275** (bottom) Dr. Dolores Piperno/ Smithsonian Tropical Research Institute; **276** Reprinted with permission from Economic Botany Vol. 49 #1, drawing by Dr. Walton C. Galinat. Copyright 1995, The New York Botanical Garden; **278** AP / Wide World Photos; **281** © Mark Richards / PhotoEdit; **282** © Pierre Boulat / Woodfin Camp & Associates; **284** Courtesy of Zhijun Zhao; **285** © Mireille Vautier / Woodfin Camp & Associates; **287** © Bettmann / Corbis; **288** © BSIP / Chassenet / Photo Researchers, Inc.; **289** © Harvey Finkle; **290** Courtesy of the Oriental Institute of the University of Chicago; **291** (both) British School of Archaeology in Jerusalem; **293** (top) Ankara Archaeological Museum /Ara Guler, Istanbul; **293** (bottom) © John Kegan / Getty Images; **295** (both) © Alan H. Goodman, Hampshire College; **296** © Sepp Seitz / Woodfin Camp & Associates; **300** © Anita de Laguna Haviland; **304** © Arlette Mellaart; **305** © Richard Reed / Anthro-Photo; **307** (top) © William A. Haviland; **307** (bottom) © Enrico Ferorelli; **308** © Anita de Laguna Haviland; **310** The University Museum, University of Pennsylvania (neg. #T4-398); **311** (top) Peter D'Arcy Harrison; **311** (bottom) Ban Chiang Project, University of Pennsylvania Museum; **312** (top left, top right) © Ronald Sheridan/Ancient Art & Architecture Collection; **312** (bottom) Negative No. 330878. Courtesy Department of Library Sciences, American Museum of Natural History; **313** © Heather Angel / Biofotos; **314** © Getty Images; **318** (both) Dr. Christopher B. Donnan / UCLA Fowler Museum of Cultural History; **319** (top, middle, bottom left) Dr. Christopher B. Donnan / UCLA Fowler Museum of Cultural History; **319** (bottom right) Studied by Duccio Bonavia, reproduction by Gonzalo de Reparaz, Painting by Felix Caycho; **322** (top) © Anita de Laguna Haviland; **322** (bottom) © William A. Haviland; **325** (top) © James Mellaart; **325** (bottom) © Victor R. Boswell / NGS Image Collection; **326** © Mohenjo/Anthro-Photo; **327** Cultural Relics Bureau, Beijing; **330** © Terry Vine / Corbis; **334** (left) © Lauré Communications/Eliot Elisofon/National Museum of African Art; **334** (right) © Jean-Pierre Hallet / The Pygmy Fund; **335** AP / Wide World Photos; **339** © Laurence Dutton / Getty Images; **340** © Lawrence Migdale / Getty Images; **341** (both) Photo © Dinodia Photo Library; **341** (right) © A. Ramey/PhotoEdit; **342** AP / Wide World Photos; **343** AP / Wide World Photos; **344** © Steve Elmore; **345** (top) © Beryl Goldberg; **345** (bottom left) © Farrell Grehan / Photo Researchers, Inc.; **345** (bottom middle) © Richard Wood; **345** (bottom right) © E. R. Degginger / Color-Pic, Inc.; **346** Royal Anthropological Institute Photographic Collection; **349** (both) Dr. Cloyce G. Coffman / Texas A & M University; **351** (both) AP / WIde World Photos; **352** © Bill Clark / The Daily Progress; **353** AP / Wide World Photos; **355** (top) © VCL / Getty Images; **355** (bottom) AP / Wide World Photos; 360 © Erich Lessing / Art Resource; **361** © Annie Griffiths Belt / NGS Image Collection; **362** © AFP / Corbis; **365** © David Young-Wolff / PhotoEdit; **366** (left) © Elizabeth Crews / The Image Works; **366** (right) © Michael Newman / PhotoEdit; **367** © Dennis MacDonald / PhotoEdit; **369** (left) © Kael Alford / Getty Images; **369** (right) © Monika Graff / The Image Works; **372** Photo by Napoleon A. Chagnon; **373** © Bettmann / Corbis; **374** © David Tejada / Getty Images; **375** Estate of Annette B. Weiner; **377** Courtesy of Phoebe Apperson Hearst Museum of Anthopology and the Regents of the University of California; **378** © Alec Duncan; **379** (left) © Bettmann / Corbis; **379** (middle, right) AP / Wide World Photos; **380** © PhotoEdit; **382** (left) © Sean Cayton / The Image Works; **382** (middle) © A. Ramey / PhotoEdit; **382** (right) © John Neubauer; **384** © Gary Conner / PhotoEdit; **386** © William Allen / NGS Image Collection; **388** © Richard Lord / The Image Works; **391** (left) © Tom Brakefield / The Image Works; **391** (right) © Reinstein / The Image Works; **392** (left) © Tim Boyle / Getty Images; **392** (right) © Reuters NewMedia Inc. / Corbis; **393** (top) © 1996 Richard Lord; **393** (bottom left) ©

1995 Richard Lord; **393** (bottom right) © Jeff Greenberg / PhotoEdit; **394** © Esbin-Anderson / The Image Works; **399** AP / Wide World Photos; **401** © Serbian TV/RL/ Getty Images; **402** © Klaus Francke / Peter Arnold, Inc.; **405** AP / Wide World Photos; **406** AP / Wide World Photos; **407** © John Chellmann / Animals Animals; **409** © Bettmann / Corbis; **412** © Natalie Fobes / NGS Image Collection; **414** © David Young-Wolff / PhotoEdit; **415** James Balog/© 1996. Reprinted with permission of Discover Magazine; **416** (top) © 1991 Richard Lord; **416** (bottom) © David Young-Wolff / PhotoEdit; **417** (left) © Mark Jenike / Anthro-Photo; **417** r © Irven DeVore / Anthro-Photo; **418** © Yogi, Inc. / Corbis; **424** © Gallo Images / Corbis; **425** AP / Wide World Photos; **427** Estate of Jerome Tiger; **428** © Cindy Charles / PhotoEdit; **430** © N. Chagnon / Anthro-Photo; **431** The Granger Collection, New York; **433** (top) © Jeff Greenberg / PhotoEdit; **433** (bottom) AP / Wide World Photos; **434** Smithsonian Intitution Photo No. 85-8666; **435** © William A. Haviland; **437** © Anthony Bannister / ABPL; **440** © David Young-Wolff / PhotoEdit; **442** © Leslie Hugh Stone / The Image Works; **445** © Mark Richards; **446** (left) Neidhardt Collection / Underwood Archives, SF; **446** (right) ©1993 Kirk Condyles; **447** © National Museum of American Art, Washington, DC / Art Resource, NY; **448** © William A. Haviland; **450** Courtesy of the University of Illinois at Urbana-Champaign; **451** © Joe Carini / The Image Works; **453** © Anthony Bannister / ABPL; **454** (top left, top right) © Anita de Laguna Haviland; **454** (bottom) © Robert Brenner / PhotoEdit; **455** © Anthony Bannister / ABPL; **457** (both) © Anthony Bannister / ABPL; **460** (top) © Paul Conklin / PhotoEdit; **460** (bottom) © 1980 James D. Nations / DDB Stock; **464** © Teas / Anthro-Photo; **465** © Adrian Arbib / Anthro-Photo; **466** © Ann Kendall / Cusichaca Trust; **467** © Dr. Cynthia M. Beall & Dr. Melvyn C. Goldstein / NGS Image Collection; **469** © D. Donne Bryant / DDB Stock; **470** Courtesy of the Department of Library Services, The American Museum of Natural History; **471** © Jeff Greenberg / PhotoEdit; **474** © 1991 Richard Lord; **478** (top) © Steven Rubin / The Image Works; **478** (bottom) Estate of Annette B. Weiner; **479** (left) © James L. Stanfield / NGS Image Collection; **479** (right) © David H. Wells / The Image Works; **480** (left) © D. Donne Bryant / DDB Stock; **480** (right) © Eric Kroll; **481** © PhotoEdit; **482** © Bruce Dale / NGS Image Collection; **483** © 1996 Joel Gordon; **485** © Anthony Bannister / ABPL; **487** © Stan Washburn / Anthro-Photo; **489** AP / Wide World Photo; **490** Estate of Annette B. Weiner; **491** © Tannen Maury / The Image Works; **492** © 1996 Steve Henrikson; **496** AP / Wide World Photo; **497** (top) © 1998 Richard Lord; **497** (bottom) Copyright © The British Museum; **499** © 1998 Joel Gordon; **500** © John Moss / Photo Researchers, Inc.; **504** © Ancient Art & Architecture Collection; **505** © James Stanfield / NGS Image Collection; **506** © Fax/ Carin Baer / Getty Images; **508** (both) Estate of Annette B. Weiner; **509** © I. DeVore /Anthro-Photo; **510** (left) © Lisa Krantz / The Image Works; **510** (right) © Warren & Genny Garst / Tom Stack & Associates; **515** © Deborah Davis / PhotoEdit; **517** ©Bill Aron / PhotoEdit; **518** © Brissaud-Figaro / Getty Images; **521** AP / Wide World Photos; **522** © Arnaldo Magnani / Getty Images; **523** © Jodi Cobb / NGS Image Collection; **524** (left) © Omni Photo / Index Stock; **524** (right) © SuperStock; **529** (top) Estate of Annette B. Weiner; **529** b © Peter Van Arsdale; **530** © John Eastcott/Yva Momatiuk / Woodfin Camp & Associates; **531** © Linda Bartlett / Photo Researchers, Inc.; **532** (left) © Glenn Russell / Burlington Free Press; **532** (right) © Jacques M. Chenet / Corbis; **536** © Lynn Abercrombie / NGS Image Collection; **538** © Bachman / Photo Researchers, Inc.; **539** (top) © Jim Varney / Science Photo Library / Photo Researchers; **539** (bottom) © Scala / Art Resource; **543** © Irven de Vore / Anthro-Photo; **544** © Zev Radovan / PhotoEdit; **545** © Aldona Sabalis / Photo Researchers, Inc.; **546** © Vanessa Vick / Photo Researchers, Inc.; **547** © John Eastcott/Eva Momatiuki / The Image Works; **549** (left) © Joe Cavanaugh / DDB Stock; **549** (right) © Robert Frerck / Odyssey; **550** (top) Courtesy of The Milwaukee Public Museum; **550** (bottom) © Stephen Trimble; **551** © Bill Bachman / Photo Researchers, Inc.; **552** Estate of Annette B. Weiner; **553** (left) © Tony Howarth / Woodfin Camp & Associates; **553** (right) © Peter Simon / Stock, Boston; **556** (left) AP / Wide World Photo; **556** (right) © Andy Levin / Photo Researchers, Inc.; **562** © Betty Press / Woodfin Camp & Associates; **564** © The British Museum; **567** (left) Culver Pictures; **567** (right) © Bettmann / Corbis; **571** Gai Ming-sheng / HK China Tourism Press; **572** Arizona State Museum, University of Arizona, Helga Teiwes, Photographer; **574** © Michael Newman / PhotoEdit; **575** Courtesy of Peggy Reeves Sanday; **577** © Donald Sanipass; **581** (top) © Anita de Laguna Haviland; **581** (bottom) © John Verelst / National Archives of Canada; **584** © Bettmann / Corbis; **585** Photo by Bortell, courtesy Museum of New Mexico Neg. #2631; **587** © PhotoEdit; **590** © David Young-Wolff / PhotoEdit; **592** (both) © Richard Hill; **593** © Daemmrich / The Image Works; **594** © Paul Conklin / PhotoEdit; **596** © Bruce Davidson / Earth Scenes; **597** (left) © Michael Newman / PhotoEdit; **597** (right) © PhotoEdit; **598** Courtesy of International Indian Treaty Council; **599** The Granger Collection, New York; **602** © David Young-Wolff / PhotoEdit; **603** © Richard Hutchings / Photo Researchers, Inc.; **605** (left) © Marc & Evelyn Burnheim; **605** (right) © Jeffrey D. Smith / Woodfin Camp & Associates; **607** (left) © A. Ramey / PhotoEdit; **607** (right) © 1997 Joel Gordon; **609** © Beryl Goldberg; **610** University of Pennsylvania Museum, Philadelphia (Neg. #69-5-10); **611** (top) © 1985 Justin Kerr; **611** (bottom) © Anita de Laguna Haviland; **613** © 1998 Joel Gordon; **616** © Jodi Cobb / NGS Image Collection; **617** © Jodi Cobb / NGS Image Collection; **618** © AFP / Corbis; **622** Documentary Educational Resources; **623** Ray Baldwin Louis; **624** © George Holton / Photo Researchers, Inc.; **627** © Bross / Anthro-Photo; **628** © Jacques Jangoux / Peter Arnold, Inc.; **629** AP / Wide World Photos; **631** Collection of The New-York Historical Society; **635** (top) AP / Wide World Photos; **635** (bottom) ©Fred McConnaughey / Photo Researchers, Inc.; **639** © Jim Bourg / Getty Images; **640** AP / Wide World Photos; **642** AP / Wide World Photos; **644** (left) © Dr. James Gibbs, Anthropology Department, Stanford University; **644** (right) © Hans Halberstadt / Photo Researchers, Inc.; **645**

© Napoleon Chagnon / Anthro-Photo; **647** © Kael Alford / Getty Images; **649** AP / Wide World Photos; **654** © Tony Savino / The Image Works; **657** (top) © Bettmann / Corbis; **657** (middle) AP/Wide World Photos; **657** (bottom) © Mike Maple / Woodfin Camp & Associates; **658** © Fujifotos / The Image Works; **659** © AFP / Corbis; **660** © Scala / Art Resource; **662** Culver Pictures; **663** © William A. Haviland; 664 © H. Gans / The Image Works; **665** © Dan Budnick / Woodfin Camp & Associates; **666** © Irven DeVore/Anthro-Photo; **670** (top) AP / Wide World Photos; **670** (bottom) © Myrleen Cate / PhotoEdit; **671** © Dirk Halstead / Getty Images; **672** (left) © Susan McElhinney / American Image Inc.; **672** (right) Courtesy of the Department of Library Services, The American Museum of Natural History; 673 AP / Wide World Photos; 674 © Dana White / PhotoEdit; **677** (top) AP / Wide World Photos; **677** (center) © AFP / Corbis; **677** (bottom) © Alain Buu / Getty Images; **679** © Ken Schles Inc. All rights reserved; **680** (left) © Craig Aurness / Woodfin Camp & Associates; **680** (right) AP / Wide World Photos; **682** © Lichtenstein / The Image Works; **684** (left) © AFP / Corbis; **684** (right) © M. Antman / The Image Works; **685** (left) © Syndey Byrd; **685** (top right) Courtesy of the National Museum of the American Indian, Smithsonian Institution, Photo No.4771; **685** (bottom right) © Anita de Laguna Haviland; **686** © Jeff Becom / Photo 20-20; **687** © Inga Spence / Tom Stack & Associates; **689** © William A. Haviland; **691** © Werner Forman / Art Resource, NY; **694** Anthro-Photo; **695** © Laura Bliss Spaan / AMIPA; **697** © Paul Souders / Getty Images; **698** (left) © Earl & Nazima Kowall / Corbis; **698** (right) © Michael Newman / PhotoEdit; **699** (left) AP / Wide World Photos; **699** (right) © Lynn Goldsmith / Corbis; **701** Courtesy of the Burke Museum of Natural History and Culture, catalog # 1163, painted skin tunic with bear design, Tlingit, Ka-gwanta-n Wolf Clan, Sitka, Alaska; **702** (top) © J. D. Lewis Williams / Rock Art Research Unit, University of the Witwatersrand; **702** (bottom) © Anita de Laguna Haviland; **703** © Scala / Art Resource, NY; **704** (top left, top right) Migraine art reproduced by permission of the Migraine Action Association and Boehringer Ingelheim.; **704** (bottom right) © Dr. Ronald K. Siegel; **705** © Larry Dale Gordon / The Image Bank; **710** © David Harvey / NGS Image Collection; **711** © Paul Chesley / NGS Image Collection; **712** © Napoleon A. Chagnon / Anthro-Photo; **715** © Stephen Trimble; **716** © SuperStock; **718** (right) © 1995 Karen Tranberg Hansen; **718** (left) © Steven Ferry / Words & Images; **720** (top) NASA; **720** (bottom) © Tony Freeman / PhotoEdit; **723** © Robert J. Gordon; **724** Chapin Library of Rare Books, Williams College; **725** (top) © Bettmann / Corbis; **725** (bottom) © Scully / Getty Images; **728** The Smithsonian Insitution Photo No.8304; **729** (bottom) © Bernard Boutrit / Woodfin Camp & Associates; **729** (top left) © Jeff Greenberg / PhotoEdit; **729** (top right) Arizona State Museum, University of Arizona, Photographer Helga Teiwes; **730** © Bettmann / Corbis; **731** (left) © Jose Guterres / Getty Images; **731** (right) © Greg Smith / Getty Images; **733** © A. Ramey / PhotoEdit; **735** (left) © Ewing Galloway / Index Stock; **735** (right) © Robert Brenner / PhotoEdit; **736** © George Mobley / NGS Image Collection; **739** © Nani Gois / Abril Imagens; **742** © Paul Conklin / PhotoEdit; **746** © Luis Marden / NGS Image Collection; **749** © Allen Green / Photo Researchers, Inc.; **751** © AFP / Corbis; **752** © Paul Conklin / PhotoEdit; **753** © Sue Cunningham Photographic; **757** (top) © Sandra Lord / Photoright; **757** (bottom) © Tom Davenport / Photo Researchers, Inc.; **758** © Bret Gustafson; **759** AP / Wide World Photos; **760** AP / Wide World Photos; **762** (right) 1987 by permission of W. W. Norton & Company, New York and Jean-Marie Simon; **763** © Karen Kasmauski / Matrix; **764** AP / Wide World Photos; **765** (left) AP / Wide World Photos; **765** (right) © Bettmann / Corbis; **768** AP / Wide World Photos; **771** AP / Wide World Photos; **772** (left) © Tony Freeman / PhotoEdit; **772** (right) AP / Wide World Photos; **773** (top) © Chuck Nacke / Woodfin Camp & Associates; **773** (bottom) AP / Wide World Photos; **775** AP / Wide World Photos; **776** © Ron McMillan / Getty Images.

LITERARY CREDITS

"Turnabout Map" © 1982, 1990 by Jesse Levine, (650) 494–7729.

Excerpt from E. E. Clark, *Indian Legends of the Pacific Northwest* © 1966. The Regents of University of California. Reprinted with permission.

Original Study: "Encountering environmentalism in rural Costa Rica." © 2000 by Luis Vivanco. Reprinted with permission.

Original Study: "Whispers from the Ice." Adapted excerpt from "Whispers from the Ice" by Sherry Simpson, Alaska, April 1995, pp. 23–28. Reprinted with permission of the author.

Figure 2.1: Grid of ancient Mayan city of Tikal. University of Pennsylvania Museum (neg. #61–5–5).

Original Study: "The Unsettling Nature of Variational Change" from "What does the dreaded 'E' Word mean, anyway?" by S. J. Gould. With permission from *Natural History,* February 2000. Copyright the American Museum of Natural History 2000. Reprinted with permission.

Anthropology Applied: "Anthropology and the Ethical, Legal and Social Implications of the Human Genome Project" by D. E. Walrath (2001). Reprinted courtesy of D. E. Walrath.

Original Study: "Culture of Chimpanzees," by A. Whitten and C. Boesch, (2001) from *Scientific American,* 284(1). Reprinted with permission. Copyright © 2001 by Scientific American, Inc. All rights reserved.

Original Study: "Will the real human ancestor please stand up?" (2001) by D. E. Walrath. Reprinted courtesy of D. E. Walrath.

Original Study: "The naked and the bipedal," (1993) by Tim Folger. Used with permission.

Original Study: "Cat in the Human Cradle" by J. A. Cavallo. With permission *from Natural History,* February 1990. Copyright the American Museum of Natural History 1990. Reprinted with permission.

Figure 7.6: Flaked stone tool production. Reprinted with the permission of Simon & Schuster Adult Publishing Group from *Making Silent Stones Speak* by Kathy D. Schick and Nicholas Toth. Copyright © 1993 by Kathy D. Schick and Nicholas Toth.

Original Study: "Homo Erectus and the use of Bamboo" by G. C. Pope. With permission from *Natural History,* February 1989. Copyright the American Museum of Natural History 1989. Reprinted with permission.

Original Study: "African Origin or Ancient Population Size Difference." Reprinted with the permission of Simon & Schuster, Inc. from *Race and Human Evolution* by Milford Wolpoff and Rachel Caspari. Copyright © 1996 by Milford Wolpoff and Rachel Caspari.

Original Study: Excerpt from "Paleolithic Paint Job" (1993) by Roger Lewin, *Discover,* 14(7), pp. 67–69. Reprinted with permission of Roger Lewin.

Original Study: "History of Mortality and Physiological Stress," excerpt from "Population, health, and the evolution of subsistence: Conclusions from the conference" by A. C. Roosevelt in M. N. Cohen & G. J. Armelagos (Eds), *Paleopathology and the origins of agriculture,* pp. 572–574 (1984). Reprinted with permission.

Excerpt from "Editors' Summation" in M. N. Cohen & G. J. Armelagos (Eds), *Paleopathology and the origins of agriculture,* pp. 594 (1984). Reprinted with permission.

Figure 12.2: Grid-map of Teotihuacan © René Millon 1973. Reprinted with permission.

Original Study: "Finding the Tomb of a Moche Priestess," by C. B. Donnan & L. J. Castillo. Reprinted with permission of *Archaeology Magazine,* Volume 45, Number 6 (Copyright the Archaeological Institute of America, 1992).

Original Study: "Race without Color," by J. Diamond, *Discover,* 15(11), 1994, pp. 83–88. Reprinted with permission of Dr. Jared Diamond.

Original Study: "The Importance of Trobriand Women" from *The Trobrianders of Papua New Guinea* by Annette B. Weiner, copyright © 1988 by Holt, Rinehart and Winston, reprinted by permission of the publisher.

Table 15.1 "Phonetic Vowel Symbols (Sapir System)" from Trager, George L., *Language and Languages,* p. 304. Copyright © 1972 by George L. Trager. Reprinted by permission of Addison Wesley Longman.

Excerpt from "Sexism" in *The Politics of Reality* by Marilyn Frye (Ed.), copyright © 1983 by Marilyn Frye. Published by The Crossing Press: Freedom, CA.

Figure 15.4 Map: Linguistic Nationalism in the United States: States with "English Only" laws. U.S. states with official English rule and year enacted. Information courtesy of James Crawford from *U.S. English.*

Original Study: "The Great Ebonics Controversy" from "Can't teach a dog to be a cat? The dialogue on ebonics" by L. Monaghan, L. Hinton, & R. Kephart. Reprinted by permission of the American Anthropological Association from *Anthropology Newsletter,* 38:3, March 1997. Not for further reproduction.

Original Study: "The Blessed Curse: Spirituality and sexual difference as viewed by Euro-American and Native American cultures," by Rhonda Kay Williamson from *The College News,* 18 (4). Reprinted by permission of the author.

Excerpt from "Being and Doing: A Cross-Cultural Examination of the Socialization of Males and Females" by Nancy Chodorow. From *Women in Sexist Society* by Vivian Gornick & Barbara K. Moran. Copyright 1971 by Basic Books, Inc. Reprinted by permission of Basic Books, a member of Perseus Books, L.L.C.

Original Study: "Gardens of the Mekranoti Kayapo," excerpt adapted from *Amazon Journey* by Werner, Dennis, © 1990. Reprinted by permission of Prentice-Hall, Upper Saddle River, NJ.

Excerpt from *A Reader in General Anthropology* by Carleton S. Coon, copyright 1948 by Holt, Rinehart and Winston and renewed 1975 by Carleton S. Coon, reprinted by permission of the publisher.

Original Study: "Prestige Economics in Papua New Guinea," excerpt from "Horticulturalists: Economic Behavior in Tribes" by Allen Johnson in *Economic Anthropology,* Edited, with an Introduction, by Stuart Plattner with the permission of the publishers, Stanford University Press. © 1989 by the Board of Trustees of the Leland Stanford Junior University.

Figure 19.1, Anthropology Applied: WHO Report on Global Surveillance of Epidemic-prone infectious Diseases from ww.who.int/emc-documents/surveillance/docs/whocdscsrisr2001.html/hiv_aids/hiv_aids.htm

Original Study: "Arranging a Marriage in India" by Serena Nanda from Philip R. DeVita (ed.), *Stumbling Toward Truth: Anthropologists at Work,* Prospect Heights, IL. Waveland 2000 pp. 196–204. Reprinted by permission of the author.

Original Study: "The Everchanging Family in North America" from *Kinship and Gender* by Linda Stone. Copyright © 1997 by Westview Press, Inc. Reprinted by permission of Westview Press, a member of Perseus Books, L.L.C.

Figure 20.4 Map: "Women's Work and Wages" from *The State of Women in the World Atlas,* 2/e by Joni Seager, pp. 68–69.

Figure 20.5 Map: "Women and Poverty" from *The State of Women in the World Atlas,* 2/e by Joni Seager, pp. 78–79.

Original Study: "Coping as a Woman in a Man's World" excerpted from *Women and family in rural Taiwan,* by Margery Wolf, with the permission of the publishers, Stanford University Press. © 1972 by the Board of Trustees of the Leland Stanford Junior University.

Original Study: "Digital revolution: Indigenous peoples in Cyberia" by H.E.L. Prins. Copyright © 2000 by H.E.L. Prins, Department of Anthropology, Kansas State University.

Figure 22.1 Chart: "Distribution of wealth 1983–1997." Reprinted from Lawrence Mishel, Jared Bernstein, John Schmitt, and the Economic Policy Institute: *The State of Working America 1998–1999.* Copyright © 1999 Cornell University. Used by permission of the publisher, Cornell University Press.

Figure 22.2 Map: "Cycle of Violence (Map)," copyright © 1997 by Dan Smith, text. Maps copyright © 1997 by Myriad Editions Ltd., from *The State of War and Peace Atlas* by Dan Smith. Used by permission of Penguin, a division of Penguin Putnam Inc.

Figure 23.2 Map: "Where the Kurds Live" from *The State of War and Peace Atlas* by Dan Smith, copyright © 1997 by Dan Smith, text. Maps copyright © 1997 by Myriad Editions Ltd. Used by permission of Penguin, a division of Penguin Putnam, Inc.

Original Study: "Limits on Power in Bedouin Society" excerpt from *Veiled Sentiments: Honor and Poetry in a Bedouin Society* by Lila Abu-Lughod, pp. 99–103. Copyright © 1986 by the Regents of the University of California, the University of California Press. Reprinted by permission.

Figure 23.3 Map: "Blood and Soil" from *The State of War and Peace Atlas* by Dan Smith, copyright © 1997 by Dan Smith, text. Maps copyright © 1997 by Myriad Editions Ltd. Used by permission of Penguin, a division of Penguin Putnam, Inc.

Table 24.1: Increase or Decrease of Selected Christian Denominations for the Past 30 Years as a Proportion of the U.S. Population from "Belief by the numbers" by R. Shorto, *New York Times Magazine,* 12/7/97, p. 60.

Original Study: "Healing among the Ju/'hoansi of the Kalahari," from *Nisa: The Life and Words of a !Kung Woman* by Marjorie Shostack. Reprinted by permission of the publisher from Marjorie Shostak, 291–293, Cambridge, Mass.: Harvard University Press, Copyright © 1981 by Marjorie Shostak.

Anthropology Applied: "Reconciling Modern Medicine with Traditional Beliefs in Swaziland": From *Anthropological Praxis* by Robert Wulff and Shirley Fiske. Copyright © 1987 by Westview Press. Reprinted by permission of Westview Press, a member of Perseus Books, L.L.C.

Anthropology Applied: "Protecting Cultural Heritage": From *Anthropological Praxis* by Robert Wulff and Shirley Fiske. Copyright © 1987 by Westview Press. Reprinted by permission of Westview Press, a member of Perseus Books, L.L.C.

Original Study: excerpt adapted from "Myths, Museums, and South African Rock Art" by T. A. Dawson and J. D. Lewis-Williams from *South African Historical Journal,* pp. 52–56 (November, 1993).

Figure 26.4 Map: States providing refuge to internatioinal refugees, from "Fear and Flight" from *The State of War and Peace Atlas* by Dan Smith, copyright © 1997 by Dan Smith, text. Maps copyright © 1997 by Myriad Editions Ltd. Used by permission of Penguin, a division of Penguin Putnam, Inc.

Figure 26.5 Map: Armed Conflict in the 1990s, from "Conflicts of Interest" from *The State of War and Peace Atlas* by Dan Smith, copyright © 1997 by Dan Smith, text. Maps copyright © 1997 by Myriad Editions Ltd. Used by permission of Penguin, a division of Penguin Putnam, Inc.

Original Study: "Violence on Indian Day in Brazil 1997: Symbol of the past and future" by R. M. Wright from *Cultural Survival Quarterly,* 21 (2), 47–49. Reprinted courtesy of Cultural Survival, Inc. www.cs.org.

Figure 27.2 Map: "Gross domestic products of selected countries and companies" from *New York Times* 12/26/99, section A pg. 1.

Original Study: "Standardizing the Body: The Question of Choice" adaptation of Nader, "Controlling Processes: Tracing the Dyanmics of Power" from *Current Anthropology,* 38–5, (Dec. 1997), pp. 715–717, University of Chicago Press. Reprinted by permission of University of Chicago Press.

Figure 27.3: "Cosmetic surgery in the U.S. 1994" from *The State of Women in the World Atlas* 2/e by Joni Seager, p. 51.

Figure 27.4 Map: Land Ownership in Central and South America, from "The Land in Whose hands? (Map)," copyright © 1997 by Dan Smith, text. Maps copyright © 1997 by Myriad Editions Ltd., from *The State of War and Peace Atlas* by Dan Smith. Used by permission of Penguin, a division of Penguin Putnam Inc.

Figure 27.5 Map: Countries with IMF/World Bank Structural Adjustment Program (SAPs) from"no free lunch" from *The State of Women in the World Atlas* 2/e by Joni Seager, pp. 80–81.

Figure 27.8 Map: Traffic of Wealth, from "Health, Wealth and Population" map courtesy of United Nations.

INDEX